Donald L. Carper

Professor of Legal Studies and Conflict Management, California State University, Sacramento

Bill W. West

Professor of Law and Real Estate, Emeritus, California State University, Sacramento

UNDERSTANDING *the* LAW

FOURTH EDITION

THOMSON

SOUTH-WESTERN

WEST

Australia · Canada · Mexico · Singapore · Spain · United Kingdom · United States

THOMSON
─────✦─────™
SOUTH-WESTERN
WEST

Understanding the Law, 4e
Donald L. Carper & Bill W. West

Vice President/Editorial Director:
Jack W. Calhoun

Vice President/Editor-in-Chief:
George Werthman

Publisher:
Rob Dewey

Sr. Developmental Editor:
Jan Lamar

Sr. Production Editor:
Elizabeth A. Shipp

Marketing Manager:
Steven Silverstein

Media Developmental Editor:
Christine A. Wittmer

Media Production Editor:
Amy Wilson

Manufacturing Coordinator:
Rhonda Utley

Sr. Design Project Manager:
Michelle Kunkler

Production House:
Lachina Publishing Services, Inc.

Internal and Cover Designer:
Kim Torbeck/Imbue Design,
Cincinnati

Cover Illustration:
© David Moore/SIS

Printer:
Phoenix Color/Book Technology
Park

For permission to use material from
this text or product, contact us by
Tel (800) 730-2214
Fax (800) 730-2215
http://www.thomsonrights.com

For more information contact
West Legal Studies in Business,
5191 Natorp Boulevard,
Mason, Ohio, 45040.
Or you can visit our Internet site at:
http://www.westbuslaw.com

BRIEF CONTENTS

CONTENTS

In the fourth edition of *Understanding the Law* we continue to provide a text that can be used in many different law courses. We still presume that the student lacks a prior law course and that this text is their first instruction specifically related to law. Our focus has been to make the text friendly, timely, and current. Our goal has been to create a textbook that is interesting and even fun as well as scholarly. Most drama is about conflict and nothing is more dramatic than law, the rationale and rules devised to address conflict.

New features include identification of Chapter Objectives at the beginning of each chapter. A detailed glossary has been a feature of this text, but terms are now also provided in the text margin when first introduced. A new appendix on how to brief a case has been added to assist those using case summaries as a critical thinking writing exercise.

We have increased the use of the Legal Focus feature, which provides background, examples, cases, and problems to break up long textbook discussion of topics that become dry if not considered with the human condition. Each Legal Focus is clearly identified in the textbook. Some problems are also actually cases, and the case classification is used when there is an available appellate court citation. Many Legal Focuses present issues that are unresolved, hopefully prompting reasoned class discussion and continued attention to the resolution of important legal issues.

We have also updated our Web site references and provided more of these references throughout the text.

To further add to this discussion we included a new section on ethics and ethical reasoning in Chapter 1 in the hopes that values when discussed on these important topics can be grounded in reason. A general review of the text heretofore found in Chapter 1 was deleted. At the suggestion of reviewers we have strengthened our discussion of alternative dispute resolution in Chapter 4. As the authors are active ADR neutrals it was a happy task. Increased coverage of personal property is provided in Chapter 10. In addition we have addressed many legal issues involving terrorism in Chapters 1, 3, and 6. We realize that during the life of this edition much will happen that will affect this discussion, but you will have a starting point to consider how the law will address this critical topic.

(S) UPPLEMENTS

INSTRUCTOR'S MANUAL/TEST BANK

The Instructor's Manual/Test Bank continues to be written by text author Don Carper. Each chapter of the manual provides a chapter overview, along with teaching suggestions. The test bank has a minimum of twenty multiple-choice, fifteen true-false, ten fill-in, and three essay questions.

EXAMVIEW

Computerized testing software contains all of the questions in the printed test bank. ExamView is an easy-to-use test-creation software compatible with Microsoft Windows.

Instructors can add or edit questions, instructions, and answers, and select questions by previewing them on the screen, choosing them randomly, or selecting them by number. Instructors can also create and administer quizzes online, whether over the Internet, a local area network (LAN), or a wide area network (WAN).

TEN COMPLIMENTARY HOURS OF WESTLAW

West's computerized legal research gives instructors and students access to U.S. Code, federal regulations, and numerous special libraries. With *WestLaw,* you also have access to Dow Jones News/Retrieval, a comprehensive source of business and financial information.

VIDEO LIBRARY

The West Legal Studies video library includes Legal Conflicts in Business, Court TV® and Drama of the Law. For further information on video supplements, go to the Teaching Resources section at http://carper.westbuslaw.com

INFOTRAC® COLLEGE

InfoTrac® is available upon request. For more information, please contact your sales representative.

TEXT WEB SITE

Visit the Carper, *Understanding the Law,* Web site at http://carper.westbuslaw.com. There you will find a link to Court Case Updates, Teaching Resources, Talk to the Author, and Product Tour, which provides a tour of the book's new and unique features.

ACKNOWLEDGMENTS

This is the first edition of this text without the moving force behind the original version of the book, Bill West, taking an active role. The first version of this text was published in 1975—almost thirty years ago, yet his contributions continue to inform and are immeasurable to this textbook. Bill was missed for many reasons, including that it was a lot more work, but most of all he was really fun to work with. I missed the passionate exchange of ideas. He was also the author who generally set the tone for the preface, and they were long ones. Also missing in this edition was Norbert J. Mietus, who worked on this textbook for more than twenty years. This is the second edition in which he did not participate and how dare he. I missed his scholarship and counsel. As the remaining primary author I have less to say in the preface, hoping I said what I wanted in the text itself.

Donald L. Carper accepts full responsibility for this edition, relieving Bill West and Norbert J. Mietus. If I accept responsibility I must also give credit to two new major contributors. Primarily responsible for the ethics discussion in Chapter 1 and for Chapter 4, Attorney–Client Relationship and Settling Disputes, was Ellen Yamshon, a mediator, attorney at law, and an adjunct instructor in negotiation and conflict resolution in the College of Business at California State University, Sacramento. Responsible for Chapter 5, Administrative Law, and the appendix on case briefing was John McKinsey, also in private practice and an adjunct instructor in legal studies in the College of Business at California State University, Sacramento. Thanks also to my colleague John LaRocco, a labor and employment law expert, for his thoughtful review and suggestions for Chapter 13, Employee and Employer Rights and Duties.

I would like to express our thanks to Rob Dewey, Jan Lamar, and Libby Shipp at West Legal Studies in Business for their support and participation in this project. I have worked for several years with Jan Lamar, and it is easy like Sunday morning. Libby was new to this text, but a pro in her job and a pleasure to work with. The capable and helpful production services were provided by Jeff Lachina and Lorne Franklin at Lachina Publishing Services. The copyeditor was Christy Goldfinch, and she was a delight. She did excellent work with a sense of inquiry and humor that made the process actually fun. Again, thanks for the help.

Our reviewers for this edition are again an eclectic group, providing helpful comments and suggestions. They are:

Judith Anshin, Sacramento City College
Scott A. Comparato, Southern Illinois University, Carbondale
Robert J. Gonzalez, American River College
James R. Ravelle, Moravian College
Marilyn R. Tayler, Montclair State University
Gay A. Young, Johnson County Community College

We wholeheartedly accept the appropriateness of their occasional plaudits, and just as completely reject each and all of their thoughtless criticisms. In truth we truly appreciate the hard work of the reviewers who give us helpful feedback on our scholarship and approach. We responded to the many helpful suggestions except when they were at odds with each other.

Previous reviews for West editions of the text have been:

Third Edition

Norma C. Connolly, Montclair State University
John L. Frank, Chippewa Valley Technical College
Terry L. Hull, Southwest Texas State University
Linda M. Moran, Santa Rosa Junior College
Gene C. Wunder, Washburn University

Second Edition

Ralph Baker, Ball State University
Thomas H.S. Brucker, University of Washington
Jack DeSario, Mount Union College
Samuel L. Jackson, American River College
Theodore S. Olin, Utica College
James C. Ray, Meredith College
Sandra W. Thompson, Georgia Institute of Technology
Perry Zirkel, Lehigh University

First Edition

Thomas M. Apke, California State University, Fullerton
Jane Bennett, Orange Coast College
Joyce Birdoff, Nassau Community College

Thomas Brucker, University of Washington
James Ford, California State Polytechnic University, Pomona
John Guarino, North Essex Community College
Susan Helf, Seattle Central Community College
Deborah Howard, University of Evansville
Mike LaFrance, Kirkwood Community College
Donald Mayer, Oakland University
Richard Mills, Cypress College
H. Randall, Kent State University
Thomas Van Devort, Middle Tennessee State University
Don Wirries, Moorhead State University

CHAPTER 1

Introduction to Law

*L*et reverence for the laws be breathed by every American mother to the lisping babe that prattles on her lap; let it be taught in schools, in seminaries, and in colleges; let it be written in primers, spelling-books, and in almanacs; let it be preached from the pulpit, proclaimed in legislative halls, and enforced in courts of justice. And, in short, let it become the political religion of the nation; and let the old and the young, the rich and the poor, the grave and the gay of all sexes and tongues and colors and conditions, sacrifice unceasingly upon its altars.

Abraham Lincoln Address before the Young Men's Lyceum of Springfield, Illinois, January 1837.

After reading and studying this chapter, you should be able to:

🏛 Provide a definition of law while understanding that the most fundamental legal concepts are susceptible to differing views.

🏛 Appreciate and recall the connection between people, historical events, and technological achievements and the law.

🏛 Understand the origins of the English common law system and its connection to the U.S. legal system.

🏛 Describe the important sources of United States law and explain how they are interrelated.

🏛 Explain the doctrine of *stare decisis* and understand how case law is related to other sources of law.

🏛 Classify the law in a variety of ways including federal and state law, criminal and civil law, private and public law, and procedural and substantive law.

🏛 Be able to define ethics and distinguish ethics from law.

🏛 Demonstrate familiarity with two forms of ethical reasoning and the ability to use them to consider an ethical problem.

🏛 Demonstrate familiarity with the terminology of court cases and how cases are reported.

Welcome to the study of law. As you leave college and begin your careers, the laws of our society will play an ever-increasing role in your lives. As educated members of the community, you will apply your understanding of our legal system in voting and in actively participating in local, state, and federal issues and affairs. From a more practical standpoint, your education about our law and legal system will help guide you toward happier and more financially successful lives. We do not assume that you are interested in becoming attorneys at law, although it is a noble calling. Instead, most of you will select from a variety of careers and lifestyles, seeking to make your lives as meaningful as possible. *Understanding the Law* is designed to help you recognize opportunities and overcome obstacles in reaching your goals.

Each individual and family engages in business activities in the sense that money is earned to buy needed and desired goods and services. Family members must be prepared to deal with a myriad of businesses as consumers, employees, and active members of communities that are involved in issues of growth and congestion. Community leaders deal with such difficult problems as neighborhood crime, traffic, homelessness, and environmental protection. Understanding the laws that affect you will not be easier in the twenty-first century.

Already you have learned something about the law, simply by experiencing life. For example, you know that intentionally injuring another person, stealing, or damaging someone else's property is unlawful. You know that in an automobile collision, the careless driver is held responsible, and when both drivers have been careless, they share the blame. You know that divorce creates issues of alimony, division of family property, and financial support for children and changes in their parental custody. You know that employers must provide safe working conditions for their employees. You know that you must conform to rules in casting your vote in elections, in registering for admission to college, in driving on public highways, and in obtaining certain drugs.

You probably could write a reasonable definition of the law. Perhaps you would correctly conclude that laws are rules that must be obeyed to avoid the imposition of sanctions (legal penalties). More precisely, the dictionary declares: **law** is a body of rules of conduct prescribed by controlling authority and having binding legal force.[1] But this traditional definition of law is static, a "snapshot" emphasizing law's nature as a set of written rules.

Consider law as dynamic, continuously changing and evolving, always responding to the needs of society for solutions to evolving new issues. There are many specific, written rules, such as speed limits. But there also are conflicts between rules and their application to changing situations. For example, consider the evolving Internet, which is changing traditional laws of privacy, free speech, and crime, as well as many rules of commerce and consumerism.

It is perfectly logical for laws to change continually in response to the evolving characteristics of and the issues within our society. That is, law changes as we change. Each new or modified law must conform to the immutable principles of our Constitution or ultimately be discarded. Thus, the laws of our society are both dynamic and predicated upon immutable principles.* The vast majority of changes in our laws do not violate the broad constitutional principles upon which our society is based. Does society change the law or does the law change society? This "Which comes first, the chicken or the egg?" variety of question is unanswerable. Consider that in some states recent changes in the law require that motorcycle riders wear helmets. Did these new laws change society? Or did society recognize a need (through its representative officials) and require a change in the

law

A body of rules of conduct prescribed by controlling authority and having binding legal force.

* Ours is a democracy in which the "immutable principles" mentioned are derived by reference to our Constitution. Not all are expressed; many are implied. For example, the much-publicized right of privacy is an unspecified constitutional principle upon which both abortion and interracial marriage have been based. These interpretative principles or laws are declared by the U.S. Supreme Court, as will be discussed more fully in Chapter 2.

law? The answer to both questions is "yes." What is important is that, either way, our legal system and laws are dynamic and respond to the legal issues that arise within our changing society. In a nutshell, the study of law is the study of a moving target. Some changes are quite immediate, as when legislatures respond to popular demands. In contrast, courts are structured to accommodate change more slowly, at a more reflective pace.

When William McKinley became president in 1897, a great industrial revolution was well underway in this country. Railroads were spreading from the east to the great cities in the west. Coal was fueling the furnaces used in making steel, which in turn was used to manufacture train rails. Following the invention of the gasoline engine, automobiles soon would become mass-produced, changing the face of our nation forever. The Wright brothers had yet to give birth to the airplane industry, and space exploration was science fiction. In the twenty-first century, we are experiencing another magnificent technological revolution, which links not seaboards but the entire world. In this modern yet still embryonic revolution, the demands upon the legal system already are reaching new heights of complexity. For example:

- The Internet is causing a re-examination of the principles of free speech and privacy and the protection of minors from sexually explicit materials.
- Applications of computer technology are rapidly changing the federal laws governing intellectual property, especially copyright and patent laws.
- The science of biotechnology is presenting our society and its legal system with momentous social and legal issues involving genetic alteration of plant and animal life, human cloning, and even the possibility of allowing parents the opportunity to produce "designer" babies. The unique products of human intervention into the natural processes of animal and plant life may be patented, thereby creating possible monopolization of some aspects of creation.
- Computer-assisted aeronautical design stands upon the threshold of HyperSoar, a commercial passenger and/or military airplane that would fly at ten times the speed of sound, leave the atmosphere after takeoff, then shut down its power and skim over the fringes of the earth's atmosphere like a flat rock skimming across the surface of a lake. Flight time between any two places on Earth could be achieved in no more than two hours; four round trips between San Francisco and London could be made each day.[2] Such a shrinking of the globe portends changes in the laws of international commerce dealing with such matters as illegal replication and distribution of products, other unfair business practices, and nearly instantaneous financial management. The merging of global cultures through such proximity in time portends legal issues of presently unimaginable dimensions.

In addition to the technology revolution, natural forces are also creating today's issues. Consider the following:

- Population continues to increase causing a multitude of social issues, and the problem is growing exponentially. For example, demands for changes in education, reapportionment, health management, and immigration policy are intensifying. Political conflicts over these kinds of issues already are so intense that, in some situations, U.S. courts are performing legislative functions following a stalemate by state officials (e.g., in management of schools, reapportionment, and even public transportation). On the one hand, our population is aging, setting the stage for fierce competition between workers and retirees for the nation's wealth and benefits. "This is a revolution in waiting that will redefine society in the twenty-first century just as baby-boomers shaped social, political and economic changes in the last half of the twentieth century."[3] Unlike the Baby Boom Generation, which came about after a surge of births following World War II, the Millennium Generation arises as much from immigration as

http://

Often when there is an Internet source available to provide additional information on a topic that is discussed in the text, we will alert you to it in the margin. The Internet makes it easier for you to have access to primary research and materials no matter where in the world they exist. Check out this site about HyperSoar:

http://www.firstscience .com/site/articles/hypersoar .asp

from the "baby boom echo" (offspring of baby boomers). On the other hand, children ages six to twelve affect the spending of an estimated $500 billion each year—by influencing "mom." The influence ranges from choosing food and restaurants to switching from the once "cool" minivans to the preferred sport utility vehicles.[4]

- Environmental issues abound from global warming to air and water pollution, presenting our society with problems it alone cannot resolve. Our legal system is already in high gear making laws to meet these forthcoming challenges.

- The terrorist attack of September 11, 2001, on the World Trade Center and the Pentagon has brought to America a multitude of social concerns with legal consequences. They include new security precautions that reduce privacy at airports, buildings, and sporting events; treatment and classification of suspected terrorists and detainees from military operations related to the "war against terrorism"; and concerns over distribution of charitable donations to family victims of the terrorist attack. Americans care deeply about these and other terrorist-related issues. And the ultimate legal resolution of these and other issues have significant legal and social implications for America.

Looking backward we see that although our legal system has resolved the issues presented by changing lifestyles, attitudes, and mores, we also see that some solutions are resting on tenuous footing, as reflected by 5–4 decisions of the U.S. Supreme Court. Although resolved by law, volatile and contentious issues such as abortion, flag burning, prayer in schools, and affirmative action are not fully resolved by society, a substantial portion of which waits for a replacement Supreme Court Justice. Others await each new election to garner a few more votes in Congress or in a state legislature to change statutes that were resolved contrary to their position on an issue. In this sense, by looking backward, perhaps you can better appreciate the importance of your participation in the future resolution of these issues.

A historical perspective can sharpen our understanding of the outlook for our laws and for our legal system in the early years of the twenty-first century. Does the outlook portend major changes, such as reform of the court structure to accommodate a more complex society? Will a new specialized U.S. Supreme Court be required? Have the issues our legal system has dealt with over the past years strained it to the breaking point? "What now?" the reasoned person might ask, as we reach warp speed. Are there new issues that should be resolved by certain institutions in society other than courts? It is said that if we ignore history we are destined to repeat it. Here we are not studying history, but we must take it into consideration in contemplating the role of law and our legal system in the early years of the new millennium.

http://

The U.S. State Department has a Web site that presents the U.S. position and response to terrorism:
http://usinfo.state.gov/ topical/pol/terror/

(L) EGAL/SOCIETAL RELATIONSHIPS OVER TIME: 1900S VS. 2000S

What do we take for granted today that was missing from our society in the early days of the twentieth century, when many of your grandparents' parents were alive? With the advantage of hindsight, we now know the problems that were presented to our legal system in the twentieth century as well as their solutions. With some foresight, we hope to paint a picture for you of the kinds of problems facing our legal system today, in the first decade of the twenty-first century. Comparing the legal/societal relationships of a hundred years ago with today's raises the question, "Is our legal system as constructed today capable of adequately fulfilling the demands our society will place upon it in the next century, or even in the next twenty-five years?" Consider the success of trial by jury over the preceding century—can you safely assume that it will be fully appropriate to our system of justice in the new millennium? In most chapters of this textbook, you will find the kinds of issues that the future holds for our laws and legal system. But first we look backward to inform our views of how our society and its legal system can interact successfully in the near future.

What was our society like only one (extended) lifetime[5] ago at the beginning of the twentieth century? With a flourishing economy fueled in part by the Klondike Gold Rush, William McKinley was re-elected president in 1900 on a platform that government should not control or discipline business. Riding the crest of victory over Spain in the Spanish-American War, Theodore (Teddy) Roosevelt became vice president. Unlike our present military capability for distance warfare, Roosevelt's "Rough Riders" fought eye-to-eye, although more U.S. soldiers died from contaminated meat than at the hands of the Spanish. On the brink of an industrial revolution and new status as a world power, changes were happening on the domestic front. Then, as now, people necessarily relied upon the ability of their laws to change responsively to their needs—and upon their legal system to oversee the process. Consider the following example of the U.S. Supreme Court in action:

LEGAL FOCUS—CASE

Minnesota law provided that "All labor on Sunday is prohibited, excepting the works of necessity or charity. . . ." Barber Petit was arrested, tried, and convicted of cutting hair and shaving beards in his barbershop on Sundays. He appealed all the way to the U.S. Supreme Court on the grounds that cutting hair and shaving beards was a work of necessity. What do you suppose was the result one hundred years ago?

Petit v. Minnesota, 177 U.S. 164, 20 S.Ct. 666 (1900).

The Court recognized the Sunday law of relaxation as "essential to the physical and moral well-being of society." The Court relied upon several precedents (prior court decisions) to the effect that shaving on Sunday was not a work of necessity. Even the House of Lords in England in earlier times had concluded that shaving customers was a worldly labor. Barber Petit lost his appeal. Most cases before the U.S. Supreme Court were far more complex than Petit's case, involving commerce, taxation, admiralty, commercial transactions, water rights, and so on. The U.S. Supreme Court was composed of nine Justices, as it is today, and the structure of lower courts remains essentially unchanged. The point remains, however, that we live in a much more complex world.

Consider the role of women on the eve of the twentieth century. Their primary work was housework and child rearing. Perhaps 20 percent of women were in the paid labor force by 1900.[6] Of those employed outside the home, the vast majority were farmhands or domestics. Other than in the states of Utah and Colorado, women did not have the right to vote. The Klondike Gold Rush had fueled a "Gilded Age" as the twentieth century began, with affluence spreading throughout many American cities. Women in the upper classes became more athletic and "outdoorsy" than before. Although still corseted, the modern woman wore only one petticoat instead of the five previously worn. Bread was purchased in shops, freeing women from the chore of baking. Dining in fancy restaurants was a primary recreation, and their men enjoyed golfing and smoking Cuban cigars as a mark of attainment. At home, Jell-O was available for dessert. Only the homes of the upper classes had bathtubs, and fewer had showers, but the twentieth century began with the expectations of more good (financial) times for our society. Trolleys (and to a very limited extent, cars) made travel easier, encouraging families from the wealthy class to move from urban areas to suburbs. The flight of people from cities to the suburbs had begun. Upper-class families sent their children to the Ivy League and other great universities. Nevertheless, women as a class were, for the most part, shortchanged in their protection by the law. For example, upon marriage a woman's legal rights to property disappeared, property ownership being vested solely in her husband.

But our law and legal system had been conceived by its founders as dynamic and, as it turned out, up to the task of coping with the dramatic changes in the extended lifetime of the twentieth century. The rights of women to vote and to own property independently were created under law, as were many other rights to the extent that few gender distinctions exist in the law today.

Consider some of the changes in our society brought about during the twentieth century, changes that placed extraordinary demands upon our legal system. Few people lived in the seven territories (Alaska, Arizona, District of Columbia, Hawaii, New Mexico, Oklahoma, and the Indian territories) in 1900, and most conveniences were found in or near the great cities. Although on the eve of an industrial revolution and as an emerging world power, in 1900, the United States had no airplanes, no spaceships, no satellites, no television sets or DVD players, no video cameras, no computers, no Internet, no color or sound movies, no suburban malls, no cellular or cordless telephones, no microwave ovens, no automatic dishwashers, no electric stoves, no trash compactors or disposals, no air conditioning, and no credit or debit cards. As for the implements of war, there were neither nuclear weapons nor submarines with inter-continental missiles to deliver them. On the other hand, Thomas Edison had harnessed electricity, with the result that the phonograph (but not stereo) and household lighting were widely available in the cities. Individual transportation was by foot, horse or horse-drawn buggy, public transportation (rail and electric trolleys), and bicycle. There were only 13,824 motorcars in a country of 76 million people with a total of only 144 miles of paved roads in the entire United States. Mass production of automobiles was soon to follow the turn of the century, creating a love affair between the public and its cars that has left a most significant impact upon the entire century, including its laws.

There were no fast-food places. The first hamburger wasn't served until the twentieth century began when, in early 1900, a man in Connecticut ground up some beef and served it between two pieces of toast without catsup or relish. Which came first, aspirin, or fast food? Aspirin had appeared a year earlier. It would be several years before vitamins were even discovered or refrigeration even invented. The towns and cities of the United States supported many small coffee-bean-roasting shops, much as Starbucks and others dot our cities today. But the coffee roasters began a steady decline into oblivion when Hills Bros. of San Francisco first began packing pre-roasted beans into vacuum tins. For almost the entire century, travelers to San Francisco would be greeted with the tantalizing aromas of coffee beans roasting at the Hills Bros.' plant. Technology already was creating its rewards and victims.[7]

Many interesting events at the beginning of the twentieth century have parallels to today's legal issues. Just before the turn of the century, Butch Cassidy and the Sundance Kid robbed a Union Pacific train in Wyoming and Gideon International began placing Bibles in hotel rooms; today, crime and religious freedom share headlines and demand solutions through new laws or even constitutional amendment (as for school prayer). One hundred years ago, the last of the Indian wars had been fought; today, Indian treaty rights to fish, gamble, and use natural resources are in the news, with proposals for new enabling laws. A century ago the first juvenile court was established in Illinois; today, attacks on schoolmates by disturbed students and juvenile gang activity prompt reactive laws. Elementary school children in Indianapolis must enter school through a metal detector to make sure no gun or knife is being brought to class[8] and convictions for gang-related crimes now are being based on out-of-court (hearsay) testimony. A plethora of court decisions have relaxed the rules to make it easier to convict "gang" members.[9]

The U.S. government was already a leading employer at the beginning of the century with a quarter of a million employees, and only one-quarter of the U.S. commercial shipping fleet was under sail power. Today, ocean pollution from petroleum-based products released from ships through disaster or otherwise continues to plague an environmentally conscious world; new laws impose severe financial penalties and require safety precautions, such as double hulls, "road maps" on the seas near coastlines, and warrantless searches of vessels.

A hurricane in Galveston, Texas, killed thousands of people in 1900, becoming at the time the worst North American disaster in history; today, natural disasters, fires, floods, hurricanes, and combinations of all occur annually. Early in this century an estimated 3,000 people were victims of an intended disaster with the September 11, 2001, crash of four planes into New York's World Trade Center, the Pentagon in Washington, D.C., and rural Pennsylvania. Each of these disasters, natural or otherwise, create financial and legal burdens of major proportions.*

At the beginning of the twentieth century, grapefruit were made to grow sweeter and gained public acceptance as a result; today, genetic engineering is modifying food products to resist pests, to gain better size and marketing durability, and to improve taste, while the legal implications of the genetic engineering of food products remains to be seen. A century ago the first drunk-driving case involved a horse-drawn taxicab driver; today, many states define drunk driving as a blood alcohol level of .08.

Obviously, most of today's necessities and conveniences were not available to our society at the beginning of the twentieth century. But neither were there federal laws prohibiting discrimination on the basis of race, religion, or gender in the workplace. Racial discrimination was alive and well at the beginning of the twentieth century. Because poll taxes and literacy tests were preconditions to voting in many states, black Americans were segregated and powerless under the law to do much about it. The constitutionality of the principle of "separate but equal" facilities based on race was well established.[10] More than one-half of the century elapsed before that doctrine was overruled, when in 1954 the U.S. Supreme Court declared that segregation was inherently unequal.[11] Although black Americans could not legally be excluded from juries by the turn of the century, many states relied upon racially selective jury selection practices. The infamous "Scottsboro Boys" case probably marks the beginning of serious changes in the law to guarantee full participation by blacks on juries. In that 1931 case, the convictions and death penalties of nine young black men for the rape of two white women by an all-white jury were overruled because of discrimination in jury selection.[12]

---

* In any disaster, legal issues include a variety of insurance coverage considerations and appropriate distribution of charitable contributions, to name but a few.

(W)HAT IS THE OUTLOOK FOR THE LEGAL SYSTEM IN THE TWENTY-FIRST CENTURY?

With the knowledge of how the law and legal system has fulfilled its responsibility to meet radically changing times during the twentieth century, what can we now foresee for the law? What can be seen is complexity brought about by our expectation that the law, lawyers, and judges will continue to accept responsibility for solutions to an increasing number of precise issues within grand problems. The single most significant reality is the likely increased role of the legal system in society, with a corresponding increase in the complexities of its procedures and the issues it resolves.

Our legal system shows no tendency to reject or limit the trend of accepting responsibilities (jurisdiction) over an increasing variety of issues. For example, in recent years courts have accepted cases involving the selection of the president of the United States and cases about discrimination against persons for reasons of health (e.g., AIDS, disability, mental illness), sexual orientation (e.g., same-sex marriage), or religion (e.g., school prayer). The courts have also overruled laws created directly by citizens through the initiative process (propositions on ballots). Many of these topics are discussed later in this text, but here it is sufficient to identify that significant problems are being addressed more by courts and the legal system than by either the legislative or the executive branches of government. We predict this trend will continue. Thus, your education about the law is more compelling than your parents' was.

There is a rationale that elected officials choose to avoid the tough and controversial issues that cost them votes, and leave these "no win" issues to the legal system where the judges are brave, if for no other reason than because the electorate participates less in their tenure. Abortion is one example where only the courts could resolve the issue, even though no express constitutional provision could be identified to support the selected result. Even the U.S. Supreme Court could muster only a 5–4 decision, demonstrating that an issue so controversial could be decided by only a single vote.[13]

In short, it is increasingly important that well-informed citizens, like yourselves, be educated about our legal system, including the role of its judges and lawyers. Otherwise, citizens risk submission through ignorance and complacency to the latest sound bite or "spin" that seeks voter approval. Your understanding of the increasingly important legal system is critical over the long run, which is precisely why it is presented to you here.

We increasingly turn to the courts to solve our problems—both public *and* private. This produces a great strain upon our legal system, evident by the growth of alternative forums for dispute resolution (discussed in Chapter 4). The point here is that the future portends increasing legal costs of doing business and of protecting consumers. These costs are indirectly reflected in the prices of products as well as taxes used to support courts, judges, and governmental offices charged with providing public/legal services.

There is no reason to suspect that the demand for attorneys (i.e., legal solutions) will lessen or that their services will cost less in the twenty-first century. Lawyers enjoy an oligarchy with the power (and willingness) to match their fees with the capabilities of their clients to pay. Increasing demand is producing more lawyers, who become safely ensconced within the parameters of existing firms, in turn, participating in an ever-wider scope of increasingly specialized tasks.

This is not to suggest that our dependence upon law, courts, and lawyers is either good or bad. It is merely a well-understood phenomenon. Educators often speak of the legal system as being composed of laws and courts. The logic is that laws are the rules of our society and courts ensure their enforcement. But what of attorneys? In reality, a person cannot hope to resolve a substantial conflict or commercial transaction without an attorney's professional help. Although citizens are entitled under law to self-representation, the reality is that to do so is ill advised for many obvious reasons. Thus, the attorney is the first person to become involved when legal issues and many business opportunities arise. Attorneys give advice, most of which is followed. They also perform other services as described in Chapter 4. The point is, attorneys must be acknowledged as an integral part of the legal system because laws and judges are powerless until attorneys bring matters into court.

We can foresee a growing population being served by expanding businesses and requiring greater governmental protection and services with expanding conflicts and issues, all requiring the services of lawyers. Do not misunderstand. Aside from the exasperation widely expressed by our society about lawyers, the law business is alive and well and adequately handling all the various clients it serves. With its ability to specialize and change to meet changing times, the prediction that the legal system (defined as to include lawyers) and the complexities it produces will continue to grow.

THE ENGLISH SOURCE OF U.S. LAW

The purpose of primitive English law was to keep the peace, and fact-finding processes were likely to provoke the population rather than calm it. So authorities avoided investigation and substituted mechanical tests that were believed to obtain the judgment of God. Among the favored tests were various ordeals an accused must suffer, including cold water, hot water, hot iron, and the morsel.[14] Imagination probably suffices to picture all but the morsel ordeal so we offer this quote from the Domesday Book of the County of Norfolk, England, describing an ordeal by morsel.

LEGAL FOCUS—EXAMPLE

"May this morsel which is given him in order to bring the truth to light, stick in his throat and find no passage; may his face turn pale and his limbs be convulsed; and an horrible alteration appear in his whole body; if he is guilty. But if innocent of the crime laid to his charge, may he easily swallow it, consecrated in Thy Name, to the end that all may know."

A Web site history of Feltwell Village, U.K., provides a vivid description of ordeal by morsel: http://www.feltwellnorfolk.freeserve.co.uk/written/trial_ordeal.htm

Before the eleventh century, England was an Anglo-Saxon society of unified and relatively prosperous people living mostly in villages. The economy was agricultural and the people were self-sufficient, growing grain, spinning wool, and even brewing beer for home consumption. Their kings headed powerful and wealthy aristocracies. Wealth was primarily tied to the landholding feudal system. Serfdom, in which people were born into vassalage and were required to work the aristocratic lords' hereditary lands, was widespread. Throughout the Saxon period, law was essentially a matter of local customs, and it changed very slowly. For the most part, long-established customs and shared values were reflected in the law, but were not recorded. Kings rarely issued laws binding the entire nation. Established legal systems provided monetary compensation for private wrongs and criminal prosecution for public wrongs. Generally, a person accused of a crime had either been caught in the act or had been found guilty in a strange proceeding during which witnesses

http://

Read about William the
Conqueror and the history of
English law at
http://www.law.cam.ac.uk/

and the accused engaged in "oath-swearing." This was a complicated procedure related more to the character of the accused than to evidence of a crime. There were no lawyers and no jury trials. Needless to say, this system was neither sophisticated nor flawless.

In 1066, William, Duke of Normandy, led 5,000 men and 2,500 cavalry across the English Channel to defeat the Saxons in the Battle of Hastings. The Duke became known as William the Conqueror. The invasion was followed by decades of regional uprisings and resistance characterized by extensive murder, oppression, famine, and fear, despite William's zeal for law, order, and justice. The Normans (Vikings who originally came from Scandinavia via northern France) were French in language,* viewpoint, and culture. Their system of law was based on the ancient Roman civil law, which was expressed mostly in detailed codes (systematic collections of rules) imposed by the ruler from above, in contrast to the Saxon practice of developing rules from below, based on customs of the people.

The Normans retained the English common law of unwritten customs, except that church courts were introduced with authority limited mainly to spiritual matters and domestic (family) relations. England gradually underwent positive changes. A sense of national unity ensued, leading to a national system of law derived from both Anglo-Saxon and Norman influences. The Normans had already been influenced by the French, and the linking of England with the European continent, effected by the conquest, led to the introduction of elements of Roman civil law. Following numerous regional battles, William became King of England and ultimately obtained the allegiance of the people. Gradually, intermarriage between the native people and the invaders became common. As before, local justice continued to be the concern of local sheriffs, and the **common law** (law applied uniformly throughout the country) was characterized even then by equality before the law (the law applied the same to every person), respect for established rights, and impartial administration of justice.

**common law: as a
system of law**

The total system of law
that originated in medieval
England and was adopted
by the United States at the
time of the American
Revolution. Expressed
originally in opinions and
judgments of the courts, it
is judge-made law that
reflects the customs and
usages of the people.
Contrasted to Roman *civil
law,* it is found throughout
the English-speaking world.
Common law is also called
unwritten law.

The king's courts dealt with civil and criminal legal matters, and new Church Courts dealt with canon law (ecclesiastical law governing internal relations of the Roman Catholic church) and all aspects of marriage and succession. Disputes between common and canon law existed in some areas, such as legitimization of illegitimate children, which was not possible under canon law. Under common law, legitimization was accomplished by subsequent marriage of the parents. This was an important matter because it affected rights of inheritance and succession to land, the foundation of wealth and power in England.

By the twelfth century, judges, who periodically visited places in the country to dispense justice, were displacing sheriffs. These "circuits" were precursors of the present U.S. circuit and district courts. The itinerant judges dealt with crimes such as murder, robbery, forgery, and arson. One judge, Glanvil, is credited with writing *Treatise on the Laws and Customs of the Kingdom of England,* the first serious book on the evolving common law. In 1215, King John was forced to accept the Magna Carta (Latin: "Great Charter"), the basis of modern English constitutional liberty, commanding free elections and reform of the courts and barring imprisonment without a trial by a jury of peers. Trial by jury had evolved into permanency by way of the Magna Carta, and ultimately was incorporated into the U.S. Constitution. The Magna Carta essentially decreed supremacy of law over personal authority of the king and his aides. It was a precursor of our constitutional democracy.

http://

One of four surviving copies
of the Magna Carta is on
display at the British
Museum in London. A brief
discussion of the Magna
Carta can be found at
**http://www.bl.uk/
collections/treasures/
magna.html**

---

* Norman French is very different from modern French.

LEGAL FOCUS—BACKGROUND

Perhaps the most famous sheriff in English history—the Sheriff of Nottingham from the tale of Robin Hood—isn't from history at all but from English folklore. Among the enduring themes from the tale of Robin Hood is a sense of outrage that arises from the abuse of power portrayed by the Sheriff of Nottingham. Although the tale of the sheriff is fiction, the position now is real and continues to this day. The current sheriff is democratically elected and the office holder in 2002, Joan Caussorn, was the fourth woman to hold the office.[15]

For several hundred years the English system of courts evolved, influenced by conflicts and political interventions. Over time, judges required formalities to be met before a matter could be brought to court. When these requirements were not met, courts were simply unavailable to a party. When the king's courts were unable or unwilling to provide a just solution to a legal problem, and a citizen (initially citizens of high status) appealed to the king, the matter would be referred to the Lord Chancellor for possible intervention. The Lord Chancellor served as the king's chief administrative officer and the position was initially staffed by high churchmen. As a man committed to justice and fairness, the chancellor was authorized to decide the cases without the assistance of a jury. This alternative court became known as a *court of equity*. An example of an **action in equity** would be a dispute over the sale of a parcel of land in which the seller refused to transfer the title. The king's courts, by tradition, could do no more than award monetary damages. The chancellor (and, later, when the administration of these hearings was delegated to junior staff, courts of equity) could and would order the seller to relinquish possession. Such decree of specific performance to this day remains an equitable remedy and is available in regular courts sitting without juries. Ultimately, jurisdictional conflicts refined the fundamental distinction between courts at law and courts in equity. This distinction endures in the U.S. today and determines important questions. However, unlike England, where courts at law and in equity were physically separated, modern U.S. courts are empowered to render either equitable or legal relief. Equity is explained further in Chapter 3.

The eighteenth century brought England from medieval to modern times. The industrial revolution greatly affected the law as England changed from an agricultural society, where land was the principal form of wealth, to a society increasingly based on factories and industrial production. Machinery produced more goods at less cost with less labor; prices dropped, resulting in greater demand for goods. England prospered as trade expanded, and the law rapidly evolved, responding with many new principles of business law. But the transition was marred by many difficulties and abuses. By the end of the eighteenth century, an eminent historian, Sir Thomas Erskine May, in these pessimistic words, described the state of the law:

> *Heart-breaking delays and ruinous costs were the lot of suitors. Justice was dilatory, expensive, uncertain and remote. To the rich it was a costly lottery; to the poor a denial of right, or certain ruin. The class who profited most by its dark mysteries were the lawyers themselves. A suitor might be reduced to beggary or madness, but his advisers revelled in the chicane and artifice of a lifelong suit and grew rich.*[16]

Over hundreds of years the common law of England had evolved into a framework of principles, found in both customs and statutes that were brought to the New World by the early colonial settlers. When the United States broke away from England after the Revolutionary

action in equity

A civil trial held without a jury when relief sought by the plaintiff is equitable in nature, such as an injunction, or a divorce or dissolution of a marriage.

http://

A discussion of ancient documents is provided by Professor Bernard J. Hibbitts of the University of Pittsburgh School of Law at **http://www.law.pitt.edu/ hibbitts/connect.htm**

http://

Lawyer Thomas P. Vincent of Northampton, Maine, provides a Web site "for all who enjoy legal history and theory." Read the Laws of the Cherokee Nation, the Code of Hammurabi, and other material that is difficult to find on the Internet at:

http://www.commonlaw. com/

common law: as a type of law

That law which comes from the common courts as opposed to a legislature or court of equity.

federalism

A government consisting of a union of more of less self-governing states under an umbrella of federal government.

http://

The U.S. federalism Web site, developed by a graduate student at George Washington University, explores the relationship between the states and the federal government.

http://www.min.net/~kala/ fed/

War, we adopted the entire body of English common law as it existed in the eighteenth century—at least to the extent it did not conflict with U.S. federal and state laws. And that is the situation today; principles of the English common law are in effect throughout the country. Only Louisiana, purchased in 1803 from Napoleon, is different, retaining a variation of the Roman civil law that was then used in France. This California statute is representative of the reception of English legal doctrine and process in the courts of the United States:

> *The Common Law of England so far as it is not repugnant to or inconsistent with the Constitution of the United States or the Constitution or laws of this state, is the rule of decision in all the courts of this state. (California Civil Code, Sec. 22.2.)*

The Revolutionary War may have eliminated the power of the king over the colonies, but not the power of English legal thought over the United States.

English common law does not rest on universal moral principles rooted in natural reason. Rather, its legitimacy arises from experience and custom and from the tacit consent of the people as evidenced from its development over a thousand years.

MODERN COMMON LAW AND *STARE DECISIS*

The term **common law** might already be confusing to you because, like many English language terms, it is used in different ways to describe different things. For example, we have been using the term to describe law common to all of England. But we have also used the term to describe a legal system derived from English legal method, and to describe law formulated by courts rather than legislatures, and to describe common law as distinguished from courts of equity. All the different expressions of the term *common law* are related. The use of the term to describe a type of legal system derives from a description of the unique nature of that legal system, the formulation of law by the courts. The distinction of law and equity (discussed in more detail in Chapter 3) derives from a historical accident within this law-making system. The uniqueness of the common law, or law developed by the courts, is what is usually meant when someone uses the term *common law*. In no other legal system do independent courts have the power to contribute to the law as they do in the common law system.

When considering U.S. court-made or case law, it is important to note the important relationship between federal and state law. Our form of government is one of shared and often overlapping power referred to as **federalism** (a union of states under a central federal government). The court systems include both federal and state courts, which function as either trial courts or appellate courts. These trial courts accept testimony and other evidence to determine guilt or innocence or to place financial responsibility. Appellate courts, on the other hand, review trial court procedures to ensure that correct laws were applied during trial. These appellate reviews, or written decisions, form the body of law also called the common law, or case law.

Both federal and state appellate courts review cases based upon the constantly evolving principles of the common law that are expressed in the written decisions of courts. Who reads these written decisions? Members of the public often learn about new, unfolding laws from television, the Internet, newspapers, and news magazines (but hopefully not from tabloids). Lawyers and scholars read and study court decisions as part of their professional responsibilities. Of course, judges read and study prior court decisions upon which they may decide the trials or cases before them.

Some principles of law derived through the common law apply to both state and federal court systems. For example, the doctrine of **stare decisis** (Latin: "to stand by things that have been settled") mandates that once a rule of law is determined to be applicable to a particular set of facts involved in a case, it will be applied to all future cases that have similar facts. This doctrine binds courts of equal or junior rank to follow in its decisions the senior court that first applied the rule or principle. Essentially, lower state courts are bound to the principles established by higher appellate courts within the same state; lower federal courts are bound to the principles established by higher appellate courts within their respective jurisdictions. (The hierarchy of courts is outlined in Chapter 3.)

This important doctrine of *stare decisis* leads to stability and predictability in the law. For example, if a high court establishes the principle that a promise to marry is not enforceable in court nor are damages allowed if broken, then routine legal research will alert all attorneys to the existence of that **precedent.** If a similar case arises, they will not waste time and money litigating the question; they know their court will be bound by the same earlier outcome under the doctrine of *stare decisis*. This doctrine is also commonly called the doctrine of precedents. Once a common law rule or principle is applied in a case it becomes a precedent and is binding on other courts in similar future cases. The appellate court's decision thus has become a part of the common law of that particular state.

Judges do not have the personal choice to disregard a binding precedent in the common law. Judges take oaths of office and are sworn "to comply with or be faithful to" the law.

LEGAL FOCUS—PROBLEM

J. Anthony Kline, a justice of a state appellate court, wrote a dissenting opinion in which, as a "matter of conscience," he refused to vote consistently with a state supreme court precedent. Does such a declaration violate the doctrine of *stare decisis*?[17]

Although the action of refusing to comply with a precedent flies in the face of the doctrine of *stare decisis,* it may be characterized as a "highly irregular and never to be lightly undertaken" exception based upon the conscience of the justice.

Stare decisis is not a straitjacket, however. If a principle has outlived its usefulness or has grown inapplicable because of changing social standards and circumstances, it may be overruled by a high court. Often a current case is not controlled by a principle previously applied in an earlier case simply because the two cases are distinguishable on their facts. The previous example of an unenforceable and uncompensable promise to marry would be distinguishable from a case where one of the prospective spouses had incurred considerable related expenses before the promise was broken. The earlier principle, therefore, would not apply to or bind the court's decision. Though the court, obviously, would not compel the parties to marry, it might establish a new principle in authorizing recovery of damages (an award of monetary compensation).

The common law of today is the body of rules derived from fundamental usages and customs of antiquity, particularly as they appeared in medieval England, and from modern judgments of appellate courts recognizing and applying those customs in specific cases. Since thousands of appellate cases are decided each year, the body of common law is enormous, even though most of these cases define no new principles. In preparing current cases, lawyers spend much time and effort searching earlier case records for principles of the common law that might be applicable. Thanks to computer technology, the task is less

stare decisis

The common-law doctrine that binds an inferior (subordinate) court to follow and apply decisions and interpretations of higher courts when similar cases arise. Also called the *doctrine of precedents.*

precedent

A court decision on a question of law that gives authority or direction on a similar question of law in a later case with similar facts. See also "stare decisis."

http://

Read the law review article "Stare Decisis in Historical Perspective: From the Founding Era to the Rehnquist Court" at **http://law.vanderbilt.edu/ lawreview/vol523/lee.pdf** physically laborious today, but the information at the attorney's fingertips is nonetheless overwhelming in volume, let alone complexity. Before they can draft formal opinions or business documents or perform advocacy, lawyers must perform legal research of the applicable common, statutory, and regulatory (administrative agency) law. Lawyers, thus, are responsible to their clients more for researching than for knowing the law. For those of you who are interested in learning more about, or in practicing, legal research, we have included a summary of basic steps and included it in Appendix D.

unwritten law

A reference to court- or judge-made law.

Originally the common law of England was called **unwritten law,** because it evolved from judicial decisions that were based on the unwritten customs and usages of the people. Moreover, the decisions and opinions of the judges were not recorded or printed in books; often judges talked with one another, exchanging their rulings through conversation. In contrast, codes and statutes (enacted by the king or a legislative body) were usually written (printed). Today, of course, most additions to the common law, made in appellate court decisions, are published chronologically in books, called **reporters,** and made available on the Internet. Such works are referred to as **case law.** If case law were unwritten, both attorneys as well as the public would be unaware of decisions that had been made and of the appellate courts' rationale for those decisions. After centuries of relying on books, many lawyers and others are no longer using books as the primary way of finding information about cases. Instead, database services and Web sites provide much of the recorded case information. The two most important legal database services providing recorded appellate court cases are Westlaw and LexisNexis.

reporter

A set of books that contain the written opinions of justices of specified appellate courts. These volumes contain the decisional, or unwritten, law. Volumes in the reporters and the cases they contain are arranged in chronological order and accessible by case name or subject matter index.

The application of the doctrine of *stare decisis* is a challenging process. For example, is a new fact situation the same as the suggested precedent, is it similar, or is it different? The adversary system allows each side a representative who argues what events occurred, what precedent should apply, and how it should apply. And what about the situation where the facts are clear, the law is clear, and the result is absurd? What precedents apply? Is the court bound to come to an unjust decision or is a decision based on settled law ever unjust?

In the search for precedent, the following possibilities exist.

case law

All reported judicial decisions; the law that comes from judges' opinions in lawsuits. Also referred to as court law, judge law, and sometimes common law.

1. The new case is identical or virtually identical to a case previously decided by a high court in the same court system. Result: Follow old decision; situation is often called a goose case or a case on all fours. This is seen as binding precedent.

2. The new case is somewhat different from a case previously decided by a high court in the same court system, but the underlying policy and rationale for the old case also applies to the new one. Result: Reason from the old case and extend the previous holding to the new facts. This is known as using precedent to extend the rule of law to new situations.

3. The new case, although having some similarity to a case previously decided case by a high court in the same court system, is not the same and the underlying rationale does not make sense in this case. Result: Distinguish new case from old case and limit the rule from the old case. This is known as using cases to limit the application of judicial doctrine.

4. The new case is identical or virtually identical to a case previously decided by a high court in the same court system but the underlying rule no longer makes sense. Result: Overrule previous precedent when strong reasons exist for doing so. This is not done often but it is consistent with the doctrine of *stare decisis.*

5. The new case presents problems that are not covered by an existing rule from a high court in the same court system. Result: Possibilities (a) case will be dismissed and facts not considered because there is not a remedy in law for every perceived wrong; (b) case will be heard and decided based upon extensions of doctrines of justice and fair-

ness, and new law and rule will be developed. The deciding court may consider precedent from other states, the federal system, or even other countries when seeking guidance as to an appropriate rule to resolve the controversy.

Ⓜ ODERN SOURCES OF U.S. LAW

Ours is a constitutional form of government. In one sense, our Constitution is the ultimate source of our laws because it contains principles by which our nation is governed. Here we are concerned with those institutions of government that create the laws of our land.

Most educated adults are familiar with the basic structure of our federal government, divided by our Constitution into the legislative, executive, and judicial branches. Knowledge of this structure facilitates an understanding of how and where our laws are made and of how they are classified for clarity and comprehensibility. State and local governments also are structured into these three branches, and they operate in a manner similar to the federal system. We explore government and these branches in greater detail in Chapters 2 and 5. Here we briefly consider the sources of our laws.

LAWMAKING BY LEGISLATORS

Legislators, both state and federal, enact laws called **statutes.*** Local legislative bodies (e.g., for cities and counties) enact laws called **ordinances.** Collectively these statutes and ordinances are called the **written law,** as contrasted to case law (unwritten law). Compilations of statutes by topic are called **codes.** For example, a state legislature may enact a statute lengthening the previous jail sentence for the crime of making an obscene telephone call. This statute will be compiled with, indexed to, and become a part of the state's "criminal" or "penal" code. There are numerous specialized codes in the states that group together statutes pertaining to particular subjects, such as the Vehicle Code, Health and Welfare Code, Corporations Code, and Business and Professions Code. These codes (often with slightly different titles) are generally available in any public law library, usually located in county courthouses.

Statutory law covers a staggering number of subjects, such as crimes, civil rights, housing, health, and indeed all matters that the legislative branch has the constitutional power to legislate upon. But it is important to understand that federal statutory law is limited to matters of federal jurisdiction.† The term *jurisdiction* refers to the power or authority the federal government is given to enact statutes under the U.S. Constitution. State statutory law is limited to matters of statewide authority; a similar limitation is true for local ordinances.

Some difficult conflicts over jurisdiction have occurred. The language in which Article I, Section 8 of the U.S. Constitution enumerates the federal government's areas of jurisdiction is open to interpretation. Some believe that the courts have interpreted it too expansively, letting the federal government intrude on states' rights. Others argue that the federal reach should be extended even further, perhaps into such matters as shelter for the homeless. (We consider constitutional law in greater detail in Chapter 2.) When conflicts

statutes

Laws enacted by Congress or by state legislatures.

ordinance

A written law enacted by a city or county. An example is a zoning ordinance that governs the use of land.

written law

The statutes and ordinances of federal, state, and local governments, and the published rules of administrative agencies.

codes

Compilations of statutes that are grouped together by subject matter, e.g., a vehicle code.

http://

For online access to the federal codes, go to the Legal Information Institute at Cornell Law School:
http://www4.law.cornell .edu/uscode/

---

* Often statutes are assigned titles, such as the Federal Racketeer Influence and Corrupt Organizations Act, called RICO.
† *Jurisdiction* refers to the subject matter for which Congress or state legislatures are empowered to enact laws. For example, Congress has jurisdiction to regulate the transportation of goods in interstate commerce; state legislatures do not. Court jurisdiction is explained fully in Chapter 3.

arise between federal and state jurisdictions, the U.S. Supreme Court makes the ultimate judicial decision through its interpretation and application of the Constitution.

Even when jurisdictions overlap—that is, when both the states and the federal government have jurisdiction—conflicts arise. The two may pass contradictory statutes. When that happens, the **doctrine of supremacy** applies, and the federal law prevails.*

doctrine of supremacy

The constitutional doctrine that applies whenever the United States and a state or local government enact conflicting laws on the same subject. Under this constitutional doctrine, the federal law prevails.

LEGAL FOCUS—PROBLEM

Amtrak, and all of its predecessors, historically has dumped raw sewage from passenger-train bathrooms directly onto the railroad tracks and roadbeds. Permission for this practice dates back to early federal laws designed to encourage railroad construction. In 1989, Florida initiated a criminal nuisance charge against Amtrak, contending it dumped sewage on fishermen while they were sitting in a boat under a railroad trestle. In retaliation for the suit, Amtrak threatened to discontinue rail service to Florida. Does the doctrine of supremacy apply?

Faced with the doctrine of supremacy, the state yielded.[18] Similar jurisdictional conflicts exist between state and local governments. For example, local governments usually exercise exclusive jurisdiction over the zoning of real estate. Zoning laws restrict how land may be used. What if a state enacted a statute that authorized state officials to rezone real estate, regardless of local government rules? Does that differ from the common practice whereby state laws require suburban communities to accept construction of prisons and of treatment centers for drug addicts? Local ordinances may reflect NIMBY ("not in my back yard") attitudes of neighborhoods, but just as state law bows to federal law, local law bows to state statutes.

Although proposed statutes are studied before their enactment, and although the end sought is usually desirable and even necessary in the minds of proponents, the validity of a statute or ordinance still remains in doubt until it is challenged by some injured party and an appropriate court determines its validity. There is a presumption that a newly enacted statute or ordinance is constitutional, and courts hold few invalid. Nonetheless, a person could be sentenced to jail for violation of a statute that later is determined to be unconstitutional and therefore void.

The question of the validity of a statute can be very complex. Is a statute or ordinance that prohibits sleeping overnight in a public place constitutional? What if its stated purpose is to maintain sanitary and safe public sidewalks and parks? But what if its true purpose is to drive homeless people out of the inner cities? Is the legal effect of the statute more or less important than its stated purpose? Sometimes the enactment of statutes that will pass constitutional muster is challenging.

case or controversy

A requirement that courts may decide only cases in which an actual conflict between persons exists.

Once the legislative branch enacts a law, uncertainty technically remains until the law is applied, then challenged in a trial, and finally judicially approved as constitutional. A court will not rule on the constitutionality of a statute or ordinance unless someone affected by its application files suit, because courts do not render decisions based on hypothetical conflicts. There must be a **case or controversy,** properly presented to a court, before judicial action will be taken.[19]

---

* Article IV: "This Constitution, and the Laws of the United States which shall be made in Pursuance thereof; and all treaties made, or which shall be made, under the Authority of the United States, shall be the supreme Law of the Land; and the Judges in every State shall be bound thereby, any Thing in the Constitution or Laws of any State to the Contrary notwithstanding."

LAWMAKING BY THE EXECUTIVE BRANCH

The executive branch of government, at the federal, state, and local levels, collaborates with the legislative branch in the adoption of statutes. However, even if the president of the United States (or a state governor), as head of the executive branch, vetoes a proposed statute, the legislators have the power to override such action, usually with a two-thirds vote. This partnership in lawmaking is part of our system of checks and balances that encourages negotiation and compromise. The executive branch can also independently make certain laws. The president, state governors, and heads of local governments all have authority to issue certain directives that have the force and effect of law.*

The president is also authorized under both the Constitution and statutes of the United States to issue executive orders consistent with legal responsibilities of the office. An example is the executive order issued on October 8, 2001, establishing the new governmental agency, the Office of Homeland Security.

> *By the authority vested in me as President by the Constitution and the laws of the United States of America, it is hereby ordered as follows:*
>
> *Section 1. Establishment. I hereby establish within the Executive Office of the President an Office of Homeland Security (the "Office") to be headed by the Assistant to the President for Homeland Security.*
>
> *Sec. 2. Mission. The mission of the Office shall be to develop and coordinate the implementation of a comprehensive national strategy to secure the United States from terrorist threats or attacks. The Office shall perform the functions necessary to carry out this mission, including the functions specified in section 3 of this order.*

Often having greater impact on day-to-day life is the lawmaking power of other federal, state, and local administrative agencies, which are specialized bodies created by Congress and by legislation at the state and local levels to regulate specific activities. Administrative agencies investigate problems within their respective jurisdictions (an executive function), make laws called rules and regulations (a legislative function), and conduct hearings (similar to court trials) to determine if their rules have been violated and, if so, what penalties should be imposed (a judicial function). There are many important federal administrative agencies, numerous state agencies in each state, and a lesser number of agencies within each sizable local government.

You have probably read or heard about such prominent federal administrative agencies as the Central Intelligence Agency (CIA), Drug Enforcement Administration (DEA), Environmental Protection Agency (EPA), Food and Drug Administration (FDA), and the National Institute of Standards and Technology (NIST). Thousands of federal, state, and local administrative agencies continue to make and enforce innumerable laws each year on myriad subjects. You will learn more about lawmaking by administrative agencies in Chapter 5.

LAWMAKING BY COURTS

Federal and state judges preside over trials to settle controversies that are brought before them by parties to legal disputes. At the conclusion of each trial, the judge renders judgment in favor of one or the other of the litigants. Sometimes these judgments are based on a jury

http://
You can find presidential executive orders in the Federal Register at
http://www.archives.gov/federal_register/

http://
The full text of the executive order establishing the office of Homeland Security can be found at
http://www.whitehouse.gov/news/releases/2001/10/20011008-2.html

* For example, in 1986 then-President Ronald Reagan ordered the random drug testing of certain employees working in interstate transportation. The subject of drug testing in other workplaces, and even in competitive sporting events, continues as an important issue.

verdict. When there is no jury, the judgment is based on the trial court judge's evaluation of the evidence and his or her application of the law to the facts as found. Most of these judgments are never appealed. They resolve specific controversies and, to that extent, usually apply existing law. Occasionally, however, if the case is the first of its kind in that jurisdiction, the trial judge may formulate and apply a new rule of common law. An appellate court may then review such a rule. All other trial courts in that jurisdiction then would follow the appellate court's decision.

Usually when judgments are appealed to appellate courts, the essential question on appeal is whether or not the trial court judge made a prejudicial error. Error exists when a trial court judge misapplies the law in the conduct of the trial. For example, a trial judge may have erred by permitting the jury to consider irrelevant evidence. Not all errors of trial courts taint the outcome of the trial: only those that reasonably could have affected the outcome of the trial are prejudicial. Much irrelevant testimony is not prejudicial because it could not reasonably have affected the jury's verdict.

When error is claimed and an appeal is taken, the appellate court may affirm the lower court's decision, reverse it, send it back for a new trial (remand), or simply modify the trial court judgment in some manner. Whichever result is appropriate, the appellate court writes and usually publishes* a written opinion that typically (1) describes the nature of the controversy, (2) states what result was reached in the lower court, (3) reveals the basis upon which the appellant is appealing, and (4) declares and elaborates on its own decision, or "holding." In its decision, the court states the applicable rules of law as well as the rationale underlying its decision.

In making rulings, appellate courts interpret and apply relevant statutory law together with appropriate rules of common law derived from prior cases under the previously discussed doctrine of *stare decisis*. If there is no controlling statute or principle of common law, which occasionally happens, the appellate court will create a new rule or extend an existing principle and apply it to the case. That new concept becomes a part of the continually evolving common law to be followed by other courts in future cases. Thus, new law is created.

Judges who purposefully expand on the law in their decisions are often referred to as **judicial activists.** Judges who narrowly interpret the law by relying heavily on the doctrine of *stare decisis* are often referred to as **strict constructionists.** Either way, the interpretations of law set forth by judges constitute "judge-made" law, or common law. Courts are reactive institutions; judges must wait for litigation to reach them before they can render a decision. Legislative bodies, on the other hand, can initiate new laws on any subject at any time they choose. Nonetheless, the judicial system has been responsible for many of the great social changes that have occurred in the United States. The following quote from political scientist Dennis D. Dorin is an enlightening remembrance that labels used by others are not necessary subscribed to by those who are so labeled.

> *I have interviewed fourteen United States Supreme Court Justices, on a spectrum ranging from "liberal" ones like Warren, Black and Douglas to "conservative" ones like Scalia and Thomas. Not one of them, I can report, has ever told me that he or she is an "activist." Not one has ever said that he or she is willing to violate the Constitution.*[20]

---

judicial activists

Judges whose judicial philosophy includes treating the law as a vibrant and active source of rules. When faced with new issues (e.g., social), such judges are likely to see the Constitution as a flexible document and *stare decisis* as challengeable when they believe important social needs must be addressed.

strict constructionists

Judges whose reading of the law narrowly interprets legal words and who subscribe to interpreting the law consistent with the believed meaning given it by the drafters.

---

* Often an appellate court rules that its decision in a particular case on appeal is not of significance generally, and orders that it remain "unpublished." Such appellate court opinions are not valid precedents and are not printed in the books, called reporters, that contain published appellate court decisions. Modern legal databases now deliver these unpublished cases. They are distinguished from reported cases by their headings, which say "unpublished," and their citations. If one is not careful, one might argue that a case is precedent only to find out it was "unpublished" and cannot be used as precedent.

[handwritten margin note: appeals—based on error of law — not error of fact!]

Not all the language used by appellate courts in their written opinions becomes part of the common law. Much of it is explanatory, analyzing the facts of the case and elaborating on various legal principles that may or may not directly apply. Legal issues addressed in the opinion that are not logically necessary to support the ruling in the case are called *dicta* (Latin: "remarks"). Being unnecessary language, *dicta* do not become part of the common law, although they may provide clues about how that judge's philosophy might be applied in future cases.

Sometimes it is quite clear which statutory language or principle of common law is applicable to a case. But the issue of how it should be applied to the specific facts may be quite complex. For example, in a murder trial there may be no disagreement about the applicability of a statute declaring that an unlawful killing with malice aforethought is murder. But the question of whether or not the particular defendant, who was severely impaired by illegal drugs at the time of the crime, can be legally capable of harboring "malice" (a state of mind prompting one to willfully kill the victim) may be open to argument. Following the trial (in which the trial court judge will have ruled one way or the other on the applicability of the issue), opposing appellate attorneys persuasively argue in favor of their contradictory positions when presenting their appeals to the court in written briefs and with oral arguments. Ultimately, an appellate court will decide the legal controversy and a precedent may be set.

Through this decisional process, both federal and state appellate judges are making new law on a daily basis. With judges throughout the country "making law," can we expect decisions to be consistent?

> [C]ritical legal scholars—or simply "crits"— . . . contend that decisions conflict with one another because they are based on different, and controversial, moral and political ideals. Lawyers cannot give a simple answer to a question, the crits say, because the legal system, like our society at large, cannot reconcile the contradictory instincts people feel when they confront social problems.[21]

Does this mean the rule of law is flexible, depending on who is declaring it? If so, does that give added significance to the political appointment process underlying the selection of judges?

To assist you in understanding the way our appellate courts make and apply the law, an edited appellate case is presented at the end of every chapter.

LAWMAKING BY THE PEOPLE

Many states have provisions in their constitutions that authorize citizens to place proposed new laws on ballots for direct vote by the people. These **initiatives** have resulted in laws approved by voters who had been disappointed by the inaction of their legislatures. To qualify proposed new initiatives for the ballot, proponents must obtain the signature of a specified number of registered voters. Many of the most widely publicized initiatives in recent times have occurred in California. Proposition 209 dismantled affirmative action programs in public employment, education, and contracting. Like statutes, initiatives must pass the test of constitutionality as determined by courts. In 1996, California voters approved an initiative to legalize the possession and use of marijuana for medicinal purposes. A federal court promptly invalidated the law based upon the supremacy clause of the U.S. Constitution—federal laws that criminalize the use of marijuana control.[22] You will learn more about the initiative process in Chapter 2.

initiative

An electoral process for making new statutes or changing the constitution by filing appropriate formal petitions to be voted upon by legislature (and governor) or by the total electorate. The initiative is not available in all states.

TYPES AND CLASSIFICATIONS OF LAW

We have briefly considered the historical sources of our contemporary law. We have also identified people and institutions that continually make and update our laws to help manage our highly complex modern society. We now turn to some definitions and classifications of U.S. law that will enhance your appreciation of its pervasiveness.

FEDERAL AND STATE LAW

We have already distinguished between common law and statutory law. Federal law consists of the U.S. Constitution, statutes enacted by Congress, treaties and presidential orders, rules promulgated by federal agencies, and decisions of federal appellate courts. State law consists of state constitutions, statutes enacted by state legislatures, rules promulgated by state agencies, and the decisions of state courts.

LEGAL FOCUS—PROBLEM

Every time you view a Web site, its contents already have been copied and stored in the random access memory (RAM) of your computer. What law would you consult to determine whether this copying is an infringement of the author's copyright protection?[23]

Copyright protection is granted to the authors of literary works by federal statutory law and federal courts have interpreted it. Thus, the question must be answered by reference to federal law.

LEGAL FOCUS—PROBLEM

Richard Perkins, a firefighter, demands financial compensation from a fertility clinic for impregnating his former wife by using frozen embryos that previously had been fertilized with his sperm. What law should he consult to determine if he can recover damages for child support and emotional distress?[24]

Liability for wrongful birth, or negligence in handling fertilized embryos, is a subject governed by state statutory and case law. This question must be answered by reference to state law.

CIVIL AND CRIMINAL LAW

Civil law is the body of law, both federal and state, that pertains to civil or private rights enforced by civil actions. For example, the laws governing contracts are civil laws. Breach of a contract may result in a civil action for money damages to reimburse the person wronged for any financial loss suffered. **Criminal law,** as contrasted to civil law, is the body of statutory law, both federal and state, that declares what conduct is criminal and prescribes penalties for its commission. For example, a statute may define murder as an unlawful killing with malice aforethought. The precise definition of "malice afore-

civil law

The branch of law dealing with civil rights and civil duties and their enforcement. Civil law also refers to the total system of law, embracing civil and criminal matters, that was used in the ancient Roman Empire and copied on the continent of Europe in modern times. In ancient times the law was defined by experts and imposed from above by the emperor. Roman civil law is contrasted to English *common law.*

criminal law

The branch of law dealing with crimes and their punishment.

thought" changes through interpretation by courts over the years, and thus courts have the continuing task of defining what conduct is criminal.

LEGAL FOCUS—PROBLEM

David Cash, Jr., entered a restroom in a gambling casino in Las Vegas a few minutes after his friend Jeremy Strohmeyer. Cash looked over a stall and saw Strohmeyer with his hand over a small girl's mouth. After telling Strohmeyer to let her go, Cash left and did not report the incident. Strohmeyer later pled guilty to rape and murder of the child and was sentenced to life in prison. Was Cash guilty of any civil or criminal offense?[25]

Like many states, Nevada did not have a statute that criminalized the failure to report a crime in progress. Thus, Cash was not guilty of any state crime. Crimes between private persons generally do not raise questions of federal law, and Cash is not guilty of any federal crime in this case. Under the common law there generally is no duty to protect strangers, and thus Cash probably is not liable for damages to the victim's parents for his conduct under the civil law of Nevada.* The law does not always criminalize immoral acts.[26]

It is common for one act or a series of acts by a person to result in both criminal and civil penalties.

LEGAL FOCUS—PROBLEM

O.J. Simpson was acquitted by jury of the crime of murdering both his former wife Nicole and Ron Goldman, a rescuer acting as a Good Samaritan. Thereafter, Simpson was sued in a civil court for the wrongful death of the victims. In the civil proceeding, the jury found Simpson responsible for the killings and liable for monetary damages. Do all criminal acts also result in civil liability for monetary damages?

No. For example, the crime of firing a handgun into the air within city limits may not injure any human, and there would be no victim to pursue a civil case. But most crimes do create victims who then are able to pursue separate civil remedies, as in the Simpson case.

The statutory law of individual states concerning crimes is collected in books often called Penal Codes. Civil laws, in general, are collected in books often called Civil Codes. You will learn about the very important differences between civil and criminal laws and trials in several future chapters.

PRIVATE AND PUBLIC LAW

Private law is the body of law regulating the rights and duties that exist between private persons ("persons" being a term that includes corporations). Contract law is an example of private law. **Public law,** on the other hand, includes constitutional, administrative, criminal,

private law

That body of law regulating the rights and duties that exist between private persons (including private corporations). Contract law is an example of private law.

public law

That body of law directly concerned with public rights and obligations, such as constitutional, administrative, criminal, and international law.

---

* Many members of the public were outraged at what they believed to be a serious moral offense by David Cash. Protesters marched at the University of California, Berkeley, where Cash studied nuclear engineering, and demanded his expulsion from the public university. The University of California student senate held a hearing and voted narrowly (10–9) to condemn Cash. The student body president vetoed the measure.

and international law, all of which are more directly concerned with public rights and obligations. Criminal law is of public concern because the next victim may be you or any other member of society. Administrative law, as will be seen in Chapter 5, protects consumers and the public from abuses by private businesses. It also protects the environment.

LEGAL FOCUS—PROBLEM

Many contend that jet skis are too noisy, leak oil and gas directly into the water, pose safety risks to bystanders, and damage natural resources. Some contend that all craft using outboard motors on America's waterways are equally offensive. Can the National Park Service (a federal administrative agency) adopt a rule with the force of law that bans the use of jet skis?[27]

Yes. Jet skis are banned at certain lakes and waterways that have been determined by the Park Service to be inappropriate for such use. Administrative agencies, such as the Park Service, continually assess the need for new regulations and create appropriate rules as required. These rules are examples of the public law of the land.

INTERNATIONAL AND DOMESTIC LAW

international law

The branch of law governing relations between and among sovereign nations.

Law that concerns relations among sovereign nations is called **international law.** Reliance upon some form of international law dates to the Roman Empire or before and is typically based on custom. The precedents relied upon in international law are the acts of independent governments in their relations with one another, including treaties. When treaties or conventions (agreements between nations such as the Geneva Convention concerning human rights) exist, they contain a procedural machinery to enforce their terms.

LEGAL FOCUS—EXAMPLE

A United States EA-6B Marine jet, practicing low-level flying, hit and severed a ski gondola cable in the Italian Alps. Twenty people were killed. The United States claimed exclusive jurisdiction of the case under the North Atlantic Treaty Organization (NATO), an international mutual defense pact. Italy, spurred by the victims' families, claimed the jet had violated NATO's mandated flight patterns and it therefore did not apply. Trial and punishment therefore should take place in Italy. However, an Italian judge threw the Italian manslaughter case out of court, ruling that there was no domestic jurisdiction because of NATO. Thus the Marine pilot, Captain Richard J. Ashby, was returned to the United States for military trial (called court-martial) where a jury of eight Marine officers acquitted him of all charges on March 4, 1999.[28]

Certain rules and principles are acknowledged in international relations. These understood rules pertain to such matters as territorial boundaries, use of the high seas, limitations on war, telecommunications, diplomatic and consular exchange, and the use of air space. The difficulty is that sovereign nations, by definition, exercise exclusive power or government within their boundaries and may or may not comply with these understood rules.

The United Nations (UN) is the primary mechanism that creates international law. It brings diplomacy, negotiation, and even propaganda to bear on world affairs. Through agreements, even military observers and peacekeepers can be organized. In 1995, the UN established an International War Crimes Tribunal to prosecute persons accused of war crimes in the Bosnian war. All members of the UN comply with arrest warrants issued by the Tribunal. Many accused persons have been arrested; others are in hiding. Thus, criminal law also can be and is a matter of international law.

Our legal system may be expected to face global problems differently than in the past, when the disputes of nations were resolved through negotiations, the United Nations, or war. During World War II, Japanese-Americans were interred because of unfounded fears of espionage and disloyalty, presenting domestic constitutional issues. In the twenty-first century, we are faced with the reality that the nature of war has changed. New electronically guided long-range missiles, so-called "Star Wars" weapons, are becoming increasingly threatening. Nuclear proliferation remains a serious challenge to international security. Moreover, weaponry now available in world markets can easily deliver genetically engineered toxins, diseases, and poisons over a wide area, resulting in the possible relaxation of domestic constitutional law, sacrificing the rights of individuals in the interest of general safety. Wars may be less likely to involve countries than to involve unidentified groups of people who, through acts of terrorism, fight for the political, financial, and religious issues they support. Thus, public security measures may involve restrictions on individual liberty by construction of fences or walls with temporary or permanent exclusion of citizens from public places. Electronic eavesdropping, by court authorization, already is being dramatically increased because it is an effective weapon against terrorists and criminals. Airport security continues to increase—and passengers are subject to warrantless searches. Many searches are based on stereotypes of personal appearances and behavior. Freedom of speech notwithstanding, jokingly mentioning a bomb while on or near an airplane is a criminal offense. Thus, international dangers affect both international and domestic law.

PROCEDURAL AND SUBSTANTIVE LAW

Procedural law consists of all the rules, or mechanisms, for processing civil and criminal cases through the federal and state judicial systems. Some cynics call it "lawyers' law" since its complexities and technicalities provide employment for attorneys.

Procedural law, in its pre-trial aspects, may dictate the dates and time limits within which papers must be filed, the size of paper to be used by attorneys, the size of print to be used, the fees that must be paid for the various documents upon filing them with the court, what information must be contained in legal papers, how witnesses and parties can be orally examined before trial, when and where the trial shall be held, what witnesses may be called, what issues may be presented to the trial court, and so on.

In its trial aspects, procedural law dictates how the jury may be selected, where the parties may sit in the courtroom and even if they may stand, what evidence may be offered to the jury, what questions may be asked of witnesses, and so on.

It is noteworthy that a separate body of procedural law governs the mechanics of processing appeals, and procedural law for civil cases differs from that for criminal cases. In short, the procedural law is as complex as it is vast, and cases that might have been won on their merits have been lost because of faulty lawyering with the applicable procedural law. A frequent type of attorney malpractice (professional negligence) involves procedural law mistakes, such as missing a critical deadline. If an attorney fails to comply with the civil procedural law, the court may, as a penalty, dismiss the case, with the result that the

procedural law

General principles and detailed rules that define the methods of administering substantive law.

attorney's client loses. If a prosecutor fails to comply with the criminal procedural law, the court may dismiss the case and set the defendant free. Some of you may already have experienced this happy event when you went to court to challenge a citation for a traffic infraction. Because the citing officer was too busy with other duties and did not appear to testify, your case was dismissed.

Procedural law is so important that it receives basic constitutional protection in the Sixth Amendment to the U.S. Constitution (made applicable to the states by the Fourteenth Amendment, as explained in Chapter 2). The Sixth Amendment, as interpreted by the U.S. Supreme Court, requires that the government provide each citizen with procedural due process in criminal proceedings, including the right to have the advice of an attorney even if the accused is indigent, the right to confront accusers in a speedy and public trial by an impartial jury, and the right to be heard and to present a defense.

LEGAL FOCUS—PROBLEM

In 1985, Charles Ng was charged with torturing and murdering a dozen people in a California cabin where they had been kept as sex slaves. Ng fled to Canada, where he was arrested. But Canada refused to return him to California because California has a death penalty. After six years, the Canadian Supreme Court ruled that Ng must be extradited to the United States to stand trial. Meanwhile, the police had inadvertently destroyed some bullets and blood samples needed in the case. One key witness had died. Ng continues to use the procedural laws to challenge every attorney appointed for him and every judge assigned to preside over the trial. The files in the case are reported to weigh about six tons—which hopefully is an exaggeration. On February 24, 1999, he was found guilty of eleven murders and sentenced to death marking commencement of the appeals process. By the time appeals are exhausted, several more years may pass. Has Ng been deprived of his right to a speedy trial?[29]

No. Charles Ng has waived his right to a speedy trial, believing, no doubt, that the passage of time was in his best interest. The public has no constitutional right to a speedy trial of criminal defendants. This case symbolizes a low point in the history of the procedural law.

Clearly the challenge of providing the mechanics for the processing of myriad cases of widely different nature has resulted in a complex body of procedural law. State and federal procedural laws are created by statute and by the courts themselves in publications called rules of court.

substantive law

General principles and detailed rules that define legal rights and duties.

The **substantive law,** as contrasted to the procedural law, defines duties, establishes rights, and prohibits wrongs. The substantive law prohibits murder, requires a real estate agent to be licensed, and imposes speed limits and registration requirements on automobile drivers. Earlier it was observed that in 1998 Nevada had no law criminalizing inaction, and therefore David Cash, Jr., was not guilty of a crime for failing to render assistance to the young girl murdered by Jeremy Strohmeyer. Such conduct is a crime in some states under their criminal substantive laws. The issue of which state's law should apply to Cash, a California resident, and the time limits within which he must be prosecuted, are questions of the procedural law.

SUBJECT MATTER CLASSIFICATION   *Categories of Law*

http://

A useful link site to various classifications of law is at **http://www.pacle.org/typesof.htm**

Law also is often classified on the basis of subject matter. Consider these representative distinct categories of law: corporate, admiralty, business, real estate, intellectual property, family, environmental, constitutional, labor, probate, corporate securities, and immigration. There are dozens of other legal specialties, and the list keeps growing. For example, a recent addition is elder law, pertaining to unique rights and duties of senior citizens.

LEGAL FOCUS—PROBLEM

Sam Kroger, seventy-five years of age and a resident of Sun City, Arizona, uses his golf cart for trips to the store and recreation center. Most residents of this retirement community also rely upon golf carts for transportation. But cars also use the roads and accidents happen. Should Kroger be required by law to equip his golf cart with seat belts, turn signals, a windshield, and mirrors?[30]

Under federal law, Sam Kroger is required to equip his golf cart as indicated. The National Highway Traffic Safety Administration (an administrative agency) has adopted rules to that effect, which some compare to similar state laws requiring motorcycle riders to wear helmets. Is it sufficient that a proposed law will, in all likelihood, protect family members from some perceived harm? Or should the potential good of a proposed law be balanced against its potential intrusiveness? But good, bad, or indifferent, golf carts are motor vehicles and, when on public streets, are subject to regulation like other vehicles.

Lawyers often refer to themselves in terms such as "trial lawyer," "corporate lawyer," "labor lawyer," or "lobbyist."* As noted in Chapter 4, when you need an attorney, you may need a specialist. Most specialists in the law have their own professional organizations, such as Trial Lawyers Associations and the National Academy of Elder Law Attorneys. A licensed attorney may practice in any field of law, but in many states the body regulating lawyers permits only those lawyers who have met certain standards of education and experience to become certified and to advertise themselves as certified specialists in the following fields: criminal law; family law; immigration and nationality law; taxation law; workers' compensation law; and probate, estate planning, and trust law. Other attorneys may practice law in those areas, but they cannot hold themselves out as certified specialists.

THE RELATIONSHIP BETWEEN LAW AND ETHICS

To state the obvious, this textbook is about the law and that is an ambitious undertaking. It is ambitious because law is about almost everything. Most of all, the law is about people and the limitations and protections on and of their choices. But the law is not the sole

---

* Not all lobbyists are lawyers, but as legislators are constantly concerned with the passage of new laws and the amendment or repeal of old laws, lawyers are especially qualified for this endeavor. Oddly enough, if they are hired and paid as legal counsel, they generally need not register as professional lobbyists and are not subject to the rules that require lobbyists to disclose sources and amounts of income received.

source of community standards or even consequences regarding these choices. It is inevitable that the study of law raises questions about the fairness of a rule of law or the lack of a rule in situations where you believe there should be law. These questions often rise from the differences between law and your moral beliefs. Although those who create law strive for fairness and justice, it is not surprising that the goal is not always met. It is thus important to be aware of ethics and morals as a separate but related topic when considering guidelines and restraints upon behavior.

We also hope that your study of law will aid you in decision-making. Is an action legal? What are the legal consequences of stated behaviors? What should you do? Concern about whether a decision is morally or ethically correct should also be an important part of decision-making. Is an action ethically correct? Which choice is the morally correct choice? We thus believe a brief discussion of ethics is worthwhile to aid in developing your decision-making ability. As an educated person you should be prepared to make, articulate, and defend the moral correctness of your decisions. Stating that an action is legally correct is usually not enough. Thus it is helpful to define some terms and provide a few examples of ethical decision-making approaches used to assist people in choosing correct or right action.

Part of one chapter in a book cannot teach a person to be ethical, but a conversation about ethics can

- Identify the nature of ethics
- Provide some useful theories and tools for personal ethical decision-making
- Provide a framework for solving inevitable conflict that results from differing moral standards and application abilities
- Provide information to help one evaluate the professional integrity of advisors and service providers (this discussion is part of Chapter 4)

WHAT ARE ETHICS?

ethics

Standards of fair and honest conduct applied to social behavior.

http://

Read more about the field of ethics at the Internet Encyclopedia of Philosophy:

http://www.utm.edu/ research/iep/e/ethics.htm

The term **ethics** has several common meanings.[31] The first is "the study of the general nature of morals and of the specific moral choices to be made by the individual in relationships with others; the philosophy of morals." This is also called "moral philosophy." A second meaning is "the rules or standards governing the conduct of the member of a profession, e.g., the legal profession."[32] Ethics is about doing the right thing when there is a sacrifice to be made. What we mean by sacrifice is that ethical behavior often entails overriding our self-interest in favor of preserving order in our society.

WHY STUDY ETHICS?

Moral issues feature again and again in the complex problems that we face in the world today. In a global economy with limited resources and unlimited consumer needs we must grapple with issues of equitable distribution of products and services. As e-communications become ubiquitous, we are faced with the challenge of interacting with people far removed from our culture, experience, and accessibility.

The world is changing so rapidly that we measure time in nanoseconds. In the new order of instantaneous exchange, it is critical to develop the ability to identify, articulate, and defend the morality of decisions. It is no longer possible to solve problems in moral isolation. Accordingly, we must develop the ability to reach rational resolutions to problems in a consistent, orderly fashion. Integrity must inform the problem-solving process; consistency must define it.

There are many obstacles to making sound ethical decisions. Faulty reasoning, false premises, hidden values, and double standards threaten the satisfactory conclusion to conflicts both complex and straightforward. Doing the right thing requires the disentanglement of a sometimes-complex web of interrelated values and viewpoints. Recognition and a more than cursory understanding of different theoretical perspectives are essential.

Most of our discussion on ethics will focus on the nature of **morals** and **moral problem solving.** However, one should be aware that the law requires lawyers and judges to obey a code of conduct (**code of ethics**) in addition to, distinct from, and even sometimes at odds with generally applicable standards of conduct. In addition, effective management of one's affairs, both personal and commercial, may require the assistance of other professional advisors such as accountants, insurance agents, and financial planners. As professionals, they too promise to conduct themselves according to a code of professional ethics. All professionals are required to vow to follow the rules of conduct of their respective professions. The discussions of legal ethics in this chapter and in Chapter 4 will serve as a guide to evaluating the professional integrity of the advisors you may hire one day.

The following incident illustrates an important ethical dilemma. We will refer to it in developing the ability to formulate a logical reasoning process for moral problem solving.

LEGAL FOCUS—PROBLEM

A young woman returns from work just after 3:00 a.m. to a typical street in Queens, New York. She parks her car and begins the 100-foot walk to her apartment building. Concerned about a man standing between her path and the apartment building, she changes course and heads in the opposite direction. She was right to be concerned; he grabs her. She screams. No fewer than thirty-eight neighbors turn on their lights and open their windows. Again she screams. "He stabbed me!" "Help!" An observer shouts, "Leave the girl alone," and the attacker walks away. Then the lights all go out and windows are slammed shut. While the victim staggers to reach the nearest apartment building the attacker returns and stabs her again. The victim yells, "I'm dying." The commotion again gets the attention of the apartment dwellers and again the attacker leaves. Again the lights go out and the windows close. The victim crawls toward the apartment house as the attacker returns again one last time to stab and kill her.

During that half hour, Kitty Genovese was stabbed three times. Had a call been made to police after the first attack, perhaps she could have been saved. (Actually, a call was made some thirty minutes after the first attack, but it was too late.[33])

Were there no good people in this Queens neighborhood in 1964? Why didn't anyone call the police or come to the young woman's rescue? Is this incident a demonstration of the sinister side of that New York community's character? Is it a symbol of a neighborhood's collective apathy? One cannot help but wonder what was going on in the minds of the thirty-eight neighbors who watched the attacks. Did they all conclude that no action was appropriate in this instance, and in that neighborhood the right thing to do was not aid someone in distress?

Although the law often provides instructions for community behavior, no New York law required any witness to report the crime to police. No New York law required any bystander to come to the young woman's aid. Absent some relationship with the woman, no one had a legal obligation to save her life. But is there a moral obligation to

morals

Values concerning right and wrong.

moral problem solving

Conflict-resolution process aimed at solving conflicts involving moral dilemmas through communication, education, and negotiation. Broad term describes interrelational rather than individual process.

code of ethics

A systematic statement of agreed-upon moral rules for a profession, business, or group.

http://

A compilation of codes of ethics for health professions can be found at the Amnesty International Web site. Use the search feature and key phrase "code of ethics" at **http://www.web.amnesty .org/**

http://

Read about the killing of
Kitty Genovese at
**http://www.lihistory.com/8/
hs818a.htm**

help an innocent victim? Although this incident occurred many years ago, it continues to be addressed in books, articles, and Web sites. Questions focus on why the neighbors did not act.

For the purposes of this text, the killing of Kitty Genovese provides a real-life situation for learning how to apply different standards of ethical behavior and reason through a moral dilemma.

THE NATURE OF ETHICAL INQUIRY

Ethical inquiry seeks to isolate the collection of moral judgments that society has made to govern behavior and to make moral judgments in daily life, in the political process, and in lawmaking.

The study of ethics is concerned not only with identification of societal values but with thinking logically about ethical challenges and developing practical approaches to moral problem solving. Other disciplines are also concerned with discovering society's moral precepts. For example, sociology and anthropology each study cultural norms.

Ethics departs from the other disciplines because ethics has another dimension. Whereas sociology and anthropology focus on identifying and accounting for societal norms, ethics goes beyond reporting. Ethics is concerned with value identification, moral problem solving, and behavior. Ethics entails action; it is not just a topic to mull or debate.[34] In short, ethics is an applied science.

Whereas anthropology and sociology would ask whether Americans believe abortion is wrong, ethics is concerned with the question itself: Is abortion wrong? Is abortion always wrong? Should abortion be banned? As a technical matter, ethics is prescriptive ("Thou shall not kill"). Anthropology and sociology are descriptive ("There is a low homicide rate in Russia").

THE OBJECT OF ETHICS

moral reasoning

A rational thought process directed at testing whether action is right or wrong. The conclusion is a determination of moral responsibility or culpability.

The object of ethics is to figure out the right thing to do. This entails perceiving ethical distinctions and making difficult ethical choices. Making ethical choices requires clear thinking. Ethicists refer to this thinking process as **moral reasoning.** Ethics is concerned with the ability to discern right and wrong, to separate the ethical questions from the facts, and to scrupulously apply the moral standard to the circumstances. Moral reasoning is a rational approach to moral problem solving and it can be learned.

ETHICAL STANDARDS

Ethics are standards of fair and honest conduct. These standards guide our behavior. They are the indications of what we must do to remain in good standing as members of a group.

Ethical standards are the basis for moral judgment and personal action. They are derived from principles of right and wrong, from religious and philosophical beliefs concerning the nature of good and evil. Courts or legislatures do not create ethical standards; these standards come from life. However, the ability to know right from wrong is not innate; it must be learned.

Our family, teachers, and peers bequeath moral standards to us. They are transferred to us though immersion in society. We perceive values through observation and imitation.

At first, we conform to moral standards because there are consequences: admonishment, punishment, and ridicule. As we mature, we internalize the moral instruction of those around us. As we become more experienced with the consequences of our behavior we decide what to believe in. We adopt some beliefs and reject others. The collection of beliefs we adopt becomes our own personal philosophy.

Ethical standards are often subjective. Since our personal philosophy is based on our unique circumstances and experiences, our ethical standards differ from those of our neighbor in some respects. Of course, universal acceptance of certain standards determines membership in a particular group.

There are ethical schools and resources available for guidance in determining ethical standards. The inquiry into the nature of "the good" is an age-old pursuit. Although there are many ethical schools of thought, our inquiry will be limited to two fundamental approaches. One approach defines ethical behavior as conforming to a set of duties. The other approach determines what is ethical or good by the consequences of any given action. We examine each of these approaches below.

Duty-Based Ethics

LEGAL FOCUS—PROBLEM

Is it wrong to cheat on an examination? Assume that no one will ever know you cheated and that cheating will help you get into a good college. Further assume that you intend to devote yourself after college to the service of others.

This question weighs the "end or consequences" of the action against the "means" used to attain the end. With **duty-based ethics,** if you believe that you have an ethical duty not to cheat or lie, these acts can never be justified by the consequences. This is true even if the consequences are charitable or desirable. In the American culture, the dominant duty-based ethical standards come from religious sources.

duty-based ethics

The doctrine that actions are morally correct if they comply with existing obligations owed another or ourselves.

RELIGIOUS ETHICS   The Western religious tradition—more specifically, the Judeo-Christian religious tradition—is rooted in the belief that certain absolute truths have been revealed through the prophets, the Torah, the Bible, and religious institutions. The "Thou shalt not's" of the Ten Commandments and Christ's instructions to help and care for others ("Love thy neighbor as thyself") are examples. These teachings establish for those who believe in them an absolute ethical duty. It is not the consequences of an act but the nature of the act itself that determines whether it is ethical.

LEGAL FOCUS—EXAMPLE

Leah Jordan decides to rob the rich to help the poor, like the English legend of Robin Hood. She has acted unethically despite her humane motive. She has "sinned" because stealing violates the Seventh Commandment ("Thou shalt not steal").

Religious ethical standards are absolute. When an act is prohibited by religious teachings it is unethical. It should not be done, regardless of the consequences. Telling a lie for the sake of gaining a promotion is unethical—even if no one is harmed by the lie and the liar's future seems more promising.

Religious ethical standards, however, also involve an element of compassion. Therefore, although it might be profitable for a business to fire unproductive employees, those employees or their families may suffer. This potential suffering is given much weight by the decision maker. A compassionate manager or employer might decide to keep the employee. Another way to increase profits might be sought.

The "Golden Rule, ("Do unto others as you would have them do unto you") also expects compassionate treatment of others—to a certain extent. This rule has been adopted in some form by most religions.

KANT AND DUTY-BASED ETHICS   A duty-based approach to ethics not expressly based on religion is characteristic of the philosophy of Immanuel Kant (1724–1804). The philosopher Kant identified some general guiding principles of moral behavior. Kant believed in the fundamental worth of human beings. He believed that each person was endowed with moral integrity and the capacity to reason and conduct their affairs rationally without resort to religious precept.

Kantian ethical reasoning gives philosophical weight to the Golden Rule. But the Golden Rule merely urges us to "do unto to others as we would have them do unto us." Kant's approach forces us to look at the larger picture and asks everyone to treat others as free individuals equal to everyone else. Thus we have the duty to treat everyone with dignity and the right to expect such treatment from others. What would society be like if everybody acted as we did? Would it be positive or negative? Kant's theory forces us to look at and evaluate, from an objective point of view, social goals as well as our personal desires and welfare when considering our behavior.

The central premise in Kantian ethics is that the morality of conduct depends on the guiding principle, not on the result or consequences of the conduct. One must follow the guiding principle no matter what the circumstance. Kant called these no-matter-what principles *categorical imperatives*. They are absolute rules.

LEGAL FOCUS—EXAMPLE

You are thinking about whether to cheat on an examination. If you agree with Kant's categorical imperative, you will decide not to cheat. If everyone cheats, an examination is meaningless. Similarly, you would not cut in line to purchase a ticket for a music concert. If everyone else cut in line, the line would disappear and chaos would result.

The strength of Kant's duty theory lies in its simplicity. The Kantian model is easily applied. Determining the absolute rule and applying it to the real-world situation is all that is required to identify ethical conduct. Predictions about how others will be affected by one's actions are not necessary although consequences do play an important role in defining the nature of conduct and formulating the categorical rule. Conduct is evaluated based on an unyielding rule: Either the rule was followed or it was not. The effect of conduct is not determinative when evaluating the moral correctness of a specific action.

PROBLEMS WITH DUTY-BASED ETHICS   The efficacy of duty-based ethics is also its major shortcoming. Duty-based theory does not give clear guidance on resolving complex ethical dilemmas. Ethical decision-making may involve fulfilling not just one ethical responsibility but several. When one ethical duty conflicts with another, you have to decide which is the most fundamental and act accordingly. Duty-based ethics provides no mechanism for prioritizing conflicting duties.

http://

The principle of the Golden Rule appears in many of the world's religions. See

http://www.fragrant.demon .co.uk/golden.html

http://

Read more about Immanuel Kant and his ethical theory at the Internet Encyclopedia of Philosophy at:

http://www.utm.edu/ research/iep/k/kantmeta .htm

Duty-based ethics has other problems. There can be disagreements about which duties exist. Different religions, while often agreeing on many things, disagree fundamentally on others. Kant's formulae are not very precise. Are there limits to obligations? If so, what are those limits? Is it morally correct to kill in order to survive? Sometimes, applying religious or Kantian ethics is difficult.

LEGAL FOCUS—PROBLEM

A business executive negotiating with another firm's representatives may feel it necessary to stretch the truth or hold back information. The reason may be to get the best deal for the executive's employer. Is this a violation of the religious teaching that one should not lie or of Kant's categorical imperative?

Yes, it is probably unethical in both religious and Kantian terms. Remember, however, that the executive also owes an ethical duty to his or her employer to make decisions that are profitable. Assume that the executive knows that, unless the deal is made, the employer will have to lay off several long-time employees. These employees depend on the firm for food on their table. Is "stretching the truth" consistent with the religious ethical duty to be compassionate toward others? Is it consistent with the Kantian imperative to act only as we would have all others act?

The executive may conclude that the ethical duty to be fully honest is more fundamental than the duty owed the business. This decision may include a personal cost, such as the loss of a raise, which may affect the executive's family. Alternatively, the executive might decide that the ethical duty owed to the business and its employees is the more fundamental one. The example illustrates that often ethical decisions are not clear-cut. Decisions involve choices, not between good and bad alternatives but between good and less good alternatives.

Utilitarianism

"Thou shalt act so as to generate the greatest good for the greatest number." This is a paraphrase of the major premise of **utilitarianism.** This philosophical theory was first developed by Jeremy Bentham (1748–1832). In contrast to duty-based moral theory, utilitarianism is outcome oriented. It focuses on the consequences of an action. It does not focus on the nature of the action itself, or on any set of pre-established moral values or religious beliefs.

RIGHT AND WRONG IN UTILITARIANISM   Under a utilitarian model of ethics, an action is morally correct or right when, among people it affects, it produces the greatest amount of good for the greatest number. When an action affects the majority adversely, it is morally wrong. Applying the utilitarian theory thus requires (1) a determination of the alternate actions available in a given situation, (2) a determination of who will be affected by these actions, (3) an assessment, or cost-benefit analysis, of the negative and positive effects of each alternative action on these individuals, and (4) a choice among the alternatives that will produce the maximum societal utility.

The major strength of utilitarian ethics is its flexible application. Duty-based ethics admits no exceptions or justifications for deviation from the moral standard. In contrast, utilitarians reject the notion that certain conduct is *always* right or *always* wrong. For example, utilitarians would deny that stealing is *always* wrong. Utilitarians consider the

utilitarianism

An ethical doctrine holding that determining right conduct is based on consequences; that the purpose of the behavior should be the greatest happiness of the greatest number.

http://

For a list of resources on utilitarianism, see
http://www.utilitarianism .com/

circumstances. A balancing of the harms resulting from unequivocal application of the moral standard is performed. Justifiable deviations are identified. Stealing would be morally acceptable if more good than harm would result from the theft. If a single mother of four, unemployed and starving, stole a loaf of bread from a supermarket, utilitarians would conclude that the theft was justified because five lives would be saved from starvation as weighed against the lost revenue (approximately $2.50) to the supermarket.

Another advantage of utilitarianism over absolutism is that utilitarianism may be applied in situations where moral standards collide. Since the practical application of the absolute duty approach offers no scheme for resolving inevitable conflict among moral standards, the conflict is irresolvable under that model.

In situations that require a choice among competing moral values, the ranking of moral values is predicated on the consequences of alternative actions. The action resulting in the greatest social benefit or the least cost to society is deemed to be the proper course. Where the practical application of duty-based ethics would produce a moral jam, utilitarian application produces a solution, however imperfect.

PROBLEMS WITH UTILITARIANISM   Utilitarianism also suffers from some problems. An accurate calculation of overall welfare, happiness, or utility requires knowledge of what the actual consequences, both negative and positive, of a given decision will be. Rarely, if ever, can all possibilities of a decision be accurately predicted. This is especially true with decisions that affect millions of people.

It is difficult to measure good and bad. What are your values? The cost-benefit method of measuring good and bad still requires the decision maker to assign values to expected outcomes. It isn't easy.

Another problem with utilitarianism is that it usually involves winners and losers. It is sometimes impossible to satisfy everyone with a policy action based on utility.

LEGAL FOCUS—PROBLEM

Tim Johnson, a manufacturer, owns many manufacturing plants. One of the plants is much older than the others. Equipment at the old plant is outdated and inefficient. The costs of production at the plant are twice that of any of Johnson's other plants. The product price cannot be increased because of competition. What should Johnson do about the plant?

In a utilitarian analysis of the problem, the costs of closing the plant, including the financial burden of laid-off employees, is weighed against the benefits of closing the plant. Benefits include the future financial security of the firm and the employees who retain their jobs at the other plants. If Johnson decides the issue from a utilitarianism perspective, he may close the plant. Closing the plant will yield the greatest benefit for the largest number of people. The winners are those helped by the decision. The losers are the workers now unemployed at the old plant.

Utilitarianism is criticized because it is an objective, calculated approach to a problem. It reduces human beings to plus and minus signs on a cost-benefit worksheet. Utilitarian reasoning has also been used to "justify" human costs that many find unacceptable.

The strongest criticism of utilitarian theory is that an end-justifies-the-means maxim supplants the moral code. **Situational ethics** is a term often used disparagingly to describe such reasoning. In other words, ethical principle is minimized in favor of net social gain.

situational ethics

Term used disparagingly to describe an "end justifies the means" maxim supplanting duty or obligation.

LEGAL FOCUS—PROBLEM

Is the execution of an innocent man ever justified? Consider the following hypothetical: An African-American man is convicted of the rape-murder of a white woman in the Deep South. Should the governor commute the sentence of this death row inmate if he is convinced of the man's innocence?

Utilitarians would say no, if allowing the convict to be put to death would prevent a riot by the white community that would likely result in the killing of innocent African-Americans. Here, execution of an innocent man would be justified under utilitarian theory because society's interest in saving more than one life (the predicted killing of innocent African-Americans) trumps the rights of the individual.[35]

There are other theories of moral responsibility, but all of them involve making difficult choices in a world in which information is imperfect. Ethical choices involve choosing between self-interest and perceived ethical obligations.

MORAL REASONING

An important learning objective of this section is to help you develop a framework for moral problem solving. The following discussion will help you organize your thinking about what your personal philosophy is and how to apply it in an orderly fashion to circumstances for which you have little or no experience.

We present a rational approach to evaluating situations, but not the answers. We offer a method, not a conclusion. It is a compass, not a roadmap: not topography, only directions.

Moral reasoning is a process of testing whether a given action is right or wrong. It also determines moral responsibility or culpability. It uses deductive logic. **Deductive logic** is a method of logical reasoning from two or more propositions to a conclusion. Inferences are drawn from a general premise to a specific premise. The argument is sound if the propositions on which the conclusion is based are true and if the inferences are valid.

Deduction may be understood as a pattern or **syllogism.** Syllogisms help to organize thinking so that a valid conclusion is reached. Syllogisms help to identify incorrect premises and flawed thinking. Moral reasoning follows the following pattern:

Proposition One   (general premise)

Proposition Two   (specific, factual or situational premise)

Conclusion   (moral determination)

The general premise is the moral/ethical standard. The situational premise is the conduct ("what happened" or "what contemplated conduct") being scrutinized. The conclusion is the product of applying the ethical standard to the conduct. It is the evaluation as to whether conduct was proper or improper as measured against the moral standard.

Consider the Kitty Genovese case under the utilitarian model and compare it with the Kantian model. Under the utilitarian model, failing to come to the rescue could be morally justified.

General premise   One should come to the rescue of helpless living beings unless doing so would cause greater harm in the community.

---

http://

A Seventh-Day Adventist look at situational ethics:

http://gospel-herald.com/ genesis_studies/ situational_ethics.htm

deductive logic

A method of logical reasoning from two or more propositions to a conclusion. Inferences are drawn from a general premise to a specific premise. The conclusion is valid if the propositions on which the conclusion is based are true.

syllogism

A pattern of deductive logic that contains a major or general premise, a minor or specific premise, and a conclusion, always in that order. The conclusion follows from the premises but is not a premise itself.

Factual premise	Coming to the rescue of a helpless woman (Kitty Genovese) while her vicious attacker was stabbing her would have resulted in a multiple murder—greater harm. [NOTE: Predicting a likely result—a multiple murder—of the asserted failure to act, here a failure to come to the rescue—is necessary to reach a conclusion in utilitarian analysis].
Moral determination	Failing to come to the rescue of Kitty Genovese was morally proper since coming to her aid would have meant more people would have been murdered.

Under duty-based models, failing to come to the rescue of Kitty Genovese is not morally acceptable.

General premise	Moral people must *always* come to the rescue of a helpless living being.
Factual premise	Kitty Genovese was helpless at the hands of her vicious attacker.
Moral determination	Since no one who witnessed the attack of Kitty Genovese, a helpless living being, came to her rescue, no witness acted morally.

Note that the different conclusions under the utilitarian and duty-based models are the result of the variation in the general premise, not a variation in the logical process. The pattern of reasoning remains the same; only the standard changed. To summarize, moral reasoning is a deductive process that follows the same pattern regardless of which ethical standard is applied: Determine the moral standard (General premise). Apply the moral standard to the situation (Factual premise). Decide whether action was right or wrong.

Individuals are not born with the ability to understand and apply moral standards.[36] People need to learn how to translate their personal philosophy into action. It requires inquiry, comparison, and reflection. It takes practice.

There are pitfalls to understanding ethics in general and moral problem solving in particular. Much of the terminology of ethics is used interchangeably. For example, the terms *morals* and *ethics* are often used synonymously. They are distinguishable, however. *Morals* are precepts or values held as beliefs. In contrast, *ethics* are the realization of those beliefs as standards of conduct or as evidenced by an act or failure to act.

Sometimes it is unclear whether one is referring to the moral standard (the rule) or the moral conclusion (the result of applying the standard to the situation). The two are distinct and especially so when one learns how to separate the steps of the moral reasoning process.

For learning purposes, it is critical to watch your language. For clarity, use vocabulary to distinguish conceptually distinct phases of the moral reasoning process and label the component terms carefully. For example, the statement "That's immoral" is an assertion that could mean the behavior is wrong. But, by what standard? It may not be a final conclusion, either. The behavior may be excused or justified.

Translating Moral Philosophy into Action

The process of moral problem solving must be broken down, step by step.

STEP ONE   First, you must break down the moral reasoning process. Separate facts from the moral premise (ethical rule or standard) and the moral premise from the moral judgment (application of the ethical rule). Be aware that moral standards are often implicit. Distinguishing among statements is helpful in separating the standard from the facts of the situation. Some statements are matters of fact. They do not assert a value judgment. Others are value laden.

Statements that reflect no value judgment are objective. They are what is so. These statements are referred to as positive or **non-normative statements.**

Statements that reflect what should be or how one should act are called **normative statements.** They tell what someone deems socially acceptable. The statement is subjective.

Practice in developing the ability to recognize one's own values and those of others begins with distinguishing between normative and non-normative statements. Again, it helps to watch your language and keep phases of the moral reasoning process separate.

Non-Normative Statements
- This legislative session, Congress lowered taxes
- The new state building has more offices than the older one.

Normative Statements
- Lowering taxes is bad because it will fuel inflation.
- Producing oil is more important than protecting the environment.
- It was not necessary to build a new state building.

It is not always easy to recognize the difference between normative and non-normative statements. One clue is that normative statements are asserted in a way that indicates both the conclusion and a justification or reason for the conclusion. The reason could be express or implied.

If we change the statement "Lowering taxes is bad because it will fuel inflation," to simply "Lowering taxes is bad," we are implying that if asked we can provide some justification for the statement.

Non-normative statements are matters of fact. They don't beg for reasons to validate their accuracy.

Another way to tell whether a sentence is normative or non-normative is to ask, "Does it tell how? Why? Why not?" If the statement expressly or impliedly answers the question then it's probably normative.

STEP TWO   Once you have isolated the moral standard, gather all relevant facts—just the facts. What happened? When? Where? Who? Be sure you have enough facts to determine the moral standard. It is critical to be accurate and complete, to use only relevant facts,[37] and to separate the facts from the moral standard.

STEP THREE   Using deductive logic, apply the moral standard to the facts of the situation. The result will be the moral determination.

This three-step process will result in a rational outcome, although it will not resolve all ethical dilemmas. Different people have differing moral philosophies and have varying abilities to solve moral problems. However, this process will help you resolve moral conflicts in a coherent, rational way. Now you are prepared to articulate, defend and negotiate for your moral conclusion. Let the moral-problem-solving process begin.

DISTINGUISHING BETWEEN LAWS AND MORAL VALUES

To answer the question of whether an action is legal does not necessarily answer the question of whether it is ethical. Furthermore, codification of moral standards does not ensure compliance, as our overcrowded prisons and clogged court calendars demonstrate. Not all

non-normative statements

Statements that reflect no value judgment.

normative statements

Statements that reflect what should be or how one should act.

moral standards are formalized or codified. Therefore, discerning between legal duties and moral obligations will simplify the moral-problem-solving process.

Many ethical decisions are made for us by our laws. In most cases law reflects many of a society's ethical values. Virtually all of what you will read in this text involves **positive law**, sometimes called *black-letter law*. Positive law tells individuals which actions are prohibited. The law gives warning that society (through government) will punish the violators. Nonetheless, simply obeying the law does not fulfill all ethical obligations. In the interest of preserving personal freedom, as well as for practical reasons, the law does not—and cannot—make all ethical requirements legal requirements.

In all societies, ethics and the law go hand in hand. Law can never operate in a vacuum. It cannot be a series of rules imposed upon society from outside the society. The law must reflect a society's customs and values. It must enforce principles of behavior that society thinks right and just. Law is thus an expression of the social forces at work in the society of which it is a part.

Criminal responsibility and civil liability imply failure to conform to a standard of conduct. Obviously, criminal responsibility and civil liability are not synonymous, and they are not coextensive with moral accountability. Significantly, moral accountability requires us to go beyond what the law requires.

In addition, the underlying rationale for criminal, civil, and moral standards and the consequences for breaching them vary in important ways.

Criminal responsibility and civil liability are legal terms describing a duty to behave or refrain from conduct the failure of which results in a penalty. Criminal responsibility is concerned with the behavior of the criminal. The penalty for criminal conduct generally involves curtailment of basic civil liberties: loss of life (death sentence), liberty (prison time), and property (fines). Criminal culpability also results in contempt for the wrongdoer. The primary justification for punishing criminals is to vindicate society's norms. Some argue that the purpose of such punishment is deterrence; some call it retribution; some believe the goal is (or should be) rehabilitation.

Civil liability is concerned with the victim. The object of civil liability is to put victims back in the positions they were in before the wrongful act, as nearly as possible. A determination that a person is liable necessitates compensation of the victim, usually in the form of monetary payment. In theory, the law's focus is on paying the victim back rather than on reproving the wrongdoer.

A moral breach may involve contempt, banishment, excommunication, or isolation. It may look and feel like punishment, but it does not entail imposition of penalty by the government.

positive law

The rules members of a society are obliged to obey to avoid punishment or penalty imposed by the government.

Ⓤ SING COURT CASES

Although case law is but one source of American law, it has a special place in the study of law. Court cases are about the actual legal problems of people. Each case is an individual drama, where parties seek help, justice, principles, and power. By reading cases a student can see the legal problems of people and how the law is used to resolve these problems.

At the conclusion of each book chapter we present a case to provide you with a real-life illustration of how courts interpret and apply the law. Other court decisions are referred to in footnotes and endnotes throughout the text, and some of the end-of-chapter problems are based on actual legal disputes. This section offers a brief introduction to case citations, the legal "shorthand" used to identify court cases.

Although the court system is discussed in detail in Chapter 3, repeating one broad distinction we discussed earlier is important. There are two types of courts, trial and appellate. A trial court is where two parties each present their version of the facts of a legal dispute and receive a decision or ruling. Appellate courts exist to review the actions of lower courts (trial or lower appellate courts) and to correct their mistakes of law.

FEDERAL COURT DECISIONS

Federal trial court decisions are published in West's *Federal Supplement* (F.Supp.). Opinions from the circuit courts of appeal are reported in West's *Federal Reporter* (F. or F.2d). Opinions from the United States Supreme Court are reported in West's *Supreme Court Reporter* (S.Ct.), the *United States Reports* (U.S.), the *Lawyers' Edition of the Supreme Court Reports* (L.Ed.), and other publications.

The *United States Reports* is the official edition of all decisions of the United States Supreme Court for which there are written opinions. Published by the federal government, the series includes reports of Supreme Court cases dating from 1791. Sample citations for federal court decisions are listed and explained in Exhibit 1-1.

STATE COURT DECISIONS

Most state trial court decisions are not published. Usually decisions from the state trial courts are filed in the office of the clerk of the court. The court clerk's job includes keeping court records and making the decisions of the court available for public inspection.

Written decisions of the state appellate courts, in contrast, are published and distributed. The reported appellate decisions are published in volumes called *Reports*. They are numbered consecutively.

State court appellate opinions also appear in regional units of the National Reporter System, published by West Publishing Company. Most libraries have the West reporters because they are published quickly and are distributed more widely than the state-published reports. Many states have eliminated their own reporters and use West's National Reporter System. The National Reporter System divides the states into the following geographical areas: Atlantic (A. or A.2d), South Eastern (S.E. or S.E.2d), South Western (S.W. or S.W.2d), North Western (N.W. or N.W.2d), North Eastern (N.E. or N.E.2d), Southern (So. or So.2d), and Pacific (P. or P.2d).

After appellate decisions have been published, they are normally referred to by:
1. The name of the case
2. The volume, name, and page of the state's official reporter (if different from West's National Reporter System)
3. The volume, unit, and page number of the National Reporter
4. The volume, name, and page number of any other selected reporter

citation, legal
Abbreviated reference to a variety of legal authorities including court cases.

This information makes up what is called the **citation.** Citing a reporter by volume number, name, and page number, in that order, is common to all citations.

When more than one reporter is cited for the same case, each reference is called a *parallel citation.* For example, consider the following case: *Quality Motors, Inc. v. Hays,* 216 Ark. 264, 225 S.W.2d 326 (1949). The opinion in this case can be found in volume 216 of the *Arkansas Reports* on page 264. The parallel citation is to volume 225 of the *South Western Reporter,* second series, page 326.

EXHIBIT 1-1: **National Reporter System—State/Federal**

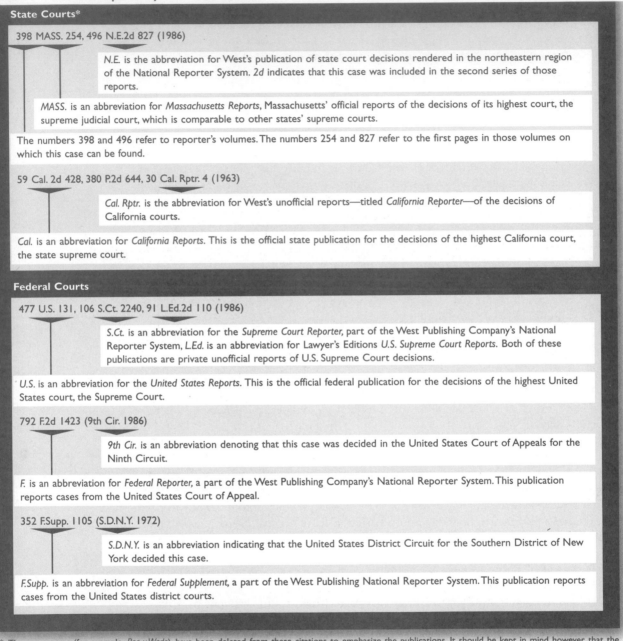

State Courts*

398 MASS. 254, 496 N.E.2d 827 (1986)

N.E. is the abbreviation for West's publication of state court decisions rendered in the northeastern region of the National Reporter System. *2d* indicates that this case was included in the second series of those reports.

MASS. is an abbreviation for *Massachusetts Reports*, Massachusetts' official reports of the decisions of its highest court, the supreme judicial court, which is comparable to other states' supreme courts.

The numbers 398 and 496 refer to reporter's volumes. The numbers 254 and 827 refer to the first pages in those volumes on which this case can be found.

59 Cal. 2d 428, 380 P.2d 644, 30 Cal. Rptr. 4 (1963)

Cal. Rptr. is the abbreviation for West's unofficial reports—titled *California Reporter*—of the decisions of California courts.

Cal. is an abbreviation for *California Reports*. This is the official state publication for the decisions of the highest California court, the state supreme court.

Federal Courts

477 U.S. 131, 106 S.Ct. 2240, 91 L.Ed.2d 110 (1986)

S.Ct. is an abbreviation for the *Supreme Court Reporter*, part of the West Publishing Company's National Reporter System. *L.Ed.* is an abbreviation for Lawyer's Editions *U.S. Supreme Court Reports*. Both of these publications are private unofficial reports of U.S. Supreme Court decisions.

U.S. is an abbreviation for the *United States Reports*. This is the official federal publication for the decisions of the highest United States court, the Supreme Court.

792 F.2d 1423 (9th Cir. 1986)

9th Cir. is an abbreviation denoting that this case was decided in the United States Court of Appeals for the Ninth Circuit.

F. is an abbreviation for *Federal Reporter*, a part of the West Publishing Company's National Reporter System. This publication reports cases from the United States Court of Appeal.

352 F.Supp. 1105 (S.D.N.Y. 1972)

S.D.N.Y. is an abbreviation indicating that the United States District Circuit for the Southern District of New York decided this case.

F.Supp. is an abbreviation for *Federal Supplement*, a part of the West Publishing National Reporter System. This publication reports cases from the United States district courts.

* The case names (for example, *Roe v. Wade*), have been deleted from these citations to emphasize the publications. It should be kept in mind however, that the name of a case is as important as the specific page numbers in the volumes in which it is found. If a citation is incorrect, the correct citation may be found in a publication's index of case names. The date of a case is also important, both to provide a check on error in citations and because a recent case is likely to have more value as an authority than earlier cases.

In cases presented in the text we provide the citation, the name of the court hearing the case, and the year of the court's decision. A few of the states—including those with more than one appellate court, such as California, Illinois, and New York—have more than one reporter for the state court opinions. Sample citations are listed and explained in Exhibit 1-1.

READING COURT CASES

The cases in this text have been reworded and condensed from the full text of the courts' opinions. For those wishing to review court cases for future research projects or to gain additional information, the following sections will help you to read and understand case law.

Case Titles

In the title of a case, such as *Adams v. Jones,* the *v.* or *vs.* stands for versus, which means "against." If the case is at the trial court level, the plaintiff—the person who files the suit—would be the first name mentioned, Adams. The second name, Jones, would be the defendant—the person who is sued. If the case is an appellate court case, however, often the original plaintiff cannot be determined from the case title. Some appellate courts retain the trial court order of names, but many place the name of the party appealing the decision first, so the case might be called *Jones v. Adams.* You must read the facts of each case carefully to identify each party.

Terminology

You will frequently find the following terms and phrases in court opinions and legal publications.

DECISIONS AND OPINIONS   Most appellate or reviewing court decisions are explained in writing. A decision contains the opinion (the court's reasons for its decision), the rules of law that apply, and the judgment. Appellate courts consist of a panel of three or more judges and there are four types of written opinions for cases decided by these appellate courts.

1. When the judges unanimously agree on an opinion, the opinion is written for the entire court and is called a **unanimous opinion.**
2. When the opinion is not unanimous, a **majority opinion** is written. This opinion outlines the views of the majority of the judges deciding the case.
3. Often a judge who feels strongly about making a point that was not made in the unanimous or majority opinion will write a **concurring opinion.** The judge agrees (concurs) with the judgment given in the unanimous or majority opinion, but for different reasons.
4. If the opinion is not unanimous, a **dissenting opinion** may be written by a judge who disagrees with the majority. The dissenting opinion is important because it may form the basis of arguments used years later to overrule the majority opinion.

JUDGES AND JUSTICES   The terms *judge* and *justice* are simply different names given to judges in different courts. All members of the U.S. Supreme Court, for example, are called justices. "Justice" is also the formal title given to judges of appellate courts. In New York, a justice is a judge of the trial court (which is called the supreme court), and a member of the court of appeals (the state's highest court) is called a judge. The term *justice* is commonly abbreviated to J., and *justices* to JJ.

A Supreme Court case might refer to Justice Kennedy as Kennedy, J.; or to Chief Justice Rehnquist as Rehnquist, C. J.

APPELLANTS AND APPELLEES   An **appellant** is a party who appeals a case to another court. An appellant is sometimes called a **petitioner,** usually when the case involves a

---

unanimous opinion

A judicial decision with complete agreement by all judges.

majority opinion

A written opinion by a judge outlining the views of the majority of the judges of the court deciding the case.

concurring opinion

A written opinion wherein a judge agrees (concurs) with the result reached by another judge, but for different reasons from those stated by the other judge.

dissenting opinion

A written opinion by a judge or judges who vote(s) contrary to the majority opinion and holding of the court.

appellant or **petitioner**

The party who appeals to a higher court for review of a lower court ruling.

appellee or
respondent

The party who, on appeal,
defends the earlier court
determination.

matter in equity. An **appellee** is the party against whom an appeal is made. This party is sometimes called the **respondent,** usually when the case involves a matter in equity.

A NOTE ON ABBREVIATIONS   In court opinions, and in other areas of this text, certain words in firm and organization names are abbreviated. Various terms for corporations, *Corporation, Company, Incorporated,* and *Limited,* for example, frequently appear in their abbreviated forms as *Corp., Co., Inc.,* and *Ltd.* Legislation and statutes are often referred to by their initials. To prevent confusion we will give the complete name of each statute when it is first mentioned in the text. We also identify how we will refer to it in the future. For example, the Uniform Commercial Code is commonly referred to as the UCC.

CASE

We provide at least one case at the end of each chapter. We briefly introduce each case but we leave the discussion of the case in the language of the court (although we have edited the court opinion for reasons of space and time). Knowing how to find and read a court opinion is an important step in legal research. A further step involves "briefing" the case to help one understand it. Legal researchers routinely brief cases by summarizing and reducing the opinions to their most important elements. A discussion as to how to brief a case and sample brief of the following case is provided in Appendix A.

ERIC J. V. BETTY M. —1

The Court of Appeals Dist. 4 —2
76 Cal.App. 4th 715, 90 Cal.Rptr.2d 549 (1999) —5

Facts: Robert brought home his new girlfriend, Helen, and her eight-year-old son, Eric, to meet his mother, father, brothers, sister, and their assorted spouses. The relationship between Robert and Helen continued and Helen and Eric were guests several times in various family homes. It was later discovered that Robert had sexually molested Eric during some of these visits at Robert's family's homes and that Robert was on parole for felony child molestation. Robert was convicted of molesting Eric and sent back to prison. Helen filed suit against Robert's family claiming they had a duty to warn her about Robert's criminal past and the potential danger to her child, and having failed that duty they were liable for monetary damages for the harm suffered by Eric. The trial court judge granted the defendant's motion to dismiss the case (nonsuit motion) after the completion of the evidentiary portion of the trial.

Justice Sills delivered the opinion of the court: When Robert was released from prison on rehabilitative parole after having been convicted of felony child molestation four years earlier, his family might have disowned him, but they didn't. They accepted him back. And when he found a girlfriend named Helen—who had an eight-year-old boy named Eric—they did not tell Helen about Robert's previous conviction, no doubt hoping against hope that he had reformed himself.

Unfortunately, and unbeknownst to any members of the family or Helen herself, Robert began molesting Helen's son early on in his relationship with her.

Facts and Litigation Background

In 1978 Robert was arrested for the misdemeanor of "annoying" a minor. He pled no contest and served six months, and was on probation for the next three years. During that time he committed one probation violation for taking four high school freshman boys to dinner without supervision. Again

he served some time in jail and was placed on probation.

Then in 1984 he was arrested for molesting a 10-year old boy. He again pled no contest, this time to a felony count. He served four years in state prison, getting out in August 1988.

In June 1989, Robert met Helen and her eight-year-old son Eric at Magic Mountain. A relationship developed between Robert and Helen, and, by Thanksgiving 1989, Robert invited Helen and Eric for an overnight stay at the home of his mother Dorothy in Big Bear so she and Eric could meet some of the rest of his family. Besides Dorothy, Robert's family consists of his father Edwin, his father's wife Betty, Robert's three brothers Frank, Phillip and Eddie.

The members of Robert's family concluded that Helen was his "girlfriend." Their relationship continued until early 1992, when Robert moved to Las Vegas.

Later that year, one of Helen's friends saw a special on television regarding convicts on parole, which showed a picture of a younger, beardless Robert and revealed that he was a convicted molester. She told Helen about the program, and a few days later, Helen took Eric to a police station. There, Helen learned that Robert had been molesting Eric. In June 1993 Robert was convicted of 23 counts of child molestation. He had never told Helen of his criminal history.

Helen, acting as guardian *ad litem* [Latin: "for purposes of the suit"] for Eric, sued various members of Robert's family. The case came to trial, during which it was learned that on several occasions Eric was molested on property owned by some of Robert's family members.

Each of the relatives had various degrees of knowledge of Robert's history. Father Edwin knew the most. He knew about the 1978 and 1984 convictions. Robert came to live with him and Betty for a short period after Robert's release from prison in 1988, and was visited by a parole officer shortly thereafter; she told Edwin that in her opinion Robert was a "pedophile." The parole officer also told Edwin that Robert had agreed to be put on a state parole rehabilitation program obligating him to report for psychiatric counseling, obtain gainful employment, not be alone with an unsupervised child, and allow for unannounced inspections of his residence.

Edwin also believed that his son was, as he would later testify in trial "truly repentant of his unfortunate situation back in 1984 that he was trying to adhere to his parole very, very vigorously." Indeed, Robert had voluntarily "participated" in the television special regarding convicts on parole against his father's advice because, as he told his father, "Dad, I want to do it to show we can succeed...."

The testimony was uncontroverted that none of the defendant family members ever told Helen about Robert's convictions.

After the evidence had been completed the trial court granted nonsuit motions made by the defendants in this appeal; Helen then filed a timely notice of appeal from the judgment in their favor. On appeal Helen now argues that the evidence was susceptible to liability based on either premises liability or general negligence theories. [We have omitted the discussion about premises liability].

Discussion

Absent a "special relationship," one cannot be held liable for mere nonfeasance, such as not protecting another from a criminal attack by a third party. (See *Totten v. More Oakland Residential Housing, Inc.* (1976) 63 Cal.App.,134 Cal.Rptr. 29 ["As a basic general principle, in the absence of a special relationship or circumstance, a private person has no duty to protect another from a criminal attack by a third person."].) The basic idea is often referred to as the "no duty to aid rule," which remains a fundamental and long-standing rule of tort law. As the Supreme Court said in *Williams v. State of California* (1983) 34 Cal.3d 18, 23, 192 Cal.Rptr. 233, 664 P.2d 137: "As a rule, one has no duty to come to the aid of another. A person who has not created a peril is not liable in tort merely for failure to take affirmative action to assist or protect another unless there is some relationship between them which gives rise to a duty to act."

[Helen's] claim essentially requires this court to depart from the rule against liability for mere nonfeasance. That rule is foundational in California tort jurisprudence. The tort law of California does not impose mandatory good samaritanism.

Helen argues that *Soldano v. O'Daniels* (1983) 141 *Cal. App. 3d 443, 190 Cal. Rptr. 310* modified the no duty to aid rule. As one commentator has noted, *Soldano* stands out as the *only* case in the United States during the thirty year period since the death of Kitty Genovese that could "be read" as adopting

a duty to aid rule, though the commentator who made that statement also noted that the "court's apparent holding [was] to the contrary." (See Payne, *Linking Tort Reform to Fairness and Moral Values* (1995) 1995 Det. C.L. Rev. 1207, 1237. *Soldano* did not abrogate the rule against liability for mere nonfeasance. Rather like Justice Scalia's observation about the famous contracts case of *Hadley v. Baxendale* (1854) 156 Eng.Rep. 145 it is an instance of a court knowing the right rule but simply not applying it correctly. The time has come to explain why the result in the case is an aberration in American tort jurisprudence.

In *Soldano* a saloon patron ran across the street to a restaurant to try to phone the police about a threat that had been made in the bar. The patron requested the bartender of the restaurant (in the fairly neutral language which the opinion used to describe the actual facts) to "either call the police or allow him to use the [restaurant] phone to call the police. The [bartender] allegedly refused to call the police and allegedly refused to allow the patron to use the phone to make his own call." The threat in the saloon eventually escalated into a lethal shooting.

The appellate court reversed the judgment entered after a summary judgment motion when the son of the man who was shot and killed in the saloon sued the restaurant across the street. The appellate court began its substantive discussion by saying the "facts" of the case before it "come very nearly within section 327" of the Restatement Second of Torts, which the court then paraphrased for the rather noncontroversial point that if you know a third person is going to render aid to another you shouldn't "prevent" that person "from doing so." The opinion then ... added the idea that you shouldn't "interfere" with another person's attempt to give aid as well as "prevent" it.

The problem with the court's analysis is that it subtly equated the concepts of prevention and interference with the fact that the bartender had *refused to allow* a saloon patron from across the street use the *restaurant's* phone. "Interference" and refusal to allow one's property to be commandeered, even for a good purpose, are simply two different things. If the English words "prevent" and "interfere" still mean anything, they necessarily convey the notion of some sort of affirmative action, not just refusal to turn one's property over to someone else.

Th[e] weighing process... has already been done by courts over the centuries in formulating the "no duty to aid" rule. We need only add that any result other than the one we reach today under the facts of this case would create intolerable conflicts of interest within families.

The judgment in favor of the respondents is affirmed. RYLAARSDAM, J., and BEDSWORTH, J., concur.

Case Notes

1. The name of the case is *Eric J. v Betty M.* Eric J. is the plaintiff, although as he is a minor his mother brought the case on his behalf; Betty M. was the first-named defendant. Other defendants are not named in the title.
2. The court deciding the case was the California Court of Appeals District 4, an intermediate-level court in the California state court system.
3. This citation is from the state of California official reporter and indicates that this case can be found in Volume 76 California Appellate Reporter, fourth series, on page 715.
4. This citation is a parallel citation to a West's state reporter and indicates this case can also be found in Volume 90 of the California Reporter, second series, on page 549.
5. The case was decided in 1999.
6. The authors prepare a short summary of the important facts, decision in the law court, and issues to be decided in the case.
7. The name of the judge or justice writing the majority or unanimous opinion and his or her recitation of important facts, history of this court case, and indication of issues in the case to be decided by the court.
8. The court addresses the legal questions posed by the case facts. This is the analysis portion of the case and the part that shows the use of prior court decisions and the specific reasoning leading to the court's ultimate decision.
9. The holding or decision of the court.
10. The remaining members of the panel concur, so this is a unanimous opinion. If one of the judges had disagreed with the result, he or she could write a dissenting opinion to explain why. A judge who agreed with the decision but not the reasons behind it could write a concurring opinion.

For Critical Analysis

1. What do you think of Robert's family's conduct? Should they have disclosed what they knew to Helen? Use both Kantian and utilitarian methods of ethical analysis to determine the duty to disclose, and compare results.
2. Is the rule determined by the court a substantive rule or procedural rule? Is this a criminal law case or civil case? Is this a state law or federal law matter?
3. Several of Robert's earlier pleas to criminal charges were "no contest." What does that mean? Why would that choice of a plea be made? Use the book index, glossary, or the Internet to find the answer.

CHAPTER QUESTIONS AND PROBLEMS

1. Consider the year 2025. What legal challenges will social and technological changes have given to society? Consider some current unresolved serious legal issues. Do you think they will be resolved by 2025?

2. Contrast statutory law and case law. How are they different? What would be some strengths and weaknesses of each form of law? Texas is one of a few states that recognize common-law marriage. Does that mean the law recognizing the marriage is statutory or case law?

3. Assume a fifty-first state called Columbia enacts the following statute sections during its 2003 session:
   a. Makes it illegal for anyone under age twenty-three to possess a can of aerosol spray paint unless that person is licensed by the state to do so.
   b. Establishes an application form and sets a filing fee to obtain a spray-paint-possessor's license.
   c. Defines the tort of spray-paint trespass and indicates the circumstances under which victims can sue and recover damages from spray-painting violators.
   d. Provides that owners whose properties are wrongfully spray-painted can sue in small claims court for damages not to exceed $25,000.
   e. Makes it a misdemeanor to sell or give a spray-paint can to any unlicensed person under age twenty-three.
   With regard to each of the above statute sections, characterize each as either civil or criminal law, public or private law, and procedural or substantive.

4. Explain to a friend the following types of court opinions: majority, concurring, and dissent.

5. Attorneys do not have a monopoly upon the legal issues within our society because everyone, individual or corporation, has the constitutional right to represent themselves without an attorney. Is this an accurate generalization?

6. Identify which of the following acts are crimes and which are civil wrongs (called torts).
   a. Dirk, brandishing a gun, robs a convenience store.

   b. Dirk captures and rapes Monica in the parking lot of a mall.

   c. Dirk shoplifts clothes from his employer's store.

   d. Dirk seduces Monica, age seventeen.

   e. Dirk carelessly drives his car into a school bus, killing one child.

   f. Dirk crudely asks Monica to engage in a sex act with him.

7. Which of the following issues would most likely be decided by both state and federal appellate courts?

   a. Proper selection of jurors.

   b. Whether or not a witness lied during trial.

   c. Whether or not a jury came to the correct decision.

   d. Whether or not certain evidence should have been produced by attorneys during trial.

   e. Whether or not the trial court judge made erroneous rulings on objections to evidence.

8. There are nine U.S. Supreme Court Justices today, just as there were in 1900 when our population was 76 million. Today the U.S. population is 270 million. Does this mean:

   a. there should be more Justices to share the workload, or

   b. that a new specialized court should be created to handle specified kinds of cases (say criminal appeals, only), or

   c. that our Justices should be paid more?

Can you think of any other possible remedy?

9. Mandy, a seventeen-year-old high school student, was spending Friday night at her friend Kristie's house. Both decided to go to a party at a fellow student's home. The parents of the host were away for the weekend. Marijuana and Ecstasy were said to have been used at the party. It was reported that Mandy told a group of friends, including Kristie, that she had taken some Ecstasy, although no one actually saw her take the drug.

Kristie went home without Mandy. As the evening wore on, Mandy complained of feeling sick. She was given lots of water to drink. (Dehydration is a common side effect of Ecstasy). Soon Mandy vomited and was moved to a bedroom to rest.

The next morning Kristie awoke to find that Mandy had not returned to sleep at Kristie's house. Kristie ran back to the house where the party had taken place. She arrived just in time to see Mandy taken away by ambulance. She was taken to the nearby hospital and pronounced dead on arrival.[38]

Who will be held responsible for allowing Mandy to die? Kristie? The students at the party? The student whose house was the site of the party? Could Kristie's parents be held responsible? The host's parents? Is there any criminal responsibility? Civil liability? Would your answer be different if Kristie gave Mandy the drug? As a matter of morality, who would be held responsible under utilitarian theory? Kantian ethics?

10. Why are the thousands of often complex state and federal appellate decisions totaling tens of thousands of pages annually printed in expensive, hardcover books to collect dust in libraries? Why are they made available on the Internet? Who reads these long and, frankly, often boring recitals of the law, precedents, and legal theory? Surely all of these volumes cannot contain only significant and important cases. Why do we need volumes on the law of the 1800s, or of the 1920s?

CHAPTER 2

Our Constitution

The layman's Constitutional view is that what he likes is Constitutional and that which he doesn't like is unconstitutional. That about measures up the Constitutional acumen of the average person.

Hugo Black, U.S. Supreme Court Justice, *New York Times*, February 26, 1971.

After reading and studying this chapter, you should be able to:

- Define "constitutionalism."

- Distinguish between natural and positive law, providing examples of each.

- Explain the concept of judicial review.

- Describe how power and authority are divided among the branches of the government under the doctrine of separation of powers.

- Explain the organization of the national government and identify important attributes of each branch.

- Understand and define "federalism."

- Identify the major processes of citizen legislation.

- Define and provide examples of police power, the supremacy clause, and the power to tax.

- Explain what the commerce clause is and describe its effects.

- Understand the nature of the Bill of Rights and provide some examples of restrictions on federal government and, through the doctrine of incorporation, state government.

- Discuss the application of the First Amendment to expressions of free speech and religion.

- Understand the major contentions involving the "right to bear arms."

- Be able to recognize and discuss the due process and equal protection clauses and the right to privacy.

Already we have identified a number of weighty issues facing our society and its legal system in the early years of the new millennium, as contrasted with the issues faced a century ago. Then, an industrial revolution was beginning within a land that was sparsely populated but fabulously rich in resources. Now, an unimaginably wider range of issues extends from implications of advancing technology to predictable social conflicts in a land with fewer natural resources and a threatened environment. Yet there is a parallel today to the future our citizens faced in the early 1900s. Then and now, our confidence in our Constitution, the form of government it commands, and the civil liberties it guarantees offset the uncertainties of the future. Then, as now, our Constitution is alive and well. What is this almost magical document?

Our Constitution is a voluntary agreement among our citizens that specifies national rules of governance and expresses our fundamental principles of justice. It also lists the inalienable rights of the people that bind them to cooperate for their general welfare. Written eleven years after the Declaration of Independence, the Constitution became operative in 1789. It is the world's oldest effectively functioning written constitution.

Our Constitution derives its legitimacy from the guaranteed right of the people to vote in the selection of their government representatives. This is also true of the written constitutions in all fifty states of the union. However, a democracy in which all of the qualified voters participate directly is obviously feasible only in very small political entities, such as some early New England towns. Our populous nation is a **republic,** meaning that its sovereign (supreme) power resides in the people but is exercised by representatives chosen through direct votes cast by qualified voters (e.g., qualified by age, citizenship, and registration) in free elections. The president and vice president are the only federal officials not elected directly; they are chosen by the Electoral College, which is, however, elected by the people.*

republic

A system of government with the supreme power in the people, exercised by representatives chosen through the votes of qualified voters.

http://

Everything you might want to know about the Electoral College is available at
http://www.archives.gov/ federal_register/ electoral_college/ electoral_college.html

constitutionalism

The principles of constitutional government; adherence to them, including, notably, restrictions and limitations on government power.

http://

Many links to important aspects of our constitutional form of government are available at the White House site:
http://www.whitehouse.gov/

arbitrary and capricious

Action taken impulsively or in bad faith and without good or valid reason.

Ⓦ HAT IS CONSTITUTIONALISM?

Constitutionalism means "a fundamental law, or a fundamental set of principles and . . . [an] institutional arrangement, which would [actually] restrict arbitrary power and ensure 'limited government.'"[1] Thus, "the governing power is limited by enforceable rules of law, and concentration of power is prevented by various checks and balances so that the basic rights of individuals and groups are protected."[2]

Constitutionalism imposes limits on the exercise of government power. Many nations have constitutions, but that does not necessarily mean their citizens enjoy the fruits of constitutionalism. For example, a constitution that permits unlimited political power, whether in the hands of one, few, or many, does not provide constitutionalism. The Fascists' constitutions of Italy and Germany in the 1930s are an example. Neither included limitations on **arbitrary and capricious** uses of political power by the rulers. Arbitrary and capricious behavior has been aptly characterized as "willful and unreasonable action taken, without consideration of or in disregard of facts or without determining principle."[3] Even a constitution that provides limited political power, but establishes no mechanism to restrain the ruler's exercise of that power, fails to provide constitutionalism. For instance, a "freedom of the press" mandate in the Argentinean constitution did not prevent Juan Peron (presi-

---

* For many years the Electoral College has interested scholars and politicians but not the general public, as the Electoral College has selected the same candidate as the popular vote. All that changed in the 2000 presidential election when Al Gore received more popular votes (50,996,582) than George Bush (50,456,062). The Electoral College vote declared Bush the winner with 271 electoral votes to Gore's 266 votes.

dent, 1945–1955) from destroying the world's largest Spanish-language newspaper, *La Prensa*, in Buenos Aires.

People enjoy constitutionalism only to the degree that their constitution limits power by specific provisions that effectively control the behavior of the ruling governors. One such control is having the judiciary serve as an enforcing watchdog on the exercise of powers by the executive and legislative branches, and even the lower levels of the judicial branch of government. The separation of powers concept is discussed more fully later in this chapter. A good example of its application occurred in 1952, when President Harry S. Truman ordered the secretary of commerce to seize and operate our country's privately owned steel mills after the United Steel Workers Union threatened to strike. Corporate managers retaliated by a "lockout" that kept the workers off their jobs. The president believed that a shutdown would impair the nation's ability to conduct the Korean War. Was the seizure order within the president's power? No. The Supreme Court held that "this seizure order cannot stand" for the following reasons:

1. The president's power, if any, to issue the order must stem either from an act of Congress or from the Constitution itself. The U.S. Supreme Court could find no congressional statute or constitutional provision that expressly authorized the president to take possession of private property as he did in the steel mill case.

2. Moreover, prior to this controversy, when the Taft-Hartley Act was under consideration in 1947, Congress had refused to adopt a law authorizing the seizure method of settling labor disputes that Truman used.

3. The order could not be sustained as an exercise of the president's military power as commander-in-chief of the armed forces. The commander-in-chief does not have the power to take possession of private property for the purpose of keeping labor-management disputes from stopping production. The nation's lawmakers, not military authorities, should regulate labor disputes, declared the Court.[4]

The power of the U.S. Supreme Court to dictate to President Truman, and have him obey, demonstrates how constitutionalism helps to protect the people of the United States from abuses of executive power, however well meant such abuses may be.

Another example of separation and limitation of power took place in 1974, when the Supreme Court ordered President Richard M. Nixon to release tape recordings of discussions concerning a politically inspired burglary in the Watergate apartment house in Washington, D.C. Initially the president refused to release the tapes, claiming as "executive privilege" the right to withhold recorded information he deemed important to the exercise of his presidential duties. The tapes showed that he had halted an FBI investigation, a serious obstruction of justice.

LEGAL FOCUS—CASE

In 1997 Paula Jones filed a civil lawsuit for money damages against President William J. Clinton, alleging sexual harassment while he was governor of Arkansas. President Clinton asserted an "executive privilege" as justification for his request to suspend the litigation until after his presidency ended. Does the U.S. Constitution provide presidents with such an "executive privilege" to delay civil litigation?

Clinton v. Jones, 520 U.S. 681, 117 S.Ct. 1636 (1997).

http://

For more information about the Paula Jones sexual harassment suit against President Clinton and its aftermath, see Court TV's Web site:

http://www.courttv.com/ casefiles/jones/

No. The president contended that ongoing civil litigation would impair his ability to lead the nation—thus, it should be suspended by "executive privilege." The president was subpoenaed (ordered by the court) to appear and testify in that litigation, and he ultimately agreed to do so. Again, the judicial branch acted as an enforcing watchdog of the exercise of power by the executive branch of government.*

WHAT IS CONSTITUTIONAL LAW?

Constitutional law in the United States has a variety of meanings. To the founders of our nation, it had to do with a concept known as **natural law**[†] and its corollary concept of **natural rights.** From the founders' perspective natural law was the higher law, in accordance with nature, applicable to all men, and unchangeable and eternal.** Natural rights are rights of human beings that exist regardless of any other law. The founders believed they had incorporated natural-law principles into the Constitution in a manner consistent with the necessities of government or positive law.[††] **Positive law** is defined as any law enacted by the sovereign (supreme power) and deemed necessary to regulate an ordered society.*** The natural-law doctrines found in the Constitution are reflected in the following fundamental beliefs, and they dictate the parameters within which legitimate governmental "positive law" must be exercised.[5]

1. The *rights of man* are inalienable and indestructible.
2. Paramount is the natural-law doctrine that the most fundamental rights of all human beings are life, liberty, and property.[6]
3. Legitimate governments are obligated (by natural law) under their social contracts (constitutions) to protect and guarantee these rights to every person within their respective jurisdictions.
4. The higher law acknowledges and promotes the principle of *private domain* into which governments should not intrude. Under this doctrine, the individual is free to do anything he chooses, unless specifically prohibited or circumscribed by reasonable positive law.[†††] This means that one may violate ethical standards, hallowed conven-

natural law

The higher law believed by some ethicists to be above and beyond man's power to change.

natural rights

Inalienable rights of every human being that exist by virtue of natural law, notably to life, liberty, and property.

positive law

Law enacted by governmental authority, such as legislatures, courts, and administrative agencies, as distinguished from natural law.

http://

See the Internet Encyclopedia of Philosophy for more about natural law as a legal and ethical theory:

http://www.utm.edu/ research/iep/n/natlaw.htm

---

* Judge Susan Webber Wright later dismissed Paula Jones' lawsuit against President Clinton before trial. "Reduced to its essence, the record taken as a whole could not lead a rational trier of fact to find for the plaintiff [Jones] and the Court therefore finds that there are no genuine issues for trial in this case." *Jones v. Clinton* No. LR-C-94-290.

† "But for natural law there would probably have been no American and no French revolution, nor would the great ideals of freedom and equality have found their way into the lawbooks after having found it into the hearts of men." See Alessandro Passerin D'Entreves, *Natural Law: An Introduction to Legal Philosophy* (London: Hutchinson and Co., 1951).

** See Marcus Tullius Cicero, *De re publica*, trans. George Sabine and Stanley Smith (Indianapolis, New York, Dobbs:Merrill, 1960). Cicero's definition of natural law reads thus: "True law is right reason, harmonious with nature, diffused among all, constant, eternal; a law which calls to duty by its commands and restrains from evil by its prohibitions. . . . It is a sacred obligation not to attempt to legislate in contradiction to this law; nor may it be derogated from nor abrogated. Indeed, by neither the Senate nor the people can we be released from this law; nor does it require any but ourselves to be its expositor or interpreter. Nor is it one law at Rome and another at Athens; one now and another at a later time; but one eternal and unchangeable law binding all nations through all time." Marcus Tullius Cicero, reported in Lactantius, *Divina institutiones*, trans. Roberts and Donaldson (1871), vi, 8, 370.

†† "They are the principles of Aristotle and Plato, of Livy and Cicero, and Sidney, Harrington, and Locke: the principles of nature and eternal reason; the principles on which the whole government over us now stands." Quote attributed to John Adams. Clinton L. Rossiter, *The Political Thought of the American Revolution* (New York: Harcourt, Brace & World, 1953), p. 53.

*** As often true with philosophies, there is an inherent conflict between the pure precept of positive law and natural law. As proffered by Thomas Hobbes (1588–1679), positive law is essential to protect people from their primitive state, so when a law is enacted, people are duty-bound to obey it. Natural law presupposes a system of law grounded on its intrinsic truth rather than on any power of compulsion, and it is held to exist irrespective of and sometimes inconsistent with man-made laws. The tension between individual belief in and respect for natural law versus the positive laws of the state is not the subject of an abstract debate. One justification often given for civil disobedience is that the violator is actually complying with a higher law, namely natural law.

††† This proscription on the law creates a conundrum. The natural right to an individual's private domain requires that the state enact a specific law before any person can be held accountable to the state for violating that law. On the other hand, because natural law exists without the necessity of any state declaration of its existence, such law could, of course, be violated without its having been declared a part of the positive law. However, the violator of the natural law may suffer from sanctions, both temporal and, some ethicists would maintain, also eternal. If nothing else, a liar, thief, or murderer, for example, may suffer the agonies of ostracism from society, and often a troubled guilty conscience that can last a lifetime.

tions, and Holy Writ, and yet not be answerable to the state unless the behavior involved has been prohibited or circumscribed by reasonable positive law. By contrast, many countries in today's turbulent world allow their citizens to do only that which is permitted by their man-made rules and decrees. All else that conflicts therewith is deemed prohibited.

5. No person is allowed to be a judge in his or her own cause.[7] Thus, a Justice of the U.S. Supreme Court who has a personal interest in a controversy under appeal before the Court will refuse to participate in the case. A long-standing philosophical bias is not a disqualifying conflict of interest.

6. No person is above the law—not legislators, not presidents, not judges.

In Chapter 1 we used the following case to describe the difference between civil and criminal law, and concluded that neither was applicable.

LEGAL FOCUS—PROBLEM

Late one night, David Thomas Cash, Jr., age nineteen, observed his friend Jeremy Strohmeyer, age twenty, escort a very young girl into a restroom inside the Primadonna casino near Las Vegas. Shortly thereafter, Cash followed them inside, where he peered over the top of a stall. He saw Strohmeyer grappling with the girl, but said nothing and left. Later Strohmeyer rejoined Cash in the casino. After discussing the killing of the girl, Cash and Strohmeyer continued their evening of conviviality and gambling. Strohmeyer ultimately pled guilty to the rape and murder of the victim, and is serving life imprisonment without the possibility of parole. Did Cash have a natural-law right to choose to assist, or to ignore, the victim?

Yes. Recall from paragraph 4 earlier: ". . . one may violate ethical standards, hallowed conventions, and Holy Writ, and yet not be answerable to the state unless the behavior involved has been prohibited by reasonable positive law." Under the natural-law principle of private domain, Cash was free either to help the victim or to ignore her plight. Nevada has no statute (positive law) that criminalizes a refusal to prevent a crime from occurring. It is unclear whether or not a law requiring citizens to intervene in criminal conduct would be constitutional.

Important elements of the natural law and natural rights were included in the second paragraph of the Declaration of Independence:

We hold these truths to be self-evident, that all men are created equal, that they are Endowed by their Creator with certain unalienable Rights, that among these are Life, Liberty and the pursuit of Happiness. That to secure these rights, Governments are instituted among Men, deriving their just powers from the consent of the governed. That whenever any Form of Government becomes destructive of these ends, it is the Right of the people to alter or to abolish it, and to institute new Government, laying its foundation on such principles and organizing its powers in such form, as to them shall seem most likely to effect their Safety and Happiness.

In January 1776, George Washington wrote of "the propriety of separation [from England on the basis of] . . . the sound doctrine and unanswerable reasoning contained in the

http://

To view the political essays that are referred to as *The Federalist Papers,* visit **http://www.bus.miami.edu/ ~jmonroe/fedindex.htm** pamphlet *Common Sense*." The author of *Common Sense*, Thomas Paine, summed up the spirit of the time in these lofty words:

> *But where, say some, is the King of America? I'll tell you, Friend. He reigns above, and does not make havoc of mankind like the royal brute of Britain. Yet, that we may not appear to be defective even in earthly honors, let a day be solemnly set apart for proclaiming the charter; let it be brought forth placed in the divine law, the word of God; let a crown be placed thereon, by which the world may know, that so far as we approve of monarchy, that in America* the law is king. *For as in absolute governments the king is law, so in free countries the law ought to be king; and there ought to be no other.*[8]

When we speak of constitutional law today we mean the fundamental law or the supreme law of the land. Constitutional principles accorded special designation as constitutional laws are (1) judicial review, (2) separation of powers, (3) federalism, and (4) civil rights and liberties. These four special categories contain the most publicized and exciting principles of constitutional law.

Ⓦ HAT IS JUDICIAL REVIEW?

judicial review

Power of the U.S. Supreme Court to declare unconstitutional an act of Congress, a presidential order, or a state law.

Judicial review is the power and duty vested in the U.S. Supreme Court to declare null and void (i.e., of no validity or effect) any statute or act of the federal government or of any state government that violates the U.S. Constitution.* Although not specifically authorized in Article III (the Judicial Article of the Constitution), some form of judicial review was presumably envisioned by framers of the Constitution. According to Alexander Hamilton, the Supreme Court is the "least dangerous branch" because it controls neither sword nor purse.[9] He said the Supreme Court and not the Congress or the president should be the custodian of the Constitution. Further, he referred to "the medium of the courts of justice, whose duty it must be to declare all acts contrary to the manifest tenor of the constitution void. Without this, all the reservations of particular rights or privileges would amount to nothing."[10]

What *judicial review* meant, however, was not articulated until 1803, in the case of *Marbury v. Madison*.[11] This case did more than validate (i.e., give legal force to) the judicial review of legislative and executive enactments and orders. Chief Justice Marshall enunciated a major power for the Supreme Court, recognizing it as the sole interpreter and custodian of the Constitution, to the exclusion of the president and Congress. With this declaration came the awesome duty of defining what the Constitution means and what it does not mean.

Although the exclusive judicial power of review has engendered heated controversy over the years, it also has been a stabilizing force for a growing and changing society. As national economic, social, and political conditions have changed, so too have attitudes and opinions of the people. This evolution is reflected in the leaders the people elect to office and in the Supreme Court Justices who are appointed. As a result, some long-standing Supreme Court decisions have been changed. What once was ruled constitutional thereafter is declared unconstitutional. For example, as the twentieth century began, racial segregation in schools was accepted and even endorsed by the "separate but equal" rule of

*Note that state supreme courts possess similar powers to nullify laws of their own legislatures that violate their respective state constitutions.

Plessy v. Ferguson.[12] In 1954, however, the "separate but equal" rule was rejected by *Brown v. The Board of Education of Topeka*.[13]

Judicial review is not the only process by which our Constitution can be changed. The people can and do make changes through the more difficult process of formal amendment. For example, women obtained the right to vote in 1920 by the Nineteenth Amendment to the Constitution, and in 1971 the Twenty-Sixth Amendment lowered the voting age in national elections to eighteen.

http://

Learn more about judicial review at
http://www.constitution center.org/sections/basics/ basic_1d.asp

WHAT IS SEPARATION OF POWERS?

Separation of powers is an indispensable element of our charter of government. The Constitution allocates powers of government according to function. The functional branches are legislative (law making), executive (law enforcing), and judicial (adjudicating).[14] Separation of powers provides an effective balance of power among the three branches of government. Different officials have unique and specific powers, and each branch operates under the direction of different persons. Each branch checks the other two to prevent them from garnering or exercising power illegally.[15] This institutional structure restrains a natural human tendency toward expansion of personal power. While preventing possible tyranny (i.e., despotic abuse of authority), the separation of powers permits officials to execute faithfully their constitutionally delegated powers.

The constitutional doctrine of separation of powers speaks of the relationships among the divisions of government. While there are indeed exclusive functions assigned to each (e.g., tax bills must begin in the House of Representatives), much of the work engaged in by the three branches of government is shared.

Congress may pass a bill; the president may sign or veto it. Congress may override the veto and enact the bill as law. The Supreme Court may strike down the statute as unconstitutional. If necessary, Congress may initiate a campaign to have the Constitution amended to accomplish the purpose of the statute, or more likely it may attempt to pass a new statute that is in conformity with the Constitution.[16] Note too that the president may be able to appoint new members to the Supreme Court (with the advice and consent of the Senate) who are sympathetic to his or her views.

separation of powers

The granting of the various powers of government among three branches so that each branch checks the other two.

http://

To view important constitutional and governmental documents or to obtain references to many, visit
http://www.lib.umich.edu/ govdocs/federal.html

LEGAL FOCUS—PROBLEM

[Assume] that President George W. Bush nominated Richard Westley to the U.S. Supreme Court. During confirmation proceedings conducted by the U.S. Senate, candidate Westley was asked, "Do you believe in the right of women to choose to have an abortion?" He answered simply, "No." The response provoked widespread public concern, and the Senate responded by killing the nomination. Should Supreme Court candidates be required to reveal their deepest personal beliefs as a precondition to appointment?

Most members of the public probably would approve of a litmus test (single-issue test that determines result) for nominees to the Supreme Court. However, over a lifetime a Justice will face an extraordinary number of important issues involving significant values, and most people, no doubt, also would prefer the appointment of highly qualified persons rather than persons sympathetic to one specific controversial issue—unless that issue was of supreme importance to the individual. The obvious conundrum typically is resolved by the refusal of candidates to respond specifically to such questions, reciting their loyalties to follow the rule of law.

It is reassuring to note that in the final analysis the power to decide most issues rests with the people, who may use their votes—"the power of the ballot box"—to elect representatives who are expected to comply with the expressed will of the people. However, the representatives are not legally obliged to do so. Even if they were, public opinion is often divided and sometimes fragmented on controversial issues.

The presidential veto procedure is prescribed by Article I, Section 7 of the Constitution, which states, "Every Bill which shall have passed the House of Representatives and the Senate shall, before it becomes a Law, be presented to the President." Thereupon, "if he approves he shall sign it, but if not he shall return it, with his Objections to that House in which it shall have originated." If, after reconsideration it is approved by two-thirds of both houses, it shall become a law. Note that "if any Bill shall not be returned by the President within ten Days (Sundays excepted) after it shall have been presented to him, the same shall be a Law, in like manner as if he had signed it, unless the Congress by their adjournment prevent its Return, in which Case it shall not be a Law."

Each year Congress presents a budget to the president for signature into law. Typically, some of the proposed expenditures in the budget are intended primarily as political patronage. These so-called "pork barrel" budget items are added by the most powerful legislators in Congress, a tactic that assists them in their reelection campaigns.

LEGAL FOCUS—PROBLEM

Congress presented the fiscal year budget for the year 2004 to the president for signature or veto. Included was an item for ten million dollars for "parks and recreation" projects in Congresswoman Peavy's hometown. For years, Peavy had been a very vocal critic of the president. Can the president approve the budget yet, in retaliation, veto the proposed appropriation for Peavy?

No. The power to make partial vetoes (called *line-item vetoes*) would have the practical effect of amending enactments by Congress. The president is not authorized by the Constitution to amend laws proposed by Congress.[17] Thus, the separation of the legislative and executive powers cannot be blurred by line-item vetoes.

HOW IS THE NATIONAL GOVERNMENT ORGANIZED?

LEGISLATIVE BRANCH (CONGRESS)

Article I of the Constitution provides the organization and functions of the legislature. The legislative branch is *bicameral* (having two parts), with an upper house (the Senate) and a lower house (the House of Representatives). Members of the Senate originally were appointed by state legislatures, but in 1913 the Seventeenth Amendment changed the system to direct selection by popular vote. The Senate has 100 members, two from each state

http://

Learn more about separation of powers at **http://www.usconstitution .net/consttop_sepp.html**

http://

Until his retirement in 1988, Wisconsin Senator William Proxmire bestowed the Golden Fleece Award for "wasteful, ridiculous or ironic use of the taxpayer's money." See a list of his top ten Golden Fleece awards at **http://www.taxpayer.net/ awards/goldenfleece/ topten.htm**

Members of the House of Representatives are elected to 435 seats that are allocated to the states on the basis of population, as determined in the decennial national census.

The basic function of the legislative branch is to enact laws. This is usually accomplished by a majority vote for or against enactment, amendment, or repeal. In both the House and the Senate, a quorum consists of a majority of the members who have been elected and sworn (i.e., taken an oath of office) to serve. Powers of the Congress are spelled out in Article I, Section 8 of the Constitution. They include the power to tax and borrow money, to regulate interstate commerce, to make laws regulating bankruptcies, to coin money, to establish post offices, to establish courts inferior to the Supreme Court, to declare war, and to govern the District of Columbia (the area of the nation's capital). However, Congress has great latitude in the detailed application of its enumerated powers by virtue of its blanket authority "to make all Laws which shall be necessary and proper for carrying into Execution" its stated powers.[18]

Once the legislature enacts a law, its job is usually done. All persons subject to the newly enacted law are then required to comply. If necessary, lower-level government officials in the executive branch (e.g., police) enforce compliance. If and when the constitutionality of a statute is challenged, the dispute may ultimately be resolved by decision of the Supreme Court.

Sometimes newly enacted laws never become law.

http://

Information about Congress is available at
http://www.house.gov/ and
http://www.senate.gov/

LEGAL FOCUS—EXAMPLE

Congress passed a law releasing alien Chinese students who were studying in the United States from the requirement of returning to China upon the expiration of their visas. (A visa is a document that grants a citizen of a foreign country legal permission to live, work, or study in the host country.) This was done because Congress believed that the Chinese government would punish most of these students for supporting the 1989 student uprising in Tiananmen Square and elsewhere in China. The proposed law was sent to the White House for signature by the president.

President George H. W. Bush vetoed the legislation on the grounds that Congress was interfering with foreign policy matters, a presidential responsibility. Moreover, the students were already protected against forced repatriation by his executive order, which directed the Immigration and Naturalization Service to extend the Chinese student visas indefinitely. When the bill was returned to the Congress, the House voted to override the veto, but the Senate did not; thus, the president's veto stood.

The only constitutional method to remove a president from office is by a congressional proceeding called *impeachment*. Impeachment is a process potentially leading to removal from office certain federal officers, including the president. The process for the president is provided for in the U.S. Constitution Article II, Section 4: "The President, Vice President and all civil Officers of the United States, shall be removed from Office on Impeachment for, and Conviction of, Treason, Bribery, or other high Crimes and Misdemeanors." Impeachment requires a majority vote in the House of Representatives. The impeached office holder is then subject to trial in the Senate with removal from office requiring a two-thirds majority vote of the Senate after trial. In 1998 the U.S. House of Representatives voted to impeach President William Jefferson Clinton for obstruction of justice and perjury relating to his conduct following the infamous "Monica Lewinsky affair." The U.S. Senate, with Supreme Court Chief Justice William Rehnquist presiding, conducted an impeachment trial. On February 12, 1999, it voted 50 to 50 and 45 to 55 on the respective charges, thereby declining to remove the president from office.

EXECUTIVE BRANCH (PRESIDENCY)

The president and vice president are each elected to a term of four years, with a limit of two consecutive full terms.* The constitutional process for choosing the chief executive and his or her running mate is cumbersome because the method is indirect, with state electors actually electing the president by casting electoral votes. The number of electors in each state is determined by the number of representatives the state has in the House, plus its two senators. These determinations were last changed after the 2000 census. Thus, currently each of seven states (Alaska, Delaware, Montana, North and South Dakota, Vermont, and Wyoming) and the District of Columbia has three votes, for a total of twenty-four; populous California alone has fifty-five; and New York has thirty-one.

In total, there are 538 electoral votes: 435 based on members of the House, 100 based on members of the Senate, and three from the District of Columbia. To win requires a majority (270) of the electoral votes. Note that presidential elections and vacancies are further regulated by technical amendments to the Constitution.[19]

The unique Electoral College has survived despite repeated efforts to alter or abolish it including the furor following the 2000 election of President George W. Bush. This survival may be because it maintains the viability of political parties, which "in turn serve to identify issues and support candidates committed to advancing identified policies and programs." A new Electoral College is created for every presidential election; that is, the people who serve as electors (casting votes) in the electoral college are different for each election.

Powers of the President

Section 2 of Article II of the Constitution specifies the following presidential powers. First and foremost, and of momentous importance during most of the twentieth century, is the power of the president as "Commander in Chief of the Armed Forces of the United States and of the militia of the several states, when called into actual service of the United States...."[20]

While Congress retains to itself the power to declare war, the power "to make war" is granted solely to the president. It was during the Civil War that the commander in chief was declared to be the sole determiner of whether the hostilities were of "... such alarming proportions as will compel him to accord to them the character of belligerent"[21] and whether he would engage the armed forces of the United States in such hostilities. Advanced technology has changed the nature of modern warfare, thus further justifying the presidential power to respond quickly with military force to a military attack without congressional approval.

The president has the duty and power to make treaties, but they must be approved by a two-thirds vote of the Senate.[22] For example, three controversial yet vitally important treaties entered into by our country in the twentieth century were the Charter of the United Nations (1945); the North Atlantic Treaty Pact (1948), which created NATO (North Atlantic Treaty Organization), a defensive military alliance; and the North American Free Trade Agreement (NAFTA) among Canada, Mexico, and the United States. All

---

* "No person shall be elected to the office of the president more than twice, and no person who has held the office of president, or acted as president for more than two years of a term to which some other person was elected president shall be elected to the office of the president more than once." (U.S. Constitution, Twenty-Second Amendment)

three of these treaties were duly voted on and approved by the Senate. The president may also sign *executive agreements*, which do not require Senate ratification. For example, during the early months of World War II, when German submarines were sinking many supply ships in an attempt to starve England into surrender, President Franklin D. Roosevelt signed an executive agreement giving the British fifty 1914-type destroyers in exchange for eight naval bases. This was entirely constitutional, despite the fact that the United States had not yet declared war on Germany.

With the "advice and consent" of the Senate, the president appoints ambassadors, public ministers and consuls, Supreme Court Justices, and presidential advisors.[23] Congress has empowered the president to choose other federal officers and commission heads. The Judiciary Act of 1789 gave presidents the power to nominate appellate and district court judges for the federal courts. Congress must approve these appointments, a function that is another example of shared power between the branches of government.

Some scholars contend that the power to nominate Supreme Court Justices, who serve for life, is the single most important power of the president.

LEGAL FOCUS—CASE

In the case of *Roe v. Wade* the U.S. Supreme Court held for the first time that women have a constitutionally protected right to choose whether or not to have an abortion. Following this declaration, the states could no longer abolish abortion within their borders. Four Justices voted against the majority in *Roe v. Wade*. Could the replacement of one Justice cause reversal of *Roe*, thereby altering or even eliminating the abortion law?

Roe v. Wade, 410 U.S. 113, 93 S.Ct. 705 (1973).

Yes. Many of the most controversial Supreme Court cases are decided by 5–4 votes. Nonetheless, presidential candidates historically have not announced the names of persons they would, if elected, nominate to the Supreme Court if the opportunity should arise. Nor do presidential candidates announce the names of possible appointees to their cabinets (department heads with the highest authority in an administration). Thus, voters make assumptions about their future based upon the campaign statements and track records of presidential candidates.

JUDICIAL BRANCH (COURTS)

Article III of the Constitution, the Judicial Article, declares, "The Judicial power of the United States shall be vested in one Supreme Court, and in such inferior courts as the Congress may from time to time ordain and establish."[24] Compared with detailed mandates given to the executive and legislative branches, Article III is sparse in providing guidance to the judiciary. Despite this lack of a closely defined role, the federal courts have become central to the doctrine of separation of powers. The U.S. Supreme Court has created and refined the "proper" place of the court within the federal government, beginning with its landmark case of *Marbury v. Madison* mentioned earlier.

The power to determine the constitutionality of federal and state legislative enactments, as well as judicial review of actions taken by the executive branch, has given the U.S. Supreme Court major responsibility for maintaining the integrity of the Constitution. The Supreme Court is commonly thought to be the branch of government least likely to be swayed by political pressures and popular whims. One reason for this is that, like all

http://

Recent treaties are all available on the Internet. For the full text of the North American Free Trade Agreement, visit **http://www-tech.mit.edu/Bulletins/nafta.html**

http://

You will find presidential executive orders in the Federal Register at **http://www.archives.gov/federal_register/index.html**

http://

You will find both pending cases and current opinions of the U.S. Supreme Court at **http://supct.law.cornell.edu/supct/index.php**

http://

Resumes of Supreme Court Justices are available at **http://supct.law.cornell.edu/ supct/justices/fullcourt.html**

federal judges, Supreme Court Justices hold office for life, contingent only on good behavior. It is not uncommon for Supreme Court Justices to remain active on the bench well beyond the traditional retirement age of sixty-five. For this reason, the Court was once referred to as "the nine old men." Currently, the Court is composed of the following Justices:

Stephen G. Breyer of Massachusetts (President Clinton, 1994)
Ruth Bader Ginsburg of New York (President Clinton, 1993)
Anthony M. Kennedy of California (President Reagan, 1988)
Sandra Day O'Connor of Arizona (President Reagan, 1981)
Chief Justice William H. Rehnquist of Arizona (President Reagan, 1986)
Antonin Scalia of Washington, D.C. (President Reagan, 1986)
David H. Souter of New Hampshire (President Bush, 1990)
John Paul Stevens of Illinois (President Ford, 1975)
Clarence Thomas of Georgia (President Bush, 1991)

All courts are empowered to issue orders to compel compliance with their rules and procedures. For example, courts authorize the issuance of subpoenas (orders to appear at a certain time and place) upon proper request by officials or lawyers (for their clients) who are engaged in litigation or investigation. Failure to comply with such a judicial order can prompt a court to hold the witness in "contempt of court." The court's penalty for contempt may range from a monetary fine to jail time.

LEGAL FOCUS—PROBLEM

In 1971 the U.S. Supreme Court approved the legality of a subpoena served upon President Richard Nixon (executive branch) to deliver to the Congress (legislative branch) certain tape-recorded conversations that Nixon most certainly knew would end his term of office. He could have refused to obey the subpoena and destroyed the tapes. If Nixon had refused to comply with the subpoena and had destroyed the tapes, what would have happened?

Most likely the Congress would have impeached President Nixon for failure to comply with a lawful subpoena approved by the U.S. Supreme Court. But it is not clear that disregard of a subpoena issued by Congress is a legal basis for impeachment. We never will know what would have happened then. But it is important to know how the three powers of government must interact, and that the gravity of the crisis then related to the president's willingness to comply with an order of the judicial branch of government. Unfortunately, uninformed citizens were destined never to understand the constitutional implications of "Watergate." Thus, they would not see the parallel in more current times.

LEGAL FOCUS—PROBLEM

In 1998 President Clinton was subpoenaed to testify before a federal grand jury, not as a witness, but concerning his personal conduct. Again, rather than create a constitutional confrontation about the obligation of a president to respond to a subpoena, President Clinton ultimately agreed to testify, and did. Could the president personally have appeared at the time and place to testify, but then refused to answer questions?

In Chapter 6 you will review the fundamental principle in our society that no person is required to testify against himself in a criminal proceeding. A person may volunteer to do so, but he or she need not. President Clinton did not assert his privilege against self-incrimination, either because there was no criminal conduct about which he was concerned or because he simply waived his right. He became the first sitting president in history to testify before a federal grand jury (by closed-circuit television). But in either case, he ultimately chose the course of former President Nixon by complying with the dictates of the subpoena.

Federal judges can be removed from their courts only by death, voluntary retirement, or impeachment by the Congress of the United States.

LEGAL FOCUS—PROBLEM

The Honorable Harry E. Claiborne, a federal district judge in Nevada, was tried and convicted of cheating on his income tax by filing a false return. He was sentenced to federal prison for two years. Upon conviction the judge refused to resign his office and continued to collect his $78,700 annual salary. He made clear his intent to resume his lifetime office after the completion of this term.[25] Can he be impeached?

Yes. Eight months after returning to his job as a judge, Claiborne was finally removed from the court by impeachment.[26] "Only thirteen federal judges have been impeached in the history of the United States, and of those, only seven were convicted."[27]

Congress is reluctant to use the impeachment procedure to remove public officials from office because it is costly, cumbersome, and time-consuming. But impeachment is the only way to remove federal judges from the public payroll even when they are proven guilty of criminal conduct. Fortunately, criminal acts by federal judges are rare.[28]

LEGAL FOCUS—EXAMPLE

U.S. District Court Judge James Ware told a conference of federal judges and lawyers a riveting story of how his brother had been killed in 1963 by a racist's bullet in Alabama on the same day of the Ku Klux Klan's bombing of a Baptist church in which four black girls were killed. Later it was discovered and widely publicized that Judge Ware's story was a lie. What punishment, if any, do federal judges receive for conduct that goes to the heart of the credibility of the courts—honesty in public life?[29]

Previous to his misrepresentation, Judge Ware had been nominated for promotion to the U.S. Court of Appeals. After publication of his falsehood, Judge Ware withdrew his nomination. He also was publicly reprimanded by a panel of federal judges who stated that his conduct "was prejudicial to the effective administration of the business of the courts." Judge Ware was not removed from office.

Under the Constitution, the Senate has the sole power to try all impeachments, and no person may be convicted without the concurrence of two-thirds of the members present. When political loyalty to the accused is involved, such a majority can be difficult to obtain unless the alleged offense is flagrant. Understandably, therefore, the practice is seldom used.

Congress sets the salaries for all federal employees, including judges. However, once the salaries for federal judges are set by Congress they can never be reduced for any reason during the tenure of judges then on the court.[30] This serves to forestall possible improper efforts to impose financial pressure on judges whose opinions are not favored. Of course, the salaries of new appointees may be lower than those of their predecessors, but this is unlikely to happen.

Reduction of salaries has been the least of the current problems for federal judges. A recent report of the American Bar Association stated, "The Constitutional guarantees of life tenure and an undiminished salary were designed to protect the independence of the Federal judiciary. In today's environment, neither guarantee is secure. While erosion of pay may not legally constitute a diminution in salary, it undermines the purpose of the guarantee of an undiminished salary. Similarly, the commitment to lifetime tenure is undermined when inadequate judicial salaries deter candidates from seeking appointment to the bench and discourage judges from remaining on the bench."[31] The Chief Justice of the Supreme Court, William H. Rehnquist, agreed stating "I consider the increase in judicial salaries to be the most pressing issue before the federal judiciary today."

W HAT IS FEDERALISM?

Federalism may be defined as a political arrangement in which two or more levels of government provide a variety of services for a given group of citizens in a specified geographic area. For example, Iowans are served by the national government and by their state government as well as by a variety of local governance structures.

Scholars estimate that more than 80,000 state and local governments* exist in the United States, each striving to meet the needs and wants of our complex, technologically driven society. This governmental profusion operates in a climate of political pressures, involving both competition and cooperation among various public officeholders. In effect, the U.S. Constitution prescribed some of this complexity when it reserved a large measure of sovereignty for each of the original thirteen states, in accordance with Article IV and the Tenth Amendment of the U.S. Constitution.

In any event, we are a people served by, but also subject to, government rule that range from taxation mandated by Congress to the narrowly defined standards for admission of toddlers to kindergarten mandated by local school boards.

The Constitution defines the boundaries between the national government and the state governments, providing that national government has only those powers delegated to it and such other powers that naturally flow therefrom. Congress shall have the power "to make all laws which shall be necessary and proper for carrying into Execution the foregoing powers."[32] Some of these powers are exclusive as to the national government, such as "to coin Money" and "to make Treaties."[33] But other powers are shared, such as taxing and spending. As noted, all other powers "are reserved to the States respectively, or to the people."[34]

Our Constitution also limits the power of the national government; for example, it is prohibited from denying a request for a **writ of *habeas corpus*** (Latin: "you have the

http://

To read some famous decisions of the U.S. Supreme Court, visit

http://supct.law.cornell.edu/ supct/cases/historic.htm

federalism

A form of government consisting of a union of more or less self-governing states under an umbrella of federal government.

http://

For various definitions of federalism, see

http://www.min.net/~kala/ fed/define.htm

writ of *habeas corpus*

[Latin: "you have the body"] A formal written order that an arrestee be brought before a court.

---

* All governments within states were (are) created by the state legislatures under provisions in their respective state constitutions. The governments of cities, boroughs, and counties are most commonly recognized by citizens. Other varieties of local governments are school districts, flood-control districts, mosquito-abatement districts, and park districts. Under their charters of government (granted by state legislatures), they have budgets, collect taxes, and perform various other government functions.

body"), a formal written order that an arrestee be brought before a court, usually to protect against abusive incarceration[35] without release on bail, pending a formal trial.

Under the Constitution, some powers are also denied to the states, such as the power to make a treaty. Finally, there are powers denied to both, such as the passage of **bills of attainder,** which are acts of the legislature punishing a named individual(s) or member(s) of a specific group without a judicial trial; and **ex post facto laws** (Latin: "after the fact"), which are retroactive laws that would punish alleged violators for acts lawful when committed, or that would increase the punishment applicable at the time the act was committed.

LEGAL FOCUS—PROBLEM

David Cash (mentioned earlier in this chapter) was not guilty of any crime by declining to rescue a young girl from his friend's murderous acts. Assume that in response to public outcry, Nevada passed a statute that made failure to assist the victim of criminal behavior a felony (i.e., a serious crime). If the state of Nevada then arrested, prosecuted, convicted, and sent Cash to jail, what, if anything, could he do?[36]

Under the preceding hypothetical example, Cash could sidestep the Nevada judicial system altogether and petition a federal court to protect him from this *ex post facto* law. The U.S. Constitution prohibits states from subjecting people to such laws regardless of the outcry or sentiment of most citizens. The federal court would order Nevada to release Cash.

WHAT CONSTITUTIONAL POWERS BELONG TO CITIZENS?

Although much power is delegated to the national government, and great power is reserved to states, it is the people who possess the ultimate power in our free society with its constitutional system. One of the great powers of the people is found in their right to vote.

Every citizen wishing to govern personally must compete with political opponents and win this privilege by receiving a majority of the people's vote. "[T]hose who make public policy [laws] in this society are privileged to do so because they have won the struggle against others who seek the privilege of making policy."[37] It is by popular vote that lawmakers and governors are chosen.

Some state constitutions give qualified voters the right and power to bypass customary law-making procedures of state and local governments and to make laws directly. This is called the **initiative process.** It enables groups of voters, if sufficient in numbers, to originate and pass statutes, ordinances, and amendments to their respective constitutions without recourse to the legislature. State legislatures may submit a **referendum** petition to voters for their approval or disapproval of an existing or proposed law. State constitutions as well as statutes can be created, amended, or disapproved through the referendum process. The **recall** petition enables voters to remove from office any elected state or local official before the expiration of his or her term. For most of the past hundred years, these three practices of direct democracy have given the people enhanced power of control over legislation and legislators.

These practices, especially the initiative process, are sometimes misused by well-financed special-interest groups, businesses, and professions to secure enactment of laws

bill of attainder

Act of the legislature inflicting capital punishment upon a named person or member of a specific group without trial and conviction. Forbidden by the U.S. Constitution.

ex post facto laws

[Latin: "after the fact"] A statute that retroactively makes previously lawful conduct a crime. Such a statute is unconstitutional.

initiative process

An electoral process for making new statutes or changing the constitution by filing appropriate formal petitions to be voted upon by legislature (and governor) or by the total electorate.

referendum

A democratic process whereby a state legislature submits (refers) proposed or existing laws to the electorate for approval or rejection.

recall

A democratic process for removing public officials from their elective positions by a vote of the people taken after filing of a petition signed by the required number of qualified voters.

that favor their own purposes. Such groups may hire public relations firms to run a campaign for passage of certain desired legislation. With the use of direct-mail fund raising, and with payments offered to "vote hustlers" for each signature obtained, the public relations firms readily qualify their initiatives for the ballot. Later, absentee ballots may be mailed to persons who have signed the petitions to make it easy for them to vote on the particular proposal.

LEGAL FOCUS—EXAMPLE

Citizens have used the initiative process to establish a statewide lottery in California, to protect the moose in Maine, to encourage the death penalty in Massachusetts, to approve the sale of wine in local grocery stores in Colorado, to abolish daylight savings time in North Dakota, and to limit rights of gays in Colorado.[38]

Critics have condemned the initiative process as it is presently used. Controversial issues make their way onto the ballot and are often written in a manner so verbose and confusing that most people cannot reasonably evaluate the relevant pros and cons or fairly understand how they should vote. The confusion frequently is increased by slick media advertising. Despite the potential abuse inherent in the initiative process, however, it has the big advantage of increasing voter interest and participation.

LEGAL FOCUS—CASE

In 1996 California voters approved by majority vote a bitterly contested initiative. The effect of Proposition 209 was to prohibit affirmative action in public education, employment, and other state programs. Lawsuits were filed in federal court by minorities affected by the change in the law on the grounds that it would deny them equal protection under the law as guaranteed by the U.S. Constitution. What was the result?

Coalition for Economic Equity v. Wilson, 110 F. 3rd 1431 (Ca.9, 1997).

In an *ex parte* (no opposition) hearing, a federal court judge initially suspended Proposition 209 pending a future trial. Shortly thereafter, a higher federal court overruled the decision, and Proposition 209 then went into effect. Thus, through the initiative process, the voter majority was able to create a new law that the state legislative branch was unwilling to enact. Neither Proposition 209 nor similar bans on affirmative action have yet to be heard by the U.S. Supreme Court.

police power

The inherent power of the government to make laws and impose reasonable regulations for the health, safety, morals, or general welfare of the public, even when this limits individual freedom.

THE POLICE POWER

Neither those who wrote the Constitution nor those who ratified it intended the national government to have authority over most details in the everyday lives of people. James Madison believed that limitation on the power of the national government was a major virtue of federalism,[39] whereby the **police power** is implicitly reserved to the states under the Tenth Amendment. The police power is the right to enact and enforce laws for the prevention of fraud and crime and to promote order, safety, health, morals, and the general welfare of the people. Both state and local governments implement police power.

LEGAL FOCUS—CASE

The Virginia state entomologist ordered Julia Miller to cut down a large number of fungoid-infected ornamental red cedar trees growing on her property. The order was made to prevent the transfer of cedar rust disease to local apple orchards. The disease did not affect the value of the cedar trees but did threaten to destroy apple crops in the vicinity. Is Miller bound to comply with the order, and if so does she have a right to compensation for the loss of value to her property?

Miller v. Schoene, 216 U.S. 272, 48 S.Ct. 246 (1928).

It is not unusual for local governments to quarantine crops, create firebreaks, and delay people to respond to important or emergency situations. Persons subject to these actions may suffer significant losses without any legal right to recover these losses from government. Julia Miller had to comply with the order and no reimbursement for her loss was required of government. "And where the public interest is involved preferment of that interest over the property interest of the individual, to the extent even of its destruction, is one of the distinguishing characteristics of every exercise of the police power which affects property."[40]

The police power is thus an essential attribute of government but is subject to the limitations of the federal and state constitutions. Under the Constitution, the national government's power to regulate, control, and circumscribe human conduct is specifically tied to one or more of its delegated powers.[41] For example, the Federal Aviation Administration was established to provide for safety regulation in the manufacture of aircraft as a "necessary and proper" extension of Congress' power to "regulate Commerce . . . among the several States," as prescribed in the Constitution:

> *The Congress shall have Power . . . To regulate Commerce with foreign Nations, and among the several States. . . . And To make all Laws which shall be necessary and proper for carrying into Execution the foregoing Powers, and all other Powers vested by this Constitution in the Government of the United States, or in any Department or Officer thereof.*[42]

WHAT IS THE SUPREMACY CLAUSE?

According to the United States Constitution:

> *This Constitution and the Laws of the United States which shall be made in pursuance thereof; and all Treaties made, or which shall be made, under the Authority of the United States, shall be the* supreme Law of the Land; *and the Judges in every State shall be bound thereby, any* Thing in the Constitution or Laws of any State to the Contrary not withstanding.[43] [Emphasis added]

Thus, the Constitution and federal laws made under it, as well as decisions of the Supreme Court of the United States, together with related supporting opinions, are constituent parts

supremacy doctrine

The judicial doctrine that holds that any state or federal law that is inconsistent with the U.S. Constitution is null and void.

of the "supreme law of the land." The significance of the **supremacy doctrine** is that it invalidates any conflicting state law by preemption, meaning that federal law takes precedence over state law in areas of control expressly delegated to the United States by the Constitution.[44]

LEGAL FOCUS—CASE

An Arizona statute made it unlawful to operate a train of more than fourteen passenger cars or seventy freight cars within the state. The law was a safety measure enacted under the state's police power. Was such state regulation of train lengths lawful?

Southern Pacific v. Arizona, 325 U.S. 761, 65 S.Ct. 1515 (1945).

No. Trains move into and out of Arizona, from and to other states. Interstate commerce is subject to federal regulation under Article I, Section 8 and the Arizona statute unduly burdened interstate transportation. If the state regulation affects interstate commerce only slightly, or if national interests are served well by it, then states may regulate the particular interstate commerce and preemption is unnecessary.

Today there is no argument about the supremacy of the national government. Most of the debate about proper state and federal roles has to do with "effectiveness": Should it be done nationally, or can it be done better locally? The availability of necessary funds and adequate resources are also important factors. States, counties, and cities that are "strapped for cash" eagerly seek federal funding for local projects such as public housing, mass transit construction, education, and indigent care. Also, major natural disasters require a national response. Federal resources are essential when local agencies are overwhelmed by major tasks of relief and reconstruction. Dramatic examples in recent years involved victims of terrorist acts in New York, Pennsylvania, and Washington D.C.; hurricane winds along the Atlantic coast; flooding rivers in the great Mississippi Valley; and earthquakes, floods, and firestorms along the Pacific coast.

WHAT ABOUT TAXES?

In the famous case of *McCulloch v. Maryland*, Chief Justice John Marshall observed that "The power to tax involves the power to destroy."[45] Although primarily revenue-raising measures, taxes also are used to influence the behavior of people and the production and distribution of goods and services. Income taxes and estate and inheritance taxes (so-called *death taxes* on the privilege of giving and receiving part of a decedent's estate) tend to redistribute wealth. So-called *sin taxes* on liquor and tobacco products presumably tend to discourage harmful use of such products. Credits against the payment of taxes otherwise due by renters tends to ease the costs of housing. Tax benefits accorded parents of dependent children tend to ease family costs. And so on.

The authority to tax is provided to the Congress in Article I, Section 8 of the Constitution.

The Congress shall have Power To lay and collect Taxes, Duties, Imposts and Excises,
to pay the Debts and provide for the common Defence and general Welfare of the

*United States; but all Duties, Imposts and Excises shall be uniform throughout the United States.**

Taxes are never popular—but, it has been said, they are the price of civilization. They are essential for the operation of government at all levels. The U.S. Constitution gives Congress "Power to lay [i.e., impose] and collect Taxes, Duties, Imposts [a generic term for taxes, usually referring to schedules of customs duties] and Excises [the term loosely applied to most taxes, including the sales tax, but excluding the income tax and the property tax]."[46]

For most employees, the personal income tax is collected by their employers, who are required to withhold proper amounts from wages or salaries earned. All wage earners are reminded of this each payday when they compare the difference between their "gross" and "net" earnings. The difference is a wide range of federal and state income taxes. Through the process of withholding income taxes, compliance and payment are comparatively simple and assured. Otherwise, at year's end taxpayers may find that they do not have enough money on hand to pay their taxes. But for persons with incomes from various investments, and for business firms, the income tax has evolved into a monstrous maze of confusing regulations. Certified public accountants (CPAs) and tax lawyers often disagree as to the proper interpretation of many clauses. Huge national CPA firms employ both accountants and tax lawyers to offer their customers full tax services. Less wealthy individuals obtain assistance in preparing their returns from tax-preparer businesses available in most cities in the United States. Computer programs also enable many people to prepare their own tax returns without professional assistance, and some file them electronically.

The income tax on individuals and corporations has become the most important single source of revenue for the federal government. It is also imposed by most states and by some local governments. Economists justify it as the most equitable, or progressive, of taxes, especially when rates are graduated, because the levy is imposed in accordance with apparent ability to pay.

In contrast, the sales tax is regressive in that it imposes a disproportionately heavy burden on persons with *low* incomes. For example, the sales tax on an automobile is the same regardless of the purchaser's income. This sum may represent a substantial percentage of one person's disposable income yet hardly be noticed by another, more wealthy individual.

It also should be noted that the ability to pay taxes is not necessarily related to income. Wealth and annual income are not the same thing. For example, large land holdings—although subject to real-property taxes—may produce no taxable income for their land-rich owners. Likewise, persons of great wealth may own tax-exempt bonds issued by the federal or state governments or other public agencies. However, the interest rate on such bonds is generally lower than rates paid by private corporate borrowers. So the owner of tax-free bonds indirectly helps to support the government. Moreover, corporations that reinvest all earnings and pay no dividends (which are taxable income) may, gradually, grow in value and increase the wealth of their shareholders, who pay no income taxes until their shares are sold, if ever, and then at reduced tax (capital gains) rates.

Obviously there is much to be considered in understanding income taxation. From a constitutional standpoint, there is no right to equality of wealth. That the more wealthy citizens may acquire more luxuries in life, or even better legal services, than less wealthy

---

* Significant limitations on how the federal government could tax were removed by constitutional amendment. "Congress shall have power to lay and collect taxes on incomes, from whatever source derived, without apportionment among the several States, and without regard to any census or enumeration," Amendment XVI (ratified on February 3, 1913).

persons is of no constitutional significance. For example, criminal defendants are constitutionally entitled to *competent* legal services, not the best available legal services nor any particular lawyer of choice.

At this book's publication, some U.S. corporations were shifting their corporate charter and business base to countries that provide more favorable tax treatment than the United States. The Corporate Patriot Enforcement Act of 2002 (H.R. 3884) was introduced by Richard Neal of Massachusetts and Jim Maloney of Connecticut to require "that corporate expatriates, who are U.S. companies in fact, must continue to pay their fair share of U.S. taxes."[47]

LEGAL FOCUS—BACKGROUND]

In May of 2002 the shareholders of toolmaker Stanley Works voted to shift the corporation's legal base to Bermuda. The move could save Stanley $30 million in annual taxes. But in a time of war and lingering economic uncertainty, there is rising pressure in Washington to stop the tax-shelter exodus. Company officials said the proposed shift would improve Stanley's ability to compete worldwide and retain thousands of jobs in the United States. In most cases, the Bermuda setup is only a shell, with the company's main operations left in this country. U.S. Rep. James Maloney, D-Conn., said before the shareholder meeting Thursday that Stanley was "engaged in a betrayal of Connecticut." "There has not been a day like this in this state since Benedict Arnold* sailed to Bermuda," said Maloney.[48]

http://

A short biography of one of the most hated Americans in history can be found at **http://www.ushistory.org/ valleyforge/served/arnold .html**

commerce

The exchange of goods or commodities for payment in cash, credit, services, or other goods.

commerce clause

A part of the U.S. Constitution that provides Congress with the power to pass laws to provide for trade with foreign countries and among states.

interstate

Activity that crosses state boundaries.

intrastate

Activity that occurs entirely within a state's boundaries.

WHAT IS THE COMMERCE CLAUSE?

In Article I, Section 8, the Constitution expressly grants the federal government the power to "regulate Commerce with foreign Nations, and among the several States, and with the Indian Tribes." This power to "regulate commerce" allows the federal government to regulate most business activities in the United States with uniform rules.

Commerce includes the buying, selling, and transporting of things of value from place to place. The Supreme Court has held that Congress through the **commerce clause** has the power to regulate any activity, interstate or intrastate, that "affects" interstate commerce. **Interstate** means any activity that crosses state boundaries. **Intrastate** means any activity that occurs entirely within a state's boundaries. Thus, Congress can pass laws that regulate intrastate commerce if, but only if, interstate commerce is affected.

LEGAL FOCUS—CASE

A farmer for several years raised "a small acreage of winter wheat, sown in the Fall and harvested in July; to sell a portion of the crop; to feed part to poultry and livestock on

---

* Benedict Arnold was an American general in the war for independence against Britain. He spied for the British and upon being discovered fled to Bermuda.

the farm, some of which is sold; to use some in making flour for home consumption; and to keep the rest for the following seeding." In the year in question the Secretary of Agriculture refused him a license to plant the wheat as his planting exceeded an acreage allotment determined under the Agricultural Adjustment Act of 1938. The farmer claims his activity is intrastate commercial activity and thus not subject to regulation by the federal government. Is the farmer correct?

Wickard v. Filburn, 317 U.S. 111, 63 S.Ct. 82 (1942).

No. The Supreme Court held that wheat production is subject to federal regulation even if it will never be sold and will be eaten entirely by the farmer's family. The Court reasoned that home use reduces the demand for wheat, which is a sufficient economic effect on interstate commerce. "The general scheme of the Agricultural Adjustment Act of 1938 as related to wheat is to control the volume moving in interstate and foreign commerce in order to avoid surpluses and shortages and the consequent abnormally low or high wheat prices and obstructions to commerce."[49]

Each state has an interest in regulating local activities. As part of their inherent sovereignty (power to govern), states possess police powers to regulate private activities to protect or promote the public health, safety, or general welfare of their citizens. For example, states have a clear interest in keeping their local roads and highways safe. However, when a state regulates the use of its roads and highways, those laws will also affect interstate commerce. A law setting a top speed on a highway affects all drivers, including interstate truckers.

If the state law affects interstate commerce, the courts may be asked to balance the state's interests with those of the federal government. The question is, does a state's exercise of its police power interfere with the federal government's right to regulate interstate commerce? Recall that the Constitution provides that when state and federal law conflict, federal law is supreme. The courts try to answer this question by balancing the interests of the state with those of the federal government. The courts will consider several factors, including the following:

- What interest is the state furthering by its law?
- Does the state law burden (make more difficult) interstate commerce?
- Is there another way the state could accomplish its purpose without burdening interstate commerce?

LEGAL FOCUS—PROBLEM

Suppose Georgia passes a law requiring use of "contoured" rear-fender mudguards on trucks and trailers operating on its highways. All other mudguards are declared illegal. In thirty-five other states, including the neighboring state of Florida, "straight" mudguards are either legal or required. There is evidence suggesting that contoured mudguards are safer than straight mudguards. Is the Georgia statute constitutional?

No. Truckers traveling through Georgia would have a problem. What is legal in Georgia is illegal in other states, including Florida, and vice versa. Clearly, the Georgia law would affect interstate commerce. Even though Georgia's purpose in passing the statute was to increase safety on the highways, a possible increase in safety would not justify requiring truckers to either avoid Georgia or change their mudguards before they pass through.

LEGAL FOCUS—PROBLEM

Kristina Shaman, a resident of Boca Raton, Florida, placed an order via the Internet with Leeward Winery in California for the delivery by mail of a case of chardonnay wine. A Florida statute provides that shipping alcoholic beverages into the state is a felony punishable by fine and jail. Can Florida constitutionally prohibit the U.S. Postal Service or a private carrier, such as United Parcel Service, from shipping alcohol interstate?

http://

For a guide to the various rules for shipping wine, see **http://www.wineinstitute .org/shipwine/analysis/ intro_analysis.htm**

At first blush, it may seem odd that a state that many consider the gateway to drug trafficking would prohibit mail-order wine sales. However, Florida and many other states have adopted such prohibitory laws.[50] These state statutes tend to push up the prices and availability of rare wines and obscure brews, thereby affecting interstate commerce. However, these laws also protect the "dry" counties in many states where all alcoholic sales are prohibited, and also inhibit sales of alcohol to minors. Yet in early 2002 two federal district courts held that a state's prohibition against interstate, direct-to-consumer wine shipments is unconstitutional.[51] Note that the U.S. Postal Service would be immune from any state penalty under the doctrine of supremacy; only the shipper and possibly the purchaser could be held responsible. Many wine-producing states have passed statutes allowing the shipment of wine only from states that also accept that state's wine.[52]

W HAT IS THE BILL OF RIGHTS?

Bill of Rights

The first ten amendments to the U.S. Constitution.

http://

For reference information regarding the U.S. Bill of Rights, use the search feature with key phrase "bill of rights" at **http://www.archives.gov/**

Bill of Rights is the all-inclusive title popularly given to the first ten amendments to the U.S. Constitution (see Exhibit 2-1). The Bill of Rights mandates specific and general restraints on the national government to protect all persons from arbitrary and capricious acts by federal officials. Thus, the Bill of Rights originally applied only as a restraint on the national government. States were bound only by provisions on civil rights if and as specified in their own state constitutions.[53]

Following the Civil War, several amendments were added to the U.S. Constitution to protect and assist the newly freed slaves. In 1865 the Thirteenth Amendment formally outlawed slavery. Previously, most African-Americans had been denied liberty despite the contrary words of the Declaration of Independence* and despite the mandate of the Fifth Amendment that "no person shall be deprived of life, liberty, or property without due process of law."[54] Three years later, in 1868, the Fourteenth Amendment reiterated the right of all persons to liberty and extended the scope of its protection by binding all state and local governments with these words:

> *No state shall make or enforce any law which shall abridge the privileges or immunities of citizens of the United States; nor shall any state deprive any person of life, liberty, or property, without* due process *of law, nor deny to any person within its jurisdiction the* equal protection *of the laws."* [Emphasis added]

The clauses guaranteeing due process of law and equal protection of the law were not defined at the time of the Fourteenth Amendment, leaving the work of definition and

---

* "We hold these Truths to be self-evident, that all Men are created equal, that they are endowed by their Creator with certain unalienable Rights, that among these are Life, Liberty, and the Pursuit of Happiness."

EXHIBIT 2-1: **Bill of Rights**

The Bill of Rights

First Amendment	Guarantees freedom of religion, speech, press, assembly and petition.
Second Amendment	Guarantees the right to keep and bear arms, because a state requires a well-equipped citizen army for its own security.
Third Amendment	Prohibits the lodging of soldiers in peacetime without the dweller's consent.
Fourth Amendment	Prohibits unreasonable searches and seizures of persons or property.
Fifth Amendment	Prohibits deprivation of life, liberty, or property without due process of law, and fair payment when private property is taken for public use, such as in eminent domain; prohibits compulsory self-incrimination and double jeopardy (trial for the same crime twice).
Sixth Amendment	Guarantees the accused in a criminal case the right to a speedy and public trial by an impartial jury and with counsel; allows the accused to cross-examine witnesses against him or her and to solicit testimony from witnesses in his or her favor.
Seventh Amendment	Guarantees a trial by jury for the accused in a civil case involving $20 or more.
Eighth Amendment	Prohibits excessive bail and fines, as well as cruel and unusual punishments.
Ninth Amendment	Establishes that the people have rights in addition to those specified in the Constitution.
Tenth Amendment	Establishes that those powers neither delegated to the national government nor denied to the states are reserved for the states.

due process

The requirement that legal proceedings (including arrest, civil and criminal trials, and punishment) comply with the U.S. Constitution and other applicable substantive and procedural laws.

equal protection

The clause in the Fourteenth Amendment to the U.S. Constitution declaring that "no state shall . . . deny to any person within its jurisdiction the equal protection of the laws."

incorporation doctrine

The Supreme Court's utilization of the Fourteenth Amendment to find Bill of Rights limitations on state and local governments.

specific application to the judicial branch. The due process and equal protection clauses have been used by the Supreme Court to restrict the constitutionally reserved powers of the states.

Simply stated, the Supreme Court defines **due process** as the equivalent of fundamental fairness and **equal protection** as the prevention of invidious discrimination (i.e., differentiating offensively or unfairly). Thus, states cannot violate the due process or equal protection guaranteed to the people, regardless of what is contained in their respective constitutions. But the application of those terms to specific examples of state action was to evolve through Supreme Court decisions through an interpretive process referred to as the **incorporation doctrine.**

INCORPORATION DOCTRINE

In its trailblazing decision in *Gitlow v. New York* in 1925, the U.S. Supreme Court announced, "[W]e may and do assume that freedom of speech and of press—First Amendment protections—are among the fundamental personal rights and 'liberties' protected by the due process clause of the Fourteenth Amendment from impairment by the States."[55]

With the *Gitlow* decision, the Supreme Court began a policy it has maintained ever since. As selected cases reach it, the Court has systematically imposed on the states most of the guarantees found in the Bill of Rights by interpreting the Fourteenth Amendment's due process clause to restrict state impositions on individual liberty. Its ongoing impact is to bind both the national and state governments to a similar standard of compliance regarding due process and equal protection.

THE FIRST AMENDMENT—AND FREE SPEECH

The **First Amendment** contains what are known historically as *primary rights*. It is no accident that this amendment begins with the phrase, "Congress shall make no law. . . ." Nor is it accidental that first among our primary rights is freedom of speech and press. They are "the matrix, the indispensable condition, of nearly every other form of freedom."[56] As Justice Hugo Black remarked, "Freedom to speak and write about public questions is as important to the life of our government as is the heart to the human body. . . . If that heart be weakened, the result is debilitation; if it be stilled, the result is death."[57] Accordingly, the Supreme Court has decided incrementally, one case after another, that the states must also guarantee to their citizens First Amendment rights of freedom of speech and press.[58]

The Court, however, has been unable to define **free speech** with precision. It has moved successively through certain legal expedients, or "tests":

1. The "clear and present danger" test under which speech could be regulated by government was explained in *Schenck*.[59]
2. The "bad tendency" test was exemplified in *Abrams*. Here the Court accorded little importance to the guarantee of free speech, focusing almost solely on the impact of the challenged speech on the war (World War I) effort.[60]
3. The "preferred position" test was articulated in Justice Harlan Stone's famous footnote in the *Carolene Products* case. Stone presented the view that free speech enjoyed a preferred position in relation to other constitutional guarantees, calling for a more precise and searching scrutiny of legislation that might curtail "political processes."[61]
4. During the Cold War of the late 1940s and the 1950s, the Supreme Court upheld the conviction of eleven leaders of the American Communist Party by enforcing the Smith Act of 1940, which made it a crime to teach or advocate the overthrow of government by force. In doing so, the Court adopted the "probability" statement of the "clear and present danger" rule, as expressed by the highly respected Chief Judge Learned Hand, writing for the lower court majority: "In each case [courts] must ask whether the gravity of the 'evil,' discounted by its improbability, justifies such invasion of free speech as is necessary to avoid the danger."[62]
5. Political dissent during the late 1960s and early 1970s found the Court using the "ad hoc balancing" test. Using the "clear and present danger" test, the Court weighed the competing interests of free speech and law and order. Every ordinance attempting to serve the interests of the state must be drawn with "reasonable specificity toward the [speech] and conduct prohibited."[63]

LEGAL FOCUS—CASE

Paladin Press published a book *Hit Man: A Technical Manual for Independent Contractors*, which provided instructions for would-be contract murderers. Lawrence Horn hired James Perry, a contract killer, to murder his ex-wife and their brain-damaged son, after which Horn expected to inherit a $2 million trust fund intended for the boy. Perry, using principles studied in the Paladin murder text, suffocated the boy and shot the ex-wife and an overnight nurse to their deaths. A sister of the ex-wife sued Paladin Press in a civil case for damages for aiding and abetting the murderer. Is the publication of an instructional book for murder protected by the First Amendment from a civil lawsuit?[64]

Paladin Enterprises, Inc. v. Rice, 940 F.Supp. 836 (D. Md. 1996), rev'd, 128 F.3d 233 (4th Cir. 1997), cert. denied, 523 U.S. 1074, 118 S.Ct. 1515 (1998).

No. The Constitution does not shield from civil lawsuits such things as bomb-making guides, assassination manuals, or similar works that exhort people to take the law into their own hands. Nor does the Constitution prevent the publication of libelous (untruthful) material and any subsequent civil lawsuits that may follow. The **prior restraint** of speech that is offensive for any reason is a judicial power that is exercised only in the most extraordinary circumstances.

The Court has been careful to protect expressive activity and symbolic speech,[65] and has ruled that burning of the national flag of the United States, as political speech, can be restricted neither by the states nor by the Congress.[66]

prior restraint

Restraints on a publication before it is actually published.

Is Commercial Speech Protected?

Commercial speech, which is defined as any communication that advertises a product or service for a business purpose to earn a profit, is also protected, but not as comprehensively as other speech.

commercial speech

Oral, written, and other forms of communication used in advertising and in other business activities.

LEGAL FOCUS—CASE

San Diego enacted an ordinance that prohibited commercial outdoor advertising signs within the city limits. Sign owners sued the city for injunctive relief, claiming that the law violated their rights under the First Amendment. Does the ordinance violate the Constitution?

Metromedia Inc. v. City of San Diego, 453 U.S. 490, 101 S.Ct. 2882 (1981).

Yes. Speaking for the Court, Justice Byron B. White stated:

> *Prior to 1975, purely commercial advertisements of services or goods for sale was considered to be outside the protection of the First Amendment.... [But] in* Virginia Pharmacy Board v. Virginia Citizens Consumer Council, *425 U.S. 748 (1976), we plainly held that speech proposing no more than commercial transaction enjoys a substantial degree of First Amendment protection. A State may not completely suppress the dissemination of truthful information about an entirely lawful activity merely because it is fearful of that information's effect upon its disseminators and its recipients....* [67]

LEGAL FOCUS—PROBLEM

U.S. Beverage Co. produced Phat Boy, an inexpensive malt liquor that was sold in bigger bottles with a higher alcohol content than competing beers. It also sported a funky red, black, and yellow label and contained ginseng, which some consider an aphrodisiac. ("Phat" is a '90s version of the word "cool.") A public interest group contended that Phat Boy was targeted to underage African-Americans, much like cigarette ads featuring Joe Camel allegedly targeted teenagers. Does the Constitution protect focused commercial advertising?[68]

Yes, but to a lesser extent than other forms of speech. When alcohol is involved in any commercial activity, the states have an additional interest in protecting the public from harm. However, the North Carolina Alcoholic Beverage Commission received no complaints from the public, and the product was promoted and sold widely, not targeted in specific neighborhoods.

IS SYMBOLIC SPEECH PROTECTED? EVEN "HATE SPEECH"?

Although originally expressed as protection for spoken, written, or printed words, the First Amendment has been appropriately construed by the Court to embrace many forms of the communication of ideas.

Motion pictures, television programs, electronic tapes and digital disks, and electronic and fax transmissions have taken their place alongside the formerly dominant person-to-person speech and printed statements. In Des Moines, Iowa, the U.S. Supreme Court upheld the right of students to wear black armbands in school to show their opposition to the Vietnam War. The conduct was "a symbolic act that is within the Free Speech Clause ... [and] was entirely divorced from actually or potentially disruptive conduct" that would interfere with appropriate discipline in the operation of the school.[69] As noted earlier, the symbolic act of burning an American flag is likewise protected under the First Amendment.

As indicated by these cases, the U.S. Supreme Court zealously erects ramparts around the cherished First Amendment freedoms to communicate.

LEGAL FOCUS—PROBLEM

Stanford University, a private institution, adopted a code stating that "one student cannot with purpose vilify another with fighting words that are ugly gutter epithets like 'nigger' and 'kike.'" The code also banned such hate-associated symbols as the swastika. Can a private university proscribe undesirable speech?

No. Stanford students challenged the code in a state superior court (trial court) where the judge granted a preliminary injunction declaring Stanford's "hate speech" ban unconstitutionally broad.[70] Basing his decision on a state law, the judge ruled that the university violated students' freedom of expression by prohibiting only certain "fighting words" linked to sex and race. Stanford defended their eighteen-months-in-the-making speech code by contending that [California's] Leonard Law, which extended free speech protections to private schools, "intruded on the university's right to govern itself and establish rules of proper behavior."[71]

In 1992, the U.S. Supreme Court unanimously condemned a St. Paul, Minnesota, ordinance that outlawed any hate-motivated expression (e.g., burning crosses, displaying swastikas) that "one knows or has reasonable grounds to know arouses anger, alarm, or resentment in others on the basis of race, color, creed, religion or gender."[72] In the **hate speech** case in question, a seventeen-year-old skinhead (i.e., an antisocial or delinquent youth who wears his hair closely cropped) was arrested after setting fire to a crude cross in the yard of an African-American family that had recently settled in a predominantly white neighborhood. Justice Antonin Scalia noted that such conduct "is reprehensible.... But St. Paul has sufficient means at its disposal to prevent such behavior without adding the First Amendment to the fire."[73] Note, however, that in the following year the Court unanimously upheld a Wisconsin statute that imposes harsher penalties on a criminal who "intentionally selects the person against whom the crime ... is committed ... because of the race, religion, color, disability, sexual orientation, national origin or ancestry of that person."[74] Most states now have similar "hate crime" penalty-enhancement laws.

In other cases, the Court has withheld the protective shield of the First Amendment from "fighting words," meaning words "which by their very utterance inflict injury or tend to incite an immediate breach of the peace" and conduct that is "directed to inciting or producing imminent lawless action and is likely to incite or produce such action."[75]

Reference in the Wisconsin statute to "sexual orientation" exemplifies increasing concern of legislative bodies and courts with the civil rights of homosexual persons, male and female. No doubt many homosexual persons have served with honor and distinction in military uniforms. In 1993 the Clinton administration took steps to permit them to openly disclose their sexual orientation. Opposition from top military commanders and others resulted in adoption of a compromise policy that is reflected in the advice, "Don't ask; don't tell; don't pursue."

LEGAL FOCUS—CASE

Master Chief Petty Officer McVeigh sent an e-mail with return address of "Boysrch," which prompted a sexual orientation investigation by the U.S. Navy. America Online revealed McVeigh's identity in violation of a federal privacy law. The Navy began proceedings to discharge McVeigh without benefits. Has the Navy violated the "Don't ask; don't tell; don't pursue" policy?

McVeigh v. Cohen, 983 F.Supp. 215 (D.D.C., 1998) and 996 F.Supp. 59 (D.D.C., 1998).

Yes. A federal judge ruled that the Navy's investigation into McVeigh's sexual orientation was a violation of the policy. McVeigh retired with full benefits and received money damages from America Online.[76]

It is noteworthy that the members of the military are controlled by the Uniform Code of Military Justice, which closely prescribes conduct within the military services. Serious issues regarding the discharge of homosexual persons from the service, of women in combat roles, and of immoral sexual behavior continue to plague the military branches.*

Certain artists and their publishers have produced paintings, photographs, magazines, books, songs, videotapes, and compact discs that allegedly violate traditional and appropriate standards of morality and decency. Probably most people are not offended because they are not within the targeted markets for most of this bizarre art. However, programs on free television and cable television now enter most homes. Increasing numbers of viewers, both old and young, find excessive violence and perceived obscenity intolerable and are

hate speech

Words spoken, written, or symbolized (e.g., by placing burning crosses on private lawns) that express irrational and false ideas that insult and demean certain persons or classes of persons.

* The president is the "Commander in Chief of the United States...." U.S. Constitution, Article II, Section 2. However, the president is not subject to the Uniform Code of Military Justice that applies to the military and prohibits, among other things, immoral sexual activity such as adultery.

demanding government imposition of restraints or standards. But the practical difficulty of imposing effective controls is readily apparent from a reading of the 1973 case of *Miller v. California*, in which the U.S. Supreme Court decreed that to be legally condemned as obscene, the material must be such that

1. the average person,
2. applying contemporary community standards,
3. would find that the work taken as a whole appeals to the prurient (i.e., characterized by lustful thoughts) interest, and
4. the work depicts or describes in a patently offensive way sexual conduct proscribed by state law,
5. and whether—taken as a whole—it is lacking in serious artistic, political, or scientific value.[77]

The inherently subjective nature of the listed criteria, coupled with potentially thousands of different problems or cases, every one of which is unique in at least some respect, makes any comprehensive policing effort predestined to fail, except in the most egregious cases.

What is known is that nearly nude dancing by females (wearing "pasties" and "G-strings") is not inherently obscene and may be expressive conduct protected by the First and Fourteenth Amendments.[78] Essentially the determination of specifically what is obscene and, therefore, may be prohibited by state or local government is made by juries on a case-by-case basis.

Symbolic speech may also sometimes be deemed offensive because of historical implications related to race, religion, or other constitutionally protected classifications.

LEGAL FOCUS—PROBLEM

The mascot of Birmingham High School in Pontiac, Michigan, is a headdressed American Indian based on Chief Pontiac, an Ottawa Indian who was an organizer of tribes against the invading English during the 1700s. The city of Pontiac is named after this chief. The high school's team name is the "Braves." In response to demands of American Indian activists, the local board of education chose to change the mascots of four high schools, including the "Mohicans" and the "Warriors." Removing the "Braves" logo from the Birmingham High School gym floor and track and purchasing new gym clothes and uniforms will cost $240,000. The activists argued that portrayal of an American Indian with a headdress is sacrilegious.[79] Does the Constitution protect the use of insulting or sacrilegious speech?

Yes. However, there may be other reasons why a public school chooses to avoid offensive language or symbols. Even if offensive speech is protected from censorship by the Constitution, that does not mean it should be employed.

FREE SPEECH AND THE INTERNET

The Internet began in 1969 as an international network of computers among the military, defense contractors, and universities conducting defense-related research. Redundant connections were established to preserve communications even if some portions of the network were damaged in a war. Today, civilian networks link with one another, allowing many millions of people to communicate and access vast amounts of information from around the world. The Internet is a unique and wholly new medium of worldwide human communication the use of which is posing new challenges to our Constitution and legal system.

Solutions to new problems, especially those involving government regulation of speech, will relate in part to the mechanics of the Internet. Approximately 143 million Americans and 400 million people worldwide were using the Internet as of September 2001.[80] Colleges and universities provide access for their students and faculty; many corporations provide their employees with access through an office network; many communities and local libraries provide free access; and computer coffee shops provide access for a small hourly fee.

The most significant category of communication over the Internet is the World Wide Web, which allows users to search for and retrieve information stored in remote computers, and sometimes to communicate back. The Web consists of a vast number of documents stored in computers all over the world. Some are files; others are more elaborate Web pages that contain links to other documents created by that site's author or to other related sites. To access a Web site, users simply type a known address into their computers or enter keywords into a commercial search engine in an effort to locate desired addresses. A particular Web page may contain the information sought by the "surfer" or, through its links, provide an avenue to other documents located anywhere in the world on the Internet. Access to most Web pages is free, although many allow access only to those who have purchased the right from a commercial provider. In this manner, any person can become a global publisher of information. No single organization controls membership in the Web, nor is there any centralized point from which individual Web sites or services can be blocked or regulated by government. According to Statistics.com, the search engine Google identified 1.4 billion unique Uniform Reference Locators (URLs) in 2002.[81]

Although the Internet is over thirty years old, it is still very young in terms of governments applying control through legal rules. The growth of Internet users with its attendant social and economic impacts make the access and control very important to people and to governments. Issues such as individual privacy, spam, identity theft, and pornography are but some of the issues that send people to government asking for rules. As electronic transmissions cross state and national boundaries, the potential legal problems are growing in number and complexity almost as fast as the Internet itself.

Among the important legal issues in the United States about the Internet are fundamental questions concerning free speech and pornography. Sexually explicit material on the Internet includes text, pictures, and chat that range from the modestly titillating to the completely explicit. Many people go looking for sexually explicit material but your authors know from experience that sometimes these sites show up in search requests for material totally unrelated to sex. In 1996 Congress adopted two acts, the Communications Decency Act (CDA)[82] and the Child Pornography Prevention Act (CPPA) in an attempt to regulate sexually explicit Internet content as it related to children.[83] The CDA attempted to prohibit the knowing transmission of obscene or indecent messages to any recipient under eighteen years of age. The Supreme Court held the CDA to be an unconstitutional infringement of free speech guaranteed by the U.S. Constitution in 1997.[84]

LEGAL FOCUS—CASE

The second act was the CPPA, which provided a federal prohibition against sexually explicit images that appear to depict minors produced without using any real children—virtual child pornography. The statute prohibited possessing or distributing these virtual images. Is the act constitutional or does it violate the First Amendment protection against free speech?

Ashcroft v. The Free Speech Coalition, 535 U.S. 234, 122 S.Ct. 1389 (2002).

The Court stated: [A]s a general principle, the First Amendment bars the government from dictating what we see or read or speak or hear. The freedom of speech has its limits; it does not embrace certain categories of speech, including defamation, incitement, obscenity, and pornography produced with real children." Among the arguments in favor of the statute was that to eliminate the market for pornography produced using real children necessitated a prohibition on virtual images. The courts response to that argument was, "The Government may not suppress lawful speech as the means to suppress unlawful speech. Protected speech does not become unprotected merely because it resembles the latter." In holding the second of the two 1996 Congressional attempts to control Internet pornography unconstitutional the Court stated the provisions considered "are overbroad and unconstitutional."

Do these two cases mean that Internet content cannot be regulated? Hardly. But the cases do make clear that constitutional freedoms such as the First Amendment make regulation of the Internet and new technologies a challenging task for the legislatures. Still improper use of the Internet by individuals, such as by publishing libelous material (civil) or by conspiring to commit criminal offenses, can result in civil or criminal penalties. Free speech does not equate to freedom from personal responsibility to comply with laws enacted under proper exercise of the police powers of the states.

LEGAL FOCUS—CASE

"Approximately 10 percent of the Americans who use the Internet access it at public libraries. And approximately 95 percent of all public libraries in the United States provide public access to the Internet." Can Congress require public libraries to provide software filters to guard against sexually explicit content as a condition to the receipt of federal subsidies?

American Library Ass'n, Inc. v. United States, 201 F.Supp.2d 401 (E.D.Pa., 2002).

The United States was sued by a group of libraries, library associations, library patrons, and Web site publishers alleging that the Children's Internet Protection Act,[85] requiring filtering of sexually explicit content, forces the libraries to violate their patrons' First Amendment rights. The court in agreeing with the plaintiffs said, "Any currently available filtering product that is reasonably effective in preventing users from accessing content within the filter's category definitions will necessarily block countless thousands of Web pages, the content of which does not match the filtering company's category definitions, much less the legal definitions of obscenity, child pornography, or harmful to minors." The U.S. Supreme Court may well consider this case during the life of this edition of the textbook.

THE FIRST AMENDMENT—AND FREEDOM OF RELIGION

It is not surprising that the Bill of Rights provides for the protection of religious liberty first, because many of the colonists came here to escape religious persecution. The First

Amendment guarantees **freedom of religion** in two ways. The First Amendment *establishment clause* prohibits Congress from establishing a religion ("Congress shall make no law respecting an establishment of religion"). Additionally, the *free exercise clause* prohibits government interference in the free exercise of religious beliefs ("Congress shall make no law . . . prohibiting the free exercise of [religion]"). Government action, both federal and state, is expected to be neutral toward religion. Regulation that does not promote religion or place a significant burden on religion is constitutional.

Religious pluralism is a hallmark of American life, together with our commitment to religious freedom. In many parts of the world, governments maintain "official" religions and official religions maintain governments. In the United States, a wall has been erected between church and state; any significant breach of that wall by either government or church, no matter how compelling, is generally suspect. Yet attempts to promote or dissuade certain religions are made from time to time in spite of the First Amendment. What should be the government's position respecting religion? The Supreme Court has answered. The First Amendment (on religion) means this:

> *Neither a state nor the federal government can set up a church. Neither can pass laws, which aid one religion, aid all religions, or prefer one religion to another. Neither can force nor influence a person to go to or to remain away from church against his will or force him to profess a belief or disbelief in any religion. No person can be punished for entertaining or professing religious beliefs or disbeliefs, for church attendance or nonattendance. No tax in any amount, large or small, can be levied to support any religious activities or institutions, whatever they may be called, or whatever form they may adopt to teach or practice religion. Neither a state nor the federal government can, openly or secretly, participate in the affairs of any religious organizations or groups and vice versa . . . the [religious] clause was intended to erect "a wall of separation between church and state."*[86]

freedom of religion

"Congress shall make no law respecting an establishment of religion, or prohibiting the free exercise thereof . . ."

ESTABLISHMENT CLAUSE

Accordingly, the Supreme Court has declared unconstitutional various state attempts to promote "religious values" in public schools under the establishment clause. In 1962, in a controversial decision (*Engel v. Vitale*),[87] the Court outlawed the recitation of a nonsectarian prayer in the public schools of New York State. The prayer was to be said aloud in class in the presence of a teacher at the beginning of every school day.* Speaking for the Court, Justice Hugo L. Black pointed out that the prayer violated the establishment clause of the First Amendment:

> *Its first and most immediate purpose [referring to the clause] rested on the belief that a union of government and religion tends to destroy government and to degrade religions. . . . [G]overnmentally established religions and religious persecution go hand in hand. . . . It was in large part to get completely away from this sort of systematic religious persecution that the Founders brought into being our Nation, our Constitution and our Bill of Rights.*[88]

The Court later said that even a one-minute period of silence for "meditation or voluntary prayer" is constitutionally impermissible.[89]

---

* Prayer prescribed by New York Board of Regents: "Almighty God, we acknowledge our dependence upon Thee, and we beg Thy blessings upon us, our parents, our teachers and our country."

FREE EXERCISE CLAUSE

The First Amendment's protection of religion is complicated because while it restricts any government establishment of religion it also restricts government from "prohibiting the free exercise" of religion. There clearly is a tension between these two admonitions. Do individuals have the right to act any way they want to on the basis on their religious beliefs? No. There is an important distinction between belief and practice. While the government lacks authority to compel you to accept or reject any religious belief, the right to practice one's beliefs does have some limitations. Through the years, the Supreme Court has followed the general principle that people are free to believe and worship as they wish so long as their conduct violates no laws that validly protects the health, safety, or morals of the community.

LEGAL FOCUS—CASE

It is the 1870s in Utah and Reynolds is a Mormon with two wives. The then territory of Utah prosecutes him for violation of a U.S. Territory statute stating "Every person having a husband or wife living, who marries another . . . is guilty of bigamy, and shall be punished by a fine of not more than $500, and by imprisonment for a term of not more than five years." Among the defenses offered by Reynolds were that the church doctrine of the time made it "the duty of male members of said church, circumstances permitting, to practise [sic] polygamy,"[90] and the First Amendment restricts government from passing a statute that prohibits the free exercise of his religion. Was he correct?

Reynolds v. United States, 98 U.S. 145, 25 L.Ed. 244 (1878).

http://

An interesting list of major religions in order of the number of adherents can be found at

http://www.adherents.com/Religions_By_Adherents.html

This United States Supreme Court case was one of the first to consider whether the free exercise clause provides a defense to a criminal act. The Court bluntly said no. "To permit this would be to make the professed doctrines of religious belief superior to the law of the land, and in effect to permit every citizen to become a law unto himself. Government could exist only in name under such circumstances."

In recent years a number of cases have raised the question of allowing free exercise of religion in public schools as a counter to public school establishment of religion. In other words; although the public school cannot encourage a religious practice, must it allow it? In 1984 Congress passed the Equal Access Act,[91] making it unlawful for any public high school receiving federal assistance (funds) to prevent student groups from using school facilities for religious activities. In addition the Religious Freedoms Restoration Act[92] was passed in 1993 stating that "governments should not substantially burden religious exercise without compelling justification."[93] These statutes have been interpreted to authorize student-initiated religious activities if other types of student-initiated gatherings are permitted. The Supreme Court had already declared constitutional student-initiated religious worship at state universities and colleges.[94]

Other activities involving religion are permissible in public schools. These include:

- Silent prayer before tests so long as other students are not persuaded to participate.
- The teaching of the history of religion as distinguished from teaching religion.
- The expression by students of their religious beliefs in the form of reports that are germane to their assignments.
- Participation in religious clubs.[95]
- The wearing of religious garb including ceremonial knives.[96]

COULD GUNS BE BANNED?

According to the Second Amendment:

> *A well regulated Militia, being necessary to the security of a free State, the right of the people to keep and bear Arms, shall not be infringed.*

When this amendment was penned, the common practice of states was to have large standing armies. There was a strong public sentiment that a large permanent army should not be part of the national government. Also, the amendment was designed to prevent Congress from disarming and abolishing state militias.

The Supreme Court has sustained this sentiment: "The Second Amendment guarantees *no right* to keep and bear a firearm that does not have some reasonable relationship to the preservation or efficiency of a well-regulated militia."[97]

States as well as the federal government may regulate some or all privately owned firearms if they so choose. According to the Court:

> *There is under our decisions no reason why stiff laws governing the purchase and possession of pistols may not be enacted. There is no reason why pistols may not be barred from anyone with a police record. There is no reason why a state may not require a purchaser of a pistol to pass a psychiatric test. There is no reason why all pistols should not be barred to everyone except the police.*[98]

How the Second Amendment should be interpreted is a contentious constitutional discussion. Strong beliefs exist on both sides of an argument as to whether restriction or control of firearms is constitutional or advisable. Proponents of gun control argue that the Second Amendment protects only a collective right to keep and bear arms in furtherance of a well-regulated militia. Most federal court opinion is on their side. Opponents of gun control argue that the Second Amendment protects an individual's fundamental right to keep and bear arms.

http://

Different perspectives on the handgun control debate can be found at **http://www.nra.org/** and **http://www.cphv.org/**

LEGAL FOCUS—CASE

Sacha Emerson sought a divorce from her husband, Dr. Timothy Emerson. As the divorce progressed she requested a restraining order (order from the court) to stop Dr. Emerson from making threatening communications or attacks on her during the divorce proceedings. The court issued the restraining order. Later a dispute occurred between the Emersons and he displayed a Beretta pistol he otherwise lawfully owned. Dr. Emerson was criminally charged with possessing firearms while subject to a restraining order in violation of a federal statute. He moved to dismiss the indictment, asserting the statute and its application to him violated his Second Amendment right to possess firearms. Was the indictment dismissed?

United States v. Emerson, 46 F.Supp. 2d 598 (N.D.Tex.1999) and *United States v. Emerson*, 270 F.2d 203 (5th Cir. Tex. 2001).

The Texas District Court agreed with Dr. Emerson and dismissed the charges. On appeal the Texas federal appellate court reversed the trial court and held "that the nexus between firearm possession by [Dr. Emerson] . . . and the threat of lawless violence, is sufficient to [suspend Dr. Emerson's] Second Amendment right to keep and bear arms."

The case is especially notable for two reasons. The first is that although the criminal charges against the doctor were upheld, the court rejected the argument that the Second Amendment protects only collective rights. Instead the court held that the right to bear arms "protects the right of individuals, including those not then actually a member of any militia or engaged in active military service or training, to privately possess and bear their own firearms, such as the pistol involved here, that are suitable as personal, individual weapons." The second reason is that as this book goes to print the case has been appealed to the U.S. Supreme Court, and the U.S. Attorney General supported the Court of Appeals interpretation of the amendment. "[T]he Second Amendment more broadly protects the rights of individuals, including persons who are not members of any militia or engaged in active military service or training, to possess and bear their own firearms, subject to reasonable restrictions designed to prevent possession by unfit persons or to restrict the possession of types of firearms that are particularly suited to criminal misuse."*[99]

FREEDOM FROM UNREASONABLE SEARCHES

The Fourth Amendment recognizes "The right of the people to be secure in their persons, houses, papers, and effects against unreasonable searches and seizures." But note that *reasonable* searches and seizures are permitted. Consequently, search warrants may be issued "upon probable cause, supported by Oath or affirmation, and particularly describing the place to be searched, and the persons or things to be seized." In two cases, *Wolf v. Colorado* (1949)[100] and *Mapp v. Ohio*[101] (1961) the Supreme Court imposed on the states the same standards of care in search and seizure procedures and the exclusion of evidence illegally obtained as that imposed by the Constitution on the national government. The Court said that citizens have a "right to privacy" and to be "free from unreasonable state intrusions.... We hold that all evidence obtained by search and seizures in violation of the Constitution is, by the same authority, inadmissible in a state Court."[102] This is known as the **exclusionary rule,** which is discussed more fully in Chapter 6.

RIGHTS OF AN ACCUSED TO DUE PROCESS OF LAW

The due process clause of the U.S. Constitution is really two clauses: the **Fifth Amendment,** which restricts federal government power, and the Fourteenth, which restricts state government power. The clauses hold that no person shall "be deprived of life, liberty, or property, without due process of law." These few words have led to millions of words by courts, lawyers, and laypeople attempting to define what due process means. Due process means government is expected to use fair and reasonable methods when exercising power over individuals, which is a matter of procedural due process. The clause has also been used to limit government exercise of power over the content of the law, which is a matter of substantive due process.

Examples of procedural due process questions often arise in the processing of individuals in the criminal justice system. Among the due process rights recognized over the

---

exclusionary rule

The court-made rule that precludes the use in criminal court proceedings of any evidence improperly obtained by the prosecution.

Fifth Amendment

"No person shall be held to answer for a capital, or otherwise infamous crime, unless on a presentment or indictment of a Grand Jury, except in cases arising in the land or naval forces, or in the Militia, when in actual service in time of War or public danger; nor shall any person be subject for the same offence to be twice put in jeopardy of life or limb; nor shall be compelled in any criminal case to be a witness against himself, nor be deprived of life, liberty, or property, without due process of law; nor shall private property be taken for public use, without just compensation."

---

* The position of the Justice Department is a significant change in its position of many years. In response the "National Rifle Association, which last summer featured a picture of Mr. Ashcroft (Attorney General) on the cover of its magazine and called him 'a breath of fresh air to freedom-loving gun owners,' lauded the Justice Department's position today." Linda Greenhouse, "U.S., in a Shift, Tells Justices Citizens Have a Right to Guns," *The New York Times*, May 8, 2002, Late Edition—Final, Sec. A; p. 1.

years is the right to be represented by a lawyer during police questioning. The right arises after one is taken into custody or otherwise deprived of freedom in any significant way. The representation by an attorney is necessary to protect against compelled testimony and self-incrimination, each a basic right mandated by the U.S. Supreme Court for compliance by federal government and all states.[103]

LEGAL FOCUS—CASE

A police undercover agent was planted in a cell with prisoner Perkins, who had been jailed for aggravated assault. Perkins was also under investigation for murder. The undercover agent asked Perkins if he had ever killed anybody. In answering the question, Perkins made statements implicating himself in the murder. Is this testimony that was given voluntarily but unknowingly by Perkins to a police officer admissible as evidence despite the way it was obtained?

Illinois v. Perkins, 496 U.S. 292, 110 S.Ct. 2394 (1990).

Yes. The Supreme Court held that an undercover officer posing as an inmate has no obligation to warn an incarcerated suspect of any constitutional rights before asking questions, even though the response could be legally incriminating.

Through a series of decisions based on Section 1 of the **Fourteenth Amendment,** the Supreme Court has imposed an obligation on the states to honor the human rights identified in the Fifth and Sixth Amendments. Included is the right to a speedy[104] and public trial[105] by an unbiased jury,[106] assuredly among the most vital of rights in a free society. To further guarantee a fair trial, the Court in other cases also incorporated the right to have **compulsory process*** for obtaining witnesses for the defense of the accused person[107] and to the assistance of professional legal counsel in all cases[108] and at all stages[109] of criminal procedures to which the defendant is subjected. An exception is made as to counsel in appellate proceedings (although, in fact, appellants are generally assisted by counsel who are paid by the state).

LEGAL FOCUS—CASE

Chicago adopted an anti-loitering ordinance intended to curb the "expanding cancer" of urban gangs. Under the ordinance, people loitering (standing) in a public place could be ordered to move along if a police officer believed one or more was a gang member. Those who refused to move along could be arrested and sent to jail for up to six months, fined $500, and ordered to perform three weeks of public service—even without proof of criminal intent. Does the ordinance as applied deprive defendants of due process of law?

City of Chicago v. Morales, 527 U.S. 41, 119 S.Ct. 1849 (1999).

Concern about criminal activity by members of urban gangs has prompted many local boards and councils to adopt ordinances designed to protect their residents. The Chicago

---

* Compulsory process means the court, at the request of a defendant in a criminal prosecution, must use its legal powers to compel the appearance of witnesses in favor of the defendant (U.S. Constitution, Sixth Amendment).

http://

No man, not even the king, is above the law. You will find the first right of an accused to trial by jury in the Magna Carta, at **http://www.archives.gov/ exhibit_hall/featured_docu ments/magna_carta/index .html**

Fourteenth Amendment

In part, "All persons born or naturalized in the United States, and subject to the jurisdiction thereof, are citizens of the United States and of the State wherein they reside. No State shall make or enforce any law which shall abridge the privileges or immunities of citizens of the United States; nor shall any State deprive any person of life, liberty, or property, without due process of law; nor deny to any person within its jurisdiction the equal protection of the laws."

compulsory process

(a) The right guaranteed by the Sixth Amendment to every person accused of a crime to require witnesses to appear in his or her favor, by court order. (b) Official action to force a person to appear as a witness in court, at an administrative hearing, or before a legislature.

ordinance is but one example. Ordinarily a person cannot be convicted of a crime by mere association and without criminal intent. In the above case the Illinois Supreme Court concluded that the Chicago ordinance did not provide sufficiently specific limits on the enforcement discretion of the police to meet constitutional standards for definiteness and clarity. In upholding the Illinois Supreme Court the United States Supreme Court stated: "We recognize the serious and difficult problems testified to by the citizens of Chicago that led to the enactment of this ordinance. We are mindful that the preservation of liberty depends in part on the maintenance of social order. However, in this instance the city has enacted an ordinance that affords too much discretion to the police and too little notice to citizens who wish to use the public streets."

The rights of persons accused of a crime are more fully described in Chapter 6.

Ⓔ QUAL PROTECTION OF THE LAW IN EDUCATION

The fourteenth Amendment of the U.S. Constitution also provides that "no state shall . . . deny to any person within its jurisdiction the equal protection of the laws," commonly called the equal protection clause. Understanding this expectation of equal treatment requires context. As college students some of you received government grants and loans, but many of you did not. Virtually no one is paying the same for their college education. Faculty, administrators, and handicapped persons probably have a better parking place at universities than others. The equal protection clause has not been interpreted to afford equality among persons; instead, it requires equal treatment of persons in similar situations. In other words, government must treat people similarly if they are "similarly circumstanced." Note again the requirement of government action, as the constitution protects against government, not private, conduct.

The Supreme Court has developed a three-stage test based on the nature of the right (e.g., to vote) or the class of individuals (e.g., gender) being affected when considering equal protection challenges. The court begins with presumption of legislative validity.

1. **Strict scrutiny test.** Is the nature of the right or the class of individuals being affected inherently suspect? Distinctions based on race, alienage, national origin, ethnicity, religion, marriage, and voting have been held inherently suspect. Government must demonstrate that any law providing for differential treatment serves a compelling state interest and is narrowly tailored to serve that interest.
2. **Intermediate scrutiny test.** Is the right or classification similar to a protected fundamental right? If so, the court provides for "heightened scrutiny." The standard has been used for gender- and legitimacy-based discrimination cases. Government must show that the discriminating law or policy bears a "substantial relationship" to an "important" government interest.
3. **Minimal scrutiny or rational basis test.** Does the challenged law involve neither a suspect classification nor a fundamental right? In that case, government need show only that the law is rationally related to a legitimate state interest. Usually classifications based on economic and social status fall within this minimal scrutiny range.

The equal right to education is arguably the first key to providing an opportunity for all students to realize their potential. The second, as shown in Exhibit 2-2, would be employment, and the third would be housing. The three are interdependent in a circular pattern:

1. Equal access to high-quality *education* provides the knowledge and skills essential for suitable *employment*.
2. Suitable *employment* provides the income required for desirable *housing*.

3. Desirable *housing* is likely to be found in neighborhoods with elementary and secondary schools that provide high-quality *education*.

And then the cycle is repeated.

To give disadvantaged minorities benefits of education that others have routinely enjoyed, the U.S. Supreme Court acted in the *Brown v. Board of Education of Topeka* cases discussed shortly. Implementation, however, has been difficult and time-consuming. At this writing, almost fifty years later, despite much progress the education problems remain. When they married, many children of older residents in large cities found more desirable housing at affordable prices in new suburban subdivisions, readily accessible by private automobiles on new superhighways. This pattern accelerated the decline of the aging city neighborhoods, which now attracted lower-income families, often minorities. Thus, the minority literally became the majority in the inner cities of a large number of metropolitan areas. Government attempts to integrate white and African-American students in elementary and secondary schools were resented by many whites (and also by some African-Americans), and in large measure were effectively frustrated by the migration to the suburbs.

The nationalization of equal opportunity continues to be a major priority of our legislatures and courts. Nowhere is this commitment by the federal government more evident than in the field of education at all levels. In 1954 a unanimous U.S. Supreme Court decreed that separation of the races in schools violated the right to *equal protection of the laws* guaranteed by the Fourteenth Amendment. Chief Justice Earl Warren declared that "segregation of children in public schools solely on the basis of race, even though the physical facilities and other 'tangible' factors may be equal, deprives the children of the minority group of equal educational opportunities. . . . To separate them from others of similar age and qualifications solely because of their race generates a feeling of inferiority as to their status in the community that may affect their hearts and minds in a way unlikely ever to be undone."[110] A year later, the Court ordered all public school districts to desegregate "with all deliberate speed."[111]

EXHIBIT 2-2: **Three Keys to Opportunity**

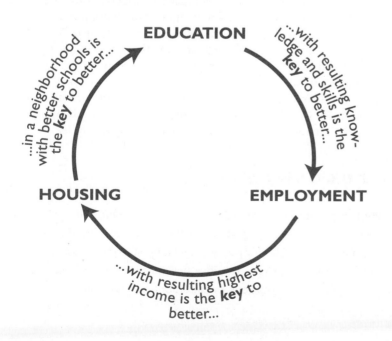

In 1976 the Court extended the principles of the *Brown* cases to private schools. It held that federal civil rights laws prohibited private nonsectarian schools from refusing to admit prospective students because they were black.[112]

Congress passed the Civil Rights Act of 1964, which is divided into subject matter sections called "titles." Title VI requires that all federal funds must be withdrawn from any school, college, or university that is guilty of discrimination on the "grounds of race, color, or national origin in any program or activity receiving federal financial assistance." (Gender, disability, age, Vietnam-veteran status, and disability of veterans were later added to the list.)

LEGAL FOCUS—CASE

Grove City College, a private, coeducational liberal arts institution, declined all state or federal financial assistance in order to preserve its autonomy. However, many of its students received Basic Educational Opportunity Grants (BEOGs) from the U.S. Department of Education. The department required every participating institution to file a report certifying that no sex discrimination existed on its campus. Grove City College refused to file the report and brought suit to prevent the department from canceling all BEOGs. What was the result?

Grove City College v. Bell, 465 U.S. 555, 104 S.Ct. 1211 (1984).

Grove City College gained a partial victory. The Supreme Court found that even though Grove City did not directly distribute the students' awards, the BEOGs clearly augmented the college's financial aid program. Therefore Grove City must assure the U.S. Department of Education that no discrimination exists in the college's financial aid program. However, the receipt of the BEOGs by some of Grove City's students was not determined to trigger institution-wide coverage under nondiscrimination statutes. Grove City challenged the conditioning of federal assistance on compliance with the nondiscrimination requirements, claiming it infringed on the First Amendment rights of the college and its students. "Congress is free to attach reasonable and unambiguous conditions to federal financial assistance that educational institutions are not obligated to accept." In other words, the college can avoid compliance requirements by not allowing students attending to accept BEOG awards. In similar cases involving tax-exempt organizations, such as religious schools, a failure to comply with legal orders to eliminate discrimination has resulted in threats from the Internal Revenue Service to remove their tax-exempt status.

LEGAL FOCUS—CASE

Bob Jones University is a private learning institution whose founding principles include a specific religious belief. BJU receives no government assistance, but the IRS denied its tax-exempt status because of the school's policy prohibiting interracial association and intermarriage. Can the IRS cause a private, religious university to pay income taxes (by denial of exempt status) while other religious organizations are exempt?

Bob Jones University v. United States, 461 U.S. 574, 103 S.Ct. 2017 (1983).

Yes. Even though all races can enroll, discrimination by racial affiliation (e.g., ban on inter-marriage) is against public policy. The state has a compelling interest in banning racial discrimination in any form. The intent of the tax law is that entitlement to tax exemption depends on meeting "certain common-law standards of charity—namely that an institution seeking tax-exempt status must serve a public purpose and not be contrary to established public policy," which could not be satisfied by less restrictive means. Loss of tax-exempt status could cause the closure of many otherwise worthwhile organizations.

Segregation in public schools due to socioeconomic factors does not, in itself, violate the Constitution. For example, in one case the Court ordered removal of a court order that required busing of students to achieve integration goals in Oklahoma City—if as much had been accomplished as was practical.[113] But schools must adopt policies that remove the effects of past discrimination. Race-neutral policies are not enough.[114] Otherwise the courts will intervene.

AFFIRMATIVE ACTION IN EDUCATION

African Americans in particular have been victims of discrimination in education, employment, and housing. **Affirmative action** is a process to eliminate continued discrimination (e.g., based on arbitrary classifications, such as race or sex) through the conscious adoption and implementation of policies favoring minorities in university admissions, public employment, and housing. Proponents argue that preferences are essential to erase the effects of prior and long-continued discrimination. Opponents argue that preferences themselves are an invidious form of discrimination—the claim is essentially that two wrongs do not make a right. There are other more sophisticated arguments concerning the possible indirect and psychological effects of preferential treatment.

Critics of racial preferences in education claim that what began as reasoned argument to overcome past discriminatory practices soon emerged as a series of numerical goals, quotas, and timetables created to bring African-Americans, Asian-Americans, Hispanic Americans, and Native Americans into the nation's colleges and universities. While there is much opposition to the way it is being done, there is no question that affirmative action is alive and well throughout the country.[115] But is it constitutional?

affirmative action

Policies and practices designed to assure employment of women and of minorities until their percentages in the work force approximate their percentages in the community.

LEGAL FOCUS—CASE

The Medical School of the University of California, Davis (UCD) set aside sixteen class admissions for minority applicants. Allan Bakke, a white male and a top undergraduate student at the University of Minnesota and Stanford University, applied for admission to the UCD Medical School and was rejected twice. On both occasions, minority students with lower admission test scores, lower grade-point averages, and less impressive interviews were nonetheless admitted.

Bakke sued the university claiming he had been rejected because of his race, in violation of the Fourteenth Amendment and of Title VI of the Civil Rights Act of 1964. The trial court and the California Supreme Court found that UCD's admission plan did indeed violate the constitutional requirement of equal protection under the law. The U.S. Supreme Court accepted the case. How should it rule?

University of California Regents v. Bakke, 438 U.S. 265, 95 S.Ct. 2733 (1978).

The U.S. Supreme Court found for Bakke* and declared the UCD admissions plan unconstitutional, thus affirming the decision of the California Supreme Court. The Court also held—with five votes and five different rationales—that ethnic diversity among medical students is an appropriate goal and therefore race can be one of the factors considered when students apply for admission.

There have been no decisions by the Court to clarify this language. In fact, United States Supreme Court Justice Byron White said recently: "Agreement upon a means for applying the Equal Protection Clause to an affirmative action program has eluded this Court every time the issue has come before us."[116]

As noted earlier in this chapter, California eliminated all affirmative action policies through the initiative process (direct vote of the people). While the U.S. Supreme Court has authorized race-conscious admissions policies, California has chosen to achieve racial balance through other practices, such as improved outreach programs to fully qualified students. Other states have variations of processes in admissions and employment to achieve racial equality.

R IGHT TO PRIVACY

The right to privacy is the right to be left alone by other persons and by government. It is generally recognized as an essential component of personal dignity, peace of mind, and independence. Nevertheless, a right to privacy has not always been implicitly recognized and respected as a constitutionally protected right. There is no reference to privacy, as such, in the Constitution or the Bill of Rights. Indeed, it was not until 1965 that the U.S. Supreme Court recognized "the new constitutional right of privacy," in the words of Justice William O. Douglas. In the case of *Griswold v. Connecticut*, the Court held invalid a Connecticut statute that made it a criminal offense for married persons to use any drug or instrument to prevent conception. The Court held that the statute violated the First, Third, Fourth, Fifth, and Ninth Amendments, plus the equal-protection clause of the Fourteenth.[117]

The nation's highest court subsequently has used the declared and implicit right of privacy to affirm (1) the right of unmarried persons to have access to contraceptives, (2) the right of persons of different races to intermarry (also protected by the due-process and equal-protection clauses of the Fourteenth Amendment), (3) the right of a woman to have an abortion under certain conditions, and (4) the right to possess obscene materials in one's home.[118]

LEGAL FOCUS—CASE

Ohio passed a law making it a crime to possess obscene materials that depict minors having sex in any form or manner. Osborne was arrested for having photographs of chil-

---

* Allan Bakke was finally admitted to UCD, received his medical degree, and continues the practice of his profession in Minnesota. In 1996 Senator Edward Kennedy declared to a Senate committee: "Dr. (Patrick) Chavis is a perfect example (of the positive results of affirmative action). He is the supposedly less qualified African-American student who allegedly displaced Allan Bakke . . . and triggered the landmark case. Today, Dr. Chavis is a successful ob-gyn in central Los Angeles, serving a disadvantaged community and making a difference in the lives of scores of poor families." Writing in *The Nation*, California State Senator Tom Hayden noted that while Allan Bakke became an anesthesiologist in Minnesota, Chavis was "providing primary care to poor women" in a mostly black community. "Bakke's scores were higher," Hayden admitted, "but who made the most of his medical school education?" In 1996 Chavis's medical license was suspended by the California Medical Board for gross negligence and incompetence in the liposuction treatment of three women—one of whom died as a result. Jeff Jacoby, *Boston Globe*, "How Affirmative Action Can Be Fatal" (New York Times Service, 20 August 1997).

dren having sex. Does Osborne have a constitutional right of privacy to possess this particular matter in his home?

Osborne v. Ohio, 495 U.S. 103, 110 S.Ct. 1691 (1990).

No. Osborne's right of privacy allowing possession of obscene materials is not absolute. The state's interest in protecting "the victims of child pornography" is paramount and sufficient to ban its possession. The U.S. Supreme Court upheld the accused's conviction.

The Court has held that the right of privacy does not extend to "places of public accommodation" and therefore adults do not have a constitutional right to acquire pornographic materials in bookstores or theaters.[119]

In *Eisenstadt v. Baird*, the Supreme Court tacitly recognized the right of heterosexual activity between consenting adults.* Does this apply to homosexual adult males? No. Georgia's statute prohibiting homosexual acts between adult males was found to be constitutional, on the grounds that the Constitution does not contain "a fundamental right to engage in homosexual sodomy,"[120] even in one's own home. Left undecided was whether a statute prohibiting sodomy between heterosexuals—husband and wife—is also constitutional.

Do "coerced" polygraph tests administered by private employers violate the right to privacy? Yes, at least in California. In a huge out-of-court settlement, the Federated Groups agreed to pay $12.1 million to job applicants forced to take polygraph ("lie detector") tests as a condition of employment.[121]

It should be noted that the reliability of lie detectors is sufficiently uncertain that they are not accepted as evidence in court over a defendant's objection. This factor of unreliability differentiates lie detector tests from others, such as blood, urine, or breath-analyzer tests.

LEGAL FOCUS—PROBLEM

Certain U.S. companies desire to sell encryption (secret code) software internationally. The software encodes e-mail and files to protect them from prying eyes. A supercomputer would need 10,000 years to break the code of a file with 128-bit encryption. The U.S. Commerce Department requires that such companies provide them with a key with which to decipher the code. Does the Constitution's right of privacy guarantee citizens and companies the right to make private and secret encoded communications?[122]

The specific issue presented may never arise because encryption software is generally available on the international market. The right of government to ban encryption software unless a key is provided involves balancing national security interests against those of privacy and free speech.

Congress long ago banned the manufacture, sale, advertisement, and use of devices intended to secretly listen to and record telephone and oral communications.[123] Yet today sophisticated electronic spy equipment is accessible in "spy shops" and from mail-order companies. A stranger can monitor conversations inside a bedroom from a mile away, and spouses can track the movements of each other in the family car. Employers can listen to

* The state could not prevent the distribution of contraceptives to college students, many of them unmarried. Sexual acts between consenting unmarried adults are still illegal in some states.

the conversations of every employee on the job. Although laws prohibiting the sale of spying equipment are on the books, lax enforcement, rapid changes in technology, and lack of public complaint have distorted (lowered) the public's expectation of privacy. Government cannot make wiretaps or otherwise perform searches without a prior search warrant, as will be discussed further in Chapter 6. But the Constitution does not guarantee a right of privacy to its citizens in the sense that they are protected from the intrusiveness of one another. The Constitution restrains only government from unreasonable intrusiveness.

D UE PROCESS AND EQUAL PROTECTION AND MEDICAL TESTING

The 1980s saw the emergence of a number of hotly contested issues pitting individual rights against the police power of the state to protect the public. State constitutions can require more stringent protective laws than are required by the U.S. Constitution. However, no state constitution or law can relax standards established by federal law, because of the doctrine of supremacy.

Among these problems, none are more difficult to resolve than the issues surrounding AIDS (acquired immune deficiency syndrome). For example, should individuals be subject to a mandatory AIDS testing program, especially those who work in certain high-risk areas or with high-risk persons? The general answer is no.*

LEGAL FOCUS—CASE

Nebraska requires state healthcare workers with the mentally retarded to submit to blood tests for AIDS. Is such a requirement an unreasonable search of a person's body?

Glover v. Eastern Neb. Community Office of Retardation, 686 F.Supp. 243, 250 (D. Neb. 1988), *aff'd,* 867 F.2d 461 (8th Cir.), *cert. denied,* 493 U.S. 932 (1989).

Yes. The Nebraska statute is unconstitutional. The Supreme Court, without comment, upheld a lower court's decision that blood tests for AIDS did violate the Fourth Amendment. For now, the Supreme Court seems content to accept the doctrine that AIDS testing must meet the same constitutional requirements of reasonableness as other warrantless search and seizure practices.

Critics of universal blood testing charge that the Fourth Amendment "right of the people to be secure in their persons, houses, papers and effects, against unreasonable searches and seizure" is violated by indiscriminate blood testing (i.e., taking blood from one's body is a "search"). However, the Supreme Court said it was not unconstitutional to take blood from a person without permission if that person is believed to be driving under the influence of alcohol. (In this case, the person in question was convicted of drunk driving on the basis of the amount of alcohol in his blood.)[124]

Another area of constitutional conflict is mandatory drug testing. The legal status of drug testing in the private sector varies from state to state. While the Supreme Court has ruled that certain government drug-testing plans are constitutional, some authorities

---

* Mandatory AIDS testing, like mandatory drug testing, involves an invasion of one's privacy that the Fourth Amendment seeks to protect.

believe that the states will have to make their own decisions about drug testing. As long as drug testing meets a "reasonableness" test as to safeguards, such as providing sufficient notice and keeping the test results secret, the business community apparently will be permitted to continue testing employees and job applicants.[125]

LEGAL FOCUS—CASE

Lawrence Berkeley Laboratory is a research institution jointly operated by state and federal agencies. Several African-American employees allege that as part of mandatory employment medical examinations, Lawrence tested their blood and urine for intimate medical conditions—namely, syphilis, sickle cell trait, and pregnancy—and that this was done without their knowledge or consent. Assuming the factual contentions are correct, would such tests violate their right to privacy as guaranteed by the United States Constitution?

Norman-Bloodsaw et al. v. Lawrence Berkeley Laboratory et al., 135 F. 3rd 1260 (C.A.9, 1998).

The court stated it did. "The constitutionally protected privacy interest in avoiding disclosure of personal matters clearly encompasses medical information and its confidentiality. One can think of few subject areas more personal and more likely to implicate privacy interests than that of one's health or genetic make-up."

C A S E

THOMAS ET AL. V. CHICAGO PARK DISTRICT

534 U.S. 316, 122 S.Ct. 775 (2002)

Facts

The Chicago Park District operates the Chicago public parks and is responsible for group use. It adopted an ordinance requiring park users to get permits before any public assembly, parade, picnic, or other event involving more than fifty people, or events using amplified sound. The applications are processed in order of receipt, and the Park District decides whether to grant or deny most applications within fourteen days. Applications can be denied on any of thirteen specified grounds. A denial requires written explanation and, when feasible, suggestions as to how to prepare a successful application. If a denial is given one can appeal to the Park Superintendent, who has seven days to respond. If the Park Superintendent denies the appeal, the applicant may seek judicial review in state court.

Petitioners have applied to the Park District on several occasions for permits to hold rallies advocating the legalization of marijuana. The Park District granted some permits and denied others. Unsatisfied, the petitioners filed suit in United States District Court, alleging that the ordinance is unconstitutional. The District Court granted summary judgment for the Park District, and the United States Court of Appeals for the Seventh Circuit affirmed.

Justice Scalia delivered the opinion of the Court.

II

The First Amendment's guarantee of the freedom of speech, or of the press, prohibits a wide assortment of government restraints upon expression, but the core abuse against which it was directed was the scheme of licensing laws implemented by the monarch and Parliament to contain the evils of the printing press in 16th- and 17th-century England. The Printing Act of 1662 had prescribed what could be printed, who could print, and who could sell. It punished the publication of any book or pamphlet without a license and required that all works be submitted for approval to a government official, who wielded broad authority to suppress works that he found to be heretical, seditious, schismatical, or offensive. The English licensing system expired at the end of the 17th century, but the memory of its abuses was still vivid enough in colonial times that Blackstone warned against the restrictive

power of such a licenser—an administrative official who enjoyed unconfined authority to pass judgment on the content of speech.

In *Freedman v. Maryland* (1965), we confronted a state law that enacted a strikingly similar system of prior restraint for motion pictures. It required that every motion picture film be submitted to a Board of Censors before the film was shown anywhere in the State. The Board enjoyed authority to reject films that it considered obscene or that tend[ed], in the judgment of the Board, to debase or corrupt morals or incite to crimes, characteristics defined by the statute in broad terms. The statute punished the exhibition of a film not submitted to the Board for advance approval, even where the film would have received a license had it been properly submitted. It was no defense that the content of the film was protected by the First Amendment.

We recognized in *Freedman* that a scheme conditioning expression on a licensing body's prior approval of content presents peculiar dangers to constitutionally protected speech. [T]he censor's business is to censor, and a licensing body likely will overestimate the dangers of controversial speech when determining, without regard to the film's actual effect on an audience, whether speech is likely to incite or to corrupt [the] morals. In response to these grave dangers of a censorship system, we held that a film licensing process must contain certain procedural safeguards in order to avoid constituting an invalid prior restraint: (1) any restraint prior to judicial review can be imposed only for a specified brief period during which the status quo must be maintained; (2) expeditious judicial review of that decision must be available; and (3) the censor must bear the burden of going to court to suppress the speech and must bear the burden of proof once in court.

[T]he licensing scheme at issue here is not subject-matter censorship but content-neutral time, place, and manner regulation of the use of a public forum. The Park District's ordinance does not authorize a licensor to pass judgment on the content of speech: None of the grounds for denying a permit has anything to do with what a speaker might say. The picnicker and soccer-player, no less than the political activist or parade marshal, must apply for a permit if the 50-person limit is to be exceeded. As the Court of Appeals well put it: [T]o allow unregulated access to all comers could easily reduce rather than enlarge the park's utility as a forum for speech.

We have never required that a content-neutral permit scheme regulating speech in a public forum adhere to the procedural requirements set forth in *Freedman*. [T]he [permit] required is not the kind of prepublication license deemed a denial of liberty since the time of John Milton but a ministerial, police routine for adjusting the rights of citizens so that the opportunity for effective freedom of speech may be preserved. Regulations of the use of a public forum that ensure the safety and convenience of the people are not inconsistent with civil liberties but [are] one of the means of safeguarding the good order upon which [civil liberties] ultimately depend. Such a traditional exercise of authority does not raise the censorship concerns that prompted us to impose the extraordinary procedural safeguards on the film licensing process in *Freedman*.

III

Of course even content-neutral time, place, and manner restrictions can be applied in such a manner as to stifle free expression. Where the licensing official enjoys unduly broad discretion in determining whether to grant or deny a permit, there is a risk that he will favor or disfavor speech based on its content. We have thus required that a time, place, and manner regulation contain adequate standards to guide the official's decision and render it subject to effective judicial review. Petitioners contend that the Park District's ordinance fails this test.

We think not. As we have described, the Park District may deny a permit only for one or more of the reasons set forth in the ordinance. It may deny, for example, when the application is incomplete or contains a material falsehood or misrepresentation; when the applicant has damaged Park District property on prior occasions and has not paid for the damage; when a permit has been granted to an earlier applicant for the same time and place; when the intended use would present an unreasonable danger to the health or safety of park users or Park District employees; or when the applicant has violated the terms of a prior permit. Moreover, the Park District must process applications within 28 days, and must clearly explain its reasons for any denial. These grounds are reasonably specific and objective, and do not leave the decision to the whim of the administrator. They provide narrowly drawn, reasonable, and definite standards to guide the licensor's determination. And they are enforceable on review first by appeal to the General Superintendent of the Park District and then by writ of common-law *certiorari** in the Illinois courts.

* * *

For the foregoing reasons, we affirm the judgment of the Court of Appeals.

For Critical Analysis

1. What was the importance of the court's determination that the Chicago Park District's procedures were content neutral?

2. Why is the court applying a federal constitution test to a state governmental entity?

3. Are the petitioners attempting to argue that actions by the Park District are a prior restraint? If so, did they succeed? Do you believe it is a prior restraint? What requirements are necessary for a prior restraint to be held valid? ∎

Bush v. Gore

531 U.S. 1046, 121 S.Ct. 525 (2000)

Facts

No matter how long you live, something new happens. The United States elections of 2000 brought something new for all U.S. citizens, an election so close that all the major television networks called the election for a candidate who is not now president. In

one of the more controversial Supreme Court cases the election was effectively decided by the Court.

"On the day after the presidential election, the Florida Division of Elections reported that Governor George W. Bush had received 2,909,135 votes and that Vice President Albert Gore Jr. had received 2,907,351 votes, a margin of 1,784 for Bush. Because Bush's margin of victory was less than one-half of one percent of the votes cast, the Florida election

---

* A writ or order by which an appellate court exercises its discretionary power to decide which lower court cases it will hear. Writs of *certiorari* are discussed in more detail in Chapter 3.

code required an automatic machine recount. The results of automatic recount showed Bush still winning the race but by a smaller margin. Gore requested manual recounts in Volusia, Palm Beach, Broward, and Miami-Dade Counties, as permitted by protest provisions in Florida's election statutes.

On November 26, the Florida Elections Canvassing Commission certified the results of the election and declared Bush the winner of Florida's twenty-five electoral votes. The next day Gore filed a complaint in Leon County Circuit Court contesting that certification. He sought relief under Florida statutes that provide that "[r]eceipt of a number of illegal votes or rejection of a number of legal votes sufficient to change or place in doubt the result of the election" shall be grounds for a contest.

On December 8, 2000, the Supreme Court of Florida ordered that the Circuit Court of Leon County tabulate by hand 9,000 ballots in Miami-Dade County. The court also ordered the inclusion in the certified vote totals of 215 votes identified in Palm Beach County and 168 votes identified in Miami-Dade County for Gore. The Florida Supreme Court noted that Bush asserted that the net gain for Gore in Palm Beach County was 176 votes, and directed the Circuit Court to resolve that dispute on remand. The Florida Supreme Court further required manual recounts in all Florida counties where so-called "undervotes" had not been subject to manual tabulation. The Florida court ordered all manual recounts to begin at once. Bush filed an emergency application to the United States Supreme Court for a stay of the Florida Supreme Court decision.

Per Curiam*

The petition represents the following questions: . . . whether the use of standardless manual recounts violates the equal Protection and Due Process Clauses. With respect to the equal protection question, we find a violation of the Equal Protection Clause.

II

A

The closeness of this election, and the multitude of legal challenges which have followed in its wake, have brought into sharp focus a common, if heretofore unnoticed, phenomenon. Nationwide statistics reveal that an estimated 2% of ballots cast do not register a vote for President for whatever reason, including deliberately choosing no candidate at all or some voter error, such as voting for two candidates or insufficiently marking a ballot. In certifying election results, the votes eligi-

---

* **Per Curiam:** A decision delivered via an opinion issued in the name of the Court rather than specific justices. Usually per curiam decisions are non-controversial and unanimous; neither was the case here.

ble for inclusion in the certification are the votes meeting the properly established legal requirements.

This case has shown that punch card balloting machines can produce an unfortunate number of ballots which are not punched in a clean, complete way by the voter. After the current counting, it is likely legislative bodies nationwide will examine ways to improve the mechanisms and machinery for voting.

B

The individual citizen has no federal constitutional right to vote for electors for the President of the United States unless and until the state legislature chooses a statewide election as the means to implement its power to appoint members of the Electoral College.

The right to vote is protected in more than the initial allocation of the franchise. Equal protection applies as well to the manner of its exercise. Having once granted the right to vote on equal terms, the State may not, by later arbitrary and disparate treatment, value one person's vote over that of another.

There is no difference between the two sides of the present controversy on these basic propositions. Respondents say that the very purpose of vindicating the right to vote justifies the recount procedures now at issue. The question before us, however, is whether the recount procedures the Florida Supreme Court has adopted are consistent with its obligation to avoid arbitrary and disparate treatment of the members of its electorate.

Much of the controversy seems to revolve around ballot cards designed to be perforated by a stylus but which, either through error or deliberate omission, have not been perforated with sufficient precision for a machine to count them. In some cases a piece of the card—a chad—is hanging, say by two corners. In other cases there is no separation at all, just an indentation.

The Florida Supreme Court has ordered that the intent of the voter be discerned from such ballots. The recount mechanisms implemented in response to the decisions of the Florida Supreme Court do not satisfy the minimum requirement for non-arbitrary treatment of voters necessary to secure the fundamental right. Florida's basic command for the count of legally cast votes is to consider the "intent of the voter." This is unobjectionable as an abstract proposition and a starting principle. The problem inheres in the absence of specific standards to ensure its equal application. The formulation of uniform rules to determine intent based on these recurring circumstances is practicable and, we conclude, necessary.

The want of those rules here has led to unequal evaluation of ballots in various respects. ("Should a county canvassing board count or not count a 'dimpled chad' where the voter is able to successfully dislodge the chad in every other contest on that ballot? Here, the county canvassing boards disagree.") As seems to have been acknowledged at oral argument, the standards for accepting or rejecting contested ballots might vary not only from county to county but indeed within a single county from one recount team to another.

The record provides some examples. A monitor in Miami-Dade County testified at trial that he observed that three members of the county canvassing board applied different standards in defining a legal vote. And testimony at trial also revealed that at least one county changed its evaluative standards during the counting process.

The State Supreme Court ratified this uneven treatment. It mandated that the recount totals from two counties, Miami-Dade and Palm Beach, be included in the certified total. The court also appeared to hold *sub silentio* that the recount totals from Broward County, which were not completed until after the original November 14 certification by the Secretary of State, were to be considered part of the new certified vote totals even though the county certification was not contested by Vice President Gore. Yet each of the counties used varying standards to determine what was a legal vote. Broward County used a more forgiving standard than Palm Beach County, and uncovered almost three times as many new votes, a result markedly disproportionate to the difference in population between the counties.

In addition, the recounts in these three counties were not limited to so-called undervotes but extended to all of the ballots. The distinction has real consequences. A manual recount of all ballots identifies not only those ballots which show no vote but also those which contain more than one, the so-called overvotes. Neither category will be counted by the machine.

That brings the analysis to yet a further equal protection problem. The votes certified by the court included a partial total from one county, Miami-Dade. The Florida Supreme Court's decision thus gives no assurance that the recounts included in a final certification must be complete. A desire for speed is not a general excuse for ignoring equal protection guarantees.

In addition to these difficulties the actual process by which the votes were to be counted under the Florida Supreme Court's decision raises further concerns. That order did not specify who would recount the ballots. The county canvassing boards were forced to pull together ad hoc teams comprised of judges from various Circuits who had no previous training in handling and interpreting ballots.

The question before the Court is not whether local entities, in the exercise of their expertise, may develop different systems for implementing elections. Instead, we are presented with a situation where a state court with the power to assure uniformity has ordered a statewide recount with minimal procedural safeguards. When a court orders a statewide remedy, there must be at least some assurance that the rudimentary requirements of equal treatment and fundamental fairness are satisfied.

Given the Court's assessment that the recount process underway was probably being conducted in an unconstitutional manner, the Court stayed the order directing the recount so it could hear this case and render an expedited decision. The contest provision, as it was mandated by the State Supreme Court, is not well calculated to sustain the confidence that all citizens must have in the outcome of elections. The State has not shown that its procedures include the necessary safeguards. The problem, for instance, of the estimated 110,000 overvotes has not been addressed. . . .

Upon due consideration of the difficulties identified to this point, it is obvious that the recount cannot be conducted in compliance with the requirements of equal protection and due process without substantial additional work.

The Supreme Court of Florida has said that the legislature intended the State's electors to "participat[e] fully in the federal electoral process." That statute requires that any controversy or contest that is designed to lead to a conclusive selection of electors be completed by December 12. That date is upon us, and there is no recount procedure in place under the State Supreme Court's order that comports with minimal constitutional standards. Because it is evident that any recount seeking to meet the December 12 date will be unconstitutional for the reasons we have discussed, we reverse the judgment of the Supreme Court of Florida ordering a recount to proceed.

* * *

None are more conscious of the vital limits on judicial authority than are the members of this Court, and none stand more in admiration of the Constitution's design to leave the selection of the President to the people, through their legislatures, and to the political sphere. When contending parties invoke the process of the courts, however, it becomes our unsought responsibility to resolve the federal and constitutional issues the judicial system has been forced to confront.

The judgment of the Supreme Court of Florida is reversed, and the case is remanded for further proceedings not inconsistent with this opinion.

It is so ordered.

Separate dissents were written by Justice Breyer, Ginsburg, Souter and Stevens.

From Justice Ginsburg's dissent, with whom Justice Stevens joins, and with whom Justice Souter and Justice Breyer join in part: "Time (ital.) is short in part because of the

Court's entry of a stay on December 9, several hours after an able circuit judge in Leon County had begun to superintend the recount process. More fundamentally, the Court's reluctance to let the recount go forward, despite its suggestion that 'the search for intent can be confined by specific rules designed to ensure uniform treatment' ultimately turns on its own judgment about the practical realities of implementing a recount, not the judgment of those much closer to the process."

Justice Souter's dissent, with whom Justices Breyer, Stevens and Ginsburg join in part: The Court should not have reviewed [this case] and should not have stopped Florida's attempt to recount all undervote ballots. If this Court had allowed the State to follow the course indicated by the opinions of its own Supreme Court, it is entirely possible that there would ultimately have been no issue requiring our review, and political tension could have worked itself out in the Congress following the procedure provided in 3 U.S.C. § 15. The case being before us, however, its resolution by the majority is another erroneous decision.

Unlike the majority, I see no warrant for this Court to assume that Florida could not possibly comply with this requirement before the date set for the meeting of electors, December 18. Although one of the dissenting justices of the State Supreme Court estimated that disparate standards potentially affected 170,000 votes, the number at issue is significantly smaller. The 170,000 figure apparently represents all uncounted votes, both undervotes (those for which no Presidential choice was recorded by a machine) and overvotes (those rejected because of votes for more than one candidate). To recount these manually would be a tall order, but before this Court stayed the effort to do that the courts of Florida were ready to do their best to get that job done. There is no justification for denying the State the opportunity to try to count all disputed ballots now.

I respectfully dissent.

Case Terms

certiorari

[Latin: "to be informed of"] A writ or order by which an appellate court exercises its discretionary power to decide which lower court cases it will hear.

For Critical Analysis

1. As Albert Gore ultimately won the United States popular vote (there is no real dispute as to this fact), why did George W. Bush become president?

2. How exactly did the Florida Supreme Court deny equal protection to Florida voters? Is there a counterargument that failure to allow a revote is a denial of equal protection?

3. One commentator wrote this about the opinion: "The complexity of the decision goes far toward explaining public apathy since the issues are too abstruse to command the comprehension, or at least capture the attention, of more than a very small number of Americans. Even among the sliver of well-informed persons who actually have read and understood the decision, the Court's divisions are more likely to reinforce longstanding attitudes and perceptions. *Bush v. Gore* has naturally helped to confirm the belief of liberals that the Court's conservatives are result-oriented. Some liberals, however, have welcomed the Court's introduction of new constitutional standards into state electoral processes." Do you agree with this observation? Why or why not?[126] ■

CHAPTER QUESTIONS AND PROBLEMS

1. Wayne Gerber, an inmate at Mule Creek State Prison, is serving a sentence of 100 years to life, plus eleven years as a habitual felon under California's "three strikes" law. Although conjugal visits are allowed in California, they are not allowed to prisoners serving life terms. As his prospects of walking among the general public are slim, so are his prospects of impregnating his wife. Gerber requested that he be allowed to package his semen in a plastic collection container and mail it to a laboratory, eventually to artificially inseminate his wife. His request was denied.

a. Does a prisoner lose all constitutional rights?
b. Does a prisoner have a constitutional right to conjugal visits? What constitutional provisions would be argued?
c. Is the warden's denial of Gerber's right to provide sperm samples a violation of the equal protection clause because the state allows conjugal visits for some prisoners but not others?

2. Organizers of the annual Fiesta Bowl football game held in Arizona proposed establishing a race-specific scholar-

ship fund for players of the competing teams. Are such scholarships unconstitutional because they are awarded only to members of one race? Would your answer be any different if the scholarships were awarded in schools that had a history of intentional racial segregation?

3. Can government constitutionally regulate the content (i.e., censor) of e-mail by banning "spam" (unwanted advertisements) and Web sex or pornography available on Web sites? What constitutional arguments would you make pro and con?

4. Do state laws that criminalize sodomy between members of the same or opposite sex violate the constitutional right of privacy? Equal protection clause? Are such laws necessary in a free society?

5. In the Seattle School District students are allowed to choose which high school they wish to attend. If too many students choose the same school the district has to turn some students away. To assist in this determination the district uses tiebreakers. The first tiebreaker tries to keep families together—a student with a brother or sister at the chosen school is given preference. The second tiebreaker tries to keep the racial mix in each high school equal to the racial mix in the district—if a school has too many white students, nonwhites are given preference, and vice versa. Is this use of race constitutionally permissible? What other selection criteria might the district use to make the decision? [*Parents Involved in Community Schools v. Seattle School Dist., No. 1*, 285 F.3d 1236 (C.A.9 Wash 2002).]

6. Several recent counter-terrorism measures raise constitutional questions. Discuss the constitutional questions that can reasonably be raised in each situation. What is the probable outcome if the challenge is made?
   a. Visitors to the United States who hold visas from Iran, Iraq, Libya, Sudan, and Syria will be fingerprinted and photographed. Visitors from other countries will not be unless the immigration service believes they represent a security risk.
   b. A presidential order allows trials by special military commissions for non-U.S. citizens who are suspected of involvement in international terrorism.
   c. Police or federal agents eavesdrop on phone calls between detained suspected terrorists and their lawyers without seeking judicial approval.

7. The City of Oakland passed an ordinance that prohibited the burning of all substances in residential yards within the city limits on days when a fire hazard warning was in effect. Violation was made a misdemeanor crime with a minimum fine of $500. Harry Haggerty, a political science major, invited student friends to his home in Oakland where, among other backyard activities, he intended to burn an American flag in protest of U.S. involvement in Iraq. If a fire warning were in effect, could Harry be convicted of the misdemeanor offense?

8. In an editorial comment, the highly respected British journal *The Economist* (27 March 1992, p. 15) opined, "Short of declaring war, nothing an American President can do has as much effect as appointing a justice to the Supreme Court." Do you agree? Why or why not?

9. The principal of Nathan Bishop Middle School in Providence, Rhode Island, invited Rabbi Leslie Gutterman to deliver prayers at the public school graduation ceremony. The rabbi agreed to deliver a nonsectarian prayer at the ceremony. Weisman, the father of a student, sued to prohibit school officials from including prayer in the ceremony. He was unsuccessful, and the ceremony took place with the Weismans in attendance. Weisman then sued to permanently bar prayers at future ceremonies, including his daughter's high school graduation. Does including a nonsectarian prayer in a public high school graduation ceremony constitute the establishment of a religion by government in violation of the First Amendment? [*Lee v. Weisman*, 505 U.S. 577, 112 S.Ct. 2649 (1992).]

10. The Legal Focus on page 64 discussed the flight of corporations to offshore tax havens to avoid federal income tax. At this writing the strategy was legal, but is it ethical? Consider the methods of ethical analysis provided in Chapter 1 in answering the question.

CHAPTER 3

The Court System

After reading and studying this chapter, you should be able to:

🏛 Explain what a "court" is and distinguish between a trial court and an appellate court.

🏛 Understand the concept of jurisdiction and explain the various types of jurisdiction. Recognize challenges to concepts of jurisdiction raised by new technologies.

🏛 Describe a typical state court system.

🏛 Describe the federal court system.

🏛 Understand how a typical civil case is processed though the court system.

🏛 Understand the nature of juries and be able to discuss jury size, jury selection, and a litigant's right to a jury trial.

🏛 Explain and provide examples of actions or causes in equity.

🏛 Understand the various ways a trial might conclude.

Sir Thomas More: The law, Roper, the law. I know what's legal and not what's right. And I'll stick to what's legal.

William Roper: Then you set man's law above God's.

Sir Thomas More: No, far below; but let me draw your attention to a fact—I'm not God. The currents and eddies of right and wrong, which you find such plain sailing, I can't navigate.

William Roper: So . . . you'd give the Devil benefit of the law!

Sir Thomas More: Yes. What would you do? Cut a great road through the law to get after the Devil?

William Roper: I'd cut down every law in England to do that!

Sir Thomas More: Oh? And when the last law was down and the Devil turned round on you where would you hide, Roper, the laws all being flat? Yes, I'd give the Devil benefit of law, for my own safety's sake.

Robert Bolt, slightly and reverently edited from his play *A Man for All Seasons*.

It is often stated and generally believed that persons residing in the United States of America are governed by law, not by people. "A government of laws, and not of men" are words written in 1774 by John Adams, first vice president and second president of the United States.[1] This means that decisions establishing and affecting rights and duties are not based on the personal values of certain individuals but rather are made by the courts according to existing rules while using fair and impartial processes. Sir Thomas More, quoted above, would no doubt approve of the United States' emphasis on established rules rather than individual discretion, but like all human creations "a government of law" is not perfect. The oft-heard condemnation of government "red tape" is sometimes a veiled criticism of the rule of law, and complaints about the law often concern the processes that are relied upon to ensure fair and impartial application of law.

Indeed, providing for the application of the **rule of law** in a fair, impartial, and consistent manner, while remaining efficient and protecting all interests, is a difficult task, especially in the United States, which contains such a diversity of ethnic origins and cultural backgrounds. Yet it is that very diversity that makes the rule of law so vitally important for the resolution of disputes with "equal justice under law" for all. The "war against terrorism" will test the United States' ability to rely on the rule of law, as individual fear and hatred can be the justification for sacrifice of rule of law and fair treatment.

> We are going to have to decide what kind of people we are—whether we obey the law only when we approve of it or whether we obey it no matter how distasteful we may find it.*

The creation, recognition, and enforcement of our rights and duties are responsibilities shared by the legislative, executive, and judicial branches of government. However, the nature and manner in which laws are made and shaped differs dramatically depending on its source. Probably no other country is more reliant on its judges and its courts than the United States. One hundred and fifty years ago, French political scientist Alexis de Tocqueville noted the unique importance of courts in the American political system. "Restricted within its limits, the power granted to American courts to pronounce on the constitutionality of laws is yet one of the most powerful barriers ever erected against the tyranny of political assemblies."[2]

Although the power of courts can and does restrict arbitrary abuse of power, bias can creep into the court system. As an example, consider the following episode in traffic court.

> The Traffic Court judge found himself facing two attorneys, both of whom he knew very well. Both were charged with speeding violations. "Gentlemen," he said, "I could not be truly objective in either of your cases, so I'm going to let you judge each other's case." Both lawyers agreed. Attorney Number One climbed to the bench. "You are charged with driving 40 in a 25 mile per hour zone. How do you plead?" he asked Attorney Number Two. "Guilty," was the response. "I fine you $50," said Number One. Then they exchanged places. "You are charged with driving 40 in a 25 mile zone," said Number Two. "What is your plea?" "Guilty," said Number One. "Then I fine you $200," said Number Two. "Hey! That's unfair," said the first. "I fined you only $50." "Yes," was the reply, "but there is too much speeding going on. This is the second case we've had like that today."

rule of law

Principle that decisions should be made by the application of established laws without the intervention of individual discretion.

http://

The Carnegie Endowment for International Peace is sponsoring an initiative called Democracy and the Rule of Law Project. Read about it at **http://www.ceip.org/files/projects/drl/drl_home.ASP**

* Harry S. Ashmore, "On integration of Little Rock High School," *Arkansas Gazette* 4 September 1957.

bias

A preconceived belief
affecting neutrality

Although the purpose of the story is to amuse, it illustrates the injustice of an inconsistent and unfair decision made by a biased judge. **Bias** is a preconceived belief about some person or fact that makes it difficult to be neutral, dispassionate, or fair in evaluating that person's rights and duties, guilt or innocence. A judge is biased when he or she has a personal interest in the outcome of a case or has reached a conclusion about a case before hearing the evidence and legal arguments.

The U.S. system of justice strives to provide both reasonable consistency and neutrality. This requires the elimination of judicial bias, including rejection of personal values that conflict with legal values. The independent neutral forum, where facts are determined and rules applied for resolving legal disputes, is the *court system*.

The role of lawyers is not to be overlooked in the operations of courts. Courts would not be effective without the service of attorneys who shape their clients' cases, present legal issues to courts, quickly object to improprieties offered by opposing counsel, and so forth. We discuss lawyers more fully in the following chapter, but here we note the dependence of our courts upon the legal profession. This always has been true. In the frontier days of the west following the discovery of gold in 1849, law and order of a sort was preserved by vigilantism. The goal of vigilantes was simple enough: to establish order and stability in mining camps, cattle towns, and the open range. The procedures of the vigilantes, unlike legal procedures today, featured simplicity and certain, severe punishment.

It was the frontier attorneys, not trained in law schools but rather by apprenticeships and experience, who encouraged and supported procedures to bring offenders into courtrooms, where fair and less arbitrary procedures could be applied. On the decline following the Civil War, vigilantism remains only as a reminder of the importance of due process brought about by court procedures that guarantee fair treatment for all. By the turn of the century, in 1900, lawyers had been educated in college and in law schools and were relied upon then, as today, to present their clients' disputes to the courts. The dependency of the courts upon the bar (the legal profession) was total then as now. Of course, there weren't as many lawyers then—according to the 1900 census, only 4,278 persons declared themselves to be practicing attorneys. Nor were there as many courts. In the year 2001 just one state, California, added over 6,000 new attorneys. Today, most of our courts are jammed with cases and more federal judges are said to be urgently needed. And with more courts handling more and increasingly complex issues, we can be assured of more attorneys.

Ⓦ HAT IS A COURT?

http://

For the ultimate directory of
state, federal, and
international courts see
**http://www.ncsconline.org/
CourtInfoPortal/index.html**

Clearly it is important and useful to know where our courts are located, how they function, and the important role they play in our society. The media has capitalized on the public's interest in courts with movies and TV shows, and the publishing industry has reaped huge rewards from novels based on courtroom activities. Significant decisions of appellate courts, especially the U.S. Supreme Court, receive widespread media coverage, and many citizens worry about the future consequences of important decisions. For example, can states provide by local statute that marijuana may be used for medical reasons? Can police use thermal imaging devices to scan a home without a search warrant? Can the Supreme Court monitor state election practices that determine the election of the United States president? Can a local public elementary school deny a religious group after-school access to school facilities if the group's activities otherwise fall within the guidelines defining the school's limited public forum? The public's acute interest in such decisions prompts lively debate on the Internet, in coffee shops, on talk radio, and so on. Because the actions of courts receive such expansive notoriety, it is obvious that you, as educated citizens, must be familiar with the functions of courts.

Courts are public facilities, available to private persons, business organizations, and government agencies, where legal disputes are heard and decided. Courts offer their tax-supported services practically free to users. Under the U.S. Constitution, courts are essentially independent of the other branches of government.* This independence protects the courts from potential interference by the executive or legislative branches.

A court is both a place and a system. It is a place where you may go to peacefully resolve your legal disputes with others ("I'll see you in court!"). The word *court* is also used to describe all the court system participants, including judges, attorneys, clerks, witnesses, parties, and the public ("Court is in session"); and sometimes only the presiding judge or justice ("If the court please, may I be heard at this time?").

Courts are also part of a system, as there are different courts for different types of legal disputes, each with different specified procedures. Some courts determine the facts of individual disputes (trial courts); others review decisions of lower courts for correctness, consistency, and fairness (appellate courts). Appellate judges, both in the state and federal systems, have the power to make new law, and do. To understand the courts, it is useful to recognize some of their different functions, including those of trial and appellate courts.

court

(a) A government body that administers justice by applying laws to civil controversies and criminal offenses. (b) The place where trials are held.

WHAT IS A TRIAL COURT?

Trial courts conduct the initial proceedings in legal disputes. These proceedings have three distinct purposes: (1) to determine the facts of the dispute ("What happened between the competing parties?"), (2) to determine what rules of law should be applied to the facts, and (3) to apply those rules to the facts.

trial court

The initial court that hears evidence and applies the law to decided facts.

LEGAL FOCUS—PROBLEM

Marya Martinez signed up for ski instruction at Heavenly Mountain in Idaho. Gary Graf, a certified ski instructor, fitted Martinez with rental skis. He then taught her how to snowplow (a beginning maneuver for turning, reducing speed, or stopping). Later that afternoon, Martinez was showing her new skills to Luther Thomas, whom she had just met during lunch. Her show was short. Martinez fell and suffered a spiral fracture of her right leg, just above the ankle. Her bindings had failed to release her boot from the skis when she fell. She sued Graf in a civil action for damages, alleging that he had carelessly adjusted the bindings too tightly. Who will win?

No one knows who will win because the facts have not yet been judicially determined. Did Graf secure the bindings too tightly? Did Martinez, or anyone else, tamper with the bindings after Graf set them? Did the bindings fail because they were too tight or because Martinez had allowed ice to accumulate beneath her boot? Were the bindings

---

* The courts are not totally independent of the other two branches. For example, the executive branch of government makes judicial appointments, collects taxes, and distributes funds necessary to pay judges and otherwise operate the judicial system. The legislative branch sets salaries and benefits of judges and often confirms judicial appointments. But it would be unconstitutional for the legislative branch to influence courts through pay or benefit cuts or other intimidating laws.

plaintiff

In trial, the person trying to recover money damages or other relief from a defendant.

damages

Money awarded by a court to a plaintiff for injury or economic loss caused by the defendant.

defendant

(a) In a civil trial, the person from whom money damages or other relief is sought by the plaintiff. (b) In a criminal trial, the accused.

lawsuit or litigation

A suit at law or in equity.

civil dispute

A lawsuit commenced for the purpose of resolving a civil conflict.

criminal dispute

A trial in which the government prosecutes a person charged with a crime.

manufactured in a defective manner? Was there a contract that disclaimed or limited Graf's liability? A civil trial will determine the answers to these and other relevant factual and legal contentions. In the trial, Martinez is the **plaintiff** (person seeking relief in a civil trial) because she is seeking to recover **damages** (money) from Graf, the **defendant** (in a civil trial, the person whom a lawsuit is brought against). The entire process, designed to resolve (i.e., decide or settle) the legal controversy, is called a **lawsuit** or **litigation.**

Martinez's attempt to collect damages from Graf is an example of a *civil dispute* (also called a *civil action* or *civil lawsuit*). **Civil disputes** are private controversies between persons.* A civil dispute is sometimes defined broadly by stating what it is not. It is not a matter involving criminal law. A **criminal dispute** (also called a *criminal action* or *criminal case*) is brought by government to determine whether an accused (also called a *defendant*) is guilty of an act committed against the public and in violation of a penal statute.

Civil matters and criminal matters are separate fields of law; in large cities, attorneys and judges often specialize in one or the other. The dependence of courts upon attorneys is such that it would be foolhardy for a civil case attorney to defend an accused murderer even before an impartial jury. There are similarities as well as differences between civil and criminal matters. Both involve formal proceedings before a court. Both are conducted to resolve disputed questions of fact and law that will, in turn, define applicable rights and duties of the parties involved. Different terminology, however, is often used. For example, a defendant found to be responsible in a civil trial is said to be *liable,* while in a criminal trial such a person is said to be *guilty.* The accused in both processes, though, is called a *defendant.*

In a criminal trial, a prosecutor (e.g., a public prosecutor or district attorney) from the local governing unit (county) represents the public on behalf of the state. If a federal crime is involved, an attorney from the Department of Justice represents the public. While government can be a party in either a civil or criminal matter, only the government can prosecute a criminal action, because *crimes*—although usually committed against private persons—are prosecuted as public offenses against all society. Procedures differ substantially in criminal actions from those used in civil actions. The focus of this chapter is on the civil court system, although we make some references to the criminal system. (See Chapter 6 for a more complete discussion of criminal procedure.)

Most court proceedings and court records are open to public scrutiny, thereby assuring us that no secret "kangaroo court" sessions take place. Court TV broadcasts trials of high interest to national, and sometimes worldwide, audiences. However, public attendance at a trial can be restricted or barred for security reasons. Sometimes one or both parties request privacy, and the court will agree when there is an overriding reason for the public to be excluded from hearing the details of the dispute or seeing witnesses whose privacy ought to be protected. Even if the proceeding is closed to the public, a verbatim transcript of the trial is prepared so reviewing courts may know precisely what was said and by whom. Moreover, the press follows important and interesting cases and often has an investigative posture when dealing with government, including courts.

LEGAL FOCUS—CASE

. . . .

The attorney general of Maryland filed a civil suit against Cottman Transmission Systems, Inc., relating to allegations of fraudulent activities. Cottman was accused of remov-

---

* The term *persons* for most situations in law encompasses artificial persons, such as government bodies and business entities including corporations, as well as humans.

ing automobile transmissions for inspection and maintenance when this costly action was unnecessary. The attorney general distributed news releases elaborating on the charges against Cottman. When the attorney general made additional claims, Cottman asked the court to close the courtroom except for parties directly involved in the proceeding. Did the court agree to do this?

Maryland v. Cottman Transmissions, Inc., 75 Md.App. 647, 542 A.2d 859 (Md., 1988).

Initially, yes. Cottman's counsel convinced the trial court judge that the press releases harmed their client's ability to obtain a fair trial, and so the public was barred. Before trial began, however, a higher court overruled this decision.

Restricting access to civil law proceedings is unusual and restricting access to criminal law proceedings is rare. The possibility of secret trials resulting in loss of individual liberty through a jail sentence is an abomination in our democracy. Equally disturbing would be the secret exoneration of a favored celebrity. Criminal proceedings may be conducted in private only in extraordinary situations that are demonstrated to, and then justified by, the trial court judge.[3]

An exception to the openness in most court cases is the juvenile court proceeding, which is conducted privately in most states to protect youthful offenders. The media typically cooperates with the juvenile courts by not publicizing the names of juveniles accused of status offenses (e.g., truancy and running away) and even conduct considered criminal when committed by adults.

As the industrial revolution progressed and spread across the country, bringing increasing opportunities for mischief by juveniles in the cities, the states began adopting laws protecting minors (under age eighteen) from the adult criminal system. Early in the twenty-first century, reconsideration of the special status for minors appears to be taking place. Many believe that people reach maturity at an age younger than eighteen, at least for purposes of the criminal law. The states are increasingly willing to treat children of sixteen, fourteen, and even younger as adults by trying and sentencing them similarly to adult criminals.

WHAT IS AN APPELLATE COURT?

Within a specified time following the trial court's final determination (a *judgment*), the losing party can **appeal,** which is a formal request to a higher court to review the trial judge's ruling. These review courts are called **appellate courts.** Consisting of three or more judges, called justices, these courts review decisions of trial court judges for substantive and procedural correctness. In civil cases, there is no automatic right to have the state's highest court consider an appeal. In criminal cases resulting in the death penalty, the right to an appellate review by the state's highest court is guaranteed. This is a safeguard against imposing an irreversible penalty without thorough review of all aspects of the conviction. Lawyers research the written opinions of appellate courts to determine what law should be applied in the trial courts to the problem facing their clients. This is one example of how trial courts depend upon attorneys.

The appellate court works from a verbatim record (court transcript) of what was said and what *evidence* was accepted in the lower court, such as photographs, models, charts, business records, contracts, and so forth. Appellate courts do not listen to witnesses, accept

appeal

Formal request to a higher court to review any action of a lower court.

appellate court

Court that reviews decisions of prior courts for substantive and procedural correctness.

briefs

Written arguments
addressed to the appellate
court.

new evidence,* make new determinations of fact, or utilize a jury. Instead, the court receives written **briefs,** prepared by lawyers, that contain legal arguments as to how the law was incorrectly stated or applied to the facts as presented to the trial court. This is an example of how appellate courts rely on attorneys. The appellate court accepts as true the facts found by the trial court, which considered all the testimony of all witnesses along with all other evidence, and upon so doing decides whether rules of substantive and procedural law were properly applied by the trial judge. However, appellate judges may also weigh, or evaluate, the factual evidence as presented in the trial court and then decide whether, as a matter of law, the facts presented were sufficient to justify the judgment.

If the appellate court concludes that the trial court erroneously applied or interpreted the law, it may modify or reverse the judgment or decision, and either enter a new judgment or *remand* (return) the case to the trial court for a new trial or other proceedings in compliance with the appellate court's instructions. In other words, the trial court is instructed to "do it right this time." Merely finding an error at the trial court level is not sufficient to overturn the trial court's judgment. If an error is minor, it is believed unlikely to have affected the case outcome. The error found must be serious, requiring correction by the appellate court in order to avoid a miscarriage of justice. Therefore, it can be concluded that when a reversal occurs, the trial court judge is deemed to have made a serious error in one or more legal rulings.

In the previously discussed *Cottman* case, the trial court judge's decision to ban the press was appealed and reversed even before the trial took place. The Maryland appellate court stated:

> To close a court to public scrutiny of the proceedings is to shut off the light of the law. How else will the citizenry learn of the happenings in the courts—their government's third branch—except through access to the courts by the people themselves or through reports supplied by the media? A . . . corporate entity involved as a party to a civil case is entitled to a fair trial, not a private one.[4]

Relative to the number of cases heard in trial court, very few cases are appealed. The cost to appeal can be prohibitive in time, money, and peace of mind. Although the parties may not be pleased with the outcome of the trial, they nonetheless have had their "day in court."

Thus, to win a corrective action by an appellate court, the appellant, the party who appeals the case to a higher court, must show that an error by the court prejudiced the appellant's cause. The appellee,[†] the party against whom the appeal is brought, will contend that no error was made, or that any error did not affect the outcome of the trial. Clearly the trial is the crucial, potent, and final source of justice for most persons involved in litigation.

WHAT IS JURISDICTION?

jurisdiction

The power of a court to
decide a controversy and
to award appropriate relief.

To understand the courts, we must understand **jurisdiction.** The power to speak the law is the broad meaning of the term *jurisdiction.* It refers to the geographic area within which a court has the right and power to operate (that is, "speak"). It also refers to the persons

---

* Examples of evidence are testimony of witnesses, photographs, documents, handwriting samples, dented fenders, and so on. In weighing the believability of testimony evidence, the jury also considers the demeanor, eye contact, dress, and mannerisms of a witness.
† In some states the party against whom the appeal is brought is called the *respondent.*

over whom and the subject matter about which a court has the right and power to make decisions that are legally binding. Obviously, the term is used many ways, but always in relation to the right and power of the courts to act. Jurisdiction is about (1) political boundaries (states, federal government, territories, foreign countries, etc.), (2) the type of dispute and dollar amount involved, and (3) persons and property. In other words, jurisdiction is about a plaintiff choosing the right place to sue and choosing the right court in that place, and about compliance with rules of fairness governing when a person must appear in court to defend his or her liberty or property.

POLITICAL BOUNDARIES OF STATE AND FEDERAL COURTS

Government power begins and ends at geographical boundaries. It is clear to most that the courts of one sovereign power ordinarily have no authority over someone present in another sovereign power, absent extraordinary reason. The United States is, however, a country with shared political boundaries, and the states are not entirely sovereign. Federalism exists in the U.S. court system as well as in the executive and legislative branches of government. Simply put, we have both federal and state court systems. There are fifty-one court systems—one for each of the fifty states, and the federal government.* They have much in common and are interrelated, but still each is an independent system.

Interestingly, a party seeking judicial resolution of a dispute often may have the choice of which court system, federal or state, he or she wishes to use. When both a federal court and a state court have the power to hear a case, they have **concurrent jurisdiction.** Which court, federal or state or both, has power or authority over a given matter is a question of jurisdiction, as provided for in the constitutions and statutes of the federal government and of the respective states.

concurrent jurisdiction

Power of more than one court to hear a case.

LEGAL FOCUS—PROBLEM

While walking along a busy street in Tallahassee, Jorge Cepada, a citizen of Florida, was struck by a crate that flew off a move-yourself rental driven by Laura Alexander. Desiring compensation for his injuries, Cepada intended suing Alexander in the convenient Florida courts. May he do so? Could he instead sue in a federal court?

When Alexander allegedly injured Cepada in Florida, the Florida state courts and the U.S. District Court had concurrent jurisdiction. An injured victim has the right to use the courts of the state where harm occurs. A plaintiff also has the right to bring suit in the courts of the state in which he or she is a resident (in this case, Cepada is a resident of Florida).

A right may also exist to use a federal court when the parties to a dispute are each citizens of different states. When such diversity of citizenship exists, a plaintiff may file an action in federal court if the claimed damages exceed $75,000. The party could also choose to file in a state court. The federal basis for jurisdiction in this example is called *diversity of citizenship* (discussed further later in this chapter). In diversity of citizenship cases, the federal court applies the substantive law of the state in which it sits, such as the state's law of negligence. Different procedural rules apply in federal civil courts than in state courts, and

* Federal courts include courts for the District of Columbia and the U.S. Territories, Puerto Rico, Virgin Islands, Canal Zone, Guam, and the Northern Mariana Islands.

attorneys are quick to seize upon advantages sometimes available in this regard. Note that diversity jurisdiction allows persons to use the federal courts when their claims are based on state law. Claims based on federal law may be filed in a federal court without the need for diversity jurisdiction.

JURISDICTION OVER SUBJECT MATTER

Subject matter jurisdiction determines which types of cases a court can hear. Probate courts—courts that handle only wills and estate matters—are examples of courts of **limited jurisdiction,** meaning courts authorized to hear limited types of cases. A court of **general jurisdiction** is a court that can hear and decide almost any type of case.

The subject matter jurisdiction of a court is usually defined in the constitutional or statutory law that creates the court. This creating law may refer to the type of case, its seriousness as reflected by the amount of money requested by the person bringing the lawsuit, or the type of relief requested of the court. For example, a court may be able to hear only cases where the damages requested are $50,000 or less, or when the court is asked to compel a person to do or not do something (an equitable remedy).

In criminal matters, the seriousness of a crime often determines which court hears a case. For example, a murder trial is held in the trial court of general jurisdiction rather than one of limited jurisdiction. Whether the proceeding is a trial or an appeal is perhaps the most obvious subject matter limitation on jurisdiction.

Venue

The proper place for trial that otherwise has appropriate jurisdiction for either a civil or criminal case is called its **venue** (French: "to come"). Venue is the local place, within the geographical boundaries of a larger political jurisdiction, where a case is most appropriately tried. Proper venue reflects a policy of closeness—that is, a court trying a suit should be close to where the incident leading to the suit occurred or close to where the defendant resides.

All things being equal, the following are typical of state venue rules:
• In divorce cases, proper venue is the county of the family residence.
• In automobile accident cases, proper venue is the county where the accident occurred or where the defendant resides.
• In breach of contract cases, proper venue is where the contract was made, or where it was breached, or where the defendant lives.
• In criminal cases, proper venue is the county in which the crime occurred or where the defendant was apprehended.

All things are not equal, however, when a significant event occurs that makes a different venue more likely to produce a just result. For example, excessive publicity in the county where a crime occurred may unreasonably prejudice an accused's right to a fair trial. Under such circumstances, courts will grant a **motion for change of venue** and order that the case be tried in a more appropriate place.

LEGAL FOCUS—PROBLEM
....

In the spring of 1992, a jury in Simi Valley, California, found four white Los Angeles police officers not guilty of using excessive force in the arrest of a black man, Rodney

---

subject matter jurisdiction

The power of a court to hear and decide cases of the general class to which the subject in question belongs.

limited jurisdiction

Limitation on a court as to the types of cases it can hear and decide.

general jurisdiction

Authorization of a court to hear and decide virtually any type of case occurring within the political boundaries of the geographical area in which it is located.

venue

The local place, within the geographical boundaries of a larger jurisdiction, where a case is generally most appropriately tried.

http://

The venue rules of the state of Ohio provide an example of state venue rules:

http://www.sconet.state.oh .us/Rules/civil/#rule3

motion for change of venue

Request to a judge by counsel to transfer the trial to a different geographic location within the jurisdiction of the court.

King. The highly publicized case involved accusations that the officers used unlawful force during King's arrest. A bystander, who had videotaped the use of force against King, made the tape available to the television media. The tape was played on television over and over, and the resulting publicity caused the police officers to request a change of venue from Los Angeles, where they argued they could not get a fair trial. The request was granted, and the trial was transferred to Simi Valley. A not guilty verdict by the Simi Valley jurors was followed by several days of rioting in southwestern Los Angeles. Many commentators announced that, in their opinions, the defendants had escaped conviction only because just 2.2 percent of Simi Valley residents are African-American. In the trial, no blacks served on the jury.*

Venue also can be changed within a single county, from one judicial district to another.

LEGAL FOCUS—PROBLEM

O.J. Simpson resided in, and was accused of committing a murder in, Los Angeles County. Ostensibly to avoid the possibility of race-based riots, the district attorney of Los Angeles personally requested a change of venue from predominantly white Santa Monica (where Simpson lived and where the murders occurred) to largely black downtown Los Angeles. Both places are within Los Angeles County. Simpson was found not guilty of the murders by the predominately African-American jury. Did the change of venue from Santa Monica to downtown Los Angeles affect the outcome of the case?

One can only speculate as to what the outcome might have been had the venue not been changed. Suffice it to say that the defense was delighted with the change in venue—the prosecuting attorneys were not consulted about the change even though their supervisor, the district attorney, made the decision.

LEGAL FOCUS—CASE

Timothy McVeigh was indicted by a federal grand jury for the planting of an explosive device in a truck next to the Alfred E. Murrah Federal Building in Oklahoma City, Oklahoma, on April 19, 1995. The explosion led to the deaths of 168 men, women, and children, and injuries to hundreds of other people. As the explosion occurred in Oklahoma City, the Oklahoma Western Federal District Court was the appropriate venue. McVeigh sought a change of venue. Why did he seek a change of venue? Why was the trial to be held in a federal rather than state court? Did he succeed in obtaining a change of venue?

United States v. McVeigh, 918 F.Supp. 1467 (W.D.Okl. 1996).

---

* After the acquittal on state criminal charges, the federal government filed federal criminal charges in Los Angeles alleging that the four police officers had violated Rodney King's civil rights. The federal jury found two officers, Powell and Koon, guilty; the two other officers were found innocent. Motions by the defendants for a change of venue in this trial were denied. The federal government does not prosecute all defendants who are acquitted of state criminal charges involving civil rights violations. It can be argued that the government makes its selection upon political bases, in cases that generate significant publicity and public outrage. Would the United States have prosecuted the police in the Rodney King case if there had been no public release of the videotape of the event?

http://

Federal venue rules for criminal matters are online at

http://www.law.ukans.edu/ research/frcrimV.htm

---

in personam jurisdiction

The power of a court over a person.

---

long-arm statute

A state law authorizing a court to hear cases brought against nonresidents under specified circumstances.

McVeigh argued that emotions would be especially high in the city where the bombing had taken place, where so many had loved ones or friends who had perished or been injured in the bombing. Federal jurisdiction existed because the bombing was of a federal building. The trial was moved to the federal district court in Denver, Colorado.

JURISDICTION OVER PERSONS AND PROPERTY

In our earlier example, if Laura Alexander can be served with a *summons*—an order informing her that a lawsuit has been filed against her—within the boundaries of Florida, the Florida state court has the power and right to hear the case. Under such circumstances, Jorge Cepada's Florida court would have **in personam jurisdiction** over Alexander, meaning power over her. The most common means of obtaining *in personam* jurisdiction in a civil case is by personal service of a summons and complaint on the defendant who is within the boundaries of the state in which the suit is commenced.

LEGAL FOCUS—PROBLEM

Assume the address given to Cepada by Alexander shows her new home is in Oklahoma, and by the time the suit is filed she lives in Oklahoma. Can Cepada still sue Alexander in Florida or must he now sue in Oklahoma?

Clearly, if the process server (a person in the business of serving summons upon defendants) can find Alexander within Florida, Cepada can sue in the Florida court. But, if Alexander had returned to Oklahoma before Cepada engaged the services of a lawyer and began litigation, the question is whether or not the Florida court could obtain jurisdiction over an Oklahoma citizen who never returns to Florida. The answer is yes, because Florida, like all states, has a **long-arm statute.**

There are two requirements before a plaintiff can get jurisdiction over an out-of-state defendant. The first is that the state must have a statute that authorizes the state to get jurisdiction under the particular circumstances. The second is a constitutional requirement that the basis for jurisdiction must satisfy procedural due process. Is it fair to require the defendant to come to the state to defend the lawsuit? Fair treatment required by due process is met by showing that the defendant has "certain minimum contacts with [the state] such that the maintenance of the suit does not offend 'traditional notions of fair play and substantial justice.'"[5]

Long-arm statutes subject nonresident defendants to local jurisdiction for wrongful activities they engage in while physically within a state even if they have left the state before they are sued. Long-arm statutes also can obtain jurisdiction over some activities of a defendant that occur outside the state but that caused harm within the state.[6] If a person drives a motor vehicle within a state, he is deemed to give his agreement to appear and answer for any harm he causes while driving in that state (called *implied consent*). Cepada won't even be required to hire a process server in Oklahoma, although that would be permissible; service of the summons by registered mail to Alexander's home would typically be adequate. Defendants also give implied consent to jurisdiction of states in which they do business. Thus, consumers in Florida can use their local courts to sue out-of-state companies who do business in their state. When defendants are not subject to long-arm statutes, plaintiffs can always sue a defendant in the state of the defendant's residence.

Although *in personam* jurisdiction is the most common way to get jurisdiction over a defendant, sometimes a dispute involves ownership or title to property. In these cases plaintiffs will seek **in rem jurisdiction** (Latin: "against a thing"). *In rem* jurisdiction empowers courts to declare rights against the world rather than just the named defendant(s). If the legal question involves ownership of real property located in Alaska, for example, the appropriate court to hear the case would be the trial court where the property is located in Alaska. Parties known to the plaintiff, who have an interest in the property, have a due-process right to receive fair notice of any proceeding based on *in rem* jurisdiction, as well as a right to participate in the case.

JURISDICTION AND THE INTERNET

The Internet is just one of the relatively new technologies to challenge settled concepts of law. The variety of exchanges and transactions on the Internet interposed on concepts of jurisdictional fairness will take some time to sort out, although the process has certainly begun.

LEGAL FOCUS—CASE

Stanley Young, the warden of Wallens Ridge State Prison in Big Stone Gap, Virginia, brought suit against two Connecticut newspapers, *The New Haven Advocate* and *The Hartford Courant,* alleging defamation (wrongful injury to reputation) for suggesting he was a racist. The Connecticut newspapers were interested in the Virginia prison system because the state of Connecticut contracted to send some state prisoners to serve their terms in Virginia. The suit was filed in Virginia, and the two newspapers moved to dismiss the lawsuit for lack of personal jurisdiction. Warden Young countered that because the articles were placed on the papers' Web sites they were accessible to Virginia residents. Was the Internet site publication a sufficient contact with the state of Virginia to satisfy the due process requirements under the Constitution?

Young v. New Haven Advocate, 184 Fed. Supp 2d 498 (w.b. Vir., 2001).

The court said yes. "The defendants published and circulated articles on their websites concerning the ongoing controversy surrounding the policy of sending Connecticut prisoners to correctional facilities in Virginia. The plaintiff was a warden in the Virginia correctional system. The allegedly defamatory news articles originated from the controversial policy and the plaintiff's relationship to the Virginia correctional system."[7] Although the law is not settled as to what Internet activities are sufficient to confer jurisdiction, this list, found in the case of *Morantz, Inc., v. Hang & Shine Ultrasonics,* is helpful.

1. [A] mere presence on the World Wide Web does not establish the minimum contacts necessary to subject a corporation to personal jurisdiction on a worldwide basis.
2. [T]he minimum contacts analysis in cases involving the Internet is conducted on a "sliding scale," on which the constitutionality of the exercise of personal jurisdiction is directly proportional to the level of commercial interactivity on a corporation's web site.
3. [A] Web site targeted at a particular jurisdiction is likely to give rise to personal jurisdiction.

in rem jurisdiction

The power of a court to declare rights against the world rather than solely against the named defendant(s).

http://

There is an excellent discussion about jurisdiction at **http://www.law.cornell.edu/topics/jurisdiction.html**

4. Court[s] will consider the quality and quantity of contacts with the plaintiff's jurisdiction to which the Internet site has given rise in determining whether personal jurisdiction may be exercised.[8]

http://

An excellent site for information about state court systems is

http://www.ncsconline.org/

How Are State Court Systems Organized?

The typical state court system consists of both trial and appellate courts. Consider the typical state court system shown in Exhibit 3-1. It has three main levels: (1) trial courts of general or limited jurisdiction, (2) intermediate appellate courts, and (3) the highest court (usually named the supreme court). Although most state court systems provide two levels of appeal, some states have but one appellate court.[†] Also, unfortunately, titles of state courts are not uniform; names of courts in one state frequently apply to quite different courts in another state. Confusion can be avoided by focusing on the function a court performs: trial or appellate.

The typical state will have a trial court of general jurisdiction, often called the *superior court*. That court may hear money matters with unlimited dollar limits and serious criminal matters. Most states have courts with limited subject matter jurisdiction, often called

EXHIBIT 3-1: A **Typical State Court System**

State Supreme Court
Highest state court. Some states call it the court of appeals, supreme judicial court, or supreme court of appeals.

Intermediate Appellate Courts
Not all states have intermediate appellate courts,

Probate Court*
This court handles wills; administration of estates, and guardianship of minors and others. Some states call it surrogate court or orphans' court.

Superior Court
Highest state trial court with general jurisdiction. Some states call it circuit court, district court, court of common pleas, or (in New York) supreme court.

Domestic Relations Court*
Some states call it family court or juvenile court.

Municipal Court*
In some states, municipal justices or magistrates hear less important cases.

County Court*
This court has limited jurisdiction in civil and criminal cases. Some states call it common pleas court or district court.

Justice of the Peace Court
Lowest state court. Limited jurisdiction in civil and criminal cases. Some states call it police magistrate court. Some states do not have this court.

* Courts of limited jurisdiction, such as probate, domestic relations, municipal, or county courts, may be separate courts or may be part of a trial court of general jusisdiction.

[†] States with only one appellate court are Delaware, Maine, Montana, Nevada, New Hampshire, North Dakota, Rhode Island, South Dakota, Vermont, West Virginia, and Wyoming.

special *inferior trial courts* or *minor judiciary courts*. A small claims court, discussed shortly, is an example of an inferior trial court of limited jurisdiction. Small claims courts hear claims involving relatively small dollar amounts. A domestic relations court, which handles only divorce actions and child custody cases, is another example of a court of limited jurisdiction. Local municipal courts handling, for example, misdemeanors and civil cases of modest dollar amounts are also courts of limited jurisdiction.

WHAT ARE SMALL CLAIMS COURTS?

Court procedures are devised to handle a great variety of legal problems ranging from the most complex to the simplest. Not surprisingly, the usual manner of handling legal matters is inefficient for small or simple cases. If you have a legal claim for $1,500 worth of minor damage to your automobile in an accident, the cost of hiring an attorney to help you recover that amount through court action would no doubt exceed your hoped-for recovery.

To promote peaceful resolution of disputes where a conventional lawsuit is prohibitively expensive, states have created a special trial court, called the **small claims court.** Jurisdiction of this court is usually limited to disputes involving small sums of money damages. They are often referred to as the *people's court,* because an average adult with limited formal education may obtain resolution of minor civil legal disputes in a speedy, informal, and user-friendly forum.

small claims court

A court with jurisdiction to decide civil controversies of a relatively minor nature.

The small claims court may be a separate court, or a designated subdivision of another court. Because it is the creation of each state, particulars vary widely. The maximum amount of recoverable damages ranges from $1,000 to $25,000, depending on the state, the most common maximum being $5,000. State legislatures frequently change the dollar limits of these courts in inflationary times to continue to provide inexpensive access to the courts for civil matters involving modest amounts of money.

http://

Look up the small claims court monetary limits for your state at **http://www.nolo.com/**

The purpose of the small claims court is the same as any other trial court: to determine facts and apply the law. However, the dynamics of the small claims court are more relaxed, proceedings are usually faster, and procedures to use the court are less complicated than those found in other courts. This is not to say it is uncomplicated or that the small claims court is a social gathering—only that it is less intimidating to the average litigant.

Most small claims cases involve disputes over money, although some are concerned with matters such as eviction from residential rentals. Divorce actions, criminal matters, and civil cases involving *in rem* jurisdiction are examples of cases not accepted in small claims court. The procedural rules differ from those of traditional trial courts. Legal documents are kept to a minimum; often the only formal document required of the plaintiff is a simple pre-printed form with boxes for checking. There are no formal rules of evidence and no juries. In the interests of economy and simplicity, most states do not permit attorneys at law to represent litigants in small claims court. Corporations are artificial, legal persons, and so when they use small claims courts to collect debts they must be represented by employees. Most states will not allow attorneys to appear for litigants even in such corporate situations unless the attorney at law is the sole shareholder or an officeholder of the corporation.

http://

Suggestions for small claims court reform can be found at **http://www.halt.org/SmallClaims/SCfactsheet.cfm**

Each party explains the dispute, calling on witnesses for corroboration or for additional facts. Each party also presents any supporting documents or other physical evidence. The judge may ask questions and then, without any elaborate commentary or research, decide the case. Sometimes the judge will rule at the conclusion of the trial, but often the judge will inform the parties of his or her decision later by mail. In some states parties can appeal the case, but in many situations the small claims court plaintiff does not have that right—use of a small claims court is deemed a waiver of the right to a jury and to appeal.

trial de novo

A new trial that takes place as if the first trial had not occurred.

http://

If you are interested in the origins of the National Judiciary, read the article by University of Chicago law professor Philip B. Kurland at **http://www.apsanet.org/ CENnet/thisconstitution/ kurland.cfm**

http://

You can obtain information on all federal courts from **http://www.uscourts.gov/**

http

Here is one of several sites dedicated to information about the kidnapping of Charles and Anne Lindbergh's baby boy, Charles Jr.: **http://www.charleslindbergh .com/kidnap/index.asp**

diversity of citizenship

A basis of jurisdiction in federal courts requiring that plaintiff and defendant be involved in an actual controversy, that they be citizens of different states, and that a minimum of $75,000 be sought in damages.

The defendant, however, generally retains a right to a **trial de novo** (*de novo* means "new" and the term means a right to a completely new trial hearing*).

Small claims courts help "the little person" get his or her "day in court" without the delays and costs that accompany use of traditional courts. However, because business firms often have a substantial number of small claims, they appear most frequently as plaintiffs in small claims court actions.[†]

Various television programs such as *Judge Judy* popularize small claims courts. Technically these proceedings are *arbitrations* (a private third party is selected by the parties to hear and resolve the dispute) rather than trials, but they illustrate the types of disputes heard and resolved in small claims courts. What they do not do is illustrate usual judicial behavior. The cases heard are chosen for entertainment value and the television judge's questions and decisions are often rendered in a sarcastic and condescending fashion.

ⓌHAT IS THE FEDERAL COURT SYSTEM?

Like the state court system, the federal court system consists of both trial and appellate courts. The two principal appellate courts are the U.S. Courts of Appeals and the U.S. Supreme Court.

FEDERAL TRIAL COURTS

The federal government has one trial court of general jurisdiction called the U.S. District Court. The country is divided into ninety-four districts. Each district consists of a number of judges doing business in a number of different courtrooms and even in different buildings. How many judges are "sitting" (i.e., conducting the court's business) is related to the population within each district. In populous areas, the districts are geographically small; in rural areas, they are large. There is at least one U.S. District Court in every state and territory in the United States.

U.S. District Courts conduct trials concerning federal matters, such as federal crimes and enforcement of federal statutes. Most federal crimes involve crimes against the government or crimes occurring on federal property. One crime, kidnapping, is a federal crime even though it does not occur on federal land. This federal law was passed after the notorious kidnapping of the son of famous aviator Charles Lindbergh in 1932. Federal jurisdiction for the crime of kidnapping is based on taking of the victim across state or country lines and the statute provides that the failure to release the victim within twenty-four hours after seizure creates "a rebuttable presumption that such person has been transported to interstate or foreign commerce."[9]

As discussed earlier it is possible to sue in a federal court even though the claim is based on state law when the plaintiff and defendant are from different states or countries. **Diversity of citizenship** jurisdiction exists when a plaintiff is a citizen of one state and the

---

* The defendant, unlike the plaintiff, did not choose the small claims court forum and usually is not deemed to have waived the right to an appeal. In the normal appeal, the trial record is reviewed to determine if the trial judge made an error. If a party has a right to a trial *de novo,* the prior court record is not considered (note that small claims courts do not keep a record of transcripts), and the defendant is automatically given a new day in court. Although the new trial occurs at a higher level court, the trial usually remains informal and is decided by a judge without a jury. See M. Barrett, The Constitutional Right to Jury Trial: A Historical Exception for Small Monetary Claims, 39 Hastings L.J. 125 (1987). See also, *Crouchman v. Superior Court,* 45 Cal.3d 1167, 755 P.2d 1075, 248 Cal. Rptr. 626 (1988) and *Iowa Nat. Mut. Ins. Co. v. Mitchell,* 305 N.W. 2d724 (Iowa, 1981).

† In number apparently about one-half the plaintiffs are businesses, according to one report. See "The Role of the Small-Claims Court," *Consumer Reports,* November 1979, p. 666.

defendant is a citizen of another state, or when one party is a foreign country or a citizen of a foreign country and the other is a citizen of the United States. The amount of claimed damages in a diversity of citizenship case must be at least $75,000.[10] In settling such controversies, the particular U.S. District Court involved applies federal *procedural law* (which involves the manner in which rights and duties are to be enforced) and the *substantive law* (which involves the defining of rights and duties) of the appropriate state, usually the state where the court is located.[11] When a federal court hears a case because of diversity jurisdiction, an example of *concurrent jurisdiction* exists because at least one state court would also have had the power to hear the case, if the plaintiff had chosen to file the case there.

LEGAL FOCUS—PROBLEM

Jorge Cepada, a resident of Florida, wishes to sue Laura Alexander, an Oklahoma resident, to collect damages for injuries and losses arising from the motor vehicle accident that occurred in Florida (see page 101). If the amount of damages requested exceeds $75,000, Cepada can sue in a U.S. District Court sitting in either Florida or Oklahoma. Can he alternatively file the case in a state court?

Yes, as noted earlier, he can. Because the accident occurred in Florida, the most convenient state court would be Florida's. Using a long-arm statute, he could get jurisdiction over Alexander through use of the mail. Cepada could also file the lawsuit in Oklahoma, Alexander's resident state, and obtain jurisdiction there. This accident provides an example of a legal dispute in which concurrent jurisdiction exists.

When cases can be tried only in federal courts or only in state courts, **exclusive jurisdiction** exists. A person filing for a discharge in bankruptcy, which is a constitutional legal right that releases one from the duty to pay one's debts, can file the petition* only in a federal court. States also have exclusive jurisdiction in certain subject matter areas—for example, in divorces and adoptions. The concepts of concurrent and exclusive jurisdiction are illustrated in Exhibit 3-2.

exclusive jurisdiction

The sole power a court has over the particular subject matter of a case.

FEDERAL APPELLATE COURTS

U.S. Courts of Appeals

The U.S. Courts of Appeals review the decisions of the U.S. District Courts located within their respective circuits. The country is divided into thirteen circuits, or geographical areas, each with a U.S. Court of Appeals. The number of judges, courtroom-building locations, and geographic size of the circuits vary greatly.[†] As with state appellate courts, the U.S. Courts of Appeals review cases brought to the court's attention by parties contending that the federal trial judge made an error of law. The federal system also has a U.S. Court of Appeals for the federal circuit, which has nationwide jurisdiction to hear appeals from all district courts in patent cases, as well as certain claims against the federal government.

---

* A petition is the appropriate filing to institute a bankruptcy proceeding.

† The Washington, D.C., Circuit is the smallest circuit in geographical size and is responsible only for the nation's capital. The largest geographical circuit is the ninth (Alaska, Arizona, California, Guam, Hawaii, Idaho, Montana, Oregon, Nevada, the Northern Mariana Islands, and Washington). The number of judges per circuit ranges from six sitting circuit court judges in the first circuit (Maine, Massachusetts, New Hampshire, Puerto Rico, and Rhode Island) to twenty-eight authorized judges in the ninth circuit. At this writing, a proposal to split the ninth circuit was under consideration by Congress.

EXHIBIT 3-2: **Exclusive and Concurrent Jurisdiction**

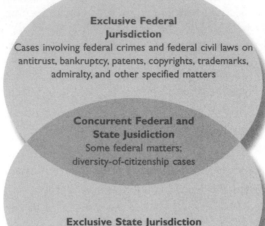

Exclusive Federal Jurisdiction
Cases involving federal crimes and federal civil laws on antitrust, bankruptcy, patents, copyrights, trademarks, admiralty, and other specified matters

Concurrent Federal and State Jusidiction
Some federal matters; diversity-of-citizenship cases

Exclusive State Jurisdiction
All mattters not subject to federal jurisdiction

Also heard before this court are appeals from specialized courts (e.g., the U.S. Claims Court and the U.S. Court of International Trade) and claims arising from decisions of federal administrative agencies.

U.S. Supreme Court

The highest level of the federal court system is the United States Supreme Court. Under the U.S. Constitution, there is but one such court. The court consists of nine Justices.* It has original, or trial, jurisdiction in rare instances—for example, in legal disputes in which a state is a party, cases between two states, and cases involving ambassadors. Most often it acts as the court of final appeal for federal Courts of Appeals and, in less frequent situations, the highest state appellate courts when they have decided cases on the basis of federal law.

Many cases compete for the attention of the U.S. Supreme Court, and in some cases the Court is required to take action (mandatory jurisdiction). An example of a mandatory case would be an appeal from either a federal or state court where the lower court has held that an act of Congress is unconstitutional. However, most appeals are discretionary (discretionary jurisdiction) and the Court is free to select which cases it will hear and decide. The selection process is accomplished by the *rule of four,* which means that the case is selected if four of the nine justices so choose. When the Court selects a case for review, it issues an order (writ of *certiorari*) to the Court of Appeals, or highest state court, requesting the record of the case. A **writ of *certiorari*** (Latin: "to be informed of") is an order by which the U.S. Supreme Court exercises its discretionary power to decide which lower court cases it will hear. To be among these cases, an important federal question must be

writ of *certiorari*

A procedural document whereby an appellate court exercises its discretionary power to accept jurisdiction of a pending case.

---

* The Constitution does not specify the number of Supreme Court Justices, and since its inception the number has varied. However, since 1869 the number has remained at nine. In 1937, an attempt was made by President Franklin D. Roosevelt to "pack the court" with six additional Justices who would presumably be sympathetic to his "New Deal" reform legislation. This maneuver was vigorously opposed and rejected by Congress.

EXHIBIT 3-3: **The U.S. Court System**

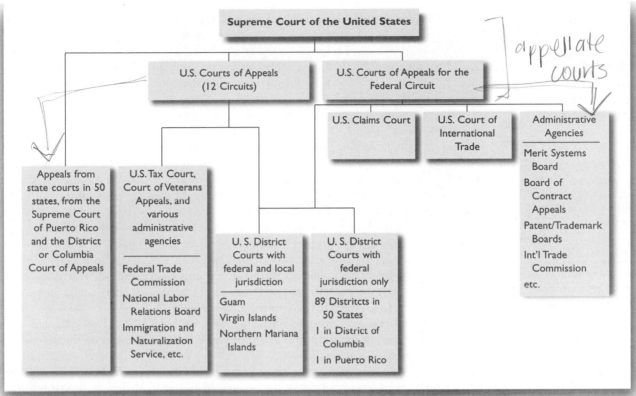

Source: Administrative Office of the U. S. Courts.

raised, such as one involving a constitutional issue (e.g., freedom of speech). When the Supreme Court declines review of a case, the practical effect is an agreement with the lower court decision, which continues binding the parties. The Court is able to hear only a small percentage of the appeals filed annually, and formal opinions are delivered in only about 115–130 cases.[12]

Exhibit 3-3 depicts the federal court structure, which, in addition to the principal courts, includes the United States Court of International Trade, United States Claims Court, and United States Tax Court. Each of these is a special jurisdiction court restricted to hearing particular types of cases.

TRIAL PROCEEDINGS

Looking back at the twentieth century, we can see that most of the dramatic changes in our legal system occurred following World War II. The first fifty years of the century saw the law functioning in a slower, if not more leisurely, way. The procedures guiding cases through courts were more relaxed by far in the first half of the century. Today, procedures are complex. Meritorious cases can be lost because of errors made in the procedures that are necessary in maneuvering a civil case through the court process. Some litigants pay their opponents a sum of money, often called "nuisance money," simply to avoid incurring the expenses that complexity always seems to create.

http://

This Web site has a lawsuit divided into five stages: investigation, notice, pleading, discovery, and trial. See the discussion of each by the law firm of Babbitt & Johnson in West Palm Beach, Florida.
http://babbitt-johnson.com/lawsuit.html

HOW IS A CIVIL CASE STARTED?

Recall the example where Marya Martinez was injured in a skiing accident that she believes would not have occurred but for the carelessness of her ski instructor, Gary Graf (page 97). If Martinez decides to sue Graf, her attorney will begin the case by filing a document called a **complaint** with the county clerk. The complaint briefly states the facts she believes justify her claim, the basis for jurisdiction of the court, and the request for damages or other relief she seeks. Martinez is the plaintiff, and the complaint is almost always prepared by her attorney, who is satisfied that she has a **cause of action** (legally appropriate basis for suing).

County clerks maintain files, generally in alphabetical and numerical order, of every case filed in their respective counties. These records are open to the public. A filing fee (from $50 to $100 or more) is charged at the time of filing. When the complaint is filed, the clerk issues a **summons** (prepared by the plaintiff's attorney) by endorsing it on behalf of the court. The summons is a notice of a lawsuit; it informs the defendant that a lawsuit has been filed against him or her in the named court and that the defendant has a prescribed time (e.g., thirty days) to personally appear or respond to the complaint. You may recall the importance of the summons in obtaining jurisdiction of the defendant, as described earlier in the case involving Jorge Cepada and Laura Alexander. If the defendant fails to respond, the plaintiff may win the case by default (forfeit), and a judgment, the final decision of the court, may be awarded to the plaintiff.

Martinez's attorney will arrange with a **process server** or a local official, such as a sheriff, to have a copy of the summons and complaint personally served on the defendant, Gary Graf, to obtain *in personam* jurisdiction. As discussed earlier, a process server is in the business of serving legal documents on defendants or plaintiffs and witnesses. If Graf cannot be found, or if he evades service of the process, he may nonetheless be served by alternative methods such as "constructive service" through a notification to the defendant by mail and the publication of a summons in a local newspaper. Serving a copy of the summons and complaint (or publication of summons) gives Graf notice that he has been sued and gives the proper court jurisdiction (or power) over his person to decide the controversy. The court, of course, must also be the appropriate forum (have jurisdiction) over the subject matter and type of dispute involved.

Upon receipt of the summons and complaint, Graf would typically hire a lawyer to represent him to uphold his interests. Graf's lawyer would file a responsive pleading, called an **answer,** with the county clerk and mail a copy to the plaintiff's lawyer. The answer is a document containing a defendant's denial and personal allegations of fact. In the answer, Graf may admit to any parts of the complaint that he believes are true and deny the rest. The complaint and answer together are called the **pleadings.**

Instead of an answer, Graf's attorney might be able to file another type of responsive document, asking for a dismissal of the complaint. This is called a **demurrer** or **motion to dismiss** and is used when the complaint, even if true, is legally insufficient to justify an answer. A **motion** is a formal request to a court for some action by the judge. The demurrer or motion to dismiss is often called a "so what" motion, as its legal effect is to say that even if all of the plaintiff's allegations are true, no legal duty was breached by the defendant. To provide an example of a motion to dismiss, let us consider an illustrative dispute.

LEGAL FOCUS—PROBLEM

Plaintiff Archibald Cantwell alleged in his complaint that the defendant professor "wrongfully, viciously, and wantonly stuck out her tongue at the plaintiff, while in class,

---

complaint

A document stating the facts constituting an alleged cause of action.

cause of action

An existing right to seek and to receive judicial relief, assuming the factual allegations of the plaintiff are true.

summons

A document issued by a clerk of the court inviting the defendant to respond to a complaint.

process server

A person who serves (delivers) a copy of the summons and complaint, or other legal document, upon a party or witness at the request of the opposing party to civil litigation.

answer

A document containing a defendant's allegations of fact in response to a complaint.

pleadings

The complaint of the plaintiff and answer of the defendant in a lawsuit.

demurrer or **motion to dismiss**

A motion filed by a defendant in response to a summons and complaint when allegations of the complaint, even if true, are insufficient to state a cause of action.

: causing great and severe mental anguish." Did Cantwell state a cause of action in his
: complaint?

No. Even if the plaintiff's claims were admitted by the defendant, there would be no legal recovery (judgment) possible for the plaintiff, simply because sticking out one's tongue is not against the law. Therefore, the defendant should file a demurrer or motion to dismiss, which would be **sustained** (agreed to) by the court, and the complaint would be dismissed. If Cantwell chose instead to file an answer, the case would continue on to trial, wasting the time of both the defendant and the court.

A demurrer can also raise procedural defenses, as, for example, a claim that the action is barred by a **statute of limitations**—a statute requiring that particular legal actions be commenced within a stated period of time. Tardy claims are barred (i.e., prohibited) by statutes of limitations even if they are otherwise meritorious. The reasoning for statutes of limitation is that memories fade and other evidence becomes scarce and less reliable, all of which diminishes the possibility of a just resolution of the dispute by a court. Such statutes also serve to eliminate what could be an ongoing threat of suit that would otherwise interfere with the defendant's life.

Once Martinez's complaint and Graf's answer are filed, the factual contentions of each party are stated on the record. Plaintiffs and defendants almost always disagree with each other's version of what had happened; these factual disagreements are much of what must be resolved at trial.

Following receipt of summons and complaint, Graf might voluntarily or unwittingly do nothing. Doing nothing is rarely a smart choice; here it would pave the way for Martinez to obtain an uncontested judgment, called a **default judgment.** As explained earlier, a judgment is a final expression by the court telling who wins and who loses. Unlike a judgment following a trial, a default judgment may be issued by the judge following a trial in which the defendant is absent, and who, it is therefore assumed, does not contest the accuracy of the plaintiff's claims. The judge simply takes minimal evidence from the plaintiff to ensure that the claim is not frivolous or improper in some respect. Following such an **ex parte** (Latin: "with one party") **trial,** which often takes only minutes of the court's time, a judgment typically is awarded the plaintiff. So, doing nothing can be a costly mistake. Even if he is going to concede fault and liability, Graf would be wise to file answer to the complaint and then try to negotiate a compromise limiting the damages he must pay or providing a reasonable payment schedule.

HOW IS A CRIMINAL CASE STARTED?

In contrast to a civil case, a criminal case is formally begun by the issuance of an **accusation,** which formally charges a specified person with commission of a particular crime. An accusation is usually initiated by the district attorney (under which circumstance it is called an **information**) or by a body called the **grand jury*** (under which circumstance it is called an **indictment**). Misdemeanor cases typically are initiated by the filing of a complaint. These terms and criminal procedures are discussed in Chapter 6.

---

* A body composed of a number of jurors that varies from state to state, sometimes six, sometimes twelve, and occasionally more than twelve. The grand jury inquires into crimes committed in the city or other geographic region from which the members are drawn, makes determination of the probability of guilt, and then issues indictments (formal accusation of crime) against supposed offenders. (24 American Jurisprudence, Grand Jury § 2.)

motion
A formal request by counsel addressed to a court or other tribunal for a particular decision or act.

sustained
Agreement by the judge with request by an attorney.

statute of limitations
A statute that bars civil or criminal proceedings unless brought within a specified period of time after the act occurred.

default judgment
Court-awarded judgment based on the defendant's failure to answer the summons and complaint or to appear at the trial to contest the claim of the plaintiff.

ex parte trial
A legal action where only one side of the dispute is heard.

accusation
Formal commencement of a criminal case by a specified public official such as a district attorney or by a grand jury.

information
An accusation of a criminal offense issued following a preliminary hearing.

grand jury
An appointed body of citizens formed both to investigate the operations of government and to issue indictments against persons suspected of criminal conduct.

WHAT ARE PRETRIAL PROCEDURES?

indictment

An accusation of felony filed by a grand jury.

alternative dispute resolution

Any of various methods of resolving disputes through means other than the judicial process.

http://

For an example of the different statutes of limitations in a state, look them up for the state of Illinois. Under Practice Areas, click on Civil Practice; at the next screen, click on Statutes of Limitations.

http://www.illinoislegalaid.org/

discovery

Group of methods used under court order during the period between commencement of a lawsuit and the date of trial to learn facts about the dispute.

deposition

Questioning of a witness or adverse party to an action, under oath, by the opposing attorney before the trial.

interrogatories

A form of discovery consisting of written questions directed to a party or witness who is expected to reply with written answers under oath.

Once a civil lawsuit begins by the filing of pleadings, a year or more may elapse before the trial. In some crowded metropolitan areas, the volume of cases filed, together with short-ages of judges and courtrooms, cause seriously congested calendars, which in turn necessi-tate undesirable delays in settling cases for trial. In rural and less populous jurisdictions, the trial may occur as soon as the opposing attorneys are prepared. In populous urban areas, delays of three to four years sometimes occur. Courtroom delay has become one of the most serious problems facing this country's legal system. In recent years, many states have begun experimenting with new administrative methods to expedite the process. Many states actively encourage alternatives to litigation, such as arbitration. The legal sys-tem is flexible enough to allow for alternatives to the courts in many situations. Alterna-tives to litigation are called **alternative dispute resolution** (ADR) and are discussed in Chapter 4.

Discovery

One of the most time-consuming, expensive, and intrusive aspects of going through civil trials today is a process called **discovery.** Discovery includes the use of a group of methods to learn facts about the dispute. Nonexistent early in the twentieth century, many believe that discovery has escalated into an arsenal of weapons that is often abused by attorneys. Should discovery be streamlined to keep pace with life and times in the twenty-first cen-tury? Many business contracts today contain arbitration agreements (discussed in Chapter 4) to avoid going to court if and when future disputes arise between the contracting persons. One major reason that many, perhaps most, financial businesses (e.g., banks, stock broker-ages) and HMOs (health maintenance organizations) choose this judicial bypass is to attempt to avoid the costs, intrusiveness, and delays associated with discovery procedures.

Although courtroom availability is the most common reason for a delay in a trial date, counsel for one or both of the parties may seek delay because more time is needed for dis-covery procedures. The stated goals of discovery are to

- Educate each party as to the facts surrounding the controversy
- Promote voluntary settlement of the controversy by revealing strengths and weak-nesses in the cases of each party
- Eliminate surprises that might otherwise arise during the trial, possibly leading to a miscarriage of justice

Depositions and interrogatories are the most common types of discovery. A **deposition** is the questioning of a witness or adverse party by the opposing attorney, long before the trial, under oath, in the presence of a court reporter and the other party's attorney. **Inter-rogatories** are a form of discovery in which written questions are directed to a party, who must then reply under oath with written answers.

LEGAL FOCUS—PROBLEM

Marya Martinez hired Sally Sharpe as her attorney in the case against Gary Graf. Sharpe's complaint and summons issued by the court were personally served on Graf. He promptly hired a lawyer, Scott Dasse, who prepared and filed an answer. Graf con-tended that he had adjusted Martinez's bindings carefully and properly and was not neg-ligent. Graf's answer also alleged that Martinez was negligent in two respects: (1) being under the influence of alcohol at the time of her injury and (2) being careless in allowing ice to form beneath her boots. The pleadings were filed, joining the issues of fact. What is the status of the proceedings?

Attorney Sharpe is seeking a money judgment against Graf to compensate Martinez for her injury on the theory that Graf was negligent. Attorney Dasse, on behalf of Graf, is contending that Graf was not negligent and that even if he was, Martinez was equally careless as to her own safety and so she should be denied a money judgment. Both attorneys will need more information in order to prepare for trial.

DEPOSITIONS   Sharpe wants to know the exact setting Graf used in adjusting Martinez's bindings; then she will seek expert advice as to the proper setting. Sharpe could mail a notice of taking deposition to Graf's attorney, requesting that Graf appear in Sharpe's office at a stated time to be questioned under oath with a court reporter present. The court reporters will use mechanical shorthand to record all testimony. In many states, electronic shorthand equipment and recording machines also are used. During this deposition, which Graf must attend, Sharpe could ask him, among other things, what setting he had used on Martinez's bindings. Of course, Graf's attorney will respond by taking Martinez's deposition.

LEGAL FOCUS—PROBLEM

At the deposition, attorney Dasse asked the following question: "Ms. Martinez, do you date frequently?" Attorney Sharpe immediately objected, shouting that she would not allow her client to be subjected to irrelevant questions by Dasse. Must Martinez answer the question?

At the deposition, Dasse cannot force Martinez to answer a question if she refuses. He could, however, seek a court order requiring her to answer the question if the question is deemed appropriate by the judge. Courts have the power to compel the parties to comply with the discovery procedures. If the order is granted and Martinez still refuses to answer, her entire case may be dismissed or another sanction (penalty) imposed. Attorney Dasse will need to explain to a judge why the question is appropriate, because its relevance to the case is not obvious.

After the deposition, the court reporter prepares a hard (paper) copy of all questions and answers. This document is made available to the witness, who makes any necessary corrections before signing and returning it. If the witness is unavailable at the trial, or is present but changes the version of the story given at the deposition, the transcript itself may be introduced as evidence and used to **impeach** (i.e., discredit) the witness. In complex cases, depositions may require several days of testimony under oath. The cost of taking depositions is a major expense of litigation and one significant reason why alternatives to litigation are often sought.*

---

* As undeniably useful as discovery is, it is costly and can be subject to abuse. Litigants can request large quantities of documents based on possible relevance, and the expense of this production of documents is borne by the person producing them. The federal courts and many state court systems are experimenting with discovery rules in an attempt to preserve discovery's value while limiting its excesses. Examples of new rules include requiring a party to provide relevant discovery without it being requested by the other party and harsher penalties (sanctions) available to the courts for instances where abuse of discovery rules exist. Some authors have suggested eliminating discovery altogether. Lorn Kieve, "Discovery Reform," *ABA Journal* 79 (December 1991), p. 11.

http://

For the different deadlines in each state for a negligence lawsuit, consult the following site, which contains excerpts from the book *Winning Your Personal Injury Claim,* by Evan K. Aidman, Esq.:

http://www.legalaidman .com/8b_state.htm

impeach

To discredit, dispute, disparage, or contradict a witness's testimony.

WRITTEN INTERROGATORIES   After the deposition, attorney Dasse thought of some additional questions that he would like to ask. He sent the following written interrogatories to Martinez through her attorney:

1. Please state the address of Luther Thomas.
2. Please state each date you visited a doctor and your total medical bill expenses.
3. Please state whether or not your medical bills are being paid by an insurance company. If so, please state the company's name and the applicable policy number.

If Martinez fails to answer the written interrogatories, Graf's attorney may seek an order from the court compelling answers. Attorneys may serve hundreds of written interrogatories in preparation of a complex case. They are less expensive than depositions because no court reporter is needed, and since they are written they tend to be more concise than the ramblings that frequently accompany oral interrogations. Furthermore, parties responding to interrogatories must search their files and records for information they "cannot recall." A disadvantage is that they allow a witness to consult with counsel and draft an answer that, while true, discloses as little as possible and states even that as favorably as possible. The questioning attorney is not present to detect signs of uneasiness and possible evasion or concealment, nor is he or she able to immediately pursue promising leads suggested by oral responses during depositions.

MOTION TO PRODUCE   The **motion to produce** may result in an order made by a judge at the request of counsel. It compels the opposing party to provide specified evidence that he or she currently controls or possesses, and that is believed to be relevant in the case.

LEGAL FOCUS—PROBLEM

Dasse believed that Martinez's diary might provide important information. He therefore filed a motion to produce with the court after his request to produce it had been refused. The motion requested an order compelling Martinez to deliver her diary to Dasse for his inspection. Will the motion be granted?

Dasse's motion will not be granted unless he can demonstrate to the court specifically what may be contained in the diary that would be relevant to the issues in the case. That appears doubtful unless, for example, Dasse can offer proof that Martinez has been deceitful and he has reason to believe that the diary would confirm the deceit.

At the time of trial, either attorney may ask the court for a **subpoena** (Latin: "under penalty"), a written order directing a person to appear in court and testify as a witness. If it is believed that the witness has books or documents needed for a full disclosure of the facts, the court may issue a **subpoena *duces tecum*** (Latin: "under penalty bring with you"), requiring that identified documents or physical evidence be brought to court.

Discovery in Criminal Matters

In a criminal case, discovery is limited because of the defendant's **privilege against self-incrimination.** (A privilege is a legal right.) This legal right, in brief, provides that a defendant cannot be compelled to testify against himself or herself in a criminal case. The privilege is derived from the Fifth Amendment to the U.S. Constitution, and it is often referred to in slang terms as "taking the Fifth."

---

http://

The law office of Myron Milch in New Jersey provides a sample order for discovery at **http://www.milchlaw.com/form7.html**

motion to produce

Request to a judge by counsel to compel the opposing party to provide specified evidence to the court.

subpoena

An order directing a person to appear at a certain time and place for the purpose of giving testimony as a witness.

subpoena *duces tecum*

A judicial order to bring specified documents or physical evidence to court.

privilege against self-incrimination

The right of any person, including one accused of a crime, to remain silent when what might be said could indicate guilt.

The government prosecutor does not have this same right, as the prosecutors are not on trial. The Sixth Amendment to the U.S. Constitution gives the accused the right "in all criminal prosecutions . . . to be confronted with the witnesses against him. . . ." Therefore, the government prosecutor must allow examination of the evidence against the defendant, including names of witnesses against the defendant. However, physical evidence (such as weapons, clothing, and stolen goods) may be impounded (seized and held) by the district attorney, pending trial. The defendant does, however, have the right to inspect all such evidence before trial. The apparent advantage of one-way discovery for the criminal defendant is more than counterbalanced by the state's greater resources to independently investigate and discover facts surrounding alleged criminal activity.

Motion for Summary Judgment

If there are no disputes over facts that need to be resolved, it is possible that the case can be decided without a trial. In a **motion for summary judgment** the moving party argues that there are no significant questions of fact and that the applicable law requires that the moving party be awarded judgment. This motion might be made to the court after discovery, when a party believes discovery has shown that there is no real dispute as to the facts. If the motion is granted, no trial takes place. The party against whom a motion for summary judgment is granted (or any other adverse order that terminates the case) would have the right to appeal.

motion for summary judgment

Request to a judge by counsel to award judgment because there are no significant questions of fact in the lawsuit.

The Pretrial Conference

Either party or the court can request a **pretrial hearing** or **conference,** which usually takes place after the discovery process is over. The conference consists of an informal discussion between the judge and the attorneys. Its purpose is to identify the matters that are in dispute and to plan the course of the trial. At the pretrial hearing, the judge may encourage the parties to settle without a trial (an out-of-court settlement). These "settlement conferences" are sometimes attended by the parties to the litigation, as well as by their attorneys. Possible "before trial" steps in a civil dispute are set forth in Exhibit 3-4.

pretrial hearing or **conference**

Hearing occurring before a trial.

> *"Jury duty [is] a bog of quicksand on the path to justice."*
> Sidney Bernard, "The Waiting Game," *New York Journal-American,* 30 December 1965.

WHAT IS A JURY?

A **jury** is a group of men and women selected according to pre-established procedures to ensure lack of bias, who are sworn under oath to inquire of certain matters of fact and declare the truth based on evidence presented to them. This broad definition of a jury includes many types of juries used in the United States including grand jury, petit jury, special jury, coroner's jury, and sheriff's jury. Our discussion focuses on those juries selected to hear and decide specific legal disputes rather than investigative juries, such as grand juries.

In the United States, litigating parties often request a jury trial. Whether the request is granted will depend on whether the requesting party has a legal right to a jury trial. Many U.S. citizens believe that they have a right to a jury trial in all legal matters, but they are wrong. Litigants do, however, have a right to a jury trial in many matters. Whether

jury

A group of men and women sworn to declare the truth based on evidence presented to them.

EXHIBIT 3-4: **Steps in a Civil Case—Before Trial**

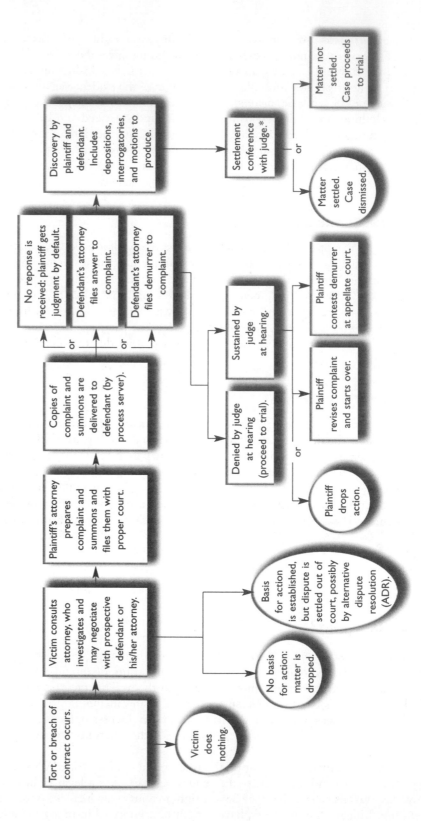

* In many states, nonbinding arbitration may be required in addition to or or in lieu of the stetclement convrence.

they have a right to jury trial may depend on whether the trial is criminal or civil, raises matters "in equity" or "law," or whether it takes place in state or federal courts.*

LEGAL FOCUS—CASE

People's Bank, a Connecticut corporation, filed an action to foreclose on a home owned by William and Nadine Podd, husband and wife, alleging the Podds failed to pay their monthly mortgage payments. The Podds requested a trial by jury. People's Bank objected. Do the Podds have a right to jury trial in this lawsuit?

People's Bank v. Podd, 1993 WL 382514 (Conn.Super.).

Any party to a civil lawsuit in the federal court system has the constitutional right (under the Seventh Amendment) to trial by jury in cases at law "where the value in controversy shall exceed twenty dollars." A right to a jury trial in a civil case in state courts is not guaranteed by the federal Constitution,[13] although state constitutions usually provide for this right. The case of *People's Bank v. Podd* was filed in a Connecticut state court, raising issues of state civil law. The Connecticut constitution provides for a right to a jury trial, but the Connecticut supreme court has held that this right exists only in those cases where a right to jury trial existed at the time of the state constitution's adoption (1812). The court concluded the action brought against the Podds was an equity action and so the state needn't provide the Podds a jury trial. We discuss equity actions in more detail later in the chapter.

The right to a jury trial is more certain in matters of criminal law. A trial by an "impartial jury" is a constitutional right (under the Sixth and Fourteenth Amendments) in any criminal matter, federal or state, where a serious penalty such as a jail sentence or imprisonment of more than six months may be the punishment.[14] Criminal defendants may waive their right to jury trials for various reasons (such as a **plea bargain,** where they admit guilt to a lesser offense than they were charged with, thereby sparing the state the expense of conducting costly trials with uncertain outcomes). A judge alone then makes the necessary findings of fact and imposes a sentence.

The televised murder trial of former Hall of Fame professional football player and movie actor O.J. Simpson in 1996 provided worldwide exposure to the role of juries in the United States. In addition to issues of selection, sequestration, crime scene visitation, and evidence tampering, viewers were presented with the possible issue of jury nullification.[†]

In usual cases a jury concludes and decides the **questions of fact**—historical events that must be proved to win a lawsuit. A jury is the **trier of fact.** For example, in a dispute about a fight between two students, Williams and Norbert, there probably will be a disagreement as to who started the altercation. A question of fact is presented and is generally answered by the jury, with a verdict in favor of the defensive fighter. If there is no jury, the trial judge decides questions of fact and is the *trier of fact.* Famous trial attorney Melvin Belli, never one for understatement, once said, "[A lawyer's] performance in the courtroom is responsible for about 25 percent of the outcome; the remaining 75 percent depends on the facts."[15]

plea bargain

A binding agreement in which an accused agrees to plead guilty if the court agrees to a specified charge and punishment in advance.

http://

Background on the O.J. Simpson murder trial can be found at the CNN Web site: http://www.cnn.com/US/OJ/

questions of fact

Circumstances or matters surrounding and involved in a case that is being tried by a court.

trier of fact

Jury or judge acting as the finder of issues of fact.

---

* Article III, Section 2 of the Constitution provides that "the Trial of all Crimes . . . shall be by Jury. . . ." The Sixth and Seventh Amendments also provide for the right to a jury trial. The Sixth Amendment, referring to criminal cases, provides that "In all criminal prosecutions, the accused shall enjoy the right to a speedy and public trial. . . ." The Seventh Amendment states, "In Suits at common law, where the value in controversy shall exceed twenty dollars, the right of trial by jury shall be persevered. . . ."

† "Jury nullification" is the power of a jury to reject the law and evidence and acquit a defendant it believes is guilty. This concept is discussed in more detail later in this chapter.

questions of law

Principles and rules of human conduct determined by the judge to be applicable in a case being tried by a court.

Questions of law are the appropriate legal rules to be applied in the trial. The judge decides or answers the questions of law in the trial. For example, in the fight between Williams and Norbert, the judge determines the legal rules appropriate to decide the case (e.g., the definitions of battery and self-defense would probably be among the legal rules applied). The judge also makes a ruling of law when allowing or disallowing certain evidence, ruling on motions, or instructing the jury which legal principles should be applied to the facts during their deliberations. A question of law, not fact, also arises whenever the constitutionality of a statute or executive action is an issue. As constitutionality is a question of law, not fact, a jury does not decide whether a statute is constitutional.

How much deference a jury must give the judge's jury instructions differs in civil and criminal cases. In a civil case, if the jury ignores the law, the judge has the duty and the power to overturn the jury verdict. The judge's power is restricted in a criminal case, although the judge can declare a defendant not guilty even if the jury decided to convict the defendant. However, in a criminal case, a judge cannot overturn a jury verdict of not guilty because he or she believes the jury is wrong or has ignored the law. This residual power of the jury in a criminal case is called **jury nullification.** Thus, for example, in a criminal case, although a jury could not find a law unconstitutional, it could legally refuse to convict a defendant because the jurors think the law is unconstitutional, or unfair, or for any other reason. A judge is not free to disregard the jury's verdict of not guilty unless the judge finds jury corruption or misconduct (e.g., one or more jurors had been bribed).

jury nullification

The power of a jury in a criminal trial to disregard the law and unanimously find the defendant innocent, although there is ample evidence to support a verdict of guilty.

LEGAL FOCUS—CASE

Defendant Douglas E. Datcher was indicted for attempted distribution of a controlled substance and related charges. A conviction on all charges could lead, under non-discretionary federal sentencing guidelines, to a minimum 25-year sentence. Datcher, believing that conviction of the offenses would mandate punishment that was too harsh, made a motion to the court to allow him to ask potential jurors during the *voir dire* process (see page 122) about their attitudes toward punishment and to argue the issue of punishment to the jury during closing argument. Should the court allow Datcher to discuss the severity of punishment when the jury's only role is to determine guilt or innocence on the charged crimes?

United States v. Datcher, 830 F.Supp. 411 (M.D. Tennessee, 1993).

The defendant's motion was partially granted. "[T]he defendant may argue possible punishment to the jury but may not *voir dire* the jury on this issue." This is so even though "that jury, upon learning of the draconian sentence hanging over his head, would deem penalty too great and thus let the defendant go free pursuant to the power of a jury nullification." This case considers the importance of a jury as a watchdog of government in a criminal case. Although the court acknowledges the inherent right of a jury in a criminal case to disregard the law, this court and others have held it improper to inform the jury that they have this power.

Prospective Jurors

The jury is a group of persons selected from a panel of randomly designated citizens of the local region to decide a particular civil or criminal case. A jury is considered the fairest instrument of justice on the theory that it tends to neutralize individual bias from the courtroom by drawing together a number of persons of diverse interests and backgrounds. No single person—not even a highly educated, coldly analytical, scrupulously honest, professional scientist—is totally objective, so it is hoped that the combination of differing perspectives will provide the balance needed for just decisions. Judges, lawyers, witnesses, scholars—and most important, litigants themselves—generally agree that the jury system works well most of the time.

Usually litigants in emotionally charged cases, both civil and criminal, prefer the consensus of a jury of their peers (equals) to the decision of one judge. On the other hand, many attorneys believe that in complex business litigation, for example, a jury can be overwhelmed and thoroughly confused by a flood of technical language. Thus, they think that in such cases their clients will fare better by waiving their right to a jury trial and relying on the expertise of the judge or an arbitrator.

It is important that the jury selection process be random. Otherwise, people would justifiably suspect its integrity. In criminal cases especially, the jury is sometimes the sole barrier between the individual and the awesome power of the prosecuting government. The selection begins with preparation of a list or panel of prospective jurors. Most states prepare such lists from voter registrations. Because minorities, the poor, and young adults do not register to vote at the same rate as the rest of the population, these groups are likely to be underrepresented on juries. For this reason, many states use other sources of names for prospective jurors, such as driver-registration records, telephone directories, hunting and fishing license lists, utility customer lists, or census rolls. Some accept volunteers for jury duty.

The Jury Selection and Service Act regulates jury selection in federal cases.[16] This act provides that names selected from voter registration lists should be supplemented with names from additional lists to help ensure selection of juries that better represent a diverse community.

Exemptions from Jury Service

A few classes of people are automatically exempt, or disqualified, from jury duty in many states. In federal courts, disqualified groups include noncitizens; minors; residents of less than one year; persons unable to read, write, and understand English; persons with mental or physical infirmities that would impair their capability as jurors; and convicted felons. States have adopted similar exemptions.[17] In addition, persons may be temporarily excused or indefinitely exempted when absence from a job or family would cause an unreasonable hardship.

It is illegal for an employer to penalize or discriminate against an employee for serving as a juror by docking vacation time.[18] Some employers continue to pay the salaries or wages of jurors, less the modest fees received from the court, but this is not compulsory. Jurors are presently paid $40 per day in the federal court system and usually less in state courts. Such small sums are inadequate pay for most jurors who are not receiving any income from their employers. Consequently, jury duty that may last for weeks or longer may mean a significant financial sacrifice. Yet jury service is a citizen's duty in a democracy. Persons refusing to serve without an acceptable excuse can be found in contempt of court, resulting in fines and/or imprisonment.*

---

* In December of 1998, a Los Angeles judge fined forty-one people $1,500 each for failing to make themselves available as jurors or appear to explain their absence. *Sacramento Bee,* December 10, 1998, p. A4.

voir dire

Process of questioning prospective jurors to ascertain whether they have any bias that would make difficult or unlikely their impartiality in determining questions of fact during a trial.

http://

A Web site for a jury consulting firm, Trial Behavior Consulting Inc., is found at

http://www.trialbehavior .com/

Voir Dire

The French phrase **voir dire** (pronounced *v'wah deer* and meaning "to speak the truth") refers to the questioning of prospective jurors to find possible bias. Understandably, attorneys try to *seat* (select) jurors whom they believe to be sympathetic to their clients' position. Thus, an accountant accustomed to arithmetic precision may not be welcomed as a juror by a defendant relying on an unverified alibi in a criminal trial, or a clerk who earns a low salary may be considered undesirable by the plaintiff in a civil action where damages sought for loss of future earning power exceed a million dollars.

In large cities, private companies are available to research potential juror lists for cases when a sizable amount of money is at stake. Such research firms provide "jury books" containing past juror voting records and other personal information. These books are sold to attorneys to assist them in identifying favorable prospective jurors. In major trials, where the stakes are high, sociologists and psychologists have been hired by lawyers to analyze the physical appearance, education, social status, economic condition, personality, and general cultural background of each prospective juror. The idea is to predict attitude and probable voting conduct in the forthcoming trial. Such assistance in jury selection raises many questions about the accuracy of character evaluation and the ethical propriety of this practice, especially if only one side has access to such information.*

LEGAL FOCUS—PROBLEM

On behalf of Marya Martinez, attorney Sharpe demands a jury trial. On the day set for trial, Sharpe and attorney Dasse meet with Judge Miller in chambers. Sharpe requests permission to personally *voir dire* the prospective jurors. Dasse does not object. Will Judge Miller grant this request?

Possibly. Historically, judges have had the power to either conduct *voir dire* themselves or to allow the attorneys to do so. Most states follow the lead of the federal court system where *voir dire* is conducted by the judge, but only after considering specific questions offered by the attorneys. Using a judge usually expedites the questioning and serves to preclude the use of inappropriate questions. Some attorneys try to argue their case in *voir dire,* which is not a valid purpose of the jury selection process.

LEGAL FOCUS—PROBLEM

Judge Miller grants Sharpe's request and orders that the two attorneys conduct the *voir dire.* One of the questions Sharpe asks each prospective juror is whether he or she has ever been a ski instructor. One person answers "yes." Is this sufficient evidence of juror bias? If so, what recourse does Sharpe have against it?

Prior experience or knowledge of a situation may or may not show that a person is biased. Everyone possesses inclinations and opinions consistent with his or her culture, education, family background, experience, and so forth, but not everyone allows these to prejudice his

---

* Legal consulting firms provide pretrial opinion polls, profiles of "ideal jurors," mock trials, and shadow juries. They also coach lawyers and witnesses and prepare designs for courtroom graphics. When such assistance is utilized, critics suggest that the jury is not composed of one's peers.

or her thinking. What matters is whether a certain experience or inclination tends to make a person unable to decide fairly a particular case. Some types of experience are more likely than others to do this. If bias is evident or likely, the judge may excuse the prospective juror using a **challenge for cause** (bias or the appearance of bias is shown). In Martinez's trial, a prospective juror who was once a ski instructor would probably not be as impartial as someone without this experience. Thus, bias is likely. The judge might properly excuse that prospective juror for cause.

There is no limit on the number of challenges for cause, which can be granted for a showing of bias. In jury selection for a trial concerning a highly publicized Brink's warehouse robbery in Boston, some 1,000 prospective jurors were excused for cause. Because of newspaper accounts over the years before the first arrest in the case, most of those excused had definite opinions as to the guilt of the defendants.[19]

Even if no bias is demonstrable, each attorney in either a civil or criminal action can challenge peremptorily (without cause) and thereby excuse from service a limited number of prospective jurors (six, for example, in civil actions, and generally more in criminal actions). The purpose of a **peremptory challenge** (dismissal of a juror for an undisclosed personal reason of the dismissing party) is to permit parties to eliminate some prospective jurors for any reason or for no reason. Some clients simply do not like the looks of a particular prospective juror. A well-known ditty goes:

> *I do not like thee, Dr. Fell;*
> *The reason why I cannot tell.*
> *But this I know and know full well,*
> *I do not like thee, Dr. Fell.*

Although no reason need be stated for a peremptory challenge, such challenges cannot be used to accomplish the illegal and impermissible purpose of excluding persons on the basis of their race or gender.* Once peremptory challenges are exhausted or waived (given up or unused), the designated number of jurors are sworn to fulfill their duty faithfully, and the trial begins. If the trial is expected to last very long, one, two, or more extra jurors (called *alternates*) are selected and remain in the courtroom throughout the trial. In the infamous criminal trial of O.J. Simpson, for the first time in U.S. history, more alternate jurors (fifteen) were selected than jurors (twelve). Alternate jurors vote only if a regular juror dies or withdraws because of illness, family hardship, misconduct, or other conflict. If by the end of a trial there are not enough jurors remaining to render a verdict, a mistrial results unless both parties agree to accept the verdict of the smaller panel.

LEGAL FOCUS—PROBLEM

A preschool molestation case in Los Angeles took more than two and a half years before the jury adjourned to consider their verdicts. By that time all six alternate jurors had replaced vacancies that occurred during trial. If the jury had lost another juror before the verdicts were rendered, a mistrial would have occurred in a trial that cost

challenge for cause

Ability to exclude a prospective trial juror if bias or prejudice is indicated.

peremptory challenge

Ability to exclude a prospective juror for any reason other than race or gender.

---

* A number of Supreme Court decisions in the 1990s changed the nature of the peremptory challenge process. It is now impermissible to dismiss a juror on the basis of race in both criminal and civil cases by either party. See *Batson v. Kentucky*, 476 U.S. 79, 106 S.Ct. 1712 (1986); *Powers v. Ohio*, 499 U.S. 400, 111 S.Ct. 1364 (1991); *Edmonston v. Leesville Concrete Co.*, 500 U.S. 614, 111 S.Ct. 2077 (1991); *Georgia v. McCollum*, 505 U.S. 42, 112 S.Ct. 2348 (1992); *Holland v. Illinois*, 493 U.S. 474, 110 S.Ct. 803 (1990); *Hernandez v. New York*, 500 U.S. 352, 111 S.Ct. 1859 (1991). In 1994, the limitation on the use of peremptory challenges was extended to make exclusions based on gender also impermissible. See *J.E.B. v. Alabama*, 511 U.S. 127, 114 S.Ct. 1419 (1994).

over $15 million. After three months of deliberations the jury reached verdicts on sixty-five counts (separate criminal charges) against two defendants. One defendant was found not guilty on all charged counts. The other defendant was found not guilty on all but thirteen counts. As to these counts, the jury was unable to reach a verdict. As the jury finished its deliberations without losing another juror, there was no mistrial.[20]

Jury Size and Vote

Since the middle of the fourteenth century, juries in England have been composed of twelve persons. Probably for that reason, laypersons as well as scholars in the United States had long assumed that the Constitution, when referring to a jury, meant a jury of twelve persons. In federal criminal court trials, twelve jurors are the required number, although criminal verdicts have been upheld with eleven jurors.[21] In civil cases, the number of jurors required has been reduced to six in many district courts. According to the U.S. Supreme Court, this reduction to six jurors in a civil case satisfies the Seventh Amendment.[22]

The U.S. Supreme Court has held that the Fourteenth Amendment does not require that state court juries (as opposed to federal ones) be composed of twelve persons in either civil or criminal cases. As few as six members have been found constitutional in a state court,[23] although a jury of five in a criminal case has been disallowed.[24] For reasons of efficiency and economy, about one-fourth of the states have reduced the size of juries to six or eight jurors in both civil and criminal matters. Currently no state provides for fewer than twelve jurors in cases where the death penalty could be imposed, although that may be constitutionally permissible.

Although the United States is indebted to England for its commitment to trial by jury, today's United Kingdom began significantly curtailing the right to juries in civil cases in 1933. This action was a response to the growing complexity of civil law and the time and expense consumed by the jury process. A civil jury is now the exception in the United Kingdom.[25]

The number of jurors required to agree on a verdict is an additional important question in American jurisprudence. Historically, to reach a verdict in criminal cases the jury vote had to be unanimous. Thus, in criminal actions one juror has been able to block the prosecutor's attempt to convict the accused. Such power is an affirmation of the importance of each juror. The requirement of the unanimous jury is the rule in federal and most state criminal prosecutions.[26] A few states allow for a guilty verdict without requiring a unanimous jury (for example, Oregon permits a conviction by ten out of twelve jurors),[27] although a unanimous vote for a verdict in a state six-person jury criminal case is required.[28] In most civil cases, however, a three-fourths majority (nine of twelve jurors) is sufficient. On the other hand, in the federal court system civil juries are required to render unanimous verdicts.*

LEGAL FOCUS—CASE

After considerable deliberation the six-person jury informed the judge they could not reach a unanimous opinion in the criminal assault and battery case against Kevin Nobles. The Palm Beach County Circuit Court judge and the attorneys for Nobles and

* Federal Rules of Civil Procedure § 48 states, "The court shall seat a jury of not fewer than six and not more than twelve members. Unless the parties otherwise stipulate, (1) the verdict shall be unanimous and (2) no verdict shall be taken from a jury reduced in size to fewer than six members."

the state discussed the limited options available, including a suggestion from Nobles' attorney that Nobles could accept a majority verdict and waive his state right to a unanimous jury rather than begin again after a mistrial. Can a defendant waive his right to a unanimous verdict?

Nobles v. Florida, 786 So.2d 56 (2001).

Keven Nobles agreed to waive his right on a day when buying a lottery ticket would have been a bad idea. The jury found him guilty by a vote of 4 to 2. On appeal Nobles argued that "the trial court erred when it accepted his request for a majority verdict because even though waivers of the right to a unanimous verdict have been accepted for super majorities of five to one, there is no authority that expressly approves a four to two majority verdict." The trial court upheld the conviction, stating, "[T]he following requirements [were] met in Nobles' trial: (1) the waiver is initiated by the defendant, not the trial judge or the prosecutor; (2) the jury has informed the court that it is unable to reach a verdict, after having had a reasonable time to deliberate; (3) the trial judge explains to the defendant his/her right to a unanimous jury verdict and the consequences of a waiver of that right; and (4) the trial judge questions the defendant directly and determines that the waiver is being made knowingly and voluntarily."*

Clearly, a reduction in jury size together with relaxed voting percentages for a verdict will do much to change the role of the jury in our society. In addition, some states are reducing the types of cases in which a jury is considered appropriate. For example, states with no-fault automobile insurance plans largely bypass the jury process in automobile-related personal injury cases. Many states have decriminalized such matters as minor traffic offenses and removed a person's right to a jury trial in such cases. In the federal system, there is a presumption that offenses punishable by incarceration for six months or less are petty offenses for which jury trials are unavailable.[29] In addition, there is an important area of U.S. jurisprudence in which the Constitution does not require jury trials and legal history has not provided them, namely all matters "in equity." Recall the Legal Focus on page 119, in which the Podds were unsuccessful in their request for a jury trial in the foreclosure action brought against them. Most laypersons are uninformed on the important subject of equity, which we address next.

WHAT IS AN ACTION OR CAUSE IN EQUITY?

The United States legal system, like that of the United Kingdom, distinguishes between what are called disputes *at law* and *in equity.* The distinction between law and equity is based not on logic but on history. As discussed in Chapter 1, in medieval times certain types of cases in England were decided by chancellors (government administrators) rather than in the king's court. The chancellors were often also religious aides to the king. In most disputes, an aggrieved person could seek and obtain monetary relief from a regular king's court. In the king's court, a judge would decide the case, sometimes with the assistance of a jury. Such were matters "at common law," and monetary damages usually were the only relief available from the king's courts.

---

* The instructions from the judge were: "It is possible to waive one's constitutional rights if the waiver is a knowing waiver. It's my understanding that after conferring with counsel, and without knowing how the jury is split in this case, that it's your desire to waive or give up your right to a unanimous verdict and to agree to a, what we call a majority verdict, which means there are six jurors, if four of them or more vote one way or another as to any count, that would be the verdict in the case. Is my understanding correct? APPELLANT: Yes, Sir." *Nobles v. Florida,* 786 So.2d 56 (2001).

A person unable to obtain relief from a regular court would appeal to the king, who would refer the citizen to the king's chancellor. As a general proposition, chancellors became involved only when there was no adequate remedy at law and when monetary damages were not sought or did not satisfy the need of the party seeking relief. These actions became known as actions "at equity." The chancellors decided matters brought before them based on their conscience, community norms of conduct, and principles of equity, or fairness.

Today, all but a few U.S. courts have combined powers of law and equity.[30] However, differences between the two methods of relief remain in the handling of certain types of disputes, available remedies, and the procedural rules applied to the actions. For example, matters involving the family were and are matters in equity, and are an example of a type of dispute heard only as a matter in equity. Thus, if a dispute involves a divorce or dissolution or marriage, adoption, name change, or juvenile problem, a court sits in equity without a jury and usually applies different procedural rules.

Other civil cases in equity based on the claimant seeking a different remedy include the following:

http://

See the discussion of equitable remedies at **http://www.west.net/ ~smith/equity.htm**

specific performance

An equitable remedy allowing a buyer to get possession and title to real property and to goods that are unique when the seller refuses to deliver under a valid sales contract.

rescission

An equitable remedy that annuls a contract and returns the parties to the relationship they had before the contract was made.

injunction

An order of a court of equity forbidding an action that is considered injurious to the plaintiff.

- An action requesting the court to order the defendant to comply with a contract by performing as promised (e.g., when the subject of the sales contract is unique, such as an original painting by van Gogh or a parcel of land), and the buyer wants performance, not monetary damages (**specific performance**).
- An action requesting the court to rescind an agreement to sell one's home, because of the undue influence of a relative (**rescission**).
- An action to bar a person from continuing to hunt unlawfully on someone else's property, or to end an unlawful strike by a union (**injunction**).

Note that in each example of equity, money damages are not sought. The monetary remedy at law was either inadequate or unavailable. However, today most courts, even in an equity action, strive to give full relief requested, including monetary damages if appropriate. Except in a few states, a modern court can grant both a remedy at law and a remedy at equity. For example, an aggrieved songwriter might be awarded an injunction barring the infringer (wrongful user) from using her copyrighted song without permission and also be given dollar damages for the prior illegal use. Examples of civil cases at law include actions to recover money for (1) injury caused by negligence of the defendant, (2) loss of earnings caused by defamation of character by the defendant, (3) money lost as the result of the defendant's fraud and deceit, and (4) profits lost due to breach of contract by the defendant. Exhibit 3-5 provides a contrast between matters at equity and at law.

However, criminal cases are not matters in equity.* There is no right to trial by jury in equity cases. The constitutional right to a jury was limited in the Seventh Amendment of the Constitution to civil matters, which are "suits at common law." The distinction between *common law* and *equity* was well known by the drafters of the Constitution. Jury trials in equity matters did not exist in England, as the chancellor relied on his own good conscience and sense of what was just. Since juries were available at law, a person who sought relief in equity waived the right to common-law procedures, including the jury. In some states, a judge in equity may use an advisory jury but is not obliged to apply its verdict.

A judge sitting in a matter in equity has awesome power. The judge is both the finder of fact and law and controls the powerful remedies available only in equity. Courts of

---

* If a juvenile commits an act that is criminal if committed by an adult, the matter will generally be considered a matter in equity. It is technically not considered a criminal matter, although a deprivation of liberty can and often does result if the minor is found responsible. Although an equitable matter, some due process protection still applies because of the potential for deprivation of liberty. However, there is no right to a jury trial. Many states provide for criminal prosecution of a minor as an adult in certain situations. If the minor is tried as an adult, the case is transferred from the court of equity to the criminal courts and all rights and jeopardies of criminal defendants apply.

EXHIBIT 3-5: **Contrast Between a Matter in Equity and a Matter at Law**

	Equity	**Law**
Subject Matter	Family law Probate Trust When remedy at law is inadequate	Everything that is not a matter in equity
Nature of Trial	No jury	Jury

Remedies	In contracts:
	   Reformation
	   Rescission
	   Specific Performance
	Injunction
	Restitution
		Money damages

equity not only provide different remedies but also often operate using different procedures and guidelines, including what are called **equitable maxims**—propositions or statements that provide a guide to a judge's exercise of his or her discretion. A few examples of equitable maxims are provided and explained in Exhibit 3-6.

Defiance of a judge's order can place a person in **contempt of court** and subject him or her to summary arrest and imprisonment. Contempt of court is willful disobedience of a judicial order or obstruction of the work of the court. Some of the most controversial cases in the history of law have involved the exercise of a judge's equitable power.

equitable maxims

General rules applied by courts to cases in equity.

contempt of court

Willful defiance of the authority of a court, affront to its dignity, or willful disobedience of its lawful orders.

LEGAL FOCUS—PROBLEM

Dr. J. Elizabeth Morgan was a party to a legal action involving visitation rights concerning her minor female child, Hilary. She maintained that the child's father had sexually abused her daughter. Although the husband strenuously denied this allegation, Morgan refused to obey an unsupervised visitation order in favor of her husband and placed the girl in hiding. Judge Herbert Dixon held Morgan in contempt of court. How could the court enforce its order?

Morgan was taken to the District of Columbia jail, where she spent the next 759 days for refusing to disclose the whereabouts of her child. She was finally released after a special law requiring her immediate release was passed by Congress and signed by then-President George H. W. Bush. As the court matter was in equity, no jury had been involved. Morgan had been jailed for her continuing refusal to follow the court's order, even though she had committed no crime.[31] During the late 1990s, Susan McDougal spent eighteen months in jail for civil contempt for her refusal to answer questions posed by Special Prosecutor Kenneth Starr about President William J. Clinton's involvement in the Whitewater Development Corporation.[32]

An even more dramatic case demonstrating the awesome power of a court of equity involved prison inmates in Texas. The United States District Court for the Southern District

EXHIBIT 3-6: **Equitable Maxims**

A maxim is a proposition or general statement. Some common maxims relating to actions in equity follow:

1. Whoever seeks equity must do equity. (Anyone who wishes to be treated fairly must treats others fairly.)

2. When there is equal equity, the law must prevail. (The applicable law will determine the outcome of a controversy in which the merits of both sides are equal.)

3. One seeking the aid of an equity court must come to the court with clean hands. (Plaintiffs must have acted fairly and honestly.)

4. Equity will not suffer a right to exist without a remedy. (Equitable relief will be awarded when there is a right to relief and there is not adequate remedy at law.)

5. Equity regards substance rather than form. (Equity is more concerned with fairness and justice than with legal technicalities.)

6. Equity aids the vigilant, not those who rest on their rights. (Equity will not help those who neglect their rights for an unreasonably long period of time.)

of Texas held that the conditions of confinement in the state violated the U.S. Constitution. To implement and ensure compliance with the court order, the entire prison system of Texas was put under the control of a Special Master of the court.[33]

Returning to Martinez's case against Graf, we can see that since it is an action at law, either party may demand a jury trial. If neither party demands a jury, the right is waived and the trial will proceed with the judge alone determining the truth of all factual contentions.

How Is a Trial Conducted?

burden of proof

The duty to produce evidence as a trial progresses.

preponderance of evidence

Standard of determining civil liability, that the weight of the evidence offered to prove a matter is more probable than not.

beyond a reasonable doubt

The quantum evidence that fully satisfies and entirely convinces the jury in a criminal trial that the defendant is guilty as charged.

After the jury is selected in a civil case, the plaintiff's attorney proceeds first because the plaintiff has the **burden of proof.** This is the duty to present evidence that supports the allegations in the complaint (the facts). In civil cases, the burden of proof is satisfied by presenting a **preponderance of evidence.** That is, according to the evidence, it is more likely than not that the allegations in the complaint are true. If the jury agrees that the plaintiff more likely than not is right, the burden is met, and they must return a verdict for the plaintiff. In a criminal case, however, the burden of proof is much greater. The state, represented by a prosecutor, has the burden of proving the guilt of the defendant **beyond a reasonable doubt.** This means the finder of fact must be firmly convinced of the defendant's guilt.* The proof of guilt must preclude any other reasonable interpretation of the facts and be inconsistent with any other rational conclusion.

* "The beyond a reasonable doubt standard is a requirement of due process, but the Constitution neither prohibits trial courts from defining reasonable doubt nor requires them to do so as a matter of course," *Hopt v. Utah,* 120 U.S. 430, 99 S.Ct. 2781 (1887). Supreme Court Justice Kennedy referred to the following "beyond a reasonable doubt" jury instruction as "clear, straightforward and accurate" in his concurring opinion in *Victor v. Nebraska,* 511 U.S. 1, 114 S.Ct. 1239, 1253 (1994): "The government has the burden of proving the defendant guilty beyond a reasonable doubt. Some of you may have served as juror in civil cases, where you were told that it is only necessary to prove that a fact is more likely true than not true. In criminal cases, the government's proof must be more powerful than that. It must be beyond a reasonable doubt. Proof beyond a reasonable doubt is proof that leaves you firmly convinced of the defendant's guilt. There are very few things in this world that we know with absolute certainty, and in criminal cases the law does not require proof that overcomes every possible doubt. If, based on your consideration of the evidence, you are firmly convinced that the defendant is guilty of the crime charged, you must find him guilty. If on the other hand, you think there is a real possibility that he is not guilty, you must give him the benefit of the doubt and find him not guilty."

LEGAL FOCUS—PROBLEM

While Marya Martinez was in the hospital, she told her father that Gary Graf took her wallet after she fell. This incensed Hernando Martinez, Marya's father, who demanded that Graf be prosecuted for theft. The criminal case came to trial months before the civil case, and the jury found Graf not guilty. Does this mean that Martinez will lose her civil case?

No. Martinez's civil case concerns the civil issue of negligence in adjusting her ski bindings. The criminal case dealt with subsequent independent, unrelated behavior. In some situations, however, a single act can result in civil liability and also a criminal penalty. For example, if Graf had deliberately struck Martinez in the face without legal excuse or justification, he should be found civilly liable for damages and criminally guilty of battery. Theoretically, though, the defendant Graf could win the criminal case and lose the civil case. Such a result could happen because of the different burdens of proof involved. Moreover, the trials take place at different times with different juries and different procedural rules. The law allows both victims (society at large and Martinez in particular) their "days in court"—society (the state) is hurt by the alleged public crime, and Martinez (a private party) is hurt civilly by the alleged private tort. Because one charge is civil and one is criminal, there is no **double jeopardy** (being tried twice for the same offense), which would be unconstitutional as violative of the Fifth Amendment.* A notorious example of this split possibility occurred after the not guilty verdict in the O.J. Simpson criminal trial. The parents of Nicole Brown Simpson and Ron Goldman sued for the wrongful death of their children. The jury in the civil case found Simpson liable (legally responsible) for the deaths.[34]

Procedures in a criminal trial are essentially the same as those for a civil case. However, under the U.S. Constitution (Fifth Amendment), a defendant in a criminal case cannot be compelled to testify. This is not true in a civil case, unless the testimony would tend to incriminate and possibly subject the defendant to prosecution for some crime.

Opening Statements

The plaintiff's attorney begins the trial by making an **opening statement**—a summary of what the plaintiff expects to prove in the trial. Then the defendant's attorney may, but need not, make an opening statement telling what the defendant expects to prove in the trial. Such statements are often used to inform the jury, in broad outline, of what they can expect to hear as the trial unfolds.

Evidence

After the opening statements, the plaintiff's attorney presents the plaintiff's **case-in-chief**. This involves calling and questioning witnesses and introducing into evidence documents, photographs, or other things that bear on the issues. **Evidence** is everything that the "finder of fact" (the jury, or judge when there is no jury) is entitled to consider in arriving

double jeopardy

A second criminal prosecution against a person for the same single offense, after the person has been found innocent of the crime in the prior trial.

http://

A story about O.J. Simpson's civil trial verdict is available at

http://www.cnn.com/US/OJ/ simpson.civil.trial/

opening statement

Summaries by counsel of plaintiff and of defendant indicating what they expect to prove in the ensuing trial.

case-in-chief

The case presented by each party in a trial.

evidence

Everything presented by disputing parties and witnesses that the "finder of fact" is entitled to consider in arriving at a determination of the facts.

---

* Separate criminal trials brought by different governmental entities even upon the same set of facts are generally not considered to be double jeopardy. For example, after the accused police officers in the Rodney King beating case were found not guilty of state criminal charges, the federal government was successful in bringing federal criminal charges against two of the officers for depriving King of his civil rights. See footnote on page 103.

at a determination of the facts. For example, the oral testimony of witnesses presented under oath is evidence; commentary of the attorney about that evidence is not. Attorneys are hired after the events in question have taken place and are thus not competent to testify as witnesses. Their role is to elicit evidence, comment on it, and argue about its significance. Of course, if the attorney's interpretation of the testimony of the witnesses is persuasive, the jury will be influenced by it.

Whether evidence should or should not be admitted is a question of law; therefore, the judge rules on all objections attorneys may make as to the admission of particular evidence. Evidence is admitted if the judge believes it will be useful in resolving issues in the case. Many rules concern what evidence is and is not admissible. For example, to be admitted evidence must be **relevant** (related to the fact in dispute). **Irrelevant evidence** (evidence not related to the fact in dispute) is not admissible.

relevant evidence

Evidence that is related to the facts in dispute.

irrelevant evidence

Evidence that does not relate to or have a bearing upon a question of fact in dispute during a trial.

LEGAL FOCUS—PROBLEM

Sharpe calls Martinez as her first witness. Martinez recites her story. Sharpe sits down and attorney Dasse begins his cross-examination. "Isn't it a fact, Ms. Martinez, that immediately before you fractured your leg you got drunk on wine with a gentleman, Luther Thomas, who you picked up in the bar?" Sharpe objects to the question. Will the judge sustain or overrule the objection?

The objection will be sustained (the judge will not allow the question to be answered). The question is compound; that is, it contains two or more questions, one concerning sobriety, the other concerning whether, and where and how, she met Luther Thomas. It also contains a conclusion, which is inflammatory: "drunk." Attorney Dasse will probably be instructed to rephrase or drop the question. The question appears to be designed more to intimidate the witness than to extract information. The ruling by the judge is a ruling on a question of law.

A better form of questioning would be as follows:

Dasse: Isn't it a fact, Ms. Martinez, that immediately before you fractured your leg you were drinking wine?

Martinez: Yes, sir.

Dasse: With whom were you drinking wine?

Martinez: Luther Thomas.

Dasse: And did you know him previously?

Martinez: No.

prima facie

[Latin for "on first appearance"] Term describing a fact presumed to be true unless disproved by some contrary evidence. With reference to a legal case, such fact will prevail unless and until contradicted and overcome by other evidence.

After Sharpe has called all of the plaintiff's witnesses and introduced into evidence all relevant documents and other physical evidence (such as the ski boots), she *rests* (ends) the plaintiff's case. The defendant may now offer a *motion to dismiss* the case, claiming that the plaintiff has failed to establish a **prima facie** (Latin: "at first sight; on the face of it") case. A plaintiff is required to offer sufficient evidence of the defendant's wrongful conduct to justify an award of monetary damages or other relief. For example, if a preponderance of the evidence proved only that the defendant "thrust his middle finger in the air as an obscene gesture," the plaintiff could not win. There was no *prima facie* case and the judge would not permit the jury to return a verdict for the plaintiff. Under those circumstances, the defense need produce no evidence and can figuratively "stick its tongue out" at the plaintiff.

A plaintiff is required to offer facts that prove a *prima facie* case before a defendant is required to respond with a defense. The court will grant a motion to dismiss only if the plaintiff has failed to produce evidence about some significant aspect of the case. If this motion is denied by the judge, the defendant's attorney may make an opening statement (provided that it was not made at the beginning of the trial).

The defendant's case-in-chief also begins by calling witnesses. Of course, the plaintiff's attorney has the right to cross-examine the defendant's witnesses immediately after their direct examination, as the defendant's attorney did when the plaintiff's case was presented. After the defense rests, the plaintiff may offer additional evidence limited to rebutting the defense, but not opening new issues. And, of course, the defense has one final opportunity to rebut, limited to whatever was presented in the plaintiff's rebuttal.

Motion for a Directed Verdict

After the parties have rested their respective cases-in-chief, either may ask the judge to decide the matter by making a **motion for a directed verdict.** This motion is a request to a judge that he or she enter the requested verdict instead of allowing the jury to present its verdict. It is based on the alleged absence of sufficient facts to allow any other verdict than the requested one. The judge could, for example, properly direct a verdict in favor of the plaintiff if, despite the evidence presented by the defendant, no reasonable person could agree with the defendant. Granting such a motion is unusual; even if the evidence appears to be legally conclusive for one party, the judge normally allows the jury to provide its independent opinion.

> *"When you have the facts on your side, argue the facts. When you have the law on your side, argue the law. When you have neither, holler."*
>
> Albert Gore Jr., Vice President of the United States (1993–2001).

Summation

After all the evidence has been offered, each attorney argues the case before the jury. In other words, each attorney tells the jury what he or she believes was proved in the trial and tries to persuade the jury to agree. The **summation** is not evidence or even a discussion; rather, it is a speech made by the attorney designed to persuade the jury. In our civil case example, the plaintiff's attorney would begin, followed by the defendant's attorney, and then the plaintiff's attorney concludes. Martinez's attorney, Sharpe, might argue as follows:

> *Ladies and gentlemen of the jury, you have heard all the evidence. It is now your duty to determine the facts. I believe we have shown by a preponderance of the evidence that the injury was caused by Mr. Graf. I remind you that Marya's medical bills were $8,742.53. She missed one month of work, at her rate of pay of $4,195 a month. She had to wear a cast from her waist to her toes for six months. What is this worth in dollars? Put yourself in her shoes—excuse me, cast. Why all this expense and all this pain and anguish? Why? Because the defendant, this careless ski instructor, Gary Graf, fastened the bindings down on Ms. Martinez's foot with unprofessional disregard for her safety and well being. The evidence is clear: Gary Graf was not thinking about bindings. Gary Graf did not pay attention to his serious duty. Gary Graf was clearly negligent. And so it is now your duty to lessen the harm he caused. Simple justice requires you to return a verdict in favor of Marya.*

motion for a directed verdict

Request to a judge by counsel to enter a particular verdict instead of allowing the jury to do so because there are insufficient facts to allow any other verdict.

summation

The review of the evidence presented to the court by each lawyer in oral argument at the close of the trial.

Attorney Dasse might argue to the jury:

Ladies and gentlemen, it is our duty to pierce the veil of emotion with which counsel is attempting to surround us. Let us look at the facts. Unfortunately, the plaintiff was injured. No one feels good about that, especially Gary Graf. However, the fact that Ms. Martinez was injured is not a reason to hold Gary Graf responsible. Skiing is a sport with risks. Marya cannot transfer responsibility for her own safety to another person if the risk materializes. Marya decided to ski. She failed to exercise the appropriate care that would have prevented her accident. Feeling sorry for her is natural. We all feel sorry for her. But this does not justify a verdict against Mr. Graf. The simple facts are that Ms. Martinez was not thinking about skiing; she was more interested in impressing her date after spending a good part of the day drinking wine. She was injured not because of any negligence of Gary Graf. Bindings don't work if they are icy, and had she been sober she would have seen the ice when she put her skis back on. She was negligent. Now she is trying to obtain a bonanza at the expense of my client, a hard-working, sincere, very professional gentleman. Ladies and gentlemen of this jury, you know your duty: return a verdict for Gary Graf.

Instructions to the Jury

After the summation, the judge will instruct the jury on the law (**jury instructions**) that must be applied to the facts that the jury decides are true. Typically, each attorney will submit proposed instructions to the judge. The judge decides on the instructions to give to the jury. The instructions might include the following, but would be considerably more exhaustive:

You are instructed that statements of witnesses, sworn to tell the truth, constitute evidence that you may consider. Comments of the attorneys are not evidence. You are instructed that if the defendant failed to use reasonable care and secured the bindings too tightly, he was negligent. You are further instructed that if the accident was caused by ice between the boot and ski, and not by the adjustment to the bindings, the plaintiff was negligent.

Deliberation and Verdict

After the instructions, the jury will retire to a private room to **deliberate,** and by vote return a **verdict,** the jury's decision. In state civil cases a three-fourths majority is a common requirement whereas in federal civil cases a unanimous verdict is required.

If the jury returns with a verdict deemed to be wrong as a matter of law, the judge in a civil case has the power to render a contrary judgment, sometimes called a judgment n.o.v., which is a **judgment *non obstante veredicto*** (Latin: "notwithstanding the verdict"). In effect, the judge is the thirteenth juror, with the power to veto the others' decision and to substitute a different one. (Recall that in a criminal case the judge cannot veto a verdict of "not guilty.")

After a verdict, the judge may grant a motion made by the losing party for a new trial. The judge will not grant a *motion for a new trial* unless some serious mistake of law (called *error*) has occurred. Sometimes the judge may think that the damages awarded by the jury are excessive or inadequate and may therefore grant a motion for a new trial unless the plaintiff or defendant, as the case may be, agrees to a modified award. To avoid the costs and uncertainties of another trial, the parties may compromise and agree to the modified award. The steps in a jury trial are identified in Exhibit 3-7.

---

jury instructions

Rules of law and charges provided by the judge to the jury for guidance in reaching a verdict.

http://

The Ninth Circuit Court of Appeals Opinions has an online "Manual of Model Civil Jury Instructions" at **http://www.ce9.uscourts .gov/web/sdocuments .nsf/civ**

deliberate

The review, discussion, and weighing of evidence presented at a trial by a jury.

verdict

The expressed decision of the jury on questions of fact submitted to it for determination, based on evidence presented during trial.

judgment *non obstante veredicto*

A decision by a judge that overrules the verdict of the jury.

EXHIBIT 3-7 Steps in a Civil Case—Jury Trial

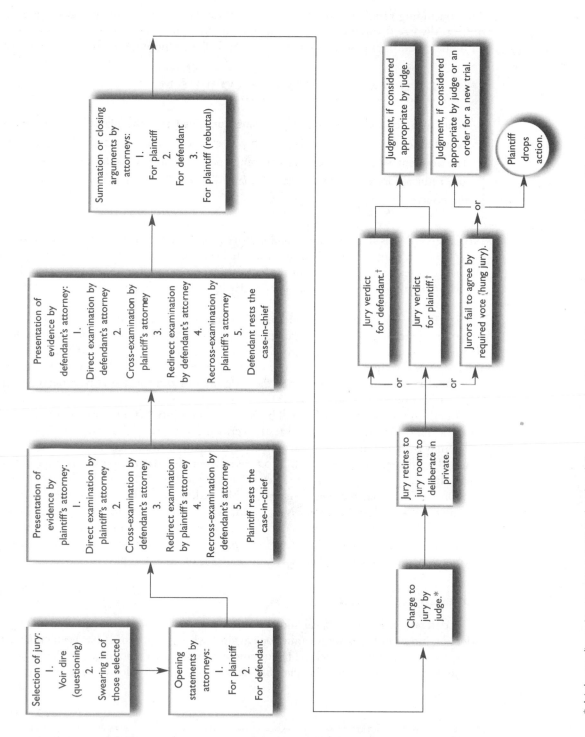

Selection of jury:
1. Voir dire (questioning)
2. Swearing in of those selected

Opening statements by attorneys:
1. For plaintiff
2. For defendant

Presentation of evidence by plaintiff's attorney:
1. Direct examination by plaintiff's attorney
2. Cross-examination by defendant's attorney
3. Redirect examination by plaintiff's attorney
4. Recross-examination by defendant's attorney
5. Plaintiff rests the case-in-chief

Presentation of evidence by defendant's attorney:
1. Direct examination by defendant's attorney
2. Cross-examination by plaintiff's attorney
3. Redirect examination by defendant's attorney
4. Recross-examination by plaintiff's attorney
5. Defendant rests the case-in-chief

Summation or closing arguments by attorneys:
1. For plaintiff
2. For defendant
3. For plaintiff (rebuttal)

Charge to jury by judge.*

Jury retires to jury room to deliberate in private.

Jury verdict for defendant.†   or   Jury verdict for plaintiff.†   or   Jurors fail to agree by required vote (hung jury).

Judgment, if considered appropriate by judge.

Judgment, if considered appropriate by judge or an order for a new trial.

or

Plaintiff drops action.

* A judge may direct a jury to return a certain verdict when, if all testimony on one side were believed, the other party nonetheless would be entitled to win.
† In rare cases, a judge may grant a judgment *non obstante veredicto* (Latin: "notwithstanding the verdict"), setting aside the jury's verdict because in the judge's opinion it is wrong as a matter of law.

HOW IS A CASE ENDED?

The concluding pronouncement of a court is its **judgment.** A judgment may declare a status (e.g., divorced), order one to do or not do something (e.g., pay money damages or transfer a title to land), impose a sentence (e.g., go to jail), or otherwise resolve a controversy.

judgment

The final determination or decision of the court as to the rights and duties of the parties in a lawsuit.

LEGAL FOCUS—PROBLEM

In an auto accident case, the jury became convinced that the plaintiff should be compensated for harm to her left leg, which was crushed and had to be surgically removed. The accident was caused by the negligent operation of a truck by the defendant. The jury returned its verdict in the plaintiff's favor for $1,300,000. Is the verdict the voice of the court?

No. The verdict is the expressed opinion of the jury. Based on the verdict, the court will usually issue a judgment for damages. As noted earlier, if the court concludes that the jury verdict is unreasonable in the light of the evidence, it can prevent a miscarriage of justice by reducing the amount of damages, ordering a new trial, or granting a judgment notwithstanding a verdict.

In divorce proceedings, the judgment of the court will be termination of the marriage. In a paternity case, the judgment of the court will be a declaration that the defendant is or is not the natural father. In a suit to end mass picketing and violence in a strike, the judgment of the court will be an injunction. In a suit to compel someone to do something that was promised by contract, the judgment of the court will be a decree of specific performance.

In criminal cases, the verdict will be guilty or not guilty.* If it is "not guilty," the judgment of the court must correspond to the verdict. However, if the verdict is "guilty," the judge may overrule the jury and acquit the defendant, or the judge may order a new trial to avoid a miscarriage of justice. In most cases, the judge has the power to impose a sentence, then suspend it, and place the defendant on probation.

Once a party has received a judgment, the judicial branch of government has completed its work, unless the matter is appealed. Sometimes a party to the action may return to court if the order of the court is not obeyed. In divorce, for example, after support payments have been ordered, either party may return and request an increase or decrease in payments because of changed circumstances, needs, or ability to pay.

Collecting a Judgment

If the defendant does not appeal and the time for appeal passes, a losing defendant is considered a **judgment debtor,** meaning one against whom a judgment has been entered but who has not paid the judgment. The judgment debtor may voluntarily pay the judgment, or pay the judgment after the plaintiff demands payment. However, if the judgment

judgment debtor

A person against whom a judgment for payment of money has been entered but who has not yet made or completed that payment.

http://

A site with excerpts from *Collecting a Small Claims Court Judgment: You're on Your Own,* by Lisa Goldoftas and Stephen Elias, Nolo Press, is found at **http://www.tenant.net/ Court/nolo/nn247.html**

---

* Of course, it is possible that a jury will be unable to reach a decision. In 1994, a pair of criminal cases captured national media attention. Erik and Kyle Menendez were accused of the first-degree murder of their parents. At the trial, the fact that the brothers had killed their parents was admitted, but both brothers defended their action on the basis of self-defense. Two juries, one for each brother, heard the case; neither jury was able to agree on a verdict. The two brothers were retried, found guilty, and sentenced to life imprisonment without the possibility of parole.

debtor fails to pay, the legal system provides a method of satisfying the debt provided the defendant has assets that can be identified and seized. State statutes generally call for payment of interest (usually at an annual rate between 6 and 10 percent) to accrue on the unpaid balance of the judgment until fully paid.

Assistance in collecting the dollar amount of the judgment is provided by the executive branch of government, usually through the office of the county sheriff or federal marshal. Officials will not do anything simply because you have won a lawsuit and have not been paid. A **judgment creditor,** one who has won a judgment but is as yet unpaid, must first provide a copy of the final judgment, identify assets owned by the judgment debtor, and give specific instructions to a sheriff or marshal before he or she will assist in collecting the judgment. The court order directing the sheriff to confiscate property of the defendant is called a **writ of execution.** Such a writ may be used to **garnish** (confiscate) part of any debt owed to the judgment debtor by others, usually unpaid wages due from the debtor's employer(s). After being paid in full, the judgment creditor must provide the judgment debtor with a signed *satisfaction of judgment* document as evidence of that fact.

Judicial means exist for compelling cooperation of the judgment debtor in identifying his or her assets—namely, by means of an **order of examination,** which is a judicially authorized inquiry about the judgment debtor's assets. Usually, the judgment debtor is either summoned to court and asked questions about assets owned or required to respond to a questionnaire about such assets. It is, however, a fact of legal life in this country that if a plaintiff wins a case but the defendant does not have sufficient assets or insurance to pay the judgment, the plaintiff will probably recover little or nothing. The U.S. Constitution (Article I, Section 8) gives Congress the exclusive right "to establish uniform laws on the subject of Bankruptcies." Under federal statutes, almost all debts, including most judgments, can be discharged by the bankruptcy of the defendant debtor. In addition, federal bankruptcy laws and state consumer statutes provide that certain property is exempt from debt collection by judicial or other means. Thus, the bankrupt is not stripped of all possessions. So analysis of the possibility or impossibility of collection should be one of the first considerations before deciding to sue, even though collection is the last step in an ordinary civil lawsuit. Possible steps in a civil dispute resolved by court action are set forth in Exhibit 3-7 on page 133.

A criminal trial is procedurally very similar to a civil trial and is explored in Chapter 6. Trial procedures in the U.S. District Courts are governed by the Federal Rules of Civil and Criminal Procedure and closely resemble state procedures.

WHAT HAPPENS IF EITHER PARTY APPEALS?

As previously discussed, procedures before a federal or state appellate court differ greatly from trial court procedures. Appellate courts hear appeals from trial courts and do not conduct trials. The only question on appeal, as a general proposition, is whether or not the law was applied correctly by the judge during the trial proceedings. Appellate courts do not consider new evidence or hear witnesses. An appellate court has several options when an appeal is filed, including refusing to hear the appeal. If it accepts the appeal and concludes the law was applied correctly at the trial court or an error was made but it did not affect the verdict, the court will **affirm** (uphold) the judgment. If the court determines that the law was applied incorrectly, it can **reverse, modify,** and/or **remand** the decision. A reversal turns the loser into the winner, a modification changes the result in a less drastic fashion than a reversal, and a remand sends the case back to the trial court with instructions for the trial court judge, such as granting a new trial.

---

judgment creditor

A person who has won a judgment but has not been fully paid.

writ of execution

Order of the court directing the sheriff to confiscate property of the defendant.

garnishment

A legal proceeding in which a plaintiff-creditor gets a court order compelling a third party to pay monies earned by the defendant to the plaintiff.

order of examination

A judicially authorized inquiry as to the assets of a judgment debtor.

affirmed

The confirmation of a lower court's judgment or order because the prior decision is deemed to be correct and free from prejudicial error.

reverse

Appellate court sets aside the decision of a lower court

modify

Appellate court alters the decision of a lower court.

remand

Appellate court sends case back to a lower court to take some further action.

LEGAL FOCUS—PROBLEM

The jury found Jack Malum guilty of cocaine possession. During the trial, the judge instructed the jury, in part, as follows: "I instruct you that a crime is committed when one attends a party at which cocaine is being used, regardless of whether or not the defendant participated in such activity." Will an appeal by Malum be successful?

Yes. An appellate court would conclude that the court's instruction to the jury was an erroneous statement of the law. Jack Malum did not receive a fair trial, because mere attendance at a party is not in itself a crime, yet the jury was told that it was.

Appellate courts consist of three or more justices. Most of their work is done in private and consists of reading *transcripts* (official copies of the proceedings in the trial court) of cases on appeal. The appellate court assumes that all facts found by the trial court are true. In order to make the court's decision, they will study the applicable law and examine briefs filed by the attorneys for the appellant and the appellee and study the applicable law. A *brief* is a written legal argument addressed to the appellate court discussing or arguing why the judgment from below should be affirmed or reversed, modified, or perhaps remanded to the trial court for further specified action. Before the appellate court makes its decision, the respective attorneys may be allowed to make oral arguments to the appellate court, within limited allotted times. The concluding steps in a civil trial are provided in Exhibit 3-8.

A SAMPLE ALMOST-UNEDITED STATE APPELLATE COURT DECISION

The case presented here is a New Jersey state appellate case. Although we provide at least one edited case at the end of each chapter, this chapter presents a virtually complete appellate case in the words of the court. Limits of space and time preclude inclusion of the full text of other cases. This is an interesting case decided on procedural grounds, and it provides an opportunity for thorough analysis.

In *Trustees of Columbia University v. Jacobsen,* a college student cross-complains when the university seeks payment of owed tuition. The student claims that the university did not provide him with wisdom and truth. He pursues his claim even after his mother paid the tuition. Consider here the function of the trial court and appellate court in this case. Also note the importance of pretrial procedures on the disposition of the case. The first part of the case identifies the pleadings made and the rulings of the trial court. The second part presents the underlying facts of the dispute. The third part presents the analysis and conclusion of the court.

EXHIBIT 3-8: **Steps in a Civil Case—After Trial**

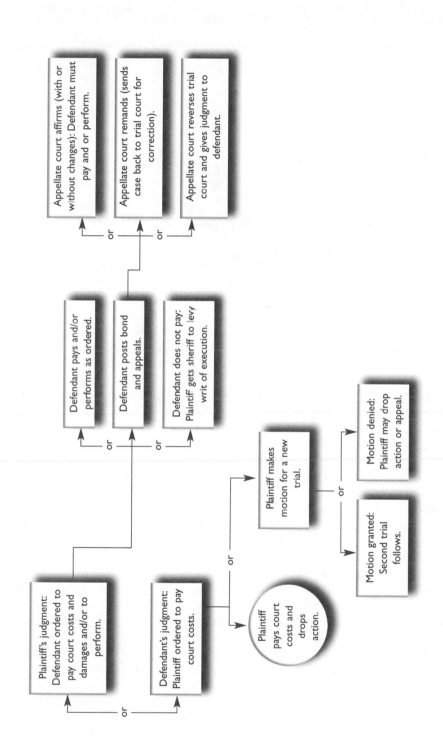

Plaintiff's judgment: Defendant ordered to pay court costs and damages and/or to perform.

Defendant's judgment: Plaintiff ordered to pay court costs.

or

Plaintiff pays court costs and drops action.

or

Plaintiff makes motion for a new trial.

or

Motion granted: Second trial follows.

Motion denied: Plaintiff may drop action or appeal.

Defendant pays and/or performs as ordered.

or

Defendant posts bond and appeals.

or

Defendant does not pay: Plaintiff gets sheriff to levy writ of execution.

Appellate court affirms (with or without changes): Defendant must pay and or perform.

or

Appellate court remands (sends case back to trial court for correction).

or

Appellate court reverses trial court and gives judgment to defendant.

CASE

TRUSTEES OF COLUMBIA UNIVERSITY V. JACOBSEN

53 N.J. Super. 574, 148 A.2d 63 (1959)

Columbia University brought suit against a student to recover money due on two promissory notes signed by the student in payment of the balance of his tuition owed. The student filed a counterclaim for deceit based on alleged false representations by the university as to what it would teach him.

Judge Goldman delivered the opinion of the court: Defendant appeals from a summary judgment of the Superior Court Law Division, dismissing his counterclaim with prejudice and denying his counter-motion for summary judgment....

I

Columbia brought suit in the district court against defendant and his parents on two notes made by him and signed by them as co-makers, representing the balance of tuition he owed the University. The principal due amounted to $1,049.50, but plaintiff sued for only $1,000, waiving any demand for judgment in excess of the jurisdictional limit of the court. Defendant then sought to file an answer and counterclaim demanding, among other things, money damages in the sum of $7,016. The counterclaim was in 50 counts which severally alleged that plaintiff had represented that it would teach defendant wisdom, truth, character, enlightenment, understanding, justice, liberty, honesty, courage, beauty and similar virtues and qualities; that it would develop the whole man, maturity, well-roundness, objective thinking and the like; and that because it had failed to do so it was guilty of misrepresentation, to defendant's pecuniary damage.

The district court clerk having refused to accept the pleading because of the amount demanded, defendant moved to transfer the action to the Superior Court. Plaintiff consented, but before an order could be entered defendant's mother paid the amount due and plaintiff thereupon discontinued its action. After transfer to the Superior Court defendant filed a supplement to this answer and counterclaim in which he [further demanded] Columbia to return the sum paid by his mother.

Plaintiff then moved in the Superior Court for an order dismissing the counterclaim and for the entry of summary judgment ... (Defendant) appeared pro se throughout the entire proceedings below as he does here.

Following oral argument the Law Division judge ... concluded that the statements attributed by defendant to plaintiff did not constitute a false representation. The judgment under appeal was then entered.

II

Following a successful freshman year at Dartmouth defendant entered Columbia University in the fall of 1951. He continued there until the end of his senior year in the spring of 1954, but was not graduated because of poor scholastic standing. Plaintiff admits the many quotations from college catalogues and brochures, inscriptions over University buildings and addresses by University officers cited in the schedules annexed to the counterclaim. The sole question is whether these statements constitute actionable misrepresentation.

... Although the remedy of summary judgment is admittedly drastic and cautiously granted ... the remedy should not be withheld where, as here, there is no genuine issue of material fact.

The attempt of the counterclaim, inartistically drawn as it is, was to state a cause of action in deceit. The necessary elements of the action are: a false representation, knowledge or belief on the part of the person making the representation that it is false, an intention that the other party act thereon, reasonable reliance by such party in so doing, and resultant damage to him.

We are in complete agreement with the trial court that the counterclaim fails to establish the very first element, false representation, basic to any action in deceit. Plaintiff stands by every quotation relied on by defendant. Only by reading into the imagined meanings he attributes to them can one conclude—and the conclusion would be a most tenuous insubstantial one—that Columbia University represented it could teach wisdom, truth, justice, beauty, spirituality and all the other qualities set out in the 50 counts of the counterclaim.

A sampling from the quotations cited by the defendant will suffice as illustration. Defendant quotes from a Columbia College brochure stating that

"... Columbia College provides a liberal arts education ... A liberal arts course ... has extremely positive values of its own. Chief among these, perhaps, is something which has been a prin-

cipal aim of Columbia College from the beginning: It develops the whole man. . . . [Columbia's] aim remains constant: to foster in its students a desire to learn, a habit of critical judgment, and a deep-rooted sense of personal and social responsibility. . . . [I]ts liberal arts course pursues this aim in five ways. (1) It brings you into firsthand contact with the major intellectual ideas that have helped to shape human thinking and the course of human events. (2) It gives you a broader acquaintance with the rest of the world. (3) It guides you toward an understanding of people and their motivations. (4) It leads you to a comprehending knowledge of the scientific world. (5) It helps you acquire facility in the art of communication. . . ."

He then cites the motto of Columbia College and Columbia University: "In lumine tuo videbimus lumen" ("In light we shall see Light") and the inscription over the college chapel: "Wisdom dwelleth in the heart of him that hath understanding." He also refers to an address of the president of Columbia University at its bicentennial convocation:

"There can never have been a time in the history of the world when men had greater need of wisdom . . . I mean an understanding of man's relationship to his fellow men and to the universe . . . To this task of educational leadership in a troubled time and in an uncertain world, Columbia, like other great centers of learning in free societies, unhesitating dedicates itself. . . ."

We have thoroughly combined all the statements upon which defendant relies in his counterclaim, as well as the exhibits he handed up to the trial judge, including one of 59 pages setting out his account of the circumstances leading to the present action. They add up to nothing more than a fairly complete exposition of Columbia's objectives, desires and hopes, together with factual statements as to the nature of some of the courses included in its curricula. As plaintiff correctly observes, what defendant is seeking to do is to assign to the quoted excerpts a construction and interpretation peculiarly subjective to him and completely unwarranted by the plain sense and meaning of the language used. . . .

At the heart of defendant's counterclaim is a single complaint. He concedes that

"I have really only one charge against Columbia: that it does not teach Wisdom as it claims to do. From this charge ensues an endless number of charges, of which I have selected fifty at random. I am prepared to show that each of these fifty claims in turn is false, though the central issue is that of Columbia's pretense of teaching Wisdom."

We agree with the trial judge that wisdom is not a subject which can be taught and that no rational person would accept such a claim made by any man or institution. We find noth-

ing in the record to establish that Columbia represented, expressly or even by way of impression, that it could or would teach wisdom or the several qualities which defendant insists are "synonyms for or aspects of the same Quality." The matter is perhaps best summed up in the supporting affidavit of the Dean of Columbia College, where he said that "All that any college can do through its teachers, libraries, laboratories and other facilities is to endeavor to teach the student the known facts, acquaint him with the nature of those matters which are unknown, and thereby assist him in developing mentally, morally and physically. Wisdom is a hoped-for end product of education, experience and ability which many seek and many fail to attain."

Defendant's extended argument lacks the element of fraudulent representation indispensable to any action of deceit. We note, in passing, that he has cited no legal authority whatsoever for his position. Instead, he has submitted a dictionary definition of "wisdom" and quotations from such works as the Bhagavad-Gita, the Mundaka Upanishad, the Analects of Confucius and the Koran; excerpts from Euripides, Plato and Menander; and references to the Bible. Interesting through these may be, they do not support defendant's indictment. If his pleadings, affidavit and exhibits demonstrate anything, it is indeed the validity of what Pope said in his Moral Essays:

"A little learning is a dangerous thing; Drink deep, or taste not the Pierian spring. . . ."

The papers make clear that through the years defendant's interest has shifted from civil engineering to social work, then to physics, and finally to English and creative writing. In college he became increasingly critical of his professors and his courses; in his last year he attended classes only when he chose and rejected the regimen of examinations and term papers. When his non-attendance at classes and his poor work in the senior year were called to his attention by the Columbia Dean of Students, he replied in a lengthy letter that "I want to learn, but I must do it my own way. I realize my behavior is non-conforming, but in these times when there are so many forces that demand conformity I hope I will find Columbia willing to grant some freedom to a student who wants to be a literary artist." In short, he chose to judge Columbia's educational system by the shifting standards of his own fancy, and now seeks to place his failure at Columbia's door on the theory that it had deliberately misrepresented that it taught wisdom.

III

In light of our conclusion that defendant has failed to state a cause of action in deceit based on fraudulent representation, we need not deal with plaintiff's further contentions that (1) even assuming an unequivocal representation by Columbia that it would teach wisdom, this amounted to nothing more than a promise to do something in the future and therefore was not an actionable misrepresentation of fact; and (2) the counterclaim is defective for failure properly to plead the particulars of the alleged fraud.

IV

In his motion to have the trial judge disqualify himself, defendant charged that the judge had rendered a premature judgment after hearing only plaintiff's side of the controversy; had needlessly added to defendant's difficulty in presenting his 'unusual case'; wrongfully claimed to be entirely familiar with the matter; and was partial to Columbia and overlooked misconduct by its attorney. To these reasons he added a suspicion that the assignment judge who had accepted his counterclaim was transferred away from the case in order to have it tried by the Law Division judge in question. These charges were set in a frame of intemperate, if not scurrilous, accusations.

There was no premature judgment. What happened was that at the first hearing on the motion for summary judgment, Columbia's attorney proceeded to make his argument and the trial judge then asked defendant if he wanted to reply. Defendant said that if there was any possibility of the motion being granted, he would want leave to file a brief. The judge then remarked that on the basis of what counsel for plaintiff had said and the papers the court had read, there was a strong likelihood of the motion being granted; and because defendant was a layman appearing pro se, the court would adjourn the matter for two weeks to give him an opportunity to prepare a brief and file affidavits. The motion was finally decided on the adjourned date.

As for the other reasons advanced by defendant, we find nothing in the record which lends them even the shadow of support.

V

In view of the entirely unjustified accusations made against the trial judge and the intemperate characterization (so admitted by defendant at the oral argument) of the proceedings below, defendant's appendix and brief will be suppressed and all copies withdrawn from the clerk's files.

The judgment is affirmed.

For Critical Analysis

1. Was there a trial in this case? Why or why not?

2. The court said the defendant appeared *pro se*. What does that mean, and what effect did it have on the case? Use the glossary and consult Chapter 4 for the answer.

3. What legal result was the plaintiff trying to accomplish by its lawsuit? The defendant?

4. Why did the plaintiff reduce its claim to $1,000?

5. Did either the plaintiff or defendant present evidence in the hearing discussed in the case?

CHAPTER QUESTIONS AND PROBLEMS

1. In regard to small claims court:
   a. Why do many states not allow attorneys to represent litigants in small claims court? (Note that in all states parties can consult counsel before and after the trial.)
   b. What are the differences between television programs such as *The People's Court* and *Judge Judy* and a typical small claims court? The success of popular television programs such as these is not without controversy. What are the pros and cons of these types of programs?
   c. What should the appropriate maximum dollar amount be for small claims court (if any)? What should be the basis for determining the appropriate jurisdictional amount?

2. While driving her car in Colorado, Pearldean Norset, a resident of Alabama, negligently struck Carl Broadnorf, a resident of Arizona. As a result of the accident, Broadnorf suffered more than $22,000 in property damage, $40,000 in medical expenses, and $15,000 in lost wages. Broadnorf wants to know whether he can obtain jurisdiction over Norset in the following courts:
   a. Federal District Court in Colorado.
   b. Alabama State Trial Court.

c. Colorado State Trial Court.

d. District of Columbia Trial Court.

e. Federal Circuit Court of Appeals for the Ninth Circuit (includes Arizona).

3. In regard to courts and trials:

a. Name each of the courts of your state and properly display them on an organization chart.

b. What are the pros and cons of permitting each side in a case to exercise one peremptory challenge of the judge assigned to the case? Would your arguments be different depending on whether the case is criminal or civil?

c. Do you believe a judge can influence a jury by such seemingly innocent conduct as smiling, eyebrow raising, grimacing, and so on during the testimony of witnesses? How can any such effect be combated?

4. Sylvester is on trial for the assault and battery of his roommate, Arnold. Sylvester hit Arnold after Arnold refused to stop playing death metal music on his guitar. Sylvester was trying to study for a test. Sylvester intends to argue self-defense, arguing a physical noise attack. One of the prospective jurors has spiked green hair and a nose ring. Suggest a strategy that would best serve Sylvester's interests in dismissing the juror. Use the correct legal terms.

5. About jury nullification:

a. What is it?

b. Are jurors instructed by the judge as to existence of the power of jury nullification? Why or why not?

c. Does the power of jury nullification exist in both civil and criminal trials?

d. Can you think of any situation where if you were on a jury you would argue for jury nullification? No matter your answer, is it ethically correct? On what basis?

6. About trial and appellate courts:

a. Define each.

b. What is the purpose of each?

c. Do juries assist both? Explain.

d. Do both exist in state and federal systems?

e. Do witnesses testify before each? Explain.

7. Thomas, William, and Ella McCollum were white defendants facing criminal charges of assault and battery against two African-Americans. Before the trial began, the prosecution requested that the court prohibit these defendants from exercising their peremptory challenges in a racially discriminatory manner. The prosecution claimed that the defendants' attorneys intended to eliminate African-American jurors from the panel through the use of peremptory challenges. The defendants argued that the law prohibiting the state from the discriminatory use of peremptory challenges was necessary to guarantee due process for a criminal defendant, but any restriction on defense use of peremptory challenges would deny defendants the right to a fair trial, The state argued that if it is prohibited from dismissing jurors on racial grounds, the defense should be similarly restrained. How did the court decide? [*Georgia v. McCollum,* 505 U.S. 42, 112 S.Ct. 2348 (1992).]

8. Walter Martin brought an employment discrimination suit against the New York Department of Mental Hygiene and Dr. Stuart Keill, a regional director of the department. Although Dr. Keill knew of the lawsuit and the nature of the claim, he was not served with a copy of the complaint and a summons. Could Martin pursue the case against Dr. Keill without such service? [*Martin v. N.Y. State Department of Mental Hygiene,* 588 F.2d 371 (1978).]

9. Martha Anderson obtained a contested divorce from her husband, Donald. The trial court judge entered judgment of divorce. Donald asked the trial court to "vacate" (rescind or erase) the judgment, but the court refused his request. On Donald's appeal, the appellate court agreed that the trial court judge was erroneous in his ruling. Does this mean that Donald and Martha are married again? [*Anderson v. Anderson,* 869 S.W.2d 289 (Mo. 1994).]

10. Joshua Southard was cited for speeding and failing to yield to an emergency vehicle. He requested a trial in the Cape Girardeu County Circuit Court and was found guilty and fined. He appealed, claiming that the circuit court lacked subject matter jurisdiction. He was correct: The appropriate court was the municipal court. However, Southard, when requesting the hearing, told the circuit court that the municipal court had previously heard his case and rendered judgment. The circuit court did have the power to hold a trial *de novo.* The prosecution argued that because Southard "stated that judgment had been rendered against him in the municipal court, he should not be allowed to take advantage of an error of his own making." Did Southard win his appeal arguing that the court lacked subject matter jurisdiction? [*City of Jackson v. Southard,* 869 S.W.2d 280 (Missouri, 1994).]

CHAPTER 4

Attorney-Client Relationship and Settling Disputes

A law firm receptionist answered the phone the morning after the firm's senior partner had died unexpectedly.

"Is Mr. Smith there?" asked the client on the phone.

"I'm very sorry, but Mr. Smith passed away last night," the receptionist answered.

"Is Mr. Smith there?" repeated the client.

The receptionist was perplexed. "Perhaps you didn't understand me. I'm afraid Mr. Smith died last night."

"Is Mr. Smith there?" asked the client again.

"Madam, do you understand what I'm saying?" said the exasperated receptionist. "Mr. Smith is dead."

"I understand perfectly," the client sighed. "I just can't hear it often enough."

Adapted from a statement made at a U.S. Senate confirmation hearing of a Supreme Court Justice.

After reading and studying this chapter, you should be able to:

- Explain the adversary system.

- Explain how an attorney qualifies to practice law.

- Discuss ethics as it relates to lawyers and judges.

- Explain how attorneys are hired and fired.

- Recognize the nature of legal malpractice.

- Recognize, explain, and distinguish the various forms of Alternative Dispute Resolution (ADR).

- Be able to discuss the pros and cons of mediation.

- Be able to discuss the pros and cons of arbitration and identify some important fairness issues related to the use of arbitration.

An ideal legal system meets the somewhat inconsistent goals of stability and flexibility. In previous chapters we have discussed constitutional law and the legal doctrine of *stare decisis,* both of which work toward balancing those two goals. In this chapter we will consider the two additional goals of an ideal legal system: understandability and accessibility. Are the laws of the country known, comprehensible, and adequate—in other words, is knowledge about United States law available to the general population and do people have access to adequate legal redress (i.e., damages or other remedy) through the legal system? After a close look at lawyers and their role in the American legal system, we will discuss alternatives lawyers might use, alternatives to the use of lawyers and, indeed, alternatives to the use of formal legal structures. Finally, we have included in Appendix D a reference to legal research methods.

Lawyers have been targets of criticism in the guise of humor, and otherwise, throughout history, but the classic quotation is undoubtedly from Shakespeare's *Henry VI, Part II:* "The first thing we do, let's kill all the lawyers."* Why is so much animosity displayed toward lawyers? In an era of political correctness where jokes and comments about gender, ethnic origin, and sexuality are considered bad form and even the basis of punishment (e.g., public apology or resignation from office), negative comments about lawyers are still common and socially acceptable. Who are lawyers, or attorneys at law, and what functions do they perform in our legal system? Is it necessary to use a lawyer to access the legal system? Before addressing these issues, the first question to ask is: What is the special importance of advocacy (i.e., pleading the cause of another person) within American jurisprudence? The answer: Advocacy is so important partly because of the adversarial nature of the American legal system.

Today, the practice of law is radically different from what it was at the beginning of the twentieth century. Consider a few of the most obvious contrasts:

- At the turn of the twentieth century, the primary reward of the practice of law was, in large part, prestige and personal satisfaction—not money.
- One hundred years ago, clients found attorneys based on reputation and by word of mouth—not by ads, promotions, flyers mailed to strangers, billboards, online solicitations, crowds of attorneys at sites of catastrophes and nearby hospitals, etc.
- Victory is paramount in the adversarial system (explained fully later in the chapter). In the early twentieth century, however, attorneys exercised professional self-restraint. Back then, winning was not the only consideration. Today, winning is sometimes valued above considerations of truth and justice.
- In years past, civility existed among the members of the bar, who took one another at their word. Today combative behavior between attorneys too often permeates the practice of law. Urban lawyers rarely, if ever, accept another attorney's word. Oral understandings must be evidenced by written memoranda. A rigorous reassessment of the rules of professional responsibility (discussed below) by the American Bar Association's (ABA) Commission on Evaluation of the Rules of Professional Conduct was prompted, in part, by persistent concerns about lawyer civility.[1]
- Lawyers formerly became partners with one another, sharing their liabilities as well as profits. Today, lawyers protect their personal wealth by forming corporations, limited liability partnerships (LLPs) or limited liability companies (LLCs).

In a nutshell, lawyering is becoming big business guided by business principles.[2]

---

* The use of this quote as a pejorative is ironic because within the context of the play, the words speak well, not ill, of lawyers. In the play, the Duke of York foments revolution through the use of Jack Cade. Cade fancies he will be king after a peasant revolution. As king he intends to be worshipped as a god, to require all in the kingdom to dress alike, to "be the parliament of England" through his mouth alone, and to require all women to surrender their virginity to him before any marriage. In the ramblings between Cade and one Dick the butcher, the environment for despotism is discussed. Dick opines that to advance Cade's evil goals, "The first thing we do, let's kill all the lawyers." Cade says, "Nay, that I mean to do."

LEGAL FOCUS—BACKGROUND

All of us have long known that there are problems in some areas of our profession which deserve and which receive criticism not only from the public but from the bar itself. The bar is the severest and most expert critic of the profession. At the same time, most citizens will acknowledge what history shows about the courageous lawyers who have been among the staunchest defenders of liberties. Virtually every advance in the cause of civil rights came at the hands of lawyers—often serving without compensation.[3]

WHAT IS THE ADVERSARIAL SYSTEM?

adversarial system

The jurisprudential system in which the parties to a legal dispute are opponents. Their attorneys advocate a great variety of theories of benefit to the cause of their clients both before and during the trial, and on any appeal.

The backbone of the U.S. legal system is the adversarial method of resolving disputes. In an **adversarial system,** parties to legal actions are opponents. The judge is independent and neutral, unlike magistrates in so-called inquisitorial systems (discussed shortly). This fairly simple concept has enormous ramifications. Courts make decisions based on facts brought to their attention by the proponents and opponents in the legal conflict. Each party is responsible for producing evidence and rules of law that support their contentions. The competitors are openly biased and partial to their side. Each asserts every possible reason to merit victory. Every theory asserted or discovered is considered and subject to attack and counter-attack. The judge acts much as a referee in a sporting contest, to ensure that the procedural rules, created to maintain civility and fairness, are followed.

Another distinguishing feature of the adversarial system is that a party must take action to get a case before the court. Legal questions are considered by a court only if a party brings a problem to the attention of the court by filing a lawsuit. Each party is independently responsible for presenting its case. Attorneys play a critical role organizing and arguing cases to the court. The moving party, or plaintiff in a civil lawsuit, must meet a required burden of proof before the defendant must respond. In a criminal case, the moving party is the prosecutor (for example, a county district attorney). He or she is from the executive branch of government, not the judicial branch.

LEGAL FOCUS—BACKGROUND

He spoke to the jurors as if he were alone with them, the way two people can be alone in a crowded public park. His notes were at the counsel table . . . but he never paused to look at them. He told the jury about the tragedies the Woburn families had endured, and then, the tone of his voice growing harsher, about W.R. Grace and Beatrice Foods.

When Schlichtmann was done, the crowd in the gallery remained quiet for a long moment. Judge Skinner broke the spell by calling a brief recess. The crowd, elbow to elbow in their seats, seemed to let out a collective breath, and began talking among themselves as they shuffled out to the corridor.[4]

The adversarial system is the essence of what many consider to be the most just legal system the world has ever known. But it also has shortcomings and critics. The merits of a legal position are not necessarily related to one's ability to persuade others, yet the adversarial system places a premium on advocacy skills. Arguments must be articulated clearly and presented in both written and oral form to convince decision makers of the merits of a case. Therefore, parties to a legal conflict generally hire advocates—lawyers—who possess the required talent.

Of course, access to the system is critically important—redress is not possible if access is denied. The means and methods used to seek legal redress are often complicated, specialized, and daunting to the casual user. Clerical personnel of courts do not assist parties to disputes. They dispense preliminary paperwork and receive new filings, but do not give any advice. If they did, they could be punished for practicing law without a license. For this reason, parties may find court clerks unhelpful and sometimes even hostile. Parties who decide to file suit without representation are doubly disadvantaged; they are ignorant of the filing process (how to get a claim before the court) and they are ignorant of the rules of engagement (procedure, evidence, and advocacy).*

The contrasting **inquisitorial system,** mentioned previously, exists in many other countries as diverse as Argentina, France, and China. Under the inquisitorial system, judges need not depend on the testimony of the parties once the matter is before the court. Judges can investigate the dispute, question witnesses, and independently seek out evidence before a trial. Although attorneys are still necessary in countries with such systems, their role and the role of a trial is often seen as less critical to the administration of justice.†

ATTORNEYS AT LAW

An **attorney at law** (also called a *lawyer*) is a person authorized by law to represent clients in legal matters. Attorneys also draft documents involving legal rights and duties and give expert advice on legal questions. Countless businesses and public organizations routinely look to lawyers for such help. More than two-thirds of the adults in the United States have consulted attorneys for assistance with personal legal problems. Most of these problems involve the preparation of wills, the purchase or sale of real property, divorce or marriage dissolution, serious personal injuries caused by other persons, consumer problems (e.g., disputes with landlords or lenders), criminal matters, or difficulties with governmental agencies.[5] Every person during her or his lifetime should anticipate direct or indirect involvement with an attorney. Accordingly, one should be familiar with the legal profession and learn how to select, retain (hire), cooperate with, and evaluate an attorney's performance.

Lawyers are trained to sort through complicated descriptions of human events to determine which facts are important. They are highly skilled at analyzing the relationship of those facts to legal rules and principles. Lawyers have the special ability to advocate positions through oral and written argument. They are expected to remain unemotional or rational enough to think clearly. On the other hand, "lawyers are accused—rightfully so—of taking simple issues and making them more complicated and of finding every possible permutation, instead of looking for the relatively straightforward answer to the problem placed before them."[6]

inquisitorial system

A legal system used in some countries that allows the judge to investigate, question witnesses, and seek out evidence before a trial.

http://

If you are curious about the law of a particular nation, satisfy that curiosity by using the Emory Law Library Electronic Reference Desk at

http://www.law.emory.edu/ LAW/refdesk/country/ foreign/

attorney-at-law

A person licensed to practice law, and usually called a *lawyer, attorney, counsel,* or *counselor.*

http://

If you are interested in law school, they are all linked at the Emory Law Library site at

http://www.law.emory.edu/ LAW/refdesk/education/ schools.html

---

* A court clerk attempting to assist a party who is not represented by an attorney might be found to be practicing law without a license in violation of state criminal statutes.
† In the interest of accuracy, it should be noted that in most modern legal systems the distinctions between adversarial and inquisitorial methods are not as great in practice as in theory. For example, in the adversary system judges do, within limits, ask witnesses questions and make limited suggestions to counsel about what evidence should be provided to the court. In inquisitorial systems, counsel represents parties, and the scope and degree of judicial inquiry are often limited.

WHO MAY PRACTICE LAW?

legal assistant

Someone with specialized training who assists an attorney. Also called a paralegal.

fiduciary relationship

A relationship between two persons wherein one has an obligation to perform services with scrupulous good faith and honesty.

Generally, only licensed attorneys may perform legal services for others, their clients. Most state legislatures have created state bar associations to regulate lawyers and the practice of law. The rules of such associations, together with applicable federal and state statutes, combine with the inherent powers of the court to regulate the legal profession. Each state sets its own qualifications for admission to practice law within its borders. However, all states permit attorneys to hire non-attorneys, often called **legal assistants,** to perform legal services under their indirect supervision. A considerable amount of legal services are actually performed by non-attorneys.

The practice of law is a licensed profession. Technical training, a commitment to public service, and a pledge to follow standards of practice distinguish a profession from a service or trade. (See Exhibit 4-1 for the commonly accepted attributes of a profession.) The practice of law is regulated in part because legal representation is fiduciary in nature. A **fiduciary relationship** is one involving a person in a position of trust who undertakes to act for the benefit of another. The attorney as a fiduciary must exercise the utmost good faith, honesty, and fairness toward that client. Licensure is designed to protect the public by seeking to ensure that every attorney is competent, honorable, and worthy of that trust reposed by the client. Offering legal services without being duly licensed as an attorney is a criminal offense. An attorney must have a separate license from each state in which he or she wishes to practice law.*

A candidate for a license to practice law must possess good moral character, complete certain minimum educational requirements,† pass an examination on the law (called a *bar examination*), and take an oath to support the law and conform to rules of professional conduct of that state. Many states also require that each attorney complete a minimum number of continuing legal education courses within a prescribed time to retain the license. A person has no inherent right to be able to practice law or to represent others in court. Only those who demonstrate moral fitness and intellectual ability are granted the privilege to practice law.

Each federal court (e.g., U.S. Supreme Court, U.S. Courts of Appeals, U.S. District Court) recognizes its own separate bar or group of attorneys permitted to practice before it. Admission is granted to attorneys licensed in the state where the federal court sits. Federal court rules impose separate pre-conditions for admission to the federal bar, although no further legal education or additional examination is required.

LEGAL FOCUS—CASE

Bonnie Cord and Jeffrey Blue, an unmarried couple, bought a home and resided together in a rural area of Warren County, Virginia. Bonnie, an attorney licensed to practice law in Washington, D.C., applied for a license in Virginia. Duncan Gibb, judge of the Circuit Court of Warren County, denied her application because her living arrangement

---

* Occasionally, an attorney will represent a client in the court of a state other than the one where he or she has a license. The attorney can do so after receiving permission from the court of that state. The granting of the right is referred to as *pro hac vice* (Latin: "for this occasion"). It is customary for a court to require that the out-of-state attorney associate with a local attorney for the duration of the case. In a 1998 California Supreme Court case, a New York lawyer was denied recovery of fees for representation of a client in a California arbitration because there was no associated California counsel. *Birbrower v. Superior Court of Santa Clara County*, 17 Cal 4th 119, 949 P.2d 1 (Cal., 1998). In recent years, attorneys, particularly those who work in-house for large companies, have questioned the propriety of state-by-state licensing of attorneys, arguing that it is in effect an illegal barrier to interstate commerce.

† The educational requirements vary depending on the state. Most states require that any person wishing to take the state bar examination must be a graduate of a law school accredited by the American Bar Association. A law school is a professional institution offering a graduate-level degree program. Today, law students must possess a baccalaureate degree to gain admission to accredited law schools.

EXHIBIT 4-1: **What Is a Profession?**

A profession is an occupation, the practice of which is based upon an understanding of the theoretical makeup of some area of learning accompanied by demonstrated abilities when applying this understanding.

Commonly accepted attributes of a profession:

- Knowledge—Specialized knowledge needed to help achieve a purpose.

- Competent Application—Usually some examination or internship to assure competence.

- Social Responsibility—Higher purpose to be achieved by practicing the occupation.

- Self-Control—Generally, group prepares and follows a code of ethics.

- Community Sanction—General community belief that the effort is professional.

Sources include: M. L. Cogan, "Toward a Definition of Profession," *Harvard Educational Review, 23* (1953), pp. 33–50; E. Greenwood, "Attributes of a Profession," *Social Work, 2* (July, 1957), pp. 45–55; and John R. Rowan, "The Basis for Social Responsibilities to Clients: Corporations as Professional Organizations," *Purdue University Calumet,* found at http://130.220.181.8/research/aapae/rowan.pdf.

"would lower the public's opinion of the Bar as a whole." Bonnie appealed to a higher court. What should have been the result?

Cord v. Gibb, 314 Va. 1019, 254 S.E.2d 71 (Va ,1979).

Bonnie won the case and her license because her conduct did not affect her fitness to practice law. The same result has been reached where an applicant disclosed a sexual preference for persons of the same sex.

With a few exceptions, no one is required to use a lawyer in a legal proceeding. A party to a case before a trial court may appear **in propria persona** (Latin: "in one's own person") or **in pro se** (Latin: "on one's own behalf"), that is, without the services of a lawyer. Generally, though, it is not advisable to go to court without a lawyer. A common saying even among lawyers is "one who serves as his own lawyer has a fool for a client!" Thus, lawyers are usually represented by another lawyer when they are sued. All of us, even lawyers, are emotionally involved in our own cases; we need educated, experienced, and rational counsel to analyze issues dispassionately and argue them persuasively before judge and jury. It is important to have an independent advocate.

> *A defendant in Superior Court decided to be his own lawyer, which some say was mistake number one. His second mistake was the first question he asked the victim: "Did you see my face clearly when I took your purse?" The sentence: Two to ten years.*[7]

An attorney's license can be suspended or revoked for failing to follow professional standards, including breaking the law, or for providing services in an incompetent and unethical fashion. However, attorneys are not required to disclose to prospective clients whether they have ever been disciplined for unprofessional conduct, whether they are under treatment for any mental or addictive health problem, or whether former clients have sued them.

in propria persona (in pro se)

Term meaning the person represents herself or himself in a legal action without the appearance of an attorney.

SPECIALIZATION

As with a license to practice medicine, a license to practice law is a broad grant of power. It permits an attorney to undertake a wide variety of legal tasks. Common sense for both lawyer and client suggests that a general-practice attorney should undertake only routine matters for a client. A complex legal problem should be referred to a specialist, who will be familiar with the intricacies, procedures, and detailed rules in that particular area of law. All areas of law practice include unwritten norms, knowledge of which allow the specialist to bring a legal problem to a faster, more satisfactory conclusion than an attorney not well versed in the particular area.

Attorneys may choose to specialize in any one or more areas, such as divorce or family law, probate and estates, criminal law, administrative law, real property law, personal injury law, small business law, and consumer law. These specialties usually correlate with the most common public needs. Other specialties include antitrust law, labor or employment law, tax law, bankruptcy law, intellectual property law, international law, workers' compensation law, water law, and elder law (a relatively new legal specialty serving America's aging baby boomers). Attorneys may also be classified as performing either transactional or litigation (court-related) services. For example, one attorney may perform transactional services such as writing wills, contracts, articles of incorporation, etc., while another performs only court cases. On the other hand, criminal lawyers are strictly litigators. A client should determine whether the attorney he or she consults has a specialty.

Many states* allow attorneys to identify themselves as certified specialists in a particular area of law if they have the requisite experience and have met the educational standards set by the state bar. In Arizona, for example, certified specialties now include bankruptcy, criminal law, family law, estates and trusts, injury and wrongful-death litigation, real estate law, tax law, and workers' compensation law.[8]

The availability of specialized legal services is determined, in part, by geography. For example, antitrust, patent, immigration, and securities specialists are found in populous urban areas, while general practitioners are usually found in suburbs and rural communities. Family, small business, criminal, and probate law attorneys are found in all communities of any significant size.

ASSOCIATIONS OF LAWYERS

A lawyer may choose to practice alone, combine with one or more other attorneys in a law partnership, or (in most states) conduct business as a professional corporation. Law partnerships and corporations currently range in size from two to more than 3,000 attorneys. The nature of the practice of law has changed dramatically in the last 70 years. The following quotation from Erwin Griswold captures some of the changes that occurred during his lifetime in the law.

LEGAL FOCUS—BACKGROUND

[G]ood openings for young lawyers were not easy to find. When I finished law school [Harvard] in 1928, I made the rounds of the New York law offices. I did receive a number of offers, but they were all at the fixed rate of $125 a month. Practically no member of my class at law school had a position at the time of our graduation. It was taken for granted that you would first take and pass the applicable state bar examination, and then knock on the doors of law offices in the city of choice and hope that some sort of an opening could be found. There was not a great deal of change until after the close of World War II.[†]

* Including Alabama, Arizona, Arkansas, California, Connecticut, Florida, Georgia, Louisiana, Minnesota, New Jersey, New Mexico, South Carolina, Texas, and Utah.
† Today it is most unlikely that a top Harvard graduate would need to go door to door to find employment. Today's starting salary would be most attractive. Erwin Griswold, *The National Law Journal*, 30 December 1991, p. 17. Adapted from the book *Ould Field, New Corne: The Personal Memoirs of a Twentieth Century Lawyer* (St. Paul, MN: West Publishing, 1991)

Most attorneys who associate with others do so in a general partnership, a limited liability partnership, or a professional corporation. When professionals, including lawyers, form organizations, they seldom gain all the advantages that exist for other businesses. For example, there are generally no restrictions on who may be a shareholder (part owner) in the usual corporation. But in a professional law corporation or limited liability partnership, non-legal professionals (e.g., legal secretaries, legal assistants, and investigators) are not allowed to be shareholders. In addition, although many business forms protect a shareholder from all personal liability for the debts of the firm, such forms will not completely protect a professional in most states. To protect the public, most states will not shield attorneys (or other professionals) from liability for errors and omissions (malpractice).*

Lawyers in all but the smallest "boutique" firms are often assisted by legal assistants or paralegals† (persons qualified to perform a wide range of administrative and semi-legal tasks), secretaries or personal assistants, investigators, and office managers.

Medium to large size partnerships include attorneys offering a wide variety of specialized legal services. On the other hand, some law firms limit their entire practice to a single specialty. For example, some firms specialize in the defense of automobile injury cases. These firms are employed by automobile insurance companies to represent their customers who are involved in automobile accidents.

Prestige within the legal community is often related to the size of the firm. The larger the firm, the greater its prestige and, usually, the higher the fees it charges the client. This phenomenon is partly the result of large, well-established firms attracting top graduates from elite law schools. Members (owners, or "equity-partners") of these firms often earn high personal incomes, serve wealthy clients, and occupy luxurious offices. The solo practitioner, rightly or wrongly, is often found at the bottom of the image and income ladder.[9] The nature of the practice of law appears to be changing drastically. While the evolution of legal practice from solo practitioners to large firms has been going on for more than 60 years,** the establishment of the megafirm with offices in different cities, states, and countries is a more recent innovation.

Certain areas of law or specialty are more prestigious than others. An example of the strong sentiments about one type of practice is expressed in the following newspaper quote from a judge (with obviously strong, but not necessarily accurate, opinions) who was contemplating his return to practice.

http://

Interested in becoming a paralegal? See The National Federation of Paralegal Associations Web site at **http://www.paralegals.org/**

LEGAL FOCUS—BACKGROUND

When he goes back into practice, Winner said he will accept any kind of case except divorce cases. "I'll represent whores, pimps, or newspaper reporters, but I'm not going to try divorce cases," he said. "There is no end to them, and no end to the calls at home. There's also no satisfactory solution to any of them. The cause of most divorces

---

* Various statutory schemes protect clients of professional corporations. One type will not allow owners to have limited liability. Another requires professional corporations or limited liability partnerships to purchase insurance against professional malpractice (errors and omissions insurance). The insurance is a condition for an initial and a continuing certification to do business. A third scheme requires all shareholders to personally guarantee all corporate obligations for malpractice as a condition for certification.

† American Bar Association definition: Persons, qualified through education, training, or work experience, who are employed or retained by a lawyer, law office, governmental agency, or other entity in a capacity or function which involves the performance, under the ultimate direction and supervision of an attorney, of specifically delegated substantive legal work, which work for the most part, requires sufficient knowledge of legal concepts that, absent such assistant, the attorney would perform the task.

** In the years immediately after World War II approximately 66 percent of lawyers in this country practiced alone. Albert Blaustein, *American Lawyer* (Westport, Conn.: Greenwood Publishing, 1972).

⋮ is that there isn't enough money, and if there isn't enough money to support one fam-
⋮ ily, there sure isn't enough money to support two."[10]

Public attorneys (e.g., district attorneys, U.S. attorneys, and county counsels) represent various local, state, and federal governments. Public defenders are also public attorneys. They are paid by local, state, and federal governments to represent indigents accused of a crime. Attorneys in public service are usually bound by the same rules of professional conduct as attorneys in private practice.* In some circumstances, public lawyers are held to a higher standard. (See the following discussion.)

Generally, the government is not obligated to provide free legal counsel to low-income people in civil matters. However, many communities have established legal aid offices. They give assistance and limited legal advice in civil matters to people who cannot afford an attorney. Representation in personal injury cases is affordable because private attorneys charge on a **contingency fee** basis. The fee, a percentage of the amount recovered, is contingent on the outcome of the case. In other words, a fee is due and payable only if the client wins. (Further discussion of attorney fees appears later in this chapter.)

The federal **Legal Services Corporation** (LSC) helps states provide legal assistance to the underprivileged through grants to local legal aid offices. "LSC's mission is to promote equal access to the system of justice and improve opportunities for low-income people throughout the United States by making grants for the provision of high-quality civil legal assistance to those who would be otherwise unable to afford legal counsel."[11] Created in 1964, the LSC has encountered some controversy since advocating for the poor often has unpopular political ramifications. Cases brought by the LSC often name other government agencies as defendants, creating political backlash and resentment.

Many bar associations and legal commentators urge lawyers to allocate part of their time to civil *pro bono publico* (Latin: "for the public good") services free of charge. Many attorneys do contribute their time and effort to serving poor people who have legal problems, but the need is far from being met to the satisfaction of all concerned. The ABA House of Delegates adopted new ethics rules requiring every lawyer to provide legal services to those unable to pay.[12] Congress and state legislatures have enacted "fee shifting" statutes to encourage attorneys to represent the underprivileged: If the attorney wins the case, the government will pay all attorney fees. Fees are quite generous in civil rights matters and government overreaching cases. Victims who do not have to pay attorney fees in advance are more likely to proceed in vindicating their rights. To some, fee shifting is the only way to protect poor people. To others, fee shifting statutes are like adding gasoline to the fires of litigation, which many believe already to be out of control.

Assistance to indigent persons accused of crimes is provided without charge through state and federal public defenders' offices. Courts appoint private attorneys when public attorneys are not available. These private attorneys are paid standardized fees by the state. Under the Sixth Amendment, legal assistance is a constitutional right of all persons accused of crimes punishable by imprisonment, even if they cannot afford to hire private legal counsel.

Some "store-front lawyers" or "law clinics" operating out of strip malls and other such quarters provide routine legal services for reduced fees. This type of law practice began in the 1970s with the relaxation of rules prohibiting advertising. These clinics often limit representation to such areas as family law, criminal defense, and probate matters. To lower costs, they take on only those matters that lend themselves to simple procedures and use of

contingency fee

A fixed percentage of the monetary recovery obtained by a lawyer for a client. It is agreed on in advance and accepted in full payment for services rendered.

Legal Services Corporation

A federally funded corporation that distributes federal tax dollars to state programs that provide legal assistance in non-criminal proceedings to persons financially unable to afford such services.

http://

The Legal Services Corporation can be found at http://www.lsc.gov

pro bono publico

When an attorney provides legal services free of charge to poor but worthy clients or causes.

---

* One exception is when an adversary extends an offer to compromise. Private attorneys are bound to disclose such vital information to their clients. A public district attorney, however, need not reveal all plea bargain offers to anyone.

standard legal forms. In recent years, many of these clinics have added other legal specialties to their services.

The cost of legal services, like the cost of medical care, has skyrocketed in recent years. For many, access to competent legal advice at an affordable rate has become elusive. Group and prepaid **legal service plans** are designed to make legal services available at reduced cost to members of associations. Increasingly, prepaid legal service plans are offered as part of employee benefits packages. These plans operate like group health insurance. Subscribers get free or reduced-fee legal services after a deductible has been met. The plans are usually limited in scope but do provide low-cost assistance for routine legal matters (e.g., simple wills, document review, and warranty enforcement). Criminal matters are generally excluded from coverage. Prepaid legal service plans have been criticized for violating attorney ethical rules (discussed next) respecting client confidentiality and for interfering with attorneys' professional judgment. However, an individual's right to obtain access to reasonable legal services has been upheld by the United States Supreme Court.[13] The criticisms notwithstanding, the dramatic growth in prepaid legal services suggests that they may be "the wave of the future."[14]

Public interest law firms became popular in the late 1960s. These firms offer assistance in particular areas such as employment, minority rights, civil rights, political rights, family law, and environmental law. Public interest law firms are often funded by grants from private charitable organizations. Public interest firms represent opposite sides of controversial legal issues.

legal service plans

Insurance plans designed to make legal services available to members of unions or other organizations, such as business firms.

public interest law firm

A nonprofit law firm that offers assistance in areas such as employment, minority rights, civil rights, political rights, family law, and environmental law.

Ⓦ HAT ARE PROFESSIONAL ETHICS?

As discussed in Chapter 1, ethics is about what is fair and just. It addresses the question: What is the right thing to do in a situation? **Professional ethics** are written rules of acceptable conduct that are adopted by and binding upon members of a professional group. They are established and enforced to protect the public and to preserve and improve the reputation of the profession. Recall that an oath to follow ethical rules is what distinguishes a profession from a service or a trade. Ethics and the law, although not identical, do go hand in hand.

Legal ethics is the set of rules promulgated by the governing bodies that regulate lawyer and judicial conduct. Legal ethics may embody moralistic choices, but not necessarily. *Rules of professional conduct* or *rules of professional responsibility* are more precise terms, as many of the rules do not directly concern moral issues. They relate to more practical aspects of legal practice such as prohibiting unauthorized practice of law. The states are responsible for regulating lawyer conduct.

As a practical matter, the legal profession is self-regulating. The various state bar associations, under the auspices of the states' supreme courts, devise and publish the ethical rules, determine admission eligibility and procedures, and decide who receives discipline and to what extent. These rules carry the force of law when they are codified by a legislature or cited by courts in opinions. A breach of these rules may lead to discipline. It may take the form of (1) disbarment, (2) suspension from practice for a stated period of time, (3) probation, or (4) reproval (formal private or public censure).

The American Bar Association is the pre-eminent source on legal ethics. Since the early twentieth century, the American Bar Association has promulgated ethical rules for legal practitioners. The first set of rules, the Canons of Professional Ethics, was introduced in 1908. It was intended as a practice guide, not a basis for discipline. A new set of rules,

professional ethics

Written rules of conduct that are adopted by and binding upon members of a professional group.

legal ethics

Rules promulgated by lawyer-governing bodies to proscribe standards of professional behavior and regulate lawyer and judicial conduct.

http://

Read about current issues
in legal ethics at a Web site
devoted to this topic
http://www.legalethics.com/

the Model Code of Professional Conduct, was introduced in 1969. It had two sets of rules: one aspirational and one disciplinary. In 1983, the American Bar Association adopted Model Rules of Professional Conduct. The aspirational component of the earlier codes was eliminated. By the summer of 2002, forty-two states and the District of Columbia adopted rules governing lawyers based, in whole or in part, on the ABA Model Rules of Professional Conduct. Almost thirty amendments to the Rules of Professional Conduct and a lack of uniformity among the states' ethics rules contributed to a growing sense that the rules were becoming incomprehensible. Meantime, monumental change occurred in the delivery of legal services. The explosion of alternate dispute resolution, the ubiquity of legal information, the instant availability of e-lawyers, and the shrinking of national borders are a few of the dramatic changes that prompted the American Bar Association to again recommend revisions to the Model Rules of Professional Conduct. The ABA Commission on Evaluating the Model Rules of Professional Conduct, nicknamed the Ethics 2000 Commission, recommended sweeping revisions. Most, but not all, of the Ethics 2000 Commission's recommendations were adopted by the ABA House of Delegates in February 2002.

LEGAL FOCUS—BACKGROUND

In the nature of law practice, however, conflicting responsibilities are encountered. Virtually all difficult ethical problems arise from conflict between a lawyer's responsibility to clients, to the legal system, and to the lawyer's own interest in remaining an upright person while earning a satisfactory living. The Rules of Professional Conduct prescribe terms for resolving such conflicts. Within the framework of these Rules many difficult issues of professional discretion can arise. Such issues must be resolved through the exercise of sensitive professional and moral judgement guided by the basic principles underlying the Rules. Such issues must be resolved through the exercise of sensitive professional and moral judgment guided by the basic principles underlying the Rules.[15]

Charging unconscionable or exorbitant fees, stealing a client's funds, improperly soliciting employment, neglecting a client's case, and misusing a client's funds are all examples of unethical conduct directly related to the attorney's profession. Other improprieties and bad behavior can also expose the attorney to ethics violations.

Attorneys may be disciplined for conduct involving *moral turpitude* (conduct contrary to justice, honesty, and good morals). Perjury, failure to pay income taxes, murder, larceny, participation in business fraud, child molestation, and sale of narcotics are all examples of crimes involving moral turpitude. Such acts subject the offending attorney to professional discipline, in addition to criminal charges and individual civil lawsuits. Disciplinary hearings may take place even if questionable conduct does not directly relate to the attorney's ability to practice law. For example, former vice president Spiro T. Agnew was disbarred following his plea of *nolo contendere* (Latin: "I will not contest it"), a special form of guilty plea, to willful tax evasion.[16]

LEGAL FOCUS—CASE

Grace Akinsanya retained [attorney] Pineda and paid him $1,500, in advance, to represent her in a real estate matter. After a few months, Akinsanya became dissatisfied with Pineda's inaction and fired him. Pineda refused to sign a substitution-of-attorney form and would not return Akinsanya's files or refund any part of the fee. Can Pineda refuse to remove himself from the case and keep the client's files?

Pineda v. State Bar of Calif., 49 Cal.3d 753, 781 P.2d 1 (Cal., 1989).

An attorney at law has no right to continue to represent a client who no longer wants the lawyer's services. Pineda finally did withdraw from the case and returned Akinsanya's files, but only after the Superior Court sanctioned (punished) him for his actions. Based on these acts and six other similar acts of failure to perform services for clients, Pineda was suspended from the practice of law for two years and placed on probation for five years.

There is an important difference between private and public attorneys. Both are ethically bound to zealously represent a client. They are advocates and the object is to win the client's case. In litigation, each attorney works with the record of historical events, which lawyers refer to as *facts.* Each must resolve all doubts about the facts (and law) in the client's favor. Significantly, a public attorney, such as a prosecutor or other government lawyer, is held to a higher standard. A government lawyer is duty bound to see that justice is carried out, not simply win the case. For example, a prosecutor must notify the defense of any obvious evidence in a criminal case that tends to show the defendant's innocence. The private attorney is not obligated in the same way. He or she is not responsible for passing judgment. However, he or she may not destroy, nor present as true, any evidence that is known to be false, nor solicit or condone perjury in order to win a case.[17]

LEGAL FOCUS—PROBLEM

Attorney Tak Sharpe represented the plaintiff in an automobile accident case that was nearing trial. To encourage a compromise, Sharpe telephoned the defendant, Sandra Broderik, instead of calling Broderik's attorney. Sharpe told Broderik that $17,500 would be a fair settlement. Broderick responded that she would prefer to discuss the matter with her attorney. Has Sharpe acted ethically?

No.[18] The Rules of Professional Conduct do not allow opposing counsel to communicate directly with another attorney's client without the other lawyer's consent. Sharpe should have telephoned Broderik's lawyer. The purpose of this rule is to prevent an opponent's lawyer from intimidating the opposition or undermining the advice given by that client's counsel.

Questions of professional ethics are sometimes very complex and susceptible to misunderstanding. The attorney's job is to vigorously represent the client while honoring the law. For example, a criminal attorney must attempt to persuade a judge and jury to free a client, even if he or she personally believes that the client is guilty of the offense. This is considered ethically correct because the lawyer's duty is to represent—not to judge—the client. Everyone is entitled to all available legal advantage. Even following conviction, the attorney will argue for probation rather than prison. A tax attorney will look vigilantly to find a loophole (an ambiguity in the law) allowing a client to reduce or avoid tax payments. This is proper, as a matter of legal ethics, so long as no fraudulent practice is involved. Congress often authorizes loopholes or tax shelters to encourage certain types of socially desirable investments. For example, Congress allows interest paid on home mortgages to be deducted from taxable income, reducing the income taxes paid by homeowners. (Of course, the taxpayer must request the deduction.)

LEGAL FOCUS—CASE

Tammy Forsberg was injured in a motorcycle accident. Her attorney, John Casey, obtained a settlement, of which her portion was $23,233. Casey paid her $5,000 and refused to pay the rest. Forsberg hired a second lawyer, James Himmel, on a contingency fee basis to recover the remaining balance from Casey. Himmel sued Casey and won a judgment of $100,000 for Forsberg. Himmel did not report Casey to the state bar. What are the ethical implications of Casey's and Himmel's conduct?

In re James H. Himmel, 125 III.2d 531, 533 N.E.2d 790 (III., 1989).

The Illinois state bar disbarred Casey for keeping Forsberg's money. Apparently, Casey had treated the money as if it were his own. He put his desire for fees above the interests of his clients and the legal system. Himmel exacerbated the misconduct by not reporting it. Under ethical rules, lawyers are required to report another lawyer's misconduct to the proper authority. The Illinois Supreme Court held that Himmel, by not reporting Casey's activities, had contributed to the misappropriation of other clients' funds. Although Himmel had practiced law without complaint for eleven years, he was suspended from the practice of law for one year.*

The public and many lawyers have trouble understanding the rules despite the continuing effort to update and clarify them. One influential source of ethical guidance is a body of published ethics opinions written by ethics committees of the American Bar Association and state or local bar associations. An ethics committee is convened to consider how the rules of professional conduct apply in a specific circumstance. The committee debates the ethical issues and writes an opinion resolving the matter. It is important to note that although influential, the opinions do not carry the force of law. Ethics Hotlines, operated by state and local bar associations, are a growing source of guidance for lawyers. Lawyers may make a confidential telephone inquiry about an ethical dilemma and receive advice on how to solve the problem. Again, such advice may be helpful, but is not binding on any court.

CONFIDENTIALITY AND THE ATTORNEY-CLIENT PRIVILEGE

attorney-client privilege

The right of a client to keep communications with his or her attorney confidential and free from disclosure.

confidentiality

A private communication with an attorney at law in which the attorney is under a duty to keep the information secret.

The **attorney-client privilege** is a rule of evidence that protects all communications between a client and his or her attorney from disclosure in a legal proceeding. An attorney cannot be compelled by statute or court order to reveal such information except in a few narrow circumstances. The client may waive the privilege but the attorney may not. The attorney-client privilege applies in all states.

The attorney-client privilege is often confused with the broader duty of **confidentiality.** The duty of confidentiality is a lawyer's ethical obligation to protect any information learned from or about a client during the course of representation. It applies in any forum or context, not just in judicial proceedings. Whereas the duty of confidentiality protects any information a lawyer learns about the client from any source from disclosure to anyone, anywhere, the attorney-client privilege protects the client's information *only* if the attorney learns it directly from the client. Some exceptions to the confidentiality rule apply. Although there is wide variation among the states, the most common exceptions are to

* The Supreme Court of Rhode Island found a similar failure to disclose to be appropriate conduct. The court noted that because of an instruction by the attorney's client not to disclose an embezzlement by a former attorney, the attorney was prohibited from disclosure under the attorney client privilege. *In re* Ethics Advisory Panel Opinion No. 92-1, 627 A.2d 317 (1993).

defend a malpractice case or fee dispute, to warn of a client's contemplated crime, and to avoid assisting with the commission of a crime.

The attorney-client privilege and the duty of confidentiality were designed to accomplish competent representation. To build a strong case, attorneys need full disclosure and open communication with their clients. Clients will share information freely with counsel only if they believe their confidences are safe.

LEGAL FOCUS—PROBLEM

A criminal defense attorney learned from his client, Derrick Dagger, that in addition to the present crime with which Derrick was charged, he previously had murdered two young girls, recently reported as missing. The lawyer even learned the specific location of their bodies. Yet the attorney did not report this information to the authorities, to the parents of the girls, or to anyone else. Did the attorney behave ethically?

Yes, according to generally understood legal ethics. An attorney cannot breach the duty of confidentiality, without the client's consent. Rule 1.6 of the ABA Model Rules of Professional Conduct prohibits a lawyer from revealing "information relating to the representation of a client unless the client gives informed consent, the disclosure is impliedly authorized in order to carry out the representation or the disclosure is [otherwise] permitted." The attorney cannot waive the privilege. However, the client may do so. Cases involving situations such as this have brought the rule to the public's attention, if not understanding, over the years.[19]

LEGAL FOCUS—CASE

An anonymous client (referred to as J. Doe) contacted an attorney following Doe's involvement in a fatal hit-and-run accident. Doe instructed the attorney to offer a plea to the prosecutor in exchange for a reduced criminal charge while Doe remained anonymous. The prosecutor refused to bargain without revelation of Doe's identity. The victim's family sued the attorney to force disclosure of the client's name. Can the family get Doe's real name?

Baltes v. Doe, 57 U.S.L.W. 2268 (Fla. Cir. Ct., 1988).

No. The Florida Circuit Court held that the information was privileged, and the attorney was not required to disclose the client's name. Courts understand the natural public resentment that arises with such rulings. Nevertheless, "if the privilege is not maintained in 'hard' cases such as this, troubled individuals with legal problems will only dare to consult lawyers in 'easy' cases—where there is little to hide in any event."[20]

LEGAL FOCUS—CASE

In 1993 Deputy White House Counsel Vincent W. Foster, Jr., met with attorney James Hamilton seeking personal legal representation. Hamilton took handwritten notes at the meeting. Nine days later, Foster committed suicide. Subsequently, a federal grand jury, at the request of Independent Counsel Kenneth Starr, issued subpoenas for the notes as part of an investigation of President Clinton and his staff. Hamilton sought to quash the subpoena, arguing that the notes were protected by the attorney-client privilege. Starr's contention was that the attorney-client privilege does not apply after the client has died, particularly if the information is relevant to a criminal proceeding. Did Starr get the notes?

Swidler & Berlin and James Hamilton v. United States, 524 U.S 399, 118 S.Ct. 2081 (1998).

No. In reversing the Court of Appeals for the District of Columbia Circuit, the U.S. Supreme Court stated, "[W]e think there are weighty reasons that counsel in favor of posthumous application [of the attorney-client privilege]. Knowing that communications will remain confidential even after death encourages the client to communicate fully and frankly with counsel. Clients may be concerned about reputation, civil liability, or possible harm to friends or family. Posthumous disclosure of such communications may be as feared as disclosure during the client's lifetime."

The privilege has not, however, been held to cover all communications in all situations; for example, there is no protection if the communication is made in the presence of others, if the communication indicates an intent to commit a future crime, or if there is a statute requiring specified communications to be disclosed.

LEGAL FOCUS—CASE

A federal law passed in 1988 requires attorneys to report the identity of any client who makes cash payment to them of $10,000 or more to the Internal Revenue Service. Attorney Robert Leventhal filed the appropriate form with the IRS indicating receipt of a payment in excess of $10,000 but did not disclose the name of the client. When ordered to complete the form, he declined, claiming such disclosures would violate the attorney-client privilege. Was Leventhal required to disclose the client's name?

United States v. Leventhal, 961 F.2d 936 (11th cir., 1992).

Yes. The federal appellate court held that the federal statute superseded both the state-created and the federal attorney-client privilege. The court also held that disclosure of the client's name was not the type of confidential communication protected by the privilege.[21]

CONFLICTS OF INTEREST

A quality attorney-client relationship depends on trust. Clients develop trust in their attorney if they believe their attorney will treat them in an honest, fair, and loyal manner. It is virtually impossible for an attorney to competently represent clients unless clients are completely candid. The natural inclination to avoid disclosing embarrassing or incriminating information cannot be overcome unless clients are confident their attorney will not use confidential information without permission. If clients believe confidences will be respected, then they will communicate openly with their attorney. A relationship of trust forms when the attorney is first engaged and continues throughout the representation and even after the representation ends.

Conflicts of interest breach this trust. A **conflict of interest** occurs when one client's interests are at odds with another's because the attorney either serves, might serve, or is tempted to serve the other. Conflicts arise when an attorney tries to serve too many masters, or when self-interest collides with clients' best interests. Any situation that compromises or has the potential to compromise an attorney's loyalty to clients is a conflict of interest. The rules of professional conduct forbid conflicts of interest. These rules are intended to foster trust in individual attorney-client relationships and to build confidence in the legal profession.[22]

Obviously, a conflict arises when an attorney seeks to be named a beneficiary in a client's will or trust. (This is called a breach of trust or breach of fiduciary duty). Attorneys may not use financial information about a client to their own advantage. Conflicts of interest can arise between two or more clients or between a new client and a current or former client. For this reason, lawyers may not represent two defendants accused of commission of the same crime. An attorney faced with a potential conflict of interest can contact the local bar association's Ethics Hotline for guidance. An advisory opinion may be published if the bar believes the issues in the case require general guidance.

LEGAL FOCUS—EXAMPLE

Problem: Several years ago, husband consulted with an attorney about a contract dispute over a used car. After the initial interview, the attorney turned the case over to an associate. The matter was heard in small claims court and a resolution was reached. Husband's wife and brother-in-law now seek the attorney's representation in a protection from abuse action and custody matter in family court. Will representation of the wife and brother-in-law create an impermissible conflict of interest? The attorney obtained no confidential information concerning any domestic matter from husband.

The Rule: Pennsylvania Rule of Professional Conduct 1.9(a), which governs conflicts of interest with former clients, provides that a lawyer who has formerly represented a client in a matter shall not thereafter represent another person in the same or a substantially related matter in which that person's interests are materially adverse to the interests of the former client unless the former client consents after a full disclosure of the circumstances and consultation.

Analysis: Since the contract matter does not in any way relate to the issues of domestic abuse and child custody, the prohibition in Rule 1.9(a) is not triggered and there is no impermissible conflict of interest. Thus, the Committee finds that the attorney is free to undertake the present representation. However, should the wife seek representation in a divorce that includes a claim for equitable distribution, and if the same used car that was the subject of the small claims action is marital property under Pennsylvania law, the rule might bar representation of the wife in the divorce action.

Edited from Opinion 2001-3 issued February 2001 from the Philadelphia Bar Association.[23]

Conflicts are created when attorneys change employers, either from one private law firm to another or from government service to private practice. The magnitude of this problem has increased with the growth in law firm size. Performing detailed conflicts checks is now critical to escaping malpractice suits and ethical rules violations. When taking on new clients, attorneys must be vigilant in determining that the new representation does not conflict with obligations owed to other clients (even previous ones). To serve the best interest of clients, even the appearance of a conflict need be avoided.

LEGAL FOCUS—CASE

Judge Bennie Boles appointed Clayton Victor to represent Larry Christopher, an indigent defendant charged with a crime. Victor asked to withdraw on the basis of a conflict of interest, stating his law partner was married to the county district attorney, Karren Price. Judge Boles held that no conflict of interest existed. Victor requested judicial review on the question. Did a conflict of interest exist?

Haley v. Boles, 824 S.W.2d 796 (Tex. 1992).

The Texas appellate court held that since indigent criminal defendants are not required to pay attorney fees, they are not free to discharge appointed counsel, even upon discovery of a conflict of interest. However, ignoring the marital relationship between the district attorney and the defense counsel would undermine public confidence in the criminal justice system. The court found this apparent conflict of interest sufficient to dismiss Haley as Christopher's counsel.

FRIVOLOUS LAWSUITS

Claims without legal justification, solely intended to retaliate or punish, are regarded as frivolous. They are costly to society. Defendants incur attorney fees and expenses. Time is wasted and minds are preoccupied unnecessarily. Courtrooms are occupied and judges' attention is diverted from valid cases. Meritless lawsuits clog the court system. Arguably, access to justice is denied when meritorious cases cannot be tried on a timely basis. Contrary to public perception, it is unethical for lawyers to file baseless lawsuits. In fact, the ABA Model Rules of Professional Conduct and states' rules prohibit attorneys from taking on any legal work of a frivolous nature.[24] A lawyer may not write a demand letter or place a telephone call on behalf of a client if there is no validity to the claim. The costs of defending a frivolous lawsuit are recoverable under statute, case law, and court rules.[25] Federal Rule of Civil Procedure 11 permits the court to sanction attorneys and *pro se* litigants for filing frivolous lawsuits. A signature on any moving paper (motions, answers, etc.) is a certification to the court that the signer believes, based on investigation, the allegations to be true. If the courts find that the suit has no basis in law or fact, it may dismiss the case and order that the defendants be paid their litigation costs, including attorney fees. Under federal statute, defendants may even recover "excess costs and attorney fees arising from vexious actions taken to escalate an otherwise valid case."[26] Plaintiffs beware: The court system may not be used to facilitate bad-faith attempts at seeking justice.

D EALING WITH AN ATTORNEY

IS AN ATTORNEY NECESSARY?

Lawyers are expected to assist with a seemingly endless stream of problems for private persons, businesses, government agencies, and other organizations. Obviously, many clients consider attorneys an essential source of information, advice, and representation in numerous situations. Nonetheless, people routinely resolve some legal problems without the assistance of an attorney. Among these are simple divorces, settlement of "fender ben-der" car-crash cases, simple handwritten wills, consumer purchase and sale contracts (such as "pink slip" certificates of vehicle ownership), and simple real estate purchase agree-ments. Numerous disputes involving small sums are within the jurisdiction of the small claims court (recall that attorneys may not appear in small claims court unless they are par-ties in a case). The Internet is a useful tool in gathering legal information. One popular legal information Web site operated by Cornell Law School reportedly receives over eight million hits a week.[27] There are excellent self-help books such as those published by Nolo Press* and legal software such as Quicken Lawyer. Unfortunately, too often persons in genuine need of legal advice or assistance fail to seek it, or delay consulting an attorney. The result may be a permanent loss of a valuable legal right. A decision about self-help should be made carefully.

Since the Internet has made legal information easily available, why consult an attor-ney? Finding the law is only one of many critical services that an attorney performs. Attorneys have legal insights that only years of study and experience can engender. In addition, attorneys are skilled orators and writers. They are expert problem solvers, nego-tiators, and advocates. Not every dispute or problem ought to be taken to an attorney. Indeed, elementary economics militates against such petty litigiousness. The potential impact of events on one's life should be considered when considering the need for an attorney's services.

Some general guidelines may help you decide whether to consult an attorney for a matter. Do consult an attorney if the matter can be characterized in any of the following ways:

1. The matter involves the risk of losing or the possibility of obtaining a sum of money that is significant to you.
2. The matter involves the risk of losing your freedom or suffering harm to your rep-utation.
3. The matter involves actual or possible physical or mental injury, suffered or threat-ened, that can be characterized as significant.
4. The matter seems very important for any other reason (e.g., a major impact on your life or that of a dependent, such as a child custody dispute).
5. The area of law is complex or you lack the time to carefully preserve or pursue your rights.

In recent years many critics have claimed that the United States has too many lawyers. The number of lawyers in our society allegedly has a negative effect on economic produc-tivity and has engendered dissatisfaction among citizens. Indeed, lawyers have the dubious distinction of inspiring an anti-fan club called HALT (Help Abolish Legal Tyranny), set off in part by dishonorable lawyer conduct. Such criticisms are difficult to evaluate because they measure productivity as a function of the number of lawyers in a country. This meas-ure is flawed because qualifications of legal practitioners vary significantly among coun-tries, making comparisons unreliable. Thus, studies purporting to measure productivity as a function of the number of lawyers are at best misleading.[28]

Given that lawyer bashing is a socially acceptable form of class denigration, why do people wish to become lawyers, and why do lawyers remain in their profession? The fol-lowing quotation from Harvey Rubenstein, President of the Delaware State Bar, offers one response.

http://

General information about legal rights and duties can be found at the Cornell legal information Web site
http://www.law.cornell.edu/statutes.html

http://

The home page for HALT says it is an "organization of Americans for legal reform." As this group has reservations about lawyers (a significant understatement), it is not surprising that the Web site provides good self-help information.
http://www.halt.org

---

* We frequently cite Nolo Press in this textbook. Nolo Press began publishing self-help legal resources in the late 1960s, and in our opinion have set the standard for accurate, easy-to-understand legal materials. As their publishing philosophy has been motivated by social goals, the materi-als they provide appear to be priced reasonably.

Why, then, do so many become and remain practicing lawyers? Maybe it is because lawyers really do take seriously their obligation to represent as best they can those who need help. Maybe it is because, once in a while, a lawyer is asked to plead a great cause that may affect the course of human events or make our society work a little better. Or maybe it is because, once in awhile, one lawyer may be the difference in one person's life. And to practicing lawyers, once in a while is enough.[29]

How Do You Find a "Good" Attorney?

http://

For selection tips and questions answered about hiring an attorney see

http://www.legalengine
.com/lawyerselectiontips
.htm

Time, energy, and resourcefulness spent finding an attorney will help create a satisfactory relationship and final result. Too often, the presence of a serious problem that prompts the search also prompts great haste in the selection process. A cavalier approach to the selection process increases the chance of retaining an attorney who may not perform as well as others who are equally qualified. An exhaustive search should not be necessary in order to avoid a "bad" attorney; to the contrary, in populous areas there are a number of qualified attorneys ready, willing, and able to perform the required service.

Paid Advertisements

In the not-so-distant past lawyers were prohibited by law and professional rules from advertising their services. Marketing legal services in this manner was considered not only unethical but also unbecoming. Many in the legal profession feared that advertising would lead to false and misleading claims. Promotional practices were thought to foster rather than resolve conflict. Many attorneys also believed that advertising tarnishes the general reputation of the profession.*

Rules of conduct regarding publicity and advertising were dramatically changed in the last quarter of the twentieth century. In 1977, the U.S. Supreme Court ruled that the public had a right to information as to the availability and cost of routine legal services, and attorneys had a right to furnish that information.[30] The Supreme Court has also held that lawyers cannot be prohibited from sending direct mail solicitations[31] and communications informing potential clients of their certification as specialists.[32]

The ABA Model Rules of Professional Conduct concerning advertising have been liberalized.[33] States have also re-formulated rules regarding advertising, although many issues are still debated. In the legal profession, claims made concerning an individual's competence or ability to achieve results is still considered unethical.

National law firms with outstanding reputations traditionally declined to advertise, but in recent years even they have begun to do so. Still, they avoid commercial television in favor of simple announcements, news releases, brochures, public television sponsorship, newsletters, and advertisements in magazines targeted to special audiences. Legal directories have been available for many years and have never been considered advertising. Bar associations, private organizations, and law firms maintain lists of attorneys, often with detailed information about each individual and areas of practice. These lists are easily accessed over the Internet. Most public libraries maintain directories of attorneys with biographical information, including practice specialties and lists of representative clients. Finally, group legal services relieve clients of the burden of finding a qualified attorney. In this sense, they serve a marketing function for member lawyers.

* "... [M]arketplace lawyer advertising, using all the sights, color, sounds, subliminal messages and not-so-hidden persuaders of commercial television, adversely affects not only the public's perception of those court officers, but also of the courts and the total judicial system." Justice Reynoldson, retired Chief Justice of the Iowa Supreme Court, "The Case Against Lawyer Advertising," *ABA Journal* 75 (January 1989), p. 60.

Word-of-Mouth Advertising

Generally, the most reliable advertising is word of mouth. However, an attorney's reputation is more than simply "good" or "bad." Better questions concerning the reputation of a particular attorney include the following:

- What is the attorney's specialty?
- How long has the attorney been in practice?
- Does the attorney have a reputation for being a problem solver? Thorough? Expensive? Aggressive? Sincere? Or any other quality thought to be appropriate or inappropriate for the case?
- Do judges and attorneys generally think highly of the individual or firm?
- Is the attorney active in the community?
- Has the attorney been disciplined by the bar or been a defendant in malpractice cases?
- Is the attorney in good health?
- Does the attorney have a reputation for consuming alcohol to excess or taking harmful drugs?
- Does the attorney usually win cases?
- Does the attorney make the fee arrangement clear?
- Does the attorney have a reputation for communicating with the client, returning phone calls promptly, keeping the client informed on case progress?
- Does the attorney work on the case personally or delegate the work to others?

The selection of an attorney should be accompanied by some introspection by the client. Clients should consider their own attitudes, goals, and objectives and, as dispassionately as possible, the nature of their claims. Some attorneys are problem solvers and others are "gladiators" (problem winners). A problem solver might complete the task in a short period of time, but the resolution may require considerable compromise on the part of the client. The gladiator might be victorious and provide more of what the client wanted (or less), but may take considerably more time and require a different emotional commitment by the client. (Fewer than 5 percent of all civil cases actually go to trial, so even gladiators typically compromise; they just do it later in the process.) The problem solver may preserve a friendly, mutually profitable relationship for the client with the other party. This is seldom possible with a gladiator who may have embarrassed, angered, or even humiliated the opposing party.

Most attorneys are listed somewhere on the Internet and in the Yellow Pages, sometimes with large ads. Such listings do not guarantee competence, however. A person with a legal problem should ask friends, family, and neighbors to recommend an attorney. Business managers, bankers, title company officers, educators, merchants, stockbrokers, insurance executives, real estate personnel and, of course, lawyers are likely to have direct communication with and know of attorneys by their reputation. Employers and government officials are also good sources.

Meeting with the Attorney

Once a prospective client gets the name of one or two attorneys as possible selections, an office appointment should be made with each by telephone. Many attorneys will consult with a prospective client for a modest fee or at no charge. It's prudent to ask how long the initial appointment will last and if there is a charge. A prospective client will have many questions about which laws apply to his or her case. Several laws may be relevant to the case, so the attorney will necessarily be noncommittal. This is to be expected, because no attorney is capable of explaining all the legal ramifications of a situation without careful research and preparation; nor is any attorney capable of predicting with certainty the outcome of any complex case.

No commitment to hire need be made at the first meeting; a simple "Thank you, I would like to consider the matter for a couple of days" permits a graceful departure. During the initial meeting, much can be learned by asking the attorney a few questions:

- Do you frequently handle cases like mine?
- Is this your specialty? If not, how many cases of this type have you handled?
- Will you be doing all the work or will other persons be involved?
- Will you refer my case to another attorney in the firm or handle it yourself?
- Will this case conflict with any of your other obligations, court calendars, or appointments?
- Is it best to settle this matter now, even at a loss, rather than to be embroiled in a lengthy legal battle?
- May I have a copy of your standard retainer agreement?
- Can you give me an estimate of my likely trial costs and fees for handling this matter to its conclusion?
- How will I be kept informed about the progress of the matter in your office?

Much can be learned about the prospective attorney by arriving for your meeting early and observing the law office in operation. Confusion and disorganization often suggest a lower quality of service. An office cluttered with files, papers, and books does not engender confidence. After you leave, will your file simply be part of the mess?

You should be aware that not all attorneys will appreciate being asked all of the questions listed above. Some will interpret your inquiries as an indication that you will be a "problem" or malcontent client. However, consumers of any service, including legal services, have the right to be informed and assured of the nature of the service they are to receive. If in the process of protecting your interests you are reasonable and courteous, a responsible attorney should not resent your questions. And if the two of you decide to do business together, you will be off to a good start, with mutual respect for each other.

Attorney Referral Services

Referral services are a means of indirect advertising. Bar associations in some communities administer attorney referral services. They are listed in telephone directories and on Web sites. The association maintains a list or panel of attorneys in various specialties. Referrals are made alphabetically or by type of case. No special qualifications are required to get on the list. Newer members of the bar, in particular, may join the panel, and possibly charge reduced rates for their services, to gain clients.

Some attorney referral services are operated by private businesses. These are quite similar to the bar panels. The service places advertisements seeking a particular kind of client; for example, a personal injury victim. Responses to the advertisement are then referred to panel members. Attorney members pay a registration fee to participate on the panel.

Public Defenders

public defender

A lawyer provided by the community for a person who is accused of a serious crime (felony) and cannot afford to hire counsel.

As noted earlier, a defendant accused of a serious crime (i.e., one for which the possible punishment is incarceration) has a constitutional right to be represented by a competent attorney at all stages of legal proceedings. If a defendant is indigent (unable to afford the services of a private attorney), the court will appoint an attorney, often called a **public defender,** to represent the accused without charge. Contrary to some popularly held views, attorneys in public defender roles generally are very competent and zealous advocates.

They are specialists. They handle a heavy caseload, develop vast experience in a short time, spend much time in court, and know the judges and court staff. Because they handle many criminal matters, they know the probable results of a plea negotiation or plea bargain. Records of numerous convictions reflect not incompetence on the part of the public defender but rather the fact that these lawyers are unable to choose their clients. Public defenders by inclination fight for the underdog, and they usually fight well. On the negative side, public defenders are often given too many cases to be able to devote the time and attention to any one case that a client accused of a crime might wish.

Solicitation

Most methods of solicitation, in which lawyers aggressively seek clients, are considered unethical. Public policy frowns on efforts to promote litigation, such as "ambulance chasing." There, an accident victim is coerced to sign a retainer agreement at a time of great vulnerability. More sophisticated forms of solicitation, through "cappers" or "runners" who frequent places such as hospitals and police stations in search of potential clients, are likewise unethical. Investigators, as well as nurses in emergency wards, have been used as cappers. They may receive an illegal referral fee from the attorney. Such payments are frequently made in cash in an attempt to prevent detection of the conspiracy and tax evasion. In most cases, direct solicitation by an attorney is unethical and should be reported to the local or state bar association.* Schemes involving cappers are illegal and should be reported to law enforcement and the appropriate bar association.

LEGAL FOCUS—CASE

Florida lawyer Shane Stafford arranged for Roy Blevins, a West Palm Beach police officer, to solicit personal injury cases for him. In an eighteen-month period, Blevins referred ten or eleven cases to Stafford, including three automobile accident cases he investigated as a police officer. Stafford gave 15 percent of his legal fees to Blevins, who received approximately $11,000 total. Is such a referral arrangement legal and ethical?

The Florida Bar v. Stafford, 542 So.2d 1321 (Florida, 1989).

This arrangement was neither legal nor ethical. The Florida Supreme Court held that "activities such as those pursued by Stafford are clearly prohibited. In recent years, perhaps no single aspect of the practice of law has received more public criticism than the unethical solicitation of clients." The court found that Stafford had violated several disciplinary rules, including asking persons to recommend him for employment, dividing legal fees with a non-lawyer, and engaging in conduct that adversely reflects on fitness to practice law. The court suspended him "from the practice of law for a period of six months and upon reinstatement to the Bar, [he] shall be placed on probation for a period of two years." Three of seven judges dissented, believing the ruling correct but the punishment too lenient: "I think in order to restore the public's faith in our system of discipline it is necessary that we rid our ranks of this type of lawyer."

* Although individual attorneys in all states are currently restricted from solicitation, the U.S. Supreme Court has ruled that the American Civil Liberties Union (ACLU) and similar organizations of attorneys may solicit directly [*In re* Primus, 436 U.S. 412, 98 S.Ct. 1893 (1978)]; that the National Association for the Advancement of Colored People (NAACP) may solicit parents of school children in desegregation cases [*NAACP v. Button*, 371 U.S. 415, 83 S.Ct 328 (1963)]; and that a union may solicit its members to funnel their injury claims to a particular attorney [*United Mine Workers v. Illinois*, 389 U.S. 217, 88 S.Ct. 353 (1967)].

How Do You Hire and Fire an Attorney?

The attorney-client relationship is determined by contract. The attorney promises to represent the client in exchange for a promise of compensation. The ABA Model Rules and many states require that contingent fee agreements be in writing and signed by the client.[34] Whether or not the law requires an agreement, the client should request a written agreement and ask that it be fully explained. An attorney has an ethical obligation to reject a frivolous case or a case raising issues where she or he lacks competence.*

The agreement will necessarily have limitations. It cannot guarantee any particular result or any particular completion date, and will usually not detail the step-by-step procedures the attorney will ultimately take. This lack of detail is not sinister, but instead realistic. Even the most common legal problem or case may entail many unpredictable complications. The client should carefully ask questions until all ramifications of the problem or case are at least generally understood.

Examples of questions a prospective client might ask include the following:

1. On what basis is the fee calculated? If hourly, is the "meter" running at the same rate while junior attorneys or paralegals are working on the case? How much library or computer research is anticipated, and at what cost? Will the fee statement be itemized as to hours spent and tasks accomplished? How often will I be billed?

   a. If the fee is contingent (client and attorney share in any recovery), are costs to be deducted from the award before or after computation of the attorney's share? If the matter is settled quickly (and so the attorney's involvement is less than was anticipated) is the fee division reduced commensurately?

   b. What happens if the lawyer's work increases greatly—for example, when a new trial is granted or an appeal must be initiated?

   c. If a flat fee is charged, how will costs be paid? What does the fee include? What happens if there is an appeal? There should be a careful delineation of the work to be performed.

2. Specifically, what important actions and events does the attorney predict, and when are they most likely to happen?

3. What are the possible outcomes of the action, good and bad? Is there any point of no return; that is, a point beyond which the client cannot practically withdraw from the matter?

4. Will there be a need to refer all or any part of the case to another attorney? If so, how will the fee and work be affected and divided?

5. What will be the means (telephone, e-mail, and letter) and frequency of communications with the attorney or secretary? Will copies of all documents and correspondence routinely be sent to the client?

A client generally has the right to dismiss an attorney at any time for any reason. Difficulty may arise with respect to how much of the fee, if any, has been earned at the time of the discharge. The rule is easy to state but difficult to apply: The attorney is entitled to be paid the reasonable value of work done before discharge. In a contingent-fee case, the attorney is entitled to be paid the agreed amount or proportionate share only if and when a recovery is obtained.

If the client is unable to pay all fees the attorney has earned up to the time of discharge, a serious conflict may arise. The attorney demands payment while the client

---

* Filing of frivolous and defamatory litigation justifies disciplinary action. The attorney is also vulnerable to a civil lawsuit for malicious prosecution, although such actions are seldom successful. See previous discussion concerning frivolous lawsuits.

demands return of all documents (the file) connected with the case. The attorney pressures the client for payment of accrued fees by refusing to release the file. In the absence of a statute giving the attorney the right to do so (called a *statutory* or *common-law retaining lien*), such conduct is illegal and probably unethical. However, many states do authorize such a lien.

A client may have difficulty hiring a new attorney for the case if one or more attorneys have been fired or have withdrawn. An attorney considering whether to accept such a case is usually suspicious of its merits and the client's emotional stability.* Care in selection of the best attorney at the beginning of the case is important for these reasons.

As a general rule, an attorney can terminate the employment relationship if there is a reasonable basis for the withdrawal. For example, the client's failure to pay the agreed fee is grounds for withdrawal. However, an attorney must (1) give reasonable notice to the client of intention to withdraw; (2) obtain court permission to withdraw if pleadings have been filed; (3) return the client's papers; and (4) refund any unearned fees. An attorney *must* withdraw from the employment when continued representation would require the attorney to violate a disciplinary rule. Other good reasons for withdrawal include failure of the attorney's health, materially affecting his or her ability to continue, or an awareness that a conflict of interest exists.

ATTORNEY FEE ARRANGEMENTS

Fees are earned based on an hourly rate (e.g., $175 per hour), a flat fee for a service (e.g., $5,000 payable in two installments), a contingency fee (e.g., 35 percent of net recovery), or a combination of these methods. Tradition, business practice, and law tie certain types of fee arrangements to certain types of legal matters. For example, the contingency fee is common in personal injury actions but is considered an unethical method of billing in a family law matter.

A **retainer fee** is an advance payment for legal services on a flat or continuing basis. A lawyer may require advance payment on any fee, and is obliged to return the unearned portion.[35] A common form of retainer is a monthly or yearly fee paid in exchange for the lawyer's promise to remain available to the client for consultation. Such agreement should be in writing and clearly define the services it covers, the term it covers, and the hourly rate at which additional services will be billed. Group legal service plans may be understood as a type of retainer. If the client seeks legal advice through the plan, minor, specified legal services will be rendered without charge. If requested services are complicated or time-consuming (such as conduct of a trial), additional charges are billed as "earned" fees. At universities and colleges it is common for the student government association to enter a retainer contract with an attorney to be available for a certain number of hours a week to assist students with minor legal problems.

Many attorneys simply will not take a case without a retainer. They are reluctant to sue a client to collect a fee because they believe doing so will create bad publicity. So they require payment up front.

Some attorneys include arbitration clauses in their fee agreements. This allows them to go after clients for unpaid fees without the negative publicity associated with a public trial. This is so because arbitration proceedings are private and arbitration awards are confidential. (See discussion of arbitration later in this chapter.)

retainer fee

(a) A sum of money paid to an attorney for a promise to remain available to the client for consultation when needed and requested. (b) Fees paid in advance that are held in a trust account to be drawn down (taken) by the attorney as work progresses.

---

* Shortly after beginning practice, new attorneys may be approached by a potential client who, with thick and tattered files, spins a tale of conspiracy, malevolence, and grievous harm. Believing they have found the case that will make their reputation, the young lawyers begin an investigation. Within a short time they find out every attorney in town is already very familiar with their client.

LEGAL FOCUS—PROBLEM

Elaine Taylor's husband Buck, a young doctor, was killed in the crash of a commercial "commuter" airplane. Buck was not in the airplane; he was in his medical office in San Luis Obispo, which was destroyed by the crash. Attorney Ian Page offered to represent Taylor on a contingent fee basis for one-third of any net recovery. Page indicated no fees would be charged "unless and until" a recovery was made. Should Taylor hire Page?

It depends. Charging contingency fees in matters where liability is clear and some recovery expected is not an ethical violation *per se*.[36] The real issue is whether the fee is reasonable and the client has been fully informed of the availability of alternative billing arrangements. In most calamitous events, there is no issue of "if" as to liability. Recovery is assured because defendants in such cases are held strictly liable. Only the amount is arguable. Obtaining a settlement will require negotiations, but one-third of, for example, a $3 million settlement is excessive for the perhaps 100 hours necessary to represent Taylor. Competent attorneys would undoubtedly take her case for $250.00 per hour with payment deferred. It could be argued that contingent fees in calamitous personal injury or death cases where liability is certain (or even probable) are unethical because clients don't fully understand the arrangement or its alternatives and the fees are excessive. It is not uncommon for personal injury attorneys to refer to such cases as "jackpots" or "retirement" cases.

A growing number of states impose maximums on the percentage that may be charged in contingency fee contracts. In New Jersey, a maximum graduated scale is used in tort cases: An attorney "shall not contract for, charge, or collect a contingent fee in excess of the following limits: 33-1/3 percent on the first $500,000 recovered; 30 percent on the next $500,000 recovered; 25 percent on the next $500,000 recovered; 20 percent on the next $500,000 recovered."[37] In California, a special limitation exists for medical malpractice cases: 40 percent of the first $50,000 recovered; 33-1/3 percent of the next $50,000 recovered; 25 percent of the next $500,000 recovered; and 15 percent of any amount on which the recovery exceeds $600,000.[38] Similar statutory limitations exist in matters processed by administrative agencies rather than by courts (e.g., veterans' benefits, social security claims, and workers' compensation cases).

The flat fee is common for certain types of routine matters such as family law, criminal law matters, real estate title searches, trusts, and wills. Business clients request competitive bidding by two or more firms, or a flat fee for matters that in the past were billed by the hour.[39] However, the hourly fee is still the dominant form of attorney billing and is used for all types of legal services.

Attorney fee agreements should describe how the fee will be calculated (hourly, flat rate, etc.) and when feasible, specify the total amount of the fee. Attorneys are free to negotiate fee arrangements with clients, so long as they are reasonable. In some instances, attorney fees are limited by statute or by the courts. Furthermore, when fee disputes arise, courts tend to give the benefit of any doubt to the client because of the usual bargaining superiority of the attorney.[40] In some states, the law presumes overreaching by the attorney if representation is begun before the fee is negotiated and the client signs a written fee agreement.[41] In such instances, the attorney is hard pressed to justify and collect more than a minimal reasonable fee.

Although attorneys are free to charge their "going rate," the client's case must not be deliberately delayed for the purpose of coercing payment of a delinquent installment,[42] nor may an attorney charge an unconscionable or clearly excessive legal fee. The attorney is subject to discipline for making such an attempt.[43]

Actual fees charged for legal services are difficult to compare because of the many factors used in setting fees in specific cases. Different fee rates exist in different parts of the country. Hourly fees are higher in large cities than in rural areas. Fees change over time and are at least somewhat related to the general economy. A flat fee for a simple divorce, with no significant property or child custody dispute, may range from $400 to $1,000; complex divorces for wealthy clients, on the other hand, may command fees in the tens of thousands of dollars. Contingency fees are rarely less than 25 percent of the net recovery or more than 50 percent. Astronomical fees in celebrated cases involving **class actions,*** national corporations, or prominent persons and politicians shed little light on fees charged for the routine legal problems of the ordinary consumer. It is, on the other hand, no doubt true that overhead costs prevent large firms from profitably handling legal matters in which small sums (less than $25,000–$50,000) are in dispute.

The following are important factors that normally are taken into consideration in setting an attorney's fee:

- The time required
- The degree of legal skill needed and novelty of the legal question presented
- The customary fee charged in the locality for similar services
- The experience, reputation, and ability of the attorney
- The amount of money involved in the case
- The result obtained for the client
- Whether or not the case precluded the lawyer from accepting other legal work
- The nature and length of the attorney's relationship with the client
- Time constraints imposed by the client
- Whether the fee is fixed or contingent

The client should understand the possible conflicts inherent in various fee arrangements. With a contingency fee arrangement, depending on how it is structured, either the attorney or the client "wants" a quick settlement while the other would be better off by proceeding through trial. In a flat-fee arrangement, the lawyer may have an incentive to dispose of the case as quickly as possible. An attorney paid by the hour might be tempted to overwork the case (i.e., with exhaustive research and discovery).

In addition, a fee charged by an attorney may be set by, or subject to the approval of, the court. An example of this would be fees of attorneys appointed to represent indigents or minors. When a fee limitation is applicable (by statute or court order), the client should ask whether the fee is prescribed or is a maximum allowed by law. In many cases, the statutory fee is a maximum and the client is free to negotiate payment of a lower fee (e.g., a probate fee).

Many countries, including Great Britain, provide that attorney fees (as well as court costs) are to be paid by the loser in a case.† In contrast, in the United States each party is usually responsible for his or her attorney fees, unless they agreed otherwise.** (The loser always pays the court costs.) The seemingly simple legal rule has very important ramifications.

class actions

When all members of a group of persons who have suffered the same or similar injury join together in a single lawsuit against the alleged wrongdoer. The group must be so numerous that it is impracticable to bring all members before the court individually.

---

*   A class action is a lawsuit brought by a plaintiff for himself or herself and all others who are similarly situated. The plaintiff represents the interests of a group which is otherwise too unwieldy for courts to handle on an individual, case-by-case basis.

† Like most things, what appears simple at first blush is not quite so. In England, the general rule is that the loser is responsible for reasonable attorney fees (and costs) of the prevailing party. However, many low-income persons in England are eligible for a government-funded legal aid program. Such persons are not subject to the cost-shifting rule.

** For example, a landlord suing a renter for past-due rent might benefit from a lease providing that the renter is to reimburse the landlord for any attorney fees incurred in collecting rent or enforcing the lease (this clause is commonly found in rental agreements). Many state statutes provide that if such a provision exists in the contract it will be construed to give the victor in the legal dispute, be it the landlord or the tenant, the right to reimbursement of legal fees. Even if a contract states that it only protects the landlord, the tenant will be awarded attorney fees if he or she wins the lawsuit. The statute trumps the contract provisions.

http://

The fee arbitration program
provided by the Georgia Bar
can be found at
**http://www.gabar.org/
feearb.asp?**

A person who is unable to settle a fee dispute with an attorney through direct negotiation should contact the local bar association. Many local bar associations sponsor attorney fee arbitration programs. Often a mutually satisfactory result can be achieved without further legal action. In California, for example, arbitration is voluntary for the client, and mandatory for the attorney if commenced by the client.[44]

LEGAL FOCUS—PROBLEM

John Tyson, owner of a Burger King franchise, wanted to fire Jason Yohn. He suspected Yohn of repeatedly failing to wash his hands after using the bathroom. A posted policy required all employees to wash their hands after using the bathroom. Tyson hired attorney Lisa Beck to advise him. Beck explained that the law had to be researched and that a written opinion would be prepared. Completely convinced of Beck's self-proclaimed expertise, Tyson left her office. Unbeknownst to Tyson, Beck assigned the Tyson file to a summer law student intern. The intern did all the research and prepared an opinion as to whether Tyson could fire Jason based upon the firm's database of hundreds of letters to previous clients on the subject of when employees may be fired. Beck glanced at the report and asked her secretary to send it to Tyson under her signature with a bill showing seven hours at $250 per hour for a total of $1,750. Beck's law firm paid its summer interns $20 per hour. Has Beck violated any ethical rules?

Tyson would have no basis to suspect that anything was out of the ordinary. Oftentimes, the lawyer with whom a client meets does not perform all the legal services for the client. As far as the billing is concerned, attorneys are free to charge whatever they choose for their services and do not routinely disclose the names of persons to whom the work is delegated. The point is that you should enter into a legal service agreement like any other service agreement, understanding your rights and being vigilant in protecting your interests.

FINANCING ATTORNEY FEES

In some instances, a client may need to borrow money to pay attorney fees. A loan may be procured from a lending institution, a third person (e.g., a relative), or the attorney. If the attorney finances the debt, the client must sign a promissory note. This arrangement may create a conflict of interest, because the attorney becomes both a creditor and agent of the client. An attorney may not use unreasonable collection methods; such conduct is unethical. Some attorneys refuse to extend credit to clients for same reason that attorneys take cases only on retainer. They do not want to sue their client.

FINANCING THE CLIENT'S CASE

As a legal case progresses, costs often are incurred long before any recovery is possible. The following are costs in a typical personal injury case:
1. *Medical examination.* The physical and sometimes mental condition of the victim is an issue in an injury case. Before trial, a physician will probably make one or more medical examinations. This procedure is distinguished from medical treatment. Some

physicians specialize in examination of injury victims (and later provide testimony in court) rather than the treatment of patients, again for a fee.

2. *Court costs.* The court charges fees (e.g., $100) to cover at least some of the administrative costs of processing the paperwork connected with litigation. Other court charges are made for such diverse items as daily fees paid to each juror in a jury trial (e.g., $20) and fees of expert witnesses.

3. *Investigation.* Most attorneys do not have the time, skill, or inclination to personally inspect the accident scene, photograph it, and talk to potential witnesses. These and similar tasks might be performed by a hired professional investigator for a fee.

4. *Discovery.* Sworn testimony is taken before a court reporter, usually in the office of the attorney who made the request. The session may be audiotaped or videotaped. Discovery is usually very expensive, involving transcription costs as well as attorney fees.

5. *Expert witness fees.* Court testimony from experts is often necessary. Experts, as distinguished from lay witnesses, are entitled to give a formal opinion about a matter within their expertise. Lay witnesses are allowed to testify only as to what they saw, heard, or otherwise experienced. In an automobile accident case, for example, one or more physicians might testify as to the nature and extent of the victim's injury. An economist might testify as to the lost wages of the victim because of the injuries. A model maker may present a replica of the intersection involved, complete with model cars and signal lights. A computer expert may devise a computer simulation of many facets of an accident. Expert witnesses are well paid for their time.

These expenses can total many thousands of dollars. Most of these expenses are incurred whether or not—and certainly long before—any recovery is awarded and received.

Under the ABA Model Rules of Professional Conduct, an attorney is permitted to "advance" litigation costs even though she or he is arguably invested in the outcome of the client's case. The attorney might be tempted to suggest an early settlement not because it is in the client's best interest, but rather to recapture costs advanced as well as to participate in the recovery.[45] In the past, American Bar Association rules permitted this practice only if the client was ultimately responsible for reimbursing the attorney. The reimbursement requirement was believed to militate against possible conflict of interest between the attorney and the client. The requirement that the client remain ultimately liable for such expenses has been eliminated.[46] The attorney's duty to require reimbursement raises interesting ethical questions. Strictly speaking, payment of court costs for the client is **maintenance,** which is maintaining, supporting, or promoting the litigation of another. Maintenance is considered unethical and illegal because it encourages litigation.

Assuming the fee is contingent and the lawsuit is successful, litigation costs may be shared by the plaintiff and plaintiff's attorney. For example:

maintenance

Assisting a party to a lawsuit with money or otherwise, to prosecute or defend the lawsuit.

Gross recovery (in damages or settlement)		$100,000
Less net litigation costs incurred by plaintiff's lawyer		
Total out-of-pocket litigation costs incurred (e.g., filing fees, investigation costs)	$(17,250)	
Portion of court costs recovered from unsuccessful litigant (e.g., jury fees reimbursed by defendant)	2,750	(14,500)
Net recovery		$85,500
Less attorney's fee (35 percent of net recovery)		(29,925)
Client recovery after deduction of all expenses		$55,575

Litigation costs may be modest in some types of cases, such as a simple divorce, while litigation costs in antitrust cases may be hundreds of thousands or even millions of dollars in celebrated cases involving major corporations.

LEGAL FOCUS—PROBLEM

Charles Hall brought a lawsuit against several defendants, alleging patent infringement regarding his waterbed innovations. To finance the lawsuit, he syndicated interests in the possible outcome of the suits. He raised $750,000.[47] May he finance his lawsuit in this fashion?

champerty

An illegal agreement with a party to a suit for a portion of any recovery in exchange for paying the litigant's lawsuit expenses.

No. The doctrine of **champerty** forbids one from financially participating in the lawsuit of another. Champerty is defined as "... a bargain by [another] with a plaintiff or defendant for a portion of the matter involved in a suit in case of successful termination of the action, which the [other] undertakes to maintain or carry on at his own expense."[48] Society's concern is that investment in cases by outsiders encourages gambling and litigation.

Ⓦ HAT IS LEGAL MALPRACTICE?

legal malpractice

Violation of a duty of due care by a professional person.

Legal malpractice is a civil cause of action that may be brought by a client against an attorney for negligence or intentional wrongdoing. Negligence arises, in this context, out of attorney carelessness or professional misconduct. A wrongful act is not sufficient to prove malpractice. The client must have suffered a loss as a consequence of the bad act. The remedy for negligence is money damages. The tort of negligence is discussed in detail in Chapter 7. In all states, attorneys have a legal duty of care to the client. The standard of care has been described in various ways, but generally an attorney is required to possess legal knowledge and skill and exercise due care and diligence. Attorney specialists are held to higher standards than other attorneys. If the attorney fails to meet the standard of care and this failure has caused the client to suffer a loss, legal malpractice has occurred.

To recover damages for attorney malpractice, the client will probably hire a second attorney to pursue the case against the first. This is undoubtedly an unpleasant prospect for a client who has already suffered a loss. A malpractice suit must be initiated within the applicable statute of limitations. This is usually within one to three years from the time of the negligent act(s).

At trial, the plaintiff must prove that, but for the attorney's negligence, the result in the earlier matter would have been more favorable to the client. The accused may deny the charge or contend, "Yes, I may have been negligent, but the result was fair, adequate, and reasonable." Legal malpractice cases are difficult to prove. Even if the client wins the case, he or she still faces the problem of collecting the judgment. Attorneys who commit serious malpractice may also be the least able to pay a sizable judgment and the least likely to have purchased adequate malpractice insurance. In many states, lawyers are not required to carry malpractice insurance, although many do. When selecting an attorney, it is reasonable and prudent to ask whether the attorney carries malpractice insurance.

It is important to distinguish between legal malpractice and disciplinary actions against an attorney. Legal malpractice actions are brought in civil court by the client seeking compensation for loss caused by the attorney's failure to exercise due care. Professional misconduct actions are brought by the state disciplinary authority, usually the state bar, seeking punishment of the attorney for ethical rules violations. The client does not normally receive any compensation as a consequence of a disciplinary action. An ethical rules violation is relevant to show failure to meet the standard of care, but it is not conclusive.

LEGAL FOCUS—PROBLEM

Mike Kline could not decide whether to consult an attorney about the neck injury he suffered when Dora Carson's car sideswiped him while he was skateboarding in a crosswalk. He had medical insurance and he expected his pain would soon stop. However, after nine months of continued distress and intermittent suffering, he consulted attorney Jules Doeshire about a suit for damages. Doeshire assured him he had a good case and prepared a contingency fee retainer agreement, which Kline signed. Several months later (thirteen months after the accident), attorney Doeshire contacted Kline and said that after further study he concluded that Kline really did not have a good case after all. "But not to worry; I won't charge you a cent," Doeshire told Kline. What should Kline do?

Mike Kline should be very suspicious and request a complete explanation of why the matter should be dropped. Kline should consult another attorney as it appears that Doeshire committed malpractice by failing to file the complaint within the statute of limitations. Once an attorney accepts a case, it is his or her obligation to comply with procedural requirements. Failure to file documents within statutory time limits is one of the most common acts of malpractice.*

An attorney is not guilty of malpractice just because a case is lost. In every case with two or more adversaries, someone must lose and someone must win. A strategic decision that subsequently turns out to be disastrous is not necessarily malpractice. The attorneys representing Texaco in the *Pennzoil Co. v. Texaco, Inc.* case were considered to be among the most able attorneys in Texas, yet Texaco lost the case at trial and suffered damages of $10.53 billion[49] (see Chapter 11).

Attorney malpractice encompasses a wide variety of negligent acts and omissions: failure to apply settled principles of law to the case, failure to protect the right to appeal, failure to draft pleadings (court-related documents) properly and promptly, failure to appear and defend, failure to assert all possible claims or defenses, failure to act in accordance with professional ethical standards, failure to present relevant evidence, lack of diligence in prosecuting a case once initiated, and mis-drafting a will. An ounce of prevention in the careful selection of an attorney is worth a pound of cure. In fairness, the following vignette is about one of the many lawyers providing public service for free. He also happens to be a lawyer professor aided by his classroom students.

LEGAL FOCUS—BACKGROUND

When an elderly couple faced eviction for amassing large amounts of clutter, Northridge professor Bruce Zucker and 10 students agreed to clean and organize the couple's longtime rent-controlled apartment to keep the pair from losing their home. And when the landlord later reneged on the agreement, Zucker took the case to trial—and the couple, who were living on a fixed income, won the right to stay put. That was just one of several recent cases in which Zucker—a full-time professor or real estate law and finance at California State University, Northridge—stepped in to assist low-income individuals in the midst of a crisis.[50]

* The American Bar Association claims that 11 percent of malpractice complaints involve failing to "calendar," or missing deadlines. W. Gates, *Charting the Shoals of Malpractice, ABA Journal 73* (July 1987), p. 82.

Ⓤ NAUTHORIZED PRACTICE OF LAW

Practicing law without a license is a crime, just as practicing medicine or dentistry without a license is a crime. Contracts for legal services by a non-attorney are void as matter of law and are unenforceable. A non-lawyer may not use the courts to collect a fee for legal services. Any payment made by the client is recoverable.

As discussed earlier in the chapter, licensure is a prerequisite to practice in all states. A person who does not have, or who fails to maintain, a license to practice law is forbidden to practice. It is sometimes difficult to decide whether a given act constitutes the practice of law or simply the performance of related activities. Different states provide different answers. For example, in some states it is common for title companies to conduct title searches when real property is sold (albeit with the aid of in-house staff attorneys). In other states, independent attorneys perform this activity. Non-lawyers (such as real estate brokers) are generally permitted to complete blanks on forms that may affect legal rights. However, these must be standard forms, and no legal advice may be offered with the forms. Accountants prepare tax returns and suggest probable tax consequences but must be careful not to interpret tax statutes, rules, or cases or render tax planning legal advice.

Today there is popular support for relaxing the historical prohibition against the unauthorized practice of law. Legal assistants, paralegals, and legal technicians should be permitted to handle routine legal matters. Legal assistants under the direction of lawyers already often perform such work. Lawyer supervision adds to the cost of such services, causing some consumers and non-lawyer providers to question whether the public is being protected or exploited. Routine matters usually include uncontested divorce pleadings, simple wills, eviction notices, simple bankruptcy filings, and probate of small estates. Exhibit 4-2 identifies the "practice of law" and other related legal work done by legal assistants under supervision of lawyers.

Exhibit 4-2: **Legal Work Permissible for Non-Lawyers under Supervision of Lawyers**

Practice of Law	Work That May Be Done by Non-Lawyers*
Accepting a case	Obtaining facts from client
Setting a fee	Communicating information to client
Evaluating the case and charting its course	Interviewing witnesses
Performing legal analysis	Performing limited legal research to assist lawyer with legal analysis
Giving legal advice	Obtaining documents (e.g., police reports, medical records, employment records, deeds, plans, probate records, weather records)
Participating in the formal judicial process (e.g., depositions, hearings, trials)	Obtaining photographs
Supervising legal assistants	Preparing summaries
	Preparing chronologies
	Preparing itemization of claims
	Preparing drafts of pleadings
	Preparing drafts of interrogatories and production requests
	Preparing drafts of responses to discovery requests
	Preparing outlines for lawyer to use in deposing witnesses
	Indexing deposition transcripts and preparing summaries of the evidence
	Preparing exhibit lists

* But performed under the supervision of a lawyer.

Source: Adapted from American Bar Association, Section of Law Practice Management, "Leveraging with Legal Assistants" (Chicago: ABA, 1993), 20.

Some critics contend that routine legal services can be delivered to the consumer at lower cost, with higher pay for the legal service technician, by eliminating a superfluous middle person—the attorney. There is, however, strong opposition to the relaxation of unauthorized-practice laws. The concern is that the dividing line between what is and what is not the practice of law will become even more confused and risky for consumers. Many do not know or appreciate the difference in the educational backgrounds of legal assistants and attorneys. Others disregard the difference and hire non-attorneys because their fees are lower. These choices can and often do compromise the consumer's ability to succeed at law. Furthermore, it is difficult if not impossible to predetermine what is simple and routine.*

Do-it-yourself probate kits (designed to assist the personal representative, executor, or administrator with necessary procedures following death) and divorce kits are not considered to be the practice of law because the information is generalized and not tailored to the needs of a particular client.[51] In recent years, many self-help books and software in a variety of legal areas have been made available.

ALTERNATIVE DISPUTE RESOLUTION

Discourage litigation. Persuade your neighbors to compromise whenever you can. Point out to them how the nominal winner is often a real loser—in fees, expenses, and waste of time. As a peacemaker the lawyer has a superior opportunity of being a good man.
Abraham Lincoln (1809–1865), U.S. president

These words of Abraham Lincoln remain true in America as the twenty-first century unfolds. They suggest that persons who are considering litigation should think twice and consider alternatives to litigation such as negotiation, mediation, and arbitration whenever possible. **Alternative dispute resolution (ADR)** is a broad term used to describe methods of resolving disputes through means other than the traditional judicial process. Today, it is prudent to include an ADR clause in all contracts, giving parties the option to use alternative dispute resolution. Or, when a dispute arises, one party may suggest an alternative to the courts to which the other party may be only too happy to agree. When clients seek the advice of counsel in a civil matter, attorneys have an obligation to inform them about the availability and appropriateness of ADR. Failure to do so may be a violation of ethical rules or the basis for attorney malpractice.

alternative dispute resolution (ADR)

Various methods of resolving disputes through means other than the judicial process.

As stated earlier, courts are available to resolve all manner of disputes, be they complicated or simple. Our courts seek to protect the fundamental liberties of free speech, press, assembly, and religion, and they are available to decide such trivia as who gets to keep the dog in a dissolution of marriage. The traditional justice system requires parties to delegate resolution authority to a judge or jury who considers the issue of law. Typically one side wins, the other loses. Often neither side is truly satisfied.[52]

Litigation is complicated and burdensome. It is costly in terms of time, money, goodwill, peace of mind, and lost productivity. Small claims courts provide relief from complicated and costly legal procedures, but only in matters involving small sums of money. There are times when it is not feasible or desirable to seek justice through the courts. Sometimes, the law fails to recognize rights or wrongs. (Recall from Chapter 1 the killing of Kitty Genovese.) These are times to consider ADR.

---

* Every attorney has been told by a client, "I just want a simple will," only to discover that either the client's circumstances or more detailed desires make that impossible.

In the latter years of the twentieth century significant developments in ADR occurred in response to lengthy court delays. Efficiency-conscious business managers have been active in the search for effective dispute resolution methods for just this reason. Businesses can suffer financial losses from delays.

One of the primary causes of court delay has been increased court filings coupled with a shortage of judges and other court personnel. Population growth, too much crime, too many persons wanting to sue, too many laws, and complex government regulations have contributed to increases in filings. Budget deficits have made it difficult to hire more judges. Criminal cases have grown faster than civil cases. Since criminal matters take priority over civil matters, judges who otherwise would be available to hear civil cases are hearing criminal cases. The increased volume of filings has greatly extended the time necessary to resolve civil disputes, especially in major metropolitan areas. The courts and legislatures have acted in response to the enormous economic, social, and emotional costs that delay imposes. A myriad of statutes and court rules at the state and federal level expressly encourage or require the use of alternative dispute resolution. Fast-track programs designed to streamline the litigation process and bring cases to trial quickly have been implemented in many court systems. They have not completely relieved the problem, however.

Although delay has provided the motivation for government to encourage the use of ADR, many believe that a common sense approach to resolving disputes suggests its use as well. Not all disputes are best resolved using litigation, which raises the important question of which methods are best for what disputes. A common saying among ADR proponents is, "The forum should fit the fuss."

LEGAL FOCUS—PROBLEM

Tanda Lee not only liked rap music, she liked it loud and late. Occupying her first house, she really appreciated freedom from repeated parental insistence that she "turn that thing down." Evan and Juanita Jenkins lived next door in the house they had lived in for forty years. After one week of 3 A.M. concerts, Evan Jenkins was unable to hide his anger. Dressed in his robe, he stormed over to Lee's house and shouted, "Turn the blessed thing off!" Lee was annoyed and shouted back, "I didn't move to get new parents. Anyway, it's a free country!" Then she turned the volume even higher. How do the Jenkinses get some sleep?

The Jenkinses have a number of legal options. They can phone the police, who will ask Lee to show more consideration for her neighbors. Lee is probably disturbing the peace, and the Jenkinses could file a criminal complaint against her. They can also seek civil redress by suing Lee, claiming nuisance, a tort. In such an action, the Jenkinses can claim money damages for past harm and request an injunction (equitable relief) prohibiting the loud music as a continuing nuisance.

The practical problem with all of these remedies is that they are costly in time, money, and tranquility. The Jenkinses could go to small claims court, where the cost of litigation is minimal, but it still will be time-consuming and a drain on their peace of mind. Moreover, courtroom resolution ignores the fact that the parties will still live next door to each other after legal actions conclude. The root of many problems referred to the courts is a defective human relationship, and such a relationship may continue and worsen after judicial intervention. The adversarial nature of a trial usually aggravates and exaggerates existing hard feelings. Neighboring parties thus often find new reasons to argue and land in court again.

Likewise, court resolution of business-related disputes may not be in the best interest of the contesting parties. Examples include consumer product disputes that affect company public relations and product reception, disputes over medical care in health maintenance organizations (HMOs), and environmental disputes that will affect community–government relations for years. With increasing frequency, business and government agencies are using ADR techniques in such cases instead of and in addition to the courts. Not only are such techniques usually easier and cheaper to use than the courts, they are more likely to lead to improved long-term understandings and harmony.

The most common types of ADR are

- Negotiation
- Mediation
- Arbitration
- Med-arb
- Private judging
- Ombudsperson
- Expert fact finding
- Early neutral evaluation
- Mini-trial
- Summary jury trial
- Partnering

Exhibit 4-3 compares the three most common types of ADR with a lawsuit.

NEGOTIATION

Negotiation is defined as two-way communication for the purpose of persuasion. It is a bargaining process in which parties plan the future, structure a transaction, or fix a

negotiation

Communication between disputing parties for the purposes of persuasion and settlement or resolution.

EXHIBIT 4-3: **Comparison of Alternative Dispute Resolution Methods with a Lawsuit**

Characteristic	Negotiation	Mediation	Arbitration	Court Trial
Private or public process?	Private	Private	Private	Public
Who decides?	Parties	Parties	Arbitrator	Judge or jury
Adversary or cooperative?	Cooperative	Cooperative	Adversary	Adversary
Elapsed time to conclusion?	As long or short as it takes	As long or short as it takes	Usually 2 to 18 months	Usually 1 to 5 years (plus appeal, if any)
Cost of process?	Low	Low	Medium to high	High
Appeal?	Unnecessary	Unnecessary	Few grounds	Full right of appeal
Procedural rules?	Decided by parties	Decided by parties	Few and simple	Complex
Need attorney?	No	No	Yes	Yes
Discovery process?	No	No	Minimal allowed	Extensive allowed
Right to jury?	Unnecessary	Unnecessary	No	Yes, in most cases
Permanent record in files?	No	No	No	Yes

problem. It is voluntary and informal. Parties communicate directly with each other or through representatives and agents. All manner of agreements and disagreements are negotiated. It is a common, everyday occurrence. Lawyers constantly negotiate on behalf of clients. Typically, by the time a dispute is referred to a lawyer, negotiation is thought to have failed. Negotiation that continues after a lawsuit is filed is then considered part of litigation strategy. There, negotiations are premised on adversarial objectives and tactics. As an ADR process, negotiation is based on a collaborative or problem-solving viewpoint. When parties approach negotiations from a collaborative perspective, the process is more pleasant, the agreement more satisfying, and the commitment to the agreement more solid.

Although we all negotiate, most people can substantially improve their negotiation skills by observing a few rules. In recent years, several books (perhaps the most significant is Fisher, Ury, and Patton's *Getting to Yes*[53]) have stressed the importance and art of negotiation. Since the point of negotiation is to persuade, careful consideration of how best to present your views and seek acceptable results is important. Thus, effective negotiation requires preparation.

Negotiation, like most skills, can be improved. Indeed, it can be continually improved. Skilled athletes do not stop trying to improve when they reach a certain level; in the same manner, one can always refine one's negotiating skills. Many effective negotiation techniques can be learned, including using supportable arguments, avoiding personalizing the dispute, giving as well as taking, and attempting to establish a relationship with the other party. The skills can be utilized in legal disputes or everyday matters. Using even a few such techniques can improve most people's success rates.

There is utility in characterizing negotiation as a form of ADR. It legitimizes informal problem solving in the eyes of clients and lawyers. It may encourage the lawyer to negotiate earlier in the dispute, perhaps even prior to filing. By doing so, the possibility of success is enhanced.

In contentious situations, parties often begin by demanding recognition of rights and a remedy of grievances by the other side. The response is generally a counter demanding similar recognition. At this point, neither party is really negotiating with the other. Neither is attempting to persuade; instead, they are talking at, not with, each other, though attempts at persuasion may follow.

In our hypothetical problem, Evan Jenkins did not try to persuade Tanda Lee to turn down the volume of her music; he issued an ultimatum. Negotiation might have been more successful. If Jenkins tried negotiating, with or without the assistance of a neutral party, and failed, he could still complain to the authorities (criminal action) and bring suit (civil action). Only if Jenkins and Lee agreed to arbitrate the claim would Jenkins irrevocably substitute ADR for the traditional trial process. In other words, Jenkins, like most persons with legal problems, would have had very little, if anything, to lose by attempting to negotiate a resolution to the dispute.

MEDIATION

mediation

The use of a neutral third party to assist parties in voluntarily resolving their dispute(s).

Mediation is a facilitative process in which contending parties negotiate their own resolution to a problem with the assistance of a third-party neutral. The process and the resolution are confidential unless the parties agree otherwise. To encourage settlement, statements made in the course of mediation are inadmissible in a subsequent adjudicative proceeding. The neutral may be an individual (mediator) or a panel of two or three members (panel). The defining feature of the mediation process is that the parties themselves determine how to structure their interactions (procedural matters) and decide the outcome (settlement).

Mediation works best when the parties participate voluntarily and in good faith. (There is precedent for mandatory mediation, but most agree that the process is less satisfying and compliance with settlements more elusive.) The mediator convenes a meeting of the parties and helps them get started. When negotiations break down, the mediator encourages the parties to keep at it. Unlike judges, who are assigned to cases at random, mediators are carefully selected by mutual agreement of the parties. Mediators are chosen for their skill in facilitating conflict analysis, bargaining, and consensus building. A mediator is not necessarily trained as a judge or even as a lawyer. In commercial cases it is not uncommon to find architects, engineers, and general contractors serving as mediators. In family law cases, the mediator may have training as a social worker or psychologist. The individual must be a good listener and an effective communicator. The parties' perception of the individual's integrity, fairness, and subject-matter expertise is critical. Significantly, the mediator has no power to impose a resolution to a dispute. This feature distinguishes mediation from trials and arbitrations. In practice, different mediators apply varying amounts of pressure to get parties to settle.

Sometimes, mediation is confused with conciliation. **Conciliation** is an ADR process, similar to mediation, in which the neutral actively attempts to get acceptance of proposals for settlement. In both conciliation and mediation, the third party attempts to lower tensions, improve communications, and explore possible solutions to a conflict. In mediation, the neutral is less involved in finding the resolution to the conflict. The mediator helps the parties develop, communicate, and bargain for solutions on their own. Theoretically, the mediator does not advocate a position. In practice, conciliation and mediation are difficult to discern because the terms are used interchangeably.

Some mediators meet with the parties separately in a private meeting called a **caucus.** Others do not. A caucus is a safe place for parties to disclose information that they would be reluctant to reveal in a joint session. It's an opportunity for parties to avoid confrontation and save face, and a way for the mediator to do a reality check—all in confidence. The mediator can act as a messenger—in a sort of shuttle diplomacy—to convey one party's concession(s) and offer to the other side. Sometimes the parties permit the mediator to divulge secrets or proprietary information. Standards of practice have been developed by service providers and professional organizations in an effort to ameliorate some of the differences in form and to gain wider acceptance of the process.[54]

Parties generally split the cost of mediation. Mediators usually charge an hourly rate for their services, although some charge a flat rate or *per diem.* Service provider organizations, such as the **American Arbitration Association (AAA),** charge an additional administrative fee, either a flat amount or tacked on to the mediator's hourly rate. In major metropolitan areas, it is possible to engage the services of a mediator at no or low cost through community-based organizations known as neighborhood dispute centers. These centers provide mediation training and services in neighbor-neighbor, landlord-tenant, and family conflicts. Although mediation has been used in labor and insurance disputes for many years, its acceptance in commercial and other types of disputes has grown significantly only since the 1980s.

The most serious barrier to use of mediation is ignorance of the features and benefits of the process. It's a challenge to get parties to agree to mediation when they have been socialized to believe that the only way to resolve a dispute, once and for all, is to let a judge or jury decide it. Attorneys are also often reluctant to mediate a case. They believe they are at a disadvantage if they mediate and later proceed to trial, because their trial strategies will be discovered during the mediation process. This perception is likely to change, however. The rules of professional conduct are being modified to expressly require attorneys to inform their clients about the advantages and disadvantages of alternative dispute resolution.

http://

JAMS, a for-profit provider of neutrals, has its own ethics standards for mediators
http://www.jamsadr.com/ ethics_for_mediators.asp

conciliation

Use of a third party to lower tensions, improve communications, and explore possible solutions to a conflict.

caucus

A private confidential meeting between disputants and a third-party neutral.

American Arbitration Association (AAA)

Private nonprofit organization organized to provide education, training, and administrative assistance to parties who use nonjudicial methods—that is, alternative dispute resolution (ADR)—for resolving disputes.

The mediation process usually involves some compromise, and people are often stubborn. They either do not want to compromise or believe no compromise is possible. This also stops parties from trying mediation. The dispute between Tanda Lee and the Jenkinses is the type that is usually best solved through mediation. A local neighborhood dispute center could be the resolution forum for a neighbor-neighbor conflict like loud nighttime music. The mutual understanding that is required for a long-term solution is seldom achieved through a criminal or civil court process. The record of neighborhood mediation on such cases has been excellent—substantially more effective than court resolution.* As observed before, the most difficult task in mediation is getting both parties to agree to use the process.

ARBITRATION

arbitration

Alternative to litigation whereby conflicting parties select a neutral third party (or parties) to hear and decide their dispute. Arbitration can be binding or nonbinding.

award

The final decision of an arbitrator or other nonjudicial officer in the resolution of a dispute.

Arbitration is the most formal of the ADR processes. **Arbitration** is a process of dispute resolution in which one or more impartial third persons (arbitrator) renders a decision after a hearing at which both parties have an opportunity to be heard. Whereas mediation is facilitative and conciliatory, arbitration is adjudicative and adversarial, like a court proceeding. Notably, arbitrators have the power to impose a resolution; they are private judges. The arbitrator conducts a hearing and acts as finder of both law and fact (as both judge and jury). Attorneys usually present their clients' case; the claimant first, then the respondent. Then, the arbitrator decides the case and issues a written disposition, known as an **award,** usually within 30 days. There is little direct negotiation between the parties.

Compared to other forms of ADR, arbitration is formal, but it is less formal than a court trial. Arbitration rules are more flexible than court rules. Procedural rules are determined by the parties. Discovery is limited and the rules of evidence are dramatically relaxed. Virtually any commercial matter can be submitted to arbitration. It is commonly used to resolve complex cases, including international commercial disputes. The number of businesses that use arbitration grows every year.

In its pure form, arbitration is a voluntary process that concludes with a final resolution of the dispute, outside the public court system. So long as there is mutual assent, the parties have wide discretion in deciding when arbitration is appropriate; who will hear and decide the case; the time and location of the hearing; what arbitration rules will apply; and whether the decision will be binding. Parties typically agree to arbitrate before a claim arises by including an arbitration clause in their contract. Parties may also agree to arbitrate after a claim arises. (Note: Arbitrations are convened less often in tort cases because parties usually don't have a prior contractual relationship). Exhibit 4-4 shows some sample arbitration clauses. Most arbitration clauses provide for binding arbitration, meaning the award is final. All state and federal courts have the power under statute to enforce an arbitrator's award, if that becomes necessary. A losing party may appeal an arbitrator's decision to a court. However, courts seldom overturn arbitration awards, except in cases of serious arbitrator misconduct, e.g., fraud or oppression. Even a clear mistake of law is not grounds for overturning arbitration award. Parties that have agreed to binding arbitration are not allowed to change their minds if they lose the case—not for any reason.

---

* See "Talk, Don't Sue," *Changing Times,* August 1986, pp. 49–52, an article that reports a settlement rate for mediation centers as high as 85 to 90 percent. Also see "Neighborhood Courts," *California Lawyer* (June 1982), p. 45, and "The Use of Mediation in the Resolution of Small Claims, Landlord/Tenant and Neighborhood Disputes," *St. Louis Bar Journal* (1986), p. 34. But also see "Mediating Neighborhood Conflict: Conceptual and Strategic Considerations," *Negotiation Journal* 3 (1987), p. 3. The authors point out that such centers often hear cases referred by the police or the courts. These agencies impose pressure to resolve the matter, but they need to monitor recurring problems to achieve success.

EXHIBIT 4-4: **Sample Arbitration Clauses**

Pre-Dispute Clause

Any controversy or claim arising out of or related to this contract, or the breach thereof, shall be settled by arbitration administered by the American Arbitration Association under its Commercial Arbitration Rules, and judgment on the award rendered by the arbitrator(s) may be entered in any court having jurisdiction thereof.

Post-Dispute Clause

We, the undersigned parties, hereby agree to submit to arbitration administered by the American Arbitration Association under its Commercial Arbitration Rules the following controversy: (cite briefly).

We further agree that the above controversy be submitted to (one) (three) arbitrator(s). We further agree that we will faithfully observe this agreement and the rules, that we will abide by and perform any award rendered by the arbitrator(s), and that a judgment of the court having jurisdiction may be entered on the award.

Reprinted with permission of the American Arbitration Association.

The parties set the rules in arbitration. They are not imposed by statute or the courts. Procedural rules apply, under statute, only by default: when parties have failed to choose which rules shall apply. The American Arbitration Association and other service provider organizations have created procedural rules and provide administrative assistance for parties seeking arbitration. Parties are free to incorporate these standardized rules in their contracts or adopt them when a dispute arises. Parties may also modify the rules or develop their own.

Unlike judges, who are assigned to cases at random, arbitrators are carefully selected by mutual agreement of the parties. Arbitrators are chosen for their integrity, fairness, and subject-matter expertise. Arbitrators are not necessarily trained as judges or even lawyers but many are. Parties may agree on any number of arbitrators; it is common to have one arbitrator in a small dispute and three arbitrators when dollar damages are high. Since arbitration awards can be binding and appeals are seldom successful, the choice of arbitrator is critical.

In common usage the term *arbitration* means binding arbitration. However, there are forms of non-binding arbitration. In addition, there are hybrids that use arbitration in conjunction with other processes. One needs to be familiar with the hybrid to discern whether the component arbitration process is binding. ADR terms are used interchangeably by practitioners, in part because the processes are so adaptable. To avoid confusion, it is important to ask if the process is binding and to watch your language.

Two common types of arbitration are court-annexed arbitration and med-arb. **Court-annexed arbitration** is a mandatory, usually non-binding process, required by statute prior to trial. Awards may be appealed and a *trial de novo* granted. Non-binding awards may become binding if neither side appeals. For example, the Hawaii court system has adopted a program of mandatory, non-binding arbitration for disputes involving less than $150,000. **Med-arb** combines mediation and arbitration in one proceeding. A neutral is appointed to mediate the dispute. If mediation fails, the neutral is authorized to resolve the dispute with a binding award. Med-arb is utilized when parties that prefer to bargain directly want assurance that if they reach an impasse, a third-party neutral will decide the case. Some believe that the possibility of proceeding to the arbitration phase of the process changes the dynamics of the mediation. Parties are thought to be less candid for fear that disclosures made during the mediation will be used against them in the arbitration. However, statements made in the course of mediation are confidential and thus protected under law.

court-annexed arbitration

A type of nonbinding arbitration required by some courts before the parties may proceed to trial.

med-arb

An alternative dispute resolution (ADR) process that combines mediation and arbitration.

LEGAL FOCUS—CASE

Greene agreed to construct a residence for homeowners Hundley and Butt. The construction contract provided that "[a]ny controversy relating to the construction of the residence or any other matter arising out of the terms of this contract shall be settled by binding arbitration . . . conducted pursuant to the Rules of the American Arbitration Association with regard to the Construction Industry Arbitration Rules." A construction dispute arose and was submitted for arbitration. After a two-day hearing, the arbitrator found for both parties and awarded $17,000 to the homeowners and $20,400 to Greene. The award lacked any explanation and the homeowners contested the award. Must the arbitrator provide support for his or her award?

Greene et al. v. Hundley et al., 266 Ga. 392, 468 S.E. 2D. 350 (Ga., 1996).

No. "[T]he Arbitration Code does not require that an arbitrator enter written findings of fact in support of an award; nor does the Code require an arbitrator to explain the reasoning behind an award." Of course, the terms of the parties' agreement to arbitrate or the applicable arbitration rules may require the arbitrator to give a reason for the decision. Some arbitrators will issue a reasoned award upon request, but they are rare.

To summarize, parties agree to arbitrate for the following reasons:

- Arbitration proceedings are private, while court actions are public. Court records are a matter of public record; arbitration awards are confidential. Sometimes parties want to handle their disputes in private.
- Arbitration is usually speedier. Rather than wait for a courtroom, the parties can schedule an arbitration to take place within a short time. Awards are typically issued within thirty days.
- Arbitrations are usually less expensive, even though parties pay the arbitrator's fees. The less formal process requires less preparation, so attorney fees are lower.
- Arbitrations are more flexible. Parties can determine the issues to be decided and set the rules.

Legal Issues in Arbitration

Binding agreements to arbitrate raise important legal issues. When parties agree to binding arbitration, parties may unwittingly waive their right to some critical traditional due process (fairness) protections. We address these issues in a question and answer format below.

An agreement to arbitrate exists but a party files a lawsuit rather than begins arbitration. What are the responding party's options? The responding party could file an answer and proceed with the litigation. If both parties agree to litigate, they are free to do so. The right and obligation to arbitrate is created by contract and not imposed by law. Parties may thus waive the right to arbitration. The respondent is more likely to respond by filing a motion to compel arbitration. The court will decide whether a valid agreement to arbitrate exists. If so, the court will stay the litigation and order the plaintiff to proceed to arbitration. Statutes exist in all state and federal jurisdictions to permit such removal of cases from courts to arbitration. The underlying purpose of these rules is to require parties to comply with their agreement to arbitrate and to encourage the use of arbitration.

You believe you have been discriminated against on the basis of religion in violation of Title VII of the Civil Rights Act of 1964. You work at a non-union company but

the employment contract provides for arbitration of all employment-related disputes. Must you arbitrate your Title VII claim? Are federal or state agencies with independent investigatory powers bound by your arbitration agreement? For many years the courts held that statutory employment discrimination claims could not be heard by an arbitrator. This is no longer the law. Today, an arbitrator can decide disputes created by common law or statute. If a claim is recognized by statute, a party's agreement to arbitrate does not waive the right of an administrative agency to pursue remedies on that person's behalf. An administrative agency may pursue a claim on behalf of a party, even if the party signed a contract or otherwise agreed to waive the right to an administrative remedy. See *Equal Employment Opportunity Commission v. Waffle House, Inc.,* 534 U.S. 279, 112 S. Ct 754 (2002) at the end of the chapter.

Can you get discovery in an arbitration process? The answer depends on whether the agreement to arbitrate provides for discovery. Most arbitration clauses are silent with respect to discovery. Sometimes the right to perform discovery is incorporated in an agreement to arbitrate by reference to the arbitration rules of a specific provider (e.g., the American Arbitration Association.) Some state statutes provide that discovery must be allowed in certain types of claims such as employment claims. If the agreement does not provide for discovery and it is not required by statute, it cannot be compelled.

Can witnesses be compelled to appear at an arbitration? In most states, arbitrators have the power to subpoena witnesses. State statutes that authorize judicial enforcement of arbitration awards also grant subpoena power to arbitrators.

Will the arbitrator provide a reasoned, written decision? The standard award states who the prevailing party is and the amount of damages. It does not explain how or why the arbitrator reached the decision. Like discovery, whether an arbitrator will write a reasoned decision depends on the terms of the agreement to arbitrate. If the agreement to arbitrate requires a reasoned award, then the arbitrator is bound to provide one. By tradition, reasoned decisions are usually provided in labor arbitrations but not in commercial arbitrations.

The arbitrator has decided the case, the award has been issued, and it is good news. You won a handsome sum. The losing party is not a good sport and refuses to pay. What do you do? The prevailing party may file a motion to confirm the award in all state and federal courts. If the motion is granted, the prevailing party may have the award entered as a final judgment. Entry as final judgment permits the prevailing party to enforce the award just as if the case had been decided by a court.

Can an arbitrator's award be appealed? Final arbitration awards may be appealed on very limited grounds, under statute. Whereas most court decisions are challenged because the trial judge made an error of law, appeals of arbitration awards are rarely successful on these grounds. To successfully appeal an arbitration award, the losing party must allege and prove that the arbitration process was unfair (e.g., the arbitrator committed fraud or oppression.) For example, a successful appeal could be based on the failure of an arbitrator to disclose a conflict of interest (prior dealings with one of the parties).

In recent years pre-dispute arbitration agreements have been subject to special scrutiny by the courts. Since arbitration is a creature of contract, parties to arbitration are free to devise the arbitration process in any way they see fit. Parties with greater bargaining power draft agreements that change the dispute resolution forum from a court to arbitration and present it to the weaker party on a "take it or leave it" basis. What appears to be a mere change in venue is a critical waiver of the weaker party's right to due process. Agreements like these, that favor the interests of the stronger party are called contracts of adhesion (see Chapter 7).

LEGAL FOCUS—CASE

Marybeth Armendariz filed a lawsuit against her employer, Foundation Health Psychcare Services, Inc. ("Foundation"), for wrongful termination under a state civil rights statute. Foundation responded by filing a motion to compel arbitration. The employment contract Armendariz had signed included a provision that required Armendariz to arbitrate any employment claims. Armendariz claimed, among other things, that the arbitration provision was not enforceable because it lacked mutuality (arbitration was compulsory if she brought a complaint against Foundation but not if Foundation brought a complaint against her), limited her ability to use discovery, limited her available remedies, and did not require a reasoned written opinion by the arbitrator. Was the arbitration clause enforceable?*

Armendariz v. Foundation Health Psychcare Services, Inc., 24 Cal 4th 83, 99 Cal.Rptr.2 745 (2000).

Armendariz argued she would be denied a fair process if the above arbitration clause was enforced, and the California Supreme Court agreed. The court found fault with an adhesion contract that lacked mutuality, did not provide for important discovery, limited the available remedies, and did not require a reasoned award. "[A]n arbitration agreement imposed in an adhesive context lacks basic fairness and mutuality if it requires one contracting party, but not the other, to arbitrate all claims arising out of the same transaction or occurrence or series of transactions or occurrences. The arbitration agreement in this case lacks mutuality in this sense because it requires the arbitration of employee—but not employer—claims arising out of a wrongful termination. The unconscionable one-sidedness of the arbitration agreement is compounded in this case by the fact that it does not permit the full recovery of damages for employees, while placing no such restriction on the employer." Many of the issues raised by Armendariz are still unsettled in other states. Not all courts have considered these issues and if they have, not all have followed the California lead.[55] Where parties have similar bargaining power and mutually negotiate the terms of the contract, the waiver of due process protections is likely to be allowed by the courts.

PRIVATE JUDGING

private judging

The use of a legally trained arbitrator who follows formal judicial procedures in hearing a case outside a court.

Private judging, also called *rent-a-judge,* allows parties to bypass the formal court system and take their cases to a private court. The proceedings have all the formalities of a public court. Private judging is permitted in all states except Illinois and Indiana, although some states may limit the issues that may be heard.[56] Cases are tried before a referee who is selected and paid by the parties. Referees are usually retired judges. In some states, including California, any member of the state bar can be a referee. Jurors can be selected from the public jury rolls to participate in such trials. State statutes authorize the referee to enter

---

* The arbitration clause read in part: "I agree as a condition of my employment, that in the event my employment is terminated, and I contend that such termination was wrongful or otherwise in violation of the conditions of employment or was in violation of any express or implied condition, term or covenant of employment, whether founded in fact or in law, including but not limited to the covenant of good faith and fair dealing, or otherwise in violation of any of my rights, I and Employer agree to submit any such matter to binding arbitration pursuant to the provisions of title 9 of Part III of the California Code of Civil Procedure, commencing at section 1280 *et seq.* or any successor or replacement statutes. I and Employer further expressly agree that in any such arbitration, my exclusive remedies for violation of the terms, conditions or covenants of employment shall be limited to a sum equal to the wages I would have earned from the date of any discharge until the date of the arbitration award. I understand that I shall not be entitled to any other remedy, at law or in equity, including but not limited to reinstatement and/or injunctive relief."

the decision in the trial court as a final judgment, if the parties choose. If so entered, the final judgment can be appealed to a state appellate court.

Private judging, much like arbitration, provides more flexibility and privacy than a court trial. With private judging, parties do not need to wait for a court date—if a referee is available, they can schedule the trial immediately. Parties are free to determine the procedural rules, but usually agree to apply the formal rules used in the public courts, including the rules of evidence. However, unlike arbitration, parties have the right to appeal adverse rulings to the appellate courts.

The use of private judging is widespread, yet is the most controversial of the ADR processes. The rent-a-judge system has been disparagingly referred to as "Cadillac justice." Since the referees are paid entirely by the disputants, private judging allows disputants to bypass the public trial calendar only if they can afford to pay the judge. Parties who cannot afford it must wait their turn in the public courts. Justice delayed is justice denied.[57] Private courts are also criticized because it is feared they may lure judges away from the public courts through early retirement. Judges are paid substantially more in fees by private clients than they earn as salaried public servants. Furthermore, hearings in private courts are not open to the public or the press. Wealthy corporations and other parties can shield their activities from the public eye and keep judgments confidential. Finally, some observers believe that this private justice system may delay or even relieve the legislature and the courts from making needed legal reforms.

OMBUDSPERSON

An **ombudsperson** or **ombud** is a consultant or permanent employee of an organization hired to resolve conflicts that arise within the organization. The concept developed in Scandinavia. There, an ombudsman was a public official appointed to investigate and hear citizen complaints against the government. In the United States, ombuds are present in both public and private institutions. The ombud investigates, proposes and advocates solutions, and often makes public his or her independent findings and recommendations. The role of the ombud, like the mediator, is to facilitate resolution through better communication among the members of the group. Neither has authority to impose a settlement. Ombuds are distinguishable from mediators in that the ombud becomes actively involved in determining the facts and advocating solutions. Whereas mediators are expected to maintain neutrality throughout their service, ombuds start out neutral but are not required to remain so. Usually, the ombud is selected by one of the disputing parties and paid solely by that party. In contrast, mediator fees are generally shared by the disputants.

ombudsperson

A proactive neutral party who investigates and determines facts and suggests resolutions to disputes.

http://

Everything you have always wanted to know about ombuds can be found at **http://www.ombuds.org/faq.html**

EXPERT FACT-FINDING

Expert fact-finding is a process by which a neutral with subject-matter expertise is appointed to conduct an independent investigation or take evidence on selected factual issues in highly technical matters. The expert does not decide the case. The sole object is to determine what happened. Like other adjudicatory processes, attorneys present evidence to the neutral. At the conclusion, the expert makes an evaluation and issues findings of fact. The findings can be binding or non-binding. Parties may adopt them in a subsequent conciliatory process or even admit them in arbitration or at trial. In a similar process, a special master, selected for his or her legal expertise, will determine the factual issues in cases set for trial. Negotiated settlements are more likely once the factual issues have been settled.

expert fact-finding

A non-binding process in which an appointed expert investigates or hears facts on selected issues. At the conclusion, he or she makes findings of fact.

EARLY NEUTRAL EVALUATION

early neutral evaluation

ADR process providing disputing parties with an early and candid evaluation by an objective observer of the merits of a case.

Early neutral evaluation is an evaluative process and typically non-binding. The objective of the process is to facilitate negotiations, not to decide the case. A third-party neutral conducts a hearing and issues an opinion as to the merits of the case and the strengths and weaknesses of evidence, and assesses the likely outcome at trial. The proceeding is not unlike a trial, but it is very brief. Oral presentations are limited to a summary of the key issues in the case. Written submissions are extremely limited in length. The attorney plays a critical role in this process. Since the proceeding is expected to be brief, the attorney must be very skilled in oral advocacy. Early neutral evaluation is appropriate for cases in which parties have valued a case unrealistically and in which fault has been established but damages are hotly contested.

MINI-TRIAL

mini-trial

A private, voluntary, informal form of dispute resolution in which attorneys for each disputant make a brief presentation of his or her best case before officials for each side who have authority to settle.

A **mini-trial** is a voluntary, non-binding process used primarily by large business organizations to better inform themselves on the merits of a case. A trial-like proceeding is conducted with high-ranking company officials who have settlement authority acting as jurors. The sides agree on rules of procedure and exchange of information, and select a neutral advisor. Attorneys for each side present a case summary to the jury. There is no examination of witnesses. As jurors, the officials hear both sides and gain insight about the dispute. Now well-informed, the parties can negotiate a settlement with or without the assistance of the neutral advisor and avoid an actual court trial. Since preparation and presentation of a case, even in summary form, can be expensive, mini-trials are used when large amounts of money are at stake.

SUMMARY JURY TRIAL

summary jury trial

A nonbinding alternative dispute resolution (ADR) process in which parties present their cases to a private mock jury, which then gives the parties an advisory verdict.

The **summary jury trial** is similar to both the mini-trial and early neutral evaluation. The object is to facilitate settlement in lawsuits that have been filed but not yet tried by providing parties with a realistic jury reaction. An abbreviated case is presented to a **mock jury.** The jury returns its verdict quickly. After the verdict, attorneys for each side are permitted to query each juror about how and why they reached their decision. Parties then negotiate a settlement, each equipped with insights gained from the jury. The process is non-binding: If a settlement is not reached, both sides have the right to a full trial.

mock jury

A panel of lay citizens selected and paid to mirror the role of an actual jury.

Procedurally, a summary jury trial is more relaxed than an actual trial. Since attorneys for the parties put on an abbreviated case, including examination of the parties as witnesses, it is more formal than a mini-trial. Summary jury trials are also more expensive than mini-trials. The presentation of a case, although abbreviated, requires more attorney research and preparation than presentation of a case summary. Also, it costs more to compensate a number of jurors as contrasted with a single third-party neutral.

PARTNERING

partnering

A teambuilding process designed to improve contract performance and reduce or eliminate contract litigation through common understanding of goals and improved communication. The process is used in large, complicated and expensive contracts with its roots in the construction industry.

Partnering is a dispute prevention process. Parties to complex undertakings such as large construction projects, land use planning, or agency rulemaking meet before commencement of the project. The objective of the meeting is to identify potential sources of conflict and design a system to resolve problems at the earliest stage possible. Partnering is similar to mediation and other dispute resolution processes in that discussions are facilitated by a third-party neutral. The key difference is that the partnering meeting is convened in advance of rather than after any conflict has arisen. Attorneys typically participate in negotiations as an advisor rather than as an advocate.

CONCLUSIONS REGARDING ADR

"The notion that most people want black-robed judges, well-dressed lawyers, and fine paneled courtrooms as the setting to resolve their disputes is not correct. People with problems, like people with pains, want relief, and they want it as quickly and inexpensively as possible."[58] People tend to accept and live more graciously with a voluntary agreement than with a court-imposed solution, which will often rankle for years. Litigation is risky, since the outcome is uncertain. It is time-consuming for attorneys and clients, and it is costly. Participants are also likely to suffer stress from drawn-out litigation. In the end, most lawsuits are settled before trial, but often after years of waiting. Litigation is necessary to vindicate rights or clarify the law, but litigation is not required to resolve all disagreements. A trial usually aggravates and exaggerates existing hard feelings. A decision to sue or defend a suit through trial should be carefully thought out. In addition to the obvious costs associated with litigation such as attorney fees, court costs, witness expenses and discovery costs, there are indirect or hidden costs that must be taken into account. Finally, the cost for the state to provide justice must not be overlooked.

LEGAL FOCUS—EXAMPLE

Kevin Banks rejected a settlement offer of $22,500 in his breach of contract and tort action against eight former associates. He believed he was entitled to $500,000 in punitive damages. The case went to trial. The "good news" was that Banks won a jury verdict of $50,000. The "bad news" was that it took three years to resolve, during which time he was unemployed. His single-minded concern with the case alienated friends and relatives. The case cost him $105,000 in litigation expenses. During the prolonged dispute, he employed seven different lawyers, one at a time—six of them quit. Despite winning at trial, he continued to be consumed by the case. He accused the judge, defendants, defense attorneys, and his own attorneys of a conspiracy against him.

Often the nominal winner is the real loser. Banks won his case, so one could assume he had been wronged. Had he accepted the settlement offer he would have had a positive net recovery, rather than a negative victory with an out-of-pocket loss of at least $55,000 (litigation recovery of $50,000 minus litigation costs of $105,000). Was his pursuit of "justice at any price" too high a personal price to pay? Some who win at trial feel vindicated despite a negative net recovery. Was the public harmed in any way?

For certain purposes, access to our public courts may be wholly inappropriate. Banks sought more than justice. He sought vengeance through the public court system in a civil matter. The civil courts are designed to shift the burden of compensating victims to the wrongdoer, not to mete out punishment. Use of our civil courts for vengeance is a breach of public trust and a squandering of public resources.

CASE

NEW HAMPSHIRE V. GORDON
141 N.H. 703, 692 A.2d 505 (1997)

In the fall of 1991, the victim, an administrator and teacher at New Hampshire Technical College in Nashua, began a consensual sexual relationship with the defendant, a student at the college. In July 1992, the victim informed the defendant that their relationship was over. In response, the defendant came to the victim's home and, after promising that he just wanted to talk to her, sexually assaulted her.

In September 1992, the defendant telephoned Judith Parys, a lawyer and his paralegal instructor at the college, and, crying, told her that he had had a relationship with the victim and "that things had gone wrong and that it was a mess." He told Parys that he was afraid the victim would have him removed from the college. Later the same day, the defendant called Parys again. He told her that "he had called [the victim] and, much to his surprise, that she had agreed to talk to him on the phone, . . . and that he didn't have to tie her up."

In October 1992, the defendant, who was shaking and looked like he had been crying, approached Parys after she finished teaching a class and told her that he had looked up the definition of rape in the New Hampshire statutes. He said that, based on the definition, "he was sure that he had raped [the victim] in the past."

The defendant was later charged with four counts of aggravated felonious sexual assault and one count of attempted aggravated felonious sexual assault. Before trial, he filed a motion in limine* to bar Parys from testifying against him, asserting that his communications with her were protected by the attorney-client privilege. The trial court denied the motion. The defendant was convicted on one count of aggravated felonious sexual assault.

Justice Broderick delivered the opinion of the court: The defendant, Steven Gordon, was convicted of aggravated felonious sexual assault after a jury trial in Superior Court. In separate but consolidated appeals, the defendant argues that the trial court erred in admitting into evidence allegedly privileged statements he made to an attorney instructor. . . .We affirm.

The defendant argues that the trial court erred in denying his motion to exclude Parys' testimony based on the attorney-client privilege. It is generally recognized that "[a]n attorney-client relationship is created when (1) a person seeks advice or assistance from an attorney, (2) the advice or assistance sought pertains to matters within the attorney's professional competence, and (3) the attorney expressly or impliedly agrees to give or actually gives the desired advice or assistance." Here, the burden of proving the existence of an attorney-client relationship lies with the defendant. The defendant conceded at oral argument that he sought no legal advice in the September 1992 phone conversations. Consequently, we need look only at the October 1992 conversation at the college to determine whether an attorney-client relationship was established and, hence, whether the attorney-client privilege applies to that conversation.

At the hearing on the motion *in limine,* the trial court heard conflicting testimony on the question of whether the defendant's conversation with Parys at the college established an attorney-client relationship. The defendant maintained that Parys told him "to go look in the [code] and, when he returned, she advised him to "back off and give [the victim] her space." Additionally, he contended that Parys offered to "make some phone calls and get back to [him]."

Parys' version of the conversation was quite different, however. She contended that the defendant informed her that "he had gone to the [code] in the law library, had looked up the definition of 'rape,' and believed that he had raped [the victim]." Rather than offering legal advice, Parys testified that because of the defendant's "rambling," she "didn't have a chance to get a word in edgewise."

The credibility of witnesses is a factual determination within the sound discretion of the trial court. "[U]nless we find that no reasonable person could have come to the same conclusion," we defer to the trial court's credibility determination. *State v. Crotty,* 134 N.H. 706, 711, 597 A.2d 1078, 1082 (1991).

The trial court's determination that the defendant "did not . . . seek advice from Parys in her legal capacity" is adequately supported by the record. Parys testified that the defendant sought "absolutely no legal advice" and that she gave none. Additionally, she testified that she informed her classes—some of which the defendant attended—that she did not give legal advice and that she believed to do so could violate the Rules of Professional Conduct.

---

* Latin: "at the threshold"; preliminary. A motion *in limine* may be made (usually at the outset of a trial) to exclude or limit the admissibility of evidence. Juries may not hear or see inadmissible evidence.

Even the defendant's own testimony does not support his argument that he sought legal advice from Parys in her capacity as an attorney. At the hearing on the motion *in limine,* the defendant read into the record his testimony from an earlier proceeding that when he spoke to Parys, he thought he was "talking to somebody in confidence. You tell somebody that you trust or that you're friendly with things that you wouldn't just openly stand out there and say. . . ." Speaking in confidence is not enough; "where one consults an attorney not as a lawyer but as a friend or as [an] . . . adviser . . . the consultation is not professional nor the statement privileged."

Moreover, the defendant's conduct at two earlier proceedings, which the trial court considered in its ruling, does not support the existence of the privilege he now seeks to invoke. Prior to the defendant's trial, Parys twice testified—at a hearing on a domestic violence petition filed by the victim against the defendant and at a judicial review board hearing at the college—about the conversations she had with the defendant in September and October 1992. According to the defendant's testimony at the hearing on his motion *in limine,* at the domestic violence hearing Parys indicated that she did not represent either party; the defendant apparently did not object. At the judicial review hearing, the defendant remarked about Parys: "I realize she's an attorney, but she's here as a witness. If she wants to play attorney, then she should represent somebody."

"A client has a privilege to refuse to disclose and to prevent any other person from disclosing confidential communications made for the purpose of facilitating the rendition of professional legal services to the client. . . ." N.H. R. Ev. 502(b). Because the defendant never established an attorney-client relationship with Parys, however, he cannot now assert the privilege as a shield against the admission of Parys' testimony.

Affirmed. All concurred.

For Critical Analysis

1. The authors of this book are attorneys. And though we are writing about the law, we do not intend to give specific legal advice to any students or other readers. Your class instructor is also likely to be an attorney. If you ask a question in class about a legal problem, or if you discuss a legal dilemma you are currently facing in a conversation with your instructor, does the attorney-client privilege arise?

2. Who holds the attorney-client privilege—the attorney or client or both? Why?

3. What additional facts might have led the court to believe a privilege existed? ■

EQUAL EMPLOYMENT OPPORTUNITY COMMISSION V. WAFFLE HOUSE, INC.

534 U.S. 279, 122 S.Ct. 754 (2002)

Waffle House fired Eric Baker when he suffered a seizure on the job within a month of being hired. He filed a discrimination complaint with the Equal Employment Opportunity Commission (EEOC) alleging that his discharge violated the Americans with Disabilities Act of 1990 (ADA). The EEOC pursued the claim and filed suit in federal court requesting injunctive relief to prevent Waffle House from discriminating against other employees now and in the future, to get Baker reinstated on the job, to collect damages on behalf of Baker, and to punish Waffle House for discriminating against Baker. Waffle House moved to stay the EEOC's suit and compel arbitration based on Baker's employment contract that required employment disputes to be settled by binding arbitration. The District Court denied

Waffle House's request for relief. The Fourth Circuit Court of Appeals also held for the EEOC but limited the EEOC to injunctive relief against Waffle House and precluded the agency from seeking victim-specific relief. The court held that the Federal Arbitration Act (FAA), which favored enforcement of private arbitration agreements, outweighed the EEOC's right to enforce private, rather than public, interests. In other words, EEOC could proceed but Baker's arbitration agreement limited Baker's recovery to that which would be determined in an arbitration.

Justice Stevens delivered the opinion of the Court: The question presented is whether an agreement between an employer and an employee to arbitrate employment related disputes bars the Equal Employment Opportunity Commission (EEOC) from pursuing victim-specific judicial relief, such as backpay, reinstatement, and damages, in an enforcement action alleging that the employer has violated Title I of the Americans with Disabilities Act of 1990 (ADA).

In his application for employment with respondent, Eric Baker agreed that "any dispute or claim" concerning his employment would be "settled by binding arbitration." As a condition of employment, all prospective Waffle House employees are required to sign an application containing a similar mandatory arbitration agreement. Baker began working as a grill operator at one of respondent's restaurants on August 10, 1994. Sixteen days later he suffered a seizure at work and soon thereafter was discharged. Baker did not initiate arbitration proceedings, nor has he in the seven years since his termination, but he did file a timely charge of discrimination with the EEOC alleging that his discharge violated the ADA.

After an investigation and an unsuccessful attempt to conciliate, the EEOC filed an enforcement action against respondent in the Federal District Court for the District of South Carolina. Baker is not a party to the case. The EEOC's complaint alleged that respondent engaged in employment practices that violated the ADA, including its discharge of Baker "because of his disability," and that its violation was intentional, and "done with malice or with reckless indifference to [his] federally protected rights." The complaint requested the court to grant injunctive relief to "eradicate the effects of [respondent's] past and present unlawful employment practices," to order specific relief designed to make Baker whole, including backpay, reinstatement, and compensatory damages, and to award punitive damages for malicious and reckless conduct..

Congress has directed the EEOC to exercise the same enforcement powers, remedies, and procedures that are set forth in Title VII of the Civil Rights Act of 1964 when it is enforcing the ADA's prohibitions against employment discrimination on the basis of disability.

The FAA directs courts to place arbitration agreements on equal footing with other contracts, but it "does not require parties to arbitrate when they have not agreed to do so." Because the FAA is "at bottom a policy guaranteeing the enforcement of private contractual arrangements," we look first to whether the parties agreed to arbitrate a dispute, not to general policy goals, to determine the scope of the agreement. While ambiguities in the language of the agreement should be resolved in favor of arbitration, we do not override the clear intent of the parties, or reach a result inconsistent with the plain text of the contract, simply because the policy favoring arbitration is implicated. "Arbitration under the

[FAA] is a matter of consent, not coercion." Here there is no ambiguity. No one asserts that the EEOC is a party to the contract, or that it agreed to arbitrate its claims. It goes without saying that a contract cannot bind a nonparty. Accordingly, the proarbitration policy goals of the FAA do not require the agency to relinquish its statutory authority if it has not agreed to do so.

[T]he statutory language is clear; the EEOC has the authority to pursue victim-specific relief regardless of the forum that the employer and employee have chosen to resolve their disputes. Rather than attempt to split the difference, we are persuaded that, pursuant to Title VII and the ADA, whenever the EEOC chooses from among the many charges filed each year to bring an enforcement action in a particular case, the agency may be seeking to vindicate a public interest, not simply provide make-whole relief for the employee, even when it pursues entirely victim-specific relief. To hold otherwise would undermine the detailed enforcement scheme created by Congress simply to give greater effect to an agreement between private parties that does not even contemplate the EEOC's statutory function.

It is true, as respondent [has] argued, that Baker's conduct may have the effect of limiting the relief that the EEOC may obtain in court. If, for example, he had failed to mitigate his damages, or had accepted a monetary settlement, any recovery by the EEOC would be limited accordingly. As we have noted, it "goes without saying that the courts can and should preclude double recovery by an individual."

But no question concerning the validity of his claim or the character of the relief that could be appropriately awarded in either a judicial or an arbitral forum is presented by this record. Baker has not sought arbitration of his claim, nor is there any indication that he has entered into settlement negotiations with respondent. It is an open question whether a settlement or arbitration judgment would affect the validity of the EEOC's claim or the character of relief the EEOC may seek. The only issue before this Court is whether the fact that Baker has signed a mandatory arbitration agreement limits the remedies available to the EEOC. The text of the relevant statutes provides a clear answer to that question. They do not authorize the courts to balance the competing policies of the ADA and the FAA or to second-guess the agency's judgment concerning which of the remedies authorized by law that it shall seek in any given case.

Moreover, it simply does not follow from the cases holding that the employee's conduct may affect the EEOC's recovery that the EEOC's claim is merely derivative. We have recognized several situations in which the EEOC does not stand in the employee's shoes. And, in this context, the statute specifically grants the EEOC exclusive authority over the choice of forum and the prayer for relief once a charge has been filed. The fact that ordinary principles of *res judicata,** mootness, or mitigation may apply to EEOC claims does not contradict these decisions, nor does it render the EEOC a proxy for the employee.

The judgment of the Court of Appeals is reversed, and the case is remanded for further proceedings consistent with this opinion.

It is so ordered.

Justice Thomas, with whom the Chief Justice and Justice Scalia join, dissenting: Because Congress has not given the EEOC the authority to usurp the traditional role of courts to determine what constitutes "appropriate" relief in a given case, it is necessary to examine whether it would be "appropriate" to allow the EEOC to obtain victim-specific relief for Baker here, notwithstanding the fact that Baker, by signing an arbitration agreement, has waived his ability to seek such relief on his own behalf in a judicial forum. For two reasons, I conclude it is not "appropriate" to allow the EEOC to do on behalf of Baker that which Baker is precluded from doing for himself.

To begin with, when the EEOC litigates to obtain relief on behalf of a particular employee, the Commission must take that individual as it finds him. Whether the EEOC or an employee files a particular lawsuit, the employee is the ultimate beneficiary of victim-specific relief. The relevance of the employee's circumstances therefore does not change simply because the EEOC, rather than the employee himself, is litigating the case, and a court must consider these circumstances in fashioning an "appropriate" remedy.

As a result, the EEOC's ability to obtain relief is often limited by the actions of an employee on whose behalf the Commission may wish to bring a lawsuit. If an employee signs an agreement to waive or settle discrimination claims against an employer, for example, the EEOC may not recover victim-specific relief on that employee's behalf.

Not only would it be "inappropriate" for a court to allow the EEOC to obtain victim-specific relief on behalf of Baker,

to do so in this case would contravene the "liberal federal policy favoring arbitration agreements" embodied in the FAA.

By allowing the EEOC to pursue victim-specific relief on behalf of Baker under these circumstances, the Court eviscerates Baker's arbitration agreement with Waffle House and liberates Baker from the consequences of his agreement. Waffle House gains nothing and, if anything, will be worse off in cases where the EEOC brings an enforcement action should it continue to utilize arbitration agreements in the future. This is because it will face the prospect of defending itself in two different forums against two different parties seeking precisely the same relief. It could face the EEOC in court and the employee in an arbitral forum.

I respectfully dissent.

For Critical Analysis

1. Waffle House requested a stay and a motion to compel arbitration. What were they asking for?

2. Do you agree with Waffle House's argument that although the EEOC was not a party to the arbitration agreement, they are still effectively bound by it (Justice Thomas' dissent)? Or do you agree with the EEOC that they are free to pursue all remedies without regard to whether an employee has signed an arbitration agreement (Justice Stevens' majority opinion)? Explain which position you agree with and why.

3. When Baker was given the pre-employment agreement with the arbitration clause, do you think he understood what he was signing? Does it matter?

4. If Baker had refused to sign the employment agreement, would he have still been hired? If he had simply struck the clause and then signed, would he have been hired?

5. Why did Waffle House require the arbitration clause in its employment contracts? Why might an employee be concerned about such a clause? Why might an employee be pleased with such a clause? ■

---

* Latin: "a matter [already] adjudicated." A party may not sue again on a matter that has been settled by judicial decision.

CHAPTER QUESTIONS AND PROBLEMS

1. The legal profession is in the process of change. Following are some questions involving changes that have impact on the public interest.
   a. Should attorneys who participate in formal courtroom trials be trained differently from other lawyers?
   b. Should charges concerning the unprofessional conduct of an attorney be heard and decided by attorneys, by non-lawyers, or by both?
   c. What limitations, if any, should be imposed on the right of attorneys to advertise for and to solicit legal business?
   d. Should there be limits to the fees charged by attorneys for legal services?
   e. Should current rules requiring all partners or owners in law firms to be lawyers be changed? Should lawyers be allowed to associate and share fees with non-lawyer professionals? Would such multidisciplinary associations benefit the general public?

2. Contingent fee arrangements are said to make legal services available to persons who otherwise would be unable to pay; but contingent fee arrangements are also said to promote litigation unnecessarily, because potential plaintiffs (victims) have nothing to lose by suing. What do you think of these contentions?

3. Our founding fathers adopted (or, more correctly, retained) the English common law after the American Revolution. However, we have consistently refused to adopt the so-called English Plan for the payment of legal fees. The English Plan requires the losing party to pay the plaintiff's and the defendant's attorney fees (as well as court costs). Presently, losers in the United States always pay court costs and their own attorney's fees (unless otherwise agreed by contract), but do not pay the attorney's fees of their opponents. Some observers strongly recommend we adopt the English Plan. Do you agree?

4. Liability insurance is available to cover potential attorney malpractice. As with most liability insurance, the premiums charged have increased significantly in recent years. Malpractice insurance coverage for attorneys is usually not required either by law or by the Professional Rules of Conduct. As in many other liability situations, those who can most afford a major loss carry ample insurance, whereas those who have little financial ability are more likely to be without insurance. Should malpractice insurance or other proof of financial responsibility be required as a condition for the practice of law? Discuss.

5. The typical arbitration clause requires binding arbitration. That means that the arbitrator's decision cannot be appealed except for very limited reasons. What are the negative and positive aspects of arbitration because of this lack of appeal? Assume that during arbitration the attorney representing one party becomes very angry, screams obscenities at the arbitrator, and finally throws the exhibits onto the floor. Can the arbitrator hold the attorney in contempt?

6. In January 1991, Gail P. Carr-Williams, an attorney licensed to practice law in Michigan, applied for admission, without examination, to the State Bar of Ohio. After an initial recommendation that Carr-Williams' application be approved, the Board of Commissioners on Character and Fitness of the Supreme Court of Ohio appointed a panel to investigate Carr-Williams' application. The panel concluded that Carr-Williams had not satisfied her federal income tax obligations for several years and owed the Internal Revenue Service approximately $98,000 in taxes, interest, and penalties. She also owed state taxes of $14,000. Should the Board of Commissioners recommend she be licensed to practice law in Ohio? [*In re* Application of Carr-Williams, 63 Ohio St.3d 752, 591 N.E.2d 693 (Ohio, 1992).]

7. Attorney Edward M. Cooperman was retained to represent a client in a criminal matter. The client signed Cooperman's fee agreement: "My minimum fee for appearing for you in this matter is fifteen thousand dollars ($15,000). This fee is not refundable for any reason whatsoever once I file a notice of appearance on your behalf." One month later, the client discharged Cooperman, but Cooperman refused to refund any portion of the fee. In the past Cooperman had been told by the local bar association grievance committee to stop using non-refundable fee agreements. The attorneys' Code of Professional Conduct and Responsibility provides that an attorney "shall not enter into an agreement for, charge or collect an illegal or excessive fee" and upon withdrawal from employment "shall refund promptly any part of a fee paid in advance that has not been earned." Did Cooperman's fee arrangement violate the code? [*Griev-*

ance Committee for the Tenth Judicial District v. Edward M. Cooperman, 83 N.Y.2d 465, 633 N.E.2d 1069, 611 N.Y.S.2d 465 (N.Y., 1994).]

8. John E. Mallard, an attorney who practiced bankruptcy and securities law, was selected by the U.S. magistrate to represent indigent inmates who were suing prison officials for maltreatment. He was compelled to represent the inmates under a federal statute authorizing federal courts to "request" an attorney to represent any person claiming poverty status. Claiming that he was not competent to handle complex trial matters, Mallard filed a motion to withdraw. The magistrate denied his request, and his appeal to the District Court and Court of Appeal was unsuccessful. Can the court compel attorney Mallard to represent an indigent civil litigant? [*Mallard v. U.S. District Court for Southern Dist. of Iowa,* 490 U.S. 296, 109 S.Ct. 1814 (1989).]

9. Richard Shapero, a Kentucky attorney, applied to the state Attorneys' Advertising Commission for approval of a letter that he proposed to send "to potential clients who have had a foreclosure suit filed against them." The letter advised the clients that federal law may prevent creditors from taking immediate action and that the recipients of the letters could call Shapero's office for free information on how to keep their homes. The commission would not approve the letter because Professional Conduct Rules prohibited direct-mail solicitation by lawyers if the mail was directed to *specific recipients* rather than to a *general group of persons* known to need the particular kind of legal services offered. The Kentucky Supreme Court affirmed the commission's finding. Shapero appealed to the United States Supreme Court, claiming that the rule violated attorneys' rights to free speech. Did Shapero succeed in his claim? [*Shapero v. Kentucky Bar Association,* 486 U.S. 466, 108 S.Ct. 1916 (1988).]

10. The Hembrees purchased a home. The purchase contract included the following clause: "Any controversy or claim arising out of or relating to this contract, or the breach thereof, shall be settled by arbitration in the city of contract origin, in accordance with the rules of the American Arbitration Association." A claim that the home they purchased had a defective roof was arbitrated and the arbitrator found for the Hembrees on the theory of implied warranty. An implied warranty is a guarantee imposed by law that the seller will stand behind the item even though the contract is silent with respect to warranties. The seller and seller's real estate agent challenged the arbitrator's award in state court. They claimed the arbitrator exceeded his authority because the contract did not expressly provide for a remedy based on warranty. They argued the arbitrator's finding was a clear error of law. Is the arbitrator's authority strictly limited to the terms of the contract? If the arbitrator is clearly wrong as to the application of law, will the award be overturned by the court? [*Hembree v. Broadway Realty Trust Company, Inc.,* 151 Ariz. 418, 728 P.2d 288 (1986).]

11. Edward Kuhnel, a correctional officer for the New York Correctional Services Department ("Department"), flew a Nazi flag from the front porch of his home commemorating the 55th anniversary of Hitler's declaration of war against the United States. His actions received a great deal of media attention. The Department suspended Kuhnel from his job for violating two sections of the Department's employee manual. Kuhnel contested his suspension and the claim was submitted to arbitration under a collective bargaining agreement. Both parties agreed that the arbitration procedure would be final and binding. The arbitrator concluded that Kuhnel was not guilty of the charges and reinstated Kuhnel with full back pay and benefits. The Department appealed. May the courts revisit the evidence and consider whether the arbitrator erred in determining the facts or applying the law? [*New York State Correctional Officers and Police Benevolent Association, Inc., v. State of New York,* 94 N.Y.2d 321, 726 N.E.2d 462, 704 N.Y.S.2d 910 (1999).]

CHAPTER 5

Administrative Law

*T*he rise of administrative bodies probably has been the most significant legal trend of the last century and perhaps more values are affected by their decisions than by those of all the courts. . . .

Justice Robert H. Jackson, U.S. Supreme Court Justice, 1941–1954

After reading and studying this chapter, you should be able to:

🏛 Define and explain the term *administrative law*. Distinguish between the two different ways in which the term is used.

🏛 Explain what an administrative agency is, how an agency gets its authority, and what the general purposes of administrative agencies are. Describe the importance of the Administrative Procedure Act and the enabling statute relative to agency authority and purpose.

🏛 Explain the importance of agency procedures.

🏛 Distinguish between an independent administrative agency and an executive department.

🏛 Identify leading administrative agencies and the areas they regulate.

🏛 Explain what a regulation is and identify the major rule-making steps required by the Administrative Procedure Act.

🏛 Describe the major investigatory methods and powers of administrative agencies.

🏛 Identify and illustrate the eleven components of a fair hearing as identified by Judge Henry Friendly.

🏛 Briefly explain the degree and type of control that each branch of the federal government has over independent administrative agencies.

🏛 Define the term *judicial review* and identify the limitations and the conditions precedent to a court reviewing administrative power or exercises of that power.

🏛 Identify and explain some methods by which the public may scrutinize agency action.

Most of us have seen recreations of dramatic courtroom showdowns and perhaps even viewed grand oratory in Congress on C-SPAN. Courts and Congress are two faces of the law, just as law enforcement is a third. There is a fourth important face to the law, the one you are most likely to encounter: administrative law. For some, this term conjures up images of powerful agencies, able to both make and execute law, and subject to less oversight and review than a court, legislature, or police officer might have. Most of us have already encountered administrative law in our life with positive and negative consequences. This chapter prepares you to better understand administrative law and its place in American governance.

We will present the structure and processes of administrative law, both in the federal government as well as in several states. A particular focus will be on the power wielded by agencies and the constraints on this power. You should come to understand why administrative law is a topic so unique and so important. Hopefully you will be better prepared to solve problems involving governmental involvement (perhaps interference) in your life and better able to obtain the services, rights, and benefits you seek from the government.

A final word before our discussion of administrative law: This chapter is mostly about process, the process that agencies use when enforcing the law. That process can deny a right or grant a privilege just as surely as any other substantive law and is an incredibly important subject. To understand its importance, you need only speak with someone who has just dealt with a governmental process and felt confused and powerless to help shape the outcome. Like trying to survive in a courtroom without understanding the complex rules for evidence and procedure, dealing with an agency without understanding how it makes decisions is an effort likely to result in frustration, anger, and long-lasting disappointment.

WHAT IS ADMINISTRATIVE LAW?

In short, **administrative law** is the law of administrative agencies, a vast portion of government sometimes called the "fourth branch of the government." Administrative law involves over 1 million federal employees and countless state agency employees. It probably affects citizens of the United States far more than judicial proceedings or legislation do. Often the term *administrative law* is used to describe two very different subjects of law. One is the law governing agency process and procedure. The other type is the law that agencies create and apply, the "substantive law" of agencies. In this chapter we focus on the process and procedure of agencies rather than on the subject matter of the laws agencies create or of the statutes that agencies enforce. Exhibit 5-1 provides examples of procedural and substantive administrative law.

AGENCY PROCESS

There is a body of law that governs how agencies can or must conduct themselves and their processes. As you will learn, policies of fairness and constitutional principles have established significant restraints and limits on agency power, particularly on the way in which an agency may act. Agencies, however, are often given significant authority to independently execute laws, make decisions, and otherwise do their business. Collectively, laws and rules governing how agencies can or must conduct themselves can be referred to as the *procedural law* of agencies.

administrative law

The body of law concerned with the power of administrative agencies. Administrative law consists of rules, regulations, orders, and adjudications. Also the composite body of substantive law created by the various administrative agencies in the performance of their assigned tasks.

http://

The administrative procedure database can be found at the Florida State University College of Law Web site

http://www.law.fsu.edu/ library/admin/

EXHIBIT 5-1: **Types of Agency Law**

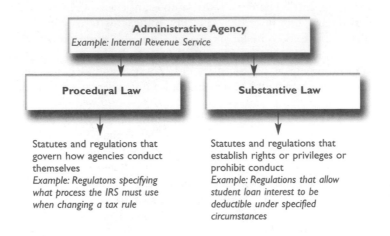

Some laws and regulations that appear procedural in nature really directly control the rights, privileges, or benefits of others. Consider the following regulation of the U.S. Department of Education.

LEGAL FOCUS—EXAMPLE

Obtaining a loan. (a) *Application for a Direct Subsidized Loan or a Direct Unsubsidized Loan.* (1) To obtain a Direct Subsidized Loan or a Direct Unsubsidized Loan, a student must complete a Free Application for Federal Student Aid and submit it in accordance with instructions in the application. . .

A strict reading of the above regulation shows that a student could be denied a loan for merely failing to follow instructions in the application! Thus, this regulation and those instructions in the loan application might be better considered as substantive in nature, not procedural. In any case, this is the realm of administrative law, where rights and benefits such as these are affected every day through the creation and application of the laws and regulations of agencies.

SUBSTANTIVE LAW OF AGENCIES

Every agency has a purpose, usually to enforce and/or apply a particular set of laws. For instance, the U.S. Securities and Exchange Commission (SEC) is tasked with enforcing, among other laws, the Securities Act of 1933. Besides that federal statute, the SEC has established **regulations** that further explain and apply the broader statute they are under, the Securities Act of 1933. The 1933 Securities Act and its associated regulations are one example of the substantive law of the SEC. The term *substantive law* here refers to the laws and regulations enforced by the SEC that describe or proscribe conduct, that allow or limit behavior. Rule 10b-5 of the Securities Exchange Act of 1934 is an example of substantive regulation.

regulations

Rules promulgated by an administrative agency under authority given to the agency by the enabling statute.

LEGAL FOCUS—EXAMPLE

Rule 10b-5—Employment of Manipulative and Deceptive Devices. It shall be unlawful for any person . . .

a. To employ any device, scheme, or artifice to defraud,

b. To make any untrue statement of a material fact or to omit to state a material fact necessary in order to make the statements made, in the light of the circumstances under which they were made, not misleading, or

c. To engage in any act, practice, or course of business which operates or would operate as a fraud or deceit upon any person,

in connection with the purchase or sale of any security.

http://

The what and why of most government agencies can be found at their Web sites. For example, see "About the SEC" at the U.S. Securities and Exchange Commission's Web site

http://www.sec.gov/

Rule 10b-5 is the so-called "Securities Fraud" regulation that some believe should proscribe the type of conduct alleged to have occurred in the Enron Corporation collapse. It is a great example of a substantive regulation that has had a colorful and rich history of enforcement. Its reach goes beyond brokers and traders and touches, theoretically, every person who buys or sells a stock or bond.

Focus on Agency Process

In this chapter we do not focus on the substantive law of agencies for several reasons. First, the substantive law of a particular agency is usually a particular topic or type of law. For instance, the SEC enforces "Securities" laws. Second, the substantive law of agencies is a topic as broad as law itself. This is because nearly every statute, state or federal, involves at least one agency in its application. In this chapter we focus on understanding agency process. Along the way we will discuss what administrative agencies are, how they are created, what they do, what they cannot do, how they affect our lives, and what we can do when we disagree with their decisions.

LEGAL FOCUS—PROBLEM

Dan and Linda Dixon bought a parcel of land on which to build their dream home. Upon retirement they met with an architect and commissioned plans. They found a contractor to build their home. Unfortunately, the land they owned had been rezoned, and they were told by the city planning commission that they had to apply for a conditional use permit (CUP), which they did. The planning commission denied their CUP application, stating that the Dixons' proposed house did not reflect the values intended for the land. The Dixons felt it would be a waste of time to appeal the decision to the City Council and engaged an attorney to file a lawsuit. Their attorney advised them that there was really nothing they could do.

The Dixons have just participated in an administrative process. Local governments also have agencies such as city planning commissions that must apply the law. The limits and powers of agencies that we study in this chapter reach down to the city level. That is one reason why understanding administrative law may be far more important than understanding trial procedures.

WHAT IS AN ADMINISTRATIVE AGENCY?

Understanding administrative law and how it affects your life requires that you first understand what an administrative agency is and what the various types of agencies are. Recall that the United States is a federal form of government, meaning it is made up of numerous governments that co-exist; namely, a federal government and fifty state governments. Each of those governments has its own body of administrative law complete with numerous agencies. In the case of the federal government, the number of agencies is too vast to cover in this chapter, even summarily. The supremacy of federal law over state law adds a layer of complexity to this as well. In any given state, there will be offices of federal agencies as well as those of the state's agencies. Some may serve similar purposes, such as environmental protection, or public health. Exhibit 5-2 depicts a simplified version of this federal/state federalism structure of administrative law.

administrative agency

Collectively, sub-branches of the executive branch of federal, state, and local governments. Administrative agencies may possess legislative, executive, and judicial powers in specialized technical areas where appropriate regulation requires action by experts.

An **administrative agency** is a sub-branch of the executive branch of the federal, a state, or a local government. Usually, federal agencies are used as examples to explain and teach administrative law. States are usually organized in a similar, if less complex, structure as the federal administrative governmental system. So it is useful to use the federal government as an introductory tool. To fully understand administrative law requires a review of state structures as well.

Two important categories of federal agencies are executive departments and independent administrative agencies. Exhibit 5-3 shows a sampling of administrative agencies within the federal government system. Exhibit 5-3 shows offices of the Judiciary and the Legislature, but those are not normally defined as agencies. The main constitutional and policy concern arises with agencies that have powers of the other branches in addition to executive power.

EXECUTIVE DEPARTMENTS

executive department

Generally, administrative bodies headed by single persons ultimately answerable to one person, the chief executive.

Some agencies are nothing more than a department of the executive branch of the federal government. These **executive departments** were created by Congress to allow the

EXHIBIT 5-2: **Federal and State Administrative Law**

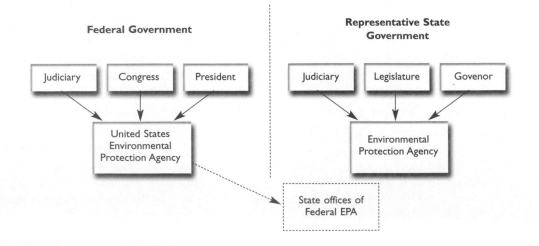

EXHIBIT 5-3: **The Government of the United States**

This chart seeks to show only the more important agencies of the government.

THE CONSTITUTION

LEGISLATIVE BRANCH

THE CONGRESS

Senate   House
Architect of the Capitol
U.S. Botanic Garden
General Accounting Office
Government Printing Office
Library of Congress
Congressional Budget Office

EXECUTIVE BRANCH

THE PRESIDENT
THE VICE PRESIDENT
Executive Office of the President

White House Office
Office of Management and Budget
Council of Economic Advisers
National Security Council
Office of Policy Development

Office of the U.S. Trade Representative
Council on Environmental Quality
Office of Sciences and Technology Policy
Office of Vice President of U.S.
Office of National Drug Control Policy

JUDICIAL BRANCH

The Supreme Court of the U.S.
U.S. Court of Appeals
U.S. District Courts
U.S. Claims Court
U.S. Court of International Trade
U.S. Tax Court
Territorial Courts
Administrative Office of the U.S. Courts
Federal Judicial Courts
U.S. Sentencing Commission

Department of Agriculture

Department of The Interior

Department of Commerce

Department of Justice

Department of Defense

Department of Labor

Department of Education

Department of State

Department of Energy

Department of Transportation

Department of Health and Human Services

Department of the Treasury

Department of Homeland Security

Department of Housing and Urban Development

Department of Veterans Affairs

INDEPENDENT ESTABLISHMENT AND GOVERNMENT CORPORATIONS.

African Development Foundation
Central Intelligence Agency
Commodity Futures Trading Commission
Consumer Product Safety Commission*
Corporation for National and Community Service
Defense Nuclear Facilities Safety Board
Environmental Protection Agency*
Equal Employment Opportunity Commission*
Export-Import Bank of the U.S.
Farm Credit Administration
Federal Communications Commission*
Federal Deposit Insurance Corporation*

Federal Election Commission
Federal Emergency Management Agency
Federal Housing Finance Board
Federal Labor Relations Authority
Federal Maritime Commission
Federal Mediation and Conciliation Service
Federal Mine Safety and Health Review Commission
Federal Reserve System
Federal Retirement Thrift Investment Board
Federal Trade Commission*
General Services Administration
Inter-American Foundation
Merit System Protection Board
National Aeronautics and Space Administration*

National Archives and Records Administration
National Capital Planning Commission
National Credit Union Administration
National Foundation on the Arts and the Humanities
National Labor Relations Board*
National Mediation Board
National Railroad Passenger Corporation (Amtrak)
National Science Foundation
National Transportation Safety Board
Nuclear Regulatory Commission
Occupational Safety and Health Review Commission*
Office of Government Ethics
Office of Personnel Management
Peace Corps

Pension Benefit Guaranty Corporation*
Postal Rate Commission
Railroad Retirement Board
Securities and Exchange Commission*
Selective Service System
Small Business Administration*
Social Security Administration
Tennessee Valley Authority
Trade and Development Agency
U.S. Arms Control Disarmament Agency
U.S. Agency International Development
U.S. International Trade Commission
U.S. Office of Special Counsel
U.S. Postal Service*

* Major administrative agency.
Source: U.S. Government Manual, 2002-2003.

http://

One example of an executive department is the National Security Council
http://www.whitehouse.gov/nsc/

president to better execute the laws of the United States. Examples include the Department of the Interior, the Department of Justice, the National Security Council, and the Department of Defense. These agencies are controlled more directly by the president and thus exist as an arm of the Executive Department. The Department of Homeland Security was a recent addition to the list of executive department administrative agencies. The executive departments that are part of the cabinet of the president of the United States are headed by a secretary appointed by the president with the advice and consent of the Senate. The president may remove department heads at will.

INDEPENDENT ADMINISTRATIVE AGENCIES

independent administrative agency

An administrative body empowered to regulate some policy area led by officials who cannot be dismissed by the president of the United States except for good cause.

Most of the agencies referred to in this chapter are not executive departments. Instead they are independent administrative agencies. **Independent administrative agencies** are governmental units with delegated powers commonly found in the other branches of government. Applying the Separation of Powers doctrine, the Supreme Court of the United States has generally allowed agencies to collect the powers of multiple branches of the federal government only when there is some guarantee of independence.[1]

Independence is established by making term appointments of the persons in charge of the agency. During the stated term, the officials or commissioners are removable only by a finding of misconduct or failure to do their job. As with executive department heads, the appointment of independent agency leadership generally is made by the executive branch (governor or president). But the executive branch's ability to remove agency heads at will (fire) is restricted by the statute creating the agency generally to reasons related to misfeasance. Moreover, a determination by the executive of good cause to dismiss is subject to judicial oversight whereas a dismissal of an executive department head is not.

LEGAL FOCUS—CASE

President Herbert Hoover appointed William Humphrey to the Federal Trade Commission for a seven-year term. Two years into the term, President Franklin D. Roosevelt, Hoover's successor as president, requested that Humphrey resign, stating, "I do not feel that your mind and my mind go along together on either the policies or the administering of the Federal Trade Commission. . . ." Humphrey declined to resign, whereupon Roosevelt wrote Humphrey, "Effective as of this date you are hereby removed from the office of Commissioner of the Federal Trade Commission." Humphrey refused to vacate his office, claiming the Federal Trade Commission Act allowed removal of commissioners only for reasons of "inefficiency, neglect of duty, or malfeasance in office." Roosevelt maintained that as president of the United States he had the inherent power to remove members of the executive branch in whom he lacked confidence. Was Humphrey allowed to remain a commissioner?

Humphrey's Executor v. United States, 295 U.S. 602, 55 S.Ct. 869 (1935).

Yes. The Supreme Court agreed with Humphrey. The court ruled that the president lacked the power to fire Humphrey, who could serve his appointed term unless found guilty of a failure to perform his job.

STATE AGENCIES

Each state has its own collection of agencies and its own rules governing them. State agencies collect the powers of one or more branches of the state's government much as federal agencies do in the federal government. Each state has its own constitution as well as statutes governing the rules for independence of and oversight of its administrative agencies. In this chapter we will touch on two state examples of administrative law, Iowa and California.

BRIEF HISTORY OF U.S. ADMINISTRATIVE LAW

The first administrative agencies were executive departments created by the first Congress to allow the president a structure to begin executing the laws of the United States. They included the Departments of State, Treasury, and War, as well as the Post Office and the Office of the Attorney General. Then, mostly in three distinct time periods, Congress added more executive departments and many independent administrative agencies. Those three time periods were characterized by significant policy dilemmas facing the United States at the time.

In the 1880s, when big business and abusive business practices surfaced as a significant problem, independent administrative agencies emerged as a new solution. The first major independent agency, the Interstate Commerce Commission, was created at that time to address problems in the railroad industry. This marked a significant step in the evolution of administrative law in the United States, as Congress experimented with powerful agencies holding multiple powers to solve regulatory problems in the growing economy and society of the United States. The Federal Trade Commission followed in 1914 to deal with business abuses, primarily anti-competitive and monopolistic behavior.

New agencies continued to appear over the next several decades. Then, during the 1930s President Franklin Roosevelt's response to the Great Depression, led to a significant addition to the ranks of administrative agencies. That era also brought an increased role of the government in providing support and services to its citizens as well as in regulating business and business transactions. Agencies created in this era include the Securities and Exchange Commission (SEC), the Federal Communications Commission (FCC), and the National Labor Relations Board (NLRB). The New Deal era embodied more than just an increase in government; it was a paradigm shift of the role of the government in regulating the economy and business and supporting workers. Administrative agencies were the workhorses for government expansion in that era.

The third wave of administrative agencies occurred during the 1960s and 1970s. Many of these agencies focused on protecting and managing the environment and its resources (e.g., the Environmental Protection Agency), ending racial discrimination (e.g., the Equal Employment Opportunity Commission), or establishing safe and stable working conditions (e.g., the Occupational Safety and Health Administration).

As the United States entered the twenty-first century, the U.S. government had evolved into a vast labyrinth of administrative agencies making up a bureaucracy that most citizens encounter on a regular basis. During the later decades of the twentieth century, **deregulation** swept through numerous industries. Deregulation symbolically means reducing the extent to which the government regulates an industry. In practice, nearly all efforts to deregulate have been in fact simply been re-regulation, that is, a change in the way industry is regulated.

deregulation

A process of eliminating, reducing, or restructuring the regulation of an industry.

LEGAL FOCUS—BACKGROUND

A recent, notorious experiment in deregulation swept through the electricity industry at the close of the 1990s. It began in California in 1997, as the largest state economy removed the utility monopoly over the generation of electricity. Left unchanged was the manner in which electricity is distributed and delivered to customers, which stayed in the hands of large investor-owned utilities. Within a few years the wholesale price for electricity soared, mysterious shortages appeared, and controversial marketing, accounting, and sales practices came to light. Other states followed suit in deregulation, but not all. Though government and business press releases and media accounts usually referred to the events as the "deregulation experiment" it was in fact a change in the way the electricity industry was regulated. As part of California's supposed deregulation, two new agencies were created, the California Independent System Operator and the California Consumer Power Financing Authority.

CREATION OF ADMINISTRATIVE AGENCIES

enabling statute

A statute that creates an administrative agency and typically also authorizes it to perform specified actions.

An administrative agency is usually created by a statute, known as the **enabling statute.** The enabling statute typically will name the agency and specify its purpose, powers, limits, and structure. The statute may call for a board or commission, or it might call for a single individual to head the agency. Some agencies are required by a state constitution. Those are usually called "constitutional agencies." Even then, the agency may be described only briefly in the state constitution, allowing state legislature the ability to better define it and modify it over time. When dealing with any particular agency, the first step should be to understand its powers and limitations, as well as its structure. Studying the enabling statute and/or constitutional authority for the agency is critical to understanding any agency.

As depicted in Exhibit 5-3, the federal government is vast and complex. As the federal government has grown, it has relied upon administrative agencies to expand its roles and responsibilities in governing the several states.

LEGAL FOCUS—EXAMPLE

In response to the terrorist attacks on September 11, 2001, Congress and the president pressed for a new cabinet-level agency, the Department of Homeland Security (DHS), to prevent future terrorist attacks. DHS, established by the Homeland Security Act of 2002, is not an independent administrative agency but, like other cabinet departments, is directly controlled by the president.

The list of administrative agencies in Exhibit 5-3 is only partial. Among other functions, administrative agencies regulate products, businesses, and transactions; protect consumers, the environment, and the economy; collect taxes; allocate welfare; explore space; collect intelligence; investigate and punish securities fraud; resolve labor infractions and disputes; and deliver the mail. Most of these agencies are independent administrative agencies that function with a head, commission, or board that can execute the laws and regulations of that agency with little concern for political consequences. Concurrent with that independence is a risk of abusive or derelict practices not easily controlled by the executive branch of the government.

ADMINISTRATIVE PROCEDURE ACT (APA)

In 1946, the **Administrative Procedure Act (APA)** established a set of rules governing most federal agency conduct.[2] The APA was enacted in response to numerous charges of inconsistent or reckless procedures and inconsistent standards being used by the numerous federal agencies created before World War II. The APA created a structure that categorized various agency conduct and set rules for each category. Agency conduct that was defined as either "rulemaking" or "adjudication" was given basic minimum requirements to ensure a fair and accurate action. Rulemaking and adjudication are explored later in this chapter. Most states have enacted laws similar to the federal APA to govern state administrative agencies.

DELEGATION OF POWER

When an enabling statute grants a power to an agency that is otherwise a power assigned to Congress in the U.S. Constitution, there is a legitimate question as to whether Congress and the president have made a constitutional delegation. The U.S. Supreme Court has ruled on this issue several times, usually allowing delegations. The most often cited case arose during the Great Depression as the New Deal sought to create numerous new administrative agencies.

LEGAL FOCUS—CASE

In the midst of the 1930s depression, Congress enacted the National Industry Recovery Act (NIRA). The NIRA authorized the president of the United States to approve codes of fair competition that had been prepared and submitted to him by trade and industry associations or had been created upon the president's own initiative. The act provided that violations of these codes would be punishable as crimes. The Schechter Poultry Corporation was held criminally liable for violation of one such code, the "Live Poultry Code." Schechter challenged the code by challenging the constitutionality of Congress's delegating to the president the power to approve codes. How did the Supreme Court rule?

Schechter Poultry Corp. v. United States, 295 U.S. 495, 55 S.Ct. 837 (1935).

A unanimous Supreme Court held that the delegation by Congress to the president in the NIRA was too broad, because it allowed the president to impose any regulation he chose. This "unfettered" power was "an unconstitutional delegation of legislative power." *Schechter* is a rare overturning of a delegation by Congress, but it helped define how and when Congress could delegate its power without running afoul of the U.S. Constitution.

Sidebar

Administrative Procedure Act (APA) of 1946

Law that mandates procedures for federal administrative agencies.

http://

You can find the Administrative Procedure Act at many sites including **http://biotech.law.lsu.edu/ Courses/study_aids/adlaw/**

The following are among the guidelines considered by the Court to determine whether a delegation is valid:

- To whom is the delegation made? Is it made to an administrative agency? Is that agency independent or is it merely an executive department? Is the delegation to state government, the president, or private industry?
- Is the delegation for a proper purpose? That is, is its purpose a legitimate exercise of government power?
- Have guidelines for delegated conduct been provided in the legislation? Are the guidelines broad or narrow in scope?
- Does the legislation provide for a fair process in creating regulations or administering tasks?
- Is the reason for the delegation an emergency?
- What is the nature of the delegation? Does it affect personal rights such as property rights?

As you learn about agency processes, note the many instances where the APA contains requirements that specifically address many of these guidelines. This is not accidental. The APA, in part, was designed to ensure that many of the constitutional fears and dangers inherent in independent administrative agencies were reduced or eliminated. For instance, the APA establishes requirements for hearings and rulemaking to help ensure fairness.

LEGAL FOCUS—BACKGROUND

The creation of the Federal Trade Commission (FTC) is an example of a lawful delegation by Congress. The FTC was created by the Federal Trade Commission Act of 1914, which prohibits unfair and deceptive trade practices. The act describes the procedures the agency must follow to charge violators, provides for the judicial review of agency actions, and grants the power to investigate and to make rules and regulations. The FTC may force a company to stop an advertising campaign if it considers the advertisements to be "unfair or deceptive" to consumers. The FTC may even require a company to make announcements or advertisements to correct the false statements made in earlier advertisements.

STATE ADMINISTRATIVE AGENCIES

California

The state of California has an administrative bureaucracy that many argue rivals the federal government. In a state famous for its protective statutes, numerous agencies exist to carry out those laws. California also has its own Administrative Procedure Act (CAL-APA). Yet another administrative agency was created just to enforce the CAL-APA, the Office of Administrative Law (OAL). Like the federal government, California has an Environmental Protection Agency (CAL-EPA), numerous other environmental protection agencies, health and welfare agencies, business and trade regulation agencies, and consumer protection agencies. In California, there is a state-equivalent agency for nearly every federal agency. In many cases, California law more strictly regulates economic transactions than federal law does. For instance, the United States Environmental Protection Agency might allow a particular chemical to be discharged into the ground whereas the California Environmental Protection Agency might prohibit it. Such duplicative state law is gener-

http://

You can consult the California Administrative Procedure Act at **http://ceres.ca.gov/env_law/apa_index.html**

ally allowed by federal statute when it does not unduly interfere with federal regulation of interstate commerce.

Iowa

California's administrative law contrasts greatly with Iowa's. Iowa has its own version of the APA, but it has a simpler and smaller labyrinth of administrative agencies. Less duplication exists with federal agencies. Still, there is a significant administrative law system within the Iowa state government. Iowa regulates business, protects the environment, and regulates its professional trades. It also has administrative agencies for building code development, organized labor, and employment disputes.

http://

You can consult the Iowa Administrative Procedure Act at

http://www.state.ia.us/ government/com/prof/ 17aindex.htm

LEADING AREAS OF ADMINISTRATIVE LAW

Administrative law touches upon nearly every aspect of government; moreover, there are several major areas in which administrative agencies of the federal and state governments do the majority of the work enforcing the law. This section introduces several substantive areas of administrative law. Every agency was created in response to a specific need. Gradually, as government regulation became more common, and perhaps more expected, the *laissez-faire* (French: "allow to act") capitalism conceived by the early economist Adam Smith was gradually replaced with a regulated economy.

BUSINESS FINANCE

By definition, in a free economy the government does not interfere in business at all. But the health and function of business can greatly affect the economy and the general welfare of the United States; left unregulated, business practices have shown themselves to be highly vulnerable to abuse and exploitation with drastic consequences for the economy as well. Since the Great Depression of the 1930s, the United States has maintained a strong regulatory oversight of the financial sector, including investment, banking, securities, accounting, and trading. Three large and important agencies in this arena are the Securities and Exchange Commission (SEC), the Commodity Futures Trading Commission (CFTC), and the Federal Reserve Board.

http://

Visit the Web site of the Commodity Futures Trading Commission at

http://www.cftc.gov/cftc/ cftchome.htm

The SEC (1934)[3] regulates organized securities markets and the securities traded there. It also thus regulates every company that uses securities for finance purposes. Because "security" is defined very broadly, the SEC reaches many investments beyond traditional securities like stocks and bonds. The SEC controls and regulates the dissemination of information by regulated companies and investigates and prosecutes violations of securities laws and regulations. Traders, brokers, and other professionals who work in securities are regulated by the SEC as well. The CFTC (1974)[4] is similar to the SEC but focuses on the commodity futures and options markets. The Federal Reserve Board (1913)[5] supervises and regulates most of the nation's banks and helps to ensure a stable money currency, to hedge against inflation, and to control the flow of money in the economy.

LEGAL FOCUS—BACKGROUND

In 2001, Enron, a large energy and technology company, collapsed under admissions of manipulating debt and hiding losses of billions of dollars. MCI, a communications company, followed suit in 2002. As this book goes to press, various government agencies are preparing indictments, civil charges, and regulatory proceedings against the companies and some of their executives. The political and economic fallout from these collapses is tremendous, and Congress is considering another round of laws to be enforced by agencies such as the SEC. Meanwhile the SEC is overwhelmed with the number of investigations and enforcements related to the business scandals.

COMMUNICATIONS

http://

Visit the Web site of the Federal Communications Commission at **http://www.FCC.gov**

The roaring economic growth of the 1990s was fueled in part by tremendous growth in the communications sector. From cellular phones to the Internet, from cable to the radio, the Federal Communications Commission (FCC) is the agency in the center of this sector. The FCC was created in 1934[6] to regulate the then-stressed radio communications business.

Much regulation of the communications business deals with the dividing up of the limited electromagnetic spectrum in the bands used for communication. In that sense cellular telephone systems are the latest growth industry that the FCC has managed. Without a regulating central agency, the communication industry would be chaos at best and war at worst. The FCC has been challenged from its beginning to keep up with technology.

Currently the Internet is not directly regulated in the United States. By virtue of regulating the telephone industry, the FCC is the closest any governmental office comes to regulating the Internet. The FCC regulates the companies that own, operate, or trade capacity in wire and radio communication systems. These include common carriers such as the telephone and telegraph services. A key function the FCC performs is the issuance of licenses to radio, telephone, and cellular telephone systems. The FCC assigns operating frequencies, where appropriate, and investigates and enforces regulations covering, for example, the use of unauthorized frequencies.

EMPLOYMENT PRACTICES

Employment law is substantially affected by administrative law. The government regulates working conditions, pay, hiring and firing of employees, health, pension and retirement benefit plans, and organized labor and its relationship with employers. Many disputes involving the employer-employee relationship are resolved through state or federal labor boards.

The National Labor Relations Board (NLRB) was created in 1935[7] to supervise the union-employer relationship. Among other functions, the NLRB is charged with preventing unfair labor practices.

Some state labor boards focus on labor disputes such as overtime pay. Employees are often surprised to find out they can file a complaint with the local labor board and have their matter heard in an administrative hearing rather than file a lawsuit.

The Equal Employment Opportunity Commission (EEOC) was created in 1964[8] to investigate and resolve complaints of discrimination filed by employees. The Employee Retirement Income Security Act (ERISA) was enacted in 1974 to regulate pension and retirement benefit plans following the prominent failure of numerous plans. The Pension and Welfare Programs Office of the Labor Department enforces ERISA.

LEGAL FOCUS—BACKGROUND

. . . .

When Enron went bankrupt in 2001, many employees had a high percentage of their 401(k) retirement accounts invested in Enron stock. (The name 401(k) refers to the section of the tax code that allows tax-advantaged retirement plans.) These plans are usually funded by the employees, but employers often contribute as well. The employer may administer the fund for the employees' benefit. Employees can choose from a variety of investment options, usually including mutual funds, money market accounts, and simple interest accounts. Many employers, like Enron, encourage employees to invest in company stock, sometimes giving incentives to do so. After Enron's bankruptcy, many employees found their retirement accounts worthless or close to it. In 2002, Congress began hearings that may lead to new restrictions on 401(k) plans. The Pension and Welfare Programs Office could add new regulations as well, by conducting rulemaking to effectuate similar restrictions. Even if Congress establishes a new statute, it is still up to the agency to create and then enforce new regulations.

ENVIRONMENT

Government protection of the environment began with agencies such as the Environmental Protection Agency (EPA), established in 1970.[9] There are numerous laws protecting the environment and restricting what individuals, property owners, and businesses can and cannot do that might affect the health of the environment. The Endangered Species Act, the National Environmental Protection Act, the Clean Air Act, and the Clean Water Act are just a few of the many statutes that obligate numerous agencies to work vigorously to protect the environment. Besides the EPA, other agencies that work to enforce these and other environmental laws include the U.S. Fish and Wildlife Service, the Bureau of Land Management, and the National Forest Service. Many state agencies are delegated authority to enforce federal environmental protection laws.

The EPA is the single agency at the core of environmental protection. Exhibit 5-4 is the formal statement of the EPA's purpose. Through the EPA and affiliated federal and state agencies, the government strives to reduce water and airborne pollution, clean up contaminated land, reduce destruction of habitat, and save species from extinction. Most of this work is accomplished by controlling development and enforcing regulations against violators. Nearly every environmental protection statute requires a tremendous amount of detail in the form of regulations to make it effective. For instance, to enforce the Clean Air Act, the EPA had to establish standards for healthy air. The agency also had to set limits for emissions of various known pollutants from sources such as refineries, boilers, power plants, and industrial processors. Even automobile emissions are subject to regulations that, among other aspects, require catalytic converters and unleaded gas.

ENERGY

The United States consumes more energy per capita than any other nation. It relies primarily upon fossil fuels (oil, natural gas, and coal) and to some smaller extent on hydroelectric dams and nuclear, geothermal, solar, and wind power. Fuel cells, which use a new technology that coverts hydrogen to electricity, have yet to make a significant contribution. The

http://

Visit the Web site of the Environmental Protection Agency at
http://www.epa.gov

EXHIBIT 5-4: **EPA Statement of Purpose**

The EPA's purpose is to ensure that:

- All Americans are protected from significant risk to human health and the environment where they live, learn, and work.

- National efforts to reduce environmental risk are based on the best available scientific information.

- Federal laws protecting human health and the environment are enforced fairly and effectively.

- Environmental protection is an integral consideration in U. S. policies concerning natural resources, human health, economic growth, energy transportation, agriculture, industry, and international trade, and these factors are similarly considered in establishing environmental policy.

- All parts of society—communities, individuals, business, state and local governments, tribal governments—have access to accurate information sufficient to effectively participate in managing human health and environmental risks

- Environment protection contributes to making our communities and ecosystems diverse, sustainable, and economically productive.

- The Untied States plays a leadership role in working with other nations to protect the global environment.

Source: See http://www.epa/gov/history/org/origins/mission.htm.

http://

Visit the Web site of the Federal Energy Regulatory Commission at **http://www.ferc.fed.us/**

United States is highly dependent on foreign sources of fossil fuels such as oil from the Middle East and natural gas from Canada and Mexico. About one-third of the oil consumed in this country is used in the transportation sector. This foreign dependency, combined with the core economic need for an adequate, safe, and reliable supply of energy, has led to creation of agencies at both the federal and state level. Further complicating the situation is that nearly all energy consumed in the United States has significant environmental injury considerations, thus drawing federal and state environmental agencies into the energy sector.

The Federal Energy Regulatory Commission (FERC), created in 1977,[10] is responsible for regulating electricity generation and transmission, numerous federally owned large hydroelectric facilities, and natural gas and oil production and transmission. Nuclear energy is regulated by the Nuclear Regulatory Commission (NRC), established in 1974.[11] The NRC licenses and supervises all non-military nuclear power plant, research, test, and training reactors. It is also responsible for regulating all medical, academic, and industrial uses of nuclear materials.

FREE ENTERPRISE AND HEALTHY COMPETITION

The United States was founded on the modern economic thought of Adam Smith. Adam Smith promoted the idea that the invisible hand of the market would naturally guide a capitalistic economy far better than the artificial efforts of government ever could. That model survived intact only briefly, as the United States steadily found circumstances where the economy was not functioning adequately. In every instance, the solution involved new laws or regulations designed to protect competition from itself.

The chief federal administrative agency tasked with protecting competition is the Federal Trade Commission (FTC), established in 1914.[12] Another agency that regulates in this area is the Securities and Exchange Commission, with its supervision of the financing of business. The primary concern of the FTC is controlling unfair competition by administering various *antitrust* statutes. Antitrust describes government efforts to control the collusion of businesses to manipulate markets; and also the development and wielding of market power by gaining monopoly status. The FTC shares responsibility with the Justice Department in this area.

LEGAL FOCUS—CASE

The Superior Court Trial Lawyers Association of Washington, D.C., (SCTLA) went on a one-month strike for higher wages (higher hourly rates). SCTLA members are criminal lawyers in private practice. They are registered with courts, indicating their availability to represent indigent defendants in cases assigned by the court.

After an investigation and hearing, the FTC ruled that the SCTLA boycott was illegal and barred any future similar action. SCTLA appealed. A federal appeals court ordered the FTC to reconsider its decision and determine if the SCTLA had sufficient control of the market to make its boycott anticompetitive. The FTC appealed to the Supreme Court of the United States. Should the FTC be compelled to reconsider its ruling?

FTC. v. Superior Court Trial Lawyers Ass'n, 493 U.S. 411, 110 S.Ct. 768 (1990).

No. The Supreme Court said, "The social justification[s] proffered for [this] restraint of trade ... do not make it any less unlawful." The Court applied the toughest antitrust rule, the *per se* (Latin: "in itself") rule. This means that the Court recognized that some business activities, such as price fixing, are so anticompetitive that they are automatically (*per se*) prohibited. Thus, these activities do not require proof that conspirators (in this case, SCTLA members) had a motive, or the power, to control the market. The Supreme Court overturned the appeals court order and upheld the FTC ruling that the SCTLA strike was inherently illegal. Therefore, evidence of SCTLA power to control the market was not required.

OTHER AREAS OF ADMINISTRATIVE LAW

Recall that administrative law is as vast as the subject of law itself. Thus, the foregoing discussion identifies only some major leading areas of administrative law. The transportation sector, medical facilities, and the licensing of the professional trades are all handled with administrative agencies. Welfare programs and other governmental benefits such as unemployment and disability insurance are supervised by administrative agencies. Suffice it to say that administrative law touches nearly every subject of law.

AGENCY POWER, PROCESS, AND ACTION

You have learned that administrative law is vast and pervasive and the agencies that create and apply the law numerous. Now we study the basic ways in which agencies perform their duties and functions. As mentioned earlier, our focus is on the federal system to explain administrative law. Most states have similar structures, processes, and rules.

Generally speaking, important agency actions are classified as rulemaking, investigation, or enforcement. Adjudication can be part of an enforcement proceeding. Exhibit 5-5 illustrates the relationship between agency actions and agency products. Rulemaking and adjudication are the two significant and powerful tools that an administrative agency wields to accomplish its purposes.

THE INDEPENDENCE OF AGENCIES

It can be said that agencies act as "judge, jury, and prosecutor," a description that well describes the independent power and action of many agencies. It also illustrates what

EXHIBIT 5-5: **Agency Authority, Purpose, and Action**

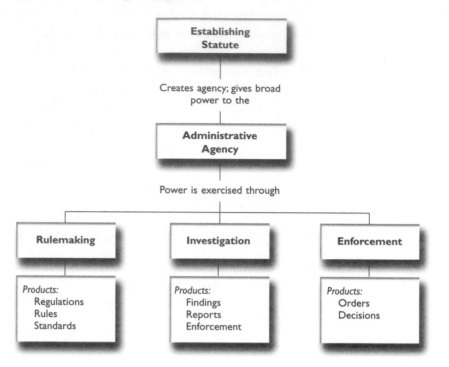

happens when powers from all three branches of the government are placed in one agency. Most independent administrative agencies and some executive departments make regulations to enforce statutes, choose how and to whom to apply those regulations, and then apply them. Agencies can fine, take property, issue permits, and give benefits to businesses and individuals. They do much of this without leaving the confines of their own buildings. Hence they operate very independently. Congress can do little to stop or control an agency's action. The president has some control over executive departments but little if any direct control over independent administrative agencies. The judiciary exercises some oversight/review of agency conduct, but as we will see later, that review is very deferential. Thus, successful interaction with administrative agencies requires good working knowledge and management of agency structure and procedure.

REGULATIONS AND RULEMAKING

Rulemaking is, obviously, the making of rules or regulations. Rules and regulations are the laws made by agencies that "implement, interpret, or prescribe law or policy."[13] Historically rules and regulations represented two distinctly different types of law. *Rules* are procedural laws that describe agency processes, such as the conduct of hearings. *Regulations,* on the other hand, are the laws that guide agency decision-making, that determine rights and duties. Today, the distinction between rules and regulations has blurred significantly in many agencies, federal and state. Agencies often create a type of regulation known as a *standard.* Standards are regulations designed to establish norms or guidelines. Another type of regulation is an *interpretive rule,* which explains how an agency interprets a rule or intends to apply it. Interpretive rules do not have the force of law that other regulations do. They do, however, have considerable weight in court, should someone challenge an agency action or decision. Courts give significant deference to agency expertise. When interpretive rules are published, courts seldom apply a different interpretation.

Below is a regulation passed by the EPA that prohibits ring carriers (the plastic that holds six-packs of soda together) unless they will degrade in accordance with specified testing standards.

LEGAL FOCUS—EXAMPLE

No processor or person shall manufacture or import, in bulk, ring carriers intended for use in the United States unless they are designed and manufactured so that the ring carriers degrade to the point of 5 percent elongation at break, when tested in accordance with [testing standards]. . . .[14]

Rulemaking has essentially the same effect as the enactment of a law by Congress and the president. For that reason, the process by which agencies establish regulations is similar to enactment of legislation including meeting minimal constitutional requirements of due process. As regulations often affect personal rights, minimum standards of fairness apply, such as requirements of notice to affected parties. Numerous other requirements apply to agency rulemaking as well. Some are of these are found in the APA and apply to most agencies, whereas some are specific to a particular agency and found in the enabling statute or other statutes.

Generally the rulemaking process contains these fundamental elements.

1. **Notice.** Agencies must inform the affected public of the intended rulemaking. The APA requires that notice be provided in the *Federal Register* including the time, place, and manner of the rulemaking proceedings.[15] The *Federal Register* is a federal government publication, usually issued daily, that administrative lawyers and researchers subscribe to and scan for matters pertinent to their clients' or their own interests. The notice must also describe the interests being affected.

2. **Public comments.** Agencies must allow for public comments, usually orally at public meetings and in writing.[16] Sometimes a statute requires that rules cannot be enacted without a public hearing. Hearings are often conducted around the country to receive comments. If a hearing is not required, the agency usually provides an address to which written comments can be sent.

3. **Publishing of the regulation.** Final federal regulations are printed in the *Federal Register,* taking effect thirty days after publication. After the thirty-day period the regulations are published in the Code of Federal Regulations (CFR). The CFR is a huge, growing document that includes all federal regulations. States often have an equivalent to the CFR for state regulations, though they are often organized very differently. States may have an equivalent to the *Federal Register* as well.

4. **Response to comments.** Sometimes agencies are required to respond in writing to significant comments made by other parties. When this is the case the agency publishes a comprehensive explanation of how each comment was addressed.

5. **Written record.** An agency may be compelled to maintain a rulemaking record in case a regulation is challenged in the courts. The regulation process results in numerous written documents including the initial rulemaking notice, comments by parties and the agency, and a final rule, sometimes with an explanation.

Exhibit 5-6 provides a general outline of the rulemaking process for the Federal Communications Commission. The specific process in each federal agency varies slightly, but stays

http://

Visit the *Federal Register* online at
http://www.gpo.gov/ su_docs/aces/aces140.html

http://

Visit the Code of Federal Regulations online at
http://www.gpo.gov/nara/ cfr/index.html

EXHIBIT 5-6: **FCC Rulemaking Process**

FCC Document

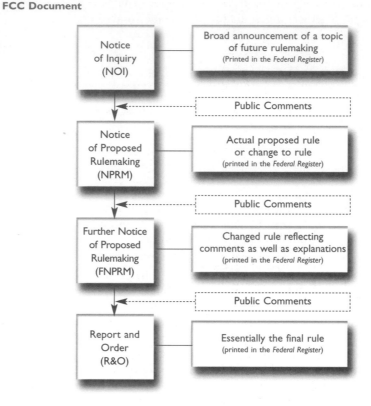

within the requirements of the APA. Each state has its own version of the rulemaking process as well. The above five components represented in Exhibit 5-6 are nearly always present, however, though perhaps with different names. Notice that public comments are invited after each step in the FCC's process. Note also the extensive use of acronyms (NOI, NPRM, etc). Administrative agency rulemaking, like many governmental activities, uses acronyms liberally. Some practitioners believe that understanding the acronyms involved in an agency process is the first step to understanding the process.

LEGAL FOCUS—PROBLEM

The Internal Revenue Service decides to create a new regulation to discourage tax evasion. The new regulation, published in the latest edition of an IRS publication, requires any taxpayer who is selected for an audit to pay the IRS $10,000. Failure to do so will be considered an admission of illegal tax evasion. An enraged taxpayer challenges the regulation in the courts. Is it an enforceable regulation?

No. A court will conclude that the regulation was not properly created. The IRS did not provide public notice and did not receive and reflect on public comments. The IRS did not tailor the regulation to reflect legitimate public concerns or respond to comments. The alleged regulation was not published in the CFR. Even if the IRS had done all of these things, it is likely a court would conclude that the regulation exceeded the authority and power granted to the IRS. Judicial review of agency action is covered later in this chapter, but this is an easy case.

Negotiated Rulemaking

Even with notice protections, the rulemaking process is often unsatisfactory to the agency or the interested parties. In some cases the overwhelming amount of written information frustrates participants. Sometimes the formulaic process of publish-comment-publish leaves interested parties feeling ignored. Often different interests make comments reflecting opposite viewpoints on numerous issues. This leaves agencies in a difficult position: they cannot satisfy all parties. The formal rulemaking process limits give-and-take dialogue that might help find common ground. The Negotiated Rulemaking Act (NRA)[17] allows an alternative method for creating regulations that is designed to increase public involvement. Under the NRA, agencies can conduct a process of **negotiated rulemaking** wherein interested parties are invited to participate in the drafting of the rule. Thus, before the proposed rule is even published the concerns of parties are already reflected in the regulation.

INVESTIGATION

The work of an administrative agency is to execute its administrative tasks. That may involve the use of investigation, prosecution, negotiation, and any number of other administrative chores. Administrative agencies frequently respond to information regarding violations of regulations. Sometimes agencies conduct inspection programs wherein all registered or licensed individuals, businesses, or facilities are systematically and regularly inspected. Often agencies simply need information in order to fulfill their administrative tasks. When agencies seek information and engage in fact-finding activities, the term *investigation* is often used.

LEGAL FOCUS—PROBLEM

A DC-10 jet crashed on takeoff at Chicago's O'Hare International Airport after its left engine and engine-support pylon dropped onto the runway. A total of 275 persons aboard the plane were killed as well as three persons on the ground. The Federal Aviation Administration (FAA), aided by investigators from the National Transportation Safety Board, immediately began exhaustive studies of other DC-10s to determine, if possible, the cause of the disaster. Was the FAA able to order all 138 U.S.-registered DC-10s grounded while conducting its investigation?

Yes, even though the loss in revenues for the affected airlines approximated $2.5 million a day. The grounding was ordered on June 6, 1979, and lasted thirty-eight days. The grounding was lifted after the FAA determined that the disaster was caused by a crack in the aft bulkhead (rear wall) of the pylon, but only after the agency had issued orders (1) to the manufacturer to redesign the pylons, (2) to the airlines to end the maintenance procedure thought to have weakened the pylons and to begin more stringent maintenance

http://

Instructions on how the public may participate in California's rulemaking process can be found at **http://www.oal.ca.gov/ document/HowToParticipate .pdf**

negotiated rulemaking

A process to bring together representatives of a rulemaking agency and stakeholders to jointly prepare the text of a proposed rule in a consensus-seeking negotiation before the agency formally submits the rule to the rulemaking process.

inspections, and (3) to manufacturers and airlines to cooperate more closely with FAA engineers and inspectors in certifying the fitness of aircraft to fly.[18]

The FAA has the power to issue emergency orders in response to an investigation. Many safety-related agencies are given such power. The ability of an agency to suddenly and so drastically affect the rights of a business owner with little or no process is obviously restricted to areas involving public safety.

When parties fail to cooperate with an agency, or when an agency believes it is necessary, subpoenas can be used. A **subpoena** is an order to produce a witness or a thing. Using a subpoena, the administrative agency can compel testimony or production of documents, papers, records, and physical objects. Failure to comply with a subpoena can lead to a contempt citation punishable by fine or imprisonment.

subpoena

An enforceable order for a witness to appear at a particular time and place to testify and/or produce documents in the control of the witness.

Search and Seizure by Administrative Agencies

Administrative agencies, like police authorities, have the power to *search and seize property*. Searches can be part of an investigation for an enforcement proceeding. Some inspections are used in place of formal processes, as when a person being inspected is shown a problem and allowed to fix it. Nevertheless, the search and seize power is useful but it clashes with a person's right to privacy, due process, and freedom from self-incrimination under the U.S. Constitution. Because of that, the Supreme Court has ruled that administrative agencies must comply with the search and seizure provisions of the Fourth Amendment.[19]

The requirements for agencies are less stringent than those for criminal warrants, and warrants are not always required. Some agencies are not required by statute to obtain a warrant. Such *warrantless searches* have been challenged in courts. The Supreme Court has held that commercial property can be searched by an administrative agency without a warrant in certain situations.[20]

LEGAL FOCUS—CASE

Craig and Marilyn Lessor of Union Grove, Wisconsin, were licensed dealers of long-eared, short-tailed lagomorphs—i.e., rabbits. Their rabbitry was subject to regulation and inspection under federal law by government agents. They were found to have unlawfully refused to allow inspections of their rabbitry on five occasions and were fined by the department secretary. The Lessors sought judicial review of the sanction, claiming that by inspecting and attempting to inspect their rabbitry without a warrant, their right to be free from unreasonable searches guaranteed by the Fourth Amendment was violated. Was a warrantless inspection of their rabbit farm lawful?

Lessor v. Epsy, 34 F.3d 1301 (7th cir., 1994).

The inspections were held to be lawful. Although the U.S. Supreme Court has yet to articulate clear guidelines for warrantless searches, generally these three guidelines apply:
1. Administrative searches of heavily regulated industries are less likely to require a warrant.[21] Industries such as nuclear power or mining fall in this category.
2. A warrantless search might be reasonable, or not even considered a search but merely an inspection.[22] In that case it is lawful. When searches are narrowly tailored to minimize the invasion of privacy or not connected to enforcement-specific efforts, they are likely to be allowed.

3. A reasonable expectation of privacy increases the need for a warrant.[23] This last guideline is the most difficult. The privacy of one's home requires the highest protection from warrantless searches, but what if a regulated business is run from one's home? Most farmers would be among those classified as having a home office.

It should be clear that these general guidelines fall far short of covering all the possible situations involving warrantless searches. For that reason, warrantless searches often create the risk for the agency that an enforcement action may be overturned. The best way to avoid the issue is to get permission to search, something the Lessors refused to grant in the above example.

ENFORCEMENT

After concluding an investigation, the agency may start an administrative action. These actions may be brought against individuals or organizations. Enforcements are used to gain compliance with the law. Sometimes enforcement does not follow an investigation. Sometimes private citizens and organizations are allowed under statute to initiate complaints precipitating the enforcement action. Usually the agency has discretion to decline a complaint or dismiss it. In any case, the enforcement is brought by the agency itself.

In enforcement actions the agency acts as prosecutor, judge, and jury. To protect persons subject to administrative investigations, there are procedural safeguards against possible abuse of power by the agency. When procedural safeguards are found inadequate, Congress may hold hearings and pass new laws constraining administrative powers. For example, in 1998 the Senate held hearings on IRS collection practices. These hearings led to new controls on IRS administrative discretion. Below is an excerpt from the reported testimony of Maureen O'Dwyer, an IRS employee.

LEGAL FOCUS—BACKGROUND

When first approached to give testimony before you, I was reluctant to do so, as I considered it to be a betrayal of my fellow employees. The IRS is an easy smear and it has been reviled both justly and unjustly in the press. From the inside looking out, it is easy to distinguish between which accusations are true, and which are not. No one has risen to the defense of the service against the unjust accusations. I did not wish to add more fuel to the already raging fire, or to further demoralize my fellow employees by disclosing any other inequitable practices of the service. But our system of taxation is dependent on the taxpayer's belief that the tax laws they follow will apply to everyone and in the belief that they will be administered impartially.

The aging returns of small taxpayers are written up unagreed and penalties are assessed.* The taxpayer will receive a statutory notice; that is, it must respond within ninety days. If the taxpayer does not respond within this time frame, it will automatically lose its appeals rights and the right to petition tax court. Understanding these procedures is difficult for the unknowledgeable, small taxpayer. Without representation, the small taxpayer is vulnerable. The results can be costly.[24]

* In general IRS-speak, an "aging return" is one filed a few years before the current date and an "unagreed" return is one that the IRS contends understated the taxes owed.

EXHIBIT 5-7: **Administrative Agency Enforcement**

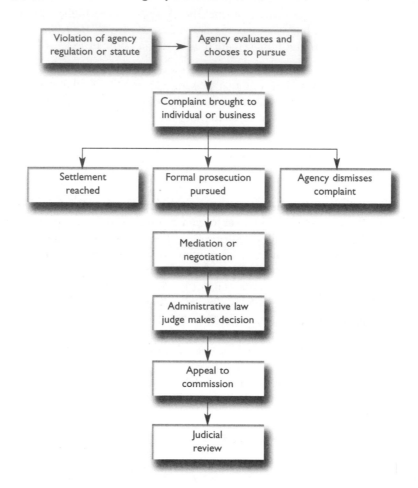

Enforcement can take one of several paths. The problem might be resolved through negotiation between the accused and the agency. It might go to a hearing before an administrative law judge (ALJ). Finally, the full commission might review the ALJ's decision or act as the decision maker itself. Every agency has its own procedures and there is significant variance in enforcement processes from agency to agency. The APA is silent on this topic, addressing only the adjudication aspect of enforcement. As a result, when an individual faces enforcement proceedings, the first step is to seek assistance from a lawyer or consult the agency's regulations, or both. In any case, the individual should become knowledgeable about the agency's procedures.

Exhibit 5-7 shows a map of a generic agency enforcement process. Many administrative law practitioners advise that someone subject to administrative action attempt to negotiate an agreement in a cooperative manner early on in the process. As agencies have huge workloads, cooperative individuals can often obtain a reasonable negotiated settlement. If that fails, most agency enforcement processes will lead to adjudication, i.e., a hearing. Sometimes alternative dispute resolution programs are offered.

ALTERNATIVE DISPUTE RESOLUTION

In the federal system, several statutes have authorized alternative dispute resolution (ADR) methods in agency processes. The 1990 Administrative Dispute Resolution Act was renewed by passage of the Administrative Dispute Resolution Act of 1996.[25] The ADR Act of 1996 expressly authorizes agencies to utilize ADR methods to supplement existing procedures. The act gives discretion to the agencies to choose how to use ADR, but does require that all federal agencies develop an ADR policy, appoint and train a senior "dispute resolution specialist," and train key employees in ADR.[26] The ADR Act of 1996 added binding arbitration as a dispute resolution method available to agencies. In the future it is likely that agency enforcement proceedings will offer negotiation, mediation, or even binding arbitration as an optional or perhaps mandatory step in the resolution processes. In any case, should ADR (if offered) fail to resolve a matter, the next step is adjudication.

ADJUDICATION

Most agencies provide a hearing as an alternative to a court action when a person is threatened with the loss of denial or some license, right, entitlement, or privilege. The agencies not only create rules consistent with their task but also enforce their rules through trial-like proceedings before an **administrative law judge** (ALJ). An ALJ is a government employee, usually an attorney, appointed to hear administrative cases.* Sometimes the appointed heads of the agency hear the cases instead of, or on appeal from an earlier decision by, the ALJ. At the state level, similar quasi-judges are often called *hearing officers* as well as ALJs.

    The APA specifies minimum requirements for these hearings but does not mandate any particular procedure. Statutes and agency regulations usually specify hearings for proceedings involving rights, privileges, entitlements, or licenses. Constitutional due process requirements can often apply requiring, at a minimum, notice and opportunity to be heard. A hearing helps ensure that those requirements have been met. Citizens, too, may request adjudication; for example, to appeal an agency's denial of their claim for government benefits (such as social security).

administrative law judge

A government employee appointed to hear and decide matters in administrative agency hearings.

LEGAL FOCUS—CASE

Kelly was a New York City resident receiving welfare benefits under the federal program Aid to Families with Dependent Children (AFDC). The New York City Social Service agency, which was responsible for administering the program, terminated her benefits. The agency told Kelly that she could request an informal review meeting and a formal hearing. She sued, claiming she had a right to a hearing *before* her AFDC benefits were terminated. Did Kelly have a right to a hearing before the AFDC benefits were terminated?

Goldberg v. Kelly, 397 U.S. 254, 90 S.Ct. 1011 (1970).

* Some ALJs are employees of the very agency prosecuting the case. When such is the case, safeguards are in place to separate the ALJ from the investigative and prosecutorial staff. Private communication between the ALJ and anyone who is a party to an agency proceeding while the matter is pending is forbidden.

Yes. The U.S. Supreme Court held that where benefits are a matter of statutory entitlement, the importance to the recipient must be weighed against the state's interest in efficient, speedy processes. As welfare benefits provide, food, clothing, and shelter, Kelly had a right to a hearing before termination. Under the Fourteenth Amendment to the U.S. Constitution, the state may not "deprive any person of life, liberty, or property, without due process of the law. . . ." Here the court held that a termination of benefits without a prior termination hearing denied Kelly due process.

Since the Kelly case, agencies have been much more sensitive to when a hearing might be required. Accordingly, agencies often offer to hold a preliminary hearing when the agency's contemplated action would deny a person some right, license, or privilege.

Many agencies use the ALJ-led hearing as a first step in the adjudication process. It is followed by a review by the head of the agency or by the full commission or board of the agency. Other agencies treat the ALJ decision as the final decision, but allow for an appeal to the head of the agency or to the full board or commission. Another variance is to assign a few members of the board or commission to work as a committee in reaching a decision. In those cases, the ALJ conducts the hearing and advises the committee members, but the ultimate decision is made by the committee. State agencies use a similar variety of approaches to adjudication.

cease-and-desist

A command from an administrative agency that the subject party refrain from specified activities.

A final order may compel payment of monetary damages, or can provide a **cease-and-desist** order to prohibit a certain activity. In the case of benefits such as welfare or unemployment, the order might reverse an agency staff's decision to deny the benefit.

LEGAL FOCUS—PROBLEM

In separate incidents over a period of several months, three employees died in a steel mill owned by USX Corp: one from burns, one from crushing, and one from suffocation. The Occupational Safety and Health Administration (OSHA), an administrative arm of the U.S. Department of Labor, was asked to investigate. After a finding of safety violations, OSHA recommended fines of $7.3 million. Does OSHA have the power to assess and collect fines without USX having an opportunity to contest OSHA's findings?[27]

No. Although the agency did have the power to impose a fine, it could not deny USX the opportunity to have a fact-finding hearing before an ALJ. At the eventual hearing, USX pleaded guilty to the violations and promised to correct the problem and follow OSHA's recommendations. The negotiated fee resulted in a much-reduced fine. Critics of such negotiated settlements are answered by OSHA's declaration that it does not necessarily want violators punished; rather, it wants the safety problems corrected. OSHA's job is to make the workplace safer, not to raise money.

Fair Hearings and Due Process

Administrative hearings are conducted much like trials. Lawyers may represent parties and evidence is presented using witness testimony, documents, and authentication. Cross-examination is usually allowed. There are significant differences, however, between a trial and an administrative hearing. Administrative hearings do not have juries. Likewise, evidence and procedural rules can be somewhat different and often slightly less formal. For instance, hearsay is often admitted.

fair hearing

An oral proceeding before an administrative agency to hear and decide some factual question related to agency action.

The APA requirements for a **fair hearing** are simple. The APA requires that each side have the opportunity to submit and have evidence considered. The APA also requires that the ALJ be neutral and unbiased.[28] Most agency regulations go farther than that, mostly to ensure a fair fact-finding process. These fairness protections are primarily driven by due process considerations under the United States Constitution.

Judge Henry Friendly, in an influential article still as timely and accurate now as when he wrote it in 1975, described eleven attributes that make up a fair hearing.[29] Not all of these attributes are constitutionally required, but many of them are what an American citizen expects as fair treatment, not only from government but also from any large organization. With some editorial license, Judge Friendly's list is reproduced with a brief discussion of how each attribute affects an administrative hearing and contrasts with court processes:

1. **An unbiased tribunal.** In a court proceeding, a tribunal is a neutral court with a judge or a jury deciding a case. In the usual administrative hearing, an agency employee who was not a party to the original decision is considered sufficiently unbiased to decide the case. Generally the hearing officer or ALJ is required to be neutral, but he or she can work for and be paid by the agency.

2. **Notice of the proposed action and the grounds for the action.** In a judicial process, a complaint and summons are used to notify the party sued of the nature of the adverse claim. In an administrative action, some additional statement is expected about what government action is proposed, along with the legal reasons for the action.

3. **An opportunity to present reasons why the proposed action should not be taken.** Fundamental to all fair processes is opportunity to tell, and justify with evidence, your view of the facts to the person making the decision.

4. **The right to call witnesses.** In a court trial, you have the right to subpoena witnesses. This means you can force a witness to attend your trial. While a party to an administrative hearing can call witnesses, they may not always be compelled to attend.

5. **The right to know the evidence against you.** A person subject to a governmental action should be aware of all evidence used by the ALJ to make the decision. A hearing officer or ALJ should not receive evidence or opinions without sharing that information with the affected party. Nevertheless, there are some administrative hearing situations where parties are not allowed to know all evidence against them. For example, a hearing to discipline a prisoner is an administrative hearing, but if testimony used to discipline the prisoner were provided to the prisoner, the adverse party, usually another prisoner, could face reprisals. For that reason, often the prisoner subject to discipline is not given complete information regarding the source and nature of the evidence.

6. **A decision based on evidence presented at the hearing.** If the decision is based on information presented at the hearing, then one has the opportunity to rebut it. If the ALJ makes a decision on facts learned outside the hearing, the claimant is denied a fair opportunity to contest the information. This right is almost always required.

7. **The right to counsel.** Most administrative hearings will allow counsel but will not pay for it. Also, unlike in court proceedings, counsel is not required to have legal training.

8. **Making of a record.** A written record needs to be available to allow a party a fair ability to contest a hearing. Administrative requirements regarding the type of record vary, whereas court records are consistently transcribed from tapes or created in shorthand contemporaneously.

9. **Statement of reasons for the decision.** If reasons for the decision are given, faulty reasoning can be challenged and appealed. A statement of reasons, even though brief, is usually expected as part of the administrative hearing process.

10. **Public attendance.** Open attendance in court trials is permitted on the general belief that the activities of government officials should be open to the public to protect individuals from possible abuse of government power. In administrative hearings, open attendance may be allowed, but often it is not.

11. **Judicial review.** As with court decisions, results of administrative hearings can be appealed. Experience has shown that courts seldom overturn administrative rulings or actions. Usually, the best chance for appeal is within the agency. When appeals are taken outside the agency, courts involved are more likely to grant relief if the agency violated due process in some way. Courts seldom challenge agency interpretation and application of the facts, because the agency is presumed to have expertise in the application of the facts presented. Nevertheless, judicial review is an important component of administrative law.

LIMITS ON AGENCY POWER

There are several restraints that counteract the broad power and independence of administrative agencies. Some of these have already been discussed, such as the limits on delegating power to agencies and the constitutional due process requirements that apply to administrative processes. Other chief restraints are political control, constitutional guarantees, laws enforcing public accountability, and—probably the most important means of controlling agency behavior—judicial review.

POLITICAL CONTROL

The separation of powers in the United States government drives a certain degree of independence in agencies, but Congress and the president still have ability to control agencies politically. One way is by amending the statute that gives an agency its power. Another avenue of control, if slower and less direct, is through the appointment process for new board or commission members. Perhaps the president's and Congress's most crucial power over independent administrative agencies is the budget process. Funding levels from year to year affect an agency's activity just as well as direct supervision can.

CONSTITUTIONAL GUARANTEES

The role of constitutional due process on agencies was described earlier. Agencies must provide notice and opportunity to be heard. They generally must receive and respond to comments when making regulations. Agencies must also respect due process in the adjudication role. Finally, as described earlier, the Fourth Amendment restricts agency search and seizure efforts.

PUBLIC ACCOUNTABILITY

Several laws hold government accountable to the public and require that it conduct itself in accordance with the law and in a manner responsible to the public's expectations. The laws discussed below are federal and apply only to the federal government, but many states have state equivalent laws for some of these federal laws.

Freedom of Information Act (FOIA)

The **Freedom of Information Act (FOIA)**[30] requires that the federal government disclose most "records" to "any person" on request. Under the act, government agencies are expected to publish most statements of policy and staff manuals that affect the public and are not already published in the *Federal Register*. Agencies are also required to state how

Freedom of Information Act (FOIA)

A federal law requiring the federal government to disclose most public records to any person on request.

http://

For additional information on the Freedom of Information Act, see http://www.usdoj.gov/04foia/

much unpublished information may be obtained and to designate a contact person in their office to handle such requests. The person requesting the information need not disclose why it is wanted. Certain records, such as information related to security risks or ongoing criminal investigations, are not retrievable. The news media and business firms make the most frequent requests under the FOIA. A refusal by a government agency to provide requested information could be challenged in court.

Government in the Sunshine Act

The **Government in the Sunshine Act**[31] prohibits secret agency meetings. It is an open-meeting law. Not only must most meetings be open for public observation, but advance notice must also be given of the meetings, along with the expected topics of discussion. Administrative hearings are not covered by the Sunshine Act, so they are often conducted in private.

Regulatory Flexibility Act

Whenever a new regulation will have a "significant impact upon a substantial number of businesses," the **Regulatory Flexibility Act**[32] requires that the agency conduct a "flexibility analysis." This means that the agency must estimate and disclose the costs of the rule on small businesses. It must also consider any less burdensome alternatives. The act requires notice to small businesses about the proposed regulations.

JUDICIAL REVIEW OF AGENCY ACTION

The courts, with their ultimate power to declare the law, provide a direct avenue for the **judicial review** of agency action. The ability of the judicial branch of government to hear complaints regarding agency actions, to review agency conduct, and to correct violations and wrongs is a critical part of the balancing of agency power with restraint. Judicial review is not an unlimited control from illegal agency processes or decisions, however, because various constraints on judicial review can limit its effectiveness.

Scope of Judicial Review

The APA allows judicial review of most agency actions.[33] That means that a court may prevent or undo any unauthorized action by an agency. Likewise, courts may compel agency action that has been unlawfully withheld. In reviewing administrative actions, courts are reluctant to review questions of fact. This deference is based partly on the judicial attitude that those who hear and see the evidence firsthand are best able to evaluate it. Also the agency is considered an expert on the topic that it hears, and as such, usually is more knowledgeable about the topic contested than a reviewing judge would be. Finally, courts generally believe that wholesale review of agency actions would destroy the value of the more efficient agency process and worsen the problem of already crowded court calendars.

A *de novo review* (new proceeding) will, however, be granted if (1) a review is required by statute, (2) the agency's fact-finding proceeding was inadequate, or (3) new facts not heard in the original proceeding are to be raised.

Standing to Sue

The challenging party must have **standing to sue.** Standing requires that a challenger have a direct stake in the outcome of the judicial proceeding. The best way to show this is

Government in the Sunshine Act

A federal law requiring that most meetings of federal agencies be open for public observation and that advance notice be given of agency meetings, listing the expected topics of discussion.

http://

For the text of the Government in Sunshine Act, see http://www.usdoj.gov/foia/gisastat.pdf

Regulatory Flexibility Act

Federal law requiring federal agencies to consider the effects of their regulatory actions on small businesses and other small entities and to minimize any undue disproportionate burden.

judicial review

The power of the courts to review administrative agency action.

de novo review

A complete reevaluation of an issue, finding, or case as if the original decision had never been made.

standing to sue

A person's right or capacity to bring a lawsuit because he or she has a legally protected interest at stake in the litigation.

http://

For more information about standing to sue, see
http://www.usdoj.gov/usao/ eousa/foia_reading_room/ usam/title4/civ00035.htm

to demonstrate that the agency's action had a substantial effect on the challenger. An injury to an economic interest, or even in some cases to an emotional, environmental, or aesthetic interest, is sufficient to show standing to sue. One reason for the requirement of standing to sue is to discourage petty lawsuits. The courts will require that a plaintiff show an actual injury by, or because of, an agency action. Protest lawsuits or lawsuits from taxpayers who are simply angry about some governmental action are dismissed because of lack of standing to sue.

LEGAL FOCUS—CASE

The trustees of the Loudoun County Public Library in Virginia instituted a policy to block access to sexually explicit material through the library's publicly provided Internet access sites. An association of library patrons, Mainstream Loudoun, challenged the regulation in court. The library trustees defended on several bases, among them that "neither the individual plaintiffs nor Mainstream Loudoun have suffered an actual injury as a result of the Policy. Specifically ... no member of the Mainstream Loudoun has attempted to access blocked Internet materials in Loudoun County libraries, or petitioned a library to unblock a blocked site." Mainstream Loudoun contradicted this claim in their complaint. Does Mainstream Loudoun have standing to sue the library trustees?

Loudoun v. Trustees of the Loudoun County Library, 2 F.Supp.2d 783 (E.D., Virginia 1998).

The court said that Mainstream Loudoun had standing to sue. Because the group's complaint contradicted the library trustees' claim, stating that several members had in fact attempted to access blocked sites, they had standing. For an association to have standing to sue on behalf of its members, "(1) its own members would have standing to sue in their own right; (2) the interests the organization seeks to protect are germane to the organization's purpose; and (3) neither the claim nor the relief sought requires the participation of the individual members in the lawsuit." All three criteria were found to exist.

Exhaustion of Administrative Remedies

Courts are reluctant to interfere with the regulatory process, preferring that the agency correct its own mistakes. Until recently, courts had been unwilling to review an action until the challenging party had exhausted all possible alternative means of resolving the controversy within the agency, known as **exhaustion of remedies.** This stance, however, has come under challenge.

exhaustion of remedies

A doctrine requiring that a person attempt all available options within an administrative agency before taking a claim to a court.

LEGAL FOCUS—CASE

R. Gordon Darby was a South Carolina real estate developer specializing in the development and management of multifamily rental projects. In the 1980s, working with a mortgage banker's plan, Darby was able to obtain mortgage insurance from the Department of Housing and Urban Development (HUD). The plan was later determined to be inconsistent with a department regulation. The assistant secretary proposed to debar (suspend) Darby from further participation in HUD programs. Darby contested the suspension, but following an administrative hearing, an ALJ upheld an eighteen-month debarment from all federal programs. Darby failed to request a review from the HUD secretary within fifteen days of receipt of the ALJ's determination. He later sought a judicial review of the ALJ's action. Did Darby's failure to avail himself of a HUD secretary review forestall his right to judicial review?

Darby v. Cisneros, 509 U.S. 137, 113 S.Ct. 2539 (1993).

No. In a decision that surprised many administrative law scholars, the Supreme Court held that, under the APA, a plaintiff need not exhaust available administrative remedies unless a statute or specific agency rule requires it, and in this case, none did. Said the Court, "It is perhaps surprising that it has taken over forty-five years since the passage of the APA for this court to definitively address this question. But where the APA applies, an appeal to 'superior agency authority' is a prerequisite to judicial review only when expressly required by statute or when an agency rule requires appeal before review and the administrative action is made inoperative pending that review."

Knowledge of the requirement is still important because the law often requires that administrative options be exhausted before seeking judicial relief at both the federal and state level.

Defenses to Agency Action

The following are the usual defenses the party might raise when seeking judicial review of an agency decision. The party's goal, of course, would be to overrule the agency determination:

* The agency exceeded the authority conferred on it by its enabling legislation.
* The agency improperly interpreted laws applicable to the agency action under review.
* The agency violated a constitutional provision.
* The agency acted in violation of the procedural requirements.
* The agency acted in a manner that was arbitrary or capricious, or constituted an abuse of discretion.
* The conclusion drawn by the agency was not supported by substantial evidence.

These criteria offer a solid base for judicial review. Other grounds for review are unlikely to suffice.

LEGAL FOCUS—CASE

Environmentalists persuaded a court to require the Nuclear Regulatory Commission to reconsider its decision to grant an operating license to the Vermont Yankee Nuclear Power Corporation. The court held that the NRC was not adequately considering the dangers of nuclear fuel reprocessing and nuclear waste management. The NRC appealed to the U.S. Supreme Court, claiming that the lower court had no power to interfere in the administrative process. Could the lower court legally interfere?

Vermont Yankee Nuclear Power Corp. v. NDRC, 435 U.S. 519, 98 S.Ct. 1197 (1978).

No. The courts do not have power to prescribe procedures that regulatory agencies must follow; at most they may analyze whether the agency followed its own procedures and gathered sufficient evidence to support its actions. This decision reflects the Supreme Court's expectation of deferential treatment toward administrative agencies.

CASE

If your university is a public institution, the due process rules applicable to administrative agencies and discussed in the chapter apply to it. If you are accused of cheating or otherwise run afoul of university administrators—or, dare we say it, professors— you can expect certain minimum protection from expulsion or other treatment detrimental to your continued beneficial enrollment. The following case discusses due process protections available in such a hearing. Consider the case in reference to the discussion of Judge Friendly's article. If your university is a private school, you will probably find that it has provided rules very similar to those available at public institutions. After all, due process protections are minimum requirements; universities whether they be public or private are free to provide more expansive protections, and they often do.

NASH V. AUBURN UNIVERSITY

812 F.2d 655 (11th Cir. 1987)

Two students, David Nash and Donna Perry, were accused of cheating on their anatomy examinations at Auburn University's School of Veterinary Medicine. At a university hearing to determine the merits of the charge, faculty members and student witnesses testified that they observed Nash and Perry examining specimens together in laboratory examinations and moving together from question to question at those exams. At the exams, Nash and Perry were seen suspiciously to signal each other and to exchange glances: on written exams, they were seen to look on each other's papers. Appellants frequently sat together at written exams in seats not assigned to them at the rear of the exam rooms. The students were suspended from the University at the conclusion of the hearing. Nash and Perry filed suit, arguing that Auburn University suspended them based on constitutionally inadequate procedures that violated their rights under the due-process clause of the Fourteenth Amendment. The U.S. District Court for the Middle District of Alabama entered judgment in favor of the university, and the students appealed. The court of appeals agreed with the district court, holding that the students were provided with a fair hearing—notwithstanding the lack of advance notice of statements from accusing witnesses and the lack of opportunity to directly cross-examine witnesses. The court also ruled that the students had been given adequate time to prepare for the disciplinary hearing.

Senior District Judge James E. Doyle delivered the opinion of the court: Appellants were advised in writing on June 6, 1985, that they were charged with a violation of the Student Code of Professional Ethics (the code) of the Auburn University School of Veterinary Medicine. They were given "at least 72 hours to prepare a defense for the charge of academic dishonesty, in that while taking examinations during the 1984–1985 school year, information was allegedly obtained in an unethical manner." Appellants appeared with counsel at the hearing

[and] objected that the notice was inadequate and too general to advise them of the charge[s]. [Counsel] requested a more specific notice and one additional day to prepare their defense. The following day each appellant received a written memorandum, dated June 11, 1985, advising them that they were charged with a violation of the code in "giving or receiving assistance or communication between students during the anatomy examination given on or about May 16, 1985." Included in the memorandum was a list of students and anatomy faculty witnesses who were expected to testify at the hearing in support of the charge against appellants.

A disciplinary hearing ... was held on June 12, 1985. Both Nash and Perry attended, in the company of their attorney. The hearing was conducted by the non-voting student chancellor of the board, in the presence of appellants, witnesses, and student justices. There was no attorney for the board present. The chancellor allowed appellants' counsel to advise his clients during the hearing, but he was not permitted to participate in the proceedings. Appellants were to be allowed to question the adverse witnesses by directing their questions to the chancellor, who would then pose their questions to the witnesses.

After all of the testimony was presented supporting the charge, appellants were granted a short recess and then given an opportunity to present their defense. Appellants were allowed to present statements responding to the charge against them and rebutting the testimony of the student and faculty witnesses. They brought witnesses in their behalf who also made statements to the board and answered questions of the justices. After all of the presentations, the board again questioned appellants and the witnesses. After the board completed its questioning, appellants were given the opportunity to question the opposing witnesses by submitting questions to the chancellor, who would then direct the questions to the witnesses. Appellants instead asked the board several questions. Appellants asked for a recess, which was denied by the chancellor, and the hearing was concluded. After deliberating in private, the board decided unanimously that appellants were guilty of the charge of academic dishonesty. The justices recommended that appellants be suspended from school, with the opportunity to apply for admission again in one year. Appellants were notified of the board's decision and recommendation.

Appellants ... appealed to the dean on June 13, 1985. Pursuant to the code, the dean referred the case to the school's faculty Committee on Admissions and Standards for its review and recommendation. On June 19, 1985, the committee held a day-long meeting to consider the appeal. The committee reviewed a copy of the materials presented to the board at its June 12 hearing and listened to an audio recording of the June 12 hearing. Appellants presented oral and written statements in their defense and answered questions from the committee. After deliberating, the committee voted unanimously to recommend that the dean uphold the board's findings and recommendation. The dean accepted the committee's recommendation and upheld the action of the board. Appellants later appealed to the president of Auburn University, who reviewed the written file in the case and concurred in their suspension.

Under the Fourteenth Amendment to the United States Constitution, no state may "deprive any person of life, liberty, or property, without due process of law...." It is alleged and not disputed that Auburn University is a creature of the state of Alabama. Further, it is assumed by the parties and by the district court that appellants have property and liberty interests in their continued enrollment at Auburn University and that their interests enjoy the protections of due process. The Procedural Due Process Claims:

"The Fundamental requirement of due process is the opportunity to be heard at a meaningful time and in a meaningful manner." *Goss v. Lopez.* What process is due is measured by a flexible standard that depends on the practical requirements of the circumstances. That flexible standard was translated by the *Goss* court to mean that high school students facing the deprivation of a property right by suspension from school must, at a minimum, "be given some kind of notice and afforded some kind of hearing." [W]e broadly defined the notice and hearing required in cases of student expulsion from college: "[A]n opportunity to hear both sides in considerable detail is best suited to protect the rights of all involved. This is not to imply that a full-dress judicial hearing, with the right to cross-examine witnesses, is required."

The adequacy of the notice and the nature of the hearing vary according to an "appropriate accommodation of the

competing interests involved." [T]hree factors are important when considering the constitutional adequacy of the procedures afforded in a given situation: First, the private interest that will be affected by the official action; second, the risk of an erroneous deprivation of such interest through the procedures used, and the probable value, if any, of additional or substitute procedural safeguards; and finally, the [g]overnment's interest, including the function involved and the fiscal and administrative burdens that the additional or substitute procedural requirement would entail. The due process clause is not a "shield ... from suspensions properly imposed," nor does it ensure that the academic disciplinary process is a "totally accurate, unerring process;" it merely guards against the risk of unfair suspension "if that may lie done without prohibitive cost or interference with the educational process."

Nash and Perry argue that [Auburn] engaged in procedures, which deprived them of constitutionally protectible rights in their continued enrollment as veterinary students. They argue that inadequate notice failed to provide them the opportunity for a meaningful response to the charge of academic dishonesty. Specifically, they claim that the interval of time between the notice and the hearing was too short, and the notice did not apprise them of the substance of the evidence against them. They argue also that the hearing was inadequate to protect their interests from erroneous deprivation in that they were denied the opportunity to cross-examine witnesses. Further, they argue that the tribunal was unfairly prejudiced by the existence and the participation of a justice with knowledge of the charge. Appellants argue also that they were denied a meaningful appeal and that the cumulative effect of these individual abridgments of their rights denied them due process of law.

1. The Notice

a. Timing:

There are no hard and fast rules by which to measure meaningful notice. "An elementary and fundamental requirement of due process ... is notice reasonably calculated, under all the circumstances, to apprise interested parties of the pendency of the action and afford them an opportunity to present their objections."

Appellants urge ... that a coercive atmosphere pervaded the June 10 hearing, providing appellants and their counsel no choice but to agree to the board's proposed timing of the restated notice and the rescheduled hearing. However, in the record of the June 10 hearing we find no evidence of coercion to give us concern that appellants' waiver might not have been knowingly given. In sum, appellants were given four days by the June 6 notice and an additional one day by the June 11 notice, for a total of about six days from the June 6 notice to prepare their defense at the June 12 hearing. Despite the severity of the charge of academic dishonesty and the severe sanction it carries, the time allowed appellants was reasonable. It enabled them to retain counsel who successfully argued in their behalf at the June 10 hearing for a more specific notice of the charge as well as for a delayed hearing. Further, appellants had sufficient time to appear at the June 12 hearing with witnesses in their behalf, bringing documentation to support their defense.

b. Content:

Appellants argue that the notice in this case was deficient because it did not advise them of the nature of the testimony to be presented against them or of the facts underlying the charge of academic dishonesty. Appellants urge that the analysis by [anatomy professor Donald] Buxton of their May 16 examination answers was persuasive, complex testimony and came as a surprise. They argue that they were entitled to a summary of the testimony expected from Buxton and the other accusing witnesses at the June 12 hearing, because only such notice would have provided safeguards against their surprise at the testimony and would have ensured them a fair opportunity to respond. Had they known of Buxton's analysis before he testified, appellants suggest they would have presented expert, statistical testimony to rebut the inference that they cheated on the May 16 neuroanatomy exam.

There is no constitutional requirement that, to provide them an opportunity to respond, appellants must have received any more in the way of notice than a statement of the charge against them. Although the June 6 notice in their case was rudimentary, the June 11 notice specified that appellants were accused of academic dishonesty on the May 16 neuroanatomy exam and it included a list of accusing witnesses. On that notice, appellants obtained the assistance of counsel and brought to the June 12 hearing students and a faculty witness who testified as to their own interpretations of appellants' conduct throughout the school year and at the May 16 exam. Appellants were present at the entire June 12 hearing to hear the evidence against them, made a cogent defense, and undertook to discredit the adverse testimony, including Professor Buxton's analysis of their exam answers.

Despite the serious charge against appellants, who were hard-working students on the threshold of their careers, and the severity of the sanction imposed on them, we find that appellants were afforded constitutionally adequate notice and were adequately prepared by the notice to defend the charge against them.

2. The Hearing

a. Right to cross-examination.

"The fundamental requisite of due process of law is the opportunity to be heard." However, the nature of the hearing "will depend on appropriate accommodation of the competing interests involved." Appellants rely on *Goldberg v. Kelly* (1970) to challenge the constitutional adequacy of their hearing on the ground they were not allowed to cross-examine the accusing witnesses. *Goldberg* taught us that "[i]n almost every setting where important decisions turn on questions of fact, due process requires an opportunity to confront and cross examine adverse witnesses." However, we have not expanded the *Goldberg* procedural requirements for quasi-judicial termination of welfare benefits in student disciplinary hearings. Where basic fairness is preserved, we have not required the cross-examination of witnesses and a full adversary proceeding. Due process requires that appellants have the right to respond, but their rights in the academic disciplinary process are not coextensive with the rights of litigants in a civil trial or with those of defendants in a criminal trial.

Although appellants were not allowed to ask questions directly of the adverse witnesses at the June 12 hearing, it is clear that they heard all of the testimony against them. Appellants were told they could pose questions of the accusing witnesses by directing their questions to the presiding board chancellor, who would then direct appellants' questions to the witnesses.

We do not suggest that the opportunity to question witnesses would not have been valuable in this case. Although an important notion in our concept of justice is the cross examination of witnesses, there was no denial of appellants' constitutional rights to due process by their inability to question the adverse witnesses in the usual, adversarial manner. . . .

3. Fairness of the Tribunal

An impartial decision-maker is an essential guarantee of due process. "[B]asic fairness and integrity of the fact-finding process are the guiding stars." Appellants argue that the board was unfairly prejudiced at the June 12 hearing by the failure of a student justice to recuse himself. Appellants argue that the active presence of one student justice unfairly prejudiced the June 12 hearing and the deliberations of the board in this case, because that justice had prior knowledge of the charge of academic misconduct against appellants. They argue that a fair hearing and an unbiased decision were not possible in their case because the justice had not recused himself.

There is no evidence in the record, however, which suggests bias on the part of the student justice in question, such that he should disqualify himself from performing his duties on the board. He was familiar with appellants' conduct and with the general comments made about them by their classmates. In his contact with some potential student witnesses prior to the June 12 hearing, he explained the method of bringing information about violations of the code before the board chancellor. We agree with the district court that just "any prior knowledge of the incident" does not disqualify a decisionmaker; neither this student justice's knowledge of the suspicions about appellants nor his contact with potential witnesses appear to have rendered him a biased decision maker or to have denied appellants a tribunal free of bias.

4. The Appeal

[A]ppellants argue that their case was given only "perfunctory, fleeting review" by the dean of the school and the president of the university, both accepting the recommendations of the board and the committee, in violation of appellants' constitutional right to a meaningful appeal. We do not agree. The possibility that an erroneous decision may have been made by the board was diminished by the extensive review by the faculty committee. To impose two additional layers of de novo review, as appellants seem to request, would not have changed the nature of their opportunity to respond to the charge against them.

The Combination of Violations

The Student Code of Professional Ethics at Auburn University School of Veterinary Medicine provides rudimentary protections for students facing suspension on a charge of academic dishonesty. As we have explained, where appellants have challenged the adequacy of the notice and hearing provided them, Auburn's procedures met the constitutional minimum, but no more. They were given notice of the specific violation with which they were charged and were allowed an opportunity to respond at a hearing before an impartial tribunal, held within a reasonable time following the notice. Appellants were allowed to speak in their own behalf, to bring witnesses to support their defense, to confront their accusers, and to appeal their adverse decision to a committee

of faculty members and then to officials of the school and the university. The judgment of the district court is affirmed.

For Critical Analysis

Considering this case and the text discussion, answer the following questions about the hypothetical Mid-State University.

1. The policies of Mid-State University provide that students who disrupt class activities are subject to expulsion. Before expulsion can occur, however, the student is entitled to a conference with the dean of students. Jim Landry is a student who has been accused of obstructing the administration of the school by engaging in a sit-in demonstration. He asserts that he is entitled to more procedural protection than afforded by the conference with the dean of students.
   a. Mid-State says that Landry enrolled at the university and therefore has waived any further protections than those granted him in the rules and regulations. Is this position well taken?
   b. Landry asserts that he is entitled to have his lawyer present during any procedures designed to expel him. Is this position reasonable?
   c. Landry states that he has the right to cross-examine the witnesses against him. Is he correct?
   d. Landry maintains that the dean of students is biased against him because of statements the dean has made to the effect that Landry is a menace and should be removed from the university. Is Landry's objection allowable?
   e. Would it make any difference to Landry if the university in question were a private rather than a public university? Restrict your answer to the right to a hearing and the general nature of such a hearing. ■

CHAPTER QUESTIONS AND PROBLEMS

1. What is the distinguishing characteristic of an independent administrative agency? What are the checks and balances on an administrative agency by the executive, legislative, and judicial branches of government?

2. Legal scholars have pointed out that "the sheer volume of law generated by all types of administrative agencies exceeds the volume produced by both the legislatures and the courts combined." Yet comparatively few cases involving the work of administrative agencies appear in the docket of the U.S. Supreme Court or in the dockets of the lower courts. Can you suggest a reason for this phenomenon?

3. Officials of the Internal Revenue Service (IRS) have repeatedly requested additional funds from Congress to enable them to audit more income tax returns and to pursue individuals who don't even bother to file tax returns. The IRS confidently predicts that additional spending would result in hundreds of millions of dollars of additional income tax revenue. Why do you suppose Congress has resisted and generally rejected such IRS requests?

4. What recourse does a citizen have when an administrative agency such as the Environmental Protection Agency, in its enthusiasm and dedication, imposes what one might consider to be unreasonable standards—for

example, for clean air, where the cost of eliminating perhaps the last 5 percent of pollution may be as high as the cost of eliminating the first 95 percent?

5. Several unrelated deaths occurred in a chemical plant owned by Rivercity Chemical Corporation over a period of several months in 1999. The Occupational Safety and Health Administration (OSHA)—an administrative arm of the U.S. Department of Labor—was asked to investigate. After a finding of safety violations, OSHA fined Rivercity $8.3 million. Does an administrative agency such as OSHA have the power to assess and collect fines?

6. Martin Mazurie, a non-Indian, operated a bar on land he owned near an Indian reservation. A federal statute authorized Indian tribes to control the distribution of alcoholic beverages on their reservations. Mazurie, after being denied a tribal liquor license, was convicted of introducing spirituous beverages into Indian country. Mazurie appealed, claiming that as a non-Indian landowner he was not subject to Indian authority and that the federal statute authorizing tribal regulation of alcoholic beverages was an unconstitutional delegation of authority by Congress to a private body. The U.S. Court of Appeals agreed with Mazurie, holding: "Congress cannot delegate its authority to a private, voluntary organization, which is obviously not a governmental agency, to regulate a business on privately owned lands, no matter where located." The Indian tribe appealed. Can Congress delegate power to an Indian tribe to regulate non-Indians on the reservation? [*United States v. Mazurie,* 419 U.S. 544, 95 S.Ct. 710 (1975).]

7. An organization of criminal-defense lawyers known as the Federal Defenders of San Diego brought suit to challenge the constitutionality of sentencing guidelines issued by the U.S. Sentencing Commission. The commission challenged the plaintiffs' standing to bring the lawsuit. The plaintiffs argued that their members appear as counsel in 60 percent of federal criminal cases that continue after an initial appearance. Do the Federal Defenders have standing to bring the lawsuit? [*Federal Defenders of San Diego, Inc., et al., v. U.S. Sentencing Commission,* 680 F.Supp. 26 (D.C. 1988).]

8. Ulmer G. Wilson, a New Orleans Realtor, was unhappy when he discovered an immobilizing "boot" on his car. A note on the car's window gave a number to call to retrieve the car. After calling, Wilson became even more unhappy. He was expected to pay $630 for previous parking violations and a $30 boot removal fee. Wilson

refused to pay and the car was stored. The decision to boot Wilson's car had been made by Datacom, a private business under contract with the city to collect unpaid parking violations, receiving commission on all it collected. The decision to boot was made by Datacom based on a city ordinance allowing for immobilization of vehicles with three or more unpaid parking violations. Wilson had at least twenty parking tickets; nevertheless, he contested the booting as a taking of his property without due process of law. He contented that the booting took place without proper notice and that Datacom's determination to boot was made by a partial decision-maker who did not offer Wilson a hearing before booting the car. Was Wilson denied his right to a fair hearing with an impartial decision-maker? [*Ulmer G. Wilson v. The City of New Orleans,* 479 So.2d 891 (1985).]

9. As a general rule, administrative searches of businesses require a search warrant. The Department of Alcohol, Tobacco and Firearms (ATF) officials inspected Colonnade Catering without either a warrant or permission. The inspection was based on information provided by an ATF agent who while a guest at a party held at the establishment noted possible violations of federal law (not paying tax on alcoholic beverages). The catering service owner claimed that the officers conducted the search in violation of his Fourth Amendment rights as they searched without a warrant or his permission. The Department of Alcohol, Tobacco and Firearms claimed that the catering service store is part of a "pervasively regulated industry" and as such there is a substantial government interest in warrantless searches. Can the department conduct the warrantless search? [*Colonnade Catering Corp. v. U.S.,* 387 U.S. 72, 90 S.Ct. 774 (1970).]

10. Save The Dolphins is a nonprofit corporation whose primary purpose is to stop the incidental killing of dolphins in tuna fishing. The National Marine Fisheries Service (NMFS) made a film on an experimental tuna-fishing cruise. Save The Dolphins requested a copy of the film under the Freedom of Information Act. The NMFS declined to release the film because at the time the film was made the government had assured tuna boat captain Medina that "the film would not be shown to anyone but those involved in the research, since the scenes therein would depict fishing trade secrets and commercial information used by Medina's crew." Will NMFS be required to make the film available to Save The Dolphins? [*Save The Dolphins v. U.S. Department of Commerce,* 404 F.Supp. 407 (N.D.Ca., 1975).]

CHAPTER 6

Crimes: Public Wrongs

*I*f there were no bad people there would be no good lawyers.

Charles Dickens, *The Old Curiosity Shop,* 1841.

After reading and studying this chapter, you should be able to:

- Be able to define the term *crime* and describe the usual elements of a criminal act.

- Define and explain *corpus delicti.*

- Explain the various crimes against the person and against property.

- Recognize various valid defenses to crimes.

- Discuss the Fourth Amendment to the U.S. Constitution and identify situations where a warrantless search might be permitted.

- Describe common procedures used in a criminal trial.

- Discuss the rights of the criminal accused, including *Miranda* warnings and the Fifth Amendment.

- Explain the various punishments available for crimes and when a punishment might be considered cruel or unusual.

No area of law provokes more intense public reaction than criminal law. And the media capitalizes on the public's interest in crime, which borders on morbid fascination. Publicized cases frequently focus on issues that are controversial, perplexing, and provocative. Unfortunately, as a result, important but controversial issues are frequently obscured by emotions.

One hundred years ago, criminal behavior reflected the times: train and bank robbery, mugging, prostitution, embezzlement, and fraud. Tammany Hall, a New York political machine noted for graft and corruption, marked the beginnings of organized crime. Every city contract and political nomination was controlled; no bridge or sewer could be repaired or brick laid without the purchased permission of Tammany Hall. But there was no widespread fear of gang crimes, carjackings, homicides in schoolyards or in courtrooms, drug crimes, terrorist bombings, or serial killers and rapists. This is not to imply that our society at the beginning of the twenty-first century is plagued with crime. But the character of criminal behavior has been modernized, reflecting the crushing growth of high-density populations within our cities, technology, the automobile, the popularization of drug use, and, according to some, television, movies, and the availability of idle time.

The impact of crime and law enforcement on our society is markedly different today than at the beginning of the twentieth century. Punishment is the direct consequence for apprehended criminals, but there also are indirect consequences of criminal law. For example, marijuana and its cousin, hemp, are illegal contraband in the United States. Thus, hemp cannot legally be grown in this country. But like soybeans, hemp can be used to produce an oil that in turn can be used in a wide variety of beneficial products, including cooking oil, cosmetics, and plastics. Hemp fiber can be used to make paper, cloth, and even structural panels stronger than plywood. Hemp seed can be ground for flour and even livestock feed. When grown in rotation with other crops, such as cotton, hemp increases their yields and reduces the need for pesticides. In short, hemp is a potentially beneficial and valuable crop that is grown successfully in other countries, such as Canada, France, Germany, and England. One professor concludes that hemp, together with wheat, rice, straw, and kenaf, could fill the growing global shortage of fiber.[1] On the other hand, hemp contains a small amount of the same chemical found in marijuana. Existence of the chemical may not be significant, but hemp looks like marijuana and would make law enforcement more difficult. Thus, some officials contend that efforts to legalize hemp are really an attempt to legalize marijuana.[2] The controversy surrounding legalization of hemp is both an example of how crime and its enforcement affect our society and an example of how the complexities of our legal system are compounding in the early years of the new millennium.

Another indirect societal consequence of modern law enforcement is the privatization of prisons. States receive competing bids from private corporations to build and manage jails or prisons. The winning bidder builds and thereafter manages a prison in exchange for a daily fee for each inmate confined. Local businesses profit substantially from nearby prisons. New jobs, increased retail sales, and new housing demand are some of the benefits. As private businesses, these jails can pay low wages to their labor force (inmates), perhaps less than one dollar per hour, to produce such products as computer circuit boards. With 1.8 million inmates in the United States, the private prison business is booming. Some accuse the prison industry of lobbying government to maintain stiff sentencing laws because more prisoners means more profits.

Opponents to the privatization of prisons argue that inmates are not treated with the minimal standards required by law and produce products in competition with union labor and private businesses. Critics compare the conditions faced by today's incarcerated labor force to the working conditions at the beginning of the twentieth century existing for chil-

http://

You may obtain current statistics on crime from the Federal Bureau of Investigation at **http://www.fbi.gov** or the Justice Department at **http://www.jrsainfo.org/**

http://

For a variety of arguments surrounding the hemp controversy, check **http://www.hemp.net/** and **http://www.crrh.org/hemptv/index2.html**

http://

For information about the privatization of prisons visit **http://www.ucc.uconn.edu/~Logan/**

dren in the nation's coal mines and for women in the textile industry. Charges are made that prisoners are mistreated to extend their sentences to the maximum permitted by law. There also have been instances of sexual and physical abuse of inmates. Proponents counter that most states require that private prisons be accredited by the neutral American Correctional Association insuring minimal standards of quality. Despite concerns, private prisons appear to be an expanding business for the new century.[3]

Society also seems increasingly willing to treat minors as adults relative to the punishments for criminal behavior. In most states, the move toward harsher treatment of juveniles is politically popular. But there is concern that juveniles in adult prisons "may be sexually and physically abused, permanently labeled as criminals, and denied access to rehabilitative services."[4]

The following questions illustrate many of the issues attracting intense public scrutiny at the beginning of the new century:

- Is society morally responsible for criminal conduct through disregard of its less fortunate?
- Is the public victimized by repeat offenders who are punished too leniently?
- Is blue-collar, back-street crime condemned while white-collar, "Wall Street" crime is implicitly condoned? Does the theft of a wallet lead to imprisonment and the theft of millions lead to fines?
- Are there different standards of justice for the rich and for the poor?
- Is capital punishment barbaric, justified, or both?
- Should so-called victimless crimes (e.g., prostitution and gambling) be prosecuted?
- Why can insanity excuse even the most heinous criminal conduct?
- Is the root cause of violent crime the creation of unwanted children in the homes of dysfunctional families? Or are the root causes moral and spiritual, or physiological and genetic, rather than social and economic?
- Are "abuse excuses" by perpetrators trivializing serious crime and producing too-light sentences?
- Are too many nonviolent offenders being sentenced to prison?
- Is an average of thirteen years on death row between original sentence and final appeal too long?
- Is criminal law being applied unfairly, producing a prison population disproportionately composed of young African American males?
- Is lawlessness encouraged by the apathy of too many citizens who, more or less unwittingly, buy stolen goods, fail to report suspicious activities in their neighborhoods, and refuse to "become involved" as informants or as witnesses in criminal trials?
- Can we afford to offer the fairness protections provided by the Constitution in our quest to protect ourselves from terrorist threats? Can we afford not to? How can we distinguish an accused terrorist from someone accused of another form of criminal activity?
- How do we bring to justice those who commit criminal acts over the Internet, sometimes from another country?
- How do we account for rapid changes in technology and biology that challenge concepts formed from the social experience of centuries?

These are not easy questions, and easy answers are not forthcoming. People like you will be required to answer these questions either by choice or by default.

This chapter will familiarize you with the pervasiveness and complexity of some of these dilemmas through a survey of selected concepts of criminal law. There are no perfect solutions or antidotes for antisocial criminal behavior, but after studying the chapter you should better understand the dynamics involved and sharpen your thinking about what might be the best ways of dealing with the problem. Crime and punishment—or what happens when prevention fails—are the subjects addressed here.

WHAT IS A CRIME?

Certain human behavior is deemed to be so offensive and objectionable that it threatens the safety or common good of society. Such objectionable and antisocial conduct is therefore prohibited by statute. A crime has occurred when a prohibitory statute has been violated.* A crime is a wrong against society, as defined by statute, and punishable by society.

Two elements must exist simultaneously before a person can be convicted of a crime: (1) a specified state of mind or intent on the part of the person and (2) the performance of a prohibited act. Even where both elements exist, there may be defenses to the criminal conduct. Criminals face a wide range of possible penalties, including monetary fines and forfeitures, incarceration, and even death, if arrested and convicted, though they sometimes are given the choice of performing some act beneficial to society, such as community service.

It is important to note the dual consequences of most wrongful behavior. That is, most crimes are also civil wrongs: A person who burglarizes a home is committing the crime of burglary, and also a civil wrong called *trespass,* and probably the civil wrong called *conversion* (theft) of another's property. In such a situation, the victim has the right to seek money compensation in the civil law whether or not society, through criminal law, punishes the wrongdoer. This principle was vividly dramatized in the mid 1990s by the globally publicized case involving O. J. Simpson.

LEGAL FOCUS—EXAMPLE

In a criminal proceeding, Simpson was found not guilty of the double murder of his former wife Nicole Brown and her friend Ronald Goldman. However, in a subsequent civil proceeding Simpson was found liable, or legally responsible, for those wrongful deaths and was ordered to pay $35 million in monetary damages to the families of the victims. Thus, the criminal law and the civil law acted independent of each other concerning a single wrong. There was no issue of "double jeopardy" in this case because double jeopardy is a safeguard that applies only to successive *criminal* trials for the same offense.

Under the U.S. Constitution, criminal statutes must describe the forbidden conduct clearly and precisely, so that all persons may know, after reasonable investigation or reflection, what is prohibited. For example, a law prohibiting "loitering," but without specifically defining the prohibited conduct, is unconstitutionally vague. The underlying principle of justice is that no one shall be held criminally liable for conduct that could not reasonably be recognized as forbidden. In general, we are entitled to a "fair warning" of the existence of a criminal law so we can avoid the behavior it proscribes. The fair warning precondition requires the following:

---

* Some criminal statutes are mandatory—for example, those that command: "You must file a tax return and pay your income taxes without evasion" or "You must serve your country if drafted in time of war." Even these can be expressed as prohibitions of antisocial conduct.

- The statute must be clear and specific. Defendants cannot be convicted of violating a "vague" statute.
- Statutes will be "strictly" construed (interpreted) by courts to limit their scope as specifically as possible. Defendants cannot be convicted of behavior that is generalized in the prohibitory statute.
- Courts cannot adopt a novel or creative interpretation of a statute to sweep certain behavior into its literal terms. Defendants cannot be convicted of behavior that would not be generally understood to fall within the scope of the statute.

LEGAL FOCUS—CASE

Tennessee judge David Lanier was convicted of violating the constitutional rights of five women by sexually assaulting them. The federal statute the judge allegedly violated provided that it is a crime to "deprive a person of rights protected by the Constitution." Under the federal statute, if the deprivation of protected rights includes bodily injury, the prison sentence is enhanced to ten years. The jury found that two oral rapes by Judge Lanier caused the victims "bodily injury" and he received a twenty-year sentence as a result of that finding. But Judge Lanier appealed, contending that he was ignorant that the words in the statute covered sexual assault. What was the result on appeal?

U.S. v. Lanier, 520 U.S. 259, 117 S.Ct. 1219 (1997).

Judge Lanier won on appeal because he could not "reasonably anticipate" that his sexual assaults would violate the statute. The U.S. Supreme Court held that the "unlawfulness must be apparent." In other words, Judge Lanier may have known that his behavior was improper, but he did not know that his sexual assaults deprived the victims of their constitutional rights. At first blush, this may appear to violate the principle that "ignorance of the law is no excuse." However, the Court ruled only that "ignorance of a *nonspecific and vague law* is an excuse."

This requirement of clarity and specificity protects citizens from being prosecuted by zealous moralists but it also often creates an opportunity for exploitation by those who exploit statutory gaps created by new challenges such as technological advance, new science, and geographical boundaries.

LEGAL FOCUS—BACKGROUND

Jim Robinson, assistant attorney general for the criminal division at the United States Department of Justice, identified three challenges to modern law enforcement in the area of cybercrime.

- Technical challenges that hinder law enforcement's ability to find and prosecute criminals operating online
- Legal challenges resulting because laws and legal tools needed to investigate cybercrime are lagging behind technological, structural, and social changes
- Operational challenges in creating a network of well-trained, well-equipped investigators and prosecutors who work together with unprecedented speed—even across national borders.[5]

Most crimes are state crimes because they violate state statutes. In terms of volume, most federal crimes involve drug offenses. Congress has the power to pass statutes criminalizing drug transactions because such transactions involve interstate commerce. Federal crimes are prosecuted in a federal court and, if conviction follows, result in confinement in a federal prison. The case involving Judge Lanier is a prosecution of a federal crime.

The difficulties inherent in clearly specifying in a statute what conduct is prohibited is dramatized by so-called "loitering" statutes. The definition of loitering has frustrated legislators who wish to prohibit undesirable conduct associated with homelessness activities such as aggressive begging, urinating in public, and sleeping on sidewalks and gang activities such as hanging out, dealing drugs, and provoking other gangs. How can such conduct be defined and then prohibited when our freedom of association, i.e., to "hang out," is protected by the Constitution? Can police logically separate harmless loitering from activity that leads to drug dealing, drive-by shootings, and other violence that the ordinance is intended to prevent?

LEGAL FOCUS—CASE

A Chicago city ordinance made loitering a criminal offense punishable by imprisonment for up to six months. To loiter under the ordinance required (1) a police officer to reasonably believe that at least one of the two or more persons present in a public place is a criminal street gang member, (2) the person to remain in place with no apparent purpose, (3) an order by the officer that all of the persons disperse and leave the area, (4) disobedience of the officer's order. Any person, gang member or not, who is found to have disobeyed the officer's order is guilty of violating the ordinance. Does the ordinance provide sufficient specificity of criminal conduct to meet constitutional requirements?

Chicago v. Morales, 687 N.E.2d 53 (Ill., 1997) and *City of Chicago v. Morales,* 527 U.S. 41, 119 S.Ct. 1849 (1999).

No. The Illinois Supreme Court held the ordinance unconstitutional and the U.S. Supreme Court affirmed. "The ordinance does not provide sufficiently specific limits on the enforcement discretion of the police to meet constitutional standards for definiteness and clarity." "It is difficult to imagine how any citizen of the city of Chicago standing in a public place with a group of people would know if he or she had an 'apparent purpose.' If she were talking to another person, would she have an apparent purpose? If she were frequently checking her watch and looking expectantly down the street, would she have an apparent purpose?"

Every criminal statute prohibits certain behavior. Most crimes require an act. That is, a person must *do* something (a guilty act) to commit a crime. Mere thoughts are not crimes. The *guilty act* requirement is based on the idea that a person should be punished only for actual harm done to society. Thinking about killing someone or stealing a car may be wrong, but the thoughts do no harm. The harm happens when thoughts are translated into action. In a few situations, *not* doing something (an omission) is a crime. This can happen when the law commands a person do something and the person chooses not to do it. Examples include failure to file a tax return or report a serious automobile accident.

A wrongful mental state, **criminal intent,** is also a usual requirement for criminal responsibility. The limited exceptions include certain types of regulatory offenses, often called **infractions** (e.g., failing to keep a restaurant kitchen adequately clean), and criminally negligent conduct, (e.g., bicycling or driving a vehicle while under the influence of

http://

A teaching plan for high school students from Street Law provides a wonderful breakdown of the issues involving loitering laws in "The Case of the Move On Law"

http://www.streetlaw.org/ chicagovmorales.html

criminal intent

The requisite guilty state of mind [Latin *mens rea,* "guilty mind"] to hold a person responsible for a particular crime.

infraction

Any minor crime (e.g., parking violation) that is not punishable by incarceration, but only by fine. Accordingly, trial by jury is not required or permitted.

alcohol). There is no universally accepted definition of criminal intent; however, generally it means evil or wrongful purpose or design. Sometimes criminal statutes require **specific intent.** Specific intent crimes require proof that an accused had a particular purpose in mind when engaging in illegal conduct (e.g., the crime of theft generally requires proof that the perpetrator intended to permanently deprive the victim of his or her property). Sometimes criminal statutes require **general intent,** which requires an intentional act but no specific knowledge of particular circumstances is required (e.g., rape and assault are usually general intent crimes).

Intent is different from **motive,** which is a need, desire, or purpose that impels a person to act. A prosecutor need not prove the existence of an evil motive; a good motive never justifies a criminal act. Thus, a "mercy killing" is a crime regardless of its underlying noble motive.

LEGAL FOCUS—PROBLEM

Marilyn Harrell, a real estate broker in Maryland, publicly admitted unauthorized diversion of $5.7 million in proceeds from sales of federally insured properties that had been foreclosed. But she insisted that the bulk of the stolen money was used to provide housing for needy families as well as food for the poor. She had been entrusted with the money by the U.S. Department of Housing and Urban Development (HUD). Are her commendable purposes a legal defense to the crime of theft (which, under these circumstances, is also called *embezzlement*)?

No. Robin Hood's classic motive to help the poor was no defense for Marilyn, who has been dubbed "Robin HUD." She was convicted and sentenced to a prison term of 46 months, which she served.[6]

Criminal negligence is conduct that is without criminal intent and yet is sufficiently careless or reckless to be punished as a crime. Driving a vehicle while under the influence of drugs or alcohol is an example of criminal negligence. Leaving a handgun in one's home that is easily accessible to a child or leaving a child for a long period in a parked car are other examples.

Violation of state food quality regulations by a restaurant is an example of a **regulatory offense,** in which proof of criminal intent is unnecessary. Failure to get a required business or professional license is also an example of a regulatory offense.

LEGAL FOCUS—PROBLEM

Derick Dagger thought about murdering his wife, Glynda, so he could inherit her money. Over a period of time, he developed and refined an elaborate scheme to commit the murder. He even wrote a step-by-step plan that he kept in his filing cabinet. Is he guilty of any crime?

No. Criminal intent in the absence of any supportive overt act (i.e., an open, outward, manifested act) is not a crime. This is true even if one confesses to such intent. The written plan could be hypothetical and is an insufficient overt act upon which to base a conviction. The desire to inherit money was Dagger's motive, but a motive is not a crime.

---

specific intent

In criminal law, the intent to accomplish the precise act and harm that the law prohibits.

general intent

In criminal law, the intent to do the prohibited act without the necessity of proving intent to cause the precise harm.

motive

A reason for committing, or failing to perform, an act. Motive is not synonymous with criminal intent. Intent is essential for proof of crime; motive is not.

criminal negligence

Conduct that is without criminal intent and yet is so careless, or occurs in such reckless disregard of another's safety, that criminal penalties are prescribed by statute.

regulatory offense

A violation of a rule promulgated by an administrative agency.

LEGAL FOCUS—PROBLEM

In furtherance of his plan, Dagger asked his lifelong friend, Patrick O'Leary, to assist him in murdering his wife. O'Leary declined to assist, but loaned his revolver to Derick for use in accomplishing the murder. Have any crimes occurred?

solicitation

The crime of encouraging another person to commit a crime.

criminal facilitation

The crime of assisting another person in the commission of a crime.

conspiracy

An agreement by two or more persons to commit a crime coupled with an overt act by one party toward commission of the agreed crime.

Yes. Dagger has committed the crime of **solicitation.** Criminal solicitation is to strongly urge, entice, lure, or proposition another to engage in the commission of a crime. O'Leary is guilty of **criminal facilitation** because he knowingly and substantially increased the probability that the crime would be committed; that is, he made it easier for Dagger to effect his plan. Unlike a gun dealer in a normal retail sale, O'Leary knew of Dagger's intended crime and voluntarily assisted in its commission.

Suppose Patrick O'Leary had responded that he would be "happy to assist in the plan." Has another crime occurred? No. An agreement to commit a crime, standing alone, is not a crime. There is a constitutional limitation in criminalizing mere thought when there is no conduct in furtherance of the conspiracy. There must be some manifestation of the conspiratorial intent by what is called an *overt act.* But suppose that O'Leary then demonstrated how to load and fire his gun, and Dagger and O'Leary agreed to divide the inheritance. Has another crime occurred? Yes. Under these circumstances, Dagger and O'Leary would be guilty of the crime of **conspiracy.** An agreement to commit a crime becomes a criminal conspiracy once a substantial act of preparation is performed by one or more of the conspirators in furtherance of their plan. Teaching how to load and use the gun is such an overt act.

LEGAL FOCUS—PROBLEM

Early that evening, while Glynda Dagger was preparing supper, Derick aimed the loaded gun at her through the kitchen window, but she kept moving, providing a poor target. He did not fire. Have any more crimes occurred?

attempt

Intention of the accused to commit a crime and a substantial step toward its commission.

Yes. Derick Dagger committed the crime of **attempt** to commit murder because he committed an act of perpetration—that is, he took a substantial step toward the commission of the crime. Because conspirators share each other's guilt, O'Leary is also guilty of attempted murder.

If Dagger and O'Leary actually did all of the assumed acts, they would not necessarily be chargeable with, nor punishable for, each separate act. Some crimes are said to be included within, and merge into, the ultimate crime. For example, the crime of solicitation would merge into, and become a part of, the ultimate crime of attempted murder, for which both O'Leary and Dagger would be guilty.

FEDERAL CRIMES

As previously noted, a crime is conduct that is proscribed by a statute enacted by the legislative branch of government. If the conduct violates a state statute, it is a state crime punishable by the state. If the conduct violates a federal statute, it is a federal crime punishable by the United States government. Examples of federal crimes are transportation of contraband (illegal property, such as certain harmful drugs) across state lines; kidnapping;

bank robbery; forgery of a federal check; violation of certain civil rights protected by federal laws; wrongful interference with, or theft of, mail; evasion of federal income taxes; theft of U.S. government property; violation of securities laws; and physical violence on government property. In recent years, Congress has stiffened penalties for drug-related and various violent federal crimes.

In a highly publicized case, police officers Stacey Koon and Laurence Powell were charged with violating a state statute forbidding excessive force while arresting suspects. A bystander videotaped the events surrounding the arrest of Rodney King, who had been fleeing the police at high speeds on a freeway. Despite the provocative video, a state jury found the police officers not guilty of violating the state statute. Soon after the acquittal Koon and Powell were charged with violating the federal Civil Rights Act of 1964 for the same offensive conduct. The federal court jury found them guilty.[7] Thus, one act can be both a state and a federal crime. Double jeopardy does not apply because the federal and state governments are separate and distinct entities under the Constitution.

WHO ARE PARTIES TO A CRIME?

To define the degree of culpability (blameworthiness) of a participant in a crime, criminals historically have been classified as either a **principal** or as an **accessory.** A principal is a person directly involved in committing a crime. An accessory is a person who helps or assists a criminal activity without being present during commission of the crime. Principals receive more severe sentences than accessories. Under such classifications, a person who actually commits the crime, such as robbing a liquor store, is a principal in the first degree. Another person not as directly involved, the driver of the getaway car, for example, is classified as a principal of the second degree. A person who participated in the planning but who was not personally present at the scene of the crime is an **accessory before the fact.** One who assists the principals in evading capture is called an **accessory after the fact.**

A recent trend in many states, as in the federal system and in California and Illinois, is to classify all participants in a crime—the planner, the actual perpetrator, and the **aider** or **abettor**—as principals. A "lookout" is aiding and abetting in a crime and would be considered a principal.[8] Anyone who knowingly hides a fugitive, under this modern view, is called an accessory.

LEGAL FOCUS—PROBLEM

In a notorious case in California in 1971, Charles Manson was charged with the murders of the pregnant movie star Sharon Tate and others. Although not present at the scene of the crime, Manson, possessing hypnotic-like powers over members of his cult, commanded certain followers to commit the atrocity. Is Manson a principal or an accessory?

Although Manson never appeared at the scene of the crime, he was convicted as a principal to the crime of murder and sentenced to death.*

---

* Manson's death penalty was reduced to life imprisonment after the U.S. Supreme Court declared the death penalty, as then prescribed, to be unconstitutional. *Furman v. Georgia,* 408 U.S. 238, 92 S.Ct. 2726 (1972). When the death penalty was later restored by corrective legislation, its impact was prospective and did not affect the life sentence of Manson, who remains in prison to the day of this writing (2003).

principal

One who is present and participates in a crime or persuades another to commit a crime.

accessory

A person who, though not present at the scene of a crime, aided and abetted the principal in its commission.

accessory before the fact

Person who encourages or assists a perpetrator of a crime but is not present at its commission.

accessory after the fact

Person who harbors, conceals, or otherwise voluntarily and intentionally aids a known perpetrator of a crime to escape arrest or punishment.

aider or **abettor**

One who encourages, incites, persuades, or sets another on to commit a crime.

The particular manner in which a state classifies participation in criminal activity is not as important to know as the fact that in all states even slight participation in the commission of a crime may subject one to grave criminal penalties.

WHAT IS THE *CORPUS DELICTI?*

corpus delicti

The two essential elements of every crime: evidence that (a) harm has occurred, (b) most probably because of a criminal act.

The *corpus delicti* (Latin: "body of a crime") sounds like but is not the body of the deceased. The term refers to two essential elements of every crime: (1) the material being, or substance, upon which a crime has been committed (as, in homicide, a dead person; in arson, a burned building) and (2) evidence of some person's criminal conduct (as, in homicide, a bullet hole in the corpse; in arson, glass fragments from a Molotov cocktail found at the scene). Evidence that a person is missing does not alone satisfy the requirement of a *corpus delicti*.

LEGAL FOCUS—PROBLEM

Margaret Lesher, widow and heiress of a $100 million estate, married professional buffalo rider T.C. Thorstenson following a whirlwind courtship. Thorstenson concealed from Lesher his previous marriage and allegations of domestic violence. Six months after their wedding, Lesher and Thorstenson were camping one evening by a desolate lake, sleeping in separate bags. In the morning, Lesher was missing. Thorstenson looked "everywhere" to no avail and then called the police. Lesher was found dead, floating in the lake near the campsite. An autopsy revealed only that Lesher had drowned. Thorstenson claimed his inheritance under Lesher's recently drafted will. Can Thorstenson be prosecuted for murder?

No. The law requires that no person be tried for any crime unless the prosecutor has established a *corpus delicti*. In the T.C. Thorstenson case, there is no clear evidence that a crime has occurred; the *corpus delicti* cannot, therefore, be established. The drowning could have been accidental.[9] However, if the corpse had a head injury apparently inflicted by a weapon, Thorstenson might be investigated and, if corroborating evidence were presented, he could be charged with and tried for **homicide** (an unlawful taking of a human life).

homicide

The killing of a human being by another human being.

LEGAL FOCUS—CASE

Goldie Millar's $340,000 ranch home was discovered burned to the ground. Her body was never found. Her grandson, Michael Pyle, lived in the vicinity and was shown to have believed that he was the sole beneficiary of her will. The sole evidence of wrongdoing was a telephone call by Pyle to his wife reporting the fire and death of his grandmother two hours before these events actually took place. Can Pyle be convicted of homicide even though no trace of Millar's body was ever found?

State v. Pyle, 216 Kan. 423, 532 P.2d 1309 (Kansas, 1975).

Yes, because neither the body of the missing person nor evidence of the means used to produce death is essential to establish the *corpus delicti* or to sustain a murder conviction. Pyle's premature display of knowledge of the fire, the fire itself, and his grandmother's absence were critical factors supporting the first-degree murder conviction. Whenever a victim's body is missing, the *corpus delicti* must be established by other evidence that a crime occurred (for example, the testimony of an eyewitness). In any crime, the *corpus delicti* must be established before a criminal prosecution can take place against anyone.

As noted, the "body of the crime" must be proven before the defendant can be prosecuted. But what if the only evidence of the "body of the crime" comes from a confession by the accused?

LEGAL FOCUS—CASE

Dennis Creutz admitted that he "might have touched" a three-year-old girl in the vaginal area but "never thought he was doing anything wrong." The only other evidence of a crime were statements from the three-year-old girl to the effect that she had been inappropriately touched with the hands and mouth of the defendant. Can the case proceed to trial?

Creutz v. People, 49 Cal.App.4th 822, 56 Cal.Rptr. 2d 870 (1996).

No. In most types of criminal cases, prosecution cannot occur unless the *corpus delicti* is established by evidence other than a confession by the accused. This prevents convictions of, among others, "crackpots" who would readily confess to anything to obtain attention and even food and shelter in a prison.

However, in crimes against minors who are too young and therefore incapable of testifying in court, confessions of the accused can be used to establish the *corpus delicti,* following which a trial can proceed. In other words, the out-of-court corroboration by a witness who is too young to testify is sufficient to justify use of a confession for a *corpus delicti.* In the preceding example, however, the mere incriminating statements of Creutz do not constitute a confession. A confession is a complete acknowledgment of guilt and must encompass all the elements of the crime. A mere admission, such as Creutz made, is not a confession and therefore cannot be used to establish a *corpus delicti.*

FELONY, MISDEMEANOR, OR INFRACTION?

States generally classify crimes on the basis of blameworthiness as either felonies or misdemeanors. The determinant is usually the gravity of the criminal act, which in turn determines the severity of the penalty imposed. Generally, a **felony** is a crime that is punishable by death or by imprisonment in a state prison for a year or longer. Sometimes felonies are divided into **capital crimes** (punishable by death or imprisonment) and **noncapital crimes** (punishable by imprisonment only). Statutes may declare that a certain crime, such as robbery, is a felony. If the statute is silent as to the gravity of the crime, but incarceration in a state prison is the prescribed punishment, the crime is a felony. Some statutes prescribe punishment as imprisonment in either a state prison or a county jail. These "wob-

felony

A serious crime (such as murder) that is punishable by death or imprisonment for more than one year.

capital crime

A crime for which the death penalty may be imposed in states where authorized and at the federal level.

noncapital crime

A homicide for which the death penalty may not be imposed even if such penalty is authorized for other crimes by the state in which the crime is committed.

blers" are public offenses that may be either a felony or a misdemeanor depending upon the actual punishment ordered by the judge.[10]

Some states have refined their system of crime classification. For example, in Illinois, murder is one separate category of felony. The penalty can be death or incarceration up to one's natural life. Various classes of less culpable crimes are as follows:

LEGAL FOCUS—EXAMPLE

Class X felonies: Examples are solicitation of murder, aggravated sexual assault, and kidnapping for ransom. Minimum sentence is six years, maximum is thirty years.

Class 1 felonies: Examples are nonaggravated sexual assault and second degree murder. Minimum sentence is four years, maximum is fifteen years.

Class 2 felonies: An example is armed escape from prison. Minimum sentence is three years, maximum is seven years.

Class 3 felonies: Examples are involuntary manslaughter, incest, and aggravated battery. Minimum sentence is two years, maximum is five years.

Class 4 felonies: An example is bigamy. Minimum sentence is one year, maximum is three years.

Actual sentences imposed in Illinois are determined by the circumstances surrounding the crime, such as whether the victim was seriously injured and whether the criminal was a repeat offender.[11]

A **misdemeanor** typically is punishable either by fine or incarceration in a jail for less than a year, or both. Some states have an additional classification for petty offenses, called infractions or **violations.** These carry no moral stigma and are punishable only by fine. Common infractions are illegal gaming, disturbing the peace, possession of alcohol by a minor, and presenting false evidence of age.[12] Illinois refines misdemeanors into three categories: Class A (e.g., prostitution, up to one year in jail), Class B (e.g., obstructing service of process, up to six months in jail), and Class C (e.g., glue inhaling, up to thirty days in jail).[13] These refinements in classification are examples of attempts to distinguish criminal acts on the basis of culpability (degree of wrongfulness), leading to appropriate differences in penalties imposed.

The U.S. Sentencing Reform Act of 1984 abolished the federal system of **indeterminate sentencing.** Indeterminate sentence statutes provide for a range of years of imprisonment (e.g., one to five years) rather than a specific period set by the judge. The indeterminate sentencing system had given federal judges broad discretion in setting the type and extent of punishment imposed. This resulted in great disparities in time actually served as well as in sentences imposed because parole boards (officials with authority to set release dates) made actual release decisions tailored to the supposed amenability of each prisoner to rehabilitation. Many prisoners resented the uncertainties surrounding the subjective nature of decisions as to their actual release dates.

Rehabilitation was a primary goal of indeterminate sentencing until the federal Sentencing Reform Act of 1984 rejected imprisonment as a means of rehabilitation. The act stated that punishment should serve the goals of retribution (punishment), education (preparation for legitimate employment), deterrence (discouragement of repetition through fear), and incapacitation (prevention of repetition through confinement). The 1984 law abolished parole (suspension of part of a jail sentence) and made all sentences determinate, with sentence reduction allowed only for credits earned by good behavior while in custody.

misdemeanor
A crime punishable by fine or by incarceration in a county jail up to a year, or both.

violations
Any minor crime (e.g., parking violation) that is not punishable by incarceration, but only by fine. Accordingly, trial by jury is not required or permitted.

indeterminate sentencing
A statute that provides for a range (such as one to five years) rather than a specific period of incarceration for a crime, the exact time to be determined by a designated authority after confinement begins.

The U.S. Sentencing Commission, an administrative agency within the judicial branch of government, now establishes binding sentencing guidelines. Under the guidelines criminal behavior is ranked in forty-three different classes of severity, with corresponding sentences that vary depending on the defendant's record of prior convictions. This federal sentencing system has been severely criticized, primarily because it provides long sentences for relatively minor drug offenses. Judges object to it because it prevents them from exercising their discretion as to sentencing. Federal and state sentences are discussed later in this chapter on page 281, under the heading "What Is the Punishment of Convicted Persons?"

The states vary widely in the severity of punishment that may be imposed by the sentencing judge for a particular crime. Some statutes prescribe determinate sentences, with a range of minimums and maximums. In all jurisdictions, a felony is substantially more blameworthy and more severely punished than a misdemeanor. It is not unusual for states to re-examine their sentencing laws in response to demand for harsher penalties for crimes and recurring questions about the nature of imprisonment.

WHAT ARE CRIMES AGAINST THE PERSON?

To be free of physical attack is of paramount value to all members of society. The right to life and physical security is the matrix of all the other inalienable rights of a person. Crimes of violence against persons therefore warrant the severest penalties. Yet violence often grows out of emotions that are difficult to control. As a result, in the United States there are distinctions in moral culpability, and they are often subtle and difficult to apply. A discussion of the general rules follows.

MURDER

Murder is the unlawful killing of a human being with **malice** (sometimes called **malice aforethought**), which denotes the highest degree of moral culpability or blameworthiness—an evil, cold-blooded state of mind. To kill with malice aforethought is to act intending to kill or to act in such a way that death or serious harm to another is virtually certain to occur (extreme disregard for human life). Both a paid killer and the person who did the hiring are examples of such a state of mind.

State laws classify murder into at least two categories—typically, murder of the **first degree** (or capital murder) and murder of the **second degree** (noncapital murder). Murder in the first degree may be punishable by death or by imprisonment for life with or without the possibility of parole. Murder in the second degree may be punishable by imprisonment for less than life.

Generally, any murder perpetrated by means of poison or torture, by ambush, during the commission of a dangerous felony (e.g., during rape or robbery), or by any other kind of willful, deliberate, or premeditated killing is murder of the highest degree. All other kinds of murder, as when some provocation exists, are deemed murder of a lesser degree. Premeditation is an important factor in determining the highest degree of murder and does not necessarily require any certain period of time to occur. A cold, calculated decision to kill may be arrived at in a short period of time. On the other hand, a sudden rash impulse, even though it includes intent to kill, is not sufficient deliberation and premeditation to render an unlawful killing as "murder one." To be guilty of a deliberate and premeditated killing with malice aforethought, the slayer

1. must have weighed and considered the question of killing, and the reasons for and against such a choice, and

murder

The unlawful killing of a human being with malice aforethought.

malice aforethought

The highest degree of criminal culpability, characterized by a cold and malignant heart and a mental predetermination to do the wrongful act without legal justification or excuse.

first-degree murder

Premeditated murder perpetrated with malice aforethought.

second-degree murder

A measurement in law of the degree of culpability of the perpetrator of a murder of less than first degree.

2. having in mind the consequences, have decided to commit, and
3. then actually have committed the unlawful act causing death.

These components are difficult to apply, as demonstrated by the following case.

LEGAL FOCUS—CASE

Ernest Martinez was at a party when he learned his live-in girlfriend had gone home with another man. Martinez ran to his apartment, climbed in the bathroom window, and chased the two out the front door into the streets. Martinez managed to hit the man on the head several times with a shower curtain rod, and then cornered his girlfriend, nude, in the rear alley. He beat her savagely until a neighbor asked what was going on. Martinez replied that he had "caught her in the act." He then dragged her back into his apartment, turned up the stereo, and beat her to death. Martinez was very jealous and often had warned his girlfriend about infidelity. Martinez contends he is guilty only of voluntary manslaughter because of the passion and rage he felt under the circumstances. How should the jury decide?

People v. Martinez, 193 Cal.App.3d 364, 238 Cal.Rptr. 265 (1987).

Martinez was found guilty of murder in the first degree on two separate theories: (1) there was evidence of premeditation and (2) his acts were murder by torture. The intervention of the neighbor coupled with the act of turning up the stereo deprived the defendant of that intensity of passion that alone could have sufficed to reduce murder to voluntary manslaughter. There had been a "cooling-off period," supporting the finding of malice.

There are three general situations in which a defendant can be convicted of murder without personally having done the killing. The major shortcoming of these rules is that a less blameless defendant may receive the same severe punishment as a hardened killer.

Vicarious Murder Rule

vicarious murder rule

A rule holding that an aider and abettor of a murder may also be guilty of the crime even though another person was the actual killer.

Assume that A, B, and C all have conspired to kill the victim, but only A pulls the trigger. According to the **vicarious murder rule,** B and C are vicariously guilty of murder in the first degree. They are aiders and abettors and, as such, considered principals. Massachusetts has adopted a "joint venture" theory of criminality in which individuals present at the scene of a crime, who know that a codefendant intends to commit the crime, and who by agreement are willing and available to help that codefendant if necessary, are equally guilty.[14]

Felony-Murder Rule

felony-murder rule

A rule in some states mandating that all participants in a dangerous felony are guilty of murder in the first degree if a killing occurs during its commission.

Assume that A, B, and C have agreed to commit an inherently dangerous felony (such as armed robbery) but do not intend to kill anyone. Nonetheless, during the robbery A shoots the victim dead. According to the **felony-murder rule,** B and C are also guilty of murder in the first degree even though they never intended that anyone be killed.* Even an aider and abettor (who, therefore, is also a principal) acting as "lookout" in the getaway car may be guilty of "murder one."[15]

---

* Some courts disfavor the felony-murder rule, although most states have some variation of a felony-murder statute. See *Suniga v. Bunnell*, 988 F.2d 664 (9th cir., 1992). Some states have reduced its classification to second-degree (Louisiana, New Hampshire, New York, and Pennsylvania) or third-degree (Maine and Wisconsin) murder. Among others, Hawaii, Kentucky, and Michigan have abolished it altogether.

Provocative-Act Rule

Assume that A, B, and C, although committing some dangerous crime, do not intend to kill anyone, and none of them pulls the trigger. Instead, A waves his gun, provoking some third party to fire a fatal bullet that kills C. A and B are guilty of murder in the first degree according to the **provocative-act rule.** This situation typically occurs with criminals fleeing the crime scene while being pursued by police. One defendant commits some act, such as firing a gun, which provokes the police to kill one of the criminals. The surviving perpetrators are guilty of murder.[16] The provocative-act rule has been rejected in some states, including Pennsylvania, Colorado, New York, and New Mexico.[17]

The preceding rules involving vicarious responsibility are intended to deter criminal activity in which there is a high likelihood of an unintentional (i.e., careless or negligent) or accidental death.

> **provocative-act rule**
>
> The rule that all participants in a dangerous felony are guilty of murder in the first degree if a lawful killing occurs in response to some threatening act by one of the felons.

LEGAL FOCUS—CASE

Fernando, a juvenile, and four other members of the "Avenue Gang" left their hideaway and drove into a rival gang's neighborhood intending to shoot "Cypress Park" members. On the first drive-by, shots were exchanged among shooters in Fernando's car, a rival gang member's car, and a nearby house. On a second drive-by, Caesar Salas, who was riding in the front passenger seat next to Fernando, was fatally hit. Of what crime is Fernando guilty?

People v. Aurelio R., 167 Cal.App.3d 52, 212 Cal.Rptr. 868 (1985).

Fernando was found guilty of murder in the first degree under the provocative-act rule. In states rejecting the rule, Fernando would be guilty of some felony other than murder.

LEGAL FOCUS—CASE

Lawrence Hernandez entered Mr. and Mrs. Wolfe's coin shop in the afternoon, brandished a gun, and robbed them of coins and currency. Hernandez did not touch either of the Wolfes, but Mr. Wolfe died of a heart attack during the robbery. Of what crimes is Hernandez guilty?

People v. Hernandez, 169 Cal.App.3d 282, 215 Cal.Rptr. 166 (1985).

Hernandez is, of course, guilty of armed robbery. In some states, he also is guilty of murder in the first degree under the felony-murder rule, which, as noted, is designed to deter negligent or accidental deaths as well as intentional homicides. If an accomplice had been waiting in the car, acting as a lookout, he would be a principal and thus guilty with Hernandez of first-degree murder.

The Malice Requirement

The presence of malice aforethought may be implied from the conduct of the accused. Without malice, there is no murder. Under such circumstances, the homicide is generally manslaughter.

LEGAL FOCUS—CASE

Robert Rosenkrantz, age 18, was a "closet" homosexual, primarily because he feared reprisal from his father and the rest of his family. His brother, Joey, discovered the truth and, along with his friend Steven Redman, revealed it to the family. Rosenkrantz, under great mental strain, purchased an Uzi semiautomatic carbine, tracked down Redman, and killed him with a fusillade of bullets. Psychiatrists agreed that Rosenkrantz was suffering from acute emotional disturbance. Rosenkrantz appealed a second-degree murder conviction, arguing he was guilty only of voluntary manslaughter because there was no evidence of malice. What should be the result?

People v. Rosenkrantz, 198 Cal.App.3d 1187, 244 Cal.Rptr. 403 (1988).

manslaughter

The unlawful killing of another person without malice aforethought. Usually classified as *voluntary* or *involuntary,* depending on the degree of culpability involved.

voluntary manslaughter

The wrongful and intentional killing of another person during the heat of passion, or under the influence of alcohol or drugs, or while engaged in some reckless and dangerous activity.

involuntary manslaughter

The unintentional killing of another person because of gross negligence, or as a result of dangerous and unlawful conduct.

vehicular manslaughter

The wrongful killing of another person by a perpetrator driving a vehicle in a reckless and dangerous manner (e.g., in some cases while under the influence of alcohol or other drug).

The second-degree murder conviction was affirmed on appeal. Malice may be implied when, as here, the jury determines that insufficient provocation existed.

The Personhood Requirement

Malice is not the only statutory requirement of murder. The unlawful killing must be of a "human being." What constitutes a human being or "person" is among the more controversial issues in law.

For purposes of the Fourteenth Amendment to the U.S. Constitution, a fetus is not yet a person. Therefore, the respective states are free to define, as a matter of state law, when life begins, for the purpose of defining the crime of murder. The vast majority of states do not consider a fetus to be a person in a criminal law context; that is, there can be no murder of a fetus. California and a minority of other states (e.g., Illinois) amended their traditional murder statutes to include a fetus as a human being.[18]

The U.S. Supreme Court has declared abortion legal throughout the country, and has also declared that the states can regulate abortions in the interest of protecting the "potentiality" of life.[19] Any distinction between a "human being" and a "potentiality of life" does not render unconstitutional the respective states' definitions of murder. The issue of abortion is discussed in Chapter 9.

MANSLAUGHTER

There are two general categories of **manslaughter,** both involving an unlawful killing of a person under some variety of emotional circumstances. **Voluntary manslaughter** is the most blameworthy because it is an intentional killing of a person. **Involuntary manslaughter** is an accidental killing. There is one further category in many states, **vehicular manslaughter,** specifically relating to deaths caused by the reckless driving of motor vehicles.

Voluntary manslaughter is an intentional killing—though without malice—in the heat of passion, as a result of severe provocation. As discussed earlier in the Rosenkrantz case, there must be a considerable heat of passion at the time of the killing from some substantial provocation. Otherwise, the homicide is murder. Robert Rosenkrantz was simply not in the heat of passion at the time of the killing. For example, he purchased the Uzi many days before the killing, allowing plenty of time to "cool off."

LEGAL FOCUS—CASE

Robert Watson, while intoxicated, ran a red light at high speed and narrowly missed hitting another car by skidding to a stop. He took off, again at high speed, and collided with a Toyota at another intersection, skidding 292 feet before coming to a stop. The driver of the Toyota and his six-year-old daughter were killed. Watson's blood-alcohol was .23 percent. Watson was charged with murder but contended he could be tried only for manslaughter because there was no proof of malice. Was Watson correct?

People v. Watson, 30 Cal.3d 290, 637 P.2d 279, 179 Cal.Rptr. 43 (1981).

No. Malice may be implied from any conduct that has a high probability of resulting in a death and when it is done in wanton disregard for human life. Watson was speeding through city streets while intoxicated, an act presenting a great risk of death. He narrowly avoided one accident, only to cause another. These factors support a finding of implied malice. The jury verdict, guilty of murder in the second degree, was affirmed.

LEGAL FOCUS—PROBLEM

Michael Costin was refereeing his son's summer hockey game when an argument ensued with Thomas Junta, a parent of one of the other players. Junta was unhappy with the on-ice roughhousing and the two had words. After the match the two men fought and Costin suffered an injury leading to his death two days later. Junta at 275 pounds outweighed Costin by 100 pounds. Prosecutors presented evidence that Junta hit Costin many times and twice slammed his head against the floor. Was the charge murder or manslaughter?

In the highly publicized Boston "sideline rage" case, Junta was charged with and later convicted of manslaughter and sentenced to six to 10 years in prison. Prosecutors charged manslaughter rather than murder because there was no indication that Junta intended to kill Costin.

RAPE

Sexual intercourse without the consent of the adult victim is the definition of the crime of **rape.** Rape statutes ordinarily apply to persons of opposite gender, while special statutes govern unlawful sexual conduct between same-sex adults. If the victim is a consenting minor, the crime is often called **statutory rape.** The purpose of statutes prohibiting sexual intercourse between adults and minors is to protect children. Presumably children cannot, because of their minority, give informed consent.

LEGAL FOCUS—PROBLEM

Mary Kay LeTourneau, age thirty-five, a popular teacher in Seattle and the mother of four children, pleaded guilty to having sex with a thirteen-year-old boy who had been a

http://

For full coverage of the "sideline rage" case, see the Court TV Web site

http://www.courttv .com/trials/junta/ 010702-PM_CTV.html

rape

An unlawful act of sexual intercourse, against the will of the victim.

statutory rape

Sexual intercourse between an adult, usually 18 or older, and a consenting minor, usually 17 or younger.

> student in her sixth-grade class. The two had originally met in her second-grade class. According to the victim, they had exchanged rings and planned the pregnancy that produced their daughter. Was LeTourneau guilty of rape?

http://

For coverage of the Mary Kay LeTourneau case, see the Court TV Web site

http://www.courttv.com/ trials/letourneau/

Yes. LeTourneau was sentenced to seven years in prison, but the sentence was suspended after six months and probation granted.[20] Promptly following her release from jail in early 1998, LeTourneau violated probation by again having sex with her underage victim. Her probation violated, LeTourneau went back to jail to finish serving her seven-year sentence, although she was pregnant. Her daughter Georgia was born in October 1998—the same month a book co-authored by LeTourneau and her underage victim was published in Europe. This bizarre case exemplifies how seriously the law recognizes the distinction between apparent and informed consent.

The crime of rape received much public attention from the 1970s through the 1990s. Generally, attention was focused on the involvement of the victim in the administration of justice; that is, how is the victim treated immediately after the crime and to what extent must the victim endure humiliating trial tactics, often dealing with prior sexual experience(s). An isolated example exemplifying attitudes that sometimes surround rape prosecutions occurred when a grand jury in Austin, Texas, declined to indict (i.e., charge with crime) an accused knife-wielding rapist because the female victim had asked that he use a condom as some protection against AIDS and other sexually transmitted diseases (STDs).[21] Speculation was the grand jury believed.

Many states have enacted **rape shield statutes** protecting victims from courtroom questioning about prior sexual experience(s) with persons other than the defendant.

rape-shield statute

A statute that protects victims from courtroom questioning about prior sexual experiences with persons other than the defendant.

LEGAL FOCUS—PROBLEM

Ignacio Perea kidnapped an eleven-year-old boy in Dade County, Florida, took him to a deserted warehouse, and raped him. Perea had a clinic receipt in his pocket indicating that he had tested HIV positive for the deadly AIDS virus. Of what crimes is Perea guilty?

A jury found Perea guilty of kidnapping (a felony discussed later in this chapter), rape, and attempted murder. This is the first time a jury had considered the AIDS virus to be a deadly weapon.[22] Other states have created new, specific crimes for those who engage in sexual contact while knowingly infected with the AIDS virus.

LEGAL FOCUS—CASE

During trial for forcible **"date" rape,** there was evidence that the victim, M., initially consented to sexual intercourse with defendant David Vela, but changed her mind during the act. She told him to "stop." Vela nonetheless forcibly continued against her will. Is Vela guilty of any crime?

People v. Vela, 172 Cal.App.3d 237, 218 Cal.Rptr. 161 (1985).

date rape

Non-consensual sexual intercourse by a friend or acquaintance.

Vela is not guilty of forcible rape because M. consented when penetration first occurred. The essence of the crime of rape is the outrage felt by the victim at being violated. If she retracts her consent during intercourse, but the male continues, she may certainly feel outrage, but of less magnitude than from nonconsensual intercourse. The male who persists once consent is withdrawn, however, may be guilty of another crime, such as assault and battery.[23]

EXTORTION

LEGAL FOCUS—PROBLEM

Autumn Jackson demanded $40 million from Bill Cosby to keep secret his alleged parenthood, and then signed a $24 million payoff agreement that was negotiated in an FBI sting. Although Jackson's mother had had a sexual liaison with Cosby approximately nine months before Jackson's birth, Cosby's paternity is denied and unproven. Is it extortion to demand money to keep quiet a fact you believe to be true?

Yes. What Jackson believed is not relevant (nor is Cosby's alleged parentage) to her wrongful demand for hush money in exchange for withholding a civil paternity claim. Note that the FBI was involved because the threat was forwarded across state lines, thereby invoking federal jurisdiction. Jackson was sentenced to 26 months in prison.[24] Notice that this example involved an attempt to extort money out of fear of publicity, not out of fear of physical harm to anyone.

LEGAL FOCUS—CASE

Richard Alday telephoned the father of a seven-year-old boy to say that he had kidnapped his son. Alday demanded $15,000, threatening that the child would be "hurt bad" unless the money was paid. Before the payment of any ransom, it was discovered that the boy had not been kidnapped but had become lost when he wandered away from the family summer cabin. Alday was arrested. During prosecution for extortion, his attorney argued that no crime had been committed because no kidnapping had occurred. Did a crime occur?

People v. Alday, 10 Cal. 3d 392, 315 P.2d 1169, 110 Cal.Rptr. 617 (1973).

Yes. **Extortion** is the crime of obtaining of money by the wrongful use of force or fear. Alday committed extortion when he tried to obtain money by threatening injury to the son. This example of threatening physical injury is unlike the Cosby example of threatening publicity. Although there was no actual kidnapping in this case, it would have been a separate crime if it had occurred.

Extortion is recognized as an inherently vicious crime. Some states confine the meaning of extortion to the unlawful taking by an official under color of his office (e.g., "pay me now or I'll have you arrested"), while **blackmail** refers to an unlawful taking of money by a private person under some threat.[25] The threat may be to accuse the victim of a crime, or to expose some deformity, previous crime, or important secret of the victim. And, of course, as in the *Alday* case, any threat to injure a person is also extortion. It is no defense to extortion that the "facts" upon which the threats were based are later revealed to be untrue. It is the threat to reveal them, if the wrongdoer is not paid, that is a criminal act.

extortion or
blackmail

Obtaining something of value from a person by force, intimidation, or undue or illegal power.

KIDNAPPING

kidnapping

The crime of unlawful seizure and transport of a victim against his or her will.

Kidnapping involves the use of force (or threat of force) in taking a person from one place to another against his or her will. Aggravated kidnapping occurs when an additional crime is involved, such as kidnapping to commit robbery, or to collect a ransom or reward, or to commit extortion. A typical sentence for aggravated kidnapping, without serious injury, is life imprisonment with the possibility of parole. Any homicide occurring during a kidnapping will trigger the felony-murder rule, enhancing the crime to murder in the first degree. Kidnapping is both a state and federal crime.

LEGAL FOCUS—BACKGROUND

The kidnapping of the infant child of Charles and Anne Lindbergh was considered the crime of the twentieth century. Colonel Lindbergh was the first person to fly solo non-stop across the Atlantic and he was a world hero to a degree that is difficult to comprehend in the twenty-first century. In 1932 his twenty-month-old son was taken out of a second story bedroom; a ransom demand was made and eventually paid. Later the infant was found dead in a decomposing state in a field only four miles from the Lindbergh home. An illegal German immigrant named Bruno Richard Hauptmann was later arrested, tried, convicted, and executed for the crime. A byproduct of the case was the federalization of kidnapping when Congress passed the "Little Lindbergh Law" making kidnapping a federal crime if the victim is taken across state lines or if the mail service is used for ransom demands.

http://

For fascinating coverage of the crime of the twentieth century see the Crime Library

http://www.crimelibrary.com/lindbergh/lindmain.htm

ROBBERY

robbery

The crime of stealing property from another person in his or her immediate presence through the use of force or fear.

Robbery is the taking of money or other personal property of another from his or her person or immediate presence by means of force or fear. A specific intent to steal is a necessary element of the crime. Robbery commands a greater penalty than theft (stealing without confrontation, discussed later) because there is a greater possibility of violence when the victim and offender are face to face. **Armed robbery** (use of a dangerous weapon) typically results in an enhanced penalty.

armed robbery

Robbery committed with the use of a lethal weapon, such as a gun or a knife.

Carjacking is the wrongful taking of control of an occupied vehicle. It is a specialized version of robbery that typically results in an enhanced penalty due to the obvious likelihood of violence and danger to society.

Recall that even an accidental killing that occurs during the commission of a dangerous felony, such as armed robbery, elevates the homicide to murder of the first degree under the felony-murder rule, and that all participants, even the getaway driver, are equally guilty.

carjacking

Taking a motor vehicle from a person by force and violence or by intimidation.

MAYHEM

mayhem

The crime of unlawfully depriving the victim of some member of his or her body; disfiguring, disabling, or rendering the member useless or otherwise permanently disfiguring the body.

The crime of **mayhem** occurs when someone gives another a serious permanent wound. A person dismembers, disfigures, or maims another person (e.g., cuts the tongue, severs a finger, puts out an eye, slits the nose, etc.). The historical definition of the crime is interesting: in essence, someone depriving another of a body part that left the person less able to fight. Thus, significantly injuring another's hand, arm, or eye was mayhem whereas scarring the face was not. The fighting distinction is no longer part of the definition.

LEGAL FOCUS—PROBLEM

Lorena Bobbitt sliced off the penis of her sleeping husband, John Wayne Bobbitt, then fled from their home and ultimately tossed his member from her car into the street. Found by a passerby, Mr. Bobbitt's member was surgically re-attached. Is the crime reduced to battery because the dismemberment was not permanent?

No. Once the crime of mayhem occurs, the success of a subsequent surgical or other repair does not reduce the crime. The permanency and nature of dismemberment may affect the penalty imposed by the sentencing judge, however.

LEGAL FOCUS—CASE

Bernie Lopez threw a beer bottle into a car, hitting Raul Morales and rendering him legally blind in the left eye. Lopez did not intend to damage Morales seriously, let alone render him partially blind. Is he guilty of battery or mayhem?

People v. Lopez, 176 Cal.App.3d 545, 222 Cal.Rptr. 101 (1986).

Lopez is guilty of mayhem. Specific intent to maim is not an element of the crime. All that is necessary is a general wrongful intent, such as Lopez had when he threw the beer bottle.[26]

ASSAULT AND BATTERY

Criminal assault is an unlawful attempt, coupled with a present ability, to commit a violent injury upon the person of another. If the assault is successful and injury results, a **criminal battery** has occurred. There can be no battery in criminal law without an assault, because battery is a completed assault. For assault, there must be a present ability to injure. A menacing gesture with an unloaded gun is not an assault in the criminal law, although the result is different in the civil law (see Chapter 7). An unloaded gun cannot injure the victim unless it is used to pistol-whip or to club. Otherwise, there is no present ability to cause physical injury. On the other hand, one who fires at a service station attendant who is protected by bulletproof glass is guilty of assault. The shooter has the ability to strike out, and by shooting does in fact strike, even though the bullets cannot reach the intended victim.[27] Waving an unloaded gun toward another person may be a lesser crime than assault, such as brandishing a firearm.

HATE CRIMES

Violence directed at victims because of their race, religion, political affiliation, or other personal beliefs (e.g., supporting abortion rights) is loosely referred to as **hate crime.** A hate crime may be a separately defined crime but usually it provides for a sentence enhancement if the elements are proven. Some states have included within their penalty enhancement laws those crimes that are based on hatred of the victim's sexual orientation. International terrorism or any antigovernment crime directed at randomly selected victims also might be classified within this category.

criminal assault

The threat of violence upon another person.

criminal battery

The unlawful application of force to another human being without excuse or consent.

hate crime

Any crime for which the motivation was persecution of a victim because of race, religion, sexual orientation, or political beliefs.

LEGAL FOCUS—PROBLEM

Pretending they were gay, Aaron McKinney and Russell Henderson lured 21-year-old University of Wyoming student Matthew Shepard from a local bar. After robbing Shepard they tied him to a fence post and beat him. He died of head injuries five days later. Would this homicide qualify as a hate crime?

Whether a crime is a hate crime depends on the motivations of the perpetrators. Was Shepard killed because he was gay or incident to a robbery? As Wyoming lacked a hate-crime statute, the prosecution charged felony murder and kidnapping. Henderson pled guilty and received two life sentences before trial. A jury found McKinney guilty of felony murder, kidnapping, and aggravated robbery. To avoid the probable finding of the death penalty, Henderson agreed to two life sentences and promised not to appeal the verdict. Dennis Shepard, Matthew's father, addressed the jurors: "This was a hate crime, pure and simple, with the added ingredient of robbery. My son, Matthew, paid a terrible price to open the eyes of all of us who live in Wyoming, the United States, and the world to the unjust and unnecessary fears, discrimination and intolerance that members of the gay community face every day." This tragedy along with several others increased lobbying efforts for hate-crime legislation.

It is believed that the number of hate groups (often identified, for example, as Ku Klux Klan, skinheads, neo-Nazis, white supremacists, and black separatists) as well the number of individuals harboring racial and government hatred is growing.[28] Many states and the federal government provide penalty enhancements for hate crimes. Opponents of hate crime legislation argue that the reason why crimes are committed does not affect the victim nor reflect the egregiousness of the act and should therefore be ignored.

TERRORISM

Terrorist activities overlap other criminal definitions and create special challenges to U.S. law enforcement. For example, a terrorist may commit murder but instead of one victim there may be a hundred or a thousand. The motivation may be political gain or revenge instead of jealousy or a desire to steal. Terrorism may be against citizens or interests of the United States in a foreign country or be by foreign nationals or U.S. citizens in the United States itself. Long-standing jurisdiction distinctions between state and federal authorities and the various federal authorities themselves (the Federal Bureau of Investigation, the Treasury Department, and the Central Intelligence Agency) are challenged by terrorist activities. Distinctions between criminal investigation and national defense become very important and perplexing. The following acts listed in the Attorney General's Guidelines on General Crimes, Racketeering Enterprise and Terrorism Enterprise Investigations assist in identifying the activities the FBI will investigate as terrorist in nature.

1) Threats or advocacy of violence or other covered criminal acts: Statements are made in relation to or in furtherance of an enterprise's political or social objectives that threaten or advocate the use of force or violence, or statements are made in furtherance of an enterprise that otherwise threaten or advocate criminal conduct:
(i) engaging in attacks involving or threatening massive loss of life or injury, mass destruction, or endangerment of the national security;

http://

For statistics and a list of federal and state hate crime laws see the Anti-Defamation League's Web site at

http://www.adl.org/

(ii) killing or injuring federal personnel, destroying federal facilities, or defying lawful federal authority;

(iii) killing, injuring or intimidating individuals because of their status as United States nationals or persons, or because of their national origin, race, color, religion, or sex; or

(iv) depriving individuals of any rights secured by the Constitution or laws of the United States.

STALKING

Stalking involves repeatedly being around or even secretly watching a person, making uninvited written or verbal communications, or making implied threats. It often involves telephone harassment or waiting for someone to appear. Victims typically are women between nineteen and thirty-nine years old and they are stalked repeatedly, some for years. Stalkers often are former husbands, boyfriends, or roommates. A new crime, whose notoriety was assured by the film *Fatal Attraction,* stalking is prohibited in all fifty states. Court restraining orders are available to potential victims before any physical harm is inflicted. Although known to be widespread (about one in every twelve women reports having been stalked), most stalking is not reported by the victims.[29]

LEGAL FOCUS—PROBLEM

Jonathan Norman was arrested for attempting to enter filmmaker Steven Spielberg's home while carrying a "rape kit" containing handcuffs and duct tape among other paraphernalia. Norman's former lover, Charles Markovich, testified that it was Norman's secret intention to bind and rape Spielberg in the presence of his wife. In defense, Norman's public defender contended that it is not a crime to have "weird thoughts" about someone famous, that Norman never entered Spielberg's property, and that when told to leave, he did. Is Norman guilty of stalking?

Yes.[30] Although conduct may fall short of an attempted crime, it nonetheless may constitute stalking under state statutes.

WHAT ARE CRIMES AGAINST PROPERTY?

ARSON

Arson is the wrongful burning of real or personal property, either intentionally or recklessly—simple negligence is not enough. It is the classic crime against property. Punishment for arson typically varies with the type of property burned. For example, arson of an inhabited structure is more serious than arson of a vacant storage building. It is not arson to burn one's own property unless there is some fraudulent purpose (e.g., obtaining casualty insurance proceeds) or damage to the property of others. In the summer of 2002 massive wildfires in Arizona and Colorado led to the arrests of forestry firefighters for the crime of arson.[31]

http://

For the complete Attorney General Terrorism Guidelines see **http://www.usdoj.gov/olp/ generalcrimes2.pdf**

stalking

An unwelcome or intrusive long-term pattern of threat or harassment directed repeatedly toward a specific individual that triggers fear or concern in that person.

arson

The intentional and malicious burning of a building or other property for unlawful purposes.

burglary

The crime of unlawfully entering premises, and structures, and vehicles with intent to commit larceny (theft) or any other felony.

home invasion burglary

The intentional breaking and entering into a person's occupied residence using violent means to take property of the occupant.

theft

The taking of property without the owners consent. Depending on the nature or value of the property stolen, it is either petty theft (*misdemeanor*) or grand theft (*felony*).

larceny

The crime of stealing property from another.

embezzlement

The crime of stealing property that, before the theft, was lawfully in the possession of the thief.

larceny by trick

Theft accomplished by deceit or subterfuge wherein the victim turns over property, especially money, to the perpetrator.

grand theft

Theft of personal property of substantial value, as declared by statute.

petty theft

Theft of a thing of little value, as specified by statute.

BURGLARY

Burglary is the unlawful entry into premises and structures with the intent to commit larceny (theft) or any other felony. Common-law definitions of crimes against property vary among the states therefore, crime statistics may be skewed because, identical terms may not indicate identical criminal acts. For example, one specialized crime triggering enhanced sentences is **home invasion burglary,** in which gang members burst into the victim's home and quickly overpower all occupants. Unfortunately a variety of other crimes usually ensue, such as murder, rape, or robbery. In some states, burglary includes breaking into a vehicle for the purpose of committing larceny or theft—crimes we will examine next.

THEFT

Theft is the modern catchall term that embraces the unlawful taking of another's personal property with the intent to permanently deprive the person thereof. It includes the common-law crime of **larceny,** which is the wrongful taking of another's property without the use of force or fear. **Embezzlement** is a common-law form of larceny in which an employee steals money from his or her employer. In embezzlement access to the money is lawful, as by a bookkeeper or government officer, but is wrongfully and secretly diverted to the personal use of the embezzler. **Larceny by trick** is the common-law crime of wrongfully obtaining property through some dishonest scam or fraudulent scheme. In all of these definitions, the modern term is simply *theft* and its definition includes the conduct previously called *larceny* under the common law.

Theft also can be defined by degree. The purpose in classifying criminal acts is to make the penalty fit the crime. **Grand theft** is a felony involving the taking of something of substantial value, as defined by statute (e.g., $400 or more in some states), or the taking of a certain kind of property, such as motor vehicles, firearms, or farm animals. Theft of personal property worth less than the statutory definition of substantial value, such as $400, is a misdemeanor and is called **petty theft.** Thus, for example, shoplifting may be either a felony or a misdemeanor depending upon the value of the stolen merchandise. Not surprisingly, grand theft results in a harsher penalty than petty theft.

RECEIVING STOLEN PROPERTY

Knowingly **receiving stolen property** is a crime. To be responsible for the offense, the accused must have known, or should have known, the property was stolen. Proof of knowledge may be inferred from the circumstances, such as adequacy of the price paid, the character of the vendor, the time and place of delivery, and so on. Ownership of the stolen property does not change; an innocent purchaser of stolen property must return it to the real owner and may seek reimbursement only from the person (generally the thief) who sold it to him or her.

LEGAL FOCUS—PROBLEM

Sam Vreeland purchased a car radio and CD player from Jaspar Malloy at the Greater Tuna Flea Market. The price was attractive, but not unusually low. Vreeland installed the unit and proudly showed it off to some of his friends at school. Donna Janeway noticed how similar the unit looked to one that had been stolen from her mother's car. She wrote down the serial number and took it home for comparison with her mother's warranty registration documents. The numbers were the same. Is Vreeland guilty of a crime? Who gets to keep the radio and CD player?

Vreeland is innocent of any wrongdoing. He did not know, and had no reason to suspect, that the radio had been stolen. Janeway's mother still owns the radio and is entitled to its return. Vreeland theoretically could sue Malloy for return of his money. More likely than not, Malloy will be gone. He may or may not be guilty of a crime, depending on how he obtained the radio.

Misuse of a credit card, issuing a check knowing there are insufficient funds at the bank, and malicious mischief (vandalism) are examples of other crimes against property. "Keying" a car (scratching its painted surfaces with a key) is an example of malicious mischief that is remarkably costly to repair. Spray-painting graffiti is another example of costly vandalism that has provoked widespread concern and public outrage.* When crimes such as these involve small amounts of money or damage, they are misdemeanors. When victims suffer significant financial loss as a result of the crime, courts usually impose a penalty and order the convicted defendant to make full restitution.

IDENTITY THEFT

LEGAL FOCUS—PROBLEM

Marsha Jones used Mari Frank's name, social security number, and driver's license number to purchase a red Mustang convertible on credit. Unfortunately, while Frank continues to defend herself from the collection agency that is attempting to collect the Mustang's price, Jones continues to possess and drive the flashy car. Is it a crime to steal another person's identity?

Yes, and it is a rapidly growing crime.[32] According to the ID Theft Data Clearinghouse, the most common types of identity theft are
- using or opening a credit card account fraudulently
- opening telecommunications or utility accounts fraudulently
- passing bad checks or opening a new bank account
- getting loans in another person's name
- working in another person's name[33]

In 1998 nine states had identity-theft statutes; by 2002, almost all states had specific identity-theft laws. In states where stealing identification is not a specific crime, other statutes may apply if the stolen identification is used to defraud a merchant. If the offense involves interstate commerce, it also is a federal crime punishable by up to fifteen years in prison.

---

receiving stolen property

The crime of knowingly receiving property of another.

http://

In 2002 the trial and conviction of actress Winona Ryder for shoplifting was big news. See the Court TV Web site for stories about her arrest, trial, and conviction

http://www.courttv.com/ trials/ryder/

http://

See the following Web site for statistics and references to your state's laws regarding identity theft

http://www.consumer.gov/ idtheft/

---

* Spray-painting graffiti in public places is a very serious crime in Singapore. In early 1994, the conviction of Ohioan Michael Fay for the offense of malicious mischief was front-page news and a matter of national television coverage. The eighteen-year-old Fay was sentenced to four months in prison and six lashes (later reduced to four) across his buttocks with a 4-foot long, 1/2-inch thick rattan cane. *San Francisco Chronicle,* 2 May 1994.

WHAT ARE CRIMES AGAINST PUBLIC HEALTH, SAFETY, AND WELFARE?

All states have adopted either the Uniform Controlled Substances Act or the Uniform Narcotic Drug Act. These laws classify drugs in schedules depending upon their harmfulness. For example, Schedule I drugs have a high potential for abuse and no generally accepted medical use. They include heroin, LSD, marijuana, mescaline, peyote, PCP, and cocaine base, as well as crack. There is an organized movement to legalize a restricted availability of marijuana on the grounds that it is a better painkiller for certain patients, such as cancer and AIDS sufferers. State laws created by the initiative process to legalize marijuana for such purpose have begun the appellate process, heading toward possible review by the U.S. Supreme Court.

Schedule II drugs, such as opium, codeine, morphine, and amphetamines, have some accepted medical use. Further down the scale, Schedule V drugs such as Buprenorphine and Lomotil have a low potential for abuse but may lead to some psychological or physical dependence.

Penalties are related to the activity (such as selling or manufacturing versus using), the class of drug involved in the crime, its quantity, previous offenses, and sale to children or around schools, and range from misdemeanors to felonies. "In the case of marijuana, an offense for trying to sell ten grams could be met with a maximum imprisonment term of less than one year in North Carolina but a term of life in Montana and Oklahoma. Similarly, a sale offense for the standard retail amounts of cocaine, ecstasy or methamphetamine could be met with a one-year imprisonment term in North Carolina but a lifetime sentence in Montana."[34]

Much controversy surrounds the implications of imposing long prison sentences for drug offenses involving the less expensive yet very potent crack cocaine. Because poor, inner-city youths are more likely to be involved with crack than more affluent adults, the overwhelming majority of those imprisoned for its use are young African American males. Are there disparate penalties for users of inexpensive drugs compared to users of expensive narcotics? Perhaps.

LEGAL FOCUS—EXAMPLE

Actor Robert Downey Jr. was arrested in 1996 when police stopped his speeding pickup truck and found cocaine, crack, heroin, and a pistol. He pleaded guilty and was sentenced to three years probation. In 1998, Downey's probation was revoked for use of drugs and alcohol in violation of the court's previous order. He then was sentenced to six months in jail. However, he received four all-day furloughs from jail to complete the movie *In Dreams*. Deputy sheriffs had been asking for and receiving autographs from Downey, posing for pictures with him, and even letting the actor buy them lunch at the movie studio. Downey also was permitted to visit a plastic surgeon after a jailhouse fight. Are these "celebrity perks" legal?

No. Judges do have discretion to tailor sentences and to modify state incarceration procedures. It is not clear whether a "furlough" to participate in a movie is a proper exercise of that discretion. The judge in the Downey case was directed by a higher court to stop further "furloughs" pending review, but Downey's sentence ended before a more definitive ruling could be made.[35] You might consider whether an inner-city African American youth, or any non-celebrity, would have received similar perks from the judge.

A few states have passed so-called medical marijuana laws. These statutes exempt patients who use marijuana under a physician's supervision from state criminal penalties.* Assuming medical use is lawful, can federal law still prohibit organized distribution of medical cannabis? The U.S. Supreme Court said there is no medical-necessity exception to the federal Controlled Substances Act's prohibitions on manufacturing and distributing marijuana.[36]

Some conduct that endangers the public health or safety is a misdemeanor.

http://

Order or download a 2002 study of the drug laws of all fifty states at **http://www.andrews.edu/ BHSC/impacteen- illicitdrugteam/chartbook .htm**

LEGAL FOCUS—PROBLEM

Marcy Allen walked through a metal detector in a public building. The bell sounded and her purse was searched. Marcy was carrying a key ring that was designed also as a can opener, windshield scraper, and hair lifter. It was in the shape of a cat head with two holes for eyes and sharp triangles for ears. By placing one's fingers through the "eyes," the key ring doubled as a sort of brass knuckles with sharp points (the ears of the cat). Allen was charged with carrying an illegal weapon. What was the result?

States prohibit the buying or possession of certain kinds of implements that can be primarily used as weapons. So-called brass knuckles and switchblade knives are examples. But what of a key ring that happens to be shaped like a cat's head and, therefore, has pointy ears? The jury sided with the state and convicted Allen of a misdemeanor. She was placed on six months probation.[37] With modern tensions it is unlikely that juries will be sympathetic to careless defendants.

Other examples of misdemeanors are (1) "rubbernecking" at the scene of an emergency when it impedes official personnel, (2) discarding a refrigerator with its door intact, (3) exhibiting the deformities of another person in exchange for money, (4) killing a farm animal while hunting, (5) operating machinery too close to high-voltage wires, (6) attaching a burning candle to a balloon and releasing it, (7) donating blood or body organs while knowingly suffering from AIDS, (8) violating laws regulating food, liquor, drugs, and cosmetics, (9) violating fish and game laws, (10) allowing animals with known vicious propensities to be loose, (11) adulterating candy with laxatives or other chemicals, (12) cutting public shrubs, (13) selling alcoholic beverages after hours, and (14) firing a pistol up into the sky within city limits. In some states, one or more of these crimes may be felonies depending upon the circumstances involved.

WHAT ARE CRIMES AGAINST PUBLIC DECENCY AND MORALS?

One of the most controversial classifications of criminal behavior involves crimes against public decency and morals. Examples in this category are unlawful sexual intercourse,

* Since 1996, Alaska, Arizona, California, Colorado, Maine, Nevada, Oregon, and Washington have adopted such laws by voter initiative. The Hawaii legislature passed a similar law in 1999.

sodomy, and oral copulation. Illinois was the first state that decriminalized sexual activities between consenting adults in private places, but some states prohibit all "unnatural and lascivious" acts whether in private or not.[38]

LEGAL FOCUS—CASE

Responding to a telephone complaint that a burglary was taking place, police burst into a home discovering, instead of a burglar, the residents John Lawrence and Tyrone Garner engaging in sodomy. They were arrested, booked, and jailed overnight for violation of the Texas misdemeanor sodomy law. Lawrence and Garner pleaded "no contest," were fined $125 each, and then filed an appeal on the grounds that the law was unconstitutional. What will be the result on appeal?

Lawrence v. State, 41 S.W. 3d 349 (2001), cert. granted, and *Lawrence v. Texas,* 123 S.Ct. 661, 2002 WL 1611564, 71 USLW 3116 (2002).

Lawrence and Garner argue that the sodomy law makes it illegal for homosexuals to engage in the identical sexual activity that is legal for heterosexuals—and therefore laws prohibiting such activity are an unconstitutional denial of due process and equal protection. Although the Texas court disagreed with this contention, the U.S. Supreme Court in December 2002 agreed to hear an appeal of the Texas decision. Until and unless the U.S. Supreme Court agrees with Lawrence and Garner, sodomy remains a crime in Texas, but not all states.

Other examples of behavior that is criminal in some, or all, states include incest (intercourse between specified classes of related persons), lewd conduct with children, adultery (intercourse between a cohabiting married and an unmarried person), obscenity and indecency, prostitution and pimping (arranging for the prostitution of another), seduction, abortion (except pursuant to law or as allowed by the Therapeutic Abortion Act), child-stealing by a parent, child neglect, failure to support a dependent, and gambling (except as specifically authorized by statute).

Sex perversion is a catchall crime that includes sodomy between consenting adults as well as lewd or lascivious acts with a child. In some states conviction of sex perversion or any other crime involving lascivious activity (such as rape, pimping, or prostitution) has for many years resulted in a continuing duty, after release from jail, to register with the local police as a sex offender. Such registration is intended to provide law enforcement with a list of "usual suspects" to be checked when sex crimes occur, but it has been difficult to enforce, is often ignored by law enforcement agencies, and has not proved to be an effective deterrent.

LEGAL FOCUS—BACKGROUND

In 1996, following the notorious murder of seven-year-old Megan Kanka, Congress passed a law encouraging states to adopt procedures disclosing the identity and residences of sex offenders. In response, the states have adopted statutes referred to as "Megan's Law." These statutes authorize law enforcement to publicize the identification and residential address of convicted sex offenders who are on parole or have served their sentences. The purpose is to protect families through disclosure. Names and addresses of convicted sex offenders are made available by CD-ROM held at local police stations, distributed by hand to households in the neighborhood, or published on the Internet; sometimes photographs are also distributed to aid identification by neighbors. Delaware requires that sex offender status be identified on drivers' licenses.

Critics of Megan's Law focus upon the fairness of subjecting persons who have served their time and paid their debt to society to a lifetime of harassment. Disclosure may prevent the former offender from retaining employment or enjoying the life available to others living in the suburbs without public shame.

There are also fears of vigilantism, and some question the potential results when sex offenders are repeatedly "pushed" from one neighborhood to another, perhaps until finally locating in the inner cities in high-density apartments and public housing. With the increased anonymity found in densely populated cities, the risk to poor children may be increased as more-affluent children in the suburbs become more protected. Regardless, the public strongly favors implementation of Megan's Law,[39] and courts have upheld its application, ruling that it does not constitute additional punishment.

http://

To check nationwide registries see the Parents for Megan's Law, Inc., Web site
http://www.parentsfor meganslaw.com/

http://

To see the impact of Megan's Law, see
http://www.vsp.state.va.us

LEGAL FOCUS—PROBLEM

Jonathan Hawes, age twenty-nine, planned to live with his mother in the small town of Dilley, about 25 miles from Portland, Oregon, upon his release from prison where he had served five years for sexually abusing two ten-year-old girls. Upon notification under Megan's Law, community members had a meeting with Hawes's mother. Tempers flared; there was talk of guard dogs, burning down the home, even killing Hawes. One resident shouted in the face of Hawes's mother, "When can I kill him?" The home where Hawes planned to live sits isolated from children in the middle of twenty-seven acres of pasture. Ultimately members of the community offered to purchase the home to get rid of Hawes, and then to sell the home later to a more acceptable person. Is Hawes legally obligated to sell and move?

No. But as his mother said, "If everyone in the community hates you, wants to sue you, wants to do you bodily harm, do you really have options"? An agreement of sale was reached and Hawes moved on.[40]

LEGAL FOCUS—CASE

John V., age sixteen, screamed obscenities at his neighbor, Nancy W., who was driving past his house. Complaint was made and John was charged with violating a statute that prohibits "offensive words in a public place which are inherently likely to provoke an immediate violent reaction." Nancy had become angry, and then furious. She was incoherent, enraged, and humiliated, although she admitted she had "flipped off" John on prior occasions. John was convicted and placed on probation. He contends the law is unconstitutionally overbroad and vague, and has appealed. What should be the result?

People v. John V., 167 Cal.App.3d 761, 213 Cal.Rptr. 503 (1985).

John lost. The right of free speech is not absolute. Not protected is speech that is lewd or obscene, profane, libelous, or insulting—"fighting" words. For fighting words to be a crime, they must be uttered, as here, in a provocative manner, so there is a clear and present danger that an immediate breach of the peace will erupt. Such words are not protected because they are of such slight social value as a step to truth that any benefit is clearly outweighed by the social interest in order and morality.[41] Obviously, these are distinctions that are difficult to make, especially on a consistent basis, if only because the circumstances vary so widely.

WHAT ARE SOME EXAMPLES OF OTHER CRIMES?

WHITE-COLLAR CRIMES

white-collar crime

Illegal acts committed usually without violence by persons of comparatively high social status and economic wealth.

The term **white-collar crime** is applied to nonviolent illegal acts committed by individuals or corporations in a business setting. Typical examples include theft, fraud, bribery, illegal kickbacks, embezzlement of money or trade secrets, prohibited "insider" information exchanges among securities dealers and corporate managers, and bid-rigging of construction contracts. There is a widespread perception that state and local prosecutors are swamped with traditional "street" crimes and display little interest in active pursuit of business crimes committed by white-collar professionals. There is another widespread perception that even those convicted of such crimes receive light sentences, and that their time is served in relatively comfortable "country-club," low-security prisons.

Although business crimes can be very complicated and difficult to prove beyond a reasonable doubt, there is reason to believe that both perceptions may change in the future as prosecutors increase their attention to white-collar crimes and ask for tougher sentencing.*

LEGAL FOCUS—PROBLEM

At age sixteen, Barry Minkow began a carpet-cleaning business in the family garage. Minkow became a youthful symbol of free enterprise by his early twenties as his company, ZZZZ Best, skyrocketed onto Wall Street and into homes across the United States through television advertising. On the way to this pinnacle of success, he swindled banks and investors out of $26 million with a pyramid of lies about company earnings and financial success. He essentially "cooked the books" of ZZZZ Best to obtain bank and investor monies. A jury convicted him of fifty-seven counts of fraud, carrying a maximum of 403 years in prison and $50 million in fines. Eleven other defendants were convicted with Minkow. Can Minkow's victims recover their losses?

The victims did initiate costly and long-lasting civil actions to recover their losses, but Minkow's financial resources made collection unlikely. The judge ordered full restitution

---

* High-profile defendants convicted of multimillion-dollar white-collar crimes involving securities include David Bloom (mail and securities fraud, eight years); Paul Bilzerian (securities and tax fraud, four years plus $1.5 million fine); Stephen Wang Jr. (insider trading, three years); and John Galanis (federal tax-shelter fraud, twenty-seven years, and state securities fraud, seven to twenty-one years concurrently). *The Wall Street Journal,* 26 October 1988 and 28 September 1989. The champion of all white-collar criminals, Michael Milken, is discussed later in this chapter.

of $26 million.[42] Victims probably can deduct their losses on their tax returns and thereby reduce the income taxes they otherwise would be obligated to pay. Thus, indirectly, all other taxpayers share the loss because they have to pay more to offset the ultimate effect of those deductions. Barry Minkow did not serve 403 years in jail—he was sentenced to twenty-five years and served seven. While in prison Minkow became a "born-again" Christian and earned a master's degree in Christian ministries. In 1997 he became senior pastor of the Community Bible Church in San Diego.

Giant corporations, as well as high-profile individuals, are more often charged with violating laws and regulations than smaller businesses and less well-known individuals are. In February 1994, General Electric and the De Beers Centenary of Switzerland were indicted for conspiracy to fix prices of industrial diamonds in world markets. These companies are the largest world users of industrial diamonds, which are used in tools, not jewelry. The De Beers group does business in just about every country in the world except the United States. In December 1994, a federal judge in Columbus, Ohio, dismissed the case, ruling there was insufficient evidence to warrant submission to a jury. The charges, although unproven, exemplify the government's enthusiasm in pursuing white-collar crime. The investigation took two and a half years of intensive efforts.[43] The 2001 bankruptcy of the giant energy firm Enron and the 2002 financial irregularities of communications giant WorldCom may provide prosecutions that will dwarf previous white-collar criminal cases.

White-collar crime can occur in securities markets where stock markets can be used by insiders (owners and managers of businesses) to raise huge sums of money from investors seeking profits.

LEGAL FOCUS—EXAMPLE

In 1988 a corporation, Bre-X, was formed by David Walsh. It was not successful until 1993, when it announced the discovery of a huge gold mine in Indonesia. The price of Bre-X stock began immediately to rise, attaining a level of $100 per share by 1996—yet no gold had been produced. Bre-X then announced that there were 40 million ounces of gold in its claim. The stock promptly soared to $281 per share. Later in 1996, Walsh and his wife Jeannette, the company secretary, began selling their stock, taking in some $20 million. In March 1997, a Bre-X geologist fell to his death from a helicopter in Indonesia—a death that was labeled a suicide. The stock crashed and became valueless by year's end. Independent tests revealed that there was no marketable gold in the mines. Mutual funds were the big losers in this white-collar fiasco.[44] What criminal laws were broken?

After accountants, securities fraud investigators, lawyers, financial market officials, and prosecutors sorted through the records and documents surrounding this huge fraud, no criminal charges were successfully concluded. Chairman David Walsh died in 1998 and Vice Chairman John Felderhof is believed dipping his toes at his oceanfront villa in the Cayman Islands, which has no extradition treaty for security violations.* The point is that white-collar crime, whether it involves fraud, embezzlement, securities violations, bribery,

---

* Bre-X is a Canadian example. A settlement to a class action lawsuit was reached in 2000 requiring Calgary-based Bresea (a sister company) to pay about $10 million to Bre-X bankruptcy trustee Deloitte & Touche. Civil lawsuits continue against company insiders.

or other crimes, can be devastating to its victims and to the public and the perpetrators often get away with it.

Tax evasion probably is the most familiar white-collar crime. Simply stated, it involves knowingly cheating on your income taxes, and it can be a serious crime—a felony. It is widely remembered that the infamous Al Capone, whose evil ways during Prohibition could not be successfully proven in court, ultimately was convicted for income tax evasion. The government pursued a less famous individual, Reuben Sturman, for some twenty-nine years, trying to convict him on obscenity charges. Sturman masterminded a pornography empire that gave him a net worth estimated by authorities at $100 million, much of which had been laundered (i.e., funneled through other organizations—in this case, through Swiss and Caribbean banks—to create the appearances of business profits). The government's first break came in 1989 when, like Al Capone, Sturman was convicted of income tax fraud and sentenced to ten years in prison. He escaped from prison in 1992, only to be caught within two months. The Internal Revenue Service took twelve years to untangle Sturman's web of dummy corporations and foreign bank accounts; but that first tax evasion conviction led to other convictions for extortion and conspiracy.[45] In 1997 he died while still in prison.[46]

In 1970, Congress passed the **Racketeer Influenced and Corrupt Organizations Act (RICO)** for use against organized crime and corruption in labor unions. Under RICO, organized crime members who are involved in an "enterprise" (the family) that engages, at least twice within ten years, in any of numerous specified criminal acts are chargeable with "racketeering."* RICO penalties include heavy prison sentences (up to twenty years) and forfeiture of any ill-gotten monetary gains.

Seizing an opportunity, federal prosecutors have utilized RICO widely against white-collar criminals, whether part of organized crime or not. RICO has been used with considerable success against violators of securities laws. For example, Michael Milken was convicted under RICO of charges of scheming to manipulate stock prices, of trading on inside information, and of defrauding customers. His employer, the investment banking firm Drexel Burnham Lambert, facing a RICO indictment, pleaded guilty to lesser charges and was fined $650 million. To qualify for a RICO prosecution, the accused must have been involved in a "pattern of racketeering activity." Abortion protesters who block access to abortion clinics can be sued by abortion-rights advocates for engaging in such a "pattern of racketeering activity."[47] The decision does not prohibit *peaceful* protests outside abortion clinics, nor stop protesters who trespass on clinic property without threatening clinic employees. Financial advisers who misrepresent money matters to their professional athlete clients also have been held to be engaging in a "pattern of racketeering activity."[48]

Federal courts have expanded the applicability of RICO to just about any collective wrongful activity, whether for economic gain or not. RICO's deterrent effect can be real. For example, actual damages can be trebled in civil cases. In criminal cases, assets of an accused can be temporarily seized before a trial begins.

MISCELLANEOUS CRIMES

Legislatures have seen fit to proscribe a myriad of activities by written laws. These miscellaneous crimes include (1) abusing animals, (2) conducting cockfights, (3) altering telegrams, (4) "beating" vending machines or pay telephones, (5) removing articles from a

---

* The list of forty criminal acts that underlie RICO includes murder, robbery, securities fraud, and use of the mail or telephone for illegal purposes. Lying twice on the telephone concerning a business contract theoretically could trigger a RICO indictment or lawsuit.

---

tax evasion

The intentional and illegal violation of federal and state tax laws.

Racketeer Influenced and Corrupt Organizations Act (RICO)

A federal law passed to control attempts by organized crime to invest money gained from illegal racketeering in legitimate business activities.

corpse, (6) loitering around public schools, (7) offering a "dead or alive" reward, (8) tattooing a minor, (9) harassing another by telephone, (10) carrying a switchblade knife, (11) committing perjury (i.e., lying while sworn to tell the truth) or suborning perjury (i.e., getting someone else to commit perjury), (12) killing protected species of birds, (13) bribing (i.e., paying money to a public official in return for some special consideration), and (14) defacing public property.

The foregoing examples are all state crimes. When criminal conduct involves interstate commerce or violates a U.S. statute, a federal crime has occurred. For example, perjury in a federal court is a federal crime. Killing certain species of birds or animals that are protected by federal laws are federal crimes.

The foregoing list shows the diversity in criminal laws deemed necessary to maintain peace and order in our politically organized, civilized society. There are thousands of miscellaneous crimes on the books, including many outdated ones that are never enforced. Regardless of the statutory blizzard of crimes on the books, ignorance of the law is never a defense. If it were, no doubt most persons accused of a crime would plead such ignorance. Generally, the rules are reasonable and conform to standards of good conduct. The human conscience, or one's innate sense of what is sometimes called "natural law," normally provides a workable guide to what is, in the eyes of society, right and lawful and what is seriously wrong, hence punishable as a crime.

WHAT ARE SOME DEFENSES TO CRIMES?

SELF-DEFENSE

Violent conduct, which would otherwise be criminal behavior, is justified when used in defense of oneself or of certain other persons. All states recognize some form of the privilege of **self-defense.**

LEGAL FOCUS—PROBLEM

Cinnamon Clark and her boyfriend, Harry Holland, were listening to CDs in her apartment. A noisy party was underway next door. Suddenly there was a banging on Clark's unlocked door, and it was flung open. There stood Butch Meen, butcher knife in one hand and beer bottle in the other. Holland's first thought was to run out the back door, but Clark grabbed her pistol from the table drawer, aimed it at Meen's heart, and stared him right in the eyes. When Meen lunged toward her, Clark, fearful of imminent and serious personal harm, killed him with a single well-aimed shot. Was the killing lawful?

Yes. The privilege of self-defense arises when one is confronted with a threat that causes a genuine and reasonable fear of imminent danger of great bodily injury. "Deadly resistance" is justified when the imminent peril is great. Since Meen held a butcher knife and bottle, Clark's fear of great and imminent harm, including possible death, was reasonable and her defense was reasonable. If Meen had retreated, stepping backward, the killing would not have been justified, and Clark would have been guilty of homicide, probably manslaughter. If Meen had lunged toward Holland alone, the killing would still be justified because she was entitled to defend Holland as well as herself.

http://

If you need a break from serious study look for stupid crimes on the Internet. Some listings are for questionable laws and others for simply stupid behavior.

http://www.courttv.com/ news/scm/ and
http://www.copzilla.com/ humor/real.html

self-defense

The legal right to use whatever force appears to be reasonably necessary to protect oneself (or specified others) from great and imminent bodily injury by an assailant.

Generally, the right to self-defense extends to members of one's immediate family or household and to others whom one is under a legal or socially recognized duty to protect. The fact that the acts occurred in Clark's apartment increases the scope of the privilege of self-defense. Defense of habitation is rooted in the ancient principle that one's home is one's castle. It does not mean that a killing is justified merely because it takes place in the home of the accused; however, when at home, one is not obliged to retreat. On the other hand, when one is outside one's house (or apartment), one might be expected to retreat if possible to do so without added risk of harm. Thus, there is a general duty to retreat rather than to kill in self-defense. Even in the home, the killing must be in defense of life or to prevent probable grievous bodily injury, such as rape.

LEGAL FOCUS—PROBLEM

John Booth was released from prison and promptly, the same day, got drunk and decided to burglarize a house. Michael Lanier, a college student, and his fiancée were upstairs when they heard glass shattering downstairs. Lanier grabbed a bat, went downstairs, and hit Booth, who was entering through the window. Immediately upon being struck by the bat, Booth began running away. Lanier chased him and continued to beat him into submission with the bat. Booth suffered a brain hemorrhage and fractured skull; his legs had been battered as well. Lanier was arrested for assault with a deadly weapon. Will the argument of self-defense work for Lanier?

The prosecutor dropped all charges against Lanier, citing (1) the outpouring of public support for Lanier, (2) the uncertainty of whether a jury from that community would convict, and (3) the fact that Lanier believed Booth to be a significant threat of death or serious physical injury.[49] As a general proposition, lethal force cannot be used to chase down an intruder who no longer poses any threat of imminent harm. But prosecutors often, as in the *Lanier* case, make the decision as to whether self-defense under all of the circumstances was justified. If Lanier had been a former convict who had served time for assault and battery on a police officer while resisting arrest for drunken driving, would the district attorney have prosecuted him for assault? If so, would that tend to suggest a dual standard of justice through selective prosecution?

Deadly force may not be used in defense against nondeadly force, such as slapping. Nor may it be used in defense of property when life is not threatened. Thus, one may not set a deadly spring gun to fire if a door or window is broken into when one is not at home. If an intruder is hurt or killed, the person who set the gun is guilty of either murder or manslaughter and is also liable in a civil action for injury or wrongful death. Whether the crime was murder or manslaughter would be determined by the presence or absence of malice in the mind of the defendant who set the spring gun.

The right of self-defense is never a "license to kill." If less than deadly force is all that is reasonably required under the particular circumstances, then a killing in self-defense becomes unlawful and punishable as a crime. Once the danger is over, there is no justification for further retaliation.

duress

Any threat of, or actual, physical harm that deprives a person of the freedom of will to choose and decide.

DURESS

Duress may negate the intent required to commit a crime. Duress is the forced participation in what otherwise would be a crime. It implies that a person's free will was overpowered, that he or she was coerced. "It is a defense that, when a defendant engages in conduct which would otherwise constitute a crime, he is compelled to do so by threat of imminent death or serious bodily injury to himself or another person or because he was compelled to do so by force."[50]

LEGAL FOCUS—EXAMPLE

Fred Salmond was visiting his wife in prison. During a routine frisk the guards discovered marijuana in his jacket. In a criminal prosecution for drug possession he claimed the defense of duress. His story was that two burly men told him to bring the drugs into the prison when he visited his wife or she would be severely beaten up. His wife had told him previously that the inmates for whom the drugs were intended were harassing her in the prison. If Salmond can convince the trier of fact that his story is true, duress should be a defense to the criminal charge.

This example also illustrates the problem that frequently confronts juries in ascertaining the truth when presented with bizarre facts. Note, however, that killing another person is never excused or justified because it was committed under duress.

IS LACK OF MENTAL CAPACITY A DEFENSE?

An insane person is not legally responsible for criminal conduct. The rationale is that our society's collective conscience does not allow punishment where it cannot impose moral blame. Nonetheless, an insane person may be committed for an indefinite period to a hospital for the insane, an approach that satisfies society's need for protection and its duty to assist those who are ill.

The historical difficulty with the defense of insanity results from the lack of a satisfactory definition of the term, coupled with clear and reliable criteria to enable juries to evaluate the mental condition and conduct of the accused. The defense of "not guilty by reason of insanity" has been eliminated by statute in Montana, Idaho, and Utah, and the U.S. Supreme Court has declined to review those laws.[51] In California, an **insanity defense** is available if the jury, in a separate trial for that purpose, determines that the defendant, by a preponderance of the evidence, was incapable (1) of knowing or understanding the nature and quality of the act or (2) of distinguishing right from wrong at the time the act was committed. In New York, a defendant is not criminally responsible if he or she lacked substantial capacity to know or appreciate (1) the nature and consequences of his or her act or (2) that such conduct was wrong.

insanity defense

A defense to a crime based on some mental disease or defect.

Juries are accustomed to determining facts (e.g., did the gun belong to the defendant or not?). But when it comes to determining the sanity of the defendant, the jury must determine the correctness of an opinion. Insanity is an opinion expressed by psychiatrists until the jury says it is a fact. It is extremely difficult to determine that a certain state of mind is a fact, and its importance is questionable if the basic goal of society is to incarcerate defendants until they no longer are a threat to society. Some argue that all perpetrators of heinous crimes are insane.

LEGAL FOCUS—PROBLEM

Defendant Jeffrey Dahmer was convicted of serial killing, of drilling holes in his living victims' heads and then pouring in chemicals to "zombify" them, of having sex with the corpses' viscera, and of keeping some body parts in his refrigerator, occasionally eating them. Should Dahmer have been punished as a criminal or treated as a desperately sick human being?

"Crazy" is different from legally insane. The Wisconsin jury trying the Dahmer case concluded that Dahmer was not insane.[52] But if Dahmer was not insane when he committed such grotesque and inhuman acts, one might ask, who *is* insane? As a matter of official policy, Wisconsin follows the Model Penal Code definition of mental responsibility: "A person is not responsible for criminal conduct if at the time of such conduct as a result of mental disease or defect he lacked substantial capacity either to appreciate the wrongfulness of his conduct or to conform his conduct to the requirements of law." Thus, Dahmer was judged able to appreciate the wrongfulness of what he did and able to refrain from doing it. The fact that he wanted to commit such "crazy" acts does not constitute legal insanity. Jeffrey Dahmer subsequently was murdered in prison.

diminished capacity

Reduced ability to exercise one's freedom of will or to choose between right and wrong.

Insanity is to be distinguished from **diminished capacity,** which involves a different mental state. Some crimes are defined to require a specific intent on the part of the defendant. For example, capital murder requires the specific intent to kill. If by reason of delusion, narcotics, or alcohol, for example, the defendant's mental capacity is diminished to the extent that there can be no specific intent to kill, there can be no capital murder. The crime may be reduced to manslaughter because of the defendant's diminished capacity.[53] This defense has been eliminated by constitutional amendment in some states. In some states, the defense of **temporary insanity** is possible, whereby the accused is innocent of the crime because of insanity, and yet, being sane after the act, need not be confined in a mental hospital.

temporary insanity

A passing or temporal mental disease or defect.

It is possible that an accused, sane at the time of the alleged crime, subsequently becomes insane. Insanity at the time of trial is not a defense to a crime committed during a prior time of sanity. However, a trial cannot proceed until the defendant is sane because a "fair" trial as guaranteed by our Constitution contemplates a rational defendant who can understand the charges against him or her and assist in a proper defense. Nor can a prison sentence be served by, nor an execution be administered to, an insane convict. In general terms, insanity suspends judicial proceedings as long as it continues. However, the defendant may be committed to a state institution for the insane until sanity is regained, at which time the criminal proceedings may resume.

LEGAL FOCUS—PROBLEM

Terrence Shulman was caught shoplifting a bottle of champagne from a supermarket. The champagne was to be a consolation gift to his girlfriend with whom he had just broken up because of his "addictive compulsive" shoplifting problem. Is kleptomania, or an "impulse control" disorder, or "addictive compulsive" behavior a defense to the crime of shoplifting?

No. There are understood to be about twenty-three million shoplifters in the United States, who steal about $25 million of merchandise each day. Few are believed to steal out of absolute financial need. Perhaps one-third steal for resale or to finance drug habits. But the vast majority of shoplifters (usually teenagers) steal as a response to personal or social pressures or in response to a compulsive impulse, such as kleptomania. The excitement created by getting away with the theft is said by many to be the one true reward of shoplifting. Because of the addictive and compulsive aspects of the crime of shoplifting, help from educational and counseling organizations, such as Shoplifters Alternative, is probably more effective than courts in reducing this crime.[54]

Criminal conduct is voluntary conduct. The defense of duress, discussed previously, is one example where participation in criminal conduct is not voluntary. Are criminal acts while asleep another example?

LEGAL FOCUS—PROBLEM

Early one morning, Kenneth Parks drove fourteen miles to attack his wife's parents while they were asleep. He killed his mother-in-law with a butcher knife, severely injured his father-in-law, and then turned himself in to police. Parks had a sleep disorder and contended that, although perfectly sane, he simply had been sleepwalking while committing the homicide and attack. Is this defense sound?

Yes, at least in Canada. The Parks case occurred in Ottawa, where a judge ruled that the acts were involuntary. His acquittal was upheld on appeal.[55] As difficult as it might be to persuade a jury, an involuntary stupor or trance, caused by some innocent involvement such as sleeping, would presumably negate the required voluntariness. In 1999 a Phoenix jury refused the sleepwalking defense and found Scott Falater guilty of first-degree murder of his wife. Apparently stabbing her forty-four times and then dragging her to their pool and holding her head under water did not fit the jury's idea of a sleep disorder.[56] Note that a stupor or trance caused by drugs is neither involuntary nor innocent if the use of the drugs is by personal choice.

WHAT IS ENTRAPMENT?

A defendant cannot be convicted of committing a crime if the government, acting through its law enforcement personnel, induced the criminal act. The defense of **entrapment** is an affirmative defense that must be proven by the defendant by a preponderance of the evidence, as in civil litigation; it does not have to be proven beyond a reasonable doubt. However, this defense is very narrow, limited in scope, and usually unsuccessful. It applies only when the conduct of the law enforcement agent was likely to induce a normally law-abiding person to commit the offense when such a person would not otherwise be disposed to do so. That is, the question is not whether the particular defendant was induced to commit the crime, but whether any reasonable, law-abiding person would have been so induced.[57] There is no entrapment when undercover agents are merely negotiating the price of, and buying, illegal drugs from the defendant.[58]

entrapment

A defense to criminal charges if the crime was induced by police encouragement, but not if police merely provided an opportunity for the accused to commit the criminal act.

LEGAL FOCUS—CASE

Joe Shapiro, operating on Whidbey Island, Washington, negotiated with Richard Russell and others for the purchase of homemade methamphetamine, or "speed." Russell needed the very scarce, but legal, chemical phenyl-2-propanone to prepare the drug, and this was supplied by Shapiro. A month after the batch was prepared and delivered, Russell was advised that Shapiro was an employee of the Federal Bureau of Narcotics. Arrest and trial followed in due course. Had Russell been constitutionally entrapped?

United States v. Russell, 411 U.S. 423, 93 S.Ct. 1637 (1973).

No. Entrapment occurs only if the government agent implants the criminal design or idea in the mind of the defendant. The U.S. Supreme Court held that Russell had a predisposition to commit the crime and that the mere affording of opportunity by Shapiro was not entrapment.

Even if the defendant is predisposed to criminal activity, the government may not engage in "outrageous" investigatory conduct, or evidence collected will be suppressed and the defendant set free.

LEGAL FOCUS—CASE

Ralph "Sonny" Barger, the recognized leader of the Hell's Angels, was convicted of conspiracy to violate federal explosives laws based upon the testimony of Anthony Tait, an FBI informant who participated in a "sting" operation (investigative activity in which a suspected criminal organization is infiltrated by a government witness). The government investigation followed the murder of a Hell's Angel by members of the Outlaws Motorcycle Club. Barger contended that the government was guilty of outrageous investigative conduct: by hiring Tait on a contingent-fee basis; by having Tait travel from city to city throughout the country, spending $150,000 of government expense money recruiting Hell's Angels to retaliate against the Outlaws by blowing up their clubhouse in Chicago; and by inciting Barger, personally, to retaliate. Should the conviction be reversed?

United States v. Barger, 931 F.2d 359 (1991).

No. The federal court acknowledged that the due-process clause of the Fifth Amendment requires fundamental fairness, and that some police conduct may be so egregious as to violate that command. But in this case the government merely responded to the real threat of gang retaliation, which could have caused great personal harm and property damage between two rival gangs with a history of violence. Barger also contended that he had been entrapped, arguing that he had no predisposition to engage in criminal activity. His predisposition was, the court held, refuted by his personal involvement in the retaliatory scheme both before and after Anthony Tait's proposed plan of action was revealed.

WHAT IS THE STATUTE OF LIMITATIONS FOR CRIME?

statute of limitations

A statute that bars civil or criminal proceedings unless brought within a specified period of time after the act occurred.

A **statute of limitations** is a legislative determination that legal proceedings in connection with various types of civil and criminal acts may not be commenced beyond specified periods of time. Accordingly, such a statute may be a valid defense for the defendant. Most criminal courts are already overcrowded with current cases. Such statutes are not intended to shield defendants from the law; rather, they prevent stale prosecutions in which witnesses' memories may have faded, making a "fair" trial exceedingly difficult, if not impossible, to obtain. Moreover, witnesses and principals may move, or die, and evidence may be obscured or lost. Furthermore, society is better served if wrongdoers resume normal, productive, law-abiding lives, without the psychological burden of possible arrest endlessly hanging over their heads.

The period of time specified in a statute of limitations commences upon commission or discovery of the offense. An accusatory pleading (indictment, information, or complaint) must be filed within the period prescribed. The statute is suspended, or tolled, by the absence of the defendant from the state; this eliminates flight as a possible method of avoiding prosecution. Although the limitation periods vary, for misdemeanors they usually are one year; for most felonies, they usually are three years. If the crime could be either a misdemeanor or a felony, depending upon the sentence ultimately to be imposed, the limitation period is typically three years. There is no statute of limitations for certain serious crimes, such as murder.*

Victim's Rights

The last years of the twentieth century witnessed a gradual but pervasive trend to elevate the rights of crime victims, even if that requires lessening the rights of the perpetrators.

> *For too long, the victims of crime have been the forgotten persons of our criminal justice system. Rarely do we give victims the help they need or the attention they deserve. Yet the protection of our citizens—to guard them from becoming victims—is the primary purpose of our penal laws. Thus each new victim personally represents an instance in which our system has failed to prevent crime. Lack of concern for victims compounds that failure.*[59]

In response to the growing concern for victims' rights, Congress enacted the Omnibus Victim and Protection Act of 1982, providing, among other things, for victim-impact statements at sentencing, protection from intimidation, restitution from offenders (e.g., return of stolen property), and a general tightening of bail procedures.

The states have not remained on the sidelines. Since 1985, there has been an explosion of new legislation and constitutional amendments supportive of victims' rights in the criminal system. Most states now require that notice be provided to all victims, or to members of deceased victims' families, prior to sentencing proceedings. During these proceedings, victims or their families may express verbally (or in writing or by videotape, if they prefer) their views about the crime, about the convicted felon, and the need for restitution. Such victim-impact statements are often provided for the judge's use in sentencing. They typically contain information about the victim's economic loss, physical and psychological injuries, and how the crime caused changes in the victim's employment.

LEGAL FOCUS—PROBLEM

Lawrence Singleton had been convicted by a Florida jury of murdering a hitchhiker he had picked up and taken to his home. Singleton claimed that the victim, Roxanne Hayes, attacked him with a knife and that he was trying to grab the weapon when the blade plunged seven times into her body. In the penalty phase of the trial, when the jury must

---

* For example, in 1983 Mary Jane Dudley Maxwell Pugh Hall (Smith) was charged with, and convicted of, the shooting murder of her husband, Donald Pugh, back in 1970. *Hall (Smith) v. Commonwealth,* 8 Va.App. 526, 383 S.E.2d 18 (Virginia, 1989). Perhaps the record for justice delayed is the case of *Mississippi v. Sam Bowers,* the 73-year-old former Ku Klux Klan Imperial Wizard who was first accused in 1966 of ordering, but not participating in, the firebombing murder of activist Vernon Dahmer. Bowers was tried four consecutive times; in each trial an all-white jury deadlocked. Thirty-two years after the murder of Dahmer, however, the prosecution, with the help of a surprise "confidential informant" as witness, obtained a guilty verdict. *New York Times,* 29 May 1998; Announcement of Anti-Defamation League, 21 August 1998. A last example is the conviction of Bryon De La Beckwith for the murder of civil rights leader Medgar Evers thirty years after his assassination.

recommend either life imprisonment or death, the assistant state attorney reached back twenty years, to 1978, to call a previous victim of Singleton's as a witness in support of the death penalty. Do former victims have the right to testify in current proceedings to help persuade the jury to render the death penalty?

Yes. Mary Vincent traveled from California to Florida to testify, and told the jury, "I was raped, and I had my hands cut off" in 1978 when she was only fifteen years old. Singleton used a hatchet and left Vincent to die in a ditch invisible to the road. Somehow, without hands, Vincent crawled up to the road, obtained help, and survived. Because Vincent survived, Singleton was hunted down and convicted. Paroled from a California prison after serving just ten years, Singleton moved to Florida because many California towns resisted his residency. The Florida jury, after listening to Mary Vincent, recommended the death penalty. Singleton died in December 2001 while on death row awaiting execution.

Some state statutes restrict plea-bargaining in cases involving violence or serious felonies. (A plea bargain is an agreement under which an accused person agrees to plead guilty to a specified offense in exchange for a court-approved sentence.) These restrictive states will not agree in advance to any particular sentence in specified types of crimes, usually involving violence, such as rape.

Some states provide victims with information about possible civil remedies against the defendant, as well as the procedures to recover compensation from the innocent-victim restitution fund. Monies are collected for these innocent-victim funds from penalty assessments and restitution fines levied against convicted persons. Victims otherwise without financial means can apply for financial assistance for medical treatment, mental health counseling, loss of income, loss of support, funeral/burial costs, and rehabilitation.

So-called **"Son of Sam" laws** impound the proceeds of sales by notorious criminals of their "story" to the media, such as movie and book rights.* Funds are escrowed until victims have had ample opportunity to sue in civil proceedings and obtain a judgment that then may be satisfied from the impounded funds. Any excess is returned to the felon. New York also created a Crime Victim's Board to administer all state programs dealing with crime victims. New York's "Son of Sam" law was later held unconstitutional,[60] but it and several other states have passed statutes since then attempting to stop convicted criminals from profiting from their criminal behavior.

Some victims are found in jail. Those are victims of a judicial system that erroneously found them guilty.

LEGAL FOCUS—PROBLEM

Freddie Pitts and Wilbert Lee, both African American, were sentenced to death by an all-white jury for the murder of two white gas station attendants. After more than thirty years in jail, nine of which were on death row, Pitts, 54, and Lee, 62, were found to be innocent. A white man, Curtis "Boo" Adams, was the guilty person.[61] As victims, can Pitts and Lee sue for compensation?

http://

For a directory of sites about victim's rights see http://dir.yahoo.com/Society _and_Culture/

"Son of Sam" law

A law that limits the ability of a criminal offender to receive profits from the recounting of his or her crime.

---

* During 1977, New York was terrorized by multiple random shootings of young women and their companions committed by a killer dubbed the "Son of Sam" by the press. The killer, David Berkowitz, sold book rights to his story. This prompted the state to enact the first "Son of Sam" escrow law. New York Exec. Law, Sec. 632-a(l), McKinney 1982.

Persons who are wrongfully convicted of a crime often do not recover compensation. As long as prosecutors acted reasonably and witnesses were truthful, there is no wrongdoer to sue. Florida, however, is an example of a state that does pay compensation in such situations. Pitts and Lee each received $500,000 as compensation for their thirty years in jail.

Some victims of crime are witnesses to its commission.

LEGAL FOCUS—PROBLEM

Gloria Lyons and Denise Jones witnessed a homicide by Charles Lafayette, a member of the "Bloods" gang. The slaying occurred during an argument over a $5 rock of cocaine. Lyons and Jones were reluctant to tell what they saw, for fear of "wearing snitch jackets," which they consider to be targets on their backs. What can the prosecutor do to safeguard these witnesses from retaliation?

Some states have witness relocation laws that provide some financial help for relocating endangered witnesses to new neighborhoods. Unfortunately, many such witnesses become lonely for and return to their old neighborhoods. The problem of witness protection in gang member prosecutions is an unresolved problem. In the preceding case, Lyons and Jones did testify; Lafayette is in prison serving twenty-five years to life. Lyons was executed in an alley within three days of testifying; Jones returned to her former neighborhood and was promptly murdered on the street. No arrests were made. The tally: One murderer in jail and two witnesses dead with their murderer(s) still on the street.[62]

http://

You may compare victim's rights laws in Alaska and Kentucky by visiting **http://www.ojp.usdoj.gov/ ovc/help/compdir/alaska .htm** and **http://www.ojp.usdoj.gov/ ovc/help/compdir/kentucky .htm**

WHEN ARE POLICE PERMITTED TO SEARCH AND SEIZE?

The Fourth Amendment to the U.S. Constitution prohibits unreasonable searches and seizures by government officials. It is aimed at protecting the privacy of people from unreasonable government intrusions, but it does not provide for any penalty against government officials when they violate its shield. However, decisions of the U.S. Supreme Court have established the so-called **exclusionary rule,** which acts as a deterrent to unreasonable police searches by prohibiting prosecutors from using improperly obtained evidence in a trial.[63]

Few rules generated more public outcry in the second half of the twentieth century than the exclusionary rule. The public heard or read that a clearly guilty person was released simply because incriminating evidence was gathered in an illegal search. To a very limited extent and subject to certain immunities, the victim of an unreasonable search may even bring a civil suit against the officer involved. Interestingly, no such rule is found in England, where relevancy remains the essential test of admissibility.

A search for, and seizure of, evidence may be authorized in advance by issuance of a search warrant. A proper judge or magistrate issues the warrant based upon "probable cause" (i.e., a reasonable ground) that incriminating evidence will be found. This may include authorization to perform electronic or telephonic eavesdropping. Warrants are granted only upon preparation of a sworn (under penalty of perjury) affidavit, which must contain the basis (such as the statement of a reliable informant) upon which the requesting law enforcement agency believes there is probable cause that criminal conduct is taking place.

exclusionary rule

The court-made rule that precludes the use in criminal court proceedings of any evidence improperly obtained by the prosecution.

A search and seizure may also be justified and legal in the absence of a search warrant when circumstances necessitate prompt, decisive action. The various states have developed many different rules with fine distinctions as to when a warrantless search is permitted. The states are free to adopt more stringent rules restricting searches than are required under federal law, but no state can permit searches that are prohibited by the Fourth Amendment. Situations in which a warrantless search may be permitted are as follows:

- **Consent.** A person may freely consent to a search. Another occupant of one's apartment may also consent to a search of shared areas within the dwelling.
- **Incident to a lawful arrest.** During a lawful arrest, a defendant is taken into custody. The arresting officer then may make a search, generally limited to an "arm's length" area in which the defendant could reach for a weapon or destructible evidence. Once at the police station, during booking procedures, the warrantless search may take the form of a strip search for weapons or contraband. In many states, a person arrested for minor, misdemeanor offenses (such as unpaid parking violations) could be strip searched at the police station. Because of the unlikelihood that such arrestees might possess weapons or contraband, however, such practices are very rare.
- **Motor-vehicle search based on probable cause.** A vehicle may be searched if there is probable cause to believe it contains contraband. Mobility of the vehicle underlies this exception to the rule requiring a search warrant in advance. Note that a traffic offense, such as speeding, may not be used as a pretext to justify a search for evidence of a different crime, but the observation of something "in plain view" is not an unreasonable search. Indeed, it is not considered a search at all and, thus, is not subject to the confines of the Fourth Amendment. For example, a handgun lying on the floor behind the front seat, if seen by the officer, would justify a search of a vehicle that had been stopped for a routine traffic offense. The only restriction on the "plain view" doctrine is that the officer must have a right to be in that place when the observation was made.

Sobriety checkpoints set up by law enforcement to detect drunk drivers do not violate the Fourth Amendment despite the absence of any individualized suspicion that a particular driver is under the influence. (DUIs refer to driving under the influence of alcohol or drugs.) Neither the magnitude of the drunk-driving problem nor the state's interest in eradicating it can be disputed. The intrusion on the privacy of motorists stopped briefly at sobriety checkpoints is slight.[64] In the state of Georgia, police make prior public announcements and then identify with large signs the sites of forthcoming sobriety checkpoints. Contraband in plain view during a sobriety checkpoint stop clearly will be admissible in evidence against the accused.

LEGAL FOCUS—BACKGROUND

The Colorado State Patrol, Colorado State Parks, and forty-eight police and sheriff's departments made 346 DUI arrests between 6:00 P.M. Friday, June 29, and 3:00 A.M. Monday, July 2, 2001, reported the Colorado Department of Transportation. The arrests included forty-two from a sobriety checkpoint in Adams County on June 29. Since the enforcement period started, the Denver Police Department made nineteen DUI arrests and the Aurora Police Department made nine such arrests. In Boulder County, the sheriff's office made ten DUI arrests and the Boulder Police Department made fourteen such arrests.[65]

LEGAL FOCUS—CASE

Officer Studnicka observed a van sitting on the shoulder of a state highway in the early evening. Thinking the van's driver might be having mechanical trouble, Studnicka made a U-turn, turned on his flashing red lights, and came to a stop at the rear of the van. When asking driver Steven Hanson for his driver's license, Officer Studnicka observed an open can of Michelob beer near the dashboard. He then asked Hanson to get out, smelled alcohol, administered an "Alcohol Sensor" test, and arrested him for DUI. The van was impounded, during which procedure 8.7 grams of marijuana was found. Hanson moved the court for an order suppressing all evidence on the grounds that an illegal seizure had occurred, in violation of his Fourth Amendment rights. What was the result?

State v. Hanson, 501 N.W.2d 677 (Minn. App., 1993).

There was an improper seizure because the flashing red lights were a clear direction to Hanson, sitting in the van, not to drive away. In effect, Hanson was detained by the flashing lights. Officer Studnicka admitted that he had no suspicion of criminal activity when he turned on the red lights. Therefore, Studnicka had improperly restrained Hanson. All evidence was ordered suppressed and the charges against Hanson were dropped. If Studnicka had not turned on the flashing red lights, the subsequent visual search would have been proper.

- **Stop and frisk based on reasonable suspicion.** If an officer has a reasonable suspicion of criminal activity, or if a dangerous misdemeanor is occurring, the object of that suspicion may be detained, questioned, and "frisked" or "patted down" for a weapon.
- **Hot pursuit.** A fleeing suspect may be pursued into a private building without a search (or arrest) warrant.
- **Emergency.** Under emergency conditions, it may not be possible to obtain a search warrant before acting. An example would be a break-in to rescue the victim of a crime, seen through the window, who is in need of immediate assistance. Other evidence of a crime in progress (such as wet blood or sounds of agony) also justify immediate action by police.
- **Open field.** An officer may search an open field suspected to contain contraband as long as there is no reasonable expectation of privacy therein. Police may trespass in a neighbor's backyard and stand on their tiptoes to visually search a defendant's backyard. The defendant's reasonable expectation of privacy, or zone of privacy, is limited to observers who happen to be less than six feet tall, or the height of the fence.[66] Observations from airplanes or helicopters (e.g., of fields suspected of being used to grow marijuana) generally do not require a search warrant. However, use of a thermal imaging device (i.e., one that registers heat from electric sun lamps) cannot be used without a warrant to detect an underground marijuana farm at a targeted property.[67]

    On the other hand, use of an infrared forward-looking device, aimed above a suspect's residence, to detect heat discharged by exhaust from lamps that might be used to grow marijuana inside the building does not violate the Fourth Amendment.[68] The difference between these two examples is that there could be no reasonable expectation of privacy regarding heat discharged from the residence through a vent.
- **Abandoned property.** An officer may search an abandoned automobile or dwelling or personal property discarded by a suspect.

LEGAL FOCUS—CASE

Jenny Stracner, a police investigator, examined the trash in a bag that Billy Greenwood and Dyanne Van Houten placed on the sidewalk near their home and discovered evidence of narcotics use. She used this evidence to obtain a search warrant of the house where quantities of narcotics were found. Was the warrantless search of the garbage constitutional?

California v. Greenwood & Van Houten, 486 U.S. 35, 108 S.Ct. 1625 (1988).

Yes. There is no reasonable expectation of privacy of trash placed outside for collection. Therefore the search does not violate the Fourth Amendment.

- **Customs and immigration.** Customs and immigration officers do not need a search warrant in certain situations. For example, searches near the border, or places of entry to the United States, are exempt from the general requirements of probable cause. That is, those officers can detain and search persons if they have a "mere suspicion." Body ("skin") searches must be based upon "real, or reasonable, suspicion," and even a body cavity search (i.e., an intrusion beyond the body's surface) requires only a "clear indication," which is much less than probable cause.[69] Conforming to a drug carrier's profile, behaving nervously, and wearing bulky clothing are typical bases for a strip search.
- **Mail to and from prisons.** Although domestic first-class mail cannot be searched without probable cause, an exception is made for U.S. mail to and from prisons, all of which is subject to search. Some states prohibit the search of prison mail that is addressed to judges or lawyers from prison inmates.
- **Searches by private citizens.** The Fourth Amendment is a restraint upon government, not upon individuals. Accordingly, evidence obtained from a search by a private citizen is admissible in court.
- **Administrative inspections.** Certain pervasively regulated businesses (e.g., food establishments) are subject to warrantless inspections by administrative personnel as part of public necessity and licensing rules, and evidence discovered during such a search is accordingly admissible, even if unrelated to the inspection.
- **Banks.** Banks and financial institutions supply information to government agencies pursuant to the Bank Secrecy Act without the necessity of a search warrant.
- **Probation and parole.** As a usual condition to the granting of probation or parole, convicted felons waive their rights to a search warrant, and searches can take place requiring no more than reasonable suspicion at any time and any place.[70]

As discussed earlier, the states are free to establish more stringent restraints upon the police than are required by the U.S. Constitution. Many states originally did further restrict their warrantless search requirements. Through adoption of victims' rights laws, as previously discussed, many states have relaxed their warrantless search rules to federal standards. In some states, federal officers continue to possess somewhat more latitude in performing warrantless searches than state officials, but this is not the modern trend. Determining the validity of a search is one of the most perplexing legal problems. It involves weighing the interests of the state in preventing crime against the interests of each person in maintaining privacy and freedom from unwarranted intrusion.

It is widely believed, and probably true, that some public officers, under the strain of daily action with dangerous and disagreeable suspects, are not always scrupulously considerate of the constitutional rights of the persons they search and arrest. Courts are reluctant to believe the stories of arrested persons when officers flatly deny those stories. Moreover, comparatively few defendants have the means or the inclination to thoroughly challenge the propriety of police conduct. However, the problem appears to have lessened with rising salary scales and better-educated law enforcement personnel.

WHAT PROCEDURES LEAD TO A CRIMINAL TRIAL?

Criminal court procedures affect the quality of justice dispensed by our legal system and so are very important. But procedural safeguards can be frightening and mysterious to non-lawyers. The professional assistance of a qualified attorney for the accused person is thus advisable as early as possible in the criminal prosecution process. As soon as an investigation has included an individual, he or she should consult an attorney. The U.S. Supreme Court has declared that every accused person who cannot afford to hire a lawyer has a constitutional right to the services of professional counsel (usually a public defender) at public expense. Persons accused of minor crimes and infractions are excluded from this constitutional protection.

A discussion follows of the procedures that face those accused of serious crimes. All citizens should be generally familiar with these procedures. Exhibit 6-1 presents the typical steps in a criminal prosecution.

ACCUSATORY PLEADING

A person suspected of committing a state or federal crime becomes an accused following the issuance of an accusatory pleading. The most common types of accusatory pleadings are **complaint, information** (or affidavit), and **indictment.** Although the federal and state systems use documents with similar names, their procedures are somewhat different.

State Crimes

In some felony cases, the district attorney will prepare a complaint and file it with a judicial officer (usually called a *magistrate*), who is authorized to issue arrest warrants. If there is probable cause for the charges made against the accused, an arrest warrant will be issued. Following the arrest, a preliminary hearing will be conducted by a judge or magistrate to determine if an information should be issued binding the defendant for subsequent trial in the designated trial court. During this period of time, the defendant may be free on bail, which is discussed later in this chapter.

In other felony cases, the district attorney will request that the local grand jury convene. This is a group of selected not random citizens like those sitting in jury trials. Following a secret session, the grand jury may issue an indictment charging the suspect with commission of a crime. The indictment is issued only if the grand jury is persuaded that there is probable cause that the defendant committed a crime. Although the grand jury hears evidence before issuing an indictment, the process has been widely criticized as being a mere "rubber stamp" procedure because the evidence in defense, if any, may be deemphasized or even withheld by the prosecutor. A commonly heard quote whose source if not meaning is in doubt is, "A good prosecutor could get a grand jury to indict a ham sandwich." Sometimes the suspect is not even aware that the grand jury proceeding is taking place. After an indictment is issued, a warrant for the arrest of the accused will follow. Trial will follow apprehension and arraignment of the defendant.

complaint, criminal

(a) A written statement filed by complainant containing facts that indicate a crime has been committed and that the accused committed it. (b) An accusation of a misdemeanor.

information

An accusation of a criminal offense.

indictment

An accusation of felony filed by a grand jury.

EXHIBIT 6-I: **Typical Steps in a Criminal Prosecution**

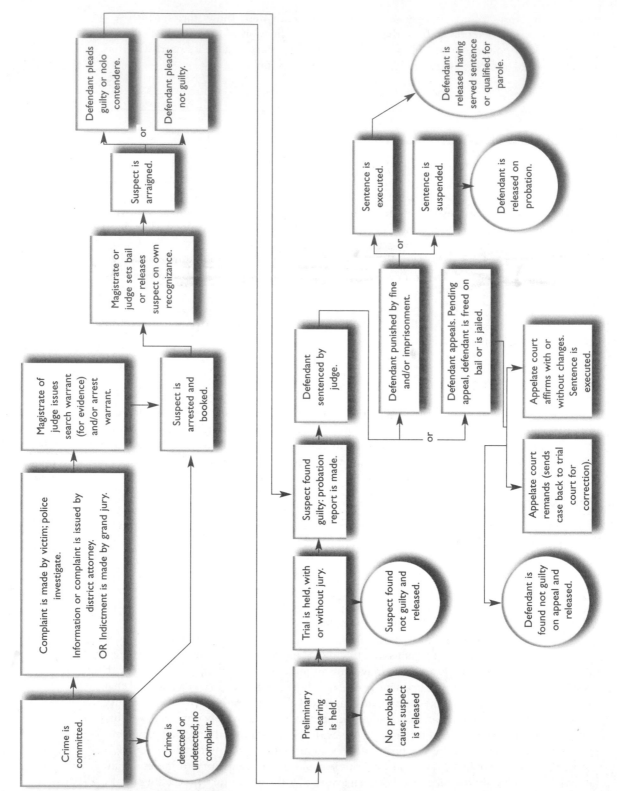

Sometimes a grand jury will identify (but decline to indict) a person as a co-conspirator with the defendant. Such an unindicted co-conspirator is neither arrested nor prosecuted, usually because of a lack of sufficient evidence to convict.

The decision to proceed against a suspect with the process of complaint/preliminary hearing/information/trial, or more directly with indictment/trial, is left to the discretion of the prosecuting attorney. Frequently, if the suspect is a prominent person or political figure, the elected district attorney may prefer the indictment procedure, thereby delegating the decision to prosecute to a body of private citizens. In either process of accusation, it is important to recognize that there must be some kind of hearing to evaluate the prosecutor's case before the defendant is held for trial. This prevents an overzealous prosecutor from arbitrarily subjecting an accused to a criminal trial.

Regardless of the name of the accusatory documents utilized in a given state, they all provide the defendant with a clear understanding of the offenses charged so he or she may prepare a defense.

Misdemeanor suspects are accused by documents usually called *complaints* rather than indictments by a grand jury.

Federal Crimes

A complaint may be prepared by a federal official (such as a U.S. marshal or U.S. attorney) and submitted to a U.S. magistrate (i.e., a judicial officer, appointed by judges of federal district courts, having some of the powers of a judge) charging that there is probable cause to arrest a suspect. A private person cannot file such a complaint but may enlist the assistance of a U.S. attorney to instigate criminal proceedings. The magistrate then may issue a warrant for the arrest of the accused. Of course, for a crime committed in their presence, law enforcement persons can make an arrest without a warrant.

After arrest, the accused must be formally charged by federal information or indictment. A federal information is prepared by the U.S. attorney to formally charge persons accused of crimes for which the penalty is one year or less in a penitentiary. More serious crimes are prosecuted by federal indictment, which is a formal charge made by a federal grand jury composed of between sixteen and twenty-three citizens who decide whether a crime has been committed and whether to institute criminal proceedings against a specific person. The federal grand jury listens to testimony and considers evidence presented by the U.S. attorney before making its decision. Many defendants waive their right to an indictment and choose to proceed by information for reasons of expediency.

Defendants accused of federal crimes are tried in the U.S. District Court before a federal judge (and jury, if a jury has been demanded and if the offense is serious enough to justify a jury). Incarceration for a federal offense is in a federal, rather than a state, penitentiary.

ARREST

After formal accusation by indictment or complaint, a warrant for the arrest of the accused is issued. To **arrest** is to take into custody for the purpose of bringing the person before a court. It is made by physical restraint or by the defendant's voluntary submission to custody.

Arrest may also occur in certain specified situations, before any accusatory pleading has been issued. This procedure differs slightly among the states. Generally, law officers may make a warrantless arrest (1) for a felony or a breach of the peace (perhaps a misdemeanor, such as simple assault) committed in their presence, (2) upon the accusation by a

http://

Professor Susan Brenner of the University of Dayton School of Law provides information on both state and federal grand juries at **http://www.udayton.edu/~grandjur**

arrest

To take a person into custody in order to charge him or her with commission of a crime.

private person accusing another of a felony, or (3) upon probable cause or official information that the person arrested has committed a felony at some earlier time.

A private person cannot obtain a warrant for the arrest of another. However, all states have retained the common-law rules, or have enacted some variation thereof, whereby a private citizen may make a warrantless arrest, known as a "citizen's arrest." Generally, such an arrest may be made for a felony committed in the person's presence or for a misdemeanor that constitutes a breach of the peace then in progress. Whenever possible, arrests should be left to trained law enforcement officers. A citizen attempting an arrest faces the problem of restraining the arrestee, the possibility of violence, and the hazard of mistake, which could lead to a civil suit and damages for the tort of false imprisonment (arrest).

An officer or citizen making an arrest may search the arrestee if reasonably necessary to prevent destruction of evidence or to detect and confiscate any weapon or article useful to the arrestee in making an escape. The search must be reasonable. Indeed, an officer is privileged to stop and frisk, by pat-down, any person being lawfully questioned as a criminal suspect. The pat-down is reasonable if it is reasonably necessary for the officer's own protection. Such a suspect, however, should not be locked in jail for questioning or investigation unless there is an adequate basis (as previously described) to make a valid arrest. There is no adequate basis for an arrest for simple failure to identify oneself or to explain one's presence satisfactorily. The circumstances determine whether there is adequate basis for arrest. For example, refusal to explain one's presence at 3:00 A.M. in a warehouse district where recent burglaries have taken place would justify **detention** pending investigation, and possibly subsequent arrest. A detention is a temporary restraint of one's liberty to permit the police to determine if there is sufficient evidence to make an arrest. For example, a person may be detained long enough to perform a computer check on vehicle registration papers, or to obtain a drug-sniffing dog, or to obtain a possible eyewitness.

An officer making an arrest may use the force reasonably necessary to accomplish the restraint. The modern view is to discourage the use of deadly force in making an arrest. A private citizen may not use deadly force in making an arrest except in the case of a violent felony (e.g., murder, arson, rape, or robbery). It is the legal duty of everyone, innocent or guilty, to submit to a lawful arrest, and improper resistance is a separate crime.

Arrests are not always necessary in situations involving misdemeanors, petty offenses, and infractions. One alternative to arrest is the ordinary traffic ticket, which is similar to the summons used in civil proceedings. The traffic violator is not a criminal and usually will appear in court after making a written promise to do so on the citation (the traffic ticket). In a growing number of misdemeanors, including shoplifting and some narcotics violations, the summons is being used instead of arrest to facilitate and streamline the procedures for handling large numbers of cases.

BOOKING

After an arrest the accused may be **booked,** which involves searching, fingerprinting, photographing, testing for alcohol or drugs, and reasonably related activities. With respect to crimes involving the operation of motor vehicles while under the influence of alcohol or drugs, states have statutes establishing prohibited levels of blood-alcohol concentration (BAC).

The practice of strip-searching arrestees for the purpose of confiscating any weapon, contraband (i.e., any property that is unlawful to produce or possess), or other evidence is often controversial. Under federal court rulings, an arrestee can be required to strip and be searched only if an officer has a reasonable suspicion he or she is concealing drugs or con-

detention

The brief stopping of a suspicious person by a police officer for the limited purpose of determining if a crime has been or is being committed in the proximity of the detainee.

booked

The administrative practice that occurs when an arrested person is brought to a police station following arrest but before incarceration in jail.

traband that cannot be discovered in a pat-down.[71] Some states prohibit strip searching in nonviolent misdemeanor cases.

The accused has certain rights after arrest, including the right to be promptly taken before a judge or magistrate, the right to be allowed bail (except in certain cases), the right to remain silent, and, in serious criminal cases, the right to have an attorney present (a telephone call, without charge, must be permitted for this purpose). The right of an accused to be promptly taken before a judge or magistrate limits the possibility of unreasonable police interrogation ("the third degree") and affords an opportunity for the accused to have bail set (if it has not already been set and stated in the arrest warrant), to have constitutional rights explained, and to have an attorney appointed if he or she cannot afford private legal services.

BAIL

An accused who is arrested is physically taken to jail. But the state has no right to punish the arrestee. Every person accused of a crime is presumed innocent under the Fifth Amendment until proven guilty beyond a reasonable doubt and to a moral certainty, and therefore is entitled to release on bail with only limited exceptions. The purpose of **bail** is merely to help assure the defendant's presence for trial. Bail refers to the security given the court by the accused to assure later appearance for trial, in exchange for immediate release from custody. The amount of bail must be specified in the arrest warrant or, if arrest is without warrant, the magistrate will set bail after the arrest and booking. The court may deny bail where there is a great likelihood the defendant will flee, as when a capital offense has been charged and the evidence of guilt is overwhelming.[72] But bail cannot be denied or set unreasonably high simply because a judge considers a defendant to be dangerous. The Massachusetts Supreme Judicial Council declared unconstitutional a statute that permitted a judge to deny bail simply because the judge believed the defendant to be dangerous. The court held that standards, such as found in the Federal Bail Reform Act of 1984, must be applied.[73]

Bail will be denied a person accused of certain extremely serious federal crimes if the government demonstrates by clear and convincing evidence, after an adversary hearing,* that no release conditions will reasonably assure the safety of the community. Bail for defendants accused of less serious federal offenses may be denied when, for example, there is a high degree of risk that the defendant will flee if released pending trial. When bail is denied, federal detainees are housed separately from convicted defendants, and other procedural safeguards apply.[74] In all cases, the policy is to be liberal in setting bail before any conviction takes place. Freedom while appealing a conviction is easily distinguishable from the situation before trial because there is no longer a presumption of innocence.

A **bail bond** is a document signed by both the accused and a bail bondsman binding them to pay to the state a specified sum if the accused fails to appear in court as directed. Bail bondsmen charge substantial fees in exchange for making such a promise, typically 10 percent of the sum specified as bail (e.g., $1,000 fee when the bail is $10,000). They rarely lose money because they secure their risk with collateral (such as stocks, bonds, mortgages, jewelry, or other valuables) and later go to great lengths to recover from the clients who "jump bail" (i.e., fail to appear in court as promised).

bail
Security posted with the court to assure that the accused, if released before trial, will voluntarily return for further criminal proceedings.

http://

Read everything you might want to know about bail from 1-800-attorney
http://www.1-800-attorney.com/li/legal_topics.cfm

bail bond
A document signed by both the accused and a bail bondsman, binding the bail bondsman to pay a specified sum of money to the state if the accused fails to appear in court as directed.

---

* The adversary hearing is a mini-trial, the purpose of which is to determine the potential danger to the community if the accused defendant is released on bail pending trial. The accused may have counsel, cross-examine witnesses, offer evidence, and so forth. There is no jury in these proceedings.

Under the Eighth Amendment, a judge or magistrate may not demand "excessive bail," but any amount may be too much for a poor person. Accordingly, at the federal level and in a number of progressive states, reforms have been enacted to permit release of the poor on their own **recognizance,** whereby the accused person simply promises in writing to appear for the trial. The court can attach other conditions to the prisoner's release, such as a promise not to contact the victim of the crime. Failure to fulfill conditions of release may lead to rearrest and may involve an obligation to pay a specified sum of money to the court.

ARRAIGNMENT

After being formally charged with a crime by the filing of an accusatory pleading (complaint, information, or indictment), the accused must be **arraigned,** meaning called into court, informed of the charge, and given an opportunity to make a response or plea. A public defender will be appointed to defend an accused who is unable to afford private counsel. In general, the defendant's plea may be either guilty, not guilty, *nolo contendere* (Latin: "I will not contest it"), or not guilty by reason of insanity. A plea of *nolo contendere* in criminal law is comparable to a plea of guilty. The only real distinction justifying its use is that a guilty plea can be used against the defendant as an admission against interest in subsequent civil litigation, whereas a plea of *nolo contendere* generally cannot. A guilty plea standing alone presumes that the defendant was sane at the time the crime was committed. Hence, the question of insanity must be raised by special plea, namely "not guilty by reason of insanity." In felony cases, a preliminary hearing (unless waived by the defendant) and trial will follow the defendant's plea. There is no preliminary hearing in misdemeanor cases. If the plea is guilty, in either a felony or misdemeanor case, sentencing will then follow.

PLEA BARGAIN

Often, following arraignment, the district attorney or county prosecutor will decide that it is in the best interests of justice to offer a **plea bargain** to a defendant. Typically, the defendant agrees to plead guilty to some crime of lesser severity than the crime specified at the arraignment. In return, a judge agrees to a specified punishment and accepts the guilty plea on that basis. Once a judge has accepted a guilty plea, the judge cannot refuse to carry through the bargain that induced the plea.[75] The government's rationale for plea bargaining is that the interests of justice are better served when the time, expense, and uncertainty of a trial can be avoided. For example, it may be uncertain whether a conviction for murder in the second degree or voluntary manslaughter can be obtained. It may be preferable to accept a guilty plea to the lesser charge than to incur the expense and difficulty of trial. There is an unending stream of cases to be disposed of, and plea-bargaining can be of benefit to the defendants—who are in jeopardy of a more severe sentence—as well as to the people represented by the prosecutor's office.

PRELIMINARY HEARING

A **preliminary hearing** is an evidentiary proceeding after a felony accusation, done before a magistrate or judge, to determine whether there is probable cause that the specified felony has been committed by the accused. The district attorney will call witnesses and

recognizance

A written promise by the accused that if released without posting bail, he or she will return voluntarily for further criminal proceedings.

arraigned

To be formally charged with a crime in a court of law and to make a plea.

plea bargain

A binding agreement in which an accused agrees to plead guilty (or nolo contendere) if the court agrees to a specified punishment in advance.

preliminary hearing

An examination in open court by a judge to determine whether sufficient evidence exists to hold the accused for trial.

present evidence in support of the charges. The accused need not, and usually does not, present any evidence because he or she is presumed innocent. However, most defendants' attorneys take advantage of the opportunity and cross-examine prosecution witnesses at length in order to learn as much as possible about the case. In some states, a preliminary hearing is not conducted after an indictment, on the theory that there already has been an evidentiary hearing. This rule is subject to constitutional question because the grand jury is a one-sided proceeding with no judge or magistrate present.

After the preliminary hearing, assuming the prosecution has presented enough evidence to justify a trial, the matter will be set for jury or nonjury trial, to determine the guilt or innocence of the defendant. Preliminary hearings are not conducted in misdemeanor cases.

WHAT ARE THE CONSTITUTIONAL RIGHTS OF AN ACCUSED?

The legislative branch of government decides what activities are criminal and therefore prohibited. Commission of a proscribed act is a crime. Of course, the legislative branch of government has no power to prohibit that which the Constitution protects, such as the expression of opinion critical of government.

The executive branch of government, in turn, has the responsibility of arresting persons reasonably thought to have committed criminal acts.

The judicial branch has the responsibility for conducting trials of the accused. In the process, it is conceivable that the executive branch or the judicial branch could treat those accused of crimes in an unfair manner, thereby increasing the possibility that innocent persons may be convicted.

To minimize this possibility, certain fundamental rights are guaranteed by the U.S. Constitution, as well as by state constitutions, to every person suspected of involvement in criminal activity. For example, there is a right to be free from unreasonable searches and seizures, as described in a prior section of this chapter.

State constitutions are free to be more demanding than the U.S. Constitution in guaranteeing such rights. Thus, in some states, persons who are accused of a crime may enjoy expanded rights of protection from unreasonable prosecutorial activities.*

According to federal law, the police cannot arrest anyone without probable cause. Moreover, that person must be informed (1) of the right to remain silent, (2) that anything said can and will be used against him or her in a court of law, (3) that he or she is entitled to the presence and aid of a lawyer during questioning, and (4) that if he or she cannot afford to hire counsel, one will be provided free of charge.[76] These **Miranda warnings** technically are not constitutional rights; rather they are "procedural safeguards" imposed by the courts to preserve the integrity of the judicial system. Therefore, if the arresting officer fails to inform the arrestee of these rights, the court subsequently may reject as evidence anything said by the defendant that is of an incriminating nature, such as a confession. Rejection of such evidence by the court may result in dismissal of the case if there is no other evidence sufficient to convict.

Miranda warnings

Warnings directed to a suspect by police before a *custodial* (while in custody) interrogation may occur.

* Persons accused of a crime in California long enjoyed broader state constitutional and statutory protections than are available to defendants accused of federal offenses. However, in June 1990, voters adopted Proposition 115, the Crime Victims' Justice Reform initiative, which literally equalized state and federal law. Affected were many criminal procedure laws, such as those instigating criminal charges, selecting jurors, conducting pretrial hearings, and even using federal law definitions of such diverse matters as "cruel and unusual punishment" and the right to privacy.

Miranda warnings are required prior to custodial (while in custody) interrogation, but not before general investigatory questioning (e.g., Where do you live? What are you doing here? How did you get here?). The warnings relate to all offenses, regardless of their gravity (e.g., for driving under the influence of alcohol or drugs). Police can detain persons, during an investigation, for a reasonable time for some reasonable purpose, without making any arrest.* This "right to detain" can be based upon a reasonable suspicion of criminal activity involving the detainee. The Miranda warnings need not be given until an arrest is contemplated. In petty misdemeanor cases or infractions (e.g., traffic violations), no arrest is contemplated, so Miranda warnings are inapplicable.

The accused is entitled to due process in all procedures following arrest. Bail, as previously discussed, is designed to prevent the punishment of one who is presumed innocent pending trial. There is a right to a speedy trial unless the defendant waives time and permits a later trial date. States typically provide that the defendant is entitled to commencement of trial within approximately sixty days of arraignment. But most defendants "waive time" to better prepare their defenses, or even simply to stall as long as possible. There is a right to be arraigned—that is, informed of the specific charges pending.

During trial, the defendant is entitled to an impartial jury and judge and is presumed innocent until found guilty. The state, representing the people, always has the burden of proof to convict "beyond a reasonable doubt." The defendant is entitled to be present in court in ordinary clothing† and is entitled to confront and cross-examine adverse witnesses, including informants.** A defendant has a right to conduct his or her own defense but must be able and willing to abide by rules of procedure and courtroom protocol. The Fifth Amendment provides that "no person shall ... be compelled in any criminal case to be a witness against himself...." This right is known as the **privilege against self-incrimination.** Accordingly, a defendant need not take the witness stand and testify in the proceeding. The prosecution must prove its case beyond a reasonable doubt without the use of the defendant's testimony.

privilege against self-incrimination

The right of any person, including one accused of a crime, to remain silent when what might be said could indicate guilt.

LEGAL FOCUS—PROBLEM

Michael Vega was charged with vehicular manslaughter. Antoinette Marie Joseph was the sole witness able to incriminate him. Just before his jury trial was scheduled to begin, Vega married Joseph, setting the stage for his wife not to testify against him. On motion of the defense attorney, Judge Carolyn Sweeney dismissed all charges, but noted that the timing of the marriage was a "terrible violation of ordinary moral decency." Was the judge correct to dismiss the case?

A variation of the privilege against self-incrimination is the privilege against incrimination by one's spouse. Thus Joseph cannot testify against Vega without his permission—an unlikely circumstance.[77]

---

* For example, detention for an hour to obtain a drug-sniffing dog is a reasonable time. *U.S. v. Campbell,* 627 F.Supp. 320 (Alaska, 1985) aff'd 810 F.2d 206 (1987).

† A defendant cannot be compelled to be tried in jail attire because it may insinuate that the defendant has been arrested not only on the charge being tried but also on other charges for which he or she is being incarcerated. The presumption of innocence requires the civilian garb of innocence.

** A defendant is entitled to confront informants who are witnesses to the crime charged, not mere tipsters. *Bradford v. State,* 184 G.A.App. 459, 361 S.E.2d 838 (Georgia, 1987). Also, a defendant charged with child abuse does not always have the right to confront the victim in open court. *Maryland v. Craig,* 497 U.S. 836, 110 S.Ct. 3157 (1990).

In trying to meet its burden of proof, the prosecution cannot suppress evidence favorable to an accused.[78] Thus, defendants may make a pretrial request for access to possibly favorable evidence. Furthermore, an involuntary confession made out of court is not admissible as evidence against the defendant, and a confession is involuntary if obtained by any form of compulsion, including false promises. Interestingly, the Fifth Amendment does not prevent police from requiring a defendant to participate in a lineup, repeat certain words that were uttered by a guilty person, submit to executing samples of handwriting, be fingerprinted, or be photographed. Both President William Clinton and defendant O.J. Simpson were required to give a sample of hair to the prosecution for DNA testing (explained in the next section). A defendant is entitled to subpoena defense witnesses and to have a "fair" trial, generally in a place where publicity about the case has not unreasonably tainted the proceedings, which must be open to the public.* Defendants may waive many of these rights if desired.

An accused cannot be placed twice in jeopardy for the same offense, but one wrongful act (such as rape) may be grounds for both criminal proceedings and a civil lawsuit for battery. A single criminal activity can involve violation of several statutory provisions and consequently result in several different crimes and punishments. The constitutional safeguard against double jeopardy protects against a second prosecution following acquittal or conviction for a single crime, and against multiple punishments by the state for that offense.[79]

A defendant cannot be convicted for violation of an *ex post facto* law—one that punishes conduct that was not a crime when committed and was only later prohibited by statute.[80]

Finally, a convicted defendant may not receive a sentence that is so disproportionate to the offense involved as to be fairly characterized as "cruel and unusual." This constitutional protection is discussed later in this chapter.

CAN INNOCENT PERSONS BE CONVICTED?

The basic purpose of the many constitutional safeguards we have considered is to minimize the risk of convicting innocent persons of crimes. In other words, the purpose is to ensure that justice is done to the extent humanly possible. To err by releasing a guilty defendant is thought to be preferable to incarcerating one who is innocent. Nevertheless, grievous mistakes are sometimes made.

LEGAL FOCUS—PROBLEM

Kirk Bloodsworth was convicted of the brutal rape and murder of a nine-year-old girl. Bloodsworth was in prison and on death row for more than eight years when serious doubt of his guilt arose from the results of recent DNA testing[†] of semen specimens, which excluded him. Should Bloodsworth be released because of these test results?

---

* Global television coverage of the O.J. Simpson murder trial prompted its label as the "Trial of the Century." Even before television was permitted in courtrooms, pretrial publicity was a significant problem. For example, Giovanni Vigliotto, dubbed the "Sicilian Seducer" for his conviction of marrying and defrauding between 82 and 105 women, received national publicity (talk shows, made-for-TV movies, and even the Guinness Book of World Records) prior to his 1983 conviction in Arizona and sentence to 34 years in prison without possibility of parole. Defense attorneys contended it was the worst case of pretrial publicity ever, a comedy of errors, but Vigliotto lost his appeal and died while in prison. *Vigliotto v. Terry*, 873 F.2d 1201 (9th cir., 1989).
† DNA is the abbreviation for deoxyribonucleic acid, which is the substance that transfers genetic characteristics in all life forms.

Bloodsworth, his innocence confirmed, was promptly released from prison.[81] Like fingerprint comparison, DNA matching is admissible in evidence, although unlike fingerprint analysis, it is not always absolutely conclusive. However, the overwhelming statistical probability of unique identification will be taken as conclusive in the minds of reasonable people. In a pioneering case, the court ruled that any evidence that was generally accepted in the applicable scientific community was admissible (acceptable) in court.[82] Thus, DNA evidence has become widely acceptable. O. J. Simpson was acquitted of the murder of two people despite DNA evidence that placed him at the scene of the crime. As a result of this acquittal, which many contend is a vivid example of jury nullification, an ongoing public resentment follows Simpson wherever he goes.

TERRORISM ISSUES

Some issues demand coverage because of their importance and timeliness and yet the complexity and uncertainty of the issues are difficult to cover in an introductory law text. Such are the legal issues raised by the war on terrorism. But a few issues can be raised briefly.

Law Enforcement or Military Defense?

Responding to Southern state complaints about military presence during the Reconstruction Era, Congress passed the Posse Comitatus Act.[83] The act separates civilian and military authority and generally forbids military enforcement of civilian laws. In recent years legislation has allowed some military involvement in border drug interdiction.[84] President Bush's November 13, 2001, Military Order directing the Department of Defense to establish military commissions to decide the guilt of non-citizens suspected of involvement in terrorist activities has raised additional legal and political questions about the long-term separation of military from law enforcement functions. "A military tribunal is a special court run by the military, not the civilian judiciary, and convened to adjudicate extraordinary cases, usually involving foreigners and usually during wartime."[85]

Due Process Protections

LEGAL FOCUS—PROBLEM

John Walker Lindh is a United States citizen detained by Northern Alliance forces in the course of the ongoing conflict in Afghanistan. Walker, formerly a California resident, had converted to Islam and then traveled to Yemen, on to Pakistan, and later to Afghanistan. Since his capture the United States charged Lindh with several crimes including attempting to provide and conspiring to provide material support and resources to designated foreign terrorist organizations, namely, al-Qaeda and Harakat ul-Mujahideen. At the time of his detention in Afghanistan Lindh alleges he was not given Miranda warnings or informed of his right to an attorney. Was he deprived of his constitutional rights?

While many observers expected that the trial of John Walker Lindh would spotlight the legal debate on what due process protections are available to American citizens accused of aid and support to terrorist activities, in July 2002 Lindh pled guilty to serving in the Taliban army and carrying weapons in doing so. In October 2002 he was sentenced to twenty years in federal prison. However, it is clear that military combatants are not entitled to the same due process protections to which criminal defendants are entitled. Traditional notions of war are challenged, however, when combatants are not sanctioned by a specific country's exercise of war power but instead are unaffiliated groups. The Uniform Code of Military Justice (UCMJ) provides due process protections, but they are less substantial than criminal law protections. The UCMJ applies to prisoners of war in custody of the armed forces, and in time of war, persons serving with or accompanying an armed force in the field.[86] But does the UCMJ apply to combatants who are members of informal combatant groups? The answer is unclear.

Immigration Law

Some persons suspected of terrorist activities are in the United States illegally in violation of United States immigration law. The Illegal Immigration Reform and Immigrant Responsibility Act of 1996 created substantial penalties for aliens who overstay their visas or enter the country illegally. In addition, violation of immigration status allows for detention of violators outside of normal criminal process.

http://

Detention standards of the Immigration and Naturalization Service are listed at
http://www.ins.usdoj.gov/ graphics/lawsregs/ guidance.htm

WHAT IS THE PUNISHMENT OF CONVICTED PERSONS?

After conviction, judges impose sentences. Some state judges have more discretion in sentencing than do federal judges, who must comply with specific guidelines. State statutes prescribe the ranges of punishments that may be imposed. To help juries determine the degree of guilt (e.g., first- or second-degree murder) and make sentencing decisions, courts allow "expert opinion" testimony on a wide range of topics, such as the psychological profile of the defendant. The personal characteristics of defendants may bear upon their personal responsibility or upon the sentence that ought to be imposed. An **expert witness** is anyone qualified by knowledge, skill, experience, training, or education to offer a useful opinion.[87] Social scientists can and do offer an array of causes for crime: low verbal I.Q. (intelligence quotient) score, low levels of certain body chemicals and elevated levels of others, the presence of the XYY chromosome pattern in men, fetal alcohol and drug syndrome, a lack of religious involvement, extreme poverty, being raised in a single-parent family, the battered woman syndrome, and more.

expert witness

Anyone qualified by knowledge, skill, experience, training, or education to offer a credible and useful opinion upon some material issue in a trial.

Imprisonment and fines are two basic forms of punishment. Either or both may be ordered, depending on the statute and what a judge (and, in some cases, a jury) decides. Misdemeanants are confined in county jail, and felons are incarcerated in state prisons. Offenders guilty of federal crimes are incarcerated in federal penitentiaries.

The highly controversial death penalty is unique among all sentences in its irrevocability and rejection of rehabilitation as a possible outcome. It is discussed in greater detail later in this chapter.

PUNISHMENT FOR MISDEMEANORS

LEGAL FOCUS—PROBLEM

Ripley Offenbach tried to shoplift a pair of jeans from a department store. He was caught, entered a plea of guilty in the municipal court, and was sentenced to sixty days in jail. While confined, can Offenbach simply loaf, eat nourishing food, and—in some jails—watch television?

Not necessarily. A prisoner is entitled to be fed, to receive medical care, and to be kept free from physical abuse* by prisoners or guards. However, there is scant management of prison guards and little solid information on abuses within prison walls.

County jail prisoners can be made to work on public roads and trails or on other jobs for the benefit of the public. Some counties have road camps for such purposes. However, commitment to such a camp, called the "farm," is selective and Ripley Offenbach, in the preceding example, may or may not be selected by jail officials. In some states, under **work furlough** programs, a prisoner in a county jail may work at regular outside employment during working hours and remain in confinement at other times. Under such programs, the sheriff collects the misdemeanant's earnings, withholding the cost of board, personal expenses, and administration and, if so ordered by the court, paying any surplus to appropriate dependents. Or, confinement may be served on weekends only. Assignments to the "farm" for work are made by the sheriff or other designated agency, whereas work furlough may be ordered by the sentencing judge.

In Illinois, misdemeanors are divided into classes A, B, and C, for which maximum sentences are one year, six months, and thirty days, respectively.[88] Most other states simply have a maximum of one year in jail; the judge specifies the exact time in accordance with circumstances surrounding the case.

Punishments can be tailored for a specific defendant and the circumstances surrounding the crime by offering probation, with conditions, in lieu of time in jail. The imposition of conditions in order to receive probation is loosely known as "creative sentencing." Conditions may involve community work, for example, but this can be rejected by a defendant who prefers to go to jail.

work furlough

A rehabilitative program for prisoners under which they may participate in part-time gainful employment even while they are serving time in a prison or jail.

LEGAL FOCUS—PROBLEM

As punishment, four crab poachers in Florida agreed to parade around town for four Saturdays wearing signs that said, "It is a felony punishable by five years in prison and/or a $5,000 fine to molest crab pots. I know because I molested one." Is this a constitutional punishment?

Yes. This unique punishment was agreed to by the defendants, who preferred it to a more traditional punishment. However, there may be a limit as to how far judges can go with their creative sentencing. Judges have assigned very unusual conditions that many find offensive, for example, that prostitutes permanently move out of the county or that the names of "johns" (men who have been convicted of soliciting prostitution) be printed in the local newspaper.

Commonly, a county jail sentence imposed by the court may be shortened for good conduct—for example, ten days off for each month of such behavior. Additional time off may be granted for satisfactory completion of work assignments and for blood donations made to a blood bank.

PUNISHMENT FOR FELONIES

Traditionally, the legislative branch of government establishes either specified periods of confinement or minimum-maximum ranges for specified offenses. For example, in Illi-

---

* Unfortunately, being raped, stabbed, or beaten has apparently become part of the penalty paid by many prisoners. With the risk of contracting AIDS, prison rape can be a death sentence, *San Francisco Chronicle*, 14 June 1994.

nois, second-degree murder warrants a sentence between four and twenty years.[89] Egregious circumstances surrounding offenses usually suggest which end of the scale will be applied by the sentencing judge.

LEGAL FOCUS—EXAMPLE

Richard Rowold fired his shotgun at a dog, missed, and accidentally shot his neighbor who was in her backyard. Rowold was convicted of criminal recklessness for injuring his neighbor and was sentenced to three years in prison. However, the sentence was enhanced to eight years because he was a "habitual offender" guilty of two previous felonies; i.e., the federal crimes of mail fraud in 1980 and fraudulent use of an access device (cable TV decoder) in 1986.[90]

Statutory penalties for crimes can and do vary widely among the states. Capital crimes (punishable by death) may be punished by life imprisonment with or without the possibility of parole, or death. Capital punishment, called the death penalty by many, is discussed later in this chapter under the heading "When Is Punishment Cruel and Unusual?" because of the controversy surrounding that issue. Under traditional statutes for noncapital felonies, a specified minimum sentence is automatically increased when certain aggravating circumstances are present. Statutes specify increased or enhanced penalties for crimes if, for example:

- The defendant has a prior conviction.
- A weapon was used during the commission of the crime.
- Great bodily harm was inflicted.
- A particular class of victim is involved (e.g., a police officer).
- The criminal motive was hatred of a protected class of persons (e.g., racial minorities).

Traditionally, three- or four-time felons face the impact of **recidivist** (repeat offender) statutes (as detailed in the discussion of cruel and unusual punishment). Some states have been echoing the former federal system by prescribing indeterminate sentences that authorize judges and parole boards to tailor the actual time served to the individual criminal. But changes in traditional sentencing formulas inevitably vary in response to ever-changing public demands. "Three strikes and you're out" has been adopted in many states in response to public outcry. The notion is that three felony convictions should result in incarceration for nothing less than twenty-five years to the maximum of life without possibility of parole.

recidivist

A repeat criminal offender.

LEGAL FOCUS—PROBLEM

Andre Wilks, age nineteen, was arrested for breaking a car window and stealing a cellular telephone. He had a juvenile record of two purse-snatching convictions, crimes committed during one spree when he was sixteen. The district attorney offered him a plea bargain of seven years in prison; if convicted by jury, he faced a three-strikes enhancement of twenty-five years to life in prison, even though it would be based on his juvenile record. Wilks, against the advice of his lawyer, his mother, his uncle, the prosecutor, and even the judge, refused to accept the offer and chose trial by jury. During trial, he perjured himself by denying everything. To his surprise and chagrin, the twelve-year old accomplice in the car burglary testified against him. Wilks was convicted by the jury. Must the sentencing judge send Wilks to prison for twenty-five years to life for stealing the cell phone?

http://

Shortly after Polly's abduction the Polly Klaas Foundation was created to aid in the search for missing children

http://www.pollyklaas.org/

The judge could "expunge" one of the prior juvenile convictions and thereby avoid the "three strikes and you're out" law. But, because Wilks showed no remorse before conviction, and because he perjured himself, he was sentenced to twenty-five years to life in prison, where he will remain until long into the twenty-first century.[91] Many states adopted "three strikes and you're out" laws in the 1990s, following the public fury over the kidnap and murder of Polly Klaas, a twelve-year-old from Petaluma, California. Polly was kidnapped from her bedroom and murdered in 1993 by a man with a long criminal record.

The publicized sentences imposed upon convicted defendants often are different from the time actually served in prison. Many contend that criminals are not serving enough time and that there is too much of a gap between sentences set by judges and the amount of time actually served. Early releases can occur for a variety of reasons, such as early parole (discussed later in this chapter), credits for time served for "good time" (prison time without disciplinary action) and even court-ordered release to relieve prison overcrowding. In reaction to public concern, more than half the states (and the District of Columbia) now require violent offenders to serve at least 85 percent of their prison sentences.

LEGAL FOCUS—PROBLEM

Ronnie Hawkins was convicted of petty theft, but it was his "third strike" and hence considered a felony. During his jury trial, although instructed by the judge to be quiet, Hawkins blurted out that he was HIV positive and was facing twenty-five years to life for petty theft—an apparent appeal to sympathy. He was considered disruptive. After his conviction, and during a sentencing hearing, Hawkins kept talking and interrupting the judge. Outraged, Judge Joan Comparet-Cassani ordered the bailiff to use a remote control device that caused 50,000 volts of electricity to surge into Hawkins. The jolt struck just above Hawkins's left kidney and continued for eight seconds, during which he "grimaced and sat stiff as a board." Can defendants be physically punished while in the courtroom even though they have not been held in contempt, are not behaving violently, or are otherwise not threatening to harm anyone?

Judges are in control of their courtrooms and can and do take precautionary steps to protect themselves and others from violence. Electronic security belts are not uncommon to restrain violent defendants. The *Hawkins* case was unusual because his disruption took the form of talking too much.[92] Restraining or subduing a defendant in court is not considered "punishment" in the same way that "punishment" follows conviction. Rather, it is physical restraint or action that serves a nonpunishment purpose; in this case, order in the court. Nonetheless, upon petition by Hawkins, a U.S. District Court Judge issued a preliminary injunction prohibiting the use of stun belts in Los Angeles courts, stating: "a pain infliction device that has the potential to compromise an individual's ability to participate in his or her own defense does not belong in a court of law."[93]

Many contend that enhancing prison sentences under three-strikes laws for nonviolent crimes is unfair and accomplishes little more than filling up the nation's prisons. Others rebut by pointing to the recent downturn in crime rates, which they suggest is the direct result of harsher sentencing policies.

Does punishment end upon release from prison? Recall the discussion earlier concerning disclosure of the identity and residential address of convicted sex offenders under state statutes known as **Megan's Law.** Does the public's fear that sex offenders are habitual also apply to other felons?

Megan's Law

A law allowing authorities to publicize information about convicted sex offenders.

LEGAL FOCUS—PROBLEM

Glenn Barker, age forty, served his sentence for murder, was released from prison, and obtained a job coaching youth basketball at the YMCA. But he was fired when police revealed his criminal record. He moved to another town, and according to his lawyer, "he's been employed, he's never had a parking ticket, and he's never been in trouble or charged. He doesn't smoke, drink, or dance the hoochie-coochie." The police then used Megan's Law as a basis to visit almost 1,000 homes distributing flyers of Barker's address and record. When does a criminal's sentence end?[94]

This is the first instance when Megan's Law has been selectively applied by police to an ex-con who was not a sex offender. Questions arise as to just which ex-cons police will choose to repeatedly expose. What are ex-cons supposed to do if they are excluded from employment and from neighborhoods? If one ex-con is exposed, should law enforcement be required to disclose all former convicts who committed similar crimes? Can police use Megan's Law as an excuse to harass selected ex-convicts?

For federal crimes, the U.S. Sentencing Commission has prepared a sentencing table. The vertical axis is divided into 43 units, each corresponding to a level of offense seriousness. The horizontal axis is divided into 6 units, each corresponding to a level of criminal history. Judges base their sentence on where the unit representing the defendant's present crime intersects with that representing his or her past record. Opponents to this mechanical procedure refer to it as "sentencing by numbers" and decry the lack of judgment it allows. This opposition, especially by some federal judges, has been vocal and abundant.[95] Under the federal sentencing guidelines, all those convicted of a felony serve some time in prison, including white-collar criminal defendants. Although mired in constitutional law litigation since its inception, all parts of the Sentencing Reform Act of 1984 have been ruled constitutional by the U.S. Supreme Court. Therefore, the act is currently applied throughout the federal court system.[96] Federal judges can and do make "upward departures" from the sentencing guidelines when warranted by the egregiousness of the defendants' offenses.[97]

Much of the objection to sentencing by numbers was highlighted in a Department of Justice study. One in five federal prisoners are "low-level" drug offenders—people with minimal or no prior criminal histories whose offenses involved neither violence nor sophisticated criminal activity. Their average sentence of seven years is reduced by good behavior to five years and nine months actually served.* These prisoners are the least likely to commit new crimes following release.[98]

In addition to fines and imprisonment, some professional persons convicted of crimes involving moral turpitude (intentionally evil) may suffer additional penalties, such as loss

http://

The entire manual—and it is a big one—of the U.S. Sentencing Commission's guidelines can be downloaded at **http://www.ussc.gov/ guidelin.htm**

---

* Even under the federal sentencing system, a prisoner can often get credit for "good time." This means that if a prisoner serves time without breaking prison rules, a certain amount of the prison sentence is deducted. The amount of deduction for good time is approximately 60 days per year.

of professional license or employment. Teachers may lose their positions if convicted of criminal sexual misconduct on the basis of unfitness to teach or for lack of moral principles. Likewise, a license to practice law may be suspended or revoked for conviction of a crime involving moral turpitude, such as income tax evasion. In Chapter 4, you already learned about lawyer discipline. Loss of professional license or position is not a substitute for a fine or imprisonment. It is an additional penalty that a professional person may suffer as the result of committing a crime.

Ⓦ**HAT ARE PAROLE, PROBATION, AND CLEMENCY?**

parole

Release from a prison on specified conditions involving good behavior.

probation

Release of a convicted criminal before sentence begins on condition of good behavior and under supervision of a probation officer. If this condition is violated, incarceration begins.

Parole, probation, and clemency are three means by which punishment is reduced or rescinded. **Parole** suspends a sentence after incarceration has begun, as distinct from **probation,** which suspends the sentence before incarceration. Either a felon in a state prison or a misdemeanant in a county jail may be paroled. Officials designated under legislative authority (parole boards) make the decision to parole. The liberty of a parolee is conditional and may be suspended or revoked unilaterally for violation of conditions specified, such as avoiding certain company (e.g., former gang members) or activity (e.g., carrying a gun). Thus, parole consists of two parts. Parole *boards* are state administrative bodies that have the authority to decide when to release prisoners. If an indeterminate sentence exists (e.g., twenty-five years to life imprisonment), the board decides the exact time for release based on such matters as "good time" credits (reductions in sentence for time spent in prison without discipline), other prison records, and recommendations from prison officials, prosecutors, victims, and the prisoner's family and friends. Even if an indeterminate sentence does not exist, such boards often set the actual date of release and provide conditions for early release from prison, set the conditions of parole (e.g., refrain from consuming alcohol and from associating with known felons), and monitor the parolee's activities while on parole. Parole officers supervise convicts after their release.

To prevent the early release of prisoners, some states have abolished parole boards. One result of eliminating early release is the swelling of prison populations. Traditionally parole officers were social workers who helped offenders find jobs. Entering the twenty-first century, parole officers are more like law enforcement officers concerned with surveillance, warrantless searches, and drug tests. Thus even more parolees are returned to prison for various offenses.*

The purpose of probation is to aid in rehabilitation. There is no absolute right to probation; it is a discretionary decision for the judge. After conviction and before sentencing, a probation officer will, at the court's discretion, thoroughly examine the defendant's background and circumstances. A recommendation to grant or deny probation is then made to the court. There are two types of probation, formal and informal. Once formal probation is granted, a probation officer supervises the defendant. If informal probation is granted, the defendant is "on his or her honor" to comply with the conditions of release. Probation depends on many events, such as compliance with all laws, search for gainful employment, restitution or return of stolen property or its value, abstention from using intoxicants, and submission to periodic tests for drug addiction.

---

* Parole boards have been abolished in Arizona, California, Delaware, Illinois, Indiana, Kansas, Maine, Minnesota, Mississippi, Ohio, Oregon, New Mexico, North Carolina, Virginia, and Washington. As noted earlier, the U.S. Sentencing Commission has eliminated parole in certain federal offenses. There is no statistical evidence that abolishing parole boards has lowered crime rates in any state—but keeping serious criminals in prison longer undoubtedly prevents some crimes. Fox Butterfield, "Parole Board Cuts Aren't a Cure," *New York Times,* 10 January 1999.

In many states statutes limit probation. Thus, probation is not allowed for certain defendants such as someone armed with a deadly weapon during a prison escape; or who committed the crimes of kidnapping, murder, or forcible rape; or who has two prior felonies. Traditional practices concerning probation are severely limited when "three strikes and you're out" legislation is adopted in a state.

When probation is granted, either the sentence is suspended pending successful completion of probation, or there is no imposition of any sentence at all during the period of probation. In either case, probation will be revoked if the defendant violates its terms or conditions. The original sentence may then become operative. However, revocation of probation may occur only after a hearing has been conducted to establish the fact of the violation. If probation is successfully completed, the defendant's conviction is legally erased.

A defendant has the right to refuse probation and accept the sentence, but that seldom happens.

In addition, there are three kinds of **executive clemency,** meaning a formal act of mercy: **reprieve** (delay in execution of judgment), **commutation** (reduction of punishment), and **pardon** (release from punishment with restoration of all rights and privileges—e.g., voting rights). Governors of states possess the power of clemency over state criminals; the President of the United States possesses the power over persons guilty of federal crimes.

LEGAL FOCUS—PROBLEM

Joseph Yandle was convicted of first-degree murder for driving the getaway car for his accomplice, who entered the Mystic Liquor store in Medford, Massachusetts, and shot the store manager to death. Yandle was sentenced to life imprisonment without possibility of parole. After twenty-three years in prison, Yandle appeared on the television program *60 Minutes* and said his crime was prompted by heroin, which he used to "numb" his memories of fighting in the Vietnam War. In patriotic response, the Board of Pardons recommended commutation of sentence; the governor agreed and Yandle was set free. Five years later it was learned that Yandle had been only a clerk in Okinawa, Japan, and had never fought in Vietnam. Yandle had lied because he "just wanted to go home." Can Yandle's commutation of sentence be revoked?

Yes. Yandle surrendered to officials and returned to custody while his commutation was in the process of revocation.[99]

LEGAL FOCUS—PROBLEM

In December 1990 Taro, a five-year-old, 110-pound Akita dog, injured Brie Halfond, a ten-year-old girl. Taro was ordered "forfeited" and killed under the New Jersey vicious-dog law. Lonnie and Sandy Lehrer, Taro's owners, began legal proceedings ultimately costing some $30,000 in fees while the state incurred twice that amount in costs plus $18,000 to house and feed Taro. Taro's fate ultimately involved the courts, the state legislature, and gubernatorial candidates and gained an international following. The legal issue was whether or not Brie had provoked Taro into the attack. The case finally

executive clemency

A formal act of kindness, mercy, and leniency by a governor or by the President in commuting a criminal penalty or granting a pardon.

reprieve

Postponement, or stay of execution (i.e., of enforcement), of the judgment after conviction for a crime.

commutation

Reduction, by a state governor or by the President, of punishment for a crime.

pardon

Release of a convicted criminal from all punishment for his or her crime through an act of the governor of the state or the President.

reached the New Jersey Supreme Court, which let stand a lower court's order to put Taro to death. Can the governor grant executive clemency to Taro?

Yes. Then-Governor Christie Whitman, fulfilling a campaign promise, used an executive order to remove a "forfeiture order" on the dog in lieu of a "pardon," which is a remedy reserved for human beings. Taro's life was spared.[100]

WHEN IS PUNISHMENT CRUEL AND UNUSUAL?

cruel and unusual punishment

Criminal punishment in which the punishment is totally disproportionate to the offense, or the prisoner is subjected to inhuman torture or merciless abuse, or the method of the punishment is unacceptable to society, or the punishment is arbitrary.

The Eighth Amendment to the U.S. Constitution prohibits government from inflicting **cruel and unusual punishment** upon persons convicted of crimes. Punishment can be cruel and unusual in any one of four ways:
1. The sentence can be totally disproportionate to the offense.
2. The prisoner may be subjected to inherently cruel abuse.
3. The method of punishment may be unacceptable to society.
4. The punishment may be inflicted arbitrarily.

LEGAL FOCUS—CASE

Defendant William James Rummel was sentenced to life imprisonment under the Texas recidivist statute. He was guilty of committing three felonies over a period of some fifteen years, as follows: (1) fraudulently using a credit card to obtain $80 worth of goods, for which a sentence of three years was imposed; (2) passing a forged check for $28.36 for which a sentence of four years was imposed; and (3) obtaining $120.75 by false pretenses, the third felony, for which a sentence of life imprisonment was required under the recidivist statute.

Under Texas law, a defendant may be paroled within 12 years if he or she earns maximum good-time credit and if the parole board and the governor approve. Defendant Rummel contended that his penalty was so disproportionate to the crimes as to violate the Eighth Amendment prohibition against cruel and unusual punishment. He appealed to the U.S. Supreme Court. What was the result?

Rummel v. Estelle, 445 U.S. 263, 100 S.Ct. 1133 (1980).

The Court upheld Rummel's sentence by a 5–4 split decision. The Court noted that although the crimes did not involve much money, the crime of obtaining $120.75 by false pretenses standing alone is a felony in 35 states. Further, his crime of passing a forged check of $28.36 would be theoretically punishable by some amount of imprisonment in forty-nine states. Thus, the Texas recidivist statute was allowed to apply.

The sentence of life imprisonment without possibility of parole for a defendant convicted of possessing a large amount of drugs (650 grams of cocaine) is not cruel and unusual punishment, according to the U.S. Supreme Court speaking in another 5–4 split decision.[101]

LEGAL FOCUS—CASE

Roger Davis was convicted by a Virginia jury of possessing nine ounces of marijuana, with a street value of $200, for distribution. He was sentenced to prison for forty years and fined $20,000. He appealed on the basis that the sentence was so disproportionate to the crime that it constituted cruel and unusual punishment. What was the result?

Hutto v. Davis, 454 U.S. 370, 102 S.Ct. 703 (1982).

The U.S. Supreme Court, in a 6–3 decision, repeated its earlier declaration that federal courts should be reluctant to review legislatively mandated terms of imprisonment, and that successful court challenges to the proportionality of particular sentences should be exceedingly rare. The sentence was permitted to stand.

Prison officials may properly use force (e.g., tear-gassing, clubbing, or even shooting) in defense of themselves or other persons. On the other hand, corporal punishment (physical injury as punishment) is constitutionally prohibited. Generally, however, the remedy for an aggrieved prisoner remains inadequate. An abused prisoner presumably can obtain a writ of **habeas corpus** (Latin: "you have the body"), a procedure prompting a court hearing, or the prisoner may sue under the Civil Rights Act of 1964 or in a common-law tort action.

habeas corpus

A legal writ or court order to release a prisoner from allegedly unlawful confinement so that he or she can appear before a court for proper remedial action. The petitioner seeks release.

LEGAL FOCUS—CASE

William McKinney, a Nevada state prisoner, filed suit against prison officials claiming that his involuntary exposure to environmental tobacco smoke (ETS) from the cigarettes of his cellmate and of other inmates posed an unreasonable risk to his health, thus subjecting him to cruel and unusual punishment. There was no claim that injury already had occurred. What was the result?

Helling v. McKinney, 509 U.S. 25, 113 S.Ct. 2475 (1993).

Justice Byron White, writing for the majority of the U.S. Supreme Court, held that McKinney was entitled to a trial on the issue of whether or not he was being exposed to unreasonably high levels of ETS that posed an unreasonable risk of serious damage to his future health. Justice Clarence Thomas, with Justice Antonin Scalia joining, dissented, stating, "I would draw the line at actual, serious injuries and reject the claim that exposure to the risk of injury can violate the Eighth Amendment."

Critics of **capital punishment** (death by execution) insist that it is not a deterrent to crime, that it is "cruel and unusual," and that it "degrades and dehumanizes" all who participate in its administration. They claim that it discriminates against the poor and minorities, citing statistics showing that most persons sentenced to die, in recent years, have been poor, male, and members of minority groups. This latter argument was especially persuasive in the decision by the U.S. Supreme Court limiting capital punishment. It held that a state may not leave the decision whether to impose capital punishment, upon a particular defendant, to the unguided discretion of a jury.[102]

If a state wants to authorize the death penalty, it has a constitutional responsibility to tailor it and apply its law in a manner that avoids any arbitrary and capricious infliction of the death penalty. The implicit assumption is that prosecutors, juries, and judges, if left to

capital punishment

Death penalty for a crime.

their own discretion, would discriminate against defendants on the basis of race. In other words, if a statutory procedure specifies the factors to be weighed and the procedures to be followed in deciding when to impose capital punishment, or specifies a mandatory death penalty for specified crimes, then capital punishment is constitutional.[103]

To sentence to death when the crime is "outrageously or wantonly vile, horrible and inhumane" is too vague because virtually all homicides fit this description.[104] Also inadequate are the words "especially heinous, atrocious, or cruel."[105] However, when "cruel" is defined to mean the defendant intentionally inflicted extreme pain or torture upon the victim, above and beyond the pain necessarily accompanying the victim's death, there is sufficient clarity of standard to justify imposition of the death penalty.[106]

Illinois authorizes the death penalty when a defendant, 18 years or older, murders a peace officer or fireman on duty, a prison guard, or multiple victims; or if he or she commits murder during the hijacking of an airplane or public vehicle, or pursuant to a contract for hire, or to prevent testimony in any criminal case.[107]

LEGAL FOCUS—CASE

Daryl Atkins was convicted of abduction, armed robbery, and capital murder. In the penalty phase of the trial Dr. Evan Nelson, a forensic psychologist, testified that Atkins was "mildly mentally retarded" with an IQ of 59 (in the lowest one percentile of the population). Nevertheless the jury sentenced Atkins to death. He appealed arguing that as he is mentally retarded a death sentence is cruel and unusual punishment. Was he correct?

Atkins v. Virginia, 536 U.S. 304, 122 S.Ct. 2242 (2002).

In this 2002 case the U.S. Supreme Court was persuaded by the fact that eighteen states had recently passed laws eliminating the death sentence for mentally retarded defendants. "We are not persuaded that the execution of mentally retarded criminals will measurably advance the deterrent or the retributive purpose of the death penalty. Construing and applying the Eighth Amendment in the light of our 'evolving standards of decency,' we therefore conclude that such punishment is excessive and that the Constitution 'places a substantive restriction on the State's power to take the life' of a mentally retarded offender."

LEGAL FOCUS—CASE

After convicting Russell Coleman of rape and capital murder, the jury was required to recommend death or life imprisonment without possibility of parole. The judge instructed the jury that the governor could commute (reduce) a sentence of life without possibility of parole, whereupon the jury recommended death. In truth, the governor does not have that sole authority and must first obtain the written consent of four state supreme court justices before reducing such a sentence. Was Russell Coleman denied a fair sentencing because of the incorrect information?

Calderon v. Coleman, No. 98-437, December 1998.

No. Arguably the jury opted for the death penalty out of fear that Coleman might someday be released from prison by the governor. However, the U.S. Supreme Court held that even if the instruction was erroneous, there was no showing that it had a "substantial and injurious" effect on the jury. Under this 5–4 split decision it is increasingly difficult for federal courts to reverse state death penalties.

Convicts may linger on death row for a dozen or more years pending the final outcome of appeals that determine the propriety of the procedures and laws applied in the original trial. Can living under the threat of a future death by execution for years itself constitute the prohibited cruel and unusual punishment? In one dissenting opinion, Justice Breyer suggested that a delay of twenty-three years between sentencing and execution may be cruel and unusual punishment.[108]

Is it cruel and unusual punishment to execute a female for a capital crime? Although executions of women are infrequent, there is no constitutional distinction between execution of a man and a woman. In 2002 there were 3,600 men and 52 women under sentence of death in U.S. prisons.[109]

The death penalty is unique among all forms of criminal punishment in (1) its rejection of rehabilitation as a fundamental purpose of our criminal justice system, (2) its total irrevocability, and (3) its conflict with our society's commitment to humane treatment of fellow human beings. Some who support it, however, ask whether there are reasonable alternatives for those few cases where death is adjudged a proper penalty. Is life imprisonment without possibility of parole, and perhaps without possibility of pardon, actually less cruel than death?

U.S. Supreme Court Justice Harry A. Blackmun voted for capital punishment throughout his legal career until 1994, when he reversed course in a case involving a man shot to death in a tavern. Blackmun, at this point, rejected capital punishment as inherently unconstitutional.* Justice Scalia, writing separately, noted that Blackmun did not select for his argument against capital punishment any of several more brutal murders pending before the Court as examples—such as the case of an eleven-year-old girl raped by four men who then killed her by stuffing her panties down her throat.[110] "How enviable a quiet death by lethal injection compared with that!" Sincerely held, yet divisive, conflicts of opinion engendered by capital punishment clearly are here to stay.

http://

For information about women on death row, see Victor L. Streib, "Death Penalty for Female Offenders, Jan 1, 1973 to Present," Ohio Northern University, available at **http://www.law.onu.edu/ faculty/streib/femdeath.pdf**

http://

For materials on the death penalty see the Death Penalty Information Center **http://www.deathpenalty info.org**

Ⓒ AN A DEFENDANT'S RECORD BE CLEARED?

State legislatures provide for the sealing (erasing) of certain criminal records as an aid to rehabilitation of defendants who have "learned their lesson." Where the sentence is probation, and the defendant has successfully completed all the requirements of probation the court may, upon motion, vacate the guilty plea or the finding of guilt and dismiss the accusation or information. Thus, most legal disabilities that arise in connection with the conviction are legally erased. Such convictions ordinarily cannot be used thereafter to enhance the penalty for a subsequent conviction, although this traditional rule may be modified by variations of proposed "three strikes and you're out" legislation.

A defendant who was under age twenty-one at the time of conviction for a misdemeanor may, upon completion of the sentence or probation, obtain an order of the court sealing all records pertaining to the conviction. Although the records are officially sealed in this manner, some applications for professional licensure inquire whether or not records

---

* Critics of Blackmun find contradiction between his rejection of capital punishment on the one hand, and his expressed pride in authorship of the majority opinion in *Roe v. Wade*, 410 U.S. 113, 93 S.Ct. 705 (1973), which legalized abortion, on the other hand.

exist and have been sealed, and, if so, what circumstance surrounded the crime. Otherwise, the defendant can answer questions as if the crime never occurred. Some types of misdemeanor records or infractions typically cannot be sealed, such as those pertaining to vehicle code violations, those involving registration as a sex offender, and those involving specified drug offenses.

WHAT SHOULD YOU DO IF ARRESTED?

A person placed under arrest, whether innocent or guilty, would be well advised to comply with the following suggestions (in the absence of more specific legal advice):

1. Do not strike an officer or resist arrest. If the officer is abusive, get the badge number and (if possible) the name. Be attentive and try to remember the specifics of the abuse involved.

2. Do not resist the officer searching you (e.g., patting down your body) and your car.

3. Do cooperate with fingerprinting and booking procedures. Even if these procedures are personally offensive, such as a strip search, no good can come from physical resistance. If given the choice between certain sobriety tests, be sure you understand your state's penalty for refusing all such tests before making that decision.

4. Do request (if not offered) the right to make a telephone call and use it to contact someone (parent, relative, friend) who can get a lawyer or assistance in posting bail and taking you home. If you cannot afford a lawyer, tell the magistrate or judge before whom you will be required to appear. You can request release on your own recognizance, and the magistrate or judge will promptly make the decision on whether to grant your request.

5. Do not respond to detailed questions—beyond such harmless basics as name, address, and telephone number—until and unless you are advised to answer by your attorney. You cannot be penalized for remaining silent. As some attorneys advise, "put a zipper on your mouth."

6. When applicable, do immediately mention to the arresting officer any physical condition requiring medication, such as multiple sclerosis, epilepsy, or diabetes.

7. Be honest in explaining in confidence to your attorney exactly what happened. Counsel is bound by law to respect this confidence, and will be better able to represent you if in possession of all the facts surrounding the incident. Your attorney cannot be compelled to reveal your conversation, even if it involves a confession of guilt.

CASE

UNITED STATES V. KNIGHTS

534 U.S. 112, 122 S.Ct. 587 (2001)

Mark Knights was convicted of a drug offense. Rather than prison he was given summary probation. The probation order included the following condition: that Knights would "[s]ubmit his ... person, property, place of residence, vehicle, personal effects, to search at anytime, with or without a search warrant, warrant of arrest or reasonable cause by any probation officer or law enforcement officer." Knights signed the probation order, which stated immediately above his signature that "I HAVE RECEIVED A COPY, READ AND UNDER-STAND THE ABOVE TERMS AND CONDITIONS OF PROBATION AND AGREE TO ABIDE BY SAME."

Three days later a Pacific Gas & Electric (PG&E) power transformer and an adjacent Pacific Bell telecommunications vault near the Napa County Airport were set on fire, causing an estimated $1.5 million in damage. Brass padlocks had been removed and a gasoline accelerant had been used to ignite the fire. This incident was one of more than thirty acts of vandalism against PG&E facilities in Napa County. Suspicion for these acts had long focused on Knights and his friend Steven Simoneau. The incidents began after PG&E had filed a theft-of-services complaint against Knights and discontinued his electrical service for failure to pay his bill. A week before the arson, a sheriff's deputy had stopped Knights and Simoneau near a PG&E gas line and observed pipes and gasoline in Simoneau's pickup truck.

After the arson, Sheriff's Deputy Hancock drove by Knights's residence, where he saw Simoneau's truck parked in front. He set up surveillance of Knights's apartment; at about 3:10 A.M. he observed Simoneau leaving the apartment carrying three cylindrical items. Simoneau walked a short distance to the Napa River, and Hancock heard three splashes. Simoneau's truck was left in the driveway and Detective Hancock observed a number of suspicious objects in the truck including a Molotov cocktail, explosive materials, a gasoline can, and two brass padlocks that fit the description of those removed from the PG&E transformer vault. Detective Hancock thereupon decided to conduct a search of Knights's apartment. Aware of the search condition in Knights's probation order, Detective Hancock believed that a warrant was not necessary. The search revealed a detonation cord, ammunition, liquid chemicals, instruction manuals on chemistry and electrical circuitry, bolt cutters, telephone pole-climbing spurs, drug paraphernalia, and a brass padlock stamped "PG&E."

Knights was arrested, and a federal grand jury indicted him for conspiracy to commit arson, possession of an unregistered destructive device, and being a felon in possession of ammunition. Knights moved to suppress the evidence obtained during the search of his apartment. The District Court granted a motion to suppress on the grounds that because the search was for "investigatory" rather than "probationary" purposes the deputy needed a warrant. The Court of Appeals for the Ninth Circuit affirmed.

Chief Justice Rehnquist delivered the opinion of the Court:
In this case, we decide whether a search pursuant to this probation condition, and supported by reasonable suspicion, satisfied the Fourth Amendment.

The Court of Appeals [held] that the search condition in Knights's probation order "must be seen as limited to probation searches, and must stop short of investigation searches."

The Supreme Court of California has rejected this distinction and upheld searches pursuant to the California probation condition "whether the purpose of the search is to monitor the probationer or to serve some other law enforcement purpose." We granted *certiorari* to assess the constitutionality of searches made pursuant to this common California probation condition.

Certainly nothing in the condition of probation suggests that it was confined to searches bearing upon probationary status and nothing more. The search condition provides that Knights will submit to a search "by any probation officer or law enforcement officer" and does not mention anything about purpose. The question then is whether the Fourth Amendment limits searches pursuant to this probation condition to those with a "probationary" purpose.

Knights argues that this limitation follows from our decision in *Griffin v. Wisconsin* (1987). In *Griffin*, we upheld a search of a probationer conducted pursuant to a Wisconsin regulation permitting "any probation officer to search a probationer's home without a warrant as long as his supervisor approves and as long as there are 'reasonable grounds' to believe the presence of contraband." The Wisconsin regulation that authorized the search was not an express condition of Griffin's probation; in fact, the regulation was not even promulgated at the time of Griffin's sentence. The regulation applied to all Wisconsin probationers, with no need for a judge to make an individualized determination that the probationer's conviction justified the need for warrantless searches. We held that a State's operation of its probation system presented a "special need" for the "exercise of supervision to assure that [probation] restrictions are in fact observed." That special need for supervision justified the Wisconsin regulation and the search pursuant to the regulation was thus reasonable.

In Knights's view, apparently shared by the Court of Appeals, a warrantless search of a probationer satisfies the Fourth Amendment only if it is just like the search at issue in *Griffin*—a "special needs" search conducted by a probation officer monitoring whether the probationer is complying with probation restrictions. This dubious logic—that an opinion upholding the constitutionality of a particular search implicitly holds unconstitutional any search that is not like it—runs contrary to *Griffin*'s express statement that its "special needs" holding made it "unnecessary to consider whether" warrantless searches of probationers were otherwise reasonable within the meaning of the Fourth Amendment.

The touchstone of the Fourth Amendment is reasonableness, and the reasonableness of a search is determined "by assessing, on the one hand, the degree to which it intrudes upon an individual's privacy and, on the other, the degree to which it is needed for the promotion of legitimate governmental interests." *Wyoming v. Houghton* (1999). Knights's status as a probationer subject to a search condition informs both sides of that balance. "Probation, like incarceration, is 'a form of criminal sanction imposed by a court upon an offender after verdict, finding, or plea of guilty.'" Probation is "one point . . . on a continuum of possible punishments ranging from solitary confinement in a maximum-security facility to a few hours of mandatory community service." Inherent in the very nature of probation is that probationers "do not enjoy 'the absolute liberty to which every citizen is entitled.'" Just as other punishments for criminal convictions curtail an offender's freedoms, a court granting probation may impose reasonable conditions that deprive the offender of some freedoms enjoyed by law-abiding citizens.

The judge who sentenced Knights to probation determined that it was necessary to condition the probation on Knights's acceptance of the search provision. It was reasonable to conclude that the search condition would further the two primary goals of probation—rehabilitation and protecting society from future criminal violations. The probation order clearly expressed the search condition and Knights was unambiguously informed of it. The probation condition thus significantly diminished Knights's reasonable expectation of privacy.

In assessing the governmental interest side of the balance, it must be remembered that "the very assumption of the institution of probation" is that the probationer "is more likely than the ordinary citizen to violate the law." The recidivism rate of probationers is significantly higher than the general crime rate. And probationers have even more of an incentive to conceal their criminal activities and quickly dispose of incriminating evidence than the ordinary criminal because probationers are aware that they may be subject to supervision and face revocation of probation, and possible incarceration, in proceedings in which the trial rights of a jury and proof beyond a reasonable doubt, among other things, do not apply.

The State has a dual concern with a probationer. On the one hand is the hope that he will successfully complete probation and be integrated back into the community. On the other is the concern, quite justified, that he will be more likely to engage in criminal conduct than an ordinary member of the community. The view of the Court of Appeals in this case would require the State to shut its eyes to the latter concern and concentrate only on the former. But we hold that the Fourth Amendment does not put the State to such a choice. Its interest in apprehending violators of the criminal law, thereby protecting potential victims of criminal enterprise, may therefore justifiably focus on probationers in a way that it does not on the ordinary citizen.

We hold that the balance of these considerations requires no more than reasonable suspicion to conduct a search of this probationer's house. The degree of individualized suspicion required of a search is a determination of when there is a sufficiently high probability that criminal conduct is occurring to make the intrusion on the individual's privacy interest reasonable. Although the Fourth Amendment ordinarily requires the degree of probability embodied in the term "probable cause," a lesser degree satisfies the Constitution when the balance of governmental and private interests makes such a standard reasonable. Those interests warrant a lesser than probable-cause standard here. When an officer has reasonable suspicion that a probationer subject to a search condition is engaged in criminal activity, there is enough likelihood that criminal conduct is occurring that an intrusion on the probationer's significantly diminished privacy interests is reasonable.

The same circumstances that lead us to conclude that reasonable suspicion is constitutionally sufficient also render a warrant requirement unnecessary.

We hold that the warrantless search of Knights, supported by reasonable suspicion and authorized by a condition of probation, was reasonable within the meaning of the Fourth Amendment. The judgment of the Court of Appeals is reversed, and the cause is remanded for further proceedings not inconsistent with this opinion.

It is so ordered.

For Critical Analysis

1. On what basis did Knights argue that a warrant was required for this search? Did the court agree with his contention?

2. Considering these facts, do you believe Deputy Hancock could have gotten a warrant? Why burden law enforcement with the delay of getting a warrant? What purpose is served?

3. Is there any limitation on the ability to conduct a warrantless search of a probationer?

4. Knights agreed to the terms of his probation. Consider the nature of this agreement: Does Knights have any realistic option rather than to agree?

5. Should the same probation principles apply to paroled convicts as well? ▩

PEOPLE V. CHEVALIER

136 Ill.2d 66, 136 Ill.Dec. 167, 544 N.E.2d 942 (1989)

This case was consolidated on appeal with a similar case (People v. Flores, *119 Ill.Dec. 214, 168 Ill.App.3d*) *because the issues on appeal are comparable. In each case, the defendant admittedly shot and killed his wife and was convicted of murder. Both contend that the evidence was sufficient to justify giving the juries permission (by appropriate instruction from the judge) to consider manslaughter as an alternative choice to murder.*

Justice Stamos delivered the opinion of the Court:
The issue common to both appeals is whether the provocation on the part of the victim was legally adequate to reduce the homicide from murder to voluntary manslaughter....

In each (case) defendant suspected his wife of marital infidelity. Just prior to the killing, the defendant and the victim had an argument, during which the victim admitted committing adultery and either disparaged the defendant's sexual abilities (*People v. Chevalier*) or flaunted the fact that she slept with her lover in the marital bed (*People v. Flores*). The victims were shot during these arguments.

In Illinois, adultery with a spouse as provocation generally has been limited to those instances where the parties are discovered in the act of adultery or immediately before or after such an act, and the killing follows such discovery. For these reasons, we hold that in each of the cases before us, the provocation claimed was, as a matter-of-law, insufficient to constitute the serious provocation necessary to reduce the homicide from murder to manslaughter.

For Critical Analysis

1. Note that during trial, the judge instructed the jury to find the defendants either guilty of murder, or not guilty. The jurors were not given the alternative of finding the defendants guilty of manslaughter. Why did the trial judge refuse to give the jury that option?

2. There are precedents in Illinois under which husbands have been found guilty of manslaughter, but not murder, for killing their wives after a confrontation about adultery. By reference to the Court's opinion, can you distinguish those precedents from the *Chevalier* case?

3. Is the practical effect of the *Chevalier* case that husbands who promptly kill unfaithful wives receive substantially more lenient sentences than those who wait a few days? Do you think the same rationale ought to apply to wives who murder their husbands following physical spousal abuse? Can you distinguish between the two kinds of situations? ▩

CHAPTER QUESTIONS AND PROBLEMS

1. Theodore Kaczynski, known as the Unabomber, pleaded guilty to killing three people and wounding twenty-three others using handmade bombs over a seventeen-year crime spree. Sentenced to life without possibility of parole, Kaczynski is in "Super Max," the Colorado federal prison designed to house "the worst of the worst." In a cell larger than his former cabin in the mountains, Kaczynski enjoys a shower, a commode, an electric lamp, a concrete desk and stool, a cigarette lighter, and a 13-inch television. He can order books, including novels. Breakfast, lunch, and dinner are delivered to his cell, and he makes limited selections from a menu. Freshly laundered clothing and bedding arrives three times a week. Although he can write to his heart's content, and receive five visitors per month, Kaczynski is isolated from other prisoners. [Cynthia Hubert, *Sacramento Bee,* 27 June 1998.]

   a. Do you think Ted Kaczynski was wise to plea-bargain for a life sentence rather than to face the risk of a death penalty from the jury?

   b. Do you think the attorney general was equally wise to offer the bargain?

   c. What changes, if any, would you recommend be made to the prison lifestyle?

2. Prison officials may deprive prisoners of any right that is reasonably related to legitimate penological interests. Thus, many states forbid beards, long hair and pony tails, earrings, and long sideburns as well as letters, numbers, and designs shaved onto the heads of inmates. Can you identify how each of the following rules may relate to a legitimate interest? Or are these simply mean-spirited attempts to make the lives of prisoners miserable?

   a. no beards
   b. no long hair or pony tails
   c. no earrings or other pierced jewelry
   d. no numbers and designs shaved onto heads
   e. no body-building machines
   f. no television

   Should exceptions be made on the basis of religion? Some Sikhs view unshorn hair as a supplication to God—cutting their hair would make them a renegade. Some Native Americans believe that long hair is a link to their ancestors. Some Muslims hold that the Koran teaches that beards are a sign of manhood. What are the implications of such exceptions?

3. George, Milton, and Fernando, all 18, decided to rob a bicyclist on a trail in the early morning in Pacific Heights. They grabbed a bicyclist who, to their dismay, promptly produced a .25 caliber handgun and shot Fernando through the heart. George and Milton jumped in their car to speed away, but promptly crashed. The bicyclist never has been found. Of what crimes are George and Milton guilty?

4. Visit the Federal Bureau of Justice Web site at http://www.ojp.usdoj.gov/bjs/welcome.html and prepare to orally describe to the class the crime statistics you find most interesting, and why.

5. Assume a violent rape occurred in a small, rural community and that DNA evidence was collected at the scene of the crime. The victim could describe her assailant only as a young Caucasian man between eighteen and thirty years of age. Assume the police then ran a local newspaper advertisement requesting that all men in the suspected category come by the station to supply saliva samples for DNA matching. Approximately 15,000 males within the suspected category were believed to reside in the nearby communities. The police intended to test all DNA samples received and to question all males in the suspected category who declined to submit samples. What issues can you identify relative to this procedure of "blanket" testing of DNA as a police procedure?

6. What percentage of prospective jurors from across the nation do you assume would be "fair and impartial" if:

   a. one of the parties in the case was a homosexual or lesbian?
   b. one of the parties was an African American?
   c. one of the parties was a Hispanic?
   d. one of the parties was an Asian?
   e. one of the parties was a tobacco company?
   f. one of the parties was a politician?
   g. one of the parties was a Muslim?

   What percentage of prospective jurors from across the nation do you assume would act on their own beliefs of right and wrong regardless of legal instructions from a judge?

   Do you believe that responses of prospective jurors about such matters would be different once they were seated and participating in the solemnity of an actual trial?

7. In this chapter you read how one act, such as the assault and battery by police upon the suspect Rodney King, could be both a state and a federal crime without violating the prohibition against double jeopardy. You may recall that officers Koon and Powell, although acquitted of a state crime, were subsequently convicted of a federal crime—for the same offensive act. Under what circumstances do you think that federal prosecutors proceed against defendants who have been acquitted in state proceedings? Should federal prosecutors proceed against everyone suspected of committing a federal crime even though they previously were acquitted by jury in a state trial? In forming your rationale, consider that every time a state police officer violates the constitutional rights of any accused, by false arrest, for example, a federal offense also has occurred (violation of constitutional rights).

8. Earlier in this chapter you read that officers in a police vehicle cannot turn on its emergency lights if they stop to assist a motorist parked at roadside. In the case example you read, Officer Studnicka turned on his flashing red lights when stopping to give possible assistance to Steven Hanson, who was parked in his van on the shoulder of the road. A beer was seen "in plain sight" of Studnicka, who then arrested Hanson for driving under the influence. A subsequent search of the van revealed marijuana. Recall that the penalty ordered by the court for the illegal detention by Studnicka was suppression of the marijuana and alcohol evidence. Thus, Hanson was set free. Do you think Hanson was allowed to take his marijuana with him from court? Do you think the ruling of the judge would have been the same if, instead of marijuana, the police found the dead body of Hanson's wife in the van with a knife sticking from her chest? Explain your answer.

9. Generally speaking, statutes—and the prosecutors, juries, and judges that enforce them—treat crimes against the person more harshly than crimes against property. The rationale is that human life is much more important than property of any description. Is there validity to the proposition that by downplaying crimes against property, society implicitly invites more serious crimes against persons? Present arguments both pro and con regarding this proposition.

10. Are you in favor of Megan's Law, which authorizes police to inform residents that a former sex offender is living in their midst? Should maps showing the specific location of residences be handed out at public expense? Should photographs be distributed for ease in identifying such persons, for example, in the local supermarket? To what other kinds of former felons should the practice be extended, if any? What constitutional issues can you identify relative to these practices?

11. On most Saturdays, Steve Mean played handball at a nearby park. He usually inline-skated via sidewalks then across a pedestrian overpass above the nearby freeway. Noticing a hole in the cagelike fencing along the overpass, Mean decided to drop a handball onto the freeway below to "see what would happen." Kristina Rey was driving to the mall when the ball struck and broke the windshield on her new Volkswagen. Startled, she jerked the wheel, sending her car directly into oncoming traffic. Rey was killed instantly when an 18-wheeler smashed into her Volkswagen head on. Of what kind of homicide is Steve Mean guilty?

CHAPTER 7

Torts: Private Wrongs

*T*hat great principle of the common law which declares that it is your duty so to use and exercise your own rights as not cause injury to other people.

Sir Charles James Watkins Williams, *English jurist.*

After reading and studying this chapter, you should be able to:

- Define a tort.

- Explain what an intentional tort is and define and identify examples of major types of intentional torts.

- Explain negligence and provide examples of negligent conduct.

- Discuss and provide examples of the elements of a negligence action.

- Discuss defenses to negligence including assumption of the risk.

- Differentiate between comparative and contributory negligence.

- Explain strict liability.

- List and explain the various types of damages.

- Identify difficulties that make the collection of damages problematic.

The twentieth century began in a gilded age of prosperity for the United States. A price was paid for the booming economy, however—an ever-increasing disparity between rich and poor, racism and sexism, and substandard housing and working conditions. The civil law system faced the challenge of resolving many new and conflicting demands. The common law of England was in general effect throughout the United States, including all of the common-law torts that, together with newly created torts, form the basis of this chapter. Our civil law tort system, today referred to by some as the "litigation explosion," was minute in scope and relatively simple just one hundred years ago. Horse-drawn-buggy crashes did not provoke personal injury litigation as we know it today.

Today, the "good life" and a "long boom" of continuing prosperity continue to be sought. Only the nature of the economic revolution has changed. The industrial revolution, fueled by the great Klondike gold rush of the 1890s, has evolved into today's scientific revolution in communications, electronics, and biotechnology. Through two world wars, a Korean "police action," and the Vietnam War, the Gulf Wars, and the war in Afghanistan, our nation remains a global economic and military power. But both the role of civil tort law* and the legal system that shapes our daily lives have changed greatly over the past hundred years. As we shall see in this chapter, tort law "tomorrow" faces—and must resolve—some very unique problems.

Today, everyone is familiar with the highly publicized awards of money to victims of a wide variety of acts that society, through its legal system, deems to be wrong or simply unacceptable. These plaintiffs (victims who bring civil actions) recover damages (money) from defendants (those held responsible) in amounts typically set by juries. Most of these monies paid to victims come from insurance companies, who expect to take in enough money from premiums to pay all claims and then, of course, to retain a profit. Sometimes, though, it is not obvious that insurance companies are involved, nor is it clearly understood who is paying their premiums.

Thus, the civil law of torts shapes our society by shifting the risk of injury from victims to others who can better afford the costs (the "deep pockets"). Certain businesses (and sometimes persons) also are punished financially for actions deemed especially wrongful. These are punitive damage cases that discourage future wrongful conduct and, as well, enrich those victims whose lawyers can successfully pursue those kinds of claims. Thus, tort law is the vehicle through which both claims for compensation by victims and demands for punitive damages are administered.

Most injuries, and hence torts, arise from the role of individuals as consumers, as commuters, and as employees. Thus, buying and using products, commuting to and from work, and being safe and humanely treated during employment are three major responsibilities of the civil tort law. We are consumers of products that may be defective, that may injure buyers and bystanders, that we may never even see (breast implants), or that may disappear (food products). Other products, such as legal, medical, and personal services, or even investments, may not be as tangible as an automobile or a coffeemaker but can still cause considerable injury and/or financial losses. We buy and equip homes with a myriad of products and store recreational "toys" in our garages, all of which can and do cause injuries. In using and enjoying the products we acquire, we can and do injure one another, as in automobile and boating accidents.

We are also employees in businesses, where we make and distribute our goods and may violate one another's rights, such as the right to be treated equally and fairly regardless

---

* The modern law of torts (Latin: "to twist") concerns compensating victims for wrongful or unacceptable conduct and sometimes for public policy reasons.

of gender, race, religion, sexual orientation, or physical condition. In other words, tort law affects our everyday conduct, making "the good life" a possible dream. It has grown and served our society along with the consumer revolution of the twentieth century.

But the tort system is less than perfect. Manufacturers, retailers, insurers, and even doctors, being frequent defendants, contend that Americans are excessively litigious, file frivolous claims, and persuade juries to award excessive damages based on sympathy and emotions rather than on hard evidence. One notorious example of this contention that has risen to urban legend status took place in the mid 1990s and involved a woman who sued McDonald's for injuries suffered when hot coffee spilled on her lap.

LEGAL FOCUS—PROBLEM

Stella Liebeck, age 79, having just purchased a cup of coffee from a McDonald's drive-through window, tried to remove its lid to add cream. The coffee spilled, burning Liebeck. Liebeck sued and recovered damages of $200,000 plus punitive damages of $2.7 million. What can we learn from this example of the tort law in action?

We can learn that the media, responding to considerable public interest, focuses upon the sensational aspects of tort cases, even at the expense of "the rest of the story." In the preceding ten years before this incident McDonald's had some 700 claims for burns. McDonald's knew that its coffee at 180–190 degrees was capable of causing third-degree burns, as it did on Liebeck. And McDonald's knew that most competitors sold coffee at the household range of 135–140 degrees. Stella Liebeck suffered third-degree burns on her buttocks, inner thighs, and genitals and required skin grafts and eight days' hospitalization. The $2.7 million punitive damage claim equaled about two days of McDonald's coffee sales. Before the trial McDonald's rejected an offer to settle for $20,000. After the large verdict, the trial judge reduced the verdict to $160,000 general and $480,000 punitive damages. There are additional important facts surrounding the matter, which may or may not change a person's mind about the fairness of the jury verdict. The lesson is that we, as educated persons, should not leap to conclusions based on media versions of tort law in action.

As noted earlier, tort laws are less than perfect. The McDonald's example is useful again. Most civil lawsuits settle after the case is initiated (and thus, after it has been reported in the media). That is, the people involved decide to resolve their dispute privately. No judge or trial is involved. Almost everyone agrees that private settlement is the preferable alternative. However, private settlements are not made public, and thus the public remains forever ignorant of how the important cases are resolved. The public seldom learns about such settlements because, as a condition of the agreement, one or both parties demand a confidentiality promise. The McDonald's "coffee" case settled out of court, and whether McDonald's eventually paid more or less to Stella Liebeck than the sums noted above is unknown to the public. It is reasonable to assume it was less.

Many aspects of the tort system create outcomes that may be less than perfect. A lay jury decides extraordinarily complex litigation. Groups of strangers scattered across the country can and do join together in "classes" of victims to right a thousand, or a million, wrongs in a single trial. The refrain "everyone is suing everyone, and most are getting big money" is common. According to this argument, the massive, mushrooming litigation explosion is said to be making attorneys rich (they generally receive one-third of recoveries) at the expense of business.

LEGAL FOCUS—BACKGROUND

A six-year-old child was killed in an automobile crash because the rear latch on a Dodge Caravan was defective; a jury returned a verdict for the parents of $262.5 million.[1] A Florida jury ordered three cigarette makers to pay $37.5 million in damages to a cancer patient. The Florida verdict was topped four months later when a California jury awarded $28 billion in punitive damages to a 64-year-old former smoker with lung cancer.[2]

What is the reason for the growth of tort law since World War II? For one, courts have been expanding the scope of tort liability, for example, by determining that manufacturers and sellers of defective products could be sued for injuries without proof of negligence or fault. We discuss "product liability" later in this chapter. New statutes passed by Congress and by state legislatures that are intended to relieve suffering and injustice are another reason for the growth of tort law.* For example, the Civil Rights Act of 1964 has been interpreted to create tort liability for a wide range of violations of civil rights. These civil rights cases occur when the wrongdoer is a government employee, such as a police officer.

LEGAL FOCUS—BACKGROUND

In response to a noise complaint, about 100 deputy sheriffs responded to a bridal shower of a Samoan-American family. A melee followed during which deputies hit partygoers with flashlights and clubs. These "torts" by police violated the civil rights of the victims. A jury returned a verdict for thirty-six plaintiffs of $16 million that, through interest while on appeal, grew to the $25 million actually paid by the County of Los Angeles.[3]

Further expansion of tort law occurred with enactment of the federal Americans with Disabilities Act. The ADA has produced lawsuits for violations of its terms. Many laws essentially benefit one group in society at the expense of another group, the latter group being better able to afford the solution. For example, businesses can afford to provide special accommodations to disabled customers who otherwise could not enjoy the same pleasures nor fulfill the same obligations of modern society without such accommodation. Thus, the tort law can and does shape social policy—indeed, some say it micromanages our lives.

In this chapter you will become acquainted with many of the rules governing the relationship between victims and the defendants who are found at fault or are held liable regardless of fault. Even your understanding of the word "fault" must be slightly revised. The "fault" upon which most of our tort system functions puts blame upon persons who fail to live up to standards that most of us regularly fail to achieve.

Private lawsuits in tort law range in importance from the trivial to the profound. Most are overlooked or are settled through negotiation. But whatever the seriousness of the disputes, they may be resolved by legal action in accordance with the law of torts.

---

* Some refer to remedial legislation as "do-gooder" laws and argue that "laws that subordinate life, liberty or property to vague notions of 'the common good' inevitably lead to injustice." *Forbes,* 5 May 1997.

tort

A private wrong committed by one person (the tortfeasor) that injures another (the victim) in person and/or property, and for which society allows the legal remedy of monetary damages.

tortfeasor

A wrongdoer who commits a private injury to another person by breaching a duty recognized by law.

intentional tort

Occurs when the tortfeasor deliberately performs a wrongful act that injures an innocent victim.

negligence

Failure to act as a reasonable, careful person would act under the same or similar circumstances, thereby causing injury that was foreseeable.

strict liability

A legal theory applicable when a defective or hazardous product is sold and the user-victim is injured.

product liability

Law holding manufacturers and sellers of goods liable to buyers, users, and perhaps bystanders for harm caused when goods are defective.

WHAT ARE TORTS AND HOW ARE THEY CLASSIFIED?

A **tort** is a private wrong (other than a breach of contract) committed by one that injures a person and/or property, for which the law allows a legal remedy (usually money damages).

The wrongdoer is called a **tortfeasor.** Sometimes two or more persons, called *joint tortfeasors,* are liable for the particular injury to one or more victims, but any one of the joint tortfeasors may be required to pay all damages suffered by the victim(s). For example, assume an automobile accident happened because a curve on a state highway was not appropriately banked and because Steve Jones was driving with unsafe tires—he failed to make the turn. Both Jones and the state are joint tortfeasors and fully responsible, but any award of money damages to an injured victim could be collected entirely from either. If Steve Jones were indigent, the victim most likely would recover all of the damages from the state with its "deep pockets."

Torts are generally classified into three groupings: intentional, negligent, and strict liability (including product liability).

An **intentional tort** occurs when a person purposely commits some act that injures the victim. As you might expect, most crimes are also torts because criminal acts are almost always intentional and cause injury to the victim. Thus, the state may prosecute the wrongdoer in a criminal action for the public wrong to society, while the victim may sue in a civil action for the private wrong. Earlier you read about this dual role in the example of O.J. Simpson, who was found not guilty of murder but civilly responsible for damages for committing the tort of battery resulting in wrongful death.

But there are significant differences between crimes and torts. In crime, the intent is evil. In torts, the intent may or may not be evil—all that is required is that the act is intended and that it causes injury. For example, a practical joke may be intended with no underlying evil motive, but if injury to a victim results, an intentional tort has occurred.

LEGAL FOCUS—EXAMPLE

Yolanda Geersan excitedly fires a pistol into the air as part of a Fourth of July celebration. Later she learns that the bullet on its inevitable descent killed a child. An intentional tort has occurred because the handgun was fired intentionally, even though Geersan lacked evil intent.

On the other hand, O.J. Simpson was found by the jury to have acted with evil intent when he committed the intentional tort of battery upon his victims. Thus, as noted, the intent behind the wrongful act necessary for tort liability may or may not be evil. Understandably, many intentional torts are not crimes because many people do not act with a *guilty mind* (i.e., with intent to commit a crime against the person or property of another).

A second kind of tort is negligence. **Negligence** means carelessness. By failing to act as a reasonable, careful person would act under the same or similar circumstances, the person inadvertently causes an injury that was foreseeable (one that a reasonable person could and should anticipate as being a possible consequence).

The third basic type of tort, **strict liability** (including **product liability**), arises when the victim need not prove that the defendant acted negligently or was guilty of an intentional tort. Indeed, strict liability is often referred to as "liability without fault." Thus, in some circumstances, the law establishes a social policy by which the risk of loss is shifted from specified victims to others in society, such as businesses, who can better afford the losses. All the victim must prove is that an injury occurred, that damages were suffered, and that the injury was caused by a product or act to which strict liability attaches, such as an airplane crash or a defective consumer product.

TORTS BY INTENTIONAL CONDUCT

It has been said that the wiles of humans are infinite. In many situations, people are motivated by greed, anger, revenge, lust, a perverted sense of humor, a distorted sense of justice, a craving for costly drugs, or a desperate quest for a quick "solution" to poverty or unemployment. So impelled, they purposely engage in antisocial conduct when they know or should know it may harm others. Deliberate conduct that is regarded by law as wrong and that causes injury to the person or property of another is an *intentional tort*. It clearly differs from negligence, which is careless, wrongful conduct. Because most persons do not deliberately commit acts that have a high probability of injury to others, intentional torts are encountered much less frequently than negligent torts. Eight of the most significant types of intentional torts are described below.

ASSAULT AND BATTERY

Assault is an intentional threat or attempt that places the victim in fear or *apprehension* of an immediate harmful or offensive touching. It is one of several intentional torts protecting against invasion of a personal interest, in this case physical and psychological well being.

LEGAL FOCUS—PROBLEM

Lon Shark was arguing loudly with "Spike" Flack over a debt. Finally, Flack said, "Listen, dork, I've paid you off. Get lost!" He turned and began walking toward his pickup. Without uttering a word, Shark grabbed a baseball bat from the ground and swung violently at Flack's head, but missed. Oblivious of the act, Flack got into his pickup and drove away. Was Shark guilty of the tort of assault?

No. Because Flack was not aware of the deadly attempt, he suffered no fear of immediate injury. Putting another person in apprehension or fear of immediate injury is the wrongful act in assault. (Note that Shark could be found guilty of the *crime* of assault, and possibly of attempted murder, neither of which requires proof of the victim's mental apprehension, as explained in Chapter 6.)

A **battery** is the harmful or offensive touching of another person without justification, consent, or excuse. A successful right hook to the jaw of someone you don't like, as well as a slap in the face, are classic examples of a battery. A left hook that misses because the victim saw it coming and dodged in time is an assault. An assault usually precedes, but is not an essential element of, a battery. Criminal sexual attacks, including rape, are also civil law assaults and batteries.

assault

The tort of creating apprehension in the mind of the victim that he or she is about to be touched in a harmful or offensive way. There is no requirement that the actor have the present ability to inflict actual harm.

battery

Any harmful or offensive touching of another human being without excuse or consent. Usually (but not necessarily) battery involves violent infliction of injury.

LEGAL FOCUS—PROBLEM

In Angola, Indiana, defendant Muir pleaded guilty to two felony counts of sexual battery, for which he was sentenced to six years in prison and fined $5,000. After the prison sentence was suspended, the victim brought a civil action for the intentional tort of battery and was awarded $17.5 million in damages.[4] Is the large judgment likely to be collectible?

Unfortunately, collection of such sizable judgments from irresponsible defendants is unlikely. Because many criminals do not have financial resources, their victims for practical rather than legal reasons do not commonly sue them. The possibility of such large judgments no doubt discourages only the more financially responsible persons in society from committing intentional torts.

LEGAL FOCUS—CASE

As part of a medical experiment, employees of the University of Chicago (in cooperation with drug manufacturer Eli Lilly & Co.) caused the drug diethylstilbestrol (DES) to be administered at its Lying-In Hospital to some pregnant patients without their knowledge. The drug was designed to prevent miscarriages. Subsequently, more than a thousand of the women alleged that their female children had suffered an increased propensity for cancer as a side effect of the drug. Were the women victims of actionable batteries?

Mink v. University of Chicago and Eli Lilly & Co., 460 F.Supp. 713 (M.D. Illinois, 1978).

informed consent

Actual and complete knowledge by a person of risks involved in a situation.

Yes. Batteries occurred because the women did not consent to the experiment. In medical practice, before administering experimental drugs, performing a surgical operation, or providing other treatment, doctors must obtain the **informed consent** of their patients. The patient must be told what risks are involved and what alternatives are available. The consent need not be in writing and may be implied by conduct. However, doctors and hospitals are increasingly concerned about lawsuits and usually do insist on written consent for any surgery. In cases of true emergency, when consent cannot be obtained, it is not required.

In the Eli Lilly & Co. case, the hospital's action was a tort, even though certainly the hospital personnel intended no harm (quite the contrary). But the act of administering the drug was intentional. Note that even if the drug had no harmful effects—indeed, even if it had beneficial effects—there would have been batteries. Such touching without prior permission would be offensive because, in the words of the *Restatement of the Law of Torts,** "it offends a reasonable sense of personal dignity."

LEGAL FOCUS—PROBLEM

Raviv Laor was going to the bathroom during a trans-Atlantic flight on Air France when a smoke alarm malfunctioned. Flight attendants, thinking someone in the lavatory was

---

* The Restatement of the Law (of Torts, Contracts, etc.) is a series of authoritative volumes written by legal scholars of the American Law Institute. In clear language, they state the principal rules of existing law in the designated area, with numerous practical examples of their application. The Restatements identify trends in the law and present suggestions for desirable changes. Judges often cite the Restatements in their opinions. In this case, *Restatement of the Law of Torts*, 2d edition (St. Paul, MN: American Law Institute Publishers, 1934) p. 19 applied.

smoking, burst in, grabbed Laor, and pulled him out onto the floor with his trousers around his ankles, exposing him to other passengers. Laor neither smokes nor drinks and opted for a non-smoking flight. He filed suit and publicly contended that the flight purser declared that "Americans are always screaming about their rights."[5] If a jury believed that Laor really was sneaking a smoke in the lavatory, would his action for battery fail?

International laws apply to international flights, and issues may arise in Laor's lawsuit about which state's laws should be applied by the federal court. But this interesting event is an example of when otherwise lawful conduct may devolve into a battery. Assuming that flight attendants lawfully can break into a bathroom under certain circumstances (such as when smelling smoke) during a flight, can they also pull a passenger off the commode and unceremoniously down onto the floor? Without some justifiable necessity for such conduct, a battery must then have occurred. A good motive is no defense to an intentional tort.

One is required to tolerate the close proximity of other persons in crowded public places. Thus, for example, bodily contact with strangers—which may be unpleasant and offensive to some sensitive individuals—is quite legal when necessary or inadvertent, as in buses and trains during rush hours, even though similar touching might be actionable battery at other times of the day.

FALSE IMPRISONMENT AND FALSE ARREST

The wrongful restraint of the physical liberty of another is called **false imprisonment.** It involves detention of the victim and restraint of his or her freedom of movement. There must be confinement within a given area, large or small, by means of physical barriers and/or physical force or threatened force. **False arrest** by an officer with legal authority (or even by one who pretends to have such authority) is a variety of false imprisonment although in some states no real distinction is made. False arrest by a police officer also may be a violation of the civil rights of the victim, a federal offense.

> **false imprisonment**
>
> The wrongful restraint of the personal liberty of another.

> **false arrest**
>
> Taking custody of another, without proper legal authority, to be held or restrained in order to answer a civil claim or criminal charge. Because this action restrains the person's liberty, it is also *false imprisonment.*

LEGAL FOCUS—PROBLEM

It did not seem like such a bad idea a few minutes before Fred Baxter merely asked Rhonda Avila to climb in the trunk to see how roomy it was in her new car. When Baxter slammed the trunk lid and left her trapped while he gathered the sales manager and the other salesmen, Avila's view of this adventure changed. She was released to the laughter of the group, and Baxter claimed his $100 prize from the sales manager for talking a customer into the trunk of her car. Does Avila have a claim for false imprisonment?

Although Avila's entry into the car trunk was voluntary, Baxter's closing the trunk and leaving her there restrained her movement without her privilege or consent. Avila's claim for false imprisonment should be successful; the more interesting question is what the extent of her damages will be.[6]

Because of the prevalence of self-service in stores where merchandise is openly displayed, the crime of shoplifting reportedly costs merchants (and ultimately consumers) billions of dollars annually. The exact figure is unknown largely because some inventory shortages are also caused by employee theft. Attempts to reduce these losses through closer surveillance and the employment of plainclothes private security personnel have brought about many arrests—and, along with them, charges of false imprisonment. Legislatures and police, however, are generally sympathetic to the plight of the storeowners. To help protect affected business firms, legislatures in many states have enacted laws that establish the **shopkeeper's privilege.** These statutes permit a retail merchant or authorized employee to detain a person if there are reasonable grounds to believe that the suspect has shoplifted and if reasonable means of detection are used. To reduce the number of lawsuits and charges of abuse of privilege, prudent store security people use minimum restraint and promptly summon official police to conduct the search and make an arrest, if justified. As a further precaution, security people usually wait until the suspect has left the store and therefore cannot claim, "I'm still shopping," when detained.

shopkeeper's privilege

Legal right of a storekeeper to detain suspected shoplifters for a reasonable time in a reasonable way when there is probable cause to believe a theft has taken place.

LEGAL FOCUS—CASE

Lucia Resendez was at Wal-Mart shopping during a lunch break when she started eating from a bag of peanuts. The source and ownership of those peanuts were the crux of a lawsuit between her and Wal-Mart. Security guard Raul Salinas saw Resendez eat the peanuts from a Wal-Mart bag that she then discarded. He watched her pay for some items but not the peanuts and she then left the store. Salinas followed Resendez and asked her to return to the store and explain her actions. Resendez complied and told him she had bought the peanuts the day before at another Wal-Mart store. Within fifteen minutes a police officer arrived to arrest her. A jury found her guilty of misdemeanor theft but the conviction was overturned for procedural reasons. She sued Wal-Mart for false imprisonment. What was the result?

Wal-Mart Stores, Inc. v. Resendez, 962 S.W.2d 539 (Texas, 1998).

The court looked at three factors to determine whether the shopkeeper's privilege applied.
1. Was the detention based on a reasonable belief that the accused had stolen store merchandise?
2. Was the detention for a reasonable period of time?
3. Was the detention conducted in a reasonable manner?

The court answered all three questions yes. Resendez was seen eating from a bag of peanuts marked with a Wal-Mart price sticker; because she did not pay for the peanuts before she left the store, probable cause existed to believe that the peanuts were stolen property. The court concluded that if a jury found probable cause to commence criminal proceedings, then reasonable cause in a civil proceeding existed as a matter of law. The court also concluded that Wal-Mart's fifteen-minute detention was not an unreasonable time and that the manner of detention was reasonable under the circumstances.

False imprisonment is also often a crime. The crime of rape constitutes two intentional torts, battery and false imprisonment. The locking of a child in a closet for an extended period may become the crime of parental abuse and the intentional tort of false imprisonment.

intentional infliction of mental distress

Outrageous conduct that causes mental, if not immediate physical, suffering by the victim

INTENTIONAL INFLICTION OF MENTAL DISTRESS

Intentional infliction of mental distress, or as some states name it, *outrageous conduct,* occurs when one intentionally acts in a manner that reasonably may be expected to cause severe mental distress to another, the victim. To be actionable, the wrongful conduct must be describable as atrocious, utterly intolerable in society, and exceeding the bounds of all decency. This kind of conduct is so extreme and outrageous that it causes severe emotional distress, even though there is no physical touching of the plaintiff (as in a battery) or apprehension of an immediate harmful or offensive touching (as in assault). Because of the absence of physical harm, or its immediate threat, such claims have formerly been rejected. Claims of mental distress that are not evidenced by some tangible injury are easy to make, yet difficult to disprove. Nevertheless, most courts now hold that in a proper case such injury is real and compensable.

LEGAL FOCUS—CASE

Mark Goldfarb, a student at Tennessee State University, was attending Professor Baker's class when an unidentified assailant surreptitiously entered the room and threw a pie that hit Baker. The professor immediately, but erroneously, accused Goldfarb of the offense. The next day, Professor Baker barred Goldfarb from the classroom and had him ejected from the building, still believing he was the culprit. Goldfarb suffered emotional distress, especially because he was an ex-prisoner attempting personal rehabilitation; the accusation of lawlessness was particularly offensive to him. Mark sued the professor for the tort of outrageous conduct. Will he prevail?

Goldfarb v. Baker, 547 S.W.2d 567 (Tennessee, 1977).

No. The conduct was not actionable because the professor acted under provocation, and his conduct, although wrong, was the product of the sudden, unjustified, and humiliating attack. This type of reflexive encounter is simply one of life's frictions and irritations for which there is no legal remedy.

LEGAL FOCUS—PROBLEM

Brendan Mcvey, age sixteen, angry because his high school girlfriend, Sara Phong, age fifteen, broke up with him, mailed a nude photograph of Phong to Chris Palermo, the editor of the school newspaper. Before it was confiscated, the photograph was shown around campus, causing Phong humiliation and distress until the school year ended. Can Phong recover damages from Mcvey and/or Palermo?

A jury certainly would agree that Mcvey's conduct was intentional and outrageous. Although Mcvey may be without funds to pay any court award, judgments may last from ten to twenty years, and sometimes more. Thus, if Phong obtained a judgment, she would be a creditor of Mcvey until he was as old as thirty-six and could, among other remedies, take part of his earnings through a procedure known as *garnishment*. Phong also may be able to convince a jury that Palermo committed outrageous conduct by permitting the photograph to be seen by others—although that is a much closer question. If Mcvey were eighteen or older, he would also be guilty of a misdemeanor crime because Phong is a minor.

The tort of outrageous conduct sometimes arises when creditors, often with the assistance of collection agencies, pursue debtors in an especially aggressive manner. The problem became so acute that in 1977 Congress enacted the **Fair Debt Collection Practices Act**,[7]

Fair Debt Collection Practices Act

A federal law that outlaws certain unreasonably harsh collection practices previously used by professional debt collectors.

which prohibits abusive tactics such as threats of violence or use of obscene language, harassing telephone calls, and publication of "shame" lists. In communicating with third parties to learn the location of a debtor, the creditor may not even state that the person owes a debt. Abused debtors may seek damages of up to $1,000 plus court costs and reasonable attorney fees. The act does not apply to creditors who do their own collecting, but under certain circumstances they may instead be subject to claims for outrageous conduct.

Torts committed by police often are characterized as violations of the victim's civil rights—but are common-law torts nonetheless.

LEGAL FOCUS—PROBLEM

Elbert Poppell opened a "swingers' club" near San Diego. Guests donated $50 to attend weekend parties where they engaged in sex on mattresses throughout the house. Some guests were married couples, others were not, still others were complete strangers. Poppell previously was denied a business license for his purple "love bus" that was outfitted with beds and a hot tub. But Poppell broke no California laws because no money was exchanged between sex partners. His business was something like renting out one motel room to a large group of "members." But the police opposed the sex club and often parked outside with lights flashing, ticketing guests for infractions such as broken taillights and illegal parking. Finally Poppell sued the City of San Diego in federal court claiming outrageous harassment. What should be the result?

A unanimous jury awarded Poppell $200,000 in punitive and compensatory damages.[8] Although the police ostensibly violated no laws, the jury believed their conduct outrageous. Would it be similar if police stopped and administered a sobriety test to every patron leaving a gay bar after midnight, but stopped none of the patrons leaving a sports bar? There undoubtedly is a strong temptation on the part of some police officers to carry out, through selective enforcement or other improper tactics, what they honestly believe is the will of the community. But the police, as well as other well-meaning persons, must express their political beliefs by working to change local laws, not by taking individual actions that may result in personal liability.

Serious actions taken to deprecate people because of their race, religion, physical characteristics, sexual orientation, etc., such as painting symbols on residences or etching epithets on plate-glass windows, usually will constitute the intentional infliction of mental distress upon the victim. As a practical matter, most victims of this tort do not file a lawsuit because the wrongdoers are insolvent as well as irresponsible.

DEFAMATION

The law imposes a general duty on all persons to refrain from wrongfully injuring another person's good reputation through false and harmful, unprivileged statements made to others. The breach of this duty is **defamation.** Breaching, or violating, this duty orally is the common-law tort of **slander;** violating it in writing is the tort of **libel.** Defamation reduces the goodwill and respect a person has previously enjoyed and may subject him or her to ridicule, contempt, or possibly hatred by others. The critical element is the effect on third parties, people in the community. Thus, there can be no civil defamation without *publication,* which means communication to at least one third party. If one

defamation

False statement injuring the reputation of the victim.

slander

Oral defamation; the speaking of false words tending to cause injury to the reputation of the victim.

libel

A false statement of fact about a person in written or other permanent form causing harm to the reputation of that person and is further communicated to a third person.

person lies about another to his or her face in private, or sends him or her a defamatory letter that only the victim reads, there is no civil defamation. If the letter is dictated to a secretary, there has been publication.

LEGAL FOCUS—PROBLEM

Anna Thompson writes Andrew Chin a private letter accusing him of embezzling funds. Edgar Peters calls Marilu Gordon dishonest and incompetent when no one else is around. All statements are false. Do these false communications result in civil liability for defamation?

No. The letter is not libel and the conversation is not slander. Neither Thompson nor Peters communicated their messages to a third party. If either Chin or Gordon later publishes the false statements, they voluntarily damage their own reputations and therefore cannot recover. If a third party, by chance, overhears defamatory statements, the courts usually hold that this is a publication. Anyone who republishes or repeats defamatory statements is liable even if that person reveals the source of the statements. Most radio stations delay the broadcast of live programs, such as talk shows, for several seconds to avoid this kind of liability.

Special state laws protect specified businesses involving perishable crops from defamatory publications. The theory is that irreparable damage is done when the crop perishes, which may be long before a trial can be obtained.

LEGAL FOCUS—PROBLEM

On her television program, Oprah Winfrey falsely warned her audience that "mad cow" disease could spread to people and, according to her guest, "make AIDS look like the common cold." Winfrey added that she was "stopped cold from eating another burger." Within days of the show, cattle prices had plummeted to ten-year lows in what was dubbed the "Oprah crash." Cattle ranchers sued in federal court for violation of the Texas "veggie" laws that protect perishable products from false statements. Are cattle a perishable product?

Perishable crops are extraordinarily vulnerable because their useful life as food is very short. Strawberries are an example of such a crop. However, the federal judge ruled that beef is not a perishable commodity, and that there was no liability for merely negligent misstatements. Thus, the cattle ranchers were required to prove, under ordinary business defamation rules, that Winfrey's remarks were deliberate or at least reckless. Oprah won the case although the "mad cow" brain disease has not been found in cattle in the United States.

Slander

A false spoken or transitory gesture about the victim is *slander*. To succeed in proving slander, the plaintiff must prove actual monetary loss, technically called *special damages* (discussed later in this chapter). However, certain types of slander are so obviously harmful to reputation that special damages are presumed to exist and need not be proved. Such cases

slander *per se*

Slander in itself; words not requiring proof of special damages.

of **slander *per se,*** defamatory as a matter of law, exist whenever the defendant falsely publishes that the plaintiff (1) has committed a crime punishable by imprisonment; (2) has an existing venereal disease; (3) is unfit for his or her lawful business, trade, profession, or office (public or private); or (4) is guilty of sexual misconduct.[9]

Not every false statement about another person is actionable, even though it may contain vituperative, derogatory, or disparaging terms.

LEGAL FOCUS—CASE

In the presence of other persons, Marjorie Taylor, a high school teacher, told Monty Standby, her principal, that he was "plain stupid ... not qualified ... a disgrace to the profession" and "just like Lee Harvey Oswald ... and Jack Ruby."* Principal Standby sued. Who won?

Stanley v. Taylor, 4 Ill.App.3d, 98, 278 N.E.2d 824 (Illinois, 1972)

Principal Standby won a jury verdict of $75,775 at the trial level. But judgment was reversed on appeal because Taylor's language was held to be not sufficiently defamatory, as a matter of law, to be slanderous. Perhaps the judge found the comparison to Oswald and Ruby, made in a fit of pique, to be so preposterous that it made the outburst laughable and not likely to damage the reputation of the principal.

LEGAL FOCUS—EXAMPLE

Tawana Brawley, age fifteen, claimed through her advisers, one of whom was the Rev. Al Sharpton, that she had been raped by a gang of white men that included state prosecutor Steven Pagones. The publicity surrounding this accusation was considerable. A grand jury later found Brawley's story to be false. Pagones sued Brawley and her advisers for slander. A jury awarded Pagones $345,000 damages against the advisers.[10]

Libel

A false written or printed communication is *libel.* As such, it historically has been considered a more durable form of defamation than slander, with a stronger, longer-lasting impact. Accordingly, the cause of action may be successful even without proof of actual, out-of-pocket special damages, such as lost wages.

LEGAL FOCUS—EXAMPLE

Britishers Helen Steel, a part-time bartender, and Dave Morris, an ex-postal worker, helped distribute a pamphlet claiming that McDonald's was cruel to animals and exploited children in its advertising, and that its low wages in Britain tended to depress salaries in the entire fast-food industry. The pamphlet contained other charges about the treatment of chickens used in McNuggets and the fat and salt content of Big Macs.

http://

The Court TV Web site provides background and coverage on the Brawley accusations and the defamation suit filed afterwards

http://www.courttv.com/ legaldocs/newsmakers/ tawana/

---

* Lee Harvey Oswald was the assassin of President John F. Kennedy. Jack Ruby murdered Oswald shortly after his arrest while he was being transferred between jails.

Many statements in the pamphlet were ultimately found to be false. McDonald's then sued Steel and Morris in what became known as the McLibel trial between David and Goliath. Without legal counsel, Helen and Dave called as expert witnesses vegetarians, environmentalists, libertarians, and animal rights activists from around the world. The English court took testimony involving some 60,000 pages of documents from 180 witnesses over 313 court days in a period of two and a half years. Lawyers for McDonald's were attired in wig and gown, as are traditional in English courts, while Helen and Dave wore jeans and sweatshirts. The McLibel trial became the longest in the history of England. At its end, the judge found that Helen and Dave had committed libel, and entered judgment for McDonald's for $96,000.[11] If McDonald's can collect none of the judgment, nor any of its huge legal fees from Helen and Dave, was the case an exercise in futility?

Sometimes considerations other than money control the decision to pursue litigation. It might be deemed sensible for a company such as McDonald's to defend its reputation and thereby to dissuade others from publicizing untrue disparaging statements. On the other hand, many believe McDonald's suffered a public relations disaster through its litigation.

Privilege to Defame Others

Truth is an *absolute* defense against a defamation lawsuit. In other words, if a statement is true, then even if it damages someone's character, it is not defamatory. Such a statement, however, may violate the person's right to privacy, which is another intentional tort discussed later in the chapter. A **privilege** may also be a defense, since it is a legal right to do something. A privilege may be absolute or conditional. An **absolute privilege** gives the holder a right to act under all circumstances. A **conditional privilege** gives the holder a right to act under certain circumstances.

ABSOLUTE PRIVILEGE   Public policy requires that certain persons be permitted and encouraged to express their ideas without restraint or fear of lawsuits for defamation. In our republic or representative democracy, legislative, executive, and judicial officers are encouraged to speak out for the common good. Legislators during legislative proceedings; judges, lawyers, jurors, and witnesses during judicial proceedings; top officials of the executive branch (notably the president and vice president, Cabinet members, and major department heads); as well as high-level officials of administrative agencies, acting in the official performance of their duties, have an absolute privilege to say anything, even if it is false, malicious, or self-serving. As noted earlier, the media (newspapers, magazines, and radio and television stations) have an absolute privilege in quoting the identified officials verbatim. Understandably, there is an absolute privilege between husband and wife for communications concerning third persons and for parents telling their children derogatory opinions about friends of the children.

QUALIFIED PRIVILEGE   A qualified privilege, or conditional privilege, exists for creditors who may, in good faith, exchange otherwise defamatory information about debtors whose creditworthiness is a mutual concern. A similar conditional privilege exists between employers with reference to qualifications of past and prospective employees. The privilege is qualified, or conditional, in the sense that the employer must act in good faith and without negligence. But note that the statements must be well-founded. Nevertheless, many employers refuse to express any opinion about the quality of performance of former employees, because of a fear of lawsuits claiming defamation. Even when one is vindicated, legal defense is costly.

privilege

A legal right to do or refrain from doing something enjoyed by only some persons or classes.

absolute privilege

Total protection from liability for defamation. Legislators enjoy it for statements made during official sessions, and judges and others enjoy it during judicial proceedings.

qualified or **conditional privilege**

A partial immunity which protects one who makes a defamatory statement in the performance of a legal, moral or social duty, to a person who has a corresponding duty or interest in receiving it.

The furor caused by defamation is better understood when one realizes that a person's reputation or good name is usually a delicate mental image in the minds of other persons in the community. It is a priceless possession available to both poor and rich, taking years to develop. Yet it is very fragile and can be shattered in seconds by one false statement. Defamation has been likened to cutting open a down-filled pillow in a violent windstorm. Fully restoring the good reputation, through denial by the victim and retraction by the liar, is like gathering up all of the thousands of tiny feathers that have scattered far and wide in the storm—impossible.

Special Status of Newspapers

A very important expansion of the right of newspapers to print libelous materials was made by the U.S. Supreme Court in 1964, in a famous case involving *The New York Times.* The Court held that the common law of libel is superseded in part by the First and Fourteenth Amendments to the U.S. Constitution, with reference to articles about public officials or public figures.[12] In effect, it gives the media a right of freedom of expression that approaches, but does not equal, the absolute privilege enjoyed by government officials as previously noted. The *New York Times* rule bars public officials or public figures from recovering for defamatory falsehoods unless they can prove the statement was made with actual malice. *Actual malice,* here, means that it was made with prior knowledge that it was false or with reckless disregard as to whether it was true or false. Moreover, the defamation must be proved by clear and convincing evidence, which is more than the preponderance-of-evidence standard usually required in civil cases. Significantly, a number of state courts have applied the rule and extended it to nonmedia defendants as well.

Some twenty-two years later, in a 1986 case involving *The Philadelphia Inquirer,* the U.S. Supreme Court reinforced free speech–free press protection of the media. It held that under the U.S. Constitution, when a newspaper publishes a speech of public concern about a *private figure,* the plaintiff bears "the burden of showing falsity as well as fault (wrongfulness) before recovering damages." Generally, if a newspaper defames someone who is a private rather than a public figure, prompt retraction and apology are mitigating circumstances that may affect the award of punitive damages. The U.S. Supreme Court, to encourage freedom of expression, has ruled that punitive damages may not be awarded to private defamation plaintiffs in actions against media defendants (e.g., newspapers and radio and TV stations) without proof of actual malice. The media defendant remains liable only for actual monetary special damages, and these are likely to be modest.

In 1990, the Supreme Court imposed a new restraint on the press. It held that statements of opinion, as well as statements of fact, can be libelous. In the words of the court, saying "In my opinion Jones is a liar" is the same thing as saying "Jones is a liar."[13] However, newspapers and other media may—without liability—publish reports containing defamatory statements that were absolutely privileged when made during legislative or judicial proceedings.

INVASION OF PRIVACY

invasion of privacy

Violation of the right of every person who has done no wrong to be left alone. Rights related to property interests in one's own person.

Most states recognize the right of privacy by means of common-law case decisions, by statutes, and by state constitutions. The *Restatement of Torts* recognizes four broad categories of **invasion of privacy** that may justify the award of damages:

1. Unreasonable intrusion on the seclusion of another
2. Appropriation of the other's name or likeness
3. Unreasonable publicity given to the other's private life

4. Publicity that unreasonably places the other in a false light before the public.[14]

In one famous case, consumer advocate Ralph Nader's privacy was violated by General Motors Corporation after he had criticized their automobiles. GMC employed persons who threatened Nader, tapped his telephone, and attempted to entice him with women—all in a futile effort to silence him.[15] In another notable case, television talk-show host Johnny Carson blocked the use of the phrase "Here's Johnny" by a corporation engaged in renting and selling portable toilets.[16] But generally, public personages, such as sports and entertainment stars, cannot claim a right of privacy in their public image, performance, or duties. Such figures usually need, want, and solicit publicity to advance their careers—thus, in effect, waiving customary rights of privacy. Some advocates suggest that celebrities ought to be protected by statute from such apparent invasions of privacy as having their photographs taken in secluded but public places through high-powered telescopic lenses, or having any obnoxious behavior in crowded public places such as restaurants or sports events be reported on.

All states, as well as the federal government, have enacted laws that supplement the tort of invasion of privacy. These include legislation concerning the wrongful opening of mail, electronic eavesdropping and telephone wiretapping, and disclosure of income taxes paid and welfare payments received. The notorious recording by Linda Tripp of private conversations she had with Monica Lewinsky in the scandal leading ultimately to the impeachment of President William J. Clinton raised the consciousness of the nation to the problem of telephonic privacy. Most states make the secretive recording of a telephone conversation a misdemeanor—although use of a cordless telephone typically results in loss of the right of privacy. The same result may follow from use of a cellular telephone because of the use of public airways for the transmission.

The tort law of privacy is not limited to celebrities. Everyone is entitled to protection from unreasonable invasions of privacy.

LEGAL FOCUS—CASE

Sylvia Nistle noticed but thought nothing of small scratches in the bathroom mirror of her apartment. Unbeknownst to her, construction workers, who were engaged in repairing the neighboring apartment, made the scratches to serve as peepholes. Nistle suffered humiliation and severe distress after learning that strangers routinely had been violating her privacy. Can she sue the landlord for the intentional tort of invasion of privacy?

Based on *New Summit Associates Limited Partnership v. Nistle,* 73 Md.App. 351, 533 A.2d 1350 (1987).

No. The next-door construction workers were not agents or employees of the landlord, who personally did not scratch the peepholes or use them. Nistle could sue the individual construction workers for the intentional tort of invasion of privacy, but they probably were without substantial wealth.

CONVERSION (CIVIL THEFT)

Any unauthorized taking of the personal property of another and wrongfully exercising rights of ownership is the tort of **conversion.** It can involve wrongfully taking such things as (1) a house trailer, (2) stock certificates sold by a broker without authorization, (3) architectural plans for a residence, even if the building is in public view, and (4) the re-recording and sale of recorded musical performances owned by a record label.[17]

conversion

Unauthorized taking of the personal property of another and wrongfully exercising rights of ownership.

LEGAL FOCUS—PROBLEM

Alexis Marks finds a valuable single-reflex camera in a leather case under a bench at Disney World in Orlando, Florida. A business card inside has the name, address, and phone number of Daniel Daze, with the words "Reward for Return." Marks recalls the ditty "Finders Keepers, Losers Weepers" from her childhood and decides to keep the camera. Has she committed a crime or a tort?

Both. Marks has committed the crime of larceny. She also is liable in damages to Daniel Daze for commission of the tort of conversion. Unfortunately for Daze, the crime and tort will probably go undetected and unpunished. Marks, the finder, is known in law as a constructive bailee of the goods. A *bailee* is a person to whom goods are entrusted for use, storage, or other purposes. The bailee has temporary possession, coupled with a duty to return or dispose of the goods in accordance with the trust. A restaurant with coat checking, a parking garage, and a laundry are examples of bailees. As a bailee, Marks should make a reasonable effort to find the owner, usually with the assistance of the local police. If no one claims the item within a reasonable time, the finder may keep the property. (See further discussion of personal property in Chapter 10.)

A brief, temporary, and unauthorized interference with the personal-property rights of another is termed a **trespass to chattel.** The owner is entitled to damages for the limited loss of possession and any actual harm to the property. But the wrongdoer is not compelled to pay the full market value. An example is the deliberate "keying" (scratching with a key) of a parked automobile (which is a tort and also the crime of malicious mischief). Repainting is costly and time-consuming, but such tortfeasors are usually juvenile "hit-and-run" types who are not likely to be caught.

trespass to chattel

A brief, temporary, unauthorized interference with the personal-property rights of another.

FRAUD

fraud

A knowingly false representation of a material fact, made through words or conduct, with intent to deceive a victim, who is induced to contract in reliance on the lie, and who is thereby injured.

misrepresentation

A false statement made intentionally, knowing it is not true. A negligent misrepresentation is a false statement made carelessly.

Fraud is a tort most frequently committed in sales of goods or services. It is also called *deceit* and sometimes **misrepresentation.** For fraud, the following elements must be present:
1. A false representation (i.e., a lie);
2. of a factual matter (not personal opinion, unless the opinion is that of an expert on the subject);
3. that is material (i.e., important enough to affect the decision of the intended victim);
4. known by the wrongdoer to be false, or made with reckless indifference as to its truth;
5. made with intent to induce action by the victim, who is unaware of its falsity;
6. and acting reasonably, the victim does justifiably rely on the lie in his or her decision; and
7. is injured as a result.

In a simple, often-repeated type of case, a seller of a used car may misrepresent the mileage,* the times and frequency of servicing and of overhaul, the number and identity of previous owners, or the number and nature of accidents, if any, in which the vehicle has

* In a gross example of this offense, Chrysler Corporation was fined $7.6 million by a federal district court judge for selling thirty previously damaged vehicles as new cars and for odometer violations. Chrysler had previously entered a plea of no contest to the criminal charges. The fine supplemented an earlier settlement of more than $16 million in a civil suit. Records showed that between 1949 and 1986, Chrysler personnel had disconnected the odometers on about 60,000 new cars that were driven for periods of one day to five weeks by Chrysler executives before being placed on sale as brand new. In the thirty specially noted cases, the cars had been damaged while being driven by the executives, and repaired before sale as new. Reported in the *San Francisco Chronicle*, 11 August 1990.

been involved. A knowledgeable car buff might not be misled, but many amateurs would buy in trusting reliance and, if victimized, could therefore sue for damages.

Fraud may also occur under a wide variety of unusual circumstances, as the following cases indicate.

LEGAL FOCUS—CASE

Peter Roberts, an eighteen-year-old sales clerk at Sears, invented a quick-release socket wrench in his spare time. He applied for and received a patent in 1965. Thereafter, Sears negotiated to buy Roberts's patent rights. He was told that (1) the invention was "not new," (2) the production cost would be 40 to 50 cents per wrench (Sears knew it would be only 20 cents), and (3) it would sell only to the extent promoted and, hence, was worth only $10,000. Roberts agreed to accept a 2 cents royalty up to a maximum of $10,000. Within days, Sears was manufacturing 44,000 of Roberts's wrenches per week. A half-million wrenches were sold in nine months. By 1975, more than 19 million wrenches had been sold for a net profit of more than $44 million, according to court records. Was Sears guilty of the tort of fraud?

Roberts v. Sears, Roebuck & Co., 673 F.2d 976 (7th cir., 1978).

Yes. A jury awarded Roberts $1 million in damages. The U.S. Court of Appeals affirmed and also authorized Roberts to rescind (set aside) his contract and sue Sears for breach of his patent. In 1982, a federal jury awarded Roberts $5 million, and the judge increased this to $8.2 million on the grounds that the infringement was willful. In 1983, this decision was overturned by the Court of Appeals, which ordered a new trial. In September 1989, 25 years after receiving his patent, Roberts and his attorney finally confronted Sears again in court. This time the trial was in its fifth day when the litigants reached a settlement agreement. At the time, a Sears spokesperson said that a term of the settlement was that neither side could comment on it.[18]

LEGAL FOCUS—CASE

Dining at Yesterday's Restaurant in Mobile, Patrick Lamey ordered the "De La Mer" omelet. Afterwards, Lamey suffered nausea, vomiting, high fever, stomach cramps, and diarrhea. He was admitted to the hospital, where his condition was diagnosed as acute gastroenteritis. He was released in a few days. Lamey had no evidence that Yesterday's had been negligent or that the food was contaminated. But the menu stated that the "De La Mer" omelet contained crabmeat and trout when in fact it contained only codfish. Can Lamey simplify the proof needed by suing for misrepresentation?

Lamey v. Yesterday's Inc., 492 So.2d 988 (Louisiana, 1986).

Yes. Lamey easily could and did prove that the menu was a false misrepresentation of a material fact, that he relied upon it, and was damaged as a result. He recovered $27,500 in damages.

Tort law protects even the naive, the trusting, and the ignorant.

LEGAL FOCUS—CASE

Soldier Steven Malandris, a truck driver in Korea, met and married Jung Ja, who was illiterate. Returning to the United States, their marriage was dominated by a quest for financial security. Malandris worked as a baggage handler for United Airlines in Colorado; Jung Ja managed their money. They lived meagerly in order to save some $60,000, which they invested in United's stock. Malandris met John Barron, an account executive for securities firm Merrill Lynch, Pierce, Fenner & Smith, Inc. (a major securities firm), who prompted him to forge his wife's name to get access to the family money held as stock and to invest it in commodity options. Barron told Malandris that there would be an "assured gain" and "no possibility" of any loss. However, soon $30,000 was gone. Jung Ja sustained permanent emotional injury, which allegedly "destroyed her ability to function as a human being." She rejected this world and lives only in anticipation of life after death. May Jung Ja recover damages for fraud?

Malandris v. Merrill Lynch, Pierce, Fenner, & Smith, Inc., 447 F.Supp. 543 (Colorado, 1977).

Yes. A six-person jury in federal court awarded compensatory damages of $1,030,000, plus punitive damages of $3,000,000.[19] When denying a motion for new trial, the judge commented, "This is not a case of a lost investment; it is the tragedy of a lost life."

LEGAL FOCUS—PROBLEM

The children of Margaret Lesher, believing that her recent husband, buffalo rider T.C. Thorstenson, had murdered their mother to obtain part of her $100 million estate, sued him for fraud. They contended that Thorstenson had intentionally concealed one of his two previous marriages, the one in which he had been accused of spousal abuse. Lesher never would have married Thorstenson, her children contended, if she had known the truth. For their part, Thorstenson's attorneys argued that Lesher told their client a lie, that she was only 55 years old.[20] Are lies told between spouses the proper basis for a lawsuit for fraud?

Lies concerning the affection one does or does not feel about the other, made just before marriage or without regard to marriage, ordinarily are not justiciable. Thus, if one person relies upon the statement "I love you" and therefore takes some action that ultimately turns out to be regrettable, there is no basis for court action. However, lies of material facts may form the basis of an action for misrepresentation or fraud, even if the consequent action was to become married. In the Thorstenson case above, the outcome is not public because the case settled out of court.

Not all misrepresentations are torts. A person commits no tort when he or she innocently does not know the information is false, but mistakenly tells you that a dog being sold to you is two years old when in fact it is five. Generally, if you are the victim of an innocent or a negligent misrepresentation, you have the option of rescinding the contract (by returning the dog and getting your money back) or renegotiating the sale price. Of course, a professional veterinarian seller who knows, or should know, the true age of the dog could be guilty of fraud under these circumstances.

Opinions of quality in advertisements and sales talks ("the finest car on the road," "enjoy the pleasure of the best in international travel," "the best in cordless telephones just got better") are actual examples of customary commercial "puffing" and are not actionable. A dissatisfied purchaser of automobile insurance claimed that the seller violated the New Jersey Consumer Fraud Act because its service did not live up to its slogan. The state supreme court disagreed, explaining that the slogan "You're in Good Hands with Allstate" is "nothing more than puffery"; there was no fraud.[21] Social fibs likewise are not actionable (e.g., "I'll be there at 5 P.M." and the person doesn't arrive until 6 P.M., or not at all).

BAD FAITH

Persons pay premiums to insurance companies, who promise in exchange to pay money when some uncertain future calamity, such as an automobile accident, death, fire, or disability, occurs. If the insured person fails to make timely payment of premiums, the insurance coverage may be cancelled. And if the insurance company fails to make a promised payment when some calamity occurs, the insured may sue for breach of the insurance contract. In the next chapter (about contracts), you will learn that punitive damages are not available for ordinary breach of contract. But some courts have imposed a duty of "good faith and fair dealing" upon insurance companies, the violation of which may subject them to punitive damages. Violation of this duty is said to be the intentional tort of **bad faith.**

The tort of bad faith in actions against insurance companies generally involves either of two scenarios.

In the first scenario, Joe Levandowski pays premiums for automobile insurance with maximum liability coverage of, say, $100,000. Suppose Levandowski is involved in a car crash that seriously injures a victim in another car. The victim sues Levandowski for $150,000 but, learning of the insurance amount, agrees to settle out of court for the $100,000. However, Levandowski's insurance company rejects the offer, choosing instead to go to trial on a "roll of the dice" to see if a jury might return a verdict of less than $100,000. Instead, the jury verdict is $150,000. The insurance company pays the $100,000 policy maximum, thinking, "Well, at least we had a chance of saving some money." But Levandowski now must pay the $50,000 personally. Levandowski's loss is caused in part by his insurance company, which violated its duty of "good faith and fair dealing" because it could have and should have paid its policy maximum to protect Levandowski. Courts in most states would permit Levandowski to sue his insurance company for "bad faith" and to recover the $50,000 above coverage limits plus punitive damages.

In the second scenario, the carrier delays payment of a legitimate claim. The reason may be to earn interest on delayed payments, a desire to gamble on a less costly award by a jury, or an attempt to induce a needy claimant to settle for less because he or she can't afford to wait or litigate. Unreasonable delay in payment of a claim violates the duty of "good faith and fair dealing" and renders the insurance company liable for general and punitive damages.[22] Some states provide for the recovery of bad faith claims by statute and provide a cap of recovery of such claims. The pertinent part of such a Georgia statute is provided here.

bad faith

The deliberate failure to fulfill some duty or contractual obligation owed to another (e.g., a purposeful failure by an insurance company to pay a lawful claim).

LEGAL FOCUS—BACKGROUND

In the event of a loss that is covered by a policy of insurance and the refusal of the insurer to pay the same within sixty days after a demand has been made by the holder of the policy and a finding has been made that such refusal was in bad faith, the insurer shall be liable to pay such holder, in addition to the loss, not more than 50 percent of the liability of the insurer for the loss or $5,000, whichever is greater, and all reasonable attorney's fees for the prosecution of the action against the insurer.[23]

In theory, courts could impose a duty of good faith and fair dealing on any contract and permit a tort recovery of damages whenever a contract is breached under egregious circumstances. So far, courts are reluctant to extend tort recovery. When calamities occur, insurance companies have a tremendous negotiating power over their dependent customers, justifying the creation of a duty of good faith and fair dealing. Most other contractual relationships are not characterized by such unequal bargaining power and dependency. In some states insurance companies have successfully lobbied the legislature or used the initiative process to limit the ability of the courts to award damages for bad faith claims.*[24]

Torts by Negligent Behavior

The Elements of Negligence

duty

The obligation enforceable in court to recognize and respect the person, property, and rights of others. Legal duty is the reciprocal of *legal right*.

Everyone has a **duty** (i.e., a mandatory obligation) imposed by law to behave with due care as a reasonable, prudent (i.e., cautious and careful) person would behave under the same or similar circumstances. If one fails to be legally careful and thus injures another's person or property, the victim may sue and recover damages from the wrongdoer for negligence.

Whether a particular act constitutes negligence depends on whether the elements of negligence exist. For that purpose we can ask these questions:

- Did the defendant owe a duty of care to the injured victim?
- Did the defendant breach that duty through unreasonable conduct?
- Did the plaintiff suffer an injury as a result of the defendant's breach of the duty of care?
- Did the defendant's breach of duty cause the victim's injury?
- Is there any social policy under which the defendant's liability ought to be cut off? For example, was the injury so remote from the defendant's act that it would be unforeseeable by a reasonable person?

Duty and Breach of Duty

The duty of care that every person owes to all others is judged by the reasonable-person test. We all are duty bound to act as carefully or prudently as a so-called reasonable person would act under all of the circumstances existing at the time. Otherwise, we may be liable to any victim we injure—if we owe that victim a duty of care and if there is no social pol-

* The California Bad Faith Bobblehead: In 1979, the California Supreme Court held that a provision of the California Insurance Code impliedly authorized a direct action against insurers by victims of unfair claims-settlement practices, including third-party claimants. *Royal Globe Ins. Co. v. Sup. Ct. (Keoppel)*, 23 Cal. 3d 880 (1979). Nine years later the California Supreme Court reversed itself with regard to third-party bad-faith claims. *Moradi-Shalal v. Fireman's Fund Ins. Cos.*, 46 Cal. 3d 287 (1988). In 1999, the California legislature effectively reversed the supreme court by passing a statute called the Fair Insurance Responsibility Act of 2000 (FAIR). FAIR restored a person's right to sue another person's insurer for the insurer's unfair claims-settlement practices. The next year two initiatives (30 and 31) sponsored by insurance companies were passed overwhelmingly by the voters, effectively reversing FAIR before it took effect.

icy cutting off our responsibility. Whether or not a defendant acted reasonably is a question for the jury (or judge when there is no jury).

Determinants of duty include the foreseeability of harm to the victim, the proximity or closeness between the unreasonable act and the injury, and the moral blameworthiness of the defendant. Also relevant are the public policy of preventing future harm; the financial burden on the defendant and the community in imposing the liability; and the availability, cost, and prevalence of insurance for the risk involved.[25] These above considerations have evolved under common law. Special rules, discussed later, have been added by state statutes.

The standard of care required is usually called ordinary care: What would a reasonable person have done under the same or similar circumstances? The law does not demand perfection. But any judgmental errors must be understandable and excusable under the circumstances. Thus, for example, a "perfect" person driving on a busy highway and caught in a sudden and unusually heavy cloudburst, or a dense dust storm, would carefully drive off the highway and onto the shoulder, and wait there for the passing storm to subside. However, practically, a reasonable person—seeing other vehicles still moving in both directions—might assume that it was safe to drive on because the storm was only momentary and would shortly end. But the storm continues. Within seconds, our driver becomes one link in a chain reaction of rear-end crashes. Was the driver negligent? A jury would probably say, "No; it was an accident."

An accident is a sudden, unexpected, unintended happening that causes injury or death and/or loss of property. It may occur under circumstances where nobody is at fault, as in an earthquake or natural landslide. However, in most "accidents," one (or more) of the parties involved is at fault because of what someone did or failed to do. Automobile "accidents" are common examples of events that are usually caused by negligence. One example of an excusable accident is when a driver unavoidably loses control of the vehicle because of the sudden attack and painful sting of a bee.

One expert on torts, Edward J. Kionka, explains that the "reasonable person . . . is not the average or typical person, but an idealized image of such a person—a composite of the community's judgment as to how the typical community member ought to behave in each of the infinite variety of circumstances and activities in which there is a potential or actual risk of harm to the actor or others."[26] Community members sit on the juries that determine how the defendant ought to have behaved; some suspect that jurors themselves might behave less carefully than the standards they impose on others.

Failure to be reasonable may be seen in an act (e.g., setting fire to a building by flicking a cigarette butt) or an omission (e.g., neglecting to put out a small fire). It may be an intentional act (pushing the "pedal to the metal"), a careless act (talking on a cell phone while driving), or a carefully performed but dangerous act (downhill skiing) that results in injury. Courts consider the nature of the act (whether it is outrageous or commonplace), how the act is performed (cautiously or carelessly), the relationship of the parties (landowner duty to trespasser), and the nature of the injury (serious or slight) to determine whether a duty of care has been breached.

The law of negligence has evolved by court decisions that arise in response to the injuries that occur as increasingly complex activities characterize our society.

LEGAL FOCUS—PROBLEM

Injo Kalen left a burning cigarette teetering on the edge of his girlfriend Amy Porubsky's ashtray, which was sitting on the arm of the couch in her apartment. While Kalen and

Porubsky were dining in the other room, the cigarette became unbalanced as it burned and fell onto the cushions, which slowly began to burn. By the time the fire was noticed and extinguished, the couch and Porubsky's cashmere sweater were destroyed, and there were large burns in the carpet and smoke damage in the apartment. What are the legal consequences of this event?

Kalen owed a duty of reasonable care to Porubsky and her landlord. That duty was breached when Kalen failed to behave as a reasonable person by leaving the burning cigarette on the edge of the ashtray. Fire from a burning cigarette is a foreseeable consequence, and the damages were the proximate result of that negligence. Therefore, Kalen is liable to both Porubsky and her landlord. Porubsky can agree to accept a specified sum from Kalen for the value of her sweater (called *damages*). Porubsky's landlord, who owns the apartment and furniture, also could settle with Kalen. But if the parties cannot settle the problem, Porubsky and/or her landlord could begin civil tort proceedings against Kalen to recover damages. If Porubsky had renter's insurance, her insurance company also would compensate her for the sweater unless its value was less than the deductible portion of coverage. Most landlords carry fire insurance and would receive compensation from their casualty insurance company for damage to the building and couch as well. As a practical matter, both Porubsky and her landlord would probably accept payments by their insurance companies and take no further action.*

CAUSATION: ACTUAL AND PROXIMATE

Common sense tells us that one should be liable for conduct that injures others only when there is a logical cause and effect relationship between the defendant's negligent act (or failure to act) and the plaintiff's injury. In most fact situations, this principle is easy to apply. But when a sequence of events and persons is involved—as is sometimes the case—the determination of cause and effect is difficult.

If a person fails in a duty of care and someone suffers injury, the wrongful activity must have caused the harm in order for a tort to be committed. In deciding whether there is causation two questions must be addressed:

actual cause

The negligent person's carelessness is the reason for the loss by the victim; in other words, when injury to person or property results from the tortfeasor's action or failure to act.

1. Is there **actual cause?** That is, did the injury happen because of the defendant's act, or would the injury have occurred anyway? If an injury would not have occurred without the defendant's act, then there is actual causation. Such causation can usually be determined by the descriptive but-for test. *"But for"* the wrongful act, the injury would not have happened.

proximate cause

An action that, in natural and continuous sequence, unbroken by an intervening force or cause, produces the injury, and without which the effect or result would not have occurred. Furthermore the result is not entirely outside the range of expectation or probablility.

2. Was the act the **proximate cause** of the injury? As a matter of social policy, how far should a defendant's liability extend or reach? The act not only was an important factor, it actually caused all the remote damages. But injuries can be so remote that, as a matter of public policy considerations of fairness, liability of the wrongdoer is simply cut off.

What if two independent forces combine to cause the injury? For example, suppose A builds an unreasonably large and roaring campfire near C's mountain cabin. B leaves an open container of gas on the ground at an adjoining campsite. Sparks from A's blazing campfire ignite B's gas can, causing a large enough fire to engulf and destroy C's cabin.

---

* In theory, either Porubsky's or the landlord's insurance company would have the right to sue Kalen for reimbursement of any claims paid. This right of an insurance company to seek reimbursement from a wrongdoer for a claim paid to their customer is called subrogation (substitution of creditors). As a practical matter, insurance companies most often do not seek subrogation, because the wrongdoer lacks financial resources.

Even if neither careless act alone could have produced that result, both A and B are liable under the *substantial-factor test,* since both contributed substantially to the destruction of the cabin and were the actual cause of the harm. The same is true if *either* careless act alone would have been sufficient to destroy the cabin.

To be "proximate," the cause need not necessarily be close or near to the resulting injury, in time or in space. But it must appear to be just and fair, and indeed feasible, to hold the defendant liable for the injury that did result.

Theoretically—tongue in cheek—we might trace all events of human history in an unbroken chain back to Adam and Eve. The injury to the plaintiff must be reasonably related to the cause (the negligent act of the defendant). If it is not reasonably related it is considered too remote. The proximate cause is the true cause "which, in a natural and continuous sequence, unbroken by any efficient intervening cause, produces injury, and without which the result would not have occurred."[27] An attempt to thoroughly define proximate cause is probably futile, but examples can help with understanding.

LEGAL FOCUS—PROBLEM

Brent Starr was testing the power of his new sports car on a clear two-lane highway in good weather. When he reached 90 mph, he lost control and the car crashed through a fence and into a high-voltage electricity pole. This caused a short circuit and power failure throughout the city of Barclay, 100 miles away. Among the many persons affected were the staff and doctors in General Hospital. Just as the power went out, surgeon Ramona Ramirez was making a critical incision near patient Albert Johnson's heart during open-heart surgery. As a result of the darkness and loss of power to essential equipment, she had to stop abruptly. The machines supplying vital oxygen and pumping blood went silent. Within minutes, Albert Johnson was dead. Is Brent Starr liable for Johnson's death?

No. Starr's wrongful conduct was the actual cause of Johnson's death. Under the actual cause test mentioned previously, it can be said that "but for" Starr's folly, Johnson would not have died when he did. But Starr's act was not the proximate, legal cause because it was too indirect and remote from the death, which was not reasonably foreseeable by Starr.

Note that Starr would be liable for the damage to the fence and to the high-voltage electricity pole. It is also possible that General Hospital could be found guilty of negligence, and therefore liable, for failing to have a standby emergency electric power source available. (This is indeed standard practice in well-run hospitals, because power failures are not uncommon. But that is another case.)

LEGAL FOCUS—PROBLEM

Brent Starr's car, after ramming the pole, caromed into the brush nearby, striking and killing Tom Sneed, who was hunting quail. Starr did not know that Sneed was hunting there. Is Starr liable for Sneed's death?

Yes. Here Starr's wrongful conduct was the actual and also the proximate or legal cause of the death. The negligent act was direct and close; there was no efficient intervening cause. With his eyes glued to the road, Starr did not even see Sneed. Under the circumstances, however, the threat of injury or death from the speeding car to any person who happened to be in any of many potentially fatal locations on or along the highway was reasonably foreseeable in the law. What people really do and do not foresee is not decisive; what is foreseeable is a matter of law.

Thus, causation, both actual and proximate, must be proved to hold a defendant liable for negligence. There is proximate causation if there is "the ability to see or know in advance ... that harm or injury is a likely result of acts or omissions."[28] If, and only if, a reasonably prudent person, under similar circumstances, could and would have foreseen the likelihood of injury from the defendant's conduct to any person in the situation of the victim, does the defendant have the duty to exercise reasonable care to refrain from such conduct. This point is discussed in practically every law school in the nation by reference to the following famous case.

LEGAL FOCUS—CASE

Standing at one end of a railroad station platform, a woman waits for her train to arrive. Suddenly there is a loud explosion at the distant other end of the platform. Vibrations resulting from the explosion cause some scales to fall on the woman, injuring her. Evidently, a railroad guard inside one car of a slowly moving train had reached out to grab a man who was running to get aboard. Another railroad guard—who was standing on the platform—gave the man a helping push from behind. The man happened to be carrying an unlabeled parcel, containing fireworks. When the parcel fell onto the railroad tracks, it exploded, whereupon Helen Palsgraf, the woman at the other end of the platform, suffered injuries. She sued the railroad for damages. The jury found the guards to be negligent toward Palsgraf, and the trial court awarded her damages against the railroad, as the responsible employer. The railroad company appealed. Should the appellate court affirm the judgment?

Palsgraf v. Long Island R.R. Co., 248 N.Y. 339, 162 N.E. 99 (New York, 1928).

No. Palsgraf's complaint was dismissed. The injuries she suffered were not reasonably foreseeable—and were certainly not intentionally inflicted—by the railroad guards. Therefore, there was no duty to her that was breached by the guards or by their employer.* To prove negligence and to collect damages, Palsgraf would have had to show that the actions of the railroad guards "had possibilities of danger so many and apparent as to entitle" her to be protected against those very actions. This she could not prove.

Without foreseeability, there is no duty to act or refrain from action. Without duty, there can be no negligence. Without negligence, there can be no fault. Without fault, there can be no liability, regardless of the extent of the injury. William Prosser and Page Keeton, leading authorities on torts, unequivocally state, "The question of foreseeability is not an element of causation and does not arise until the issue of causation has been determined."[29] Another legal scholar, Leon Green, properly points out that "Causation is a neutral issue, blind to right and wrong ... but in absence of causal relation plaintiff has no case, and all other inquiries become moot."[30] After all, the linkage of cause and effect in any series of

---

* The legal doctrine of *respondeat superior* (Latin: "let the master answer") holds the employer responsible to third parties for the acts of employees done in the course of, and within the scope of, their employment. The doctrine is discussed in Chapters 10 and 13.

events may be coldly analyzed and *objectively* determined. Thereafter, one may inquire into whether any involved person (e.g., the defendant) *subjectively* could have and should have foreseen any of the described events or injurious effects.

Returning to Brent Starr's predicament in the earlier example, he could and should have foreseen that a person, such as Tom Sneed, might be in the bushes near the highway, perhaps hiking, hunting, resting, or bird-watching. But he could not reasonably have foreseen the tragic sequence of events in the hospital, nor could he have foreseen countless other resulting events at great distances from the scene of the crash, in areas served with electricity by the power line.

In summary, to prevail in a negligence action the plaintiff must present a preponderance of evidence proving

1. existence of a legal duty to the plaintiff, and
2. breach of that duty by the defendant's action or failure to act, with
3. resulting legal causation, actual and proximate, of an alleged injury, which
4. justifies the award of damages in court.

Remember that the weight of required evidence in civil negligence cases is not as demanding as in criminal cases, where the trier of facts must be convinced of their truth beyond a reasonable doubt. The weight of the plaintiff's evidence must be such that what is alleged is more believable, more convincing, more probable than not.[31]

LEGAL FOCUS—PROBLEM

Deborah Gaines arrived at the Preterm Health Services clinic to obtain her scheduled abortion. While sitting in the waiting room, John Salvi III opened fire and killed two receptionists. Gaines left unharmed, but was "emotionally messed up" and could never return to any clinic for an abortion. The two guards on duty at Preterm also were emotionally traumatized. Gaines later gave birth to Vivian, who is learning disabled and hyperactive. Gaines has sued Preterm and the owner of the building for negligence that wrongfully caused the birth of Vivian. Gaines seeks damages with which to properly raise Vivian. The security guards also have sued Preterm for negligence. Was the claimed negligence (failure to provide safe premises) the proximate cause of the birth of Vivian?[32]

There was sufficient time following the Salvi shooting for Gaines to obtain an abortion at a different clinic. But, according to her lawsuit, she was "too emotionally upset" to do so. Unsafe premises may cause the foreseeable result of injury to the customer. But it is quite different to argue that unsafe premises may foreseeably result in the birth of a loving child.

LEGAL FOCUS—PROBLEM

Chicago police were pursuing a car over a traffic violation. The speeding car crashed, killing Jamil Khouri, severely injuring his son Omar, and slightly injuring his daughter Ahlam. The Khouri estate and family sued the City of Chicago as employer of the police who, it was claimed, negligently pursued the traffic violator whose car was in the fatal crash. Is the act of pursuing a fleeing criminal the proximate cause of injury to an innocent bystander?

The City of Chicago settled the case, paying a total of more than $5.1 million to the Khouri family. After that case, the United States Supreme Court ruled that the police were not responsible for the death of a passenger on a fleeing motorcycle who was killed when it crashed. The Court established a new rule that police essentially are not negligent nor is their conduct the proximate cause of resulting injuries during pursuits of suspects unless the actions of the police are so egregious that they "shock our conscience."[33] The U.S. Supreme Court had jurisdiction because the action was pursued as a violation of the federal civil rights of the deceased.

LEGAL FOCUS—PROBLEM

Mukesh Rai, a devout Hindu, after ordering a bean burrito from Taco Bell, discovered to his dismay that he was eating beef, in violation of a fundamental religious principle. Rai contends that Taco Bell was negligent and must pay for psychiatry costs, for a trip to England for a purification ceremony with Hindu masters, for a trip to India for the ultimate purification of bathing in the waters of the Ganges River, and for emotional distress, pain, and suffering.[34] Assuming that Taco Bell was negligent, were the damages claimed foreseeable?

On the one hand, there was a breach of contract when Rai did not receive the product he ordered. But damages from breach of contract are restricted to foreseeable and quantifiable monetary damages. The measure of damages in torts, as will be discussed later in this chapter, is more generous in that nonquantifiable losses, such as pain and suffering, are compensable. Still they also must be foreseeable. In today's multicultural society, is it unreasonable to require national retail organizations to be aware and protective of the differing religious and other beliefs, customs, and activities of customers?

LEGAL FOCUS—CASE

Darrell Parsons was riding his horse Poco along a bridle path when a garbage collection truck in a nearby restaurant parking lot picked up and emptied its trash-filled bin. The clanging noise spooked Poco, who began spinning, bucking, and finally bolting. Parsons was injured when he landed on the ground. Parsons sued the Crown Disposal Company for his injuries. What was the result?

Parsons v. Crown Disposal Company, 15 Cal. 4th 456, 936 P. 2d 70, 63 Cal.Rptr. 2d 291 (California, 1997).

The case was thrown out of court summarily and never reached the jury. Appeals continued until the case reached the California Supreme Court some six years after the incident. The defense attorney asked rhetorically, "Why should we be liable if a horse operates like a horse and a trash truck operates like a trash truck?" If you believe the answer to this case was easy, you may be surprised to learn that two dissenting justices on the five-member court believed that the victim was entitled to a trial.

LEGAL FOCUS—PROBLEM

Tired from an afternoon of drinking beer with friends while watching the Buffalo Bills on TV, Will Brown was driving home. While passing down a street where homes were scattered among small warehouses, he didn't notice a fairly large, dilapidated cardboard carton near the gutter in the road ahead. Weaving slightly, Brown's car hit the cardboard box. To his dismay and horror, he saw in his rear view mirror that the carton had concealed a child. Kathy Wellington, age three, had been walking on the curb, holding the carton over her head. She had evidently stumbled into the street, and the carton covered her completely. Her death was mercifully sudden. Kathy's parents now seek to hold Brown liable. Will they prevail?

No. Although Brown's clearly negligent conduct was the actual cause of Kathy's death, he is not liable. While it is foreseeable that a pedestrian might be in the vicinity, it is not foreseeable that a tiny person would be inside an old cardboard carton in the street.

INTERVENING CAUSES AND SHARED RESPONSIBILITY

An **intervening cause** is an independent force (either an act or a failure to act) that comes or happens after the defendant's negligent conduct has commenced. The natural sequence of events that could have caused an injury does not in fact take place. Instead the end result is an injury that could not have been reasonably foreseen. Therefore, the original wrongdoer is not liable in damages.

> **intervening cause**
>
> A cause of an accident or other injury that legally excuses the wrongdoer who originally sets a series of events in motion.

LEGAL FOCUS—PROBLEM

Danny Dimmwith foolishly keeps a can of gasoline in the trunk of his car, thereby creating risk of a foreseeable injury from explosion or fire. Now lightning strikes the car, exploding the car's built-in gas tank as well as the portable can. Nearby pedestrians are injured. Is Dimmwith liable to the victims?

No. The lightning, an unforeseeable natural phenomenon at that time and place, intervened, and the actual cause of the injuries from the explosion was the lightning.

Sometimes intervention of a human actor expands the scope of a negligent wrongdoer's liability. Consider the following hypothetical situation.

LEGAL FOCUS—PROBLEM

Isaac York and Thor Waller are among a group of teenagers who walk to the end of a pier along the Atlantic coast in Florida. Waller objects when York engages in horseplay, but York persists, and with a quick push accidentally sends Waller into the deep water. Waller can't swim. He flounders, but is rescued by Connie Himaet and is revived by prompt resuscitation. Himaet was also injured when a high wave tossed her against the piling of the pier. Is York liable for the injury to Waller? To Himaet?

York is liable for injuries to Waller for negligently pushing him off the pier. He also is liable to Himaet under the doctrine that "danger invites rescue." Thus, the intervention of "Good Samaritan" Himaet expanded York's liability.

Whereas the law does not ordinarily require that a person "the Good Samaritan" intervene (no legal duty), what happens if they choose to do so? At common law if one undertakes a duty then the law expects that they be careful under the circumstances, and failing that they are liable for their own negligence. This can happen, as it did when the U.S. Coast Guard temporarily abandoned a search for a fisherman who subsequently died on a life raft five days after his boat had sunk. The death resulted because the USCG had negligently fouled up its own rescue-message transmission.[35]

To deal with the moral dilemma of no liability if you do nothing but liability if you try but fall short in the quality of assistance rendered, most states have enacted some type of so-called **Good Samaritan laws.** These statutes shield doctors and others from liability they may incur to an injured person when they stop along the way and render emergency aid. Obviously if all goes well no protection is needed for the volunteer but if the provided assistance aggravates the person's injuries then the Good Samaritan statute provides immunity from liability. These statutes vary from state to state as to who is covered and in the protection provided. Some state statutes protect any emergency volunteer and other state statutes protect only named emergency providers such as doctors, nurses, police, and firefighters; furthermore, some statutes distinguish between free assistance and paid providers. Volunteers are still expected to use reasonable care under the circumstances but they cannot be found liable if they fail to do so.

Good Samaritan laws

Refers to statutes today that protect volunteers from liability for ordinary negligence while aiding persons in need.

LEGAL FOCUS—EXAMPLE

Utah Statutes 78-11-22. Good Samaritan Act.

A person who renders emergency care at or near the scene of, or during an emergency, gratuitously and in good faith, is not liable for any civil damages or penalties as a result of any act or omission by the person rendering the emergency care, unless the person is grossly negligent or caused the emergency. As used in this section, "emergency" means an unexpected occurrence involving injury, threat of injury, or illness to a person or the public, including motor vehicle accidents, disasters, actual or threatened discharges, removal, or disposal of hazardous materials, and other accidents or events of a similar nature. "Emergency care" includes actual assistance or advice offered to avoid, mitigate, or attempt to mitigate the effects of an emergency.

These immunity statutes generally do allow recovery by the injured person if the Good Samaritan is grossly negligent in the assistance provided. A wrongdoer is guilty of **gross negligence** "when he inflicts injury intentionally or is so utterly indifferent to the rights of others that he acts as if such rights did not exist."[36] Good Samaritan statutes are just one form of statutory immunity; there are many others. The state of Maryland purportedly has twenty-four separate statutory immunities in the Maryland Annotated Code protecting individuals for their negligent acts.[37] Included within other immunity protections are state officers and employees acting within the scope of their employment. These other immunity protections also do not protect against grossly negligent acts.

gross negligence

The failure of even slight or scant care.

VIOLATION OF A STATUTE AS PROOF OF NEGLIGENCE

Legislation—at the federal, state, and local levels—often describes standards of conduct designed to prevent injuries. Violation of such statutes may be a tort. In most states when a court determines that the particular statute applies to the facts of a case, its violation is *prima facie* (Latin: "on first appearance") negligence. An example would be harm flowing from exceeding the well-posted speed limit on a winding mountain road. Unless the defendant produces evidence that excuses the violation, negligence is conclusive. A possible excuse would be a sudden emergency, such as unexpected brake failure caused by another's defective repair. The application of this rule is called **negligence** *per se.*

PROFESSIONAL MALPRACTICE

Few areas of legal conflict have caused as much heated debate as **malpractice.** Malpractice is negligence committed by a professional person. It is the failure to use that degree of care, learning, and skill ordinarily possessed and applied by the average prudent member of the profession in the same locality. Thus, a general practitioner of law or medicine in a small town is not expected to have the skills or facilities of a group of specialists in a large city.

Physicians and surgeons have been the prime targets of plaintiffs, but dentists, lawyers, accountants, architects, and engineers have comparable professional duties to those they serve and are increasingly being sued. Lawsuits have also been brought against other similar public-service types, such as pharmacists, chiropractors, insurance and real estate agents, and investment advisers. Some contend that many doctors routinely order costly laboratory tests and X-rays, even when they are not essential for proper patient care, as "security blankets" to help protect themselves against possible lawsuits.

Harvard University researchers examined some 31,000 medical records in a four-year-long study of malpractice (conducted in fifty-one hospitals in New York State), with results disclosed in 1990. They found 1,133 "adverse events" ranging from patients falling down to patients being infected during surgery. Twenty-five percent of the adverse events could be traced to negligence, yet only one lawsuit was filed for every 9.6 cases of detected negligence. If these figures are extrapolated to the entire total of 2.7 million patients who were hospitalized in New York State during 1984, about 100,000 patients were injured by improper medical treatment, and as many as 7,000 died.[38]

Thus, it could be that medical malpractice suits are less frequent than they should be, not the other way around.

PREMISES LIABILITY

The common-law duty of care that is owed to all persons generally is modified relative to the owners or occupiers of property. Owners and occupiers of real property (land and buildings) owe special care to certain classes of potential victims. We review the duties owed by landowners to those who **trespass,** by homeowners to guests, and by businesses to their customers.

Trespassers on Land

Adult trespassers to real property are by definition uninvited, generally unexpected, and unwanted. To them, minimal duty is owed—the owner (or occupier) must not set traps or spring guns to thwart or hurt trespassers or burglars, nor otherwise intentionally harm them. A landowner need not warn trespassers of dangerous natural conditions, but if trespassers are known to be on the premises the landowner has a duty to warn of unforeseeable man-made risks (e.g., an attack guard dog).

negligence *per se*

The unexcused violation of a statute or ordinance which is automatically deemed to be negligent conduct without argument or proof as to the particular surrounding circumstances.

malpractice

Violation of a duty of due care by a professional person.

trespass

Wrongful interference with the real or personal property of another.

LEGAL FOCUS—PROBLEM

It was the first day of the summer holiday. Jimmy Parker and Tom Rouble, both ten years old, rode their bicycles into the country. They spotted an unattended tractor near the road, on the farm of Jensen Dairy, Inc. Tom said, "Let's see if we can start it!" Within minutes they were over the fence and fiddling with the controls of the machine. The engine started and in a sudden forward lurch, Jimmy was thrown off and broke his arm. Is Jensen Dairy liable?

attractive-nuisance doctrine

The doctrine under which minors who trespass may collect damages if attracted onto the defendant's premises where they are injured by a man-made instrumentality that has special appeal to children (such as a railroad turntable or an unfenced swimming pool).

Young children are an exception to the rules regarding trespassers. When children trespass because of natural curiosity about an **attractive nuisance** and are injured, the owner is liable. The tractor could be considered such an attraction. A common attractive nuisance is a swimming pool. Many cities now have ordinances that specify the type of fencing that must safeguard pools from trespassing children. Attractive nuisances that are highly dangerous to children have included the second floor of a house under construction, from which a seven-year-old girl fell; an abandoned, burned-out semitrailer, with melted remnants of red-taillights, that fell on an eight-year-old boy; and an open sewer drain where a nineteen-month-old child was found drowned.[39]

In deciding whether the attractive-nuisance doctrine applies, courts consider (1) whether the defendant knew, or should have known, of the likelihood of trespassing children, and of the unreasonable risk of death or serious injury to them from an artificial (i.e., man-made) condition; (2) whether the children, because of their youth, do not realize the risk involved; and (3) whether the benefit of maintaining the condition, coupled with the burden or cost of eliminating the hazard, is slight compared to the risk to the children.

LEGAL FOCUS—CASE

Pacific Bell installed two public telephone booths on the sidewalk within twenty feet of the parking attendant's booth for the adjacent parking lot. The telephone booths attracted young drug dealers who loitered nearby often harassing passers-by. Pacific Bell refused to relocate the booths after Alfonso Martinez, parking attendant, complained. After Alfonso was robbed and shot in the hand and back, he sued Pacific Bell on the theory that the telephone booths were an attractive nuisance. Does Pacific Bell, under any theory, have a duty to protect a nearby parking attendant from harm by third parties?

Martinez v. Pacific Bell, 225 Cal. App. 3d 1557, 275 Cal.Rptr. 878 (1990).

Even if telephone booths were an attractive nuisance, Pacific Bell would not be liable for the wrongful acts of those who were attracted to the area. These criminals were not children and they did not injure themselves. As to the parking attendant, Pacific Bell had no special duty to someone working on the adjoining property.

Guests of Homeowners

licensee

A person who enters another's land with permission (implied or express) of the owner or possessor, for the visitor's convenience.

Anyone who is on or inside a homeowner's property with implied or express permission is a **licensee.** Social guests, U.S. Postal Service employees, public utility employees (e.g., meter readers), and building and health inspectors are licensees. Generally, the occupier of land owes the licensee a duty of reasonable care, but has no duty to inspect premises for dangerous conditions that are not obvious. However, once dangers are known, they must be repaired or the licensee must be warned.

Police officers and firefighters are licensees under a special rule called the *fireman's rule*. Probably the vast majority of fires are caused by negligence; and once started they also threaten the property of neighbors. Thus, public policy generally bars suits by firefighters for injuries suffered in performing their work in an emergency situation. But the owner is duty-bound to warn the firefighters of any known hidden hazards, if there is an opportunity to do so. Failing this duty, the owner would be liable for injuries to the firefighter.

Many homeowners erroneously believe they will be held liable for any injury that occurs on their property. But homeowners have no duty to warn of a condition of which they are unaware. If a social guest stumbles on concrete stairs leading to the front door, there is no liability. On the other hand, if a social guest slips on a throw rug that carelessly was placed on a newly waxed hardwood floor, there may be liability for failure to warn of the rather obvious danger.

Customers in Business Premises

Shoppers and customers in retail stores and patrons of restaurants, hotels, theaters, and amusement parks are called property **invitees.** They are there for business purposes and the owner or occupier of the premises is seeking to earn a profit from their presence. To them, the owner owes a high duty of care for their safety. He or she must routinely inspect for dangerous conditions and either correct them or clearly warn the invitees.

If a homeowner invites guests to a "lingerie party" hoping to make sales, the guests likewise have become business invitees to whom a high duty of care is owed.

invitee
One who enters another's land with the permission (implied or express) of the owner or occupier, for a matter of business benefiting the owner or occupier

LEGAL FOCUS—PROBLEM

Viola Velour was walking in the aisle of a supermarket, wearing her new high-heeled pumps for the first time. Suddenly, her left ankle twisted, and she tumbled to the floor. As she fell, she grasped at an empty shopping cart nearby, and it came down on her head. The impact broke her dentures and caused a painful, unsightly gash in her face. She sued the owner of the supermarket for damages. Is there liability?

No. Velour was an invitee, but the market is not an insurer of her safety. The accident resulted from her inability to use high-heeled shoes safely. To recover damages, she would have to prove that (1) the premises were in a dangerously defective condition; and (2) this condition was the result of the store owner's conduct, or that it existed long enough for the owner to be alerted and to correct it; and (3) the usual rules of causation were satisfied.

Sometimes produce in markets ends up on the floors, causing slippery spots. Customers who fall and are injured may bring "slip and fall" suits, which are fairly common. The question always arises as to the frequency with which the market inspects the floors for such spots and cleans them. A market is not reasonably required to inspect the floors every five minutes, and thus a "slip and fall" can occur under circumstances when the market simply is not negligent.

See an interesting article by Warren Richey in *The Christian Science Monitor*, "Banana-Peel Lawsuits: Beyond Slapstick"
http://www.csmonitor.com/durable/2000/02/16/p2s1.htm

THE INJURY REQUIREMENT AND DAMAGES

There is no negligence if no one is injured. To recover damages (receive compensation), a person must have suffered some loss, harm, wrong, or invasion of a protected interest.

Essentially, the purpose of tort law is to compensate people for legally recognized injuries that result from unreasonable behavior. If no harm or injury results from a given action, there is no tort. Thus, the drunk driver of a speeding vehicle may be negligent, but until injury occurs there is no tort. This is different from a crime, which does not usually require an injury.

LEGAL FOCUS—PROBLEM

Patricia Burns, who had advanced multiple sclerosis, claims that her doctor, Thomas Hanson, negligently failed to detect her pregnancy in time for her to obtain an abortion. She thus gave birth to Molly, whom she loves very much. But Burns requires substantial funds (she asks for $1.6 million) to assist her with hiring in-house childcare and other workers to help her raise the healthy Molly.[40] Is having a healthy child a "wrongful birth" for which damages should be allowed?

In this case, the jury returned a verdict for the doctor. However, the trial judge refused to permit Burns to testify to the jury that she would have had an abortion if she had known promptly of her pregnancy. The difficulty is, of course, in defining a new life as a measure of damages suffered by the parent. On the other hand, if a doctor commits negligence that proves to be disruptive and costly to the victim, shouldn't there be compensation? And if so, by what standard should the amount of damages be measured?

LEGAL FOCUS—BACKGROUND

Issues surrounding difficult legal and moral choices are worldwide problems for decision makers. French courts in the early twenty-first century concluded that physicians could be liable for wrongful birth. One case involved doctors who had negligently failed to warn an expectant mother that pre-natal scans showed that her baby had Down syndrome. The doctors were held liable for the full amount of the child's care after the mother claimed that had been aware of the child's condition she would have had an abortion.[41] In February of 2002 the French parliament limited "wrongful birth" lawsuits against doctors. "Under the new law, a person can sue a doctor for damages from failing to detect a disability in the womb, but only if it is a 'blatant error' on the doctor's part." The parliament also limited damages so parents can no longer receive compensation for the extra costs of raising a child.[42]

res ipsa loquitur

A doctrine under which negligence is inferred when the instrumentality causing the injury was under control of the defendant and an injury occurred that normally would not occur in the absence of negligence by the defendant. This doctrine is frequently relied on by victims of medical malpractice.

WHAT IS A *RES IPSA LOQUITUR* CASE?

In negligence lawsuits the injured victim is required to prove that the defendant has breached a duty. In certain situations, however, courts infer that the duty was breached. In this type of case, the burden shifts to the defendant, who must prove that he or she was not negligent. In other words, negligence can be found in situations lacking direct evidence of wrongdoing. This inference of the defendant's breach of duty is called the doctrine of **res ipsa loquitur** (Latin: "the thing speaks for itself").

The *res ipsa loquitur* doctrine applies when both of the following conditions exist:

1. The event is one that ordinarily does not occur without someone being negligent.
2. The agency or instrumentality creating the injury is under the exclusive control of the defendant.

LEGAL FOCUS—PROBLEM

Mike Hubell is walking on the sidewalk alongside a building with a penthouse apartment on the tenth floor. The penthouse has an open terrace with a railing 3 feet high and 6 inches deep, decorated by a line of potted plants on the railing. Hubell is knocked unconscious when he is hit on the head by a potted plant. It is later proven that the pot that hit him is similar to others on the penthouse railing, where one pot is missing. Hubell is unable to prove how the pot happened to fall on him. Is this a *res ipsa loquitur* case?

This is a classic situation for application of the doctrine that "the thing speaks for itself." The pot evidently came from that penthouse terrace, which was under the exclusive control of the occupants of the apartment. It would not ordinarily have fallen unless someone was either careless or, possibly, intended to be funny.

The doctrine has been applied by patients after undergoing surgery. If the patient suffers an injury that ordinarily does not occur without negligence (as when a sponge is not removed from the surgical area), the doctrine can be used to shift the burden to the defense to show they were not negligent. Thus as the burden of proof shifts, the surgeon, surgical nurses, staff, and others will have to sort out the events among themselves.

LEGAL FOCUS—CASE

Seventy-eight-year-old Margaret Frostick was admitted to Porter Memorial Hospital for a right carotid endarterectomy. (Ouch!) Anesthesia was given to permit the patient to be in a sedated state but still be responsive. Supplemental oxygen was given to her through a mask. During surgery the oxygen mask caught on fire and Frostick's face and chest were burned as a result. Not surprisingly she sued the medical providers. Is she entitled to an instruction of *res ipsa loquitur* against the medical providers?

Gold v. Ishak, 720 N.E.2d 1175 (Indiana, 1999).

The court of appeals held that the plaintiff had presented evidence that the oxygen mask was "under the exclusive control of the Medical Providers and that the fire was such that the ordinary course of things would not happen if those who used these devices exercised proper care. The conditions surrounding the surgery have met the underlying elements of the doctrine of *res ipsa loquitur,* and therefore, the inference of negligence is applicable."

WHAT ARE DEFENSES TO NEGLIGENCE?

Under certain circumstances, a defendant who might otherwise be liable because of his or her negligence can avoid payment of all or some of the damages by proving that the injured victim did one of the following:

- Assumed the risk

- Also was negligent and, in most states, is entitled only to reduced damages, if any, under the doctrine of *comparative negligence*
- Also was negligent and therefore, in a few states, is entitled to no damages under the doctrine of *contributory negligence*

These three defenses are discussed next.

Assumption of Risk

A person who voluntarily puts himself or herself in a risky situation, who knows the risk involved, and who is then injured is not allowed to recover damages. This is the defense of **assumption of risk.** A plaintiff who knows and appreciates a given risk may assume it, thereby absolving the defendant of liability if injury results. In sports, especially, the hazards may be serious for both spectators and participants, and both may assume the risks of customary hazards of such games as baseball, basketball, football, and hockey.

In contact sports, participants assume the risk of injuries that are common and expected, even when an opponent is violating a rule of the game (e.g., when a jockey carelessly changes lanes during a horse race—a violation of a "foul riding" rule). But this does not give the contestants a *carte blanche* (French: "blank check") waiver of all violations of the rules. Conduct that is substantially outside the ordinary play of the game, especially if it is intentional, may give rise to tort liability.

To prove that a potential plaintiff had knowledge of the risk undertaken, many activity providers will require each participant to sign a document that explains the hazards of a particular activity. (The clause may also serve as a contract waiver of that person's legal rights; we will discuss such waivers in Chapter 8.) Whether the document effectively waives legal rights or not, it can clearly establish knowledge of the risk and establish the doctrine of assumption of risk.

Comparative and Contributory Negligence

Almost all states have adopted the rule of **comparative negligence,** under which a victim who is negligent may nevertheless recover damages from a defendant who is more negligent. Damages allowed are simply reduced in proportion to the amount of negligence attributable to the plaintiff. In other words, liability for damages is allocated to the parties in proportion to the fault each contributed to causing the injury, as determined by the jury (or judge when there is no jury).

LEGAL FOCUS—PROBLEM

T. Ray Vitesse was driving home in his heavy-duty pickup truck at dusk on a residential street, about an hour after sunset. He had several beers that afternoon. He later claimed he was not drunk, although he had forgotten to turn on his headlights. It was raining heavily at the time, and he felt mellow and refreshed as the raindrops splashed on his face through an open window. "Just cruising along" at only 10 mph over the posted speed limit (of 25 mph), his reverie suddenly ended as he crashed into the left side of Art Aritroso's sedan. Aritroso was backing out of his driveway, but had failed to look both ways and hadn't turned his lights on until he was in the street. Vitesse suffered no injuries and his truck required no repairs, but Aritroso's sedan was extensively damaged and he was badly injured. Aritroso sued and the jury decided that his negli-

assumption of risk
When a plaintiff with knowledge of the facts of a dangerous condition voluntarily exposes himself or herself to the particular risk of injury.

http://
Scuba diving is so much fun it seems like it should be illegal. It is legal, but it is also a dangerous sport. The National Association of Underwater Instructors (NAUI) provides an assumption of risk document for those who want to learn how to scuba dive through a NAUI program.
http://www.naui.org/pdffiles/Standard Waiver_01-02.pdf

comparative negligence
Negligence of the plaintiff that does not bar recovery of damages but may reduce the amount of recovery proportionally.

gence constituted 25 percent of the total. Aritroso's damages total $100,000. How much is he entitled to under the comparative-negligence rule?

The total damages recognized are reduced by the amount of the plaintiff's negligence, as long as it is not as great as the defendant's. Under this process, Aritroso would get $75,000 (100 percent—25 percent – 75 percent). He would have received $51,000 if his negligence had been 49 percent (100 percent—49 percent – 51 percent), but nothing if it had been 50 percent or higher. (This is the case in Wisconsin, one of the first states to adopt comparative negligence.) In a number of states, however, under the "pure" comparative-negligence rule, contributory negligence never bars recovery. Damages are reduced in proportion to the amount of the plaintiff's negligence. In those states, even if his negligence had been 99 percent, Aritroso would nevertheless have received $1,000 (100 percent – 99 percent = 1 percent).

Previously, the rule of **contributory negligence** generally determined whether damages could be awarded at all for negligence. If two persons were involved in an accident and both were negligent, neither could recover any damages. Contributory negligence was held to be a complete bar to a negligence lawsuit. This was the rule even if one party "contributed" almost all of the negligence. Determination of contributory negligence is a question for the trier of fact. Not infrequently, a jury will temper strict application of the rule with compassion and common sense, and simply overlook minimal amounts of negligence by an otherwise deserving plaintiff. Moreover, the contributory negligence of a plaintiff is no defense for a defendant found guilty of willful and wanton misconduct (acting with reckless disregard for the plaintiff's safety, as by drunk driving).

This harsh rule of contributory negligence originated in England and was commonly applied in the United States during the 1800s, when railroads were first introduced. "Establishment-oriented" courts were interested in helping the new industry, and they applied the doctrine as a matter of law to collisions at grade crossings. The doctrine survived into the twentieth century and frequently blocked recovery of damages in automobile accident cases (where it is not unusual to find at least some negligence on the part of both drivers).* Modernly most states have abandoned the doctrine of contributory negligence in favor of comparative negligence.

Is the failure to use an automobile seat belt or shoulder harness (or airbag that inflates upon impact) evidence of contributory negligence? This issue is somewhat confusing. Belts generally reduce the severity of injury, but in some cases can cause internal injury. However, there is no documented proof that any person has died in a fiery accident because he or she could not unbuckle the seat belt. Indeed, the crash victim, if belted, is more likely to be conscious and better able to escape. If in the driver's seat, he or she is more likely to minimize further damage by maintaining better control of the car. Most states have mandated by statute the installation of seat belts, but not all require their use. Moreover, there is really no logical connection between a collision and the failure to use a seat belt. Consequently, most jurisdictions, including those of such populous states as Florida, New York, and Texas, have ruled that failure to use a seat belt does not constitute sufficient negligence to bar the plaintiff's lawsuit.[43] In some states such failure is negligence that may reduce damages if expert testimony proves how much less the injuries would have been had the belt been used.[44] A further discussion of negligence pertaining to automobile accidents is included in Chapter 10.

contributory negligence

The negligence of a plaintiff that helped to cause a tort. In states accepting the doctrine a contributory negligence plaintiff is usually barred from claiming damages if injured.

---

* A few states apply the doctrine of "last clear chance" to deny recovery if, despite the negligence of the defendant, the injured victim had the last clear chance to avoid the injury but failed to do so. Thus, a driver who foresaw an approaching car straddling the white line, and who reasonably could pull over to the right, but who continued ahead with a resultant crash, would have had the last clear chance to avoid the injury and thus could not recover damages.

STRICT LIABILITY TORTS

As a matter of public policy, certain businesses are required by law to compensate persons who are injured by their products, services, or activities. In these situations, the victimized plaintiff need not prove intent or negligence—the defendant is liable even if not at fault. This is true, for example, in the comparatively rare cases where the defendant keeps a wild animal, with dangerous propensities, that injures someone. Circus and carnival elephants, lions, and tigers may have been trained or tamed, but they remain wild. In contrast, some wild animals—such as deer, oxen, and monkeys—are excluded if they have been domesticated to live peaceably in the service of humans. Nevertheless, the owner of domestic animals, including dogs, is strictly liable for injuries inflicted by the animal if the owner knows of their dangerous propensities. Thus, a guard dog known to be vicious is not entitled to a first "free bite."

Of course, the owner of an ordinary dog or cat, one not believed to be abnormally dangerous, would be liable if he or she directed the animal to harm another or negligently failed to prevent the harm. Animal behavior is often unpredictable and uncontrollable, and it is difficult to prove prior knowledge of viciousness. Therefore, some thirty states have enacted statutes that impose strict liability on owners of dogs that injure others, or specify that negligence need not be proved (e.g., as in roving dog cases and when leash laws are violated).

Certain activities are deemed to be so hazardous as to justify imposition of strict liability on the person so engaged. Examples of such ultrahazardous activities are fumigating buildings with poisonous gases and blasting with explosives in populated areas. Operating a nuclear reactor is another example of an ultrahazardous activity. To date, there has been no Chernobyl-type disaster with loss of life in the United States. Nevertheless, Congress has responded to the potential threat with the Price-Anderson Act of 1957, which placed a liability limit on the nuclear power industry of $710 million in damages, with any additional claims to be paid by the federal government. The limit was raised in 1988 to $7.1 billion and extended to cover university research reactors, nuclear weapons plants, and nuclear waste repositories.

WORKERS' COMPENSATION

Another important category of strict liability is imposed on employers when a worker is injured or killed on the job. In all states workers' compensation insurance laws now cover most employees, although farm or agriculture workers and domestic servants in homes are still often excluded. Under **workers' compensation,** workers receive (1) all medical treatment necessary to cure or provide relief from effects of employment-caused injuries or illness, (2) temporary or permanent disability payments, (3) vocational rehabilitation and retraining benefits when unable to return to the former job, and (4) legal assistance without charge. The benefit payments are not lavish, but they are reasonably certain, and the injured worker is not required (nor, indeed, permitted) to sue in court to obtain prescribed benefits. Claims are, however, subject to review and approval in special administrative hearings.

Requirements for a successful workers' compensation claim are simple (at least in theory). (1) The claimant must be an employee; (2) the injury must be a work-related one; and (3) the employee must file a timely claim.

If someone other than the employer is responsible for the workplace injury, the worker may be able to sue and recover damages without limit in a conventional negligence action. A typical example would be when the injury is caused by defectively

http://

The Centers for Disease Control and Prevention tells us that every forty seconds, someone in the United States seeks medical attention for a dog bite-related injury

http://www.cdc.gov/ ncipc/fact_book/ 14_Dog_Bite_Injuries.htm

http://

One of several sources providing information on the Price-Anderson Act is the Nuclear Information and Resource Service at

http://www.nirs.org/ reactors/ThePriceAnderson Actfactsheet1001.htm

workers' compensation

Medical treatment, rehabilitation benefits, and disability payments for workers injured on the job.

designed or built equipment that was used on the job. The injured worker cannot sue his or her own employer, but can sue the third-party equipment manufacturer. Also, coworkers may be liable for injuries caused by intentional attacks or by willful or wanton negligence. Limited circumstances under which workers' compensation benefits would be denied are when the injury was the result of voluntary intoxication on the job or was intentionally self-inflicted, or when the injured worker was the aggressor in a fight.

Generally, workers' compensation is the exclusive remedy available against the employer in covered businesses.* This is a major practical improvement over the old common-law rules, which permitted the worker to sue his or her employer—a costly and seldom prudent thing to do. For starters, the worker (if still alive) could be fired. Thereafter, in court, the employer could avoid liability by proving that either (1) the worker knew the hazards involved and assumed the risk (perhaps in exchange for a higher wage); or (2) the worker was guilty of contributory negligence; or (3) a coworker's negligence caused the accident.

LEGAL FOCUS—PROBLEM

It was a glorious spring day as Willie Jon Fisher climbed to his workstation 125 feet above the bay. As a steelworker, he was paid premium wages for assuming the risk of his hazardous job on the new Silver Gate Bridge. In a burst of youthful exuberance, he removed his hard hat, waved to his pal Don Jones twenty feet above, and danced a quick jig on the beam where he stood. Jones shouted, "Simmer down and get to work!" But Willie fell, hitting a cross beam before the safety net caught his unconscious body. His injuries were permanent and he never returned to the job. Does his carelessness preclude his recovery of benefits?

No. Any covered employee injured on the job is entitled to benefits under the state's workers' compensation law.

At the beginning of the twentieth century, workers did not enjoy much protection under law. There was no workers' compensation, no safety laws governing workplaces, and no state fair employment agencies to assist workers. There weren't even any child labor laws, and thousands of children worked for almost no wages in the coal mines of Pennsylvania. There also was no minimum wage.

Pressures to speed up production have accounted for more accidents on the job in recent years. Increasing numbers of workers have filed successful claims for mental stress and for strain injuries caused by repetitive hand motions. Many workers complain about aching wrists, carpal-tunnel syndrome (from the Greek *karpes,* "wrist"), and sore fingers incurred in garment factories, meat-packing plants, post offices with letter-sorting machines, newspaper offices with video display terminals, supermarkets with bar-code scanners at checkout counters, and offices with the ubiquitous keyboards. Employers complain that healthcare and workers' compensation premiums have risen, and workers complain that benefit payments are too low. Fortunately for employers, insurance premiums are a deductible business expense, and they can pass the cost along to their customers. On the receiving end, no federal income tax is assessed on workers' compensation insurance benefits (although social security disability payments may be subject to income tax).

http://

An example of a state workers' compensation scheme can be found at the Iowa workers' compensation Web site **http://www.iowaworkforce .org/wc/index.html**

* An uncommon exception would be when the employer fraudulently conceals a hazardous working condition, such as the presence of asbestos particles. In such a case, substantial damages may be claimed by the injured worker in a separate action. See *Johns-Manville Products Corp v Contra Costa Superior Court,* 27 Cal.3d 465, 612 P2d 948 (1980).

DEFECTIVE PRODUCTS THAT CAUSE INJURY

Every year, millions of consumers are injured and thousands are killed by familiar products used in daily life. Usually, there is nothing wrong with the product, but the user has been careless or has failed to follow instructions for proper use and maintenance. Examples include trucks and automobiles; power boats; skis, bats, hardballs, and other sports equipment; guns and firecrackers; knives; and patent and prescription medicines. The most innocent-appearing and useful product, however, may in fact be lethal. For example, a child's pajamas may be made of highly flammable chemical fabric; a sleek sedan may have a steering mechanism prone to failure; and a wonder drug that prevents miscarriages may cause cancer in any female child born to the patient.

Under common-law rules, a person injured by a defective product may recover damages by proving that the product was negligently made. The negligence may be in the design, a lack of safety features, faulty materials or manufacture, or a failure to explain proper use and maintenance. Proving negligence in such cases is usually extremely difficult and costly, and often near impossible. The suspect product may be made with thousands of interrelated component parts; these may have been assembled many years before, in a factory located thousands of miles away, possibly in a foreign land.

An injured plaintiff might also allege a breach of a contractual warranty (see Chapter 8). However, there might be no warranties, or they may have expired, or recovery may be barred by failure to give proper prompt notice of the breach. Moreover, limited warranties often provide for no more than repair or replacement of the product if defective, or at best for a refund of the purchase price.

LEGAL FOCUS—BACKGROUND

In 1962, the California Supreme Court provided a new legal solution to the deficiencies of negligence and warranty theories by defining the new tort of strict liability for the manufacturer when a defective product is sold that injures a user. In this case, the product involved was an ingenious multipurpose power tool that could be used as a saw, a drill, and a wood lathe. It was purchased by the plaintiff's wife. Later the plaintiff bought the attachments necessary to use the tool as a lathe to trim a large piece of wood. He had worked on a piece of wood several times without difficulty when it suddenly flew out of the machine and hit his forehead, causing a serious injury. Experts testified that an inadequate set of screws had been used by the manufacturer to hold parts of the machine together, and the machine's normal vibration caused the screws to be loosened, which brought about the accident. The court held, "A manufacturer is strictly liable in tort when an article he places on the market, knowing that it is to be used without inspection for defects, proves to have a defect that causes injury to a human being."[45]

The *Restatement of Torts* expanded the strict product liability doctrine to include "injuries to any user or consumer or to his property," but qualified it by providing that the seller must be "engaged in the business of selling such a product ... in a defective condition unreasonably dangerous to the user or consumer" and that it "is expected to and does reach the user or consumer without substantial change in the condition in which it is sold."[46] Many other jurisdictions, including such populous states as Illinois, Pennsylvania, and Texas, have adopted the rule. Contributory negligence of the plaintiff does not defeat his or her case. However, some states, using comparative negligence, allow a reduction in damages. In some jurisdictions, if the product was produced in accordance with the then-existing state of the art, the injury-causing design is not considered a defect.

The rule of strict liability for defective products shifts the burden of resulting injuries from the user to the manufacturer. Intermediaries such as wholesalers and retailers are also held responsible as they are better equipped to pursue the manufacturer. The manufacturer may purchase added insurance, which becomes a routine cost of production. But in any case, producers of products can pass along added costs to all customers in the form of slightly higher prices. Manufacturers are encouraged, moreover, to be more careful in product design, pre-sale testing, inspection, quality control in production, post-sale follow-up of performance, and prompt recall and repair when defects are disclosed. In recent years, many automobile models have been recalled for appropriate modifications to forestall costly strict liability litigation.

The following is a selection of products for which liability has been imposed.

- Accutane (an anti-acne drug linked to birth defects)
- All-terrain vehicles
- Bendectin and other teratogens (chemicals linked to birth defects)
- Chymopapain (a drug used to treat herniated disks)
- Dalkon shield (contraceptive device associated with inflammatory disease and spontaneous abortion in users; removed from the market in 1974)
- Aspirin (lack of warning labels relating a child's use of aspirin to Reyes syndrome).
- DES (a drug used to prevent miscarriages but discontinued because of increased risk of cancer in women who had fetal exposure)
- Halcion (a drug used to induce sleep)
- IUDs (a contraceptive device)
- Silicone gel breast implants
- Tobacco products
- Vehicle transmissions and gas tank placement
- Vehicle tires

LEGAL FOCUS—BACKGROUND

Dow Corning Corporation helped develop and sold tens of thousands of silicone gel breast-implant devices. Thousands of women sued in a class action contending that their breast implants were defective, leaking silicone into their bodies and impairing their immune systems. Dow Corning, disputing the injuries, filed for bankruptcy due to the crush of claims. Later, under federal bankruptcy court rules, Dow Corning settled the cases, agreeing to pay $3.2 billion to those women who were injured by its product.[47]

Class actions are procedural devices whereby groups of injured persons who are similarly situated can obtain redress in a single lawsuit, rather than filing hundreds or even thousands of separate cases. The silicone gel breast-implant case is an excellent example of how large groups of victims are handled by the civil-law tort system. Shortly after the Dow Corning settlement, a court-appointed panel of neutral scientists concluded after two years of study of more than 2,000 cases that there is no credible evidence that breast implants cause disease.[48] Silicone gel implants were introduced in the 1960s, and more than a million women had the procedure until it was banned by the U.S. Food and Drug Administration in 1992.

class action

When all members of a group of persons who have suffered the same or similar injury join together in a single lawsuit against the alleged wrongdoer. The group must be so numerous that it is impracticable to bring all members before the court individually.

http://

An interesting page on a report of the United Kingdom Independent Review Group on silicone breast implants can be read at

http://www.silicone-review.gov.uk/

The largest and most notorious cases of strict liability in the early years of the twenty-first century involve tobacco products. Smoking presents many dilemmas to society. There is no longer a debate that smoking is addictive (as are many other substances) and that it carries a high probability of contributing to lung diseases, especially cancer. Individuals generally cannot successfully sue cigarette companies effectively because of the difficulties in engaging enough experts to prove causation. While it is one thing to show statistically that smoking contributes to lung cancer in the population, it is quite another thing to show that smoking (and not something else) caused an individual's lung cancer. Meanwhile, taxpayer-funded (via Medicaid) hospitals incur substantial costs in treating persons afflicted with diseases that likely were caused or exacerbated by cigarette smoking. Given these premises, almost all states joined together in filing litigation against the nation's four largest cigarette manufacturers.

LEGAL FOCUS—BACKGROUND

The tobacco industry settled lawsuits filed by most states by agreeing to pay about $206 billion as reimbursement for the Medicaid payments that had been incurred caring for patients of smoking-related diseases, and for future such costs through 2025. The states will receive portions of the $206 billion each year.[49] Tobacco manufacturing companies agreed to pay the states a portion of their proceeds from cigarette sales. The states represented that they will use the money to pay some hospital and other expenses of those who are afflicted with tobacco-related diseases and who are unable to care for themselves. For example, California is slated to receive $23.9 billion each year, although estimated health costs of smoking-related diseases there is $42.5 billion each year. Furthermore, there is no requirement that the money actually be spent on smoking-related deaths. Thus, the settlement, spread out over more than twenty-five years, is a social policy akin to a "user tax" whereby cigarette users provide the funds with which to care for the illnesses created by cigarettes. Other provisions in the settlement restrict the kinds of advertising that will be permissible (no cartoon ads).

Immediately following the settlement, and to nobody's surprise, tobacco manufacturers announced a substantial price increase in cigarettes to offset the costs of the settlement. Since the price increase, Internet cigarette sales—some advertising no sales tax, discount prices, and free shipping—have been booming, as have sales of black-market cigarettes bought in low-tax states. Professional smuggling of "tax-free" export cigarettes has increased.[50]

LEGAL FOCUS—PROBLEM

Marie Schwartz's husband brought a wrongful death action against Philip Morris after Schwartz died of lung cancer. She had smoked Merit cigarettes for twenty-three years, having chosen the brand as a "low-tar alternative" that she hoped would help her quit. Her husband argued that Merits had kept her from giving up cigarettes entirely and were the cause of her lung cancer. He also argued that Philip Morris had engaged in deceitful practices to suggest the low-tar cigarettes were a safer and healthier alternative in order to keep smokers as customers. Philip Morris claimed that Schwartz knew smoking was dangerous and that when she still chose to smoke she assumed the health risks. What was the result?

In the 2002 Oregon case the jury found for the plaintiff and awarded $168,000 for compensatory damages and punitive damages of $150 million: $115 million for fraud, $10 million for strict liability, and $25 million for negligence.[51] The case has been appealed by Philip Morris.[52]

Cigarettes are distributed in a huge global market. The world's largest study of smoking deaths reveals that China makes up twenty percent of the world's population but smokes thirty percent of the world's cigarettes. Two-thirds of Chinese men under age twenty-five smoke. Globally, a record four million people will die of smoking-related illnesses in the year 2000.[53]

Everyone knows that guns can cause injury. According to the Centers for Disease Control, 28,874 persons died of gun-related injuries in 1999.[54] Under what circumstances might a gun manufacturer be held responsible for a defective gun?

LEGAL FOCUS—PROBLEM

Michael Soe, age fourteen, took his father's Beretta 92 Compact L handgun from a camera bag and replaced its loaded ammunition magazine with an empty one. Unbeknownst to Michael, a cartridge remained in the gun's chamber. Michael then, while playing with the gun, shot his best friend Kenzo Dix in the heart, killing him instantly. Kenzo's parents sued Beretta Corp. for $7.5 million on the theory that the red dot on the gun's barrel that is raised one millimeter when a cartridge is in the chamber was too subtle and inadequate a warning. Beretta blamed Michael's father for keeping the gun readily available and loaded. Beretta argued that a defense verdict would mean "personal responsibility is still a healthy concept in this society." Was the gun defective?[55]

This was the first jury trial involving the question of whether or not a handgun is defective in its design or warnings. In the Kenzo Dix case, the jury returned a verdict for Beretta. Many other similar suits are pending in the United States with several having been decided against the plaintiffs.

The City of Chicago filed a lawsuit against gun manufacturers to recoup the cost of urban gun violence. The contention is that guns are inherently defective products, unreasonably dangerous to the public health, much like cigarettes. Chicago also alleges that gun makers and dealers design, market, and sell easily concealable guns that are tailor-made for street warfare and not for sport. Such guns are sold in stores just outside Chicago, so the guns can easily be taken within the city's limits. Over twenty cities including New Orleans, Miami, Boston, Atlanta, and Los Angeles have filed similar lawsuits based more or less on the cigarette litigation.

Statutes of Repose

A **statute of repose** is a special statute of limitations that applies to specified defective products. Statutes of limitation (discussed fully later in this chapter) set time limits within which lawsuits must be commenced. Because knowledge that a product is defective may

http://

Updated information on tobacco litigation is available at

http://www.lawpublish.com /tobacco/

http://

For the pro side of gun litigation, see

http://www.jointogether.org/

http://

For the con side, see

http://www.nra.org/

statute of repose

A type of statute of limitations that specifies an absolute time from the date of sale during which the cause of action must be brought to collect damages for defects in the product.

not arise for many years, there is a public policy to extend the time within which victims may instigate their lawsuits for injuries they may sustain. However, it would be unfair to businesses to allow an unlimited number of years to pass before claims are asserted. Statutes of repose are a compromise of the interests of consumers on the one hand and of manufacturers and sellers on the other. A statute of repose cuts off liability for a defective product following a specified number of years following its manufacture or sale, regardless of when the victim's injury occurs or is discovered. Statutes of limitation, on the other hand, do not begin to run until an injury has been discovered, or should have been discovered by a victim using reasonable care. There is no federal statute of repose. State statutes vary, but all cut off the time allowed for specified lawsuits pertaining to, for the most part, consumer products.

In addition to consumer products, statutes of repose may apply to medical and legal malpractice, to workers who are injured in the workplace, and even to renters who are injured by a defective product that is installed in their apartment. In malpractice cases, when they are applicable, statutes of repose typically cut off liability of the physician regardless of when the defect or harm is discovered by the victim. Thus, the "clock starts running" for possible liability for malpractice from the date the injury was inflicted. For example, one state's statute of repose cuts off medical malpractice lawsuits if they have not been commenced within five years of the physician's negligence, regardless of when the harm was discovered.[56] The clock starts running for construction or architectural design defect cases from the date of completion of the project, regardless of when the victim is injured.

LEGAL FOCUS—PROBLEM

Tom Urquhart worked for the Acme Excavating Company performing maintenance duties on heavy equipment. In September 2002, a steel roller on a hydraulic conveyor that was transporting rock broke free, causing a large rock to severely break Urquhart's right leg. The conveyor was manufactured in 1972 by Zeland Equipment Co. and sold to Acme in 1985. Urquhart was covered by workers' compensation insurance and received medical and other financial assistance. His attorney advised him to sue Zeland under a defective product "strict liability" theory. Can Urquhart recover damages from Zeland?

The statute of limitations is usually one year from the date of the injury, so Urquhart has until September 2003 to commence litigation. But thirty years have elapsed since the conveyor was built by Zeland Equipment Co. and seventeen years since it was sold to Acme. If there were a twenty-five-year statute of repose, Urquhart's case would be barred. If the allowable period was twenty years, then Urquhart could sue Acme for product liability.[57]

Most statutes of repose are applied to lawsuits brought upon the theory of a defective consumer product. For example, Oregon cuts off a manufacturer's liability for a defective vehicle after eight years with only limited exception.[58] Victims generally have been unsuccessful in claiming that statutes of repose deny them equal protection of the law if their claim is barred at any time within the useful life of the product.[59]

WHAT ARE DAMAGES?

The word *damage* is often used to mean the loss caused by an injury. Perhaps just as often it is used to mean the injury itself (to a person, his or her property or rights). In the law, however, the plural word *damages* means the money awarded by a court to a plaintiff in a civil action for loss and/or injury caused by a defendant's wrongful conduct. Damages may be awarded for a breach of contract, in order to put the plaintiff in the position he or she would have been in had the contract been performed as promised (see Chapter 8). They may also be awarded to a plaintiff because of a tort; for example, an injury suffered in an accident caused by the defendant's negligence. The money received reimburses the plaintiff for medical bills (of doctors and hospital), property loss (a "totaled" car), lost wages, and/or future "lost" income that cannot be earned because of the plaintiff's injuries. Damages also are designed to compensate for physical impairment (e.g., spinal injury or broken arm), mental anguish, and/or pain and suffering (both present and prospective, because they are expected to continue into the indefinite future).

COMPENSATORY DAMAGES

Compensatory damages are also called *actual damages* because they consist of money awarded to the plaintiff for real (i.e., actual) loss or injury.

If two or more tortfeasors are responsible for a given injury, each is fully liable to pay the entire amount of any judgment, but of course the plaintiff is entitled to only one full recovery. In most states, a tortfeasor who pays all or more than his or her share of the damages is entitled to contribution or partial reimbursement from the other wrongdoers. Compensatory damages may consist of two types of compensatory damages, special (or economic) and general.

Special or Economic Damages

Special damages are often called *economic damages* or *out-of-pocket costs* because they can be specified and precisely measured in terms of money. Common examples are the cost of a hospital stay, income lost because of absence from work, and the cost of repairing a car that was rear-ended. In awarding special damages for anticipated future losses, a jury may award the present value of such future sums, using an appropriate discount interest rate. The plaintiff gets a sum of money that, if invested at the selected interest (discount) rate, will grow over the years to precisely the amount that had been determined to be the total future monetary loss. Since World War II, inflation has caused a continuing decline in the purchasing power of the dollar. This fact of life may also be taken into consideration in calculating future expenses resulting from the injury. Special damages are the actual result of the particular loss or injury; they flow from it naturally and proximately because of the unique combination of circumstances in any given case.

General Damages

General damages, the second kind of compensatory damages, are also the actual and proximate result of the particular loss or injury. General damages compensate victims for other than out-of-pocket monetary losses suffered. Prime examples include compensation for pain and suffering and compensation for mental distress caused by physical injuries.

LEGAL FOCUS—PROBLEM

Annette Blenker, thirty-seven, was shopping at Berry's Market when a six-pack of long-necked beer bottles fell on her foot—she was wearing socks and sandals. Two months later she contacted Berry's and complained of her injury. She then sued for $2.5 million.

compensatory damages

Amount awarded by a court to make good or replace the actual loss suffered by a plaintiff.

special damages

Amount awarded by a court to pay for monetary out-of-pocket losses resulting from the specific or special circumstances of the plaintiff (e.g., for medical expenses, loss of wages, and destruction of property).

general damages

Amount awarded by a court to pay the plaintiff for nonmonetary losses (e.g., pain and suffering) that resulted from an injury, without reference to any special circumstances of the plaintiff.

> According to her claim, Annette suffers from a rare nerve disorder that leaves her in constant pain. She walks on crutches, takes painkillers, and has trouble sleeping. Her doctors report that she is likely to suffer from RSD (reflexive sympathetic dystrophy) for the rest of her life. She consulted eleven different doctors, including podiatrists, neurologists, anesthesiologists, an orthopedic surgeon, and a psychiatrist. What is the proper amount of damages?[60]

The jury returned a verdict to Blenker of $388,000 for past and future economic damages and $87,000 for her pain and suffering. Jurors found no negligence in stacking the beer, but found that the store employees failed to preserve an in-house videotape of the incident and that the store neglected to have a written policy on how to handle injured customers. The owner of Berry's Market was "shocked" at the verdict and cites it as an example of "lawsuit abuse" and the need for "tort reform." His expert witness testified that Blenker's pain may be psychosomatic (bodily symptoms caused by mental or emotional disturbance).

In certain cases, a plaintiff may recover special and general damages for personal loss suffered as the result of harm done by the defendant to a third party, such as a spouse or child. For example, a spouse may recover for loss of **consortium** with the injured or deceased mate. *Consortium* includes companionship, affection, and sexual relations. Damages for consortium have not been recoverable by unmarried persons, regardless of the intimacy or duration of the relationship.

In early common law, if a victim died because of someone's tortious conduct, the death terminated all claims for damages. Today, however, **wrongful-death statutes** compensate immediate dependent relatives for loss of companionship and financial support resulting from the death. The award may be as high as millions of dollars, such as when the victim is a highly paid executive who leaves a surviving dependent spouse and children. On the other hand, the death of a single person with no children or other dependents could result in no cause of action. However, some states have **survivor statutes** that provide that a decedent's cause of action survives the death. It is owned by the decedent's estate, rather than by the surviving dependents (if any). Damages recovered by the estate are then distributed in accordance with the decedent's last will or by intestate distribution (see Chapter 14).

PUNITIVE DAMAGES

In certain cases, the civil law resembles the criminal law in sanctions imposed. It punishes especially blameworthy wrongdoers who intentionally hurt other persons. It does this by awarding **punitive damages** (also called *exemplary damages*) to the victim, in addition to compensatory damages. The purpose is not to enrich the plaintiff, who has already been fully compensated for his or her loss or injury; rather, the purpose is to punish and make an example in order to deter the wrongdoer and others from a repetition of the offense.

Punitive damages are not awarded in breach-of-contract cases, unless they involve an intentional tort by the defendant, such as fraud or bad faith. They are awarded "where the wrong done . . . was aggravated by circumstances of violence, oppression, malice, fraud, or wanton and wicked conduct . . . and are intended to solace the plaintiff for mental anguish, laceration of his feelings, shame, degradation, or other aggravations of the original wrong, or else to punish the defendant for his evil behavior, or to make an example of him."[61]

Generally, punitive damages are available in cases of intentional tort, such as assault and battery, defamation, and fraud. They may also be awarded (1) in product-liability cases, but only those in which the defendant acted despicably with willful and conscious disregard of the rights and safety of others; (2) in premises-liability cases, in which a tenant of an apartment building is the victim of criminal attack when the landlord knew of

---

consortium

The reciprocal legal right of companionship, cooperation, aid, affection, and sexual relations of each spouse from and to the other.

wrongful-death statutes

A law allowing the heirs of a deceased person to sue whoever caused the decedent's death, and to collect any court-awarded damages. The damage sued for is the damage to the heirs for the loss of the loved one's life.

survivor statutes

Law allowing a lawsuit even after the death of the victim perhaps permitting recovery for damages to the victim.

punitive damages

Amount awarded by a court, to the victim of an intentional tort, in addition to compensatory damages; designed to punish the tortfeasor and serve as an example to others.

the danger of such attacks yet failed to take corrective action (e.g., by excluding unauthorized persons or preventing their access); and (3) in cases in which the defendant consumes alcohol to the point of intoxication when he or she plans to later operate a motor vehicle, and thereby harms another.[62]

Punitive damages have been likened to fines imposed on convicted criminals. But critics point out that fines are always paid to the state, and thus benefit all of society. By the same logic, they say, punitive damages should be paid to the state, for the benefit of all. At the time of this writing, a number of states take a portion of punitive damages awarded in civil cases.* Constitutional challenges to this scheme have been upheld by the U.S. Supreme Court.[63] Most states, however, do not take any portion of the civil recovery. In a case involving a gold scam in Texas, the trial court judge approved an award of $75 million in compensatory damages and $100 million in punitive damages to the three victims. Although affirming the result on appeal, one justice of the Texas Supreme Court made the following observation:

> I write separately to recommend that the Legislature enact a law apportioning one-half of punitive damage awards to the State. Presently, plaintiffs receive the entire award of punitive damages in Texas. For example, in this case three plaintiffs will share $100 million in punitive damages even though they were fully compensated for their injuries when the trial court awarded them more than $31 million in actual damages and $43 million in attorneys fees. Yet, the primary purposes for awarding punitive damages are to punish a defendant for reprehensible behavior and to deter similar conduct in the future. [citations] Also, punitive damages are generally awarded in situations in which the defendant's conduct has damaged society as a whole as well as the individual plaintiff. [citations] Thus the goal in awarding punitive damages is not to compensate the victim. Actual damages perform that function. Nevertheless, our law creates a windfall for plaintiffs by allowing them to recover the entire award of punitive damages. I question whether this is a wise public policy.[64]

LEGAL FOCUS—EXAMPLE

Municipalities often raise capital to build public improvements by issuing (selling) bonds to investors. These bonds create debts for the municipality; investors are the creditors. Monthly interest is paid to the investors as their bonds are repaid. Banks, acting as trustees, offer the administrative service of receiving monthly bond payments and then distributing them to the rightful bond owners. Over the years some payments on bonds are unclaimed by bond owners. Patrick Stull, manager of the corporate trust department for Bank of America, noticed that unclaimed bond payments were being taken by the bank instead of being returned to the municipalities. In 1995, after being discharged, Stull filed a "whistleblower" lawsuit alleging that his discharge was retaliatory. "Whistleblower" laws protect employees who "blow the whistle" on fraudulent or illegal activities. Stull was joined by defrauded bond issuers and the City of San Francisco who filed suit against Bank of America. The key issue in the case was whether or not Bank of America deliberately siphoned off the cash or simply could not keep its bookkeeping straight. Facing this issue, Bank of America, denying any wrongdoing other than poor

* For example, Florida, Georgia, Illinois, Iowa, Missouri, New York, Oregon, and Utah take a portion of punitive damage awards.

⋮ bookkeeping practices, settled the case by payment of $187.5 million to the various
⋮ plaintiffs. What role did punitive damages play in this settlement?

If a jury had believed that Bank of America, with its sophisticated computer systems and accounting staff, could not have made such an obvious and huge error, and therefore the bank was deliberately stealing money, it may have awarded punitive damages in an astronomical amount. The threat of punitive damages often influences the decision to settle.[65] Generally, punitive damages may not be awarded in the absence of compensatory damages.

Judges or juries determine the proper amount of punitive damages by considering the nature and gravity of the offense as well as the defendant's ability to pay and the amount of compensatory damages awarded. Damage awards that are grossly inflated as a result of prejudice against large corporations, or passion, are typically substantially reduced or even rejected on appeal.

LEGAL FOCUS—PROBLEM

⋮ In a widely publicized case in 1989, a Los Angeles jury awarded the male lover of actor
⋮ Rock Hudson $14.5 million in compensatory damages and $7.25 million in punitive
⋮ damages, in an action against the estate of the deceased star. The jury found that Hud-
⋮ son, who died of AIDS, was guilty of conspiring with his personal secretary to keep the
⋮ fatal affliction secret so that the plaintiff would continue his sexual relationship with the
⋮ movie star. Is an award of damages justified?

Yes. However, the trial judge reduced the compensatory damages to $5 million and the punitive damages to $500,000, saying he would order a new trial on damages if the plaintiff refused to accept the reductions.[66]

NOMINAL DAMAGES

nominal damages

Insignificant amount (such as $1) awarded by a court when the defendant has violated the rights of the plaintiff but no monetary loss has been suffered or can be proved.

A victim who has suffered no actual loss or injury may recover **nominal damages** (usually $1). The awarding of nominal damages recognizes a technical injury when there is no actual loss by the plaintiff. An example might be a "Peeping Tom" whose gaze caused no monetary loss to the plaintiff. Ordinarily if there is not harm there is no tort, but if the conduct is particularly wrongful the victim's recovery of nominal damages will support an added award of punitive damages.

W HAT BARRIERS CAN PREVENT COLLECTION OF DAMAGES?

A person with a good cause of action may fail recovery if (1) litigation is not commenced promptly, and thus the victim is barred from suing by an applicable statute of limitations or (2) a judgment is obtained from a judgment-proof defendant.

STATUTES OF LIMITATION

Statutes of limitation "wipe the slate clean" for a wrongdoer after specified periods of time have elapsed without the filing of a lawsuit by the victim. These statutes specify the period of time during which the victim must formally initiate an action for legal relief, or, in the case of a crime, during which the government must prosecute the accused. (Chapter 6 more fully discusses statutes of limitations for crimes.)

It is strategically counterproductive and ethically questionable to keep a potential civil lawsuit or criminal indictment hovering over a wrongdoer indefinitely. It discourages personal reform and tends to limit the individual's peace of mind as well as his or her social and economic productivity.

Statutes of limitation are designed to prescribe reasonable periods of time during which civil claims for damages may be filed. Normally, persons become aware of the breach or injury within the specified time and are expected to sue for damages within that time. With the passage of time, evidence is lost, memories fade, witnesses move away or die, and it becomes very difficult, if not impossible, for a court to determine "the whole truth."

In most jurisdictions, an action to recover damages for a tort injury must be commenced within one year from the date of commission of the negligent tort. The period is generally the same for intentional torts, except for fraud. The defrauded victim may not even be aware of the injury until much later, and so the time limit is usually three years from time of discovery of the fraud. Generally, in medical and legal malpractice actions the statutory time does not begin to run until the plaintiff becomes aware of the injury suffered. Statutes of limitation are tolled and "the clock stops" while the defendant is out of the jurisdiction and during a plaintiff's minority. Recall the earlier discussion of statutes of repose: Even though repose statutes are usually for a longer period of time, they begin to run as soon as the negligence occurs and thus they will often terminate a right to sue earlier than a shorter statute of limitations will.

In certain types of cases, the doctrine of strict liability effectively supersedes traditional statutes of limitation, allowing a suit for damages many years after the allegedly defective product was sold. This is permitted even if the product, when sold, had been manufactured conscientiously and was of acceptable quality as measured by the state of the art at the time. Because lawsuits are now being filed under principles of strict liability well beyond the statutory periods of limitation, substantial damages awarded to plaintiffs have been affecting the price and availability of domestic products. There is a considerable political movement favoring "tort reform" that focuses upon elimination of stale cases, punitive damage limitations, and other issues.

It is noteworthy that the statutory time limit for breach of contract (see Chapter 8) is typically two years for oral contracts and four years for written contracts and credit accounts. With crimes (see Chapter 6), the statutory periods of limitation reflect the gravity of the offenses. For felonies, three years from the date of commission is typical; for misdemeanors, one year. For murder, there is no time limit.

JUDGMENT-PROOF DEFENDANTS

Another barrier to collection of damages is that, even if found liable, the defendant may be **judgment-proof,** i.e., without sufficient liability insurance (if any) or other resources to pay. However, under state laws a judgment survives for years, perhaps ten on average, and may be renewed or extended for a like period. Meanwhile, the judgment continues to

judgment-proof

Financial condition of a person who lacks the assets to pay any judgment rendered against him or her.

grow from the effect of accruing interest, typically at 10 percent. Earnings made and other assets acquired by the debtor (e.g., through gifts or by inheritance) during the life of the judgment may be levied on by the unsatisfied judgment creditor. A *levy* is a process whereby a court official confiscates assets of a judgment debtor to satisfy the judgment. The creditor must first locate the debtor and identify the property to be confiscated—an easier task now that computer-assisted asset-search services are readily available. Nonetheless, socially irresponsible debtors often "skip," sometimes leaving the city, state, or country and providing no forwarding address. The difficulty the FBI has in tracking down "most wanted" criminals suggests the cost and practical impossibility of locating and collecting money from a determined "skip." Thus, winning a money judgment in court is not an assurance the winner will collect.

C A S E

Randi W. v. Muroc Joint Unified School District

14 Cal.4th 1071, 60 Cal.Rptr.2d 263 (1997)

Robert Gadams sought assistance from his placement office at Fresno Pacific College, where he had received his teaching credential. Former employers were asked to provide references.

One former employer, Mendota School District, provided a letter of recommendation prepared by an official, Gilbert Rosette. Rosette's recommendation to Fresno Pacific College's placement office noted Gadams's "genuine concern" for students and his "outstanding rapport" with everyone, and concluded "I wouldn't hesitate to recommend Mr. Gadams for any position." Rosette allegedly knew, but did not mention, Gadams's history of improper contacts with female students. The contacts included hugging some female junior high school students, giving them back massages, making "sexual remarks" to them, and being involved in "sexual situations" with them.

Another former employer, Tranquility High School District, provided a letter of recommendation prepared by an official there, Richard Cole. Cole's recommendation to Fresno Pacific College's placement office was positive, but he did not mention information he allegedly possessed about Gadams while he was employed at Golden Plains Unified School District. Specifically, Cole knew that Gadams had been the subject of various parents' complaints, including charges that he "led a panty raid, made sexual overtures to students, sexual remarks to students. . . ." Nonetheless, Cole recommended Gadams for "almost any administrative position that he wishes to pursue."

Yet another former employer, Muroc Unified School District, provided a letter of recommendation prepared by an official there, David Malcolm. Malcolm's recommendation to Fresno Pacific College's placement office was positive. Malcolm described Gadams as an "upbeat, enthusiastic administrator who relates well to the students" and recommended him for "an assistant principalship . . . without reservation." Malcolm allegedly knew that during Gadams's employment, disciplinary actions were taken against him for "sexual touching" of female students that caused him to resign.

Robert Gadams then was hired by Livingston Union School District as vice principal. Randi W., thirteen, a student at Livingston Middle School, was in Gadams's office when he offensively "touched, molested, and engaged in sexual touching" of her.

Randi W. brought suit against the school districts that recommended Gadams for employment on the theory, among others,

that they were negligent for failing to disclose negative background information in their letters of recommendation to the placement office that provided them to her school's district.

The trial court dismissed the negligence aspect of Randi's action on the basis that the recommending school districts did not owe any duty to protect Randi because their recommendations were made only to a placement office.

Associate Justice Chin delivered the opinion of the court: . . . [N]o California case has yet held that one who intentionally or negligently provides false information to another owes a duty of care *to a third person* who did not receive the information and who has no special relationship with the provider. . . .

Although the chain of causation leading from defendants' statements and omissions to Gadams's alleged assault on plaintiff is somewhat attenuated, we think the assault was reasonably foreseeable. . . . [D]efendants could foresee that Livingston's officers would read and rely on defendants' letters in deciding to hire Gadams. Likewise, defendants could foresee that, had they not unqualifiedly recommended Gadams, Livingston would not have hired him. And finally, defendants could foresee that Gadams, after being hired by Livingston, might molest or injure a Livingston student such as [Randi W.]. . . .

As for public policy, the law certainly recognizes a *policy of preventing future harm* of the kind alleged here. One of society's highest priorities is to protect children from sexual or physical abuse. [citations] Defendants urge that *competing social or economic policies* may disfavor the imposition of liability for misrepresentation or nondisclosure in employment references. They observe that a rule imposing liability in these situations could greatly inhibit the preparation and distribution of reference letters, to the general detriment of employers and employees alike. We have recently stated that "when deciding whether to expand a tort duty of care, courts must consider the potential social and economic consequences." [citations] Defendants argue that a rule imposing tort liability on writers of recommendation letters could have one very predictable consequence: employers would seldom write such letters, even in praise of exceptionally qualified employees. In defendants' view, . . . an employer would be better advised . . . merely to confirm the former employee's position, salary, and dates of employment.

In response, plaintiff asserts it is unlikely that employers will decline to write reference letters for fear of tort liability, at least in situations involving no foreseeable risks of physical injury to someone.

. . . [W]e hold . . . that that the writer of a letter of recommendation owes to third persons a duty not to misrepresent the facts in describing the qualifications and character of a former employee, if making these misrepresentations would present a substantial, foreseeable risk of physical injury to the third persons.

Note: The case was returned to the Superior Court for trial by jury. The decision of the justices was split 4–3 on other issues in the case, but all agreed upon the portion quoted above in which new tort law was created.

For Critical Analysis

1. Suppose an employer knew that an ex-employee had an arrest record of assault and battery that grew from a bar fight. Must the employer reveal that information every time a prospective employer asks for references? Or must only sexual offenses be reported? Would the complete withholding of such information violate the duty "not to misrepresent the facts"? Isn't failure to reveal some fact as damaging as misrepresenting it?

2. Would the former employers in the Randi W. case have escaped liability if they had reported only the dates of Robert Gadams's employment? Or, to escape liability, must they reveal whatever sordid details they possess to future employers? What if the information the former employers passed on was only rumor and unsubstantiated reports—could Gadams sue them for libel?

3. If the former employers reported the unsubstantiated information they possessed to all future prospective employers of Gadams, whether schools or any other businesses, would anybody employ him? Is it fair to warn only prospective employers who ask for references, and not others who accept prospective employees at their word? If your answer is "no," would you recommend publishing the names of such persons in some database available to all future employers? ■

DEBRA AGIS ET AL. V. HOWARD JOHNSON CO. ET AL.

371 Mass. 140, 355 N.E.2d 315 (1975)

Debra Agis, a waitress, sought to recover damages for mental anguish and emotional distress from her employer and the manager of the Ground Round (a Howard Johnson Restaurant). On May 23, 1975, Agis's manager had called the waitresses of the restaurant together and informed them that "there was some stealing going on," but that the identity of the person or persons responsible was not known, and that until the person or persons responsible were discovered, he would begin firing all the present waitresses in alphabetical order, starting with the letter "A." He then fired Debra Agis.

Agis filed a complaint stating that as a result of the manager's action she suffered emotional distress, mental anguish, and loss of wages and earnings. Her husband, James Agis, also brought suit for loss of the services, love, affection, and companionship of his wife.

The defendants moved to dismiss the complaint, alleging that even if everything the plaintiffs alleged were true, no action can be brought for emotional distress unless actual physical injury occurs.

The Superior Court agreed with the defendants and dismissed the complaint. The plaintiffs appealed.

Justice Quirico delivered the opinion of the court: This case raises the issue whether a cause of action exists in this Commonwealth for the intentional or reckless infliction of severe emotional distress without resulting bodily injury. Counts 1 and 2 of this action were brought by the plaintiff Debra Agis against the Howard Johnson Company and Roger Dionne, manager of the restaurant in which she was employed, to recover damages for mental anguish and emotional distress allegedly caused by her summary dismissal from such employment. Counts 3 and 4 were brought by her husband, James Agis, against both defendants for loss of the services, love, affection, and companionship of his wife. This case is before us on the plaintiffs' appeal from the dismissal of their complaint.

The complaint alleges that, as a result of this incident, Mrs. Agis became greatly upset, began to cry, sustained emotional distress, mental anguish, and loss of wages and earnings. It further alleges that the actions of the defendants were reckless, extreme, outrageous, and intended to cause emotional distress and anguish. In addition, the complaint states that the defendants knew or should have known that their actions would cause such distress.

The defendants moved to dismiss the complaint on the ground that, even if true, the plaintiff's allegations fail to state a claim upon which relief can be granted because damages for emotional distress are not compensable absent resulting physical injury. The judge allowed the motion, and the plaintiffs appealed.

Our discussion of whether a cause of action exists for the intentional or reckless infliction of severe emotional distress without resulting bodily injury starts with our decision in *George v. Jordan Marsh Co.* (1971). While in that case we found it unnecessary to address the precise question raised here, we did summarize the history of actions for emotional distress and concluded that the law of the Commonwealth should be, and is, "that one who, without a privilege to do so, by extreme and outrageous conduct intentionally causes severe emotional distress to another, with bodily harm resulting from such distress, is subject to liability. . . ." The question whether such liability should be extended to cases in which there is no resulting bodily injury was "left until it arises," ibid., and that question has arisen here.

In the *George* case, we discussed in depth the policy considerations underlying the recognition of a cause of action for intentional infliction of severe emotional distress with resulting physical injury, and we concluded that the difficulties presented in allowing such an action were outweighed by the unfair and illogical consequences of the denial of recognition of such an independent tort. In so doing, we examined the persuasive authority then recognizing such a cause of action, and we placed considerable reliance on the Restatement (Second) of Torts § 46 (1965). Our examination of the policies underlying the extension of that cause of action to cases where there has been no bodily injury, and our review of the judicial precedent and the Restatement in this regard, lead us to conclude that such extension is both warranted and desirable.

The most often cited argument for refusing to extend the cause of action for intentional or reckless infliction of emotional distress to cases where there has been no physical injury is the difficulty of proof and the danger of fraudulent or frivolous claims. There has been a concern that "mental anguish, standing alone, is too subtle and speculative to be measured by any known legal standard," that "mental anguish and its consequences are so intangible and peculiar and vary so much with the individual that they cannot reasonably be anticipated," that a wide door might "be opened not only to fictitious claims but to litigation over trivialities and mere bad manners as well," and that there can be no objective measurement of the extent or the existence of emotional distress. There is a fear that "[i]t is easy to assert a claim of mental anguish and very hard to disprove it."

While we are not unconcerned with these problems, we believe that "the problems presented are not . . . insuperable" and that "administrative difficulties do not justify the denial of relief for serious invasions of mental and emotional tranquility. . . . That some claims may be spurious should not compel those who administer justice to shut their eyes to serious wrongs and let them go without being brought to account. It is the function of courts and juries to determine whether claims are valid or false. This responsibility should not be shunned merely because the task may be difficult to perform."

Furthermore, the distinction between the difficulty which juries may encounter in determining liability and assessing damages where no physical injury occurs and their performance of that same task where there has been resulting physical harm may be greatly overstated. "The jury is ordinarily in a better position . . . to determine whether outrageous conduct results in mental distress than whether that distress in turn results in physical injury. From their own experience jurors are aware of the extent and character of the disagreeable emotions that may result from the defendant's conduct, but a difficult medical question is presented when it must be determined if emotional distress resulted in physical injury. Greater proof that mental suffering occurred is found in the defendant's conduct designed to bring it about than in physical injury that may or may not have resulted therefrom." We are thus unwilling to deny the existence of this cause of action merely because there may be difficulties of proof. Instead, we believe "the door to recovery should be opened but narrowly and with due caution."

In light of what we have said, we hold that one who, by extreme and outrageous conduct and without privilege, causes severe emotional distress to another is subject to liability for such emotional distress even though no bodily harm may result. However, in order for a plaintiff to prevail in a case for liability under this tort, four elements must be established. It must be shown (1) that the actor intended to inflict emotional distress or that he knew or should have known that emotional distress was the likely result of his conduct; (2) that the conduct was "extreme and outrageous," was "beyond all possible bounds of decency" and was "utterly intolerable in a civilized community;" (3) that the actions of the defendant were the cause of the plaintiff's distress; and (4) that the emotional distress sustained by the plaintiff was "severe" and of a nature "that no reasonable man could be expected to endure it." These requirements are "aimed at limiting frivolous suits and avoiding litigation in situations where only bad manners and mere hurt feelings are involved," and we believe they are a "realistic safeguard against false claims...."

Testing the plaintiff Debra Agis's complaint by the rules stated above, we hold that she makes out a cause of action and that her complaint is therefore legally sufficient. While many of her allegations are not particularly well stated, we believe that the "[p]laintiff has alleged facts and circumstances which reasonably could lead the trier of fact to conclude that defendant's conduct was extreme and outrageous, having a severe and traumatic effect upon plaintiff's emotional tranquility." Because reasonable men could differ on these issues, we believe that "it is for the jury, subject to the control of the court," to determine whether there should be liability in this case. While the judge was not in error in dismissing the complaint under the then state of the law, we believe that, in light of what we have said, the judgment must be reversed and the plaintiff Debra Agis must be given an opportunity to prove the allegations which she has made.

Counts 3 and 4 of the complaint are brought by James Agis seeking relief for loss of consortium as a result of the mental distress and anguish suffered by his wife Debra. There is no question that an action for loss of consortium by either spouse may be maintained in this Commonwealth where such loss is shown to arise from personal injury to one spouse caused by the negligence of a third person. The question before us is whether an action for loss of consortium may be maintained where the acts complained of are intentional, and where the injuries to the spouse are emotional rather than physical.

Traditionally, where the right to sue for loss of consortium has been recognized, intentional invasions of the marriage relationship such as alienation of affections or adultery have been held to give rise to this cause of action. We see no reason not to apply the same rule to the tort of intentional or reckless infliction of severe emotional distress. Similarly, the fact that there is no physical injury should not bar the plaintiff's claim. In [a previous] case, we hinted that "psychological injury" could provide the basis for a consortium action. In addition, the underlying purpose of such an action is to compensate for the loss of the companionship, affection, and sexual enjoyment of one's spouse, and it is clear that these can be lost as a result of psychological or emotional injury as well as from actual physical harm.

Accordingly, we hold that, where a person has a cause of action for intentional or reckless infliction of severe emotional distress, his or her spouse also has a cause of action for loss of consortium arising out of that distress.

The judgment entered in the Superior Court dismissing the plaintiffs' complaint is reversed.

For Critical Analysis

1. Debra Agis was fired because her last name began with the first letter in the alphabet. She was not accused of being a thief. This event was held to be sufficiently outrageous conduct to justify an action for damages, punitive damages (as an intentional tort), and for loss of consortium by her husband. Would a racial epithet be as outrageous? What about a disparaging remark about one's weight? Or skin complexion?

2. Under the *Agis* case, are all chain restaurants liable for damages each time their managers, who are distant from company headquarters, say or do something that upsets an employee? What limitations upon this liability can you identify in the *Agis* case? What limitations would you impose as judge? Employers are liable for the wrongful acts of their employees that are done in the course and scope of their employment. Are franchise restaurants "employees" of the franchising company, or are they "independent contractors" for whom no liability is incurred? ■

CHAPTER QUESTIONS AND PROBLEMS

1. Sarah Gramling, an expert in the use of explosives, obtained a city permit to level a ten-story building in the center of town by implosion. The explosives were carefully placed throughout the structure so that it would collapse inwardly and leave a heap of rubble on the site. Unfortunately, for unknown reasons, one charge on the third floor caused fragments of brick, concrete, and glass to fly outward. As a result, extensive and costly damage was done to plate glass in nearby buildings and to parked automobiles in the vicinity. There were also personal injuries. Is Gramling liable, even though she acted with a city permit and there was no evidence or claim of negligence?

2. Assume a jury rules that John Forsyth was driving negligently and caused an automobile crash that injured the plaintiff.
   a. Does moral fault attach to Forsyth?
   b. Would your answer above be different if John were uninsured and unable to pay the judgment? If your answer is yes, what is the fault, driving negligently or being uninsured?
   c. Assuming Forsyth had adequate insurance, what consequences does he personally suffer as a result of his negligence? Does the accident go into his permanent employment records? Into a national database of negligent drivers? Or can he conceal it in all of his future personal transactions?
   d. Can society reasonably expect Forsyth to become a more careful and accident-free driver following his first accident?
   e. Is the law of negligence more about social policy or more about providing for compensation to injured persons?

3. Nick Dekker went into the Black Oak Restaurant for dinner. When leaving, he mistakenly took George Walton's hat from the coat rack and walked out the door. Walton observed the incident, ran outside, and yelled "Stop thief!" just as Dekker was driving out of the parking lot. Walton jumped into his own car and gave pursuit. He overtook a car driven by a man who looked like Dekker, although it was really Ferdinand Sinzant. Walton pulled alongside and forced Sinzant onto the shoulder of the road by easing his car along the front left side of Sinzant's car. When the cars stopped, Walton leaped out and smashed Sinzant in the mouth, knocking him unconscious. He put Sinzant into his car and drove back to the restaurant, where he phoned the police. When the squad car arrived, Sinzant regained consciousness, and Walton said, "Arrest this man, he's a thief!" The police refused to make the arrest because they had not observed any crime. However, they advised Walton that if he made a citizen's arrest, they would book Sinzant. Walton thereupon placed Sinzant under arrest. Meanwhile, Harry Hightower was injured when his car ran into, and badly damaged, the left rear of Sinzant's car, which was protruding slightly into the street with its lights out. At the time of the accident, Hightower was under the influence of marijuana. What torts have occurred?

4. During a wild party on the Fourth of July, Harry Hammer went outside and fired his 9mm pistol several times into the dark Los Angeles sky. Unfortunately, unlike the fabled arrow shot into the sky, Hammer's bullet descended, hitting and penetrating Penelope Marsh's head and causing her modest but permanent injuries. Following the incident, Marsh lacked enthusiasm, complained of headaches, and was easily frightened by loud noises. Hammer had homeowner's liability insurance that would cover his negligent acts, and a good, permanent job paying him $8,000 a month. Would Hammer's insurance policy pay for Marsh's injuries? Could Marsh obtain punitive damages from Hammer?

5. Vera Babbitt, a mischievous prankster, called and told her friend Michelle Fleischer that her fiance Gary Dunn was in a booth at the Hardball Sports Bar making out with an old girlfriend. Before Babbitt could explain her message was a joke, Fleischer slammed down the telephone, jumped into her RV, and sped off to catch Dunn in the act. Unfortunately, Fleischer cut off another driver and caused an accident, seriously injuring Billie Bellweather. What tort liabilities have arisen and against whom?

6. Harriet Robicheaux made a batch of brownies and donated them to the Girl Scouts to be sold as part of a fund raiser. Unfortunately, several purchasers of the brownies became ill and died. Does the product-liability rule establish that Robicheaux is strictly liable for all injuries caused by the brownies?

7. Assume that a state enacted the following statute: "There shall be no recovery of damages based upon the commission of ordinary negligence." What ramifications can you think of that might flow from this statute?

8. Johnson entered the defendant's store carrying her small child in an infant seat. When she tried to leave the store, she was stopped in a public place by a security officer who said that another employee had reported seeing her steal the infant seat. To show ownership, Johnson pointed to cat hair, food crumbs, and stains on the seat. After a twenty-minute delay, the security officer apologized to the defendant and permitted her to leave. The trial court dismissed her action for false imprisonment, and Johnson appealed. Did the defendant have probable cause to detain Johnson, and was the twenty-minute detention of Johnson reasonable in these circumstances? [*Johnson v. K-Mart Enterprises, Inc.*, 98 Wis.2d 533, 297 N.W.2d 74 (Wisconsin, 1980).]

9. Peter Wallis, a real estate broker, contends that before having sex, his girlfriend Kellie Clarke represented that she would use birth-control pills. But Clarke purposefully got pregnant, according to Wallis. He is suing Clarke for fraud and for conversion (civil theft) for wrongfully acquiring and misusing his sperm. Clarke contends that she was using birth-control pills and that his sperm given during sexual intercourse was not stolen or misused and should be considered a "gift" in the law. Clarke refused to obtain an abortion, moved out of their apartment, and gave birth to their daughter, Taylor. Has Clarke converted Wallis's sperm? Assuming that Wallis is correct in his contentions, what legal damages has he sustained?

10. The Carters traveled to a concert at the Birmingham Civic Center and checked into the Birmingham Civic Center Travelodge. That afternoon, they purchased fast food and went back to their room to eat, relax, and enjoy a romantic interlude away from home. The wall on one side of the room was covered by a mirror. Concerned about noises (not theirs) while they were enjoying the room, the Carters investigated and discovered a large hole in the wall behind the mirror. It would be possible for someone to look into their room from the adjoining room. Without specific proof that anyone observed the Carters, could they recover for invasion of privacy? [*Carter v. Innisfree Hotel, Inc.,* 661 So.2d 1174 (Ala.,1995).]

11. Wanda Birdsong went shopping at the Hopkinsville, Kentucky, Wal-Mart. She bought some items and began to exit the store along with several other customers. A theft control device set off a sensor alarm. A Wal-Mart employee asked all the customers to re-enter the store and, after inspecting their bags, she asked them to walk through the sensor alarm one at a time. The only one who triggered the sensor alarm a second time was Birdsong. After a second search Birdsong was asked to pass through the alarm a third time. Again the alarm was activated. Birdsong claims that the Wal-Mart employee then told her to sit down and stay at an area near the front door entrance where a shopping cart was placed to block her from leaving. A supervisor then determined that Birdsong's purse was tripping the alarm, whereupon Birdsong volunteered to let them search the purse. The Wal-Mart employees declined, saying they were not allowed to do so. Birdsong claims she was detained another fifteen minutes until the store manager arrived and told her she was free to go. Birdsong claims that she was detained a total of forty-five minutes and that she was humiliated by her placement at the front of store. Wal-Mart claims her detention lasted no more than thirty minutes and was reasonably conducted. Would the shopkeeper's privilege protect Wal-Mart from Birdsong's false imprisonment and intentional infliction of emotional distress lawsuit? [*Birdsong v. Wal-Mart Stores, Inc.,* 74 S.W.3d 754 (Ky.App., 2001).]

12. Identify the tort that corresponds to each of the following crimes:
    a. Date rape
    b. Robbery
    c. Murder
    d. Manslaughter by vehicle
    e. Physical child abuse by a parent
    f. Burglary
    g. Shoplifting a dress
    h. Crawling over a backyard fence and peeping through a bedroom window
    i. Posting a naked picture of a former lover on the Internet
    j. Practicing medicine without a license

CHAPTER 8

Contracts: Enforceable Agreements

The modern mystics of muscle who offer you the fraudulent alternative of "human rights" versus "property rights," as if one could exist without the other, are making a last, grotesque attempt to revive the doctrine of soul versus body. Only a ghost can exist without material property; only a slave can work with no right to the product of his effort.

Ayn Rand, *Atlas Shrugged,* 1957.

After reading and studying this chapter, you should be able to:

- Define a contract and distinguish a contract from a tort, a crime, and a non-legally binding moral obligation.

- Appreciate the importance of legally binding obligations in the U.S. and world economy.

- Understand the importance of the Uniform Commercial Code in business transactions and especially Article 2 (sales), in commercial transactions.

- Identify and discuss the various elements necessary to form a contract, including competent parties, offer and acceptance, genuine assent, consideration, legality, and proper form.

- Discuss contract rights of parties in privity and third parties.

- Identify important issues involving performance of contract obligations, including satisfactory performance, substantial performance, breach, and discharge.

- Identify contract remedies including compensatory damages and equitable remedies.

- Identify selected consumer protection statutes and the social ills they are intended to protect consumers from.

- Identify express and implied warranties, including warranties of title, encumbrance, infringement, merchantability, and fitness for particular purpose. Appreciate the power and limitations of attempted exclusion of warranties.

The law of contracts reflects our social values (commitment), interests (consumerism), and expectations (keeping promises) every day. How do people in our society make promises or commitments that are legally binding? What excuse justifies breaking a legal commitment? Are there promises that are contrary to public policy and, therefore, void or invalid? If a promise violates the interests of society at large, will courts enforce it? If a child or an incompetent person makes a promise, will it be enforced? Answering these and other related questions is what contract law is about.

Through contracts, parties can create a greater degree of certainty as to the possible occurrence of future acts. The parties can create rights and duties upon which each might rely. Parties to contracts can also agree upon what are acceptable standards of conduct and how each party might be expected to behave relative to situations that may or may not occur.

LEGAL FOCUS—PROBLEM

Joseph Yonan needs 3,000 pumpkins for his inner-city pumpkin patch by late September to celebrate the Halloween season. He is acquainted with Paula Felps, a local farmer, who is interested in selling the pumpkins. How can Yonan increase the probability of getting the pumpkins he needs when he needs them at a price he can afford?

A contract entered into with Felps in July for a September delivery of those pumpkins will increase the likelihood that Yonan will have the pumpkins when and where he needs them and at a price he can afford. Felps, on the other hand, no longer must worry about selling her "ripe" pumpkins. If Felps fails to make delivery, Yonan will have rights against her to make good any loss because of her failure to perform. The parties can arrange by the contract who is responsible for delivery, the expected grade and condition of the pumpkins upon arrival, whether the sale is for credit or cash, and on and on.

Contract law allows parties to make enforceable promises. If you think about it, you will realize that many promises people make do not create legal obligations. Sometimes the promises create moral rahter than legal obligations. A moral obligation defines what you should do. Failure to perform a moral obligation, such as an agreement to give a friend a ride, does not usually create a legal liability. Sometimes promises create both a moral and a legal obligation (as when a friend promises to pay you for gas expenses to drive her to a neighboring city).

LEGAL FOCUS—PROBLEM

Rosalie Chu invited an acquaintance, Jonathan Kaplan, to a fund-raising dinner dance featuring the governor at the Pilothouse Restaurant on the Delta King in olde towne Sacramento. Kaplan accepted the offer and, eager to please Chu, spent $750 lavishly preparing for the evening. He got a haircut and purchased a new jacket, new shoes, and flowers. On the evening of the dance, Kaplan arrived at Chu's house and found out that she had gone out of town for the weekend. Kaplan is considering suing Chu for breach of contract to recover his expenses. Does he have a lawsuit?

Agreements to go on dates are not contracts; they are social arrangements. Although Chu may have breached a moral obligation, she is not required to pay Kaplan's expenses even though she did not keep the date.

One short, snappy definition of a **contract** is "an agreement that can be enforced in a court." The definition is accurate and easy to remember but not especially helpful. The authoritative *Restatement of Contracts** expands the definition of a contract to say it is "a promise or a set of promises for the breach of which the law gives a remedy, or the performance of which the law in some way recognizes as a duty."[1] Contracts are the intelligent response to the human need to get things done with the cooperation of other human beings. They reflect the fact that in our technologically advanced civilization, marked by specialization and division of labor, with individuals highly dependent on each other, "No man is an island, entire of itself."[2] The U.S. Constitution expressly provides that "no State shall . . . pass any . . . Law impairing the Obligation of Contracts."†

Ordinarily, a contract is made when two (and sometimes more than two) parties exchange binding promises. In a promise, each party declares that she or he will (or will not) take a specified action in the future.

If the contractual promise is not performed, the contract has been breached, and the party who failed to keep the promise must compensate the party to whom the promise was made. The non-performing party is usually required to pay money damages for failure to perform. In some situations, money damages cannot make the victim of the failure to perform "whole," and so a court of equity may require actual performance of the promised act. In either case, the law seeks to give the party the benefit of the promise that was made. Understandably, punitive damages are not awarded; there is no crime and no tort, and generally no moral stigma attaches to the breach of contract. When a contractual promise is breached, in the vast majority of cases the parties agree to some acceptable alternative without litigation and the payment of damages.

Most people keep promises because of a sense of duty. Furthermore, keeping their promises is usually in the self-interest of both parties. Often the **promisor** (the person making the promise) and the **promisee** (the person to whom the promise is made) are not aware of the rules of contract law. They may rely on the good faith—the honesty and fairness—of the other persons who are involved. In business situations, however, parties should follow the rules of contract law carefully to avoid potential misunderstandings and disputes.

contract
A legally enforceable agreement to do or not to do a specified thing.

promisor
The person who makes a contractual promise.

promisee
The person to whom a contractual promise has been made.

A N OVERVIEW OF THE PROMISES WE LIVE BY

Contracts are generally entered into privately, between private parties creating essentially private law. Government agencies—local and federal—are not directly involved unless the government is itself a party to the contract. Of course, this happens often in our time of big government. Collectively, government is the nation's biggest employer, always under contract. It is the biggest buyer of goods and services, all under contract. It is also true that government statutes and court decisions prescribe the rules for creation, performance, and enforcement of contracts.

THE EVER-PRESENT CONTRACT

Contracts are legally binding links between producers and consumers throughout the world. They are the promises that are exchanged (and generally faithfully kept) to do the

---

* A Restatement is a treatise on law written and periodically reviewed by legal scholars. See Appendix D for further explanation.

† U.S. Constitution, Art. I, § 10. In the famous Dartmouth College case, the first Chief Justice of the U.S. Supreme Court, John Marshall, held that a charter of incorporation granted by King George III to Dartmouth College in 1769, which gave its trustees the right to govern the college forever, was indeed a contract. As such, it could not be rescinded, as was attempted by the New Hampshire state legislature, which had voted to transfer control of the college to a new board of overseers. *Dartmouth College v. Woodward*, 4 Wheaton 518 (1819).

many things that get the world's work done. Literally billions of contracts are made and performed every day, often facilitated by the use of a common medium of exchange (money or credit).

Consider some ramifications of contracts in operation. Many millions of workers are employed under oral or written contracts. They work under contracts at every stage of production and distribution of goods and services. Each person contributes to the total effort that provides all of us with food, clothing, shelter, transportation, utilities, and entertainment. The seemingly limitless range of human needs and wants are thereby met through the fulfillment of contracts. The vast and incredibly complex public infrastructure of roads, highways, airports, harbors, schools, museums, fire and police departments, and sewage and refuse treatment and disposal systems has been constructed and is maintained by means of contracts. With relatively few exceptions, these binding agreements are performed without litigation. Were any substantial fraction of all contracts disputed, the country's court system would be overwhelmed and rendered inoperative. This is a tribute to the fundamental integrity and intelligence of most people. The widespread use of standardized contracts, common trade practices, and the uniformity and repetitiveness of most business dealings, of course, also explain it. People generally act with enlightened self-interest, serving the needs of others while gaining benefits of the contracts for themselves.

Examine the book you are reading—the paper, the ink, and the printing. Identify, if you can, the contracts involved in cutting trees, grinding them into pulp, and transforming the pulp—with the aid of water, chemicals, and heavy machinery—into rolls or sheets of paper. Don't overlook all the workers involved at each step, and the contracts they perform each day. Recognize the various transportation and communication facilities utilized from start to finish. Take any one of the above contract leads and pursue it to its sources; for example, the mining of minerals to produce the steel for the saws, trucks, ships, and other machinery. It is impossible to identify all the contracts that were involved, directly and indirectly, in placing this book at your disposal. One can convincingly argue that an incredibly complex yet effective network of contracts has integrated all human activity in our civilized, interdependent society.

WHAT IS THE UNIFORM COMMERCIAL CODE (UCC)?

Elements of contract law vary from state to state and among major types of business enterprise. Many contracts are based on the common law, notably personal service agreements. Specialized statutes affect contract rights and obligations in security markets (for stocks and bonds), corporate financial transactions, and real estate dealings. But, overall, most contracts involve the sale/purchase of **goods** (i.e., all movable personal property that consists of things—other than money and securities), and these contracts are governed by the **Uniform Commercial Code (UCC).***

In the twentieth century, a movement began to create various "uniform" acts or codes to make laws more consistent throughout the fifty states. The most pervasive and thus most significant uniform code is the UCC, which has been adopted, at least in part, by all fifty states as part of their statutory law. Because the UCC does not attempt to answer every contract question, generally accepted common-law rules still provide answers to most contract questions.

---

goods

Tangible, movable personal property.

Uniform Commercial Code

A uniform code drafted by the National Conference of Commissioners of Uniform State Laws governing the conduct of business, sales, warrenties, and other commercial matters.

http://

The full text of the Uniform Commercial Code can be found at

http://www.law.cornell.edu/ ucc/ucc.table.html

---

* The UCC, as amended, replaced seven other "uniform" acts and a variety of other legislative acts governing commercial activities. Currently, the following articles constitute the bulk of the official text: (1) General Provisions; (2) Sales; (2.A) Leases; (3) Commercial Paper; (4) Bank Deposits and Collections; (5) Letters of Credit; (6) Bulk Transfers; (7) Warehouse Receipts, Bills of Lading, and Other Documents; (8) Investment Securities; (9) Secured Transactions; Sales of Accounts and Chattel Paper.

An important thing to know about any investigation of commercial law is whether the UCC governs a contract. Article 2 (Sales) is the most important part of the UCC for our discussion of contracts. Article 2 defines the rights and duties of contracting parties if the subject matter of the contract is a sale of goods. A **sale** is a transfer of ownership of goods in exchange for a price. Nonsale transfers of personal property, leases, are covered in Article 2A of the UCC.

Also important to note is the emergence of expanded world markets and the law related to international sale transactions. The *United Nations Convention on Contracts for the Sale of Goods* became part of the law of the United States in 1988.* The convention applies to sales entered into by citizens of any two of the signatories, and it deviates from the UCC in some details. For example, unlike the UCC, the convention provides that any sales contract may be oral, whereas under the UCC, contracts for the sale of goods in excess of $500 must be evidenced by a written document. However, the contracting parties may expressly opt out of all or any part of this United Nations law.

sale

A contract in which title (ownership) of property passes from seller to buyer. Possession usually transfers at the time of sale.

How Are Contracts Classified?

Generally, just two parties are involved in a given contract, but there may be multiple parties when appropriate. One person (and a "person" could be a corporation or partnership), the **offeror,** makes an offer to a second person, termed the **offeree.** The offeree may then respond to the offer with an acceptance. In effect, each party promises to do (or in some cases, promises *not* to do) something the other party wants to have done (or not have done). Generally, no special words need be used. Often there is preliminary negotiation or bargaining. With a few exceptions (discussed later in this chapter), the contract may be oral, written, or implied from conduct and/or from some custom or usage of the particular trade; the agreement may also result from a combination of these methods of expression. Contracts may be classified as to method of expression, parties bound, legal effect, and extent of performance. A summary of these classifications is represented in Exhibit 8-1.

offeror

In contracts, the party who makes an offer.

offeree

In contracts, the party to whom an offer is made by the offeror.

Method of Expression

Any person capable of reading this sentence has probably been a party to countless contracts. The agreements may have been **express,** when made in words spoken or written, or they may have been **implied in fact,** when manifested in conduct or body language (e.g., an arm waved at a vendor in a stadium during a football game followed by the toss of money and a return toss of a bag of roasted peanuts). Contracts often are neither simply express or implied but combine express and implied terms.

Sometimes the law will imply and enforce an obligation even when there is no true agreement either express or implied between the parties. Such an obligation is called a **quasi-contract.** The law creates a quasi-contract when, under the circumstances, there would be unjust enrichment of one person unless he or she was required to pay value for a benefit received from someone else. The law provides that recovery in court is the reasonable value of the benefit received. Thus, a person may be required to perform as though a contract exists, even though no promise was made and no intent to be bound was manifested. A fairly common example of how a quasi-contract may come into being follows.

express contract

An agreement stated in words, spoken or written.

implied in fact contract

Contractual agreement manifested by conduct or body language (e.g., purchase of items from vendors in noisy stadiums during sporting events).

quasi-contract

Not a true contract, but an obligation imposed on one party to prevent unjust enrichment of another. Also called "implied in law contract."

* Among the other countries that have adopted this convention are Australia, Canada, France, Germany, Italy, Mexico, Sweden, and Switzerland.

EXHIBIT 8-1: **How Are Contracts Classified?**

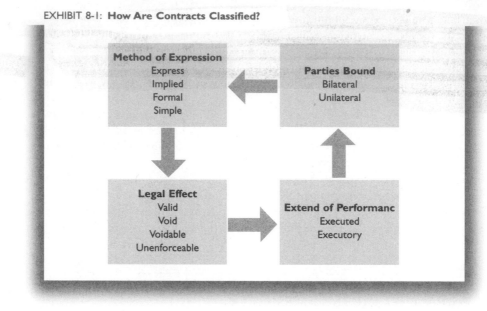

Method of Expression
Express
Implied
Formal
Simple

Parties Bound
Bilateral
Unilateral

Legal Effect
Valid
Void
Voidable
Unenforceable

Extend of Performanc
Executed
Executory

![icon] **LEGAL FOCUS—EXAMPLE**
....

A surgeon stops her car at the scene of an automobile collision. She gives needed emergency aid to an unconscious victim at the accident. There was no agreement, yet the doctor has a legitimate claim in quasi-contract for the reasonable value of her services. In contrast, a passer-by with some knowledge of first aid who performed similar services is not entitled to any payment. Such an act would be that of a helpful volunteer, not of a professional who is customarily paid for such services.

Generally, the parties to an express contract or an implied in fact contract can use any language they please. In some cases, however, statutes prescribe the terms and exact language. Examples are negotiable instruments such as bank checks and promissory notes. These special types of contracts are called **formal contracts;** other types of contracts are called **simple contracts,** whether they are oral or written.

Parties Bound

In most contracts, both parties exchange legally binding promises. Such an agreement is a **bilateral contract;** that is, a promise made in exchange for another promise. For example, Dawn Summers agrees to try to find Angie Gagliano's dog during a 24-hour period in exchange for Gagliano's promise to pay $50. If Summers looks for the dog as promised, she is entitled to collect the $50 whether or not she succeeds in her search. Note that at the time the contract is created neither party has performed the promise they made to the other. In contrast, an offer for a **unilateral contract** is actually a potential agreement. One party makes a promise or offer to induce some completed *act* by another party. For example, Brandon Tore promises to pay $50 to anyone who will find and return his dog, dead or alive. No one is legally obliged to join in the search, nor is Tore obliged to pay unless the requested act is done and the dog is returned.

---

formal contract

Agreement that must use prescribed language or be in prescribed form.

simple contract

All oral and written contracts that are not classified as formal contracts.

bilateral contract

Agreement in which both parties exchange binding promises.

unilateral contract

A contract in which the promisor seeks performance of a requested act. Upon performance of the act, the contract is formed and the promisor is obligated to fulfill his or her promise.

LEGAL FOCUS—EXAMPLE

In May 1927, Charles A. ("Lucky") Lindbergh became the first person to fly across the Atlantic Ocean solo and nonstop from New York to Paris, using a single-engine monoplane, "The Spirit of St. Louis." Lindbergh was responding to a unilateral contract offer made by a St. Louis businessman to pay $25,000 to the first person(s) to perform the feat. After he was aloft and on his way (a substantial effort to perform), the offer could not be revoked or cancelled. Once the offeree has clearly started to perform, the law requires that the offeree have a reasonable time to complete the act, even though the offeree is not legally obliged to finish.

LEGAL EFFECT

If a contract complies with all essential elements (described in the next section), it is a **valid contract.** Sometimes the attempt to create a contract may be totally ineffective, and so there is no contract; in such a case, there is a **void agreement.** An example is an agreement to commit a crime or a tort. Sometimes an essential element of a valid contract is missing, and a party to the contract has the power to perform or withdraw without liability. Such contract is said to be **voidable.** For example, a minor (under age 18) may generally invalidate or avoid a contract even if freely and intentionally made. A parent or guardian may also take such action on the minor's behalf.

Finally, some contracts are valid yet **unenforceable.** A proper contract claim for money or performance may have become stale and unenforceable because enforcement was not sought before the time provided under the statute of limitations had passed. For example, a creditor may have a right to be paid the balance due on a retail store credit account. The typical statute of limitations requires that such creditors sue within four years of the due date, otherwise collection is barred.

EXTENT OF PERFORMANCE

If a contract has been fully performed by both parties, it is an **executed** contract. Sometimes parties to a contract say that they have "executed the agreement" when they have simply signed the written contract. But the parties must perform the promises contained in their contract before it is truly an executed contract.

If something remains to be done by either or both parties, it is an **executory contract.** Often sales contracts for goods, such as automobiles, are coupled with warranties as to performance for specified periods of time or extent of use (e.g., warranty for three years or 30,000 miles, whichever comes first). Although the basic contract may be executed, obligations created by the warranty remain for the specified time. Also, as noted in Chapter 7, if the user is injured by some defect in the product, the manufacturer may be strictly liable in tort for damages whether or not the warranty period has expired.

What Are the Requisites of a Valid Contract?

There are six requirements for a valid contract: *competent parties* who make a *mutual agreement* with *genuine assent* supported by *reciprocal consideration* and which is legal in *formation and execution* and in the *form prescribed by law.* Let us examine each requirement.

---

valid contract

An agreement that complies with all requisites of the law for enforceability.

void agreement

Without legal force or binding effect.

voidable contract

An agreement that may be legally enforced or may be rejected by a party. For example, a contract between a minor and an adult is voidable or valid at the option of the minor.

unenforceable contact

A contract that was initially valid but can no longer be enforced, e.g., because of the running out of a statute of limitations.

executed contract

A contract that has been fully performed by both parties.

executory contract

A valid contract in which something remains to be done by either or both parties.

COMPETENT PARTIES

competent parties

Parties who are legally qualified (i.e., have the capacity) to make a binding contractual agreement.

The first essential for validity is **competent parties,** meaning that the parties who contract must have *legal capacity* to do so. The law generally expects that human beings will act as rational beings with freedom of will or of choice among alternative courses of action. Thus, the apparent agreement of a party may be negated by (1) infancy or minority (under age 18 in most states), (2) incapacitating mental condition that prevents the person from knowing the nature and consequences of a contract, or (3) incapacitating intoxication (from alcohol or drugs). Although most persons have full capacity (i.e., legal qualification or power) to contract, a large number do not. The law denies them the rights that flow from contracting, primarily to protect them from the burdensome duties of performance in foolish or improvident agreements. The restrictive denial also serves to protect them from possible exploitation by unscrupulous persons who might take unfair advantage of their ignorance, naivete, or incapacity.* In all three basic types of incapacity, the contract made is usually voidable, but only at the option of the incompetent person (or parent or guardian in control). The agreement is sometimes but seldom absolutely void. It is occasionally valid. Exhibit 8-2 illustrates the parallel status of minors, the mentally incompetent, and intoxicated persons.

Exception for Necessaries

necessaries

Goods and services ordinarily required by and appropriate to an incompetent person's station in life, yet not available and/or not provided by parent or guardian.

An agreement to purchase goods or services that are **necessaries** is enforceable as a quasi-contract. In such a case, no valid contract exists, but a contractual remedy of reasonable compensatory damages is allowed to prevent unjust enrichment of the person who received the necessaries. Only the fair price would have to be paid, which might be different from the bargained-for price. Necessaries include such things as food, clothing, shelter, and medical care at the level the person is accustomed to. They must be truly needed, yet not be available from or provided by the parent or guardian of the incompetent.

Many business firms aggressively promote sales of cars, audiovisual and electronic equipment, and other items to minors, especially teenagers. They do this knowing that most of the purchases will not be returned even when the legal right to do so exists. To many teenagers, nothing is more precious than the freedom and independence provided by their very own car. Such persons are not likely to return cars, or indeed any other deeply coveted products, and demand refunds. Moreover, such items are usually acquired with parental knowledge and often with parental financial assistance. For big-ticket items, prudent retailers often require parental acknowledgement or approval and financial responsibility (e.g., by cosigning a promissory note or security agreement).

MUTUAL AGREEMENT

objective theory of contracts

A theory that the words and conduct of an offeror mean whatever a reasonable person in the offeree's position would think they mean, as opposed to what the offeror may have actually meant.

The second essential of a valid contract is self-evident: The parties must come to a mutual agreement. There must be an offer by one and an acceptance by the other. There must be an agreement of the parties to the same thing. This is sometimes referred to as a "meeting of the minds." This subjective concept, however, is not strictly true. The law requires external or objective manifestation, in words or actions, of willingness to deal. Intent is decided by the **objective theory of contracts.** A party's intent to enter into a contract is judged by outward objective facts; persons are bound by what they express, either by their

* In a few instances, the restriction is a form of punishment (as where prisoners are barred from most contract activity) or national defense (as where enemies in times of war are barred from contracting with American citizens).

EXHIBIT 8-2: **General Patterns of Effects of Incapacity on Agreements**
(caveat: in some states variations exist in definitions and effects)

Contracting Party	Valid Contract	Voidable Contract	Void Agreements
Minor	• *All* contracts, if married. • *All* contracts, if emancipated.* • *All* court-approved contracts. • Contract to enlist in armed service (at age 17). • In some states, contracts for loans incurred to pay for necessaries, including education and medical care.†	• *Most* contracts. • To avoid liability, any goods received must be returned if still available. • *Some* states do no require a full refund even if goods cannot be returned, and even if minor lied about age; in most states the minor may disaffirm the contract, but is liable for any depreciation and wear and tear or use. • The contract may be ratified or avoided within a reasonable time after person reaches majority age.	• *Some* attempts to contract e.g., an apparent contract to name an agent or to dispose of real property.
Mentally Incompetent person	• *All* contracts, if person is merely neurotic. • *All* contracts made during a lucid interval of full sanity.	• *All* attempts to contract made when person is entirely without understanding. • Any goods received must be returned, unless they are no longer available and other party acted in bad faith.	• *All* attempts to contract, if person has been judicially declared insane and a guardian has been appointed.
Intoxicated person	• *All* contracts, if the person is sober enough to understand the nature of the contract (even if he or she would not have made the contract if sober).	• *All* attempts to contract made when person is too intoxicated to understand the nature of the contract. • Avoidance, to be effective, must be prompt after regaining sobriety and learning of the agreement.	• *All* attempts to contract, if person has been judicially declared a victim of habitual intoxication and a guardian has been appointed.

* Living separate from consenting parents and managing own financial affairs.
† In most states this will be a quasi-contract rather than a "valid" contract.

words or by their conduct. Internal, subjective thoughts remain secret. Before, during, and after an agreement of any complexity is entered, the parties seldom disclose the full content of their mental thinking about the terms of the contract.

The Offer

Three elements are necessary for an offer to be effective:
1. The offer must manifest an intention to be legally bound.
2. The terms of the offer must be reasonably definite and certain so a court can fashion a remedy.
3. The offer must be communicated to the offeree.

LEGAL FOCUS—PROBLEM

Adam Steinberg and three other students ride to college each day in June Naylor's new-to-her automobile. Her car is worth $8,000. One cold morning just after everyone got into her car, it would not start. Naylor yelled in anger, "I'll sell this car to anyone for $20!" Steinberg immediately dropped $20 in her lap. Does Steinberg, the offeree, have a contract with Naylor and a right to the car? Did Naylor, the offeror, intend to create a contract?

offer

A promise by one person (the offeror) to do or to give consideration (something of value) in exchange for sought-for consideration through acceptance by another person (the offeree).

For a valid **offer,** the person making the offer must manifest intent to be bound, to make a business agreement, a contract. The offer must be serious, not in obvious jest or in panicky fear. Naylor's expression is obviously made in anger, excitement, or jest, and it does not meet the objective-intent test. Since the offer is not effective, Steinberg's attempt to accept does not create an agreement. Likewise, an invitation to a social engagement or date is not a legal offer. If accepted, either party may cancel it without legal liability.

Most advertisements by custom are not legal offers to sell; instead, they are considered to be invitations to the world to come in and make offers to buy, to negotiate. Thus, under contract law an advertiser generally cannot be compelled to sell goods on the terms stated in an ad. Of course, if the ad is deliberately false or misleading, the advertiser may be liable for a tort or criminal act or may be in violation of some other duty as an advertiser. Catalogs, price lists, circulars, and other pricing vehicles used by companies are treated in the same fashion as advertisements.

LEGAL FOCUS—EXAMPLE

You put an ad in the classified section of the local newspaper offering to sell your favorite guitar for $75. Seven people call and "accept" your "offer." If the ad is truly an offer, you would be bound by seven contracts to sell your guitar. But since initial advertisements are treated as invitations to make offers rather than as offers, you would have seven offers to choose from. You could accept one without assuming any liability for the six you reject.

The offer must be reasonably definite and certain. In case of a dispute, a court must be able to determine what the parties agreed to do.

Among the terms the court expects to find in a valid offer are
* Parties—who and how many
* Subject matter—what and how many
* Time of performance—when, delivery terms, warranties
* Price—how much and when to be paid

Many common contracts are considered sufficiently definite and certain even though important terms are left unsettled. An example is a contract where one is hired to work and the duration of the employment is not stated; such a contract is considered an employment at will. Also, contracts for the professional services of a doctor, dentist, lawyer, or accountant are often made without clear knowledge of the full scope of the time and effort that will be needed, and so no fixed fee is given. In these situations, when the price is finally set it must be reasonable in light of all the circumstances. When such uncertainty is troubling or unacceptable, one can insist on a specific figure or an hourly rate, stated in advance.

Finally, the offer must be communicated to the person to whom is it made, the offeree. Only the offeree or an authorized agent of the offeree may accept. In daily life, the parties to contracts usually identify themselves more precisely than as offeror–offeree. They may be known as university–student, seller–buyer, doctor–patient, employer–employee, lawyer–client, landlord–tenant, bailor–bailee, and so forth.

The Acceptance

To create a contract, the offeree must accept the offer by making a positive response to the offeror. General rules of contract law require that **acceptance** be a mirror-image response to the offer. It must be a timely, responsive, and unequivocal affirmation of a desire to enter into the contract on the terms of the offer. It also must be communicated to the offeror or to the offeror's authorized agent.

acceptance

Affirmative response to the terms of an offer, creating a contract.

Under the Uniform Commercial Code, the rules of acceptance for contracts involving the sale of goods are more flexible as to what constitutes an acceptance. For all types of transactions, the courts look for a timely response showing that the offeree wishes to be contractually bound.

Under the UCC, an offer to make a contract for the sale of goods is "construed as inviting acceptance in any manner and by any medium reasonable in the circumstances."[3] Generally, unless otherwise specified, the offeree may accept by the same or faster means than were used by the offeror. Today many communications of offers and acceptances are made by telephone, fax machines, e-mail, or overnight express delivery services. When an offer is made by U.S. Postal Service mail, the offeror impliedly authorizes the offeree to respond by mail, unless otherwise specified.[4] The acceptance is effective, and a contract arises, when the acceptance is properly posted (i.e., placed in the custody of the U.S. Postal Service with the correct address and proper postage), even if the letter of acceptance is lost in transit. The rule is often called the *deposit acceptance rule* or *mailbox rule.** Similarly, if private overnight express delivery services are used, the acceptance is effective when the offeree gives the document to the delivery service.

How Long Does an Offer Last?

An offer, once made, does not last forever. It is ended by the *lapse of time,* if specified (e.g., "Let me know before Friday the 27th"). If no time is stated, then it ends after a reasonable time—an elastic concept that varies with the circumstances (e.g., a farmer's offer to sell fresh strawberries may be good for a few hours; an offer made in June to sell loads of firewood may be good for several months).

An offer is also ended by the destruction of the subject matter.[5] For example, Annabel Leeds offers to sell her pickup truck to Salix Waukem. Before Waukem accepts the offer, the truck is damaged beyond reasonably practicable repair. Death or mental incompetence of either party also precludes acceptance and ends the offer.[6]

LEGAL FOCUS—PROBLEM

Saturday, Fred Arthur mailed Kim Trang an offer to sell his car for $1,000. On Monday, Arthur changed his mind and, not having heard from Trang, sent her a letter revoking

---

* Restatement (Second) of Contracts, § 30, provides that an offer invites acceptance "by any medium reasonable in the circumstances," unless the offer is specific about the means of acceptance. Under § 65, a medium is reasonable if it is one used by the offeror or if it is one customary in similar transactions, unless the offeree knows of circumstances that would argue against the reasonableness of a particular method (the need for speed because of rapid price changes, for example).

his offer. On Wednesday, before she had received Arthur's letter of revocation, Trang mailed a letter of acceptance to Arthur. Trang demands that Arthur sell his car as promised, but Arthur claims that no contract exists because the offer was revoked prior to Trang's acceptance. Is Arthur correct?

revocation

The taking back of an offer.

No. As previously noted above, when an offer is made by mail, a contract exists when the acceptance is properly posted. In sharp contrast, although the offeror may notify the offeree at any time that the offer is revoked, such **revocation** is generally effective only upon receipt by offeree. If this were not so, the offeree could never be sure that an offer received in the mail was still open to acceptance. Trang's acceptance was sent by an authorized and reasonable means (the same means used by Arthur) before she received or was aware of the attempted revocation of the offer. Because of the deposit-acceptance rule, the acceptance was good when sent.

If a week was originally specified "to let you think it over," the offeror can nevertheless generally revoke the offer, without liability, before acceptance. Remember that promises are enforceable only when a contract is formed, so a promise to keep an offer open can usually be broken without recourse. To avoid such possibility, the offeree may pay the offeror to keep the offer open for an agreed length of time by entering into an **option contract.*** An enforceable option is a separate related contract. The option contract gives the offeree a fixed time to accept the offer. During this period, the offeror does not have the legal right to revoke. The offeree pays the offeror something of value to create the option contract. An option contract is often used in the negotiation of real estate sales.

option contract

The right to purchase property at an established price at any time within a specified period. The optionee (potential buyer) pays option money to the owner in exchange for this right.

Subsequent incompetence, or even death, does not terminate an offer made in an option contract (unless the offeror's personal performance is essential).[7] In such cases, generally a personal representative fulfills the contract, as by delivering goods or paying the price.

http://

Option contracts are the subject matter of major trading bodies such as the Chicago Board of Trade
http://www.cbot.com/

Now the offeree–option holder knows that he or she has the agreed-on option time to reflect, look at alternatives, or arrange financing. If the offeree–option holder decides to accept the original offer, any money paid for the option might be applied to the purchase price, if the parties had so agreed. If he or she rejects the offer, the offeror simply keeps that money as compensation for keeping the offer open.

The parties may haggle over the terms of the contract. In doing so, an unequivocal rejection of the offer by the offeree would end it. The rejection may take effect immediately, if made during oral negotiations; if mailed, unlike an acceptance it is effective only when received. Similarly, a *counteroffer* terminates an offer.[†] Noncommittal words such as, "Your price sounds too rich for my diet, but let me sleep on that offer," would have no effect. Understandably, death or insanity of either party, or destruction of the subject matter, ends the offer.

RECIPROCAL CONSIDERATION

When a man keeps hollering, "It's the principle of the thing," he's talking about the money.

Frank Hubbard, American humorist, 1868–1930

---

* As to contracts involving the sale of goods, a merchant may make a binding firm offer to keep the offer open for a stated time up to three months. It is not essential that the offeree pay for such a right, but the agreement must be in writing and signed by the merchant (UCC § 2-205). This rule does not apply to casual sellers of goods.

† It is interesting to note that between merchants, an acceptance may be valid and binding on both parties "even though it states terms additional to or different from those offered or agreed upon. . . ." However, this provision of the UCC, § 2–207, is subject to a number of conditions that effectively maintain the offeror's control and ability to require that acceptance comply with his or her terms if there is to be a contract.

The third requisite of a valid contract is the presence of *reciprocal consideration.* **Consideration,** in this context, is simply the value given in exchange for a promise or an act. The parties "bargain for," that is, freely negotiate, an exchange of promises and/or acts whereby each party ultimately enjoys some legal benefit and each suffers some legal detriment. Each party gives; each party receives. What is given and received must have legal value; generally it need not be equal or adequate by any other person's standards of valuation. Thus a promise of a gift is not legally enforceable because the donor is promised nothing of legal value in return. To say "Gee, thanks!" or "I love you!" is not consideration.

> **consideration**
>
> The price or inducement (for example, reciprocal promises) to enter a contract.

Recalling that in a bilateral contract each party is both promisor and promisee, study the following explanation of consideration provided by the *Restatement of Contracts.* Consideration may be (1) a return promise (e.g., to pay money or to give some service or property), (2) an act other than a promise (as in unilateral contracts), (3) a forbearance (where one party refrains from doing what he or she has a legal right to do), or (4) the creation, modification, or destruction of a legal relationship (where, e.g., the parties agree to become associated as business partners).

LEGAL FOCUS—PROBLEM

Jerry Revcik says to Max Harris, "If you paint the garage green, I will pay you $100." Harris paints the garage green. Can Harris legally require Revcik to pay the $100? Is consideration present?

The answer to both questions is yes. The act of painting the garage is the consideration requested and in this case given in return for Revcik's promise to pay.

LEGAL FOCUS—PROBLEM

Suppose instead that Revcik says to Harris, "In consideration of your not being as wealthy as my other friends, I will pay you $500 next Tuesday." Can Harris legally require Revcik to pay him the $500? Does consideration exist?

No. Revcik's promise is not enforceable, because consideration is absent. Harris did not pay anything (give consideration) for the $500 promised. Jerry simply stated his motive for an intended *gift* to Harris. Note that use of the term *consideration* does not, alone, mean that consideration was given. Consideration is the sweetener that induces both parties to perform as promised. It conforms to the natural and customary human tendency to expect to receive something in exchange for something given, unless a gift is intended.

In so-called illusory agreements there is no reciprocal consideration and therefore no contract. Examples are when the parties "agree to agree," or when a supplier agrees to sell all goods of a given type that the buyer "may want," which may actually be none at all. This is distinguishable from a deal where the seller agrees to sell and the buyer agrees to buy all of the specified type of goods that the buyer may actually and measurably need or require during a stated period of time.

Similarly, there is no consideration when the promisor is already bound to do the act (e.g., when a police officer, for a promised fee, agrees to try to apprehend a burglar) or when some past consideration is involved (e.g., when A rescues B from drowning and *subsequently* B promises to pay A $5,000).

Under some special circumstances, consideration is not required as a matter of public policy. An illustration is a pledge or charitable subscription to a church or nonprofit hospital or school. The pledge states that it is for the purpose of erecting a library building, and it is made, in part, to induce others to contribute. Such a promise is legally binding in most states, even if the donor gets no valuable consideration in return. However, the charity must act in reliance on the pledge, for example, by contracting for construction of the new facility. Likewise, no consideration need be given by a creditor for a new promise by a debtor to pay a debt that has been barred by the statute of limitations.

LEGAL FOCUS—PROBLEM

Debra Muller borrows $500 from Tyrone Carter. She gives Carter a promissory note in which she promises to pay Carter the $500 with yearly interest of 7 percent one year from the date. A year passes, and no payment is made. Four more years (the statutory period of limitations for written contracts) pass, and still no payment is made. Carter has thereby lost the legal right to compel payment through court action. A year later, Muller has pangs of conscience and sends Carter a letter apologizing and promising to pay the note in full. Is this promise enforceable?

Yes, this promise revives the debt, even though Carter gave no new consideration. But if Muller verbally agreed to pay the debt, it would not be revived. An oral promise lacks the evidentiary value of the written note. A partial payment, identified as such by the debtor, would also revive the debt. Carter now has four more years in which to seek payment by court action.

GENUINE ASSENT

genuine assent

When consent of both parties to be bound by a contract is freely given and is not negated by fraud, duress, undue influence, and/or certain mistakes.

The fourth essential of a valid contract is that the agreement be made with the **genuine assent,** or real consent, of both parties. Assent is negated when either party acts under duress or because of undue influence. Assent, although given, is also fatally flawed if it resulted from fraud or certain types of mistakes.

Duress

duress

Any threat of, or actual, physical harm that deprives a person of the freedom of will to choose and decide.

Duress happens when one party is prevented from exercising judgment and free will by some wrongful act or threat of the other party. It could result from threat of imprisonment (e.g., "I'll keep you locked up until you sign this contract!") or of physical injury to the other party or to a close relative or friend (e.g., "Sign here or I'll bash you so hard you'll never ever sign anything again!"). In addition, blackmail to induce consent to a contract is duress. The victim of the duress can generally choose to carry out the contract or to avoid the entire transaction, although duress involving a serious threat of violence leads to no contract at all, a void agreement. A threat of criminal prosecution would be duress; not so the comparatively common threat of civil suit to collect a debt. Why the difference? The first is a form of extortion or menace; the second is the voicing of a legal right to sue for money owed.

Economic need is generally not a basis for a finding of duress, even when one party charges a very high price for an item the other party needs. If the party charging the price also creates the need, however, economic duress may be found.

LEGAL FOCUS—PROBLEM

The Internal Revenue Service assessed a large tax and penalty against Sam Thompson. Thompson retained Earl Eyman to represent him to reduce the tax and penalty. The last day before the deadline for filing a reply with the IRS, Eyman refused to represent Thompson. He said he would reconsider if Thompson signed an agreement to pay a much higher fee than previously agreed. Is the agreement enforceable?

No. Although Eyman threatened only to withdraw his services, something he could legitimately do if done in proper time, he delayed his withdrawal until the last day. It would have been practically impossible at that late date for Thompson to get adequate representation elsewhere. Because Thompson was forced into signing the contract or losing his right to challenge the IRS assessment, the contract is voidable by him.

Undue Influence

Although peaceful and more subtle than duress, **undue influence** has the same effect: depriving a party of freedom of will in choosing a course of action. Wrongful persuasion and persistent pressure accomplish it. Typically, the wrongdoer asserts his or her position or authority or exploits the victim's misplaced confidence in the wrongdoer's apparent good faith and wisdom and, for example, obtains property from the victim at a price well below fair market value.

http://

See a different definition of duress in Rupp's Insurance Glossary
http://www.nils.com/rupps/duress.htm

undue influence

Wrongful persuasion, often by a fiduciary or other trusted individual, which deprives the victim of freedom of will in making a contract.

LEGAL FOCUS—EXAMPLE

When Mabel Taylor reached her eightieth birthday, she was no longer able to drive her car. Her nephew, Johnny Ray, convinced Taylor that she should sell him the car for $50. Ray told Taylor that if she did not agree then he would no longer visit her. The actual value of the car was $7,000. This agreement is not enforceable because Ray is taking advantage of his special relationship with Taylor.

A suspicion of undue influence arises when parties are in a confidential or fiduciary relationship. Examples include that of parent and child, client and lawyer, guardian and ward, conservator and elderly conservatee, and principal and agent. Because one party relies so heavily on the other, the law requires the utmost good faith, scrupulous honesty, and full disclosure by the dominant party in dealings between the parties. To overcome a presumption of undue influence, the dominant party should make a full disclosure of all relevant facts; insist that the other party get the advice of qualified, independent counsel; and make honest, fair contracts.

Fraud

The essential elements of **fraud** are (1) false representation, a lie, (2) of a material (important) (3) fact (generally not a personal opinion, unless an expert is expressing it) (4) known to be false (or made with reckless indifference as to its truth or made with blameworthy ignorance of its falsity), (5) made with intent to deceive the victim and induce the victim to contract, as a result of which (6) the victim is deceived and contracts in reliance on the lie, and (7) the victim is thereby injured.

fraud

A knowingly false representation of a material fact, made through words or conduct, with intent to deceive a victim, who is induced to contract in reliance on the lie, and who is thereby injured.

LEGAL FOCUS—PROBLEM

Peter Pride, proprietor of "Cars You're Proud to Own," sold a used car to Lilly Lee, a first-car buyer. Pride, who knew otherwise, said the car had one previous owner (actually, there had been two); had never been in an accident (actually, a rear fender, the trunk, and a bumper had been replaced after a collision); and had the original paint (the car had been repainted). The odometer showed 52,000 miles, and Pride said the engine had been overhauled (in fact, the odometer had been turned back from 66,000 miles, and the engine had been given only a tune-up). Pride also claimed the car had new tires (they looked new to Lee but were actually retreads). Pride claimed the car was worth $12,000 but since he was trying to reduce his inventory, he'd let Lee "steal it" for only $8,500. Relying on Pride's sales pitch, Lee bought the car for the asking price. She soon learned that in its actual condition, it was worth no more than $4,500. Is Peter Pride guilty of fraud? If so, what can Lee do?

http://

The Office of the Florida Attorney General has a good site for information about fraud in consumer contracts

http://www.myfloridalegal.com/

Yes, Pride is guilty of fraud. He made a series of misrepresentations of fact, known to be false, intending to deceive Lee and to induce her to buy. Lee was deceived and, relying on the lies, bought the car to her injury. She paid more than she would have had she known the truth.

Lee has several options. She could *rescind* (cancel or undo) the contract, return the car, and demand a full refund of her $8,500. In addition, she could sue in tort for compensatory and punitive (or exemplary) damages. In a minority of states, Lee's compensatory damages would be the *out-of-pocket loss* suffered (i.e., the difference in value between what she gave—$8,500—and the value of what she got—$4,500—or a net $4,000). In most states, her compensatory damages would be the difference between the value of what she received ($4,500) and the value of performance as misrepresented by the defendant Pride ($12,000), or a net $7,500. In either case, in most states Lee could also sue for punitive damages in addition to the compensatory damages because of Pride's intentional tort of fraud. Here the jury might award as much as $50,000 or more.[8]

LEGAL FOCUS—PROBLEM

Tom Cullen contracts to purchase a hearing assistance dog from Manny Estacio. The dog is blind in one eye but when Estacio shows the dog, he skillfully conceals this fact by turning the dog's head so Cullen cannot see the defect. All of the dog's senses are important in fulfilling the hearing assistance tasks. Is this concealment fraud?

Yes, this knowing concealment constitutes fraud. Another example of misrepresentation by conduct is the false denial of knowledge or information concerning facts that are material to the contract when such knowledge or information is requested. It is important that a purchaser ask many questions.

The use of deception to extract money or property from others is unfortunately not new or uncommon. And new forms of doing business attract the unscrupulous as well as the adventuresome who try new and old schemes with new features to mislead the trusting and naïve among us. Use of the Internet and mobile phones are among those business ventures of which consumers need be wary.

LEGAL FOCUS—EXAMPLE

A $3.50 "rebate" check was sent to millions of small businesses and consumers. The check came with an attached form that looked like an invoice and used terms like "reference number," and "discount taken," making it look like there was a previous business relationship. Upon cashing the check the consumers were unknowingly agreeing to allow the defendants to become their Internet service provider, and the defendants placed monthly charges of $19.95 to $29.95 on the consumers' telephone bills. They also made it very difficult to cancel future monthly charges and receive refunds. A judge found ". . . that, as a matter of law, check/invoice combinations that do not clearly and conspicuously disclose the effects of cashing the check and/or clearly state the check is an offer for the sale of Internet services on the face of the document constitute material representations that are likely to mislead consumers acting reasonably under the circumstances."[9]

http://

A good site for information about fraud on the Internet and telemarketing is at the National Fraud Information Center of the National Consumers League
http://www.fraud.org/

Mutual Mistake

When both parties have an erroneous idea or understanding about some fact that is an important element of the contract, there is a **mutual** or **bilateral mistake** that generally renders their agreement void, or voidable by either party. When both parties are mistaken about a material (i.e., important) fact, either party may rescind (i.e., cancel or annul the contract without liability). If the error were not obvious, the same court would not excuse the mistaken party.

mutual or **bilateral mistake**

Where both parties to a contract labor under the same error about an important fact in their agreement.

LEGAL FOCUS—CASE

Defendant Wichelhaus contracted to buy 125 bales of cotton from plaintiff Raffles. They agreed that the cotton would come from Bombay, India, to Liverpool on the ship *Peerless*. Buyer Wichelhaus reasonably thought the goods would arrive on a ship named *Peerless* that was scheduled to sail in October. Seller Raffles reasonably thought of another ship, which also happened to be named *Peerless*, but which was scheduled to sail from Bombay in December. When the cotton finally arrived, much later than expected by Wichelhaus, he refused to accept or pay for it. Was Wichelhaus legally bound by the alleged contract?

Raffles v. Wichelhaus, 159 Eng. Rep. 375 (1864).

No, according to this landmark old English case. Acting in good faith, the parties referred to different ships, sailing at significantly different times. The mutual mistake of fact rendered the agreement voidable. Note that different opinions as to value (e.g., of a parcel of land, a jewel, or a share of stock) or expectations of future value do not affect the validity of the contract. Likewise, a **unilateral mistake** (by one party) about value, expectations, or the applicability of a statute, such as a zoning law, generally does not affect the contract. However, suppose one party is mistaken or errs in submitting a bid on a construction job. The other party recognizes the obvious error but says nothing, and quickly signs the contract. A court of equity would permit the mistaken party to withdraw without liability.

unilateral mistake

A situation in which one of the parties to a contract labors under some error about an important fact in the agreement.

LEGAL FOCUS—PROBLEM

Jane Collins contracts to purchase one of two antique washing machines owned by Mike Heimer. Collins thinks she has purchased a white one, a premier model. Heimer thinks she has purchased the beige one, his less valuable washing machine. Does a contract exist?

No. Collins and Heimer have made a genuine mutual mistake of fact. Collins believes the contract subject matter is the white washing machine, while Heimer believes it is the beige one. Nothing is more material than the subject matter of the contract. Since both parties are mistaken about the subject matter, no contract exists.

LEGAL FOCUS—PROBLEM

Suppose instead that Collins contracts to buy the white washing machine, believing it to be worth $1,000 when it really is worth only $250. Can Collins escape the contract because of her mistake?

No. Collins's mistake is one of value or quality, not fact. A mistake of this nature does not normally affect the enforceability of the contract.

LEGALITY IN FORMATION AND EXECUTION

As the fifth and, in many cases, the final requisite for validity, the contract must be legal in its formation and in its proposed execution. Generally, an agreement may fail to qualify because it is either (1) contrary to some statute or (2) contrary to public policy (i.e., prevailing community standards as to what is contrary to the public good, or commonweal).

Violations of Statutes

The gangland expression "There's a contract out on him" refers to an agreement to kill a designated victim. Such agreement is obviously illegal and void. The same summary condemnation would apply to any agreement to commit a tort. Not so clear is the legal status of agreements (1) to gamble or conduct illegal lotteries, (2) to practice a trade or profession without a license, (3) to engage in profit-seeking business on Sundays, and (4) to charge interest rates that might be usurious. Consider the confusing status of these practices.

GAMBLING   Traditionally, gambling agreements, lotteries, and games of chance have been illegal when they involve three elements: (1) some payments by the gambler (2) for a chance (3) to win some prize. However, many states now have certain legal forms of gambling. Pressure to raise public revenues in recent years has led to this legalization (according to some observers, a highly regressive form of taxation). Critics object to such activity as economically wasteful (unless one regards the dubious entertainment effect to be a valuable product). They say that the gullible and the ignorant thereby squander money that would be better spent for necessaries, and that gambling promoters cynically pander to greed and unfounded hope by suggesting that "you, too, can get rich quick," despite astronomical odds against such a result.

http://

For a listing of what gambling is legal within each state's borders, see http://www.naspl.org/programs.html

Sometimes it is difficult to distinguish a gambling contract from the risk-sharing inherent in most contracts.

LEGAL FOCUS—PROBLEM

Jaime Zavala takes out a life insurance policy on an acquaintance, Pete Botello. Zavala names himself as the beneficiary (the person to be paid) under the policy. Is this a legal contract or a gambling agreement?

The life insurance policy contract appears legal; however, Zavala is simply gambling on how long Botello will live. To prevent this type of contract, only someone with an **insurable interest** is allowed to recover on an insurance contract. An insurable interest exists when a person has a real economic risk related to the property or person insured. If your watch is stolen or damaged, for example, you suffer a real loss. If someone else's watch is stolen or broken, you may feel bad, but you suffer no direct economic loss. Thus, you have an insurable interest in your watch, but not in the other person's. Zavala cannot collect on an insurance policy on Botello's life (or home or auto) because he does not have an insurable interest in Botello or his property. If Zavala were a part owner in Botello's automobile, however, he could legally collect on an insurance policy on the auto because he has a property interest.

If an insurance company is aware that a person applying for insurance lacks an insurable interest, the company should refuse to sell the policy. An insurer that sells a policy unaware that the holder lacks an insurable interest will claim lack of insurable interest as a defense to a claim for payment upon learning the truth. An innocent claimant will get a return of the premiums paid but not a payment on the policy.

LICENSING   Many professions and trades require a license to practice (engage in business). Traditionally, the legitimate objective of such licensing laws has been to protect the public against unqualified practitioners. Critics complain the real objective is to limit entry in order to reduce competition in service and price. Nevertheless, contracts made by unlicensed persons are generally unenforceable; they cannot collect for services rendered. However, when the true objective of the licensing is to raise government revenues, failure to obtain a license does *not* render the contracts of the parties unenforceable or void. This would be true of a license required of all profit-making business firms in a city.

insurable interest

A sufficient interest in property to where its loss or destruction would cause an economic loss to the owner or possessor.

http://

See one state's (Missouri) grounds for refusal, revocation, or suspension of licenses required for enforceable contracts at **http://www.moga.state.mo .us/statutes/C300-399/ 3370630.htm**

LEGAL FOCUS—CASE

Paris was a real estate broker licensed in the state of Georgia. Paris contacted Cooper, a Florida resident who was interested in purchasing some Gulf County, Florida, acreage. Paris visited the property in Florida, helped prepare Cooper's written offer of purchase, worked with Cooper's attorney on the sales contract, and attended the closing of the sale in Panama City, Florida. As a result of this sale, Paris received a $315,070 commission. Can Cooper recover the commission on the basis that the contract is unenforceable because Paris was not licensed to conduct real estate transactions in Florida?

Cooper v. Paris, 413 So.2d 772 (Fla. App., 1st Dist., 1982).

Yes. An agent must have a real estate license to represent a client in a real estate transaction and expect to collect a fee. Such licenses are granted by each state to protect the citizens of that state. A license in Georgia does not authorize the agent to practice in Florida. The agent could not collect the commission, and if the commission had been paid, the client could sue for its return.

BLUE LAWS   In some states, strong support continues for traditional observance of the Sabbath as a day of rest and worship as mandated by the Mosaic Code.[10] Accordingly, **blue laws*** restrict the right to make or perform various contracts on Sundays. When such laws have been challenged as a violation of the First Amendment respecting establishment of religion, the U.S. Supreme Court has refused to interfere. Such observance is justified for needed rest and relaxation, the Court's reasoning goes; any day of the week could be designated for the purpose.

USURY   Most states regulate the maximum rates of interest that may be charged for certain loans of money. *Usury* is the practice of charging excessively high rates on loans. Today most states maintain some control over how much interest may be charged, but, for example, they allow rates as high as 40 percent a year or more on loans of no more than a few hundred dollars made by pawnbrokers and small loan companies. The extra interest charge is justified by the higher unit cost of processing such loans and by a higher risk of defaults by borrowers. The availability of such loans also helps to keep the borrowers out of the clutches of loan sharks, who may charge interest rates of 100 percent a year or more. Civil sanctions for usury vary among the states. In some states, the usurer is barred from collecting either principal or interest; in others, only the principal is payable; and additional variations exist. But observers suggest that many violations are unreported, often because of ignorance or fear of violent retaliation.

The purchase of goods on credit, subject to a carrying charge (some states call it **interest**) on the unpaid balance, has not been considered usury because there is not a direct loan of money. However, as this practice has become very widespread, legal limits are now often imposed on the percentage rate that may be imposed. The typical carrying charge (or "interest rate") approaches and sometimes exceeds 20 percent a year. This is a heavy levy, in light of the fact that the ordinary saver seldom earns as much as 3–5 percent in a bank savings account. Note that the federal **Consumer Credit Protection Act of 1968** (often referred to as the **Truth in Lending Act**) requires a full disclosure of the terms of contracts for sales on credit or for loans.[11] But it does not set any ceiling at the federal level on the rate of interest that may be charged, nor does it limit the price that may be charged for the goods or services sold.

Violations of Public Policy

Some agreements are obviously contrary to public policy and therefore illegal and void. The list includes attempts to obstruct justice in court by bribing jurors, paying a witness to lie under oath (this is the crime of **subornation of perjury**), or paying a witness more than the modest legal fee prescribed by statute. (Note that counsel may engage experts for both the plaintiff and the defendant, to study and render their opinions about facts of the case. They are often called on to testify during the trial. Such expert witnesses may legitimately receive fees for their services far in excess of payments made to other witnesses.) Also included in attempts to obstruct justice is paying bribes to influence legislators, adminis-

---

blue laws

Statutes that regulate or prohibit commercial activities and amusements on Sundays.

interest

The price, usually expressed as an annualized rate (percentage), for use of a sum of money (principal) obtained from a lender.

Consumer Credit Protection Act of 1968

Federal law requiring full disclosure to borrowers or consumers of the cost of credit as an annual percentage rate (APR) and in total dollars. This act is also known as the Truth in Lending Act.

http://

The charging of interest is an important moral issue in some religions. Read about interest and the Koran at **http://www.moslem.org/library/articles/interest.htm**

subornation of perjury

Crime of persuading another person to commit perjury.

---

* Blue laws originally referred to strict rules in colonial New England that outlawed such practices as working, dancing, and drinking intoxicating liquors on Sundays. The term now refers to statutes that regulate commercial activities and amusements on Sundays. In contrast, "blue sky laws" regulate the sale of stocks and bonds and are designed to prevent fraudulent sale of securities worth no more than patches of blue sky.

trators, and judges. Banned also, by the Federal Foreign Corrupt Practices Act, are bribes to obtain contracts with foreign governments.[12]

Lobbying, properly practiced, is vital to the democratic process of legislation. Lobbyists outnumber legislators in Congress and in most statehouses. They are usually employed under contracts with special-interest groups to persuade legislators to vote in a certain way on legislation. To many persons, "lobbyist" is a term of infamy, no doubt because the practice of lobbying has too often in the past been corrupted by bribery or veiled purchases of favors. Nevertheless, lobbyists serve a useful purpose in providing important information on the pros and cons of present and proposed legislation. Any person may lobby on his or her own behalf; however, federal and state statutes generally require that persons who lobby for other individuals or groups must register, identify their clients, and disclose the source and amounts of payments received and dispensed.

Agreements that restrict trade and competition are generally illegal. Such contracts, called **covenants not to compete,** often violate one or more federal or state statutes and are often construed as common-law torts as well. These restraints of trade are against the public interest, which favors free competition. There are two major potential exceptions to this rule of illegality:

1. When the restraint of free trade is part of an otherwise enforceable contract for the sale of a business and where a partner agrees not to compete in anticipation of dissolution of a partnership
2. When a new employee agrees, as part of the employment contract, not to accept another employment position with any other employer who is a competitor of the present employer

To be legal, such agreements must involve a legitimate business need and can be no more extensive in time, scope, and distance than reasonably necessary to protect the future related interests of the protected parties (i.e., the buyer of the business and the first employer). Courts also consider the effect of enforcement of such agreements on the public good—the restriction on the freedom to purchase goods and services cannot be excessive and is balanced against the contracting party's legitimate business need.

A promise by a person selling a business not to open a competing business close to the old one is an example of a covenant not to compete. A shoe retailer selling her business might appropriately agree not to open a competing business anywhere in a sparsely populated county for perhaps a year; a seller of a company manufacturing heavy-duty earthmoving machines, headed by a brilliant inventor whose unique products are sold worldwide, might properly agree not to open a competing business anywhere for three or more years. Thus, the buyer properly gets the benefit of the price paid for the goodwill* value of the going concern.

In employment contracts, it is common for middle-level and upper-level managers to be asked to agree not to work for competitors or start new competing business firms for a specified time after leaving the current employment relationship. Such non-compete clauses in employment contracts are subject to even more scrutiny than those in the sale of business. The restriction on competition must be reasonable; be necessary to protect confidential information or trade secrets obtained during employment; and not be any greater than necessary to protect a legitimate business interest.

lobbying

Efforts by individuals and representatives of special-interest groups to persuade legislators (and sometimes administrators) to enact, amend, or rescind specified laws.

covenant not to compete

A promise not to engage in a competing business or profession. Such covenants are generally illegal unless part of an otherwise enforceable contract for the sale of a business or for employment. In such case, they are legal only if they are drafted to be reasonable regarding time, scope, and geographic area, and are necessary to protect the interests of the contracting parties.

* Goodwill is the valuable intangible asset of a business that is developed over a prolonged period of time through successful contractual relations with satisfied customers and suppliers. Thus, an established business with goodwill normally enjoys higher profits than a new business of the same size but lacking such goodwill.

LEGAL FOCUS—CASE

Thomas Rector and four other employees of Paramount Termite Control Company agreed not to compete with their employer if they quit. The agreement stated they would refrain for two years after leaving Paramount employment from soliciting "business from any customer of Paramount where the purpose thereof is to provide the services of pest control with which customer the employee established contact while in the employ of Paramount at any time during the two years next preceding the termination of the Employment Agreement." The restriction covered the geographic areas the employees serviced as Paramount employees. Later, the employees resigned from Paramount and began working for a Paramount competitor that solicited business in the counties prohibited by the noncompetition agreement. Paramount sought to enforce the promise. Did Paramount succeed?

Paramount Termite Control Co. v. Rector, 238 Va. 171, 380 S.E.2d 922 (Virginia, 1989).

Yes. The Supreme Court of Virginia declared the restriction on competition was reasonable in time (two-year period) and in the geographic area covered. The court applied three criteria: (1) From the standpoint of the employer, was the restraint greater than necessary to protect a legitimate business interest of the employer? (2) From the standpoint of the employee, was the restraint reasonable—not unduly harsh and oppressive in limiting the employee's ability to earn a living? (3) Was the restraint reasonable as sound public policy? The court concluded that the restraint was no greater than reasonably necessary to protect Paramount's legitimate business interest. The five employees "had frequent contacts with Paramount's customers" and "were familiar with Paramount's methods of estimating the cost of its work, its specifications for doing the work, and its techniques of pest control." The court also found the geographic restriction reasonable, as it applied only to those counties in which the employees had previously worked and not in all counties within the state. Finally, because there was sufficient competition in the area, the court held the restrictions did not unreasonably restrain trade or violate public policy.

In a few states, such as California, non-compete agreements in employment contracts are not enforceable.* But in such states an out-of-state corporate employer may provide that the contract is to apply the law of the corporate home state where such clauses are enforceable rather than the state where the contract is illegal. Although the enforceability of such a tactic is doubtful, the employer will often go to great lengths to protect their interests.

http://

Find additional information about employee non-compete agreements at **http://jobsearchtech.about .com/library/weekly/ aa042202.htm**

What Is the Effect of Illegality?

An illegal agreement is void, and courts will normally not aid either party to the transaction in any way. Exceptions are made and damages in tort or other relief may be awarded (1) when the violated law is intended to protect one of the parties (this is true, for example, when one party is the victim of usury), (2) when the parties are not equally blameworthy (e.g., when one party is the victim of fraud in illegal securities dealing, or when one party acts under duress or undue influence), and (3) when one of the parties repents and withdraws before the time set for performance (as in illegal bets over the outcome of a football game).

---

* California Business & Professions Code § 16600 declares that every contract by which anyone is restrained from engaging in their lawful trade, business, or profession is to that extent void. It is permissible to restrict use of trade secrets and an employer's confidential information.

FORM PRESCRIBED BY LAW

The last requisite of a contract requires that contracts be in the form prescribed by law to be enforceable. This requirement exists only for those contracts for which statutes have created this as an additional requirement. Such contracts may be deficient in form, yet otherwise be valid. Thus, if the party who is entitled to raise the issue of form does not object, the contract may be routinely performed (executed) by both parties. After the contract is performed, the question of proper form is usually moot (no longer open to argument).

> *A verbal contract isn't worth the paper it's written on.*

Samuel Goldwyn, movie producer, 1882–1974

What Is the Statute of Frauds and Perjuries?

By statute, certain specialized contracts must contain prescribed language. This is true of fire and homeowners insurance policies. It is also true of contracts for loans and for sales of goods on credit under the Truth in Lending Act. But the most important legislation governing form in contracts was originated in 1677 in the English **Statute of Frauds and Perjuries.**[13] In essence, this statute provided that certain designated important contracts, to be enforceable in court, must (1) be in writing and (2) be signed by the party against whom enforcement is sought, or by his or her agent. Note that no problem as to form arises if the party *seeking* to enforce the contract has not signed. Such party could simply and promptly sign the document if the other party points out the lack of a signature.

The English statute is the original model for many versions adopted in most American states, all designed to prevent parties from subsequently fraudulently misrepresenting the actual terms of their agreements.

Writing important agreements encourages more careful draftsmanship and thus reduces potential misunderstandings and costly litigation. The requirement of a signature permits free and open negotiation and exchange of unsigned tentative drafts of the contract without fear of unintended or premature commitment. Including a sentence requiring the losing party, in case of litigation, to pay all court costs and reasonable attorney fees of the winner can discourage breaches of contracts and spiteful lawsuits. Better still, the written contract can provide for arbitration or some other specified alternative method of dispute resolution (see Chapter 4). Although the Statute of Frauds should encourage careful draftsmanship, any writing satisfies the requirement if it sufficiently expresses the agreement. Of course, the party against whom enforcement is sought must sign it. The writing could consist of a memorandum or letter(s), for example.

The following rules are better understood if certain technical words are first defined. The word **property** has a double meaning. It usually means the thing that is owned; in a strict legal sense, however, *property* means the rights of the owner to possess, use, and dispose of that thing. Property is broadly classified as real or personal. **Real property** is the land and things "permanently attached" to the land, such as buildings. It includes rights to airspace above the land, to water on the surface, and to the materials below the surface (e.g., oil, gas, and minerals). **Personal property** includes all movable property other than land. Both real and personal property appear in tangible and intangible forms. **Tangible property** has physical existence—it can be touched or seen. In contrast, **intangible property** has conceptual existence; an example is your reputation. Examples of *tangible real property* are the ground or land and buildings erected on the land. An example of *intangible real property* is an easement. An *easement* is the right to use another person's real property within prescribed limits and without removing anything from the property. An

---

Statute of Frauds

A state statute requiring certain types of contracts to be evidenced by a writing and to be signed by the party to be charged, or by her or his authorized agent.

http://

See the interesting article by Lloyd Rain about the origin and persistence in America of the Statute of Frauds
http://www.naeb.org/ Purchasing_Link/ Commentaries/Nov2002_LR _Commentary.htm

property

Anything that may be owned.

real property

Land and things permanently attached to it. Includes air space above, surface water, and subsurface waters, gases, and minerals.

personal property

All property that is not real property, i.e., property other than land and things permanently attached to it.

tangible property

Property that has physical existence and can be touched. An automobile is tangible personal property; a house is tangible real property

intangible property

Property recognized by law even though it has no physical existence.

example would be an easement to go across another's land to get to the shore of a lake or river. Examples of *tangible personal property* include this book, your watch, and a Big Mac at McDonald's. Examples of *intangible personal property* are the copyright on this book, the design patent on your watch, and the goodwill enjoyed by owners of McDonald's fast-food restaurants. Under the UCC, a sale "consists in the passing of title from the seller to the buyer for a price."[14] The person who has *title* owns the property. Personal property is discussed further in Chapter 9 and real property in Chapters 11 and 12.

What Contracts Must Comply with the Statute of Frauds?

The Statute of Frauds applies to the following kinds of contracts:

• *A contract for the sale of land or an interest therein.* Some states also require a lease for more than one year to be in writing. Thus, a month-to-month lease, or a lease of as long as one year, is valid even if oral. Under what is called the *equal-dignities rule,* the real estate broker's employment agreement (sometimes called a *listing*) to search for a purchaser of real property must also be in writing and properly signed.

• *A contract for the sale of tangible goods for the price of $500 or more.* Under the UCC, *goods* "means all things . . . which are movable . . . other than the money in which the price is to be paid, investment securities . . . and things in action" (which are rights to recover personal property or money by means of a trial or other judicial proceeding) "also . . . the unborn young of animals and growing crops and other identified things attached to realty."[15]

Certain important exceptions are made to this rule by the UCC. An oral contract for goods priced at $500 or more is nevertheless enforceable "if the goods are to be specially manufactured for the buyer and are not suitable for sale to others in the ordinary course of the seller's business." An example would be a unique and elaborate cabinet made with costly imported woods to hold a variety of audiovisual equipment, complete with a wet bar and built-in refrigerator. Before notice of repudiation of the contract is received, the seller must have "made either a substantial beginning of their manufacture, or commitments for their procurement." Further more, the buyer is bound "with respect to goods for which payment has been made and accepted or which have been received and accepted." Finally, the buyer is bound who "admits in his [her] pleading, testimony, or otherwise in court that a contract for sale was made."[16] The contract in such case would be enforceable, but only for the quantity of goods admitted.

LEGAL FOCUS—BACKGROUND

The UCC provides a special rule for merchants. Assume that between merchants a writing in confirmation of the sales contract and sufficient *against the sender* (who has signed) is received within a reasonable time, and the recipient has reason to know its contents. This will satisfy the requirement of a signed writing against the recipient (even though he or she has not signed), unless the recipient gives written notice of objection to its contents to the sender within ten days after it has been received.[17]

• *A contract that is not to be performed, and cannot possibly be performed within one year from the date of the agreement.* In calculating the time, the law ignores fractions of days, including any fraction of the date of the agreement. Thus, an oral contract for one year, to begin tomorrow, is enforceable. If it is to begin two or more days hence, it must be in writing and signed.

LEGAL FOCUS—PROBLEM

Samer Jamal is set to graduate from college. An employer orally contracts with Jamal to employ him for two years at $2,000 per month. Is this contract required to be in writing?

Yes. Because the terms of the contract exceed one year, this contract must be proved by written evidence to be enforceable. The oral agreement is insufficient proof of the existence of the contract. The one-year period begins to run the day after the contract is made, even if performance is not expected to begin until later.

- *A secondary, or underlying, contract* under which one person promises to pay or answer for the debt or duty of another, if such person fails to perform, or one in which an executor or administrator of an estate promises to pay a debt of the estate with his or her own money.
- *A promise made in consideration of marriage* (e.g., "If you marry me, I will support your parents until they die"). Note that a contract to marry, and the actual contract of marriage, may be and usually are expressed orally: "Will you marry me?" "Yes." "I now pronounce you husband and wife."
- *For the sale of kinds of personal property not otherwise covered* (in an amount or value beyond $5,000).[18] This provision does not apply to contracts for the sale of goods, securities, or security agreements, all of which are covered separately.[19]

Sufficiency of the Writing

The Statute of Frauds does not require a complete written contract signed by both parties. The statute can also be satisfied with a far less extensive writing—a memorandum. The memorandum can consist of any confirmation, invoice, sales slip, check, or telegram. Such items, singly or in combination, may be writings sufficient to satisfy the Statute of Frauds. Requirements of the statute for the memorandum are as follows:

- It must be signed by the party against whom enforcement is sought.
- It must contain at least the essential terms of the contract.

It is not required that both parties sign the memorandum. The essential signature is the signature of the person against whom enforcement is sought (person being sued).

LEGAL FOCUS—PROBLEM

Shelly Moon agreed to lease Eric Almendral's house for three years for $600 a month rent. Moon found an old standard-form lease, filled out the terms, signed it, and gave it to Almendral saying, "Please sign this lease, Eric." Almendral responded that he had changed his mind and now would like $750 a month rent. Can Moon enforce Almendral's oral promise to lease the property for three years at $600 a month? Does the lease she signed satisfy the Statute of Frauds?

Moon cannot enforce Almendral's promise as a lease for a three-year term must be in writing to be enforceable. Although Moon prepared the lease, Almendral did not sign it, and he is the party against whom enforcement is sought. In other words, for a party to enforce a contract, the writing must be signed by the other party. Thus, it is possible for a contract to be enforceable by one party, but not by the other.

The signature can be placed anywhere on the writing. It need not be at the end. And a signature can be initials or even a mark rather than a full name. The law does not require a witness, although without a witness it is hard to prove who created a mark and whether the mark was intended as a signature. Moon could have made a deposit by check (noting purpose of the payment on the check) and then Almendral's signature as an endorsement would undoubtedly have satisfied the Statute of Frauds.

D IRECT INVOLVEMENT OF THIRD PARTIES IN CONTRACTS

THIRD-PARTY DONEE AND CREDITOR BENEFICIARIES

privity of contract

Applies to a direct contractual relationship between parties, as exists, for example, with a consumer-buyer dealing with the retail-seller but not with the wholesaler or manufacturer of the goods.

third party beneficiary

A third party who receives the benefit of a contract between two other persons.

If a contract is valid and legally enforceable, attention turns to the rights and duties of the parties. The relationship created between parties to a contract is called **privity of contract.** Parties in privity of contract have rights and duties because of the contract. Usually, third parties not in privity have no rights under the contract.

Most bilateral and unilateral contracts directly involve only the two original contracting parties. However, from the very inception of their agreement, one party may name and provide for a **third-party beneficiary.** For example, a parent in a contract for ordinary life insurance may name a child as a beneficiary of the policy. Since the main purpose is to confer a gift upon a third party, the child who has paid nothing therefore qualifies as a *donee beneficiary.*[20] As such, the child may enforce the contract and collect the proceeds of the policy upon the death of the parent. If the main purpose of the promisee buying the policy is to pay a debt or extinguish an obligation owed to a third party, then the third party is a *creditor beneficiary.*[21]

LEGAL FOCUS—PROBLEM

When Ricky Nikkel sold his gift and novelty shop to Lisa Oddeon, there were accounts payable (money owed to creditors) on the books with a total of $12,000 owed to five suppliers. Oddeon agreed to pay the balance due as part of the purchase price of the shop. Thus, the five suppliers were third-party creditor beneficiaries in the sales contract, and they have legal claims under the contract against Oddeon.

Beneficiaries of contracts (whether donee or creditor) can sue to enforce a contract that was made purposely for their benefit. Not all persons who benefit from contracts are given the right to enforce beneficial promises, however. The courts distinguish between intended beneficiaries (who can sue to enforce the contract) and incidental beneficiaries (who cannot).

An incidental beneficiary is a person who benefits from a contract but is not named and has no legally enforceable rights or duties under the contract. An example would be the benefit that people enjoy when the government builds a road under contract, or when private developers build a shopping center. Probably everyone has been an incidental beneficiary in many contracts.

assignment

The transfer of some or all rights under a contract to another person.

ASSIGNMENT OF CONTRACT RIGHTS AND DELEGATION OF DUTIES

After a contract has been made, the original parties generally may transfer their contractual rights and duties to others. The transfer of a right to a third person is an **assignment.**

When rights under a contract are assigned, the rights of the *assignor* (the party making the assignment) are usually ended. The third party—the *assignee,* the party receiving the assignment—has a right to demand performance from the other original party to the contract, the *obligor.* Most rights can be freely assigned, but there are exceptions. For example, unless otherwise agreed, one may not transfer rights to personal services. Also, a transfer of rights may not be made if it could materially increase the burden of performance on the other party to the contract. Thus you cannot transfer your fire insurance policy to someone who buys your house, nor your automobile insurance to someone who buys your car. Indeed, such contracts specifically prohibit assignment to another party.

Parties can also transfer duties. Duties are not assigned, they are *delegated.* Normally, a **delegation** of duties does not release the party making the delegation (the *delegator*) from any obligations. If the party to whom the duty has been delegated (the *delegatee*) fails to perform, the delegator—who is the original obligor—must perform. No special form is required to delegate duties. In special situations, as where they involve uniquely personal services, the duties may not be delegated. Thus without consent of the patient, a surgeon may not transfer an accepted duty of performing an operation.

Valid transfers of contractual rights and duties occur with regularity. A common example that often involves multiple transfers is a contract for the construction of a private residence.

> **delegation**
>
> Transfer of some or all contractual duties to another person.

LEGAL FOCUS—PROBLEM

On June 1, 2000, Able Construction Company, a general contractor, agreed to build and sell a particular house to Susie Baker on land it owns, for a contract price of $250,000. Promised delivery date is on or before November 1, that year. Daniel Able and a small crew of his employees prepare the site and lay the foundation. In separate contracts, on and after June 8, 2000, Able delegates all other construction work to independent contractors who are trade specialists in their fields (carpentry, plumbing, electrical work, painting, and so forth) for various prices. Able remains liable to Baker for the completed job as promised. On July 1, 2000, Baker learns that she is to be promoted and transferred by her employer to another city. Therefore, she sells the house to a friend, Jessica Newcomer, on August 10, 2000. She does this by assigning her rights and delegating her duties in the project to Newcomer. These contracts are graphically portrayed in Exhibit 8-3.

Note that Able might have assigned the right to part of or the entire $250,000 price to a bank for a construction loan. Also, both Baker and Newcomer could have negotiated separate loan contracts, with the house as security, to finance the purchase (see Chapter 12). Note, too, that Baker might have asked Newcomer to pay more or less than $250,000, but the parties agreed to the transfer at the original price.

HOW ARE CONTRACTS DISCHARGED?

The customary and usual way of discharging contracts is by **performance.** The reciprocal rights and duties of the parties are legally terminated when the parties have done what they have promised to do. Sometimes the performance is not precisely as promised, but the minor deviation may be a good-faith oversight or failure. In the house-construction example,

> **performance**
>
> That which each party to a contract promises to do.

EXHIBIT 8-3: Example of Contract with Subsequent Delegation of Duties and Assignment of Rights

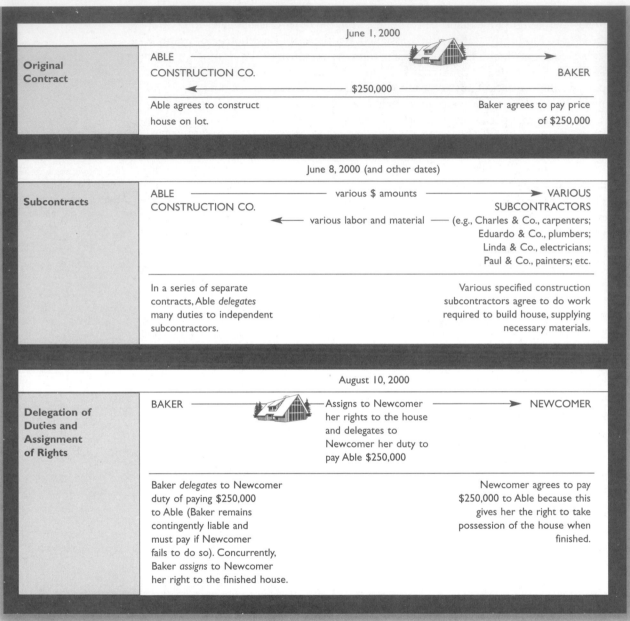

substantial performance

When a party to a contract honestly performs most essentials of the contract, but there is some minor omission or deviation which can be corrected, or compensated for in a reduction of the price.

assume the paint used was the proper quality and color but the wrong brand, or the garage door may have been a half-foot wider than specified. The buyer must still "perform" by paying for such **substantial performance** by the general contractor, but may deduct an appropriate amount because of any deficiency in the builder's performance. The buyer need not pay extra for any improvements "volunteered" by the builder. Often businesspersons as well as ultimate consumers will accept an alternative or a variation of a promised performance simply because the deviation is not significant or does not reduce the value of consideration received. To insist on absolute compliance may end a mutually beneficial relationship.

Rather than engage in costly and acrimonious arguments and litigation, a party may **waive** (give up) or renounce legal contract rights. For example, an employer may do so when an employee under a year's contract quits without just cause after a month or two. Occasionally, a party will agree to accept some substitute for the original promised consideration.

LEGAL FOCUS—EXAMPLE

Malcolm Defft, a dentist, never refused to treat a patient, regardless of his or her ability to pay promptly for the service. When the charges for dental care of Earl Gartner, an unemployed gardener, and his wife Hildy reached $600, they offered to redo Defft's lawn and trim all the trees and bushes on his lot in full payment or satisfaction of the debt. Defft agreed. This was an executory *accord.* When the work was completed, the debt was discharged by *accord and satisfaction.*

An accord is an agreement to perform an act to satisfy an existing contractual duty. A satisfaction is the performance of the accord agreement. For a contract to be discharged by **accord and satisfaction,** the parties must agree to accept a performance different from the performance originally promised. An accord and its satisfaction, or performance, discharge the original contractual obligation. Until satisfaction, the parties do not give up the rights they had before the accord.

LEGAL FOCUS—EXAMPLE

Peter Benton gets a judgment against Kris Lorie for $6,000. Later, both parties agree that the judgment can be satisfied (paid) by Lorie's transferring her motor home to Benton. This agreement to accept the motor home instead of $6,000 in cash is the accord. If Lorie transfers her motor home to Benton, the accord agreement is fully satisfied, and the $6,000 debt is discharged. If Lorie refuses to transfer her motor home, the accord is breached. Since an original obligation is merely suspended in an accord, Benton can bring a lawsuit to enforce the judgment for $6,000 in cash.

In the hypothetical house construction, buyer Baker's contractual obligation might have been discharged if Able, the general contractor, had agreed with Baker and Newcomer to a **novation** (i.e., substitution of a new contract, debt, or obligation for an existing one between the same or different parties). Typically, a new contract is created with the same terms as the original one, but the novation substitutes a new party and discharges one of the original parties by agreement of all three parties.[22] This would allow Newcomer to be substituted for Baker in the contract. The bank that lent the construction money to Baker undoubtedly required her to sign a promissory note agreeing to pay. Had the bank deliberately marked the note "Cancelled" or destroyed it—a very unlikely possibility—the debt would have been discharged by *cancellation.* Similarly, any deliberate important change in a promissory note or other written contract by a party to the contract is a **material alteration,** and discharges the contractual obligation of the other party.

When there is a material (important) **breach,** or failure or refusal to perform a contract, the victim may cancel the contract with no liability and sue for damages. The right

---

waive

To give up a right.

accord and satisfaction

A party agrees (by accord) to accept some substitute for the promised performance of a contract, which is then provided (the satisfaction).

novation

A three-party agreement in which a creditor accepts a new party who agrees to assume the debt and to release the prior debtor.

material alteration

Any deliberate, unilateral (by one of the parties), important change that is made in a written contract, without legal excuse.

breach

Failure without legal excuse to perform a promise made in a legally binding agreement.

to sue, if utilized successfully, may be superseded by a judgment of the court. This, too, serves to discharge the contract, but by operation of law. Other means of discharging a contract by operation of law include (1) subsequent illegality—as when the Eighteenth Amendment prohibited "manufacture, sale, or transportation of intoxicating liquors"; (2) bankruptcy (the debts are not extinguished, but they cannot be enforced unless reaffirmed by the debtor with approval by the court); (3) running of the statute of limitations (again, the debts are not extinguished, but they cannot be enforced unless reaffirmed by the debtor); (4) literal impossibility (as where a contract requires personal service and the individual dies); and (5) commercial impracticability, where "performance as agreed has been made impracticable by the occurrence of a contingency the non-occurrence of which was a basic assumption on which the contract was made."[23] Outbreak of war, surprise discovery of solid granite throughout much of the anticipated site of an underground garage, and a major earthquake are examples of circumstances in which performance might be excused because it has become commercially impracticable.

Circumstances can be such that both parties "want out." In such a case, a voluntary **rescission** is mutually agreed on. Anything already received is returned, and the previous situation is restored.

rescission

The unmaking of a contract by the mutual agreement of the parties.

What Remedies Are Available for Breach of Contract?

Vigorous contract activity is essential to a healthy economy. Through its laws, society seeks to encourage people to enter contracts and to perform as promised. Failure to do so is not conducive to goodwill and continued relations. But a breach of contract is not a crime and, except in unusual circumstances (e.g., when there is a breach of covenant of good faith and fair dealing), it is not a tort. In a sense, contracting parties can usually regard a breach as a possible alternative to performance; it is surely not morally reprehensible if the victim of the breach is promptly "made whole" by being provided with money or some alternative performance that offsets any loss suffered.

If litigation becomes necessary, the defaulting party is generally obliged by a court to pay **compensatory damages**, sufficient to place the victim in essentially the same economic position or condition that would have resulted from performance of the contract. Only if the agreement were corrupted by a related tort, such as fraud, would punitive damages be awarded.

compensatory damages

In the case of a breach of contract, this amount is equivalent to the actual dollar loss suffered because the defendant did not perform as promised.

LEGAL FOCUS—EXAMPLE

Pete Armond agreed to sell his used Harley-Davidson motorcycle to Candy Bushnell for $6,500. When Armond changed his mind and refused to complete the deal, Bushnell promptly bought a comparable model for $7,500 from Pat Caldwell. Armond is liable to Bushnell for $1,000 in compensatory damages. If Bushnell was lucky enough to find a similar model priced at $6,000, she could still sue for *token or nominal damages* (typically for $1). Armond would also be liable for court costs, but not for Bushnell's attorney's fees, unless that was provided for in the original sales contract.

Sometimes, the parties to a contract specify in advance what the damages shall be in case of breach. Such **liquidated damage clauses** are often used in contracts for the construction of public buildings or commercial structures where damages are difficult to determine and prove. Courts will enforce such terms as long as the damages are not in fact penalties. They must be reasonable in the light of the anticipated or actual injury or harm caused by the breach.

liquidated damages

Amount of damages that contracting parties have previously agreed would be fair payment in case of breach. This amount will be unacceptable by a court if it is so large as to constitute a penalty.

LEGAL FOCUS—EXAMPLE

When Metropolitan College contracted for its new classroom buildings (price $6 million), the general contractor promised to have it ready for occupancy two years thereafter, when the fall semester would begin on August 28. A liquidated damage clause called for the payment of $600 per school day (Monday through Saturday) of delay in completion beyond the promised date of August 28. Losses incurred would include rental costs for temporary portable buildings and the monetary value of burdens imposed on students, faculty, and staff from overcrowding and required reassignments. Therefore, this clause would be enforceable.

In some cases where money damages are inadequate, courts provide an *equitable, non-monetary remedy*. For example, since every parcel of land is unique, a buyer of land can compel delivery of possession by the owner who promised to sell. So, too, with unique works of art. For example, in 1989, an unidentified Japanese bidder at an auction agreed to pay $45.9 million for *Pierrot's Wedding*, a masterpiece from Pablo Picasso's famed "blue period."[24] Under U.S. law, a seller who refuses to deliver such a painting could be compelled to do so by a buyer who obtains a *specific performance decree* from a court of equity. Of course, if the painting has already been sold to another person who, unaware of the prior contract, bought in good faith and received good title, the victimized buyer would have to be satisfied with a money judgment. When appropriate, courts of equity may also issue *injunctions* (sometimes called *restraining orders*), which may prohibit a defendant from doing a specified act or command the defendant to do some positive act.

LEGAL FOCUS—PROBLEM

The talented and temperamental opera star Matilda Nocallara contracted—a full year in advance—to perform at a gala concert in New York City. The event was promoted by Joy Jordane. A month before the scheduled date, Nocallara told Jordane that she was "indisposed" and planned instead to make "a less strenuous television appearance" that week in Los Angeles. What did Jordane do?

Jordane obtained an injunction from a court of equity, forbidding Nocallara to perform in Los Angeles on the day of the scheduled concert. The court would not directly compel her appearance in New York because that would smack of involuntary servitude and would be difficult to enforce. In addition, the court would award Jordane dollar damages if Nocallara failed to keep her New York commitment.

Ⓦhat Special Protection Is Provided for Individual Consumer Contracts?

"Some devices, such as battery-operated toys costing $39.95, break down almost instantly upon exposure to the Earth's atmosphere. Other devices, such as stereo systems owned by your next-door neighbor's 13-year-old son who likes to listen to bands with names like 'Nerve Damage,' at a volume capable of disintegrating limestone, will continue to function perfectly for many years, even if you hit them with an ax."

Dave Barry, humorist

adhesion contract

A contract drafted by a dominant party and then presented to the other party—the adhering party—on a "take it or leave it" basis.

caveat emptor

[Latin for "let the buyer beware"] A phrase meaning that before purchase a buyer should investigate and then rely on his or her own judgment regarding obvious or readily discoverable shortcomings of the goods or services.

caveat venditor

[Latin for "let the seller beware"] A phrase meaning that a seller should exercise appropriate care to assure that goods sold (or services rendered) are of fair value and suitable for human use, or be subjected to possible legal sanctions.

Everyone is a consumer for some of their contracts. The most common consumer contracts are sales (purchase) agreements. Purchases are often made on credit, involving separate contracts to permit payment over extended periods of time. Sellers (i.e., manufacturers, wholesalers, and retailers) are generally more knowledgeable about their products and services than are most consumers. Moreover, sellers are more likely to have the assistance of attorneys in drafting contracts.

When one party has vastly superior bargaining power over another, they often draft their contracts without consultation with the other party. These contracts are called **adhesion contract,** defined as a contract drafted by a dominant party and then presented to the weaker party—the adhering party—on a "take it or leave it" basis. If the powerful party used their bargaining advantage to include unfair and/or surprising terms in the contract, a court has the power to consider such terms or the entire contract unconscionable and refuse to enforce it as against public policy. Unconscionable clauses, those that "shock the conscience" of a court, are more likely to be found in adhesion contracts than contracts where the parties truly bargained over terms.

▶ LEGAL FOCUS—PROBLEM
....

A welfare recipient with a fourth-grade education agrees to purchase a refrigerator under a two-year installment contract with a high but legal interest rate. The total price of the refrigerator is $2,500. The same type of refrigerator usually sells for $400 on the market. Is it possible that this contract is unconscionable?

Some courts have held this type of contract to be unconscionable, even though courts generally do not inquire into the adequacy of the consideration. To tell the consumer, "*Caveat emptor*—let the buyer beware," is no help when the buyer lacks the knowledge needed to evaluate the goods (be they simple clothing or complex electronic gear).

Over the years (dating back at least to 1906, when the federal Pure Food and Drug Act was enacted), government at all levels has been involved in protecting consumers against unfair practices of a comparatively small group of unethical businesspersons and firms that are always present somewhere in the marketplace. In the 1960s and 1970s, several important federal consumer protection bills were added. Although abuses continue, three broad categories of legislation (before-sale laws, during-sale laws, and after-sale laws) have given meaningful "teeth"—such as fines and prison terms—to the admonition, "*Caveat venditor*—let the seller beware."

BEFORE-SALE LAWS

Before-sale laws regulate the design, composition, and production of products for sale. They embrace such elements as quality, safety, purity, description, and packaging. For example, before-sale laws require emission devices to be installed in automobiles to reduce air pollution and tamper-proof packaging for over-the-counter drugs.

Since 1972, the Consumer Product Safety Commission (CPSC) has been charged with overseeing the safety of all consumer products other than autos, trucks, airplanes, boats, food, drugs, and cosmetics (which are the concern of other federal agencies).

http://

The U.S. Consumer Product Safety Commission Web site is at
http://www.cpsc.gov/

LEGAL FOCUS—BACKGROUND

John D'Angelo, owner and president of Utility Free Inc., a Colorado-based distributor of alternative energy products, was sentenced to nearly two years in jail for violating two laws enforced by CPSC. D'Angelo pled guilty to fifteen counts of improperly shipping hazardous substances, including a highly corrosive, clear electrolyte solution. In December 1993, fifteen-year-old Justin Pulliam mistook the solution for water because D'Angelo had shipped it in a reused plastic one-gallon milk container that lacked appropriate warnings. The teenager drank it and died two weeks later from internal injuries.[25]

Probably the most important task of the CPSC is recall or corrective action orders on products produced and/or sold in the United States.

The Pure Food and Drug Act of 1906 is a legislative landmark in the area of consumer before-sale health protection. It marked the beginning of federal regulation of food and drugs in the United States. What caused the congressional action was the public outrage generated by a novel. Upton Sinclair's *The Jungle,* published in 1905, was an exposé of the Chicago meatpacking industry. The story was so revolting that no one who read it could remain unaffected. President Theodore Roosevelt demanded an immediate investigation of the Chicago meatpacking houses, supposedly after reading the following paragraph:

> *There was never the least attention paid to what was cut up for sausages; there would come all the way back from Europe old sausage that had been rejected, and that was mouldy and white—it would be dosed with borax and glycerine, and dumped into the hoppers, and made over again for home consumption. There would be meat that had tumbled out on the floor, in the dirt and sawdust, where the workers had tramped and spit uncounted billions of consumption germs. . . . It was too dark in these storage places to see well, but a man could run his hand over these piles of meat and sweep off handfuls of the dried dung of rats. These rats were nuisances, and the packers would put poisoned bread out for them; they would die, and then rats, bread and meat would go into the hoppers together. This is no fairy story and no joke; . . . there were things that went into the sausage in comparison with which a poisoned rat was a tidbit.[26]*

President Roosevelt ordered an investigation and the labor commissioner confirmed Sinclair's observations. Both the long-stalled Pure Food and Drug Act and the Meat Inspection Act were passed immediately.

Under the authority of the federal Nutrition Labeling and Education Act of 1990, the Food and Drug Administration now requires that nutritional information (per serving) be provided on labels on canned and packaged foods. Examine the label on a can of your favorite soup, for example, and note the detailed listing of quantities therein of calcium, various types of fat, cholesterol, sodium, vitamins, and minerals. For many consumers, such information can literally be a lifesaver.

DURING-SALE LAWS

http://

The Federal Trade Commission provides a very helpful Web site at **http://www.ftc.gov/**

During-sale laws regulate truth in advertising, extension of credit, and contract terms and language. The Federal Trade Commission, created under the Federal Trade Commission Act of 1914, was originally primarily concerned with enforcement of the federal antitrust laws (i.e., the Sherman Anti-Trust Act of 1890 and the Clayton Act of 1914). The FTC sought to prevent among business corporations unfair methods of competition that could lead to monopolies. More recently, the FTC has also been active as the principal federal agency regulating advertising.

LEGAL FOCUS—BACKGROUND

On September 21, 1998, Judge Wilkie D. Ferguson, Jr., in U.S. District Court, Florida, granted the FTC's request for a stipulated final order and permanent injunction against National Scholarship Foundation (NSF) to forbid advertising of student scholarship services. The FTC complaint stated that NSF sent hundreds of thousands of postcards to potential college students and their families to solicit NSF's scholarship search services. When a consumer called the listed 800 number, a company representative told the caller that NSF could guarantee $1,000 worth of free grants and scholarships for a student if the caller paid a fee. In addition, the $189 fee would be refunded to anyone who did not receive $1,000 or more in scholarship money through NSF within one year. The FTC charged that in fact NSF did not fulfill its promise to find sources for its customers that led them to $1,000 minimum scholarship(s) and that the service provided was generally worthless. In addition, according to the FTC, NSF rarely honored its refund guarantee.[27]

Consumer Credit Protection Act of 1968

Federal law requiring full disclosure to borrowers or consumers of the cost of credit as an annual percentage rate (APR) and in total dollars. This act is also known as the Truth in Lending Act.

The most important section of the **Consumer Credit Protection Act of 1968** is known as the *Truth in Lending Act,* which requires a full disclosure of the comparative costs of buying goods for cash or on credit. On credit sales and loans of money, the creditor must disclose, in writing and in advance of signing, the total dollar finance charge and the effective annual percentage rate (APR) of the interest or finance charge. Sellers may not mislead gullible customers, for example, by quoting a credit cost of "only 1.5 percent a month." They must disclose that the equivalent interest cost per year is 18 percent. The act also provides for a three-day "cooling-off" period when a consumer agrees to borrow on the security of a second mortgage on a home. Under the law, the borrower may rescind and get back any money delivered to the creditor as long as he or she does it within the three days. The act places no limit on the rate or amount of interest or carrying charge, although some consumer advocates think it should.

The cooling-off rule of the Truth in Lending Act does not apply to first mortgages (or first deeds) on homes, because such credit has not generally been the basis for exploitation of unsophisticated homeowners in need of funds and because the interest rates have been reasonable. The three-day cooling-off period is a narrow exception that allows a party to escape a contract acceptance. Unfortunately, many consumers who have heard of the "three-day rule" think it applies to all consumer contracts. It does not.

Traditionally, *garnishment* (attachment of the salary or wages of a defaulting debtor) has been a principal remedy for unpaid creditors. To use this remedy, the creditor gets a court order (called a *writ of execution*) directing the debtor's employer to pay a certain portion of the employee's wages directly to the creditor until the judgment is paid in full. Sometimes employers fired workers who got into such financial trouble. Under the federal Consumer Credit Protection Act, normally the amount garnished may not exceed 25 percent of the worker's weekly take-home pay, or $60, or the amount by which the take-home pay exceeds 30 times the federal minimum wage, whichever is least. The act further provides that an employer may not discharge an employee simply because wages have been garnished for any one indebtedness.

The federal **Credit Card Act of 1970** controls certain practices of credit card companies. A consumer must apply for a credit card; it may not be thrust on the consumer without such request and consent. Moreover, the cardholder's liability for unauthorized use of the card by a thief or dishonest finder is limited to a maximum of $50 per card. And even this limited liability can be imposed only if all of the following apply:

- *The cardholder requested and received the credit card, or signed or used it, or authorized another person to do so.*
- *The card issuer provided a self-addressed, pre-stamped notification to be mailed by the cardholder in the event of loss or theft of the card.*
- *The card issuer gave adequate notice of the $50 liability.*
- *The card issuer provided positive means of identification (for example, signature or photo of the cardholder on the card).*
- *The unauthorized use took place before the cardholder notified the issuer that such use might take place.*

The **Fair Credit Reporting Act of 1970** as amended (FCRA) regulates the conditions under which disclosure of personal information may be made to third parties by consumer reporting agencies. For example, the consumer must give consent before a credit report can be released to an employer or potential employer. And before an adverse employment action can be taken based on such a report, the consumer must receive a copy of the report. Although the act does not restrict the amount or type of information that can be collected, it does give consumers the right to check their credit files for accuracy. The opportunity is provided to correct or explain inaccurate information, and the credit agency is under a duty to remove inaccurate or incomplete information. The national bureaus are required by law to have a joint reinvestigation system so (in theory) a consumer trying to correct an incorrect credit report does not have to deal with all national providers. Violations of FCRA are enforced by the Federal Trade Commission.

The **Equal Credit Opportunity Act of 1974** forbids discrimination in extension of credit because of sex, marital status, race, color, religion, national origin, or advanced age; because the applicants get all or part of their income from a public assistance welfare program; or because the applicant has in good faith exercised a right under the Consumer Credit Protection Act.

In the past few years, the use of debit and ATM cards has increased significantly. A **debit card** deducts the amount of a purchase directly from your checking account. Its use is not dependent on any coding. An ATM card is used in an automated teller machine (thus the ATM acronym) which may access a credit or a debit account to complete banking inquiries and fund transfers between accounts. Its use requires a code (Personal Identification Number, or PIN). Technically an ATM card is subtype of debit card. Although

Credit Card Act of 1970

Federal law that regulates issuance and enforcement of credit cards.

Fair Credit Reporting Act of 1970

A federal law that enables consumers to check and correct credit information about themselves in the files of credit-reporting companies.

http://

The three major credit reporting agencies where you can find out your credit history for a fee are Equifax
http://www.equifax.com/
Experian
http://www.experian.com/
and TransUnion Corp
http://www.transunion.com/index.jsp

Equal Credit Opportunity Act of 1974

Federal law that forbids discrimination in the extension of credit because of sex, marital status, race, or other specified qualities of the applicant.

debit card

A card that allows customers access to their own funds immediately, through various electronic means.

the use of these cards is pervasive, consumers appear to lack a good understanding of their legal significance.

Although they often look like credit cards, these cards are very different. Debit cards draw against an account the user has with a financial institution or a prior payment of money the user has made to the card issuer. They do not involve an extension of credit. Instead of "pay later," they represent "pay now."

Few of the consumer protections available when credit card disputes arise apply to debit card use. The transactions are essentially cash transactions. If the debit card is stolen, federal law limits the holder's maximum liability to $50 if the card loss is reported within two days of discovery. After two days liability increases to $500; if the card loss is not reported within 60 days, the liability can be unlimited. In addition, because the money is taken directly from an account, checks can bounce with all attendant costs perhaps even before the consumer knows there is a problem. With a credit card a bill is received; if charges are unauthorized the consumer still has the money while working on the problem. With a debit card you are working with your bank to get your money back.

Because debit card use provides a greater profit to banks than ATM use many banks have sent debit cards to their customers in exchange for ATM-only cards. Although disclosures accompany these transactions, most consumers don't appreciate the distinction between an ATM card and a debit card that also acts as an ATM card. Many debit card providers provide more favorable terms to their customers than the law requires. As debit cards carry significant additional risk over ATM cards or credit cards, be careful and shop around.

AFTER-SALE LAWS

After-sale laws regulate credit billings, methods of debt collection, and warranties. The **Fair Credit Billing Act of 1974** is a response to problems that result when clerks with computers electronically provide invoices that may be erroneous. Consumers who believe (1) an accounting error has been made by the issuer of a credit card; (2) goods or services have not been delivered or accepted; (3) credit extensions have not been made or have been made incorrectly; or (4) payments or credits have been recorded incorrectly may notify the creditor in writing within sixty days after the issuer mailed them the first bill with the error. The creditor (or issuer of the card) must investigate and respond promptly, normally within thirty days of receipt. Within ninety days, the creditor must either eliminate the error or explain why it believes the bill was correct.

After notification, the creditor is temporarily barred from pressing for payment or reporting to a credit bureau, although statements may continue to be sent. Consumers are legally obligated to pay any part of the bill not in dispute. If the creditor admits an error, it cannot impose finance charges on the disputed amount. The creditor must submit a correct written notice of what is owed, and consumers must be given the usual time to pay before any finance charges or late-payment charges may be assessed. If it turns out that there was no error, consumers must pay finance charges on the disputed amount and make up any payments missed. The debtor who is not satisfied with the creditor's explanation is allowed a minimum of ten days after receiving the explanation in which to protest. Thereafter, whether or not such protest was made, the creditor may sue or use other collection procedures. If there was a second protest, however, the creditor who notified credit bureaus and other creditors must mention the dispute and inform the debtor of the identity of the addressees.

Failure to comply with the stated rules makes the finance charges and first $30 of the disputed amount uncollectible, even if later events prove there was no creditor error.

http://

Read all about debit cards at the National Consumers League Web site at **http://www.nclnet.org/debitbro.htm**

Find out what to do if you lose your ATM or debit card at **http://www.ftc.gov/bcp/conline/pubs/credit/atmcard.htm**

Fair Credit Billing Act of 1974

A federal law that permits users of credit cards to challenge correctness of charges, without penalty.

The **Fair Debt Collection Practices Act of 1977** outlaws a variety of unreasonably harsh tactics used in the past by overly aggressive debt collectors. Banned are late night and early morning telephone calls, the use of obscene and abusive language, threats to notify employers, false representation as police or official government agents, harassment with repeated phone calls, and similar unsavory behavior. Nothing in the law prevents creditors from using legitimate methods and conventional legal remedies to collect overdue debts.

WHAT WARRANTY PROTECTION DO YOU HAVE AS A CONSUMER?

A **warranty** is an assurance, promise, or guarantee by one party that a particular statement of fact is true and may be relied upon by the other party in a commercial transaction. Some warranties are implied by law and exist even if nothing is said about them; other warranties are expressed and may be oral, but are usually stated in the written contract. An **express warranty** can exist even if a seller did not intend to make one.

Although warranties can arise in a variety of commercial situations, coverage in this chapter focuses on the assurances given in the sale or lease of goods under the UCC. The UCC does not require that the seller "use formal words such as 'warrantor guarantee' or that he has a specific intention to make a warranty." It is necessary only that a reasonable buyer would believe that a particular representation was part of the bargain. An **implied warranty** is one that the law implies from the nature or circumstances of the transaction.

Although warranties can arise in any sales or lease transaction, it is important to distinguish between merchants and casual sellers. A **merchant** is a professional seller who deals in goods of the kind, or otherwise by occupation holds himself or herself out as having knowledge or skill peculiar to the practice or goods involved in the transaction.[28] Casual sellers are ordinary laypersons disposing of things they own.

Either a merchant or a casual seller may explicitly make the following express warranties:

- **Warranty of conformity to description, sample, or model.** All goods supplied must conform to the sample or model shown at the time of the sale, or to the specifications provided.
- **Warranty of conformity to seller's statement or promise.** The seller who openly states or writes a factual assertion about the goods is bound by that assertion.

In addition to express warranties, sales by either a merchant or casual seller create each of these implied warranties:

- **Warranty of title.** The seller has the title to the goods as claimed and the right to transfer or sell them.
- **Warranty against encumbrances.** The goods delivered will be free of liens or encumbrances—creditors' claims—of which the buyer is not aware at the time of contracting.
- **Warranty of fitness for a particular purpose.** If the buyer indicates the purpose for which the goods are needed and then relies on the seller's selection, the goods will be reasonably fit for the intended stated purpose.

LEGAL FOCUS—PROBLEM

When Peggy Butler visited Mac's Sport Shack, she told the salesperson that she was planning a backpack trip into the Great Smoky Mountains. Butler insisted on being outfitted

---

Fair Debt Collection Practices Act of 1977

A federal law that outlaws certain unreasonably harsh collection practices previously used by professional debt collectors.

warranty

Assurance given by the seller of goods concerning the title to, or the quality or performance of, the product sold.

express warranty

A warranty given by a seller to a buyer orally or in writing.

implied warranty

A warranty implied by actions or law whether or not it is specifically mentioned in a contract.

merchant

A businessperson who regularly deals in goods of the kind involved in a sales or lease contract.

http://

A Businessperson's Guide to Federal Warranty Law can be found at **http://www.ftc.gov/bcp/conline/pubs/buspubs/warranty.htm**

with "Pathfinder" brand moccasin boots and a "Kozy" brand sleeping bag. After several days in the wilderness using this gear, she realized that neither product fit her needs. Her ankles were swollen, and she caught pneumonia. Is Mac's Sport Shack liable on a breach of warranty of fitness for a particular purpose?

No. A warranty is not given when the buyer insists on a particular brand, as here. Possibly Butler could hold the manufacturers liable if they had made express warranties as to the goods and these warranties were breached.

Merchant sellers alone make the following two additional implied warranties:

- **Warranty against infringement.** The goods sold are delivered free of any rightful claim of a third party under patent, copyright, or other legal protection.
- **Warranty of merchantability.** This is an extremely important warranty, promising that the goods are fit for the ordinary purposes for which such goods are used. Thus, a rocking chair (or stereo or toaster or umbrella) should function as such and last a reasonable length of time (which might be many years) under ordinary use.

LEGAL FOCUS—EXAMPLE

Goods that fail the warranty of merchantability include light bulbs that explode when switched on, pajamas that burst into flames at slight contact with a stove burner, high-heel shoes that break off under normal use, and shotgun shells that explode prematurely.

Contracts for sale or lease of used or secondhand goods involve only such obligation as is appropriate to such goods. This obligation includes the customary implied warranty of merchantability, but the price, age, and condition of the goods at the time of the sale are considered in determining the scope of the warranty. Obviously, such a warranty may be of little value to the buyer, especially if the goods are worn out or in poor condition.

LEGAL FOCUS—EXAMPLE

You need a gallon of paint to match the color of your bedroom walls, a light shade somewhere between coral and peach. You take a wall chip sample to your local hardware store and request a gallon of paint of that color. Instead, you are given a gallon of bright blue paint. The salesperson has not breached any warranty of implied merchantability—the bright blue paint may be of high quality and suitable for interior walls. The clerk has, however, breached an implied warranty of fitness for a particular purpose.

Ⓜ AY A SELLER DISCLAIM ALL WARRANTIES THAT OTHERWISE PROTECT THE CONSUMER?

A seller or lessor may generally *disclaim* (limit or negate) all warranties. Fortunately, because of competitive pressure, this seldom happens. To exclude the implied warranty of merchantability, the seller must conspicuously mention *merchantability* in the **disclaimer** or notice of exclusion. A statement that the goods are sold "as is" or "with all faults" also serves to exclude all implied warranties. However, the UCC provides that **consequential damages** may *not* be limited or excluded if the exclusion is **unconscionable** (i.e., against public policy). Limitation of such damages "for injury to the person in the case of consumer goods is prima facie unconscionable. . . ."[29] Also, if the goods are defective, the seller may be liable for damages under the tort doctrine of strict liability (see Chapter 7).

Formerly, sellers were often shielded from liability by legal requirements of *privity,* meaning that the plaintiff buyer seeking to enforce a warranty must be the party who contracted with the defendant seller. Thus, a consumer might sue a retailer who sold the defective product to him or her, but not the much wealthier manufacturer who made it. Most states have modified or rejected this archaic doctrine and hold all merchants or manufacturers in the chain of distribution liable for any breach. The UCC has extended the warranty protection beyond the buyer to include all members of the buyer's family or household and any of the buyer's guests, where they might reasonably be expected to use such goods and where the defective goods cause physical injury.[30] But in most states, innocent bystanders and others who are injured by a defective product must seek recovery on some other basis, such as strict product liability of manufacturers and intermediaries in a tort action, as noted previously.

LEGAL FOCUS—PROBLEM

While trying to persuade Marjorie Ayers to buy an expensive personal computer system, Leon Cannon said that all parts were guaranteed and would be replaced without any charge if found defective within five years. The written purchase contract that Ayers later signed spoke of only a one-year warranty against defects in materials and workmanship. Moreover, it said that the customer would have to pay for half of the usual labor charge. Which warranty terms actually apply to the purchase?

The one-year warranty terms apply—unless the buyer can satisfy a judge of the lie, or that she was the victim of mistake or fraud, or that the written contract was incomplete. This is the result of the **parol evidence rule,** which presumes that the contracting parties have included all previous desired oral or written understandings in their final, integrated written agreement.[31] Thus, it is not enough for a consumer to get all-important contracts in writing; one should also make sure that the writing includes all desired terms and any oral assurances and that they are stated correctly and completely, including a clear statement of any warranty protection. The parol evidence rule is discussed in more detail in Chapter 10.

The federal **Magnuson-Moss Warranty Act of 1975,** designed to help protect ultimate consumers of personal, family, or household goods costing $10 or more, has added the concepts of *full* and *limited* warranties.[32] Under the act, no one is required to give a written warranty, but the seller who elects to do so must label it as either full or limited. If it is a *full warranty,* the seller agrees to fix the product within a reasonable time and without charge if it proves to be defective. If it cannot be fixed or if a reasonable number of attempts to fix it prove unsuccessful, the buyer has the choice of a full cash refund or a free replacement. (Some states have added *lemon laws,* which clarify and strengthen this rule.) No time limit may be placed on a full warranty, but if an otherwise full warranty has a time limit, it may be described, for example, as a "full five-year warranty." The seller must label any warranty that does not provide full protection a *limited warranty.* A warranty

---

disclaimer

A written or oral statement stating that a warranty does not exist.

consequential damages

Amount awarded by a court to make good or replace indirect but foreseeable economic loss resulting from a party's breach of contract.

unconscionable

A bargain so unfair to a party that no reasonable or informed person should agree to it and a court may decline to enforce.

parol evidence rule

The rule that when contracting parties have put their complete agreement into writing, no prior or contemporaneous oral or written terms may be unilaterally added later to change the written contract, absent proof of fraud, mistake, or illegality.

Magnuson-Moss Warranty Act of 1975

Federal law that protects ultimate consumers of personal, family, and household goods by defining effects of full and limited warranties.

would be limited if, for example, the buyer had to pay any fee or transportation charge in order to utilize it. Implied warranties (e.g., of title or of merchantability) may not be disclaimed if any written warranty is given, but they may be defined and limited.

Typical language in an express warranty given by a representative manufacturer of consumer goods states that the product is warranted "against any defects due to faulty materials or workmanship for a one-year period after the original date of consumer purchase." In fairness to manufacturers, it should be noted that a warranty extended beyond the stated short period can be very costly to service. Buyers who neglect their possessions and fail to follow recommended maintenance schedules take unfair advantage of warranties. Yet all buyers pay for the added protection that most do not need, because the added cost is distributed over the price in all sales. A better alternative for some may be the purchase of "extended warranty protection" for an additional period of time for an additional charge.

The Federal Trade Commission (FTC) has independently imposed further regulations in cases where the consumer good costs more than $15. The seller is required to disclose the name of the warrantors, the nature and limitations (if any) of the warranty, and the fact that the buyer has legal rights to specified procedures for the enforcement of the warranty.

CASE

HAMER V. SIDWAY
124 N.Y. 538, 27 N.E. 256 (1891)

At a family celebration, in the presence of witnesses, William E. Story, Sr., promised to pay his nephew William E. Story, 2d, $5,000 if he would refrain from drinking, using tobacco, swearing, and playing cards or billiards (all legal activities for the nephew at that time) until he turned twenty-one. The nephew assented and fully performed the conditions of the promise. When he reached twenty-one, not quite six years later, he wrote a letter to his uncle, explaining that he had performed his part of their agreement and was thereby entitled to the $5,000. The uncle wrote a letter in response, reaffirming his promise. Unfortunately for the nephew, his uncle died some twelve years later without having paid him any money. The nephew assigned his claim to Hamer (the plaintiff in this case), but Sidway, the executor of the uncle's estate and the defendant in this action, rejected the claim. The executor's refusal was based on his belief that there was no consideration for the uncle's promise to pay because the uncle received no benefit from the nephew's perform-ance. The following opinion of the New York Court of Appeals is a landmark statement on the rules of consideration, made in an interesting factual context. Keep in mind that $5,000 in 1891 is equivalent to about $100,000 today.

J. Parker wrote the following: The uncle received the letter, and a few days later he wrote and mailed to his nephew the following letter:

"Dear Nephew: Your letter of the 31st ult. came to hand all right, saying that you had lived up to the promise made to me several years ago. I have no doubt but you have, for which you shall have five thousand dollars, as I promised you. I had the money in the bank the day you was twenty-one years old that I intend for you, and you shall have the money certain. Now, Willie, I do not intend to interfere with this money in any way till I think you are capable of taking care of it, and the sooner that time comes the better it will please me. I would hate very much to have you start out in some adventure that you thought all right and lose this money in one year. The first five thousand dollars that I got together cost me a heap of hard work. You would hardly believe me when I tell you that to obtain this I shoved a jack-plane many a day, butchered three or four years, then came to this city, and, after three months' per severance, I obtained a situation in a grocery store. I opened this store early,

closed late, slept in the fourth story of the building in a room 30 by 40 feet, and not a human being in the building but myself. All this I done to live as cheap as I could to save something. I don't want you to take up with this kind of fare. I was here in the cholera season of '49 and '52, and the deaths aver-aged 80 to 125. . . .

"Mr. Fisk, the gentleman I was working for, told me, if I left them, after it got healthy he proba-bly would not want me. I stayed. All the money I have saved I know just how I got it. It did not come to me in any mysterious way, and the reason I speak of this is that money got in this way stops longer with a fellow that gets it with hard knocks than it does when he finds it. Willie, you are twenty-one, and you have many a timing to learn yet. This money you have earned much easier than I did, besides acquir-ing good habits at the same time, and you are quite welcome to the money. Hope you will make good use of it. I was ten long years getting this together after I was your age. Now, hoping this will be satisfactory, I stop. One thing more. Twenty-one years ago I bought you 15 sheep. These sheep were put out to double every four years. I kept track of them the first eight years. I have not heard much about them since. Your father and grandfather promised me that they would look after them till you were of age. Have they done so? I hope they have. By this time you have between five and six hundred sheep, worth a nice little income this spring. Willie, I have said much more than I expected to. Hope you can make out what I have written. Today is the sev-enteenth day that I have not been out of my room, and have had the doctor as many days. Am a little better today. Think I will get out next week. You need not mention [this] to father, as he always worries about small matters.

Truly yours, W. E. STORY. P.S. You can consider this money on interest."

The nephew received the letter, and thereafter consented that the money should remain with his uncle in accordance with the terms and conditions of the letter. The uncle died on the 29th day of January, 1887, without having paid over to his nephew any portion of the said $5,000 and interest. . . .

The question which provoked the most discussion by counsel on this appeal, and which lies at the foundation of plaintiff's asserted right of recovery, is whether by virtue of a contract, defendant's testator, William E. Story, became indebted to his nephew, William E. Story, 2d, on his twenty-first birthday in the sum of $5,000. The defendant contends that the contract was without consideration to support it, and therefore invalid. He asserts that the promisee, by refraining from the use of liquor and tobacco, was not harmed, but benefited; that that which he did was best for him to do, independently of his uncle's promise—and insists that it follows that, unless the promisor was benefited, the contract was without consideration—a contention which, if well founded, would seem to leave open for controversy in many cases whether that which the promisee did or omitted to do was in fact of such benefit to him as to leave no consideration to support the enforcement of the promisor's agreement. Such a rule could not be tolerated, and is without foundation in the law. The exchequer chamber in 1875 defined "consideration" as follows: "A valuable consideration, in the sense of the law, may consist either in some right, interest, profit, or benefit accruing to the one party, or some forbearance, detriment, loss, or responsibility given, suffered, or undertaken by the other." Courts "will not ask whether the thing which forms the consideration does in fact benefit the promisee or a third party, or is of any substantial value to any one. It is enough that something is promised, done, forborne, or suffered by the party to whom the promise is made as consideration for the promise made to him." Anson, Cont, 63. "In general a waiver of any legal right at the request of another party is a sufficient consideration for a promise." Pars. Cont. "Any damage, or suspension, or forbearance of a right will be sufficient to sustain a promise." 2 Kent, Comm. (12th Ed.)

Pollock, in his work on Contracts (page 166), after citing the definition given by the exchequer chamber, already quoted, says: "The second branch of this judicial description is really the most important one. 'Consideration' means not so much that one party is profiting as that the other abandons some legal right in the present, or limits his legal freedom of action in the future, as an inducement for the promise of the first." Now, applying this rule to the facts before us, the promisee used tobacco, occasionally drank liquor, and he had a legal right to do so. That right he abandoned for a period of years upon the strength of the promise of the testator that for such forbearance he would give him $5,000.

We need not speculate on the effort which may have been required to give up the use of those stimulants. It is sufficient that he restricted his lawful freedom of action within certain prescribed limits upon the faith of his uncle's agreement, and now, having fully performed the conditions imposed, it is of no moment whether such performance actually proved a benefit to the promisor, and the court will not inquire into it; but, were it a proper subject of inquiry, we see nothing in this record that would permit a determination that the uncle was not benefited in a legal sense. . . .

The order appealed from should be reversed, and the judgment of the special term affirmed, with costs payable out of the estate. All concur. [Hamer, the nephew's assignee, was found entitled to the $5,000 plus interest.]

For Critical Analysis

1. If "drinking, using tobacco, swearing and playing cards or billiards" were illegal for minors in New York at the time of William Story, Sr.'s offer, would consideration have been present?

2. Why do you suppose the nephew didn't demand payment from his uncle at the time he received his uncle's letter?

3. Could Sidway (the executor) argue that the Statute of Frauds applies in this case? How would Hamer counter that claim? ■

LUCY V. ZEHMER
196 Va. 493, 84 S.E.2d 516 (1954)

This is a suit to compel specific performance of a land purchase contract claimed by defendant sellers to have been entered into as a joke. The circuit court entered a decree dismissing the suit, and purchasers appealed. The Supreme Court of Appeals held evidence showed that the contract represented a serious business transaction and good-faith sale and purchase of the farm, that no unusual circumstances existed in its making, and that purchasers were entitled to specific performance. This is another landmark contract case. In it, the court discusses the contract rules governing the manifestation of intent to contract and the contractual capacity of parties negotiating a contract while sipping distilled spirits.

J. Buchanan delivered the opinion of the court: This suit was instituted by W. O. Lucy and J. C. Lucy, complainants, against A. H. Zehmer and Ida S. Zehmer, his wife, defendants, to have specific performance of a contract by which it was alleged the Zehmers had sold to W. O. Lucy a tract of land owned by A. H. Zehmer in Dinwiddie county containing 471.6 acres, more or less, known as the Ferguson farm, for $50,000. J. C. Lucy, the other complainant, is a brother of W. O. Lucy, to whom W. O. Lucy transferred a half interest in his alleged purchase.

The instrument sought to be enforced was written by A. H. Zehmer on December 20, 1952, in these words: "We hereby agree to sell to W. O. Lucy the Ferguson Farm complete for $50,000, title satisfactory to buyer," and signed by the defendants, A. H. Zehmer and Ida S. Zehmer.

The answer of A. H. Zehmer admitted that at the time mentioned W. O. Lucy offered him $50,000 cash for the farm, but that he, Zehmer, considered that the offer was made in jest; that so thinking, and both he and Lucy having had several drinks, he wrote out "the memorandum" quoted above and induced his wife to sign it; that he did not deliver the memorandum to Lucy, but that Lucy picked it up, read it, put it in his pocket, attempted to offer Zehmer $5 to bind the bargain, which Zehmer refused to accept, and realizing for the first time that Lucy was serious, Zehmer assured him that he had no intention of selling the farm and that the whole matter was a joke. Lucy left the premises insisting that he had purchased the farm.

W. O. Lucy, a lumberman and farmer, thus testified in substance: He had known Zehmer for fifteen or twenty years and had been familiar with the Ferguson farm for ten years. Seven or eight years ago he had offered Zehmer $20,000 for

the farm, which Zehmer had accepted, but the agreement was verbal and Zehmer backed out. On the night of December 20, 1952, around eight o'clock, he took an employee to McKenney, where Zehmer lived and operated a restaurant, filling station and motor court. While there he decided to see Zehmer and again try to buy the Ferguson farm. He entered the restaurant and talked to Mrs. Zehmer until Zehmer came in. He asked Zehmer if he had sold the Ferguson farm. Zehmer replied that he had not. Lucy said, "I bet you wouldn't take $50,000 for that place." Zehmer replied, "Yes, I would too; you wouldn't give fifty." Lucy said he would and told Zehmer to write up an agreement to that effect. Zehmer took a restaurant check and wrote on the back of it, "I do hereby agree to sell to W. O. Lucy the Ferguson Farm for $50,000 complete." Lucy told him he had better change it to "We" because Mrs. Zehmer would have to sign it too. Zehmer then tore up what he had written, wrote the agreement quoted above and asked Mrs. Zehmer, who was at the other end of the counter ten or twelve feet away, to sign it. Mrs. Zehmer said she would for $50,000 and signed it. Zehmer brought it back and gave it to Lucy, who offered him $5 which Zehmer refused, saying, "You don't need to give me any money, you got the agreement there signed by both of us."

The discussion leading to the signing of the agreement, said Lucy, lasted thirty or forty minutes, during which Zehmer seemed to doubt that Lucy could raise $50,000. Lucy suggested the provision for having the title examined and Zehmer made the suggestion that he would sell it "complete, everything there," and stated that all he had on the farm was three heifers.

Lucy took a partly filled bottle of whiskey into the restaurant with him for the purpose of giving Zehmer a drink if he wanted it. Zehmer did, and he and Lucy had one or two drinks together. Lucy said that while he felt the drinks he took he was not intoxicated, and from the way Zehmer handled the transaction he did not think he was either.

December 20 was on Saturday. Next day Lucy telephoned to J. C. Lucy and arranged with the latter to take a half interest in the purchase and pay half of the consideration. On Monday he engaged an attorney to examine the title. The attorney reported favorably on December 31, and on January 2 Lucy wrote Zehmer stating that the title was satisfactory, that he was ready to pay the purchase price in cash and asking when Zehmer would be ready to close the deal. Zehmer replied by letter, mailed on January 13, asserting that he had never agreed or intended to sell. Mr. and Mrs. Zehmer were called by the complainants as adverse witnesses. Zehmer testified in substance as follows: He bought this farm more than ten years ago for $11,000. He had had twenty-five offers, more or less, to buy it, including several from Lucy, who had never offered any specific sum of money. He had given them all the same answer, that he was not interested in selling it. On this Saturday night before Christmas it looked like everybody and his brother came by there to have a drink. He took a good many drinks during the afternoon and had a pint of his own. When he entered the restaurant around eight-thirty Lucy was there and he could see that he was "pretty high." He said to Lucy. "Boy, you got some good liquor, drinking, ain't you?" Lucy then offered him a drink. "I was already high as a Georgia pine, and didn't have any more better sense than to pour another great big slug out and gulp it down, and he took one too."

After they had talked a while Lucy asked whether he still had the Ferguson farm. He replied that he had not sold it and Lucy said, "I bet you wouldn't take $50,000 for it." Zehmer asked him if he would give $50,000 and Lucy said yes. Zehmer replied, "You haven't got $50,000 in cash." Lucy said he did and Zehmer replied that he did not believe it. They argued "pro and con for a long time," mainly about "whether he had $50,000 in cash that he could put up right then and buy that farm."

Finally, said Zehmer, Lucy told him if he didn't believe he had $50,000, "you sign that piece of paper here and say you will take $50,000 for the farm." He, Zehmer, "just grabbed the back off of a guest check there" and wrote on the back of it. At that point in his testimony Zehmer asked to see what he had written to "see if I recognize my own handwriting." He examined the paper and exclaimed, "Great balls of fire. I got 'Firgerson' for Ferguson. I have got satisfactory spelled wrong. I don't recognize that writing if I would see it, wouldn't know it was mine."

After Zehmer had, as he described it, "scribbled this thing off," Lucy said, "Get your wife to sign it." Zehmer walked over to where she was and she at first refused to sign but did so after he told her that he "was just needling him [Lucy], and didn't mean a thing in the world, that I was not selling the farm." Zehmer then "took it back over there ... and I was still looking at the dern thing. I had the drink right there by my hand, and I reached over to get a drink, and he said, 'Let me see it.' He reached and picked it up, and when I looked back again he had it in his pocket and he dropped a five dollar bill over there, and he said, 'Here is five dollars payment on it. . . .' I said, 'Hell no, that is beer and liquor

talking. I am not going to sell you the farm. I have told you that too many times before.'"

The defendants insist that the evidence was ample to support their contention that the writing sought to be enforced was prepared as a bluff or dare to force Lucy to admit that he did not have $50,000; that the whole matter was a joke; that the writing was not delivered to Lucy and no binding contract was ever made between the parties.

It is an unusual, if not bizarre, defense. When made to the writing admittedly prepared by one of the defendants and signed by both, clear evidence is required to sustain it.

In his testimony Zehmer claimed that he "was high as a Georgia pine," and that the transaction "was just a bunch of two doggoned drunks bluffing to see who could talk the biggest and say the most." That claim is inconsistent with his attempt to testify in great detail as to what was said and what was done. It is contradicted by other evidence as to the condition of both parties, and rendered of no weight by the testimony of his wife that when Lucy left the restaurant she suggested that Zehmer drive him home. The record is convincing that Zehmer was not intoxicated to the extent of being unable to comprehend the nature and consequences of the instrument he executed, and hence that instrument is not to be invalidated on that ground. . . . It was in fact conceded by defendants' counsel in oral argument that under the evidence Zehmer was not too drunk to make a valid contract.

The evidence is convincing also that Zehmer wrote two agreements, the first one beginning "I hereby agree to sell." Zehmer first said he could not remember about that, then that "I don't think I wrote but one out." Mrs. Zehmer said that what he wrote was "I hereby agree," but that the "I" was changed to "We" after that night. The agreement that was written and signed is in the record and indicates no such change. Neither are the mistakes in spelling that Zehmer sought to point out readily apparent.

The appearance of the contract, the fact that it was under discussion for forty minutes or more before it was signed; Lucy's objection to the first draft because it was written in the singular, and he wanted Mrs. Zehmer to sign it also; the rewriting to meet that objection and the signing by Mrs. Zehmer; the discussion of what was to be included in the sale, the provision for the examination of the title, the completeness of the instrument that was executed, the taking possession of it by Lucy with no request or suggestion by either of the defendants that he give it back, are facts which furnish persuasive evidence that the execution of the contract was a serious business transaction rather than a casual, jesting matter as defendants now contend.

If it be assumed, contrary to what we think the evidence shows, that Zehmer was jesting about selling his farm to

Lucy and that the transaction was intended by him to be a joke, nevertheless the evidence shows that Lucy did not so understand it but considered it to be a serious business transaction and the contract to be binding on the Zehmers as well as on himself. The very next day he arranged with his brother to put up half the money and take a half interest in the land. The day after that he employed an attorney to examine the title. The next night, Tuesday, he was back at Zehmer's place and there Zehmer told him for the first time, Lucy said, that he wasn't going to sell and he told Zehmer, "You know you sold that place fair and square." After receiving the report from his attorney that the title was good he wrote to Zehmer that he was ready to close the deal.

Not only did Lucy actually believe, but the evidence shows he was warranted in believing, that the contract represented a serious business transaction and a good faith sale and purchase of the farm.

In the field of contracts, as generally elsewhere, "We must look to the outward expression of a person as manifesting his intention rather than to his secret and unexpressed intention. The law imputes to a person an intention corresponding to the reasonable meaning of his words and acts. . . ."

At no time prior to the execution of the contract had Zehmer indicated to Lucy by word or act that he was not in earnest about selling the land. They had argued about it and discussed its terms, as Zehmer admitted, for a long time. Lucy testified that if there was any jesting it was about paying $50,000 that night. The contract and the evidence show that he was not expected to pay the money that night. Zehmer said that after the writing was signed he laid it down on the counter in front of Lucy. Lucy said Zehmer handed it to him. In any event there had been what appeared to be a good faith offer and a good faith acceptance, followed by the execution and apparent delivery of a written contract. Both said that Lucy put the writing in his pocket and then offered Zehmer $5 to seal the bargain. Not until then, even under the defendants' evidence, was anything said or done to indicate that the matter was a joke. Both of the Zehmers testified that when Zehmer asked his wife to sign he whispered that it was a joke so Lucy wouldn't hear and that it was not intended that he should hear.

The mental assent of the parties is not requisite for the formation of a contract. If the words or other acts of one of the parties have but one reasonable meaning, his undisclosed intention is immaterial except when an unreasonable meaning which he attaches to his manifestations is known to the other party. . . .

The law, therefore, judges of an agreement between two persons exclusively from those expressions of their intentions which are communicated between them. . . .

An agreement or mutual assent is of course essential to a valid contract but the law imputes to a person an intention corresponding to the reasonable meaning of his words and acts. If his words and acts, judged by a reasonable standard, manifest an intention to agree, it is immaterial what may be the real but unexpressed state of his mind. . . .

So a person cannot set up that he was merely jesting when his conduct and words would warrant a reasonable person in believing that he intended a real agreement. . . .

Whether the writing signed by the defendants and now sought to be enforced by the complainants was the result of a serious offer by Lucy and a serious acceptance by the defendants, or was a serious offer by Lucy and an acceptance in secret jest by the defendants, in either event it constituted a binding contract of sale between the parties.

Defendants contend further, however, that even though a contract was made, equity should decline to enforce it under the circumstances. These circumstances have been set forth in detail above. They disclose some drinking by the two parties but not to an extent that they were unable to understand fully what they were doing. There was no fraud, no misrepresentation, no sharp practice and no dealing between unequal parties. The farm had been bought for $11,000 and was assessed for taxation at $6,300. The purchase price was $50,000. Zehmer admitted that it was a good price. There is in fact present in this case none of the grounds usually urged against specific performance.

Specific performance, it is true, is not a matter of absolute or arbitrary right, but is addressed to the reasonable and sound discretion of the court. . . . But it is likewise true that the discretion which may be exercised is not an arbitrary or capricious one, but one which is controlled by the established doctrines and settled principles of equity; and, generally, where a contract is in its nature and circumstances unobjectionable, it is as much a matter of course for courts of equity to decree a specific performance of it as it is for a court of law to give damages for a breach of it. . . .

The complainants are entitled to have specific performance of the contracts sued on. The decree appealed from is therefore reversed and the cause is remanded for the entry of a proper decree requiring the defendants to perform the contract in accordance with the prayer of the bill. Reversed and remanded.

For Critical Analysis

1. Why does the court require objective intention to contract? The contrasting term to *objective* is *subjective,* meaning "peculiar to a particular individual." Why isn't

subjective intent preferable; after all, if you want to know what someone means, can't you ask them?

2. Can you identify three separate contentions Zehmer makes to defend against Lucy's action? Why were they unsuccessful? Do you agree with the court's ruling?

3. Lucy testified that there had been an oral agreement to buy the farm for $20,000 "seven or eight years before." Why do you suppose Lucy had not sued to enforce that agreement? ■

CHAPTER QUESTIONS AND PROBLEMS

1. Regarding the elements of a valid contract:
   a. What are the five, and sometimes six, elements that are said to be essential for a valid contract?
   b. In which of the six elements does the law permit performance or execution at the option of one of the parties who might have legally withdrawn without liability? Explain.

2. Regarding breach of contract:
   a. Is breaching a contract comparable in moral culpability and legal effect to committing a tort or committing a crime? If not, how do these actions differ?
   b. Under what circumstances can a party who breaches a contract also be guilty of committing a tort?

3. Identify three contracts you have experienced or observed. Select one that is expressed in writing, one expressed orally, and one implied in fact from conduct. Classify each as to parties bound, legal effect, and extent of performance.

4. Clearly distinguish between a valid contract, a voidable contract, and a void agreement. Provide an example of each type of agreement and demonstrate how the court would treat each of your situations if they were litigated.

5. When is an acceptance to an offer sent by mail effective to form a contract if the acceptance was returned by mail?
   a. When it arrives at the offeror(s)?
   b. When you decide you intend to accept?

   c. When the acceptance is given to the secretary to mail?
   d. When your check clears the bank?
   e. When your letter of acceptance is mailed?
   f. What are the legal consequences, if any, if a timely sent, properly addressed and stamped letter is lost by the postal service?

6. Anne Marcie and Bob Bruce entered into a binding bilateral contract. The terms of the contract included that Marcie was to build a hang glider for Bruce, and that Bruce was to pay Marcie $18,000 upon its completion. After formation of the contract, Bruce decided he did not want the hang glider; because the contract was advantageous, however, he assigned all of his rights thereunder and delegated his duty of payment to his friend Marc Shadoe. Shadoe paid Bruce $1,400 for the transferred right and immediately informed Marcie of the assignment. After Shadoe took delivery of the glider, he fled without paying Marcie. He was last seen by reliable sources gliding into Canada singing, "I did it my way." Characterize the contractual relationships of the parties and explain their respective rights.

7. Evelyn Millie, a university psychology professor, says to her students, "All of you have worked hard, and if you continue to perform at a high level, I will pay for a pizza party for the class at the end of the year—if I think it is warranted." The students insist that they continued to "work hard," and they claim that the class grades "are high," but Millie gives no party. Can the students enforce Millie's promise?

8. Plaintiff, a minor, alleged that his grandfather Schultz had made an oral contract with the plaintiff through his mother. In this alleged contract, Schultz agreed to give the plaintiff certain real estate if the plaintiff's mother would name the plaintiff after him. The plaintiff's parents accepted the proposal, since they had in fact already named their son after Schultz. However, Schultz never arranged for the title of the property to pass to the plaintiff. He did deliver possession of the real estate to the plaintiff's parents. The plaintiff requested that the court determine that he is the absolute owner of the real estate. Was the alleged contract between Schultz and the plaintiff's mother supported by consideration and therefore enforceable? [*Lanifer v. Lanifer,* 227 Iowa 258, 288 N.W. 104 (Iowa, 1939).]

9. When Tom Trousseau loaned Bob Barrow $100, he asked for an IOU. Barrow took a business card from his wallet and scribbled these words on its back: "IOU, old pal Tom, one hundred bucks," signed and dated it, and gave it to Trousseau. Is the card an enforceable written contract?

10. Defendant Robert Martin gave his American Express credit card to E. L. McBride, a business associate, for use in a joint business venture. McBride had returned the card to Martin and then disappeared. Martin claimed he orally authorized McBride to charge up to $500 on the card. But McBride had actually charged approximately $5,300 to Martin's card. Martin also testified that he had previously sent a letter to plaintiff American Express asking them not to allow total charges on his account to exceed $1,000. Under the Truth in Lending Act, is Martin liable for $50 or $5,300? [*Martin v. American Express, Inc.,* 361 So.2d 597 (Alabama, 1978).]

11. This quote appeared in a recent law review article: "Parties to modern form contracts sometimes interact with one another in the same way a parent of an autistic child interacts with that child. When a licensor offers a software license with the assertion that it will infer acceptance of all the license terms if the licensee removes the power cord from its plastic wrapper, the licensor is drawing an inference from the licensee's behavior just as doubtful as the inference a hopeful parent draws from an autistic child's apparently knowing response to the parent's statement." (James J. White, 45 Wayne L. Rev. 1693 (2000).) How do modern methods of commercial communication relate to the old rules of offer and acceptance?

CHAPTER 9

Family Law

*L*ove, the quest; marriage, the conquest;
*d*ivorce, the inquest.

Helen Rolland, *Reflections of a Bachelor Girl,* 1903.

After reading and studying this chapter, you should be able to:

- Discuss what legal topics fit within family law.

- Describe the typical legal requirements of marriage.

- Discuss domestic partnerships.

- Describe the legal rights and obligations of marriage.

- Describe the common attributes of marital and community property.

- Discuss tort immunities of family members.

- Discuss the legal duties of parents and issues establishing maternity and paternity.

- Identify legal issues surrounding adoption.

- Discuss major issues regarding juvenile justice and protection of minors.

- Distinguish an annulment from a divorce and indentify the grounds for each.

- Discuss issues surrounding alimony, property distribution, and child custody.

- Discuss marital property contracts and their likely enforceability.

Unquestionably some aspects of family law will affect your life. The legal implications of living as a family can and do involve a wide variety of laws. There are many examples with which to demonstrate the complexities existing between families and laws, beginning with the very definition of marriage.

LEGAL FOCUS—PROBLEM

Some clergy in the Methodist church perform "holy union" ceremonies for same-sex couples. Other pastors with a more conservative or fundamental view of the Bible vehemently object to this practice and threaten to withdraw from the church. Do these ceremonies create marriages?[1]

Legal marriage must be created in conformity with state laws, all of which, for example, require marital licenses and that members be of the opposite sex. However, same-sex "marriages" or "unions" create families that are, in many states and in many ways, protected by law. For example, in those states, sexual orientation is not a valid basis for a landlord to refuse to rent living space.

Family law is designed to protect family values. But differences of opinion as to those values can be significant. For example, in many states the family is thought to be protected by the criminalization of adultery. The federal government rewards families with certain tax benefits and provides financial and other assistance (e.g., withholding of income tax refunds) to states that have difficulty tracking down parents who are delinquent in child support payments. A variety of criminal and civil laws protect the family from abusive treatment. Clearly a well-informed citizenry must understand the essentials of family law.

Entering the twenty-first century, we find family law facing what promises to be the most controversial issue ever—the genetic alteration of humans, which offers prospective parents the choice of specific characteristics in their offspring (so-called designer babies). Already thorny issues of custody and the use of frozen and fertilized embryos following death or divorce have arisen in this blend of moral and legal issues.

In this chapter you will learn about additional laws designed to protect family values as well as the potential involvement of family law in your daily lives. Family law governs the legal relations of the basic social unit, the family. In general, family law has very little to do with happy families. Rather, family law is about protecting the family unit, especially children. Family law begins with rules expressed in state statutes designed by legislatures to protect the family institution. There are rules defining marriage, the mechanics of divorce, the basis for division of family assets upon divorce—all are set forth in state statutes. Wide variations exist in family law from state to state because legislative viewpoints reflect substantially different cultural and societal values. Understandably, these viewpoints often clash on the very sensitive and important principles applicable to the family. Religious beliefs, for example, probably conflict more frequently with family law than with any other categories of law.

As in other areas of law, when disputes arise between family members, we rely upon lawyers for assistance in presenting our family issues to judges and courts for resolution. These "divorce" lawyers present family law issues to judges (without juries, as family law is "in equity") for resolution. These judges, who typically specialize in domestic matters, rely heavily upon the recommendations of social service experts for such sensitive issues as child custody following the breakup of the marriage.

Lawyers often joke amongst themselves about their availability for our legal problems "from the cradle to the grave." In this book the distressing legal issues related to "the grave" are appropriately covered in our final chapter (pun intended). In this chapter you will discover that our need for family law begins long before "the cradle." Our law increasingly is focusing upon protection of the fetus during pregnancy. The primary issue in society involving the unborn fetus has been the right of females to choose abortion. By the turn of the twentieth century, virtually every state had a law prohibiting or restricting abortion. It is noteworthy that women also did not have the right to vote. It was not until 1973 that the choice to abort a nonviable fetus became guaranteed under the U.S. Constitution.* But the issue of protection of the fetus is changing. Abortion no longer is the single issue.

Again we note the mushrooming complexities within our huge and diverse society. Looking forward, there is a scientific opportunity to "modify" or "adjust" a fetus before or after conception. Harnessing the human gene creates opportunities and challenges in family law that make the issue of abortion pale in comparison. There are emerging constitutional issues in family law, such as those presented by the demand for same-sex marriage, which would allow equality in taxation and financial benefits that traditional couples currently enjoy.

Already the law authorizes a variety of surrogacy arrangements under which persons otherwise incapable of having their own progeny can be rewarded. But legal issues defining the rights of the "natural" parents who are different from the "birth" parents continue.

At the beginning of the twentieth century, many children were called upon to work long hours for little pay and with little regard for their workplace safety or health. Facing the new millennium, we find that children are protected from abusive employment, but too many remain in need of protection from abuses by their parents, from other adults, and even from themselves. Child abuse is a violation of both criminal and family law, and is found in both of those chapters in this textbook. The scope of protective laws and issues cover a vast range of problems, from censorship of the Internet to the exclusionary zoning of "adult" bookstores; from sex, gore, and alcohol on TV to metal detectors in grade schools. This area of family law is rich with controversy, with prospects for new legal solutions undoubtedly eluding us well into the twenty-first century.

Most rules of family law are found in the civil law. But some are also found in the criminal law because certain conduct involving family members is so reprehensible that society, through legislation, expresses its disapproval by imposing criminal penalties. Child abuse and spouse-beating are examples of such conduct. Both criminal and civil statutes exist to protect and enhance marriage and the family. Examples of criminal laws designed to protect the family include those proscribing adultery, bigamy, seduction accomplished by false promise of marriage, and incest (i.e., sexual intercourse between individuals who are so closely related to each other that marriage is forbidden by law). Examples of civil laws relating to the family declare that upon termination of the marriage, courts may distribute the family property equitably (in accordance with applicable state law) and define and order the continuing support rights and duties of family members.

There is hardly an area of law more relevant to each of us than family law. Even if it does not touch one's life directly, its societal effects are felt by all.

http://

For access to various state family law statutes, uniform laws, and other information visit

http://fatty.law.cornell.edu/ topics/divorce.html

A promise to "love, honor and cherish as long as we both shall live" is in fact easily and frequently revocable today. It is lamentable that many decide to live together without benefit of such vows and many who take them soon forget them. However, we are concerned here with legal, not moral obligations.

Associate Justice Haden, California Court of Appeal, speaking for the court in the case of *In re Marriage of Wilson*, 201 Cal.App.3d 913, 247 Cal.Rptr. 522 (1988).

---

* A fetus is viable when it theoretically could survive independent of its mother. In 1973, the law described viability as beginning after the first trimester (three moths). *Roe v. Wade*, 410 U.S. 113, 93 S.Ct. 705 (1973).

Is the Federal Government Involved in Family Law?

Although there is no national (federal) marriage or divorce law, a family member may become involved in a matter involving federal jurisdiction. For example, if American citizen Bruce Brown, husband and father, entered the United States at Nogales, Arizona, with contraband, such as marijuana, he would have committed a federal crime. If Brown is jailed, the question of how his family would then be supported would be determined by principles of family law in the state of his residence. In addition, some federal laws are designed to protect the family when issues involving more than one state are raised. For example, the Child Abuse Prevention and Treatment Act of 1984 encourages states to adopt remedial statutes; the Omnibus Budget Reconciliation Act of 1981 provides for interception of income tax refunds payable to parents who are delinquent in their support obligations; the Parental Kidnapping Act of 1984 provides special penalties for "child-snatching" parents; and more recently the Uniform Interstate Family Support Act of 1992 streamlines the forced collection of support and establishes a commission to further study the problem. Also, the U.S. Supreme Court has held that former spouses who reside in different states may sue each other in federal court for damages (but not for divorce, alimony, or child custody).[2] There is an emerging trend of federal courts accepting jurisdiction in family law matters that extend across state lines.[3] In the following case, a federal court applied the Illinois law regarding a breach of promise to marry.

LEGAL FOCUS—CASE

Sharon Wildey, an attorney, sued her fiancé Richard Springs, III, for damages for ending their seven-week engagement, which had followed a whirlwind romance. She sued in federal court on the basis of diversity of citizenship. Sharon claimed she suffered depression and lost income by giving up her main client. Richard told Sharon that she could keep the $19,000 engagement ring and offered her $10,000 cash to help her "get through these times." She was thrice divorced and had four children; Richard was once divorced and had fathered three children. At the close of trial, Sharon's attorney asked the jury for damages of $365,000. What result do you predict?

Wildey v. Springs, 840 F.Supp. 1259 (N.D. Ill., 1994).

The federal court jury awarded Sharon $93,000 for pain and suffering, $60,000 for lost income, and $25,000 for counseling. This case was exceptional because few states permit legal actions seeking damages for breach of promise to marry on the general grounds that "pillow talk" cases ought not be resolved in court.

No one doubts the sincerity of the intentions to protect families that underlie new federal laws. But many such national laws fail to live up to their expectations when adopted. For example, federal law now bars the sale of cigarettes to persons under eighteen years of age, yet minors are still able to purchase them in four out of every ten attempts.[4] Are the new taxes on cigarettes likely to reduce their consumption by minors or more likely simply to raise funds? Alcohol has similarly been banned, yet there is a perceived need for federal laws to reduce driving under the influence and to protect the fetuses of minors from the alcohol syndrome.

What Is Marriage?

[W]hilst marriage is often termed by text writers and in decisions of courts a civil contract . . . it is something more than a mere contract. The consent of the parties is of course essential to its existence, but when the contract to marry is executed by the marriage, a relation between the parties is created which they cannot change. Marriage remains largely a matter of status, although that status is today more ambiguous than in the past. [From Maynard v. Hill, 125 U.S. 190, 8 S.Ct. 723 (1888)]

marriage

Legal union as husband and wife.

Marriage is a status, the legal union of husband and wife, entered into by means of a contract that is enforceable by courts. The legal relationship of marriage is based on state rather than federal law. When the status is created, the law grants enforceable rights to the parties and also imposes various mutual duties or obligations. Such official governance of the relationship is justified because marriage is recognized as essential for healthy, viable families and therefore the foundation of a healthy, viable society.

LEGAL FOCUS—PROBLEM

Alexis McVey and Martin Neiderhasen were exchanging wedding vows when Neiderhasen collapsed. He died of cardiac arrest in the ambulance. During their courtship, neither prepared a last will. Does McVey have any legal rights to inherit from Neiderhasen?

McVey has no rights of inheritance unless their vows were completed and their marriage proclaimed. The law treats McVey and Neiderhasen just as it does any other unmarried persons. Neiderhasen parents would inherit from him. If the marriage existed for only a moment, McVey would have significant rights to his property in all states. This seemingly absurd hypothetical is based on an actual dispute between an alleged spouse and her bridegroom's parents.

Statutes regulate the lawful creation of marriage. In most states, a license between adults is prescribed for marriage. Parental consent is required for a minor (person under eighteen years of age) to obtain a marriage license, but in special situations (e.g., pregnancy out of wedlock), some state courts are authorized to approve the marriage of underage persons. In Maryland, only parental consent is required for marriage of an underage pregnant girl.

LEGAL FOCUS—PROBLEM

With her parents' blessings, Tina Akers and her boyfriend, Wayne Compton, went to the courthouse, obtained a license, and were married. Compton is twenty-nine years old while Tina, eight months pregnant, is thirteen. Is this a new legal family or an example of parental child abuse or predatory and even pedophiliac sexual abuse and statutory rape?[5]

In Maryland, Tina and Wayne Compton and their newly born son, Austin, are a legal family. In other states, Wayne would have been charged with a crime and the marriage would not have been valid. Tina's father had married his wife Nancy when she was sixteen. They had eight children before their divorce. Although the marriage of very young teenagers was commonplace at the turn of the century, that practice gradually ended and largely disappeared following World War II.*

All states prohibit marriage between members of the immediate family (ascendants-descendants, i.e., parent and child) and siblings (brother and sister) on moral and genetic grounds. Most also prohibit uncle-niece or aunt-nephew marriages, and some extend the prohibition to first cousins. A few continue to proscribe matrimony for certain relationships of affinity (e.g., stepfather-stepdaughter). Statutes typically require that a person entering marriage be of sound mind—not be insane, an idiot, an imbecile, or a lunatic—although doctors have difficulty diagnosing mental illness, and there is confusion as to what such terms mean in law. Most states used to require a health examination showing freedom from certain venereal diseases as a precondition for issuance of a marriage license. But that requirement has been eliminated in the vast majority of states. Solemnization is generally required by either a civil (justice of the peace or judge) or religious (minister, priest, rabbi, or the like) authority.

LEGAL FOCUS—PROBLEM

Pauline Bradshaw, while planning her marriage to George Hall, became curious about whether she will be legally required to take and use George's surname. Is a wife legally required to take her husband's surname?

No. Wives customarily have taken the surname of their husbands in the United States. But this custom is not required by law. Many women choose to use both family surnames in combination. Thus, Pauline could choose to be known as "Pauline Bradshaw-Hall." Pauline could choose to retain her name as Pauline Hall; George could change his name from George Hall to George Bradshaw.

COMMON-LAW MARRIAGE

In 14 states,† a **common-law marriage** may arise when a man and a woman continue to live together as husband and wife but without legal formalities (health examination, marriage license, and proper solemnization). For a common-law marriage to exist, the parties must be legally qualified to marry, must cohabit and create the public impression that a marriage exists, and must intend that it exist.[6]

LEGAL FOCUS—BACKGROUND

Sandra Jennings and actor William Hurt had a three-year intimate relationship while living in Manhattan. New York state does not recognize common-law marriages. But Jennings and Hurt spent five weeks in South Carolina during Hurt's filming of *The Big Chill*. After they ended the relationship, Jennings sued Hurt in a New York court claiming that a common-law marriage, by mutual agreement, had existed under South Carolina's law.

http://

A list of the marriage laws of all states can be found at **http://fatty.law.cornell.edu/topics/Table_Marriage.htm**

common-law marriage

The bond formed when a man and a woman live together in the manner of a husband and a wife for the number of years prescribed by state law, though without observing the legal formalities of marriage. This is a legal form of marriage in some states.

---

* For example, country music star Loretta Lynn married at 13 and was a grandmother by 29.
† Alabama, Colorado, Georgia, Idaho, Iowa, Kansas, Montana, Ohio, Oklahoma, Pennsylvania, Rhode Island, South Carolina, Texas, Utah, and the District of Columbia.

But Hurt often expressed his desire not to marry, and evidence of any agreement contrary to that desire was lacking. Jennings lost her case and appealed, contending, among
other things, that the trial court wrongfully excluded Hurt's diaries from evidence. She
also lost the appeal, prompting her attorney, Richard Golub, to publicly declare that the
trial court judge, a woman, was so in love with Hurt that Jennings never had a chance.[7]

The law clearly requires considerable evidence in support of any determination that a
common-law marriage exists. But once the common-law marriage is created, it is treated
by the laws the same as all other conventional marriages. The vast majority of states do not
permit cohabiting as a legal method of establishing a (common-law) marriage. In other
words, most states do not provide for common-law marriage.

However, Article IV, Section 1 of the U.S. Constitution provides: "Full faith and
credit shall be given in each State to the public Acts, Records, and judicial Proceedings of
every other State." Accordingly, states that do not themselves permit common-law marriages must recognize as valid a common-law marriage that was legally created elsewhere.

THE "MARVIN MARRIAGE"

LEGAL FOCUS—CASE

Michelle Triola met actor Lee Marvin during the filming of *Ship of Fools*. The couple soon
moved into the same household. Lee divorced his estranged wife, Betty, but in 1970 left
Triola to marry his childhood sweetheart, Pamela Feeley. Triola sued for a share of Marvin's considerable earnings as well as compensation for the earnings she allegedly sacri-
ficed for Marvin's sake in giving up her career as a singer. Under Triola's theory, she
would have shared one-half of Marvin's earnings from *Ship of Fools* while his estranged
wife would receive the other one-half as community property. What was the result?

Marvin v. Marvin, 134 Cal.Rptr. 815, 18 Cal.3d 660, 557 P.2d.106 (California, 1976).

Triola ultimately lost her case. But the celebrated trial between Michelle Triola and Lee
Marvin highlighted a trend, in segments of our society, toward living together without the
formality of a traditional marriage. The historical attitude of the courts had been to give
no protection to either party of a so-called meretricious (based on pretense) relationship.
Thus, upon separation, neither "pseudo-spouse" could obtain a share of the other party's
earnings or accumulated wealth, or receive payments of alimony for continued support.
Any contract that purported to create property or support rights in another in exchange
for participation in a meretricious relationship was declared void as against public policy.

Departing from tradition, the California Supreme Court held that adults who live
together and engage in sexual relations are, nonetheless, competent to contract to pool (i.e.,
combine) earnings, or to keep earnings and other property separate. The court stated that
such an agreement might be express, implied (inferred from conduct), or based upon
"some other tacit understanding." However, the contract could not be based on the
exchange of sexual favors. The California Supreme Court remanded the case to the trial
court to determine if such an agreement existed between Triola and Marvin. The trial
court rejected Triola's contention that a contract existed, but awarded her $104,000 for
rehabilitative compensation, called "palimony" by the media. That award subsequently
was reversed on a second appeal because there was no evidence of a contract, and Michelle
ultimately received nothing.[8]

A rash of similar lawsuits followed in California, setting a trend for courts in other states to grant relief to "discarded" companions when existence of a contract could be proved. But most state legislatures have been reluctant to enact protective laws for cohabiting persons, usually citing public policy as a reason for discouraging cohabitation without marriage. In effect, some courts have discarded public-policy objections and recognized the economic value of the pseudo-spouse as a homemaker. Thus courts in many states now protect cohabitants by awarding division of property or payment of support through enforcement of an express (written or oral) or implied (inferred) agreement.[9] Some states continue to deny all relief to cohabitants on the grounds of public policy.[10]

In recent years the legal status of non-married couples has made a major public policy shift, although it appears much of what has happened has not received publicity commensurate with its historic importance. Three groups have provided the impetus towards marital-type recognition for non-married couples. First, the number of cohabiting heterosexual couples has increased since the 1980s. Second, senior couples (many of whom are widows or/and widowers) who in the past might have married do not for Medicare, social security, estate tax and income tax reasons. Third, the gay rights movement has sought either the right to marry or an alternative to marriage for committed same-sex couples.

DOMESTIC PARTNERSHIPS

Married couples receive many financial benefits that are not available to unmarried couples who may have financial interdependence, shared living arrangements, and a commitment to mutual caring and love. Are such couples entitled to equal protection under law through equal access to financial benefits? A few states* and Canadian provinces and several cities in the United States and Canada have, by statute or ordinance, created "**domestic partnerships**" under which non-married couples can qualify for marriage-like benefits that had previously been reserved for heterosexual married couples. These laws vary significantly, as some restrict coverage to gay couples and others allow gay and opposite-gender couples to qualify. Some laws require or allow registration with the law-making body as a pre-condition to inclusion in the law's benefits and others do not. Coverage of these laws is often restricted to public employees. Benefits may include health insurance, bereavement leave, annuity and pension rights, and housing rights (as in rent-controlled apartments). Proponents are lobbying to expand these benefits to include adoption and inheritance rights, federal income tax equality, and veteran's benefits. Similar coverage is provided by over four thousand corporations to the domestic partners of their non-married employees.[11]

Opponents claim that a sexual relationship should not be a precondition to receiving such benefits nor are any of the typical characteristics of a loving marriage. Theoretically, they argue, an elderly woman and her live-in nurse could qualify, or even a pair of fraternity brothers living as roommates.

GAY MARRIAGE

State laws traditionally restrict marriage to a man and a woman. Proponents of same-sex marriages argue that the heart of the public contract is an emotional, financial, and psychological bond between two people. That the two people cannot bear children is not relevant because no civil marriage license is granted on the condition that the couple bear children.

domestic partnerships

Unmarried couples who live together and seek economic and noneconomic benefits available to married couples.

http://

A helpful site for information on domestic partnerships can be found at **http://www.lambdalegal .org/cgi-bin/iowa/issues/ record?record=3**

---

* California, Connecticut, Maine, Massachusetts, New York, Oregon, Rhode Island, and Vermont.

LEGAL FOCUS—CASE

Nina Baehr and Genora Dancel applied for but were denied a marriage license in Hawaii. In court, they argued that they had a fundamental right to marry that was protected by the same constitutional right of privacy that legitimized abortion. Are Nina and Genora correct?

No. However, the Hawaii Supreme Court did rule that by restricting marriage to opposite-sex couples only, a sex-based discrimination occurred that violated the Hawaii Constitution unless the state could demonstrate a "compelling interest" to do so. More than a dozen states immediately enacted definitions of marriage excluding same-sex couples as "against public policy." The fear was that if same-sex marriages became legal in Hawaii, then under the full faith and credit clause of the U.S. Constitution, all other states would be required to recognize such marriages, just as they must recognize common-law marriages. Congress acted promptly by adoption of the Defense of Marriage Act of 1996, which sought to relieve states of any obligation to recognize same-sex marriages from other states. A number of states already have acted to prohibit same-sex marriages. And, in 1998 the people of Hawaii voted to change their state's constitution to ban same-sex marriages.[12]

In 1989 Denmark became the first country to legalize same-sex unions, called registered partnerships. Norway and Sweden soon followed suit. In 2000 the state of Vermont became the first and so far only state to create a legal entity called civil unions for members of the same gender. The requirements of a civil union under Vermont law include that the parties (1) be over 18, (2) not be a party to another civil union or a marriage and (3) be of the same sex and therefore excluded from the marriage laws of Vermont.[13] The Vermont law bestows the rights and duties of marriage to civil unions. A "'civil union' means that two eligible persons have established a relationship pursuant to this chapter, and may receive the benefits and protections and be subject to the responsibilities of spouses."[14]

The legal issues and social questions being raised by same-gender unions are significant and complicated. The quest for recognition of marital rights raises issues of adoption, child and partner support, health insurance, and property rights to name but a few. Among the victims of terrorist crimes of September 11, 2001, were gay partners; those who lost their partner have requested that they be treated as spouses. Because same-gender relationships violate many people's personal and religious beliefs, resolution of these issues is likely to be very contentious.

A civil union created in Vermont can be between citizens of other states and indeed other countries. What happens when these couples go back to where they live? Will the states or countries recognize the civil union legal status? Does the full faith and credit clause of the Constitution require sister states to recognize the Vermont civil union?

http://

The Vermont Guide to Civil Unions is online at **http://www.sec.state.vt.us/ otherprg/civilunions/ civilunions.html**

LEGAL FOCUS—CASE

Glen Rosengarten filed an action in Connecticut to dissolve a civil union created in Vermont with Peter Downes. Connecticut law does not provide for civil unions and the lawsuit was filed claiming jurisdiction as a family law matter. Will the Connecticut court recognize the Vermont civil union and accept jurisdiction to dissolve it?

Rosengarten v. Downes, 802 A.2d 170 (Conn. App., 2002).

The Connecticut court dismissed the lawsuit holding that it was not a family relations matter under Connecticut law and that the court had no subject matter jurisdiction to dissolve a civil union. The court addressed the Constitutional question of full faith and credit and added: "[W]here statute or policy of the forum State [where the lawsuit is brought] is set up as a defense to a suit brought under the statute of another State . . . the conflict is to be resolved, not by giving automatic effect to the full faith and credit clause and thus compelling courts of each State to subordinate its own statutes to those of others but by *appraising the governmental interest of each jurisdiction and deciding accordingly.*"[15] Cases addressing enforcement issues of the Vermont civil union statute in other states will continue to raise difficult and important issues of constitutional law.

WHAT ARE THE LEGAL CONSEQUENCES OF MARRIAGE?

OBLIGATION OF SUPPORT

The marital relationship implies a continuing and mutual obligation of support. Support includes food, shelter, clothing, medicine, and usually a wide range of consumer goods, all appropriate to the family's wealth and established standard of living. Management of the family budget is left to the wise or unwise (and sometimes spiteful) management of the spouses. It is a crime for parents to willfully fail to support their children. Moreover, some states have enacted statutes requiring adult children who have the financial means to support their indigent parents who receive government assistance. But courts seldom become involved in support disputes unless the marriage in question is in the process of dissolution or divorce. You will see, later in this chapter, that the family's budget (standard of living) before divorce is relevant to the issue of how much support (called *alimony*) should be imposed by law for the period following divorce.

LEGAL FOCUS—PROBLEM

Robert Hamilton became disabled and could not work. His wife, Sally, a trained legal secretary, had been serving as housewife and homemaker. Sally declared that she would not seek gainful employment to support her husband and would henceforth terminate the marriage. Is Sally required to go to work to support Robert if the marriage remains intact? If it is terminated?

Yes, Sally will be required to apply her earning skills in support of her husband whether or not the marriage remains intact. Also, in this hypothetical case, she could be required to use property owned in her name for his support. However, Sally would not necessarily be indentured for life; courts will terminate lifetime support in many circumstances. At some point, the balance of equities would weigh in favor of public support of the disabled Robert, and Sally would be released from that obligation.

The specific criteria often used by courts in setting the amount of required support following termination of the marriage, and the length of time support must be paid, are reviewed later in this chapter.

PROPERTY RIGHTS

The legal rights of the spouses to their marital property (assets of the family, as defined by statute) vary depending upon the applicable state law.

http://

For a chart of state marital property law see

http://www.abanet.org/family/familylaw/table5.html

separate property

Property owned by a marital partner separate from the spouse, either brought into a marriage at the outset or acquired during marriage by gift or inheritance.

marital property

Property acquired during marriage in a marital property state.

community property

All property acquired (in a community property state) by the husband or the wife during marriage other than by gift or inheritance, and other than as profits or income from separate property.

commingling

The mixing together of community property and separate property to the extent that the properties cannot be traced back to their original status. Commingled property becomes totally community property.

Marital Property States

Under original common-law theory, title to all property owned by a woman was automatically vested in her husband upon marriage. During marriage, the wife owned no property. Marriage created one entity: the husband. A creditor who successfully sued the wife received a judgment against the husband, and thereby reached all of the family's nonexempt assets.

Today most states have adopted a form of marital property law that distinguishes between separate and marital property. **Separate property** is property acquired before marriage or during marriage by gift or inheritance.[16] The husband and wife are "partners" in all other property acquired during marriage, and that property is called **marital property.** Property earned (i.e., wages) by one spouse during marriage is marital property even if held in one spouse's name in a separate account. As you read below about community property states and compare it to marital property states, the two types of property ownership will sound very much alike. For our purposes the most important distinction occurs upon divorce. In a marital property state, courts are expected to divide the property equitably, but not necessarily equally. In a community property state the family property is considered equally owned and thus is awarded 50 percent to each spouse. More information about marital property division upon divorce is explained later in this chapter.

Community Property States*

All property acquired by the husband or the wife during marriage, other than by gift or inheritance, is **community property.** Unless agreed otherwise, the respective earnings of husband and wife during marriage are owned equally when received. Upon dissolution, accumulated earnings, as with all other community properties, are divided equally between the spouses because the ownership of community property is equal. Whereas most United States law is based on English law, the civil law systems of Spain and France are the origin of community property law in the United States.

As stated earlier, separate property is property either brought into the marriage or acquired during marriage by gift or inheritance. Separate property retains its separate character as long as independent records are kept. For example, cash kept in a separate savings account will retain its separate property classification. **Commingling** of separate property and community property occurs when the two are so combined that they cannot reasonably be traced back to their original status. In such cases, the separate property has been transmuted into community property and has lost its former status. An example is cash brought into the marriage and subsequently combined in the family checking account with monthly community earnings. The status of property as separate or community can also be altered by an agreement between the spouses.

---

* Community property states are Arizona, California, Idaho, Louisiana, Nevada, New Mexico, Texas, Washington, and Wisconsin, and the territory of Puerto Rico. In 1998 Alaska adopted the Alaska Community Property Act, which allows couples to agree to be subject to community property rules. See Jonathan G. Blattmacher et al., "Tax Planning with Consensual Community Property: Alaska's New Community Property Law," *Real Property, Probate and Trust Journal* 33 (1999), p. 615.

LEGAL FOCUS—BACKGROUND

How romantic can you get? Not only did she consent to marry, but C.V. brought to the marriage her two mules. As the marriage and affection grew so did the mules. But a third party, Stringfellow, came between the two—not romantically but economically. Stringfellow successfully sued C.V.'s husband, but when he found the husband's coffers bare he sought to satisfy the judgment by levying upon C.V.'s mules. Stringfellow claimed the increase in value from $35 to $75 was due to the husband's care and thus was community property. The Texas Supreme Court sided with C.V., declaring that the animals were the same ones owned by her at her marriage. "She does not hold her separate property by so precarious a tenure as to depend upon the fluctuations of weight or the prices in the market."[17]

Marriage property issues can arise in many ways, and state marital law is not as uniform as in other law areas. Issues of property can be raised by creditors, gifts to others, death, and divorce, and treatment of the property is influenced by how the question arises. In this brief discussion community property and marital property sound very much alike. Like much in the law the devil is in the details and much detail is sorted out in the dissolution of a marriage, where the differences in treatment of the two types of marriage property are considerable.

Gifts of Marital Property

MARITAL PROPERTY In a marital property state, property is not classified as marital property until some event that requires a classification, such as a divorce or death. At the time of the event all existing property is classified as either marital or separate property. As a general rule, an asset transferred before the need to classify it is no longer eligible as marital property. In other words, gifts of property before a divorce or probate proceeding usually are not recaptured in the marital estate.[18] The major exceptions to this general rule are when a transfer results in dissipation, waste, or conversion of assets with the intent to deprive the marital estate.

LEGAL FOCUS—EXAMPLE

James A. Szesny appealed from an order of the divorce court that found him solely responsible for over $82,000 in marital debt. The court found that during the marriage he went out at night without his wife and child; that he belonged to a health club; that he opened charge accounts without his wife's knowledge or permission; that he spent money on clothing for himself and at fine restaurants; that he gave money to his mother; that he borrowed money but did not use it to reduce the marital debt; and that he "in effect kited his account in consumer debts." The trial court also found that Taryn Szesny spent minimal amounts on clothing, ate in fast food restaurants, and in one year was responsible for less than one-twelfth of their total expenses. In upholding the trial court's determination the court stated, "Dissipation can occur prior to dissolution. The key is whether one spouse uses marital property for his or her own benefit for a purpose unrelated to the marriage."[19]

COMMUNITY PROPERTY   Because both spouses own an undivided one-half interest in the community property, neither spouse can defeat the other's ownership rights by giving it away without consent.

LEGAL FOCUS—PROBLEM

In Bellevue, Washington, George Thompson was enamored of his secretary, Vickie Ehlers, and gave her a Jaguar XJS purchased with earnings from his accounting business. When his wife, Betty, learned of the gift, she insisted that the car be taken from Ehlers. Can this be done legally?

Yes. Whenever either spouse gives away community property without the other's consent, the injured spouse can ask the court to set aside the transfer of property and order the property returned to the community. However, if the automobile was "given" to the secretary in exchange for services legitimately rendered, then the "gift" would be in the nature of a bonus, or wage, and would not be set aside. Realistically, in the preceding hypothetical example, the marriage probably would have deteriorated to the extent that Betty Thompson would pursue a dissolution (divorce) rather than continue the marriage while pursuing a lawsuit to return an improper gift from the community. In any divorce decree the court, in dividing the community property equally, would give Betty "credit" for her one-half value of the XJS.

Creditors of the Family

MARITAL PROPERTY   The extent to which creditors of one spouse can reach the family's marital property varies from state to state. Under the Uniform Marital Property Act (UMPA), which has been adopted only in Wisconsin but which has influenced other marital property states, all marital property can be reached by the creditors of either spouse. Courts in Maine have ruled in the absence of statute that all marital property can be reached by creditors of either spouse during the marriage.[20] This rule reflects the trend. But courts in many states continue to rule that creditors of one spouse can reach only marital property that is held in that spouse's name. These states hold that property rights generally are based upon who holds title to the property, and creditors can reach only property held in the title of the debtor. However, even in these states property owners cannot change the title to property simply to avoid the claims of creditors. Such transfers can be set aside as fraudulent.

COMMUNITY PROPERTY   Unpaid creditors who obtain a judgment against either the husband or wife can reach all nonexempt community property to satisfy their claims. Property declared "exempt" by statute cannot be taken from anyone by any creditor (sufficient monies to obtain the necessaries of life are an example of exempt property). Accordingly, if a husband wrongfully punches a letter carrier, for example, severely injuring that person's eyesight, the victim can receive payment of the court judgment from the accumulated earnings of the defendant's wife, or from any other nonexempt community property. Of course, the husband's separate property would be liable for his torts committed during marriage and his personal debts incurred before his marriage; his wife's separate property would not. Reciprocally, the wife's separate property would be liable for her torts or other debts before marriage; her husband's separate property would not. However, either spouse's marital earnings may be diverted from the marriage and taken to satisfy premarital debts. To this extent, one does "marry" the preexisting debts of the spouse.

One spouse is not responsible for the crimes or torts of the other, and separate property is immune from fines or civil judgments against the other. Indirectly, of course, the innocent spouse is hurt if a fine is paid from community property or if, as a result of confinement, community property is not earned. Marriage does not shield one's separate property from his or her own creditors.

CIVIL LAWSUITS BETWEEN FAMILY MEMBERS

One traditional concept embodied in the common law has been that marriage melded a man and woman into a single legal entity. It logically followed that one spouse could not sue the other spouse, other than to dissolve the entity (as through divorce). This common-law rule, called **spousal immunity,** prohibits actions between spouses for torts, such as negligence and assault and battery. A justification for this immunity is to protect domestic tranquility. This doctrine does not prevent a victimized spouse from obtaining a divorce on grounds of adultery or extreme mental cruelty, but it does insulate many types of wrongful and abusive conduct by a family member. Consequently, the doctrine of spousal immunity currently is yielding to modern concepts and modifications by the courts (and legislatures) to permit lawsuits between spouses in various situations and provide more equitable property distributions upon divorce.

Wives have successfully sued husbands for both compensatory and punitive damages for wife-beating (recovery, $360,000); for intentional infliction of mental distress where a husband tried to hire a hit man (i.e., professional killer) to kill his wife (settled for a six-figure sum); for fraudulently undervaluing and selling marital property worth $800,000 for a price of $45,000 (recovery, $240,000); and for emotional distress when a husband had temper tantrums, doled out stingy amounts of cash, made his wife wear cheap clothes, and belittled her in front of their daughter (recovery, $362,000, forcing husband into bankruptcy).[21]

spousal immunity

A doctrine of the common law that tort actions between spouses are prohibited because of a public policy to protect the harmony of the marital relationship from adversarial and disruptive legal proceedings.

LEGAL FOCUS—CASE

Shortly after her whirlwind courtship and wedding to Samuel B. McNeill III, Jo McNeill falsely told her husband that she was an attorney, had a master's degree in accounting, was suffering from cancer, and had an outstanding premarital judgment against her that could affect their assets. In reliance on these false statements, Samuel deeded title of his separate property, an exclusive waterfront home in Huntington Beach, California, into their joint names. Later, Jo falsely told Sam that she had only 90 days to live, encouraged him to put "their" assets into trust, and then gave him documents to sign that, in reality, transferred all of his assets to her. Soon thereafter the marriage deteriorated and Sam moved into a small rental cottage in Los Angeles near his work. Upon discovery of the truth, Sam sued his wife for fraud, and also sought recovery of his property. What was the result?

In re Marriage of McNeill, 160 Cal. App. 3d 548, 206 Cal. Rptr. 641 (California, 1984).

The trial court ruled in favor of Sam. Misstatements of affection or feelings generally are not actionable, but none of the false statements made by Jo McNeill concerned her feelings about Sam. On appeal, the judgment was upheld. Children also may sue their parents in many states. For example, a daughter was permitted to sue her father for assault and rape;[22] a child sued her mother for negligently failing to buckle the child's seatbelt;[23] and a child injured *in utero* successfully sued her mother for negligence in jaywalking.[24] But the state of Florida, applying the doctrine of parental immunity, rejected a child's civil lawsuit for sexual abuse.[25] Maryland continues to apply parent-child tort immunity doctrine to actions based on negligence.[26] These actions between spouses, as well as lawsuits between children and their parents, are called *domestic torts.**

Some argue that permitting lawsuits for injuries from domestic torts simply places another weapon in the hands of embittered and vengeful spouses. It drags soap operas into public courtrooms, implicitly forces the government (through its courts and legislatures) to prescribe what constitutes "normal" or "acceptable" interpersonal conduct, and exacerbates the litigation explosion. Others respond that spousal immunity should not be a shield against penalties for abusive conduct that would be compensable if the parties were strangers. The question of what conduct ought to be compensable is not easy to answer. In the following example, actions are based upon the intentional infliction of mental distress by one family member on another.

LEGAL FOCUS—CASE

A family court judge found that Mr. Hakkila's behavior in demeaning his wife, screaming at her, locking her out of the house and refusing to have sex with her was "... beyond the bounds of decency ... atrocious ... utterly intolerable" and constituted compensable negligent and intentional infliction of emotional distress. Should Mr. Hakkila be ordered to pay damages to his wife?

Hakkila v. Hakkila, 112 N.M. 77, 812 P.2d 132 (New Mexico, 1991) (cert. den. June 4, 1991).

The case against Mr. Hakkila was thrown out on appeal. In New Mexico, family members can sue one another but only if the wrongful conduct is sufficiently outrageous: "... "the threshold of outrageousness should be set high enough ... that the social good from recognizing the tort will not be outweighed by unseemly and invasive litigation."[†]

Why must intentional conduct between spouses be outrageous to justify civil liability? Presumably the law should not require a degree of civility between spouses that is beyond their capacity. People need to vent to some extent. About half of the states where the question has arisen have honored emotional-distress cases between spouses.[27] The other half of the states require extraordinarily outrageous behavior or the lawsuit is rejected.[28]

There is also new attention to lawsuits by children against abusive parents, even when many years have elapsed since the alleged wrongful conduct. Many states hold that actions by children are not barred by the statute of limitations because it does not begin to "run" until adult survivors of child abuse overcome their memory blocks and discover (usually in

---

* There are significant financial advantages for attorneys who, in addition to accepting divorce cases (which are not usually lucrative), also take a related domestic tort case in which substantial contingent fees may be earned. Seizing the opportunity while the law evolves, lawyers are filing tort suits across the country, for intentional and negligent infliction of emotional distress; assault and battery; the transmission of or fear of transmission of sexual diseases; child-snatching; false imprisonment; defamation (libel or slander); fraudulent concealment of personal attitudes, beliefs, or physical condition; and hiding assets during divorce proceedings. *The National Law Journal,* 23 September 1991. Attorneys may be expected to pursue only those defendants who have the means to pay judgments. Homeowners insurance policies will probably soon exclude domestic tort liability from coverage. Consequently, victims in wealthy families may benefit more from the recognition of domestic torts than victims in poor families. Stated bluntly, wealthy wrongdoers may be punished by monetary judgments, while judgment-proof poor wrongdoers escape unscathed.

† That the husband insulted his wife in front of her friends by calling her an obscenity, mistreated her physically, locked her out of the house after she ripped the buttons off his shirt, called her "stupid" and "insane," and blamed their poor sexual relationship on her was held insufficiently outrageous to justify liability.

psychiatric or psychological therapy) the acts that took place when they were young children. Even grossly negligent conduct by mothers during pregnancy (e.g., drug, alcohol, or nicotine abuse or rejection of prenatal care) may also give rise to civil judgments for damages in favor of the injured children.

Sexual abuse and severe physical abuse of a child are serious crimes discussed later in this chapter. Child abuse also is a domestic tort that, like other civil cases, may be proven by a "preponderance of the evidence." This burden of proof is much easier to meet than the proof "beyond a reasonable doubt" that is required for conviction in criminal cases. Perhaps the most perplexing dilemma clouding this particular domestic tort is how to identify and reject unjustified claims for damages sought many years following commission of the alleged acts. Such claims are based upon "recovered memory" that is recovered, perhaps after many years, during psychiatric therapy. The issue of the reliability of such recollections, the possibility that they were suggested rather than recollected, as well as the possibility of false claims are among the most difficult issues in such cases.

Claims of child abuse, made during contested custody proceedings (as distinguished from claims made during civil litigation) are discussed later in this chapter.

Not all abuse within families is by parents, nor are all civil lawsuits between family members designed to obtain money.

LEGAL FOCUS—PROBLEM

Merle Haggard, at the time age sixty, famous for singing "Okie from Muskogee" and "Workin' Man Blues," received a "continuous barrage of threats against his safety" from his then thirty-nine-year-old son, Marty. Marty believed that Merle "owed him and his mother a lot of money." What civil remedy is available to protect the senior Haggard?

Haggard obtained a restraining order from court barring Marty from harassing or even coming near him. Violation of such an injunction would be a contempt of court, for which jail is the usual sanction.[29]

WHAT LAWS GOVERN PARENTHOOD?

PRENATAL LAWS

Perhaps the most controversial issue in family law is the question of abortion. Until 1973, an overwhelming majority of states prohibited abortion unless necessary to preserve the life or health of the mother. In that year the leading and much-publicized case of *Roe v. Wade*[30] was decided by the U.S. Supreme Court. It held that a pregnant female, married or single, in consultation with her physician, has an unqualified, absolute right to have an abortion during the first trimester (three months) of her pregnancy. This right cannot be vetoed by the natural father, by a parent, or by a husband. During the second trimester the right continues, but the abortion procedures may be regulated by the state, if it chooses, in ways that are related to maternal health (e.g., hospitalization). During the final trimester and when the fetus has become viable (capable of continuing its existence outside the womb naturally or by use of artificial life-support systems), the state may, if it chooses, prohibit abortion unless it is necessary for the health or preservation of the life of the mother. In the more recent *Webster* case, the U.S. Supreme Court held that a state may withhold the use of public employees and facilities to perform or assist abortions that are not necessary to save the mother's life.[31] Also, while *Roe* held that there is a compelling state interest in protecting a fetus (through regulation) once it has become viable, in *Webster* the Court held that a state may regulate abortion before the fetus is viable by requiring medical tests to determine if the point of viability has occurred.

In 1990, the U.S. Supreme Court upheld (1) an Ohio law requiring an unmarried minor to notify at least one parent of her intended abortion and (2) a Minnesota law requiring an unmarried minor to notify both parents. The Court ruled that both laws were constitutional.[32] In both states, a minor may bypass parental notification by obtaining a judge's order. In 1992, the U.S. Supreme Court declared that although a state cannot prohibit an abortion before a fetus is viable, it nonetheless can require that candidates for abortion first consider information about available and legal alternatives. Although states can regulate abortions before viability, the Court stated that they cannot do so in a way that "places a substantial obstacle in the path of a woman's choice."[33]

LEGAL FOCUS—BACKGROUND

The Supreme Court in *Stenberg v. Carhart* (2000) began its opinion noting the impossibility of its task. Whereas most institutions of government can pass on controversial issues, the court is not free to do so. "We again consider the right to an abortion. We understand the controversial nature of the problem. Millions of Americans believe that life begins at conception and consequently that an abortion is akin to causing the death of an innocent child; they recoil at the thought of a law that would permit it. Other millions fear that a law that forbids abortion would condemn many American women to lives that lack dignity, depriving them of equal liberty and leading those with least resources to undergo illegal abortions with the attendant risks of death and suffering. Taking account of these virtually irreconcilable points of view, aware that constitutional law must govern a society whose different members sincerely hold directly opposing views, and considering the matter in light of the Constitution's guarantees of fundamental individual liberty, this Court, in the course of a generation, has determined and then redetermined that the Constitution offers basic protection to the woman's right to choose."[34]

http://

Information on both sides of the abortion debate is available on the Internet
http://www.naral.org/ and
http://www.prolifeinfo.org/

The mechanical trimester analysis of *Roe* has shifted to the moment of viability, which because of medical advances may occur earlier, at perhaps 23 to 24 weeks, or even earlier. Whenever it occurs, the attainment of viability is an important fact, although in *Stenberg* the U.S. Supreme Court held unconstitutional a Nebraska law making criminal the performance of dilation and evacuation (D&E) abortion. The Supreme Court held that restrictions on methods of abortion must be specific and must not ban the most commonly used and safest methods. In addition any statute banning abortion must contain an exception for the woman's health.

All of the U.S. Supreme Court decisions authorizing abortion have been 5–4 votes. In theory, the appointment of a single justice could shift the majority vote the other way.

PATERNITY

A legitimate child enjoys rights and sometimes duties* of support; possesses rights of inheritance; and typically carries the father's surname. Such a child is the issue of his or her natural, married parents. Historically, an illegitimate child was a child born of an unmarried mother or born of an adulterous, incestuous, or bigamous relationship. Statutes today are inclusive and tend to resolve any doubt in favor of legitimacy through application of a legal presumption of legitimacy.

The Uniform Parentage Act, last revised in 2000, has been adopted in some form by about one-third of the states and has influenced law in many others. The Uniform Parentage Act provides that a child born during a marriage or within 300 days after termination of the marriage is the child of the birth mother and her husband. A man is also presumed to be the father of a child if: before the child's birth, he and the mother marry; or after the birth of the child, he and the child's mother marry and he voluntarily asserts his paternity of the child; or he agreed to be and is named as the child's father on the child's birth certificate; or he promised in a record to support the child as his own. The presumption of **paternity** may be rebutted only by adjudication.

The presumption of legitimacy is difficult to overcome and usually will depend on the husband's showing of impotency or on a blood-typing analysis, which all but conclusively proves that the husband could not be the child's father. With modern blood-typing techniques and analyses, experts can establish statistical probabilities as to whether or not a suspect could be the natural father. Such tests also can show a high probability that a specific man is the father. Every state has statutes providing for the admissibility of specified genetic tests in paternity cases.[35] Blood tests are not absolutely conclusive. In one case, the defendant contended that he had never even met the mother of the child he was accused of fathering even though blood tests revealed he had a 99.99 percent probability of paternity. The court believed the persuasive man.[36] DNA testing is even more conclusive.

paternity

Establishing the father of a child. Often determined by a lawsuit to prove that a named person is the father of a child.

LEGAL FOCUS—PROBLEM

Four poor children born out of wedlock to different mothers had their paternity established by DNA "sibling" testing of one another. Their deceased father was Larry Hillbloom, who crashed at sea leaving no DNA readily available. Hillbloom had sex with the teenage mothers of the half-brothers and -sisters while he was on various other trips to the South Pacific. Hillbloom's will left everything to the University of California at Berkeley—nothing was said about any children. Can the illegitimate children inherit?

Yes. Both legitimate and illegitimate children (once paternity is established) inherit in California unless specifically disinherited in the will. Not mentioning is not disinheriting. Thus, the four South Pacific children each received $90 million.[37]

The basic handicaps of an illegitimate child are financial. Until paternity is established by a court, the child does not inherit as an heir and has no right to paternal support.

There is a trend to equalize the rights of illegitimate (whose paternity is established) and legitimate children. (Adopted children are treated under the law the same as natural

---

* As previously noted, in some states adult children are required to support their indigent parents who are receiving public assistance. There is no common-law duty of a child to support a parent.

children.) This trend reflects the facts that increasing numbers of children are born out of wedlock and that such children are innocent of any wrongdoing. Thus, the U.S. Supreme Court has held that states may not discriminate against illegitimate children and that states must require that natural fathers support both their legitimate and illegitimate children.[38] Nor may a state create a right of action in favor of legitimate children for the wrongful death of a parent and exclude illegitimate children from the benefit of such a right.[39] And illegitimate children may not be excluded from sharing equally with other children in the recovery of workers' compensation benefits for the death of their parent.[40]

Custody of a child conceived out of wedlock remains with the mother as long as she is a suitable person. Otherwise, custody may be awarded to another suitable person, including the natural father.

Some states (such as California) have adopted statutes that permit the illegitimate child with ascertained paternity to inherit from his or her father. In the absence of such a statute, the illegitimate child will inherit only from his or her mother.

Legal rights for nonmarital offspring have little meaning unless the natural father becomes identified. Statutory presumptions create paternity in many cases, but the mother or child may need to bring a civil paternity action to establish the child's natural parentage. Usually the mother testifies to the requisite act of intercourse. Proof that an unmarried mother had sexual intercourse with other men during the period of possible conception is admissible; however, testimony concerning the mother's sexual activities before or after the time of possible conception cannot be considered by the jury.

If the mother prevails and paternity is established, the court's judgment will include an order of periodic support and reimbursement of her medical costs, expenses of pregnancy, and attorney fees. Once paternity is established, all states authorize their courts to order the payment of support because of state interest (welfare authorities may have the burden of support if the natural father is not held responsible). A few states also confer inheritance rights upon a child legitimated by a paternity proceeding. But note even though a child has inheritance rights, any child may be intentionally disinherited by the will of his or her parent. (See Chapter 14 for a more complete discussion of inheritance and disinheritance.)

http://

There are many resources available concerning the topic of adoption. See

http://www.adoptex.org/,
http://www.adopting.com/,
http://www.adoption.org/

SURROGATE-MOTHER CONTRACTS

To obtain a biologically related child, a husband and wife may desire to artificially inseminate a contracting **surrogate mother,** who agrees to carry the fetus until birth and then relinquish her parental rights to the biological father. The natural father's wife then adopts the child. One type of surrogacy arrangement is gestational surrogacy, where the surrogate mother is not genetically related to the child. A fertilized egg is transferred into the surrogate mother's uterus to gestate until birth. The fertilized egg may or may not be genetically related to both the husband and wife who may have used the sperm or egg of a donor.

surrogate mother

A female who is artificially inseminated, carries the fetus to term, and who then relinquishes her parental rights to the biological father. Surrogacy services are performed pursuant to a contract in return for money.

LEGAL FOCUS—CASE

In 1985, William Stern and Mary Beth Whitehead entered into a surrogacy contract. It stated that Stern's wife, Elizabeth, was infertile, that they wanted a child, and that Whitehead was willing to serve as the mother with Stern as the father. The contract provided that Whitehead would become pregnant (through artificial insemination, using Stern's sperm), carry the child to term, bear it, deliver it to the Sterns, and thereafter do what-ever was necessary to terminate her maternal rights so that Mrs. Stern could thereafter adopt the child. Stern agreed to pay $10,000 to Whitehead.

On March 27, 1986, Baby M was born; on March 30 she was delivered to the Sterns. Later that day, Whitehead underwent an emotional crisis; she was deeply dis-turbed, disconsolate, and stricken with unbearable sadness. She had to have her child. Fearing that she might commit suicide, the Sterns returned Baby M in exchange for Whitehead's promise to return the child in one week. The struggle over custody then began in the courts, and Melissa (Baby M) was returned to the Sterns pending final out-come of the litigation. Whitehead was permitted limited visitation.

The trial court ruled in favor of the Sterns. Whitehead appealed. What was the result?

In re Baby M, 217 N.J. Super. 313, 525 A.2d 1128, reversed at 109 N.J. 396, 537 A.2d 1227 (1988).

The supreme court of New Jersey held that the surrogacy contract conflicted with the state's adoption laws, especially in calling for the payment of money and by providing for the irrevocable agreement of the natural mother to terminate her parental rights to facili-tate the adoption. Also, the contract's basic premise, that the natural parents can decide in advance of birth which one is to have custody of the child, conflicts with the law that the child's best interests shall determine custody. Therefore, the court reasoned, the contract was void and unenforceable. The court then decided that custody with the Sterns was in the best interests of Melissa regardless of the invalidity of the contract. Whitehead lost cus-tody but was awarded visitation rights.

After *In re Baby M,* legislatures in a number of states barred or severely limited the enforceability of surrogate contracts.[41] Assisted reproduction and gestational agreements still became commonplace in the 1990s, and the Uniform Parentage Act (2000) provides for gestational agreements. "A prospective gestational mother, her husband if she is mar-ried, a donor or the donors, and the intended parents may enter into a written agreement providing that: (1) the prospective gestational mother agrees to pregnancy by means of assisted reproduction; (2) the prospective gestational mother, her husband if she is married, and the donors relinquish all rights and duties as the parents of a child conceived through assisted reproduction; and (3) the intended parents become the parents of the child."[42] In 2002 about 20 percent of the states had laws allowing surrogacy contracts.[43] Another 20 percent either ban surrogacy contracts or ban payment exceeding expenses. The New York statute is representative: "Surrogate parenting contracts are hereby declared contrary to the public policy of this state, and are void and unenforceable." Law in the area of human reproduction is clearly still seeking consensus.

LEGAL FOCUS—CASE

Crispina and Mark Calvert entered into a contract with Anna Johnson, who agreed to have their embryo (created by the sperm and egg of the Calverts) implanted into her uterus and to bear the child. The Calverts agreed to pay Anna $10,000 and to purchase a life insurance policy on Anna's life for this service. Several months into the pregnancy, Anna claimed that she had "bonded" with the fetus and filed suit to be declared the legal mother. What was the result?

Johnson v. Calvert, 5 Cal. 4th 84, 851 P.2d 776, 19 Cal. Rptr. 2d 494 (California, 1993).

http://

For reference materials about surrogacy arrangements and sample contract forms visit **http://www.opts.com/** and **http://www.surromoms online.com/**

The California Supreme Court held that the law recognizes both genetic consanguinity (of the same blood) and giving birth as two means of establishing a mother and child relationship. In this case, the two means did not coincide in one woman. Anna Johnson's attorney argued that the birth mother had the better case because the donor of the fertilized egg had never been pregnant and had never given birth. But the court decided that the one who intended to bring about the birth of a child that she intended to raise as her own (Crispina Calvert in this case) is the natural mother.

In vitro fertilization (IVF) takes place in a petri dish (a glass dish with an overlapping cover for the culture of microorganisms), following which the fertilized egg is placed into the mother's uterus. It also is possible to freeze the fertilized embryo and implant it in the distant future.

LEGAL FOCUS—CASE

Maureen Kass, 39, could not have children naturally because while in her mother's womb, she was exposed to the drug DES. Maureen and her husband, Steven, caused five of her eggs to be artificially fertilized by his sperm, and then frozen. They signed a contract stating that, upon divorce, the eggs would be donated to research and ultimately destroyed. But following their divorce, Maureen changed her mind; Steven objected, saying he did not want to have a child by his former wife. Maureen contended that the law should protect her maternal rights to her fertilized egg. Who wins?

Kass v. Kass, 91 N.Y.2d 554, 686 N.E.2d 174 (N.Y., 1998).

The New York Court of Appeals upheld the contract. The issue would not be so clear if there had been no contract to uphold. A male has no legal right to object to an abortion of the embryo; should he have a right to object to its gestation and birth before it has been implanted into a womb?

Cryopreservation of sperm makes artificial insemination possible without having to match ovulation cycles with sperm donations. The storage of large numbers of sperm samples permits infertile couples to select donor characteristics to assure a closer match to the sterile husband's own makeup. Selection can be based on race, height, body type, eye color, intelligence, religious background, and even national origin.[44] Because fertilized embryos can be frozen, for perhaps 100 years, women do not need to be subjected to surgery each time they need to get an egg—a dozen or more can be retrieved at one time.

At the beginning of the twenty-first century, there were an estimated 9,000 embryos stockpiled in the country's freezers. The number is much larger now. Some of these fertilized eggs are forgotten or abandoned. Legal issues arise when storage bills are not paid. What if one or more of the donors dies? Can abandoned embryos be foreclosed upon and be given or sold in the open market? One set of "test tube orphans" (fertilized embryos) are residing in a deep freeze in Australia; its donors died in a plane crash leaving a multi-million-dollar estate to their children, if they are ever born.[45]

Today a thriving surrogacy industry exists in this country, and thousands of IVF children have been born. Typically, these surrogacy arrangements involve fertilization of the woman's own egg with a male client's sperm. However, many arrangements, like the Crispina and Mark Calvert case, involve a couple's renting of a womb for nine months to produce their baby.

Legal issues presented in such cases concern validity of the underlying contracts, forfeiture of parental rights by surrogate mothers, assurance of adoption by wives of the natural fathers, the best interests of the children, inheritance rights following the intestate death of either of the biological parents, and commercialization of the whole process.

In addition to the legal issues, surrogacy raises many fundamental social, medical, and moral questions: Is surrogacy an acceptable positive solution to the problem of female infertility? Or is it an unnatural arrangement, and in effect a "forced baby sale" exploitive of poor women, even if they are paid for their cooperation? Should similar questions be asked about the use of fertility drugs, which have resulted in multiple births, even the birth of octuplets (eight siblings)? Later in this chapter we will consider whether or not the legal problems created by the use of human surrogates can be sidestepped by the use of artificial wombs.

PARENTING BY SAME-SEX COUPLES

LEGAL FOCUS—BACKGROUND

Steven Lofton is a registered pediatric nurse who has raised three foster children, including John Doe ("Doe"), since infancy. All three of Lofton's foster children tested positive for HIV at birth. While the other two foster children developed AIDS, Doe no longer tests positive for HIV. For the past ten years, Lofton has cared for his foster children full-time, administering medications and looking after them when they were sick. He has an Outstanding Foster Parenting award from a child placement agency. Doe was released for adoption in 1994, and Lofton applied to adopt. However, under Florida law, Lofton was automatically disqualified because he is gay.

Same-sex couples or gay persons are allowed to adopt a child in most states but in one state, Florida, a statute specifically bans gays from adoption: "No person eligible to adopt under this statute may adopt if that person is a homosexual."[46] A challenge to the statute was filed in 1999 arguing that it violates the constitutional rights of children who need homes and gay people who want to adopt by denying each the equal protection of the law when the denial is based solely on sexual preference. In upholding the state statute the Federal Southern District of Florida stated, "In areas of social . . . policy, a statutory classification that neither proceeds along suspect lines nor infringes fundamental constitutional rights must be upheld against equal protection challenge if there is any reasonably conceivable state of facts that could provide a rational basis for the classification."[47]

When adoption occurs, the law applies the same parenting rules that apply to all natural parents.

PARENTAL RIGHTS AND LIABILITIES

Freedom from governmental involvement in family affairs is a fundamental value in our society. While not explicitly stated therein, the U.S. Constitution implies a right to marry, to establish a home and bring up children, to educate one's children as one chooses, and to privacy—that is, to be let alone by the government in the private realm of family life. Parents thus have a constitutional right to autonomy in rearing their children, and the state cannot interfere except under "clear and convincing" proof of severe child abuse or abandonment.[48] Parents also must exercise reasonable care, supervision, protection, and control over their minor children. Willful failure to do so may be a crime, a variation of the misdemeanor called contributing to the delinquency of a minor.[49] The *Restatement of Torts* describes "a duty to exercise reasonable care so to control his minor child as to prevent it from intentionally harming others. . . ."[50] Parents are not criminally responsible for negligent parenting if they make reasonable efforts to control their children, but are unable to do so. There is no crime (or civil liability) visited upon parents for their children's general incorrigibility and bad disposition.

In general, parents have the right to custody of their minor children and are free to raise them as they see fit. Does the following case fly in the face of this rule?

LEGAL FOCUS—PROBLEM

Gregory Kingsley, age twelve, was living happily with his foster parents, George and Lizabeth Russ, who had eight children of their own. George Russ had noticed Gregory while visiting the Lake County Boys Ranch, and soon applied to be his foster parent. (A foster family usually provides a temporary haven for a child until the child can be reunited with his or her family.) Before long, the Russes applied to formally adopt Gregory, but his natural mother, Rachel, objected. Gregory then contacted and hired his own attorney, Jerri Blair, to "sue his parents for divorce" so he could be legally adopted by the Russes. What was the outcome?

The State Circuit Court in Orlando, Florida, allowed Gregory Kingsley to "divorce" his natural parents, freeing him for adoption by George and Lizabeth.[51] However, this case does not contradict the broad rights of parents to raise their children as they see fit. The reality of the Gregory Kingsley case is that his parents, for various reasons, were not raising him at all.

GENETIC ENGINEERING AND FAMILY PLANNING: LEGAL ISSUES

You most certainly will be affected by and participate in society's response to what many refer to as the "Biotech Century."* The accelerated pace of scientific discovery in biotechnology is the direct result of the marriage of the genetic and computer revolutions. The computer is being used "to decipher, manage and organize the vast resource of the biotech economy."[52] It is estimated that biological knowledge is currently doubling every five years; in genetics, the quantity of information is doubling every twenty-four months.

The U.S. Department of Energy funded the Human Genome Project, which in June 2000 provided a working draft of the entire human genome sequence.[53] Private companies working alone and in cooperation with the Genome Project are racing to use the information in an amazing variety of applications. Among the current and potential uses of genome research are in the fields of molecular medicine, microbial genomics, risk assessment, bioarchaeology, anthropology, evolution and human migration, DNA forensics (identification), agriculture, livestock breeding, and bioprocessing.

Private biotech corporations are interested in the potential profits from new medicines and vaccines that can be produced once the genetic code of disease is identified.[†] Driven by the rush to create and to monopolize the profits flowing from new discoveries, private

http://

For background as well as timely information on the Human Genome Project, visit its Web site at
http://www.ornl.gov/hgmis/

---

* Biotechnology is the use of the data and techniques of engineering and computer technology for the study of living organisms.
† For example, the full genetic sequence of chlamydia, the most common bacterial sexually transmitted disease in the United States and a leading cause of infertility, has been identified and published. A vaccine for disease is now within sight.

business will provide new medicines and vaccines promising longer and healthier lives for families. Agricultural products that are improved (e.g., made disease-resistant) through genetic engineering also hold the promise for huge profits, and indirectly affect families through healthier children. Already there are thousands of genetically altered food products in the markets of the world. But here we are concerned with the laws and issues that are more directly surrounding the family. This rapidly developing science will begin affecting the family and family law in the early years of this century.

CURING CHILDREN THROUGH DRUGS AND TRANSPLANTS

Already, human genes have successfully been spliced into animal embryos, reducing the future risk of human rejection of transplanted organs from fully grown animals. It has become possible to produce cows that provide human milk (milk containing the human-like serum albumin) and pigs that grow human-like organs minus the pig gene that promotes human rejection when transplanted when needed.[54] Mice, rabbits, sheep, and cows have been genetically engineered to carry human genes, useful for producing various medicines. Private corporations hold patents to these human-animal combinations called *chimeras.* The next step already has occurred. A human cell's nucleus has been implanted into a cow's egg—its own nucleus was sliced off. A hybrid cell, part human and part cow, was thus created and grew, quickly becoming more human-like as the human nucleus took control. Even though the hybrid is in the form of cells, the concept of half-human creatures stirs deeply felt beliefs.[55] Recently, patents have been requested on the process of mixing human cells with the cells of chimpanzees and pigs. A true chimera, one that is perhaps 30 percent human, is the goal. But at what point do constitutional rights kick in? The patent office has publicly announced that it will not grant patents on any "monsters." Patent law scholars have publicly responded that there may be no choice under existing law. Many patents already have been granted on animals engineered to contain some human genes, cells, and tissues.[56]

For family members, what are the potential consequences of creating chimeras? A staggering number of pharmaceutical products are in the pipeline, ranging from anti-cancer to anticlotting drugs. One transgenic goat alone, "Grace," is valued at $1 million, the most valuable goat in history, for the anti-cancer drug it produces. Immediately after the cloned sheep "Dolly" was born, a second cloned sheep with a human gene, "Polly," was born. Animal clones could be used to harvest organs for human transplantation; carrying human genes, these organs will be less likely to be rejected by their recipients. These animals would serve as "factories" for needed drugs and body parts. (More than 100,000 Americans die annually when no suitable organ is available.) Thus, there will be new cures and repairs for babies and children unless new family laws intervene. Should new family laws be adopted to restrict the dimensions of such human/animal combinations, or would this be futile in a global research environment?

"DESIGNER" BABIES IN THE FUTURE?

Ethical and legal issues arise when a human egg is fertilized in a petri dish and then is permitted to divide and grow in the dish before implantation into a surrogate's womb. What legal issues will arise when potential parents engage the services of geneticists to obtain "designer babies"?

With *in vitro* fertilization already an established process, genetic changes could be made in embryos outside the womb to correct deadly diseases, enhance mood, modify behavior, or change intelligence and physical traits. The "enhanced" embryo then would be planted in its mother's womb. The mapping of the entire human genome will allow the characteristics associated with specific genes to be studied and modified in the laboratory. The result: "designer babies." Even though environmental factors bear strongly on behavior, so also do genetics, as demonstrated by twins who have been raised in radically different environments.[57]

Human genome mapping, reproductive technologies, and genetic manipulation are by their nature the tools of *eugenics* (the movement to improve the human species through hereditary measures via "proper" mating). Eugenics was a popular movement at the beginning of the twentieth century, until it later was twisted by the insanities of Adolf Hitler. It was popularly believed that heredity was more influential than economic, cultural, or social factors in determining human behavior. Theodore Roosevelt was a believer:

> *I wish very much that the wrong people could be prevented entirely from breeding; and when the evil nature of these people is sufficiently flagrant, this should be done. Criminals should be sterilized and feeble-minded persons forbidden to leave offspring behind them . . . the emphasis should be laid on getting desirable people to breed.*[58]

Indeed, many states enacted laws mandating sterilization under specified circumstances of family members who were criminals or "idiots." Today, "[g]enetic engineering is a technology designed to enhance the genetic inheritance of living things by manipulating their genetic code."[59] Like it or not, you are on the threshold of a new eugenics society. In germline therapy, genetic changes are made in the sperm, the egg, or in embryonic cells after fertilization and are carried on to future generations. Whatever is excised by genetic surgery is gone forever from the heredity of that future family. Genetic therapy that prevents the inheritance of some negative characteristic by future generations will likely be the first to be developed.

LEGAL FOCUS—PROBLEM

In 2010, Jean Luc Gelé and his bride Kristie Moore consider and then decide not to obtain a genetic review of their *in vitro* embryo before it is implanted. They choose to let "nature run its course." Their son Injo is subsequently born with a lifelong defect that easily could have been deleted from the fertilized egg by simple gene surgery. Are Gelé and Moore civilly liable to Injo for negligently failing to obtain genetic screening?

In considering your answer to his hypothetical, do not assume the family members are angry with each other. Sometimes family suits are designed to obtain payment from an insurance company, as when a minor/passenger sues the parent/driver who is covered by insurance. Clearly, family law will be faced with difficult issues.

Parents in Massachusetts sued their doctor for his inability to extract fluid from the wife's uterus that would have revealed the presence of Down's syndrome. Had they known, they would have aborted the fetus.[60] Would prospective parents abort a fetus that was predisposed to obesity? More than one-half of all adults and more than 25 percent of all children are overweight or obese.[61] If lifelong illnesses are to be prevented by gene surgery, what about less serious characteristics? Would prospective parents choose to genetically eliminate myopia, dyslexia, left-handedness, or shortness? Already, sex screening is well established and opportunities sometimes are taken through abortion to achieve gender balance in the family. Would these families choose gene therapy to improve the physical characteristics of their babies, to produce "designer babies"? Such designer babies may be available only to the wealthy, who may also opt for gestation in an artificial womb to avoid the unpleasantries of pregnancy.*

Should children have the legal right to be told of changes made to their genetic sources? For many years, many children have had genetic roots different from their parents, because of adoption or sperm donation. Today, egg donation also is in widespread use, allowing women to overcome infertility in this fashion.[†] Do their children know? An overwhelming majority of parents of children conceived through sperm donation have not told their children, and many of those who have reportedly regret it.[62] So far, children do not have a legal right to know the truth. In some states, such as New York, the identities of sperm and egg donors are not disclosed to recipients—but records are maintained.

CLONING BABIES

For centuries, science has been domesticating, breeding, and hybridizing animals and plants. But nature always has imposed limits on combinations of species. Today, microscopic bits of DNA from two species that could not mate in nature can be spliced together to create new life forms, to modify existing life forms, or to produce biological chemicals, such as insulin. In 1997, a scientist replaced the DNA in a normal sheep egg with the DNA from the mammary gland of an adult sheep. The splice worked—the egg grew and was then transplanted into the womb of a surrogate sheep, who bore Dolly, the famous cloned sheep. Thus, the DNA of an existing adult sheep was recreated in a newly born sheep that was gestated by a surrogate. Simply substitute the word "human" for "sheep" in the preceding sentence and you describe one of the most perplexing legal problems facing the family in the foreseeable future—human cloning.

In November of 2001 scientists at Advanced Cell Technology in Worcester, Massachusetts, announced that they had cloned the first human embryo. In Congress the House of Representatives had passed legislation that made all types of human cloning a federal crime[63] but the bill is still pending in the Senate.[64] Cloning is specifically forbidden by law in many countries including England.[65] However, England's law covers "reproductive cloning," not "therapeutic cloning." Therapeutic cloning is legal for scientists who have been granted a state license.[66]

Concern about cloning is complicated by the different types of cloning. *Embryo cloning* occurs where cells are removed from a fertilized embryo and encouraged to develop into one or more duplicate embryos. Twins or triplets are formed, with identical DNA. *Adult DNA cloning* is what many think of when the term *cloning* is used. This type of cloning intends to produce a duplicate of the existing animal. This is the technique used to clone Dolly and other mammals. The DNA from an ovum is removed and replaced

---

* Scientists theorize that early in the coming century a fetus will be grown in a totally artificial womb, from conception to birth, permitting a more predictable and safe environment and making genetic corrections easier. This process would add a new dimension to surrogacy contracts that could involve many presently unimaginable legal issues. Theoretically, a couple would contract to have either her or another woman's egg fertilized by either his or another male's sperm and gestated until birth in a rented glass womb. Thus, a true "test tube baby" is on the horizon.

  By suppressing development of parts of such an embryo in an artificial glass womb, it may be scientifically possible to gestate body parts for future medical reasons, such as transplanting to humans. Because such organs would not have a head or nervous system, the applicability of law and the Constitution may be avoided. And even if new laws prohibit such research in the United States, the likelihood of such global research is substantial. Rather than suppress parts of such an embryo in an artificial glass womb, what if the contributor of the egg chose to "abort" or terminate the "test tube baby"? Such a woman then would have no claim to the right of privacy to deal with her own body—rather she would be in the constitutional shoes of the male who merely contributes sperm outside his body. Thus, such a gestating embryo may have constitutional protection in its own right.

† In vitro fertilization raises myriad legal issues when fertilized eggs stored in banks are abandoned by their owners, or when disagreements arise between their owners relative to their ultimate disposition. These issues already are in our courtrooms. In one bizarre example, a fertility doctor, Lillian Nash, erroneously transplanted the embryo of an African-American couple into Donna Fusano's uterus along with an embryo created by Donna and her husband, who are Caucasian. Twin boys were born, one black, whose custody has been volunteered to his genetic parents. Litigation is pending. Michael Grunwald, "Embryo Mix-Up Is Double Trouble," *Washington Post,* 31 March 1999.

http://

The Americans to Ban
Cloning Web site
**http://www.cloning
information.org/**

A more favorable stance is
taken by the Federation of
American Societies for
Experimental Biology
http://www.faseb.org/

A discussion distinguishing
between types of cloning
can be found at
**http://www.religious
tolerance.org/clo_ther.htm**

with the DNA from a cell removed from an adult animal. The fertilized ovum (pre-embryo) is implanted in a womb and allowed to develop into a new animal. The last type is *therapeutic cloning*. This procedure begins like adult DNA cloning but stem cells are removed from the pre-embryo with the intent of producing tissue or a whole organ for transplant back into the person who supplied the DNA. The pre-embryo dies in the process.[67]

Given the opportunity, would family members be willing to pay to clone themselves? To produce genetically identical children? If a fetus is not protected by the Constitution, then presumably it has no legal standing to object to its alteration. Or does it? What if, following legal separation, one parent chooses to genetically alter the embryo and have it transplanted in a surrogate mother? These unanswered questions are only meant to typify the many and esoteric kinds of family law issues that will be surfacing in the early years of the new millennium.

STATE PROTECTION OF MINORS

My mother loved children—she would have given anything if I had been one.

Groucho Marx, 1895–1977

Involvement of the state in family affairs is a modern trend. The purpose is protection of those family members who are least able to protect themselves. Out-of-wedlock births have contributed to a growing number of single-parent families, often requiring tax-supported public assistance. The state steps in when special needs arise, for example, to protect family members from serious harm caused by drug addiction or venereal disease, or in complications from difficult pregnancies. Finally, the state now engages in "co-parenting" through official acceptance of teenagers' decisions with regard to abortion and contraception.

Still another area of government protection of minors involves parental misconduct. Historically, parental immunity was considered necessary to preserve family harmony. For example, children could not sue their parents for personal injuries caused by parental negligence. In modern times, though, insurance covers damages caused by the negligent driving of the parent—at no apparent risk to family harmony. Thus, as indicated earlier in this chapter, parents are liable to their children for serious misconduct, parental immunity being a rapidly fading concept.

As a general common-law rule, parents are not liable for torts of their children causing injury to third persons. However, nearly half of the states have statutes creating parental liability up to certain specified limited amounts, often up to $20,000 or thereabouts, for their children's torts. Thus, in California, for example, parents would be responsible up to $25,000 for windows broken, cars keyed, or graffiti done by their minor children.[68] Some states require a showing of willful conduct by the minor before their parents are responsible, up to a statutory maximum amount of money. Many states also create parental liability for malicious mischief when their children damage school or other public property.

LEGAL FOCUS—PROBLEM

Antoinette Walker is a police officer in Oakland, California, with responsibility to recruit new officers. She left her loaded handgun on her bedroom dresser where it was found by her ten-year-old son, who shot and wounded his twelve-year-old brother. No adult was at home. What family law issues have arisen?

Antoinette could be charged with a crime—either misdemeanor or felony negligence in leaving a firearm readily available to minors. Handguns can be disabled by parents using trigger locks or simply by keeping them under lock and key. No crime was charged, however, raising the issue of selective enforcement—would an ordinary citizen have been prosecuted?[69] The father, Antoinette's separated husband, could sue in civil court for money damages or even to contest the existing custody arrangement. The wounded son may be entitled to recover damages from his mother for negligence. None of these events, however, took place in this family tragedy, as often they don't. Family law has implications for much injurious behavior amongst family members, but only when victims make complaints and attorneys bring their cases to court. Unfortunately, many abuses exist within families that are known only to the victims and perpetrators.

Some children need protection from each other. Metal detectors are widely used in junior and senior high schools in major metropolitan areas. Some schools use screening in elementary schools. The policy is believed to be needed to protect students, teachers, and staff.[70] When minor students commit serious crimes against other students, especially involving guns or knives, they are prosecuted in juvenile court, the same as with off-campus crime. But lesser antisocial behavior among students, such as physical bullying, is ignored by the law. Such bullying, if occurring between strangers at a downtown mall, for example, would be a criminal assault and battery. Persistent schoolyard abuse (e.g., pushing and slapping or teasing about physical or mental characteristics) can be more damaging to its victims than isolated incidents off-campus. Yet such incidents largely are ignored by police and left for administrative discipline by school officials.

State statutes impose the obligation on parents to support their children until majority, or until earlier emancipation when the minor child becomes self-supporting. However, some states provide for postminority (over age 18) support by order of the divorce court or by statute.* Even when postminority support is not required, states will enforce marital agreements that call for such support. The general purpose of postminority child support is to pay for college education. In most states, child support is a joint obligation, although it may be apportioned between the parents according to their respective financial circumstances. It is a crime to willfully fail to support a child, and almost all states have computerized methods for tracking down deadbeat parents. But finding deadbeat parents is not the only problem. Often there simply isn't enough money to go around.

LEGAL FOCUS—PROBLEM

Keith Jackson was elected school board president in San Francisco, overseeing 64,000 students and a $530 million budget. He receives $500 per month for his services. He had previously been hired by the district attorney to "track down deadbeat dads," but that job, for some unknown reason, lasted only three days. Keith is divorced and has two sons, ages six and twelve, for whom the court has ordered $643 monthly child support. Keith is in arrearage of more than $5,000 and is falling further behind each month. Should a father run for an elected office that pays less than a court order for support, or should he obtain employment that pays enough for child support?

* California, Colorado, Illinois, Indiana, Iowa, Mississippi, Missouri, New Hampshire, New Jersey, New York, Oregon, Pennsylvania, South Carolina, and Washington.

A court could order Jackson to search for a job that pays adequately for child support, and jail him if he refused. Public service as an elected official is important, but perhaps it is not as indispensable as being a supportive father.[71] The issue of child support is covered more fully later in this chapter.

Most parents choose to provide for their children, "the natural objects of their bounty," by will. However, a parent may intentionally disinherit his or her child (or children) completely, even if the child is a dependent minor of tender years. This rule of absolute testamentary freedom originated in the common law. Nevertheless, state statutes commonly provide that the child gets a share of the parental estate unless it is absolutely clear that the disinheritance was planned. In other words, disinheritance of a child cannot occur through oversight by a parent. If a disinherited child is mentioned in the will (for example, when a child is left a nominal amount), it is clear that the disinheritance was intentional and it will be upheld.

EMANCIPATED MINORS

emancipated minor

A minor legally allowed to handle his or her own financial affairs.

The term *emancipation* means setting free. Therefore, an **emancipated minor** is "set free" from his or her parents. This means that the parents no longer have responsibility for or control over their emancipated child. Thus, parents also are set free, so to speak. Following emancipation, parents no longer have a legal duty to support or care for that child. Emancipated minors take on all of the rights and responsibilities of adults except for certain ones, such as being able to legally purchase alcoholic beverages. Nor is such a minor necessarily deprived of the benefits of juvenile court, discussed in the following section.

A number of states recognize the status of emancipation based on lawful marriage of the minor, or service in the military, or simply for becoming self-supporting. Some states provide a judicial procedure for declaration of the emancipated status.

LEGAL FOCUS—PROBLEM

In the fall of 1998, 17-year-old Dominique Moceanu, a member of the 1996 gold medal U.S. Olympic gymnastics team, filed suit in Texas requesting, among other things, future independence from her parents, saying they squandered her fortune and oppressed her for years. "I want whatever I have earned to be under my control so I know how my earnings are being used, and I want to be able to train and compete in the sport I love for the right reason—because I love it—not because my father tells me I have to make more money." Has Moceanu stated sufficient grounds to become emancipated?

Yes. Before trial, Moceanu and her parents settled the lawsuit and her parents agreed to the emancipation. The settlement was approved by court.[72]

JUVENILE COURT PROTECTION

I've been struck by the upside-down priorities of the juvenile-justice system. We are willing to spend the least amount of money to keep a kid at home, more to put him in a foster home, and the most to institutionalize him.

Marian Wright Edelman, American lawyer

Unfortunately, children sometimes are forced to live without adequate, or any, parental supervision; consequently, many become delinquent or even incorrigible. Legislatures have created juvenile court systems to protect minor children as well as the public in such situations. Unknown at the turn of the twentieth century, juvenile law and courts have burgeoned, especially following World War II. Today there is much sentiment that juvenile laws and courts are too lenient and that more minors who engage in vicious crimes ought to be treated as adults.

Children are not under the jurisdiction of juvenile courts simply because they are minors (under age eighteen); rather, juvenile courts become involved only when necessary. For example, minor children who need proper parental care or who are destitute (with no home and without the necessaries of life) are within the jurisdiction of the juvenile court system. They can be declared "dependents" of the court, which then is free to make a wide variety of possible orders for their care, supervision, custody, and support. A dependent child may be taken from the custody of his or her parents and, for example, be placed in a foster home (as in the Gregory Kingsley case, discussed on page 422) or the home of a relative, or be subject to any other arrangement deemed by the court to be in the child's best interest.

Also subject to the jurisdiction of juvenile courts are minor children who commit acts that would be crimes if done by adults. Because juveniles may be confined against their will, they are entitled to many constitutional protections. For example, a minor in juvenile court has the right to representation by an attorney (without charge, if the minor is indigent) and cannot be compelled to be a witness against himself or herself. The burden of proof is the same as in criminal cases—generally, that is, "beyond a reasonable doubt." However, no right to trial by jury exists in juvenile court, nor is there a right to bail (although prehearing release is common).

Ordinarily, juvenile court hearings are not open to the public. If the accused person is found to have committed the charged offense, the court will declare the minor a ward of the court. Juvenile courts can make various orders, such as probation, fines, or commitments to juvenile homes, ranches, camps, or special jails for youthful offenders.

Parents can and do take control of unruly, out-of-control children who are truants from school and otherwise incorrigible by hiring "professional escorts" (moonlighting police and probation officers) to take their children to "behavior modification" camps in other locations, sometimes as far away as Jamaica. These children can be taken against their will because parents have the right and responsibility to determine what is best for their children.

Under specified conditions (usually the passage of a specified number of years), juvenile courts will officially seal all records pertaining to a minor's case. The minor then officially has no criminal record and will not be handicapped in the future when seeking employment.

Not all juvenile offenders are processed by juvenile courts. The nature of some youthful offenders, and the severity of their alleged misconduct (such as homicide, armed robbery, or rape), may lead the juvenile court to reject jurisdiction, thereby compelling the minor to stand trial as an adult and face harsher criminal procedures and possible penalties.

SEXUAL ABUSE OF CHILDREN

Sexual abuse of a child is a serious felony that is difficult to detect, usually occurring in complete privacy. The victimized child may be the only witness and may be reluctant or unable to testify adequately. Forced testimony by a child in open court may result in the child's suffering serious emotional distress that may adversely affect both the child and the usefulness of the information obtained. The scope of the problem in the United States is subject to considerable debate. One expert describes the public response as "sex-abuse hysteria," whose manifestations are overreacting, seeing danger when it does not exist, dramatizing, and so on.[73] Countering that argument is the Third National Incidence Study of Child Abuse and Neglect, completed in 1996, which showed "a sharp increase in the scope of the problem, whether maltreatment is defined using the Harm Standard or the Endangerment Standard."[74]

Nearly all of the states have adopted statutes designed to protect child witnesses from further harm caused by the humiliation and stress of testifying in open court. To balance the goals of protecting the child and the constitutional rights of the accused, various techniques are evolving to obtain testimony from involved children outside the presence of the alleged abuser. For example, out-of-court statements (hearsay evidence) made privately by children to mental health or child protection professionals, who often use anatomically correct dolls, sometimes can be used in court.* This procedure assists many children who are unable to recall, report, or evaluate events accurately. Critics, however, point out that some experts, with the best of intentions, may come to faulty conclusions based on interpretations of the manner in which children manipulate dolls. Additional protective procedures include closed-circuit testimony from a private room, videotaping of such out-of-court testimony, and allowing admission of hearsay evidence that otherwise would be excluded from the trial. But some of these protective laws may clash with the Sixth Amendment to the U.S. Constitution.

The Sixth Amendment grants an accused the right to confront all witnesses. Thus, the U.S. Supreme Court has denied the use of a screen in court to shield a child from visual contact while testifying.[75] But one exception to the right to eye-to-eye confrontation between the accused and the child while testifying in court has been approved by the U.S. Supreme Court. A 5–4 majority of justices held that the Sixth Amendment does not invariably require face-to-face confrontation between a defendant and an adverse witness. It concluded that public policy, including the interest in protecting child witnesses from trauma, can justify an exception to the normal "preference" for face-to-face confrontation. The Court upheld a Maryland statutory scheme permitting a child to testify from outside the courtroom via closed-circuit television.[76]

Note that protection of the child from confrontation with the accused is a different problem than closing the trial to the public and press. Court proceedings almost always are open to the public; however, under appropriate circumstances, a judge can close the courtroom to protect a child from serious emotional injury.

Recall from Chapter 6 that proof of guilt in criminal cases must be "beyond a reasonable doubt." Moral certainty has been removed. Such a high standard of proof is not easily met with testimony that is incomplete, inconsistent, or even contradictory. The age and maturity of a child can make prosecution especially difficult in sexual abuse cases. The best example of the difficulties in determining the guilt or innocence of the accused is the notorious *McMartin* case (one of the longest and most costly criminal trials in U.S. history), in which one defendant was found not guilty of molesting numerous children while responsible for their care in a preschool.[77] The jury in the three-year trial deadlocked on certain charges against the other defendant, and a retrial limited to those charges again resulted in a hung jury. Clearly emotions were very high, perhaps bordering on hysteria, in the local community, and the consequences were very serious with regard to everyone involved in such difficult, complex, and bewildering litigation.

http://

For information and extensive resources concerning child abuse, see

**http://www.child-abuse
.com/**

For discussions about adults who were abused as children and statistics about abuse, see

**http://www.jimhopper.com/
abstats/**

For definitions and statistics on child abuse see

**http://www.calib.com/
nccanch/pubs/sag/define
.cfm**

---

* Admission into the record of such hearsay evidence is proper only when the "totality of circumstances" surrounding the testimony render the witness particularly worthy of belief. Out-of-court hearsay was ruled not admissible where the doctor conducted an interview without a videotape, asked leading questions, and had a preconceived idea of what the child should be disclosing. *Idaho v. Wright,* 497 U.S 805, 110 S.Ct. 3139 (1990).

In civil law divorce and child custody proceedings, more relaxed procedures and reduced standards of proof are applicable. For example, there is no right to trial by jury in divorce or custody matters.* Civil remedies also are quite different than criminal penalties for sexual abuse of a child. Whereas jail is the probable result of a criminal conviction for child abuse, a court order that all child visitation be supervised is one possible result of a civil proceeding. Monetary damages are another possible result of a civil remedy, as previously discussed.

The social and legal aspects of child abuse are rapidly evolving and few conclusions can accurately be drawn at the time of this writing.

LEGAL FOCUS—BACKGROUND

Vulnerable children with self-image problems get real pleasure and support from a song written in 1998 by songwriters Steven Seskin and Alan Shamblin. The song "Don't Laugh at Me" was recorded by several singers including Brad Paisley and Peter, Paul, and Mary. After hearing the song, Peter Yarrow of Peter, Paul, and Mary was so moved that he established the Don't Laugh at Me Project. Children suffering from self-image problems, which often include victims of sexual abuse, children with disabilities, and children subject to bullying, have benefited from the song and project activities. See http://www.dont-laugh.org/ and http://www.steveseskin.com/laugh.html for further information.

MATERNAL ABUSE DURING PREGNANCY

The U.S. Constitution has been interpreted to guarantee women the right to choose to abort their fetuses under most circumstances at any time before viability (the first moment following which the unborn child could survive without its mother). The right of privacy also guarantees women the right to live their lives during pregnancy any way they please—with certain reservations. There is no constitutional right for women to live their lives during pregnancy in such a way that their future children predictably will be harmed.

LEGAL FOCUS—PROBLEM

Government fliers distributed at her high school warned Shirley Pinker that drinking alcohol during pregnancy was likely to cause serious health defects to babies. Several years later, she began drinking whiskey heavily during pregnancy. Has Pinker committed a crime?

If Pinker were a resident of South Dakota, she could be made to attend a hearing (without a jury) and then be ordered by a judge to a detox center for days or to a treatment center for months. Fetal alcohol syndrome can leave its victims mentally and physically disabled for their entire lives, and the law in South Dakota has intervened to protect these unborn family members. Fetal alcohol syndrome affected about 0.5 to 2 children per 1,000 births in the United States during the 1980s and 1990s.[78] It is about twenty times more prevalent in South Dakota (and some other states) and among certain ethnic groups.[79]

* Only Texas permits trial by jury in divorce cases.

The most pervasive abusive behavior by pregnant women consists of drug and alcohol use. Perhaps 11 percent of fetuses in the United States are exposed to illegal drugs.[80] This complex issue involves weighing the interest of society in healthy fetal life versus the mother's right to freedom of movement during part or all of her pregnancy. Earlier in Chapter 6, we mentioned the conflicting efforts of states to criminalize such behavior. The difficulties of such a family law are described in the *Johnson* case found at the end of this chapter.

Here the issue arises in the context of civil proceedings to confine abusive mothers in treatment centers, hospitals, or even the homes of relatives. Proposed laws are pending in a dozen or more states that would legalize the involuntary commitment to some kind of treatment facility for most or all of the gestational period of drug or alcohol abusers. But what about pregnant women who make other choices that adversely affect their fetuses, such as poor food and medicine choices, poor or no prenatal care, and even smoking? Is a civil proceeding to incarcerate a person a veiled device to avoid the constitutional rights enjoyed by those accused of crime? Some states proposing incarceration of future mothers put the matter under jurisdiction of the juvenile court, where many rules are different and where trial by jury is not available. However, most constitutional rights are not suspended simply because the juvenile court has jurisdiction. How can society prevent the birth of "cocaine babies"? Can the unborn fetus be confined in a place where it is safe from abuse by its mother, such as a health institution, a foster home, or even the home of a responsible friend?

LEGAL FOCUS—CASE

Darlene Brown was pregnant with a viable fetus and critically needed a blood transfusion, which she refused on religious grounds. Brown's refusal threatened the life of her unborn baby. Can the court order Brown to submit to a blood transfusion to save her viable fetus?

In re fetus Brown v. Darlene Brown, 228 Ill. Dec. 525, 294 Ill. App. 3d 159, 689 N.E.2d 397 (Illinois, 1997).

No. At the turn of the twentieth century, fetuses were protected by the laws making abortion illegal. As the twenty-first century approaches, the right of women to an abortion has been established. How that right will be reconciled with the rights of fetuses to be born free of harm from drug use or other abusive conduct by their mothers is evolving. In addition, thirty-three of the states proscribing child abuse provide exceptions on religious grounds for behavior or conditions that would otherwise be abuse. The Georgia statute is one example: "No child who in good faith is being treated solely by spiritual means by prayer in accordance with the tenets and practices of a recognized church or religious denomination by a duly accredited practitioner thereof shall, for that reason alone, be considered to be an 'abused' child."[81]

How May Marriage Be Terminated?

Dissolution (Divorce)

divorce

Termination of a marriage relationship by court judgment. Divorce is called *dissolution* in some states.

As there is a need for marriage, so is there a need for **divorce** (also called *dissolution of marriage*). Divorce ends the marriage but it does not necessarily terminate spousal responsibilities that arose from the marriage, such as the duties of child support and alimony. Divorce requires court proceedings, in which a judgment (or decree) in dissolution is rendered. Legislatures have traditionally permitted divorce for an "innocent" spouse from a "guilty" spouse; this "fault" basis of divorce, in some form or other, is still in effect in some states. However, all states also provide for some variety of **no-fault divorce**.[82]

In response to widespread disenchantment with fault systems of divorce, many states adopted some variety of no-fault divorce exclusively. The prevailing no-fault system requires proof of two elements: a breakdown of the marriage and the objective fact of physical separation of the spouses for some specified period of time, such as six months. This separation period offers the added benefit of preventing overly hasty divorces. Some states also retain the fault basis of divorce in order to provide immediate relief in severe cases or to allow judges to award unequal distributions of marital property. (Distributions of property and rights to spousal support upon divorce are covered separately later in this chapter.) A breakdown is established by testimony that the marriage is irretrievably broken because of the attitude of one or both spouses or because of a long physical separation without a resumption of cohabitation. Following appropriate evidence of a breakdown, divorce is then available.

A primary advantage of no-fault divorce is that spouses are not required to "air their dirty laundry" in a courtroom, detailing each other's alleged misdeeds. Furthermore, private detectives are unnecessary to track spouses thought to be unfaithful. In fault systems, on the other hand, the stakes can be much higher because the more innocent spouse can benefit through uneven distribution of marital property and perhaps through award of a larger amount of support.

Under no-fault systems, an "innocent" spouse cannot prevent a divorce from occurring. People cannot be locked into marriage. But people facing divorce can use the law in retaliation.

no-fault divorce

A divorce granted by a court without either party having to prove fault in the other party.

http://

You have to love the Internet. This site provides links to divorce law of all 50 states

http://www.split-up.com/ main/law.htm

LEGAL FOCUS—PROBLEM

The divorce proceedings by Donna Carroll, of Janesville, Wisconsin, prompted her husband to file criminal charges of adultery. This did little to save the marriage, but did cause Donna to perform 40 hours of community service. Facing a criminal trial, up to two years in jail, and as much as a $10,000 fine, Donna entered a plea bargain. Can the threat of criminal adultery charges be used by spouses to obtain larger divorce settlements?

Yes. Adultery is still a crime in many states, including New York, Massachusetts, Connecticut, and Michigan. In Maryland, adultery is a misdemeanor punishable by a $10 fine. Enforcement of adultery statutes seldom occurs until a spouse brings charges during no-fault divorce proceedings.[83] However, there is a fine line between using legal proceedings as a club and the crime of extortion. (You may recall from Chapter 6 that the coercion of money under threat of harm is a felony called extortion.) Adultery can be committed only with a member of the opposite sex so a gay affair would not be adultery.

Some states permit civil remedies for alienation of affection. A third party can be sued by one spouse for "alienating" the affections of the other spouse—usually through sexual intercourse. While the "alienated" spouse may also be guilty of the crime of adultery, the third-party interloper may be civilly liable in damages. This kind of "heart balm" lawsuit may be more of a vindication than a realistic legal remedy.

LEGAL FOCUS—EXAMPLE

Dorothy Hutelmyer sued secretary Lynne Cox for wrecking her marriage by sleeping with her husband Joseph. Dorothy was awarded a jury verdict of $1 million as damages, even though Lynne testified that Joseph's marriage already was wrecked as evidenced by a lack of sexual relations for the preceding seven years. The North Carolina jury apparently rejected that contention in making the award. Adulteress Cox was broke, and even though she subsequently married Joseph Hutelmyer, he is not liable for her debts.[84]

Recall our discussion of the modern trend to permit suits for damages in domestic torts. Critics of this development argue that they are "putting the fault back into no-fault divorces." Indeed, the family "dirty laundry" (e.g., wife-beating) can be aired in court as the basis for tort litigation, even if it is shielded from the court by no-fault divorce laws. Of course, this criticism applies only to a limited number of divorce cases where the alleged spousal misconduct is egregious enough to justify the filing of a separate domestic-tort lawsuit.

Although no-fault divorce is generally available throughout the states, new schemes to strengthen the marital vows have been proposed. The current "quickie divorce" system, according to proponents of these plans, promotes irresponsibility because spouses can "walk away" from their marriages very easily. Nearly one in two marriages can be expected to end in divorce. Children of broken homes are more likely to do poorly in school, suffer relationship problems, have babies out of wedlock, and get in trouble with the law. Not all sociologists agree with these conclusions, but there is a national movement afoot to make divorce more difficult. A two-tier system under which no-fault divorce would not be available if minor children were involved has failed to become law in any state—but is pending in some state legislatures. States are also considering longer pre-divorce waiting periods.

covenant marriage

A type of marriage where couples agree to certain marital promises and limitations on their ability to terminate the marriage. States allowing covenant marriage provide it as optional.

Another scheme called the **covenant marriage** has been adopted in Arizona, Arkansas, and Louisiana. Louisiana's covenant marriage, requires couples to engage in premarital counseling and a mandatory two-year waiting period before divorce. Opponents refer to this as cheapening the institution of marriage by offering the choice of a "lite" or full-blown version. In Arizona, parties that select covenant marriage status agree to pre-marital counseling and a significant limitation on grounds for any divorce. Among the grounds available is "divorce by persuasion," under which both parties need agree to the divorce. If one spouse disagreed, the other would have to purchase a ticket out through financial incentives or failing that, revert back to a "fault" basis for divorce.

LEGAL FOCUS—BACKGROUND

The Arizona covenant marriage requires among other things the following declaration of spouses wishing such a marriage. "We solemnly declare that marriage is a covenant between a man and a woman who agree to live together as husband and wife for as long as they both live. We have chosen each other carefully and have received premarital counseling on the nature, purposes, and responsibilities of marriage. We understand that a covenant marriage is for life. If we experience marital difficulties, we commit ourselves to take all reasonable efforts to preserve our marriage, including marital counseling."[85]

Although a couple may obtain a divorce without the services of an attorney, it is usually desirable to hire one where there are substantial family assets or liabilities that must be distributed, or if child custody or visitation rights are contested. Many persons with limited assets and no children obtain uncontested divorces by filling out appropriate forms without the assistance of any attorney. But there are many divorce attorneys in the world today, responding to a felt need. Unfortunately, this area of law is rife with opportunities for unethical behavior by attorneys. The very nature of divorce renders the clients extraordinarily vulnerable, emotionally as well as financially. The topic of legal ethics has been discussed in Chapter 4, but it is appropriate to note here that at least one state—New York—has by court rule adopted special ethical standards for divorce lawyers. One rule prohibits charging "up-front" nonrefundable fees. Such fees, collected before representation is undertaken, necessarily tend to dissuade the client from discharging the lawyer even if he or she is doing a poor job. Another clause prohibits so-called "couch fees," i.e., sexual favors from the client during representation. Yet another important clause requires written, instead of verbal, fee agreements. Contingent fees in divorce cases have long been prohibited, but are permitted in domestic tort cases. The expenses and problems of a contested divorce is captured well by Arlington, Virginia, family law attorney John Crouch, who on his Web site answers the question "How much does a divorce cost, for ordinary people?"

LEGAL FOCUS—BACKGROUND

This following is a quote from attorney John Crouch answering the question "How much does a divorce cost, for ordinary people?"

Not counting what it does to the standard of living, and having to pay support, and the expenses of visitation, you can get [a divorce] for under $10,000 per spouse in lawyer fees if you're lucky and if both the spouses and their lawyers are reasonable and fair. But you really can't predict that. In fact, it is considered unethical for a divorce lawyer to even give a client an estimate, because it's so out of control. Either side can pull all kinds of stuff in court that just makes both the lawyers waste time until one client runs out of money. I just finished one case where they settled, but then the husband had to spend $70,000 just to enforce the settlement agreement!

A custody fight is more like $25,000 to $35,000 apiece. And the thing with custody cases is that no matter how reasonable one side is, how much you give up in order to stay out of court, the other side can always demand more until you have to choose between fighting and never seeing your kids. Also, after the settlement or the court decision, either of you can come back to court the next year to try the case all over again. And you may be fighting about visitation arrangements until the children are grown.[86]

ANNULMENT

Annulment is a declaration by a court that a purported marriage does not exist and never existed because of some defect present at the time of the marriage ceremony. Examples of such serious defects that could exist at the inception of the apparent marriage are incest, bigamy, mental incapacity, physical incapacity to consummate the marriage, insanity, and consent to marry resulting from fraud, dare, or intoxication.

When a defective marriage exists, only the innocent victim has the option to annul and must do so promptly upon discovery of the defect. False statements (e.g., that one is pregnant or that one will attempt to have a child) justify an annulment; less significant false statements (e.g., that one is rich or that one is a virgin) do not.

Even though a marriage is annulled, in the eyes of the law a child conceived prior to the annulment is deemed to be a legitimate child of the marriage that legally never existed.

LEGAL FOCUS—PROBLEM

On the second day of Mardi Gras in New Orleans, Carl Seither, 21, met Maria Escovedo, 17, at a Dixieland jazz concert. Within a week they were madly in love and decided to marry and begin a family of six children. They promptly applied for a marriage license and discovered that Louisiana enforced a three-day waiting period between the license and marriage dates. Impetuous, they drove to Texas and got married, although Escovedo had to lie about her age on their license. Within weeks, as their passions were cooling, Seither revealed that he "hated" children and that the divorce from his former wife was not yet final. What would Escovedo's attorney advise her?

Escovedo's lawyer would observe that Seither's lie about children was material and sufficient basis to annul the marriage. Further, a declaration that the marriage was void also was possible because Seither's divorce was not final. Although without significance in most states, Seither was guilty of bigamy. Escovedo also committed a crime when she lied about her age, but the court would not refuse to grant an annulment for that reason. Most likely, Escovedo would not be prosecuted for that misdemeanor. Seither also committed the intentional tort of fraud and could be sued civilly by Escovedo. If she could persuade a jury that she suffered substantial mental distress, such as humiliation and loss of sexual naiveté because of Seither's wanton and malicious lies, Escovedo may recover substantial compensatory and punitive damages.

"BED AND BOARD" SEPARATION, SEPARATE MAINTENANCE, OR LEGAL SEPARATION

Many states provide for a partial termination of marriage. **Separation** *a mensa et thoro* (Latin: "from bed and board") allows the spouses to live apart without fixing desertion upon one or the other. Support obligations are established and property is divided by the court. However, the couple is not divorced and neither can remarry. This remedy of **divorce from bed and board** derives from early English law when divorce was not available. The remedy is appropriate where the spouses (1) do not intend to remarry, (2) desire a complete settlement of their economic affairs, (3) want to preserve entitlements under certain public laws (e.g., social security), and (4) are opposed to divorce on religious grounds. Separate **maintenance** and **legal separation** are very similar to "bed and board" separation and provide the same benefits to the couple, except that property division normally is not adjudicated

separation

The status of spouses who are by judicial decree living apart, i.e., no longer cohabiting.

divorce from bed and board

A modification of the spousal relationship in which the parties are forbidden to cohabit but do not dissolve the marriage. Support may be paid, and property is divided as in a divorce.

maintenance

Payment by one spouse to the other spouse following dissolution of their marriage. Term used interchangeably with *alimony*.

legal separation

A court order permitting spouses to live apart with necessary related orders for child custody and child support, support of the wife (or husband), and division of property (as in dissolution), but the marriage endures

WHAT ARE A SPOUSE'S RIGHTS AND DUTIES UPON TERMINATION OF MARRIAGE?

MAINTENANCE (ALIMONY)

Upon termination of the marriage by divorce, maintenance (often called *alimony* or *support*) may be ordered by the court in both dollars per month and in duration of payments. Rehabilitative, or limited-term, alimony terminates at the end of a specified time period, during which the recipient seeks education, training, or experience to become self-supporting.[87] Permanent alimony or maintenance is indefinite in duration. Many couples who divorce arrive at a mutual agreement as to maintenance and thereby avoid the time, expense, and uncertainty of a court's decision. (Note that such marital agreements are subject to approval by the court.) But if the former spouses cannot agree, the judge, sitting as a court of equity and hence without a jury, considers all relevant factors and makes the award.

In 1979 the Supreme Court "de-sexed" alimony and held that gender-based alimony statutes were unconstitutional.[88] Alimony is required from either spouse if the other is in genuine need. One is in need, for example, if she (or sometimes he) cannot be self-supporting or if there is a child whose situation precludes employment by the parent with custody. Generally, marital fault is not a factor in determining whether or not alimony should be awarded, although some states specifically consider fault.*

The amount of alimony is related to the needs of the spouse receiving it and the ability of the other to pay. The following factors are considered by courts in setting and terminating alimony:

- Financial condition of the spouse seeking support as well as the ability of the other to pay
- Length of the marriage
- Age, health, education, and station in life of the parties
- Occupations, vocational skills, and employability of the parties
- Needs and opportunities for future income of the parties
- Contributions of each in acquiring or maintaining marital property (including noneconomic contributions)
- Need of a custodial parent to occupy the marital home
- Tax consequences involved

LEGAL FOCUS—CASE

Thomas Wilson had been married about four years when his wife, Elma, was injured in a fall. Her injuries resulted in a permanent neurological deficit. She lacked "social judgment, common sense, and social intelligence." Two years later, the Wilsons agreed to divorce. Elma received $500 per month for two years, plus medical insurance for the same time. After those two years, Elma asked the court to extend alimony, anticipating

---

* Alabama, Connecticut, Florida, Georgia, Idaho, Louisiana, Michigan, Missouri, New Hampshire, North Carolina, North Dakota, Pennsylvania, Rhode Island, South Carolina, South Dakota, Tennessee, and West Virginia either take "fault" into consideration in setting the amount of alimony, or accept it as a bar altogether. See e.g., *Mathews v. Mathews*, 614 So.2d 1287 (Louisiana Ct. App., 1993) and *Cantwell v. Cantwell*, 334 N.C. 162, 432 S.E.2d 357 (North Carolina, 1993).

further brain surgery and continued unemployment. The court extended alimony for one year, following which Elma asked for another extension, claiming no improvement in her condition or employment potential. What should the court order?

In re the Marriage of Wilson, 201 Cal. App. 3d 913, 247 Cal. Rptr. 522 (1988).

The trial court terminated the alimony, noting the shortness of the marriage and weighing society's obligation to assist Mrs. Wilson against Mr. Wilson's continuing obligation. In affirming the judgment, the appellate court observed that Mrs. Wilson was not a "displaced homemaker" but a "middle-aged bartender" with adult children. It further said, "While no one will dispute Elma's tragic disability, the clear trend is for trial courts to consider the totality of circumstances (in terminating support). . . ."

In the 1970s, the push for equality between the sexes resulted in a shift of state laws from permanent to rehabilitative alimony. But regardless of notions of equality, the reality often is that some women, especially those in their forties and fifties, could not go back to school and become doctors or lawyers and compete with their former husbands' earning capacity. As a result, such displaced homemakers often suffer a severe drop in their standard of living following divorce. Many such women lack marketable job skills or even knowledge about the changing workplace. Moreover, they often face illegal gender and age discrimination. For these reasons, courts in Ohio, Maryland, Louisiana, New York, Pennsylvania, and Florida have begun to require permanent, rather than limited-time, alimony awards. Contrary opinions are offered that alimony should not be a "perpetual pension." Some believe that permanent alimony ought to be awarded to older women in marriages of long duration, but not to younger women who are capable of becoming self-supporting.

When circumstances change, alimony may be modified (even terminated) by petition to the court, which retains continuing jurisdiction until alimony is finally terminated. As previously noted, all relevant factors are considered by the court when hearing a petition to modify.[89] Often the changing factors relate to changes in the relative financial conditions of the former spouses. For example, a former husband can be reluctant to support his ex-wife while she is living with another man. Generally, cohabitation with another person in itself is not a sufficient basis for terminating alimony.[90] However, some states do provide for modification or termination of alimony under such circumstances.[91] These laws are equally operative if a former wife is paying support to her ex-husband.

LEGAL FOCUS—CASE

Dentist Hall agreed to a divorce settlement in which his wife received the home, furnishings, and vehicle totaling more than $100,000 in value, plus annual alimony of $15,000. Three years later, he petitioned the court to terminate alimony due to changed circumstances. Robert Jones, who was sharing Hall's former home with his former wife, contributed nothing toward rent or maintenance, and engaged in sexual intercourse with her. The trial court terminated the alimony on the grounds that Hall should not be compelled to "support his divorced wife and her paramour in idleness and fornication." What was the result on appeal?

Hall v. Hall, 25 Ill. App. 3d 524, 323 N.E.2d 541 (Illinois, 1975).

The judgment was reversed. Alimony may not be utilized as a club to regulate the ex-wife's sex life. On the other hand, the court did remand the case to the trial court for a reduction in alimony.[92]

Fourteen states allow payment of spousal support in a lump sum.[93] In these states, the spouse may pay the total support obligation at the time of the divorce. Although the payment burden could be steep, completed payment usually extinguishes any future support obligation or risk of modification of the support order. New Mexico's statute is representative: "a single sum to be paid in one or more installments that specifies definite amounts, not subject to any contingencies, including the death of the receiving spouse."[94]

The obligation of permanent alimony ends with the death of either spouse. Remarriage of the spouse receiving alimony also automatically terminates the duty to pay.

PROPERTY DIVISION IN EQUITABLE-DISTRIBUTION STATES

A divorcing couple can reach an agreement about how to divide their property and debts and a judge will normally incorporate their agreement in the final divorce decree. But if the couple cannot agree, they can submit their property dispute to the court, which will use local state law to divide the property. Remember most states are marital property states and these states provide for an "equitable" distribution of marital property upon divorce, either in the form of property division or maintenance. Note that equitable distribution in a marital property state does not mean equal distribution. The process is in three steps: 1) identification of marital property, 2) valuation of the assets, and 3) distribution to each spouse.

LEGAL FOCUS—CASE

James Long sued Sandra Long for a divorce, alleging incompatibility. The wife counterclaimed, alleging incompatibility and alleging adultery. She sought alimony, a division of the marital assets, and attorney fees. A judgment of divorce was entered, alimony was granted, and property was divided. The husband moved to set aside the property division arguing that the trial court had abused its discretion in awarding the wife over $2 million in marital assets. The wife moved to set aside the trial court's property division because she received an unequal share of an estate valued at over $5 million. Should the judgment be set aside because it is unequal?

Long v. Long, 824 So. 2d 778 (Ala., 2001).

Remember that in equitable distribution states, marital distributions need not be equal, just equitable. The Alabama Appellate Court upheld the trial court's decision, making these points. 1) The trial court is presumed correct because they are in the unique position of observing the witnesses to assess their demeanor and credibility. 2) Matters of alimony and property division are within the trial court's discretion, and its rulings are to not be disturbed except for abuse of discretion. 3) Awards of alimony and property division are interrelated, and the entire judgment must be considered in determining whether the trial court abused its discretion. 4) A division of marital property in a divorce case does not have to be equal, only equitable, and a determination of what is equitable rests within the sound discretion of the trial court.

The doctrine of equitable distribution awards a marital interest in all assets that were acquired with a material economic contribution by both spouses regardless of which spouse holds legal title. Savings or acquisitions from salaries or interest income and investment proceeds are obvious examples of marital property. One important property interest typically considered to be marital property is pensions earned during the marriage, with an important caveat: The U.S. Supreme Court held that military pensions cannot be awarded to divorcing spouses; otherwise important "military personnel objectives" would be threatened. For one example of such objectives, retirement (pension) payments are similar to a retainer, because retired military personnel may be required to return to duty at any time.[95] As a result of this decision, Congress enacted the Federal Uniformed Services Former Spouses' Protection Act (FUSFSPA)[96] which gave states the choice of whether or not to treat military pensions as marital property, with up to 50 percent of the pension going to the non-military spouse if the marriage has lasted ten years or more. Most states do consider military pensions as marital property. However, some married veterans are entitled to either pension or disability payments, and since the former are taxable income and the latter are not, these veterans often elect disability pay. To the chagrin of some, disability pay cannot be considered marital property.

LEGAL FOCUS—CASE

The O'Briens' married life began in 1971. The action for divorce came during the holiday season of 1980, two months after the husband received his medical license. The New York trial court found that the wife contributed 76% of the family income while the husband did post-graduate work, and attended medical school in Guadalajara, Mexico, and in New York. At the time of the divorce the couple had few assets—or did they? Is the prospective value of the husband's career marital property?

O'Brien v. O'Brien, 66 N.Y.2d 576, 498 N.Y.S.2d 743, 489 N.E.2d 713 (New York, 1985).

It is also not clear whether one spouse should be awarded a property interest in the professional license or degree of the other. How should an advanced degree, such as a master's in business administration (MBA), or a professional license, such as a license to practice medicine, be treated upon divorce? Can they be assigned a dollar value and equitably distributed or divided? Suppose one spouse sacrifices his education to put his wife through medical school. Upon a divorce immediately following the wife's graduation, should the husband be awarded half of the dollar value of the degree or license? If so, how should it be valued? In the above New York case it was held that a husband's medical license was marital property under the state's equitable distribution law. Following that decision, New York's highest court held that an academic degree obtained during marriage is also marital property subject to equitable distribution.[97] In the states that equitably distribute marital property, division of property is based upon such factors as length of the marriage, the parties' abilities to support themselves, and the property and income that was obtained during the marriage. Thus, a spouse has claim to an expected future stream of earnings resulting from an investment, or perhaps from an advanced degree.

In North Carolina, professional degrees and licenses are separate property, but their value is taken into consideration in dividing marital property.[98] In Kentucky, a professional degree or license is considered in determining the standard of living to be maintained in setting alimony.[99] But it also has been widely held that college degrees and professional licenses are property rights that are not capable of being owned by a community (in marriage) and are not subject to distribution upon divorce.[100] In Utah, the goodwill of a solo practice dentist is not marital property,[101] nor is the goodwill of a CPA (certified public accountant) in Texas.[102] However, in most states "professional" goodwill, which may be defined loosely as enhanced earning power based upon special talents, reputation, business referral base, or uniqueness of services offered, is marital property that can be and is divided upon divorce.

In some states, restitutional alimony instead of property division may be awarded to reimburse one spouse for contributions made to the other in earning a professional degree.[103]

In many states, the nonmonetary contributions of a homemaker are considered to be the equivalent of the wage earner's monetary contributions. The starting point in making an equitable distribution is a presumption that equality is equity: an equal division is the most just.

LEGAL FOCUS—CASE

For 32 years, Lorna Jorgenson Wendt ran the household and raised the Wendts' two daughters. Her husband Gary, 55, chairman of GE Capital Services, testified that Lorna had no interest in business or his problems. Connecticut is an "equitable distribution" state and the divorce judge must decide the worth of a stay-at-home wife. Lorna said, "I worked hard and I was very loyal." Gary said, "I worked hard. She didn't." The Wendt estate was valued as high as $100 million. What should the judge award to Lorna?

Wendt v. Wendt, 1998 WL 161165 (Conn. 1998).[104]

Lorna was awarded a multimillion-dollar home in Stamford and a vacation home in Key Largo; $252,000 a year payable in monthly installments; and half of all stocks, bonds, and cash, all totaling about $20 million. In a community property state, Lorna would have received precisely one-half the total value of the family assets.

LEGAL FOCUS—CASE

Sam Burgess's premarital house appreciated in value during his marriage with Sally. On the advice of her attorney, Sally Burgess agreed to quitclaim deed all her right, title, and interest, if any, in the house to Sam for a payment of $10. Did Sally lose her marital interest in the house?

Burgess v. Burgess, 710 P.2d 417 (Alaska, 1985).

No. The court ruled that all increase in value of a premarital house is a marital asset if the nonowner spouse takes an active role in its upkeep and management. The court will not uphold an unconscionable agreement.

Assets, such as a promissory note requiring payment of money to the spouses, must be distributed to comply with the court's ordered distribution. One asset that may be distributed in kind is a cryogenically preserved (frozen) preembryo.

LEGAL FOCUS—CASE

When Junior L. and Mary Sue Davis divorced, they owned seven cryogenically preserved preembryos. Ms. Davis desired to carry the preembryos to term; Mr. Davis objected and did not want to become a father against his will. The trial court ruled that the preembryos were human beings and awarded custody to Ms. Davis. During lengthy appeals, Ms. Davis remarried and changed her mind, desiring to donate the preembryos to another couple. Who should receive the preembryos, and why?

Davis v. Davis, 842 S.W.2d 588 (Tennessee, 1992).

In a case of first impression, the Tennessee Supreme Court ruled against Ms. Davis, saying that preembryos do not enjoy protection as "persons" under federal law. "[There are] two rights of equal significance—the right to procreate and the right to avoid procreation. The equivalence of and inherent tension between these two interests are nowhere more evident than in the context of *in vitro* fertilization. None of the concerns about a woman's bodily integrity that have previously precluded men from controlling abortion decisions is applicable here. If the state's interests do not become sufficiently compelling in the abortion context until the end of the first trimester, after very significant developmental stages have passed, there is no state interest in these preembryos. Ordinarily, the party wishing to avoid procreation should prevail, assuming that the other party has a reasonable possibility of achieving parenthood by means other than use of the preembryos in question. If no reasonable alternatives exist, then the argument in favor of using the preembryos to achieve pregnancy should be considered. However, if the party seeking control of the preembryos intends merely to donate them to another couple, the objecting party obviously has the greater interest and should prevail."[105]

The trend is to minimize relative fault of the spouses as a factor in property division.[106] However, many states consider economic fault (e.g., dissipation of marital assets pending divorce) in making an equitable division.[107] The criteria used in most states in making an equitable distribution of marital property between the spouses are comparable to the factors (previously listed) that are relied upon in setting alimony awards. Food stamps, other government assistance, and child support payments are not considered income to the recipient parent and therefore are not included as factors in dividing marital property.[108]

PROPERTY DIVISION IN COMMUNITY PROPERTY STATES

LEGAL FOCUS—BACKGROUND

"If America is really looking for a uniform system of marital property rights that completely incorporates the partnership theory of marriage, eventually all states will have to abandon elective or forced share law and adopt some sort of community property system."[109]

As stated earlier, community property is all property acquired by the husband and the wife during marriage other than by gift or inheritance. Community property must be distributed equally because each spouse is the "owner" of an undivided one-half interest. This is the most important distinguishing characteristic between community property and equitable distribution states.

Upon divorce, the court allocates the net value of each one-half interest to each spouse.* If the community property cannot be physically distributed equally, it may be sold and the cash proceeds divided, or a promissory note may be made from one spouse to the other to equalize the values received from an unequal physical distribution. (A physical distribution of assets is called a *distribution in kind*.) As discussed earlier, professional licenses or degrees may be marital property (in both equitable distribution and community property states) and are good examples of property that cannot be distributed in kind.[110]

In some community property states (e.g., Washington and Texas), the court may divide the marital property in any manner it deems "just and equitable," not necessarily equally.[111] An unequal distribution of community property may act as a substitute for alimony.

All property either brought into the marriage or acquired by gift or inheritance is separate property, as mentioned earlier. Separate property is not typically subject to distribution by the court upon divorce and neither are its passive earnings (such as interest) if they are maintained separately with proper records. In a few states, however, all marital property is subject to distribution by the divorce court.

CHILD CUSTODY

The legal standard for court award of child custody and visitation rights is the "best interests of the child." Often, parents are sensitive to their child's needs, and so they agree on custody and visitation. In such instances, courts normally comply with the parents' joint request. However, when both parents demand custody or argue about visitation rights, the court must attempt to determine the best interests of the child and make appropriate orders.

The Uniform Marriage and Divorce Act specifies several factors including the following for determining custody arrangements in the best interests of the child: (1) the wishes of the parents and the child; (2) the child's adjustment to his or her home, school, and community; and (3) the mental and physical health of all individuals involved. Although courts consider the wishes of the child, they weigh their importance by the child's age and maturity. It is not appropriate to ask a child in open court which parent he or she chooses to live with because it is not reckoned to be in the child's best interest to have custody turn on the transitory desires of a child.[112]

Children may be the parties most affected by divorce; they are undoubtedly the least able to protect their own rights, especially since the court receives most of its information about finances and emotional trauma from the parents. For this reason, one theory holds that children ought to be independently represented by their own attorney. Advocates of this theory applaud the case of Gregory Kingsley, previously discussed, who successfully "divorced" his parents by using his own attorney. A contrary theory holds that the illusion of power created by one's own attorney might be inimical to children's emotional well-being. Courts have the power to appoint a special guardian *ad litem* (Latin: "for the purpose of the suit") to protect the interests of the child. In Alaska and Wisconsin, courts have directed such guardians to vigorously advocate for the children in custody disputes.[113]

---

* Wisconsin modified its community property laws in 1986 by adoption of the Uniform Marital Property Act. What was "community property" is now called "marital" property, but like community property, each spouse owns an undivided one-half interest. What was "separate" property is now called "individual" property. But the treatment upon dissolution or divorce is much the same as the other community property states.

The granting of meaningful visitation opportunities may be expected to temper the impact of a change in custody unless visitation is used by a vindictive spouse as a weapon to prolong the agonies of divorce for all concerned. In such situations, the court may prohibit visitation or strictly limit its terms.

When divorced parents reside in different communities, split custody—where one parent has custody during summer, the other during the school year—may be an effective alternative.

Joint custody, in which the parents share responsibility for the child, became the most widespread choice of courts in the 1980s. Many state legislatures expressed a preference for joint custody in their statutory guidelines under the theory that, ideally, children need two actively involved parents in their lives.

joint custody

Responsibility shared by both parents, following a divorce, annulment, or separation, to guide and support their child(ren).

LEGAL FOCUS—PROBLEM

Matthew Anderson and Margie Stavros have court-ordered joint custody of their only child, Roger. Living within the same city, both parents share all important issues, such as those created by religion, school, and sports activities. Roger lives with Mom Monday–Thursday and with Dad Friday–Saturday. Sundays are alternated. Anderson earns more than Stavros and pays monthly child support. This arrangement is working smoothly and both parents remain flexible. What happens when Stavros wants to move away to live with her new boyfriend, and to take Roger with her?

This hypothetical example shows both the benefits and the possible disadvantages of joint custody. When parents cooperate and circumstances permit, joint custody is very effective in providing the parental guidance needed by children. When parents are emotionally antagonistic, judges sometimes are asked to establish the specific custody changes on each vacation or holiday and to otherwise resolve normal parenting issues. The hiring of lawyers to formally dispute child custody issues further depletes the family funds available for the children. When one parent moves far away, the children necessarily lose the stability of a two-parent family. The emotional costs to the children and parents, as well as the financial costs, can be ruinous. Judges cannot be expected to solve all parenting issues by court orders. The toll upon children from marriages gone wrong cannot be measured or cured by the application of family law. Simply stated, children are not best served when joint custody is awarded to parents who continue their bitterness and disagreements after the divorce. In keeping with this experience, many states now have neither a preference nor a presumption for joint custody awards.[114] The key to effective joint custody is joint cooperation between the parents.

Virtually everyone agrees that a mutually acceptable custody and visitation arrangement is the best method of minimizing the traumatic experience of divorce upon children. One method of achieving agreement is through mediation. Recall that mediation uses a professional and neutral third party who attempts to assist in the reconciliation of opposing views. Often mediation is the only way divorcing parents can reach agreements. Studies indicate that children of mediated divorces appear to adjust better and their parents appear to retain less hostility.[115] Indeed, many states have adopted mediation proceedings that are required whenever child custody is disputed.[116] One concern about mandated mediation programs is that husband and wife may not have equal bargaining power, and one may give away some of his or her rights in reaching an agreement. This inequality may be especially significant where full disclosure of financial matters is not enforced as rigorously as it is in court proceedings, where formal discovery procedures are available.

All rational attempts to base custody fairly in the best interests of the child are made difficult, if not impossible, when false charges of child abuse are made by one parent, and/or the child, against the other parent (usually the father). The false charging of child abuse is referred to as the Parental Alienation Syndrome (or PAS). In PAS, the "mother and children become so intent upon driving away the father that they launch a campaign of disparagement that can include falsely accusing him of sexually abusing his offspring."[117] Of course, false charges can be made by a husband against a wife as well.

CHILD SUPPORT

In addition to custody orders, the court granting a divorce must make orders providing for the future support of the minor children. Statutory guidelines for setting the appropriate amount of child support presently exist in most states as a result of adoption by Congress of the Family Support Act.[118] State statutes typically consider the following factors:

- Child's necessities
- Parent's standard of living and circumstances
- Financial status of the parents
- Earning capacity of each parent
- Future educational plans of the child
- Child's age
- Earning ability and fiscal resources of the child
- Duty of each parent to support other people
- Value of care given by the custodial parent

States also frequently take into consideration the need for and cost of day care. Most of the criteria listed relate to finances—but the legal obligation of support cannot exceed the financial capacity of the parent to pay it. One criterion listed credits the custodial parent with the monetary value of the care he or she gives. Would the value of that care be greater if the custodial parent—if a woman—were a "homemaker" mom or a "career" mom? What is the monetary value of daily love and affection? These examples of questions, and others that may occur to you, help explain the variable degree of subjectivity underlying support awards.

Original support orders can be modified by petition to the court when circumstances change. A frequent argument is that remarriage constitutes a significant change in circumstance. Allocation of the earnings of an ex-spouse between a former family and a second-marriage family can be a very sensitive issue. Traditionally, the common-law position has been that children should not be made to suffer from the existence of a new family in their father's (or mother's) life. The modern view is contrary: Remarriage may constitute a changed circumstance sufficient to justify a reduction in child support payments. And as remarriage can affect an ex-spouse's ability to pay child support, so may a change in career. Sometimes a new career will offer lower wages (necessitating a reduction in child support) in exchange for higher potential earnings in the future.

Collection of child support payments is far more difficult than ordering them. When the parent who is delinquent in making child support payments (the obligor) resides in the same state as the child, the custodial parent has several options: Legal procedures (often called the *levy of a writ of execution*) are provided for taking the delinquent parent's assets, including bank accounts and real property. However, certain portions of the debtor's assets are exempt from execution and cannot be taken. Legal procedures necessary to obtain relief by writ of execution can become so complex as to be ineffective, especially when the debtor does not have substantial assets. If the delinquent parent is employed, a wage assignment is an alternative. Under this legal mechanism, a portion of the parent's wages are withheld from weekly or monthly earnings and are forwarded to the custodial parent.

A judgment ordering the payment of child support also can be enforced by contempt proceedings when the failure to support is willful. Theoretically, an obligor who has the ability to pay the ordered child support but purposefully fails to do so can be jailed for contempt, that is, for violating the court's order. However, courts are reluctant to jail an employable parent. Jail precludes employment and contributes to an already crowded correction system. On the other hand, the threat of jail, or a short sentence for contempt of court, may act as a catalyst in encouraging a delinquent obligor to make the required child support payments.

When the parent who is delinquent in making child support payments resides out of state, another difficult problem exists. How can the custodial parent enforce the payment of child support by a former spouse who resides in another state? To alleviate this problem, all states have adopted the Uniform Child Custody Jurisdiction and Enforcement Act (UCCJEF). This law streamlines procedures and closes loopholes that had evolved under prior law. Under the uniform law, the prosecutor in the local state (residence of the custodial parent) initiates a formal legal proceeding in the foreign state (residence of the delinquent obligor), which will be prosecuted in the foreign state by its local prosecutor. The court in the foreign state enters a support order there and enforces it under local laws (including the issuance of a writ of execution or contempt of court proceedings, if appropriate). Monies collected in the foreign state are forwarded to the custodial parent.

If the failure to make support payments is a crime,* the foreign court can extradite (return) the delinquent obligor to the local state for criminal prosecution. The Child Support Recovery Act of 1992[119] made the willful failure to pay child support for more than one year a federal crime. This remedial legislation also created the National Commission on Child and Family Welfare, which has many enumerated duties relating to child custody, visitation, and domestic violence.

When court-ordered child support payments become delinquent, they do not disappear; rather, they accumulate and may be collected at any time in the future, in the same manner that other money judgments are collected, such as by levy of writ of execution to take assets or portions of the debtor's wages. Nor are accumulated child support liabilities discharged (eliminated) if the delinquent father successfully petitions for bankruptcy.

Even with existing legal remedies that are available to enforce child support (and alimony) payments, collection remains a serious problem in most states. It is widely acknowledged that custodial parents generally receive inadequate child support regardless of court orders.

antenuptial, premarital, or **prenuptial agreement**

A contract whereby two persons who are contemplating marriage specify certain future mutual rights and obligations as marriage partners. These binding contracts are also called *premarital agreements* or *prenuptial agreements.*

How May Family Law Be Modified by Contract?

Premarital Agreements

A marital contract made before marriage is called an **antenuptial, premarital,** or **prenuptial agreement.** This type of agreement should be in writing to facilitate enforcement, and some states require that it be witnessed by a third person or notary public. They are

---

* The willful (deliberate) failure to supply necessaries of life to a child, without any excuse, is a crime. The elements of the offense are that the defendant (1) has the ability to pay, (2) willfully fails to pay, (3) there are known past due (child) support obligations, (4) which have remained unpaid for longer than one year or total more than $5,000, (5) for a child who resides in another state. 18 U.S.C. § 228.

increasingly popular as more and more persons prudently seek to establish and fix, before their nuptials, property division and/or support payments in the event that the marriage ends in divorce. Especially when either spouse has a disproportionately large estate of separate property, the premarital agreement can help to resolve future potential misunderstandings without costly litigation.

In response to this need, all states recognize premarital agreements. Approximately half of the states have adopted some version of the 1983 Uniform Premarital Agreement Act. Theoretically, premarital agreements can deal with (1) property and support rights during and after marriage, (2) the personal rights and obligations of the spouses during marriage, or (3) the education, care, and rearing of children. But the most common subjects of marital agreements are property divisions and support rights upon death or divorce. Furthermore, any contractual provision regarding the treatment of minor children is subject to modification by the court.

In most states, upon death of a spouse, the surviving spouse has an elective right to choose between inheriting under the decedent's will or rejecting the inheritance and taking instead a portion of the decedent's estate as provided for by statute. Premarital agreements may alter this option. On the other hand, this "elective" choice is not available in community property states because the surviving spouse is protected through ownership of one-half of the community property. But this community property ownership interest can also be altered by premarital agreement. Even states that do not permit contracts that alter the incidents of divorce do permit contracts that alter property distributions upon death of one spouse. (Inheritance is fully discussed in Chapter 14.)

Upon divorce, premarital agreements can alter court determinations concerning both property division and continuing support (alimony or maintenance). However, prenuptial agreements are void, as a matter of law, to the extent that they adversely affect the rights of minor children. Agreements affecting custody, care, or education of minor children can be valid but are subject to approval by the court. The court will void agreements if they adversely affect the children's best interests. Although about one-half of the states authorize premarital agreements that alter the legal incidents of divorce, some will not enforce agreements affecting support (alimony, maintenance, or child support).

LEGAL FOCUS—PROBLEM

Arlene Van Zandt, a talented and promising young actress, had received her first multi-million-dollar contract to perform the lead in a major movie production. She also was contemplating marriage to Bud Waleska, her off-again, on-again childhood sweetheart, who was a professional boxer with a low earning potential. Van Zandt decided to confer with an attorney concerning preparation of a premarital agreement. What might such a contract accomplish?

If Van Zandt and Waleska lived in a community property state and did not have a premarital agreement, Waleska would become the "owner" of one-half of Van Zandt's earnings after the marriage and would be entitled to his one-half of all community property acquired with her earnings upon any future divorce. This result could not be altered by the divorce court. A contract, on the other hand, could provide that all of Van Zandt's earnings would remain her separate property, and that upon divorce Waleska would be entitled to a cash payment of, say, $100,000. In an "equitable distribution" state, the court would allocate Van Zandt's earnings based on the factors discussed earlier in this chapter.

But Van Zandt and Waleska also could agree in equitable distribution states that $100,000 would be distributed to Waleska upon any future divorce—and that would resolve the issue. In some states, Van Zandt and Waleska could agree that, upon any divorce, Van Zandt would pay alimony to Waleska in some specified amount for some specified time. Courts, however, would not enforce such a promise that attempted to set support payments unless it was fair under all the circumstances. An agreement would not be necessary relative to distribution of assets upon Van Zandt's unexpected death. That matter should be covered by her last will, a topic we consider in our final chapter.

LEGAL FOCUS—CASE

She met him in Montreal in the summer of 1987. The meeting led to telephone calls and a fall visit and a later move to his Phoenix home before marriage in February 1988. The day before the Las Vegas marriage both signed a premarital agreement stating in part that "all the earnings and accumulations resulting from the other's personal services, skill, efforts and work, together with all property acquired with funds and income derived therefrom, shall be the separate property of that spouse." In the property settlement portion of a dissolution action against baseball mega star Barry Bonds, Susann (Sun) Bonds sought to have the agreement set aside arguing it was unfair, she did not understand it when she signed it, and she was not represented by counsel. Was her argument a home run?

In re Marriage of Bonds, 24 Cal. 4th 1, 5 P.3d 815, 99 Cal. Rptr. 2d 252 (California, 2000).

Like most baseball pitchers, a unanimous California Supreme Court gave Mr. Bonds a free pass in its interpretation of the Uniform Premarital Agreement Act. The court held that "although persons, once they are married, are in a fiduciary relationship to one another," the same confidential relationship does not exist before marriage. As to the fairness of the agreement the court concluded that substantial evidence existed that Sun Bonds voluntarily signed the agreement and that she had ample opportunity to get independent legal advice, and that it was her duty to protect her interests, not her fiancé's. Prenuptial agreements can be updated during the marriage to reflect the desires of the spouses as their circumstances change from time to time, but during the marriage, a fiduciary responsibility would exist rising fairness issues that does not exist before the marriage.

As distinguished from prenuptial agreements, contracts made during marriage are called simply *marital contracts,* or *separation agreements* if they are entered while contemplating a forthcoming divorce. Marital contracts are intended to resolve the same sorts of future problems as premarital agreements, and receive comparable enforcement by the courts.

Courts will not enforce marital contracts of any kind that they conclude are unconscionable (unjust, unfair, or excessive). Preceding marriage, there often is unequal bargaining power between the prospective spouses, and the opportunity for overreaching (taking unfair advantage) may be available. Contracts signed immediately before the marriage ceremony may be voided by the court but like the Bonds case they may also be enforced. A contract prepared by the attorney of only one of the party should at least be reviewed and approved by counsel of the other party before signing. Legal representation minimizes the possibility of unfair overreaching and a possible subsequent declaration of invalidity by a court. This procedure also increases the likelihood that all assets will be disclosed and taken into consideration before the contract is signed. Because there is a public policy against divorce, courts will not enforce premarital agreements that are unconscionable or that promote divorce. A premarital agreement drafted so as to absolve a breadwinner from all obligations after divorce would, no doubt, be declared unconscionable and therefore unenforceable. But note that in recent years at least a few cases have upheld premarital contracts that have waived a spouse's right to spousal support if a divorce occurs.[120] As a general rule, courts are more likely to enforce premarital agreements that affect property rights than those that affect support rights.

SEPARATION AGREEMENTS

As noted previously, a marital contract made during marriage, but when a divorce or dissolution is contemplated or is occurring, is called a *separation agreement*. These agreements are enforceable if each spouse fully discloses to the other all financial information and if its provisions are not unconscionable. Public policy favors private settlement of disputes, and courts will usually approve separation agreements as a part of the divorce proceedings. Parties to separation agreements should obtain legal counsel before signing because ramifications of such contracts are not readily apparent to, or understood by, a lay person. For example, will payments from one spouse be taxable income to the other? Will agreed-upon support payments be subject to future modification by the court in case of changed circumstances (e.g., an unanticipated disability)? What would be the effect of a bankruptcy on the contractual obligations? Will the support provisions be enforceable by contempt powers of the court? What effect will a subsequent marriage of either spouse have upon the earlier separation agreement? The answers to these questions, as well as many others, may differ based on the needs and desires of the separating spouses and the law of the particular state. Accordingly, couples usually require the services of a qualified attorney to achieve results that are fair to both parties.

COHABITATION AGREEMENTS

Unmarried persons who live together as husband and wife may desire to protect their respective financial interests by entering into a *cohabitation agreement*. The first obstacle facing such a couple is the long-standing refusal of courts to enforce any contract purporting to exchange property for sexual favors.[121]

LEGAL FOCUS—CASE

Mary Mullen orally agreed to "quit her job and be available to travel" in exchange for a man's promise to "take care of her for the rest of her life." Is the agreement enforceable?

Mullen v. Suchko, 279 Pa. Super. 499, 421 A.2d 310 (Pennsylvania, 1980).

Yes. The contract services do not necessarily include sexual favors. In a few states, such as New York, an agreement for a lifetime of support requires a writing. In still other states, the contract could be interpreted as including sexual favors and therefore violates public policy.

LEGAL FOCUS—CASE

Michele, 20, orally promised to "account to" Charles, 80, "all of her waking moments; to be at his beck and call as he should desire," for which services he would pay her $1,000 a month for the rest of her life. Is this contract enforceable?

Rubenstein v. Kleven, 261 F.2d 921 (1st Cir., 1958).

This contract would not be enforceable in most states because it implies compensation in exchange for sexual favors, in violation of public policy. Public policy will not condone a contract that impliedly calls for the exchange of sexual favors.

The preceding examples demonstrate the difficulties in establishing consistent laws for the enforcement of cohabitation agreements. Cohabitation agreements that do not contemplate the exchange of property for sexual favors are enforceable in most states, whether express (written or oral) or implied. You may recall the case involving Michelle Triola and Lee Marvin from earlier in this chapter (page 406). There, the court was willing to enforce even an oral agreement concerning financial support. But Triola was unable to produce any evidence of such an agreement.

To increase the probability of enforcement of such an agreement, the parties would be well advised to obtain legal counsel for each person, fully disclose their respective financial resources, provide for a reasonable distribution of their properties upon any future parting of their ways, and express it all in writing.

C A S E

JOHNSON V. STATE OF FLORIDA
602 So. 2d 1288 (1992)

Jennifer Johnson gave birth to a boy whose urine contained benzoylecgonine, a breakdown product of cocaine. Fifteen months later Jennifer gave birth to a girl who also tested positive for a cocaine derivative in her urine. Florida has a statute that states: "....it is unlawful for any person 18 years of age or older to deliver any controlled substance to a person under the age of 18 years.... Any person who violates this provision ... is guilty of a felony in the first degree." Johnson was convicted on two counts of delivering a controlled substance to her children. The theory of the prosecution was that Jennifer Johnson "delivered" cocaine to her two children via blood flowing through the childrens' umbilical cords in the sixty- to ninety-second period after they were expelled from her birth canal but before their umbilical cords were severed. Johnson could not be prosecuted for giving birth to a drug-dependent child because that is not a crime in Florida. Nor does Florida have a criminal statute prohibiting in utero transfers of controlled substances. Johnson's convictions were appealed to the Florida Supreme Court.

Opinion of the Court: Justice Harding delivered the opinion of the Court.... There can be no doubt that drug abuse is one of the most serious problems confronting our society today.... Of particular concern is the alarming rise in the number of babies born with cocaine in their systems as a result of cocaine use by pregnant women. Some experts estimate that as many as eleven percent of pregnant women have used an illegal drug during pregnancy, and of those women, seventy-five percent have used cocaine. Report of the American Medical Association Board of Trustees, Legal Interventions During Pregnancy, 264 *Journal of the American Medical Association* 2663 (Nov. 28, 1990). Others estimate that 375,000 newborns per year are born to women who are users of illicit drugs. American Public Health Association 1990 Policy Statement. It is well-established that the effects of cocaine use by a pregnant woman on her fetus and later on her newborn can be severe. On average, cocaine-exposed babies have lower birth weights, shorter body lengths at birth, and smaller head circumferences than normal infants. 264 *Journal of the American Medical Association* 2666 (Nov. 28, 1990). Cocaine use may also result in sudden infant death syndrome, neural-behavioral deficiencies as well as other medical problems and long-term developmental abnormalities. American Public Health

Association 1990 Policy Statement. The basic problem of damaging the fetus by drug use during pregnancy should not be addressed piecemeal, however, by prosecuting users who deliver their babies close in time to use of drugs and ignoring those who simply use drugs during their pregnancy. Florida could possibly have elected to make *in utero* transfers criminal. But it chose to deal with this problem in other ways. One way is to allow evidence of drug use by women as a ground for removal of the child to the custody of protective services, as was done in this case....

At Johnson's trial, Dr. Tompkins testified that a mother's blood passes nutrients, oxygen and chemicals to an unborn child by a diffusion exchange at the capillary level from the womb to the placenta. The umbilical cord then circulates the baby's blood (including the exchange from its mother) between the placenta and the child. Metabolized cocaine derivatives in the mother's blood thus diffuse from the womb to the placenta, and then reach the baby through its umbilical cord. Although the blood flow is somewhat restricted during the birthing process, a measurable amount of blood is transferred from the placenta to the baby through the umbilical cord during delivery and after birth.... Dr. Stephen Kandall, a neonatologist, testified for the defense ... that it is theoretically possible that cocaine or other substances can pass between a mother and her baby during the thirty-to-sixty second period after the child is born and before the umbilical cord is cut, but that the amount would be tiny.

.... [I]n my view, the primary question in this case is whether [the statute] was intended by the Legislature to apply to the birthing process. Before Johnson can be prosecuted under this statute, it must be clear that the Legislature intended for it to apply to the delivery of cocaine derivatives to a newborn during a sixty-to-ninety second interval, before severance of the umbilical cord. I can find no case where "delivery" of a drug was based on an involuntary act such as diffusion and blood flow.... My review... leads me to conclude in this case that the Legislature expressly chose to treat the problem as a public health problem and that it considered but rejected imposing criminal sanctions....

.... The California Medical Association has noted: While unhealthy behavior cannot be condoned, to bring criminal charges against a pregnant woman for activities which may be harmful to her fetus is inappropriate. Such prosecution is counterproductive to the public interest as it may discourage a woman from seeking prenatal care or dissuade her from providing accurate information to health care providers out of fear of self-incrimination.

The conviction of Jennifer Johnson was reversed.

Not all state courts agree with the Florida Supreme Court. In 1992, Cornelia Whitner was sentenced to eight years in jail after her baby was born with traces of cocaine in its system. The South Carolina courts relied on a statute prohibiting child "endangerment." Other states rely upon drug laws, charging that women were delivering drugs through the umbilical cords, as in the Johnson *case. The South Carolina Supreme Court ruled that a viable fetus is a person under the meaning of the child abuse law—thus a child had been endangered. See also the cases cited in endnote 49 supra.* [New York Times, *31 October 1997.*]

For Critical Analysis

1. What are the pros and cons of the position that a woman has either or both a natural law right or a right of privacy under the U.S. Constitution to control her body as she pleases both before and during her pregnancy?

2. If a theory of criminality in a proposed law is to be based on a child abuse statute, how would you define the term "criminal abuse"? For example, would you include smoking, abusive smoking, or prolonged exposure to secondhand smoke during pregnancy? Of accepting employment that meant standing at an assembly line for eight hours each work day? Of neglecting to obtain prenatal care? Of getting drunk?

3. If a theory of criminality in a proposed statute is to be based on a statute prohibiting the supplying of illegal drugs, how would you describe the extent of drug use that constitutes the crime? Would you include the occasional use of marijuana? Of cocaine? Of a misused prescription drug? Or would you reserve the determination until the newborn baby's blood could be tested? If so, would that be gambling with the health of the child? ◼

IN THE MATTER OF ALISON D. V. VIRGINIA M.

77 N.Y.2d 651, 572 N.E.2d 27 (1991)

Alison and Virginia were living together in a home they owned. Intending a permanent relationship, they decided to become parents. Virginia was artificially inseminated and gave birth to a boy, ADM, in 1981. It was explicitly planned that the child would be theirs to raise together, and both were known to the boy as "Mommy." After two years, Alison and Virginia separated and terminated their relationship. For several years, Alison contributed child support and enjoyed visitation with ADM while he was living with Virginia, his biological mother. Ultimately, Virginia severed all ties between ADM and Alison, prompting Alison's request for court-ordered visitation on the grounds that she was a parent entitled to visitation within the meaning of the term "parent" as used in Section 70 of the New York Domestic Relations Statute.

PER CURIAM

. . . . (Alison) claims to have acted as a "de facto" parent or that she should be viewed as a parent "by estoppel." Therefore, she claims she has standing to seek visitation rights. These claims, however, are insufficient under section 70. . . ."It has long been recognized that, as between a parent and a third person, parental custody of a child may not be displaced absent grievous cause or necessity." (citations to precedents). To allow the courts to award visitation—a limited form of custody—to a third person would necessarily impair the parents' right to custody and control. (Alison) concedes that (Virginia) is a fit parent. Therefore she has no right to petition the court to displace the choice made by this fit parent in deciding what is in the child's best interests. Accordingly, the order of the Appellate Division should be affirmed, with costs.

KAYE, J. (dissenting): The Court's decision, fixing biology as the key to visitation rights, has impact far beyond this particular controversy, one that may affect a wide spectrum of relationships—including those of long-time heterosexual stepparents, "common law" and non-heterosexual partners such as involved here, and even participants in scientific reproduction procedures. Estimates that more than 15.5 million children do not live with two biological parents, and that as many as eight to ten million children are born into families with a gay or lesbian parent, suggest just how widespread the impact may be. (citations).

But the impact of today's decision falls hardest on the children of those relationships, limiting their opportunity to maintain bonds that may be crucial to their development. The majority's retreat from the courts' proper role—its tightening of rules that should in visitation petitions, above all, retain the capacity to take the children's interests into account—compels this dissent. . . .

Most significantly, Virginia M. agrees that, after long cohabitation with Alison D. and before ADM's conception, it was "explicitly planned that the child would be theirs to raise together." It is also uncontested that the two shared "financial and emotional preparations" for the birth, and that for several years Alison D. actually filled the role of co-parent to ADM, both tangibly and intangibly. In all, a parent-child relationship—encouraged or at least condoned by Virginia M.—apparently existed between ADM and Alison D. during the first six years of the child's life.

While acknowledging that relationship, the (majority) nonetheless proclaims powerlessness to consider the child's best interest at all, because the word "parent" in the statute imposes an absolute barrier to Alison D.'s petition for visitation . . . . I cannot agree that such a result is mandated by Section 70, or any other law. . . .

For Critical Analysis

1. The court considered visitation as a "limited form of (parental) custody" to which Alison was not entitled under the statute. Under this theory, does a mother give a limited form of parental custody each day to a day care provider? Or is visitation something less than an intrusion into parental custody? Can you make an argument that visitation is only a change in physical, but not necessarily parental, custody?

2. Which view, the majority or dissenting, is more progressive given what you have learned about the future impact of surrogacy and genetic engineering upon the family? Does the majority, in effect, treat any person who is not a biological parent of a child as a "third person"? Can you formulate an argument in support of the dissent that considerations other than the biological relationship may serve the best interests of a child?

CHAPTER QUESTIONS AND PROBLEMS

1. Family law is in a state of change because of rapidly evolving social patterns. For example, there is an emergence of "informal marriage" (cohabitation with express or implied contract) alongside formal marriage (ceremonial or statutory). The domestic partnerships of gay persons also are a variety of "informal marriage." Both varieties of relationships, formal and informal marriage, often are terminated by choice, creating special legal consequences. Although you probably have not studied all the implications that can flow from marriage, from your generalized knowledge try to compare the implications of both types of relationships (formal marriage and cohabitation) on the following criteria:
   a. Federal and state income taxes
   b. Selection and use of surname
   c. Child support obligations
   d. Credit extension
   e. Expense of creating or ending the relationship
   f. Mutual support obligations
   g. Vicarious tort liability
   h. Recovery for lost consortium, or wrongful death
   i. Privilege not to testify against one another
   j. Immunities for sex crimes between spouses
   k. Division of assets upon death or termination of relationship
   l. Inheritance rights, absent a will
   m. Costs and coverage of health or life insurance
   n. Social security benefits
   o. Privacy in business matters upon termination of marriage
   p. Workers' compensation benefits
   q. Care for a dying loved one

2. It has been said that divorce is "the great American tragedy." Among measures suggested to reduce the divorce rate are higher age requirements for marriage, computerized analysis of personalities and backgrounds of prospective spouses, longer mandatory waiting periods after a marriage license is obtained, mandatory "marriage license training" (including instruction in the financial, social, psychological, and sexual aspects of marriage), trial marriage for a probationary period, and government

day care centers for infants and preschool children to free mothers from the burdens of child care. What do you think should be done, if anything?

3. Which of the following promises are enforceable if contained in a premarital agreement?
   a. Wife waives any claim for support upon any future divorce.
   b. Husband agrees to raise children in a specified religion.
   c. Both agree to a specified variety of sexual activities with a specified frequency.
   d. Husband agrees to transfer certain valuable property to wife immediately upon marriage.
   e. Wife agrees that husband may have custody of the children, if any, upon any future divorce.

4. What legal rights accrue in your state to an unmarried woman who lives with a man for 13 years "as husband and wife" who then is abandoned? Does it make any difference if she had received an oral promise of future support? What if they had a child? You may either refer to a legal encyclopedia in your library or surf the Web. In either case, search under the subject index of "cohabitation," "same-sex marriage," and "domestic partnerships."

5. Does someone have a legal right to know that she is not genetically related to her father because her mother's egg was fertilized *in vitro* at a sperm bank? Should someone have a legal right to know the name of his genetic parent? Do you apply the same rationale to donors who someday want desperately to find their genetic children, perhaps to leave them millions of dollars?

6. What legal problems can you think of that might arise if a surrogate mother changed her mind immediately following birth and refused to release her child to the natural father, as she had contracted to do? For example, what if she moved to another state and assumed a new identity and life—would she be guilty of child-snatching (kidnapping by a relative) or only responsible for breach of contract? Would your answer change if the surrogate mother was genetically related to the child (via her egg with *in vitro* fertilization)? Do any legal problems come to mind if a surrogate mother aborts the contracting parties' fetus?

7. Sharon Bottoms and April Wade were living together in a lesbian relationship. Sharon's mother, Kay, sought court-ordered custody of Sharon's two-year-old son, Tyler, on the grounds that Bottoms's relationship with Wade made her an unfit mother. What should be the result? Are children raised in a homosexual family thereby disadvantaged in some way?

8. Suppose that John and Mary Powers arrange to have their fertilized egg, or preembryo, frozen for future use. Suppose John is killed in an airplane crash. Should Mary have the legal right to bring the preembryo to birth? To hire a surrogate mother for that purpose? To have genetic surgery performed upon it to change its future behavioral characteristics? To donate it to gene research? To donate it to another couple? What should be the rights of the genetic donors to custody of a preembryo?

9. If one spouse puts the other spouse through medical school by working and by delaying his or her own formal education, and if divorce occurs soon after the doctor completes residency, how might a court's judgment take these factors into consideration? What difference would it make if divorce occurs *before* the medical license is obtained?

10. Should divorcing spouses be permitted to bring tort actions against each other for precisely the same conduct that would entitle strangers to sue each other? Can you think of any conduct between spouses that arguably should not justify a domestic tort? Should the same rules of liability between spouses be interpreted to include liability between parents and their children?

11. Pat Price, Sean's spouse, charges several purchases that remain unpaid. Creditors seek payment from Sean's separate property. Is Sean liable? Does it make any difference if the charges are for necessities?

CHAPTER 10

Owning and Operating Motor Vehicles

*E*verything in life is somewhere else, and you get there in a car.

E.B. White, *One Man's Meat,* 1944.

After reading and studying this chapter, you should be able to:

🏛 Explain the nature of a contract to buy an automobile.

🏛 Discuss the warranties arising in a sale or lease of a motor vehicle and how such warranties are disclaimed.

🏛 Explain what a lemon law is and how it might affect a vehicle contract.

🏛 Define product liability and different theories used to bring a product liability claim.

🏛 Explain the nature and importance of automobile registration.

🏛 Explain the application of negligence to motor vehicle incidents and accidents.

🏛 Define DUI and identify some of its legal ramifications.

🏛 Define a bailment and describe various bailment situations.

🏛 Define a common carrier.

🏛 Describe a financial responsibility law.

🏛 Identify the basic types of automobile insurance coverage.

🏛 State the legal requirements of an enforceable gift.

🏛 Distinguish between the legal requirements of ownership by possession, production, gift, and inheritance.

🏛 Distinguish between lost, abandoned, and mislaid property.

How people transport themselves and their products from one location to another is a major concern in all societies. Public policy issues arising from transportation questions compete with other major issues in the twenty-first century. Where shall we live relative to where we work? How are goods best distributed in a worldwide market? What are the costs of different transportation systems? How much environmental harm is caused by pollution and how can it be minimized? Are large and efficient mass transportation systems economically feasible?

Automobiles are the most valuable item of personal property owned by most Americans. No other widely owned, mass-produced and distributed products are more costly than automobiles, trucks, and mobile motorized variations. No other item of personal property is as subsidized through public expenditures such as highways and fuels and through tolerance for air and surface pollution.

Many of the issues that existed when automobiles were introduced are repeating today—with competition between automobiles powered by electricity and by other fuels (then, by gasoline, coal, or oil-fired steam; now by ethanol, natural gas, or one-half electricity and one-half gasoline). Although there were few gasoline-powered vehicles, most people in the major cities had seen them maneuvering through horse-clogged streets. A new independence and freedom was promised. "Trains kept their own schedules and never took you quite where you wanted to go, and horses got hungry, cold and tired. The auto was nothing but a dumb machine, but that was part of the joy."[1] One of the earliest proposed settlements from a crash was proposed by financier William K. Vanderbilt, who was "taking his father for a spin down the main street in New York, [when] he almost killed them both" in a collision with a "fishwagon." Vanderbilt promptly offered to compromise the case: "I'll settle for everything, my good fellow." What Vanderbilt meant was that he would pay for disposal of one horse and purchase of another.[2] Even in 1900, with perhaps 8,000 *handmade* cars in the entire nation, there were fatal accidents with pedestrians, prompting public outcries for "mancatchers" on the front of cars. The *New York Times* was calling for driver education, while the age of motor vehicle crashes and litigation was begun.

The competition between gasoline and other fuels for vehicles is intensifying as the twenty-first century begins. Several global manufacturers already are offering selections of electric vehicles, part gasoline and part electric cars, and natural gas alternatives to the public. We expect that the gasoline-powered automobile with its considerable impact on the environment will fade away in the twenty-first century as we return, in a sense, to where we were with electric carriages silently meandering around our largest cities.

There may be substantial impacts upon the vehicle laws brought about by changing from gasoline to other less offensive fuels. For example, cars can have useful life expectancies of twenty and more years. Can government enact laws that keep older cars, sometimes called gross polluters, off the highways? Or must these owners be compensated for their losses as the changeover to electricity or other fuel becomes mandated?

Few human-made objects have had as extensive and intensive an impact on the law as the automobile. The registration of vehicles, collection of tens of millions of dollars in fees, and licensing of drivers are monumental recurring tasks mandated by state statutes. Comprehensive vehicle codes govern rules of the road. Administrative agencies regulate vehicle manufacturers with particular emphasis on safety and fuel consumption. Other administrative agencies evaluate the environmental impact of new building construction to anticipate the effect on traffic flow and volume. Executive and legislative branches of the government, especially at the federal level, continue to struggle with the problem of maintaining a fuel supply for a nation on wheels. Collectively, millions of workers manufacture the vehicles, fuel them, service them, use them as tools, and ultimately dispose of them as scrap—a sizable problem in itself. International disputes often revolve around trade issues related to import and export of automobiles.

There is no body of law called motor vehicle law. However, previously discussed areas of law such as contracts, torts, and crimes have application to motor vehicles. We will also introduce personal property law emphasizing its relation to motor vehicles. The application of all these different areas of law to one type of personal property highlights both the rules and the importance of this type of property.

Owning a Motor Vehicle

Property is an aggregate of rights to a thing which are protected and guaranteed by government, including and especially ownership. Property is classified in many ways, most importantly as either real or personal. **Real property** is land and almost everything permanently attached to it, such as buildings, fences, trees, and roads. (See Chapters 11 and 12 for an in-depth discussion of real property.) An automobile is a form of **personal property.** Personal property* is property not permanently attached to land, such as vehicles, merchandise in stores, food products, skis, boats, and backpacks. The general idea is that if property is not land or that which is permanently affixed to land, it is personalty (personal property), which is often referred to as property that can be easily moved. That mental image usually works until one tries to move a filled waterbed.

Ownership of personal property occurs many ways. Personal property can be created, for example when you create a painting or a clay pot. It can be transferred to another by gift. It can be bought, traded for, and found. In the case of motor vehicles, ownership usually results from a purchase.

property

The legally protected rights and interests a person has in anything with an ascertainable value that is subject to ownership.

real property

Land and things permanently attached to the land.

personal property

Movable property; any property that is not real property.

Is a Special Contract Required to Purchase a Motor Vehicle?

The sale of a motor vehicle is an ordinary contractual transaction subject to the law of contracts relating to personal property. The contract involves a sale of goods (tangible personal property) and is subject to the Uniform Commercial Code (see Chapter 8). The UCC relaxes some of the otherwise formal rules of common-law contract formation and performance and motor vehicle sales law is mostly uniform throughout the states.

Motor vehicles, of course, usually cost more than $500, and so the Statute of Frauds applies to such purchases. Thus to provide evidence of an executory contract there must be a writing signed by the party to be obligated. This requirement is usually met with a standard form contract prepared by commercial sellers. Standardized (pre-printed) form agreements, including automobile sales contracts, are adhesion contracts. Recall adhesion contracts are drafted by a dominant party and then presented to the other party—the adhering party—on a "take it or leave it" basis. Unconscionable clauses, those that "shock the conscience" of a court, are more likely to be found in adhesion contracts than contracts where the parties truly bargain over terms. If language in an adhesion contract is ambiguous, courts will often interpret the language to favor the buyer, the party who did not draft

---

* During the first one-half of the twentieth century, items of personal property, such as couches, were called chattels. Thus, when you borrowed money to purchase furniture for your home you would sign a document called a chattel mortgage giving the creditor rights to repossess (or foreclose upon) the furnishings. This terminology has been abandoned in some areas of the United States.

the contract. Nevertheless, the buyer should be aware that the contract is written primarily to protect the interests of the seller, and is unlikely to have ambiguous terms or clauses. (See additional discussion of Statute of Frauds, adhesion contracts, and unconscionable clauses in Chapter 8.)

LEGAL FOCUS—PROBLEM

The trunk of the car seemed too small to Bill Clark as he viewed the car he was thinking about buying. The salesperson, Frank, assured him there was adequate room in the trunk for luggage for a family of four. Frank also said: "If there isn't enough room, bring the car back and we will install a luggage rack." Bill signed a standard form automobile purchase contract that did not include any reference to the luggage rack. A few months later, Bill, unable to load four suitcases in the trunk, returned to the dealership expecting a new luggage rack free of additional charge. Does Bill have an enforceable right to a luggage rack?

Bill's claim would be thwarted by the parol evidence rule.* This rule holds that when people have signed a contract as their final and complete expression of intention (integrated contracts), then neither party may introduce in court any evidence of prior or contemporaneous oral or written material that adds to or modifies that written contract. The rule does not apply to less formal contracts—those not portending to be the final and complete expression of the agreement. However, standard form automobile purchase contracts do purport to be final and complete agreements. The lesson is clear and crucial: If important promises are made to you (e.g. warranties, credit terms, additional equipment), be sure they are included as part of the written contract.

In motor vehicle sales transactions, there are standard sales customs and techniques, and some states regulate contracts written by commercial sellers. A complete discussion of the mini-culture of "list price," "5 percent over invoice," and "clearance sales" are beyond the scope of this text. However, buyers are well advised to consult reliable sources for help in selecting the appropriate vehicle (especially if previously owned), and for information on negotiating the best deal.†

The Statute of Frauds and parol evidence rule also apply to purchases from private owners. If there are warranties, any other promises, or an extension of credit, a written contract should be prepared containing these terms and the signatures of both the seller and the buyer to satisfy these requirements.

WARRANTIES FOR MOTOR VEHICLES

The seller of a new motor vehicle transfers title with any express warranties made and with several implied warranties. Recall from Chapter 8 that express warranties are created by statements of fact made by the seller about quality, condition, description, and performance potential.

---

* Legal scholar John Murray suggests the parol evidence rule would be better understood if it were called the "Rule against Contradictory Integrated Writings." We think if you already understand the concept he is right, but if you don't understand it is unlikely this different phrasing will help.

† Every April, Consumers Union's magazine *Consumer Reports* publishes an issue devoted to selecting and buying new and used cars. Several helpful books describing car salesperson tactics are also available to assist the buyer of automobiles.

LEGAL FOCUS—PROBLEM

Praneel X. Singh expressed his interest in the new model SRV. Steve Walters, the number one salesperson at Autoworld, claimed, "This is the best new vehicle to be introduced in forty years." Is Walters's statement an express warranty?

Walters's *opinion* that the vehicle is "the best new vehicle to be introduced in forty years" is not a warranty; it is **puffing,** the word used to describe normal sellers' exaggerations about goods for sale. Similarly, statements such as, "It's worth a fortune" or "Anywhere else you'd pay more for it," do not usually create warranties. Whether the buyer's reliance on the seller's statement is reasonable is often the controlling factor. For example, a salesperson's statement that a car "will never break down" and "will last a lifetime" is so improbable that no reasonable buyer should rely on it. The how and where of the statement is also important in determining the reasonableness of the buyer's reliance. For example, it is generally more reasonable for a buyer to rely on a statement made in a written advertisement than on a salesperson's oral statement.

Also recall from Chapter 8 that *implied warranties* are warranties that arise in a sales transaction unless specifically disclaimed. The most important implied warranties in automobile sales transactions are usually the warranty of title, the warranty against encumbrances and the warranty of merchantability. The **implied warranty of title** promises to the buyer that the seller possesses good title to the motor vehicle and can rightfully transfer title to the buyer. The **implied warranty against encumbrances** promises the buyer that the title to the vehicle is free of secured debt (no creditor has a right to the vehicle for failure to pay off a loan). The implied warranty of merchantability refers to quality and is a promise that a vehicle is of usual and customary quality and as such is fit for its ordinary and intended use. Implied warranties of merchantability are made only by merchants. Of course, an auto dealer is a merchant. Given the value of a motor vehicle and its intended use, the implied warranty of merchantability is very extensive, unless limited by the seller. As you will see and should note, implied warranties of quality are almost always limited in some fashion by the seller.

LEGAL FOCUS—PROBLEM

When Betty Orra bought her new automobile, she expected 100,000 or more miles of carefree motoring. She carefully maintained and serviced her vehicle. The car was sold with a written warranty from the dealer that included this language: "This warranty is in lieu of and excludes all other warranties, express or implied, including the warranty of merchantability." The warranty covered defects in materials or workmanship "for one year or 12,000 miles, whichever occurs first." Did Orra lose anything when she received this warranty?

Yes and no. The dealer statement is an attempted **disclaimer** sufficient to deny an implied warranty of merchantability in most contracts except those involving consumer goods. An automobile for personal use is certainly consumer goods. A disclaimer is a specific statement indicating a particular warranty does not exist or limiting the warranty as to nature or duration. In a transaction for consumer goods, you can make a total disclaimer of the implied warranty of merchantability, but not a partial disclaimer. Total exclusion of an

puffing

Seller's talk; claims about the quality of goods, usually exaggerated; not considered fraud.

implied warranty of title

An implied warranty to a buyer that the seller has and is transferring good title.

implied warranty against encumbrances

An implied warranty in the sale of goods that goods are delivered free from any security interest or other lien of which the buyer has no knowledge.

disclaimer

A written or oral statement stating that a warranty does not exist. Negation or limitation of a warranty in the sale or lease of goods.

http://

Research purchase options at *Consumer Reports, Popular Mechanics,* and *Motor Trend*

http://www.consumer reports.org/, http://www. popularmechanics.com/, http://www.motortrend .com/

implied warranty of merchantability requires specific, legally acceptable language of disclaimer. The most common methods of a total disclaimer for an implied warranty of merchantability are (1) use of the terms "as is" or "with all faults" or (2) a statement that no other warranty, including that of merchantability, exists. The dealer did not use the "as is" form of disclaimer but relied on the alternative method. Although in a non-consumer transaction this disclaimer would be effective, the federal Magnuson-Moss Warranty Act preempts the UCC in consumer transactions involving warranties.

The federal Magnuson-Moss Warranty Act[3] (see Chapter 8) allows sellers of consumer goods to limit, but not eliminate, warranties of merchantability if any express warranty is given. Thus, the dealer cannot disclaim the warranty in the manner attempted. A merchant cannot give an express warranty and include an "as is" clause to eliminate the implied warranty of merchantability. Under Magnuson-Moss, a seller making an express warranty in a sales contract is not allowed to disclaim or modify either the implied warranty of merchantability or the implied warranty of fitness for a particular purpose. However, sellers can impose a time limit on the duration of an implied warranty. The time limit must be no less than the duration of the express warranty. Any limitation must also be reasonable, conscionable, and stated in clear and conspicuous language on the face of the warranty. All motor vehicle manufacturers provide express warranties, and the implied warranty of merchantability is often limited in time as part of the express warranty provision in the sales contract.* An acceptable limitation might read, "Any implied warranty of merchantability or fitness for a particular purpose applicable to this vehicle is limited to the duration of this written warranty."

Thus, Betty Orra did not lose her implied warranty of merchantability, but its limitation to 12 months was effective. The extent of the express warranty, both as to scope of coverage and length of coverage, is a very important issue when determining which motor vehicle to buy and how much to pay.

Motor vehicle dealers often offer (at an additional cost) extended warranties to vehicle buyers. These warranties typically extend the time and expand the coverage provided by manufacturer warranties. These policies can be purchased from companies other than the original dealership and often at more favorable prices. Before deciding whether to purchase an extended warranty, one should become an informed consumer by studying the need for the product and the available extended warranties and prices. There are substantial differences in price, scope, and length of coverage, and possible restrictions on who may service the vehicle.

A manufacturer providing a written warranty is also required to comply with Magnuson-Moss and applicable state laws. Magnuson-Moss does not require that the manufacturer or seller provide a warranty, but it does govern the wording of and extent of warranties when express warranties are given. If a seller makes an express written warranty involving consumer goods costing more than $10, the act controls how the warranty is to be given. Any warranty under the act must be labeled as "full" or "limited." In addition, if the cost of the goods is more than $15, the warrantor (the person making the warranty) must make certain disclosures in language that is easy to understand. The disclosures must state the names and addresses of the warrantor and must identify the product warranted, the procedures for enforcement of the warranty, and any limitations on warranty remedies.

A *full warranty* may not cover every problem arising from use of a consumer product, but it must give the buyer rights to free repair or replacement of any defective part. If the product cannot be repaired within a reasonable time, the consumer can choose a refund or

http://

Nolo Press can provide answers to many of your warranty questions. Go to the homepage and enter "warranty" in the site search engine
http://www.nolo.com/

http://

A discussion of automobile service contracts is at
http://www.ftc.gov/bcp/conline/pubs/autos/autoserv.htm

---

*   Some states have statutes that further restrict the ability of a seller to disclaim or limit implied warranties in consumer transactions. These state laws are upheld as long as they add to those rights provided by Magnuson-Moss

a replacement without charge. The warranty does not cover damage that is caused by the consumer. A written consumer warranty that does not meet all the requirements of a full warranty is a *limited warranty*. The seller must state clearly that only a limited warranty is given. The Federal Trade Commission has the power to enforce many provisions of Magnuson-Moss and may sue businesses that fail to honor their written warranties.

Used cars purchased from dealers also carry implied warranties of merchantability because the dealers are still merchants even though the goods are used. Used cars purchased from private parties do not carry any warranty of quality unless made expressly by the non-merchant seller (get these assurances in writing). Remember that the implied warranty of merchantability is disclaimed by the words "as is." This is true even under Magnuson-Moss as long as no express warranty of quality is given.

What Are Lemon Laws?

LEGAL FOCUS—PROBLEM

Maggie O'Malley was very excited when she bought her new convertible Aardvark Seven from Autoworld. She drove it off the lot and headed toward Slim's Health Club to show it to her friends. Two blocks from the dealership, the engine died. The car needed to be towed back to Autoworld. A very angry O'Malley was not mollified when the sales representative said, "We'll be happy to repair or replace that cracked engine block." O'Malley snapped back, "I expect to get a new and different Aardvark Seven. I am a consumer who won't be satisfied with a lemon." Will O'Malley get a new car or must she allow the repair or replacement of the engine block?

The legal question is, did the dealership perform its contractual obligations when it delivered the vehicle? If the delivery is legally sufficient, Autoworld need only honor the warranty—either repair or replace the defective part. If, however, the delivery is insufficient under key UCC provisions, Autoworld must replace the defective car with a new one.

O'Malley had a right to inspect her purchase before accepting it and becoming obligated to pay its purchase price. What is considered an appropriate inspection depends on the circumstances and the nature of the goods. In this situation, although O'Malley received and took possession of the vehicle, a normal inspection would not have shown that the engine had a cracked block. Since she discovered that the vehicle was nonconforming almost immediately after receipt, she can return it and argue reasonably that she never really accepted it. O'Malley really did indeed get a lemon[4] (sour deal), and she has a legal right to a full refund or a new vehicle under the UCC.[5]

There are additional rights under the UCC that may also be claimed to assist a buyer when there is a major and initial contract breach by the seller. Perhaps even if O'Malley accepted the vehicle after a careful inspection, she could revoke her acceptance and enjoy the same rights (of replacement or full refund) as if she had rejected it initially. It is necessary that she revoke within a reasonable time after she discovers (or should have discovered) a sufficient reason for revocation, and before there is any substantial change in the condition of the goods (not caused by the defect).[6]

Most problems with new cars are not as dramatic or immediate as the problems suffered by O'Malley. All states have passed so-called **lemon laws** to provide protection for angry consumers who are dissatisfied with extensive warranty work and instead demand

http://

Access the various state lemon laws from the Car Talk Web site of Tom and Ray Magliozzi (aka "Click and Clack, The Tappet Brothers"), renowned hosts of a radio program on auto care

http://cartalk.cars.com/
Got-A-Car/Lemon/

lemon laws

Statutes designed to assist the buyer of seriously defective goods to obtain a replacement or full refund.

a new car or their money back. A lemon law provides that if a car is determined to be a lemon, the dealer must refund to the customer the purchase price of the car, plus sales tax, registration, and license fees, minus a reasonable allowance for use.[7] The problem, of course, is to define a "lemon" with sufficient precision and to enforce consumers' rights in a fair and prompt manner.

A lemon is often defined as a major problem not permanently fixed after a reasonable number of attempts (i.e., four or more), or if a car is out of service for repairs for a certain number of days within a certain period (i.e., thirty calendar days during a twelve-month period). The covered period in different states ranges from the written warranty period, or twelve months to two years; sometimes coverage is based on miles driven (for example, 18,000 miles). Many lemon laws allow for the use of ADR methods, such as non-binding arbitration, to assist in the resolution of the dispute (see Chapter 4).

LEGAL FOCUS—CASE

John L. Hughes's new 1990 Dodge Caravan qualified as a lemon. His first year of ownership required seven separate trips to the dealer to repair transmission defects. Attempts to get Chrysler to replace the car within the time provided by the lemon law were unsuccessful. Hughes filed a lawsuit. The court entered judgment for Hughes in the amount of $74,371, double the amount he paid for the vehicle and attorney fees. Do lemon laws always provide for a recovery that exceeds the price of the vehicle?

John L. Hughes v. Chrysler Motors Corp., 197 Wis. 2d 973, 542 N.W.2d 148 (Wis., 1996).

Wisconsin does but most states do not. The Wisconsin statute specifically allows a court to award twice the customer damages plus attorney fees. The court opinion recites the transactional dilemma well: "We realize that car manufacturers do not deliberately set out to manufacture a lemon. Quite the opposite. In fact, it is in their own best interest not to do so. However, an unfortunate fact of life, seemingly as inevitable as night following day, is that occasionally a 'lemon' will slip through the line. And when that happens, another unfortunate fact of modern-day life is that the cost to the unlucky consumer who purchases that 'lemon' is far more than the cost of the car: interrupted, delayed, or even cancelled schedules; the time and the trouble, as well as the anxiety and stress that accompany those changes; the apprehensions that result every time the consumer gets back into that automobile wondering 'what next?' Dependability is a prime objective of every new car buyer. When that is taken away, the loss is far greater than the cost of the car. It is this fact that the legislature recognized when they enacted the lemon law. Its principal motivation is not to punish the manufacturer who, after all, would far prefer that no 'lemons' escape their line. Rather, it seeks to provide an incentive to that manufacturer to promptly return those unfortunate consumers back to where they thought they were when they first purchased that new automobile."

WHAT ARE AUTOMOBILE LEASES?

Leasing has become a popular alternative to purchasing a vehicle. Technically, a "lease" is a common-law **bailment** for use. A bailment is a common legal relationship created when personal property is temporarily delivered into the care of another without transfer of title. Thus, a bailment is created when you lend your car to a friend and any personal property can be bailed. The legal specifics of bailment are discussed later in the chapter.

http://

The Better Business Bureau administers a program to help automobile manufacturers and individual customers resolve disputes concerning alleged manufacturing defects
http://www.bbb.org/complaints/BBBAutoline.asp

bailment

A delivery of personal property to another by which that person has the right to temporary possession. Often, though not always, bailment is created by contract.

Virtually every study and analysis concludes that buying an automobile is less expensive than leasing over the full term of ownership.[8] However, monthly costs of leasing are reasonably low and the lease deposit is small, leaving the impression of a lower cost. Many consumers are also happy that at the end of the lease the car is simply returned to the dealer, or lessor. Although strings are attached to the car's return, most people view them as a very distant and unimportant problem. A person contemplating a lease should consider:

- What is the term of the lease and what are the front-end, monthly, and back-end charges?* What additional charges, such as responsibility for repair, are occasioned by what events?
- What limitations are imposed on total miles driven during the lease? What extra costs are incurred if the mileage limit is exceeded?
- What warranty is offered with the leased automobile?
- How and at what cost can the lease be terminated before it expires?

Anyone who leases an automobile should realize that the usual and normal costs of automobile ownership still exist in a lease. For example, costs such as license registration, liability and property insurance, emission certificates, gasoline, and maintenance remain costs of the buyer or lessee and are not changed by the normal lease. Also, bailment law and lease contracts require that personal property be returned in good condition. Thus, while an owner may neglect an automobile, a lessee does so with peril. There will undoubtedly be additional costs at lease return for excess mileage or wear and tear. Some leases contain important options at the end of the lease. If the car is worth more or less than a specified amount at the end of the lease, the consumer will receive a credit (unlikely) or pay a differential (likely) to guarantee the leasing company from any unpredicted depreciation or loss in value.

Leases are covered by Article 2A of the Uniform Commercial Code. Article 2A provides rules similar to provisions in the sales code for contract formation, performance, and warranties. Special protection under the UCC is provided for consumer leases which are defined as "a lease that a lessor regularly engaged in the business of leasing or selling makes to a lessee who is an individual and who takes under the lease primarily for a personal, family, or household purpose."[9] Some states provide that a consumer lease cannot exceed a maximum amount but states with a maximum have varied the amount.[10]

The federal Consumer Leasing Act also covers personal property leases lasting more than four months if the total contractual obligation does not exceed $25,000. The act requires the lessor to make several disclosures to the lessee:

- Total amount of any upfront payment
- Number and amount of monthly payments
- Payments for other fees, such as registration and taxes
- Any penalty for default or late payments
- The annual mileage allowance and the amount of extra charges for exceeding the allowance
- What counts as excessive wear and tear
- If you can end the lease early, and if so are there any extra charges
- Provisions for purchase at lease conclusion, and for what price
- Any responsibility for the difference between the estimated value of the auto and its market value at the end of the lease
- Any extra payments at the end of the lease

http://

Order or read online "A Consumer Guide to Vehicle Leasing" at **http://www.federalreserve .gov/pubs/leasing/**

---

* A "back-end" charge refers to costs the consumer pays at the end of the lease.

Some consumers who use their automobiles in their businesses, such as traveling salespersons and real estate agents, assume that they obtain tax benefits by deducting from their taxes the full amount of lease payments, plus all other related expenses. However, the tax laws do not play favorites with leased automobiles. Owners can also deduct their business travel expenses, including interest payments, and can depreciate (deduct) the cost of their vehicles gradually and proportionally over the years. Many states levy a "use" tax against buyers in lieu of the sales tax they would otherwise pay if they had purchased the vehicle.

LEGAL FOCUS—CASE

Potente leased a new Peugeot through Peugeot Motors of America, Inc (PMA). A few months later, after experiencing problems with the vehicle, he sought relief under Ohio's "lemon law." PMA moved for summary judgment on the lemon law claim, arguing that Potente, as lessee, had no standing to bring an action under Ohio's lemon law. What was the result?

Potente v. Peugeot, 62 Ohio Misc.2d 335, 598 N.E .2d 9907 (1991).

The court held that any consumer entitled to enforce contract warranties against the manufacturer had the right to enforce the state lemon laws. "A lease agreement which extends the manufacturer's warranty and the ability to enforce the warranty to the lessee falls within the protective ambit of Ohio's Lemon Law." Most state lemon laws do extend to automobile leases, but not all.

WHAT ARE AUTOMOBILE RECALLS?

Even after motor vehicles are sold, manufacturers have a continuing obligation to ensure their safety in normal use. Under federal law, manufacturers are required to notify consumers and the National Highway Traffic Safety Administration (NHTSA) of discovered safety defects and how they propose to eliminate or "cure" them. Recalls can be voluntary or mandated by the NHTSA. The manufacturer generally has the option of repairing the defect, replacing the vehicle, or refunding the price paid. Obviously, repairing the defect is the usual means of correction chosen by the manufacturers.

Recalls are common and usually only noticed by affected parties. However, some notices are accompanied by significant media attention because of the number of vehicles involved or because they involve a significant risk to life Problem standard equipment Firestone Tires on some Ford vehicles got such attention in 2000. "On August 9, 2000, Firestone recalled all of its ATX and ATX II tires of the P235/75R15 size manufactured since 1991. It also recalled Wilderness AT tires of that size made at its Decatur plant, for a total of 14.4 million tires. On May 22, 2001, Ford announced a tire replacement program that includes all other Firestone Wilderness tires on certain Ford, Mercury, and Mazda SUVs and light trucks. This replacement action totals approximately 13 million tires."[11] See Exhibit 10-1 for the Firestone recall notice. The problems with the Firestone tires were not confined to the United States as other countries complained about defective tires. Venezuela's consumer protection agency said defects in Firestone tires on Ford motor vehicles were linked to at least 46 deaths in that country.[12]

http://

Compare what you know about automobile safety in the U.S. with automobile safety information in Japan

http://www.osa.go.jp/anzen/ indexe.html

EXHIBIT 10-1: **Firestone Recall Notice**

NHTSA CAMPAIGN ID Number: 00T005000
Component: TIRES: TREAD
Manufacturer: BRIDGESTONE/FIRESTONE, INC.

| Year: All years | Make: FIRESTONE | Model: WILDERNESS AT | Recall Date: 08/10/2000 |

Type of Report: Tire

Potential Number of Units Affected: 14400000

Defect Summary:
TIRE DESCRIPTION: FIRESTONE WILDERNESS AT, SIZE P235/75R15, PRODUCED AT THE DECATUR, ILLINOIS TIRE PLANT AND ALL FIRESTONE RADIAL ATX AND RADIAL ATX II TIRES, SIZE P235/75R15. OPERATION OF THESE TIRES AT LOW INFLATION PRESSURES, HIGH SPEED, AND IN HOT WEATHER, CAN CONTRIBUTE TO SEPARATION OF THE TIRE TREAD.
Consequence Summary:
IF THE TREAD SEPARATES FROM THE TIRE, THE DRIVER CAN LOSE CONTROL OF THE VEHICLE, POSSIBLY RESULTING IN A CRASH CAUSING INJURY OR DEATH.
Corrective Summary:
THE REPLACEMENT/REIMBURSEMENT PROGRAM FOR THIS CAMPAIGN EXPIRED ON AUGUST 29, 2001. HOWEVER, CUSTOMERS SHOULD CONTACT FIRESTONE CUSTOMER SERVICE AT 1-800-465-1904 FOR POSSIBLE ASSISTANCE.

PRODUCT LIABILITY

LEGAL FOCUS—BACKGROUND

In early 1993, the National Highway Traffic Safety Administration requested that General Motors recall 4.7 million pickup trucks equipped with side-saddle gasoline tanks. "Since the side-saddle trucks were introduced in 1973, their gas tanks have sometimes ripped open and exploded in side-impact collisions. The GM trucks are 2.4 times as likely as pickups made by Ford Motor Co. to be involved in deadly crashes with fires, NHTSA says. This translates into about five deaths a year out of more than 40,000 on the nation's highways." GM was the defendant and loser in two cases with multimillion-dollar product liability verdicts based on accusations of defective side-saddle gasoline tanks. In GM's defense, the NHTSA acknowledged that the vehicles passed all NHTSA safety tests in existence at the time the vehicles were manufactured. On December 2, 1994, four days before a public hearing to consider making the recall mandatory, the government dropped its recall effort. In exchange, GM agreed to spend $51 million on a variety of vehicle safety programs.[13]

Manufacturers and sellers of goods, including automobiles, can be held liable to consumers, users, and bystanders for physical harm or property damage caused by the goods. This liability is called **product liability.** Legal theories of product liability include the contract theory of warranty and dual tort theories of negligence and strict liability (Chapter 7).

product liability

A general area of law holding manufacturers and sellers of goods liable to buyers, users, and perhaps bystanders for harm caused when goods are defective.

Product Liability Based on Warranty

An important part of product liability law is the breach of warranty theory. A person suffering physical injury or injury to other property because of substandard goods can seek recovery based on breach of warranty. The general rule is that consumers, purchasers, and even users of goods can recover from any seller for losses resulting from breach of implied and express warranties. In other words, most parties who are injured by goods can sue any seller of the goods, including the manufacturer on warranty theory.

This extensive right to recover is an exception to the usual requirement that a party be in *privity* of contract (direct contract relationship) with another to sue on a contract theory. The UCC has addressed the problem of privity by eliminating the requirement of privity for certain types of injuries and for certain third party beneficiaries.

Product Liability Based on Negligence

In Chapter 7, we discussed *negligence* as a failure to use the degree of care that a reasonable, prudent person would have used under the circumstances. If a seller does not exercise reasonable care and injury results, he or she is liable for negligence. A manufacturer must exercise due care to make a product safe. This due care must be exercised in all aspects of manufacturing the product. It includes product design and selection of the materials to make the product. It includes appropriate production, assembly, and testing of the product. It includes placing adequate warnings on the label to inform the user of potential dangers of which he or she might not be aware. And it extends to the inspection and testing of any purchased products used in the final product sold by the manufacturer. The failure to exercise due care is negligence. A manufacturer is liable to any person who is injured by a negligently made (defective) product. The manufacturer is liable for harm regardless of whether a sale or a contract to sell was involved.

Product Liability Based on Strict Liability

Under strict liability (introduced in Chapter 7), persons are responsible for their products regardless of the intentions or the exercise of reasonable care. The doctrine of strict liability applies to manufacturers, wholesalers, and retailers (also processors, assemblers, packagers, bottlers, and distributors) of personal property. A product may be defective because of production errors, design deficiencies, improper packaging, or failure to warn of dangers or to provide safety devices or instructions. A seller of any product in a defective condition that is unreasonably dangerous is subject to liability for physical harm caused to the ultimate user or to his property if (1) the seller is in the business of selling such a product and (2) the product is expected to and does reach the user without substantial change from the condition in which it was sold. See Exhibit 10-2 for the requirements to prove strict product liability.

Thus, under this theory, in any action against a manufacturer or seller, the plaintiff need not show how the product became defective. The plaintiff must, however, show that at the time of the injury, the condition of the product was essentially the same as it was when it left the hands of the defendant manufacturer or seller. All courts extend the strict liability of manufacturers and other sellers to injured bystanders.

LEGAL FOCUS—PROBLEM

The motor of a car exploded, producing a cloud of steam. The steam caused a series of multiple collisions, since it prevented other drivers from seeing well. Is the automobile manufacturer liable for injuries caused by the explosion of the car's motor?

EXHIBIT 10-2: **Requirements of Strict Product Liability**

The basic requirements of strict product liability are as follows:

- The product is sold in a defective condition.

- The defendant is in the business of selling that product.

- The product is unreasonably dangerous to the user or consumer because of its defective condition.

- The plaintiff (who need not be the purchaser) must suffer physical harm to self or property by use or consumption of the product.

- The defective condition must be the proximate cause of the injury or damage.

- The goods were not substantially changed from the time sold to the time of the injury.

Yes, since the car motor was determined to be defective and the cause of the harm to the innocent third parties. Strict liability has also been expanded to include suppliers of parts and lessors of movable goods. Liability for personal injuries caused by defective goods extends also to those who lease such goods. Most courts hold that a leasing agreement creates an *implied warranty* that the leased goods will be fit for the duration of the lease. Under this view, if a Rent-a-Car Company leases an improperly maintained automobile, a passenger who is injured in an accident can sue the Rent-a-Car Company. (Liability here is based on the contract theory of warranty, not tort, because the lease is an ongoing contract.)

Frequently, a product injures a person because he or she did not use it carefully. Misconduct or misuse by a claimant can be a defense to reduce the claimant's recovery or to deny it altogether.

REGISTRATION OF MOTOR VEHICLES

The government requires that ownership of most types of motor vehicles be registered and that formal documents of ownership be properly executed. Similar requirements do not exist for most other types of personal property, such as stereos and backpacks (nor for guns, although that has been proposed by gun-control advocates).

Advantages of Registration

Registration provides a method by which a state government can ensure vehicle owner compliance with safety and environmental requirements. To be registered initially, the vehicle must comply with minimal safety and pollution standards governing brakes, lights, and exhaust emissions. Registration of ownership also ensures orderly transfer of title. By requiring presentation and release of the certificate of ownership signed by the seller, the buyer has a better assurance of receiving good title and becoming the true owner. If the vehicle is stolen, the certificate of ownership and registration facilitates identification and restitution to the rightful owner. If a vehicle is involved in an accident in which property is damaged and/or a person is injured or killed, vehicle license numbers help trace the party responsible and facilitate follow-up measures. The issuance and renewal of the certificate of registration also serves as a convenient means of raising tax revenues for a variety of purposes, including highway construction and maintenance. Moreover, annual motor vehicle registration lists also aid selection of jury panels and the collection of unpaid traffic fines.

Licensing and Registration Procedures

Generally, a state will issue two certificates to the owners of motor vehicles: a certificate of ownership, or title, showing who owns the vehicle; and a certificate of registration, permitting operation of the vehicle on the highways of the state. License plates, or annual renewal tags, are also issued in conjunction with the certificate of registration.

With a few exceptions, such as U.S. government vehicles, a motor vehicle is licensed in the state where it is usually driven. When you move to another state, your vehicle registration generally remains valid for a limited period of time (30 to 90 days) before a local vehicle registration and license is required. At the time of yearly license registration, states commonly provide for emissions control device inspections and sometimes vehicle safety inspections. Some states require that the primary driver of the vehicle offer proof of financial responsibility (e.g., through ownership of an automobile liability insurance policy) before vehicle license plates are renewed.

Special laws also govern the vehicle and driver when traveling in foreign countries; information about these laws should be obtained from the country where you intend to travel and reviewed with a knowledgeable travel agent before departure.

Many counties and cities require the registration and periodic licensing of bicycles. The money generated from bicycle licensure is commonly used to maintain records that facilitate the recovery and return of stolen bikes.

LEGAL FOCUS—PROBLEM

Kitty Horrigan was carefully riding her new imported British motorcycle along a city street when Dick Guarno negligently lost control of his automobile and crashed into her. Guarno now claims Horrigan was also guilty of negligence because she failed to register her motorcycle as required by law. Is it considered negligence to drive an unlicensed motor vehicle on a public road?

registered owner

The buyer of a car on credit, who, as the equitable owner, gets possession and use of the vehicle while making payments.

legal owner

An owner who has legal title, for example, as security for repayment of a loan or payment of the purchase price of real property or personal property, such as an automobile.

equitable owner

An owner who has possession and use of the property although someone else may retain the legal title.

No. Horrigan's failure to register her motorcycle had nothing to do with Guarno's negligence and will not prevent her from recovering damages for her injuries.[14] Horrigan is guilty of the infraction of driving an unregistered vehicle on a public street. Failure to sign title over to a new owner when delivering possession of a motor vehicle may leave the original owner liable to strangers who are injured by the motor vehicle in a later accident. Some states provide that the registered owner is liable (usually limited to some specified amount) for damage caused by the negligence of any authorized user of the vehicle.

Usually, a certificate of ownership of a newly purchased vehicle lists two owners: a **registered owner** and a **legal owner.** Most automobiles are purchased on credit, and the lender retains a security interest in the vehicle. The purchaser-borrower is the registered owner (also called the **equitable owner**), with an ownership interest in the vehicle to the extent that the loan has been paid. Persons who refer to their equity in a vehicle mean the difference between the automobile's market value and the amount still owed to the lender. The lender (or creditor), having advanced the purchase money or sold the car on credit, retains a security interest in the vehicle and remains the legal (technical) owner until the loan is paid in full. A legal owner is generally not responsible for the manner in which the equitable owner uses or misuses the vehicle. The legal owner is primarily concerned with timely monthly payments. The lender's singular interest is in protecting the value of the collateral, increasing the probability that the loan will be repaid in full. For protection in the event that the car is damaged or stolen, the lender (legal owner) requires the equitable owner to carry adequate collision and comprehensive automobile insurance. The former covers damages to the vehicle caused by collision, the latter covers theft of the vehicle or damages caused by vandals. Careful and socially responsible owners also carry liability insurance to protect themselves from liability for possible injuries to others.

Because a registered owner has potential tort liability, it is very important to change registration simultaneously with the transfer of the vehicle. Requirements for a valid transfer of registration vary from state to state. It is common to require both a signed transfer of a certificate of ownership ("pink slip") and a notification to the department of motor vehicles requesting a change in the registered owner of the vehicle. The seller should file the notice of change of ownership, transferring potential liability to the buyer along with the ownership.

Each automobile has a unique 17-character Vehicle Identification Number (VIN) found on vehicle dashboards and title documents. VIN numbers have enabled the creation of a new and useful national business. Carfax has created a national registry of historic information about most automobiles in the United States and Canada. Carfax claims a database of "two billion unique records compiled from hundreds of separate data sources including motor vehicle departments in the United States and Canada, vehicle inspection stations, auto auctions, fleet management and rental agencies, automobile manufacturers and fire and police departments." Use of the VIN information database can disclose the following critical information about a vehicle:

- Totaled in an accident/Salvaged
- Flood damage
- Odometer rollbacks
- Lemon histories
- Junked titles
- State emissions inspection results
- Lien activity
- Vehicle use (taxi, rental, lease, etc.)

WHEN AND HOW MAY AN AUTOMOBILE BE REPOSSESSED?

It is unusual for people to have sufficient cash to buy an automobile outright. Yet, sellers still wish to sell automobiles and buyers still wish to buy them. Article 9 of the UCC provides a way for sellers to grant credit with low risk. Payment is guaranteed, or *secured,* by the car being purchased by the debtor. This is a type of **secured transaction,** meaning any transaction regardless of its form that is intended to create a security interest in personal property.

The importance to the creditor of being a secured creditor cannot be overemphasized. State laws that protect debtors generally do not hamper secured creditors. They have a preferred position if the debtor becomes bankrupt. Business as we know it would not exist without secured transaction law.

If the debt is paid, full legal ownership is returned or transferred to the purchaser. If, however, the debt is not paid, the creditor may exercise a right to seize or repossess the vehicle. Failure to pay a credit debt is called **default.** After default, a secured creditor can sue to collect the balance due on the debt, or enforce a security interest in the car by any available judicial process. The most common remedy is to take back the collateral. The debtor may simply return the collateral at the request of the secured party or the creditor may surreptitiously confiscate the car. When the secured party seizes the collateral, care must be taken to assure that no *breach of the peace* (as determined by state law) occurs. In other words, the creditor or the creditor's agent cannot forcibly enter a debtor's home, garage, or place of business without the permission of the debtor.

Check out the services and prices available at the Carfax Web site **http://www.carfax.com/**

The Florida Attorney General's Office provides advice on "How to Protect Yourself: Automobile Repossession" at **http://legal.firn.edu/consumer/tips/tipautor.html**

secured transaction
Any transaction, regardless of form, that is intended to create a security interest in personal property.

default
Failure of a party to do what is legally required.

LEGAL FOCUS—PROBLEM

Max Fisher borrowed money from Acme Finance Company to purchase a car. Fisher gave Acme a security interest in the car to protect Acme from the possibility that Fisher would fail to pay his debt. After Fisher stopped making payments on the car, Acme sent Ben Travis to seize it. Travis sneaked onto Fisher's property in the dead of night and made his way up the driveway where the car was parked. Travis jimmied a window of the car, hot-wired it, and drove it off. Is this a lawful repossession?

It appears to be a lawful repossession, as there was no confrontation with Fisher and no breach of the peace. And although Travis did go onto Fisher's property, he did not forcibly enter any building. However, to avoid possible confrontations with defaulting debtors, most car repossessions occur when the car is parked on a street or in a parking lot.

The secured party can sometimes keep the goods in satisfaction of the debt by following strict notice requirements under the UCC. Alternatively, the secured party can resell the goods and apply the proceeds (money received from the sale) toward the debt. Proceeds from a sale of retaken collateral must be applied in the following order:

1. Reasonable expenses stemming from the retaking, holding, or preparing for sale are covered first. When authorized by law and if provided for in the agreement, these can include reasonable attorneys' fees and legal expenses.
2. Satisfaction of the balance of the debt owed to the secured party.
3. Payment to owners of other security interests who have made a written demand received by the secured party before the proceeds has been distributed.
4. Return of any surplus amount received from the sale to the debtor.

Often, after proper disposition of the collateral, the secured party has not collected all that is owed by the debtor. Unless otherwise agreed, the debtor may be sued for any deficiency.

The debtor may be able to exercise the right of *redemption* of the collateral. The right of redemption is the right to have the collateral returned to the debtor. Redemption obviously must occur before the secured party disposes of the collateral. The debtor can exercise the right of redemption by paying the underlying debt. All expenses related to the enforcement of the security interest by the secured party also must be paid.

DRIVING A MOTOR VEHICLE

WHY MUST DRIVERS BE LICENSED?

LEGAL FOCUS—PROBLEM

Colleen Callahan's license to drive had been revoked for proper cause. (She had been convicted of speeding on three occasions within eighteen months.) She resented this interference with her freedom of movement and decided to drive anyway—but with extra care to avoid any trouble. As luck would have it, while driving safely and in compliance with the rules of the road, another motorist negligently ran a red light and rammed into her car. Will her lack of a driver's license have any effect on civil and criminal court proceedings?

No and yes. Unless there is some cause-effect relationship between the lack of the driver's license and the accident, the lack of license is immaterial. Callahan's rights in a civil action for damages resulting from the accident are not affected by her lack of a driver's license. However, she would be guilty of the offense of driving without a license, and for this she could be fined and/or jailed.

Driving is a privilege, not a constitutionally protected right,[15] and is regulated by state or local government as an exercise of government police power.* Prospective drivers must demonstrate an ability to drive in traffic and must understand the rules of the road. A license to drive may be suspended or revoked for violating the rules of the road, or even for an inability to demonstrate financial responsibility after an accident. Demerit points are assigned for each infraction, and a person's license can be suspended or revoked if too many points have been accumulated in a specific time period. Point systems vary from state to state. Exhibit 10-3 shows an example of the South Dakota Driver's License Point System. Many states have much more complicated charts.

EXHIBIT 10-3: **South Dakota Point System**

South Dakota Point System
Effective July 1, 1986

Conviction	Points
Driving While Intoxicated	10[†]
Reckless Driving	8
Eluding/Attempting to Elude	6
Drag Racing	6
Failure to Yield Right of Way	4
Improper Passing	4
Driving Wrong Side of Roadway	4
Stop Sign/Light Violation	3
Other Moving Offenses	2

[†] State Law requires revocation of license for Driving While Intoxicated

Any operator who accumulates fifteen (15) points in any twelve (12) consecutive months, or 22 points in any 24 consecutive months is subject to Driver License suspension.

Periods of Suspension

First Suspension . . . . 60 Days Maximum
Second Suspension . . . . 6 Months Maximum
Subsequent Suspension . . . . 1 Year Maximum

Source: http://state.sd.us/dcr/dl/sddriver.html

---

* Some states use driver's license statutes as a means of regulating behavior not directly related to driving a vehicle. For example, Wisconsin allows any municipal court to suspend a driver's license for nonpayment of any fines. In Kentucky, students who quit high school or have an academic deficiency lose their right to drive unless this would cause a family hardship. S. Garfield, "What License for DMV," *Sacramento Bee*, 27 March 1994.

Auto insurance companies check government records for information about the driving records of people who apply for insurance or have policies with the company. The insurance companies routinely charge higher premiums or cancel coverage after one or more "moving" violations (an infraction based upon the car's motion). The individual must then purchase a minimum coverage policy at a premium price under what is called an *assigned-risk program*. Most states have an assigned-risk program under which insurance companies are required to sell insurance to high-risk drivers on a rotating basis. They are allowed to charge higher premiums to cover their risk.

Computer tracking has assisted some states in collecting payments for unpaid parking tickets. The department of government that renews vehicle registrations is kept informed by computer and simply withholds new license plates or tags until all fines are paid.

Generally, any competent adult may qualify for a driver's license upon passing a written test, a driving test, and a vision test. A minor of proper age (typically 16) may also qualify, but often must, in addition to the requirements for an adult, complete a driver education and/or driver training course. Several states have recently changed their laws on initial youth licensing to provide for a graduated licensing procedure consistent with driving schemes in New Zealand, Australia and Canada. The significant requirement of the model law is a mandatory learner permit for at least six months, followed by at least six months in an intermediate licensing phase restricting night driving.

Some states require that parents sign and verify a minor's application and consent to be responsible for harm caused by their child while driving on a highway. Fortunately for most parents, this liability is usually limited. The amount of liability is often tied to the state's financial responsibility laws (e.g., $15,000 for injury or death, payable to any one person, and $30,000 payable to any number of persons, plus $5,000 for property damage as the result of any one accident for which their minor child is found to be legally responsible).[16] The requirement that an owner purchase insurance may be mandated by statute; if not, prudence and concern for others who may be injured by a child's negligence would dictate that a parent purchase at least the minimum coverage.

Parental liability for a child's damages caused with motor vehicles deviates from the general rule that parents are not vicariously responsible for their child's torts. Of course, parents are liable if the wrongful conduct of the child was committed at the parent's command, or in the course of the parent's business. In recent years, some states have extended the motor vehicle exception to include limited liability of parents for the willful misconduct of minor children.[17] Even in states where statutes create this parental liability, the minor wrongdoer is likewise liable. Realistically, however, the minor usually lacks the financial resources to pay the injured victim. Moreover, in cases of negligence the minor could escape a heavy judgment by bankruptcy, unless drunken driving caused the accident.

WHAT STANDARD OF CARE DOES THE LAW PRESCRIBE FOR DRIVERS?

The standard of care necessary when operating a motor vehicle is one example of the rules of negligence discussed in Chapter 7. The duty to act as a reasonable person requires that you, whether on or off the highway, refrain from carelessly injuring others. The question always is, were you as careful as a hypothetical reasonable person would have been under all circumstances surrounding the event? This broad duty may be violated willfully or negligently. Comparatively few people injure others willfully, with deliberate intent to harm. Such conduct could be criminal, and could result in a civil action for punitive damages as well as compensatory damages. In one case, the court said:

http://

For a list of states that follow the model law, as well as a state-by-state rundown of Youth Driver Laws, see the Institute for Highway Safety site at **http://www.highwaysafety.org/**

Here there is testimony from which the jury could find that defendant saw plaintiff 196 feet away in the paved portion of the roadway, and neither slowed nor sounded his horn. There is also the testimony that defendant's car swerved toward plaintiff immediately before the impact. Thus the evidence could support a jury finding that defendant was guilty of willful or wanton misconduct.[18]

From time to time, most of us are careless. We fail to exercise reasonable care. We do not behave as an ordinary, prudent man, woman, or child of comparable age should behave under the same or similar circumstances. If someone is injured as a result of our negligence, we are generally liable for monetary damages. In the preceding case, there is some evidence of the intentional tort of battery.

Sometimes, of course, we may injure someone while we are acting without negligence or willful intent to harm. Then there is no liability. Such an injury could happen in a pure accident, a casualty that is sudden, unexpected, unforeseeable, and unplanned—perhaps the result of an unknown cause or the unpredictable result of a known cause. There is no liability, for example, when an injury results from a natural calamity (a violent storm) or from the victim's own carelessness (when a person, walking along while reading a paper, steps off a curb into a stream of traffic and is suddenly injured or even killed).

LEGAL FOCUS—PROBLEM

Robby Drexhage was driving on a freeway with his girlfriend, Karen DeWitt, at his side, bragging to her about his car and about himself as a "hot driver." Suddenly, without notice to her or signal to other drivers, he accelerated within seconds to 95 mph. Visible ahead, moving at different speeds in three lanes, were about a dozen other vehicles. Drexhage rapidly passed them all, weaving skillfully from outside to inside lanes and back again. There were no highway patrol officers in sight, he was not arrested, and he did not cause an accident. Has he breached any legal duty?

Yes. He breached his general duty to drive as an ordinary prudent person exercising reasonable care for the safety of the lives and property of others. He did not respect the rights of his date and all others on the highway. He breached specific duties to drive within the speed limits, to refrain from weaving in and out of traffic lanes, and to signal before changing lanes. Most criminal breaches of duty while driving go unpunished; fortunately, most such breaches do not cause injury to others. Drexhage committed no torts because there were no injured victims.*

MUST DRIVERS STOP AT ACCIDENT SCENES?

LEGAL FOCUS—PROBLEM

Gus Shikel, an expert in first aid, was driving along a lonely country road when he came upon the scene of a one-car accident. The wrecked vehicle had collided with a utility

---

* Although not stated in the example, the conduct of Drexhage's high-speed maneuvering probably caused serious apprehension of serious physical injury in the minds of other drivers and of DeWitt as well. These victims could sue Drexhage for the intentional tort of assault and, although there were no physical injuries, could recover damages for mental distress and possibly punitive damages as well.

pole. Inside were two adults and a child, all unconscious or in shock. One was bleeding profusely. Not wanting to get involved, Shikel drove on. Was he legally obliged to stop and render aid?

Not in most states. We visited the issue of strangers failing to help Kitty Genovese in Chapter 1 and David Cash failing to help a young girl in deadly peril in Chapter 2. Generally, the law does not require one to be a good neighbor. The victims were strangers to whom Shikel legally owed no duty. The same result would apply in most states if Shikel were a medical doctor. Shikel's retreat is likely an ethical violation, but not a legal one. However, if Shikel had in any way caused or contributed to the accident (as by drifting across the center line and forcing the oncoming driver into defensive maneuvers that resulted in the crash), he would be obligated to stop and would be criminally and civilly responsible for failure to do so.

In any event, if he does stop—and one hopes that he would—and renders first aid, under the common law he has the duty to provide help with reasonable care under emergency situations. Conceivably, if one stops and renders aid, injured persons could sue the person providing assistance if that person failed to exercise reasonable care and thus aggravated the injuries. Such lawsuits are rare and recovery rarer still but they create the anomaly that ethical behavior creates a legal peril that unethical behavior does not.

As discussed in Chapter 7, most states have specially enacted **Good Samaritan statutes** to shield volunteers from actions for ordinary negligence. North Carolina has a typical statute, stating that no person shall be liable for damages for injuries or death claimed to result from the rendering of first aid or emergency healthcare treatment when the circumstances require prompt decisions and actions, and when the necessity is "... so reasonably apparent that any delay ... would seriously worsen the physical condition or endanger the life ... " of the patient.[19] As stated in Chapter 7, immunity is not available when the act is gross negligence, wanton conduct, or intentional wrongdoing. Nor does the statute relieve persons of liability for damages "... while rendering healthcare services in the normal and ordinary course of a business or profession."[20]

DOES A TRAFFIC CITATION PROVE CIVIL LIABILITY FOR AN ACCIDENT?

LEGAL FOCUS—PROBLEM

Kevin Harper was driving on the wrong side of a two-lane highway when he was involved in a head-on collision with Lisa Bowden. Bowden was proceeding legally in the opposite direction. Harper was cited by the state patrol for violation of the vehicle code. Is he guilty of negligence *per se* (Latin: "of itself") because he was apparently violating a statute at the time?

Probably. **Negligence *per se*** means that proof of the act establishes the duty. Violation of a statute raises a *prima facie* (Latin: "at first sight") **presumption** or inference of negligence. Presumptions are important rules of which permits a court to assume a fact is true it is shown by a greater weight of evidence that assumed truth is disproved. If the plaintiff proves that the statute was violated and caused the accident, and the defendant introduces

---

Good Samaritan statute

Statute that protects volunteers from liability for ordinary negligence while aiding persons in need.

---

negligence *per se*

(a) The unexcused violation of a statute or ordinance that is automatically deemed to be negligent conduct without argument or proof as to the particular surrounding circumstances. (b) Certain conduct that is deemed negligent because of its obvious breach of duty.

---

presumption

A rule of law permitting one to assume a fact is true until such time as there is a greater weight of evidence which disproves or outweighs the assumed fact.

no contrary evidence, then the defendant is negligent. Violation of the statute must bear some relationship to the accident and be the cause in fact and proximate cause of the accident. For instance, violation of a statute requiring the driver to be licensed would not bear any relationship to Kevin's accident and would not be its cause. However, violation of a statute established to protect against driving the wrong way down a road and injuring others driving on the proper side of the road would be negligence *per se.* That very type of harm occurred, and it appears Kevin is liable.

Although difficult to do, a presumption of negligence can be rebutted by proof of excuse or justification. It is possible that Kevin diverted his car because of conditions beyond his control (such as an object in the road, an unforeseeable failure of his steering mechanism, a sudden heart attack, or an illegal action by another car squeezing by on his right side).

ARE OWNERS LIABLE FOR NEGLIGENCE OF OTHER DRIVERS?

Clearly an owner-driver is liable for injuries to others caused by his or her own negligent driving. Under the principle of **vicarious liability** (liability for acts of another), the owner may also be liable for harm caused when someone else is the driver, if one of the following conditions applies:

vicarious liability

The responsibility of one person for the wrongful acts of another.

- The driver is the employee or agent of the owner, and is acting within the scope of his or her employment. See the discussion of the doctrine of *respondeat superior* in Chapter 13.
- The owner is negligent in lending or giving the car to someone who is not qualified to drive or is known by the owner to be an unsafe driver. The owner is also negligent if he or she lends or gives an automobile to another in a condition (e.g., with faulty brakes) that makes it unsafe to drive.
- In a number of states,* owners are responsible whenever a member of their immediate family or household drives and a third party is injured because of the negligence of the driver. This is called the **family purpose doctrine.**
- In several states, parents or guardians who sign a minor's application for a driver's license become liable for damage caused by the minor's negligent operation of the vehicle. As discussed earlier, there are usually dollar limits to the amount of this liability.
- Many different variations and combinations of state statutes impose liability when an owner permits another to use the vehicle (called *permissive use*). In several states, owners are liable when a person they allow to use the vehicle negligently injures a third party.† In a few states, owners are liable only for permissive use when they have furnished a car to a minor who negligently injures a third party.** As noted earlier, there often are limits on the extent of liability under these statutes.

family purpose doctrine

A law in some states that holds the owner of a motor vehicle vicariously responsible whenever a member of his or her immediate family or household drives and a third party is injured because of the negligence of the driver.

If the driver is an employee of the owner and is acting within the scope of employment, the owner-employer is liable without limit under the doctrine of *respondeat superior.* A driver, even though an employee, is always liable (without limit) for his or her own torts.

LEGAL FOCUS—PROBLEM

Walter Johnson was driving down Main Street on his way to deliver a package for Race-horse Delivery Service. Unfortunately, Johnson was distracted for a second and ran into the rear of Marisa Woode's new Saturn automobile. Luckily, Woode was not hurt, but the car was damaged and repairs cost $3,000. Who is legally responsible for the harm to Woode's car?

Johnson is, of course, liable for his own negligence. Walter Johnson was also an employee of Racehorse and he injured another while driving the automobile on company business. As Johnson was within the scope of his employment, Racehorse Delivery Service is also liable under the doctrine of *respondeat superior*. Woode can sue both or either Johnson and Racehorse, but she can collect her actual damages only once.

LEGAL FOCUS—PROBLEM

Karl Mellon parked his car in the street and ran into the post office to mail a parcel. In his haste, he forgot to remove the ignition key. When he returned, the car was gone. The police later reported that his stolen car had been in a collision with a motorcycle, injuring its rider, Joanna Denton. Denton later sued Mellon. Is he liable?

No.[21] Although leaving the key in an unattended car is negligent and, in some states, a violation of a statute, the owner has no duty to protect the public from unexpected and illegal activities of thieves. The theft and negligent use of stolen property is an intervening and supervening act. A contrary argument can be advanced that Mellon's carelessness created a danger and a result that was predictable. However, most states have rejected such an extension of liability to a careless automobile owner theft victim.

LEGAL FOCUS—CASE

Luella Wilson, a 91-year-old Vermont grandmother, enjoyed her own home, friends, and family and had more than $500,000 in the bank. She lent her grandnephew, Willard Stuart, money to buy a car. After a night of drug and alcohol use, he was involved in a serious accident. A passenger in his car, Mark Vince, was paralyzed from the waist down and lost a leg. Stuart had no driver's license, no assets, and no automobile insurance. The victim sued Wilson, alleging that she knew Stuart did not have a license and used drugs and that she was therefore negligent in lending him the money to buy the car. Luella did not appear at the trial because she was ill. What was the verdict?

Vince v. Wilson, 151 Vt. 425, 561 A.2d 103 (Vermont, 1989).

The jury held for the plaintiff against Luella Wilson in the amount of $950,000. This case of negligent lending attracted considerable attention and was appealed. The Vermont Supreme Court did not reverse the trial court verdict, but did order a new trial to determine whether the automobile dealership and the salesperson who sold Stuart the car should share Wilson's liability. At the new trial, the parties reached an out-of-court settlement, with the plaintiff dismissing his claim against Wilson.[22] The out-of-court settlement relieved Wilson of her liability, but it did not change the rule of law in this case, which found liability for a person other than a driver in a case of negligent entrustment (loan of the car or in this case the means to get the car).

A common extension of liability to persons who neither own nor were driving the car involved in an accident occurs under a **dramshop statute,** a state law making it a crime for a tavern proprietor or employee to serve intoxicants to an obviously drunk patron or someone under the legal drinking age. Injured victims of accidents caused by these patrons have successfully sued the bars and restaurants when they can prove that a dramshop statute was violated.[23] A few cases have found liability against social hosts of parties where intoxicating beverages or drugs were served and shortly afterward the guests were involved in automobile accidents.[24] Wisdom and prudence dictate: If you drink, don't drive. Arranging for a designated driver, one who does not drink alcoholic beverages or take any mood-altering substances, avoids the problem. Furthermore, as a host or hostess, do not have "open bars" or serve drinks of alcoholic beverages to the point of intoxication of your guests.

ARE DRIVERS LIABLE FOR INJURIES TO GUESTS IN THEIR CARS?

Generally, a driver has a responsibility not only to persons outside the vehicle but also to passengers inside the vehicle. The duty is that of ordinary and usual care for the safety of others. Issues of comparative negligence and assumption of the risk must also be considered when appropriate. In years past a driver usually could not be held liable to guest passengers for injuries caused by the driver's ordinary negligence, because of special protective statutes called **guest statutes.** Today, only a minority of states have retained guest statutes.[25] Idaho's guest statute is representative of the content of such protections for motor vehicle drivers.

> *LIABILITY OF MOTOR OWNER TO GUEST*
>
> *No person transported by the owner or operator of a motor vehicle as his guest without payment for such transportation shall have a cause for damages against such owner or operator or for injuries, death or loss, in case of accident, unless such accident shall have been intentional on the part of the said owner or operator or caused by his intoxication or gross negligence.*
>
> *The provisions of this section shall not relieve a public carrier or any owner or operator of a motor vehicle while the same is being demonstrated to a prospective purchaser of responsibility for injuries sustained by a passenger being transported by such public carrier or by such owner or operator.*[26]

Proponents of guest statutes argue that when the drivers are insured, there can be collusion in staged accidents to defraud insurance companies. Even in the absence of fraud, a negligent driver who is a relative (e.g., a parent) of the guest (e.g., a child) who receives dollar damages would indirectly profit from his or her own negligence. Guest statutes also prevent possible fraudulent claims by guests who may be the only witnesses to a single-car accident. Texas courts have upheld the Texas guest statute, holding that the legislature is justified in seeking to prevent possible fraudulent claims against insurers.[27]

As social views have changed, most states have abolished guest statutes. The rationale for change has been that the recovery will probably come from an insurance company, and

dramshop statute

A state law making it a crime for a tavern proprietor or employee to serve intoxicants to an obviously inebriated customer.

guest statutes

Law that pertains to guests of a driver of a motor vehicle. In some states a guest cannot sue the driver if injured, unless the driver is guilty of intoxication, willful misconduct, or gross negligence that causes the accident and resulting injury or death. In other states a guest may sue the driver for ordinary negligence.

if you buy insurance to compensate strangers whom you might injure, you probably would want to have the same protection for relatives and friends who are your guests.

Even when a state has a guest statute, liability exists when the plaintiff can prove that death or injury resulted from intoxication or willful misconduct of the driver. Thus, in our earlier example, Luella Wilson's nephew Willard Stuart, who was high on drugs and alcohol, was not protected from the lawsuit by a guest statute. He was, however, judgment-proof, which led the injured plaintiff to seek other possible defendants who were not judgment-proof.

DRIVING UNDER THE INFLUENCE (DUI)

People who drive under the influence (**DUI**)* of mind-altering chemicals are a major social problem in the United States. Drunk driving is the major cause of accidents on the highways and is an ingredient in most fatal accidents. The NHTSA reports that of the 38,386 vehicle occupant fatalities suffered in 2001, 17,488 were alcohol related. In addition, DUI has been identified as the crime most often committed by otherwise law-abiding persons. "The vast majority of Americans occasionally drive after drinking. Alcoholics who have access to a car habitually drive after drinking."[28] "About 1.5 million arrests are made annually for driving under the influence of alcohol or narcotics (1 in every 121 licensed drivers)."[29]

Several organizations try to protect the rights of people who are victims of such criminal activity. These organizations include MADD (Mothers Against Drunk Driving) and SADD (Students Against Drunk Driving). They have had a significant effect on public attitudes and on the enactment of laws concerning driving under the influence. In the past decade, all fifty states have joined in making twenty-one the minimum age for purchasing alcohol legally. The penalties for DUI have increased with longer jail sentences, driver's license revocations, and bigger fines.

LEGAL FOCUS—PROBLEM

Several friends were at Lawrence Harberson's apartment celebrating the end of the school year. Beer was flowing freely. Harberson, a 260-pound star tackle on the college football team, had just finished his first 12-ounce beer when he opened a second. Waving the beer can, he jumped into his car and rammed the pedal to the metal, burning tire rubber as he sped off to collect his girlfriend Marcie Jasper at the nearby airport. While en route, he was stopped by a highway patrol officer for exceeding the posted speed limit by 20 mph or more. Is he also guilty of driving under the influence of alcohol?

Probably not, although he could be required to demonstrate his sobriety. One beer is not likely to intoxicate or adversely influence a 260-pound person's body mechanisms. However, he could be cited for carrying an open container of alcoholic beverage in his car. It is also true that alcohol affects persons, genders, and those using medications differently.

When stopped under suspicion of intoxication, a driver is required to submit to a **field sobriety test.** It is a preliminary test at the scene, where the driver may be asked to walk a straight line, stand on one foot, or perform some other similar act. A person who appears

DUI

Violating the law by driving while one's judgment and ability to react are impaired by alcohol or other mind-altering drugs.

http://

"Mothers Against Drunk Driving (MADD) is more than just a bunch of angry moms. We're real people, moms, dads, young people, and other individuals just trying to make a difference. We are determined to stop drunk driving and to support victims of this violent crime."

http://www.madd.org/home/

http://

The National Clearinghouse for Alcohol and Drug Information provides an alcohol impairment chart at http://www.health.org/nongovpubs/bac-chart/

field sobriety test

A simple test used to determine the reactions of a motor vehicle driver who is suspected of driving under the influence of alcohol or another drug. The test is administered at the scene of the arrest.

* Also referred to as Driving While Intoxicated (DWI)

intoxicated may be taken to a police station and asked for a sample of breath, blood, or urine to be analyzed for alcoholic or drug content.

Refusing to submit to a chemical test by exercising your constitutional right against self-incrimination may cause forfeiture of your driver's license. Every person who accepts a license to drive impliedly consents to sobriety tests upon police suspicion, with probable cause, of the driver's intoxication. The driver has a right to a proper warning of the possible effect of the law, and a right to a court or administrative hearing, before the license is revoked.

The percentage of drugs in the blood system necessary to classify a person as DUI has been lowered in most states in recent years. In most states driving with a blood-alcohol concentration of 0.8 or above satisfies the crime; a diminishing number require .10 or more. It need not be proven that the driver is intoxicated. Driving with a blood-alcohol content level at or above the stated percentage is a violation of law and therefore cannot be contested. Most states have per se laws. *Per se* is Latin for by itself. In other words it need not be shown that a person is impaired; instead, having the prohibited blood alcohol content while driving completes the crime. The means of measurement varies, but almost all states provide for blood, breath, or urine tests or some combination of tests. In several states, the percentage standard is much lower for minors than for adults, and sometimes evidence of any consumption of alcoholic beverage leads to an automatic suspension of the driver's license.

Criminal penalties for driving under the influence can be severe. In a representative state, a jail sentence of from two days to six months is imposed if one is convicted two or more times for drunk driving within five years; a judge who fails to send the defendant to jail must write a formal opinion justifying such leniency. It is also common that a first conviction leads to an automatic driver's license suspension of 90 to 120 days. A fine of from $500 to $2,500 or more is also assessed. Under certain circumstances, the vehicle may be impounded or even forfeited. In addition, the defendant's automobile insurance premiums will rise. A single DUI can lead to cancellation of insurance and an inability to rent an automobile when out of town or on vacation for up to three years after conviction. It is clear that the cost of DUI starts at about $5,000 the first year (not including court costs and attorney's fees) and continues for several years while your new insurance company surcharges coverage premiums.* Deaths resulting from a DUI can subject the wrongdoer to various degrees of homicide charges—usually vehicular homicide, but convictions have included second-degree murder.

It should be noted that the legal tolerance of drinking while boating has lessened in many states in recent years. In 1998, Georgia's new tougher boating law provides for a loss of boating privileges, up to a $1,000 fine, and one year of jail upon conviction of the first offense.

http://

State law facts regarding DUI/DWI laws as of January 2003 can be found at **http://www.hwysafety.org/ safety_facts/state_laws/ dui.htm**

http://

We have discussed the judicial and administrative expenses and penalties in DUI cases. You can examine some of the nonjudicial costs of a DUI **http://alcoholism.about .com/library/weekly/ aa082797.htm**

LEGAL FOCUS—BACKGROUND

Unfortunately, bad decision-making by people who drink is not confined to automobile drivers. Two pilots, Thomas Cloyd and Christopher Hughes, just wanted to carry their coffee through the security checkpoint but security personnel had other plans. While

---

* The California State Automobile Association estimated at least $5,000 for a first-time DUI. Included in the costs is the fine (typically $390 to $1,700), attorney's fees, courts' assessment fees, raised insurance premiums, court-ordered educational programs, and vehicle and impoundment fees. *Via*, November/December 1998, p. 11. Coors' Sacramento, California, Drive Sober Campaign estimated a similar figure in this ad: "Your first DUI: 1 hour in cuffs, 4 hours in jail, 3 hours getting your car back, 2 days at the DMV, 2 days community service, 15 weeks of DUI classes, 4 months without your license, 2 nights DUI victim impacts sessions, 7 years with 2 points on driving record, 3 years probation, plus $5,249 in fees, assessments, and fines." *Sacramento News and Review*, 17 December 1998.

discussing their differences security smelled alcohol on their breath. The pilots continued to the America West plane but air traffic controllers ordered the aircraft back to
the gate before it could take off on a scheduled flight to Phoenix. They were arrested
after tests showed Cloyd's blood-alcohol level was 0.091% and Hughes' was 0.084%.
Both pilots have had their licenses revoked by the Federal Aviation Administration and
were fired by America West. They are awaiting trial for operating an aircraft while intoxicated and driving under the influence.

"The Almost Drunken Skies," ABCnews.com, July 1, 2002.

MUST OWNERS MAINTAIN THEIR VEHICLES IN GOOD REPAIR?

Owners of motor vehicles are legally required to maintain them in safe operating condition. One appellate court stated this generally applicable duty in the following words:

> *Generally speaking, it is the duty of one driving a motor vehicle along a public high-
> way to see that it is properly equipped so that it may be at all times controlled to the end
> that it be not a menace to the safety of others or of their property. The law requires that
> such a vehicle be equipped with brakes adequate to its quick stopping when necessary
> for the safety of its occupants or of others, and it is equally essential that it be main-
> tained in such a condition as to mechanical efficiency and fuel supply that it may not
> become a menace to, or an obstruction of, other traffic by stopping on the road. But if
> the person in charge of such vehicle has done all that can be reasonably expected of a
> person of ordinary prudence to see that his vehicle is in proper condition, and an unfore-
> seen failure of a part of his equipment occurs, it does not necessarily follow that he must
> be deemed guilty of negligence as a matter of law.*[30]

A driver is not liable for injuries suffered by strangers from an unforeseeable mechanical
failure of his or her automobile. Furthermore, if the driver is injured, he or she might
recover damages from the manufacturer (or an intermediary) on the theory of strict product liability. The driver must prove that the defendant placed the product (automobile or
component part thereof) on the market, knowing that it was to be used without inspection
for defects by the consumer. The driver additionally must show personal injury as a result
of a defect in the design or manufacture of the article while it was being used properly.
There can be no recovery, however, if the driver was aware that such defect made the article unsafe for its intended use.

LEGAL FOCUS—PROBLEM

When Alberta Ayers stopped for a cup of coffee at the Summit Cafe, she mentioned a
"short pedal" on the hydraulic brakes of her heavy-duty truck. She had to "pump" the
brake pedal to get a braking response. Nevertheless, after her coffee break she proceeded down the mountain road until the brakes did not hold and the rig went out of
control, ultimately careening over the side of the road and landing 200 feet below. Was
the manufacturer or seller of the truck or of the brakes liable?

No. Even if the brakes were defective in design or manufacture, Ayers knew of the condition and was negligent by returning to the highway, especially in the mountains without
a checkup, adjustment, or repair.

Both federal and state governments assist owners by prescribing a variety of safety standards for motor vehicles.[31] Not only are manufacturers required to manufacture motor vehicles meeting minimum safety standards, but also in recent years many states (through court opinions and legislative statutes) have increased the responsibilities of drivers for their own safety.[32] The most common personal safety equipment is the mandatory use of safety seat belts. With respect to motorcycles, protective headgear must be worn while driving.

The driver of a rented vehicle is generally not responsible for the vehicle's condition, except for obvious and/or known dangers that create an unreasonable risk of harm to the driver or others. Examples of such dangers include missing headlights or brakes that obviously need to be adjusted or repaired. The operator of a leased vehicle, unlike a rented vehicle, is treated the same as an owner-driver.

ARE THERE SPECIAL LAWS FOR RENTED VEHICLES?

When you rent an automobile, you contract for the use rather than the ownership of personal property. The legal term for this relationship is a *bailment,* which, as explained earlier, is a temporary right of possession of the goods of another. In a sale or a gift, title is transferred; in a bailment, possession is transferred, but not title. Any personal property can be bailed and automobile rentals are bailments. The rental car company is a **bailor,** and the renter a **bailee.** Although bailment law has very well-defined rights and duties, the most important determinant of the relationship is the language of the rental agreement, which is the controlling written contract.

Most bailments are created by agreement, but not necessarily by contract. For example, if you loan your bicycle to a friend, a bailment is created. However, as there is no payment it is not a contract. Most bailments are, however, based on contract (e.g., the delivery of your sleeping bag or dress to the cleaners for dry cleaning).

bailor

One who transfers temporary possession of personal property to another, the bailee.

bailee

One who rightfully receives temporary possession of personal property from another, the bailor, in a bailment.

Elements of a Bailment

For a transfer of property to be a bailment, the following three conditions must be met.
1. **Personal property** Bailments involve only personal property. A bailment of your luggage is created when it is taken to an airline. The airline passenger is not subject to a bailment. Real property cannot be bailed; thus, renting a house is not a bailment.
2. **Delivery of possession** The property must be transferred to the bailee. There are two requirements for effective delivery. (1) The bailee must be given both exclusive possession and control over the property, and (2) the bailee *must knowingly* accept the personal property.

LEGAL FOCUS-PROBLEM

Millie Banks took Billie Saven out to dinner at an expensive restaurant. Upon arrival at the restaurant, Banks turned over her car to the parking attendant, who parked the car. Did a bailment of Bank's car occur?

Yes, valet parking is usually a bailment. Self-parking is not. The difference is who controls the car keys. If Banks parked the car herself, locked it, and kept the keys, it is considered a lease of space. The owner of the parking lot is a *lessor* and Banks a *lessee* of the space. Self-service parking lots are generally not considered bailments because the parking lot owners do not take control or possession of the automobile. Even if a bailment exists, the bailee often will limit or disclaim liability by posting signs and including disclaimer language on the claim ticket.

3. **Bailment agreement.** A bailment agreement can be *express* or *implied.* A written agreement is usually not required for a bailment. It is, however, a good idea to have one when valuable property is involved. Remember that not all bailment agreements are contracts. If you loan your next door neighbor your hedge trimmer, it is an agreement and a bailment, but it is not a contract unless the neighbor pays for the use.

A bailment agreement expressly or impliedly expects the return of the property to the bailor. An agreement might provide for the return of the property to a third person, or for disposal by the bailee. The bailee is expected also to return the identical goods given by the bailor. In certain types of bailments only equivalent property must be returned, for example a bailment of *fungible,* uniformly identical, goods.

LEGAL FOCUS-EXAMPLE

Holman stores his grain (*fungible goods*) in Joe's Warehouse. At the end of the storage period, the warehouse does not have to return the exact same grain. The warehouse bailee must, however, return grain of the same *type, grade,* and *quantity.*

Laws relating to rental car bailments vary significantly among the states, but two rules are uniform. The first uniform rule is that the rental car company has a duty to provide a vehicle that is safe to use and in good driving condition. A bailee has rights both in contract and tort if harmed because of a breach of this duty. Second, the bailor has a right to expect the car to be returned in the same condition in which it was rented, minus ordinary wear and tear. The bailee is responsible for harm to the car even if it was not the bailee's fault. Rental companies suggest special collision insurance (called *collision damage waivers*) to cover this risk. As this insurance is very costly (rental companies make a sizeable profit with this add-on fee), many states have restricted rental car company practices promoting such special coverage.[33] If you have collision insurance on your own automobile, your policy typically will cover this risk (minus the deductible) on any rental car (however, check your specific policy to determine your specific coverage). Credit card companies often provide collision waiver coverage as an important fringe benefit for their customers. Of course, for the benefit to apply, the customer must use the credit card when renting the vehicle.

LEGAL FOCUS—PROBLEM

Joua Landini landed at Metropolitan airport and walked over to the Maxi Car Rental agency to pick up his reserved auto. After he provided his license and credit card to the rental company, the agent refused to rent him an automobile. She told Landini that the two speeding violations found when she did a computer search of his driving disqualified him from renting from Maxi. Landini insists that Maxi rent him a car, arguing that the search was an invasion of his privacy.

The rental company has a legitimate interest in public information, which lets it determine the level of risk it takes when renting to a particular customer. If the renter has certain types of recent traffic violations or a certain violation "point level," the rental company may refuse to rent or may charge a higher rental amount. This has become a common business practice of rental car companies, and neither court case nor legislation has yet successfully curbed this practice.

ARE THERE SPECIAL LAWS FOR COMMON CARRIERS?

A **common carrier** of passengers agrees to transport, in exchange for money, anybody applying for passage, assuming there is available space and no legal justification for refusal.[34] Bus lines, taxicabs, railroads, airlines, and subway systems are all classified as common carriers. Common carriers are required to be licensed and are regulated by federal, and sometimes state, agencies. Regulations usually cover routes, safety measures, operating methods, rates, passenger contracts and treatment, and luggage handling. At the heart of the relationship are two legal concepts: (1) specific obligations or duties are owed to passengers created by a contract of transport and (2) general duties are also owed as a matter of public policy. These general duties are independent of private contract and arise from the carrier's position as a public utility.[35] These common carrier legal duties are very important for passenger safety and baggage care.

LEGAL FOCUS—CASE

Mark Oglesby and Mark Finken, both seventh graders, were riding on the Milwaukee County bus. A group of about twenty youths stormed the bus, some entering through its windows. The hoodlums demanded money of Finken; when he refused, they beat him. Oglesby and Finken eventually were able to flee the scene. During the entire course of events, the bus driver, although watching in her rear-view mirror, made no attempt to intervene. Did the bus driver breach a duty owed Oglesby and Finken?

Kasanof v. Embry-Riddle Co., 157 Fla. 677, 26 So. 2d 889 (Florida, 1946).

Yes. Common carriers are responsible for the safety of their passengers. Because common carriers are open to everyone, the public reasonably expects to be safe. Although the carriers are not insurers of the passengers' safety, their duty is described as either high, or the highest, duty of care. This duty includes inspection of equipment, safe means of access and departure, use of protective restraints such as seat belts in airlines and possibly even in buses,[36] and protection from fellow passengers.[37] In the preceding case, the court stated, "It was reasonable to infer . . . that the assault would not have occurred had the driver ordered the youths off the bus for their rowdiness, warned them, or notified them she was summoning the police."[38]

A common carrier is also responsible for the safe transport and return of a passenger's baggage, as covered by that passenger's ticket or fare. If there is no extraordinary excuse (such as confiscation of the baggage by police), the carrier is responsible for loss or damage to the baggage, without proof of fault. Statutes regulating baggage transport typically provide that although liability may not be eliminated, it may be limited by contract to certain defined amounts. Such partial disclaimers are allowed as long as the passenger is given the right to have the monetary limit raised after paying an additional fee. As baggage transport contracts generally include a disclaimer, it behooves the passenger to protect valuable goods through a suitable declaration of higher value and payment of an additional fee.

http://

The driving record requirements at the world's largest automobile rental company can be accessed here
http://www.hertz.com/ servlet/ByrServlet? MOVE_TO=3

common carrier

A carrier that transports for payment all persons who apply for passage, assuming space is available and there is no legal excuse for refusal.

http://

A discussion of airline passenger rights can be found at
http://flyana.com/index.html

A recurring complaint about airline travel is the "bumping" of passengers (leaving them behind) with confirmed reservations. Airlines do not guarantee their schedules and, following deregulation of the industry in the 1980s, many consumer protections for passengers have been left to carrier discretion. Department of Transportation regulations do require airline companies to ask passengers for volunteers to stay behind for compensation. However, the regulations do not specify compensation, which is up to airline discretion. If sufficient volunteers are found, the problem is solved; if not, then there are several possibilities depending on when the bumped passengers will ultimately arrive at their destination. Although there are some mandated rules for bumping passengers, much of what the airline does will be its own choice.

WHAT IS THE FINANCIAL RESPONSIBILITY LAW?

LEGAL FOCUS—PROBLEM

Jill Searle and Bob Ranney were in an automobile collision that occurred when their speeding cars collided at the campus entrance on the way to morning classes at Nashville University. The collision created a terrible traffic jam, and several hundred students missed their first morning class. Many regarded the event as a festive occasion because no one was hurt and everyone had an excuse from class. Each car sustained at least $500 worth of damage. Searle and Ranney notified their respective insurance companies and relaxed with the thought that both had adequate coverage. Have they overlooked anything important?

financial responsibility law

A statute requiring that after an automobile accident of specified severity, any driver not covered by insurance must post specified cash or equivalent bond.

http://

Read about the Iowa Motor Vehicle Financial Responsibility Law at **http://www.dot.state.ia.us/ mvd/ods/financial.htm**

Yes. Although proof of insurance is important and notifying their insurance companies is wise, they must also notify the state about the accident. Tennessee, like most states, has a **financial responsibility law.** Such laws require that within a set period each driver involved in an automobile accident, regardless of fault, must provide proof of financial responsibility and also report to the state any accident that causes more than a modest amount of property damage (such as $1,000) or in which someone is injured (no matter how slightly) or killed. The financial responsibility requirement is usually met by purchase of a minimum amount of automobile insurance. Drivers who do not have automobile insurance usually must either pay a cash deposit or post a bond. The cash deposit or bond (a form of guarantee) is proof of financial responsibility.

Failure to report a serious accident (e.g., $1,000 damage, injury, or death) can lead to suspension or revocation of your driver's license. If you do not have insurance and cannot establish financial responsibility, your driver's license will be suspended in most states until proof is presented. The minimum financial responsibility requirements vary among the states. A common required amount is $25,000 for injury to or death of any one person in any one accident, $50,000 for injury to or death of more than one person, and $10,000 for property damage. Many states have compulsory insurance laws in addition to financial responsibility laws. All states have at least one or the other.[39] Insurance salespersons and brokers should know your state's minimum coverage requirements.

Financial responsibility requirements, as the name suggests, are designed to provide some assurance that persons who use the highways and negligently injure others will pay resulting claims. Damages awarded by a court may far exceed the statutory responsibility limits. Furthermore, since financial responsibility need not be demonstrated until after an accident has occurred, there is no guarantee that any particular driver is complying with the law. Indeed, socially irresponsible persons who violate the rights of others are the least likely to buy the needed insurance. Even states that require motor vehicle insurance are left with many liability issues unresolved. The minimum coverage required is typically low, unregistered (and uninsured) automobiles are still driven, and unlicensed (and uninsured) drivers still drive.

LEGAL FOCUS—PROBLEM

Negligently backing his car and house trailer from a parking spot across a mountain road, Malcolm Maclede caused a major accident in which three persons were seriously injured and two $27,000 automobiles were totally wrecked. Medical expenses alone exceeded $70,000 within a year, and one victim had to be confined to a bed, presumably for the rest of her life. All three victims were adults with families, and none could work for a year or longer. Maclede had the minimum insurance coverage required by the financial responsibility law. Is Maclede guilty of a crime? Will he lose all his assets in civil litigation? Can he escape punishment through bankruptcy?

Maclede is not guilty of a crime because he was not criminally negligent. If he had been intoxicated, and had any of the victims died he would have faced manslaughter and possibly even murder charges (see Chapter 6 for examples). He will, no doubt, lose all of his assets not otherwise subject to preexisting creditors' claims, unless he is very wealthy. He can escape his civil liability through bankruptcy, but all his nonexempt assets could be seized. **Exempt assets** are assets that every debtor is permitted to keep, such as an inexpensive automobile, personal clothes and effects, tools of his or her trade, a television, and a residential homestead. The moral is that all drivers should carry adequate public liability coverage for bodily injury to others as a matter of prudent self-interest as well as of social justice and concern for other human beings.

exempt assets

Property that a debtor can protect against seizure resulting from execution of judgment by a judgment creditor or a trustee in a bankruptcy distribution.

Purchasing Automobile Insurance

Owners of a car absolutely, unequivocally, and without reservation need to protect themselves against losses that may arise from, for example, a collision, vandalism, or theft, and especially against the overwhelming losses that could arise from injury to oneself or others as a result of an auto accident. The typical family automobile insurance policy covers the named insured (and spouse, if any) and residents of the same household (including children, even when they are temporarily away from home, as when attending a distant school). The policy also covers other persons when they are using the vehicle with the permission of the named insured. Persons in the household other than the named insured cannot give permission to others to use the family car with continuing coverage by the policy. When an insured person drives another owner's car with permission, the driver's policy provides additional supplementary coverage if the owner's policy is insufficient to cover a valid claim or judgment.

http://

A short discussion of various forms of automobile insurance coverage terms can be found at **http://www.insurance.ca. gov/index.html**

WHAT TYPES OF AUTOMOBILE INSURANCE ARE AVAILABLE?

LEGAL FOCUS—PROBLEM

When Tosh Takimota celebrated his twentieth birthday, his parents gave him his first new car. "Remember," his father said, "you won't be driving one horse, you'll be driving 150 of them. That can be worse than a stampede. So before you use these keys, let's see our insurance agent and make sure you're adequately covered." What sort of insurance coverage does Takimota need?

Tosh needs all four basic types of automobile insurance—liability, medical-payments, uninsured-motorist, and physical-damage—to meet the hazards caused by motor vehicles and those who drive them.

Liability Insurance

liability insurance

Coverage sold to protect against claims based on the insured's negligence which has caused bodily injury or property damage to the claimant.

A policy of **liability insurance** (also called personal-liability or *PL insurance*) will pay a specified amount of money for bodily injury and property damage (also called *PD insurance*) to other persons occurring for which any insured is legally responsible. If your state mandates that all drivers have insurance coverage, this is the coverage required. Personal-liability and property-damage coverage compensates others who are injured by the negligence of the insured. Personal-liability coverage pays claims against the insured for losses resulting from the injury or death of the victim(s). Property-damage coverage pays claims resulting from damage to the car or other property of the victim(s). PL and PD coverage can be purchased in most states with a single liability limit, such as $50,000. In other words, the insurance company provides $50,000 coverage for both personal and property losses suffered by injured victims. Some policies are written with "split limits," such as $10,000/$20,000/$5,000 (that is, in any one accident the company pays up to $10,000 for injury or death to any one person or $20,000 to all persons, and $5,000 for property damage).

Medical-Payments Insurance

medical-payments insurance

Coverage available in conjunction with automobile insurance—for example, to pay medical, surgical, dental, and funeral expenses suffered by the insured or any member of the insured's household who is injured while occupying or being struck by an automobile.

Medical-payments insurance covers medical and funeral expenses incurred by the insured and others riding in the car. Payments are made without reference to fault. If the named insured or family members are injured by a motor vehicle while they are pedestrians, or if they are injured while occupying another motor vehicle, they also will be protected by this coverage.

If a person already has adequate health insurance, this additional coverage may be unnecessary. Of course, guests in the insured's car may not have health insurance, and for their sake this comparatively inexpensive coverage should be considered.

LEGAL FOCUS—PROBLEM

Stranded in downtown Atlanta without his wallet, which had been picked from his pocket, Dean Labordee desperately needed a ride to the airport for a return flight to Detroit. (His airline ticket was safely tucked in his breast pocket.) Frantically, he "hotwired" the first idle car he came upon (an Oldsmobile owned by Than Turner) and headed for the airport. Labordee had been drinking, and within a block he crashed into a telephone pole. Before it was all over, his medical payments totaled $18,789. Will Thad Turner's medical-payments policy (limit $20,000) have to cover Labordee's damage?

No. In order for Turner's medical-payments insurance to apply, he must have given the driver, Labordee, permission to use his vehicle. Labordee did not have Turner's permission; he had stolen Turner's car. Labordee's own medical-payments coverage is inapplicable, as is the rest of his automobile insurance policy, because, as a thief, he was using a vehicle without a reasonable belief of permission. However, if Labordee also carried ordinary health insurance, his medical expenses would be covered.

Like other forms of automobile insurance a certain limit of coverage will identify the responsibility of the insurance company. The limit applies to each covered person in the accident.

Uninsured-Motorist Insurance

This type of insurance pays for injuries and/or property damages to the insured, family members and guests in a covered vehicle resulting from accidents involving hit-and-run drivers and uninsured or underinsured drivers.

LEGAL FOCUS—PROBLEM

Pedro Perez was at the wheel of his car, patiently waiting for a green light, when he was rear-ended with a horrendous crash. He was wearing a shoulder harness, but his neck and back were snapped in a violent whiplash. Although conscious, he was dazed and could not identify the hit-and-run driver or car that backed off, made a U-turn, and then sped away. What type of automobile insurance protects Perez in this situation?

Perez can recover his medical expenses and his property damages up to the agreed limits under **uninsured-motorist insurance.** For a relatively modest premium, this policy typically pays between $15,000 and $25,000 for bodily injury suffered by the insured as a result of being struck by a hit-and-run driver who escapes without being identified, or by an identified but uninsured or judgment-proof driver who is at fault. Some states require uninsured-motorist insurance to be included in all PL/PD policies.

Physical-Damage Coverage

Two types of insurance are available to pay for damages to your own automobile in excess of any agreed deductible. Most physical-damage coverage is divided into two parts: collision and comprehensive. **Collision** pays for damage to the insured's motor vehicle caused by a collision, no matter who is at fault. If the other party was at fault, your automobile insurance company will have a right of **subrogation.** Subrogation is the right to succeed to or substitute for the rights of another. In insurance law, if the insurance company pays a claimant, it has the right to reimbursement from the wrongdoer.

Comprehensive (also called *other-than-collision loss*) protects against any losses to the insured's vehicle except those caused by collision. Thus, comprehensive applies if the vehicle is stolen, vandalized, or otherwise damaged (as by fire, earthquake, flood, or sandstorm). The policy does not pay for loss caused by theft of personal effects (e.g., clothing,

uninsured-motorist insurance

Automobile insurance that protects against the risk of loss from bodily injury and property damage suffered by an insured driver because of the negligence of either an uninsured, an underinsured, or a hit-and-run driver.

collision insurance

Automobile insurance that protects against the risk of loss from damages to one's own automobile in a collision regardless of who is at fault.

subrogation

The substitution of a third party for the creditor in a claim against a debtor.

comprehensive insurance

Automobile insurance that protects against losses from having one's car stolen or damaged other than by collision (e.g., by falling trees, sandstorm).

cameras, or luggage) left in the vehicle or for the theft of radio or stereo equipment, although these may be covered by special endorsement or addition to the policy.

WHO IS PROTECTED BY AUTOMOBILE INSURANCE?

LEGAL FOCUS—PROBLEM

Sally and Ben McFarland have a teenage daughter, Karen. All drive the family car. Are all covered by the couple's automobile insurance policy?

Yes, if the insurance company is properly informed that everyone drives the family car. As all family members are likely to be significant drivers, the insurance company has a right to be told which members of the family drive in order to properly estimate its risk and charge the appropriate insurance premium (price paid for the policy). With respect to an owned automobile identified in a policy, the following persons are normally insured:

- The named insured and spouse, if residing in the same household.
- Declared residents of the same household. (This applies even if the person is temporarily away from the residence; for example, if Karen goes to school in another state.)
- Other persons who use the automobile with the permission of the named insured. This coverage is provided to nonresident drivers who infrequently drive the insured vehicle.
- Other persons who might be liable because of negligence of the insured. This could be the employer of the insured, if Sally or Ben McFarland got into an accident while on company business.

Under most policies, if you sell your car and buy another, your automobile coverage continues for at least thirty days, or at most until the next policy anniversary date. Thus, you are fully protected in case you are in an accident during the short transition period. However, the company should be notified promptly so it can make the necessary changes to your policy, including an adjustment in the premium.

LEGAL FOCUS—PROBLEM

While on vacation in Glacier National Park, Nelson Salbeck borrowed a four-wheel-drive vehicle from some friends and took off on a cross-country trip. Does his automobile insurance policy cover him while he drives the borrowed vehicle?

non-owned automobile

An automobile or trailer not owned by, or furnished for, the regular use of the named insured.

http://

Auto insurance laws can be found at **http://www.bbb.org/library/autoins.asp**

Yes. Salbeck and relatives who reside in his household are all covered when they drive non-owned passenger automobiles with the permission of the vehicle's owner. A **non-owned automobile** is defined as an automobile or trailer not owned by, or furnished for, the regular use of the named insured. Insurance carried by the owner of the vehicle provides the basic coverage. Salbeck's insurer would pay only amounts in excess of the owner's policy limits.

LEGAL FOCUS—PROBLEM

When Nelson Salbeck came home, he learned that his adult son, Jack, who still lived with his parents, had bought a new car with a manual gearshift and had insured it in his own name. Salbeck asked if he might try it out; Jack said yes, and Nelson took off. He had an accident in which the car was damaged, and both a pedestrian and Nelson were injured, all because of his negligence in shifting gears. Did Nelson's insurance cover him?

Nelson's insurance would be secondary or excess. The son's car does not fit the definition of non-owned since a resident relative, the son, owns it. However, since Salbeck drove with his son's permission, the son's policy will cover the accident. Unfortunately, this might be much less coverage than he considers adequate; he is vulnerable to a sizable claim for damages by the pedestrian. An exception to this rule exists if Salbeck borrows his son's car while his own is being serviced or repaired. The son's car would then be considered a temporary substitute automobile, and both policies would cover the loss.

LEGAL FOCUS—PROBLEM

Aaron Dittmar bought a stand-alone trailer for camping trips and mounted a light trail motorcycle to the rear of the trailer. Are these vehicles covered by Dittmar's automobile insurance policy?

The trailer is covered, without an added premium, for PL and PD only if it is designed for use with a private passenger automobile and is not used for business or commercial purposes. Motorcycles, dune buggies, all-terrain vehicles (ATVs), mopeds, motor homes, and other similar vehicles are generally excluded from coverage unless specially added to the policy. Of course, individual policies may be written directly for a motorcycle or other vehicle.

A policy effective within the United States generally does not cover the insured in other countries unless specially endorsed in exchange for an extra premium. Most U.S. policies apply to travel while in Canada, but U.S. drivers need to carry proof of insurance coverage while driving there. Most U.S. insurance is not sufficient in Mexico. Before driving in Mexico, a driver should purchase a policy covering Mexican travel. Such policies are sold in both countries. It is extremely important that you review your automobile liability and property-damage coverage with your insurance agent before you leave to travel by car in foreign countries. Otherwise, you could be burdened with a non-covered judgment and might even be jailed pending trial because of lack of local insurance to cover possible damages.

WHAT IS THE INSURANCE COMPANY'S DUTY TO THE INSURED?

The insurance company is obligated under the policy to act fairly towards its insured in handling their claims. They are expected to pay rightful claims up to the policy limits and provide legal defense to the insured against claims made which are covered by the policy. The cost of defending claims is covered under the policy over and above any policy limits.

WHAT IS NO-FAULT INSURANCE?

No-fault is a type of insurance requiring each driver to look to his or her own insurance carrier for reimbursement of losses after an accident. Injured victims cannot sue negligent drivers. Under no-fault, every driver is required to buy insurance. After an accident, each company pays the physical injury damages suffered by its insured up to some prescribed

no-fault

A type of automobile insurance, generally mandatory for all motorists in adopting states, that provides benefits to the insured, regardless of fault of parties to the accident.

limit, regardless of fault. The label "no-fault" means that the insured will be paid even if he or she caused the accident. There are different versions of no-fault insurance, but in its purest conceptual form neither party may sue the other, nor may the insurance companies sue by right of subrogation after making payment. With pure no-fault, the insured may not recover any damages for pain and suffering, which is often the largest portion of jury verdicts. If there is a dispute as to the proper amount of damages to be paid, an administrator decides after a hearing. Each party collects from his or her own company for medical or funeral expenses and lost wages (usually for a limited time), both for themselves and for other occupants of the cars.

No-fault insurance replaces the typical method of establishing responsibility for wrongs related to automobile accidents. It replaces the tort fault system and thus it is a system itself. The closest existing parallel is workers' compensation insurance, which replaced the fault system for most work-related injures. All the states that have adopted no-fault systems have implemented modified versions of the pure concept. For instance, in a modified plan if an accidental death, permanent injury, or disfigurement results, or if medical expenses exceed a specified minimum (such as $2,500 or $5,000, or 90 days of disability), it is called the "threshold for suit." When the "threshold" is met, the general prohibition against suits is waived. If it is then proved that the other party's negligence caused the accident, a larger sum may be recovered, including all special damages (for medical expenses, loss of wages, or destruction of property) and payment of general damages for pain, suffering, and disfigurement.

Massachusetts pioneered no-fault in 1971 and several states followed with a variety of no-fault plans. Some states have adopted plans and then abandoned or modified them.* Other states have considered the idea but rejected it. At the federal level, repeated unsuccessful efforts have been made to enact a comprehensive national plan, excluding only those states that have acceptable equivalent plans. Individuals who are not satisfied with recovery schedules under no-fault can, of course, buy additional health or medical-payments, accident, and disability insurance coverage for themselves. Most no-fault plans exclude property damage, so drivers should continue to buy such protection, both comprehensive and collision.

CAN AUTOMOBILE INSURANCE PREMIUMS BE MINIMIZED?

 LEGAL FOCUS—PROBLEM

Tim and Jane Quinn are graduate students working at multiple jobs to support themselves and their infant child. Every dollar is important in the family budget. They wonder how they can economize on insurance for the car they are buying. They know that if either of them negligently injures or kills another person while driving, they would be hard-pressed to pay a judgment that could be for hundreds of thousands of dollars. Even if they could clear themselves of such a judgment by bankruptcy, they do not want to lose all of their savings, let alone hurt others and have no hope of making good the loss. Also, they do not want a discharge in bankruptcy on their credit records. What automobile insurance should they buy?

---

* States with some type of no-fault plan as of 2002: Colorado, Florida, Hawaii, Kansas, Kentucky, Massachusetts, Michigan, Minnesota, New Jersey, New York, North Dakota, Oregon, Pennsylvania, and Utah, and the territory of Puerto Rico. Some other states have laws that allow policyholders to obtain compensation for auto accidents from their own insurers. Connecticut, Georgia, Nevada, and Pennsylvania are examples of states that have repealed no-fault plans. The Illinois Supreme Court declared an Illinois plan unconstitutional.

The Quinns have limited freedom of choice if they are buying their car on credit. A lender seller will insist that the buyers carry collision and comprehensive insurance until the vehicle is paid in full. Because of the Quinn's fear of incurring a huge debt in damages, they decide to add personal-liability and property-damage coverage to their automobile insurance package. They find that they can substantially increase the amount from a basic 10/20/5 to 100/300/50 for perhaps only 40 percent higher premiums. This "bargain rate" for the larger amount of coverage is economical for insurance companies because most claims are for small amounts. Yet, it is also better for the policyholder, because the big risk is a financially devastating judgment.

In three to five years, when the car is paid for,* the Quinns can drop the expensive collision and comprehensive coverage, because even total destruction of the car would not be a catastrophic loss. At the least, they should then contract for the maximum **deductible.** Thus, they would pay, perhaps, the first $500 cost of any damage to the car, the deductible. The premiums would then be lower. Indeed, if a loss occurs, it might be wise to make no claim unless the damage far exceeds the deductible, because the company might raise the premium the year following the claim. After a series of small claims, some companies cancel policies at renewal time. In some states, statutes or administrative bodies limit insurance companies' right to raise premiums or cancel policies.

The Quinns can also save on automobile insurance now by driving carefully and avoiding moving violation citations, which lead to rate increases and cancellations. An insurance company may legally refuse to insure an applicant for any reason related to the hazard insured against: a bad driving record because of accidents that are the fault of the driver, moving traffic violations, employment in a line of work with an unfavorable loss experience (such as bartending, barbering, acting, or soldiering), physical or mental handicaps, or a reputation of being a *deadbeat* (slow-pay or no-pay debtor).

A person who cannot otherwise get insurance may qualify for a risk assignment policy (or assigned risk). Most insurance companies supply policies on a risk assignment basis as a condition of state law for handling other, less risky business. Under risk assignment plans, companies may be required to accept the unwanted business on a rotating basis in proportion to the volume of policies voluntarily sold in the state by each firm. The plans usually provide minimal coverage at very high premiums.

Companies often offer significant discounts to young men and women who have successfully completed approved driver education courses. Insurance company records show those who have received such training are less likely to be involved in accidents. Some companies give discounts to drivers who do not drink or smoke, who travel very little and do not commute to work, or who drive compact cars. Young drivers may qualify for discounts if they are superior students on the scholastic honor roll or maintain a "B" average. Insurance companies have evidence that such persons have fewer accidents, and so the rate discrimination is legal.

WHAT SHOULD YOU DO IF INVOLVED IN AN ACCIDENT?

The following suggestions are made to help protect your legal rights in the event that you have an accident while driving a car. More important, they may help to protect human lives, including your own.

1. If your car is not stopped by the accident, park it in a safe place, immediately ahead of the accident area and preferably off the highway. To hit-and-run is a serious criminal offense and morally wrong. If possible, post someone to warn oncoming vehicles,

deductible

A provision in an insurance policy whereby the insured bears modest losses up to a prescribed sum (e.g., $50, $100, or a little more) in exchange for reduced premiums.

---

* The Quinns might avoid this expensive coverage by buying a good used car for cash. The first year's depreciation in value is highest; money can be put into a savings account and in five or six years be enough to pay cash for a new car.

place warning flares, or do both. If you hit an unattended car or damage other property, leave your name, address, telephone number, and automobile license number on a note inside the car or under the windshield wiper.

2. Provide first aid to anyone injured if you are qualified to do so. Do not move anyone unless absolutely necessary, lest you aggravate injuries.

3. Call, or have someone call, for an ambulance, if necessary. As soon as practical, see a doctor if you or others have been injured. This is important because some serious injuries are not immediately apparent.

4. Call, or have someone call, the highway patrol or local police when anyone is injured or killed, or if there is serious property damage. Get the name or number of the officer who investigates the accident. Although the officer's name will be on the police report, you will not receive this report for several days. Persons protecting your interests (e.g., your insurance company or your attorney) will want to begin their investigation of the accident immediately.

5. Even before the police arrive, write down (or have someone else write down) the vehicle license numbers, names, addresses, and phone numbers of all witnesses (they might leave the scene after a few minutes). Get the same information from the driver and occupants of the other vehicle. Also ask the other driver for the name of his or her insurance company.

6. Do not admit responsibility for the accident. Any such admission of fault would be later held against you in court. Right after an accident is not the time to make dramatic conclusions, especially since they may be wrong.

7. Notify your insurance company if the other party is injured or has suffered property damage, and/or if you intend to submit a claim for personal injuries and/or damages to your car.

8. As soon after the accident as possible, write down the full details of what happened immediately before, at the time of, and immediately after the accident. A map or sketch of the scene may help. Note the weather and road conditions, visibility (sun, moon, lights), time, speed estimates, and skid marks. If you can, get pictures of the cars and any skid marks.

9. If the accident was serious, have your family contact an attorney as soon as possible. If you do not have an attorney, find one. (Methods of attorney selection are discussed in Chapter 4.) The attorney may have a professional photographer take pictures of the scene, including skid marks, aided by your notes of the event.

10. Notify the appropriate government agency, using its preprinted forms, to comply with the state's financial responsibility law.

11. If an insurance claims adjuster for the other driver contacts you or your family, refer them to your attorney. Be careful not to admit fault to the adjuster, who openly or with concealed equipment may be recording any conversation. Do not make any settlement until you know the extent of your damages. You cannot know that information until after you have been released by your doctor and have received legal advice. If you are an innocent victim of another driver's negligence, you may be entitled to damages sufficient to cover (a) medical and hospital expenses, present and future; (b) damage to property (car, clothing); (c) loss of wages, actual and prospective; and (d) payment for pain, suffering, and disfigurement. When damages are high, you are well advised to hire an attorney. Even after the attorney's fee, you will probably receive a sum larger than any direct offer from an insurance claims adjuster.

12. You will probably want to have your damaged car repaired. The insurance company may require two or more written estimates from reliable repair shops. The insurance company will pay you on the basis of the lower estimate. If it seems that a defect in

your vehicle caused the accident, consult your attorney before you repair the car. The attorney may arrange to have an expert examine the suspect parts to preserve them as evidence.

OTHER METHODS OF ACQUIRING OWNERSHIP OF PERSONAL PROPERTY

As discussed earlier in the chapter, ownership of personal property can occur in several ways. These methods include possession, purchase, production, gift, will or inheritance, and accession. Property can also be acquired when it is lost, abandoned, or mislaid. Purchase is the most likely method for a motor vehicle although other methods are possible. We will discuss these other methods of personal property ownership even though they occur more commonly with other types of personal property than motor vehicles.

POSSESSION

The person who finds abandoned property generally becomes the owner of it. A person who finds lost property may become the owner of that property if the true owner does not come forward. The first person to take possession of a wild animal normally owns it.

PRODUCTION

Production—the fruits of one's labor—is another means of acquiring ownership of personal property. For example, writers, inventors, and manufacturers all produce personal property and get title to what they have produced.

GIFTS

LEGAL FOCUS-PROBLEM

Katrina Brown's favorite aunt, Valerie Karnes, tells her when she graduates from college she is going to give her a new Ford Mustang convertible. What rights if any does Brown have to the new car upon her graduation?

In the movie *Field of Dreams,* a mysterious voice said to an Iowa farmer, "If you build it, he will come." The reference was to a baseball field and the "he" was the ghost of the former baseball great, Shoeless Joe Jackson. Brown is in the same position as that Iowa farmer. If the farmer built the field and Joe didn't come, there would be nothing he could do about it. To say it another way, "Katrina will own it, if she gives it." Aunt Valerie has made a gratuitous promise and the Mustang does not become Brown's until and unless Karnes delivers it to her.

A **gift** is a voluntary transfer of property ownership. The very essence of a gift is giving someone something without expecting anything in return. A promise to make a gift is not enforceable. The gift must be actually delivered to be an effective transfer of ownership. The person giving the gift is called a **donor.** The person receiving a gift is called a **donee.**

gift
A voluntary transfer of property ownership by one under no duty to transfer the ownership.

donor
A person who makes a gift in life or by will.

donee
The person to whom a gift is made in life or by will.

LEGAL FOCUS-PROBLEM

Linda Ector wishes to make a gift to Patricia Nguyen of some old rare coins stored in a safety deposit box at the Lone Star Savings and Loan. Ector is the donor. The intended beneficiary of Ector's generosity, Nguyen, is the donee. How can Ector effectively transfer ownership of the rare coins to Nguyen?

There are three requirements to an effective gift: donative intent, delivery, and acceptance.

donative intent

Present intent to make a gift.

1. *Donative intent.* There must be evidence of the donor's intent to give the donee the gift. **Donative intent** is determined from the language of the donor and the surrounding circumstances. Ector can tell Nguyen that she wishes to give her the coins. Writing down her intention provides even better proof.
2. *Delivery.* Delivery is giving up *complete control and dominion* (ownership rights) over the subject matter of the gift. Delivery is obvious in most gift situations. In the gold coin example, delivery could take place several ways. Ector could go get the coins and deliver them to Nguyen. Ector may, however, be reluctant to take the coins out of the bank. When a physical object cannot be delivered, a symbolic, or *constructive,* delivery is sufficient.

constructive delivery

Acts that are the equivalent of actual delivery such as delivering the key to the safety deposit box with the present intent to give the person the contents of that box.

   Constructive delivery is a term describing acts that the law holds to be equivalent of a real delivery. In our rare coin example, the delivery of the key to the safety deposit box to Nguyen would be a constructive delivery of the contents of the box. The delivery of intangible property—such as stocks, bonds, insurance policies, contracts, and so on—is always accomplished by symbolic, or constructive, delivery.

3. *Acceptance.* The final requirement of a valid gift is acceptance by the donee. This rarely presents any problems since most donees readily accept their gifts. The courts generally assume acceptance unless shown otherwise.

WILL OR INHERITANCE

Ownership of personal property may be transferred by will or by inheritance under state statutes. (See Chapter 14.) These transfers are called *bequests* (personal property), *devises* (real property), or *inheritances* (any or all property rights transferred on death).

ACCESSION

accession

"Adding on" to the value of personal property by either labor or materials.

Accession means "adding on" to something. It happens when someone adds value to a piece of personal property by either labor or materials. The installation of a stereo system in an automobile adds value to the automobile and becomes part of it.

   If accession occurs without the permission of the owner, the ownership rights in the improved property usually depend on the good faith of the improver. If the improver is a wrongdoer, most courts will not allow him or her to be reimbursed for the value added. For example, if a car thief put new tires on a stolen car, he or she would not be paid for the value of the new tires.

LEGAL FOCUS-PROBLEM

Roberto Juarez is walking in a large country field. He discovers a huge stone shaped somewhat like a horse lying near a fence. Juarez works on the stone for twenty-seven weeks. He eventually transforms it into a replica of the Lone Ranger's horse, Silver. Juarez's artist friends are very impressed and convince him to move the stone horse to a gallery. The gallery appraises the art at $50,000. The owner of the field where Juarez found the stone now claims title to it. Who gets the statue of Silver? Who is that masked man, anyway?

Juarez should get title to the stone statue because the changes he made greatly increased its value and the accession was performed in good faith. Juarez is, however, responsible for paying the owner of the field the reasonable value of the unaltered stone. If the increase in value is not significant, the original owner would keep title to the property. Many courts require the original owner to compensate an honest mistaken improver for the value he or she has added to the property.

CONFUSION

Confusion is the mixing of one person's personal property with another's, resulting in the goods becoming indistinguishable. This frequently occurs when the goods are **fungible.** "Fungible" means that each individual item is identical to every other item; this is the case with grain and oil. For example, if two farmers put their number 2–grade winter wheat into the same silo, confusion occurs.

    If the confusion of goods was done to deceive or take advantage of another, the innocent party gets title to the whole. If the confusion occurs as a result of agreement, an honest mistake, or the act of some third party, the owners share ownership as *tenants in common.*

confusion

Mixing of one person's personal property with another's, resulting in the goods becoming indistinguishable.

fungible

Each item of personal property is identical to every other item.

MISLAID, LOST, AND ABANDONED PROPERTY

If you find someone's property, it is important to learn whether the owner mislaid, lost, or simply abandoned the property because it effects who has what rights to the property. We define and discuss each below.

Mislaid Property

LEGAL FOCUS-PROBLEM

While at the movie theater, Dawn Waller went to the concession stand to purchase some popcorn and a cola. She accidentally left her gloves on the concession stand. The next day she realized they were gone. What are Waller's rights to a return of her gloves?

mislaid property

Property that has been
voluntarily placed
somewhere by the owner
and then forgotten.

Property that has been voluntarily placed somewhere by the owner and then forgotten is **mislaid property.** Her gloves are mislaid property. Assuming the theater employees found the gloves, Waller has a right to the return of the gloves. The theater owner has the duty to care for the goods in a reasonable way. The finder does not get title to mislaid property; instead he or she becomes an *involuntary bailee.* The law presumes the true owner will return for the property.

Lost Property

lost property

Property that is
involuntarily left and
forgotten.

Property that is involuntarily left and forgotten is **lost property.** The finder of the property can claim title to the property against everyone but the true owner. If the true owner demands that the lost property be returned, the finder must return it. The finder, however, has better title than anyone else.

If the finder knows who the true owner is, the property should be returned to him or her. Failure to return such property is the tort of *conversion* (see Chapter 5). Many states require the finder to make a diligent search to locate the true owner of lost property.

estray statutes

Laws requiring finders of
lost personal property to
report their discovery to
authorities.

Many states have **estray statutes** to encourage and aid the return of lost property. A common estray statute requires finders to report their discovery, whereupon the county clerk will advertise that property is found to try to find the owner. After a specified time, if the true owner does not claim the property, the finder becomes the new owner.

Abandoned Property

**abandoned
property**

Property discarded by the
true owner, who has no
intention of reclaiming it.

Property discarded by the true owner, who has no intention of reclaiming the property, is **abandoned property.** Generally, the person who finds the abandoned property gets title to it. This title is good against everyone, *including the original owner.* If the finder is trespassing and finds abandoned property, title belongs to the owner of the land.

CASE

JAMISON V. THE PANTRY, INC.

Court of Appeals of South Carolina, 301 S.C. 443, 392 S.E.2d 474 (1990)

After attending a football game, Willis DeBruhl, a minor, drives to a convenience store and buys some beer. It is illegal in South Carolina for a minor to purchase alcohol. He apparently returns to the car and shares the beer with his buddy. Sometime later, DeBruhl is involved in a head-on collision with another vehicle, killing himself and the driver of the other vehicle and injuring passengers in that vehicle. An action was brought on behalf of the deceased driver and passengers against the convenience store. The trial court granted a directed verdict for the defendant on the grounds that the plaintiffs failed to prove that "any beer purchased at The Pantry was ever consumed prior to this accident [and] that any beer purchased from The Pantry was [a] proximate cause of the accident in question." The plaintiffs appealed.

GOOLSBY, Judge: These personal injury actions against The Pantry, Inc. arise out of an alleged unlawful sale of beer. The actions were consolidated for trial. The trial court directed a verdict in The Pantry's favor. The question on appeal concerns only the sufficiency of the evidence as to proximate cause. We reverse and remand.

The three complaints, among other things, allege that The Pantry sold beer to Willis Dean DeBruhl, a minor, that DeBruhl's consumption of the beer resulted in a head-on collision that injured Jamison and Kyle Ruff and fatally injured Opal Ruff, and that the sale of the beer by The Pantry was a proximate cause of the collision and of the injuries the collision brought about.

At trial, the trial judge granted The Pantry's motion for a directed verdict, finding simply that "as a matter of law there [is] insufficient evidence to submit the case to the jury." The grounds for The Pantry's motion were that Jamison and the Ruffs failed to prove that "any beer purchased at The Pantry was ever consumed prior to this accident [and] that any beer purchased from The Pantry was [a] proximate cause of the accident in question."

In determining the question of whether the trial judge properly granted The Pantry's motion for a directed verdict, we are required, as was the trial judge, to view the evidence and all reasonable inferences that can be drawn therefrom in the light most favorable to Jamison and the Ruffs and if there

is even a "scintilla of evidence" tending to prove the allegations of the complaints, the motion should have been denied. Because a direction of a verdict is not favored, a case must be clear, certain, or indisputable to warrant a trial judge's granting of a motion seeking a directed verdict.

A review of the evidence and its reasonable inferences in the light most favorable to Jamison and the Ruffs follows.

On September 5, 1986, Mark Uggiano talked to DeBruhl, a nineteen-year-old, at a high school football game and arranged to meet him after the game at The Pantry. Thirty or forty minutes after leaving the game, Uggiano met DeBruhl and Richard Derodo in Dusty Bend at The Pantry, a convenience store. DeBruhl, who was not intoxicated at the time, bought a case of beer from The Pantry.*

*We infer from the following that DeBruhl was not intoxicated:

> Q. (By Mr. Hardaway): Did you see Willis Dean DeBruhl on September the 5th, 1986?
> A. (By Mr. Uggiano): Yes, sir.
> Q. When did you first see him?
> A. I saw him at the football game at Camden High.
> Q. Did he appear to be drunk?
> A. No, sir, he didn't.
> Q. When you saw Willis Dean DeBruhl at The Pantry when he came there that night, describe what he looked like then.
> A. Nothing out of the ordinary, same way.
> Q. Was he drunk?
> A. Not that I could tell.

And from the following:

> Q. (By Mr. Pulliam): . . . In your opinion, as an eyewitness, was he drunk or intoxicated when he went into [The] Pantry?
> A. (By Mr. Uggiano): As far as I know, no.

The beer, which The Pantry was licensed to sell, was put into a paper bag and DeBruhl carried it to his car. DeBruhl got into the car and handed the beer to Uggiano who sat on the back seat. The beer DeBruhl purchased was the only beer in the car.**

**We infer from the following that the beer bought by DeBruhl from The Pantry was the only beer in the car:

Q. (By Mr. Hardaway): Was there any particular reason for ya'll to meet at this particular Pantry?

A. (By Mr. Uggiano): To buy beer so that we could head out to sorority night.

Q. How much beer did he buy?

A. A case.

Q. How much beer did Willis Dean DeBruhl buy that night?

A. I only saw a case.

Q. (By Mr. Mathews): Now, when Dean went into The Pantry and he came back out, did he give you something in the back seat?

A. He gave me the beer.

Q. Did you see any other beer in the car at that time?

A. No, sir. I didn't.

Q. (By Mr. Hardaway): When ... Willis Dean DeBruhl bought that beer and brought it back to the car, was there any other beer in the car?

A. Not that I could see.

Q. Were there any other coolers in the car?

A. Not that I know of.

At 10:45 P.M., a mile from The Pantry, DeBruhl's car collided head-on with another car. The collision killed both DeBruhl and the driver of the other car, Opal Ruff, and injured the passengers in her car, Jamison and Kyle Ruff. DeBruhl was the at-fault driver.

A highway patrolman found opened beer cans inside the car, along with unopened beer cans in a paper bag and inside an ice chest. DeBruhl's blood alcohol level was determined to be .135. This amount of alcohol is sufficient to bring a person under its influence to such an extent as to impair the person's faculties. (A person is under the influence of alcohol or drugs when the ingestion of alcohol or drugs results in the impairment of the person's faculties.)

We think the evidence just recited supports the inferences that DeBruhl purchased beer at The Pantry no later than about 9:58 P.M., or approximately 47 minutes before the accident at 10:45 P.M., that the beer sold DeBruhl by The Pantry was the only beer in the car, that DeBruhl consumed from the opened cans found in his car some of the beer purchased from The Pantry, and that his consumption of the beer caused him to be under the influence of alcohol and impaired his driving ability.***

***We determined the time this way: the game ended at approximately 9:30 P.M.; a quarter of high school football is 12 minutes; Uggiano left the game either at the end of the third

quarter or at the start of the fourth; assuming it actually took only 12 minutes to play the 12-minute quarter, which is highly unlikely, Uggiano left the game at approximately 9:18 P.M.; and he met DeBruhl at The Pantry 30 or 40 minutes later, or at approximately 9:48 or 9:58 P.M. Had it taken longer than 12 minutes to play the fourth quarter, then Uggiano, obviously, would have left the game earlier than approximately 9:18 P.M. and would have met DeBruhl earlier than approximately 9:48 or 9:58 P.M. Viewing the evidence as suggesting that Uggiano left the game at approximately 9:18 P.M. and not earlier favors The Pantry and not Jamison and the Ruffs.

We also think the evidence just recited supports the inference that The Pantry's sale of beer to DeBruhl, a minor, in violation of Sections 61-9-40 and 61-9-410 of the South Carolina Code of Laws* was a proximate cause of the injuries suffered by Jamison and the Ruffs. It was reasonably foreseeable that a nineteen-year-old who was sold a case of beer by a convenience store in violation of statutes would consume a portion of the beer, would become intoxicated, would drive an automobile, would collide with another vehicle, and would injure or kill someone.

A jury issue existed, therefore, regarding whether The Pantry's sale of the beer to DeBruhl in violation of Sections 61-9-40 and 61-9-410 was a proximate cause of the injuries sustained by Jamison and the Ruffs.

REVERSED AND REMANDED

SANDERS, C.J., and SHAW, J., concur.

For Critical Analysis

1. Willis DeBruhl was the negligent driver; why is The Pantry the defendant?

2. The case was reversed and remanded in favor of the plaintiffs—is the case over?

---

* Section 61-9-40 of the South Carolina Code of Laws (1976) (Rev.1990) provides in part as follows:
(A) It is unlawful for any person to sell beer ... to a person under twenty years of age and effective September 14, 1986, under twenty-one years of age. Any person making such unlawful sale must be, upon conviction, fined not less than one hundred dollars nor more than two hundred dollars or imprisoned not less than thirty days nor more than sixty days, or both, in the discretion of the court....
Section 61-9-410 provides in part as follows:
No holder of a permit authorizing the sale of beer ... or any servant, agent, or employee of the permittee shall knowingly do any of the following acts upon the licensed premises covered by the holder's permit:
(1) sell beer or wine to a person under twenty years of age and effective September 14, 1986, under twenty-one years of age;....
A violation of ... the foregoing provision[ ] is a ground for the revocation or suspension of the holder's permit.

3. Assuming that DeBruhl has automobile insurance, what type of coverage applies to this type of claim? If his policy limits are less than damages proved, would his estate be personally liable? His parents?

4. Assume that when DeBruhl purchased the beer from The Pantry he used a fake identification that showed he was of legal age. Would it make any difference as to the case against The Pantry? ■

CHAPTER QUESTIONS AND PROBLEMS

1. Scott Noojin had not quite mastered the stick shift in his new four-wheel-drive truck. While parking in a shopping center lot, he shifted into forward when he wanted reverse. With a sickening crunch, his truck rammed into the side of a new limousine, causing $5,000 in damages. His own vehicle needed $2,000 in repairs. Scott purchased his car with a loan from Schools Credit Union. Since he had repaid only 25 percent of the loan, Schools Credit Union was listed as the legal owner of the truck. Who is liable for the damages to the limousine?

2. Darryl Galloway is fourteen years old, but he has been driving autos, trucks, and all-terrain vehicles on his family's 3,000-acre cattle ranch for more than five years without a driver's license. Sometimes he drives on a neighbor's land and sometimes on nearby U.S. forest service land. Is he or are his parents guilty of violating the state's vehicle code?

3. A driver was seated behind the steering wheel of her car, which was stopped in the fast lane of the highway. The car started drifting backwards, its transmission in neutral, while the driver was trying to start the car. Officers tried without success to find out what she was doing. A field sobriety test showed probable cause for a breath test, which she failed with a .13 reading. What criminal offenses might the driver face, if any? [*People v. Garcia,* 214 Cal. App. 3d. Supp.1, 262 Cal. Rptr. 915 (Calif., 1989).]

4. As Alyse Brooks was easing from her tight parking space in the three-story "Park Yourself" garage, she creased the side of the neighboring vehicle, a 1975 Pinto, with her front bumper. She stopped, looked, and left, thinking it was an old car not even worth spending the $100 it would take for repairs. Has Brooks violated any law?

5. David Kelynack was the proud purchaser of a new Yamaha motorcycle from Anderson Vehicle Sales with a six-month limited warranty. About two and a half months and 3,115 miles after the purchase, a tapping noise in the engine caused Kelynack to bring the cycle in for repairs. The seller agreed that the repairs were under warranty, but through misdiagnosis, a wait for parts, and another wait for additional parts, the cycle was in the shop for two months. At that time, Kelynack informed Anderson Vehicle Sales that the limited warranty was inadequate and he was exercising his right to revoke under the UCC. Three and a half months after repairs began, the cycle was as good as new. Could Kelynack revoke his acceptance and demand his purchase price returned? [*Kelynack v. Yamaha Motor Corporation,* 152 Mich. App. 505, 394 N.W.2d 17 (Mich., 1986).]

6. Following an extra-inning baseball game thousands of fans were pouring onto the local highways, where visibility was poor due to fog. On the main highway, thirty-seven vehicles smashed into one another in a massive chain collision. If it is established that Douglas Burham, driver of the second car in line, was at fault because he rear-ended the first car, is he liable for damages to all the other damaged vehicles?

7. Lisa Dunning borrowed John Brady's car with his permission. Due to carelessness in making a U-turn, Dunning was involved in a collision. The driver of the other vehicle was faultless and neither his person nor his heavy-duty truck suffered damage. Brady's car needed $1,500 worth of bodywork. Both Dunning and Brady have collision insurance coverage, each providing for a $250 deductible. Which policy, if either, will pay for Brady's loss?

8. Joann Earley liked Ford Grenadas so well that she purchased a used one three years newer than her previous Grenada. Within three days the car needed valve work, relocation of the radiator, and various other repairs. O'Neal Ford agreed to make these repairs under a limited guarantee that appeared in the contract of sale. Earley sent O'Neal Ford a letter revoking acceptance under rights provided by the UCC and requested a return of her payments. Can a buyer revoke acceptance of a used car under the UCC? Does the fact that she was given a limited warranty prohibit her claim of revocation? [*O'Neal Ford, Inc. v. Earley,* 13 Ark. App. 189, 681 S.W.2d 414 (Ark., 1985).]

9. D. J. Parthworthy owned the Old Eagle Tavern, located with a beautiful view overlooking Deadman Canyon. One Saturday night the bartender, Tran Ong, was serving Craig Hamada "Long Island Iced Teas" (an especially potent alcoholic drink) from 8 P.M. until 2 A.M. Ong knew that Hamada would have to drive some fifteen miles to get home. Hamada left for home at 2 A.M., after "one more for the road," and had gone only two miles before crashing into an oncoming car driven by Toni Shelia. Shelia was killed; the relaxed Hamada was uninjured. Shelia's mother brought a wrongful death action against Craig Hamada, Tran Ong, and the Old Eagle Tavern. Discuss.

10. You intend to drive your automobile into a foreign country for a four-month vacation. What legal issues regarding the car's use should you consider prior to your trip?

11. Leases defined as consumer leases often are limited to a $25,000 maximum in order for the special protections to occur. Are dollar limitations for such qualification good public policy? Is that amount sufficient?

12. Does your state have a point system for driver license suspension or revocation? Check the Web to see.

CHAPTER 11

Renters and Landlords

A ngry landlords respond with stories of 'scumbag' tenants.

Headline in April 9, 2002, edition of *The Dominio,* a New Zealand newspaper.

After reading and studying this chapter, you should be able to:

- Compare the advantages and disadvantages of renting your dwelling.

- Identify the legal terms used in real estate leases.

- Identify the legal rights and duties of landlords and tenants.

- Describe the legal requirements and types of real estate leases.

- Discuss major issues in leases such as deposit or security use and return, eviction, habitability, and quiet enjoyment.

- Discuss legal theories for landlord liability for injuries of the tenant on the premises.

- Distinguish and explain subletting and assignment of apartment leases.

- Use the guidelines for tenants to make good choices and create a positive landlord/tenant relationship.

Many of you are renting an apartment or sharing a rented home during your years at college. Most of you will probably rent housing for some time after college while saving for a down payment to buy a home. What are your rights as a renter, and what duties do you owe the owner (called the landlord)? There are many questions that should be asked by prospective residents before signing a lease and committing to a rental unit. Can the landlord raise the rent? What if your landlord does not fix a leaking roof? If your belongings are stolen from your apartment, are you legally entitled to receive compensation from the landlord? Must your landlord provide safe living accommodations? Can your landlord secretly enter your apartment in your absence? Are you entitled to know what crimes have occurred in the rental premises before you sign a lease? What happens if you break your lease?

LEGAL FOCUS—PROBLEM

Jamie O'Quinn moved into an apartment near the university she was attending. O'Quinn did not know, did not ask, and was not informed that the prior resident in her unit had been evicted for failure to pay rent following his arrest on charges of forcible rape. She also did not know that the apartment door lock had not been changed. Does the law require landlords to provide new door locks when apartments are rented to new tenants?

No. But if O'Quinn had asked, the landlord would have been placed in the precarious position of either lying or telling the truth and re-keying the apartment. If the landlord opted to lie, and if O'Quinn became the victim of a crime following an entry into her apartment, the landlord would then be liable for substantial compensatory and punitive damages. The important laws pertaining to renters and landlords are outlined in this chapter.

Like others around the world, millions of Americans live in dwellings they do not own. This circumstance continues into the twenty-first century. Called **tenants,** these people rent their living quarters, mostly in cities and suburban areas.

Around one hundred years ago, young people were migrating from rural America, from their farm homes with nearby churches and stores. Although there were tens of thousands of farmers who grew most of what they ate and traded for the rest—horseshoes, nails, sugar, salt—the call of the cities was compelling. Electrification was years away for most farms, while city lights symbolized a new promise. Furthermore, increasing crop production drove prices down while railroad freight rates rose, forcing many to migrate to cities such as New York, Kansas City, and Chicago. These rural migrants were joining the droves of European immigrants—500,000 in 1900 alone.

The big cities offered crowded rooming houses, apartments, high-density tenements, "flophouses," cellars, and hotels, and even lesser accommodations to their immigrants and residents in slums. Individual sleeping spaces might be rented in an apartment, with four men sleeping "broadside" on a sofa, their legs extending out onto chairs. Of course, there were luxurious apartment suites in the exclusive neighborhoods, but rural migrants could not even dream of living in such splendor. "To the people of soil, the cities, with their saloons, gambling halls, and masses of foreign people speaking strange tongues, seemed the source of much that was wrong with contemporary America, and these godless places were . . . luring away innocent country children with promises of easier money and a more stimulating way of life."[1] Unwelcome, rural migrants were "having difficulty dealing with their new image as backward rubes, hayseeds, or country bumpkins, butt of the jokes of

tenant

A party to a lease who pays rent to the landlord in exchange for the possession and use of real property (e.g., a person who rents an apartment).

smooth-talking, unscrupulous city folk who mocked them as allegedly bereft of intelligence, sophistication, or any sense of fun."[2] And they were forced to live in the most dreadful conditions imaginable. For example, around 1900, more than 2.5 million head of livestock would be butchered in Kansas City—with nothing wasted. "But the grime, the noise, and the stench from the stockyards intruded into every corner of the town," penetrating tenements everywhere. Even in the midst of such filth could be found "'squatters shacks' surrounded by refuse and smoky, evil-smelling fires."[3]

New York was the first city to appoint a Tenement Commission to solve the problems of renters who were jammed into squalid, disease-infested apartments with six or more people in windowless rooms, with peeling walls and leaking pipes. Many cities today have such commissions responsible to administer laws, such as rent controls, that are designed to protect renters. The plight of the poor who rent was, and some believe still is, unfortunate. But as you will learn, renters today are protected by legal rights that were unknown at the beginning of the twentieth century. Rent gouging at the turn of the century set the tone for future conflicts between landlords and their tenants. That issue continues today, but expressed as a landlord's right to a fair return on the investment. Regardless of how the issue is expressed, its solution, satisfactory to both sides, continues to elude society.

Why do people rent their living accommodations? Lack of funds to buy is usually the primary reason, although personal preference influences many. In some desirable areas home prices have escalated to the extent that fully employed families cannot afford to live close to downtown employment centers. These families must therefore either choose to rent in unglamorous, high-density apartment buildings or commute to suburban areas where home prices are lower. As a result, many choose to buy and commute rather than to rent and walk or take public transportation.

Traditionally it has been understood that the financial benefits of renting are poor. The rent that tenants pay edges upward, reflecting continuing inflation (or, more precisely, the rising costs of new construction and increasing expenses of operation and maintenance). As the demand for apartments increases, new construction must occur or vacancies become impossible to find; rents respond accordingly by increasing further.

The cost of home ownership also is high, largely because of population increases and demographic shifts that occur as more people become parents and new buyers in the housing marketplace. Many young people in metropolitan areas who desire to own their homes cannot qualify as purchasers because of the prices and high down payments required. These reluctant renters contribute to overall low vacancy rates, and thus to the economic pressure for higher rents. One result of demand for home ownership in urban locations has been the conversion of apartment units into condominiums, thereby further reducing the number of apartments available for rent. See Exhibit 11-1 for a chart comparing advantages and disadvantages of renting versus buying.

When housing shortages intensify, causing rents to escalate, a clamor for government remedial action is heard. Some local governments, especially in crowded metropolitan areas and university towns, respond with rent controls; others restrict condominium conversions. Government-subsidized apartment building programs for poor families are demanded in populous areas. In response, some frightened communities curtail the rental housing supply by enacting growth-limitation laws, out of fear that any new growth will disturb existing lifestyles and may reduce property values in the city's core or vicinity. Subsidized high-density housing also requires expanded public services (e.g., police and fire protection and community services) financed, at least in part, by higher taxes. So the desire to avoid higher taxes fuels the resistance to uncontrolled growth, even though new development contributes to the revenues of local governments in many ways (e.g., property tax and sales tax revenues).

EXHIBIT 11-1: **Advantages and Disadvantages of Renting**

Advantages	Disadvantages
Little or no responsibility for maintenance	No tax benefits
Easier to move	No building of equity
	No control over rent increases
	Possibility of eviction

Rent

Source: Adapted from a comparison chart provided by Ginnie Mae (http://www.ginniemae.gov), a wholly owned corporation within the Department of Housing and Urban Development (HUD).

As we shall explain more fully in the following chapter about home ownership, the traditional economic benefits of home ownership may be in sharp decline in response to new characteristics of employment in the new millennium. Renters traditionally lament that each month they are "throwing their money away" while home owners are "buying equity." Renters may take some solace in our observation that the efficacy of this classic theory is in doubt in the early years of the twenty-first century.

The overall inventory of available housing, and the laws that guarantee at least minimum health and safety standards to renters, have improved indescribably since 1900. Suburban apartment buildings are characterized by many amenities, such as recreational and laundry facilities. However, much substandard housing still exists, usually within our great cities, much of which is rented to the elderly and the poor.

From the foregoing it should be clear that laws affecting housing necessarily reflect some kind of social policy. Almost everyone agrees that the housing industry, both rental and homeowner, must be regulated by law—the most notable of which is called **NIMBY** (not in my back yard).

Unfortunately, the relationship between tenants and the owners of rental properties, legally called **landlords,** often is characterized by misunderstanding, controversy, and even ill will. Many of the legal problems experienced by these parties may be anticipated simply from the nature of the relationship. Landlords desire to control rent and maintenance standards and to choose selectively from among tenant applicants who, in turn, rely on civil rights and consumer laws for protection against discrimination. Tenants also benefit from the forces of competition when vacancy factors are high and landlords accordingly are anxious to rent.

Once in occupancy, tenants do not have any compelling economic incentive to maintain the rented premises. They have no proprietary interest in the property; all monetary

NIMBY

Not in My Back Yard—The response that planners often hear to the proposed location of less than desirable social programs or buildings.

landlord

The owner of residential property who leases it to a tenant, or renter, in exchange for rent.

benefit goes to the landlords. And landlords have an incentive to maintain their rental premises only if the expenditures are covered by rental receipts. Rising maintenance costs, taxes, and utility charges lead to rent increases, which can be onerous for the poor and create hostility even in tenants who are well able to pay. No tenant appreciates a rent increase. Moreover, tenants often are considered, by some, to be in a lower social position because they rent rather than own. This erosion of self-esteem is heightened by the insecurity caused by the landlords' continuing ability to remove tenants under certain circumstances.

Sometimes the economic realities of housing favor the landlord, and some landlords lacking common decency take advantage of tenants who are unlikely to take advantage of available legal protections.

LEGAL FOCUS—EXAMPLE

Moving day came, but Cheryl Daniel never received the key to her newly rented apartment in south Sacramento's Franklin Villa. The landlord, she said, "told me to go in through the window." So Daniel crawled through a side window, into a place filled with piles of trash, wires jutting from electrical sockets and mold in the refrigerator. Upstairs, the electricity didn't work at all. "I had no choice," said Daniel, 32, who had paid $1,000 for the apartment two months earlier from her wages as a temporary worker. Daniel had been staying in a Stockton motel with her two teenage daughters. "I'd run out of money and I had no place to go," she said, "so I came into this filthy, nasty apartment."[4]

The law governing the landlord-tenant relationship evolved from concepts, now archaic, that related to an agrarian, feudal society in England. Those concepts are largely irrelevant to the relationship as it is, or as reformers think it should be, in our urbanized, egalitarian democracy. For example, in the eyes of the law, a **lease** of a dwelling historically was considered primarily a conveyance of a property interest, not a traditional contract with reciprocal rights and duties. Accordingly, the landlord owed no continuing duty of maintenance because the tenant had the right of exclusive possession of the "leasehold" or "property." Thus, repairs had to be made by the tenant if they were to be made at all. The rule of *caveat emptor* (Latin: "let the buyer beware") clearly applied to tenants.

In modern times, though, legislatures and courts increasingly approach the landlord tenant relationship in a more enlightened manner. For example, most states now consider a lease to be primarily a contract with reciprocal rights and duties. Thus, a landlord now may be required by law to repair and maintain the rented premises. In most states, legislatures have adopted comprehensive statutory schemes that have replaced or modified the historic common-law rules. The following laws now in effect in many states exemplify significant departures from the common law:

- The landlord must maintain the premises in *habitable* (reasonably livable) conditions, unless the tenant agrees otherwise. The tenant's agreement cannot be coerced.
- If the landlord fails to maintain the premises, the tenant, under specified conditions, may do so—spending (typically) up to one month's rent, which then may be deducted from the next installment of rent due.
- The landlord cannot evict a tenant in retaliation for exercising any tenant right; if the attempt is made, the landlord may be held liable for punitive damages up to a specified cap (of perhaps $1,000).
- Landlords must refund **security deposits** promptly (often within two weeks of vacancy). The deposits may be retained by the landlord only to repair or clean the

lease

A contract, usually written, by which the relationship of landlord and tenant is created, and a property interest is created.

security deposit

A lump sum of cash paid by a tenant to his or her new landlord as security that the tenant will pay rent as agreed and will not damage the rented premises.

premises, and then only by following procedures typically set forth by statute. Statutory damages may be imposed for a failure to comply with these laws. Nonrefundable security deposits are not legal in modern law.

- Charges by the landlord for cleaning or damage repair, if withheld from security deposits, must be itemized and explained. The landlord typically has the burden of proving, in court, the reasonableness of each levy contested by the former tenant.
- Landlords owe their tenants and perhaps their guests a continuing duty of safety under certain circumstances.

LEGAL FOCUS—PROBLEM

Richard Cory, in Unit 5 of Shady Tree Apartments, had plugged a portable space heater, television, and hot plate for coffee into a long extension cord that was designed for low amperage use, such as a radio. It was plugged into the bedroom socket. Hours after Cory fell asleep with all three appliances on, the electric socket overheated and started a fire. There was extensive damage before the fire was extinguished, partly because the nearby fire extinguisher in the hallway was not operative. What liabilities have arisen?

Tenants, as well as landlords, are obligated by law to use reasonable care. In this example, Cory's negligence was primarily responsible for the fire damage. He is lucky that other tenants were not injured or even killed. The landlord, however, must share liability to the extent the damages are attributable to negligently maintaining the fire extinguisher.

Unfortunately, rental property reform has evolved slowly, which has led to various disruptive developments: organizations of militant tenant groups, legislatively imposed rent controls, and increasing reluctance of investors and lenders to become involved in the purchase or operation of rental properties in certain geographical areas, thus aggravating the shortages of needed housing (especially for low- and moderate-income tenants). Another trend has been the willingness of public interest attorneys to misuse procedural laws to further exacerbate the landlord-tenant relationship. Even with reform, the amounts of money in dispute are relatively small and many tenants simply move away without claiming or enforcing their rights.*

Many apartments are constructed especially for low-income renters. These apartments are subsidized under programs authorized by the U.S. Housing Act. Administered by the Department of Housing and Urban Development (HUD), these programs seek to improve landlord-tenant relations in many ways, e.g., by eliminating onerous clauses from its leases and rental agreements. For example, *distraint clauses* (which authorize the landlord to seize the tenant's property for unpaid rent) and *exculpatory clauses* (which immunize the landlord from responsibility for all injuries or losses caused by negligence), discussed later, have been eliminated from standard HUD leases. Even so, tenants of public housing projects still must rely on state law to protect other basic legal rights as renters.

Clearly there are opposing public policy issues, e.g., housing for everyone in our nation and respect for property rights of owners of rental properties. Legislatures and enlightened courts will no doubt continue the movement toward uniformity in landlord-tenant laws of the various states. Meanwhile, prospective tenants need to bargain carefully and effectively with landlords to minimize the risk of possible future costly conflict. It is important to

* The 1990 movie *Pacific Heights,* widely available in video rental stores, captures the essence of combative relationships between renters and landlords in an emotionally charged and entertaining fashion.

understand that state laws protect you primarily after you become a tenant. It is the responsibility of prospective tenants to fend for themselves in negotiating rental terms and in obtaining the often specific and detailed protections that are provided by state statutes. Without any doubt, an "ounce of prevention" in making rental commitments is worth a "pound of cure" for both landlords and their renters.

THE CONFLICTING PERSPECTIVES OF RENTERS AND LANDLORDS

After all, the three major sources of apartments are death, divorce, and transfer.

Cornelius Gallagher, New York City Real Estate Agent

The landlord and tenant are involved in a business relationship. One must accept this fact in order to understand landlord-tenant law. The landlord's primary concern is that total rent received be sufficient to cover all cash outlays, including periodic major expenditures to replace carpets and appliances, to repair roofs, and to repaint building interiors and exteriors. As cash outlays rise with inflation, pressure grows to raise rents sufficiently to cover these outlays. The renters of modern projects often enjoy rising incomes and are able to pay higher rents, with the result that the owners' project continues to appreciate in value. (Note this declaration pertains primarily to multifamily projects renting to more affluent segments of society.)

Millions of other dwelling units are rented by low-income persons who cannot afford any increases in their rent, which already represents a formidable portion of their total income. Some multifamily dwellings languish in disrepair and gradually become uninhabitable. Mainstream thinking is that laws designed to force landlords to spend money for adequate maintenance and repair would actually hurt low-income tenants, who could not afford to pay necessary resulting increases in rent. They would be forced to move, possibly onto the streets, joining the growing ranks of the homeless. This conundrum prompted the production of huge housing projects for low-income renters under government subsidies.

Typically, the owner, especially of a large apartment complex, hires an on-site manager to handle the day-to-day business of the apartment—collecting rent, paying bills, maintaining the building, or employing others to perform some, or all, of these tasks. The on-site manager, or *resident manager,* is the person with whom the residents must deal, at least initially, in solving whatever problems arise. Unfortunately, some resident managers try to do as little work as possible in exchange for the customary rent-free apartment and small salary. Thus, tenant complaints may fall upon "deaf ears" where the owner-landlord is a passive investor, secure in anonymity and absence from the premises.

Owners of larger complexes frequently hire property management firms that specialize in managing apartments. These organizations supervise the resident manager, the collection of rents and payment of bills, and maintenance and repairs. They often charge a percentage of the gross rent collected for their services, which tend to be more systematic and efficient than those found in owner-supervised projects.

The manager, whether an individual or a professional organization, is the owner's agent, and agency law governs the relationship (see Chapter 13). It extends to all activities connected with the conduct of the rental business, including the receipt of notices and complaints. It therefore is a wise policy for tenants to make complaints in writing to the resident manager, retaining a copy for themselves as well.

The nature of the rental business obviously places the landlord and tenant in conflicting financial positions. On the one hand, as owner of the property the landlord is in the superior position, having both business experience and the availability of professional help from attorneys and accountants. On the other hand, government regulation, modernization of applicable state laws, and enlightenment of the renting public has done much to equalize the strength of the parties. But to bargain effectively over the terms of a lease, a tenant should understand what terms are negotiable and what potential problems can be solved in advance. Unfortunately, the bargaining power is often so lopsided in favor of the landlord that the tenant has little choice but to "sign on the dotted line" or "keep on looking." This is so because most consumer protection laws become operative only after one becomes a tenant—the negotiating process is left to the prospect and landlord. Often the landlord presents a form lease full of disclaimers and frequently printed in difficult-to-understand legalese: a classic *adhesion contract* (discussed in Chapter 8). Many state laws protect tenants from unfair provisions within the leases they sign, on the basis of public policy. State laws are found in statutes and in the common-law decisions of courts.

LEGAL FOCUS—PROBLEM

Kristin Benet moved into the Berkshire Arms apartment complex during registration week at the University of Washington. Vacancies at rental rates that Benet could afford were scarce, and she was especially pleased to be able to walk to school because she did not own a car. Harry Hammer, the owner and manager, began "hitting" on Benet the day she moved in. At first, Hammer made remarks about her "fine body" and what a "sensational lover" he was, and how "she could have the time of her life with him." Week after week the harassment continued, becoming more graphic in its innuendos and more threatening to Benet. Fearing the need to abandon her coveted apartment, Benet visited the campus legal adviser, Sherlock, and asked what she could do, if anything. Sherlock advised her that apartments were not businesses and tenants are not employees, therefore the sexual harassment laws did not apply to protect her. Until she was "assaulted" or "battered" by Hammer, there was nothing she could do. Was Sherlock right?

Sexual harassment against persons in their homes may be more oppressive than at their workplaces, but it is far less protected under law. Being forced to abandon a desirable apartment or home is a considerable loss. But what statutory laws protect Benet from Hammer's obnoxious behavior? Federal laws apply to larger employers whose business affects interstate commerce. State employment laws protect *employees* of local (intrastate) businesses, and many extend specified protections to tenants. Under the common law, if the harassment became very obnoxious and offensive, Benet could bring an action for the tort of intentional infliction of mental distress and seek punitive damages as well as compensation for her anguish.

LEGAL FOCUS—PROBLEM

Sidney Chaudhry owns the Laguna Apartments, an exclusive oceanfront complex. Appealing to upper-class retirees, Chaudhry charges high rents and restricts the behavior of his tenants with clauses in the lease agreements and in exhaustive written "rules." These rules are intended to assure privacy, to maintain the quiet and peaceful co-existence of the tenants, and to preserve the aesthetics of the structures. One of the restrictions prohibits the installation of any kind of antenna or satellite dish on the balconies or in the patios of apartments. Chaudhry also is the principal shareholder of the local cable TV corporation that services his apartments. Stanley Craig, a Silicon Valley technocrat, installed a satellite dish in his Laguna Apartments patio to assist him in his work. Chaudhry, after repeatedly demanding removal of the dish, instigated eviction proceedings. Can Chaudhry evict Craig?

No. Despite Craig's agreement not to install any antennae, his behavior is protected by rules of the Federal Communications Commission. The FCC, a federal administrative agency, bans the blanket prohibition of viewers to use competing technologies. Reasonable rules of how such a satellite dish may be used would be appropriate. Under the doctrine of supremacy, the rules of the FCC supersede all contrary state laws or private contracts, such as Chaudhry's lease.[5]

Ⓦ HAT KINDS OF LEASES ARE AVAILABLE?

A lease transfers possession of a dwelling or apartment unit from the owner (called **lessor** or landlord) to the renter (called **lessee**) in exchange for **rent.** With a lease, the landlord transfers to the tenant the exclusive right to use and possess a designated space (apartment unit) for a period of time in exchange for a promise to pay rent periodically. A lease usually is, and always ought to be, in written form. Leases for more than one year (or three years, in some states) must be in writing and signed by the obligated party to be enforceable under state statutes of frauds. Ideally, both parties should sign. However, no law is violated if a landlord and tenant choose to abide by an oral lease, even though it may be unenforceable if taken to court. If there is no complaint, there is no consequence. A lease contains the mutual promises of the parties. Because a lease involves both the transfer of a property interest (possession) and reciprocal agreements, it is both a conveyance of a property interest and a contract.

A resident's occupancy (or tenancy) commonly is called a lease if it continues for a fixed period of time (e.g., "I have a one-year lease"). On the other hand, if the tenancy is agreed to last indefinitely, usually renewing automatically from month to month, it commonly is called simply a **rental agreement** (e.g., "I have a month-to-month rental agreement"). Technically, both tenancies are created by a lease and are called a *tenancy for years* and a *periodic tenancy,* respectively. Both types are discussed later in this chapter.

LEGAL REQUIREMENTS OF A LEASE

A lease document must (1) express the intention to establish the relationship of landlord-tenant; (2) state that exclusive possession transfers to the tenant at the beginning of the lease term; (3) provide for the landlord to retake possession of the property upon termination of the lease; (4) describe the leased premises, usually with its street address and unit number; and (5) provide for the length of the lease (its term), the amount of rent, and payment dates. Most lease documents are supplied by landlords who obtain them from trade associations or from purveyors of business forms. In addition to the minimum legal requirements of a lease, as noted previously, most lease forms contain many

lessor

A party to a lease who receives rent from a tenant in exchange for the possession and use of real property by the tenant. The lessor is more commonly called the *landlord.*

lessee

A party to a lease who pays rent to the landlord in exchange for the possession and use of real property, such as a person who rents an apartment. The lessee is more commonly called the tenant.

rent

The tenant's payment to the landlord for the tenant's use of the landlord's real property.

rental agreement

A contract, usually written, between a landlord and tenant. Technically it is a lease.

difficult-to-understand clauses regarding legal remedies for the landlord. Prospective tenants are well advised to read lease forms completely and to insist on clarification of any words and phrases they do not understand. But realistically, most prospective tenants will gloss over most of this "fine print" and trust that they are adequately protected by law. At the end of the chapter a checklist is provided for prospective tenants to help them in negotiating with landlords about the standardized or customized forms.

There are four types of tenancies: (1) a tenancy for years, (2) a periodic tenancy, (3) a tenancy at will, and (4) a tenancy at sufferance. All except a tenancy at sufferance involve the transfer of the right to possession. The owner or lessor (landlord) conveys the property to the lessee (tenant) for a certain time. The tenant has a qualified right to exclusive possession. The tenant's right to exclusive possession is qualified by the landlord's right to inspect the premises to assure that the tenant is properly caring for the property.

TENANCY FOR YEARS

tenancy for years

Tenancy for a specified time period stated by express contract.

The unique characteristic of a **tenancy for years** lease is that it is always for a stated period of time, usually one year.* The main advantage of such a lease to the lessee-tenant is that all terms, including the amount of rent and duration of occupancy, are fixed by the lease and cannot be changed by the lessor-landlord until the lease expires. However, the lease may authorize the landlord to change the detailed *operating rules* for the rental premises during the period of the lease. For example, the hours during which a swimming pool may be used may be changed during the leasehold. Nonetheless, the tenant can rely on a fixed, or predictable, rent for a stated period while enjoying occupancy of the dwelling.

The main disadvantage to tenants is the inability to move during the lease term without ensuring that the landlord will continue to collect the agreed-upon rent. Likewise, a main advantage to the lessor is that rental income is uninterrupted for the term of the lease; there will be no need to advertise the premises or to prepare them for another resident. This is a significant advantage, since new tenants rarely can be found to replace departing tenants precisely when vacancies occur. Consequently, even brief periods of vacancy, during which apartments are readied and replacement tenants are sought, contribute to a *vacancy factor*. When tenant turnover is high, vacancy factors are larger and the financial return to the owner is less.

A disadvantage to the owner is that the rent is locked for the duration of the lease and cannot be increased to reflect increases in operating expenses. However, some landlords include an adjustable rent feature in their leases that limit annual increases to some percentage, say 4 percent, as an alternative to an absolutely fixed amount of rent. Or, in very long-term leases, the rent may fluctuate with a standard cost-of-living index. This protects landlords from a decline in their net cash flow caused by increasing operating expenses. And tenants thus know they will, or may, face an increase in rent each year, but at least it is limited in amount.

PERIODIC TENANCY

periodic tenancy

Tenancy for a period often determined by frequency of rent payments; automatically renewed unless proper notice is given.

A **periodic tenancy** is modernly commonly called a *month-to-month tenancy* because most landlords prefer to do business on a monthly basis rather than, for example, a weekly basis. The defining attribute of a periodic tenancy is that the agreeement states a measuring

---

* Technically, a lease for a fixed period of time is called an *estate for years*, even when it terminates in less than one year. Thus, a six-month lease creates an estate for years, also called a tenancy for years.

period. For example, Landlord agrees to lease a unit in Rivercity Acres to tenant on a month-to-month basis. The characteristic of a month-to-month tenancy is that it continues indefinitely for successive monthly periods until properly terminated, again in writing, by the lessor or the lessee.

At common law, to terminate a periodic tenancy the landlord or tenant must give one period's notice to the other party. If the tenancy is month to month, one month's notice must be given. If the tenancy is week to week, one week's notice must be given. State law often provides the notice that is required to end a periodic tenancy and it might require a minimum notice period no matter what the expressed term in the lease. In 2002, California statutory law was changed to require a minimum notice of sixty days in many rental situations before a landlord can terminate a tenancy without cause.*

The main advantage of a month-to-month tenancy to the resident is the freedom to vacate without further liability for rent by giving a relatively short notice. The main advantage to the landlord is the freedom to increase the rent or to evict a "problem" tenant by giving the same short notice. The tenant who is faced with an unacceptable rent increase may choose simply to move elsewhere.

TENANCY AT WILL

If a landlord rents an apartment to a tenant "for as long as both agree," the tenant receives a **tenancy at will.** At common law, either party can terminate the tenancy without notice. This type of estate may come about when a tenant keeps possession after the termination of a tenancy for years with the landlord's consent. Before the tenancy is converted into a periodic tenancy (by the periodic payment of rent), it is a tenancy at will. The death of either party terminates a tenancy at will.

tenancy at will

Tenancy for as long as both parties agree; no notice of termination required.

TENANCY AT SUFFERANCE

If a tenant remains in possession after another form of tenancy ends without the owner's permission, a **tenancy at sufferance** is created. A tenancy at sufferance is not a true tenancy, as it is created by a tenant wrongfully retaining possession of property. The tenant is, however, in a different position from a trespasser, someone with no right to be on the property. A trespasser can be summarily arrested; a tenant at sufferance must be evicted. The eviction process provides protection for the person accused of wrongfully possessing the property that is unavailable for the trespasser.

tenancy at sufferance

Continued possession of land by a tenant without legal right.

ⓁAW AND PUBLIC POLICY IN THE LANDLORD-TENANT RELATIONSHIP

Under basic principles of contract law in former years, landlords were generally free to rent to whomever they pleased upon whatever terms they pleased. Of course, then and now, the marketplace dictates a cap on maximum rent, since it must be competitive if

---

* The law will require an owner of a residential dwelling to give at least sixty days' notice to a tenant of intent to terminate the lease or thirty days' notice if the tenant has resided in the dwelling for less than one year. The law only applies to a few specified California cities including Los Angeles. California SB 1403 (2002). The bill had popular political support after a Japanese investor gave thirty days' notice to around 1,000 Northern California tenants, most of whom were in single-family dwellings. A public uproar ensued. See James Sterngold, "30-Day Notice for a Mass Eviction," *New York Times*, February 21, 2002.

rent control

A law that places limits on the amount of rent a landlord can charge for an apartment.

vacancies are to be minimized. But in addition to market forces, some metropolitan areas now have comprehensive **rent-control** or rent-stabilization laws that regulate increases of rent and criteria for eviction.*

Rent control repeatedly has been ruled constitutional despite the contention that it constitutes the compulsory "taking" of private property without "just compensation." The constitutionality of rent control depends upon the actual existence of a housing shortage with its concomitant ill effects. Under those circumstances, rent control is deemed to be a rational curative measure. Opponents of rent control contend it is a disguised tax on landlords, discriminating unfairly against them by taking their wealth to subsidize renters, a burden that should be imposed on the total society. Still others argue that rent controls result in the deterioration of rental units because artificially low rents are not sufficient to cover the increasing costs of maintenance and repairs. The buildings are not maintained and often are finally abandoned and permitted to become veritable urban wasteland.

Almost all rent-control laws exempt new construction from coverage to avoid the possibility of discouraging new residential developments. Landlords can recapture some of their losses from rent control by setting very high rents for new tenants when vacancies occur. For example, university towns such as Berkeley, California, are characterized by rental accommodations because streams of students come and go on a regular basis. Thus, strict rent control, called "vacancy control," under which landlords cannot raise the rents on newly vacated apartments to their market value, has been in effect in Berkeley for more than 25 years. This has angered landlords and triggered attempts to preempt the Berkeley city laws with a new state law permitting increases to market value of all vacancies. The landlords were successful: In 1999 a state law preempted local rent control, allowing landlords throughout California to raise the rents on vacant units to market demand.[6]

Under one alternative to rent control, government agencies make direct cash subsidies (e.g., through rent vouchers) to qualified low-income renters who can then pay market rental rates. This alternative shifts the burden of subsidized housing from landlords to taxpayers in general. Needless to say, landlords prefer voucher systems to rent control.

The landlord is generally free to include in the lease noise limitations, parking regulations, restrictions on wall hangings, restrictions on the number of guests and frequency of parties, and so on. Some landlords are strict in such matters, others lax. Renters generally are informed about restrictions when their tenancy begins, although the enforcement policy often is not spelled out. Nevertheless, the remedy available to the landlord for violation of such rules is the same as for nonpayment of rent: eviction, plus monetary damages when appropriate.

The power of the landlord to exclude prospective tenants is not without limitation. Although illegal for many years, racial discrimination in housing still exists. This phenomenon is attributable to weak enforcement as well as to apparent regional preferences for segregated lifestyles by persons of different races. The Fair Housing Amendments Act of 1988[7] has been hailed as the strongest modern legislation to combat housing discrimination. Its primary weapons include the possible award of generous damages (no limit is specified), as well as necessary reasonable attorney fees, coupled with an overall expanded role of the federal government for proven, illegal discrimination. New classes of persons now protected from exclusionary discrimination are children, the physically disabled, and the mentally impaired. AIDS sufferers also are protected. Qualified senior citizen complexes may discriminate on the basis of age. Traditional protection from discrimination in

---

* Restrictions on eviction are necessary to prevent landlords from avoiding rent restrictions by periodically evicting tenants for no reason, and then renting to new tenants at increased rates. Valid cause to evict in jurisdictions that regulate eviction would include such defaults as failure to pay rent or deliberate damage to the premises.

housing is continued in the categories of sex (gender), race, color, religion, ancestry, and national origin. Other areas of historical discrimination that are ignored by the act are lack of wealth (minimum income restrictions), marital status (unmarried couples), family size (separate bedrooms for each child), and sexual preference (homosexual relationships). However, state civil rights or human rights laws now protect some of these categories.* California long has protected against discrimination on the basis of sex (gender), sexual orientation, race, color, religion, ancestry, national origin, blindness or other physical disability, and children.[8]

Certain possible terms of leases or rental agreements generally are declared to be against public policy and unenforceable by landlords. Nonrefundable security deposit clauses[†] and exculpatory clauses—explained later in this chapter—are examples.

LEGAL FOCUS—CASE

Timothy Whalen, attorney at law and former state legislator, owns the Shannon Rose Apartments in Billings, Montana. John Taylor, a 48-year-old janitor, was renting an apartment from Whalen. When Taylor was late for the payment of rent, Whalen changed Taylor's locks, refused to accept the late rent when Taylor returned, and gave him a small part of his deposit. Taylor moved to the Esquire Motor Inn that night. Whalen personally moved into Taylor's apartment, and then sued him for damages and attorney fees. Taylor countered, asking for damages and possession, but was confronted with a clause in the rental agreement that said: *Acceptance of a refund of deposit shall constitute a full release of landlord from any claims of tenants whatsoever.* Is Taylor's claim for damages for wrongful eviction waived?

Whalen v. Taylor, 925 P.2d 462 (Montana, 1996).

No. Such a waiver is against public policy. Under the Montana statutes, Taylor was entitled to three months' rent because attorney Whalen used the clause knowing it was illegal. Furthermore, Whalen was evicted from the apartment and possession was awarded to Taylor. How this interesting example ultimately worked out is not public information. Presumably Taylor moved back in. Under these circumstances Whalen would, no doubt, be tempted to serve Taylor with a thirty-day notice to vacate—a normal eviction procedure. However, attorney Whalen might then face an action by Taylor for retaliatory eviction, a variety of wrongful eviction that is discussed later.

Unfortunately, a tenant may unwittingly sign rental papers that include an unenforceable provision and submit to its consequences not realizing the lease provision is not enforceable. For example, an unsophisticated or illiterate tenant who agrees in a written contract that the security deposit is nonrefundable might fail to request the deposit. The unscrupulous landlord who obtained the illegal waiver is not likely to volunteer a refund that the tenant doesn't request.

Prospective tenants always should read and obtain explanations for the lease and rules forms with which they are presented. For example, many states require the landlord to pay interest on the amount of security deposit that is refunded at the end of the lease term. However, a trusting tenant who does not understand this benefit may simply not receive it. Thus, a tenant should ask at the beginning about the landlord's policy in this regard and a record should be made of the answer.

Legal Remedies for Landlords

Substantive and procedural law benefits and protects landlords over tenants, creditors over debtors, lenders over borrowers, and the poor are seldom among the favored parties.

John Turner, former Attorney General of Canada

Damages and Eviction

abandonment

When a tenant leaves rented premises with no intent to return or to honor legal obligations under the lease.

If a tenant fails to pay rent (defaults) and leaves the premises (**abandonment**) the landlord may sue the tenant for accrued rent and damages. Damages may include the cost of repairs for physical damage to the premises, as well as the rent the landlord would have received if the tenant had completely performed the rental contract. In a month-to-month tenancy, for example, the landlord is typically entitled by state statute to one month's notice of the tenant's intention to terminate (not necessarily on the first day of the month) and is also entitled to receive rent for that full period. Reciprocally, the tenant has the same legal right to receive notice of the landlord's intention to raise the rent or to terminate the lease.

In a tenancy for years (a lease with fixed term), the landlord is entitled to rent payment for the entire unexpired portion of the lease term. However, the landlord would have to deduct from that amount any rent actually received from any successor tenant. In other words, the landlord is not entitled to obtain double rent for the premises: once from the tenant who abandoned and once again from a replacement tenant. As a practical matter, a tenant who simply "buys himself out of the lease" by paying rent for the full unexpired term would be unlikely to learn if his former landlord in fact collected double rent. Sometimes landlords do not sue for damages because their defaulting tenants "skip" leaving no forwarding address, or are without financial resources and are therefore "judgment-proof." Many rental agreements also include a provision allowing the landlord to recover reasonable attorney fees incurred in settling the matter after abandonment.*

When the tenant remains in possession after default in the payment of rent, the situation becomes more complex. The tenant may have defaulted in the payment of rent because of some personal circumstance, and remained in possession simply because there was nowhere else to go. Or, the tenant may have defaulted in rent because of what the tenant believed was just cause, such as a continuing failure of the landlord to maintain habitability (e.g., to repair the heating system). Regardless of why the tenant-in-possession defaulted in the payment of rent, the landlord will typically seek to reclaim possession by evicting the tenant.

forcible eviction

An illegal eviction technique, by which a landlord confronts a tenant, forcibly removes all personal items, and changes locks on the unit.

Under common-law rules, a landlord could forcibly evict (expel) tenants who were in default and then literally throw their possessions into the street. **Forcible eviction** is now prohibited in all states.

---

* In many states, the inclusion of a clause giving a landlord the right to recover attorney fees in a lease dispute is interpreted, as a matter of law, to allow for the recovery of reasonable attorney fees by the prevailing party, landlord or tenant.

LEGAL FOCUS—PROBLEM

Shariya Williams was two months behind in the rent for her one-bedroom apartment near Brigham Young University. Her landlord, Sahun Hong, waited until she left for school and then, by prearrangement, opened her apartment with his master key and caused two workers to box all of her possessions. Five mover's boxes containing all of Williams's belongings were carefully set on the ground outside her former apartment. Hong changed the lock to the apartment. When Williams returned after classes and discovered what had happened, Hong was nowhere to be found. Has Williams been lawfully evicted for nonpayment of rent?

No. The self-help remedy of **peaceable eviction** is also prohibited in all states. Although the landlord is entitled to possession of the property ultimately, statutory remedies compel the landlord to follow court procedures. In this case, Williams could sue her landlord for *wrongful eviction* and, in many states, could recover punitive damages even though she was behind in her rent. Note that Williams's situation is different from those situations where tenants abandon their rental unit and leave their personal property behind.

peaceable eviction

An improper eviction technique by which a landlord surreptitiously enters the absent tenant's apartment, removes the tenant's belongings, and changes locks to the unit. It is peaceable in the sense that no eye-to-eye, person-to-person confrontation takes place, as in a forcible eviction.

LEGAL FOCUS—PROBLEM

Salvatore Smith rented a small apartment in Butte, Montana. He lost his job and was looking for work and missed his December 1 rent payment. Landlord Gene Dudley repeatedly demanded the overdue rent, threatening eviction. Smith, finding no work, traveled to Chicago to visit his niece and to look for work over the Christmas holiday. When the rent was due again on January 1, a bitter cold front had hit the area, dropping temperatures to 20 degrees below zero. Dudley, angry about the late rent, turned off the heat to Smith's apartment and left a note on the table that said: "no rent—no heat." Smith, returning on January 5, abandoned the freezing apartment within days and took up residence in a downtown homeless shelter. Can Dudley sue Smith for the unpaid rent?

Yes. However, the apartment was not habitable from the date the heat was cut off. Thus, no rent would accrue for that period. Also, to Dudley's chagrin, Smith, like Williams in the previous example, could sue for wrongful eviction. Landlords cannot indirectly evict a tenant by cutting off services, such as water, heat, electricity, and so forth. Unless a tenant voluntarily complies with a request or demand to vacate the premises, court remedies must be obtained. As a practical matter, it would be very unlikely that Dudley would pursue litigation against the insolvent Smith.

All states provide for statutory remedies that enable a landlord to resolve the problem of a defaulting tenant who remains in possession. These proceedings generally are *summary proceedings,* and different terms for the process are used in different states. Other common titles are **unlawful detainer,** *dispossessory warrant* proceedings, and *forcible entry* proceedings.

Uniformly, the purpose of summary proceedings is to secure possession of the premises quickly, pending any subsequent and time-consuming litigation concerning collection

unlawful detainer

A statutory remedy for a landlord to evict a renter who has defaulted in the payment of rent or who has broken the terms of the lease in some other manner. It is not a full-blown trial on all issues before a jury.

of unpaid rent, forfeiture of deposits, or monetary damages. Because summary proceedings for eviction are so important, involving a person's shelter, most states

grace period

A period of time during which a tardy payment on a debt, a home-purchase mortgage, or rent will be accepted without penalty. The grace period is the time between the due date of a payment and the delinquent date, following which a penalty may be assessed.

- Require a notice to precede the litigation, giving the tenant a **grace period** to cure the default
- Make trial by jury available to decide disputed factual contentions, although this option imposes expenses upon the tenant and landlord and practically requires hiring attorneys
- Permit the tenant who acted in good faith to continue occupancy by paying all overdue rent and court costs even after loss of the case
- Give the proceedings priority of hearing time on court calendars, which are frequently crowded

Eviction, when decreed by the court, is effected by the marshal, sheriff, or other designated officer who physically removes the tenants (if necessary) and places their personal belongings, if abandoned, in a municipal warehouse or other designated place. Personal property may be redeemed by the tenant upon payment of storage fees. Some states give landlords a *lien* (a formal, legal claim) on all of the tenant's property abandoned in the apartment. The practical effect is to guarantee the landlord that the value of the property ultimately will be applied to unpaid rent as well as to storage costs. However, the landlord must instigate court proceedings to cause the property to be sold.

Although the disposition of abandoned personal property may sound unreasonably harsh at first blush, the tenant has the opportunity and responsibility to make other arrangements. Only under exceptional circumstances are valuable goods left behind by an evicted tenant. Warehouses that store belongings must be paid for their services, and usually enjoy a statutory **possessory lien** to help assure payment of storage fees through sale of the goods, if necessary. Either way, the handling of such a tenant's property is unpleasant for all persons who are involved.

possessory lien

A lien that empowers a creditor to retain possession of the collateral until the debt is paid or until it is sold to the highest bidder in accordance with law.

The typical defense to a summary proceeding for eviction is exemplified by the tenant who testifies: "Yes, I admit I did not pay the rent. But that was because the toilet does not work," or "There's a big leak in the roof." This response may or may not be a proper defense to the eviction proceedings, depending on who has the duty to repair and maintain under the contractual terms of the lease, or under applicable statutes. Unfortunately, most tenants are not adequately informed as to the laws of their state and do not know whether they can successfully resist eviction on the grounds that the premises are not habitable. The tenant facing summary eviction is in a difficult position. It is possible to simply appear in court at the designated time and testify as to the conditions that render the premises uninhabitable. But many lease forms provide for the recovery of attorney fees in addition to rent and court costs. In some metropolitan areas, public interest attorneys are available through nearby law schools or legal aid services, but they are restricted to low-income tenants. Hiring a private attorney is an expensive proposition, although specialists can be identified from advertisements and may be reasonably priced due to the volume of these routine cases they handle. Unfortunately, many tenants with proper defenses of non-habitability probably give up the fight and simply move on.

On the other hand, landlords can be made to suffer from "tenants from hell" who do not pay their rent on time or at all. Many public interest lawyers are experts in resisting evictions, both properly and improperly. It is unethical for an attorney to use legal procedures to stall an eviction that is legally justified, and court-ordered sanctions (monetary fines) can be imposed to punish such unethical behavior. But as a practical matter, it is almost impossible to determine if an attorney is employing judicial tactics for ethical or unethical reasons.

SECURITY DEPOSITS

LEGAL FOCUS—BACKGROUND

In June 2002 the following appeared in *The Buffalo News:* "Nick Sidoti's nose itched at the rancid smell. A stench of urine, smoke, mold and spoiled food hung in the air as cut-up winter blankets filtered the cold spring sunlight through the windows. The Riverside neighborhood apartment was littered with garbage bags, uneaten food, glasses filled with furry mold, empty beer bottles and an open box of macaroni and cheese. In the bedroom, a pristine Holy Bible sat beside a table of burnt marijuana stems. Sidoti, the landlord, took a good look around. "I hate to say this," he said, "but this is not bad."[9]

Security deposits are lump-sum cash payments commonly demanded by landlords to protect them from various forms of loss that may result when a renter defaults, or if unpaid rent is due when the lease ends. The legal right to the return of a security deposit depends on how it is characterized by the court interpreting the documents involved. It may be considered (1) an advance payment of rent, (2) a bonus for the landlord for renting to the tenant, (3) liquidated or agreed-upon damages that may later be owed to the landlord, or (4) security for the tenant's performance. Let's look at each of these interpretations.

LEGAL FOCUS—BACKGROUND

"Security deposit" means value given, in money or its equivalent, to secure the payment of rent by the tenant under a leasehold agreement or to secure payment for damage to and cleaning of the leasehold premises. If a leasehold agreement or an agreement incident thereto requires the tenant or prospective tenant to provide or maintain in effect any deposit to the landlord for part or all of the term of the leasehold agreement, the deposit shall be presumed to be a security deposit. A fee or charge for cleaning and damages, no matter how designated, is presumed to be a security deposit. [Montana Statutes 70-25-101 (4)]

http://

See the legal uses for security deposits listed according to Montana law
http://www.mv.com/ ipusers/nhpoa/mtdepo.htm

First, the deposit may be designated as an advance payment of rent (called *prepaid rent*), usually for the first and last month of the occupancy. It serves to give the landlord security because the tenant has something to lose if the premises are abandoned. In such event, the rental unit is paid for while the landlord locates another tenant. But advance rent is rent; it cannot be retained by the landlord as compensation for damage or cleaning.

Another use of the security deposit is as a "bonus," or "key money" paid to a landlord when desirable rental quarters are hard to find. It is owned by the landlord and is not refundable under any circumstances.

A third use is as **liquidated damages,** an amount of money the parties agree will compensate the landlord for any property damages that may occur in the future, whether or not the actual amount for repairing the damage turns out to be more or less. Liquidated damage clauses are seldom found in leases because state laws limit their use, for example, to situations where actual damages would be very difficult to prove.

On the other hand, a security deposit is commonly used as a security fund held by the landlord to be applied against any actual losses incurred by the landlord from any default

liquidated damages

Amount of damages that contracting parties have previously agreed would be fair payment in case of breach. This amount will be unacceptable by a court if it is so large as to constitute a penalty.

by the tenant. Any portion of the security deposit in excess of actual damages must be refunded to the tenant; if actual damages exceed the amount of deposit, the tenant remains liable for their payment.

The prospective tenant should insist that a clearly understandable provision in the lease explains the ultimate disposition of the security deposit. Although a true security deposit (as distinguished from prepaid rent) is the tenant's money until properly applied to damages, the landlord is not, in most jurisdictions, obligated to pay any interest on it to the tenant.

Disputes often arise in connection with the return of security deposits because of disagreement as to the condition of the premises at the beginning and at the end of the term. Also, there can be differences in opinion as to what constitutes ordinary wear and tear, which is generally defined as deterioration attributable to the passage of time and reasonable use by a tenant rather than abuse or wrongful conduct.

LEGAL FOCUS—PROBLEM

Harry Okamoto, Sally Broome, Kristina Duval, and Jocelyn Powers rented a home in the neighborhood of the university they were attending. The home was owned by an elderly widow who had moved to an apartment in a nearby city to be closer to her children following the death of her husband. The rent was mailed to her each month. After Okamoto and his roommates moved out at the end of their two-year lease, they wrote and asked for return of their $1,000 security deposit. A rental management company reported to the widow that paths were worn in the carpets, the paint around all light switches and door handles was scratched and stained, grease spatters on the walls around the kitchen stove and sink were permanent, there were permanent water stains on the drapes caused by outside sprinklers that had been showering the open windows, the toilet was "running" constantly and two faucets were dripping, the linoleum in the kitchen and bathrooms was curling at the edges and needed replacement, there was a hole in a window screen, and there was water damage to the subfloor around the shower in each bathroom. Can the widow use the security deposit to repair the items?

ordinary wear and tear

Deterioration in a residential rental property that is attributable to the passage of time (e.g., fading of draperies) and not to abuse by the tenant.

Probably not. All of the items would ordinarily and gradually occur in any house occupied by four college students. These kinds of deterioration are called **ordinary wear and tear** in the law. Over time, interior paint will fade, discolor, and even crack; carpets will wear down, especially in high-traffic areas; curtains will sag, lose their shape, and discolor from the sun's rays and from oxidation; sediment in water will accumulate around rubber washers and cause faucets to leak; caulking around showers and tubs will discolor, crack, and ultimately leak; wood surfaces around door handles and cupboard pulls will mar from fingers and fingernails, and so forth. Sprinkler damage is not the tenant's responsibility, nor is the window screen damage unless caused by one of the tenants. Tenants are not legally responsible for correcting these types of damage.

Examples of damage beyond ordinary wear and tear, which usually are indeed the tenant's responsibility, include cigarette burns on furniture, permanent stains on carpets, chipped porcelain in sinks, burns on rugs and floors from fireplace embers, broken windows or damaged light fixtures, scratched and gouged walls, animal urine on carpeting or flooring, and graffiti on walls and ceiling.

Dirt is not damage, nor is it ordinary wear and tear and so it is considered differently for purposes of security deposits. However, at the end of a rental tenancy, the tenant is legally obligated to leave the premises just as clean as when the tenancy began. If the tenant breaches this legal obligation, the landlord may use the security, i.e., cleaning, deposit to make the premises just as clean as when the tenancy began. The landlord cannot rightfully retain security deposits to make the premises cleaner than when the tenant took possession, even if the deposit is labeled a "cleaning deposit" in the paperwork. Sometimes the distinction between cleanliness and damage is fuzzy, as when an oven has been used but left without cleaning over a long period of time, or when toilet bowl stains become permanent from lack of periodic cleaning. If the security deposit is inadequate to return the premises to as clean a condition as when the tenancy began, the tenant remains liable for any additional money that may be required.

Generally, the landlord and tenant are free to contract as they please. However, because of their unequal bargaining power, courts will not enforce certain terms that frequently appear in landlord-tenant agreements because they are "against public policy." For example, a security deposit that is agreed to be nonrefundable nonetheless must be refunded to the extent it is not applied to some proper purpose, such as the repair of damage to the apartment.

http://

Read advice from Pine Tree Legal Assistance in Maine on how a tenant can get a deposit back
http://www.ptla.org/ securitydeposit.htm

LEGAL REMEDIES FOR TENANTS

IMPLIED WARRANTY OF HABITABILITY

Under archaic principles of common law, a landlord had no continuing duty to maintain the rented premises; the tenant had the duty to maintain and repair. Under modern law, the landlord does have a continuing duty to provide and to maintain habitability and to make repairs unless otherwise provided in the lease agreement.[10] This duty, called the **implied warranty of habitability,** means that the landlord guarantees that there are no concealed defects in the facilities (i.e., those that are vital to the use of the premises for residential purposes) because of faulty original construction or deterioration from age or normal usage. This warranty applies to the condition of the premises at the time the rental arrangement is made.

implied warranty of habitability

(a) An implied guarantee in a lease that there are no concealed defects in the rented premises existing at the beginning of the lease term. (b) An implied obligation upon a landlord to maintain leased premises in a condition fit for use and enjoyment by the tenant through the term of the lease.

LEGAL FOCUS—CASE

Becker fell against an untempered, frosted-glass shower door in the apartment he rented from IRM Corp. Becker broke and lacerated his arm. The landlord was not aware the doors were made of untempered glass, and therefore was not aware of any risk to tenants. Becker sued under a theory of strict product liability, arguing that the landlord should be held liable just like the manufacturer of any defective product. What was the result?

Becker v. IRM Corp., 38 Cal.3d 454, 698 P.2d 116, 213 Cal. Rptr. 213 (California, 1985).

Becker won in a 1985 case in which the California Supreme Court agreed that landlords were strictly liable (without fault) for damages caused by products in the apartments they rented. Courts in other states balked and refused to apply this new interpretation of law. Later the California courts abandoned the rule, ruling that a tenant *cannot* reasonably expect that the landlord will have eliminated defects of which the landlord was unaware and which would not have been disclosed by a reasonable inspection. Thus, the implied warranty of habitability does not support an action for strict liability. In the *Becker* case, even if the landlord had inspected the apartment, the untempered type of glass would not have been apparent. The landlord therefore was not negligent, and Becker would lose if the case arose today.[11] Still, a landlord must exercise due care in the management of the rental property to avoid foreseeable injury to tenants and others.

The implied warranty of habitability gives a tenant a reasonable expectation that the landlord has inspected the rental dwelling and corrected any defects disclosed by that inspection that would render the dwelling uninhabitable. The tenant further can expect that the landlord will maintain the property in a habitable condition by repairing promptly any conditions of which the landlord has actual or constructive notice that arise during the tenancy. Some states, however, reject the implied warranty of habitability.

LEGAL FOCUS—CASE

Robert Flain, visiting a friend who rented a home in Casper, Wyoming, fell down the rickety stairs leading to the basement and was seriously injured. There were no handrails on the dimly lit stairs. Flain sues the landlord for bodily injury from negligence. Can Flain win his case?

Ortega v. Flain, 902 P.2d 199 (Wyoming, 1995).

Not in Wyoming, which follows the old common-law rule under which a landlord owes no duty of care to tenants or their guests. Wyoming is a "Let the Tenant Beware" state, unlike the vast majority of states that have established an implied warranty of habitability. Under the modern rule, a jury would have decided whether the condition of the staircase violated an implied warranty of habitability. Even in Wyoming, the landlord owes a duty of reasonable care in maintaining the premises over which control is retained, such as hallways and parking lots.

Under the more modern view, the landlord is responsible for necessary maintenance and repairs arising during the lease term (e.g., stopped-up toilet, broken air conditioner, burned-out water heater, leaky faucet). However, the parties are free to include a provision in their lease specifying that the tenant will make specified or all repairs. Unfortunately, in part due to their unequal bargaining power, the lessee-tenant frequently agrees to make all repairs, thereby effectively canceling any implied warranty of habitability. Unless so specified, the landlord has an ongoing duty to make repairs. Repairs made necessary because of the negligence of the tenant are, of course, the responsibility of the tenant.

Generally, the warranty of habitability applies to major physical defects in the property that affect the tenant's quality of life (e.g., a serious leak in the roof). The landlord has a reasonable time to repair such major defects. A defect that is merely unattractive or annoying, such as a crack in a wall, probably will not violate the warranty. Unless the crack is a structural defect or affects the residence's heating capabilities, it generally is not serious enough to make the property uninhabitable. In deciding whether a defect violates the landlord's warranty, courts may consider the following:

- Did the tenant cause the defect, or is the tenant otherwise responsible for it?
- How long has the defect existed?
- What is the age of the building? A newer building is expected to have fewer problems.
- What is the defect's impact—present and potential—on the tenant's health, safety, and activities, such as sleeping and eating?
- Is the defect in violation of housing, building, or sanitation codes?

The landlord is responsible for maintaining common areas, such as halls, stairways, and elevators. This duty requires repair of defects of which the landlord has actual knowledge and of those the landlord should know about.

Tenants have duties also. Lease agreements contain clauses requiring tenants to comply with the law and incorporate rules that purport to regulate conduct. The state has an obligation to provide for the health, safety, and welfare of the public, and thus has an interest in tenant life. State statutes[12] may require tenants to keep premises as clean and sanitary as conditions of premises permit (slum property less sanitary than a suburban garden apartment); to dispose of all rubbish and trash; to pay for any fumigation necessary for removal of any infestation caused by the tenant (e.g., cockroaches, fleas, lice); to properly use all plumbing, heating, and appliances; to not intentionally trash the premises (doing so may be a crime); and to not engage in or permit drug-related activities in the premises. As a practical matter, police are not aware of any tenant violations until some commotion occurs, or until a landlord calls them to press criminal charges.* The police power also extends to homeowners, but in a slightly different way. For example, municipal ordinances ordinarily require trash to be disposed of, limit the kinds of animals owned (public health hazard), limit noise levels, and prohibit certain activities (practicing with firearms). But the renters in apartments may be more closely regulated because of the high density and, hence, close proximity of families, the semipublic nature of the premises that can themselves invite mischief, as well as the property interest of landlords.

As already noted, courts and state legislatures consistently have been abandoning the old common-law rules and have been imposing certain duties upon landlords to maintain and repair their premises reasonably, unless otherwise agreed. In this way, the common law is continually expanding, meeting new and changing circumstances.

The **covenant of quiet enjoyment** is a duty implied by law and declared by courts to be an incident of the landlord-tenant relationship. The historical covenant merely provides that the tenant will not be put out of possession (i.e., evicted) by any act or failure of the landlord. Courts have extended this principle so that any substantial interference with the tenant's use of the premises is considered a violation of the implied covenant of quiet enjoyment.

covenant of quiet enjoyment

A promise usually implied from the landlord that others will not interfere with the tenant's right to occupy the premises.

LEGAL FOCUS—PROBLEM

Brenda Castro and Julie Madison, MBA students, were roommates at Shady Tree Apartments, which were managed by Marta Johnson. Billy Baba, who lived next door, hosted loud and boisterous "Monday night football" parties; on Friday nights, he threw wild and noisy "TGIF" parties. As many as twenty to thirty people routinely attended these parties, which lasted until long after midnight. After their repeated complaints to Johnson that they couldn't sleep or study, Castro and Madison suddenly broke their one-year lease and moved out. Seven months remained on their lease and their rent was $1,200 per month. Can Johnson sue Castro and Madison for the unpaid rent?

Not if Castro and Madison provide documented strong evidence of the offensiveness of Baba's parties. The law treats certain serious and wrongful conduct, or neglect by a landlord, as a **constructive eviction,** which is equivalent to an actual wrongful, physical evic-

constructive eviction

Indirect eviction of a tenant by means of the landlord's failure to correct an intolerable interference or defects in the premises, which effectively drives the tenant out.

---

* Recall from Chapter 6 that the attempt to obtain a monetary advantage by threatening prosecution of a crime is a variety of the felony called extortion. There is a world of difference between calling the police and threatening to call the police unless monetary restitution is made.

tion. Violation of the covenant of quiet enjoyment is one example of wrongful conduct or neglect. Madison and Castro could sue their landlord Johnson for tort damages (including, e.g., mental distress and suffering) and moving costs on the theory of a wrongful eviction. Some courts would award them damages for any increase in rent they were required to pay for a similar apartment. In some states they could ask for punitive damages, although the failure to provide peace and quiet doesn't appear to be particularly egregious conduct. Note that Castro and Madison would have no basis to sue Baba for damages. Baba was committing no tort even if he was breaking the published rules of the apartment by hosting noisy parties.*

Less egregious conduct by a landlord also may be considered a constructive eviction, i.e., a violation of the covenant of quiet enjoyment. For example, in cases where a clogged sewer pipe caused foul odors, where there was lack of heat, and where the landlord permitted occupants of other parts of the buildings to carry on lewd activities, courts have found a violation of the implied covenant of quiet enjoyment. These examples do not mean that occasional noise is prohibited. But when persistent offensive and disturbing conduct reaches the level of a constructive eviction, the tenant becomes free to abandon the premises without further responsibility for rent and may sue the landlord for wrongful eviction. In most states, the tenant must vacate the premises before suing for a constructive eviction.[13]

In addition to this developing private duty upon landlords to maintain rental premises, most cities and towns have housing ordinances designed to protect the health, safety, and welfare of renters and the public and to prevent the deterioration of dwellings to substandard or slum conditions. These ordinances may impose alleged hardships upon landlords, but they are constitutional exercises of the police power. Typically, for example, these ordinances require that flush toilets, lavatory sinks, bathtubs and showers, kitchen stoves and refrigerators, heating systems, and similar essentials be maintained by the landlord in good operating order.

Failure to comply with housing codes or ordinances may subject a landlord to government sanctions. But the landlord's obligation is to the municipality and not to the tenant, who, accordingly, cannot bring an action to enforce such codes and ordinances. The tenant is entitled to complain to the appropriate local official and wait for administrative enforcement of the housing code.

retaliatory eviction

An eviction carried out by a landlord primarily for revenge, or retaliation, against a particular tenant who has in some way angered the landlord.

A **retaliatory eviction** (an eviction for revenge) occurs when a landlord evicts a tenant because the tenant insisted upon enforcement of some right, such as by complaining to a local official of a building code violation. Most states, by statute, specifically prohibit retaliatory evictions and provide remedies for occasions when they occur. Aggrieved tenants, however, must prove by a preponderance of the evidence that the eviction was motivated by revenge and not for valid reasons.†

Many housing codes impose reciprocal duties of cleanliness and housekeeping upon the tenant, but enforcement is rare, as the landlord usually is reluctant to register a complaint that will invite inspection of the premises by an official.

If the landlord fails to maintain the premises, what remedy is available to the tenant? Under such circumstances, and depending on the terms of the lease and the state statutes involved, one of the following situations exists:

- The landlord is breaching an implied warranty of habitability or an implied covenant of quiet enjoyment (whether the duty was created by court decision or by statute).

---

* Some cities have adopted "noise" ordinances that make persistent noise-making (above a specified decibel level) an infraction punishable by fine. At some level of boisterousness, party-making may constitute the misdemeanor crime of disturbing the peace. Under the common law, persistent excessive noise may be declared a civil nuisance and enjoined by a court of equity.

† The obvious defense for an aggressive "landlord's attorney" to assert in a case for retaliatory eviction is that the tenant broke the lease or violated the rules and deserved eviction. This explains why some apartments have very strict rules that are enforced only when necessary to get rid of an undesirable tenant.

- The landlord is violating a term in the rental agreement or lease.
- The tenant has the duty to repair and there is no remedy against the landlord.

If the landlord persists in violating a duty to maintain or repair, the tenant is free to declare the lease terminated and abandon the premises. This breach of duty will be a good defense for the tenant in any action the landlord might later pursue seeking unpaid rent.

More likely, however, the tenant desires to remain in possession as originally agreed, and simply wants the landlord to fulfill the duty of maintaining, and if necessary repairing, the premises. Most states require the tenant to pay the rent and then sue for *redress*. Damages recoverable for breach of the covenant of quiet enjoyment or the implied warranty of habitability are measured by the difference between the rental value of the premises actually received and the rental value if the premises had been as "covenanted" or as "warranted." Thus, the costly testimony of expert witnesses as to their opinion of these values may be necessary. Such a suit brought in small claims court may also instigate a retaliatory eviction by the landlord and, thereby, escalate the legal proceedings beyond the willingness of the tenant to proceed. Unfortunately, there often is a practical side to legal remedies that oftentimes look better on paper than they turn out to be when applied in real life.

In most states, legislators have created new remedies for tenants. Some statutes permit the tenant to make necessary repairs and deduct their cost from the rent. The amount of the deduction from rent due usually is limited to a maximum of one month's rent. This remedy of "repair and deduct" is subject to various procedures and limitations. Some states have permitted **abatement,** temporary suspension of the duty of rent payment, as long as the premises remain uninhabitable.

A tenant facing eviction because of a failure to pay rent may admit the charge, but may claim legal justification because of the landlord's failure to maintain the premises. Where an implied warranty of habitability or an expanded covenant of quiet enjoyment exists, the tenant's contention is "relevant" and may constitute a valid defense to the summary proceedings for eviction. Every prospective renter should inquire as to which party will have the duty to maintain and repair. Where feasible, the tenant should negotiate to impose that burden upon the landlord, and have it stated in the terms of the lease; otherwise, the tenant should give long and careful thought to the potential financial burdens of making periodic repairs before blithely assuming that responsibility.

As noted earlier, some real estate scholars believe that forcing landlords to repair and maintain will hurt low-income tenants who are unable to afford increases in rent levels. However, the U.S. Department of Housing and Urban Development (HUD) now is extensively involved in financing and maintaining low-rent housing.

abatement

The suspension of the duty of rent payment while the premises are uninhabitable.

LANDLORD NEGLIGENCE CAUSING BODILY INJURY

The laws of torts apply to landlords and tenants just as they do to everybody else. Thus, if a landlord punches a tenant in the nose, a battery has occurred. But unlike other common situations, such as strangers driving automobiles on a freeway, landlords are in a special position of trust and responsibility for the safety of their tenants. In legal terms, landlords owe a duty of reasonable care for the safety of their tenants. States may adopt statutes that declare a specified duty of a landlord. For example, in California apartment landlords have a duty to install and maintain deadbolt locks and must provide locking devices on windows and on all exterior doors that lead to common areas, such as lobbies.[14]

The specific duties of landlords that are required by law often become an issue when tenants are injured by the criminal activities of third persons. On the one hand, landlords are not police officers and have no general responsibility to protect the public or tenants from criminal acts. However, landlords do have the duty to take all reasonably necessary management steps to protect tenants from unreasonable risks of criminal activity.

LEGAL FOCUS—CASE

Marisela Gomez, age twelve, was waiting for an elevator in the lobby of the 150-unit apartment building in New York City where she lived. She saw a man enter through the back door of the lobby, which was always ajar because it did not fit in its frame correctly. The man entered the elevator with Gomez and several other people, but he did not push a button to select a floor. When Gomez exited the elevator, the man followed, forced her to the building's roof, and then raped her. Gomez sued the landlord for negligently failing to maintain the back door. The trial court dismissed her case on the basis that there was no evidence the assailant was an intruder. The assailant could have been another tenant, and thus the broken door would not be the proximate cause of the crime. The fact that no one recognized the assailant is not sufficient proof that he was an intruder—in a large apartment building nobody would recognize every tenant or tenant's guest. Gomez appealed. What was the result on appeal?

Gomez v. New York City Housing Authority, 92 N.Y.2d 544, 706 N.E.2d 1163 (New York, 1998).

Gomez won on appeal. The court was persuaded that the man was an intruder because he made no attempt to conceal his identity although he knew there were other tenants about, who might recognize a neighbor. The fact that the assailant did not push an elevator button also caused the court to view him as an intruder (although a tenant rapist who was following Gomez would also not know which button to push until she got off the elevator). The court held that a jury could find the landlord liable to Gomez for the negligent failure to maintain a properly locked rear door. The entrance of a criminal through an unlocked door is reasonably foreseeable, at least in high-crime areas. If doors to the lobby of the building never were locked, and if that fact was made known to prospective tenants, there would be no liability for the crimes of third parties (unless locked doors were required by statute). But, by providing locked doors, the landlord was obligated to keep them operating in good repair.

LEGAL FOCUS—CASE

Norma Burgos lived in a mid-rise apartment building with 25 units. One evening she opened her door into the common area hallway, only to be accosted by two unmasked men who, after pushing her back into her apartment, beat and robbed her. She sued her landlord for negligence in failing to maintain functioning locks on any of the three entrances—the front door, back door, or roof door. The landlord defended on the basis that there was no proof that the assailants were "intruders" and thus no evidence that the unlocked doors were the proximate cause of Burgos's injuries. Who wins?

Burgos v. Aqueduct Realty Corp., 92 N.Y.2d 544, 706 N.E.2d 1163 (New York, 1998).

Burgos wins. Because the assailants were unmasked, the court reasoned, they probably were not residents of the building. Burgos does not need to prove absolutely that the assailants were strangers who gained access through the unlocked doors—only that it is more likely than not. Thus, the liability of a landlord in New York City under these circumstances depends on whether or not an assailant is wearing a mask. The premise is that tenants (for whom there would be no liability) would wear masks to avoid recognition, while strangers who entered through an unlocked door would not bother.

As noted above, landlords are not guarantors of the safety of tenants from criminal acts by third persons. But when criminal acts are foreseeable, a landlord can be held liable for failing to take steps to prevent a crime, such as by failing to install sufficient exterior lighting. Whether or not criminal acts were foreseeable is influenced by the existence of similar criminal acts on or near the premises.

LEGAL FOCUS—PROBLEM

Norm Bates owns Bates Garden Apartments, which are managed by Bryan Walker. There are four buildings, a swimming pool, laundry room, and extensive landscaping. On the day that Amiee Morris asked for and received a rental application for Unit #15, the following circumstances existed:

- A pardoned sex offender and stalker was living in Unit #13.
- Over the preceding two years, no fewer than six master keys had become misplaced, stolen, or kept by former gardeners or maintenance workers.
- The few night lights above the parking area were out of order.
- The chlorine level in the pool had not been checked for three months and the sides were slimy to the touch.
- Bates had received an annual notification that the drinking water serving the area was below federal minimum guidelines.
- There was lead in the hot water piping and in the paint used in most apartment units.
- The four apartment buildings, built by Bates's father some twenty-five years earlier, had asbestos insulation.
- The complex was located in an earthquake and flood zone, and renter's insurance therefore was more costly than otherwise.
- There were no safety locks on the sliding glass doors that led from bedrooms to patios.
- Last year there had been a murder in Unit #15 involving a teenage gang member.
- Homicide police had visited the previous month inquiring about the tenant who lived in Unit #17. They assured Bates that the tenant was not a suspect yet.
- The manager, Walker, once had been convicted of voluntary manslaughter but had fully served his three-year sentence. Bates was unaware of this fact, and also had no knowledge of the history of the gardener who carried a master key and hung out in the apartment workshop all day.
- The locks on Unit #15 had not been rekeyed during the residency of the preceding three tenants, the most recent of whom had been evicted for verbally harassing other tenants.

> Which of the preceding circumstances does the law require landlords to reveal to prospective tenants?

This example is not as bizarre as it may first appear to be. The laws safeguarding prospective buyers of homes are more protective than the laws safeguarding prospective renters. As you will learn in Chapter 12, although the laws of the states are not uniform, taken together they require disclosure to the buyer of most of the preceding circumstances. These same states do not require such advance disclosures to renters.

Although Morris may not have been told of these strange circumstances before she rented, she is owed reasonable care by her landlord. To put it differently, suppose that Morris rented Unit #15 and subsequently was gravely injured as the proximate result of action related to any of the listed circumstances. Could she sue and recover damages from Bates for negligently failing to inform her? The general answer is yes, even though she was not informed of the circumstances at the outset. Let's consider some laws that apply differently to renters than to buyers:

- Home sellers must inform buyers of convicted sex offenders who are neighbors, or minimally how the buyers can learn the residence of nearby offenders. State legislators someday may apply Megan's Law (discussed in Chapter 9) to renters.
- Home sellers in many states must inform buyers of earthquake and flood zones, of water quality, of the presence of lead or asbestos, and even whether or not water heaters are strapped to walls. Although ignored now, can it be too far in the new millennium before courts will protect prospective tenants with comparable zealousness?
- In Minnesota, owners of apartments are required by law to screen prospective managers and cannot hire persons who have been convicted of, for example, stalking, rape, or murder.* Can we expect other states to follow suit? Of course, homeowners do not have managers, but many are subject to homeowner associations. Should they be screened?
- As already noted, deadbolt locks often are required by law on apartments, as are smoke alarms, and locks on windows and doors to outside entrances to common areas. Homeowners must also install smoke alarms but are free to provide whatever other security devices they choose.
- Home sellers in some states must inform buyers of any unnatural deaths that have occurred in the home (other than by AIDS), such as by murder or suicide. Renters need not be informed even though they are just as likely to be affected psychologically as buyers.

In considering whether or not the law ought to protect renters to the same degree as it protects buyers, ask yourself whether you, as a renter, feel entitled to be informed of the items listed in the Bates Garden Apartments example. Under law, the landlord makes an implied (unwritten) representation that the premises are fit for use as a dwelling. Are the Bates Garden Apartments fit? There is a pertinent distinction between the nature of disclosures to buyers on the one hand and to renters on the other. Buyers are concerned about matters that affect the value of the home they are about to purchase, while renters are not. Renters are more concerned with disclosures that pertain to their safety and enjoyment of the premises. Perhaps that distinction will influence the evolving laws concerning what information landlords must provide to prospective renters.

There are unique risks of harm, especially to females, from living in apartments that typically do not have "neighborhood crime watch" programs, that are located in high-density

---

* The Kari Koskinen Manager Background Check Act was adopted in response to the murder of Kari Koskinen by her apartment manager, who, unbeknownst to her, was a convicted felon.

locations that often provide housing for the more transient and less affluent members of society, and that may be more likely to house convicted sex offenders than residential neighborhoods.

LEGAL FOCUS—PROBLEM

Rosa Hidalgo, a very meticulous person, lived alone in a one-bedroom apartment near Sacramento State University, where she was a sophomore. The apartment manager, Ben Willard, 23, had a long history of sex-related accusations, including peeping, stalking, and flashing, while he was a juvenile. Willard had been suspected, accused, investigated, and warned but never convicted. One afternoon Hidalgo returned home from school and soon developed a sense of uneasiness—it was as if something in her apartment was not precisely the way it had been left. The next day Hidalgo left concealed threads and buttons balancing on dresser drawers—when she returned, her greatest fears were realized—the buttons and threads had fallen. Someone had been in her dresser. What legal remedy does the terrified Hidalgo have?

None, as a practical matter. Hidalgo is unaware of the suspicious circumstances surrounding Willard, who may be innocent. Although Hidalgo has been injured mentally, an attorney would be very unlikely to sue the landlord on the basis of a general suspicion with the hope of finding evidence later. Unlike Morris in the preceding Bates example, Hidalgo had no tangible evidence nor physical injury to support a claim of wrongdoing upon which a case could be filed. Testimony might show that Willard had been negligently hired, or that the master keys had been carelessly managed, or that the locks on Hidalgo's door had not been changed. But without additional evidence, a lawsuit would be unlikely.* This dilemma points out the vulnerability of tenants, like Hidalgo, whose regular comings and goings are obvious to persons on the premises who possess master keys.

Recognizing the opportunity for abusive violations of tenant privacy, some states have enacted statutes addressing the problem. For example, Minnesota adopted the Tenant's Right to Privacy Act, under which a $100 fine, payable to the tenant, is imposed for each illegal entry.[15] Apartment managers are entitled to enter and inspect the premises, or to make repairs, but only after reasonable notice is given to the tenant. Thus, statutes restricting entries by landlords may do little to help in situations like Hidalgo's where an illegal entry is intended for illegal purposes. It would not be illegal or necessarily negligent for the apartment owner to hire someone with Willard's background as apartment manager. Minnesota also requires the screening of applicants for apartment manager jobs and makes it illegal to hire convicted felons. But even that law would not disqualify Willard.

LEGAL FOCUS—PROBLEM

Hei Ainy Lai owned a vicious dog, a Doberman, which she believed was necessary for her protection while she was in her apartment and outside while jogging. She paid additional

* You may recall that attorneys can obtain information by using written interrogatories and depositions. But those devices are available only after civil litigation has been commenced. Attorneys ethically cannot use a lawsuit as a device to search for evidence to justify the filing of the case. If that were done for Hidalgo, and if Willard were innocent, and if the keys had been properly maintained, the attorney personally might be held accountable by a lawsuit for malicious prosecution—a serious intentional tort.

rent each month for the privilege of keeping the dog. While the dog was exercising on the apartment lawn, it attacked and severely injured Albert East, a guest who was visiting his girlfriend who also lived in the complex. East sued the landlord for his injuries, primarily because Lai carried no personal liability insurance. What will the result be?

East probably will win if the landlord knew, or should have known, the dangerous propensity of the dog.* As soon as an animal's dangerous propensity is known, a prudent landlord should request the tenant to immediately remove the animal from the premises. If the tenant fails to act, his or her lease should be terminated by the landlord to avoid injury to others as well as personal liability. While eviction proceedings are underway, the landlord should seek the assistance of local officials and, if reasonably necessary under the circumstances, warn other tenants and others likely to be endangered, such as postal employees. The landlord would be wise to include a provision in the lease agreement that if pets exhibit any dangerous tendencies, they must be removed within a few days or the tenant shall be evicted. Some landlords refuse to rent to tenants with animals. The landlord is not responsible for injuries caused by tenants' pets that previously have exhibited no dangerous propensities, or are not inherently dangerous.

LEGAL FOCUS—CASE

Lewis Crowell's father rented an apartment from the Dallas Housing Authority. The apartment contained a defective gas heater that leaked carbon monoxide gas. The lease contained an exculpatory clause stating the landlord would not be liable for any negligence. The father died of carbon monoxide poisoning and the son sued the landlord. Is the clause enforceable? In other words, is the landlord relieved from legal responsibility?

Crowell v. Housing Authority, 495 S.W.2d 887 (Texas, 1973).

exculpatory clause

Provision in a contractual agreement (e.g., a lease) by which a party agrees not to hold the other party responsible for his or her negligence.

An **exculpatory clause** is a provision in a lease or rental agreement under which the tenant agrees that the landlord shall not be liable for negligence. At common law, through the use of exculpatory clauses, landlords could effectively escape liability for personal injuries caused by their negligence in maintaining the premises or caused by physical defects in the premises. Liability could not be avoided for willful or wanton misconduct, for this would be against public policy. Legislatures in most states now prohibit broad exculpatory clauses, or severely limit their scope, and courts in the remaining states have modernized the common law by ruling that exculpatory clauses are often unenforceable, being against public policy. In this Texas case the court held the exculpatory clause void against public policy and allowed the son to recover for the loss of his father.

ASSIGNING AND SUBLETTING

sublease

The transfer by a tenant of less than the full, unexpired term of the lease to a subtenant.

A lease may prohibit the future transfer of possession of the rented premises by the resident to a substitute tenant. Such a transfer is either an assignment or, more commonly, a **sublease.** An assignment is the transfer of the full unexpired term of the lease, while a sublease

---

* Lai is, of course, liable for the damages caused by her dog. If the landlord were held responsible and paid the claim, he or she could seek indemnification from Lai. But the problem is a practical one—with no liability insurance, the tenant is judgment-proof.

is the transfer of less than the full term. The distinction, although potentially important, is ignored for the purposes of this discussion.

The lessor usually does not want another person, of unknown desirability as a tenant, to appear suddenly as a subtenant. On the other hand, a tenant who has permission to assign has a practical escape route from the lease if it becomes necessary (e.g., when a change of employment occurs). A typical compromise is for the lessor to permit an assignment or sublease "subject to approval." If such a term is provided in the lease, the approval must not be unreasonably withheld by the lessor. Solid reasons to withhold approval of a prospective substitute tenant would be a poor credit record or a history of evictions from prior rental units. Following a proper assignment, the former tenant may be released from liability for future rent, although this is not necessarily so. For example, a tenant may choose to sublease to a new, substitute tenant but at a slightly reduced rent. The landlord, presented with a request to approve this arrangement, would no doubt ask the original tenant to remain responsible on the original lease and to personally make up any discounted rent. The landlord is legally bound to be reasonable in approving proposed subleases but is not required to accept discounted rent or any other material alteration in the original lease.

LEGAL FOCUS—PROBLEM

Jill Newton, Maria Medina, and Crissy Bell, juniors at Lighthouse University, signed a lease on a three-bedroom condominium at the beginning of the school year. They agreed to share the $1,200 per month rent plus all utilities equally. Consider each of the following situations:

1. Bell needed to drop out of school for a quarter, but intended to return for the following quarter.
2. Bell flunked out of school and needed to return to her hometown.
3. Bell developed personality conflicts with her roommates and wanted out of the lease so she could move into campus housing.

What are Bell's options under each of the three scenarios?

Under the first alternative, Bell could *sublease* to a substitute tenant who would agree to pay Bell's share of the rent and utilities. The landlord could refuse to permit the sublease, but only for good reason, such as if the proposed sublessee had a history of damaging apartments and fighting with landlords about repairs. Bell would remain responsible for her share of the rent, and could continue making payments personally while collecting from her sublessee. Or Bell could permit her sublessee to make payments directly to her roommates. If Bell's subtenant agreed to pay only $350 rent each month, Bell would be responsible to make up the $50 per month deficiency. This arrangement would at least minimize her loss. Bell would return at the end of the sublease and resume her living arrangement with her roommates.

Under the second alternative, Bell could *assign* her lease to a substitute tenant who could agree to pay Bell's share of the rent and utilities until the end of the lease. Bell would have no right to return and resume living in the premises following assignment of the entire unexpired term of her lease. The landlord could, but need not, release Bell from the lease completely. Otherwise, the same consequences follow that pertain to the first alternative.

Under the third alternative, Bell has the power to simply move out and abandon her lease. However, she cannot "abandon" or avoid her legal obligations to pay rent. If Newton and Medina paid the entire $1,200 each month, they would have the right to sue Bell to recover rent (and utilities) they paid on her behalf. The landlord could evict Newton and Medina if they paid only $800 rent each month. Each individual tenant is fully responsible for the entire rent; if all the rent is not collected, the remedy of eviction is available to the landlord.

Under all three alternatives, Newton and Medina would have a very significant interest in the course of action Bell selected. They would have to live with any substitute tenant and would undoubtedly be concerned about Bell's willingness to continue her obligations to pay the rent. Proposed roommates are well advised to consider the impact of possible future changes in their circumstances.

How Can a Renter's Problems Be Minimized?

The bargaining power of renters may be slight in communities where vacancies are scarce. Lease and rental agreement forms are commonly supplied by the prospective landlord and favor the owner's legal position. And landlords tend to know more about the applicable laws and customs. How then may a prospective tenant minimize the risk of controversy, litigation, and victimization? Here are some suggestions:

- **Calculate the economics of the transaction.** In addition to the rent, the prospective tenant should inquire about all expenses that will be involved in the rental. Each utility service paid by the tenant (which may or may not include water, gas, electricity, sewage, heating oil, garbage and trash collection, and telephone) should be estimated. Increased commuting costs (in time and money) should be estimated. What penalty, if any, is levied for a tardy rent payment? Are rents increased each year, and if so, by how much? Ask when the last rent increase was made. Consider asking for a longer-term lease to protect against future increases in rent, provided you are reasonably sure you won't be under pressure to move because of a job change or family situation. It sounds simple, but many make the mistake of miscalculating their total housing cost. Don't bite off more than you can comfortably chew.

- **Clarify the landlord's interpretation of the future disposition of all required security deposits.** Often the landlord's forms are not sufficiently clear as to how security deposits are to be used. Ascertain how any deductions, if applicable, are to be calculated; when deposits will be refunded; what the landlord means by ordinary wear and tear; and whether full refunds will be made if there is no damage and the premises are left as clean as when you moved in. Ask when the dwelling was last painted on the inside, and who will be responsible for repainting, and when. Is interest paid on returned deposits? Make thorough notes while obtaining this information. Take date-stamped photos. On important items, later send the landlord a memo stating your understanding of the oral agreement, and keep a copy.

- **Ask about security and prior criminal activity in the building and vicinity.** Everyone expects to be safe and secure in his or her "castle." Unfortunately, some areas are more vulnerable than others to burglaries or even felonious assaults and rapes. The inquiry may prompt the installation of deadbolt locks, window security pins, exterior lighting, or other apparatus designed to reduce the chance of such occurrences, if they have not been previously installed. Although it is true that landlords could lie about this unfavorable information, they are unlikely to do so. If proven, such a lie would subject the landlord to the risk of substantial punitive damages that may not be covered by liability insurance. Landlords are reluctant to accept such serious risks.

- **Ask about master keys and authorized entry.** Many leases and rental agreements do not mention the circumstances under which the landlord may enter the rented premises in the absence of the tenant. Entry should be authorized for an emergency (e.g., a broken water pipe), but otherwise prior notice should be given to the tenant and an appointment made at a mutually convenient time, and for agreed-upon purposes. This discussion should lead to the question of who has a master key and when the locks were last changed. It is not a major task to adjust a lock to reject prior keys. The landlord's manager or agent customarily will have a master key for emergencies. But there is no good reason why the gardener's master key that fits the maintenance shop must also fit your entry door.
- **Ask who has the duty to make needed repairs within the dwelling.** The landlord should regularly have assumed, or should now agree to assume, the responsibility for making all repairs required as a result of normal wear and tear. The tenant should be required to make only those repairs necessitated by the tenant's negligence (e.g., carelessly allowing a spoon to lodge in a garbage disposal) or willfulness (e.g., throwing a beer bottle through a window).
- **Prepare a thorough inventory of the rented premises and their contents** (see Exhibit 11-2). Before moving into the rented apartment or dwelling, inspect the premises for both cleanliness and damage. List your findings room by room. Be accurate and do not exaggerate, a tactic that most likely would serve little purpose other than to anger the landlord. As soon as the inventory is prepared, deliver a signed copy to the landlord (or agent) and obtain a signed copy in return. Keep your copy with your valuable papers for future reference. If the landlord challenges the accuracy of the information, suggest a confirming joint inspection. Sometimes color snapshots are useful, especially if the premises are furnished.

EXHIBIT 11-2: **Inventory of Rented Premises and Their Contents**

Room	Damage	Cleanliness
Kitchen	Chip in counter near stove burners	Dust and debris behind refrigerator
		Linoleum clean but not waxed; several cuts and loose patches
		Encrusted stains in oven and on stove top
Living Room	Electrical outlet cracked	Windows spotted and streaked with dirt
	Hole in ceiling from former hanging object	Stain on carpet near front entry, about one square foot
	Holes in wallboard from picture hangers	
	Carpet torn near entry into kitchen	

Landlord _____

Tenant _____

- **If extraordinary unanticipated expenses compel a tardy payment of rent, advise the landlord in advance.** Often, late charges will be waived in exchange for such prompt and courteous notice; indeed, the desired mutual respect in your landlord and tenant relationship may even be strengthened. A partial payment of rent on time is recommended.
- **Upon departure at term's end, compare the premises to the inventory and ask for a joint inspection with the landlord.** The best times for discussing the condition of the premises (for cleanliness and for damage) are the day of arrival and the day of departure. Comparison of the premises to the previously prepared inventory helps to avoid misunderstandings and disputes. Usually, an agreement can be made on the spot as to the ultimate disposition of the security deposit.

The foregoing suggestions have been arranged in checklist form for quick review (see Exhibit 11-3).

In the event these suggestions do not prevent a serious misunderstanding with the landlord, the best recourse is ADR (alternative dispute resolution), if available. If not, take the matter to the appropriate court, usually a small claims court. In many states, no attorney is necessary to do this, and whatever assistance is required may be obtained from a designated clerk or administrative official. All documents should be available for the court, including your personal notes taken at the time the lease was negotiated and the inventory prepared upon taking occupancy. This procedure is relatively inexpensive and will usually result in a satisfactory solution for the well-prepared tenant who has a valid claim. The successful tenant, depending on the state, may recover attorney fees (if they were actually paid) and double or triple the amount of deposits wrongfully retained by the landlord. In some states, landlords successfully avoid small claims suits by concealing their identity and address, which makes the service of process practically impossible. Only the resident manager is known to the tenant. But a persistent tenant can obtain needed information from the local tax assessor's office or from the record of fictitious business names maintained by the clerk of each county, which lists the true names of owners. In other states, the apartment manager is the agent for accepting process (service of small claims court papers), and that solves the problem. You should ask for this information when initially renting the apartment.

The specific laws governing renters and landlords vary from state to state in considerable detail. We have included a representative sample of them to broaden your understanding and sharpen your analytical skills. However, we believe the information contained in Exhibit 11-3 is so valuable to you that we recommend you reproduce it for use in the future when renting accommodations.*

---

* West Legal Studies in Business authorizes each purchaser of *Understanding the Law* to make one reproduction of the material contained in Exhibit 11-3 for personal use.

EXHIBIT 11-3: **Suggestions for Prospective Renters**

BEFORE SIGNING A LEASE, FIND OUT ABOUT:

Projected expenses (Stay within your budget!)

- What are the personal expenses connected with living in the rental unit?
- What cash is due upon moving in (eg., prepaid rent, cleaning deposit, security deposit, telephone deposit)?
- What are the average utility rates? Are additional deposits required?

Deposits

- What is the disposition of all deposits at the end of the lease? Is a full refund possible?
- Is interest paid on deposits? Are deposits held in a separate account?
- Will your landlord or manager inspect the premises with you on the day of your departure at the end of the lease?

Condition of premises

- What is the condition of each room: ceiling, walls, drapes, carpet, and all doors?
- What date was the unit last painted, the drapes cleaned, and the carpets professionally shampooed? Who pays for these items if they are necessary at the end of the lease?
- What is the operating condition of each appliance? (Check them out.)
- How does your landlord define "ordinary wear and tear"? Who is expected to pay for it at the end of the lease?
- How clean does the landlord expect the unit to be at the end of the lease? (Tell him or her that you will prepare a room-by-room checklist for both of you.)
- Are all light bulbs new? Who must replace them? Are any exterior lights wired into the tenant's system, with the cost of electricity added to the tenant's electrical bill?
- What are policies regarding alterations, hanging framed paintings, pictures, bookcases, decals, adhesive shelf paper, etc.?

Safety

- Under what circumstances will the landlord enter your apartment in your absence?
- Who has master keys? When were the locks last changed? Are there deadbolt locks in the entry doors?
- What security measures are in effect? Is there a roving security patrol?
- Are fire extinguishers provided in or near your prospective unit?
- How soon do police and firefighters respond to a call in that area?
- What lighting exists in and around the unit at night? Are the parking areas well lit at night? (You should visit the prospective unit in the middle of the night to see for yourself.)
- What security problems have there been in the past? Assaults, burglaries, or thefts from cars?
- What is the policy about confidentiality of your rental application?
- Who are the neighboring tenants? Have there been any prior noise, safety, or other problems with them, or with traffic on fronting or nearby streets during rush hours?
- Are there safety pins or other devices for securing sliding glass doors?
- Are all windows equipped with screens? Are they in good condition?

Rights and responsibilities

- What are the rules of the rental property regarding television and stereo use, swimming, parking, guests, parties, laundry facilities, and the like?
- Under what circumstances may a tenant break the lease? What about a job change, flunking out of college, illness, marriage, divorce, or birth of a child?

EXHIBIT 11-3: **Suggestions for Prospective Renters** (continued)

- Does a tenant have the option to substitute another person as tenant? What are criteria for the landlord's approval of a sublease, if required?
- When is the rent due? What is the delinquent rent penalty? What excuses are acceptable for late payments of rent without incurring any penalty, such as a check lost in the mail, a bank error, or an illness?
- In student housing, or other joint housing arrangements, is each of several roommates fully responsible for rent? (All occupants should sign the lease.)
- Who is responsible for repairs (e.g., roof leaks, plumbing failure, sewer drain blockage, and garbage disposal and appliance breakdowns)? Has there been a history of such problems in your prospective unit?
- Who is to be telephoned if problems arise late at night, or on Sundays or holidays?
- What is the name and address of the owner (with the understanding that you Will deal directly with the manager without disturbing the owner)?
- Who pays for utilities (electricity, gas, water, sewer, and refuse disposal)?
- What are the rules concerning pets?

In case of disputes

- Will any disputes be handled by ADR or by court action?
- Will tenant's attorney's fees be paid by the landlord if the tenant wins in a court preceding? And vice-versa?

UPON SIGNING A LEASE AND BEFORE MOVING IN, DO:

- Make and date written notes of your understanding of your conversations with the landlord. Carefully enumerate subjects that do not appear to be covered in your lease.
- Prepare a detailed list of any damages on the premises (e.g., chipped counters, stains, cuts or tears in the carpeting, cracks around door handles, tears or bends in screens, caulking cracks and stains in the bathroom, stains in the drapes, stains around heating and air conditioning vents, cracks in windows, and so forth). Be thorough, because when you leave, the landlord will assuredly be.
- Prepare an inventory of all furniture and items on the premises, noting the condition of each.
- Prepare a list on cleanliness of the unit, room by room. Pay special attention to the kitchen appliances and bathroom facilities.
- Deliver a signed copy of these lists (but not your notes) to the landlord. Invite verification by personal inspection. Obtain a signed copy for your records.
- Keep yourself from being lulled into complacency by the personality of the landlord. After all, landlords change periodically, and you may be dealing with a different face when checkout time comes.

BEFORE MOVING OUT, DO:

- Make the unit as clean as it was when you moved in, or hire a professional cleaner to do so.
- Compare the original damage list to-the unit's present condition, Arrange for repairs, or bargain with the landlord for an agreed-on amount of deduction from deposit.
- Insist on a personal inspection of your unit by the landlord 'in your presence, Make notes of what is said, If possible, get the landlord to admit that the place is clean and the damage is as you indicate.
- Give your new mailing address to the landlord for your refund; ask when you can expect to receive it.

C A S E

MARINA POINT, LTD. V. WOLFSON

California Supreme Court, 30 Cal. 3d 721, 180 Cal. Rptr. 496 (California, 1982)

A landlord refused to rent an apartment to any family with a minor child. The landlord contended that middle-aged persons, having worked long and hard, having raised their own children, and having paid both their taxes and their dues to society, deserve to spend their remaining years in a relatively quiet, peaceful, and tranquil environment of their own choice. This right is lost in the presence of children, who are rowdier, noisier, more mischievous, and more boisterous than adults.

The trial court agreed, holding that the exclusionary rental policy was reasonable and not arbitrary, and therefore not barred by a state statute that prohibited arbitrary discrimination in business establishments. On appeal, a majority of the California Supreme Court reversed the trial court and held the exclusion improper.

Justice Tobriner: .... [T]he basic rights guaranteed by (the California civil rights statute) would be drastically undermined if, as the landlord contends, a business enterprise could exclude from its premises or services entire classes of the public simply because the owner of the enterprise had some reason to believe that the class, taken as a whole, might present greater problems than other groups. Under such an approach, for example, members of entire occupations or avocations, e.g., sailors or motorcyclists, might find themselves excluded as a class from some places of public accommodation simply because that, as a statistical matter, members of their occupa-

tion or avocation were more likely than others to be involved in a disturbance.... [T]he exclusion of individuals ... on the basis of class or group affiliation basically conflicts with the individual nature of the right afforded by the (civil rights statute) of access to such enterprises.

... [T]he exclusionary practice at issue in this case is clearly distinguishable from the age-limited admission policies of retirement communities or housing complexes reserved for older citizens. Such facilities are designed for the elderly and in many instances have particular appurtenances and exceptional arrangements for their specified purposes.

Judgment reversed.

For Critical Analysis

In the foregoing case, there was no issue concerning due process or equal protection under the U.S. Constitution because there is no "state action" in the apartment rental business. The rule of the Marina Point case has been extended to apply to nonprofit homeowners' associations that attempt to restrict condominium occupancy to adults. On the one hand, exclusion of children as a class is not permitted. On the other hand, however, housing accommodations exclusively for the elderly are permitted. What is the difference? ■

NEW HAVERFORD PARTNERSHIP V. STROOT

772 A.2d 792 (Delaware, 2001)

Elizabeth Stroot and Joletta Watson were tenants at the Haverford Place apartments in the early 1990s. They had continuing problems with water leaks and mold in their apartments, and as a result both women's general health deteriorated. Numerous complaints failed to motivate the landlord to correct the problem. Plaintiffs' experts examined the mold and the tenants' doctors offered testimony that both tenants suffered permanent health damage from their exposure to the mold. The jury awarded Stroot

$1,000,000 for personal injuries and $5,000 for property damage, and Watson $40,000 for personal injuries. Each award was reduced by 22 percent for contributing negligence. The landlord moved for remittitur,* arguing it owes no common-law duty to maintain the apartments. The landlord has appealed.

* A judge's order reducing a judgment awarded by a jury.

BERGER, Justice. We hold that the Landlord Tenant Code imposes a duty on landlords to maintain the leased premises in a safe, sanitary condition and that an injured tenant may recover for personal injuries sustained as a result of landlord's negligent failure to do so. We also find no abuse of discretion in the trial court's contested evidentiary rulings or in its decision denying remittitur. Accordingly, we affirm.

Factual and Procedural Background

Stroot, whose health problems were more severe, was a 33 year old graduate student when she and a friend moved into a third floor apartment at Haverford Place in August 1992. Stroot immediately noticed mold around the windows and in the bathroom. Although she attempted to remove the mold by washing the affected areas with bleach, the mold kept returning. There also were leaks in Stroot's bedroom ceiling and in the kitchen sink and bathroom.

Stroot complained to the management and was told that the problem was caused by the upstairs tenants taking "sloppy" showers. Although the landlord made some effort to fix the upstairs shower, nothing was done to Stroot's apartment and the bathroom ceiling kept getting worse.

On the evening of May 16, 1994, Stroot's bathroom ceiling collapsed and water from the ceiling flooded her bathroom floor. The drywall debris and the exposed ceiling area were covered with black, green, orange and white mold. According to Stroot, the room was filled with a strong, nauseating odor. When she called maintenance, she was told that they could not do anything until the next morning. Stroot closed the bathroom door and slept in her apartment that night. By the next morning, she could not breathe. Stroot called her doctor, who told her to get an ambulance and go the hospital. When she was released later that day, Stroot decided that she could not continue to live at Haverford Place.

Stroot has suffered from allergies and asthma since childhood. As a result, she has required hospitalization and strong medications, such as prednisone, periodically. But the frequency and severity of her medical problems increased significantly after she moved to Haverford Place. During the 21 months that she lived at Haverford Place, Stroot was forced to go to the emergency room seven times for asthma attacks. In addition, she spent a total of nine days as an inpatient and received intravenous steroids twelve times.

[Discussion of tenant Watson's problems with mold are omitted.]

Plaintiffs offered the opinions of several experts to support their claims. Dr. Yang, a mycologist and microbiologist, inspected Haverford Place, took bulk samples and air samples, and interviewed residents. He opined that there was excessive and atypical mold growth in the apartment buildings; that it was caused by long term leaks; and that the widespread mold contamination posed a health risk to tenants. Dr. Johanning, a physician board-certified in environmental and occupational medicine, gathered similar data at Haverford Place. He also took blood samples from plaintiffs. Based on his analysis of this data, Johanning opined that the high concentration of toxic mold at Haverford Place significantly and permanently increased the severity of Stroot's asthma. He also opined that Stroot's cognitive deficits, diagnosed by Dr. Gordon, were caused by exposure to excessive and atypical molds. Johanning testified that Watson developed an allergy to Penicillium and permanent upper respiratory problems as a result of her exposure to the same molds.

Dr. Gordon, a neuropsychologist who has studied cognitive defects associated with exposure to atypical molds, evaluated Stroot and concluded that she suffers from significant cognitive impairment in the areas of attention, concentration, memory and executive functions. Gordon opined that these problems are permanent and were proximately caused by Stroot's exposure to atypical molds. Dr. Rose, a physician who is board-certified in pulmonary, occupational and environmental medicine, examined Stroot and opined that Stroot developed osteopenia as a result of her increased steroid usage while at Haverford Place. Dr. Rose also opined that Stroot's steroid usage increased her risk of developing tuberculosis.

Michael Lynn, an architect and partner in a real estate due diligence firm, performed a limited property condition assessment at Haverford Place. He noted standing water, roof joists covered with fungus, water-damaged dry wall covered with mold, and other evidence of excessive moisture. He opined that the deferred maintenance on the buildings was excessive and that landlord's failure to maintain the buildings was the proximate cause of the unhealthy and unsanitary conditions he observed.

Discussion

Landlord argues that its conduct does not give rise to any of the three causes of action that plaintiffs were allowed to present to the jury. [Also], Landlord complains that the jury verdict was so excessive as to shock the conscience and should have been reduced on its motion for remittitur. Each will be considered in turn.

Tort Liability of Landlord

Plaintiffs pursued three theories of tort liability: (i) ordinary or common law negligence based on Landlord's alleged failure to maintain safe and sanitary conditions in the apartments; (ii) negligence *per se* based on alleged violations of the New Castle County Code; and (iii) negligence *per se* based on alleged violations of the Landlord Tenant Code. The jury verdict form required a separate finding for each of the asserted forms of negligence, and the jury found for the plaintiffs on all three. Landlord argues that it has no duty that would support a claim for common law negligence, and that the statutes at issue do not give rise to a claim of negligence *per se*.

Landlord bases its common law negligence argument on the fact that, before the Landlord Tenant Code was enacted in 1972, landlords had no duty to maintain their buildings in a safe and sanitary condition. Although the Landlord Tenant Code imposes such a duty, Landlord says that the statute cannot be used to support a claim of common law negligence. Plaintiffs' only recourse, according to Landlord, is the Landlord Tenant Code, which purportedly abolishes all tort liability unless a plaintiff can establish negligence *per se*.

Landlord offers no authority for this position, which seems to be based on a misconception as to the meaning of the phrase "common law negligence." To state a claim for negligence one must allege that defendant owed plaintiff a duty of care; defendant breached that duty; and defendant's breach was the proximate cause of plaintiff's injury. The duty owed may be one recognized at common law or one imposed by statute. In either case, the elements of the negligence claim are the same. The phrase "common law" negligence is sometimes used, as it was in this case, to differentiate between ordinary negligence and negligence *per se*. It does not prevent a plaintiff from relying on a statute as the source of defendant's duty.

In sum, we find no error in the trial court's decision allowing plaintiffs to pursue an ordinary, or common law, negligence claim. Moreover, since the jury found in favor of plaintiffs on this claim, we need not address Landlord's arguments with respect to negligence *per se*. Assuming, without deciding, that it was error to allow the jury to consider the two negligence *per se* claims, they were duplicative of the ordinary negligence claim and the error, if any, was harmless.

Motion for Remittitur

Landlord argues that the amounts awarded to Watson and Stroot were so excessive that they shock the conscience. It points out that Watson's medical complaints were relatively mild and she had no observable symptoms after leaving Haverford Place. Stroot incurred $28,810 in medical expenses and suffered aggravation of her asthma and allergies. Her cognitive deficit, according to Landlord is mild and her increased risks of osteopenia and tuberculosis were not quantified. At best, according to Landlord, these injuries could support an award of $250,000, not the $1,000,000 set by the jury.

The trial court carefully considered these arguments:

The presumption in Delaware is that a jury verdict is "correct and just." A Motion for Remittitur ... may be granted ... only with great reluctance. This Court has the authority to grant a new trial if it finds that the verdict is based upon "passion, partiality, prejudice, mistake or misapprehension on the part of the jury." It has also been held that a verdict will not be set aside unless it is "so grossly excessive as to shock the Court's conscience and sense of justice; and unless the injustice of allowing the verdict is clear."

* * * * * *

The jury obviously accepted Dr. Johanning's and Dr. Rose's medical testimony in this case that despite other triggers which could cause her to have an asthma attack, Stroot's asthma was nevertheless significantly exacerbated or worsened by her exposure to microbial contamination at the apartment complex, and that her need for medication increased significantly after she moved to Haverford Place. The Court is satisfied that Stroot showed to a reasonable degree of medical probability that her asthma symptoms decreased, but did not return to her pre-exposure baseline, after she left the apartment complex.

* * * * * *

The Court also finds that the medical and scientific evidence presented at trial established ... that [Stroot's] osteopenia is causally related to her increased steroid use not only while living at Haverford Place, but also after she moved out. The evidence ... also showed that Stroot's increased need for steroids to suppress the asthma has increased her risk for developing active tuberculosis.

Further, the jury may have also chosen to accept Dr. Wayne Gordon's testimony ... that ... Stroot's cognitive deficits in three areas—attention, concentration, and executive functioning, were proximately caused by her long-term exposure to microbial contamination at Haverford Place.

* * * * * *

Given the permanent nature of Plaintiffs' injuries as well as the physical and emotional pain and suffering Stroot and Watson will have to endure for the remainder of their lives, the Court does not find the $1,000,000 verdict to Stroot, or the $40,000 verdict to Watson unreasonable, nor is its conscience shocked.

We accept the trial court's well reasoned analysis.

Conclusion

Based on the foregoing, the decision of the Superior Court is affirmed.

For Critical Analysis

1. The landlord in this case would have violated what duty owed the tenant?

2. The court opinion does not disclose the reasons for the reduction of damages based on plaintiff's contributory negligence. What do you suspect was the basis for the jury's reduction of damages?

3. What self-help remedies would the tenants have had in most states?

4. Why do you suppose the tenants didn't simply move?

5. What is the treatment of mold and other similar conditions such as lead paint in your state?

6. Can a landlord legally reject as a tenant anyone who takes prednisone, who has been asthmatic since childhood, like Stroot? ■

CHAPTER QUESTIONS AND PROBLEMS

1. Arlene Hart, Sherry Francis, and Marguerite Bradley, college students, are roommates in an apartment they leased for one year. Their rent is $900 a month. If for an important reason (e.g., an ill family member, failure from school, or marriage) the women need to break their lease six months before its termination, may they do so? What are the consequences of "breaking" their lease? If only Bradley needs to leave, and the other two desire to remain, what are the probable consequences?

2. Several tenants, including Dorothy Detling, sued their landlord, C. E. Edelbrock, for damages, alleging that their leased premises were infested with rodents and roaches, were missing screens, and had exposed electrical wiring. They also alleged that the heating boiler was defective, that rubbish was strewn in passageways, and that the common area stairs were unstable. Does the landlord have a duty to prevent these kinds of conditions from occurring, or are such repairs and maintenance tasks the responsibility of the tenants? If you conclude that the landlord was at fault, must these tenants move out of the premises because they have been constructively evicted? [*Detling v. Edelbrock,* 671 S.W.2d 265 (Missouri, 1984).]

3. Assume that a landlord who was angry because a tenant's rent was unpaid entered the tenant's apartment with a master key, placed all of the tenant's possessions in a refuse-disposal container, and changed the locks on the door. What would be the tenant's legal remedy? Assume that a landlord's agent (i.e., an apartment manager) wrongfully entered and snooped through the tenant's

personal belongings, but did not steal or damage anything. What would be the tenant's legal remedy?

4. Note that you have special permission to make a copy of Exhibit 11-3 without infringing on the publisher's legal copyright. Please make your personal copy now or at your earliest convenience. Even though you are probably settled in for the semester or school year, it is not too late to benefit from a careful, conscientious application of the questions in the exhibit to your own present living accommodations if you are currently a renter.

   Make the effort and take the time to ask and to answer every one of the questions that is applicable to you. (Ideally, of course, we wish you could have done this before you signed your lease or rental agreement.) After you have answered as many questions as you can (always in writing), talk to your landlord and, in a friendly manner, ask her or him to help you answer the remaining questions. (Blame us, the authors, for this assignment if any blame is forthcoming.)

5. Angela Jendralski, bitten by her neighbor's monkey, sued her landlord for damages for negligence. The apartment lease forms did not allow the keeping of animals except small, caged birds. What should the result be? Would your answer be different if the lease permitted all pets? [*Jendralski v. Black,* 222 Cal. Rptr. 396 (1986).]

6. What arguments can you make to support the notion that tenants should earn interest on the portion of their security deposits that is refunded? Can you think of any opposing arguments?

7. Before making an apartment available for rent, the landlord legally must take which of the following actions?
   a. Provide a freshly painted unit
   b. Provide the unit with sterilized bathroom facilities
   c. Rekey the entry locks to the unit
   d. Deflea and deodorize the unit if a cat or dog had been kept in the premises
   e. Provide a clean oven
   f. Arrange for repair of all damages done by the previous tenant
   g. Disclose to prospective tenants any security problems that have occurred in the complex
   h. Provide the unit with a fire extinguisher

8. If a landlord files a court action against a former improvident tenant for unpaid rent and for damages to the rental unit, and obtains a judgment for damages, how can the landlord "get blood out of a turnip"?

9. Notes jotted down on paper are not a contract and are not clauses in a written lease or rental agreement. Why then should prospective tenants who ask pertinent questions of a landlord who is offering rentals make written notation of the answers received?

10. Robert Calef leased a house from David West in the city of Flint, Michigan. Seven weeks into the lease term Calef claims he tripped and fell when he stepped into a snow-covered hole located in the front yard. Calef claims that the hole had been created by West's removal of a fence post in the lawn. As the hole had been covered by snow during Calef's entire occupancy he was unaware of the hazard. Suffering injuries including fractured humerus and ribs. Calef claims the landlord had a duty to warn him about the dangerous condition. West sought summary judgment based on an exculpatory clause signed by Calef. Does the exculpatory clause bar the claim by the tenant? [*Calef v. West,* 652 N.W.2d 496 (Mich. App., 2002).]

CHAPTER 12

Home Ownership

*M*id pleasures and palaces though we may roam, Be it ever so humble, there's no place like home.

John Howard Payne

After reading and studying this chapter, you should be able to:

🏛 Compare advantages and disadvantages of home ownership.

🏛 Identify the various types of homes available.

🏛 Distinguish between the various types of agreements with real estate agents and brokers.

🏛 Understand the important considerations to keep in mind when buying or selling a house.

🏛 Understand the major legal considerations in a home sale contract.

🏛 Identify and distinguish among the various methods of financing available for home sale contracts.

🏛 Explain the legal ramifications of foreclosure and transfer of real estate security mortgages.

🏛 Identify the important aspects of the escrow process, including title insurance.

🏛 Distinguish between the various methods of joint title ownership.

🏛 Identify the types of real property deeds.

🏛 Explain how real property is taxed.

🏛 Identify important attributes of fire insurance.

🏛 Identify important attributes of CC&Rs and other neighbor-to-neighbor legal issues.

A few years after college, almost all of you will be pursuing "the American dream of owning your own home." How do you locate, finance, and purchase a home? How large will your monthly payments be? Can your monthly payments increase? What happens if you miss a payment? Do you need the services of a real estate broker or sales agent when buying? When selling? Should you transfer credit card debt to a new home-equity loan? Can two unrelated persons qualify for home financing?

LEGAL FOCUS—PROBLEM

Joe and Stephanie DiMarco and their two young children purchased a lovely home in the suburbs for $325,000. They were unaware that a neighbor, Joshua Cox, previously had been convicted for a violent sexual assault upon a minor, had served five years in prison as a result, and had been released only two months before the DiMarco family arrived. Was the seller obligated to tell the DiMarcos about the neighbor?

The twentieth-century principle of "let the buyer beware" has been changing to "let the seller beware," at least in regard to home purchases. The new trend is that sellers must reveal all relevant known information that might bear upon the decision to purchase a home. The current address of felons who have been convicted of specified violent sexual assaults is public information—but must sellers tell prospective buyers? The answer is uncertain, but with the trend as a guide, the most probable answer is that the DiMarcos should have been told by the seller. We consider the practices, economics, and laws affecting the "American dream" in this chapter.

Most people want to own their own home. This dream has become a reality for a majority of the U.S. population, but remains beyond the reach of others. In most areas of the country, home prices have gone up sharply during the first years of the twenty-first century to levels too high for many would-be buyers. But permanent federal and state programs designed to bring home ownership within the financial means of moderate- and low-income families promise to extend their success well into the new millennium. Of course, many renters could afford to purchase homes but choose to rent for personal reasons, such as freedom from the responsibilities of home ownership.

There are two traditional kinds of benefits of home ownership: amenity and economic. We begin by examining these characteristics separately. Exhibit 12-1 provides a comparison of advantages and disadvantages of homeownership.

http://

For population, housing, and a wealth of similar statistical information, begin at the U.S. Census Bureau home page at
http://www.census.gov/

CHARACTERISTICS OF HOME OWNERSHIP

Home is the wallpaper above the bed, the family dinner table, the church bells in the morning, the bruised shins of the playground, the small fears that come with dusk, the streets and squares and monuments and shops that constitute one's first universe.

Henry Anatole Grunwald, "Home Is Where You Are Happy," *Time,* July 8, 1985

EXHIBIT 12-1: **Advantages and Disadvantages of Home Ownership**

Source: Adapted from a comparison chart provided by Ginnie Mae (http://www.ginniemae.gov), a wholly owned corporation within the Department of Housing and Urban Development (HUD).

Ⓐ MENITIES

amenities

Features that increase the attractiveness or value of real estate.

Amenities are conveniences that flow from living in a single-family residence, or home. The kinds of available amenities changed dramatically in the last hundred years. In 1900, the homes of average Americans did not contain indoor plumbing; cooking was done on oil- or wood-fueled stoves; and there was no electricity in the rural and farm areas. There were no refrigerators, no microwave ovens, no washing machines, no hot showers, no garages for cars and storage. There was no wall-to-wall carpeting, fiberglass insulation, or water-based paint. Of course, the affluent in their mansions were the first to receive the amenities of electricity, indoor plumbing, water closet toilets, and central heat. Upscale Victorian homes and mansions were well-equipped and beautiful—ordinary homes were merely functional. But for average Americans, home ownership offered far more amenities, space, and privacy, not to mention a greater sense of satisfaction, than was enjoyed by dwellers of rented apartments and rooms.

Today, most American homes feature extensive creature comforts such as swimming pools and entertainment centers—amenities far beyond the imaginations of your grandparents in their day, but with which you are quite familiar. Homeowners today enjoy the option of selecting a neighborhood with compatible people, away from congestion, street noise, and commotion. Home buyers may make their choice based on the quality of schools or a host of other intangibles that contribute to an improved lifestyle. Home ownership usually provides a safer environment for children and adults alike.

Even renters enjoy far more amenities than before, with common-use swimming pools, tennis courts, workout facilities, laundry rooms, and game rooms with televisions and computers. Modern apartments are more spacious, better lit, and fully equipped with modern appliances and creature comforts such as central heating and air conditioning. Renters argue that they have an additional amenity—the absence of mowing, trimming, weeding, cleaning rain gutters, waiting and paying for roof and plumbing repairs, and painting. These renters-by-choice are proof that one person's delight is another person's agony.

ECONOMICS

Single-family homes in New York generally come in two price ranges: expensive and unbelievably expensive.

Michael deCourcy Hinds in an article for the *New York Times*

Economic aspects of home ownership partly offset the benefits from amenities. Sometimes furnishing a house may involve credit purchases at high consumer interest rates. Acquiring a home in a suburban area usually boosts the costs of commuting, including higher automobile insurance rates. For example, a no-car or one-car family renting an apartment in the inner city may need two cars if they move to a home in the suburbs. In crowded metropolitan areas, such as the New York City and San Francisco Bay areas, many persons take public transportation or commute fifty miles or more, enduring gridlock on highways for the privilege of living in an affordable suburban house with a yard.

In addition to large outlays of money when the home is acquired and furnished, the monthly expenses may prove burdensome. Homeowner's insurance, utility bills, property taxes, and repair and maintenance expenses must be paid in addition to principal and interest on the mortgage loan. Most of these expenses are included in the rent of the apartment dweller, but in reduced amount because of the economies of scale of multiple units.

Along with the considerable monthly expenses of home ownership, there is compelling evidence that in the early years of the new millennium the traditional economic advantages of home ownership may be diminishing. If correct, this is a dynamic new aspect in home ownership. Traditional economic benefits of home ownership consist of (1) increasing value, called *appreciation,* (2) equity buildup as mortgage debt is paid off, and (3) tax benefits from deducting interest and property tax expenses. Appreciation and equity buildup are depicted in Exhibit 12-2.

Although the effect will be discussed in more detail later, notice that equity buildup from the systematic repayment of the mortgage debt occurs with significance only after about six to eight years. Furthermore, appreciation usually begins in earnest after five or so years, in part because transaction costs (sales commissions) consume about 6 percent of the home's value when it is purchased. Because of the slow start of both equity buildup and appreciation, the economic benefits of home ownership become attractive only after five or more years elapse from the date of purchase.

At the beginning of the twenty-first century, changes in traditional employment also are occurring. For example, unlike your grandparents and parents, who may have held only one or two different jobs during their working years, it is likely that you will change jobs perhaps frequently. The transitory nature of the modern work force is the product of many new changes. For one example, consider that many jobs in technology change as its science changes. Also consider that companies downsize for modern efficiencies, sometimes taking employment across our country's borders in search of cheaper labor. Some companies expand by opening new plants and even administrative centers overseas for

EXHIBIT 12-2: **The Economics of Home Ownership**

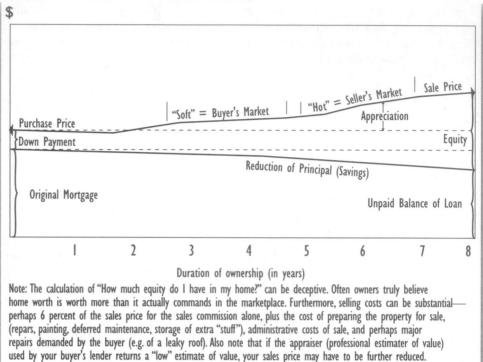

Note: The calculation of "How much equity do I have in my home?" can be deceptive. Often owners truly believe home worth is worth more than it actually commands in the marketplace. Furthermore, selling costs can be substantial—perhaps 6 percent of the sales price for the sales commission alone, plus the cost of preparing the property for sale, (repars, painting, deferred maintenance, storage of extra "stuff"), administrative costs of sale, and perhaps major repairs demanded by the buyer (e.g. of a leaky roof). Also note that if the appraiser (professional estimater of value) used by your buyer's lender returns a "low" estimate of value, your sales price may have to be further reduced.

economies. In other words, the work force is becoming globalized, shifting and moving to meet necessary economies and the needs of opening markets. At the same time, we have become a service/technology/communications economy with frequent employee turnover and "outsourcing" (hiring contractors for specific tasks instead of employees). Furthermore, the two-income family is now well established, and one spouse's job change can force the other to change jobs as well.

None of the foregoing was occurring at the beginning of the twentieth century. On the contrary, America was a melting pot of labor with more jobs of all descriptions available for the new European immigrants who were flooding our borders every year. In some industries, children would follow in the footsteps of their fathers at the plant and begin their own lifetime jobs. Today, however, our nation is rapidly changing from a manufacturing economy often characterized by lifetime employment in huge plants. A major consequence of changing jobs every five to eight years on average is that the traditional economic benefits of home ownership—equity buildup and appreciation—will essentially cease to exist.

We will consider other examples of this unhappy phenomenon in later sections of this chapter dealing with property taxation, other new financial burdens, and transaction costs (burdens placed upon sellers)—all of which are helping to erode traditional twentieth-century economic benefits of home ownership. Thus, for many, the benefit of home ownership may well be primarily amenity, not economic, benefit. Those modern and mobile persons will consider the opportunity of *renting* single-family homes to obtain all of the amenities of home ownership.

How Do You Find Homes Available for Sale?

Most homes are in subdivisions, a term that derives from the real estate business of dividing a tract of land into separate lots that are suitable for individual ownership of new homes. Served by common sewer trunk lines, water and electric delivery systems, and interior streets, the subdividing of land through economies of scale has made home ownership a financially realistic option for most Americans. Two general categories of homes that are located in subdivisions may be available: pre-owned or newly constructed.

New Subdivision Homes

New subdivision homes are houses built mostly by one company offering a limited variety of floor plans. They may be constructed before being offered to buyers, or be sold before construction by display of model homes to prospective buyers. Some companies catering to more affluent customers offer custom homes that are built according to floor plans selected by each buyer. New subdivisions are often called *planned developments* because they offer a common design and architectural scheme with common areas shared by all homeowners, such as large entry streets with beautiful medians and, sometimes, gates, interior parks, and common landscaping. These planned subdivisions typically are governed by a **homeowner's association (HOA)** composed of residents who volunteer or are elected by owners within the subdivision. Monthly fees are collected from owners within the subdivision and are used to maintain the common facilities. Rules also are designed and enforced to maintain property values in the subdivision. For example, the parking of RVs, boats, or disabled cars on interior streets often is prohibited. There are differing views of the role of HOAs, and they are discussed later in this chapter under "Help from CC&Rs."

One advantage to buying a new subdivision home is that the developer-seller probably will offer a financing package (prearranged loan terms) for qualified (in terms of creditworthiness) buyers, sometimes at very favorable interest rates. One disadvantage is that the character of the neighborhood is not established because many homes are new or practically new, or may not be constructed until after the purchase is made. Subdivisions do evolve by gradually reflecting the nature of the persons and families that buy and then maintain the houses.

Developers of new subdivision homes usually advertise heavily in local newspapers. Prospects who visit a new subdivision are usually given written data and shown furnished model homes. Once the decision to buy is made, the developer-seller provides many services to the buyer, assisting with the necessary paperwork and otherwise making the purchase experience as simple and expeditious as possible.

Pre-Owned Subdivision Homes

Homes in mature subdivisions may have been sold several times over the years. With the average length of employment shortening to perhaps seven years on average, it follows that in the twenty-first century homes will be owned by families for fewer years than ever before. Mature subdivisions offer well-defined benefits because their character has become stabilized. Subdivisions become neighborhoods with well-known characteristics that influence the prices charged by sellers. Most available homes that are for sale are pre-owned.

Prospective buyers of pre-owned subdivision homes typically rely upon the services of real estate sales companies who hire sales agents to assist buyers and sellers. Prospective buyers often telephone for appointments with real estate companies whose signs they have

homeowner's association (HOA)

Association of people who own homes, condominiums, or cooperatives in a given area, formed for the purpose of improving or maintaining the quality of that area.

http://

For information about the management of planned developments and other residential developments with common areas, from the perspective of the community association, visit the national headquarters of community associations at **http://www.caionline.org/**

seen in front of homes that are for sale in the desired area. Sales agents then provide prospective buyers with information about homes that are for sale in the area. Once a home is selected, the sales agent assists the buyer in consummating the purchase.

CUSTOM HOME

A person who wants to build a custom home must do the preliminary work of locating an available lot. Some custom home builders have plans and lots available in new subdivisions and will build a custom home, provided it meets certain standards consistent with other houses in the area. Otherwise, the services of an architect or building designer, as well as those of a building contractor—someone licensed by the state to supervise all aspects of home construction—and lending institution must be obtained. Persons desiring a custom home can obtain names of builders from advertisements in the Yellow Pages and local newspapers as well as by contacting local architects and savings and loan associations for recommendations. Many prospective buyers of custom homes tour desirable areas of the community and obtain leads as to architects and contractors from homes that are under construction or already built. The choice of contractor should be carefully made, preferably after interviewing previous customers of each contractor under consideration.

You should understand that building contractors are supervisors who usually perform no personal construction services. Rather, they select and hire subcontractors to grade the lot, pour the concrete foundation, frame and plumb the structure, etc. Perhaps that is why they are also called "general" contractors—they act as generals commanding the workers. The general contractor you hire may not know any of the subcontractors who will perform the actual construction services. Thus, quality can vary widely. Furthermore, all subcontractors have the right to put liens or claims, called **mechanic's liens,** on your property if the building contractor you hired fails to make all payments. Mechanic's liens protect claims of persons who improve property by giving them claims on the owner's property. If unpaid, the owner of the property is liable to the workers even if the owner already has paid the general contractor for the work done. Because the law does not require the building contractor even to visit your home while it is being constructed (although most do), you may rightfully come to feel neglected and even abused. These few summary points should serve to etch in your mind this rule: *Always* obtain the assistance of an attorney who has considerable experience in construction law and litigation before hiring any building contractor.

OTHER AVAILABLE HOMES

Three other types of homes are available in both the new and pre-owned markets: the cooperative apartment, the condominium, and the manufactured (mobile) home.

Cooperative Apartments

For **cooperative apartments,** a corporation is formed to acquire land and erect a multi-family (apartment) building. Interested persons buy sufficient shares of capital stock in the corporation to obtain rights to proprietary leases that entitle them to live in one of the units and to use the common areas (such as stairs, elevators, swimming pools, parking spaces, and gardens). The corporation arranges for a single mortgage loan on the property and pays taxes and other costs, allocating proportional responsibility to the resident shareholders. Any owner of shares may sell the shares and assign the lease to someone else, who is then entitled to reside in the seller's unit. Shares offered for sale often are advertised for direct sale or submitted to sales agents in the area.

mechanic's lien

A legal claim of a contractor or material supplier who helped or supplied materials to construct, improve, or repair a building.

http://

For a wealth of practical and current housing information, begin at the public Web page of the National Association of Home Builders (NAHB) at **http://www.nahb.org/**

cooperative apartment

A residential multi-unit building whose title is held by a trust or corporation that is owned by and operated for the benefit of persons living within the building.

Condominiums

The **condominium** is a more common variety of home ownership than the cooperative. Each owner of a "condo" receives a deed conveying title to a particular unit and arranges individual financing for its purchase. Only the areas used in common are owned in common, typically by a corporation whose stock is owned by the unit owners. In some condominiums, the common areas are owned as a *tenancy-in-common* (a form of co-ownership) among all the unit owners. The corporation hires professionals to maintain the building exteriors and common areas, and the owners share the related costs. Condominiums vary in type from townhouses with common walls to the John Hancock skyscraper in Chicago, with commercial establishments on lower floors and residences on upper floors.

All condominiums are governed by a homeowner's association (HOA) with a set of corporation by-laws and rules. Buyers should carefully read all applicable governing rules, making certain there are no surprises (e.g., no dogs allowed in common areas) that would make their purchase undesirable.* Pre-owned condominiums are advertised individually and also offered through multiple-listing services as with single-family detached residences.

Condominiums are especially attractive to people who must (or prefer to) travel extensively because all exterior maintenance is performed by the HOA. Many condominiums offer as many amenities as typical homes, or even more. For example, many offer common areas that include pools, spas, workout facilities, dog runs, etc. Historically, condominiums have not appreciated as rapidly as single-family homes. But recall, those people who must move every five to eight years from single family-homes may not enjoy any significant appreciation either.

condominium

A residential or business building in which individuals own, and receive title to, separate units or apartments.

Manufactured Homes

Manufactured homes are constructed in a factory and delivered to a lot oftentimes in a specially designed subdivision or park. Their lineage comes from what were once called mobile homes. The initial appeal has been the construction savings offered by factory efficiencies. Over the years costs of manufactured homes have been modest. In recent years the variety and sophistication of manufactured homes is such that some units are now quite large and no longer just budget items.

Special concerns exist for some manufactured-home owners. After the homes are placed on a site, owners usually have no expectation of moving them. In recent years more of these homes are being placed on homeowner property, but many manufactured homes are still placed in residential parks where the space is rented. When these homes were truly mobile the problems of eviction from a rented space meant hooking up the unit to the automobile and moving it to a new site. With newer manufactured homes moving the unit is a dramatic and expensive undertaking.

manufactured home

A single-family house constructed entirely in a controlled factory environment, built to the federal Manufactured Home Construction and Safety Standards.

LEGAL FOCUS—BACKGROUND

"A mobile home, also referred to as 'type of manufactured housing,' may not be very 'mobile,' however, once it is installed on a site. A mobile home owner can be in the odd position of owning his or her home but renting the land upon which it sits if the home is located in a mobile home, or manufactured housing, park. Manufactured housing parks

* State laws require the seller of a condominium to submit copies of specified documents, such as by-laws, rules, and restrictions, to the buyer before the sale is complete to reduce the risk of unpleasant surprises later.

straddle a complex intersection of statute, common law, culture, zoning laws, and economics. Legal questions involving manufactured housing parks can be complicated because of competing, and seemingly irreconcilable, legal doctrines."[1]

To assist with the trauma of possible undesired moves, one state enacted a statute requiring owners of mobile home parks to pay toward their tenants' relocation costs if their park is closed. Regardless of its helpful intent, the statute was declared unconstitutional.[2] Many states do, however, provide protections to tenants of such residential parks. Such laws restrict landlord reasons for eviction from such parks and allow residents time to "correct" the reason for the eviction. For example, before a tenant can be legally evicted from a manufactured housing park in New Hampshire the resident must be notified that he or she has:

- Thirty days to pay any rent owed
- Sixty days to comply with any local, state, or federal law that has been violated
- Sixty days to repair any damages to the leased property
- Sixty days' notice for repeated "breaches of the peace"
- Sixty days to comply with park rules
- Eighteen months to vacate due to a condemnation or a change in the use of the park's land.[3]

http://

For a wide selection of information, search the Web under "manufactured homes." Many manufacturers and sales companies from around the nation promote their products online and provide useful data.

Because these homes come in a variety of sizes and are less expensive per square foot than other types of housing, they have a special appeal for budget-minded couples, both young and old. Financing is typically available only for shorter terms than customary for mortgage financing of conventionally built homes. The term of the loan may be as short as seven years with larger down payments (as much as one-third of the purchase price) than for standard homes. Dealers of mobile homes typically advertise in Yellow Pages, in local newspapers, and on the Web.

Because of poor construction in the early years of the industry, as well as hard sale tactics, the entire manufactured home industry is regulated by federal statutes.[4] Related types of homes gaining acceptance in some areas of the country are prefabricated and kit homes. The idea is to produce part or most of the components inexpensively on an assembly line, then to ship the components to their final site for assembly. Manufacturers need to be careful to comply with local building codes and zoning requirements.

WHAT FACTORS INFLUENCE HOME SELECTION?

Location, location, location.

Real estate axiom

Within the price range permitted by the buyer's budget, the most important factor in selecting a particular house from those available is usually its location. Location influences commuting time to work and shopping areas, availability of police and fire protection, utility services, refuse and sewer disposal facilities, school districts and houses of worship, ambulance and medical care services, access to public transportation and highways, and proximity to public and private recreational facilities. Specific location can determine whether the home is in the path of community decline or growth; whether the neighborhood is deteriorating; whether surrounding properties are of comparable value; whether local traffic, noise, or commotion is excessive; whether airplanes fly low patterns overhead; whether factories with fumes, smoke, and noise are nearby; whether television reception is poor in the area or cable is available; whether neighbors are likely to be compatible socially and economically; whether there are deed restrictions and zoning regulations that increase or decrease values; whether ground waters are clean; whether high-voltage overhead electrical cables are nearby; whether the building is in a flood plain or vulnerable to earthquakes, and so forth. Some of these issues are not as obvious in their implications as you may think.

LEGAL FOCUS—PROBLEM

It is well established that electric power lines create electromagnetic field radiation (called EMFR); on the other hand, the effects on humans living nearby are in dispute. Most studies have focused on neighborhood electric power lines, which probably should be avoided if possible. Even so, EMFR, to a lesser degree and only for intermittent periods, is also created by home appliances, such as electric razors, hair dryers, toasters, food mixers, vacuum cleaners, electric radios, electric garage openers, cell phones, and, of course, computers.[5]

Another significant criterion for evaluating a house is the configuration of the house itself. Does the lot drain well? Is it located on a corner? Where does the sun shine in the morning and afternoon? Is there sufficient privacy? How old is the house? Are bathrooms and kitchen up-to-date and functional? What is the condition of the electrical system, the plumbing, and the heating and cooling systems? When must the roof be redone? Is the house well insulated? Does the house contain asbestos, radon gas, or lead in its paint or plumbing systems? Are the rooms adequate for storage, furniture, and appliances? A myriad of other common-sense questions should be considered. If you lack the necessary expertise to ask and answer such questions, get assistance from someone who knows how to help you. **Home inspection services**—professionals who evaluate and report upon all important aspects of a house—are widely available to assist buyers in making good decisions and are available by referral from sales agents or through advertisements in the Yellow Pages. (The legal obligation of sellers to reveal certain characteristics of their homes to prospective buyers is discussed later.) Prospective home buyers should remember one axiom of business: "Money is made on the buy"; in other words, buy wisely, and even if you do not plan to move from the house in the foreseeable future, "well bought is half-sold."

FIXER-UPPERS

A special category of pre-owned home may be appealing to certain budget-minded buyers who are handy with tools. **Fixer-uppers** are properties whose building and landscaping have been allowed to deteriorate to some considerable degree. These properties are often sold through foreclosure sales and at auctions by government agencies. Although the price for a fixer-upper may seem very attractive, prospective buyers must be careful to ensure that no serious and prohibitively expensive structural defects exist that make even the most modest price unacceptable. If the home suffers only superficial or limited deterioration, obsolescence, and disrepair, it may be a bargain for buyers who have the skill and the will to do most of the cleaning, painting, repairing, and planting themselves.

home inspection services

Professional businesses that inspect residential properties to discover any defects that might influence the decision of a prospective buyer either to buy or to offer a lower price.

http://

For information about home inspection services, begin with the National Association of Certified Home Inspectors (NACHI) home page at **http://www.nachi.org/**

fixer-upper

A property whose building and landscaping have been allowed to deteriorate to some considerable degree.

How Do Real Estate Agents Serve Buyers and Sellers?

Inequality of knowledge is the key to a sale.

Deil O. Gustafson, real estate executive

The real estate business is composed of *brokers* and *sales agents*.

Real estate brokers must obtain a state license that authorizes them to hire sales agents. Brokers need not be but often are corporations that hire many agents to perform the necessary services to sellers and buyers. Brokers act as managers and rarely meet with buyers or sellers, whose personal contact almost always is with a sales agent. **Real estate agents** also are licensed by the state, and perform all of the day-to-day services and provide information as necessary to bring sellers and buyers of homes together and to make sales transactions happen. The success of home purchasers and sellers is affected by the services they receive from real estate sales agents, and their role cannot be ignored.

Sales agents seldom receive salaries from the brokerage firms that employ them. Instead they receive a portion, say 50 percent or more, of the sales commissions they generate. Thus, if a sales agent produces a commission of $18,000 by handling a home sale with a price of $300,000 (a 6 percent commission), he or she will be paid $9,000 by the broker, who will retain the other one-half. Top sales agents command commission splits with their brokers of 60 to 80 percent.

Service to Sellers

An owner desiring to sell usually hires a real estate brokerage company by negotiating with a sales agent. The owner understands that all future dealings will be directly with the sales agent—none with the broker. The employment of the agent, who is called the **listing agent,*** is accomplished by using a form of employment contract that usually is presented to the homeowner by the agent. The employment contract, or listing, serves to hire the real estate broker (acting through the sales agent) to hunt for a suitable buyer.

The effect of the standard employment contract, or listing, subject to many regional variables, is that the prospective seller and the real estate agent exchange promises as follows: Seller promises to pay a commission of a negotiable percentage (often 6 percent) of the actual sales price if an acceptable offer to purchase is made by a qualified buyer (regardless of who finds the buyer) within a prescribed time period (often three to six months). The real estate broker promises to use "diligence" in hunting for a buyer. It is difficult, if not impossible, to prove in court that an incompetent agent failed to "use due diligence" in hunting for a buyer. That is why few sellers who become disenchanted with their listing agents sue them in court.

---

real estate broker

One who acts as an intermediary for real estate transactions on behalf of others for a fee or commission.

real estate agent

A person licensed by the state to negotiate the buying and selling of real property while employed and supervised by a licensed real estate broker.

http://

For information about real estate sales occupations, see at the Occupational Outlook Handbook provided by the Federal Bureau of Labor Statistics

http://www.bls.gov/oco/ocos120.htm

listing agent

An employment contract between the owner of real property and a licensed agent authorizing the latter to hunt for a buyer of the property on specified terms.

---

* The term "listing" is a word of art the original source of which has eluded your authors. Colloquial information suggests that it originally referred to a "list" of homes that were available for sale in an area—the composite list being called "multiple listing." As a verb, "listing" meant adding a new seller's home to the list. An agent who persuades a new seller to engage his or her services uses a "listing agreement" and then is referred to as the "listing agent" or simply the "lister." The price the new seller hopes to obtain is called the "listing price." All of these usages appear to be accurate except when used to describe the listing agreement, which as indicated in the text is actually a variety of employment contract—a more daunting phrase.

LEGAL FOCUS—PROBLEM

Samuel and Kimberly Yamshon signed a standard exclusive listing with Acme Real Estate for the sale of their home on specified terms. Shortly thereafter, at a social gathering, they met a couple—the Auburns—who were interested in buying a house similar to the Yamshons'. The Auburns came by and decided to make an offer to purchase it in an amount that was satisfactory to the Yamshons. Samuel telephoned their agent to cancel the listing because they had found their own buyer. Their sales agent, Jasdeep Saltsman, responded: "Fine, you may mail me a check for the 6 percent commission you owe." Do the Yamshons owe a commission even though their sales agent did no work and did not find the buyer?

Yes. The commission is owed because the variety of employment contract known as an **exclusive listing** requires payment of a commission regardless of who finds the buyer. Sometimes owners find their own buyers, sometimes buyers simply appear on their own accord, sometimes other sales agents find buyers, and, of course, sometimes the hired agent finds a buyer. In each of these situations, the commission is owed to the exclusive listing agent. The Yamshons would not owe any commission if they had asked for and signed a different kind of employment contract—an "exclusive-agency." **Exclusive-agency listings,** under which owners who find their own buyers do not pay commissions, are widely available to new sellers who are smart enough to ask for them. Such a listing is preferable from the seller's standpoint because, through luck or accident, a buyer may be found or appear without any agent.

As noted, listing agents promise to use diligence in hunting for a suitable buyer. This is accomplished by submitting data about the new seller's home to a regional database called the **multiple listing service.** All real estate brokers subscribe to this service and thereby gain access to specific data (address, square footage, number of baths and bedrooms, all amenities, etc.) about all homes in the region that are on the market. Thus, the subscribing broker has available for the firm's sales agents all of the information necessary to present to prospective buyers. Putting a home "into multiple listing" alone probably satisfies the promise by the listing agent to use due diligence. As a result, some "listing agents" never perform additional services to find a suitable buyer—a practice that always angers sellers who wait expectantly for "action" on their listings.

Although the terms of the agreement between the seller and the listing brokerage firm are completely negotiable, as a practical matter most sellers routinely accept the deal as proposed by the listing agent. Curiously, real estate agents customarily do not promise to spend any specified amount of money on advertising, but prudent sellers can negotiate for that useful provision.

At the time a new seller hires a sales agent, a "listing price" will be agreed upon and stated in the listing form. Some agents earn the initial goodwill of prospective sellers by suggesting a very high "listing price," creating the impression that the home is worth more than might be the case. When the broker finds a purchaser who is willing to buy at a price lower than the listing price, and the owner accepts the offer, the owner cannot refuse to pay the commission on the grounds that the broker failed to find a buyer at the listed price. Acceptance of the lower price effectively amends the listing (or employment contract) to provide for a commission based on the actual sales price. Indeed, the only reason to include a listing price in the listing agreement is to provide a measure of damages the agent might obtain if the seller should fire the agent and withdraw the residence from the

exclusive listing

Employment contract in which the owner of real property agrees to pay a licensed agent a certain commission regardless of who finds the buyer to whom the property is sold. Also called an *exclusive right to sell.*

exclusive-agency listing

Employment contract between an owner of real property and a licensed agent in which the owner may find a buyer and sell the property without liability for payment of commission, but must pay the listing agent if that agent—or any other licensed agent—finds the buyer.

multiple listing service

An organization of real estate brokers who exchange information about listings of property they have obtained.

http://

For multiple listings on the
net see Homeseekers for
national listings

**http://www.homeseekers
.com/indexhs.htm**

For an example of a regional
service, see GreatHomes.org

http://www.greatHomes.org/

market during the listing period. Absent a listing price, the discharged agent would be entitled to damages equal to the reasonable value of the services rendered to the date of termination. With a listing price, the discharged agent is entitled to damages equal to a stated percentage, often 5 percent, of the listing price. Thus sellers would be better off with no listing price in the listing agreement.

Recall that the listing agreement is a fully negotiable employment contract. Before hiring a real estate broker to sell your home, you are well advised to negotiate for some, if not all, of the following provisions:

- The right to pay no commission if you find your own buyer. Often a potential buyer may transfer to your workplace or surface through recommendations of your friends and acquaintances.

- A short listing period, perhaps as little as thirty days, with the understanding it will be extended in thirty-day increments if the agent is satisfactorily "pushing" the property. Remember, once your agent is hired, you have no legal right to end the listing early. How can you be sure your agent will provide good service?

- A reduced commission, perhaps 5 or even 4 percent, if the property is readily saleable and market conditions are good. Always calculate what percentage of your equity a 6 (or other) percent commission of the sales price represents. You will be surprised, and probably shocked. Use this information in negotiating for a reduced commission percentage rate.

- Restrictions on when sales agents and their prospects will be permitted to enter the house, especially if you are still residing there. You can require the presence of your agent on each occasion your house is shown to others. (The sign in front of your house can read "shown by appointment.") Or you can accept a lock box arrangement whereby any agent can enter at any time.

- A specified advertising budget, to be paid by the agent. Your Sunday newspaper carries many real estate advertisements, because they are effective. Make sure an ad for your house is professionally made and will appear there. Line ads are not considered expensive, and you could make your negotiations with the agent in this regard very persuasive by offering to pay half the budget. If one agent refuses to advertise, consider listing with a competing agent, of which there always are many. The more unique your home, the more useful are tailor-made advertisements.

- Electronic advertisements, including interior and exterior photographs, are becoming more popular and more effective as their availability gains recognition and acceptance. From the seller's standpoint, they can't hurt and will be offered by some agents in the area, especially if demanded during the negotiating process.

In addition to negotiating the terms of the listing agreement, and at the same time, prospective sellers should fully discuss each of the following matters with prospective listing agents:

- Ask for a sample of text of different advertisements that will be published in identified newspaper(s). Also ask for samples of information sheets that are placed in dispensing boxes in front of houses next to their proper "For Sale" signs. Ask how the information sheets will be distributed, and make sure they will contain all the relevant information about nearby shopping, transportation systems, schools, churches, parks, police and fire stations, and so forth.

- Whether there will be an agent tour, and what steps the listing agent will take to ensure that most of the other agents in the area will attend the agent tour.

- How and when the house will be shown to potential buyers by all other agents. You do not want to have agents arriving with prospective buyers at unexpected times during your daily routine.

- A list of all repairs thought necessary to put the house in condition for sale. Also, obtain advice with regard to what disclosures about the condition of the house you will need to make in contracting with a buyer. (More about sellers' disclosures will be discussed later in this chapter.) If it will take you two weeks to get the house ready for sale, then sign the listing in two weeks.

- The lowest price you should consider accepting. This will be useful later when your agent begins bringing you offers to consider. Do not disclose to your agent the actual lowest price you would accept, or any other information that might suggest you have an urgent need to sell.

- Estimated net cash proceeds from escrow, assuming various sales prices. This will avoid any surprises from exaggerated expectations concerning how much cash you ultimately will receive.

- The highest reasonably possible selling price, and how it was derived. Have the agent provide a list of all sales of comparable homes in your area within the past twelve months, indicating which ones were handled by the subject brokerage firm. This information is easily obtained by sales agents. Agents tend to specialize by geographical area (their "farm"), and agents who work successfully in your area will probably get better results sooner than agents who customarily work other areas.

- Whether the seller will be permitted to hold any earnest money deposit received, and if not, why not. If it is deposited in an escrow or trustee account, it will be difficult for the seller to obtain it if the sale is not consummated. And will any earnest money deposit be restricted to a certified check or money order? If not, why not? How will the earnest money deposit be divided if the prospective buyer defaults (backs out) before escrow closes?

- How much effort the agent who signs the listing personally will expend. Will your agent accompany potential buyers or simply send them by? Or will your agent rely on other agents to sell the property, while spending his or her time obtaining new listings? Will your agent "qualify" each and every prospect to make sure they are financially able to buy your home, rather than simply curious "lookers"?

- Whether an immediate termite inspection is advisable. If major repairs need to be made, shouldn't you know that before signing a contract obligating you to sell? If not, why not? Similar concerns exist about the condition of the roof or about major structural problems.

- What current terms of financing are available for a buyer of your home. Should you offer an assumption of the existing loan and carryback of some of the unpaid balance? If financing is not available for the potential buyers of your home, should you consider a lease-option and make a quick deal? What will you owe your agent if you make a lease-option during the listing period? If you handle a lease-option arrangement, is it excluded from the listing?

- Whether an open house is necessary. (Many agents conduct open houses primarily to obtain listings from other persons in the neighborhood who may be considering selling. This technique is especially attractive to a modestly successful agent who happens to land one upscale listing. It may produce other upscale listings and generate considerable profits.) Most prospects do not spend hours slowly driving around the city hoping to see "open house" signs on desirable homes. Rather, they seek counsel from sales agents who know what's available and who can show the house to the prospect.

- Precisely what the broker intends to do, step by step, in diligently hunting for a buyer. Will your agent exchange referrals with other brokers nationwide? Are new employment centers opening that may provide clues about potential buyers moving into your area? Will a handsome flyer or prospectus about your house be prepared and widely distributed to all other agents in the community?

554 Unit 2 *Application of Law to the Individual*

A candid discussion of these topics with the prospective agent will illuminate many areas of concern and forestall potential misunderstandings.

Finally, do not sign a listing agreement before obtaining the names and current addresses/telephone numbers of two or more former sellers. Ask the references if they were satisfied with the negotiating process; if they felt pressured to drop their price; if they thought the agent was working hard for them all the time; if they were surprised by closing costs and repairs they had to make; and if they would hire the agent again. In addition to obtaining references from former employers, you might consider asking prospective agents for their résumés, indicating their education and work experiences. After all, you routinely are asked as much when applying for employment positions.

The greatest benefits from hiring an agent to assist in the sale of your home is the experience of the agent (1) in directing you how to prepare your home for sale, (2) in knowing and explaining the market data in general and how it specifically affects the price of your home, and (3) in aggressively urging all other agents in the community to show your home to their prospects and providing them with a professional brochure of its features.

There are risks in hiring a listing agent. Your property may be placed in multiple listings and be quietly forgotten, with your agent doing nothing more than hoping that some other agent somewhere will stumble upon it (out of the thousands that are multiple-listed). If your agent knows what your absolute lowest possible acceptable price is, that too often will be the top offer you will receive. If your agent knows that your job has changed and you are desperate to sell, that information may find its way to prospective buyers who then will "bottom fish" (offer below-market prices). If no prospects appear as the weeks and months drift by, you cannot fire your listing agent for inactivity. If your listing agent is not competent and experienced, you may face problems with disclosing or withholding material information, with obtaining a reasonable termite clearance, and with demands by prospective buyers for repairs, fix-ups, and other costly changes. Care in employing a listing agent should be no less than the obvious care required in employing any professional person who will be charged with important responsibilities on your behalf.

SERVICE TO BUYERS

Real estate sales agents are authorized by law to solicit for new "listings" from prospective sellers. This often is referred to as the "listing" function. These agents often send flyers to homeowners asking if they will be selling soon and recommending themselves as agents. Sales agents also are authorized to take prospective buyers to and show homes that are on the market but that were listed by other agents, even from competing brokerage companies. This often is referred to as the "selling" function. By tradition, the commission paid by the seller is split evenly between the brokers in charge of the listing and selling functions.

It is important to distinguish between these two functions, and to understand how the seller's commission is distributed. An example may clarify this distinction.

LEGAL FOCUS—PROBLEM

Sam Seller employed Larry Lister of Cold Realty to hunt for a buyer for his home on Shady Tree Lane, and promised to pay a 6 percent commission if a ready, willing, and able purchaser was found who agreed to pay a $200,000 purchase price. Sallie Saleslady noticed Seller's home in the electronic multiple listing service while she was sitting at her desk at Tigar Realty Co. Saleslady thought this might be the right home for Betty Buyer, with whom she had been working, and arranged to show Seller's home to her.

Buyer loved the home and asked Saleslady to prepare an offer to purchase and handle all the necessary details. As a result, Buyer bought Seller's home and a commission of $12,000 was payable. Who gets the money?

In the listing agreement, Seller promised to pay the brokerage firm, Cold Realty, the $12,000 commission. But since the buyer was found by Tigar Realty Co., it received half, $6,000, directly from Cold Realty. Cold Realty splits 50–50 with its agents, and so paid Lister $3,000, his share. Tigar Realty, however, had agreed to a 60–40 split with its leading producers, and so paid $3,600 to Saleslady for her efforts in finding the buyer, and kept $2,400 for itself. Thus it is said that finding a listing is worth half of the commission while finding a buyer is worth the other half. Saleslady was representing the buyer, Buyer, against the best interests of Seller who, nevertheless, ends up paying her fee. Thus it is said that the buyer ordinarily pays no commission.*

With the understanding of how both listing and selling agents are paid, we can consider what services are provided.

The *listing agent* provides specific information about the homes for sale to the multiple listing service; causes a For Sale sign to be displayed on the property; prepares a flyer or brochure for distribution to other agents who farm (specialize in) the area; and organizes an agent's tour of the home featuring refreshments and a semi-party atmosphere. The home then is officially on the market. Interested persons may respond to the sign in the front yard and telephone the listing agent. The listing agent then becomes a selling agent, like Sallie Saleslady, and shows the house. If that buyer makes a purchase, it is called a *double-ender* because the listing agent and the selling agent are one and the same person, who collects "both ends" of the commission, or $6,000 in our preceding example. The agent in a double-ender is a *dual agent* representing both the seller and the buyer. This fact must be disclosed to the parties because there is a serious conflict of interest and the temptation is great for the agent to, for example, recommend a speciously low purchase price to the seller. On the other hand, an interested buyer might telephone any brokerage company in town, and one of their salespersons will show the house, just as Sallie showed the house that had been listed by Larry.

In either of the preceding situations, the agent representing the buyer (called the *buyer's agent*) will prepare a written offer to purchase. The buyer's agent will negotiate with the seller's (listing) agent by exchanging counteroffers. Once a real estate purchase agreement is signed by seller and buyer, the agents will play a less active role. The agents will assist in arranging for a home inspection, a termite inspection, and any other service providers who may be needed. Sellers and buyers typically rely on their agents for a wide variety of suggestions and information, but should also read all documents and give the transaction the personal attention that its importance deserves.

Real estate brokerage companies, seizing an opportunity presented by the Internet, are offering concierge services to buyers and homeowners for no charge. Also called "home provider" services or "home-link," the concierge service provides homeowners with references to all kinds of service providers, for repairs, cleaning, gardening, child care/house sitting, or perhaps legal, accounting, or any other service—all at discount prices. Home products also may be obtained through these services. Service providers pay real estate brokerage companies a fee, anywhere from $500 to $15,000 every three months, to place an

http://

For a sample of a dual agency consent agreement see the Connecticut Association of Realtors' site at

http://www.ctrealtor.com/forms/consentagreement.htm

http://

For consumer protection information about home ownership, buyers may visit http://www.ftc.gov/

A home buyer "inspection kit" is available from http://www.freddiemac.com/

---

* Although the buyer pays no cash to any agent in the transaction, the buyer is paying the sales price. If the sales price was "inflated" by $12,000 in this example, the economic "loss" of the commission would fall upon Betty the buyer. For those of you who enjoy financial analysis, note that most of the purchase price is financed over many years—thus, Betty's economic "loss" is spread over the same period of time. The word *loss* is in quotation marks because it is descriptive—there is no loss when a valuable service is received for a fair price paid.

advertising banner on the company's Web site. Thus homeowners have a single source to find a provider for any service or product that is desired. Real estate companies expect to attract new listings, produce advertising income, and obtain referral fees from providers. Consumer advocates express concern that the quality of services and products referred to homeowners may be lacking.[6]

How Is an Offer to Purchase a Home Made?

An offer to purchase real property, such as a home, should be made in writing. Otherwise, under the Statute of Frauds, it is unenforceable should either party dispute its terms or even deny its existence. The offer must state essential terms, such as a description of the property, the purchase price, and payment terms. The offer is usually made on a form document called a **purchase agreement and deposit receipt,** or simply *deposit receipt.** The deposit receipt is a standard form with many blanks to be completed by the buyer with the assistance of the real estate agent. The deposit receipt cannot be drafted by the real estate agent because that would constitute the illegal practice of law. But filling in blanks in a form contract is permitted.

    The process of negotiating back and forth on behalf of the seller and buyer, thereby avoiding the intransigence that typically is created by eye-to-eye dealings, is the single most valuable service provided by agents. Some contend that preparation of the written purchase agreement is the primary service rendered for sellers and buyers, but attorneys could easily be hired to perform that service for considerably less than a real estate commission—and may even recommend that the contract be bypassed. The role of attorneys in sales transactions is discussed later in this chapter.

What Is the Effect of an Accepted Offer?

When a written purchase contract is prepared for and signed by the buyer, it becomes a formal offer to purchase[†] and is delivered to the seller's agent.

    A good-faith deposit made by the buyer usually accompanies a purchase agreement. In theory, the deposit is to assure the seller that the buyer is not a mere "tire kicker" and intends to purchase the property. **Liquidated damages** are an amount of money agreed upon between contracting parties to fairly represent all losses of the innocent party if the contract is wrongfully broken. Such a provision is common and eliminates the necessity of litigation, since a solution already has been agreed upon. The earnest money serves as liquidated damages in the event of a broken contract. If the buyer wrongfully fails to complete the purchase, the deposit can be retained by the seller as liquidated damages for the breach of the contract of purchase. There is no legal requirement that a buyer include a deposit with the offer, but it is a customary sign of serious intent and ability to buy, and a seller would most likely refuse to accept an offer without one. Often the earnest money deposit will approximate 1 percent of the purchase price. But, there is one "fly in the ointment" for the seller who attempts to retain the earnest money deposit after a buyer defaults.

---

purchase agreement and deposit receipt

A contract by which a seller agrees to sell, and the buyer agrees to buy, a specified parcel of real property at a specified price and upon specified terms.

liquidated damages

Amount of damages that contracting parties have previously agreed would be fair payment in case of breach.

---

* The term "deposit receipt" is a misnomer because, once signed by the parties, it is a binding contract between seller and buyer. A purchase contract also serves the dual role of acting as a receipt for any refundable "good faith deposit" that may accompany it, hence the derivation of its euphemistic phrase "deposit receipt."

† An offer confers upon the seller a power to create a binding contract, simply by acceptance (signing the offer). Usually, the seller will make a responsive counteroffer, and after reciprocal negotiations a final contract will emerge.

LEGAL FOCUS—PROBLEM

Sam Seller signed a contract to sell his home to Betty Buyer. A $1,500 earnest money deposit had accompanied the deposit receipt and was on deposit at the Acme Escrow and Title Company. Then Buyer found a home she liked better and bought it. Seller never saw her again. A few days later Seller telephoned Acme and asked them to send the now-forfeited $1,500 deposit to him. To his dismay, Acme declined and referred him to the listing agent, Wade Larry. Seller immediately called Larry asking about the money. What do you suppose Larry said?

In all likelihood, Larry said, "Like it says in the listing, I get one-half of the forfeited deposit money for my troubles in finding the buyer." Seller learned, by reference to the listing contract, that Larry was indeed entitled to one-half of the money for finding the "deadbeat" buyer. If Seller had bothered to read the listing form before signing it, he could have deleted that provision.

LEGAL FOCUS—PROBLEM

Audra Acquirer made a written, signed offer to purchase Tom Holden's home. Holden signed and returned the offer, thereby creating a binding contract. Subsequently, pending "close of escrow" (the usual moment when ownership passes to the buyer), Holden refused to complete the transaction. Acquirer believed that Holden did this because he found out that his house was worth a lot more money than his selling price. Acquirer contacted her attorney. What advice will she receive?

Acquirer's attorney will advise her that she has two legal remedies. In the first, she can proceed "in equity" and request the court to order Holden to comply with the agreement. This remedy is called *specific performance* and is available when dollar damages would be inadequate. Money damages would be inadequate here because every parcel of land is considered by the courts as unique (no two parcels can be in the same place) and cannot be substituted for in the marketplace, as can, for example, an automobile. If Acquirer won such a lawsuit, the court would order Holden to convey ownership as promised. Acquirer, of course, would have to pay the price, as promised.

In the alternative remedy, Acquirer can sue "at law" and request the court to assess damages against Holden in an amount equal to her out-of-pocket expenses plus the benefit of her bargain, if any. (This "benefit of the bargain" could be the difference between the low purchase price of the home and its higher fair market value.) Acquirer's choice of remedy—to sue for the property or the money—would depend primarily on how unique the property was to her and what amount of monetary damages she could expect to recover.

In addition, and as a separate matter, if Holden had "listed" the property with a real estate brokerage firm, he would be obligated to pay the firm a commission, even though the sale was never completed. This is so because the broker had found in Acquirer a "ready, willing, and able buyer" who had signed a written offer to buy on terms originally specified by the seller. Listing agreements typically contain language protecting real estate agents from nonpayment by sellers who change their minds and withdraw their properties from the market either before or after signing sales contracts. If sellers want an "out" in their listing agreements, they must negotiate for them before they are signed.

WHAT ARE DISCLOSURE LAWS?

In the common law, the seller of a home is not required to disclose patent (visible) defects to a buyer, the theory being that the buyer should be alert enough to see and discover such defects. Latent (hidden) defects that were known to the seller need not be revealed; if asked, the seller cannot lie, but ordinary sales "puffing" is legal. In a general sense, the common law holds "let the buyer beware." Under this version of the common law, many cases evolved that distinguish between those lies by sellers for which there was liability, and those for which there was not.

LEGAL FOCUS—PROBLEM

C. J. Thomas and his wife Joan were home when their real estate sales agent brought a prospective buyer, Art Shab, for a viewing. During introductions, Shab asked whether the neighbors ever made unusually loud noises or otherwise caused problems, and whether the house was insulated. Thomas answered that the neighbors "were quiet" and "yes, the building was well insulated." In truth, as Thomas knew, the neighbors were extremely boisterous, often screaming profanities at each other in the early hours, and their children were known to break neighborhood windows with BB guns, empty garbage cans over neighbors' fences, and race their motorcycles up and down the street. Likewise, as Thomas also knew, the house was not insulated. Shab purchased the home and shortly thereafter learned the truth about the neighbors and the insulation. He contacted his attorney seeking to revoke the purchase, claiming fraud. Will Shab succeed?

Shab will succeed with the fraud claim if the seller (1) made a representation (2) of a material fact, (3) knowing the statement to be false, (4) which asserted fact was reasonably relied upon by the buyer, and (5) induced the buyer to consummate the purchase. Under the common law, the falsehood concerning the "quiet neighbors" is irrelevant because it is only a personal opinion. What is admirable to some is anathema to others. However, the presence or absence of insulation is a fact. If the absence of insulation would be obvious (patent) to an ordinary layman, Shab would again be out of luck—a buyer cannot close his or her eyes to the obvious and then complain after the sale. But the presence or absence of insulation is usually not readily ascertainable. Therefore, Shab may pursue either of two common-law remedies. He may seek to recover the cost to cure the defect (by installing insulation) as compensatory damages, and he could also seek, and might receive, an additional sum as exemplary or punitive damages because of the intentional deception or fraud by Thomas.* Alternatively, Shab may rescind the purchase, give up possession of the house to Thomas, and receive reimbursement for his down payment and other monies expended in the purchase. This is the remedy authorized by the New York court in the *Stambovsky* case included at the end of this chapter.

Note that the remedies available to Shab are based on the common-law tort called fraud (also called deceit). Some states have modern disclosure statutes, discussed shortly, that change the common law under which Thomas would be responsible for both misrepresentations.

---

* Some states, such as Washington, do not permit the award of punitive damages. Punitive damages were explained fully in Chapter 7.

Following are examples of statements of personal opinion, often exaggerated. A seller may make them to a prospective buyer without fear of liability for damages or of a demand for rescission:

- "This house is really worth much more than I'm asking."
- "This is the finest home in the area."
- "This is the best-constructed home you will ever live in."
- "Will taxes go up in this neighborhood? Never!"
- "The value of this house will increase at least 5 percent per year."

Statements such as the following *may* justify a rescission or action for damages, if they are false:

- "A new roof was installed on this house two years ago."
- "During the rainy season, all excess surface water drains off almost immediately."
- "There are no termites, no dry rot."
- "The foundation was not damaged by the earthquake."
- "There is no asbestos in the house."

A more difficult question arises when a seller, knowing of some important latent defect such as a fractured foundation, simply doesn't say anything to the prospective buyer. No lies are told, but important information is withheld. Under the common law and in some states, a seller has no general duty to speak. The rationale is that the buyer is free to investigate and to inquire; if asked, the seller's answers must be truthful. The problem is that most buyers are not qualified or prepared to ask all possibly relevant questions. For example, how many buyers would be likely to ask if there is radon gas emission within the premises or if the neighbors have threatened to sue about location of the new backyard fence, or if there is landfill on the property?

There is a new trend under which state laws require sellers to disclose increasing amounts of information, not limited to the traditional material questions of fact. The real estate industry largely favors this trend. Why would an industry favor laws that increase the disclosure burdens (and liabilities) of their customers-sellers? Licensed real estate agents carry information back and forth between negotiating buyers and sellers who almost never meet eye-to-eye. Salesmanship and negotiating success require that agents serve as buffers between and out of the presence of sellers and buyers, alternately conveying persuasive information back and forth. Thus, when buyers believe they have been lied to by the seller, they normally sue the sales agents as well, contending that the agent also knew, or should have known, of the false information. The National Association of Realtors (NAR) is a huge trade association that exists for the purpose of serving its members. In so doing it continually lobbies for new laws to protect its members from lawsuits, among other things. Thus, it favors laws that shift burdens of disclosure from sales agents to sellers by creating legal defenses for agents. This influence, and the push for consumer protection, have created a recent trend called "let the seller beware." Under relatively new laws, all sellers of homes are required by statute to disclose a great deal of specific information about the property they offer for sale. In theory, the buyer is entitled to be informed of virtually anything that may influence the value or subjective desirability of the property about to be purchased. Thus informed, the real estate agent is off the hook and unlikely to be sued after a buyer discovers some bothersome defect. Sellers, however, can be and are sued if they fail to disclose all specified information or if their disclosures are inaccurate.

The trend of law requires the seller to disclose, in writing and as soon as practicable before close of escrow, information that he or she either knows or can ascertain. For example, one category of disclosure requires preparation of a checklist of items on the premises, such as a range, dishwasher, washer/dryer hookup, burglar alarm, and so forth. Another category of disclosure requires notice to the buyer if any of the systems or appliances are not in good working order. Yet another category requires notice of any defects or malfunctions in the roof, ceiling, floor, foundation, driveway, plumbing, sewer/septic system, etc. A final category calls for disclosure of general knowledge the seller has about any easements, absence of a building permit for any additions that have been made, a landfill under the house, settling or sliding incidents, flooding or drainage problems, zoning violations, and even neighborhood noise problems. Furthermore, both the seller's agent and any buyer's agent must inspect the property and report to the prospective buyer any problems they observe. Unlike the seller, if the agent does not observe a defect, he or she is not responsible to discover and disclose it.

If the seller is negligent or dishonest in making any disclosure that later comes to the buyer's attention, a suit for money damages is authorized by statute. The sale, however, cannot be rescinded (undone).[7]

LEGAL FOCUS—PROBLEM

Brent and Lorri Lanfield, having lived frugally for several years while accumulating sufficient money for a down payment, purchased their first home from the Maxwell family. A month after escrow closed, while Lorri was mowing the lawn, a next-door neighbor dropped by, introduced himself, and asked, "Did you know that the Maxwells' grandson committed suicide in the upstairs bedroom of your new house?" The Lanfields were shocked by this discovery, and in the ensuing weeks became increasingly ill at ease because of it. They consulted Monica Smith, attorney at law, for advice. Should the law provide the Lanfields with a remedy against the Maxwells?

It is unfortunately true that occurrence of a human being's death in a house can have an adverse effect on its future resale value. In times past, for some people, a house wasn't a home unless and until both births and deaths had occurred within its walls. Today, rightly or wrongly, knowledge of a death by suicide may affect potential buyers differently than natural death from old age. Death on the premises from any cause may adversely affect the willingness of some people to purchase the property. Under common-law principles, the Maxwells probably had no duty to reveal the fact of their grandson's death because it was not a material defect in the real property as distinguished from the subjective attitudes of members in the buying public. For example, nondisclosure of a nearby tuberculosis (TB) clinic provides no common-law remedy for a buyer who is distressed by its presence and who would have offered less purchase money if the truth had been known. TB clinics do not distribute contagion and subjective thoughts to the contrary are irrelevant. However, in states where the common law has been modified by comprehensive disclosure statutes, sellers must disclose the occurrence of prior deaths (statutes differ and may exclude certain types of deaths) or face the likelihood of an action for damages measured by the impact of such fact upon the market value of the property.

LEGAL FOCUS—PROBLEM

Justin and Michelle Goodbright, with two daughters ages eight and ten, were especially attracted to the excellent schools that were located near the Waterford subdivision. After searching for months, they finally found and purchased a custom home at 2204

Almond Court for $345,000. Unbeknownst to them, Rodney Weasel, a former convict who was twice convicted of sexual offenses involving minor children, was living nearby at 2214 Almond Court. Was the seller, or the seller's agent, required to inform the Goodbrights of this, to them shocking, bit of information?

Under Megan's Law, as discussed earlier in Chapter 6, police routinely notify residents in neighborhoods of the residency of sexual predators. Notification is passive in some communities (available by telephone) and active (delivered door-to-door) in others. A seller may or may not be aware of the nearby residence of a sexual predator. Furthermore, if such a disclosure is made to a prospective buyer like the Goodbrights, surely the sale will not occur. Should the financial ramifications of where a sex predator chooses to live fall upon the shoulders of his neighbors? Should an agent, who is in the business of knowing what is going on relative to market values in the area, be excused from responsibility to tell buyers while the seller is not?

Relative to Megan's Law, the National Association of Realtors lobbies for laws that straddle the fence by requiring disclosure to the buyer only of the police telephone number (or other source) to obtain the addresses of sexual predators. If prospective buyers ask the real estate sales agent who is showing the home, "Are there any sexual predators nearby?" the NAR position is to answer, "You can check by calling 555-6463 or by ..." After doing this, no further disclosure need be made.

Future homeowners and sellers should be alarmed that the value of all homes in the vicinity would drop substantially on the happenstance of a convict moving nearby. If the notoriety through posting of pictures and shunning, if not ridicule, drives convicts from subdivisions in the suburbs, the problem may be transferred to renters. That is, convicts may be effectively pushed into the large, highly populated and densely housed cities, as renters, where their anonymity is possible. Under that scenario, the attendant risks of harm will have been shifted from the children of homeowners in the suburbs to the children of renters in the cities.

How Can a Buyer Finance Purchase of a Home?

Few buyers have the cash to pay the entire purchase price of a home. Even if they do, they may prefer to make a relatively low down payment and borrow the balance of the purchase price, because they can then invest the rest of their savings elsewhere. The assumption is that with climbing wages or salaries, it is progressively easier to pay off the fixed amount of the loan as time goes by.

Buyers desiring to borrow money to purchase a home will be required to sign, and to be legally bound by, two very important documents: the promissory note and the mortgage.

The Promissory Note

A **promissory note** evidences the loan (see Exhibit 12-3). It is signed by the borrower, called the **maker,** and delivered to the lender, called the **payee,** when the sale is completed. As evidence of the debt, the note contains important information pertaining to the loan. The note is not a contract; rather, it is evidence of the existence of a debt. The most important information it contains is
* The names of the maker and the payee
* The amount of the debt

promissory note

A written promise to pay to a named person or to the bearer of the note a certain sum of money in the future.

maker

The creator of a promissory note.

payee

Person in whose favor a check, draft, or promissory note is drawn.

EXHIBIT 12-3: **Example of Promissory Note for $200,000**

PROMISSORY NOTE SECURED BY DEED OF TRUST

$200,000   June 1, 200__

FOR VALUE RECEIVED, I PROMISE TO PAY TO _____ (the lender/payee) _____, OR ORDER, AT _____ (lender's address) _____ THE PRINCIPAL SUM OF $200,000, WITH INTEREST FROM THIS DATE UNTIL PAID AT THE RATE OF _____ PERCENT A YEAR ON THE BALANCE REMAINING FROM TIME TO TIME UNPAID. PRINCIPAL AND INTEREST SHALL BE DUE AND PAYABLE IN MONTHLY INSTALLMENTS OF $_____ OR MORE,* COMMENCING ON THE _____ DAY OF _____, 200__, AND CONTINUING THEREAFTER UNTIL THE PRINCIPAL AND INTEREST ARE FULLY PAID.

UPON ANY DEFAULT IN THIS NOTE OR IN THE TERMS OF THE DEED OF TRUST SECURING THIS LOAN, THE UNPAID PRINCIPAL AND ACCRUED INTEREST SHALL AT ONCE BECOME DUE AND PAYABLE, WITHOUT NOTICE, AT THE OPTION OF THE HOLDER OF THIS NOTE.

MAKER AGREES TO PAY COURT COSTS AND REASONABLE ATTORNEY FEES INCURRED BY PAYEE IN CONNECTION WITH THE ENFORCEMENT OF THIS NOTE.

IF ANY MONTHLY INSTALLMENT IS RECEIVED BY PAYEE MORE THAN 10 DAYS AFTER ITS DUE DATE, LATE CHARGES OF _____ PERCENT OF SAID PAYMENT, BEING THE SUM OF $_____ EACH PAYMENT, ALSO WILL BE DUE AND PAYABLE.

PRIVILEGE IS RESERVED TO MAKE ADDITIONAL PRINCIPAL PAYMENTS NOT TO EXCEED A TOTAL OF $_____ IN ANY TWELVE-MONTH PERIOD DURING THE FIRST 36 MONTHS OF THIS LOAN.

_____
/s/ Maker

* The phrase "or more" gives the borrower the option to make additional payments of principal. Technically, if the phrase is not included in the note, the loan is said to be "locked in," meaning that the borrower cannot make larger or additional monthly payments to retire the debt earlier. However, most states have declared that "locked in" home-purchase loans are against public policy, and unenforceable; therefore, lenders customarily add a provision, such as found at the bottom of this exemplar note, specifically authorizing additional principal payments in specified amounts.

collateral

Money or other property made available as security by a debtor to a creditor, through physical possession or legal right, to guarantee repayment of a loan.

foreclosure

Process by which secured real property is confiscated at the direction of the unpaid creditor and sold to the highest bidder.

mortgage (or real mortgage)

The contract in which the buyer of real property typically gives a lender a lien or claim against the real property which serves as collateral for a loan of money, often borrowed to pay part of the purchase price.

mortgagor

The borrower of funds secured by a mortgage.

mortgagee

The lender of funds secured by a mortgage.

- The interest rate
- The amount of the monthly payments (of principal and interest)
- The due date of payments
- The delinquency date of payments after which a penalty is charged
- The penalty for delinquent payments
- The obligation of the debtor to pay creditor's collection and attorney fees, if applicable

THE MORTGAGE

The lender will not trust the borrower as the sole source for repayment of the loan. Too much money is involved. The lender will require the home to be put up as **collateral,** or security. If the borrower defaults (fails to make the proper monthly payments in repayment of the loan), the lender may take the home, sell it, and apply the proceeds of the sale to pay off the balance of the loan. This procedure is called **foreclosure.** The document that establishes the home as collateral is called a **mortgage.** The borrower or debtor is called the **mortgagor;** the lender or creditor is called the **mortgagee.*** Most home loans are paid

* Not all states use the mortgage, or real mortgage as it is sometimes called. Other states use a "deed of trust" to accomplish the same result. The debtor is called the trustor and the lender the beneficiary. Even in these states, the deed of trust is often referred to as a mortgage. There are technical differences between mortgages and deeds of trust that need not concern home buyers and sellers. Both documents allow lenders to foreclose upon a home as indicated above.

on time, although the national rate of foreclosures fluctuates considerably from year to year. In years of recession, like 2003, the foreclosure rate increases.

When the home mortgage loan is completely paid off by the homeowner, the lender will return the mortgage to the borrower, who then may "burn the mortgage" or, perhaps, frame it. In the case of a **deed of trust,** the full repayment will be evidenced by a deed of reconveyance, or simply "recon" as it is called.

WHAT IF A HOME OWNER DEFAULTS ON MONTHLY LOAN PAYMENTS?

Upon default by the owner, the lender may simply do nothing for a while, giving the homeowner extra time to pay, or may start foreclosure proceedings. Both deeds of trust and mortgages contain many formal promises of the homeowner, such as to pay property taxes as they come due, to keep casualty insurance in force, to maintain the property, and to comply with all applicable laws. The mortgage lenders require these promises because they may have to foreclose on the property in the future and want it to be in good condition at that time.

A breach of any of these promises or of the promise to make monthly payments is called a *default,* for which the lender's basic remedy is foreclosure. Lenders do not like foreclosure any more than borrowers do. As a practical matter, long before foreclosure will be commenced by an unpaid lender, many attempts will be made to help solve the debtor's financial problem. See Exhibit 12-4 for advice on avoiding foreclosure.

If the remedy of foreclosure becomes necessary, most lenders will choose foreclosure by private sale, which is called **nonjudicial foreclosure,** under which no court proceedings are necessary. Mortgages (and deeds of trust) contain a provision, called the *power-of-sale clause,* that authorizes a private foreclosure sale without court supervision. The date and place where the foreclosure sale will occur must be advertised in a local newspaper, and a notice will be posted in the county courthouse. Before the sale, the homeowner may reinstate the loan by paying all delinquent monthly payments as well as late-payment charges and any costs and fees to date. This valuable **right of reinstatement** exists even though the borrower may have agreed within the terms of the promissory note that upon default the entire unpaid balance becomes immediately due and payable. Such a provision is called an **acceleration clause** (because the loan due date is accelerated to the present), but its impact is overridden by the right of reinstatement.

If the defaulting homeowner does not reinstate (or, alternatively, completely pay off) the loan, a **foreclosure sale** will occur after about four months from the date the borrower's default was formally recorded. At the sale, the trustee accepts the highest cash bid and conveys title to the successful buyer by deed. If no bidders offer cash in at least the amount of the unpaid balance of the mortgage loan, the lender will bid its debt, that is, cancel its loan in exchange for ownership of the property. Thus, the lender either obtains payment of its loan in full from some cash bidder, or cancels its loan and acquires ownership of the house.

Houses owned by institutional lenders that have been acquired through foreclosure are called **real estate owned** (REOs) and make attractive purchase opportunities for home buyers. Oftentimes institutional owners of REOs will provide buyers with attractive financing to complete the purchase, as well as keep the price at an attractive level. These REO owners are not in the business of owning homes and thus will work with interested home buyers who may "take them off our hands."

Sometimes homes are sold, before foreclosure occurs, for less than the unpaid balance of their original mortgages in what are called **short sales.** A short sale is any sale during

---

deed of trust

A deed used by a borrower (called *trustor*) to transfer the legal title to real property to a disinterested stakeholder (the *trustee*) to hold as security or collateral for the benefit of the lender (the *beneficiary*).

nonjudicial foreclosure

The involuntary sale, without court proceedings, of an owner's real property to raise money to satisfy the unpaid balance of the loan that is in default.

right of reinstatement

The right of a defaulting debtor to reinstate the loan by payment of all money due for prior months including late charges, even though the note and mortgage declare that the *entire* unpaid balance is immediately due in full upon any default.

acceleration clause

A provision in a loan agreement that allows the lender to declare the entire unpaid balance due and payable immediately if a given event occurs.

foreclosure sale

Sale of a debtor's real property to raise cash with which to reduce or retire the unpaid debt. A foreclosure sale may be of two varieties, by a court official following judicial foreclosure or by a trustee following nonjudicial foreclosure.

EXHIBIT 12-4: **Avoiding Foreclosure**

Avoiding Foreclosure

- ■ Immediately contact your lender to discuss any problems regarding mortgage payments.
- ■ Marshall your assets to pay your mortgage payments. Consider drawing on emergency funds.
- ■ Read all important documents and pay attention to communications from your lender.
- ■ Contact local government or government approved counseling programs to consider all your options and receive explanations about the foreclosure process and your rights.

real estate owned

Institutional lenders, such as banks and savings and loan associations, sometimes receive title to properties secured by loans that are in default, following foreclosure sales.

short sale

The sale of property (such as a home) for less than the unpaid balance of a loan in which the property serves as security.

deficiency judgment

Judgment against a debtor for the unpaid balance still due after repossession and resale of goods that were sold on credit, or after judicial foreclosure of a real estate mortgage.

judicial foreclosure

The forced sale, following a court proceeding, of an owner's real property to raise money to satisfy the creditor's claim for the unpaid balance of the loan that is in default.

right of redemption

Right of a debtor to recover, within one year, the property sold at a judicial foreclosure sale.

foreclosure where the asking price is less than the unpaid amount of the mortgage on the home. Short sales were frequent in the early 1990s when home prices fell, leaving many people saddled with homes worth less than the mortgages they owed. Many simply "walked away," leaving the banks with the choice of proceeding through foreclosure and then selling the homes as REOs, or simply accepting short sales during foreclosure to cut their losses.

Homeowners who are not making their monthly mortgage payments receive advance notice of the date and place of their foreclosure sale, and are entitled to remain in possession of the home until the sale takes place and a new owner of the property takes possession.

Proceeds of foreclosure sales go to the creditor to satisfy the homeowner's debt. Any excess (unlikely) belongs to the homeowner whose home was sold. But if there was any significant potential excess (i.e., equity) at the time of the foreclosure sale, it is likely the homeowner would sell the property and pay off the loan rather than suffer foreclosure.

The creditor may be entitled to a **deficiency judgment,** a court judgment against the debtor for the difference between the unpaid mortgage balance and the fair market value of the property. This represents the amount of money lost by the creditor as a result of the foreclosure. But such a judgment can be obtained only through a court-ordered and supervised foreclosure called **judicial foreclosure,** and most lenders prefer nonjudicial foreclosures by private sale because they are quicker, are less expensive, and don't require the services of an attorney. Furthermore, following judicial foreclosure, the debtor has one year within which to reclaim the property—called the one-year **right of redemption**—by fully reimbursing the person who made the winning bid at the judicial-foreclosure sale. So the only advantage to a judicial foreclosure is the possibility of a deficiency judgment, which could be uncollectible anyway (because the debtor lacks funds or assets).

Sometimes borrowers facing foreclosure offer a deed to the property to the lender to avoid the bad-credit implications of foreclosure. Such a deed is called a *deed in lieu of fore-closure.* Although these are more common in commercial property finances, they can offer advantages and disadvantages to other borrowers and lenders. From the homeowner's perspective, a deed in lieu of foreclosure can avoid the impact of a foreclosure upon his or her credit history. On the other hand, unless otherwise agreed, possession must be given immediately to the lender instead of several months later, following foreclosure sale. A deed in lieu of foreclosure also cancels any possibility of a deficiency judgment by the lender. From the lender's perspective, one advantage is that the delay and possible deterioration of the property while foreclosure is pending are avoided. If no deficiency judgment is possible or desirable, the deed in lieu of foreclosure should be satisfactory. However, the lender acquiring title by a deed in lieu of foreclosure takes the property subject to any junior liens, such as a mechanic's lien, an unpaid home-equity loan, or a carryback mortgage, that are on the property. Such liens would be wiped out if title were obtained by foreclosure sale. The decision to use a deed in lieu of foreclosure should be supported by professional advice.

State **homestead** laws* do not apply to home buyers who fail to make payments required under purchase-money mortgages. Rather, these laws are designed to protect the family home from other, unsecured creditors. State homestead laws vary in many details, including the scope of protection they afford homeowners.† The purpose of all homestead laws is to protect a family's ability to obtain a place of residence free from the threat of existing creditors.

TYPES OF FINANCING

There are three general sources of financing available for home buyers: new financing, assumption of existing financing, and seller's financing. We discuss these alternatives in order.

New Loans

Several different types of new, or original, loans are available to persons who desire to purchase a home. Most loans are made by savings and loan associations, banks, mortgage brokers, and mortgage bankers. **Mortgage brokers** prepare loan packages (applications and other documents) for borrowers, which they send to other lenders who actually advance the funds and make the loan. These brokers often work with a pool of many lenders and try to find the most attractive loan terms for borrowers. **Mortgage bankers,** on the other hand, make loans that they may later resell for cash, which is used again as working capital.

All lenders supply the information and forms necessary to apply for a mortgage loan. Usually loan application fees, and sometimes appraisal charges, must be paid even if the applicant fails to qualify for, or abandons, the loan commitment. A loan commitment is a lender's written agreement to make a loan to the borrower upon specified terms and conditions. But lenders do not ordinarily make loan commitments until the buyer has signed a purchase agreement. Then the prospective lender can have the home appraised and make other lending evaluations. However, it is increasingly popular for prospective buyers to get either **pre-approved** or **pre-qualified** for financing. For pre-approval, lenders will require a credit check and often written verification of employment. Pre-qualification is an estimate of the borrowing power of the prospective buyer based upon hypothetical information. Neither is a legal commitment by the lender to make a loan. Only a written loan commitment is binding. However, pre-approval and pre-qualifying are useful because they tend to assure sellers that the buyer is financially able to purchase the home that is for sale.

Loan terms are said to be completely negotiable, but in reality lenders advertise the terms of loans they are willing to make and rarely depart from such limitations. Nevertheless, those astute borrowers who take the time to comparison-shop for available financing will often save a considerable sum of money. Many mortgage brokers and even lenders advertise online the up-to-the-hour terms of available loans and offer assistance in making applications. Lenders compete aggressively to make loans to home purchasers, who are well advised to shop and to fully discuss the opportunities with their sales agent.

---

homestead

A declaration of a debtor's exemption in a specified amount of the equity of the homeowner's residence from levy and execution by a creditor.

http://

For current mortgage information visit
http://www.interest.com/

mortgage broker

A person licensed to engage in the business of bringing together borrowers and lenders of mortgage funds. Mortgage brokers typically are paid a commission based upon the volume of loans they originate.

mortgage banker

A business that makes real estate loans with its own capital, as well as with institutional funds, and then sells the loans in the secondary mortgage market.

pre-approved

A conditional offer to lend a given amount at a stated interest rate.

pre-qualified

An educated guess about how a much person can borrow based on information that person has provided.

---

* State homestead laws currently in force should not be confused with a series of United States Homestead Acts beginning in 1862, which gave clear title to 162 acres of federal public land to any person who occupied and cultivated the land for five years. By the 1950s, the federal government had thus given away about 250,000,000 acres of land west of the Mississippi River.

† For example, in California a creditor can cause a forced sale of the debtor's family home, but the first net proceeds (above the purchase-money mortgage) up to $75,000 for most married couples and $125,000 in a few situations go to the debtor and can be used to purchase a substitute home. Any excess goes to the creditor. See California Code of Civil Procedure, § 704.730. In Florida, on the other hand, regardless of the value of the residence, no sale can be forced during the lifetime of the debtor. O. J. Simpson moved from California to Florida and purchased an expensive home before the conclusion of the civil trial that assessed damages of $35 million against him for the wrongful deaths of Nicole Simpson and Ronald Goldman.

Fannie Mae (FNMA)

Nickname for the Federal National Mortgage Association, a corporation created by the National Housing Act to establish a secondary mortgage market by purchasing existing home-purchase mortgages.

Freddie Mac (FHLMC)

Nickname for the Federal Home Loan Mortgage Corporation, a corporation that participates in the secondary mortgage market by buying and selling conventional, FHA, and VA (Veteran's Administration) mortgages.

Ginnie Mae (GNMA)

Nickname for the Government National Mortgage Association, a federal corporation that purchases mortgages in the secondary mortgage market.

http://

See how Fannie Mae, Freddie Mac, and Ginnie Mae help low- and moderate-income families achieve home ownership

http://www.fanniemae.com/

http://www.freddiemac.com/

http://www.ginniemae.gov/

conventional loan

A home-purchase mortgage the repayment of which is not guaranteed by an agency of the federal government.

Once loans are made (or "originated") in the primary market—that is, the market composed of savings and loan associations, banks, and others that issue new loans—they are sold to buyers in the secondary mortgage market, which is a market of agencies and buyers who are competing to purchase new loans. Selling home loans gives lenders the cash with which to make additional new loans to buyers in the primary mortgage market. The major buyers in the secondary mortgage market are government-enacted agencies known widely by their nicknames, **Fannie Mae (FNMA), Freddie Mac (FHLMC), and Ginnie Mae (GNMA).** * Since these buyers purchase home mortgages, they can specify the terms of the loans that they will purchase, by interest rate, length for repayment, loan-to-value ratio, qualifications of borrower, etc. Nonconforming loans will not be purchased. Institutions then will make only those kinds of loans they can sell in the secondary market. These guidelines by mortgage buyers are regularly reviewed and updated to keep pace with changing market conditions and emerging social policies.

Buying loans is one way these three agencies—FNMA, FHLMC, and GNMA—fulfill their responsibility to stabilize the mortgage-money market. For example, when money is "tight" (difficult to borrow and with rising interest rates), these agencies purchase loans from lenders, thereby making more cash available to them for new loans. When money is "loose" (easy to borrow and with declining interest rates), these agencies will sell loans at attractive prices, thereby taking money out of effective circulation. Such transactions help prevent wide fluctuations in interest rates that would endanger the health of the economy.

Well-informed real estate agents check the fluctuations in the mortgage markets every day, and especially keep abreast of trends, all to help home buyers and sellers make smart decisions.

CONVENTIONAL LOANS   A **conventional loan** is one in which the terms are not directly influenced by government regulations or subsidies. The bank that is not going to sell its mortgages can make the loan on any terms it desires. Such a lender is called a **portfolio lender** because the loan is retained in the lender's own portfolio of outstanding loans. Lenders usually require a larger down payment for these loans than for loans to be sold.

Most conventional loans are, however, sold in the secondary market, in which case the buyer must qualify for the guidelines of Fannie Mae or Freddie Mac. These guidelines declare that if the down payment is less than 20 percent, the buyer must purchase **private mortgage insurance (PMI)** to guarantee the loan purchaser against loss in case of default by the homeowner/borrower. The premium for PMI is collected monthly along with principal and interest payments. Thus, PMI achieves the same security for the ultimate holder of the home buyer's mortgage loan as does government insurance, as explained shortly. In effect, mortgage buyers invest in risk-free mortgages—they are paid either by the homeowner or by an insurance company.

Redlining is a prohibited practice by a few lenders designed to avoid making loans to minority persons. The word is derived from a practice of drawing red circles on maps around minority neighborhoods, especially any areas in which repayment histories have been poor. Excuses are used to justify avoiding making loans in those redlined areas.

FEDERAL HOUSING ADMINISTRATION (FHA) LOAN   In a **Federal Housing Administration (FHA) loan,** repayment is insured by the U.S. government, and so the lender (or current mortgage holder) is not likely to lose its money. In a sense, the U.S. govern-

* Federal National Mortgage Association, Federal Home Loan Mortgage Corporation, and Government National Mortgage Association, respectively. These quasi-governmental agencies buy and sell mortgages to influence interest rates and to provide for the availability of funds for new mortgage lending. For example, if Fannie Mae announced that it would purchase mortgage loans made to recent college graduates for 100 percent of the purchase price of homes they bought, with interest at 6 percent, banks would immediately make such loans. Thus, public policy is influenced by the secondary mortgage market.

ment "cosigns" the borrower's loan. Since the loan is insured, lenders are able to accept transactions where the down payment is as little as 3 percent of the purchase price. The FHA establishes limits on the amount of loans it will insure. These loan "ceilings" vary by metropolitan area, ranging in amount from $144,336 in low-cost housing areas to $261,609 in expensive areas. These ceilings on single-family loans change from time to time.

Prospective home buyers may request an FHA loan application from any authorized FHA lender, such as most savings and loan associations, banks, and mortgage brokers. All real estate sales agents keep informed as to the FHA loan ceilings.

VETERAN'S ADMINISTRATION LOAN   In a **Veteran's Administration (VA) loan,** repayment to the lender is guaranteed by the U.S. government because the borrower is a qualified veteran. No down payment is required for these loans unless the price paid for the home exceeds its "reasonable value" as determined by the VA appraisal (a professional estimate of value). In such cases, the excess must be paid in cash by the veteran. The VA does not have loan ceilings, but lenders adhere to guidelines set by Ginnie Mae and Fannie Mae.

SELECTING THE BEST NEW FINANCING   The principal sources of all of these loans are savings and loan associations, commercial banks, and mortgage brokers who represent insurance companies, pension funds, and a variety of other organizations. The terms of available loans, such as their interest rates, change from time to time, and differ somewhat between lenders. A prudent buyer will shop for a lender willing to offer the most advantageous package of terms. Real estate sales agents are familiar with aggressive (very competitive) lenders in the area and ought to be consulted, as well as one or more mortgage brokers. As indicated earlier, many lenders are online with up-to-date financing packages. Generally, borrowers seek the highest **loan ratio** (lowest down payment), longest loan repayment period, lowest interest rate, and lowest loan charges. The reasons why borrowers usually seek these terms are described in the following paragraphs.

Veterans may qualify for a VA loan or, in many states, for state assistance. In California, a direct loan is obtainable from a state agency. Although the interest rate for such loans fluctuates with the cost of money to the state, it is generally far below the conventional loan market rate. Oregon and Wisconsin offer their veterans a benefit in the form of a loan repayment guarantee, but not a direct loan. Veterans almost always will receive better deals under VA programs than from other lenders.

Some of the factors a borrower should consider in determining which loan is best are the repayment term (longer is usually better), interest rate (the lower the better), qualification requirements (the more relaxed the better), and amount of the loan (the larger the better). We have suggested what is "better" only as a general guide; obviously, what is better for you will depend on your particular situation.

Loans where the interest rate remains the same during the life of the loan are called **fixed-rate mortgages.** Types of loans where the interest rate may (will) fluctuate are called **variable-interest-rate mortgages (VIRMs),** also called *adjustable-rate mortgages (ARMs).* Borrowers should examine carefully what caps, or limits, are placed on periodic fluctuations. Caps may restrict how high the interest rate can ultimately go, how much it can increase at any one adjustment, and how often adjustments can be made. Careful borrowers understand the parameters of any ARM they are considering. All real estate sales agents should be able to explain the pros and cons of an ARM given the prevailing interest rate at the time the information is requested.

REPAYMENT TERM   The longer the time span during which the loan must be repaid, the lower the monthly payment. For example, the monthly payment to **amortize** (pay off)

---

portfolio lender

A lender of home-purchase funds that does not expect to sell its mortgages in the secondary mortgage market. Because such lenders keep their loans within their own portfolio of loans, they can be more flexible (liberal) in the terms of the loans they offer prospective home buyers.

private mortgage insurance (PMI)

Insurance to protect a lender in the event that a borrower defaults in the repayment of a mortgage loan.

redlining

An illegal lending practice identifying minority or low-income neighborhoods where repayment histories have been poor and then denying or restricting loans to persons in that area.

http://

For general information about discrimination in housing or lending, visit the home page of the U.S. Department of Housing and Urban Development (HUD) at

http://www.hud.gov/

Federal Housing Administration loan (VIRMs)

A loan in which the lender is insured by the Federal Housing Administration, with the borrower paying the mortgage insurance premium.

http://

Look up the FHA loan limits in your county/state

https://entp.hud.gov/idapp/html/hicostlook.cfm

Veteran's Administration loan

A home-purchase mortgage loan made to any eligible veteran by the federal Veteran's Administration. The VA was established in 1944 by the Serviceman's Readjustment Act to assist veterans in becoming homeowners.

loan ratio

The ratio of a prospective loan amount to the appraised value of a home. Also called the *loan-to-value ratio.*

fixed-rate mortgage

A traditional home-purchase mortgage in which the interest rate and the monthly payment do not fluctuate during the life of the loan.

variable-interest-rate mortgage

A home-purchase mortgage and promissory note in which the interest rate may fluctuate, up or down, in sync with a published index. Also called adjustable-rate mortgage.

amortize

Repayment of a note secured by mortgage through agreed-upon monthly payments of principal and interest over the life of the loan.

an 8 percent loan of $100,000 over fifteen years is $955.70. In addition to principal and interest of $955.70, the borrower also must pay property taxes and casualty insurance (both discussed later). Lenders often require those payments on a monthly basis, which are then held in "impound accounts" until remitted to the appropriate insurance company and tax collector. Principal, interest, taxes, and insurance are often referred to by the acronym **PITI.** If PMI (private mortgage insurance), discussed earlier, is required by the lender, its premium is also tacked onto the monthly payment.

The same $100,000 loan repaid over a thirty-year period at 8 percent interest requires a monthly payment of $733.80, which is $221.90 a month less than the fifteen-year loan. These "savings" in monthly payments are offset by the increased amount of total interest that must be paid because of the longer-term loan. For example, the purchaser of a $115,000 home who borrows $100,000 of the purchase price at 8 percent will pay $172,026 ($955.70 × 12 × 15) over fifteen years, whereas the total cost would be $264,168 ($733.80 × 12 × 30) if the term of the $100,000 loan were thirty years. This $92,142 difference is interest paid because of the longer term. The example given is intended only to demonstrate the change in monthly loan payments when the term of the loan is extended from 15 to 30 years.

There are distinct advantages in taking a loan with a longer term, particularly for the younger family:

- The longer repayment term gives young buyers extra cash in early years while their family increases in size and cost of support.
- The young buyer's income is probably rising, so postponed payments will be easier to make in the future.
- Any inflation provides "cheaper" dollars in greater numbers, which helps pay off the loan later.
- Buyers might otherwise need to rely on costlier installment credit (18 percent or more a year) to buy goods wanted now and services needed now if extra cash goes into larger payments on the home.
- The tax deduction for interest paid on the mortgage remains available over the longer term. But note, it is more profitable to pay no interest than to obtain a tax deduction for interest that is paid.

A long-term loan can, of course, be paid off much earlier if the borrower chooses to make extra principal payments each month. Most loans permit an additional payment of principal each month without penalty. After five years of payments, there typically is no limit on the size of extra principal payments that may be made. The longer-term loan gives the borrower the choice, whereas a shorter-term loan requires the larger payment each month regardless of changing financial circumstances.

There are limits on the available term, typically thirty years for FHA and VA loans. Conventional lenders who sell their loans in the secondary mortgage market also are limited to thirty-year terms; however, loans allowing up to forty years for repayment are possible with portfolio lenders.

INTEREST RATE   The price of borrowing money is **interest.** The higher the interest rate, the higher the monthly payment (which includes both principal and interest). For example, a real estate loan of $100,000 over thirty years at 8 percent interest requires a monthly payment of $733.80. If the interest is reduced to 7 percent, the monthly payment decreases to $665.31, a savings of $68.49 each month. Thus, the total payments under the 8 percent loan would be $264,168 ($733.80 × 12 × 30) and only $239,512 ($665.31 × 12 × 30) for the 7 percent loan, a savings of $24,656. Exhibit 12-3 gives a more complete idea of monthly payments necessary to amortize (pay off) various loan amounts, to be repaid over thirty years,* with interest rates varying, for example, at 7 percent, 8 percent, and 9 percent (payments for property taxes and insurance are not included).

Although interest payments on home loans are tax-deductible, interest payments (or carrying charges) on consumer loans or credit purchases for cars, furniture, and so forth, are not—unless financed with a **home-equity loan,** a consumer loan secured by the equity in a home. This explains the popularity of home-equity loans.

Increased pressures for realistic financing, with monthly payments within the average budget, as well as for stability within the mortgage markets, have resulted in new variations of loans. As noted, the adjustable-rate mortgage (ARM) provides for the periodic increase or decrease in interest rate depending on prevailing interest levels. Because lenders of ARMs are protected against being locked into a low rate should prevailing rates increase, they are willing to begin the loan at an interest rate lower than is available for fixed-rate mortgages. These "teaser" rates may last for only a year or two before automatically "triggering" up to the market rate. If market interest rates decrease, the borrower is protected against being locked into a higher rate. In recent years with historically low fixed-rate mortgages the difference between ARMs and fixed-rate mortgages has been minimal.

Borrowers of fixed-rate mortgages found themselves locked into an unfavorable position in the last years of the twentieth century as interest rates plummeted. As a result, in recent years there has been a blizzard of refinancing in which these borrowers obtained much lower interest rate loans. A refinancing occurs when a homeowner replaces the existing mortgage with a new mortgage at a lower interest rate, and sometimes for a greater amount of money that produces cash for other purchases or needs or even for investment. In refinancing, many of these smart borrowers switched to fixed-rate loans, capitalizing on very attractive interest rates that cannot rise regardless of prevailing rates. Interest rates fluctuate upward and then downward over time, making the question "Should I apply for a fixed-rate or a variable-rate mortgage?" impossible to answer with scientific precision. Everyone desires a VIRM when interest rates are falling and a fixed-rate mortgage when interest rates are rising. At the writing of this edition, 2003, fixed-rate mortgages are available at less than 6%. No one should accept a VIRM when fixed rates are this low.

To avoid the possibility that the monthly payment may become unbearably high, the loan contract can call for maintenance of the same monthly payment even when the interest rate automatically increases in step with the relevant index, simply by extending the term of the loan. Other VIRMs may maintain the same monthly payment, even though the variable interest rate has increased, by adding the monthly difference owed but unpaid to the unpaid balance of the loan. This is called **negative amortization** because the unpaid principal balance of the loan is actually getting larger each month. If you don't pay what you owe this year, you end up owing more next year. Consequently, the owner's equity is decreasing each month, unless the amount of negative amortization is exceeded by gains in appreciation.

Another variation is the **graduated-payment mortgage,** where early payments are kept artificially low (through reduced interest rates), then increased later to artificially high levels (above-market interest rates). This arrangement is geared to young persons who are beginning their careers. Much of the interest is deferred to later years when income has risen and interest can be repaid without undue hardship.

* As noted earlier in this chapter, most homeowners no longer live in one home for thirty years, making payments on the same mortgage until it is paid off. But homeowners who move ordinarily resume monthly mortgage payments on each successive home they purchase, and thus do make mortgage payments for thirty years or even longer. On average, in our highly mobile society, most new home buyers will move between five and eight years after purchasing a home.

PITI

An acronym for *principal, interest, taxes,* and *insurance,* which represent the four basic repetitive expenses of buying real property with borrowed funds.

interest

The price, usually expressed as an annualized rate (percentage), for use of a sum of money (principal) obtained from a lender.

home equity loan

A loan for any purpose, (e.g., to pay off credit card balances that carry higher interest rates, or to pay for college tuition, a new car, a vacation, or home improvements) that is collateralized by a mortgage on the borrower's home.

negative amortization

A monthly increase in the unpaid principal balance of a mortgage loan resulting when the borrower does not make the required monthly interest payments in full.

graduated payment mortgage

A home-purchase mortgage and promissory note that features artificially low monthly payments for the initial few years as an inducement for borrowers whose incomes and creditworthiness are expected to improve in the future.

Yet another variation is the rollover mortgage, where an existing mortgage loan is replaced entirely, every three to five years, as agreed, with a new loan at then-current interest rates. The borrower usually is not charged loan fees or processing costs for the new loan. Lenders can be and are very creative in tailoring new loans to the perceived needs and desires of new home buyers. Pressure on the housing supply, and financing availability, will no doubt prompt new government subsidy programs and private sector financing ingenuity. Whatever happens, the purchase of living accommodations will continue to be the most significant financial undertaking and legal contract transaction entered into by most adults.

POINTS AND ANNUALIZED PERCENTAGE RATE   Interest rates should not be confused with loan charges, called **points,** which are one-time charges made by a lender at the time the home loan is made (originated). These charges are computed much like any percentage commission. They have ranged from about 0.5 percent to 3 percent. Thus, two points on a $100,000 loan would mean a charge of $2,000. Points are said to be a payment designed to bring the effective, or true, profit of the loan in line with prevailing interest rates. They also serve to generate cash for the lender to pay a loan broker's commission. Often the seller pays the points to the lender in order to avoid losing the sale, because on FHA and VA loans the buyer-borrower cannot be charged more than one point, which is considered a **loan origination fee.** This limitation reduces buyers' closing costs (which are discussed in detail later); but sellers who can do so may boost their sales price to make up the difference, thus indirectly passing this added cost to their buyers.

To show borrowers more clearly what their borrowing costs are, points are computationally treated as additional annualized interest. Thus, an 8 percent loan (with no points charged) may have an 8.75 percent **annualized percentage rate (APR)** if points are charged. When shopping for loans, prospective borrowers should compare the APRs of loans, and not their stated interest rates. All lenders must, by law, provide to prospective borrowers the APRs of each of their available financing packages.

AMOUNT OF LOAN   The greater the amount of money that can be borrowed to purchase a home, the lower the required down payment. Lenders will loan up to a specified percentage of the **appraised value** of the home—that is, the value assigned by a professional appraiser chosen by the lender. Conventional lenders might lend up to 90 percent of the appraised value and require the borrower to guarantee its repayment through the purchase of private mortgage insurance (PMI). Thus, to purchase a home appraised at and selling for $250,000, a loan of $225,000 can be made, requiring a $25,000 down payment.* Other portfolio lenders may require a larger down payment. FHA loan limits are adjusted from time to time by government regulation, but always are more liberal than conventional loan limits. For example, the FHA typically permits (will insure) loans with as little as a 5 percent down payment. Current FHA and market data may be obtained from any real estate sales agent or lending institution. Online mortgage services, mentioned earlier, also publish the terms of available financing.

LOAN QUALIFICATION REQUIREMENTS   To obtain a loan to purchase a home a borrower must meet creditworthiness criteria set by the lender. For a conventional loan, for example, a lender may require that monthly payments of principal and interest not exceed 40 percent of the borrower's total monthly income. Spouses or unrelated co-owners of a home may pool their respective incomes and credit standings to qualify for a loan. For government-subsidized loans, such as FHA and VA loans, qualifications are set by administrative regulation. Furthermore, purchasers of mortgages in the secondary mortgage

points

A one-time charge made by a lender when a home loan is originated. One point is 1 percent of the loan.

loan origination fee

A lump-sum fee paid by a mortgage borrower to the lender, who in turn pays all or a portion of it to the mortgage broker who introduced the borrower to the lender.

annualized percentage rate

The rate of interest a borrower is paying to a mortgage lender when points and lender's fees are considered as interest rather than mere expenses of the transaction.

appraised value

Opinion of a real estate expert "professional appraiser" of the fair market value of property, usually stated in a formal writing.

http://

To learn about appraisers, visit
http://www.asc.gov/

---

* The actual cash requirements of the buyer will be somewhat higher than $25,000 because of closing costs, which are explained later.

market dictate borrower-qualification requirements as a precondition to purchase of their loans. The process of evaluating a borrower's qualifications for a specified loan is called **loan underwriting.** All of these qualifying rules use ratios that compare the borrower's anticipated monthly housing expense and total monthly obligations to monthly gross income.

Mortgage borrowers must have good credit histories or their applications will be denied. Often, loan applicants are categorized by *alphabet lenders* as either A, B, C, or D, depending on their credit histories. B and C borrowers have histories reflecting significant financial problems (missed payments), but they are not "deadbeats" (persons with disastrous credit histories). When even regional recessions occur, tens of thousands of homeowners may slip from category A to categories B and C. Unfortunately, these rating changes occur to victims of corporate downsizings, plant closings, regional economic slumps, and similar catastrophes that do not truly reflect upon their character as borrowers. B and C borrowers can qualify for mortgage loans, but will face higher than usual loan-to-value (LTV) requirements, meaning that larger down payments are required (e.g., 25 percent for B and 35 percent for C applicants). To assist these borrowers, many lenders typically permit a larger percentage of their income to be absorbed by monthly payments (up to 45 and even 50 percent is common, whereas category A borrowers cannot commit more than 38 percent of their income to PITI). This permits credit-impaired B and C borrowers to qualify if they are willing to commit both a larger down payment and a substantial portion of their income to home ownership.

Qualifying criteria often change, but current requirements are readily available free of charge from offices of real estate brokerage firms, mortgage brokers, banks and savings and loans, and online mortgage information providers.

Assumption of Existing Loan

The obligation of an existing mortgage may be transferred from the debtor (homeowner who desires to sell) to another person (a prospective buyer) who desires to become obligated to its monthly payments. This transfer of obligation is called an **assumption of mortgage.**

Equity is the market value of a property minus the unpaid balance of loans against it. Frequently, sellers of a home have only a small equity in their property. In such a situation, the purchasers may not need to borrow directly; rather, they may desire to assume the loan of the sellers, especially if its interest rate is attractive.

LEGAL FOCUS—PROBLEM

Laura Shields wanted to sell her home for $200,000. She still owed $176,000 against it as represented by a promissory note payable to the bank. The note was secured by a deed of trust on the home. Mark Hendricks offered to buy the house by paying Shields $24,000 for her equity and by assuming her loan for the balance of the purchase price. Shields contacted her attorney, Colleen Strong, to find out what would happen if she accepted Hendricks's offer and if, at some future time, Hendricks failed to make his newly assumed monthly payment. What would attorney Strong advise her?

Shield's attorney would advise her that when Hendricks assumed the bank loan, he would become a debtor of the bank. The bank could either accept him as the sole debtor, and

loan underwriting

The process of evaluating the acceptability of a prospective borrower's loan application.

assumption of mortgage

An agreement by one person (usually a buyer) to *assume* (i.e., take upon himself or herself) all the obligations of an existing secured real property loan of another person (usually the seller).

equity

The net interest of a homeowner in the property, representing the excess of the value of the property over loans or other legal claims outstanding against it.

release Shields from the loan, or keep both as debtors. In either case, if the bank is not paid each month on time, the trustee (or mortgagee) can cause the house to be sold at public auction with the proceeds going to the bank in satisfaction of the debt. This may not bother Shields since she already would have received $24,000 for her equity; however, her credit rating could be affected adversely if the bank foreclosed in the future since her name would remain on the defaulted note. In addition, if the loan were federally insured, such as an FHA loan, and the sales price at foreclosure was less than the unpaid balance due on the loan, Shields could be made to pay the bank any deficiency (unpaid balance) on the loan remaining after a foreclosure sale. For this reason, most sellers whose mortgage is being assumed by a buyer request a release of liability from the lender at the time of the sale. A release will be given by the lender only if the assuming purchaser has a satisfactory credit record, or if the loan balance is small compared to the value of the security (the house). Generally speaking, it is easier for a prospective buyer to qualify for assumption of an existing loan than to qualify for a new loan.

Some states have **anti-deficiency laws** that apply to conventional purchase-money loans, which are any loan the proceeds of which are used by the borrower to purchase a home. As their name implies, anti-deficiency laws prohibit the collection of any deficiency by the creditor following foreclosure sale. A deficiency would arise if the proceeds of the foreclosure sale were less than the amount then owed on the defaulted loan, plus certain costs. These debtor laws date back to the Great Depression of the 1930s, when many people lost their homes and substantial equities through foreclosures but ended up still owing money to their lenders. If a home is fully paid for, and then a mortgage is given for a loan, this statutory protection generally is not available. No doubt legislators believe such borrowers are not vulnerable seekers of shelter, but sophisticated borrowers for profit.

For the same reason, **construction loans** for the purpose of building a house generally are not protected, nor are **refinance loans** that are taken out to replace an existing loan. Another type of unprotected loan is the currently popular home-equity loan, whereby a homeowner borrows for miscellaneous purposes, such as traveling, paying tuition, or buying expensive consumer goods. As noted earlier, interest within limits on home-equity loans is tax-deductible whereas interest on consumer debt is not, which helps explain their popularity. Note, though, that income tax laws change frequently; professional advice always should be obtained before making financial decisions based upon supposed tax consequences. As stated, these home-equity loans are subject to deficiency judgments if a foreclosure sale should fail to generate enough cash to pay them off in full.

Most mortgages cannot be assumed without the consent of the mortgagee (beneficiary) because they contain **due-on-sale clauses** that trigger payment of the entire unpaid balance upon any sale of the home. However, assumption is permitted by lenders if the buyer (who is assuming the existing mortgage) agrees to pay an assumption fee, and often an increased interest rate if the loan has a fixed rate. Financing the purchase of a home by assuming its existing mortgage is one alternative that sometimes is attractive, and sales agents often promote the possibility of a loan assumption as an additional selling point for their listings that have assumable mortgages. But at other times loan assumption is less appropriate than new financing.

Seller's Financing

Sometimes prospective buyers do not have sufficient funds for a substantial down payment, or are unable to qualify for a new loan under then-existing underwriting (borrower qualification) requirements. As an alternative to "hard" money loans from institutional lenders in which cash is borrowed for the purchase price, a "soft" money (paper) loan from

anti-deficiency laws

State laws protecting a homeowner from payment of any deficiency (or unpaid balance) if a mortgage foreclosure sale fails to produce sufficient money to satisfy the underlying debt in full.

construction loan

A short-term real estate loan, secured by mortgage, intended to finance building costs.

refinance loan

A loan, secured by mortgage, the proceeds of which are used primarily to pay off, or retire, an existing mortgage loan. Refinancing occurs when interest rates drop, encouraging homeowners to pay off existing high-interest-rate loans with new lower-interest-rate loans.

due-on-sale clause

A clause found in most promissory notes secured by home-purchase mortgages that accelerates the due date of the loan to the date the home is sold.

the seller may be appropriate. Soft money here refers to simply paying the purchase price by giving the seller a promissory note for the amount owed. The seller takes on the role of a creditor; receives a note secured by deed of trust; and conveys title to the buyer. This kind of transaction gave rise to the sagacious wives' tale "Buy with paper—sell for cash."

CARRY BACK MORTGAGE FINANCING   Sellers of homes that are free and clear of any loans may themselves finance, or "carry," their buyers, which is called **carry-back mortgage financing.** In this situation, the buyer usually makes a small down payment and signs a promissory note in favor of the seller. The seller, like a bank, will not be content with the mere promise of the buyer to pay the unpaid balance but will want the home as collateral. The seller will then require the buyer to execute a carry-back mortgage (or deed of trust).

If the buyer fails to make payments when due, the trustee (or mortgagee) will sell the property in a foreclosure auction and apply the cash proceeds to satisfying the defaulted debt. This would be a purchase-money mortgage (or deed of trust), and the seller could not obtain a deficiency judgment against the buyer-debtor if the proceeds of sale were inadequate to pay off the loan. The seller would simply absorb any such loss.

CREATIVE FINANCING   Sometimes a seller will finance a portion of the sales price (say, 30 percent), accept cash (say, 10 percent), and transfer the existing mortgage loan (say, 60 percent) to the purchaser who assumes the existing mortgage. This is an example of a combination carry-back mortgage and assumption transaction, often called **creative financing.** The carry-back mortgage accepted by the seller as part of creative financing is a **second mortgage** (entitled to any proceeds at foreclosure sale only if the institutional first mortgage is paid in full). Second mortgages can be risky for the lender, who, in this instance, is the seller. One reason why buyers may suggest creative financing is because they are unable to qualify for new financing. Sellers should consider whether they want to accept credit risks that well-managed financial institutions will not accept. When creative financing is agreed to and an existing mortgage is assumed, institutional lenders normally will charge an assumption fee and increase the existing interest rate in the assumed loan. Their risk is less than the seller's because of their lower LTV ratio and first priority to foreclosure proceeds. Generally, assumption fees and interest rate hikes are not attractive to most buyers; on the other hand, it is easier to qualify to assume an existing loan than it is to qualify for a new loan. Creative financing is most popular when it is offered by sellers as a sales inducement in a sluggish real estate market.

CONTRACT FOR DEED OR INSTALLMENT-LAND CONTRACT   As an alternative method of financing, the buyer and seller may enter into an **installment-land contract,** also called a **contract for deed.** Under this arrangement, the seller will not immediately convey title to the buyer, who simply moves in and begins making monthly payments. Rather, title is retained by the seller until the buyer has made monthly payments for many years. This method is used when a buyer cannot qualify for a loan and has no money for a down payment. In these circumstances, the buyer simply makes monthly payments to the seller for, say twenty years, at which time the seller conveys title to the buyer in exchange for payment of the balance of the purchase price.

From the buyer's standpoint, this generally is not a good way to buy a home, but when no other financing is available, it does solve the immediate problem. This type of transaction may be tempting to a budget-conscious buyer because closing costs can be eliminated, no legal assistance is necessary, the cost of title insurance (discussed later) may be avoided, and appraisal fees and lender's up-front fees (points) are avoided. Even the down payment may be small. However, some of these are false savings—the seller may inflate the price of the house as compensation for the other munificent terms offered to the buyer.

carry-back mortgage financing

A credit sale of real property where the seller takes a promissory note and security in the property (mortgage) from the buyer.

creative financing

Any financing for the purchase of a home in which the seller accepts a note secured by mortgage for all or part of the purchase price.

second mortgage

A mortgage on real estate already subject to an earlier mortgage; the holder of the second mortgage has rights subordinate to those of the holder of the first mortgage.

installment-land contract

A method of selling real property in which the seller retains title during the years that the buyer in possession is making monthly payments.

contract for deed

An installment sales contract whereby the buyer, although in possession of the premises, promises to make monthly payments for years before title is conveyed from the seller by deed.

The buyer under a contract for deed who fails to make a monthly payment theoretically may be evicted, as would a defaulting tenant, and would have no asset to show for the payments made to date. Because the buyer did not receive title, there is no apparent need for the seller to foreclose and regain title. Simple eviction theoretically is a potent remedy for the unpaid seller.

However, if payments have been made regularly for a long time under an installment-land contract, a court of equity, in the vast majority of states, will require the seller to recognize that the buyer has acquired some reasonable amount of equity in the property. This remedy, however, requires a lawsuit by the buyer, who could be out of possession of the residence pending the litigation. Following litigation, there would be a foreclosure sale; any balance received in excess of the unpaid balance on the contract would go to the defaulting buyer.[8] As a practical matter, buyers under land contracts who have been in possession for only a short period probably will not profit from a lawsuit to establish an equity in the property, because most payments during early years go primarily to interest and do not reduce the principal amount of the loan very much.

LEGAL FOCUS—PROBLEM

Rossi Wareham owned a cabin that was situated on five acres in the mountains. His listing agent, Larry Bingham, advised him to sell under a land contract for a small down payment of $1,000, thereby eliminating appraisal fees, title insurance premium, points, and most other closing costs so the property would attract a wider number of possible buyers. A buyer made an offer to pay $150,000 (which was a good price) with $3,000 down payment, interest at 8 percent, and principal and interest payable at $1,100 per month for ten years, at which time the unpaid balance would be paid in full. Following Bingham's advice, Wareham accepted the offer while unaware that the buyer, Hammer Studkin, was a leader of the Hell's Angels. Studkin and his buddies moved in and never made a monthly payment. Seven months later, and the day before Wareham's lawsuit for eviction was due to be heard in court, Studkin leased the premises to Irwin Goodheart for one year, for $10,000 rent, all paid in advance. Goodheart moved in; Hammer and his buddies moved out; and the judge ruled that eviction was not a proper remedy because Studkin was an "owner" and not a mere "tenant." Wareham consulted his new attorney, Colleen Strong. What advice would Strong give Wareham?

This hypothetical situation illustrates many of the problems that can be encountered when using an installment-land contract. Studkin was buying the property and had the right to lease it to a third person, such as Goodheart. His transaction netted him seven months of occupancy and a net cash profit of $7,000 ($10,000 prepaid rent less $3,000 down payment). The original down payment was much too small, as Wareham discovered; his out-of-pocket losses were not nearly covered. It is doubtful that Wareham can evict Goodheart if he leased the premises in good faith. Attorney Strong probably would advise a lawsuit be filed against the real estate agent, Bingham, for negligence in recommending acceptance of the deal. However, it is doubtful that Strong would take the case on a contingency. She also would be unlikely to sue Studkin, who, if he could be found and served with the lawsuit papers, would probably be judgment-proof. Strong might recommend a **quiet title action** (declaration as to who owns real property) to achieve clear title in Wareham's name, and possibly to force a negotiated settlement with Goodheart. But she would, no doubt, ask for a substantial retainer fee before commencing such a lawsuit.

quiet title action

Action "against the world" initiated by a person who claims ownership of a particular parcel of real property.

What should Wareham have done? If he used the land contract method, he should have received a larger down payment, prohibited leasing of the premises, and posted the premises with a form declaring the "owner's nonresponsibility" for any third-party claims, as for repairs or for possession by a subtenant. Better yet, he should have sold the premises in a more orthodox fashion. For example, if the premises had been leased with an option to buy, as discussed next, Wareham could have simply evicted any occupant in the ordinary manner of all evictions.

Generally speaking, both parties to a land contract should proceed very carefully and receive professional advice.

Lease with Option to Buy

A buyer who has inadequate funds for a down payment and who may have difficulty qualifying for a new loan may sometimes be able to purchase a home by leasing it with an option to buy. This gives the renter an absolute right to purchase the property at a future date at a fixed price upon established terms. The renter who would like to buy now hopes to be better able financially to complete the purchase a few years in the future. A typical lease would be for five years. A portion of each month's lease payment would be "credited" to and earmarked as down payment on the purchase price. This gradual buildup of equity helps reduce or even eliminates the need for a down payment when the option is exercised. Any appreciation in the value of the residence above the agreed-upon option price would further benefit the buyer. Meanwhile, lease payments are made, equity is growing, and opportunity exists for the buyer to enjoy his or her future home while saving for a down payment. The seller, on the other hand, receives the advantage of delaying income taxes by delaying the sale to some future year, and receives tax deductions permitted for rental property (depreciation, interest, taxes, maintenance if applicable, insurance, supplies, and so forth) while waiting. Because a future sale already is in the works, a real estate commission may be avoided. What is more, tenants with an option to buy probably will be excellent residents, making improvements and caring for the property as if it were their own.

Leases with options to buy can be a panacea for buyers and sellers alike. Lease-option forms are readily available from stationery stores and sellers of legal forms. But like most transactions involving a considerable sum of money, precautions should be taken by both parties. For example, if the seller should go into bankruptcy or foreclosure during the term of the lease, and consequently be unable to deliver title in the future, the tenant-buyer could lose his or her rent credit. Professional legal assistance is advisable before entering a lease-option purchase contract.

Ⓦ HAT IS ESCROW?

To complete the purchase of a house, many things need to be done at the same time. At the moment title passes, the buyer wants to be certain that title insurance and fire insurance (discussed later) are in effect; the seller wants to receive the amount of the sales price; the lender wants the promissory note and mortgage or deed of trust; the real estate broker wants the earned commission, and so forth. Because it would be impractical for all these persons to meet and hand some documents out with the left hand while simultaneously taking other documents in with the right, the practice of hiring a third-party intermediary (called the **escrow agent,** or simply **escrow**) developed.

http://

For general information about real estate issues, visit the 'Lectric Library at **http://www.lectlaw.com/ tlat.htm**

escrow agent

A person paid to perform all the administrative tasks necessary to close a real estate escrow.

escrow

An arrangement common in real estate transactions whereby the buyer and seller (and/or the borrower and lender) designate a neutral third party as an agent to carry out instructions for gathering and distributing documents and funds as necessary.

Title companies, escrow departments of banks, escrow companies, and sometimes real estate brokers and attorneys may act as escrow agents. The escrow agent collects the required monies and documents from all the interested persons as necessary, and then, at the close of escrow, disburses and distributes them to the appropriate persons. Close of escrow is execution of the contract; title is conveyed to the buyer and cash is delivered to the seller, and so forth.

Each party interested in a real estate transaction signs escrow instructions that are prepared from standard forms by escrow agents, or by attorneys for the parties. The escrow instructions command the escrow agent as to what each person will put into escrow and what is expected out of it upon its close. For example, in simplified form, the seller may instruct the escrow officer as follows: "I hand you a duly executed grant deed that you are authorized and instructed to record and deliver to the buyer upon the receipt on my behalf of $175,000, the sales price." The escrow agent who complies with all of the instructions will not be liable for any losses suffered by any of the parties.

LEGAL FOCUS—CASE

On or about December 4, 1998, Darryl S. Anderson agreed to sell and Kathy Falcon and Adam Ferrecchia agreed to buy real estate for $99,000. The sale agreement called for a closing date of January 22, 1999, with "time being of the essence." The agreement also contained a mortgage contingency clause wherein the buyers agreed to make diligent efforts to obtain FHA financing for up to $96,000. It was also agreed that if the buyers failed after diligent efforts to obtain financing they were entitled to a return of the $5,000 deposit. They were however, required to notify the seller in writing by January 4, 1999, of failure to get financing. Furthermore under the contract if the buyers failed to comply with the contract they would forfeit the $5,000 deposit as liquidated damages. The buyers did not get financing and also failed to notify the seller by the agreed date. Both the seller and buyer are demanding the $5,000 from the escrow agent. What is the escrow agent to do?

Kotseas v. Anderson, 13 Mass. L. Rptr. 232, 2001 WL 881471 (Mass.Super., 2001).

The escrow instructions must dovetail or the escrow cannot close. For example, if a mistake is made such that the instructions direct the escrow agent to accept $175,000 for the seller but for the buyer to pay only $172,000, there is a conflict and the escrow cannot close. Sometimes, errors are made and instructions of the buyer and seller conflict as to how some of the money should be disbursed by the escrow officer. Or situations arise such as the above where the parties make conflicting demands on the escrow agent. Facing conflicting demands or instructions that do not dovetail, the escrow officer may file a court action called **interpleader,** deposit the contested funds with the clerk of the court, and withdraw completely, leaving the buyer and seller with the problem of settling their dispute in court. The rationale is that the escrow officer is a mere stakeholder who is obligated to follow instructions as received and when instructions conflict, the stakeholder should be allowed to withdraw. In the above Massachusetts case the escrow agent filed an interpleader action and the court awarded the remainder of deposit after costs of escrow to the seller.

The escrow officer is a disinterested stakeholder owing allegiance to neither seller nor buyer. Therefore you should not rely upon escrow agents for advice about the merits or

interpleader

A legal proceeding to resolve conflicting claims (e.g., to funds in an escrow account).

consequences of any real estate transaction. In fact, escrow agents are reluctant to say anything to anybody that might be construed as advice. This "mere stakeholder" concept is so clearly defined in the law that even if an escrow officer knows that the buyer is about to be defrauded in a transaction pending in escrow, nothing can be said and no warning can be given. The theory underlying such law is that if escrow officers were permitted to offer advice or suggestions, it would lead to claims of negligent advice (malpractice), bias, and deal-wrecking by disappointed consumers. As a practical matter, sellers and buyers do sign many important papers (standard forms) in the presence of the escrow agent, who generally explains their meanings. These papers include written escrow instructions, deeds, and even promissory notes and mortgages provided by the buyer's lender. Do buyers and sellers rely upon escrow agents? Most do.

In some states, such as New York, attorneys commonly perform all services necessary to close escrow, that is, they serve as escrow officers. More commonly, banks, professional escrow companies, or title companies provide escrow services. Escrows charge fees for their services—it is up to the parties to negotiate how they will be allocated between buyer and seller. Usually the parties agree to allocate escrow costs "in accordance with the customs and practices" of the county.

CLOSING COSTS

Buyers and sellers negotiate how to share a variety of costs that are necessary to close escrow when homes are sold. This array of expenses commonly is called **closing costs.**

closing costs

Charges for various services that arise in connection with the purchase and sale of a home.

LEGAL FOCUS—PROBLEM

Michelle Chen was buying Henry Foster's home for $225,000. She had arranged financing of $200,000 from a savings and loan association and anticipated putting down $25,000 of her savings to make the purchase price. Will she be required to pay more than $25,000 into escrow?

Yes. The seller will likely have prepaid real property taxes and fire insurance premiums, some amount of which will have to be reimbursed by the buyer. Thus, if seller has prepaid say $1,000 for the period that extends six months after the close of escrow, the buyer must reimburse that sum. The buyer is responsible for property taxes following the sale.

The same sort of allocation results with prepaid casualty (fire) insurance. Furthermore, the buyer will probably pay the cost of a boundary survey if needed, termite inspection, loan fees (points), and perhaps title, notary, and recording fees. All of these costs and more make up what are commonly called closing costs. Some participants call them garbage fees.

It is customarily the responsibility of the seller to pay any transfer taxes (taxes imposed upon the transfer of ownership of real property, based upon its sales price) and to pay for any corrective repairs determined to be necessary because of damage by termites or dry rot (wood damage from water penetration). Almost all details of the purchase of a home are appropriate matters for inclusion in the contract between seller and buyer, and are freely negotiable. Real estate sales agents should be capable of estimating closing costs for their clients.

THE LEGAL SIGNIFICANCE OF CLOSE OF ESCROW

The term *close of escrow* already has been defined as the final distribution of cash and documents to the seller and buyer. At the close of escrow, the deed to the buyer and mortgage to the lender are recorded in the official records of the county. **Recordation** is a process by which a county official date and time stamps deeds and mortgages, then files copies in the official records. These records are open to the public and are the records relied upon by attorneys or title companies when a title search is made. The original documents are returned to the parties.

Prior to close of escrow, the buyer has promised to buy, the seller has promised to sell, the lender has promised to lend, the broker has earned a commission, and so forth. All of these contractual promises are executory, that is, still to be performed. Upon the close of escrow, the buyer has received title to and possession of the home and is its owner; the seller has sold, received the net purchase price, and no longer owns any interest in the property; the lender has made the loan, which the buyer has promised to repay; the broker has received the agreed-upon commission. Most of the promises have been executed or performed. Sometimes, in complicated transactions, the parties will be present with their attorneys at a final meeting called the closing. Many of the documents will be reviewed for the last time and then signed. Although the transaction is completed at close of escrow, the buyer, as borrower, must of course continue to make future payments on the loan as required by the note.

Although it is possible to agree that the seller will retain possession for a period subsequent to close of escrow, or that the buyer will move into the home before close of escrow, these terms are invitations to trouble. The best practice is to have a final walk-through just prior to close of escrow, and to have possession change immediately thereafter. The purpose of a walk-through is to ensure that the condition of the property is the same as it was when the agreement to purchase was made.

In brief, the sale is a *fait accompli* (French: "fact or deed accomplished," presumably irrevocably) when escrow closes. However, some rights and responsibilities linger beyond close of escrow. For example, buyers and sellers continue to have the right to sue each other for fraud or deceit up until the statute of limitations extinguishes their claims. But generally speaking, most buyers and sellers consider the transaction completed when escrow closes.

recordation

The act or process of recording title to real property in a public registry.

abstract of title

A chronological history of recorded documents that affect the title to a parcel of real property.

standard title insurance

Customary title insurance coverage that does not include the special coverage included within the more expensive American Land Title Association policy, which includes physical inspection of the premises as well as a review of the official records in a title search.

Ⓦ HAT IS TITLE INSURANCE?

In some states, such as New York, attorneys perform title searches and render legal opinions regarding the quality of title to property. These opinions are called **abstracts of title.** In most states, however, title insurance companies guarantee property purchasers that they have accurately searched the public records. **Standard title insurance** is a policy of insurance whereby the owner of a home may ensure that there are no surprises lurking in the official records that pertain to his or her newly acquired property. The insurance covers a narrow range of losses, up to a specified face amount of the policy. Title insurance is unlike any other variety of insurance, such as life insurance, where the event of loss is unpredictable. Title insurance does not insure against unpredictable losses. Rather, it insures against losses that may occur from the failure to reveal to the owner any recorded documents—which should have been found absent negligence by the title insurance company.

At the time the title insurance policy is issued, the owner is given a list of recorded documents pertaining to the property, which might include earlier deeds, mortgages, and liens. As briefly noted earlier, recorded documents have been physically date-time stamped and copies have been filed in the public records, indexed alphabetically by the surnames of the parties to the document. You can visit the recorder of your county and examine any recorded document. The process of recording permanently establishes the sequence in which the documents pertaining to a particular parcel of real property were recorded (date-time stamped). In general, claims that are first in time are first in right, so such formal recording in the official records obviously is important.

The accuracy of the list of recorded documents is guaranteed by the policy of title insurance. Losses arising from something in the public records that was somehow not found by the title insurance company (and therefore not placed on the list) are made good by the title insurance company. Losses therefore are unlikely. Visions of a senior attorney wearing a green visor while hunched over a desk under a dim light, diligently searching through piles of documents hunting for some defect in the title to real property, are dated to the beginning of the twentieth century. Technology, especially microfiche and the computer, have revolutionized the process of title searching. Title companies have been indexing all recorded documents in huge databases, making their existence accessible in every branch office.

In addition to the accuracy of a list of recorded documents, standard coverage title insurance covers a few losses that may arise from matters not readily ascertainable from the official records, such as forgery of a deed in the chain of title, lack of capacity of parties who are grantors (perhaps through mental incompetency), or lack of delivery of a deed to a former owner. Losses from forgery are unlikely because documents must be **notarized** (signed in the presence of an official who is called a notary public) before being recorded. Losses from lack of capacity of previous owners also are unlikely because court judgments declaring a person incompetent (lacking in capacity) are available in official records. Nor is lack of delivery of deed a likely defect since the law presumes delivery whenever a document, such as a deed, is recorded.

notarized

Signed in the presence of a person licensed by the state to perform identification services as a notary public.

LEGAL FOCUS—PROBLEM

Percy Fairchild bought a one-acre homesite in the country, on which he planned to build a home and enjoy a "gentleman's farm" with an extensive garden and a variety of animals. In connection with the purchase he acquired a standard policy of title insurance. Thereafter, he began leveling the land for a foundation for his home and outbuildings. He promptly was served with a lawsuit in which a neighbor to the rear, Georgette Simpson, was the plaintiff. Simpson alleged that she owned an easement (right to use) across the middle of Fairchild's lot because she had used it for fifteen years for access to the county road. She requested the court to enjoin the construction to protect her easement. Fairchild asked his lawyer to cross-complain against the title insurance company for the apparent defect in his title. Will he win?

Fairchild will probably lose his case with Simpson and will certainly lose his cross-complaint against the title company. Among defects in title that are *not* covered by standard title insurance are unrecorded **easements,** i.e., legal rights to use the land of another that are not recorded in the official records. Some easements are prepared by deeds and are recorded in

easement

The right to use the real property of another for a limited purpose (e.g., access to a beach or public road).

prescriptive easement

An easement, usually of access, over the land of another person, created by a continuous, open (visible) use without the consent of the landowner for a long period of time, usually five years or more in most states.

extended coverage

Coverage for title defects as described within the American Land Title Insurance form of insurance contract.

American Land Title Association insurance policy

A standardized form of extended title insurance coverage that is more comprehensive than the customary policy.

adverse possessor

The creation of ownership of real property through its possession for a prescribed number of years without the consent of its owner.

the official records. But many easements do not appear in the public records. They are created by adjacent landowners who repeatedly use neighboring land for access over many years. These **prescriptive easements** are not evidenced by any documents, and therefore do not appear in the public records. In Simpson's case, the court would not bar Fairchild from any use of his land but could order him to make suitable some portion of his land for continued periodic access by Simpson. It is important to note that if a defect is disclosed by the title insurer in its policy, any losses from that defect are not covered by insurance. That is, the risk of loss is that the insurer (title company) will negligently overlook a recorded document, and thus fail to inform the insured (home owner) of its existence.

Other exclusions from coverage in standard title insurance policies are boundary discrepancies and errors about how many acres or square feet are contained within the parcel.

Many lenders require **extended coverage** insurance (also called an **American Land Title Association insurance policy**) against loss from any defect, including such unrecorded matters as the presence of tenants or adverse possessors who may assert a future claim of ownership in the property. An **adverse possessor** is anyone who physically occupies and pays taxes on someone else's property for a number of years, such as five, under some color or claim of ownership. Such interlopers can be awarded ownership rights by judicial proceeding even though they never paid a cent for the property. Extended insurance (ALTA) costs more than standard coverage because the title insurance company must make an on-site physical inspection in addition to the customary search of the official records. Presumably such an on-site inspection would reveal to the title insurer that someone is adversely possessing the property or encroaching its boundaries, causing that fact to be noted as an exception to coverage and thereby placing the risk of loss upon the buyer. As a practical matter in the buying and selling of homes, adverse possession would be extraordinarily unlikely and on-site inspections are not made.

Unfortunately for home buyers, the premium charged for title insurance is a function of the sales price of the insured property, not a function of the insurer's risk. That is, the premium is calculated as a scaled percentage of the purchase price of the home each time it sells, whether or not there is any increased risk of loss to the title insurance company. Therefore, the buyer of a new subdivision home faces a purchase price that already includes the accumulated costs of premiums for title insurance that were paid by the developer and again by the builder. The buyer must pay again for title insurance that already has been twice paid for, all on the same lot and all, perhaps, in the same year.[9] Should the buyer resell the home immediately, the next buyer would face another title insurance premium based on the new purchase price. This layering of premiums without commensurate risks of loss has prompted title insurers to offer discounts on homes that are repeatedly sold within a short time.

Title insurance premiums are a major part of closing costs in the sale of every home. Buyers and sellers are free to negotiate as to who will pay the title insurance premium, and are well advised to do so. Any thoughts of avoiding the purchase of title insurance should be set aside because mortgage lenders require it as a condition to making their loans.

Role of Attorney in Home Transactions

On the one hand it would be prudent to simply advise all prospective sellers and buyers of homes to consult with an attorney to draft or at least to review all documents involved. However, it is unrealistic to engage the services of an attorney for each step in the process, which occur at different times and places. As a general proposition, most buyers and sellers of homes do not consult attorneys; rather, they rely upon the advice and recommendations of their real estate sales agents who, in turn, rely upon standard forms and customs and practices they have followed for years. And yes, many sellers and buyers end up unhappy or even outraged by how they feel mistreated following a home purchase. The more costly the transaction, the more likely the services of attorneys should be considered.

LEGAL FOCUS—PROBLEM

Dave and Kathy McDaniel were in the market for a home priced around $285,000. While deciding whether to buy a pre-owned or newly built home, they contacted their attorney, Colleen Strong, for advice about available financing. What would attorney Strong's advice likely be?

Their attorney would probably advise the McDaniels that financing is primarily an economic, not a legal, question. The most knowledgeable persons concerning the availability of home loans and their terms are found in real estate sales and loan brokerage firms. Additional useful information is obtainable from local banks, savings and loan institutions, and the Federal Housing Administration (FHA). Attorney Strong might properly suggest, however, that she review all significant documents before they are signed. Sales agents loathe the involvement of attorneys, who never seem to be available at critical times when the parties are ready to sign a document and who raise many questions, some of which may create buyers' or sellers' remorse. Agents often refer to attorneys as "deal killers." Nonetheless, Strong might review any purchase agreement.

The advice of attorneys always is essential in complex arrangements in which one party is in a position to take advantage of the other. The hiring of a building contractor to build a custom home is one important example that was emphasized earlier.

Because most questions that arise in buying homes are simple and repetitive, real estate agents develop considerable expertise and are usually qualified to assist buyers in the preparation of purchase agreements without the need for legal assistance. However, agents are primarily in the business of selling and are not qualified or authorized to render legal opinions to prospective buyers or sellers. A prudent buyer who asks questions and receives fuzzy, nonresponsive, or incomplete answers would be well advised to obtain legal assistance before signing any contracts. Fees for contract review are likely to be modest because attorneys can perform such routine services in a short time—if that is their specialization.

One decision that more often than not should be carefully made, perhaps requiring the services of an attorney, concerns choice in legal form of title, which we consider next.

How May Title to Your Home Be Held?

A home without a cat—and a wellfed, wellpetted and properly revered cat—may be a home, perhaps, but how can it prove title?

Mark Twain [Samuel Langhorne Clemens] (1835–1910), in *Pudd'nhead Wilson and Those Extraordinary Twins*

Title may be held (1) by one person that is termed in **severalty,** (2) by two or more persons (co-owners) as **tenants in common,** (3) by two or more persons (co-owners) as **joint tenants**

severalty

Separate or individual ownership of property by one person or ownership as separate property by a married person.

tenants in common

A form of co-ownership of property by two or more persons. Upon the death of any co-owner, his or her percentage interest passes by intestate succession or by last will.

joint tenants

A method of co-ownership of property by two or more persons. Upon the death of any co-owner, his or her percentage interest goes to the surviving joint tenant(s) regardless of the decedent's last will. This right of survivorship is the basic incident of joint-tenancy ownership.

tenancy by the entirety

A form of co-ownership of property between husband and wife in some states. As with joint-tenancy ownership, the spouses have a right of survivorship.

with right of survivorship, or (4) by two or more persons (co-owners) as partnership property. About half the states permit a variation of joint tenancy between husband and wife called **tenancy by the entirety.** Some states (Arizona, California, Idaho, Louisiana, Nevada, New Mexico, Texas, and Washington) have community property and a few have marital property, both a variation of co-ownership by married couples.

When two or more persons decide to purchase a residence, a decision must be made as to the legal form of joint ownership to be used.

LEGAL FOCUS—PROBLEM

Robert and Clarissa Ramirez, a married couple, were buying their first home. Just before close of escrow, they were advised by their real estate agent to take title in joint tenancy.* Should they do so? What alternatives should they consider?

Owning a home in joint tenancy is a common form of ownership by married couples. Upon the death of one joint tenant, transfer of ownership to the survivor is expedient because the property need not go through probate (discussed in Chapter 14). Joint tenancy property is not affected by a will, and may be vulnerable to death tax problems in large estates.

In some states, the Ramirezes would probably take title as tenants by the entirety, with essentially the same effect as if they were joint tenants. In any of the states where available, they might consider taking title as community property, so that each spouse's one-half share could be disposed of by will, if so desired. Community property ownership also offers income tax advantages to the surviving spouse when his or her highly appreciated house is sold following the other's death. One community property state, Washington, requires that married couples own their home as community property.

If two or more unrelated persons decide to pool their resources in order to improve their quality of life by purchasing a home, they would, no doubt, prefer to retain the right to individually will their undivided interests to their respective relatives or loved ones. They would accordingly select the tenancy-in-common form of home ownership.

LEGAL FOCUS—PROBLEM

Jinna Roberts and Kathy Jennings, unrelated, owned Sky High Ranch as joint tenants. Upon learning that their respective interests would go to the survivor of them regardless of their respective wills, they decided to change their ownership form. May they do so?

Yes. Roberts and Jennings can simply convey the property to themselves as tenants in common. Then both may will their respective equal shares to anyone they choose. For example, if Roberts should die without leaving a will, her undivided one-half interest would go to her closest surviving heirs. Such surviving heirs would, under law, become tenants in common with Jennings.

---

* This advice is dangerously close to constituting the unauthorized practice of law. A more prudent agent would provide his or her clients with published materials generally describing the alternatives available and add that they should obtain any further advice from an attorney. Even the publishers of "how-to" legal books, such as Nolo Press, have been challenged by lawyers for engaging in the practice of law. As a practical matter, agents often respond, "I cannot give you legal advice, but I can say that most of my clients choose joint tenancy."

A **deed** is the document that transfers or conveys title (ownership) of real property from one person to another. A valid deed must contain the following:

- The names of the seller (grantor) and the buyer (grantee)
- Words evidencing an intent to transfer title (e.g., I hereby "grant," or "convey" to)
- A legally sufficient description of the real property deeded
- The grantor's (and usually the spouse's) signature(s)

Finally, to be valid, a deed must be delivered from the grantor to the grantee. Most deeds are recorded in the official records of the county in which the property is located, and must be recorded if title insurance is to be purchased. But unrecorded deeds are legally valid.

Typically, a **quitclaim deed** is used to change the manner in which title is held. It is a deed by which a person merely gives up any claim he or she may have to the named property. The transferor makes no promises or warranties to the transferee about the condition of the property or quality of title conveyed. A quitclaim deed seems strange to most people. After all, what value is a deed where the person transferring title to you does not promise ownership? Actually, quitclaim deeds are used often in situations where ownership rights are uncertain, and serve to clarify title in the official records. The quitclaim deed is appropriate when land is transferred by gift or to clear some possible "**cloud on title**"—some obstacle to clear title, such as an old abandoned leasehold that might otherwise be the basis for a later lawsuit.

In contrast to a quitclaim deed, a **warranty deed** is used for transfers of real property by sale. By its use, the grantor impliedly makes certain covenants or promises:

- The grantor has full ownership of the exact interest being conveyed.
- The property is free of liens or claims of third persons except as disclosed in the deed.
- The title will not be challenged by third persons.
- The grantor will execute any further documents that may be required to perfect the grantee's title.

In states where title insurance policies provide considerable assurance that there will be no surprises found in the official records, the simple **grant deed** is commonly used. By use of the word "grant," the grantor (seller) impliedly warrants that (1) he or she has not previously conveyed the property to someone else and (2) the estate (ownership) conveyed is free from prior encumbrances by the grantor, unless disclosed.

Married persons can change the form of ownership of property held as community property to tenancy-in-common or joint tenancy, or vice-versa, by deed. Under some circumstances, courts have held that even though held in joint tenancy, the husband and wife actually intended to and did hold the property as community property. The result of such a ruling is a tax advantage, in that surviving owners of community property pay considerably less income tax on any future sale than do surviving joint tenants.

S ELLING YOUR HOME YOURSELF

Some homeowners desire to sell their home without using an agent in order to avoid paying the negotiable sales commission, which often is 6 percent of the sales price. If a home sells for $300,000 and there is a mortgage outstanding with unpaid balance of $280,000, the owner's equity is $20,000. A 6 percent commission equals $18,000 (.06 x $300,000), which equals 90 percent of the owner's equity ($18,000/$20,000). For this reason, some homeowners do not hire sales agents.

A property whose seller does not utilize agents is referred to as a *FSBO* ("for sale by owner") pronounced somewhat disrespectfully as "fizzbo."

---

deed

Any document used to transfer any ownership interest in real property. Many types of deeds are used in a variety of property transfers.

quitclaim deed

A deed to real property in which the transferor conveys whatever ownership interest he or she may possess, which may be none.

cloud on title

Any dormant or actively pursued claim to the possession of or title to real property that is unresolved or contested.

http://

See a copy of a quitclaim deed at **http://www.ilrg.com/forms/quitdeed.html**

warranty deed

A type of deed with several warranties implied by law to protect the buyer.

grant deed

A document that conveys the ownership of real property, and impliedly warrants that the grantor has not previously conveyed the property to another and that the property is free from undisclosed encumbrances.

Selling without an agent is not as easy as it might seem at first blush, because of the lack of cooperation of real estate agents. They will take their prospective buyers to listed homes, which if purchased will produce a commission, and will avoid non-commission-paying FSBOs. But selling without an agent is realistic under certain circumstances.

FSBO sellers cannot place their houses in the privately owned multiple listing service. But FSBO sellers can create a beautiful and informative brochure describing all of the amenities of the house and of the neighborhood. Or a Web site can be created complete with photographs and information about schools, shopping, transportation, etc. Most sellers can arrange for effective advertising simply by consulting with specialists at the local newspaper. If the property is on a street with significant traffic flows, even if only at certain hours, a suitable "for sale" sign might be posted.

Once a buyer is obtained, all the paperwork necessary (escrow instructions) can be accomplished by the title company or escrow company that is selected to close the escrow. Once the escrow instructions are prepared and signed, they constitute a legally binding contract.

Pending preparation of the escrow instructions and before they are signed, the parties should hire an attorney to prepare a purchase agreement, if they want one. Generally it is in the seller's interest not to have such a contract, because the seller without a contract can continue to receive offers that might be higher or more favorable. In short, the seller's property is not technically "off the market" until a contract is signed. Signed purchase agreements protect buyers and agents more than sellers.*

Problems face FSBOs in preparing their property for sale; in determining the highest price they might receive; in dealing face-to-face with buyers who expect to benefit from dickering about the price; in separating qualified buyers from "lookers"; and in retaining confidence in their ability to handle the sale in the face of many licensed agents who may contact them attempting to obtain a listing. But the problems can be solved and the benefits to the seller can be substantial, especially in a seller's market (i.e., where the demand for homes exceeds the available supply, and properties offered for sale are promptly sold).

A FSBO can pass along some of the commission savings to his or her buyer (e.g., through price reduction or inclusion of items of personal property), thereby making the deal especially attractive.

open listing

Employment contract in which the owner of real property agrees to pay a commission only to the agent who produces a ready, willing, and able buyer.

A more effective possibility for a seller who hopes to save on the costs of selling is to make an **open listing** under which one-half of a normal commission is offered to be paid to any agent who brings a buyer to whom the property is sold. An open listing can be created by making the statement on the sales brochure, on a Web page, on the sign in the front yard, or by any other form of communication. Because agents who bring buyers typically produce only one-half of the total commission (the other one-half, or 3 percent, going to the listing office), they will respond to open listings for, typically, 3 percent. Thus, in the preceding example, the seller would pay a commission of $9,000 instead of $18,000.

HOW IS A HOME TAXED?

A home may be located within the boundaries of both a county and a city as well as within various municipal taxing districts, all of which may impose taxes on property to finance

* The effect of a real estate purchase agreement is that the seller's property is "off the market" and subsequent, more lucrative offers must be rejected. The deal may linger on for longer than anticipated, all the while "handcuffing" the seller. Meanwhile, all the buyer has at risk is an earnest money deposit, which sometimes is represented by an uncashed check. Even then the deposit is refundable under most circumstances. Thus, the seller has great risk from such a contract while the buyer has little or none.

schools, colleges, flood control districts, mosquito abatement districts, air pollution control districts, parks, water systems, sewers, and so on. Generally these needs are expressed in a combined budget, which reflects the money local government must obtain from its residents in order to function for another fiscal year.

Taxation of real property, including homes, is the principal method by which local governments obtain needed funds. Theoretically, all properties are taxed in proportion to their current values, whether they are residential, commercial, industrial, or whatever. The county assessor appraises each property at its **market value** (called *full cash value*) and declares a uniform fraction of that amount to be its **assessed value.** Some states assess at full cash value. These values are approximations of fair market values because assessors cannot possibly keep all properties within a jurisdiction currently appraised on a year-to-year basis.

Whether a full cash value or fractional assessment (some arbitrary portion, or fraction, of full cash value) is used has no effect on the amount of property tax paid by the homeowner. These "assessed" values are listed on the assessment roll.

The applicable combined budget is then divided by the total assessed value of all taxable property in the county to arrive at the property tax rate—the percentage that must be applied to the assessed value of each parcel of taxable property in the county to determine how much its share of the entire budget should be.

In this way, property owners are taxed in proportion to the value of the property they own. A property worth 30 percent more than another property will be liable for 30 percent more in taxes, if both are within the same municipal taxing districts. Also, a home worth $275,000 will be liable for exactly the same amount of tax as a service station worth $275,000, if both are within the same districts.*

Owners who believe their taxes are unfairly high in comparison with similar properties may informally request a reappraisal by the tax assessor, or formally appeal to the specified appeals body (such as the local Board of Equalization). If unsuccessful here, they can appeal to a court, but courts generally do not overrule administrative agencies, especially on matters of taxation.

If government expenditures (initially proposed in budgets) increase, property taxes increase. If government expenditures are constant, total tax revenues are constant, regardless of whether assessed values increase or decrease. If government expenditures decrease, property taxes decrease, regardless of whether assessed values increase or decrease.

$$\frac{\text{Total expenditures, i.e., the budget}}{\substack{\text{Assessed value, all}\\ \text{taxable property combined}}} = \frac{\text{Tax}}{\text{rate}} \times \frac{\text{Your assessed}}{\text{value}} = \frac{\text{Your}}{\text{tax}^{\dagger}}$$

Of course, any individual's property may be reappraised and if its assessed value goes up, its specific tax bill will rise. Conversely, a person whose property goes down in assessed value in relationship to other properties will pay a lower tax. Increases or decreases in assessed values or tax rates have nothing to do with increased total taxes, which can occur only when government expenditures increase. In other words, if all assessed values rise, but budgeted expenses remain constant, total taxes collected will remain constant. Rising and falling property taxes are a function of rising and falling combined county budgets.

market value

The price property would bring if offered for sale in a fair market (not at auction or in a forced sale) by a willing and fully informed (but not compelled) seller, after ample time to find a willing and fully informed (but not compelled) buyer.

assessed value

The value assigned to real property by a local official called an *assessor* for the purpose of levying a property tax.

---

* Some states, following California's lead, have adopted property tax limitations that apply to older but not recently sold properties. Therefore, a home that recently sold for $250,000 may be chargeable with more property tax than a home or service station also worth $250,000 but which has been owned a number of years. In effect, new homeowners subsidize owners who have owned their homes for some years. This result of higher taxes for newer homes of comparable values is another example of how the traditional economic benefits of home ownership are eroding in the early twenty-first century.

† Notice that so long as all property is assessed upon the same basis, whether that basis is full cash value, 25 percent of full cash value, or 10 percent of full cash value, the particular basis used in your community will not affect the amount of tax paid by any one homeowner.

Typically, all assessed values in a county are increased annually by some percentage to reflect estimated general inflationary pressures. A constant tax rate thus will produce an increase in the budget, producing, in turn, higher taxes for everyone's property.

Not all real estate is subject to property taxes. Property owned by any type of governmental organization is exempt from taxation. Thus, when private property is acquired by local government, as for a public park or school, property tax collections are reduced. If total expenditures are to be maintained, or increased, the remaining private property must contribute more to taxes assessed and collected. Federal lands and the lands under highways and streets are all exempt from taxation. Rising property values automatically provide increases in funds for local governments when tax rates are constant; thus, inflation fuels local budgets. If the preceding statement is unclear to you, reconsider the preceding formula for how your property taxes are computed.

Property taxes typically are paid twice a year, in December and April, although they accrue daily. Some lenders require their borrowers to pay taxes monthly, along with their payments of principal and interest. These lenders then forward the collected property taxes to the local tax collector twice a year. The funds collected monthly are held in an **impound account** by the lender until disbursed to the tax collector. A small amount of interest is paid to the borrower by some lenders for these prepayments of taxes. The reason lenders prefer impounds is that it gives them an assurance that the homeowner has set aside enough money to pay the taxes when due. When negotiating for a home mortgage, borrowers can ask that they pay all property taxes and insurance bills directly, avoiding the impounding process. This gives the homeowner use of the cash until the periodic tax and insurance bills arrive.

WHAT IS FIRE INSURANCE?

A private home is the costliest single asset the typical adult is likely ever to acquire. The greatest hazard both buyer and lender face is the possibility that a fire may break out and damage or completely destroy the building and contents. To protect their respective interests, both lenders and buyers generally agree that the latter shall purchase appropriate casualty (fire) insurance. Casualty insurance on a home is generally provided in what is called a **homeowner's policy.** Essentially, the basic policy covers the dwelling, together with equipment and fixtures, such as heating and air conditioning equipment and the contents, including furniture, clothing, and other household goods. Coverage also exists for loss of use of the home following a casualty, and often medical benefits. Homeowner's policies also contain liability coverage protecting against, for example, injuries to guests. Additional coverage, such as for damages from windstorm, hail, an explosion, or earthquake or flood, is available for added premiums.

WHAT IS NEIGHBOR LAW?

Disputes between neighbors frequently center around noise, encroachments of tree roots and limbs, boundary lines, and obstructions of views. Various laws, both statutory and common law, comprise **neighbor law.**[10] Court decisions are infrequent largely because the picayune nature of many neighbor squabbles does not justify spending the substantial sums that are required to pursue formal litigation remedies. Neighbor disputes, however,

---

impound account

An account held by a mortgage lender in which to accumulate sufficient funds to pay all annual property taxes and property and liability insurance premiums.

homeowner's policy

Insurance that typically covers losses of the homeowner's property from specified casualties, such as fire and water damage, as well as the possible liability of the owner for specified damages he or she may cause to another person through negligent behavior (other than with a motor vehicle or boat).

neighbor law

The body of laws and rules found in state statutes; in county and city ordinances; in covenants, conditions, and restrictions (CC&Rs); and in court decisions that govern the legal issues that arise between residential neighbors.

are notable for their intensity and longevity. Lawyers and judges alike prefer to remain uninvolved, knowing that even after a court rules the neighbors will find something else to fight about. Most neighbor quarrels are resolved by local officials in small claims courts (fully discussed in Chapter 3), and many are resolved by simple resignation and tolerance of annoyances that are part of "life." Renters, of course, simply move.

HELP FROM LOCAL OFFICIALS

Many common neighbor disputes have been anticipated and are regulated by local ordinance. Ordinances prohibit allowing city property to become blighted (in a condition of disrepair), and they often prohibit the accumulation of weeds, debris, rubbish, etc. Anti-blight ordinances may apply to fences, sidewalks, windows, and driveways as well as structures. Graffiti may be considered a form of blight. Some local ordinances address possible public health problems, such as garbage, debris, and weeds or other rubbish that encourages the breeding of rats and insects or are conducive to fires. Offended neighbors can obtain assistance from city officials, who will compel repairs of unsightly messes or impose fines upon persons responsible. Local ordinances also prohibit unreasonably loud noises, sometimes applying to such activities as late-night basketball, blaring outdoor stereos, and even screaming and fighting neighbors. Police can be called to enforce such ordinances. What is reasonable sound is sometimes determined by measurement of decibels and their relationship to the time of day ("quiet times" may be included within the ordinance) and the type of applicable zoning. Some states have criminal statutes prohibiting noise that is so loud that it "disturbs the peace."

The traffic, crime, and fear engendered by continuous drug dealing in a house also may be prohibited by ordinances that provide neighbors with small claims court remedies against landlords and owners of such nuisances. Courts have imposed damages upon landlords of such crack houses and this ultimately leads to evictions to forestall future penalties.

Local ordinances also impose restrictions on irresponsible animal owners. Under the common law the owner of an animal, such as a dog, is absolutely liable for damages caused when it bites someone. Ordinances often make illegal continuous dog barking and howling and require leashes when dogs (and sometimes cats)[11] are off their owner's property. Offended neighbors can seek assistance from city officials to enforce "pooper scooper" ordinances if they are in effect, or can sue for trespass if they aren't. The number of dogs and cats per household also is often regulated. In at least one instance, the number of geese that can be kept (often as substitutes for watch dogs) also is regulated.[12]

Local zoning ordinances also regulate how property may be used. Zoning laws typically prohibit running a business at a residence if it attracts customers and creates traffic. Persons who perform "outsource" work at home do not violate residential ordinances unless repeated customer and car traffic is thereby generated. Even running garage sales every weekend is probably illegal in most residentially zoned communities. Ordinances also regulate the use and storage of motor vehicles. For example, recreational vehicles (RVs) sometimes must be shielded by fencing or vegetation. Cars cannot be stored in driveways in a state of disassembly and disrepair for indefinite times, under many ordinances. And most communities prohibit the continuous parking of cars on public streets.

HELP FROM CC&Rs

Condominium projects and planned unit subdivisions are regulated by deed restrictions, called **covenants, conditions, and restrictions (CC&Rs).** These restrictions are binding

---

CC&Rs

A written set of limitations, in deeds or other recorded documents, on the future use of real property.

http://

According to its Web site, "Community Associations Institute (CAI) is the only national organization dedicated to fostering vibrant, responsive, competent community associations."

http://www.caionline.org/

upon the owners and occupants of homes within the subdivision. The purpose of the CC&Rs is to maintain property values within the community and to contribute to a safe, neat, and pleasing environment.* A wide range of neighbor disputes may be solved by application of the CC&Rs to the problem. For example, CC&Rs almost always cover noise problems, regulate the time of day when swimming pools may be used, restrict when basketball may be played and whether a court may be lighted, and so on. Colors of fences as well as their style, height, material, and location are usually regulated, both by local ordinance and by applicable CC&Rs.

When a dispute arises, the CC&Rs include a mechanism, or procedure, by which complaints can be brought to the attention of the homeowner's association (HOA).

Earlier in this chapter a general comparison of the amenities between owning and renting a home was presented. Homeowner's associations and the rules they enforce are considered by many to equal, or at least to resemble, the restrictive rules found in apartments. In other words, the owned home is less like a "castle" and more like a rented apartment.

LEGAL FOCUS—PROBLEM

Phyllis Hammond was living in Taromina, a 92-unit oceanfront co-operative in Florida, when its HOA ended its ban on cats. Hammond scurried out and bought a 10-pound cat named Sam for $100. Weeks later the co-op board of directors reinstated its prior ban on cats as pets, and ordered Hammond to get Sam out of her one-bedroom apartment. Legal battles ensued, and before long Hammond, who was living on a modest pension and social security, had spent $8,063, mostly in attorney fees; the co-op board had spent $11,000. The governing rules provided that in legal skirmishes, the prevailing party was entitled to reimbursement of attorney fees from the losing side. In disgust, Hammond offered to get rid of Sam, sell her apartment, and end the dispute if each side would pay its own attorney fees. The board refused, "on principle" according to its lawyer.[13] How can Hammond end the dispute?

Hammond cannot end the dispute. All too often, attorney fees become the tail that wags the dog (or cat, in this situation) in litigation. HOA rules typically provide that the prevailing party is entitled to recover attorney fees, which may greatly exceed the amount in controversy, as the Hammond case demonstrates. Because of the frequency and ferocity of litigation between owners and HOAs, California requires that such disputes be submitted to non-binding arbitration before litigation can be pursued. The theory is that the non-binding arbitration decision will give the parties third-party input that may lead to some compromise.

---

* Nationwide, more than 231,000 developments are governed by community associations. Developers create community associations in nearly all new developments to manage and levy fees for common facilities and obligations such as road and landscaping maintenance. Some provide for the collection of monthly fees from each lot owner specifically to fund roving patrols who assist the publicly funded police in maintaining security within their borders. To some homeowners, these associations are overbearing mini-governments without checks and balances. Typically, elections are conducted periodically and only homeowners can be elected to serve on an association's governing board.

HELP FROM COURT

Many people develop zealously protective attitudes about their trees. As trees grow, their limbs may extend across lot lines, offering both their fruit to the neighbor (sometimes welcome) as well as their dripping sap, falling leaves and limbs, and bird droppings (seldom welcome). Furthermore, your neighbor's trees can be counted on to clog up your rain gutters and downspouts (never welcome). Roots can and do extend across lot lines, and sometimes even a tree's trunk will cross the line. Any physical protrusion across a boundary line is called an **encroachment.** Problems arise when neighbors want to cut limbs off their neighbor's tree, or cut the tree down entirely, especially if its roots are uprooting the fence, driveway, or even a nearby structure. Of equally provoking concern is loss of sunlight, allergic reaction to drifting pollen, and, of course, loss of an ocean, valley, or mountain view. The location of a tree's trunk determines its ownership. If the trunk overlaps a lot line, it is jointly owned by both homeowners whether they like the idea or not. If a wrongdoer (whether or not a neighbor) kills a landowner's tree, the victim may recover compensatory damages (cost of replacement or diminution in value of the land, plus out-of-pocket costs) and punitive damages if applicable. Many states have adopted statutes prescribing damages for crimes against trees, doubling or trebling compensatory damages and sometimes permitting the recovery of attorney fees.[14] In some states wrongful tree killing is a crime, a misdemeanor punishable by fine and/or imprisonment.[15]

In the common law there is a right of self-help. Under the doctrine of self-help, a person has the right to personally secure or enforce some legal right so long as no violent confrontation is involved.* But, in a modern application of the rule, neighbors can simply cut off any encroaching limbs or roots of trees. This conduct may offend the tree's owner, but it is permitted in all states under the common law. However, the trimming is generally at the neighbor's expense, and cannot result in killing the tree—if it does die, the neighbor can be sued for damages for loss of the tree. This is noteworthy because some trees can add a substantial amount to the value of a home. In most states, the neighbor has no other remedy than to trim the tree back to the boundary, unless real damage has been caused (for example, by partially falling onto the roof.)† When substantial injury has occurred, or is threatened, the encroaching tree qualifies as a **nuisance.** Any unreasonable interference with the use and enjoyment of real property is called a nuisance, and it may be enjoined by court (through its issuance of an injunction) and/or damages may be awarded. Tree owners clearly must keep their trees from becoming a nuisance, i.e., from encroaching on and damaging their neighbors' property.

The owner of a fruit tree owns its fruit, even if the fruit is growing on a limb that is overhanging the boundary fence. This rule makes it clear that the public cannot legally pull off a road to pick fruit from orchard trees that overhang onto the public right of way. If the owner of a fruit tree desired to enter upon the neighbor's property to retrieve fruit, the issue of trespass would arise. It is unclear whether the law would uphold an owner's fundamental right to exclude persons from the property, or would create a limited right in the owner of a fruit tree to trespass on another's property to retrieve fruit.

encroachment

Construction (e.g., building or fence) or vegetation (e.g., tree limb or ground cover) that physically intrudes upon or overlaps the real property of another.

nuisance

Any unreasonable and continuous interference with the use and enjoyment of real property.

---

* The classic example of the mostly outdated rule of self-help is the right to trespass (go onto another person's property) to retrieve a stolen horse, so long as a violent confrontation can be avoided. It is usually preferable to summon and rely upon proper officials to execute the law.

† California, Louisiana, and Washington permit suits against owners of encroaching trees even if no serious damage has occurred, on the theory that such trees are a private nuisance.

LEGAL FOCUS—PROBLEM

Janice Turner was angry that her neighbor's Strawberry Blush cling peach tree was overhanging the fence. She said nothing to her neighbor, Baylor Scott, during the following months. In August the tree was laden with beautiful ripe fruit, much of which was clinging to the limbs overhanging Turner's property. Turner then smugly trimmed the limbs back to the fence line and, after the limbs were severed, picked the peaches, canning some and simply enjoying the others. Scott learned of the timely trimming and sued in small claims court for the value of the peaches Turner had taken. What arguments support each side, and what decision should the judge make?

Turner would argue that she exercised her common-law right of self-help by trimming the encroaching limbs back to the property line. Scott might counter that her real intention was to steal his fruit. He could argue that the limbs and fruit remained his property even after they were trimmed, and that Turner is guilty of the tort of conversion. (Conversion was explained in Chapter 7.) The law on this point is nonexistent; the judge would simply have to make a decision without the benefit of the doctrine of *stare decisis*. What decision would you make as judge?

Homeowners enjoy sunlight, free-flowing breezes, and sometimes good views. However, in the common law there is no right to light, air, or view, which may be impaired from growing trees (or even buildings) on neighboring property. This harsh rule has been modified by local ordinances in some areas near the ocean or with other scenic-view potential. These ordinances do not prohibit growing trees that may someday obstruct a neighbor's view. The court is authorized to balance the owner's rights with the desirability of a view for the neighbor, whether or not trimming to the extent of providing a filtered view, or even topping or windowing (cutting out a window to provide a partial view) would be a satisfactory solution. CC&Rs also may regulate the protection of views from growing trees.

Disputes in connection with fences, as noted above, may be resolved by resort to local officials, who will enforce ordinances regulating fences, or by resort to HOA officials, who will enforce applicable CC&Rs. Sometimes, however, a property owner will erect a spite fence, creating a dispute that will require going to court for relief. Any fence that is built to annoy or vex a neighbor, and that has no reasonable value to its owner, is called a **spite fence.** Many states have statutes defining spite fences as nuisances and authorizing lawsuits for their removal and recovery of damages.[16] Proof that a fence is intended to annoy or vex may be easier to produce than it seems. Often a spite fence is deliberately made to look like a monstrosity, to further annoy the neighbor. The existence of ongoing hostility between the neighbors is evidence of a malicious intent. If a fence does not contribute materially to needed privacy, or does not effectively fence anything inside, or does not effectively stop intruders, strong evidence exists that it is a spite fence. Made-up reasons, such as "needed to support my climbing roses" are not likely to be persuasive. Courts can order the removal of spite fences and award compensatory damages, and even punitive damages in outrageous cases.

Neighbor disputes can make life less enjoyable. Prospective home buyers are well advised to extend their inquiries beyond the four corners of the lots they are considering for purchase. Much about the neighborhood can be learned from asking nearby residents pertinent questions. Letter carriers also are available for questions, and often are experts in any

spite fence

A fence erected primarily to vex, annoy, or "spite" a neighbor.

ongoing neighborhood disputes. The location of trees, condition of fences, establishment of boundary lines through survey, as well as a late-night visit on Friday or Saturday can all contribute to making a well-informed purchase.

Sometimes families rent homes in subdivisions in which most homes are owned. This situation can exacerbate problems on occasion when renters are less concerned than owners with long-term neighbor relations. Some think that renters are less likely to maintain proper outside appearances of the home they rent, as by storing old vehicles or making repairs in front or by not picking up loose papers, etc. Owners of homes that are rented also often are accused of ignoring exterior appearances through marginal landscaping services, deteriorated paint and roof conditions, and permissiveness toward all **blight.** Blight in real estate refers to any condition that negatively affects property values in a neighborhood. Examples of blight include foil in or bars over windows; toys constantly left asunder; motorcycles on lawn areas; moss growing on roofs; cracked windows; makeshift visible repairs; exposed garbage cans; etc. Neighbors who are offended by nearby blight have little recourse in the law, no recourse in CC&Rs if none are applicable, and little assistance from government officials unless more serious violations of law also are taking place.

Sometimes the American dream can become an American nightmare—it pays to be a smart buyer.

blight

An extremely adverse condition affecting the value of real property such as disrepair or garbage in the yard.

CASE

STAMBOVSKY V. ACKLEY

169 A.D.2d 254, 572 N.Y.S.2d 672 (New York, 1991).

Jeffrey Stambovsky, the plaintiff, was horrified to discover that the house he contracted to buy was widely believed to be possessed by ghosts. These ghosts had reportedly been seen by the defendant seller and members of her family on numerous occasions over the nine years prior to the sale of the house. The defendant had reported the presence of ghosts in both a national publication (Readers' Digest) *and the local press. The plaintiff buyer, a resident of New York City, did not know about the "reputation" of the house in Nyack Village, where the house was located. Plaintiff brought this lawsuit to rescind the contract to buy the house and to have his down payment of $33,000 returned to him. The New York trial court dismissed the plaintiff's lawsuit before the trial, holding that the doctrine of* caveat emptor *applied to real estate transactions and thus Stambovsky was expected to investigate any facts important to him in a sale. Stambovsky appealed. On appeal, Stambovsky argued that the seller, Ackley, who knew about the ghosts, had a responsibility to tell him the house was haunted. The appellate court agreed and held the plaintiff had a right to pursue his lawsuit and have a trial.*

Justice Rubin delivered the opinion: The unusual facts of this case, as disclosed by the record, clearly warrant a grant of equitable relief to the buyer who, as a resident of New York City, cannot be expected to have any familiarity with the folklore of the Village of Nyack. Not being a "local," plaintiff could not readily learn that the home he had contracted to purchase is haunted. Whether the source of the spectral apparitions seen by defendant seller are parapsychic (paranormal psychological phenomena, e.g., telepathy or clairvoyance) or psychogenic (originating in the mind), having reported their presence in both a national publication (*Readers' Digest*) and the local press (in 1977 and 1982, respectively), defendant is estopped to deny their existence and, as a matter of law, the house is haunted.

More to the point, however, no divination is required to conclude that it is defendant's promotional efforts in publicizing her close encounters with these spirits which fostered the home's reputation in the community. In 1989, the house was included in a five-home walking tour of Nyack and described in a November 27th newspaper article as "a riverfront Victorian (with ghost)." The impact of the reputation thus created

goes to the very essence of the bargain between the parties, greatly impairing both the value of the property and its potential for resale. The extent of this impairment may be presumed for the purpose of reviewing the disposition of this motion to dismiss the cause of action for rescission . . . and represents merely an issue of fact for resolution at trial.

While I agree with supreme court that the real estate broker, as agent for the seller, is under no duty to disclose to a potential buyer the phantasmal reputation of the premises and that, in his pursuit of a legal remedy for fraudulent misrepresentation against the seller, plaintiff hasn't a ghost of a chance, I am nevertheless moved by the spirit of equity to allow the buyer to seek rescission of the contract of sale and recovery of his down payment.

New York law fails to recognize any remedy for damages incurred as a result of the seller's mere silence, applying instead the strict rule of *caveat emptor.* Therefore, the theoretical basis for granting relief, even under the extraordinary facts of this case, is elusive if not ephemeral. "Pity me not but lend thy serious hearing to what I shall unfold." [William Shakespeare, *Hamlet,* Act 1, Scene V (Ghost)]

From the perspective of a person in the position of plaintiff herein, a very practical problem arises with respect to the discovery of a paranormal phenomenon: "Who you gonna call?" as the title song to the movie *Ghostbusters* asks. Applying the strict rule of *caveat emptor* to a contract involving a house possessed by poltergeists conjures up visions of a psychic or medium routinely accompanying the structural engineer and Terminix man on an inspection of every home subject to a contract of sale. It portends that the prudent attorney will establish an escrow account lest the subject of the transaction come back to haunt him and his client—or pray that his malpractice insurance coverage extends to supernatural disasters. In the interest of avoiding such untenable consequences, the notion that a haunting is a condition which can and should be ascertained upon reasonable inspection of the premises is a hobgoblin [a goblin or gremlin or elf that is mischievous but not malicious] which should be exercised from the body of legal precedent and laid quietly to rest.

It has been suggested by a leading authority that the ancient rule which holds that mere nondisclosure does not constitute actionable misrepresentation "finds proper application in cases where the fact undisclosed is patent, or the plaintiff has equal opportunities for obtaining in formation which he may be expected to utilize, or the defendant has no reason to think that he is acting under any misapprehension" [Prosser, *Law of Torts,* § 106 at 696 (4th ed., 1971)]. However, with respect to transaction in real estate, New York adheres to the doctrine of *caveat emptor* and imposes no duty upon the vendor to disclose any information concerning the premises ... unless there is a confidential or fiduciary relationship between the parties ... or some conduct on the part of the seller which constitutes "active concealment. . . ."

Caveat emptor is not so all-encompassing a doctrine of common law as to render every act of nondisclosure immune from redress, whether legal or equitable. "In regard to the necessity of giving information which has not been asked, the rule differs somewhat at laws and in equity, and while the law courts would permit no recovery of damages against a vendor, because of mere concealment of facts under certain circumstances, yet if the vendee refused to complete the contract because of the concealment of a material fact on the part of the other, equity would refuse to compel him so to do, because equity only compels the specific performance of a contract which is fair and open, and in regard to which all material matters known to each have been communicated to the other." [*Rothmiller v. Stein,* and cases cited therein] Common law is not moribund. *Ex facto jus oritur* (law arises out of fact). Where fairness and common sense dictate that an exception should be created, the evolution of the law should not be stifled by rigid application of a legal maxim.

The doctrine of *caveat emptor* requires that a buyer act prudently to assess the fitness and value of his purchase and operates to bar the purchaser who fails to exercise due care from seeking the equitable remedy of rescission. . . . It should be apparent, however, that the most meticulous inspection and search would not reveal the presence of poltergeists at the premises or unearth the property's ghoulish reputation in the community. Therefore, there is no sound policy reason to deny plaintiff relief for failing to discover a state of affairs which the most prudent purchaser would not be expected to even contemplate. Where a condition which has been created by the seller materially impairs the value of the contract and is peculiarly within the knowledge of the seller or unlikely to be discovered by a prudent purchaser exercising due care with respect to the subject transaction, nondisclosure constitutes a basis for rescission as a matter of equity. Any other outcome places upon the buyer not merely the obligation to exercise care in his purchase but rather to be omniscient with respect to any fact which may affect the bargain. No practical purpose is served by imposing such a burden upon a pur-

chaser. To the contrary, it encourages predatory business practice and offends the principle that equity will suffer no wrong to be without a remedy.

Defendant's contention that the contract of sale, particularly the merger, or "as is" clause, bars recovery of the buyer's deposit is unavailing. Even an express disclaimer will not be given effect where the facts are peculiarly within the knowledge of the party invoking it. . . . Moreover, a fair reading of the merger clause reveals that it expressly disclaims only representations made with respect to the physical condition of the premises and merely makes general reference to representations concerning "any other matter or things affecting or relating to the aforesaid premises." As broad as this language may be, a reasonable interpretation is that its effect is limited to tangible or physical matters and does not extend to paranormal phenomena. Finally, if the language of the contract is to be construed as broadly as defendant urges to encompass the presence of poltergeists in the house, it cannot be said that she has delivered the premises "vacant" in accordance with her obligation under the provisions of the contract rider.

Application of the remedy of rescission, within the bounds of the narrow exception to the doctrine of *caveat emptor* set forth herein, is entirely appropriate to relieve the unwitting purchaser from the consequences of a most unnatural bargain.

The court reinstated the cause of action for rescission of the contract of purchase.

All concurred except J. P. Milonas and J. Smith, who dissented in an opinion by Justice Smith: I would affirm the dismissal of the complaint. . . . The parties herein were represented by counsel and dealt at arm's length. . . . There is no allegation that defendants, by some specific act, other than the failure to speak, deceived the plaintiff. . . . Finally, if the doctrine of *caveat emptor* is to be discarded, it should be for a reason more substantive than a poltergeist. The existence of a poltergeist is no more binding upon the defendants than it is upon this court. Based upon the foregoing, the motion court properly dismissed the complaint.

For Critical Analysis

Early in his opinion, Justice Rubin made the following statement: ". . . . defendant (seller) is estopped to deny their (the ghosts') existence and, as a matter of law, the house is haunted."

1. Does this mean that all future buyers must be told the house is haunted because, as a matter of law, it is? Or does this rule apply only to the seller in this case?

2. Is this case precedent for the rule of law that whenever a person behaves as if a situation is true, that the law holds the person to that situation even if it's false? Can you think of limitations or qualifications that ought to limit such a rule of law?

3. New York follows the common-law rule of *caveat emptor* (let the buyer beware). Did the majority opinion discard the rule, as suggested by the dissenting justices, or did it distinguish the rule in some way? ■

VAN CAMP V. BRADFORD

63 Ohio Misc. 2d 245, 623 N.E.2d 731 (Ohio, 1993).

Buyer filed her complaint alleging that the defendant's seller and real estate agent and broker knew of the unsafe character of the residence and neighborhood, failed to disclose, and concealed these material facts, which would have influenced her decision to buy the property. Plaintiff sought damages from all defendants for mental stress and anguish, for the decreased value of the property, for fraud and negligence, and for equitable relief.

The defendants filed for summary judgment, arguing that the doctrine of caveat emptor *is a complete defense in a suit seeking recovery for the "stigma" attached to or the "psychological impairment" of a piece of property. Defendants also claimed that a cause of action for property defects that are neither a physical or legal impairment does not exist in Ohio.*

The trial court held that: (1) latent nature of alleged stigmatizing defect in property which resulted from rape in residence rendered defense of caveat emptor *inapplicable; (2) material issue of fact as to whether purchaser in fact inquired regarding safety of premises precluded summary judgment; and (3) real estate agents had no affirmative duty to speak up and disclose knowledge of crimes simply because they were in room at time inquiry regarding safety of residence was made.*

Ordered accordingly.

MICHAEL J. SAGE, Judge

I

This case arises from the sale of a residence located at 6027 Arcade Drive, Fairfield, Ohio. On or about October 30, 1991, a renter's daughter was raped at knifepoint in the residence owned by defendant Bradford. On or about December 20, 1991, another rape occurred in a neighboring home. That same day, defendant Bradford listed the house for sale with defendant Realty World.

Plaintiff Kitty Van Camp submitted a written offer to purchase the home on February 4, 1992. Before closing and during a walk-through inspection of the premises with defendant Bradford and defendant Patton (listing agent) and defendant Hoff (co-operating agent) present, plaintiff noticed bars on the basement windows. In response to plaintiff's inquiry regarding the purpose and necessity of the bars on the windows, defendant Bradford stated that a break-in had occurred sixteen years earlier, but that there was currently no problem with the residence. Plaintiff stated that she would like to remove the bars for cosmetic purposes, but Bradford advised her not to do so, as it was in plaintiff's best interests to leave the bars in place.

The closing on the property took place on February 21, 1992. At this time, the perpetrator of the crimes was still at large. While moving into the home, a neighbor informed plaintiff that the daughter of the last occupant had been raped in October, and that another brutal rape had occurred shortly before Christmas, in 1991. Two more rapes occurred in June and August 1992 at a nearby home. Plaintiff's house was burglarized on April 8, 1992, and threatening phone calls were received by plaintiff in July 1992. Police reports submitted by plaintiff confirm that all of these crimes did in fact take place.

Plaintiff, after being informed of the rapes in her home and the surrounding neighborhood, confronted defendant Campbell (owner of Realty World) who acknowledged that he, defendant Patton, and defendant Hoff were all aware of the rapes, including the rape at the subject property.

II

The rule that a seller is generally under no duty to disclose material facts about the subject matter of a sale unless a specific exception exists originates from the doctrine of *caveat emptor*. At least since 1956, the principle of *caveat emptor* has been consistently applied in Ohio to sales of real estate relative to conditions discoverable by the buyer, or open to observation upon an investigation of the property.

[In 1979], however, the Supreme Court of Ohio held that latent defects do give rise to a duty on the part of the seller, and constitute an exception to the application of *caveat emptor*. When latent defects are coupled with misrepresentations or concealment, the doctrine of *caveat emptor* does not preclude recovery for fraud. Fraudulent concealment exists where a vendor fails to disclose sources of peril of which he is aware, if such a source is not discoverable by the vendee. Thus, the Supreme Court of Ohio held that the plaintiffs could sue for termites discovered after the real estate agent made the representation that the house was a "good solid home," especially since the seller was personally aware of the problem prior to the sale. The nature of the defect and the ability of the parties to determine through a reasonable inspection that a defect exists are key to determining whether or not the defect is latent.

In contrast to the national trend, Ohio has recently upheld the doctrine of *caveat emptor* with regard to real estate sales. Conditions traditionally limiting the application of the doctrine, however, were also vigorously upheld in the court's opinion: the property defect must be open to observation or discoverable upon a reasonable inspection, the purchaser must have an unimpeded opportunity to examine the property, and the vendor may not engage in fraud. The court held that, unlike a latent defect, the structural defect of the basement wall at issue was "highly visible," and the corrective I-beams supporting the wall were open to observation by the plaintiffs.

With the recent enactment of R.C. 5302.30, the Ohio legislature has taken a bold step toward ameliorating the harsh application of *caveat emptor* in even patent defect real estate transactions. For sales conducted on or after July 1, 1993, the statute requires a seller of residential property to provide each prospective buyer, or his/her agent, with a prescribed disclosure form regarding various aspects of the property. Even though the official disclosure form has not yet been formally established, preliminary drafts indicate that its purpose is to disclose material matters regarding not only the physical condition of the property, but also title, survey and other matters. If the seller fails to provide the disclosure form, the statute grants the buyer the powerful remedy of rescission. With this initiative, the Ohio legislature has seriously undermined the doctrine of *caveat emptor* as previously applied.

Virtually all of the case law regarding the buyer's duties under *caveat emptor* focuses on physical property defects. Thus, the case at bar is unique in that it presents issues regarding duty and liability for a so-called psychological defect in the property, namely, that the property was rendered unsafe for habitation by the plaintiff due to the serious crimes that had occurred in and near the residence.

The stigma associated with the residence at 6027 Arcade Drive is analogous to the latent property defects that have become an exception to the strict application of *caveat emptor*. Due to the intangible nature of the defect at issue here, a prospective buyer would have been unable to determine from a walk-through of the house in 1992 that it was the site of a serious, unsolved violent crime. Clearly, any psychological stigma that may be attached to a residence is even more undiscoverable than the existence of termites in a home, or a

defect in the title to the property, both of which have been deemed latent defects despite the fact that they could have been discovered through a professional inspection or title search.

Defendants' argument that the defect at issue here was readily discoverable lacks merit. Checking police records in order to ascertain the relative safety of a neighborhood or a particular residence would not be an action undertaken by even the most prudent of purchasers. When viewed in conjunction with a potential misrepresentation or concealment on the part of defendant Bradford regarding the relative safety of the home, the latent nature of the defect at issue here renders the defense of *caveat emptor* inapplicable.

III

The case *sub judice* raises the question whether Ohio should recognize a cause of action for residential property tainted by stigmatizing events that have occurred on and near the premises. The only reported case involving a psychological property defect was heard in California and involved a house that had been the site of multiple murders ten years prior to its sale to the plaintiff. The Third District held that the plaintiff buyer did have a cause of action capable of surviving the seller's motion to dismiss. The determinative issue in that case was whether the failure to disclose the murders was material.

The California court "saw no principled basis for making the duty to disclose turn upon the character of the information," and held that the failure to disclose the murders was a material fact that could conceivably depress the value of the property.

IV

Clearly defining the cause of action for stigmatized property is necessary in order to protect the stability of contracts and prevent limitless recovery for insubstantial harms and irrational fears: misrepresentation, concealment or nondisclosure of a material fact by a seller of residential property in response to an affirmative inquiry is evidence of a breach of duty on the part of the seller. After inquiry, if the buyer justifiably relied on the misrepresentation or nondisclosure, or was induced or misled into effecting the sale to his/her detriment and damage, the buyer has met the burden of proof required to withstand a summary judgment motion.

When a seller receives an affirmative inquiry regarding the condition of a piece of property, the buyer is entitled to a truthful answer. One who responds to an inquiry is guilty of fraud if he gives equivocal, evasive or misleading answers calculated to convey a false impression, even though the answer may be literally true. Responding honestly to an affirmative inquiry regarding the condition of a residence is a lighter burden than the voluntary disclosure of a defect mandated by *caveat emptor*, particularly when knowledge of a stigmatizing defect is within the ready personal or actual knowledge of the seller at the time of the inquiry.

A seller who is under a duty to disclose facts and fails to do so will be held liable for damages directly and proximately resulting from his silence. A person injured by fraud is entitled to such damages as will fairly compensate him for the wrong suffered. As an additional safeguard, objective tangible harm must be demonstrated to still the concern that permitting cases of this nature to go forward will open the floodgates to rescission on subjective and idiosyncratic grounds.

V

The defendants in this case have argued that the prevailing trend across the nation regarding property disclosure is evidenced by the nondisclosure statutes that have been enacted in twenty states and the District of Columbia. Defendants also contend that these statutes imply that a cause of action for tainted property in Ohio is necessarily barred.

These statutes generally state that sellers of real estate are not liable for failing to disclose stigmatizing events, such as the fact that a homicide, suicide, felony or death by AIDS occurred in the residence. Ohio has not adopted a nondisclosure statute of this nature.

It is the opinion of this court that the nondisclosure statutes as enacted in other states still require a good faith response to an inquiry regarding a potential psychological impairment: these statutes were enacted solely to insulate sellers from liability for any failure to *voluntarily* and automatically disclose information regarding potential stigmas associated with property. As aptly stated by Representative Prague during the public hearings discussing Connecticut's newly adopted nondisclosure statute, "It seems to me that anybody selling a house would have to answer truthfully when a buyer asks a question. I mean, why should we tell you what the realtor should say or shouldn't say, or should reveal and shouldn't reveal. He should reveal anything that is asked of him."

VI

A cause of action for stigmatized property, as previously defined and limited, is warranted in the case at bar. At this point, it is necessary to analyze the elements of the cause of action for stigmatized property in the context of the defendants' summary judgment motions.

A motion for summary judgment shall be granted when there is no genuine issue of any material fact and the moving party is entitled to judgment as a matter of law. It must be awarded with caution, resolving doubts and construing evidence against the moving party, and granted only when it appears from the evidentiary material that reasonable minds can reach only an adverse conclusion as to the party opposing the motion.

Construing the evidence in the light most favorable to the plaintiff, the court finds that the plaintiff has met her initial burden of proof. The court must accept plaintiff's evidence that a rape occurred in the residence at 6027 Arcade Drive, and that several other crimes occurred in close proximity to the property. Further, the court must accept plaintiff's allegation that all of the defendants involved knew that these crimes had occurred, yet failed to disclose this knowledge to the plaintiff.

Reasonable minds could construe the plaintiff's question regarding the bars on the basement windows as an affirmative inquiry directed at ascertaining the safety of the premises, and defendant Bradford's statements regarding the reason for the bars to be a misrepresentation or a nondisclosure of their current purpose. Upon the plaintiff's inquiry, defendant Bradford was simply required to tell the truth. A more difficult case would arise had there been no evidence to indicate that the plaintiff had solicited information regarding the safety of the residence.

Numerous questions of material fact remain regarding the conversation that took place between plaintiff and defendant Bradford, and these questions preclude a granting of summary judgment. [D]efendant Bradford's motion for summary judgment is hereby DENIED.

By contrast, however, the court finds as a matter of law that the inquiry of plaintiff was directed solely to the homeowner, defendant Bradford: she alone responded to plaintiff's question regarding the safety of the residence. The real estate defendants had no duty to affirmatively speak up and disclose their knowledge of the crimes simply because they were in the room at the time the inquiry was made. Had the real estate agents similarly misrepresented or failed to disclose a material fact upon an inquiry directed to them, summary judgment in their favor would not be warranted. Even construing the facts in the light most favorable to the plaintiff, however, the court must nevertheless find that this factually distinguishable situation simply did not transpire in this case. Thus, since reasonable minds could come to but one conclusion regarding the evidence, and that conclusion is adverse to the plaintiff, the summary judgment motions of defendants Realty World, Campbell, Patton, and defendants West Shell and Hoff are hereby GRANTED.
So ordered.

For Critical Analysis

1. Distinguish latent from patent defects. Which type is discussed in the case? Explain.

2. Was the response by the seller to the buyer about the reason for the bars on basement windows made before

the contract to buy the house was entered into or was it made afterward? Should that make a difference? Did it?

3. Whose real estate agents were being sued? The seller's or buyer's? Does it make any difference?

4. Is the treatment of *caveat emptor* consistent in the prior case of *Stambovsky v. Ackley*?

5. Would you analyze this case differently if you were applying ethical rules rather than legal rules?

6. When was the Ohio disclosure statute enacted relative to this case? Is that important? Why? ■

CHAPTER QUESTIONS AND PROBLEMS

1. What is the amount of the standard real estate commission charged by brokerage firms in your community? Assume you own a home in which your equity is $25,000, and that you are about to sell for $125,000. If your agent's commission rate is 6 percent, what is the commission rate expressed as a percentage of your equity? How much difference in effort do you suspect a sales agent expends in listing a home in which the owner has a $50,000 equity? What conclusions can be drawn from your analysis? Would a prospective seller be wise to engage the services of a listing agent on an hourly basis? Why or why not?

2. What specific services are rendered to a homeowner by a licensed real estate agent who has "listed" the property?

3. What questions should you ask the seller, or the seller's agent, before buying a house for your personal residence?

4. In 1950 Michael and Albina Klos purchased a lot from the Molenda family, who continued to live right next door. Rather than survey the property, the buyers and sellers paced off the lot and placed stakes in the ground as boundary markers. After Mr. Molenda's death in 1983, his widow hired a surveyor to determine the exact property line. The property line turned out to be 30" closer to the Kloses' house. Mrs. Molenda immediately dug up 30" of the Kloses' grass and erected a fence on the true property line. Should the court require dismantling of the fence and award ownership of the 30" strip to the Kloses? [*Klos v. Molenda,* 355 Pa. Super. 399, 513 A.2d 490 (Pennsylvania, 1986).]

5. If you were selling your home, and a prospective buyer offered a very attractive price, and suggested the use of a land contract with only $1,000 down payment, what factors would you take into consideration?

6. If you were applying for a loan at a savings and loan association for the purpose of buying a home, which three of the following factors would be the most important to you?
   a. A relatively low interest rate.
   b. A relatively long repayment term.
   c. The right to prepay principal payments without penalty.
   d. A relatively low "late payment" penalty.
   e. The right to have someone else assume your loan without any assumption fee and without any increase in the interest rate.
   f. The absence of the requirement that you pay the lender's attorney fees incurred by the lender because of your default in making monthly payments.
   g. The absence of an acceleration clause that made the entire unpaid balance of the loan due upon any default in monthly payments.

7. As a prospective buyer of your first home, what disadvantages would there be in leasing with an option to buy?

8. Would you prefer to finance the purchase of your home with a fixed-rate mortgage or with a variable-rate mortgage that begins with an interest rate one full percentage point rate lower than the former? Why?

9. Would you prefer to own a single-family detached home or a condominium? What are your perceptions of the advantages and disadvantages of each?

10. What is the primary reason you hope to be a homeowner in the future? If you will buy and sell a home on five different occasions over your working career, would you still prefer to be a homeowner? Explain.

CHAPTER 13

Employee and Employer Rights and Duties

*I*m a great believer in luck, and I find the harder I work the more I have of it.

Thomas Jefferson, 1743–1826

After reading and studying this chapter, you should be able to:

- Discuss and define the types of employment classifications: principal/agent, employer/employee, and employer/independent contractor.

- Explain and provide examples of the doctrine of *respondeat superior*.

- Identify the groups protected under the Civil Rights Act of 1964. Distinguish between disparate impact and disparate treatment theories of discrimination.

- Understand the nature of sexual harassment and the difference between *quid pro quo* and hostile environment sexual harassment.

- List necessary steps to a Title VII claim.

- Identify employer defenses to Title VII claims.

- Define a disability and suggest the limits of reasonable accommodation for the ADA.

- Understand the development of different legal theories regarding wrongful termination.

- Identify basic rights and duties of employees.

- Discuss the distinction between at will and just cause employment.

- Identify some major legal issues of employee welfare in wages, retirement, family leave, privacy, and safety.

- Identify and discuss the major federal statutes affecting the labor/management relationship.

- Define "collective bargaining" and understand its ramifications. Understand the difference between a union and a non-union workplace.

- Discuss the importance and limitations of arbitration clauses in employment contracts.

In George Washington's time, approximately 90 percent of all Americans could be classified as farmers. In 2001, our estimated total population exceeded 284 million and included a civilian labor force of 142 million workers. Of that number, less than three percent worked in farming, forestry, or fishing. Thus, our agricultural revolution has enabled 1 percent of our population to produce more than enough food to feed the nation. The industrial and agricultural revolutions of the last hundred or so years shifted most people into urban areas, where manufacturing and various service activities expanded. In more recent times, mechanization, automation, robotization, and siliconization has reduced the need for factory workers and miners.

At the beginning of the twentieth century, workers had to adjust to new types of machines, ones they did not understand. Instead of the steam engine, which mechanically inclined workers could observe and figure out, the internal combustion engine befuddled many. A greater challenge to understanding was electrical machines, which operated quite differently from the earliest machines; how and why these contraptions worked was past the understanding of most laborers. Most of us have long since reconciled everyday dependence on a world we don't quite understand. Pictures are transmitted to satellites and received in homes through cable or satellite receivers with hundreds of viewing options available. We can log on to the Internet and find out how to safely thaw the frozen turkey in time to save Thanksgiving dinner. We can record movies for our own use and make phone calls from almost anywhere in the world, including Mt. Everest.[1] In 1899, only the wildest ranting of a mad scientist or science fiction writer could have predicted the cooperative construction of a space station by several countries. Yet just when we have become somewhat comfortable with machines we don't understand, the pace of change again appears to be accelerating. Silicon-based technology and biomedical research are making groundbreaking advances almost weekly. The details make little sense to most people. However, workers in both the early 1900s and 2000s face a future with rapid change and exciting new possibilities.

THE CHANGING WORK ENVIRONMENT

Dramatic realignments in work have occurred in this century. In April 2002, 31 percent of American workers were in managerial and professional occupations; 28 percent in technical, sales, and administrative support; 14 percent in service occupations; 10.5 percent in precision production, craft, and repair; 12.5 percent in operating, fabricating, and labor; 2.5 percent in farming, forestry, and fishing; and 6 percent unemployed. In the Bureau of Labor Statistics' *Occupational Outlook Handbook* (2002–03 edition) the jobs with the highest predicted growth rates all require a college degree and relate to the computer industry. They include database administrators, computer support specialists, computer scientists, computer engineers, and systems analysts. Among the next several areas of predicted employment growth are in the health industry and relate in part to a growing aged population. College degrees were rare a hundred years ago, but now they are necessary for most of the best employment opportunities.

The pace of change in science and technology has increased in recent decades, stimulated by discoveries and inventions best exemplified by the computer. Among the most evident effects of this accelerated pace of change in employer–employee relations has been corporate downsizing: cutbacks in numbers of middle-level managers and lower-level line workers. This has been made possible by machines and technology that improve efficiency in all steps, from accounting through production, warehousing, and marketing. Concurrently the internationalization of much business has greatly expanded

http://

Read the latest edition of the Occupational Outlook Handbook at http://www.bls.gov/oco/

world trade and intensified competition. The Bureau of Labor Statistics tells us that in 2001 more than 19.8 million persons did some work at home as part of their primary job; instead of agriculture, repair work, or production, however, most of these workers were in white-collar occupations. We enter the workforce armed with knowledge from the recent past that many common jobs may soon disappear and new job titles may require tasks and functions that today are unknown.

How Does the Law Affect Workers and the Workplace?

Legislation and court decisions affect or control a wide range of issues concerning employment.

- **Who may work?** Labor of persons under eighteen years old is limited and strictly regulated under federal and state laws. Thus, persons age sixteen or seventeen are barred from hazardous work, including driving motor vehicles, mining, logging, and wrecking. Persons age fourteen or fifteen may work in some office or sales jobs and in retail, food service, and gasoline service, but not during school hours or in such a way as to interfere with school. Under specified conditions, persons of any age may deliver newspapers; act in movies, theater, radio, or TV; and work on any farm owned or operated by their parents. The secretary of labor prescribes other regulations.[2] Many laws are designed to prevent discrimination in hiring, training, promoting, and dismissing employees simply because of their race, color, gender, national origin, religion, disability, or advanced age (forty to seventy).[3]

- **What work may be done?** By statute, scores of occupations from commercial aviator to X-ray technician require a license obtainable only by persons who have prescribed education and experience and pass qualifying examinations. Many are required to continue formal education to keep their skills current.

- **When may the work be done?** Generally, at least one day in each week is set aside for rest and recreation. Legal provision of this day of rest has been upheld by the U.S. Supreme Court as a valid state exercise of the police power in the interest of public health and general welfare. (Reasonable exceptions to Sunday closing laws permit sale of commodities necessary for health and recreation. This does not violate the equal protection or due-process clauses of the Fourteenth Amendment.)[4] Annual vacations of one week or longer are not required by law but are generally provided as a fringe benefit. Most states, by statute or executive proclamation, observe some ten federal holidays that are legally designated by the president and Congress. Many states add one or more local legal holidays of their own.

- **Where may the work be done?** Extensive legislation and administrative regulations prescribe minimal acceptable environmental conditions in workplaces.[5] Some twenty-five states (including California, Florida, Illinois, Michigan, New York, and Pennsylvania) have **right-to-know laws.** These require disclosure to workers of information about any hazardous chemical substances they are likely to be exposed to on the job.

- **How may the work be done?** The Occupational Safety and Health Administration (OSHA) has a mission to ensure safe and healthful workplaces in America. The agency states that since its inception in 1971 workplace fatalities have been cut in half, and occupational injury and illness rates have declined 40 percent while the number of U.S. workers has doubled. In 2000 over 90,000 workplace inspections took place by either federal OSHA or state OSHA programs.

http://

Visit the 'Lectric Law Library's "Lawcopedia" on employment and labor law at

http://www.lectlaw.com/ temp.html

right-to-know laws

Federal and state laws requiring that information be collected and distributed about possible exposure to hazardous chemicals.

- **How many consecutive hours of work may be required in certain occupations?** Regulations control the maximum number of hours that bus drivers and airline pilots can be on duty without time off for sleep.
- **How much must be paid for labor?** At both the federal and state levels, minimum wage laws have been in effect since the Great Depression. They are coupled with regulations of the maximum hours of work that employers may demand without the payment of "time-and-a-half" for overtime.[6]
- **Do workers have the legal right to unionize?** Federal and state laws guarantee most workers the right to organize into unions of their own choice, and require employers to bargain collectively with the representatives of such unions over wages, hours, and a broad spectrum of conditions of employment.[7]

The law's concern with the employment process is pervasive. It precedes hiring, applies during employment, continues through dismissal, and extends into retirement. Our public education system provides lifelong learning opportunities that facilitate useful employment. Without proper knowledge and skills, one is likely to be underemployed or unemployed throughout one's life. Legal involvement continues when jobs are lost because of an economic recession, and public funds pay unemployment compensation.[8] Some workers wrongfully dismissed from employment may sue for damages under developing tort law.

LEGAL CLASSIFICATION OF EMPLOYEES

The world of work has been a prime concern of lawmakers over the centuries. Rules enforceable in court enable businesses to fulfill their needs of providing goods and services to many customers. They also govern the employer–employee relationship, of which there are three basic types: principal–agent, employer–ordinary employee, and contracting employer–independent contractor.

PRINCIPAL–AGENT RELATIONSHIP

Agency is described in technical language by the authoritative *Restatement of Agency* as "the fiduciary relation, which results from the manifestation of consent by one person to another that the other shall act on his behalf and subject to his control, and consent by the other, so to act."[9] In less arcane terms, this means that the principal is a special type of employer who hires an **agent** to act for the **principal** in negotiating and transacting business with customers. The agent receives and accepts authority from the principal to carry out the principal's business as directed.

Agents may be authorized to make contracts with customers on behalf of their principals. When made, the contracts are treated as legally binding between the customer and the employer, although negotiated by the agent. If every business customer had to deal directly with the owner, business as we know it could not exist. Agency law enables a business owner (as principal) to employ any number of persons (as agents) to enter into contracts with third parties for the sale or purchase of goods and/or services on behalf of the principal. Because an agent can legally bind his or her employer (the principal) to contracts that are made, the law declares the agent to be a *fiduciary* and imposes a high obligation of trustworthiness upon the agent.

A **fiduciary** relationship exists when the law requires one person to treat another with the most scrupulous good faith and honesty (e.g., an attorney toward a client, a trustee toward a beneficiary in a trust, and a partner toward another partner in a partnership).

agency

Relationship in which, by mutual consent, an employee (the agent) is authorized to represent and bind an employer (the principal) in business dealings with third parties.

agent

A person employed by a principal to deal with third parties and to make contracts binding the principal to the third parties. An agent is a fiduciary of the principal.

principal

The person who empowers an agent to enter contract(s) on her or his behalf.

fiduciary

Someone who has an obligation to act with scrupulous good faith and honesty toward another.

Obviously, a key to the expansion and success of business is to find and retain competent, honest, and industrious agents. The following hypothetical example illustrates how an agent may perform legal acts that bind the principal.

LEGAL FOCUS—PROBLEM

Bruce Henning is hired as the booking agent for a rock group, the Understanding Slugs. He negotiates and signs a contract for the group to appear in one evening performance at the Wisconsin State Fair in Milwaukee. Two months before the show date, Henning informs the Milwaukee producer that the group cannot appear as scheduled because "they'll be tied up in a two-week appearance in Vegas—a big break we just can't walk away from." Are the Understanding Slugs liable to the Milwaukee producer for damages for breach of the earlier contract?

Yes, the group is liable. They are legally bound by the acts of their agent just as is the Milwaukee producer is liable under the contract to the group. Following are highlights of the agency relationship:

- Agency is a relationship between two persons: the *principal,* or employer who wants to get something done, and the *agent,* or employee who is authorized by the principal to do the specified job as a representative of the principal.
- The relationship is always *consensual.* Both principal and agent must expressly or impliedly consent to the relationship. For example, as a favor Juanita agrees to act as Lou Hockley's agent to buy two tickets to the big game. Hockley reimburses Feria for the price paid, but gives her no more than a "thank you" for the service. (Had Feria bought the tickets without Hockley's consent, he would have no obligation to pay.) The relationship is also usually—although not always—*contractual,* meaning that generally both parties gives and receives consideration (see Chapter 8). For example, under an employment contract, Craig Marks serves as Molly Moore's agent (sales representative) in the Chicago territory. Marks makes contracts on Moore's behalf and binds her to perform. She pays him a salary and/or commission for his services.
- The agent represents and acts on behalf of the principal in dealings with third parties. The resulting contract is legally binding on the principal, provided the agent acted within the scope of his or her authority as given by the principal. Usually the agent is not bound to the third party to perform the contract.
- However, an agent who acts beyond the scope of his or her authority is personally liable to the third party. If in doubt as to the nature and scope of the agent's authority, the third party should check directly with the principal, asking (1) Is he/she your agent? and (2) What is your agent's authority (e.g., to sell, to buy) and on what terms? The law holds that generally a third party has a duty to verify that an agent has the authority that he or she claims.

LEGAL FOCUS—PROBLEM

The hospital workers were excited to find that former Major League Baseball pitcher Mickey Lolich was checking into St. Joseph's Medical Center. When the healthcare workers checked the identity of their patient, they found out it was not Lolich but someone named Leroy Fulton. Is Mickey Lolich liable for the health bills incurred by Leroy Fulton in his name?

http://

See the 'Lectric Law Library's discussion of agency at **http://www.lectlaw.com/def /a026.htm**

If an agent exceeds his or her authority, the principal is ordinarily not liable. It is then also true that if a person attempts to pass himself or herself off as someone else, that person is liable but the "real" person, in this case Lolich, is not. Apparently, Leroy was also bumming beers and giving autographs. Don't assume that someone is who he or she claims to be without carefully checking. Leroy was arrested on suspicion of forgery and theft.[10]

- The agent, in effect, walks in the shoes of the principal, even when out of the principal's presence. The principal has the continuing right to control the agent, but while alone, the agent may make a foolish contract and the principal must honor it as long as the agent's acts were authorized. Note that even if the agent violates explicit orders, the principal would be liable to affected innocent third parties (e.g., the agent sells goods below a minimum price set by the principal, or grants credit in violation of stated company policy). The principal is likewise responsible for most torts the agent committed while within the scope of authorized behavior under a doctrine called *respondeat superior* (discussed shortly).

- An official notice (e.g., legal summons and complaint) given to a duly authorized agent is legally deemed to be a notice to the principal. Also, the agent is duty bound to perform as promised and to use reasonable care (which could be appropriate skilled care, as when the agent is a lawyer or real estate broker).

- Agency is a fiduciary relationship in which the agent must act in scrupulous good faith and honesty toward the principal, always placing the interests of the principal first. He or she must be loyal, never serving two adverse parties (e.g., the buyer and the seller in a transaction) at the same time, unless both are fully informed and give consent. Of course, an agent may be employed by a group of associated principals. Also, an attorney at law may be employed by two or more persons to prepare a partnership agreement as long as all clients give their informed consent, and the attorney treats them with impartiality and balanced fairness. Any agent must account to the principal for all receipts and disbursements and must never keep a secret profit.*

EMPLOYER–ORDINARY EMPLOYEE

An ordinary **employee** is a person hired to perform services for another, the employer, and the employee's physical conduct is controlled by, or is subject to control by, the employer. As mentioned, the employment relationship is a contractual relationship. Employees who transact business with third parties have a dual status; they are both ordinary employees and agents.

employee

A person who agrees by contract to perform work as directed and controlled by an employer in exchange for compensation (usually consisting of wages or salary and fringe benefits).

LEGAL FOCUS—PROBLEM

Donna Hunt owns a dress shop. She employs Myra Feldman, Roxanne Peters, and Nita Travis as salespeople and Kari Hudspeth as an in-house accountant. Hunt is the employer, and Feldman, Peters, Travis, and Hudspeth obviously work for her. Which of the employed parties are employees and which are agents? Are the terms mutually exclusive?

Feldman, Peters, Travis, and Hudspeth are all employees. All are also agents. The classifications are not mutually exclusive and many employees are agents and vice-versa. The key to an employer–employee relationship is the extent of the employer's right to control the employee's acts. Ordinary employees often lack independent business discretion. The

---

* The burden of the fiduciary obligation is upon the agent and operates to safeguard the principal. The principal, although not a fiduciary, is still expected to deal fairly. For example, a company (the principal) must account to the agent for all receipts and commissions owed.

salespeople in the dress shop are told how to handle and display merchandise and how to record sales. When they actually sell the dresses, however, they act as agents as well as ordinary employees because they have been given the authority by Hunt to sell goods to customers. These sales are contracts between the customers and Hunt. Hudspeth, the accountant, has no authority to sell dresses but undoubtedly represents her employer in other ways. An employee is not an agent if she lacks authority to contract for or represent the employer to others. Obviously most employees are also agents in some respect.

The employer is liable to third parties for injuries caused by the negligence of employees while they are acting within the scope of their employment under a common-law doctrine called **respondeat superior.** This legal doctrine imposes vicarious—that is, indirect—liability on an employer for the wrongful acts of an agent or employee that occur while the agent or employee is on the job. Vicarious liability occurs even though the employer has not been careless. Because liability exists even without the fault of the employer, the doctrine is similar to the theory of strict liability in tort.

The discussion in this text refers to employer and employee, but the terms *principal* and *agent* and even *master* and *servant* are also often used when discussing *respondeat superior.* If the appropriate control over the actor by the employer exists and the act is in the scope of employment, then liability exists, despite any inconsistency in the use of terms.

The doctrine of *respondeat superior* is justified by three supporting theories. The first concerns the issue of control. An employer has the right to control the acts of the agent or employee and is thus responsible for injuries arising out of such service. The second theory is economic in nature. Since the employer profits from the employee or agent's service, he or she should also suffer the losses. The third reason is practical and is referred to as the *deep-pocket theory.* The employer is more likely to be able to pay for the losses than the employee and/or agent. In other words, the employer usually has more money; this is where the saying "the employer has the deep pockets" comes from.

It is important to note that there are limitations on the employer or principal's vicarious liability. An employer is responsible only for the wrongful conduct of an employee/agent occurring in the scope of the employment. Generally, the act must be of a kind the worker was employed to do. It must also have occurred within authorized time and space limits and must have been activated, at least in part, by a purpose to serve the employer.

There are several questions used to determine if the employee's act occurred within the scope of employment. The answers assist a court or jury in determining whether the employee was on the job for purposes of the doctrine of *respondeat superior.*

- **Did the employer authorize the act?** If the answer is yes, then the act is probably within the scope of employment.
- **What were the time, place, and purpose of the act?** If it occurred on the worksite, then the employee was probably on the job. An employee commuting to or from work is generally not acting within the scope of employment.
- **Was the act one commonly performed by employees for the employer?** If yes, the employee was acting within the scope of employment.
- **To what extent was the employer's interest advanced by the act?** If the act would ordinarily benefit the employer, then the employee was acting within the scope of employment.
- **To what extent were the private interests of the employee involved?** If the act was primarily to benefit the employee, then perhaps the employee was not on the job. For example, an employee takes a break during the day and goes downtown to shoot a game of pool. An accident occurs while driving to the pool hall. The employee is probably not within the scope of employment.
- **Did the employer furnish the means or instrumentality (for example, a truck or a machine) by which the injury was inflicted?** If the employee is using the employer's truck, he or she is more likely to be considered within the scope of employment.

respondeat superior

(Latin: "let the master answer") A legal doctrine holding employers liable for injuries caused third persons by their employees who were negligent while acting within the course and scope of their employment.

http://

The National Labor Relations Board's Web site includes a great gateway list for information about just about every type of employment-related issue **http://www.nlrb.gov/ helpdesk.html**

- **Did the employer expect that the employee would do the act?** Had the employee done the act before? If the answer is yes to both questions, the employee is more likely to be within the scope of employment.
- **Did the act involve the commission of a serious crime?** If the act is a serious intentional wrong, the employee is not usually considered to be within the scope of employment, unless the employer requested or might reasonably expect that the employee would perform that wrongful act.

LEGAL FOCUS—PROBLEM

Walter Johnson was driving down Main Street on his way to deliver a package for Racehorse Delivery Service. Unfortunately, Johnson was distracted for a second and ran into the rear of Felicia Fresno's new Lexus automobile. Luckily, Fresno was not hurt, but the car suffered $10,000 in damages. Who is legally responsible for the harm to Fresno's car?

Johnson is, of course, liable for his own negligence. Because Johnson was an employee of Racehorse and because he injured another while driving the automobile on company business, Johnson was within the scope of his employment, making Racehorse Delivery also liable. Although Fresno can sue both Johnson and Racehorse, she will collect her actual damages only once; she will not receive twice that amount.

Many state and federal employment laws apply to employer–employee relationships. These laws cover such issues as Social Security, withholding of income taxes, workers' compensation benefits, unemployment compensation, workplace safety laws, employment discrimination, unionization, and the like. These laws do not apply to employer–independent contractor relationships, discussed next.

CONTRACTING EMPLOYER–INDEPENDENT CONTRACTOR

Independent contractors are not ordinary employees; they are engaged to accomplish some task, such as to build a warehouse. The party who contracts for their service has little control over how the job specified in the service contract is performed. The *Restatement of Agency* 2d § 2 defines an independent contractor as

> [A] person who contracts with another to do something for him but who is not controlled by the other nor subject to the other's right to control with respect to his physical conduct in the performance of the undertaking. He may or may not be an agent.

If someone is an independent contractor rather than an employee, then the doctrine of *respondeat superior* does not apply, certain tax obligations of the employer do not arise, and obligations under various employment laws such as the Civil Rights Act of 1964 do not arise.* In determining whether someone is an employee or an independent contractor, the following questions are important:

- **What control does the employer exercise over the details of the work?** Little or no control suggests the worker is an independent contractor.

independent contractor

A person who is hired to do a specific job, and who retains control over how that job is done.

---

* Thus, when interviewing lawyers or real estate agents who are to be hired, a prospective client can ask questions that would not be permissible if directed to candidate employees. "Are you married?" "Have you been arrested?" "Are you a Democrat?" "Do you believe in equality of the sexes?" "Do you contribute to the ACLU (American Civil Liberties Union)?" would all be legal questions to ask. Furthermore, the hiring principal could discriminate for or against candidates based on the answers to those questions. Interestingly, candidates to be engaged as independent contractors rarely even submit résumés to their prospective principals.

- **Does the employed person work in an occupation or business distinct from that of the employer?** A different business suggests an independent contractor.
- **Is the work usually done under the employer's direction, or by an unsupervised specialist?** Little or no supervision suggests an independent contractor.
- **Does the employer supply tools or equipment required at the place of work?** Not supplying tools or equipment suggests an independent contractor.
- **How long is the period of employment?** The shorter the period, the more likely that the employed person is an independent contractor.
- **What is the method of payment—by time period or upon completion of the job?** Payment upon completion suggests an independent contractor.
- **What degree of skill is required of the person employed?** A high degree of skill suggests an independent contractor.

How the employer or employed person for that matter refers to the relationship is not determinative or even particularly important. In other words, calling someone an independent contractor does not make that person an independent contractor. Building contractors and their subcontractors are examples of independent contractors. A property owner does not control the specific way in which either of these professionals performs the work. Truck drivers who own their equipment and hire out on an *ad hoc* basis are independent contractors. However, truck drivers who drive company trucks are usually ordinary employees. Collection agents and real estate brokers are usually independent contractors when hired to collect a debt for a business or sell a house for a homeowner. They are also employees for the collection agency and the real estate company unless the business is a sole proprietorship.

The relationship between a contracting employer and an independent contractor also may or may not be an agency relationship. Attorneys are often independent contractors who advise their clients and who also act as agents when they negotiate contracts on behalf of their clients with third parties.

The fact that the contracting employer has little or no control over the way in which the independent contractor does his or her work emphasizes the responsibility of the independent contractor to perform that work competently, although not as fiduciaries.

Yellow page community directories list many such independent contractors, from accountants to locksmiths to word-processing specialists. Many operate sizable firms, and employ their own staffs of ordinary employees and agents. What is their appeal? Usually they are experts in their specialized fields, and they perform jobs (such as painting houses) that are required only occasionally by the persons who employ them. An employer who hires independent contractors is relieved of the burdens of hiring and maintaining such specialists in a permanent workforce. Eliminated also are troublesome and costly chores of record keeping, payment of wages and workers' compensation insurance premiums, and the provision of fringe benefits such as medical insurance. However, as noted below, the relationship can be misused. The nature of the relationship is ultimately determined by its legal characteristics, not how the parties designate it. In other words, as stated above, simply being called an independent contractor does not necessarily make one an independent contractor. The relationship may instead really be an employer-ordinary employee relationship with its attendant consequences.

http://

The IRS rules for determining independent contractor status can be found at

http://www.irs.gov/pub/irs-pdf/p1976.pdf

LEGAL FOCUS—BACKGROUND

In 1989 the General Accounting Office estimated that the U.S. government was losing between $1.6 billion and $8 billion annually because some employers failed to withhold taxes from paychecks of ordinary employees who were improperly classified as independent contractors. Construction companies were major offenders. Legally, when the employer controls the location, the hours, and the quality of work, the individuals are in fact ordinary employees, and the employer must withhold and transmit their income and Social Security taxes.[11]

http://

Questions about hiring household workers are answered by HomeWork Solutions, Inc.:

http://www.4nannytaxes .com/faq.htm

In the early months of President Clinton's first term, another employee tax problem surfaced when it was determined that certain prospective presidential appointees had failed to pay Social Security taxes for their domestic help, presumably because of ignorance of the complex applicable law. Further investigation disclosed that the practice was widespread. It was estimated that three-quarters of all household employers had failed to pay applicable Social Security and Medicare taxes. The law passed in 1950 required such payments for domestic workers who earned more than $50 in a three-month period, or more than $200 in a year. In 1994, Congress approved a new "nanny tax" law that permits affected employers to pay their household employees' Social Security taxes as part of their own annual 1040 income tax returns, rather than file separate quarterly reports as in the past. The tax is payable on any domestic helper's wages that currently exceed $1,300 a year, which is substantially more than the former threshold of $50 a quarter.[12]

Is There a Constitutional Right to Work?

Do you have a constitutional right to work for pay? The answer is no. The U.S. Constitution does not recognize any right to work for pay. In 1946, however, Congress enacted the Employment Act, which was a philosophical commitment to provide full employment by "all practical means" for persons who are able, willing, and seeking to work. Initially, these practical means included a federal job-finding program under the leadership of the U.S. Training and Employment Service; the gathering and interpreting of economic data; the advising of the president and Congress via the Council of Economic Advisers; and the strategic use of the fiscal weapons of federal taxing and spending, as well as the federal monetary weapons of controlling the supply of money and credit through actions of the Federal Reserve Board of Governors.*

The United States has never achieved 100 percent employment. The reasons are numerous. Federal Reserve measures are limited in their accuracy and effectiveness. Some jobs are seasonal, as in farming and professional sports. Also, every year thousands of high school and college graduates attempt to enter into, and must be absorbed by, the full-time job market. Additionally, the supply and demand for products and services are in a constant state of flux in our competitive business world, and countless variables affect the nation's economy. A theory, which has gained support in recent years, is that there is, in fact, a natural and unavoidable rate of unemployment.†

---

* Controls available to the Federal Reserve Board of Governors include (1) changing the discount rate (interest) charged to member banks when they exchange promissory notes for cash (a lower rate releases more money into the economy), (2) buying or selling U.S. government securities (buying them from member banks releases more money into the economy), and (3) increasing or decreasing the reserves that member banks must maintain (lowering the reserves releases more money into the economy).

† This theory is advanced by Edmund Phelps in his book *Structural Slumps: The Modern Equilibrium Theory of Unemployment, Interest, and Assets* (Cambridge, MA: Harvard University Press, 1994). Phelps refers to a rate below which unemployment cannot fall without causing the economy to "overheat" with higher prices. That, in turn, brings on adjustments or corrections in the economy. These then push unemployment back up again.

LEGAL FOCUS—PROBLEM

Laura Lanier was pleased and honored when she was discharged from the U.S. Army, but now she needed a job in the private sector and could not find one. She heard that her state had enacted a "right-to-work" law, and so she went to a state employment office, described her skills as a truck driver, and demanded a job. "It's my legal right," she said. Must she be employed?

No. *Right-to-work laws,* which have been enacted in 21 states,* in no way guarantee every able and willing person a job. The term was coined to gain voter support for legislation outlawing union shops (discussed later in this chapter). Many believe that such laws are actually designed to weaken unions rather than to protect jobs or an authentic right to work. In states with right-to-work laws, a worker is not obligated to join or to pay dues to a union in order to get or keep a job. Note, however, that even in states without such laws, most workers do not belong to unions. In the preceding situation, Lanier, as a veteran, may legally be given preferential treatment in competition with non-veterans for federal civil service jobs. (Many states and local governments allow some such bonus.) Thus, five points may be added to a veteran's score on qualifying tests for federal jobs, and ten points may be added if the applicant has a service-connected disability and was disabled while in uniform.

Laws Against Discrimination

LEGAL FOCUS—PROBLEM

Employees in G. R. Coleman's machine shop in a small New England town reflected the social makeup of the community. All were white, Anglo-American, Protestant, male, and highly skilled. Coleman was proud of his business and its products, and he ascribed much of its success to the homogeneity of the workforce. He therefore refused to hire Samara Fuguady when she applied for work in the mechanical drafting department. A native of southern Egypt, she was a naturalized American citizen, had extremely dark skin, and was a practicing Muslim. Fuguady had ten years of experience and excellent references. "It's not that I'm prejudiced," Coleman said, "but your presence would be disruptive and no one would be happy—least of all you." Is Coleman within his legal rights in refusing to hire Fuguady?

Civil Rights Act of 1964

Federal law (specifically Title VII) that makes it unlawful for employers of fifteen or more persons, engaged in interstate commerce, to discriminate with respect to employment against any individual because of such person's race, color, religion, sex, or national origin.

No. The **Civil Rights Act of 1964 (Title VII)** makes it unlawful for an employer "to fail or refuse to hire or to discharge any individual, or otherwise to discriminate against any individual, with respect to compensation, terms, conditions, or privileges of employment because of such individual's race, color, religion, sex, or national origin."[13] A group of peo-

---

* Alabama, Arizona, Arkansas, Florida, Georgia, Idaho, Iowa, Kansas, Louisiana, Mississippi, Nebraska, Nevada, North Carolina, North Dakota, South Carolina, South Dakota, Tennessee, Texas, Utah, Virginia, and Wyoming.

ple defined by one or more of these criteria (race, color, gender, national origin, or religion) are referred to as a **protected class.** Coleman is using color, national origin, gender, and/or religion as a reason to not hire Fuguady—a clear case of illegal discrimination.

Title VII covers all employers and labor unions affecting interstate commerce with 15 or more workers, and all employment agencies. It applies to all state and local governments. A special section of the law forbids discrimination in most federal government employment. Many states have passed legislation prohibiting discrimination among employers with fewer than fifteen employees. Discrimination is prohibited whether intentional or unintentional. To deal with the variety of complaints of discriminatory treatment the following typology has evolved.

TYPES OF DISCRIMINATION

- **Disparate treatment** is intentional discrimination, and it may be proved by either direct or circumstantial evidence. "The employer simply treats some people less favorably than others because of their race, color, religion, sex, or national origin. Proof of discriminatory motive is critical, although it can in some cases be inferred from the mere fact of differences of treatment."[14]
- **Disparate impact** discrimination occurs when an employer uses a rule or practice that although appearing neutral adversely affects or excludes a protected group. "If the inquiry in a disparate treatment case focuses upon the existence of discriminatory intent, the inquiry in a disparate impact case is generally directed toward the business justification for the disputed employment test or practice."[15]

Under Title VII, as amended, discrimination in employment practices is permitted only if in conformance with a bona fide (1) pre-act seniority system, (2) merit system, (3) system that measures earnings by quantity or quality of production, or (4) system that is based on the results of a professionally developed ability test (or criteria) not designed or intended to discriminate on any of the barred bases, provided that the test is *job-related,* meaning that persons who do well on the test do well on the job, and vice-versa.

To win a case, a plaintiff generally needs to satisfy three steps:
1. The plaintiff must prove a *prima facie* (on its face) case of discrimination.
2. The burden then shifts to the defendant to show some legitimate, nondiscriminatory reason for the employee's treatment or that its impact is a business necessity for the test or practice.
3. If a legitimate reason is shown, the plaintiff can counter that the reasons offered by the defendant were not the true reasons for the employer actions, but were pretext for discrimination.[16]

Remedies available to a successful plaintiff include reinstatement or hiring or front pay (future lost earnings for one not rehired), a court order to eliminate discriminatory practices, and a restoration of lost wages and damages. Although punitive damages are available, there is a statutory cap on total damages based on the number of employees working for the employer ($300,000 maximum for an employer of 500 employees). The prevailing plaintiff in a Title VII action is ordinarily entitled to recover attorney's fees and costs.[17] A prevailing defendant also can claim attorney fees and costs, but "a plaintiff should not be assessed his opponent's attorney's fees unless the court finds that his claim was frivolous, unreasonable, or groundless, or that the plaintiff continued to litigate after it clearly became so."[18]

protected class

A classification of persons defined by one or more of these criteria: race, color, gender, national origin, age, or religion.

disparate treatment

Less favorable treatment on the basis of race, color, religion, gender, age, or national origin.

disparate impact

An ostensibly neutral employment criterion that has an adverse discriminatory impact upon a protected group.

http://

Fill in the hiring statistics to find statistical information about hiring practices for purposes of disparate impact

http://www.hr-software.net/ EmploymentStatistics/ DisparateImpact.htm

http://

All the information you wish to know about the EEOC is at its Web site at
http://www.eeoc.gov/

THE ROLE OF THE EEOC

Congress made important amendments to the Civil Rights Act of 1964 with the Equal Employment Opportunity Act of 1972. For the first time, the federal Equal Employment Opportunity Commission (EEOC) was given power to bring civil actions itself to eliminate violations of the law. Formerly, it had to rely on informal methods, such as conferences and conciliation, which an employer could ignore.* The individual victim often was unwilling or financially unable to take the grievance to court. Government was also added as a covered employer.

Title VII charges must generally be filed with the EEOC within 180 days of the alleged discriminatory act. In states or localities where there is an antidiscrimination law and an agency authorized to grant or seek relief, a charge may be presented to that state or local agency instead of to the EEOC (the time requirements may differ). Strict time frames govern filing charges of employment discrimination: failure to file timely undermines the ability of the EEOC to act and may terminate an injured victim's right to file a private lawsuit. Filing a complaint with the EEOC or appropriate state equivalent and complying with EEOC rules is required before filing a private lawsuit.

LEGAL FOCUS—PROBLEM

Hazel Mortensen believed the promotion given Jack Hall should be hers. There are no high-ranking female executives in her company and she thinks the reason is a systematic preference for males in executive positions. If she were right, this would be a violation of law. Mortensen was thinking about filing a lawsuit against her employer, but her employment contract contained an arbitration clause. Assuming the arbitration clause is fair and enforceable can the EEOC bring an action against the company on Hazel's behalf or is arbitration her sole way to enforce the law?

http://

The Department of Labor's "Employment Law Guide" with laws, regulations, and technical assistance services can be found at
http://www.dol.gov/asp/ programs/guide.htm

The EEOC can still bring the action in its own name and recover damages on behalf of someone subject to illegal discrimination in violation of the Civil Rights Act.[19] "[T]he EEOC is authorized to bring suit in its own name and . . . the EEOC has the prerogative, as a federal enforcement agency, to decide what relief is appropriately sought in a particular action brought by the EEOC. The Supreme Court rejected the argument that the EEOC is a mere proxy for the individuals for whom it seeks relief in its actions, ruling that the EEOC is the 'master of its own case' and can decide to bring a claim for monetary damages in court, even though the individual for whom the EEOC seeks relief would be required to pursue his or her own claim in arbitration."[20]

RACE AND COLOR DISCRIMINATION

A company's standards, policies, or practices for selecting or promoting employees are illegal if they discriminate on the basis of race or color. Discrimination in employment conditions and benefits are also illegal. For example, an employer cannot grant higher Christmas bonuses to whites than to blacks.

---

* The authors of this text are proponents of alternative dispute resolution, such as mediation and conciliation, but acknowledge that adversary alternatives such as lawsuits are necessary if ADR does not work. This is particularly true in situations with significant power imbalances.

LEGAL FOCUS—CASE

Julie Deffenbaugh, a white manager of the jewelry department at Wal-Mart in Arlington, Texas, began dating Truce Williams, a black sales associate in another department. The store manager saw them together after work, obviously as a couple. The store manager told Deffenbaugh that she "would never move up with the company being associated with a black man and that Wal-Mart frowned upon fraternization with[in] the company." Deffenbaugh responded that her personal business was not the company's concern, "because it did not affect [her] job performance." Later her supervisor fired her, purportedly for shopping while on company time. Prior to the discovery of the interracial relationship, Deffenbaugh's employment record was spotless. Deffenbaugh sued Wal-Mart, claiming that she was discharged because she was dating a black male. Wal-Mart claimed that Deffenbaugh was not a member of a protected class because she was white and could not sue on the basis of Title VII. What was the result?

Deffenbaugh-Williams v. Wal-Mart, Inc., 156 F.3d 58 (5th Cir., 1998).

Deffenbaugh's jury verdict of $19,000 in compensatory damages was upheld, and a punitive damage award of $75,000 was allowed. Title VII prohibits discrimination in employment premised on an interracial relationship. "A reasonable juror could find that Deffenbaugh was discriminated against because of her race (white), if that discrimination was premised on the fact that she, a white person, had a relationship with a black person." A more complicated case and one more representative of the type of discrimination that African-Americans have been subjected to is the case of *Roberts v. Texaco*. In 1996 this case, which involved the revelation of audiotapes featuring Texaco executives discussing the hiding of evidence and speaking of blacks in a disparaging way, made headlines nationwide. The case was settled for $176.1 million.[21] The Texaco settlement was bypassed three years later when Coca-Cola agreed to pay the highest amount in history to settle a racial-discrimination lawsuit. They agreed to pay $192.5 million including about $40,000 apiece to former and current black employees. "The lawsuit, filed in April 1999, accused Coke of erecting a corporate hierarchy in which black employees were clustered at the bottom of the pay scale, averaging $26,000 a year less than white workers."[22]

A leading U.S. Supreme Court case unanimously held that it is a violation of the Civil Rights Act of 1964 for an employer to require a high school diploma and a passing score on a general intelligence test for employment or promotion when neither can be demonstrably related to job performance.[23] This finding of disparate impact discrimination opened the door to some minority and non-minority members who lack the benefit of high school education but are willing and capable workers. Moreover, the Court held that employment and personnel management practices, procedures, or tests neutral on their face and even neutral in terms of intent are not maintainable if they operate to "freeze" the status quo of prior discriminatory employment practices. Thus, disparate hiring of relatively few women or minorities is illegal unless truly necessitated by lawful business purposes or requirements.

It does not matter whether or not an employer intends to discriminate in its hiring practices. If the requirements for employment operate to exclude minority groups and are unrelated to job performance, the requirements violate Title VII.[24] The would-be employee need prove that the employer's policy has a disparate impact on qualified women or minorities in the particular workforce (*not* in the much wider labor market). To overcome these

http://

Garland's Digest on Employment Discrimination Law can be found at **http://www.garlands-digest.com/sample/recentcases.html**

facts, the employer must then prove that the practice is required by business necessity and is essential for the job, a heavy burden of proof.[25] The employer, however, is not compelled to hire and promote to meet specified quotas under 1991 amendments.

NATIONAL-ORIGIN DISCRIMINATION

It is unlawful under Title VII to discriminate against any employee or applicant on the basis of national origin. National origin includes birthplace, ancestry, culture, and linguistic characteristics common to a specific ethnic group. The Immigration Reform and Control Act of 1986 (IRCA)[26] also prohibits discrimination based on citizenship. The IRCA covers employers of four or more employees and proscribes discrimination against any person (other than an unauthorized alien) in hiring, discharge, or recruiting or referring for a fee because of national origin or citizenship status.*

LEGAL FOCUS—PROBLEM

Kwame Maafo, a Ghanaian-born black man, was employed in the laundry at Rivercity Resort Hotel. He made several unsuccessful attempts to transfer to the accounting department. Maafo had completed high school in Ghana and studied business at several universities in the United Kingdom. After emigrating to the United States, he also took classes at two community colleges and completed 30 units at State University in pursuit of a bachelor's degree in finance. Rivercity told Maafo that his accent was a barrier to all positions in the accounting department. Maafo filed a discrimination claim. Is an accent sufficient reason to deny Maafo the transfer?

In order to succeed with a defense based on accent and English usage, Rivercity must show that Maafo's accent or manner of speaking would have a detrimental effect on job performance (that clear enunciation was a requisite job requirement and Maafo did not meet that requirement). A legitimate nondiscriminatory reason to not hire the applicant must be shown. In the case upon which this hypothetical is based, the court found that the plaintiff "speaks fluent, understandable English. His speech was clear and understandable during a whole day on the witness stand during which he underwent probing cross-examination." The hotel lost the case.[27]

Whereas discrimination against a person on the basis of national origin is illegal, it is also illegal to hire an alien who is not authorized to work in the U.S. All employers (agricultural and nonagricultural) are prohibited from knowingly employing aliens not legally entitled to work in the U.S. The definition of "knowingly hiring" has been greatly expanded in recent years. The applicable law now states: "Knowing is defined as including not only actual knowledge, but also constructive knowledge—knowledge which may fairly be inferred through notice of certain facts and certain circumstances which would lead a person, through the exercise of reasonable care, to know about certain conditions."

In the aftermath of the September 11, 2001, bombings, individuals of Middle Eastern or Asian descent (and some seen by others as similar in appearance) have been subject to

---

* While the IRCA prohibits discrimination on the basis of citizenship, it also requires verification of legal status of all workers. Employers are required to check workers' documents to confirm the identity and work eligibility of all persons hired. The U.S. Immigration and Naturalization Service (INS) requires employers to (1) hire only those persons authorized to work in the United States, (2) ask all new employees to show documents that establish both identity and work authorization, and (3) complete the INS Employment Eligibility Verification Form I-9 for every new employee—U.S. citizens and noncitizens alike.

various forms of backlash. Most of the reported situations that have made the national newscasts have not involved employment, but the Civil Rights Act applies to many discrimination situations including racial profiling. In June 2002 the ACLU and the American-Arab Anti-Discrimination Committee filed lawsuits claiming discrimination on the basis of appearance and national origin on behalf of five plaintiffs who were trying to take airline flights. One of the plaintiffs is a native of Guyana; check your world maps for how close Guyana is to the Middle East or Asia.

LEGAL FOCUS—BACKGROUND

Four civil rights lawsuits filed across the country today accuse American, Continental, Northwest, and United Airlines of blatant discrimination against five men who were ejected from flights based on the prejudices of airline employees and passengers and for reasons wholly unrelated to security. Four of the passengers are United States citizens and the fifth is a permanent legal resident; two of the five are of Arab descent. Michael Dasrath, 32, a U.S. citizen born in Guyana, had taken his seat in first class when he noticed a woman glaring at him and several other passengers seated nearby. He heard her tell the captain, "Those brown-skinned men are behaving suspiciously." Moments later, he, Edgardo Cureg (a permanent legal resident of Filipino descent), and another man were removed from the plane. "I was working in Manhattan on September 11 and I will never forget the horror of that day," said Dasrath. "But ejecting me from a flight to make a passenger feel better isn't going to make anyone any safer."[28]

RELIGIOUS DISCRIMINATION

Title VII prohibits employers from discriminating on the basis of an employee's religious beliefs. Prohibited discrimination may be overt and blatant or a more subtle failure to reasonably accommodate an employee's religious beliefs. The plaintiff must establish four elements of a *prima facie* case of discrimination: "(1) he is a member of or practices a particular religion; (2) he is qualified to perform the job at issue; (3) he has suffered some adverse employment action; and (4) someone outside the protected class of which he is a member was treated differently."[29] Plaintiff must show that he possessed a bona fide religious belief that was not reasonably accommodated.

LEGAL FOCUS—CASE

Officer Angelo Rodriguez, a patrol officer in the Chicago Police Department (CPD), was among those assigned to guard an abortion clinic during various demonstrations. A life-long Roman Catholic, Officer Rodriguez believed clinic activities to be wrongful, and he requested that he not be assigned to guard the clinic. Rodriguez was offered a transfer to a district without an abortion clinic, but he refused. Thereupon, CPD refused to exempt Rodriguez from the duty, claiming department policy prohibited an officer from refusing any assignment. Must the employer agree not to assign Officer Rodriguez to such duty as an accommodation to his religion?

Rodriguez v. Chicago, 156 F.3d 771 (7th Cir., 1998).

The court held for the Chicago Police Department. "Because the CPD provided Officer Rodriguez with the option of transferring to a district without an abortion clinic and such a transfer would have eliminated the conflict between his job responsibilities and his religious beliefs, we conclude that the City has satisfied its duty of reasonable accommodation under Title VII."

LEGAL FOCUS—PROBLEM

The Blessed Mary Catholic Hospital hired Kobe Jackson to work as a lab technician. Some time after Jackson was hired he became a born-again Christian. He then began to supplement the blood and urine tests he administered to patients with attempts to convert them to his view of Protestant Christianity. Hospital administrators asked him to stop but he kept on spreading his message. He was fired. Can he claim protection under the Civil Rights Act for religious discrimination?

The Civil Rights Act requires employers to reasonably accommodate employees but does not require any and all accommodations. The accommodation need not be what the employee demands, and it need not be the least burdensome one to the employee.[30] The Blessed Mary Catholic Hospital has a right to restrict Jackson's behavior on the job and perhaps even his on-site activities during his break or lunch time.[31] When he refused his instructions the hospital was within its legal rights to fire him. In particular a religious institution can discriminate by hiring only members of its own religion even for secular (not religious) positions (e.g., receptionist or gardener). The religious institution can also discriminate on the basis of conduct or views inconsistent with a religion's tenets and teachings.

GENDER DISCRIMINATION

The Equal Employment Opportunity Act of 1972 (EEOA), amending the Civil Rights Act of 1964, dramatically changed employment law relating to women. Before 1972, state law often prohibited the employment of women in certain jobs ostensibly for their own protection. For example, many state statutes barred women from working at night, working as a bartender, or working more than a certain number of hours per day or week. The EEOA struck down most of these limiting laws. Employers are forbidden to classify jobs as male or female and they cannot have separate male and female seniority lists.

LEGAL FOCUS—BACKGROUND

Some 115 female flight attendants brought a class action suit against Pan American World Airways, Inc., in 1984. The women had been suspended, denied promotion, or fired for being overweight. The airline had used different tables of heights and weights, classifying men under the heading of "large frames" and women under "medium frames." The difference between the two sexes was 11 pounds for a person 5'7" tall. Did the corporation's standards discriminate illegally against women?

Yes. The federal district court in San Francisco found the weight standards discriminatory against the female employees, while reserving the issue of damages for later determination.

Pan American began an appeal, but dropped it in 1989. Without admitting bias, it agreed to pay the attendants $2.35 million. It also adopted a more flexible weight policy with a new "large frame" category for women. Under it, a 5'7" woman of medium frame should weigh 139 pounds; for a 5'7" woman with a large frame, the acceptable weight could be as much as 150 pounds. Moreover, the attendant could add up to three pounds upon reaching the age of thirty-five, and again at ages forty-five and fifty-five.[32]

A defense to a sex discrimination case is the existence of a **bona fide occupational qualification (BFOQ).** A BFOQ is a job requirement that, although discriminatory, is essential to the job in question. The BFOQ defense is available for gender, age, religion, and national origin discrimination but never for discrimination based on race or color.

bona fide occupational qualifications (BFOQ)

Selection criteria that serve a legitimate business interest, which is justified although it has a disparate impact.

LEGAL FOCUS—CASE

Four male corrections officers at the Women's Community Correctional Center (WCCC) on the Island of Oahu filed a Title VII sexual discrimination claim after the WCCC assigned only female correction officers to six of forty-one available watch posts. The WCCC claimed that gender was a BFOQ because the protested watch sites were shower and toilet areas and the purpose of the restriction was to protect female inmates and to prevent allegations of sexual misconduct. Is gender a BFOQ in this case?

Robino v. Iranon, 145 F.3d 1109 (9th Cir., 1998).

The court said yes. "Each designated female-only post is residential and requires the ACO [Adult Corrections Officer] on duty to observe the inmates in the showers and toilet areas for the prison's own security or provides unsupervised access to the inmates. The state's legitimate penology interests outweigh whatever interests the male ACOs may have in standing the watches of their choice. Viewing the evidence in the light most favorable to the plaintiffs, the defendants have met their burden of demonstrating that their policy is reasonably necessary to the operation of the WCCC. The defendants have established these six female-only posts are a reasonable response to the concerns about inmate privacy and allegations of abuse by male ACOs."

The following case illustrates how the well-intended protection of one group can hurt another.

LEGAL FOCUS—CASE

Johnson Controls, Inc., of Milwaukee, produces batteries. The manufacturing process exposes workers to levels of airborne lead considered harmful to a fetus and may cause birth defects. In 1982, Johnson instituted a program banning women from all jobs in the division where the airborne lead level was 25 micrograms per cubic meter or higher, unless they presented a doctor's certificate of sterility. It also barred women from jobs where the lead level was below 25 micrograms if the jobs could lead to promotion to more dangerous areas. Female employees working in the lead division were transferred to other divisions without loss of pay or seniority. The United Auto Workers union claimed that this was illegal sex discrimination and filed a complaint with the Equal Employment Opportunity Commission on behalf of seven involuntarily transferred women. A federal civil rights suit followed, and the district judge awarded summary judgment to Johnson Controls without trial, although a 1982 amendment to Title VII (the Pregnancy Discrimination Act) declared that "women affected by pregnancy or childbirth . . . shall be treated the same for all employment related purposes . . . as other persons not so affected but similar in their ability or inability to work." The UAW appealed. What was the outcome?

United Autoworkers v. Johnson Controls, Inc., 499 U.S. 187, 111 S.Ct. 1196 (1991).

The U.S. Supreme Court reversed the trial court, stating, "The PDA's (Pregnancy Discrimination Act) amendment to Title VII contains a BFOQ standard of its own: unless pregnant employees differ from others in their ability or inability to work, they must be treated the same as other employees. . . . Title VII and the PDA simply do not allow a woman's dismissal because of her failure to submit to sterilization."

Sexual Harassment

Sexual harassment in the workplace is a form of illegal gender discrimination that has garnered much publicity in recent years. Sexual harassment, a type of Title VII violation, occurs when job opportunities, promotions, and the like are given on the basis of sexual favors. Harassment also occurs when an employee is subjected to a work environment where the employee must put up with sexual comments, jokes, or physical contact that is sexually offensive.

The EEOC has defined two types of sexual harassment in its guidelines:
1. *Quid pro quo.* "Unwelcome sexual advances, requests for sexual favors, and other verbal or physical conduct of a sexual nature constitute 'quid pro quo' sexual harassment when (1) submission to such conduct is made either explicitly or implicitly a term or condition of an individual's employment, or (2) submission to or rejection of such conduct by an individual is used as the basis for employment decisions affecting such individual." This form of harassment usually involves a supervisor/subordinate relationship because it requires the authority to grant an employee help in return for the unwelcome advance or punishment for the lack of cooperation.
2. **Hostile environment.** Conduct in a hostile environment "has the purpose or effect of unreasonably interfering with an individual's work performance or creating an intimidating, hostile, or offensive working environment." The EEOC considers several factors to determine whether a hostile environment exists for either gender: "(1) whether the conduct was verbal or physical or both; (2) how frequently it was repeated; (3) whether the conduct was hostile or patently offensive; (4) whether the alleged harasser was a coworker or supervisor; (5) whether others joined in perpetrating the harassment; and (6) whether the harassment was directed at more than one individual. No one factor controls. An assessment is made based upon the totality of the circumstances."[33]

LEGAL FOCUS—CASE

Rena Weeks began work as Martin Greenstein's secretary on July 23, 1991. Greenstein was a partner at Baker & McKenzie, the world's largest law firm. "On August 8, the Thursday of her third week at the firm, Weeks had lunch with several persons, including Greenstein, at a local restaurant. As they left the restaurant, Greenstein gave her some M & M candies, which she put into the breast pocket of her blouse. As they walked to Greenstein's car,

http://

The law firm of Morgan, Lewis and Bockius, with offices in several states and countries, provides a newsletter with brief well-written discussions of current trends in employment law

http://www.morganlewis.com/

sexual harassment

A form of illegal gender discrimination wherein (1) job opportunities, promotions, and the like are given on the basis of sexual favors or (2) the employee is subjected to a work environment where the employee must put up with sexual comments, jokes, or physical contact that is sexually offensive.

quid pro quo

(Latin: "something for something") Expression used in sexual harassment situations when sexual favors or demands are a term or condition of an individual's employment, or the basis for employment decisions affecting such individual.

hostile environment

Conduct by others in the workplace that has the purpose or effect of unreasonably interfering with an individual's work performance or creating an intimidating, hostile, or offensive working environment.

Greenstein pulled Weeks back, put his arm over her shoulder, put his hand in her breast pocket and dropped more candies into the pocket. He then put his knee in her lower back, pulled her shoulders back, and said, 'Let's see which breast is bigger.'" Is this behavior actionable sexual harassment for Greenstein and his employer, Baker & McKenzie?

Weeks v. Baker & McKenzie, 63 Cal. App. 4th 1128, 74 Cal. Rptr. 2d 510 (California, 1998).

A San Francisco jury said yes, awarding Weeks $50,000 in compensatory damages. They said yes to this jury instruction: "Has plaintiff Rena Weeks proved by clear and convincing evidence that defendant Baker & McKenzie (a) had advance knowledge of the unfitness of defendant Martin R. Greenstein and with a conscious disregard of the rights or safety of others continued to employ him, or (b) ratified the conduct of Mr. Greenstein which is found to be oppression or malice?" The jury awarded Weeks $7.1 million in total punitive damages.* The trial court judge reduced the punitive damage award to $3.5 million, an amount later upheld on appeal. In upholding the punitive damage award against Baker & McKenzie, the court stated, "In all events, there is substantial evidence that at the time Weeks was hired, Baker & McKenzie and its relevant managing agents were well aware that Greenstein was likely to create a hostile work environment for women, and that Baker & McKenzie consistently failed to take measures reasonably designed to protect women from Greenstein's abuse. The failure to place reports of Greenstein's misconduct in his own personnel file so as to warn future supervisors of that conduct in and of itself demonstrates a conscious disregard for the rights and safety of other employees. No formal action was taken by the firm to prevent Greenstein from creating a hostile work environment."[34]

Treating people in a nondiscriminatory fashion is clearly a laudable goal, but difficulty among people of good will can still arise. An employee wrongfully accused of discriminatory treatment may be discharged without a full and accurate investigation in order to protect the employer from sexual harassment claims.[35] Except in limited circumstances, the wrongfully accused employee has no legal recourse.†

The risk and complexity of civil rights lawsuits leads defendants to settle cases out of court. In 1992, State Farm Insurance settled a class action sex-discrimination lawsuit for $157 million to be paid to 814 women plaintiffs. The federal district court had previously ruled that State Farm had engaged in discriminatory practices. The court approved an agreement between State Farm and aggrieved employees whereby the company agreed that for the next ten years at least 50 percent of all sales agents hired would be women, to help remedy past violations. This affirmative action remedy was based on evidence of discriminatory practices that had occurred between 1970 and 1974, a period during which State Farm had hired 586 agents in California, but only one was a woman. Many women had applied for positions, but had been rejected. One of the witnesses who worked as an insurance agent's assistant testified that when she applied for a sales agent job, she was told that a college degree was a prerequisite. Yet at that time State Farm was hiring male sales agents who did not have college degrees. Later she was told that State Farm would not hire women as agents. At the time this settlement was the largest in the history of civil rights litigation for any type of discrimination. Divided by the number of plaintiffs, however, the average award shrank to $19,287.

---

* A discerning reader might note that the damage total in this case exceeds the maximum provided under Title VII of the Civil Rights Act. Rather than filed as a Title VII case, it was pled under the California Civil Rights Law, which lacks the federal damage limitation. The Fair Employment and Housing Act (FEHA) Gov. Code, § 129000 et seq.

† Employees protected by a just cause provision of a labor contract are among those with some protection. In union contracts, issues of employee discipline including discharge usually provide for a grievance mechanism, which culminates in a neutral arbitration. In the usual labor contract, an arbitrator decides if the employee was a harasser and if discipline is consistent with fair treatment under the contract.

LEGAL FOCUS—CASE

Joseph Oncale worked as a roustabout for Sundowner Offshore Services on an oil plat-form in the Gulf of Mexico. On several occasions, he was forcibly subjected to sex-related, humiliating actions against him by three of his eight-man crew in front of the others. Two of the employees, Danny Pippen and John Lyons, also "physically assaulted Oncale in a sexual manner, and Lyons threatened him with rape." Oncale complained to a supervisor but no help was forthcoming. Oncale quit and then filed a complaint against Sundowner alleging that he was discriminated against in his employment because of his sex, forcing him to resign. Is same-sex sexual harassment a form of discrimination protected by Title VII of the Civil Rights Act?

Joseph Oncale v. Sundowner Offshore Services, Incorporated, et al., 523 U.S. 75, 118 S.Ct. 998 (1998).

Yes. Title VII's prohibition of discrimination "because of . . . sex" protects men as well as women[36] but the Oncale case raised a different issue because the alleged harassment was same-gender in this case male on male. The court found that distinction unimportant. "We see no justification in the statutory language or our precedents for a categorical rule excluding same-sex harassment claims from the coverage of Title VII. As some courts have observed, male-on-male sexual harassment in the workplace was assuredly not the principal evil Congress was concerned with when it enacted Title VII. But statutory pro-hibitions often go beyond the principal evil to cover reasonably comparable evils, and it is ultimately the provisions of our laws rather than the principal concerns of our legislators by which we are governed. Title VII prohibits 'discriminat[ion] . . . because of . . . sex' in the 'terms' or 'conditions' of employment."

EQUAL PAY FOR EQUAL WORK

LEGAL FOCUS—PROBLEM

Disappointed in her quest for civilian employment after leaving the Army, Laura Lanier enrolled in a private business school. Within a year, she was qualified as a computer operator. A wholesale hardware supply house hired her to work in its inventory con-trol department. Her performance and output soon equaled that of several male com-puter operators who had been with the company for periods ranging from three to ten years. All of the men were paid more than Lanier. Was this a violation of federal equal pay legislation?

No. The federal Equal Pay Act of 1963 specifically prohibits wage discrimination on the basis of gender for equal work in jobs that require equal skill, effort, and responsibility and that are performed under similar working conditions. However, the law permits inequality in pay on the basis of (1) seniority, (2) merit, (3) quality or quantity of produc-tion, or (4) any factor other than gender (e.g., a shift differential, a higher rate maintained for an employee reassigned to a lower-rate job because of "exigencies of the employer's needs," different level of responsibility, a training program, or higher sales commissions because of higher profits on goods sold). The employer must, however, act in good faith

http://

The Institute for Women's Policy Research (IWPR) is an independent, nonprofit, scientific research organization that focuses on public policy issues of importance to women, including employment, poverty and welfare, family, and health

http://www.iwpr.org/

without unlawful discrimination in assignment and evaluation of work. Thus, in Lanier's case, there was no violation if the pay differentials were based on seniority.

For a variety of reasons, certain jobs tend to be held mostly by women—and most of these jobs pay less than most jobs held by men. When different pay scales are based on differences in work performed, there is no unlawful discrimination under present laws. However, under the theory of **comparable worth,** jobs that have equal social and economic value should be paid equally. Thus, it is said, the services of a registered nurse who helps to keep you alive are worth at least as much as those of a licensed electrician who helps to provide light and power in your hospital room. The problem is that it is extremely difficult to measure with precision and fairness all the elements and variables that should determine the dollar value of different jobs at different times in different places. Presumably, the economic forces of supply and demand should automatically decide the question. Realistically, this function of the free market is distorted by such factors as traditional attitudes, long-established seniority rights, union pressures, government licensing regulations, and willingness or ability to make a commitment to long-term, full-time, career-type employment.

The Canadian province of Ontario passed a statute in 1987 designed to introduce comparable-worth standards to both government units and private companies with at least ten employees. It requires employers to define job classes by grouping positions with similar qualifications and duties that are recruited and paid in similar ways. Jobs are ranked in terms of skill, effort, responsibility, and working conditions. For each female-dominated class (60 percent or more), the employer must seek a comparably rated male class. If the women are paid less, they must get a raise. Although comparable worth has been advanced for several years as mandated under the equal pay statute, the doctrine has not been accepted in the United States courts.

The Institute for Women's Policy Research has created a composite index considering several women's issues including employment and earnings, political participation, and economic autonomy. It then ranked the various states on the criteria. The five best states in 2000 were Connecticut, Vermont, Washington, Hawaii, and Colorado. The five worst were all southern states: Mississippi, Alabama, Tennessee, Arkansas and Kentucky.[37]

AGE DISCRIMINATION

LEGAL FOCUS—PROBLEM

Harry Rockwell lost his job with the Majestic Admiral Products Corporation when he was forty-five years old. A friend told him about a similar job that had just become available in the Crescent Moon Company because of the death of the incumbent. When Rockwell applied, the personnel manager said, "You are eminently qualified for the assignment, except that you're too old. We're looking for a bright young college graduate with maybe five years of experience. We want him or her to grow with the company." Does Rockwell have any legal recourse?

Yes. Three years after the Civil Rights Act became law, Congress passed the **Age Discrimination in Employment Act of 1967 (ADEA),** which prohibits "arbitrary age discrimination in employment" of persons forty years of age and older. It makes it unlawful for an employer in interstate commerce to fail or refuse to hire or to discharge any indi-

comparable worth

The theory that the same wage or salary should be paid for jobs that have equal societal and economic value based on such factors as required preparation, skill, effort, responsibility, and working conditions.

http://

For a longer explanation of comparable worth see **http://www.payequity research.com/worth.htm**

Age Discrimination in Employment Act of 1967

Federal law that added "advanced age" (over age forty) to attributes listed in the Civil Rights Act of 1964 that may not be used negatively in employment decisions.

vidual, or otherwise to discriminate against persons with respect to compensation, term, conditions, or privileges of employment, because of age. This law also applies to employment agencies and unions. It permits discrimination when age is a bona fide occupational qualification, and it recognizes the right of companies to discipline or even discharge a person for good cause.

LEGAL FOCUS—CASE

A fifty-four-year-old plant manager who earned $15.75 an hour was temporarily laid off when the company plant was closed for the winter. When spring came, a forty-three-year-old worker who earned $8.05 per hour replaced the manager. The older manager, who had worked for the company for twenty-seven years, was not given a chance to accept a lower wage rate. Was the action of the company permissible under the ADEA?

Metz v. Transit Mix, Inc., 828 F.2d 1202 (7th Cir., 1987).

No. The court, which referred to the firm's dismissal of the manager as "industrial capital punishment," held that the manager's termination in these circumstances violated the ADEA.

The ADEA applies to "a person (including a corporation) engaged in an industry affecting commerce who has twenty or more employees for each working day in each of twenty or more calendar weeks in the current or preceding calendar year."[38] If the older manager had refused the pay reduction, the result would have been different.

An "'employee' means an individual employed by any employer except that the term 'employee' shall not include any person elected to public office in any State or political subdivision of any State by the qualified voters thereof, or any person chosen by such officer to be on such officer's personal staff, or an appointee on the policymaking level or an immediate adviser with respect to the exercise of the constitutional or legal powers of the office."[39] "The law also provides for mandatory retirement of certain executives over the age of sixty-five under certain conditions.[40]

LEGAL FOCUS—CASE

In Missouri, four judges were appointed to preside over state courts under the Missouri Non-Partisan Court Plan. They had been retained in office through elections, but became subject to mandatory retirement at the age of 70 under a provision of the Missouri State Constitution. Must they retire?

Gregory v. Ashcroft, 501 U.S. 492, 111 S.Ct. 2395 (1991).

Yes. The U.S. Supreme Court held that the judges qualified as appointees on the policymaking level because performance of their duties required "discretion concerning issues of public importance." Moreover, the Court said that if the Congress had wanted the ADEA to apply to state judges, it could have plainly said so.

The ADEA is joined by the Workers Benefit Protection Act,[41] making it illegal for a business to use a worker's past-forty age as the basis for discriminatory treatment in awarding employee benefits.

Almost all states have enacted their own laws barring employment discrimination on the basis of race, sex, religion, national origin, and advanced age. Most states call for equal pay for equal work and also follow the federal model of protecting the employment rights of handicapped persons. Also, the developing tort law of wrongful dismissal (discussed later in the chapter) sometimes protects permanent employees against arbitrary discharge without good cause.

WHAT IS MEANT BY "AFFIRMATIVE ACTION" IN EMPLOYMENT PRACTICES?

Because of many years of discrimination in employment against women and minorities, government administrators have made special efforts to provide these groups with more opportunities for gainful employment. By threatening to terminate lucrative supply and research contracts, federal government agencies have often pressured companies to adopt **affirmative action programs.** Essentially, these programs require positive efforts to hire and promote minorities and women, in percentages reflecting the makeup of the surrounding communities (sometimes referred to as the "potential applicant pool"). These efforts might include special outreach programs (recruiting), special training, and preferential hiring. Some have claimed this is **reverse discrimination** against qualified nonminority male employees and applicants. The presumption has been that such persons are better able to fend for themselves in the job market. It should be noted that Title VII neither requires nor denies affirmative action as a remedy for discriminatory practices.

No provision of Title VII provides for affirmative action; instead, it is a judicial remedy and sometimes administrative decision to correct historic discriminatory practices. Opponents of affirmative action say that the Civil Rights Act of 1964 calls for neutrality, with no discrimination for or against anyone. Proponents argue that with neutrality, corrective action might take several generations, and that is too long to correct historic discrimination.

The Supreme Court has not been as helpful as it might in determining the legality of affirmative action, perpetuating a contentious political debate over its efficacy and legality. In 1979, the Supreme Court gave its stamp of approval to a private, voluntary arrangement negotiated by the Kaiser Aluminum and Chemical Co. with the United Steelworkers Union. This program set up a skilled craft-training program with half the slots arbitrarily reserved for blacks and half for whites. At the time, although there was a 30 percent black population in the geographical area of the plant, fewer than 2 percent of the skilled craftworkers were black. Brian Weber, a white, was passed over for skilled craft training and challenged the company and union plan as discriminatory. He lost.[42] The Court's approval of this private, voluntary affirmative action plan to correct manifest racial imbalance automatically legitimized some 175,000 similar plans already in existence at that time, and others that have been added since then. Moreover, one effect was to shield such employers from charges that the plans impliedly admitted prior bias for which they could be sued.

LEGAL FOCUS—CASE

Among seven finalists seeking promotion to road dispatcher, Diane Joyce had a lower score than Paul Johnson on qualifying tests and interviews. However, as not one of the 238 job positions of the pertinent job classification was held by a woman, the employer (Transportation Agency of Santa Clara County, California) voluntarily adopted an affirmative action program and promoted Joyce to the position. Johnson claimed this violated

http://

A time line of affirmative action programs can be found at
http://www.inmotion magazine.com/aahist.html

affirmative action programs

Programs that require preference in hiring be given to some statutorily protected group.

reverse discrimination

Label given to the results of affirmative action programs by opponents who claim that such programs discriminate against male and white workers.

his rights under Title VII, and the trial court agreed. The Court of Appeals reversed, and Johnson appealed to the U.S. Supreme Court. How did it rule?

Johnson v. Transportation Agency, Santa Clara County, California, 480 U.S. 616, 107 S.Ct. 1442 (1987).

The judgment of the Court of Appeals was affirmed. The Court opined that the employer had acted reasonably in considering Joyce's gender because of "'a manifest imbalance' that reflected underrepresentation of women in 'traditionally segregated job categories.'" She was one of seven applicants, all classified as "qualified and eligible," and the agency director was authorized to promote any one of the seven. Johnson remains an employee who may seek other promotions in the future.

Amendments to Title VII in 1991 highlight the legal ambiguity of affirmative action: "Nothing in the amendments made by this Act shall be construed to require or encourage an employer to adopt hiring or promotion quotas on the basis of race, color, religion, sex or national origin: Provided, however, that nothing in the amendments made by this Act shall be construed to affect court-ordered remedies, affirmative action, or conciliation agreements that are otherwise in accordance with the law."[43] In 1996, California voters passed a constitutional amendment by initiative, Proposition 209. The key provision of the initiative is "The state shall not discriminate against, or grant preferential treatment to, any individual or group on the basis of race, sex, color, ethnicity, or national origin in the operation of public employment, public education, or public contracting." Court challenges to the initiative have been unsuccessful.[44] The effect of the initiative has been the curtailment of affirmative action programs like the one found in the preceding case.

LEGAL FOCUS—CASE

Cheryl Hopwood, a white Texas resident, applied for admission to the University of Texas School of Law, one of the nation's leading law schools. She was denied admission although her application credentials were impressive, including a 3.8 undergraduate grade-point average and a 160 score on the Law School Admissions Test (83rd percentile). She sued, claiming she was "subjected to unconstitutional racial discrimination by the law school's evaluation of [her] admissions applications." The University of Texas School of Law admissions process separated the files of black and Mexican American applicants and enrollment decisions were made separately, accepting GPA and test scores lower than Hopwood's. Was Hopwood successful in her lawsuit?

Hopwood v. Texas, 78 F.3d 932 (5th Cir., 1996) Cert. denied 518 U.S. 1033, 116 S.Ct. 2581 (1996).

Whether she was successful or not depends on what you mean by success. The Federal Court of Appeals held that the "University of Texas School of Law may not use race as a factor in deciding which applicants to admit in order to achieve a diverse student body, to combat the perceived effects of a hostile environment at the law school, to alleviate the law school's poor reputation in the minority community, or to eliminate any present effects of past discrimination by actors other than the law school." Hopwood, however, was not admitted to the school and she received only minimal damages although she was awarded attorney fees and costs. Further court proceedings found that she failed to establish by a preponderance of the evidence that she would have been offered admission to the law school under a constitutional admissions process.[45] Although the Supreme Court declined to hear an appeal of the *Hopwood* case as this edition goes to print the Supreme Court agreed to consider two University of Michigan affirmative action cases. In these cases the 6th U.S. Circuit Court of Appeals upheld the University of Michigan Law School's admissions practices allowing race and ethnicity to be considered to achieve a diverse student body.[46]

AMERICANS WITH DISABILITIES ACT

The **Americans with Disabilities Act of 1990 (ADA)** was hailed as a declaration of independence for some 43 million disabled Americans at the time of its enactment. The ADA applies to both the public and private sectors and went well beyond prior existing protective legislation at the state and federal levels. The ADA applies to practices in employment, public and private accommodations, transportation, and telecommunications facilities. Business firms and other establishments must improve access for the disabled if "readily achievable" without "undue hardship." This hardship could involve the nature and cost of the accommodation in comparison to the overall size of the firm and its financial resources.

Employers with fifteen or more employees are legally forbidden to discriminate in employment of disabled people who are capable of performing the essential functions of the job and are expected to make reasonable accommodations if necessary to allow them to do so. The ADA does not require employment of anyone who is unqualified for the job, nor does it require preferential treatment for the disabled.

Definition of Disability

Determining what is a disability deserving of legal protection and defining reasonable accommodation have been among the most difficult tasks since enactment of the ADA. The definition of disability used is very different from that used in workers' compensation, Social Security, and other laws providing benefits for persons with a determined disability. Under the ADA, an individual with a disability is a person who:

1. "has a physical or mental impairment that substantially limits one or more major life activities;
2. has a record of such an impairment; or
3. is regarded as having such an impairment."

Major life activities are activities that an average person can perform with little or no difficulty such as walking, breathing, seeing, hearing, speaking, caring for oneself, learning, and working. Title II of the ADA provides that "no qualified individual with a disability shall, by reason of such disability, be excluded from participation in or be denied the benefits of the services, programs, or activities of a public entity, or be subject to discrimination by such entity."

LEGAL FOCUS—CASE

Rock Island County Metro Link has a federally required reduced fare program that makes transportation services available at a reduced rate for persons with disabilities. The application form for this program states, "Applicants do not qualify if their sole disability is . . . AIDS. . . ." Howard Hamlyn has AIDS, which has caused him to have significant difficulty

http://

For a webcast provided by The Institute for Rehabilitation and Research on the definition of disability under the ADA go to
http://www.ilru.org/online/archive/2002/be03-20-02.html

Americans with Disabilities Act of 1990 (ADA)

Federal law that bars discrimination in the employment of capable handicapped persons by both private and public employers, and that requires reasonable accommodations for their special needs.

walking more than one block and boarding or alighting from a standard bus. Is Rock Island's exclusion of AIDS from the reduced fare program illegal under the ADA?

Hamlyn v. Rock Island County Metro Mass Transit Dist., 986 F.Supp. 1126 (C.D. Ill., 1997).

Yes. AIDS is considered a disability under the ADA. In the court's opinion, it is undisputed that the AIDS infection renders Hamlyn physically "unable . . . to utilize mass transportation facilities and services as effectively as persons who are not so affected." This exclusion is discriminatory under the ADA. "An individual with epilepsy, paralysis, a substantial hearing or visual impairment, mental retardation, or a learning disability would be covered, but an individual with a minor, nonchronic condition of short duration, such as a sprain, infection, or broken limb, generally would not be covered."[47]

LEGAL FOCUS—CASE

Ella Williams was an assembly line worker for a Toyota manufacturing plant in Kentucky. She developed carpal tunnel syndrome in both wrists and tendonitis in her neck, shoulders, and arms as a result of the use of certain tools used in performance of her job. At first Toyota accommodated her condition as she was given two of the simpler jobs at the plant. Later on, Toyota asked her to perform some additional tasks, which she was unable to do because of her carpal tunnel syndrome and tendonitis. She requested that, as an accommodation, her job be modified to include only the tasks she was previously performing. Toyota denied this request. As a result, Williams was ultimately forced to resign. She sued Toyota, claiming violation of the ADA. At trial Williams conceded she could still brush her teeth, wash her face, bathe, tend her flower garden, fix breakfast, do laundry, and pick up around the house. Was Toyota required to make the requested employment accommodation?

Toyota Motor Mfg., Kentucky, Inc. v. Williams, 534 U.S. 184, 122 S.Ct. 681 (2002).

Despite the court ruling in *Williams v. Toyota*, repetitive strain injury is a real problem in the modern workplace. Read about it at http://www.engr.unl.edu/ee/eeshop/rsi.html

No. The Supreme Court stated that the ADA requires plaintiffs to show a substantial impairment limiting major life activities occurring at home as well as work. The critical question should be "whether the claimant is unable to perform the variety of tasks central to most people's daily lives." Major life activities include those that an average person can perform with little or no difficulty such as walking, breathing, seeing, hearing, talking, learning, reading, taking care of oneself, lifting, sitting, standing, and working.

Reasonable Accommodation

A qualified employee or applicant with a disability is one who with reasonable accommodation can perform the essential functions of the job in question. Reasonable accommodation may include, but is not limited to:

- Making existing facilities used by employees readily accessible to and usable by persons with disabilities
- Restructuring jobs, modifying work schedules or loads, or reassigning to a vacant position

- Acquiring or modifying equipment or devices; adjusting modifying examinations, training materials, or policies; and providing qualified readers or interpreters

Reasonable accommodation may be necessary to apply for a job, to perform job functions, or to enjoy the benefits and privileges of employment that are enjoyed by people without disabilities.

An employer does not have to provide a reasonable accommodation that would cause an **undue hardship** to the employer. The EEOC provides the following factors to determine undue hardship:

- The nature and cost of the accommodation needed
- The overall financial resources of the facility making the reasonable accommodation; the number of persons employed at this facility; and the effect on expenses and resources of the facility
- The overall financial resources, size, number of employees, and type and location of facilities of the employer (if the facility involved in the reasonable accommodation is part of a larger entity)
- The type of operation of the employer, including the structure and functions of the workforce, the geographic separateness, and the administrative or fiscal relationship of the facility involved in making the accommodation to the employer
- The impact of the accommodation on the operation of the facility.

"An employer is not required to lower production standards to make an accommodation. An employer generally is not obligated to provide personal use items such as eyeglasses or hearing aids."[48]

LEGAL FOCUS—CASE

Michael Salley began working at Circuit City as a video sales counselor. Within two years, he became a store manager. Circuit City had a drug policy providing that managers "will work to ensure that employees are free from the effects of alcohol and illegal substances, whether consumed on or off Company property." Within a year of becoming a store manager, Salley told a superior of his significant drug activity and addiction, but said it was a thing of the past. Salley was assured that no action would be taken against him. Unfortunately, he suffered a relapse into drug and alcohol addiction. Circuit City discovered his drug use and other apparent violations of company drug policy, including missing work time because of drug use and alleged drug involvement with a subordinate, whose drug use he failed to report. Circuit City fired Salley two days after he signed a statement admitting his misconduct. Was Salley's firing in violation of the ADA?

Salley v. Circuit City Stores, Inc., 160 F.3d 977 (3rd Cir., 1998).

No. While an employer is required to reasonably accommodate a person with a disability (drug addiction is a protected disability), it is not required to tolerate disobedience and violation of company rules. "[F]or purposes of [the ADA], the term 'qualified individual with a disability' shall not include any employee or applicant who is currently engaging in the illegal use of drugs, when the covered entity acts on the basis of such use." The employee poses a hazard to the public and fellow employees. The court upheld Salley's dismissal,

http://

For a discussion of reasonable accommodation see
http://www.eeoc.gov/facts/accommodation.html

undue hardship

An action or accommodation that is excessively costly, extensive, substantial, or disruptive, or would fundamentally alter the nature or operation of the business.

stating "an employer may hold an alcoholic or drug-dependent employee" to the same qualification standards for employment or job performance and behavior that such entity holds other employees, even if any unsatisfactory performance or behavior is related to the drug use or alcoholism of such employee. "[No] reasonable jury could conclude that Salley was discharged for his disability rather than his drug use and concomitant violations of Circuit City's drug policy."[49]

LEGAL FOCUS—CASE

Mario Echazabal worked for independent contractors at an oil refinery owned by Chevron U.S.A. Inc. He applied for a job directly with Chevron but an employment medical examination showed he had suffered a hepatitis C illness, which had damaged his liver. Chevron's medical staff was concerned that further exposure to toxins at Chevron's refinery would make his condition worse. Echazabel did not get the job at Chevron, and to make matters worse Chevron asked the independent contractors to reassign him. They instead let him go. Echazabal sued under the ADA. Chevron defended claiming that an EEOC regulation allowed it to refuse to hire someone whose disability on the job would pose a direct threat to other workers' health. Echazabal claimed the EEOC regulation was not consistent with the ADA. Who is correct, Chevron or Echazabal?

Chevron USA, Inc. v. Echazabal, 536 U.S. 73, 122 S.Ct. 2045 (2002).

Oil Company 1, Mario 0. The United States Supreme Court unanimously held that the ADA permits the EEOC's regulation allowing Chevron to refuse to hire someone for a task that endangers the workers' health.

> *"If Typhoid Mary had come under the ADA, would a meat packer have been defenseless if Mary had sued after being turned away?"*[50]

The ADA expressly recognizes an employer's right to adopt an employment qualification barring anyone whose disability would place others in the workplace at risk.

An employer is not expected to make accommodations that will impose an undue hardship on the operation of the employer's business. Undue hardship has been defined to mean "an action that requires significant difficulty or expense when considered in relation to factors such as a business' size, financial resources, and the nature and structure of its operation."[51]

As with other protected classes, certain questions and tests are prohibited. Among prohibited questions are those asking about the existence, nature, or severity of the disability. Job-related questions are allowed, such as: Can you keyboard or work with the newest Rivercity software? Passing a medical examination may be a pre-hiring qualification for a job as long as it is required of all applicants for the same job and is somehow job- and business-related. Although inquiries by the employer are generally prohibited, an individual wishing an accommodation for disabilities must let the employer know that an adjustment or change at work for a reason related to a medical condition is needed.

Exhibit 13-1 lists the major federal statutes prohibiting employment discrimination.

EXHIBIT 13-1: **Major Federal Statutes Prohibiting Employment Discrimination**

Equal Pay Act	1963	Protects men and women who perform substantially equal work in the same establishment from sex-based wage discrimination
Civil Rights Act as Amended (Title VII)	1964 1972 1982 1991	Prohibits employment discrimination based on race, color, religion, sex, or national origin
Age Discrimination in Employment Act as Amended (ADEA)	1967 1990	Protects individuals who are forty years of age or older from employment discrimination
Americans with Disabilities Act (ADA)	1990	Prohibits, employment discrimination against qualified individuals with disabilities
Immigration Reform and Control Act (IRCA)	1986	Requires employers to assure that employees hired are legally authorized to work in the United States and prohibits discrimination based on citizenship

Source: Adapted from American Bar Association, Section of Law Practice Management (Chicago: ABA, 1993).

WHAT ARE THE BASIC DUTIES OF EMPLOYEES?

DUTY TO FOLLOW LAWFUL INSTRUCTIONS

LEGAL FOCUS—PROBLEM

Two weeks after being employed as a deckhand on Plato Pamasi's 180-foot yacht, *The Invincible,* Jake Morgan refused to obey an order of Chief Mate Ben Blight to swing over the side on a rope ladder and scrape and repaint a rusted section of the hull. Morgan argued that nothing had been said about such dirty and potentially dangerous duties when he was hired. Moreover, he said, "I'm too tired. Why don't you do it?" May he be fired without recourse?

Yes. Scraping and painting are customary duties of deckhands. This was reasonably implied, if not explicitly expressed, in their employment agreement. The agreement could have been expressed in words (spoken or written) or implied from conduct of the parties, or from customs of people in that occupation. Also, being too tired during working hours is no excuse for refusal to do a job. An employee is duty bound to obey reasonable orders and to comply with reasonable rules. Failure to follow a lawful order is insubordination, which is grounds for discharge or other discipline. However, one cannot be required to do anything that is illegal, immoral, or contrary to public policy, nor can one be compelled to do work not covered by the employment contract. A worker may refuse to perform work that appears to be unreasonably dangerous.

LEGAL FOCUS—CASE

Two workers were instructed to clean a wire mesh screen suspended about 20 feet above the shop floor. The cleaning process required that the workers step above the screen to remove objects that had dropped onto the screen from overhead conveyor belts. Ten days before, a coworker had fallen to his death while doing similar work. The day before the same two workers brought alleged unsafe conditions to the attention of the company. After the workers refused the work instructions written reprimands were placed in their employment files and their pay was docked. The workers claimed they had the right to refuse work under these conditions without workplace penalty.

Whirlpool Corporation v. Marshall, Secretary of Labor, 445 U.S. 1, 100 S.Ct. 883 (1980).

The U.S. Labor Department and later the Supreme Court agreed with the workers' position, claiming authority to limit the employers discretion under OSHA (the Occupational Safety and Health Act), which seeks to guarantee a hazard-free working environment for employees.

DUTY OF CARE

Every employee is duty bound to use reasonable skill in performing assigned work, to perform it conscientiously (i.e., to do "an honest day's work for an honest day's wages"), and to do nothing contrary to the interests of the employer. For example, one may not sabotage equipment, steal supplies, or sell company secrets to competitors.

LEGAL FOCUS—PROBLEM

Ed Block was a stationary engineer in charge of a battery of boilers at the Metropole Chemical Works. Safety valves would prevent a major explosion, but the equipment could be seriously damaged even if the fail-safe devices worked perfectly. All controls had to be closely monitored and regulated. One day Block's wife left him after a prolonged argument over their son, who had been arrested on a narcotics possession charge. Perhaps understandably, but not excusably, Block had consumed a large bottle of bourbon before he went to work on the swing shift. Within an hour, he was sound asleep at the control panel. The boilers soon overheated and shut down automatically. Repairs would cost at least $5,000, to say nothing of the cost of disrupted production and spoiled goods in process, worth perhaps another $50,000. Is Block liable for the loss?

Yes. Theoretically, an employee may be charged with the cost of the employer's products he or she spoils or the value of equipment damaged either intentionally or through negligence.

Practically, most employers seldom go beyond dismissing the errant employee. They absorb such spoilage costs as part of the price of doing business, and pass them along to consumers in higher prices for finished products. Insurance sometimes helps cover the costs.

DUTY OF LOYALTY

Loyalty is a fundamental duty in an employment relationship. The employee has the duty to act to benefit the employer. He or she may not act for his or her personal interests or for those of a third party at the detriment of the employer, and doing so is a conflict of interest.

The duty of loyalty also means that any information or knowledge learned through the employment relationship is confidential. It is a breach of loyalty to disclose such information during the relationship and even after it ends. An example of confidential information would be a list of customers that belongs to the employer.

An employee hired to sell something cannot also be the buyer unless the employer specifically agrees to it. If an employee is selling an employer's product, he or she must report to the employer the true and accurate price obtained for the goods. If an employee's job is to buy goods or services for the employer, he or she cannot falsely report what was paid or pay an excess amount and then receive a return of some of the excess payment from the seller. In short, the employee's loyalty must be absolute. The actions must not result in any secret profit for the employee.

LEGAL FOCUS—EXAMPLE

Aztec Petroleum Corporation arranged to have Merle Douglas buy oil and gas leases on the company's behalf. In return for his services, Douglas was paid $5,000 plus a royalty interest in the leases purchased. Douglas purchased several leases for Aztec. He told Aztec that he paid more for the leases than he actually did. Through various tricks, Douglas kept much of the money Aztec gave him to pay for the leases. Douglas used the money for personal purchases, including two new cars and a boat. When Aztec refused to grant Douglas the promised royalty interest in the leases, Douglas sued. Because Douglas had breached his fiduciary duty (specifically the duty of loyalty) to Aztec, Aztec was not required to pay him any royalty.[52]

WHAT ARE THE BASIC RIGHTS AND COMMON BENEFITS OF EMPLOYEES?

Every employee is entitled to compensation for services as agreed on with the employer. If no figure is specified, the prevailing or customary wage applies, or whatever would be reasonable under the circumstances. Sometimes, as in many sales jobs, pay in the form of commissions is related to particular performance, such as a specified percentage of all sales made. A common variation is a contract that calls for payment of a minimum base salary, or "draw," to be offset by commissions earned. The employee retains any excess commissions. State laws commonly require payment every two weeks, or sometimes weekly.

AT WILL AND JUST CAUSE EMPLOYMENT

An employee is neither a slave nor an indentured servant bound to remain for a prescribed time. One has the power to quit at any time—simply leave the job. But there is no legal right to quit when to do so breaches a contract that one has made to work for a specified period of time. For this reason, an employee who quits without good cause before the contract ends may be liable for damages but won't be forced to continue services. This is an example of having the power to do something but not the right. In legal terms, the courts will not stop the employee from breaching the contract but instead will hold him or her responsible for any damages the employer suffers. Realistically, employers seldom sue their rank-and-file employees. A lawsuit is costly, other employees resent it, and any sizable judgment won often is uncollectible.

LEGAL FOCUS—PROBLEM

Sean Yashima was the star reporter for a leading Jacksonville, Florida, television station. Although pleased with his work he wanted desperately to accept an offer from a Seattle television station to anchor the weekend news. Yashima is an on-the-rise newsreader and this was an opportunity to move from the fifty-third largest television market to the twelfth. Sean is in the eighteenth month of a three-year contract with the Jacksonville station. Can Yashima accept the new offer?

Yashima is an exception as an employee because most employees do not have term-of-time contracts. Because Yashima does have a term-of-time contract, he cannot accept the new offer unless the Jacksonville station releases him from his contract obligation. A highly valued employee who quits before the expiration of a specified term of a written contract to take a better job elsewhere cannot be compelled to return to his or her job. But a court of equity might grant the first employer an injunction barring the employee from working for anyone else during the contract term. To defy the court order would mean citation for contempt and a possible fine, as well as a judgment for damages.

The second employer might also be guilty of the tort of interference with a contract or an economically advantageous situation. Some authors call this a *contort*—a contract tainted by a tort. The tort is **interference with an economically advantageous relationship** and is defined as the knowing and wrongful interference with the performance of an existing valid contract. Generally, there must be a contract in existence between two parties, and the defendant must induce one of the parties to breach the contract. Thus, a computer software manufacturer might wrongfully induce a talented software designer to breach a fixed-term employment contract with the plaintiff and join the defendant's staff at a higher salary.

interference with an economically advantageous relationship

A knowing and wrongful interference with the promised performance of another person's contract.

LEGAL FOCUS—BACKGROUND

In the early 1980s Texaco and Pennzoil competed over which suitor would buy Getty Oil. Texaco and Getty Oil reached an agreement. But shortly thereafter Pennzoil sued Texaco claiming that Texaco had prevented the performance of a binding "agreement in principle" between Pennzoil and Getty and had committed intentional interference with contractual relations. Although there was no formal written contract between Pennzoil and Getty, they had been engaged in a serious business relationship with a reasonable expectation of successful completion The 1984 trial led to the largest civil award in world history, with a Houston jury awarding Pennzoil $7.53 billion in compensatory damages and $3 billion in punitive damages.*

Employment At Will

Instead of term-of-time contracts, most employment contracts are informal stating no definite period of time. They also usually lack detailed express agreement as to the rights and duties of the parties. Such employment contracts are called **at-will employment.** Each party is free to terminate the relationship at any time without liability (other than payment by the employer for services rendered to date, or sometimes to the end of the pay period). Under such contracts employers generally can fire or let employees go at will and employees have the right to quit at will without liability.

In the last sixty years major changes have occurred in the at-will employment doctrine. Among the changes to the doctrine are union contracts, federal and state statutes, public policy, implied contracts, and tort claims. Of course, contracts for a specified term (like Sean Yashima's) have always been an exception to the at-will doctrine. Specified term contracts in business usually exist only for top leadership, such as corporate presidents. The at-will doctrine still is an important part of employment law. However, as we discuss below, the firing of most employees can no longer be for any reason.

> **at-will employment**
>
> A term used, for example, to indicate that an employment contract may be terminated at any time by either the employee or the employer without any liability (beyond payment for services rendered up to the time of departure or discharge).

Union Contracts

Most unions have successfully bargained for a **just cause** provision in employment contracts. A just cause clause in a contract means that the employer must have a legitimate provable reason to fire or perhaps even discipline any employee. The just cause provision thus limits the employer's ability to fire at will. Often fired union employees have a right to an independent arbitration to examine the employer's reason for the firing or discipline and decide whether a firing was legitimate.

> **just cause**
>
> An action based on reasonable grounds and fair treatment; lawful reasons for taking an action.

Federal and State Statutes

As discussed earlier in the chapter federal statutes restrict an employer's ability to fire at will. Title VII of the Civil Rights Act of 1964, for example, prohibits discrimination on the basis of race, color, national origin, religion, and sex. An employee fired for discriminatory reasons has legal rights against the employer. Other federal statutes protect against discrimination on the basis of age, disability, or pregnancy.

State statutes also often prohibit discrimination and may provide additional remedies for employees. Sometimes these laws prohibit other types of discrimination, such as discrimination based on sexual preference, or they prohibit firings because employees are requested or required to perform public responsibilities.

---

* The Texas Intermediate Court of Appeals affirmed the judgment but reduced the punitive damages to $1 billion. In April 1987, Texaco filed for bankruptcy in a Chapter 11 proceeding (which allows temporary freedom from creditor claims while the company formulates a strategy to pay its debts), delaying payment of the judgment and permitting continued operations while avoiding forced liquidation (i.e., selling all of its assets and paying all debts to the extent possible). After the Texas Supreme Court affirmed the judgment that November, Texaco planned to appeal to the U.S. Supreme Court. However, on Christmas Day, Pennzoil agreed to accept Texaco's "final settlement offer" of $3 billion—still a colossal penalty (20 percent of Texaco's total net worth, and three times the net worth of Pennzoil). The case is the subject of a best-selling book by James Shannon, *Texaco and the $10 Billion Jury* (New York: Prentice Hall, 1988).

LEGAL FOCUS—EXAMPLE

Many states have laws that forbid an employer from firing an employee for certain specified public policy reasons. Examples include situations where an employee is called for jury service, subpoenaed as a witness at a court or legislative proceeding, or called to serve in the National Guard.

Civil service statutes protect also over half of the fifteen million public workers, county, state, and federal. Civil service statutes require just cause before an employee is fired. Your professor probably has tenure, which is a form of just cause protection.

Public Policy

Sometimes firing an employee violates a judicially recognized public policy. Many states will not allow an employee to be fired for performing an act encouraged by public need. An employee should also not be fired for refusing to perform an illegal or wrongful act. For example, employees who are discharged after refusing to lie in court about illegal company practices such as illegal price fixing have successfully challenged the employer's action.

What public policies are significant enough to warrant protection by the courts? This is a difficult question. The courts answer the question on a case-by-case basis. Employees fired because they file a workers' compensation claim have been protected. In states that lack specific laws protecting workers who serve on juries, courts have found such a firing to be a violation of public policy. Perhaps the most interesting application of the public policy exception is the protection of workers who act as **whistleblowers.** A whistleblower is someone who tells the public or the authorities about illegal or other wrongful activities in his or her organization.

whistleblower

A person who makes a disclosure about improper conduct by an organization or organization officer or official.

Implied Contract Theory

A few courts have found that an implied contract may exist to protect employees from arbitrary firing. The court may find that the acts of the employer and employee have created the contract. An employee fired in breach of these implied terms can sue for breach of contract.

LEGAL FOCUS—EXAMPLE

An employer's handbook or personnel bulletin may state that, as a matter of standard practice, workers will be dismissed only for good cause. If the employee is aware of this policy and works for the company relying on it, an implied contract may exist. The handbook or bulletin supplies the terms.

Oral statements, job evaluations and other acts may also lead to an implied contract. This theory is most likely to be successful in cases involving long-term employees where the work relationship has existed for ten, fifteen, and even twenty years.

Tort Theory

In a few unusual cases, employers who fired an employee have been found to have committed a tort. If the firing is done in an abusive manner, an employer's acts might be found to be either the tort of intentional infliction of emotional distress or defamation.

LEGAL FOCUS—CASE

A restaurant had suffered a theft of supplies. The manager gathered the employees together at a special meeting. At the meeting he announced that he would start firing waitresses alphabetically until the thief was identified. The first waitress, Debra Agis, was fired. She sued the restaurant claiming she suffered emotional distress as a result of her firing. Do these facts support a tort claim?

Agis v. Howard Johnson Co., 371 Mass. 140, 355 N.E.2d 315 (1976).

Yes. Recall this end-of-chapter case from Chapter 7 where the highest court of Massachusetts said the manager's acts were actionable as the tort of intentional infliction of emotional distress.

Discharge is legal if it is for good cause (e.g., insubordination or intoxication of the worker on the job, or lack of business, or bankruptcy for the employer).

Despite all these legal theories an employee who has been wrongfully discharged often faces difficult obstacles to meaningful relief. One commentator stated, "The average employee who has been wrongfully terminated has as much chance of getting a jury trial as sprouting wings and flying to the moon."[53] While this is an exaggeration it is certainly true that significant barriers exist to successful plaintiff resolution of such cases.

WHAT IS THE MINIMUM WAGE?

The Fair Labor Standards Act of 1938 (FLSA) set a minimum standard hourly wage for industrial workers engaged in interstate commerce, and set the maximum workweek at forty hours. The wage rate has been periodically increased (it was 25 cents in 1950, for example); since September 1997, the rate has been $5.15 for all workers who are at least twenty years old. Persons under twenty may be hired for ninety days for no less than $4.25 an hour. The act is complex, with exemptions and exceptions specifically detailed in the law (e.g., employers of tipped employees [those customarily receiving $30 or more a month in tips] may consider those tips as part of the wages and may pay as low as $2.13 per hour). Among those employees exempt from minimum pay requirements, as well as overtime provisions of FLSA, are executives, professional employees, academic employees, farm workers on small farms, casual babysitters, and administrative employees.

Legally an employer must withhold federal income taxes (and, in some states, state income taxes) and Social Security taxes and pay them directly to the appropriate government agencies. By agreement with the employee, deductions are also common for such purposes as buying insurance, government savings bonds, or company stock; paying off company credit union loans; paying union dues; or putting money into savings accounts. The law also mandates record keeping requirements for employers to ensure their compliance with the FLSA.

http://

Find minimum wage information at the Department of Labor's Web site
http://www.dol.gov/

http://

For a fact sheet on child labor provisions of the FLSA, see
http://www.dol.gov/esa/regs/compliance/whd/whdfs43.htm

If wages are not paid, an employee has the right to sue for money owed. Special legislation in most states and under federal bankruptcy laws gives the employee a preference or priority over the employer's other creditors.

LEGAL FOCUS—PROBLEM

Darleen Gorski was employed as a sales engineer by the Apogee Corporation at a salary of $3,500 a month plus a commission of 5 percent of all net sales made in excess of a minimum specified at the beginning of each year. The company supplied her with a car and agreed to pay all expenses of its operation and maintenance. (Apogee had so many agents on the road that it set aside the equivalent of premiums on automobile insurance and was thus self-insured.) At the end of the first month, Gorski submitted an itemized bill of $409 for gas and oil and $1,175 to cover the cost of replacing wheels and tires and a tape deck that had been stolen. Were the items claimed by Gorski collectible as part of her compensation?

No. Although Gorski was entitled to both sums, technically the $409 was reimbursement for expenses properly incurred, and the $1,175 was indemnification for a loss suffered. Neither is compensation for services rendered; neither is includible in taxable income.

WORKING CONDITIONS

Occupational Safety and Health Act of 1970 (OSHA)

A federal law to assure safe and healthful working conditions by authorizing enforcement of health and safety standards.

http://

The most often cited OSHA violations by size of business can be found at **http://www.osha.gov/oshstats/std1.html**

Every employee is entitled to reasonably safe working conditions. The federal **Occupational Safety and Health Act of 1970 (OSHA)** broadly requires the employer in interstate commerce to furnish employment and a place of employment that are free from recognized hazards that cause or are likely to cause death or serious physical harm. The enforcement arm of the act is the Occupational Safety and Health Administration (OSHA). According to OSHA, since its 1970 charter the workplace death rate has been cut in half; still, about seventeen Americans die every day on the job.[54]

The law extends to such diverse items as equipment, protective clothing, vapor and noise levels, and in-plant health facilities. The law requires that companies log injuries and correct unsafe conditions as well as notify employees of their rights to bring notice of unsafe conditions to the attention of OSHA. It provides for inspections, investigations, issuance of citations, judicial review, and penalties for violations. All states have a variety of similar local regulations governing production in intrastate commerce.

LEGAL FOCUS—PROBLEM

Carlos Gutierrez preferred to be a low-profile employee. However, in a previous job he had been a safety inspector and his new employer, Rivercity Cleaners, appeared to be in clear violation of several OSHA safety standards. After his supervisor refused to act, he notified the appropriate state OSHA. They inspected Rivercity and found violations related to protective equipment, portable fire extinguishers, electrical components and equipment, and walking-working surfaces. Rivercity fired Gutierrez for disloyalty. Does Gutierrez have any remedy?

Yes, he does. OSHA prohibits retaliation against workers who exercise their right to report unsafe working conditions. Workers must contact an OSHA office almost immediately after learning of the alleged discriminatory action in order to protect their rights. OSHA will investigate the complaint and upon finding merit will order reinstatement or other remedies. The Department of Labor reached settlements with various employers involving forty-one workers in New York and New Jersey who reported workplace hazards and were discharged or otherwise penalized as a result. "Under the terms of settlement agreements reached between employers and the U.S. Labor Department's Occupational Safety and Health Administration (OSHA), the forty-one workers received a total of $211,231 in back wages. Other remedies included reinstatement, restoration of vacations and 401K benefits, informal negotiated settlements between the complainants and their employers, and the requirement that employers display posters on the rights of employees."[55]

FRINGE BENEFITS

An employee has no constitutional right to fringe benefits, but legislation, competition, and union pressure have made them an integral part of most employment contracts. Such benefits are provided in addition to the regular wage or salary. Social Security, no doubt the most important fringe benefit, is mandated by the Social Security Act of 1935. Financed by taxes paid by both employers and employees, the massive Social Security program provides benefits to more than 40 million persons, a growing number that includes retirees (who generally start receiving pensions at the age of sixty-five), dependent survivors of insured persons, and qualified disabled workers and disabled dependents. It also encompasses the Medicare program of health benefits for qualified retirees, their dependents, qualified disabled persons under sixty-five, and qualified workers and their dependents of any age that need dialysis treatment or a kidney transplant.

Since the Social Security Act was enacted in 1935, people are living longer and are having fewer children, with the result that more and more people are withdrawing benefits while fewer and fewer are contributing. Further, Congress has repeatedly increased benefits, extending them to additional groups and requiring increased payments to compensate for increases in the cost of living. As a result, to keep the program economically viable well beyond the year 2003, changes have been made and more will surely be made—in Social Security taxes levied, in benefits paid, and in income taxes on benefits received by wealthier recipients.

Many private and public employers supplement Social Security retirement benefits with their own pension, stock-purchase, and profit-sharing plans. Some provide a simplified employee pension (SEP) plan, whereby they contribute to the employee's individual retirement account (IRA). Paid vacations and holidays and paid or subsidized medical and dental insurance are very valuable fringe benefits for most employed persons. Some employers also offer a variety of less significant benefits. These include life insurance; legal aid plans; sick leave; prenatal, child, and elder care; maternity and paternity leave; adoption assistance; social, recreational, physical fitness, and continuing education programs; and employer-assisted housing. The dollar value of fringe benefits often equals as much as 20 to 30 percent of the monetary wages paid. The appeal of fringe benefits is enhanced by the fact that most are tax-free to the employees and tax-deductible as business expenses to the employers.

RETIREMENT BENEFITS

In every state, society intervenes when a worker is hurt on the job by providing for compensation under applicable workers' compensation laws (see Chapter 7). The worker who is permanently disabled, on or off the job, may qualify for Social Security disability payments, as may the worker's dependents. Upon reaching retirement age, the worker qualifies for Social Security benefit payments, and dependent survivors of a deceased worker may qualify for survivors' benefits under Social Security.[56] If a private employer has voluntarily provided a private pension to supplement Social Security retirement payments, the worker is again protected by the federal **Employee Retirement Income Security Act (ERISA),**[57] which regulates **defined benefit plans.** A defined benefit plan is one where the amount of the employee's retirement income is a promised fixed dollar amount or an amount determined in advance by a benefit formula. Under ERISA, the Pensions Benefit Guaranty Corporation (PBGC) was created "to guarantee payment of basic pension benefits earned by about 44 million American workers and retirees participating in more than 35,000 private-sector defined benefit pension plans."[58] Reserves come from insurance premiums paid by the participating private employers.

Employee Retirement Income Security Act (ERISA)

Federal legislation regulating private pension plans that supplement Social Security.

defined benefit plans

Plans that provide for the payment of determinable retirement income benefits.

http://

Technical and planning information on Roth IRAs for practitioners and consumers can be found at
http://www.rothira.com/

LEGAL FOCUS—PROBLEM
....

Durango Apparel, Inc., a corporation with manufacturing plants in Tennessee and Kentucky, had a pension plan covering more than 7,000 workers. The company filed for bankruptcy in March of 2001. The pension plan had assets of about $15 million and projected benefit liabilities totaling around $40 million. Will the workers' claims for pension benefits be lost in the bankruptcy proceeding?

No. The PBGC took over the underfunded pension plan in March of 2002 to protect the workers benefits. Although individuals were subject to a maximum pension benefit under federal law, PBGC projected that most workers and their dependents would receive full benefits.[59]

Individual Retirement Accounts (IRAs)

Federally authorized private pension plans in which qualified employees contribute a certain percentage of their income, tax-free, to their retirement accounts until retirement.

Roth IRA

A form of Individual Retirement Account authorized by federal law that allows a taxpayer to contribute after-tax dollars to the account so that earnings are not taxed when withdrawn.

Individual Pension Plans

Because many private employers do not provide pension plans to supplement Social Security, the federal Internal Revenue Code allows qualified workers to individually set aside a certain percentage of earned income, tax-free until retirement, in conventional **Individual Retirement Accounts (IRAs)** and **Roth IRAs.** IRAs are accounts that individual workers select and fund with pretax dollars. The employee gets a present tax break on the invested amount and a continuing income tax break on income earned over the years in the IRA account. However, income taxes are paid on the account principal and earnings when withdrawn after retirement. Thus the regular IRA is a tax deferred account.

A Roth IRA is very different, first because the income used to fund the account is after-tax income. Like the regular IRA, earnings on the account are not subject to income tax before retirement. The second big difference is the after retirement treatment. Whereas income in a regular IRA's account is subject to income tax when withdrawn, a Roth IRA is free from any income tax obligation upon retirement. With a Roth IRA, the income is tax exempt.

Which is best? Variables such as tax rates (current and future), eligibility requirements, and account fees and so on make the answer dependent on the individual employee's situation.

LEGAL FOCUS—BACKGROUND

Finley Cory invests $250 a month in a Roth IRA starting at the age of twenty. He waits until age sixty-five to make withdrawals and the investment earns a 6 percent return compounded monthly. What will his tax-free investment be worth?

The power of compounding is astounding. After forty-five years, Cory's $250 a month investment ($135,000 total invested) in a tax-free Roth IRA would be worth $688,998. In all likelihood, as his income increases, Cory would invest additional funds in the account and the amount available at age 65 would be much greater. And if he waited until age seventy to retire, he will be almost a millionaire ($946,797) on this $3,000 a year investment alone.

Some employers contribute to their employees' retirement through **401(k) plans.** With these plans companies may deposit cash or stock bonuses to a trust account for their employees' benefit. Also the employee may fund these plans solely or partly through salary reduction. These deposited amounts are not taxed and like IRAs accrue income without tax consequences until distribution at retirement. Employees often have investment choices for the funds in these accounts; a popular choice has been stock in the company in which they work.

401(k) plans

Retirement savings account taking its name from the Internal Revenue Code of 1978. The plan is funded by employee contributions and (often) matching contributions from the employer. Contributions are taken from pre-tax salary, and the funds grow tax-free until withdrawn.

LEGAL FOCUS-BACKGROUND

The 2001 collapse of Enron Corporation, an energy provider company, has caused many employees to rethink investment in company stock and Congress to consider limitations on how much employer stock should be in a 401(k) account. Sixty percent of Enron's 401(k) plan was invested in the Enron shares, which fell to 26 cents from a peak of $90 in the previous year.[60]

Self-employed persons may establish SEP-IRA or Keogh retirement plans, which serve the same purpose as IRAs or 401(k)s. All of these private arrangements provide retirement funds in addition to the maximum Social Security payments, which are meant to lay a minimum "floor" rather than an ideal customized "ceiling" for retirement needs.

FAMILY AND MEDICAL LEAVE

The **Family and Medical Leave Act of 1993 (FMLA)** requires employers with fifty or more employees to grant employees leave for certain family purposes related to child care and family health. All public agencies (state and local government) and local education agencies (schools) are covered even if they have fewer than fifty employees. The act allows an employee to take up to twelve weeks' leave in any twelve-month period but does not require that the leave be paid, although the employer must continue any provided health benefits. The employer may require the employee to use paid benefits as part of the leave (e.g., the employee has three weeks of vacation available). Among the reasons deemed proper for family leave are

- Caring for a child newly placed with the employee for adoption or foster care

Family and Medical Leave Act of 1993 (FMLA)

A federal law requiring employers with fifty or more employees to grant employees leave for certain family purposes related to child care and family health.

- Caring for an immediate family member (spouse, child, or parent—but not a parent-in-law) with a serious health condition
- Being unable to work because of a serious health condition

After any leave is taken, the employee must be restored to the same or similar position in the company.

LEGAL FOCUS—CASE

Juanita Caldwell is a single mother with three children working for a Kentucky Fried Chicken franchisee. Before the events in question, records suggest she was an excellent employee. On Saturday morning her three-year-old son, Kejuan, developed a high fever, pain in his ears, and congestion, later diagnosed as a ear infection. Caldwell promptly notified her supervisor before the start of her morning shift that she would be absent attending to Kejuan. Her supervisor approved the absence. When she returned for her next regular shift on Monday morning, the restaurant manager abruptly fired her without stating a reason. Caldwell sued, arguing that her termination violated the FMLA. The district court granted her employer a summary judgment, concluding that although the act generally protects employees when the immediate family members have a "serious health condition," Kejuan's condition did not qualify. Caldwell appealed. Was her appeal successful?

Caldwell v. Holland of Texas, Inc., 208 F.3d 671, 676 (8th Cir., 2000).

Yes. The Court of Appeals reversed the trial court and remanded the case back to the trial court for further proceedings. The FMLA provides that a "serious health condition" occurs, under the regulations, when the family member suffers an "illness, injury, impairment, or physical or mental condition" that requires "inpatient care" or "continuing treatment" by a health care provider. "FMLA's purpose is to help working men and women balance the conflicting demands of work and personal life. The law requires courts to consider the seriousness of the afflicted individual's condition because the law was designed to prevent individuals like Juanita Caldwell from having to choose between their livelihood and treatment for their own or their family members' serious health conditions. Upon examining the seriousness of Kejuan's ear infection, which required surgery to prevent deafness, we hold that there is at least a question of fact as to whether Kejuan's condition was 'serious' under the regulations." The standard for one's own serious health condition is higher than that for a family member's serious health condition. Specifically, you may take leave to care for a family member who merely has a serious health condition. Your own health condition must be such that you are unable to perform the functions of your position.

LEGAL FOCUS—PROBLEM

ACME Company provides in its employee handbook that the Family and Medical Leave Act applies to the company's employees. An employee seeking leave is denied it and the company claims as a defense to that it employs fewer than fifty employees. Is this a good defense?

Yes. Federal statutes apply to companies according to the jurisdictional requirements of the statute. As the act applies only to employers with fifty or more employees, FMLA does not apply to ACME Company. "The agreement between the parties that ACME would comply with the requirements of the FMLA does not bring the parties within the Act itself, because to do so would effectively enable them to contract around the Court's lack of subject matter jurisdiction. Although such an agreement may have enhanced the terms of the contractual relationship between the parties, it does not provide the federal courts with jurisdiction to hear cases under the Act."[61]

Exhibit 13-2 lists major federal statutes protecting employee safety, financial security, and family interests.

PRIVACY RIGHTS

New technology can alter old habits and customs within a short time. For example, the introduction of computers and the Internet into our lives has aided business but at the expense of legal and ethical tradeoffs. Many find the tradeoffs disturbing, particularly in relation to privacy rights.

Computers make it possible to accumulate, store, and retrieve vast amounts of information. Virtually all institutions with which we deal—insurance companies, mail-order houses, banks, and credit card companies—gather information about us. They store that information in their computer files. Government agencies such as the U.S. Census Bureau, the Social Security Administration, and the Internal Revenue Service also collect and store data.

These businesses and agencies collect information on income, expenses, marital status, and other personal history and habits. Frequently, this personal information finds its way to present or potential employers. Seldom—if ever—do most persons give permission for, or even know about, the use of this information.

In recent years, the right to privacy has become a significant employment issue. As in many other areas of social life, the law attempts to balance competing interests to arrive at fair policies. Employers are interested in minimizing employee theft, loss of trade secrets, and misuse of company property while maximizing productivity; employees are interested in being treated with respect and dignity. Employers today must be careful not to violate their employees' rights to privacy and personal security. Areas of concern include drug testing, lie-detector tests, and electronic monitoring. Employees must realize that they have limited privacy rights at the workplace. Personal e-mail, items kept in their desks, phone conversations, and the like may be subject to company monitoring and retrieval.

EXHIBIT 13-2: **Selected Federal Statutes Protecting Employee Interests**

Occupational Safety and Health Act (OSHA)	1970 1998	→	**Promotes safe and healthful working conditions for workers**
Employee Retirement Income Security Act (ERISA)	1974	→	**Protects workers who have worked for substantial periods under pension plans**
Family and Medical Leave Act (FMLA)	1993	→	**Provides unpaid leave for serious personal or family health problems**

Drug Testing in the Workplace

Drug and alcohol abuse has been estimated to cost industry between $50 and $100 billion in absenteeism, impaired performance, and accidents each year. Naturally, employers are concerned about a decline in job performance and other harm resulting from drug abuse. Some employers therefore test employees to uncover drug use. But the tests are not always reliable. Even when tests are accurate, a question exists as to whether they violate employees' right to privacy.

If the employer is a government agency, testing is subject to the requirements of the U.S. Constitution. Employees have a Fourth Amendment right to be "secure in their persons . . . against unreasonable searches and seizures." So the administration of drug tests is constitutional only if there is a reasonable basis for suspecting the employee's use of drugs—or if drug use in a particular government job could threaten public safety.

LEGAL FOCUS—CASE

The Department of Transportation required employees working on oil and gas pipelines to submit to random drug testing. All employees were subject to the rule whether they were suspected of drug use or not. Does the Department of Transportation's drug-testing rule violate employees' constitutional rights?

Electrical Workers Local 1245 v. Skinner, 913 F.2d 1454 (9th Cir., 1990).

No. The government's interest in promoting public safety was held to outweigh employees' privacy interests. Government also requires such testing for safety-sensitive occupations such as air and rail travel.

Constitutional limitations do not usually restrict private employers. However, some state constitutions and statutes do restrict and regulate private drug testing. Some collective-bargaining agreements regulate drug testing, specifying when and how it is or is not permitted. It is often required for participants in important competitive sporting events, such as track and field meets and certain Olympic events.

LEGAL FOCUS—PROBLEM

Donna Moran's employer maintained a drug-free workplace, requiring all employees to be subject to a random drug-testing program. Moran, a mechanical engineer and fifteen-year employee, was asked to report immediately for a urinalysis drug test. She refused and told her supervisor she had no intention of being tested and did not believe in the program. After additional unsuccessful attempts to get Moran to comply, the company fired her. Moran sought unemployment insurance and was denied because she lost her job because of "willful misconduct." Moran claims that the drug-testing policy is a humiliating invasion of her privacy and was adopted without the consent of the employees. Did the company have the right to require Moran to take the drug test, and can unemployment benefits be denied her?

Yes and yes. Moran's reasons for declining the test are unknown, but the cost is clear. In the case upon which this scenario is based, the company's drug-testing program was upheld and the denial of unemployment compensation was deemed proper. "The avoidance of injury, as well as concern for vicarious liability that can accrue to the employer, are legitimate interests of the employer that must be accorded substantial weight. Appellant's objection that [the employer] adopted the testing program without having obtained the employees' consent is groundless. The creation of rules and requirements that govern the workplace is the prerogative of the employer. . . . We conclude that the testing program of [the employer] was narrowly tailored to meet the employer's needs and that it did not unduly intrude on appellant's privacy interests. Hence, it was reasonable. Appellant's failure to cooperate with the program was without good cause. Willful misconduct was properly found, and the denial of unemployment benefits was, therefore, proper."[62]

Lie-Detector Tests

At one time, many employers required job applicants and employees to take lie-detector tests (also called *polygraphs*) to determine if the individual was honestly answering questions asked by the employer. Many employees considered these tests to be an invasion of their right to privacy and their privilege against self-incrimination. Other critics believe lie-detector tests create a dangerous fantasy that the truth can be ascertained, because most experts seriously doubt the tests' accuracy.

In 1988 Congress passed the Employee Polygraph Protection Act, which severely restricted the use of polygraphs. This act prohibits certain employers from (1) requiring, suggesting, requesting, or causing employees or job applicants to take lie-detector tests; (2) using, accepting, referring to, or asking about the results of lie-detector tests taken by employees or applicants; and (3) taking or threatening negative employment-related action against employees or applicants based on results of lie-detector tests or because they refused to take the tests.

Some employers are exempted from these prohibitions, notably federal, state, and local government employers, certain security service firms, and companies manufacturing and distributing controlled substances. Other employers may use polygraph tests when investigating losses attributable to theft, including suspected embezzlement and theft of trade secrets. In all cases where lie-detector tests are still permitted, however, stringent procedural requirements are imposed on employers. Employees may always refuse to submit to polygraph testing, but this may make them vulnerable to dismissal for good cause.

Monitoring Job Performance

Another workplace privacy issue involves the monitoring of employees' performance by employers. Today, some employers electronically monitor employees' use of computer terminals or company telephones. Some employers use video cameras to evaluate employees' performance.

Current federal law recognizes the right of employers to listen in on telephone conversations to monitor employees' performance, but state laws vary. An employer may often avoid state laws by simply informing employees subject to monitoring that the company may be listening. In areas such as this, there is very little case law, and an employer may wish to consider carefully whether the need to monitor employees' performance outweighs the employees' right to privacy, as well as the possible negative effect on general employee morale and productivity. If the company's monitoring is formally challenged, a court will balance the purposes of the search against its effect on the employee's privacy. The existence of other available methods for accomplishing the employer's goals will be considered as alternatives.

http://

Find the Employee Polygraph Protection Act by searching the U.S. Code at the U.S. House of Representatives Office of the Law Revision Counsel site

http://uscode.house.gov/ usc.htm

LEGAL FOCUS—PROBLEM

Fred Meyer's employer had assured all employees that their e-mail communications would not be accessed and used by the employer against its employees for disciplinary reasons. Meyer sent several work-related e-mails to his supervisor. The messages also included threats to "kill the backstabbing bastards" and referred to a planned holiday party as the "Jim Jones Kool-Aid affair." Meyer was fired. He sued, claiming his termination violated "public policy which precludes an employer from terminating an employee in violation of the employee's right to privacy as embodied in Pennsylvania common law." Was Meyer's lawsuit successful?

No. In the case on which this hypothetical is based the court found for the employer, stating, "We do not find a reasonable expectation of privacy in e-mail communications voluntarily made by an employee to his supervisor over the company e-mail system notwithstanding any assurances that such communications would not be intercepted by management. Once plaintiff communicated the alleged unprofessional comments to a second person (his supervisor) over an e-mail system, which was apparently utilized by the entire company, any reasonable expectation of privacy was lost. Significantly, the defendant did not require plaintiff, as in the case of a urinalysis or personal property search, to disclose any personal information about himself. Rather, plaintiff voluntarily communicated the alleged unprofessional comments over the company e-mail system. We find no privacy interests in such communications."[63]

RIGHTS REGARDING UNIONS

Have workers always had the right to join with coworkers in unions? The answer is no. The history of relations between labor and capital is long and stormy. More precisely, in many cases, it is a record of relations between union leaders selected by workers and professional managers hired by the investors who are the owners of capital. In 1806 a group of Philadelphia boot and shoemakers (called *cordwainers*) who joined together were found guilty of common-law criminal conspiracy and were fined.[64] In another classic case about thirty-five years later, *Commonwealth v. Hunt,* the Supreme Court of Massachusetts rejected the idea that a combination of workers was criminal simply because of their concerted action. The proper test, the court said, was the purpose of the combination; if intended "to induce all those engaged in the same occupation to become members," it was lawful. "Such an association might be used to afford each other assistance in time of poverty, sickness, or distress; or to raise their intellectual, moral, and social condition, or to make improvement in their art; or for other proper purposes."[65]

Nevertheless, **unions** continued to be harassed by court action instituted by employers who resisted any erosion of their decision-making power. For example, the federal Sherman Anti-Trust Act of 1890 was enacted to protect trade and commerce against unlawful restraints and monopolies of business firms, but was also applied by courts to unions. Injunctions were often used to restrain concerted labor activity such as **picketing** (patrolling outside a business location to encourage workers to join the union, to gain recognition from the employer, or to gain sympathy and support from third parties during a strike). But the pendulum eventually did swing in the opposite direction to favor labor

union

Association of workers formed to bargain collectively with employers over wages, hours, and conditions of employment.

picketing

Patrolling by strikers or sympathizers, generally at the entrances to a business plant, during a labor dispute.

and union organization. For example, in 1940 the Supreme Court recognized peaceful picketing as a form of free speech protected by the First Amendment. In 1988, the Court upheld a local law that banned picketing in front of any particular or private home, but marching through a residential neighborhood or in front of an entire block of homes is not prohibited.[66]

STATUTES GOVERNING LABOR–MANAGEMENT RELATIONS

During the Great Depression (1929–1939), many new socioeconomic laws were enacted as part of the New Deal of President Franklin D. Roosevelt. In the labor field, two important laws survived challenges to their constitutionality: the Anti-Injunction Act and the National Labor Relations Act.

The **Anti-Injunction Act of 1932** (popularly known as the Norris–La Guardia Act, after its prime movers) restricts the issuance of injunctions by the federal courts against unions peacefully striking in labor disputes.[67] Together with the Clayton Act of 1914, it effectively exempts unions from prosecution as monopolistic trusts or conspiracies in restraint of trade. The Norris–La Guardia Act also outlawed **yellow dog contracts,** under which an employee—as a condition of employment—agrees never to join a union. (See Exhibit 13-3.)

The **National Labor Relations Act of 1935 (Wagner Act)** recognizes the right of private sector employees to form, join, or assist unions and to bargain collectively with employers through representatives of their own choosing.[68] **Collective bargaining** is the right given to a union to bargain with the employer over the terms of employment, including wages, hours, job security, and benefits covering all members of the worker group. Once a union is recognized as the bargaining agent of a group of workers, the union has the exclusive authority to bargain for all members of the group. Accordingly, an employee is no longer free to bargain individually with the company. The recognized union not only has the right to bargain on behalf of all members of the group, it has a duty. It cannot refuse to represent a worker in the group even if he or she is not a member of the union. The pejorative term used by union members for such non-members is *freeloader.* The Wagner Act listed and outlawed five **unfair labor practices** of employers:

- Interference, restraint, or coercion with the organization or practice of union activities
- Wrongful domination of unions
- Encouragement or discouragement of unions by discriminating against union members

Anti-Injunction Act of 1932 (Norris–La Guardia Act)

Federal law that restricts the issuance of injunctions in labor disputes, outlaws yellow dog contracts, and exempts unions from legal attack as monopolies.

yellow dog contracts

An employment contract in which a worker agrees not to join a union.

http://

The National Labor Relations Board administers the National Labor Relations Act by monitoring elections, preventing unfair labor practices, and performing other adjudicatory functions. Visit the NLRB at

http://www.nlrb.gov/

National Labor Relations Act of 1935 (Wagner Act)

A federal law that recognizes the right of workers to organize into unions of their own choice, and the duty of employers to bargain collectively with the unions over wages, hours, and conditions of employment. It provides a list of unfair labor practices by management.

EXHIBIT 13-3: **Yellow Dog Contract**

I, Alexander Krakner, in consideration of employment with Hardly Caring Corporation (HCC), covenant that I am not a member of a union nor have I ever been a member of a union. I further agree that while I am employed at HCC I will not become a member of a union nor will I assist or otherwise consort with those who purport to represent unions or are involved with any attempt to unionize HCC. I further agree that I will bring to the attention of HCC any contacts by a union of me or the names of any employees who I find out are engaging in union activities. I expressly agree that any violation of this agreement gives HCC the right to terminate my employment immediately.

Date: 11/17/30

Alexander Krakner, employee
Leavin Nutin Toochance, President of HCC

collective bargaining

The process of negotiation by representative(s) of the employees' union and representative(s) of an employer for an employment contract that provides terms and conditions of employment.

unfair labor practices

Certain practices of employers and unions that are prohibited by federal or state law.

Labor-Management Relations Act of 1947 (Taft-Hartley Act)

A federal law that lists unfair labor practices of unions. It outlaws the closed shop and the secondary boycott.

closed shop

A place of employment where workers must join a union before they can be hired. Made illegal by the Taft-Hartley Act.

secondary boycotts

Occurs when striking workers picket or use other pressure against a neutral third party who supplies or buys from the struck employer.

open shop

A company or department where union membership is not requirement to get or keep a job.

- Refusal to bargain with the union
- Discrimination against any employee seeking protection under the act

LEGAL FOCUS—PROBLEM

Antonio Mondalli and Jack Smith were the two youngest and toughest workers at the Iceberg Cold Storage and Ice Company. When their request for a wage boost to match community levels was denied, they started to persuade other workers in the plant to join them in forming a local union or affiliating with the Teamsters Union. When Artemus Finley, owner-manager of Iceberg, heard of the talk, he promptly fired Mondalli and Smith. Do they have any recourse under the law?

Yes. They can file a complaint with the nearest office of the National Labor Relations Board. For intrastate businesses, in some states they could apply to a comparable state board. In either case, the board could order their reinstatement with back pay.

The Pendulum Swings the Other Way

Some critics claimed that in applying the Wagner Act, the National Labor Relations Board favored the revitalized unions unfairly. And so the pendulum eventually swung back with law that restrained unions (but did not deprive them of their basic rights). The **Labor-Management Relations Act of 1947 (Taft-Hartley Act)**[69] amended the Wagner Act and added a list of unfair labor practices of unions, including, most notably, coercion of employees in their right to join or to refuse to join a union. It outlawed the **closed shop,** which mandated that one must belong to the union before getting a job, and it banned **secondary boycotts,** in which pressure is brought by striking workers against neutral third parties who supply or buy from the affected employer. For example, workers on strike at a furniture factory may not legally picket the independent retail stores that sell the furniture.

In an **open shop,** a union may be recognized as the sole bargaining agent for all employees in the particular group or bargaining unit, but no workers are required to join the union.

LEGAL FOCUS—PROBLEM

Although a union had been selected by a majority of the workers in his department, Virgil Redman refused to join. There was no union-shop agreement, and he insisted on making his own "deal with the boss." "After all," he said, "I've been doing it that way for more than thirty years. We're both satisfied. I don't intend to stop now." May Redman make his own contract with his employer governing his compensation and other terms of employment?

No. When a union is designated as the bargaining representative for workers in a given unit, collective bargaining requires the union to represent all workers in that unit, including nonmembers. This is true even when only a bare majority of eligible workers participated in the representation election, and consequently only a minority of the total workers voted for the union. The same phenomenon can be found in political and campus elections when there is a light turnout.

Legal Injunctions

The Taft-Hartley Act reintroduced the injunction against strikes, but made it available only at the request of the National Labor Relations Board or of the president of the United States in cases of disputes that endanger the national health and welfare. After an eighty-day cooling-off period in such cases, during which time the issues are investigated and reported on by a public board, the strike may resume—to be ended possibly by government seizure and operation under an act of Congress. This extreme option is very seldom utilized. Courts may also issue injunctions against illegal strikes or lockouts and illegal activity in connection with either, such as mass picketing or violence in a strike or lockout.

LEGAL FOCUS—PROBLEM

Loren Hilton was a rugged individualist, and as a matter of principle he opposed joining any mutual help organization. He was also a highly skilled toolmaker. Some time after Advanced Avionics Corporation hired him, the company signed an agreement with the toolmakers' union that called for a union shop. Must Hilton now join the union if he wants to keep his job?

Yes. In a **union shop** an employee must join the union within thirty days after being hired. It is legal under the Taft-Hartley Act although, as noted before, some states have enacted "right-to-work" laws that outlaw this limited approach to union security and stability. Employers who accept the union shop reason that if they have to deal with a union, it may as well include all workers in the bargaining unit. There is likely to be less internal discord, and the union leaders, feeling more secure, are less likely to make outrageous demands or promises to justify their existence. Also, since the union provides benefits, the members understandably believe all workers should share the costs; thus, those who do not join the union are regarded contemptuously as freeloaders.

A variation of the union shop is the **agency shop,** in which all employees in the bargaining unit (nonmembers as well as members) support the union by paying a representative fee (usually a little less than union dues) as a condition of employment. Nonmembers must accept the union as their agent to conduct negotiations with the employer and to conclude employment contracts on behalf of all the employees within the bargaining unit. Many public-employee labor unions have agency-shop agreements that apply to nonmembers. The union cannot use any of such agency-shop dues for activities not directly related to collective bargaining.

The **Labor-Management Reporting and Disclosure Act of 1959 (Landrum-Griffin Act)** is sometimes called the bill of rights of union members, because it guarantees their right to participate in union affairs, protects their freedom to speak up in union meetings, and requires that they be kept informed about the union's financial condition.[70]

LEGAL FOCUS—PROBLEM

Raul Keroupian had joined the union at his plant shortly before the day of the meeting at which officers were to be selected. When nominations were made from the floor,

---

union shop

A place of employment where newly hired workers must join the union within thirty days of being hired.

agency shop

A company or department in which all employees in the bargaining unit must pay union dues (or some comparable fee) irrespective of whether they are union members.

http://

The National Right to Work Legal Defense Foundation is a nonprofit organization providing legal assistance to employees who claim their rights have been violated by compulsory unionism abuses. Visit its Web site at **http://www.nrtw.org/**

Labor-Management Reporting and Disclosure Act of 1959 (Landrum-Griffin Act)

Federal law that mandates open, democratic internal government of unions.

⋮ someone moved to elect the entire incumbent slate by acclamation. Keroupian swallowed nervously, then stood up and said, "I don't think we can do that; it would be illegal." There were hoots and catcalls from the back of the room. Was he correct?

Yes. Among other things, the Landrum-Griffin Act prescribes that every local labor organization must elect its officers at least once every three years by secret ballot among the members in good standing.

Exhibit 13-4 lists the major federal statutes pertaining to labor-management relations.

Do Most Workers Engage in Strikes?

Only about 15 percent of the private workforce belong to unions and unions normally call strikes, so that means that most workers do not engage in strikes. A **strike** is a concerted refusal by employees to perform the services for which they were hired. Strikers do not quit permanently; they consider themselves employees and plan to return to their old jobs when the strike ends. By then, they hope, their employer will have acceded to all or some of their demands. The strike is the ultimate weapon of unions, just as the ultimate weapon of employers is the **lockout**—a shutdown of operations in response to union activity or demands. Neither tactic is used casually or frequently, although the strike is much more common.

The number of major work stoppages in 2001 was historically very low, according to the U.S. Department of Labor's Bureau of Labor Statistics. There were twenty-nine major work stoppages during 2001, idling 102,000 workers.[71] The percentage of days lost in 1997 was less than 0.005 percent compared with 0.3 percent in 1947 when the data was first collected. The peak percentage of work stoppage was in 1959 with 0.43 percent.

strike

A concerted refusal by employees to perform the services for which they were hired, generally in order to gain recognition of a union, or improvements in wages, hours, or conditions of employment.

lockout

A shutdown of operations by an employer in response to union demands or to achieve other changes in an employment contract.

EXHIBIT 13-4: **Major Federal Labor Law Statutes**

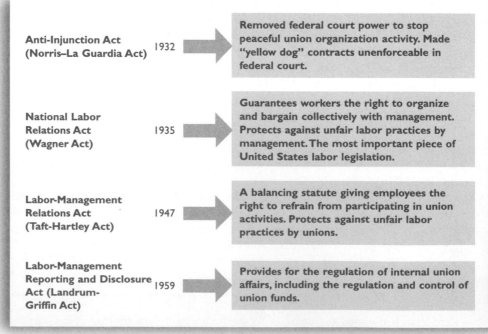

Anti-Injunction Act (Norris–La Guardia Act)	1932	Removed federal court power to stop peaceful union organization activity. Made "yellow dog" contracts unenforceable in federal court.
National Labor Relations Act (Wagner Act)	1935	Guarantees workers the right to organize and bargain collectively with management. Protects against unfair labor practices by management. The most important piece of United States labor legislation.
Labor-Management Relations Act (Taft-Hartley Act)	1947	A balancing statute giving employees the right to refrain from participating in union activities. Protects against unfair labor practices by unions.
Labor-Management Reporting and Disclosure Act (Landrum-Griffin Act)	1959	Provides for the regulation of internal union affairs, including the regulation and control of union funds.

Source: Adapted from American Bar Association, Section of Law Practice Management (Chicago: ABA, 1993).

What Kinds of Strikes Are There?

LEGAL FOCUS—PROBLEM

Pat McGillicuddy was unhappy with the wages, hours, work schedule, plant rules, heating and lighting of the workroom, fringe benefits (there were none), and supervision at his place of employment. One day, after weeks of grumbling and complaining to his coworkers, he got up from his workbench, put on his coat and hat, and shouted so that all in the large room could hear, "I strike!" Then he walked out the door and started to picket in front of the building. Was he on strike?

Because there was no union ordering the strike nor combined action by a group of workers, McGillicuddy was not on strike. It is an individual's protest, and his employer can take the action to mean that he has quit and can be replaced.

When there is a union and it orders all members to walk out in an **economic strike** (over wages, hours, or conditions of employment), the employer may legally hire **strikebreakers** as permanent replacements. After the strike is over, however, if the jobs again become available (which is unlikely) the employer must rehire the strikers, provided they have not taken substantially equivalent permanent jobs elsewhere (which by the time the job becomes available is usually the case). On the other hand, when the strike is an **unfair labor practice strike** prompted by one or more unfair labor practices of the employer, the striking workers retain full rights to their jobs and must be restored to them when the strike ends. Moreover, the offending employer must pay back wages to the strikers.

LEGAL FOCUS—PROBLEM

The Snug Fit Shoe Corporation had a three-year contract with its production workers under a collective-bargaining agreement. The union vote approving the contract had been very close, and initial dissatisfaction had gradually turned into outspoken protest. After sixteen months, the workers defied their leaders and announced through a spokesperson: "We're on strike. To prevent strikebreakers from taking our jobs, we're going to stay right here in the plant." A sit-down strike had begun. Friends and relatives brought the strikers' sleeping bags and food for a long stay. Was the strike legal?

No. **Sit-down strikes,** in which workers retain possession of the employer's property, are illegal.[72] Moreover, this was a **wildcat strike,** one that is in violation of the contract and of the union's own rules. As such, it constituted an unfair labor practice on the part of the workers, and the employer could hire permanent replacements for the strikers, who could be evicted by the police and be subject to punishment.

Arbitration of Employment Disputes

Collective-bargaining agreements often provide for arbitration of disputes arising during the term of the labor agreement. For example, a common provision in a labor contract

---

economic strike

A strike in which workers seek a change in wages, hours, and/or conditions of employment.

strikebreakers

Persons hired to take the place of workers who are out on strike. If it is an economic strike, the strikebreakers may be retained as permanent replacements

unfair labor practice strike

A strike in which the workers are protesting an unfair labor practice of their employer.

sit-down strike

Illegal strike in which strikers remain in their places of employment but refuse to work.

wildcat strike

An unlawful strike of union members that takes place without the approval of the union leaders.

restricts management discretion in employee discipline and termination. The provision establishes that no discharge or discipline can occur except upon a showing of "just cause" (a limitation upon the common-law "at will" doctrine) and in a specified fashion. If the subject union member is displeased with the discipline, he or she can grieve under agreed processes, which ultimately lead to a hearing by a neutral arbitrator.

LEGAL FOCUS—CASE

The manager of safety and security at a convalescence hospital became aware that "S," a PBX operator with some receptionist responsibilities, was wearing nose jewelry, namely a small silver hoop in her left nostril. The manager informed "S" not to wear this at work other than on breaks and lunch periods. An accommodation was later reached allowing "S" to wear a Band-Aid over the small hoop while working. "S" believed that the Band-Aid over her nose hoop violated provisions of the collective-bargaining agreement, and she filed a grievance. The case went to arbitration. How did the arbitrator rule?

103 Lab. Arb. (BNA) 988 (1994).

http://

The American Arbitration Association has an excellent Web site for information about employer/employee arbitration labor and otherwise at
http://www.adr.org/

Most disputes involving discipline over unusual hairstyles, body piercing, and clothing choices are resolved in the employer's favor. The employer's right to set dress standards is allowable management discretion unless it is a subterfuge for prohibited discrimination. In this case, the arbitrator noted that the company had dress guidelines prohibiting extremes in jewelry. The arbitrator gave great "deference to management's interpretation and application of its dress and grooming standards. [The company] did not violate the Agreement when it prohibited the Grievant from wearing a ring or hoop through her nose while on duty as a PBX Operator. Therefore, the grievance shall be denied."

Whereas arbitration in union–labor contracts is common, is it common in nonunion employment situations? Until recently, the answer was no.

LEGAL FOCUS—CASE

Interstate/Johnson Lane Corporation (Interstate) hired Robert Gilmer as a manager of financial services in May 1981. Gilmer was required by his employer to register as a securities representative with the New York Stock Exchange (NYSE). His registration application provided for arbitration of any controversy arising out of a registered representative's employment or termination of employment. Interstate terminated Gilmer's employment at age sixty-two. Thereafter, he filed a charge with the EEOC and brought suit in the District Court, alleging that he had been discharged in violation of the Age Discrimination in Employment Act of 1967 (ADEA). Interstate moved to compel arbitration. Was Gilmer forced to arbitrate his ADEA claim?

Robert D. Gilmer v. Interstate/Johnson Lane Corporation, 500 U.S. 20, 111 S.Ct. 1647 (1991).

He was. Gilmer argued that U.S. Supreme Court precedent provided that employees were free to file civil rights suits without regard to agreements to arbitrate such claims and that Congress intended to protect ADEA claimants from a waiver of the judicial forum. The

Court held otherwise, stating that earlier cases were restricted to collective-bargaining employment contracts. "An important concern therefore was the tension between collective representation and individual statutory rights, a concern not applicable to the present case. Finally, those cases were not decided under the FAA [Federal Arbitration Act], which reflects a 'liberal federal policy favoring arbitration agreements.' Therefore, those cases provide no basis for refusing to enforce Gilmer's agreement to arbitrate his ADEA claim." The U.S. Supreme Court required Gilmer to submit all his claims (including ADEA) to compulsory binding arbitration.

After the *Gilmer* case, courts began to uphold agreements to arbitrate non-union employment disputes.[73] Substantial concern about arbitration of employment disputes was raised by the National Employment Lawyers Association, which argued that such agreements lacked true consent by the employee and often limited employee rights. A special task force composed of individuals representing management, labor, employment, civil rights organizations, private administrative agencies, government, and the American Arbitration Association drafted "The Due Process Protocol for Mediation and Arbitration of Statutory Disputes Arising Out of the Employment Relationship." The Due Process Protocol "recognizes the dilemma inherent in the timing of an agreement to mediate and/or arbitrate statutory disputes" but does not take a position on whether an employer can require a pre-dispute, binding arbitration program as a condition of employment.[74]

The *Gilmer* case technically did not deal with an employment contract, although it appears no one except perhaps the U.S. Supreme Court believed that. Gilmer's arbitration agreement was in a securities exchange registration form, not an employment contract. Because of this, the Court did not address at that time the specific language of the Federal Arbitration Act (FAA), which states it does not apply to contracts of employment of "seamen, railroad employees, or any other class of workers engaged in foreign or interstate commerce." Ten years later the Court held that the FAA does apply to all employment agreements, except those covering employees engaged in transportation. Companies can now ask their employees to waive their right to go to court and rely exclusively on arbitration to resolve workplace bias claims.[75] As discussed on page 611 the arbitration clause does not preclude the EEOC from pursuing a claim on behalf of an employee.[76]

LEGAL FOCUS—EXAMPLE

Greg Hendrickson was delighted to begin work for LA Billboards, Inc. Like most employees he paid little attention to his six-page employment contract. Three years later he was fired after he complained to his boss about business practices he said violated local ordinances. When Hendrickson contemplated filing a lawsuit for wrongful termination, he read his contract more carefully. The employment contract not only required he arbitrate any dispute but it forbade recovery of punitive damages and discovery. In addition, it ordered the payment of a nonrefundable $500 filing fee; that the matter be heard on the other coast at the company home office; that any back pay recovery to be capped at $2,000, and that the employee share the costs of the arbitrator and the arbitration hearing room. Lastly, the arbitrator was to be selected from a list provided by LA Billboards. Oops.

Signing an arbitration clause may be nothing more than changing forums, which, although important, does not necessarily affect fundamental rights. On the other hand, giving up remedies and rights in the process could also be part of the contract. What restrictions might be enforceable is still in contention in United States courts, but it is clear that LA Billboards went too far. In the 2002 case *Circuit City Stores, Inc. v. Adams,*[77] the 9th Circuit Court of Appeals held that the Federal Arbitration Act, although allowing for the enforcement of employment arbitration clauses, does not allow enforcement of an unconscionable agreement. The contract in the *Circuit City* case was replete with "objectionable provisions pervading the entire contract." The court instructed employers that to be enforceable, a contract must:

- Provide for neutral arbitrators
- Provide for more than minimal discovery
- Require a written award
- Provide for all of the types of relief that would otherwise be available in court, and
- Not require employees to pay either unreasonable costs or any arbitrators' fees or expenses as a condition of access to the arbitration forum.[78]

PRICE WATERHOUSE V. HOPKINS
490 U.S. 228, 109 S.Ct. 1775 (1989)

Ann B. Hopkins worked for five years as a minor manager in the Washington, D.C., office of Price Waterhouse, a major accounting firm, when she was proposed as a candidate for partnership. Of the 662 partners in the firm at that time, seven were women. Of the thirty-two partners who submitted comments, thirteen supported her bid, three recommended it be placed on hold, and eight recommended that she be denied partnership (the remaining eight said they had no informed opinion about her). The firm's Admission Committee and its Policy Board placed her candidacy on hold. Hopkins brought a sex-discrimination charge against the firm under Title VII of the Civil Rights Act of 1964. The District Court ruled in her favor, and the Circuit Court of Appeals affirmed in part, reversed in part, and remanded the case to the District Court. The case came to the U.S. Supreme Court on certiorari. In a 6–3 vote, the Supreme Court approved the findings of the District Court but remanded the case for determination under the proper standard of evidence (i.e., by a preponderance of the evidence).

On remand, the District Court again held Price Waterhouse liable and ordered the firm to accept her as a partner, retroactive to 1982, and to pay her $371,000 in back salary and interest. When Price Waterhouse again appealed, the District of Columbia Circuit Court of Appeals again affirmed.

Justice Brennan wrote the opinion: The partners in Hopkins' office praised her character as well as her accomplishments, describing her in their joint statement as "an outstanding professional" who had a "deft touch," a "strong character, independence and integrity...." Evaluations such as these led [trial] Judge Gesell to conclude that Hopkins "had no difficulty dealing with clients and her clients appear to have been very pleased with her work" and that she "was generally viewed as a highly competent project leader who worked long hours, pushed vigorously to meet deadlines and demanded much from the multidisciplinary staffs with which she worked...." On too many occasions, however, Hopkins' aggressiveness apparently spilled over into abrasiveness.... Both "[s]upporters and opponents of her candidacy," stressed Judge Gesell, "indicated that she was sometimes overly aggressive, unduly harsh, difficult to work with and impatient with staff."

There were clear signs, though, that some of the partners reacted negatively to Hopkins' personality because she was a woman. One partner described her as "macho;" another suggested that she "overcompensated for being a woman;" a third advised her to take "a course at charm school." Several partners criticized her use of profanity; in response, one partner suggested that those partners objected to her swearing only "because it's a lady using foul language." Another supporter explained that Hopkins "ha[d] matured from a tough-talking somewhat masculine hard-nosed [manager] to an authoritative, formidable, but much more appealing lady [partner] candidate." But it was the man who, as Judge Gesell found, bore responsibility for explaining to Hopkins the reasons for the Policy Board's decision to place her candidacy on hold who delivered the coup de grace: in order to improve her chances for partnership, Thomas Beyer advised, Hopkins should "walk more femininely, talk more femininely, dress more femininely, wear make-up, have her hair styled, and wear jewelry...."

The Court of Appeals affirmed the district court's ultimate conclusion, but departed from its analysis in one particular: it held that even if a plaintiff proves that discrimination played a role in an employment decision, the defendant will not be found liable if it proves, by clear and convincing evidence, that it would have made the same decision in the absence of discrimination.... Under this approach, an employer is not deemed to have violated Title VII if it proves that it would have made the same decision in the absence of an impermissible motive, whereas under the district court's approach the employer's proof in that respect only avoids equitable relief. We decide today that the Court of Appeals had the better approach, but that both courts erred in requiring the employer to make its proof by clear and convincing evidence....

We have, in short, been here before. Each time, we have concluded that the plaintiff who shows that an impermissible motive played a motivating part in an adverse employment decision has thereby placed upon the defendant the burden to show that it would have made the same decision in the absence of the unlawful motive. Our decision today treads this well-worn path....

In saying that gender played a motivating part in an employment decision, we mean that, if we asked the employer at the moment of the decision what its reasons were and if we received a truthful response, one of those reasons would be that the applicant or employee was a woman. In the specific context of sex stereotyping, an employer who acts on the basis of a belief that a woman cannot be aggressive, or that she must not be, has acted on the basis of gender. . . .

The very premise of a mixed-motives case is that a legitimate reason was present, and indeed, in this case, Price Waterhouse already has made this showing by convincing Judge Gesell that Hopkins' interpersonal problems were a legitimate concern. The employer instead must show that its legitimate reason, standing alone, would have induced it to make the same decision. . . .

The courts below held that an employer who has allowed a discriminatory impulse to play a motivating part in an employment decision must prove by clear and convincing evidence that it would have made the same decision in the absence of discrimination. We are persuaded that the better rule is that the employer must make this showing by a preponderance of the evidence. . . .

Although Price Waterhouse does not concretely tell us how its proof was preponderant even if it was not clear and convincing, this general claim is implicit in its request for the less stringent standard. Since the lower courts required Price Waterhouse to make its proof by clear and convincing evidence, they did not determine whether Price Waterhouse had proved by *a preponderance of the evidence* that it would have placed Hopkins' candidacy on hold even if it had not permitted sex-linked evaluations to play a part in the decision-making process. Thus, we shall remand this case so that that determination can be made. . . .

In finding that some of the partners' comments reflected sex stereotyping, the district court relied in part on Dr. Fiske's expert testimony. . . .

Indeed, we are tempted to say that Dr. Fiske's expert testimony was merely icing on Hopkins' cake. It takes no special training to discern sex stereotyping in a description of an aggressive female employee as requiring "a course at charm school." Nor, turning to Thomas Beyer's memorable advice to Hopkins, does it require expertise in psychology to know that, if an employee's flawed "interpersonal skills" can be corrected by a soft-hued suit or a new shade of lipstick, perhaps it is the employee's sex and not her interpersonal skills that has drawn the criticism. . . .

We hold that when a plaintiff in a Title VII case proves that her gender played a motivating part in an employment decision, the defendant may avoid a finding of liability only by proving by a preponderance of the evidence that it would have made the same decision even if it had not taken the plaintiff's gender into account. Because the courts below erred by deciding that the defendant must make this proof by clear and convincing evidence, we reverse the Court of Appeals' judgment against Price Waterhouse on liability and remand the case to that court for further proceedings. It is so ordered.

For Critical Analysis

1. Is this case about sexual harassment or gender discrimination? What is the difference?

2. Does this case suggest to you that if your reason for a particular decision is nondiscriminatory that liability could still occur if your explanation suggested discrimination is involved?

3. Preponderance of the evidence and clear and convincing evidence are both discussed as burdens of proof. Which standard does the court ultimately require and for what and why? Does this decision favor the employer or the employee?

4. Do we know the ultimate result of this controversy from this opinion? Explain.

RAYMOND J. GONZALES V. SOUTHWEST SECURITY AND PROTECTION AGENCY, INC.

Court of Appeals of New Mexico, 100 N.M. 54, 665 P.2d 810 (1983)

Raymond Gonzales, assaulted by security guards at a wrestling match, brought this action against the city, the sponsor of the wrestling match, the security company, and the individual security guards for damages resulting from false imprisonment, battery, and negligent hiring, training, supervising, and retaining of certain personnel. The District Court entered judgment in favor of the plaintiff against the security company and certain guards. The security company appealed, claiming that the doctrine of respondeat superior *did not apply when employee torts were intentional and that Southwest Security was not independently negligent. The Court of Appeals held that (1) as the guards' conduct was naturally incident to the company's business, the company was properly held liable for intentional torts committed by the guards, and (2) substantial evidence supported findings that the company was negligent in equipping, training, supervising, and retaining the guards, and that its negligence caused the patron's injuries.*

Judge Lopez wrote the opinion of the court: Plaintiff sued for damages resulting from false imprisonment, battery and negligent hiring, training, supervision and retention of certain personnel. A bench trial was had and plaintiff was awarded $15,000.00. Defendant appeals. We affirm.

Plaintiff, Raymond Gonzales (Gonzales), sued the City of Albuquerque (City), Fundamentals, Inc. (Fundamentals), Southwest Security and Protection Agency (Southwest) and five security guard employees of Southwest. The suit arose out of an episode where Gonzales received injuries while attending a wrestling match sponsored by Fundamentals. The match was held in the civic auditorium owned by the city, which it rented to Fundamentals. Southwest was hired by Fundamentals to provide security services for the event.

Gonzales sustained a broken jaw and lost four teeth in an incident involving five of Southwest's security men. He claims he was handcuffed by the security men, taken to a small room in the auditorium and beaten. The incident occurred as Gonzales and a friend were leaving the auditorium and a woman accosted him for having thrown beer during the matches. Security guards intervened and told Gonzales and his friend to leave. Once outside the auditorium the woman again accosted Gonzales's friend, setting off a substantial disturbance. When the security guards arrived Gonzales was a bystander. Nevertheless, the guards threw Gonzales to the ground, handcuffed him and took him to a

small room where he was beaten. Throughout the incident Gonzales apparently was calm and did not provoke the guards.

Default judgment was entered against Southwest employees Mike and Alex Sedillo and David Chavez. At trial the City, Fundamentals and Southwest employee Ysidro Victor Vigil were found to be free of fault. Judgment in favor of Gonzalez was entered against Southwest and its employee Denny Sanchez. Southwest appeals.

On appeal Southwest contends (1) that it should not be held responsible for the intentional torts of its employees; and (2) that substantial evidence does not support the trial court finding it negligent.

Point 1: An Employer's Liability for the Intentional Torts of Its Employees. An employer is liable for the intentional torts of its employees if the torts are committed in the course and scope of employment. Whether an employee's conduct is within the course and scope of employment is a question of fact. In the case at bar, the question is whether the security guards' imprisonment and battering of Gonzales was within the course and scope of their employment. In resolution of this question we note that local decisions exist regarding an employee's intentional torts; however, none address the activity of private security personnel.

The definition of "the course and scope of employment" is variable. [The court has] adopted the following test of whether conduct was within the course of employment: "... an act is within the 'course of employment' if (1) it be something fairly and naturally incident to the business, and if (2) it be done while the servant was engaged upon the master's business and be done, although mistakenly or ill advisedly, with a view to further the master's interests, or from some impulse of emotion which naturally grew out of or was incident to the attempt to perform the master's business, and did not arise wholly from some external, independent, and personal motive on the part of the servant to do the act upon his own account."

In addition to the test delineated above, the instant case requires additional considerations because of the nature of Southwest's and the security guards' work. The Restatement of Agency addresses the use of force as follows: A master is subject to liability for the intended tortious harm by a servant to the person or things of another by an act done in connection with the servant's employment, although the act was unauthorized, if the act was not unexpectable in view of the duties of the servant. Restatement (Second) of Agency § 249 (1958). Comment c to § 245 adds the following: c. Nature of employment. Whether or not an employment involves or is likely to lead to the use of force against the person of another is a question to be decided upon the facts of the individual case. To create liability for a battery by a servant upon a third person, the employment must be one which is likely to bring the servant into conflict with others. The making of contracts, or the compromise, settlement, or collection of accounts, does not ordinarily have this tendency. On the other hand, the employment of servants to guard or to recapture property, to take possession of land, or to deal with chattels, which are in the possession of another, is likely to lead to altercations, and the master may become liable, in spite of instructions that no force shall be exerted against the person of the possessor.

In this case Southwest provided the security personnel with uniforms, handcuffs, guns, night sticks and the authority to keep peace. Evidence at trial showed that Gonzales's injuries were inflicted, at least in part, by a guard's use of a nightstick. Moreover, Gonzales was handcuffed during the beating. We therefore have a situation where not only did Southwest's employees beat a person, but the beating was facilitated by instrumentalities provided by Southwest.

According to the foregoing facts and authority, we conclude that the trial court properly determined that the guards' conduct was naturally incident to Southwest's business. The trial court also properly determined that the guards' conduct substantially arose out of an attempt to perform Southwest's business. Finally, from our review of the record, we hold that substantial evidence supports the trial court's finding that Southwest was liable for its employees' intentional torts.

Point 2. Whether Substantial Evidence Supports Finding Southwest Negligent. Southwest contends the trial court's finding of negligence is not supported by substantial evidence. [In the New Mexico Supreme Court decision in *F & T Co. v. Woods* (1979)], the court held that defendant could not be liable for negligently hiring or retaining an employee because there was no showing that defendant's omissions proximately caused plaintiff's injuries. The principle [sic] reason proximate causation was lacking was because defendant's employee was acting outside the scope of employment, without defendant's authority and without instrumentalities provided by defendant, when plaintiff was harmed. In the case at bar, however, we have held that the guards were acting within the scope of their employment, and were using instrumentalities provided by Southwest, when Gonzales's injuries occurred. We therefore begin with a vast factual disparity between *F & T Co. v. Woods* and the case at bar.

The specific error alleged by Southwest is that the guards' intentional torts were neither foreseeable nor the cause of Gonzales' harm. While the terms "foreseeability" and "proximate causation" evade precise definition, the meaning of these terms is well known in the law. The existence of causation is ordinarily a question of fact. In the case at bar the court concluded that Southwest negligently equipped, trained, supervised and retained the guards, and that Southwest's negligence was the cause of Gonzales's harm. These conclusions were based on the following findings:

12. Southwest Security did not adequately investigate the background and the character of the individual Defendants herein prior to hiring them as security guards.

13. Southwest Security did not adequately supervise their security guards in general and in particular on the evening of August 19, 1979.

14. Southwest Security failed to adequately train the security guards in the use of weapons such as clubs and handcuffs which were provided to Mike Z. Sedillo, Alex Sedillo, Denny Sanchez and David Chavez.

15. Southwest Security failed to adequately instruct its employees in the proper method of restraining and arresting individuals.

16. There was at least one other prior beating of an individual by employees of Southwest Security and in particular Mike Z. Sedillo which occurred [sic] at a wrestling match and Southwest Security was or should have been aware of such incident(s) and failed to take appropriate action to avoid further incident(s) of this nature.

17. The negligence of Southwest Security as specified above proximately caused the damages which resulted to Raymond J. Gonzales.

The findings quoted above are supported by evidence in the record. Testimony at trial revealed that Southwest's guards previously had mistreated people, that supervisors or owners of Southwest knew or should have known of such treatment, and that Southwest knew violence was pervasive at similar events held in the auditorium. From these facts we conclude that substantial evidence supports the trial court's findings that Southwest was negligent and that its negligence caused Gonzales's injuries.

The judgment of the trial court is affirmed. Appellate costs are to be paid by Southwest.

For Critical Analysis

1. Employers are not usually liable for an employee's intentional torts. What about this situation persuaded the court to hold the employer liable?

2. Did the court hold Southwest liable under the doctrine of *respondeat superior* and also hold them negligent? If these are different theories, explain the difference.

3. Could Southwest sue the security guards for any payments they are required to make to Gonzales? Explain your answer.

4. What precautions can a company such as Southwest Security and Protection Agency employ to avoid or reduce liability in the future? ◼

CHAPTER QUESTIONS AND PROBLEMS

1. Problems abound in the area of employment. The following questions involve some of the more difficult and challenging ones. What are your suggestions for answers and solutions?
   a. Do minimum-wage laws discourage employment of young persons, especially the unskilled, and thus encourage idleness and crime? Should the minimum-wage laws be eliminated or modified for minors and young adults?
   b. Subtle illegal discrimination because of sex, color, religion, age, and national origin still exists in many places. How can it be further reduced or eliminated? How can victims of discrimination facilitate that elimination?
   c. Should the federal government be the employer of last resort for those who cannot find jobs in the private sector? What meaningful work could such persons do?
   d. Should all states enact right-to-work laws?
   e. Should labor strikes and management lockouts be forbidden, and labor–management disputes be settled by compulsory arbitration?
   f. Are unions obsolescent or obsolete? If not, why, when, where, and how should union membership be encouraged? Should employers be required to rehire all strikers (after the strike is ended), even in an economic strike?
   g. Should comparable-worth laws be enacted at the federal and state levels? Would women be the only beneficiaries of such legislation?
   h. Since people live longer now than when the Social Security Act was enacted in 1935, should the normal retirement age be advanced from 65 to 70?
   i. Should racial and other special interest or minority quotas and affirmative action policies for employment and educational (e.g., college admission) opportunities be legally forbidden?
   j. The Civil Rights Act is silent as to gay rights. Does the federal statute provide civil rights protections to gays?

2. Generally, an employer has the right to fire an employee at will, even as the employee has the right to quit at will. Both parties by means of an express written and signed agreement can negate these rights, as, for example, when a college football coach is hired "for three years." An employer's power to fire may also be limited if there is an implied agreement not to discharge without cause. How could such an implied agreement be created?

3. A probationary police officer in the Globe, Arizona, police department was fired. The officer sued the city for wrongful discharge, claiming he was terminated because he had discovered that a man who had been arrested and convicted and was now serving time for vagrancy was doing so under a law that had been repealed. The officer told a court official of the situation, pointing out that the detention was illegal. The judicial official informed the police chief. The chief fired the officer, saying he did not appreciate "big city cops" coming to Globe to tell him how to run his department. A probationary civil service employee may generally be dismissed at will; a "just cause" need not be stated or proved. Was this firing nevertheless a wrongful discharge? [*Wagner v. City of Globe,* 150 Ariz. 82, 722 P.2d 250 (Arizona, 1986).]

4. Consider the following ethical issues:
   a. Is it legal for an employer to require an employee to lie when dealing with customers in order to make a sale?

b. Should an auto mechanic be required by his employer to replace parts prematurely in order to boost the income of the shop?

c. A carpet installer is asked by a customer to by-pass his employer and install a carpet on his own time.

d. The boss's son is making unwanted and unpleasant comments about his sexual intentions toward you. You keep it to yourself because you fear nothing will be done if you report the incidents.

5. Carolyn Garcia, nurse extraordinaire, was fired from her River County health clinic job when she refused to distribute "morning after" pills to patients. These pills are an emergency contraceptive medicine used to end a pregnancy in a manner similar to a miscarriage. Garcia sued River County alleging religious discrimination under Title VII of the Civil Rights Act and a violation of her First Amendment rights to free speech and religious practice. Do you think she prevailed in her lawsuit?

6. Delta Bibby had worked as a dental assistant in Dr. Harley Hayes's dental practice for three years. When Delta became pregnant she approached Dr. Hayes about a leave. He scheduled an appointment to discuss the leave but when Bibby arrived, Dr. Hayes gave her a check for two weeks' severance pay and asked for the keys to the office. Bibby asked Dr. Hayes why she was being fired. He replied: "My wife's jealousy has really gotten out of hand. She thinks I got you pregnant and she said either I let you go or forget the marriage. Sorry, but you have to go." Bibby and the dentist were innocent of any wrongdoing. Does Bibby have a gender discrimination case?

7. After a strike was legally called, Phil Thornbush joined coworkers on "picket duty" at their place of work, an intrastate business. There was no violence, and only two picketers at a given time marched in front of the plant, day and night. Thornbush and his partner were arrested and convicted under a state statute that made loitering and picketing a misdemeanor. They appealed, claiming the state violated their federal constitutional right to free speech. Should the convictions be reversed?

8. Several types of discrimination fall within the prohibitions of various civil rights acts. Which of the types of discrimination do you think occasion the most complaints by alleged victims?
a. race
b. gender
c. national origin
d. age
e. disability
f. religion

9. Two days after starting a new job Dourly Popper was fired. He claims it was because he reported for jury service on the third day of work. His supervisor said it was because he refused to work overtime the first time he was asked. Can a probationary employee successfully sue for wrongful termination? What are his chances?

10. April Barber, an agent employed by Prototype, Inc., was driving her own car and rushing to an important luncheon meeting scheduled with a prospective customer. She saw the amber light in the signal ahead, but to stop and wait would delay her at least four minutes, and she was already late. So she pushed the accelerator down, even though the light had changed to red, and raced ahead at 50 mph through the intersection—*almost*. Before she got across, her car collided with Fred Lamare's truck, which had legally entered on the far right side. Lamare was injured and the truck was demolished.
a. Is Barber's employer, the principal Prototype, liable?
b. Would the employer be liable if Barber were an ordinary employee?
c. Would the employer be liable if Barber were an independent contractor?
d. Would your answer be different in a, b, and c above if April were violating not only the speed limit but also Prototype's explicit orders not to go faster than 35 mph in town?
e. Is Barber personally liable to Lamare?
f. Is Barber personally liable to Prototype?

CHAPTER 14

Wills, Trusts, and Probate

*I*n youth my wings were strong and tireless,
But I did not know the mountains.
In age I knew the mountains,
But my weary wings could not follow my vision—
Genius is wisdom and youth.

"Headstone of Alexander Throckmorton," *Spoon River Anthology*,
Edgar Lee Masters, 1864–1950

After reading and studying this chapter, you should be able to:

🏛 Define estate planning and describe the major concerns one should attend to in planning an estate.

🏛 Identify the major taxes and expenses that accompany transfers of property by gift of death.

🏛 Identify the requisites of and the different types of valid wills. Understand the reasons why a person creates a will.

🏛 Describe challenges that can be made to a will.

🏛 Understand probate and describe its positive and negative aspects.

🏛 Explain how property is distributed if a person dies without a valid will.

🏛 Describe advance directives, living wills, directives to physicians, and durable powers of attorney for health care.

🏛 Discuss the legal concepts of suicide and euthanasia and understand the moral debate over end-of-life issues.

🏛 Identify the legal requisites of different types of trusts, including living trusts.

🏛 Describe the use of conservatorship and guardianship.

Unfortunately, not all of the significant events in our lives are pleasant. Death must some-day come to family members and others we love, including ourselves. But life goes on, and the law provides means of assuring survivors that important financial matters of the deceased are properly handled. Are you prepared to share in these responsibilities? Who should have a will? How do you create a will? Do you need the services of an attorney to prepare a will? Should property be left equally, share and share alike, to heirs? When is a trust helpful in preparing for the financial aftermath of death? Is an attorney needed when a family member dies? Under what circumstances can a will be contested? How are family assets taxed when death occurs? What is a living will? A living trust? Can you leave instructions to prevent hookup to life support systems if you suffer a stroke or are in an automobile accident and become too incapacitated to make such a decision?

LEGAL FOCUS—PROBLEM

Mary Trimble, age eighty-seven and bedridden, had been suffering from a painful, debilitating illness for two years. Medical opinion was that she would never improve. She asked her physician to help her commit suicide by lethal injection. She also asked her husband to take whatever means he could to end her life as mercifully as possible. Can Trimble's physician or husband legally give her the relief she seeks?

No. Almost every state prohibits assisted suicide, and the U.S. Supreme Court has ruled that there is no constitutional right to die.[1] This situation is quite different from those in which the patient previously has signed a written directive that he or she desires that life support equipment be avoided, or even removed once hooked up. Many believe that laws should be expanded to include the choice of physician-assisted suicide.

In this chapter we present the challenging laws of estate planning and probate matters. To most of us the subject of death is unpleasant, so we avoid discussing it. We are, of course, willing to acknowledge that death happens. But it happens "to others, not to me! At least not yet!"

The inevitability of one's death should be calmly recognized as a reason for appropriate planning starting at least by midlife. By law, upon death, title to assets of the **decedent** (a more technical and less personal way of saying that a person has recently died) must go to someone, generally through the procedures of a probate court. It is true that "You can't take it with you!" But with prudent planning, and using such legal instruments as a will and perhaps a trust, you can arrange to have your property distributed consistent with your wishes. Moreover, your foresight can guarantee that your **heirs** (those who are legally entitled to your estate if you leave no will), as well as other intended beneficiaries or "objects of your bounty" will receive more, and that the government death-tax collectors will receive less. The topic is important.

One hundred years ago, only the rich needed to do estate planning (wills and trusts), but today its importance has increased for the rich and middle class alike. In the early years of the twenty-first century, taxes are a significant potential burden on the passing of wealth to heirs, and many Americans have estates substantial enough to desire protection from high federal tax rates. In Congress elimination of estate taxes has become a recurring theme, and recent legislation provides for a yearly reduction and elimination of some of these estate taxes by 2010 and a reinstituting of the taxes in 2011 unless Congress continues

decedent

A deceased person.

heirs

Persons designated by law to receive the estate of a decedent who leaves no will.

the elimination.* The issue of whether estate taxes are good taxes that should remain a permanent source of government revenue is a political issue, not a legal one, and the ultimate resolution is anybody's guess. The complexity of the political fallout is, however, a legal and financial issue.

In 1900, there was no federal income tax or federal estate and gift tax. Many of the legal methods used in estate planning discussed in this chapter existed in the late nineteenth century, but many did not. There were no living wills, medical directives, A and B trusts for tax planning, or "Avoid Probate" seminars and self-help books. And to advocate legally assisted suicide would itself have been suicidal. Property that might be transferred in the year 2005 will include such items as a computer, automobile, airplane, Microsoft common stock, high-definition television set, vacation-share condominium, and cryo-freeze container complete with instructions. These gifts will not be found if you search the probate records of early 1900 wills. Instead, you will find horses, wagons, guns, family Bibles, books, tools, and (if lucky) the family farm. An attorney at the beginning of the last century needed to ask clients the names of all of their children born of any marriage or born outside of marriage (the last part asked with great delicacy). An attorney today must now ask clients about frozen eggs and sperm when trying to establish potential heirs and estate claims. What will the attorneys of the year 2101 need to ask?

WHAT IS ESTATE PLANNING?

Estate planning is an ongoing analysis of what a person owns or expects to own (assets), and what he or she owes to others (liabilities). It involves short-range tactics and long-range strategies to maximize benefits for the individual and the estate (and dependents) while still alive, and for the heirs and other beneficiaries who will own the estate after the individual's death. As personal income and expenses change, and as needs and wants also change over the years, the estate plans must change as well, or they can cause more harm than good. For example, estate plans typically must be adjusted following a divorce, the birth of a child, the receipt of a substantial inheritance, or changes in the number and circumstances of intended beneficiaries. An estate plan may involve continuing education, investing, saving for major purchases, borrowing for such things as a residence, and providing for retirement.

Estate plans usually include the following four major objectives:

- **To provide for the financial needs of the planner while alive.** If married, the financial needs of the spouse and other dependents are also an important concern.
- **To reflect the desires of the planner.** That is, the plan should provide appropriately for beneficiaries who are thought to be deserving, and possibly charities, while excluding potential beneficiaries who are deemed undeserving or not in need.
- **To minimize or legitimately avoid taxes.** Taxes include (a) income taxes payable both during life and after the planner's death, and (b) estate and inheritance taxes (**death taxes**) payable after the planner's death.
- **To minimize or avoid the delays, costs, and publicity of probate. Probate** is the process of proving the validity of a will in court, coupled with the ability to monitor the administration of the decedent's estate.

---

* The Economic Growth and Tax Relief Reconciliation Act of 2001 provides for reductions in taxes until 2010 and then an elimination of the estate tax in 2010. However, the law is subject to a sunset provision that repeals the law in 2011 unless a further law extends its repeal. It might be referred to as a Congressional sleight of hand.

http://

A general Web site with links to estate planning sites on the Internet is **http://www.estateplanning links.com**

estate planning

The process of arranging a person's property and estate, taking into account the laws of wills, taxes, insurance, property, and trusts so as to gain maximum benefit of all laws while carrying out the person's wishes for use of the property during his or her lifetime and disposition of the property upon his or her death.

death tax

Taxes imposed on the estate of the decedent (that is, an *estate* tax on the privilege of giving) and on the gifts received by the donee(s) (that is, an *inheritance* tax on the privilege of receiving).

probate

The process of proving the validity of a will in court, coupled with the related matter of administering the decedent's estate.

Even for persons of modest wealth and income, the importance and value of proper estate planning cannot be overstated. All aspects of such planning have legal consequences, but our focus is on the transfer of property to others before or after death, and on trusts and wills as they relate to probate.

WHAT TAX BURDENS CAN THE ESTATE PLANNER REDUCE OR AVOID?

At least until 2010 the federal government imposes a death tax or **estate tax** on the total net assets of a person at death. Thus, it is a levy on the giving of property to others after death. A declining number of states also levy death taxes.* A few state governments impose these death taxes as a transfer tax on the estate on the property transferred at death. More states impose an **inheritance tax** upon the receiving of property from the estate of a decedent. The individual who inherits the property pays state inheritance tax. Inheritance and estate taxes together are called death taxes, as mentioned earlier.

Inheritance tax rates vary from state to state. The inheritance tax rate increases or decreases depending on the amount received and the relationship of the recipient to the decedent (spouses and close relatives pay less than friends). Many states, including California, Colorado, Florida, Illinois, Minnesota, Texas, and Washington, impose no death taxes.†

Most modest estates are distributed free of federal tax. Large estates are heavily taxed, although appropriate estate planning can reduce and even eliminate this burden. The highest tax after deduction of an **estate tax exemption** is 49 percent in 2003 declining to 45 percent in 2009 before elimination in 2010. (See Exhibit 14-1 for estate tax exemptions by year.) Wealthy persons avoid taxes (both income and estate) by making exempt gifts, by utilizing trusts, and by making thoughtful wills. Wills and trusts are also used to direct property to preferred persons, called *beneficiaries*. The most common type of tax-reduction trusts are marital trusts and generation-skipping trusts, both of which are described later in this chapter.

EXHIBIT 14-1: **Estate Tax Exemptions and Highest Tax Rate**

Year	Estate tax exemption	Highest estate rate
2003	$1 million	49%
2004	$1.5 million	48%
2005	$1.5 million	47%
2006	$2 million	46%
2007	$2 million	45%
2008	$2 million	45%
2009	$3.5 million	45%
2010	Estate tax repealed	Estate tax repealed

estate tax

A tax imposed by the federal government and some states on the privilege of giving property to another person after death of the donor.

inheritance tax

A tax imposed by most states on the privilege of receiving property from a decedent.

http://

Answers to frequently asked questions on estate and gift taxes are available at the Nolo Press Web site at http://www.nolo.com/chunkEP/ep70-74.html

estate tax exemption

A sum of money tha be transferred witho implications. Once th amount is exceeded, are imposed on any additional transferre amount.

* Connecticut (phasing out in 2005), Indiana, Iowa, Kentucky, Tennessee, Louisiana (phasing out in 2004), Maryland, Nebraska, New Hampshire, New Jersey, Ohio, Oklahoma, and Pennsylvania.
† Even the states that have no death taxes generally impose a death tax on estates that are subject to federal estate tax. The tax imposed takes advantage of a credit allowed for state death taxes under the federal law. The net effect on a person's estate has been nil, as the amount paid the state is deducted from the amount that would have otherwise been paid the federal government. The federal Economic Growth and Tax Relief Reconciliation Act of 2001 will phase out this credit in 2005. Some believe states may reenact estate taxes to recover anticipated loss of tax revenue in response to the federal law change.

Tax laws clearly affect behavior. The government often encourages certain conduct through enactment of particular tax laws (e.g., property tax and mortgage interest deductions encourage home ownership). Tax laws also stimulate the creative energies of tax advisors, who seek ways to reduce tax burdens for their clients. Not all such tax-avoidance behaviors are desired by those who draft tax laws. The result is that every few years tax laws are amended to encourage some social policies and to discourage others.* It is an oft-repeated ritual of Congress.

TAXES ON LIFETIME GIFTS

Until repeal (assuming it really happens) federal estate taxes provide for a **unified estate and gift tax**.[2] In other words, both estate and gift taxes have the same tax rates and exemptions. By imposing a federal tax on gifts, federal law prevents a person from avoiding payment of death taxes by making large gifts, especially "deathbed gifts." This tax system requires the taxpayer to keep track of larger gifts and combine the total value of these lifetime gifts with the value of property transferred at death. Taxes are based on the total value of these gifts, after deduction of a *unified credit* (exemption). As of 2003, the unified credit effectively allows all types of gifts totaling $1 million in property value before the individual's estate is taxed. Once $1 million is transferred by gift or will, the estate tax is imposed. Starting in 2004 the estate tax exemption increases to $1.5 million, but the gift tax exemption remains at $1 million. Thus beginning in 2004, property transferred at death has a preferential tax treatment compared with lifetime gifts.

In reality most gifts are totally free of tax. An individual may make annual tax-free gifts of up to $11,000 to each of any number of *donees* (recipients of gifts). Such gifts are called *exemptions*. A husband and wife together may give $22,000 each year. If a gift is $11,000 or less, the gift has no federal tax consequences, and need not be declared. Use of the tax-free exclusion allows a considerable amount of money or property to be given tax-free over time.

> **unified estate and gift tax**
>
> A federal tax levied on the transfer of property through an estate at the time of death or on a taxable transfer by gift. The estate or the donor is responsible for payment of the tax. A unified credit is available to be applied against the transfer tax.

LEGAL FOCUS—EXAMPLE

Over a period of fifteen years, Clint and Mary Hamilton gave each of their three children the maximum tax-free gift each year ($11,000 each, or $22,000 together): three children times $22,000 per year tax-free gift times fifteen years equals $990,000 of tax-free gifts. Moreover, they can continue such tax-free giving as long as they live.

MATTERS CONCERNING WILLS

WHAT IS A WILL?

A man who dies without a will has lawyers for his heirs.

Anonymous

---

* One such loophole (a legal method to avoid taxes that was not planned by legislators) was the transfer of property to children through an irrevocable but temporary trust called a Clifford Trust. The transfer was irrevocable for at least ten years, during which time the income belonged to the child and was the child's taxable income (at a much lower rate). After ten years, the property would return to the donor. The Tax Reform Act of 1986 closed this loophole by taxing income from a Clifford Trust to a child under fourteen at the same rate as the donor would be taxed.

will

Legal expression (usually in writing, signed and witnessed) of a person's directions as to how property owned is to be disposed of after death.

testate

The legal status of a person who has died leaving a valid will.

intestate

The status of a person who has died without leaving a valid will.

testator

(a) Person who makes a valid will. (b) Person who dies leaving a valid will.

devise

A gift of real property by will.

bequest or **legacy**

A gift of personal property by will.

executor

A person named by a testator to dispose of her or his estate after death as directed in the will and in compliance with law.

administrator

A person appointed by a court to supervise disposition of the estate of a decedent who dies without leaving a valid will.

marital deduction

A tax deduction allowing a surviving spouse to receive an estate from the deceased spouse free of federal estate tax.

A **will** is the proper written legal expression of a person's wishes for the distribution of his or her property after death. A person who dies with a will dies **testate;** without a will, **intestate.** Upon death without a will, state statutes control the distribution of property. Generally statutes prefer descendants to ascendants. In other words, children or grandchildren, instead of parents or grandparents, will inherit from the deceased. If there are any lineals (grandparents, parent, child, grandchild, etc.), then collaterals (aunts, uncles, siblings, or cousins) will not inherit. If a person dies without any heirs whatsoever, not even distant cousins, the decedent's assets escheat (transfer) to the state—usually the state of the decedent's permanent residence—to benefit the public in general.

A person who dies leaving a will is called a **testator.** The court responsible for administering any legal problems surrounding a will is usually called a *probate court* and sometimes a *surrogate* or *chancery court.* A gift of real estate by will is a **devise,** and a gift of personal property by will is a **bequest** or **legacy.** When someone dies, a personal representative settles affairs of the estate. An **executor** is a personal representative named in a will. An **administrator** is the personal representative appointed by the court for someone who dies without a will. An administrator may also be appointed if a person fails to name an executor in a will, or names an executor who lacks the capacity to serve, or writes a will that the court refuses to admit to probate (because, for example, it was not properly witnessed). A will that is "admitted to probate" has been accepted by the court as the valid last will of the decedent.

A will is a conditional document. Although valid when properly created, it has no immediate legal effect. It becomes operative at the testator's death. Hence, the will "speaks upon the author's death." Therefore, if the testator destroys it, or writes a more recent will, the older will is automatically nullified. This conditional feature makes a will a unique document, adding importance to proving its validity (a process called *authentication*) after the death of the testator.

To be valid, wills normally must strictly follow state statutory requirements regarding both the right and the process of making a will. A will can serve other purposes besides the distribution of property; it can recommend appointment of a guardian for minor children or incapacitated adults, and it can nominate a personal representative to settle the legal affairs of the deceased. Indeed, a well-drafted will provides many important advantages:

- **Property is distributed as the testator wishes.** Gifts may be made to charities, to distant relatives, to friends, or to employees. Some beneficiaries may receive more, some less. Unique assets, such as family heirlooms, go to specified donees (beneficiaries).
- **The possibility of a disaster that kills both husband and wife, and possibly one or more children, can be anticipated and accommodated.** Although unlikely, this is a danger that is increased by modern means of transportation. A properly drafted will can eliminate multiple costly, tax-burdened probates that may be required when couples or adult family members die in close succession over a period of days or weeks from injuries sustained in a common calamity.
- **Death taxes may be avoided or reduced.** This is accomplished by taking the **marital deduction** (tax deduction allowed a surviving spouse that is not available to single persons) or by utilizing appropriate trusts. Also, the will may direct the executor to pay inheritance taxes, as well as estate taxes from the *residuary property* (property not specifically identified and given to a beneficiary) of the estate. Therefore, assuming assets are sufficient, gifts to named beneficiaries will not be reduced by death taxes.
- **Confusion is minimized when specific property owned by the testator is identified, and beneficiaries are correctly designated.** The will also minimizes the possibility of lawsuits among contending claimants—for example, a claim that "He gave it to me before he died."
- **The testator may nominate appropriate guardian(s) for minor children and their** estates. The will may name both a guardian of the person (handles personal decisions

in lieu of parent) and a guardian of the estate (handles the child's assets). Nominations by a testator are generally honored, but the welfare of the child (or children) is the primary concern of the court. If a natural parent survives, this problem does not arise. If there is no nomination, the court makes the appointment independently.

- **A personal representative (usually called an executor) may be designated in the will to handle the estate.** Otherwise, or if the nominated executor refuses to serve, the probate court will name an administrator. A statutory commission, or fee, is ultimately payable to the personal representative from the assets in the estate,* although it is very common for the personal representative to waive the fee if he or she is also the principal beneficiary under the will.

If a will does not waive it, a **fidelity bond** is required. A fidelity bond insures against losses caused by the dishonest performance of duties by a personal representative (or by a guardian of the children, if any is named and accepts the task). While this provides added protection, it is an expense to the estate. However, it often is prudent to require the posting of a fidelity bond for estates that consist of large amounts of cash. The judgment of trustworthy persons can be affected through control of large sums of cash, as opposed to other "less liquid" types of assets such as real property, automobiles, jewelry, or investments. Such a bond may be unnecessary altogether when the estate consists of no liquid assets or the executor is also the sole primary beneficiary. Also it is common advice that if a person is not trustworthy enough to be appointed without a bond, he or she should not be appointed.

- **The will can give funeral instructions,** although this can and should also be done in a letter of "last instructions" (described next), separate from the will and immediately available to a close relative or friend upon death.

Accompaniments to Wills

Ideally, a personal or family balance sheet, listing assets and liabilities, should accompany a will and be updated periodically. A **letter of last instructions,** as mentioned above, should also be prepared. This letter is not binding on the executor, but it is helpful in disclosing the location of assets and liabilities. It can indicate how the testator would like matters requiring immediate attention, such as a donation of body organs under the Uniform Anatomical Gift Act, to be handled. Note that letters of last instructions, or even explanations for survivors, can be prepared by the testator in many ways: in writing, in an audio recording, or even in a video recording. These instructions are not legally binding, but can be useful in explaining why, for example, someone was disinherited.

Types of Gifts by Will

Gifts by will can be specific, general, or residuary. A *specific* devise or bequest describes particular property—for example, a bequest of an inscribed gold watch or a collection of rare books. A *general* bequest usually specifies a sum of money but does not single out any particular item of property. Sometimes a will provides that any assets remaining after specific gifts are made, and after debts are paid, are to be distributed through a **residuary**

---

fidelity bond

A bond insuring against losses caused by a fraudulent performance of duties by a personal representative.

http://

More detail about this chapter's topics can be found in "Crash Course in Wills & Trusts," by Michael T. Palermo, Attorney at Law; Certified Financial Planner

http://www.mtpalermo.com/

letter of last instructions

A document prepared by a person instructing his or her personal representative (executor or administrator) as to the nature and location of assets and liabilities and suggesting appropriate action to be taken immediately after death.

residuary clause

Any part of the will that allocates property not expressly disposed of by other provisions of the will.

---

* It is important to note that the statutory fees to both personal representatives and their attorneys who assist them during probate proceedings are maximums, not prescribed fees. That is, beneficiaries can encourage competitive bids from probate attorneys as an additional way to maximize the estate. Personal representatives often waive fees because such fees are taxable income. If they otherwise inherit the property, there may be a lesser tax or no tax.

clause. Such a clause is useful because the testator can never be exactly sure what property will remain following payment of debts and taxes. Sample gift clauses in a will follow.*

- *A specific bequest.* I give my grandfather's gold ring with the initials GSH to my son, Scott Bradshaw of Mountain Oaks, Colorado.
- *A general bequest.* I give the sum of ten thousand dollars ($10,000) from my account number ZXY1117865 in First Hoosier Bank to the American Cancer Society, 1244 Normal, Decatur, Indiana.
- *A specific devise.* I give my real property situated in Shorewood County, Milwaukee, Wisconsin, and commonly known as 1278 University Lane, to my sister, Carolyn A. Hamilton.
- *A residuary gift.* I give the residue of my estate, both real and personal property, to my wife, Patricia A. Jenkins-Bradshaw.

How Does One Create a Valid Will?

A will must comply with statutory formalities that are designed to ensure that the testator understood his or her actions at the time the will was made. These formalities are intended to help prevent fraud. If not precisely followed, the will is void. The decedent's property is then distributed according to state laws of intestacy.

Three types of wills are generally recognized as valid: formal (or witnessed) typed or printed wills; informal (or holographic), handwritten wills; and, in a very limited situation almost never applicable, oral wills.†

What Is a Formal or Witnessed Will?

formal will

A typewritten or computer-printed will executed in compliance with law and signed or acknowledged by the testator in the presence of witnesses who also sign the document.

The **formal will** is usually drafted by a lawyer and is generally prepared on a computer, word processor, or typewriter. It must be signed at the end (subscribed) by the testator. The subscription must be made in the presence of witnesses, or in their presence the testator must acknowledge that the will was previously made by him or her or under his or her direction. Most states require the following to create a valid formal will.

1. **The testator must have testamentary capacity.** The testator must be of legal age and sound mind *at the time the will is made.* The legal age for executing a will varies, but in most states eighteen is the minimum age. Thus, a will of a twenty-one-year-old decedent, written when she was sixteen, is invalid.

The concept of "being of sound mind" refers to the testator's ability to formulate and understand his or her plan to distribute property, coupled with intent that the will put into effect the distribution plan. Although the testator must be competent when executing the will, illiteracy or physical or mental infirmity caused by old age (such as senility) do not necessarily prevent the making of a valid will. Where there is physical or mental infirmity, it is advisable to have a medical doctor as one witness who can testify that the condition did not affect the soundness of the testator's mind at the execution of the will.

---

* These gifts are examples assuming the testator owns and has the right to give away this property through the will. For example, in a community property state, a spouse has the right to will only his or her share of community property and all of his or her separate property.
† An oral will, also called a nuncupative will, is valid only when the testator is in fear of imminent death (e.g., an accident victim with fatal injuries). Under a typical statute, two persons must hear the orally expressed intentions. Most states limit the property that a testator may dispose of in this manner to personal property of no more than a small designated sum (usually $1,000). Because of these limitations and special requirements, nuncupative wills are seldom used. Nuncupative wills are recognized in Georgia, Indiana, Kansas, Louisiana, Mississippi, Missouri, Nevada, New Hampshire, North Carolina, Ohio, Tennessee, Texas, Vermont, and Washington.

LEGAL FOCUS—PROBLEM

Michael Taylor signed a new will three days before he died of AIDS. The new will left most of his $3.5 million estate to a charitable trust for the decorative arts. The next largest gift was to his companion, who was to receive property worth about $400,000. His eighty-seven-year-old mother challenged the will. What is the result?

A San Francisco superior court jury held that Taylor, in a weakened condition in the final days of his illness, was subjected to undue influence by his companion. He lacked the freedom of will necessary to express his true intent, and the will was declared void.[3]

2. **The will must be in writing.** The writing itself can be informal as long as it complies with statutory requirements. A will can be handwritten in crayon or ink. It can be written on a sheet or scrap of paper, on a paper bag, or on a piece of cloth. A will also can refer to a memorandum that, although not a will, contains information necessary to carry out the will.

LEGAL FOCUS—PROBLEM

Fran O'Hehir's will directed that a sum of money be divided among a group of charities named in a memorandum that she gave to Bob Meehum the same day she signed her will. Can the charities obtain their bequest?

http://

See the actual wills of famous people on this Court TV Web site at

http://www.courttv.com/ legaldocs/newsmakers/ wills/

The list of charities is legally included or "incorporated by reference" into the will, but only if it was sufficiently described when the will was signed. This practice is not desirable and should be avoided because of the opportunities it presents for error or even fraud.

3. **The will must be signed by the testator.** It is a fundamental requirement in almost all jurisdictions that the testator's signature appear at the end of the will. Each jurisdiction dictates what is a legally sufficient signature. Initials, an "X" or other mark, and words like "Mom" have all been held valid when shown that the testator intended them to be a signature.

4. **A formal will must be witnessed.** A will must be witnessed by at least two witnesses or it is invalid.* The number of witnesses, their qualifications, and how a will should be witnessed are set out in state statutes. Most states require that a witness be disinterested—that is, not a beneficiary under the will. There are no age requirements for witnesses, but they must be mentally competent.

   The purpose of statutes that require witnesses is to verify that the testator actually executed (signed) the will and had the required intent and capacity at that time. A witness does not have to read the contents of the will. Typically, the testator and witnesses must all sign in the sight or the presence of one another. The act of witnessing the signing of a will and thereafter signing the will to that effect is called **attestation**.

5. **Sometimes a will must be published.** A will is **published** by an oral declaration by the maker to the witnesses that the document they are about to sign is his or her "last will and testament."

Will formalities are strictly enforced by probate courts and provide added assurance of validity. After all, the testator is dead when the will "speaks," and not able to challenge

attestation

The act of witnessing the signing of a document and thereafter signing, as evidence that you have witnessed it.

published

A legal rule of wills in some states requiring a declaration by the maker of the will to the witnesses that the document they are about to sign is indeed his or her will.

---

* Vermont requires three witnesses.

fraudulent claims. If witnesses are also dead at that time and cannot supply appropriate affidavits (sworn statements in writing), their handwriting on the will may be authenticated by other means. This complication is usually avoided through the use of witnesses who are younger than the testator.

One variation of a formal will is a **statutory will,** a standardized form of will authorized by the state, with blanks to be completed by the testator. Statutory wills were devised to provide for the simple and usual circumstances of persons who may otherwise die intestate. States authorizing such wills commonly provide that no changes to the pre-printed form are permitted.*

Wills can be complicated or simple. The will in Exhibit 14-2 is the actual complete will of the retired Chief Justice of the United States Warren E. Burger, now deceased. Because of the size of his estate and the lack of planning and appropriate assignment of executor powers, his heirs undoubtedly lost substantial amounts of money to taxes and administrative costs. The irony of his lack of careful planning is real and instructive.

statutory will

A form will authorized by state law with blanks to be completed by the testator.

What Is a Holographic Will?

holographic will

An unwitnessed will. States that allow such a will usually require it to be written in longhand by the testator, signed, and dated.

An exception to the formal witnessed will exists in many states. A **holographic will** is a type of self-prepared will written, signed, and dated with a complete date, all entirely in the handwriting of the testator. About half the states[†] recognize this type of will, although

EXHIBIT 14-2: **The Last Will and Testament of Warren E. Burger**

LAST WILL AND TESTAMENT OF WARREN E. BURGER

I hereby make and declare the following to be my last will and testament.

1. My executors will first pay all claims against my estate;

2. The remainder of my estate will be distributed as follows; one-third to my daughter, Margaret Elizabeth Burger Rose and two-thirds to my son, Wade A. Burger;

3. I designate and appoint as executors of this will, Wade A. Burger and J. Michael Luttig.

IN WITNESS WEREOF, I have hereunto set my hand to this my Last Will and Testament this 9th day of June, 1994.

/s/Warren E. Burger

We hereby certify that in our presence on the date written above WARREN E. BURGER signed the foregoing instrument and declared it to be his Last Will and Testament and that at this request in his presence and in the presence of each other we have signed our names below as witnesses.

/s/Nathaniel E. Brady residing at 120 F St., NW, Washington, DC

/s/Alice M. Khu residing at 3041 Meeting St., Fall Church, VA

---

* The National Conference of Commissioners of Uniform State Laws approved a Uniform Statutory Will Act providing a simple will statute that could be adopted by interested states. Four states adopted the statutory will including California (Probate Code § 6200 et seq.), Michigan (Comp. Laws Ann. § 700.123c), Maine (Rev. Stat. Ann. Tit. 18-A, § 2-514), and Wisconsin (Stat. § 853.50 et seq.). No state has adopted a statutory will since the mid-1980s and it appears the National Conference no longer is actively promoting this Uniform Act.

† Alaska, Arizona, California, Colorado, Idaho, Kentucky, Louisiana, Maine, Michigan, Mississippi, Montana, Nebraska, Nevada, New Jersey, North Carolina, North Dakota, Oklahoma, South Dakota, Tennessee, Texas, Utah, Virginia, West Virginia, and Wyoming.

the exact requirements often vary slightly. If the will is appropriately witnessed and other formalities are observed, the document is considered a formal will even though handwritten by the testator.

LEGAL FOCUS—PROBLEM

Dave Decker, married to Dora May Decker and father of one child (female) named Dora June Decker, decided to make a holographic will. He carefully wrote on a blank sheet of paper, "I give all I own to Dora." He signed and dated the paper. As an afterthought, he took the document to his office and asked his friend, Arthur Bamish, to sign and date his paper as a witness. Is the document a valid will?

No, the will is not valid in this particular case. In many states, a person may prepare a valid holographic will without witnesses, in one's own handwriting, signed and dated by oneself. Even if Decker's state is one of these, his will is nevertheless invalid. Why? Decker's wife and daughter were both named Dora. When he dies, the probate court cannot be sure to whom he intended to leave his property. Consequently, his will is void because of the uncertainty as to the identity of the beneficiary. Such ambiguity invalidates a will.*

Dave Decker also failed to meet an additional requirement of some states: that he declare to the witnesses that it is a will and specifically ask them to serve as witnesses. Decker did not tell his witness, Bamish, that the document was his will, nor did he sign, or acknowledge his signature, in Bamish's presence. (Recall that witnesses must sign in the presence of the testator. Some states also require that witnesses sign in the presence of each other.)

In most states that permit holographic wills, requirements must be followed precisely. A major objection to the holographic will is the absence of witnesses. Probate courts are concerned, among other things, with the possibility of forgery and undue influence. As holographic wills are usually not witnessed, there is little protection against forgery or undue influence. Probate judges have ruled many attempted holographic wills invalid because they were partially typed (thus not entirely in the handwriting of the testator) or not dated.

A few states, including Colorado and California, have liberalized the requirements for a holographic will, allowing typed or printed provisions ". . . if the signature and the material provisions are in the handwriting of the testator."[4] Even where holographic wills are legally acceptable, the wisdom of preparing one is questionable. Many people fail to express their intentions clearly. They also may fail to take advantage of readily available techniques to minimize estate taxes and other costs (such as appropriate executor powers and waiver of bond). A person who insists on proceeding without professional legal assistance would be well-advised to study one of the self-help books containing standard forms and provisions.

[An] individual, trying to avoid leaving anything to her daughter (a drug addict), carefully specified each piece of property in her will and which heir was to receive it. However, after writing her will, she received a large inheritance from her father. Because the inheritance was not listed in her will, under the intestacy laws of the state of Texas, the

---

* Once a will is invalidated, state laws substitute a statutory will for the testator, more formally called statutes of succession. Under a state statutory will or law of succession, either the wife will inherit all the property, or both the wife and daughter will share in Decker's estate in a specified proportion depending on the nature of the state's property law and the statutory will.

inheritance passed to her daughter—clearly not her intent. These are. . . . horror stories I have come across that could have been prevented if the people involved had consulted an attorney rather than written their wills.

Daniel Palmer, Attorney at Law, Texas[5]

LEGAL FOCUS—CASE

Shortly after Christine McCarthy and Stephen Kapcar married in 1972, Kapcar named McCarthy as beneficiary of an Aetna Life Insurance Co. group life insurance policy. Within a year of the marriage, Kapcar was diagnosed with multiple sclerosis. He developed severe tremors, underwent brain surgery to alleviate the tremors, and became legally blind in 1974. Within a few years they separated and in 1978 Kapcar divorced McCarthy. Neither the divorce decree nor a property settlement mentioned the Aetna policy. Kapcar died in 1984 a quadriplegic, having spent the last seven years of his life unemployed and living with his father. According to the terms of a holographic will written in 1977, Kapcar stated that "I will all my personal belongings, stock certificates, bank accounts, insurance benefits, and any other earthly belongings to my father. This will voids my previous will bequeathing my belongings to Christine B. Kapcar." Kapcar never changed the named beneficiary (Christine) on the Aetna policy. Christine claimed the proceeds of the insurance policy. Did the holographic will transfer the interest in the life insurance policy to Kapcar's father?

McCarthy v. Aetna Life Insurance Co., 92 N.Y.2d 436, 704 N.E.2d 557, 681 N.Y.S.2d 790 (New York, 1998).

The admonition that people should seek legal counsel to prepare wills is not made simply to line lawyers' pockets with gold. Any competent attorney would have asked questions about Kapcar's assets, including life insurance policies, and Kapcar would have been directed to change the beneficiary according to his wishes. The predictable result in this case was that the self-prepared will was insufficient to change the beneficiary in the life insurance policy, and the divorced wife prevailed over the faithful father. "To hold that a change in beneficiary may be made by testamentary disposition alone would open up a serious question as to payment of life insurance policies. It is in the public interest that an insurance company may pay a loss to the beneficiary designated in the policy as promptly after the death of the insured as may reasonably be done. If there is uncertainty as to the beneficiary upon the death of the insured, in all cases where the right to change the beneficiary had been reserved there would always be a question as to whom the proceeds of the insurance should be paid. If paid to the beneficiary, a will might later be probated designating a different disposition of the fund, and it would be a risk that few companies would be willing to take. . . ."[6]

HOW DOES ONE REVOKE A WILL?

The maker of a will may revoke it at any time during his or her lifetime. Revocation can be partial or complete, and it should follow certain specified formalities. A testator can revoke a will by a physical act such as intentionally burning, tearing, canceling, obliterating, or destroying it. Having someone else destroy the will at the maker's direction and in the maker's presence also revokes the will. The intention to destroy the will is essential.

Another writing, called a **codicil,** may also revoke a will. A codicil is a written instrument, separate from the will, that amends or revokes provisions in the will. A codicil makes it unnecessary to redraft the entire will if its maker wants to change only part of it. A codicil can also be used to revoke an entire will. In either case, the codicil must be created with the same formalities required for the will, and it must refer to the will.

A second or new will can be executed to revoke the first. The second will must use specific language, such as "This will hereby revokes all prior wills." If the first will is not revoked, then some courts will admit both wills into probate. The second will is treated as a codicil. It is good idea to keep copies of prior wills—but they should be clearly marked and preferably initialed and dated to indicate that they are revoked and superseded by the will executed on (name the date).

codicil

A document prepared to change but not revoke an existing will.

CAN A PROBATE COURT DISTRIBUTE PROPERTY CONTRARY TO THE TERMS OF A WILL?

In most states, a failure to provide for a spouse or child can partially revoke a will, in which case a probate court can compel distribution of an estate contrary to the stated terms of a will. A **pretermitted heir** is a child either unintentionally left out of a will or born after the will is made. Most states have pretermitted heir statutes that give to a pretermitted child a statutory share of the testator's property. This statutory share overrides the will, unless the child received some gift in the will, or his or her exclusion was deliberately, expressly, and clearly made. If a child (or grandchild, if the child has died and there is a surviving grandchild) is not mentioned in the will, and no provision was made for the child outside the will, the law assumes that the omission was a mistake. A parent testator may ignore and exclude a child in his or her will, but must do so expressly. Likewise, in some states spouses can be omitted from receiving the decedent's property only if the will specifies that such omission of the spouse is purposeful.

pretermitted heir

A child who was not specifically provided for in life and was not mentioned in his or her parent's will.

Sometimes a testator identifies a specific gift of property in a will, but then disposes of it before the will "speaks." For example, the testator wills his savings account at the Texarkana Bank of Austin to Johnny Raye, but when the testator dies, no such account exists at the Texarkana Bank of Austin. Even if an account can be found at another bank in Austin the gift will fail. The executor is powerless to substitute other property to Johnny Raye. Instead, the property will be distributed as otherwise specified in the will (e.g., in a residual disposition clause). This is called **ademption:** disposing of something given to a donee in a will. Thus, the provision in the will is inoperative and impossible to carry out. The person for whom the gift was originally intended does not receive it, even though the will was not revoked.

ademption

The elimination of a specific gift of property listed in a will because it no longer exists.

LEGAL FOCUS—CASE

Jason Fuller claimed that although he was found guilty of first-degree murder, technically he did not kill his grandmother because his girlfriend did. Can a beneficiary speed up a gift in a will by accelerating the testator's death, or as Sam Spade would say it, "Can you do the person in and still inherit"?

Estate of Walker v. Russell Eastern Star Home of Colorado, Inc., 847 P.2d 162 (Colorado, 1992).

Because a will is a document subject to change at the whim of the testator, it has been the subject of much intrigue in fiction, and in life (or in death—pardon the pun). A potential heir can be written out of a will anytime the testator wishes. States have passed laws to protect individuals from impatient and evil beneficiaries. For example, anyone convicted of a crime that caused the death of a testator cannot receive benefits under the will. Fuller's claim was based on the court narrowly construing a so-called "slayer statute."* "We conclude that the term 'kills' as used in [the statute] refers to a person who causes the death of another by bringing about that effect."

Probate court is the place of proving the validity of a will. It is also where wills are challenged or contested. The usual grounds for challenging a will are

- The testator lacked capacity.
- The testator was subject to undue influence.
- The will was not properly executed.
- Someone defrauded the testator into executing this particular will.

To discourage will contests, will drafters often include a *no-contest* or *incontestability clause* in the will. Such a clause might read:

> *If any beneficiary under this Will in any manner, directly or indirectly, contests or attacks the Will or any of its provisions, any share of interest in my estate given that contesting beneficiary under the Will is revoked and shall be disposed of as if that contesting beneficiary had died before me.*

Such a clause discourages beneficiaries from asserting frivolous will-contest lawsuits. However, when an entire will is ruled invalid, the incontestability clause as well as all other provisions is rendered void. The estate therefore would be distributed by intestate succession, or in some cases by the terms of a prior will.

What If the Testator Is the Victim of Undue Influence?

Valid wills express the maker's intention to transfer and distribute his or her property after death. If it can be shown that the will was the result of improper pressure brought by another person, the will is void because it does not truly express the maker's intention.

undue influence

Wrongful persuasion, often by a beneficiary or other trusted individual, that deprives the victim of decision-making freedom in making a will.

Undue influence is sometimes inferred by the court if the testator ignores his or her blood relatives, who are normally the "natural objects of his bounty," and instead names a nonrelative as a beneficiary. The likelihood of undue influence is greater if the beneficiary is a person who was in constant close physical contact with the deceased and therefore able to influence the making of the will. When a nurse or friend who cares for the deceased during a comparatively short span of time before the death benefits to the exclusion of close family members, questions of undue influence inevitably arise. Even a spouse may be suspected of undue influence if children from a former marriage are excluded.

---

* The Colorado law applied to Fuller provides an example of a slayer statute, § 15-11-803, C.R.S. (1987 Repl. Vol. 6B). (1) A . . . devisee who kills the decedent and, as a result thereof, is convicted of . . . the crime of murder in the first or second degree or manslaughter, as said crimes are defined in Sections 18-3-102 to 18-3-104, C.R.S., is not entitled to any benefits under the will or under this article, and the estate of the decedent passes as if the killer had predeceased the decedent. Property appointed by the will of the decedent to or for the benefit of the killer passes as if the killer had predeceased the decedent.

LEGAL FOCUS—PROBLEM

J. Seward Johnson died in 1983 from prostate cancer, leaving his entire estate to his wife of twelve years, Barbara Piasecka Johnson. Mrs. Johnson had worked as a chambermaid and cook at the Johnson mansion before their marriage in 1971. Mr. Johnson's six children by a prior marriage contested the will, claiming that their father had been the victim of undue influence by his wife and had been "terrorized" into signing the will just before his death. The estate valuation exceeded $500 million. Did the children succeed in their will contest?

After a four-month legal battle in New York's Surrogate Court, the parties reached an out-of-court settlement. Mrs. Johnson received $350 million, and the remainder was divided between the children and a charitable oceanographic research foundation that had been founded by the testator in 1971.[7]

Will-signing ceremonies are sometimes videorecorded to show that the ritual prescribed by law was correctly followed. Such records also provide evidence as to the demeanor (behavior and possibly competence) of the testator and have been used effectively to defend challenges to the validity of wills.[8]

WHAT HAPPENS TO THE ESTATE OF A PERSON WHO DIES WITHOUT LEAVING A WILL?

Each state regulates how property shall be distributed when a resident of the state dies without leaving a will. Such laws attempt to carry out the presumed intent and wishes of the decedent. These statutes are called **intestacy laws** and, as briefly noted earlier in the chapter, provide for the distribution of property to designated heirs.

The rules of descent vary from state to state. The law always provides that the debts of the decedent must first be paid with assets of the estate. Then there is usually a special statutory provision for the rights of the surviving spouse and children. When no children or grandchildren survive the decedent, the surviving spouse gets the entire estate.

intestacy laws

Statutory prescription for distribution, among heirs, of the estate of a decedent who has died leaving no will.

LEGAL FOCUS—EXAMPLE

Freddie Allen dies intestate and is survived by his wife, Della, and his children, Duane and Tara. Allen's property passes according to intestacy laws. After Allen's outstanding debts are paid, his widow will ordinarily receive one-third to one-half interest in the property; Duane and Tara will receive equal shares of the remainder.

State distribution laws specify the order in which heirs of an intestate have claims against the estate. When there is no surviving spouse or child, then the grandchildren, brothers and sisters, and, in some states, parents of the decedent follow in that sequence to receive the entire estate.

Because state laws differ so widely, few generalizations can be made about the laws of descent and distribution. It is necessary to refer to the exact terms of the applicable statutes to answer questions about intestate distribution in any given state. Exhibit 14-3 shows a typical pattern of intestate distribution of property (in this case, in Indiana).

EXHIBIT 14-3: **Intestate Distribution of Property under Indiana Law**

Deceased	Survived by	Spouse	Parent(s)	Child(ren)	Siblings (Brothers & Sisters)	Grandparents
Husband or Wife	Spouse only	All Property				
	Spouse and one or more children	1/2[a]		1/2[b]		
	Spouse, children, and parent(s)	1/2		1/2[b]		
	Spouse and parent(s) only	3/4	1/4			
	Child(ren) and parent(s) only			All property		
Widow, Widower, or Single or Divorced	Child(ren)			All property		
	Child(ren) and parent(s)			All property		
	Parent(s) only		All property			
	Parent(s) and siblings[c]		1/2		1/2[b, c]	
	Siblings				All property[b]	
	Grand-parents only					All property
	No spouse, parent issue, siblings or grand-parents[d]					
	No relatives[e]					

[a] Limitations exist for a childless spouse when children by the dependent's prior marriage survive.

[b] Descendants of a deceased take the deceased person's share.

[c] Assumes both parents are living and there are two or more siblings. Each parent takes as a sibling but receives at least one-fourth interest. For example, one parent and one sibling each would receive one-half share. If there are one parent and six siblings, the parent would get one-fourth and the six siblings would divide the remaining three-fourths share.

[d] All property to aunts and uncles. If an aunt or uncle is deceased but leaves a surviving child, the child or children receive the aunt or uncle's share.

[e] All property goes (escheats) to the state.

Source: Indiana code. § 29-1-2-1.

MATTERS CONCERNING PROBATE

Is it the eccentric nature of the customers or the probate system itself that generates so much attention? I think it is a little bit of both.

Probate Judge Pat Gregory, Harris County, Texas[3]

WHAT IS PROBATE?

Probate is a court proceeding where wills are proved to be valid or invalid and where estates of decedents are administered and ultimately properly distributed. Probate serves several useful purposes. It provides an opportunity for unsecured creditors of the decedent to submit claims for payment from the estate. If they fail to submit a claim, they risk having their debts canceled, with no future claims against the beneficiaries of the estate.* Death taxes are also normally paid as part of the probate process. If the court finds a valid will, the net assets (after all debts and liabilities of the decedent are paid) are distributed to named beneficiaries. If there is no valid will, the probate court will accomplish similar tasks by complying with the state's law of intestate succession. Probate laws vary from state to state, although eighteen states have adopted a Uniform Probate Code. Note that applicable death taxes are payable whether or not there is a probate proceeding.

CAN PROBATE BE AVOIDED?

Probate has important disadvantages. It takes time: generally a minimum of six months, often one to two years, sometimes longer. During this time, title to property is uncertain, as it is not yet transferred to the beneficiaries pending proof of the will and payment of the debts of the estate. The trauma of a loved one's death may be exacerbated by the inability to use assets that the survivor badly needs. Appropriate planning and a well-chosen executor advised by a competent lawyer should minimize or eliminate problems caused by probate delay. In addition, the facts about the estate and its disposition become a matter of public record. If the probate is of the estate of a prominent person, famous or infamous, information about the estate and beneficiaries is often publicized in the media.

Probate fees are payable to the personal representative (executor or administrator) and to the attorney who handles the estate. Sometimes the executor is a principal or sole beneficiary and will waive probate fees (which are taxable as earned income for income tax purposes) to increase the inheritance (which may be tax-free depending on size, or may be taxable at death tax rates that are lower than the executor's income tax bracket).

In California, the following percentages of the probated estate's gross value are the maximum fees that may generally be received by both the executor and the attorney:[10]

4 percent of the first	$15,000
3 percent of the next	$85,000
2 percent of the next	$900,000
1 percent of the next	$9,000,000
0.5 percent of the next	$15,000,000

A reasonable amount to be determined by the court of any amount over $25,000,000.

In some states, statutory maximum fees are higher than California; in other states, they are lower. The amount of the lawyer's fee is negotiable and an executor may reach an agreement in which the attorney agrees to accept a fee less than the statutory amount. However, the statutory fee is typically the amount paid. Costs of appraisal, tax returns, and property management are extra. If unusual or extraordinary services are provided, such as defense against a claim that the will is invalid, a court will usually allow a higher fee. If a state does not provide a statutory fee, the usual practice is for the attorney to bill by the hour.

Many states have laws that allow distribution of assets without probate proceedings. Less formal methods of transferring title are used for estates with small property values. In some states, for example, merely filling out standard forms can transfer savings and

http://

Find out if your state has adopted the Uniform Probate Code
http://www.law.cornell .edu/uniform/probate.html

http://

Read about probate in Texas at the Web site of the Texas law firm of Barnes and Karisch P.C. at
http://www.texasprobate .com/

---

* Secured debts (for example, a note secured by a testator's real property) remain secured. In other words, the beneficiary who receives the property receives it subject to the security interest held by the creditor.

checking accounts, title to cars, and certain other property. And summary proceedings are often available when there is only one heir, notably a spouse. Most states provide for a Transfer on Death (TOD) of securities free of probate under the Uniform Transfer-On-Death Security Registration Act. The securities need to be held in an account that provides for this type of transfer, and the specific details must be carefully planned.* California, Missouri, and Ohio offer car owners the ability to name a beneficiary on their certificate of title, allowing the vehicle to bypass probate. With TODs, the beneficiary has no rights as long as the donor is alive. The donor is free to sell or give away the car, or name someone else as the beneficiary.

A majority of states provide for **family settlement agreements**—private agreements among the beneficiaries. Once a will is admitted to probate, the family members can agree to settle among themselves the distribution of the decedent's assets. However, a court order is still needed to protect the estate from possible future claims of creditors and to clear title to estate assets.

The use of summary procedures in estate administration saves time and money. The expenses of a personal representative's commission, attorneys' fees, and appraisers' fees can thus be eliminated or at least minimized.

Some persons with larger estates (not eligible for summary procedures) nonetheless try to avoid probate and its related costs. With proper estate planning, the size of the probate estate may be substantially reduced. The following are types of property transfers that bypass probate:

- Undivided interests in property owned by the decedent in joint tenancy (or tenancy by the entireties) goes to the survivor(s) without probate under the right of survivorship (see Chapter 12).
- In community property states, only one-half of the community property will go through probate, since the surviving spouse already owns the other half.
- Life insurance proceeds are paid directly to beneficiaries, unless the estate is named as the beneficiary (e.g., to provide cash for payment of death taxes, thus avoiding forced liquidation of other assets, such as equity in a business).
- Certain U.S. government bonds are paid directly to the person listed on the front of the bond as POD ("paid on death").
- Property previously transferred to an *inter vivos trust* (discussed later in the chapter) is not probated.

Not all of these methods are suitable for every estate, but they are alternatives to probate administration.

WHAT ARE THE DUTIES OF AN EXECUTOR?

LEGAL FOCUS—PROBLEM

One day Robert Yu received the sad news of the death of his wealthy uncle, Wilbur Yu. A few days later he received some good news and some bad news. The good news: He was

family settlement agreement

A law of probate in some states allowing family members to agree to settle among themselves the distribution of a decedent's assets.

* Alaska is one of the states that has a TOD statute. Two important sections are provided as an illustration. AS § 13.33.307. Ownership On Death of Owner: On death of a sole owner or the last to die of all multiple owners, ownership of securities registered in beneficiary form passes to the beneficiary or beneficiaries who survive all owners. On proof of death of all owners and compliance with any applicable requirements of the registering entity, a security registered in beneficiary form may be reregistered in the name of the beneficiary or beneficiaries who survived the death of all owners. Until division of the security after the death of all owners, multiple beneficiaries surviving the death of all owners hold their interests as tenants in common. If no beneficiary survives the death of all owners, the security belongs to the estate of the deceased sole owner or the estate of the last to die of all multiple owners. AS § 13.33.309. Nontestamentary Transfer On Death: (a) A transfer on death resulting from a registration in beneficiary form is effective by reason of the contract regarding the registration between the owner and the registering entity and AS § 13.33.301-13.33.310 and is not testamentary. (b) AS § 13.33.301-13.33.310 do not limit the rights of creditors of security owners against beneficiaries and other transferees under other laws of this state.

named a beneficiary in his uncle's will and was to receive 1,000 shares of IBM common stock. The bad news (or so he regarded it): He was named executor of his uncle's will. Should he accept the appointment?

Probably yes. If Yu declines, the court will appoint a substitute administrator. If he accepts the nomination, an attorney he selects to handle the estate in probate court will do the legal work and will guide him in the proper performance of his duties. Both Yu and the attorney will be entitled to payment authorized by statute, plus compensation for extraordinary time or expenditures (e.g., defending or pursuing litigation on behalf of their estate, or negotiating sales of real property). This compensation is usually adequate and even generous, at least for larger estates. Compensation is usually limited by statute based on the gross value of the estate (total value of assets without regard to liabilities). Executor and attorney fees are often the same for a complicated estate consisting of various business and assorted assets as they are for an estate consisting of one bank account, if the values of each estate are the same. This anomaly flows from the misunderstanding of most executors that the maximum attorney fees provided by statute are the standard fee. In fact, a lower fee can be paid if agreed to between the executor and the attorney.

LEGAL FOCUS—BACKGROUND

Baseball Hall of Famer Ted Williams of the Boston Red Sox died in July 2002. Immediately after his death, tribute to his skills lost news space to a story about his body being stored in a chamber of liquid nitrogen (cryonics).* Apparently Williams had been frozen at the request of his son, John Henry, and his daughter Claudia. His other daughter, Bobby-Jo, was reportedly appalled, claiming his will and professed wishes called for cremation. Probate is where the final decision will be made, but the executor of his will makes the initial call. Once a body is cremated, cryonics no longer matters even to the most optimistic futurist. One article quoted friend Bob Breitbard as saying, "Ted was an American icon. It's terrible, this talk. You don't put an icon on ice."[11]

The duties of an executor are important and generally include the following. Note that many of these services are provided by the lawyer employed by the executor to assist with administration of the estate.
1. Complying with decedent's special instructions for funeral and burial
2. Locating witnesses to the will
3. Notifying heirs (i.e., persons who would get the estate if there were no will) and beneficiaries named in the will, preferably meeting with them, if convenient
4. Arranging for bond, if necessary, to cover faithful performance of his or her duties as executor
5. Notifying the post office to send the decedent's mail to the executor and discontinuing telephone and other services as appropriate
6. Opening a bank account for the estate
7. Assisting the attorney in identifying creditors and arranging for payment of debts
8. Identifying, inventorying, and safeguarding all probate assets (obtaining appropriate insurance and preventing relatives from plundering estate assets, if necessary)

---

* "Cryonics is basically the science of turning us humans into popsicles upon our death with the hope of reviving us in the future and restoring us to our former, healthy selves again. Just after death, 'patients' who elect to take a shot at immortality are stored in a chamber of liquid nitrogen to prevent further physical decay." Adam Thierer, "Could Ted Williams Hit .400 Again in the Future?" *TechCentralStation*, 12 July 2002.

9. Reviewing nonprobate assets (joint tenancy and trusts) for appropriate action to ensure legal transfer

10. Offering the will for probate in court and being formally appointed by the court as executor (referred to as *receiving letters testamentary*)

11. Reviewing and taking appropriate action regarding the decedent's financial records: leases, mortgages, notes, life insurance policies, pensions, social security, stocks, bonds, saving accounts, checking accounts, etc.

12. Collecting any dividends, interest, and/or rent and paying any rent, interest, insurance premiums, or other obligations

13. Having assets appraised when advisable or required

14. If decedent had a business, acting to continue proper operation if feasible and appropriate, or to sell and liquidate if necessary

15. Publishing statutorily required notice to creditors and reviewing and paying claims

16. Keeping detailed records of receipts (income) and disbursements (expenses and debt payments)

17. Determining cash requirements for taxes (income and estate), probate expenses, valid claims, and cash bequests, and deciding which assets are to be used or liquidated for these needs

18. With the aid of an accountant, filing income tax returns (final return of decedent, tax returns for the estate while administration continues) and death taxes (inheritance and/or estate) and making necessary payments

19. Preparing a final estate accounting to submit to the court (listing assets, receipts, disbursements, sales with gains and losses, and reconciliation of beginning and ending balances)

20. Transferring title to real and personal property to beneficiaries (and sometimes trustees) in accordance with the probate court decree of distribution under the will, obtaining receipts for them

21. Obtaining formal court approval of the settlement of the estate and final discharge as the executor.

WHAT IS THE UNIFORM PROBATE CODE?

A Uniform Probate Code (UPC) has been adopted in whole or in substantial part by eighteen states, including Arizona, Colorado, Florida, and Michigan.[12] Under the UPC, a person must be eighteen or older and of sound mind to make a will. The will must be in writing and signed by the testator (or in the testator's name by someone else in the testator's presence, by his or her direction). Two competent witnesses must witness the will. They need not be present when the testator signs, but must be present later when the testator acknowledges the signature on the will. The code permits holographic wills.[13] A major goal of the creators of any uniform code is that it be adopted by most states in order to provide uniform law throughout the country. Because of the mobility of our society, compelling arguments exist for uniformity in probate law, yet the goal of general acceptance of the UPC remains elusive.

http://

A reference to state-specific advance directives can be found at Partnership for Caring at

http://www.partnership forcaring.org/Advance/ index.html

WHAT ARE LIVING WILLS AND OTHER ADVANCE DIRECTIVES?

The population of the United States is aging primarily thanks to some remarkable advances in pharmacology and in medical practice as well as diet. Increases in the number of aged persons influences social, political, and economic policy and related law. There has been a growing acceptance of a document called a **living will,** which allows an individual to instruct his or her family, and medical personnel, about the medical procedures to follow—or more particularly, to abstain from—under specified circumstances.

LEGAL FOCUS—CASE
....

Twenty-five-year-old Nancy Cruzan lapsed into a permanent coma after an automobile accident. Five years after the accident, Nancy's parents sought a court order to remove a feeding tube from Cruzan, who had been existing in a vegetative state since the accident. Without medical assistance, Cruzan would die. Were her parents able to get the order from the court?

Cruzan by Cruzan v. Director, Missouri Dept. of Health, 497 U.S. 261, 110 S.Ct. 2841 (1990).

After several years of court battles, a Missouri circuit court in 1987 granted Nancy Cruzan's parents' wishes and the feeding tubes were removed. Twelve days after the court order, Cruzan died. Among the reasons for the long court battle was the absence of any written evidence as to what Cruzan's desires might be. A living will would have provided the written evidence that her parents lacked.

All states now have passed statutes providing for **advance medical directives (AMD),** instructions to others about the care they wish, or do not wish, to receive if they become terminally ill or incapacitated. **Incapacity** is the lack of legal capacity to make important decisions. It can result from a serious illness, an accident causing a coma, or even old age if coupled with Alzheimer's disease. The most common AMD is the living will.

The term *living will* is misleading because a living will has nothing to do with the transfer of property after death. A less confusing term used in many states is **directive to physicians,** which in most states has an identical meaning. A related directive is the durable power of attorney for healthcare, discussed later. Whatever the name, it is a document directed to physicians to consider the ill or injured person's wishes regarding the use of life-support systems. All states provide for living wills, but the requirements vary. (A living will should not be confused with a living trust, which is discussed later in the chapter.)

Some living will statutes require that the living will be created after a patient has learned of a terminal illness but not before. This type of living will obviously would not have assisted Cruzan's parents, because her condition occurred without notice or time to plan. Also, Cruzan was not just permanently ill; she was brain dead in a permanent coma.

Living wills must be witnessed by two or more disinterested (meaning free from any selfish motive or interest) persons, and prepared using a specific format or form.[14] If a form is legally invalid in execution, it may still be used in court to show the desires of the ill person if he or she is unable to testify.

A **durable power of attorney for healthcare** is a more flexible document than the living will. It authorizes another person to make healthcare decisions for a person who is incapacitated. It is one type of power of attorney. A **power of attorney** is a common legal document allowing the creator, a principal, to empower another (agent) to act on his or her behalf, usually in regard to financial and property decisions. These documents can authorize another to perform any act that the principal could otherwise do. They also can be limited in scope to authorize specified and limited acts, such as selling specific shares of stock. Note that the person nominated is known as the *attorney-in-fact,* and he or she need not be and usually is not an attorney at law. (The term *attorney* literally means "representative.") An ordinary power of attorney ends with the *incapacity* or death of the person giving the power; it automatically terminates at that point. The powers granted by a durable power of attorney, however, do not end with the incapacitation of its creator.

---

living will

A document, usually authorized by state statute, that directs any attending physician to comply with the wishes of the drafter regarding the use of life-support systems in the treatment of a terminal illness.

advance medical directives (AMD)

Instructions prepared in advance of a life-threatening condition as to what care should be given or not given in the event of incapacitation.

incapacity

Lack of legal capacity to make important decisions.

directive to physicians

A signed document communicating the signer's wishes regarding the use of life-support systems in the treatment of a terminal illness.

durable power of attorney for healthcare

A document authorizing another person to make healthcare (and sometimes other) decisions for a person even after he/she has become incapacitated.

power of attorney

A document authorizing another person to act as one's agent. A general power of attorney authorizes the agent (called the *attorney-in-fact*) to do all acts not prohibited by law for another (called the *principal*).

A durable power of attorney can be created in some states to authorize financial decisions, as well as healthcare decisions, but here we are discussing the *durable power of attorney for healthcare,* a phrase describing a document that limits the attorney-in-fact to healthcare decisions. Such durable powers of attorney are often created to be "springing" documents, written so as to provide power to the designated representative only upon the occurrence of a healthcare crisis. In other words, the power is given to the attorney-in-fact only upon the occurrence of certain specified events or conditions.

In any form, a durable power of attorney gives the attorney-in-fact, usually a close relative or friend, the power to make healthcare decisions for a person who becomes incapacitated through serious illness, accident, or any other means. The decisions authorized include life-and-death decisions such as whether to order the withdrawal of life-support systems for the incapacitated party. The durable power is not necessarily restricted to life-and-death health decisions, however. For example, if a person who is incapacitated needs elective surgery, the durable power of attorney may allow the designated person to approve of the surgery.

A durable power of attorney for healthcare typically requires the signature of at least one disinterested witness, and must contain exact, approved statutory language. Often the signature of the creator of the power must be attested and certified by a notary public.*

As with a living will a durable power of attorney can be revoked by the principal creator at any time before incapacity. Note that the durable power of attorney differs from the living will in two important ways: (1) it can be created at any time—one need not be terminally ill—and (2) it delegates very extensive and critical decision-making powers to another person. Therefore, that person should be selected carefully. While these documents are well-advised and useful, they should be created with great care and thoughtful consideration.

LEGAL FOCUS—PROBLEM

Mabel Bradshaw was elderly and concerned about being able to handle her affairs in the future. She wished to grant a power of attorney to her daughter Ann, who could then manage her property and make decisions about her medical care if she, Bradshaw, became incapacitated. Would you advise Bradshaw to create a power of attorney or a durable power of attorney?

Bradshaw's wishes suggest that a durable power of attorney is more appropriate. This will permit her daughter to handle her healthcare decisions and to make decisions about her property and investments should she become unable to do so.

LEGAL FOCUS—CASE

A petition to remove the life-support system for George Vogel was accompanied by this affidavit of Dr. Jonathan Sumner: "George Vogel suffered a major stroke that has left him in a vegetative state. He can move, but has no awareness; he further has no intellectual

---

* As law in this area is still developing, it varies from state to state. Specific state statutes must be consulted before creating either a living will or durable power of attorney. Considerable thought need also be given to the selection of the attorney-in-fact. He or she should be someone you trust implicitly and who knows and is willing to abide by your wishes in trying times. In both the living will and either type of durable power of attorney, the instructions can be as detailed for the attorney-in-fact as one might wish, including exactly what to do in a variety of circumstances.

function. He is being kept alive solely by the use of a gastric tube through his nose in which material, in the consistency of eggnog, is fed into his body. George Vogel is not aware of his surroundings, nor is there any possibility that he will ever be in any other state other than the vegetative state that he presently suffers." Testimony was also offered by his sister-in-law that Vogel, prior to his recent illness, had said "he did not wish to be kept alive by having tubes inserted into his body and that he would not wish to be kept alive solely by artificial means." A non-physician guardian appointed by the court opposed the petition, stating that Vogel was neither brain dead ("his brain stem is operative") nor terminally ill. Vogel had not prepared any advance directive and he was not otherwise terminally ill. What was the order of the court?

Vogel v. Forman, 134 Misc.2d 395, 512 N.Y.S.2d 622 (New York, 1986).

The court denied the petition, stating, "A distinction must be drawn between those who are unable to care for themselves due to infirmities of illness, age or other physical disabilities and those who are brain-dead or terminally ill, without hope of recovery and are being kept alive solely by use of artificial means made available by the techniques of modern medicine and technology. [I]t is a function of humanity to care for those who are unable to care for themselves by reason of illness, age or infirmities." Clearly the legal response to Vogel's condition would have been different had he prepared an appropriate advance directive.

In 1991 the federal government passed the Patient Self-Determination Act, which requires that, before being admitted to certain healthcare facilities participating in Medicare or Medicaid (including hospitals), patients must be informed of the right to execute advance directives and have an opportunity to inform the healthcare facility of their wishes regarding heroic measures to sustain life.[15]

States are establishing, and liberalizing, their statutes involving living wills and durable powers of attorney to allow persons greater flexibility.* Issues involving death are understandably difficult and sensitive creating disagreements among those with different values. Requirements for the creation and use of the document will undoubtedly continue to vary until a greater consensus emerges as to the proper way to deal with issues of natural death.[16]

DOES A TERMINALLY ILL PERSON HAVE THE LEGAL RIGHT TO COMMIT SUICIDE?

LEGAL FOCUS—BACKGROUND

In the later years of the twentieth century Dr. Jack Kevorkian, a retired pathologist and advocate for physician-assisted suicide, became a focal point for much of the debate

---

* Together, living will statutes and durable powers of attorney are often part of a "Natural Death Act" or "Rights of Terminally Ill" statute. Some states provide that family members or close friends can make medical decisions for incompetent patients who have not provided advance directives. Also, approximately twenty states provide for non-hospital do-not-resuscitate orders. The typical DNR order is written on an official form provided by the state department of health. Upon presentation to a paramedic, emergency room technician, or any other health professional, all resuscitation efforts must be stopped.

about assisted suicide. He admittedly assisted in the suicide of several terminally ill patients. At least one source has credited Dr. Kevorkian with assisting in the death of over 130 persons. He was charged with various homicide offenses in his home state of Michigan, with the charges usually being dropped or, in three instances, resulting in an acquittal by jury. In November 1998, the CBS television program *60 Minutes* used videotape provided by Dr. Kevorkian showing his participation in the death of Thomas Youk, a terminally ill fifty-two-year-old ALS patient.* Youk was wheelchair bound, fed through a tube, and forced to use a machine to help him breathe, waiting to die an agonizing death when he requested that Dr. Kevorkian terminate his life. Millions of Americans witnessed physician-assisted suicide in prime time. This portrayed act led to Kevorkian's second-degree murder conviction in March of 1999 and a sentence of ten to fifteen years in prison. In October of 2002, the U.S. Supreme Court denied certiorari, refusing to review Dr. Kevorkian's conviction. Kevorkian will become eligible for parole on his seventy-ninth birthday in 2007.

The issue of whether **suicide** (the taking of one's own life) is morally correct is one of many issues upon which Americans lack consensus. Most religions and certainly legal rules generally label it a wrongful act. Currently no state in the United States explicitly condones suicide; and only one state, Oregon,[17] provides for legalized assisted suicide. Oregon voters narrowly passed the Oregon **Death with Dignity Act** on November 4, 1994. The act has been challenged by various groups since its passage. On November 6, 2001, U.S. Attorney General (AG) John Ashcroft issued a federal order prohibiting the use of controlled substances under the Oregon Death with Dignity Act. Controlled substances were used by doctors to assist patients in hastening their death, so the order made the behavior illegal and seriously undermined the Oregon Death with Dignity Act. The AG order was challenged and on April 17, 2002, the U.S. District Court–Oregon issued a permanent injunction against the Attorney General leaving physician-assisted suicide (with controlled substances) in place.[18] At the time of writing this edition the issue is far from permanently resolved. No other state has passed a Death with Dignity Act although such a law came close to passing in Hawaii in 2002.

Euthanasia, also called mercy killing, is the affirmative act of bringing about the immediate death of another, allegedly in a painless way; it is generally administered by one who thinks that the dying person wishes to die because of a terminal or extremely painful disease. The advance directives discussed earlier provide that only extraordinary and heroic measures to resuscitate can be refused or continued. Euthanasia involves an aggressive act of putting the patient to death without his or her prior authorization, an act most likely to be treated as some form of criminal homicide. The Oregon Death with Dignity statute is effectively a law legalizing euthanasia for the first time in the United States. A few other countries such as the Netherlands provide for legal euthanasia.

LEGAL FOCUS—CASE

Washington law provides that "[a] person is guilty of promoting a suicide attempt when he knowingly causes or aids another person to attempt suicide." Such promotion is a

---

http://

For information about Dr. Jack Kevorkian's participation in assisted suicide and his conviction, see Public Television Service, Frontline coverage **http://www.pbs.org/wgbh/pages/frontline/kevorkian/**

suicide

The intentional killing of oneself.

Death with Dignity Act

A state statute that allows competent, terminally ill adult patients to obtain a physician's prescription for drugs to end their life.

http://

Read the text of the Oregon Death with Dignity Act at **http://www.rights.org/deathnet/ergo_orlaw.html**

Read the chronology of events surrounding the passage and implementation of the Oregon Death with Dignity Act at **http://www.dwd.org/law/chronology.asp**

euthanasia

The act of allowing one to die by withholding extraordinary medical measures, or putting to death by painless means a person suffering from an incurable disease or condition of an extremely painful nature.

---

* ALS is commonly referred to as Lou Gehrig's disease, a severe and progressive disorder of the nervous system for which there is no cure.

felony punishable by up to five years' imprisonment and up to a $10,000 fine. Four Washington physicians who treat terminally ill patients, along with three gravely ill plaintiffs (since deceased) sued the Washington State Attorney General, claiming that Washington law has kept the physicians from assisting these patients in ending their lives. This legal barrier violated "a liberty interest protected by the Fourteenth Amendment which extends to a personal choice by a mentally competent, terminally ill adult to commit physician assisted suicide." Was the claim successful?

Washington et al. v. Glucksberg et al. 521 U.S. 702, 117 S.Ct. 2258 (1997)

The U.S. Supreme Court considered this important issue in 1997 and rejected the plaintiffs' arguments.[19] The Court acknowledged the blurring of the issue given that Washington had in 1979 passed a **Natural Death Act** allowing the "withholding or withdrawal of life sustaining treatment" at a patient's direction and providing that such an act "shall not, for any purpose, constitute a suicide."[20] In rejecting the physicians' arguments, the Court recognized that "for over 700 years, the Anglo American common law tradition has punished or otherwise disapproved of both suicide and assisting suicide."[21] "The history of the law's treatment of assisted suicide in this country has been and continues to be one of the rejection of nearly all efforts to permit it." "[We] conclude that the asserted 'right' to assistance in committing suicide is not a fundamental liberty interest protected by the Due Process Clause. Throughout the Nation, Americans are engaged in an earnest and profound debate about the morality, legality, and practicality of physician-assisted suicide. Our holding permits this debate to continue, as it should in a democratic society."[22] The Court noted that since the enactment of Oregon's Death with Dignity Act, which legalized physician-assisted suicide, several other states had considered similar proposals, though none had been enacted.[23]

Natural Death Act

A statute that allows a person with a terminal condition to request a physician to remove life support.

http://

Web site of National Death with Dignity Center
http://www.deathwith dignity.org/index.htm

Matters Concerning Trusts

Put not your trust in money, but put your money in trust.

Oliver Wendell Holmes, Jr., 1841–1935
(Associate Justice of the United States Supreme Court, 1902–1932)

What Are Trusts?

LEGAL FOCUS—PROBLEM

Marisa Fabor and her husband, Brandon, are worried. They fear that when their children, Kathy and Tom, inherit the family farm, they will sell it and squander the proceeds within a short time; the children "simply do not know the value of a dollar." What can the Fabors do to keep their children from squandering their inheritance?

One solution is the creation of a **trust.** This is done by transferring legal title to property from the owner (called a **settlor** or sometimes called the *trustor* or *donor*) to another (called

trust

A legal relationship in which one party (called trustor, settlor, or donor) transfers legal title in property to a second party (trustee) for the benefit of a third party (beneficiary, or donee).

settlor

A person who establishes a trust. A settlor is also called a *trustor*.

trustee

A person who holds property in a trust for the benefit of another, the beneficiary.

beneficiary

A person or entity who is to receive assets or profits from an estate, trust, insurance policy, or other device when there is distribution.

http://

Read about trusts at this Cornell Law School Web site

http://www.law.cornell.edu/ topics/estates_trusts.html

a **trustee**) to hold for the benefit of, and someday distribute to, the specified **beneficiary.** A trust becomes a separate legal entity, governed by its trustee. Thus, the trustee is anyone who holds property for the benefit of another, called the *trust beneficiary*. In the preceding situation, Marisa and Brandon would be the settlors, Kathy and Tom would be the beneficiaries. The person or business firm selected by Marisa and Brandon to manage the trust would be the trustee. They could select themselves as co-trustees and name others as successor trustees upon their deaths.

How property is to be distributed is determined by the settlor and stated in the trust document. The trustee receives possession and legal title to the property for the duration of the trust, until it is distributed to the beneficiaries. Pending distribution, the beneficiary owns the *equitable title* to the property, which is a beneficial interest but without the right to possess or transfer the property. A trust can be created for any legal purpose consistent with public policy. Its essential elements are as follows:

1. The settlor must be competent to create a trust.
2. The settlor must intend to create a trust.
3. The trust must be created for a proper purpose.
4. Money or property sufficiently identified to allow title to pass must be transferred to the trust.
5. A beneficiary must be designated.
6. Although a writing is not absolutely required to create a trust, it is expected.
7. The trust instrument should name a trustee with appropriate capacity.

If the Fabors transfer their farm to the First Bank of Minnesota, in trust, for the benefit of their children, the couple will have created a trust. This arrangement is illustrated in Exhibit 14-4.

A frequent use for trusts is to provide funds for a child's education. These trusts are created both in wills and as *inter vivos* trusts. The amount of assets or cash necessary to accomplish the purpose of this trust obviously changes over time. If Yale is your child's goal (or the parent's), note that the estimated cost of tuition and room and board for attending Yale for one academic year in 2002–03 was $35,370. Tuition and fees cost was $27,130. If you could find a working time machine and travel back to 1900, you would

EXHIBIT 14-4: **Trust Arrangement**

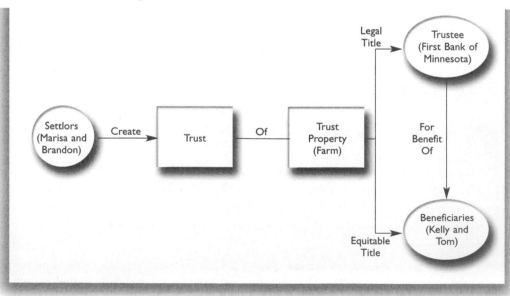

find Yale's tuition a more reasonable $155 per year; room rent, $200; board, $200; books, $35 to $45; subscriptions, society dues, etc., $100; and clothing and incidentals, $150—making a total of $850.[24]

WHO MAY BE A TRUSTEE AND WHAT DOES A TRUST COST?

Any settlor who creates a trust may serve as his or her own trustee. However, unless the trust is a living trust, the settlor usually chooses a competent and trustworthy relative or friend or a commercial trust company with its staff of experts. In addition, many financial corporations, such as banks, offer their services as commercial trustees. Anyone nominated as a trustee is free to decline to serve. If a successor or alternate is not named in the trust document, the court will usually name a trustee.

If compensation is not mentioned in the trust document, the trustee has a right to be paid for his or her services. The fees are determined consistent with state law or as allowed by the probate court. The settlor can provide in the trust document how, or even whether, the trustee is to be paid for services. If the court sets the fee, it will determine what is reasonable in view of the size of the estate, time required to administer it, services performed, and results achieved.

In trusts created during the settlor's life, like Marisa and Brandon Fabor's, the fees are negotiated. Common percentages are three-fourths of one percent of the fair market value of real estate and obligations secured by real estate, and three-fifths of one percent of the fair market value of other assets in the trust estate. The percentage may be less for a very large trust (e.g., one with assets in excess of $1 million). Corporate trustees frequently charge one-tenth of one percent as an "acceptance fee" when the trust takes effect, and a one percent "distribution fee" for all amounts they distribute. Trustees, like attorneys and personal representatives in probate proceedings, are also entitled to extra compensation for special services and expenses, as for defending the trust in a lawsuit.

WHAT ARE THE DUTIES OF A TRUSTEE?

The trustee is a fiduciary to the beneficiary of the trust; that is, the trustee owes to the beneficiary a duty of highest care, honesty, and loyalty. The legal responsibilities of trustees are the same in both *inter vivos* and testamentary trusts, discussed shortly.

A trustee is duty bound to manage the assets of the trust properly. The trustee is accountable to the beneficiaries and must invest the property carefully. As a fiduciary, the trustee may not personally profit from the trust, other than by the payment provided for services rendered.* Trustee duties are specified in state statutes, but they are often modified or further explained by the trust document.

ARE THERE DIFFERENT TYPES OF TRUSTS?

There are two general categories of trusts that are commonly used in estate planning. **Inter vivos** (Latin: "among the living") **trusts** are those created before death, such as the Fabors. *Inter vivos* trusts may be *revocable,* meaning they can be terminated (i.e., legally erased) at

inter vivos **trust**

A trust created during the lifetime of the settlor.

---

* Payment for duties performed as a trustee is obviously not considered a conflict of interest. Also, if the trustee is a beneficiary of the trust, receiving benefits from the trust consistent with the trust terms does not violate the duty of the trustee.

any time, or *irrevocable,* meaning they are permanent. A second general category of trust is the testamentary trust, which is created by will and which becomes effective upon the death of the testator.

IRREVOCABLE *INTER VIVOS* TRUSTS

irrevocable trust

A trust that cannot be terminated or revoked by the settlor who created it.

If the trust is an **irrevocable trust,** it cannot be revoked, nor can the property be returned to the settlor. Income from the trust is taxable to whoever receives it. Thus, shifting it in trust to someone in a lower tax bracket can reduce the amount of tax paid on one's income property. An **irrevocable *inter vivos* trust** can also keep property out of a settlor's estate at death and avoid the cost and delay of probate.[25] A marital life estate trust (to be discussed later) may also limit payment of death taxes.

irrevocable *inter vivos* trust

A trust created and having operative effect during the trustor's life that cannot be terminated or revoked by the trustor who created it.

In the trust example, Marisa and Brandon Fabor (settlors) can name themselves as trustees, or they could name another person or a bank or trust company to perform the task.* The Fabors could create a trust with provisions that become operative upon the death of the surviving spouse, including the following:[†]

- The children shall receive a limited amount of income from the trust as spending money, but most of their needs shall be paid for directly by the trustee (to shield such funds from possible creditors of the children).
- The children cannot give away or sell their rights in the trust.
- Creditors of the children cannot reach the trust principal.
- The trustee may spend part of the principal of the trust, if necessary, for the welfare of the children (using discretionary power to "invade the corpus" or use the "body" of the principal amount, in addition to interest or profit earned on the principal).
- The trustee shall transfer 25 percent of the trust to each child when he or she attains age 30 and the balance at age 40. (The ages used here are arbitrary. The parents, reflecting their opinion of when their children will have matured and could safely be given the assets, could select any age. Also, the trustee could be given the power to decide the time for appropriate distributions within some constraint.) Alternatively, the parents could direct that the principal remains intact and go to the then-living grandchildren. This would eliminate a possible levy of estate taxes on the trust assets when their own children—the initial beneficiaries—die.

A major disadvantage of the irrevocable trust is that it cannot be changed to meet new circumstances. A will can be changed frequently to reflect new thoughts about how assets ought to be distributed upon death (of course, after death a will is irrevocable). And that distribution could be made under the terms of a testamentary trust included in their wills.

REVOCABLE *INTER VIVOS* TRUSTS

revocable *inter vivos* trust

A trust created and having operative effect during the trustor's life that may be terminated or revoked by the trustor who created it.

The Fabors may be reluctant to make the trust irrevocable, because they might need the money for themselves before they die. Therefore, they might create a **revocable *inter vivos* trust.** Here they can change the terms, or beneficiaries, or completely terminate the trust at any time, regaining full control over the principal. All trust income would be taxable to them as owners, however, and the value of the trust principal would be taxed as part of the estate of the spouse who is last to die. Death taxes would not be affected one way or the other by this trust. On the other hand, the trust assets will not be probated if the trust exists, is funded, and is not revoked prior to their deaths.

* Professional trustees charge fees for their services, and their use may not be appropriate except in very substantial trusts.
† These provisions create a type of spendthrift trust that is discussed on page 690.

WHAT IS A LIVING TRUST?

The **living trust** is a popular term for a type of *inter vivos* trust designed to avoid probate. A person may desire to avoid probate because of its costs, and also to maintain privacy in the settlement of family affairs. The living trust is often less expensive than probate, and it is private. However, a living trust will not by itself reduce death taxes.

With the living trust, the settlor transfers all of her or his property into a revocable living trust. To illustrate, assume that the trust is created jointly by husband and wife; the settlors can be joint trustees, or one alone may serve as the trustee. During their lives, they each may be the beneficiary of the trust. At the death of the first settlor, certain benefits of the trust shift to one or more other person(s), and the surviving settlor becomes the sole trustee, perhaps with the power to name a co-trustee.

LEGAL FOCUS—PROBLEM

Don and Pat Lee have a gross estate of $900,000 and a net estate (after payment of debts) of $800,000. They wish to avoid probate expenses for whichever of them is the surviving spouse. Ultimately, they wish to minimize shrinkage of estate assets for their only child, Kelly. They decide to create a living trust. Will it accomplish their goals?

Yes. They create a living trust, transferring all or most of their property into the trust. For example, if they own real property, their ownership interest is conveyed by deed to the trust. Thereafter, the trust is legal owner of the real property. Other property, stocks, bonds, and pension contracts are also transferred to them as trustees of the trust.

The Lees name themselves co-trustees with the surviving spouse also named as the successor trustee, anticipating the inevitability of death. (They might name additional successor trustees as well.) They also name the beneficiary (or beneficiaries) who will receive distributions from the trust after the death of the settlors. At the death of the first spouse, the property remains in the trust and the trust becomes irrevocable as to the decedent's property. At the death of the second spouse, the property is distributed to the named beneficiary (or beneficiaries) in compliance with the terms of the trust.

Thus, the costs directly attributable to probate are not incurred. Deciding the cost savings, however, can be tricky and misleading. In California, for example, fees for an executor and an attorney to probate an estate with a gross value of $450,000 would be $20,300. (See the earlier discussion about probate fees.) However, the fee savings are probably overstated. It is common and usual when the executor is the heir for executor fees to be waived, and if all or most of the property is community, and the spouse is the heir, he or she may elect an alternate procedure to probate, which eliminates most of the fees. When the property is probated at the time of Pat's death (assuming that her gross estate now totals $900,000), the probate fees would be $38,300. (An assumption is made that Pat has lived within her income and the estate is larger because Pat received Don's property.) It should be noted that the executor might waive his or her $19,150 executor fee, so again the probate costs are probably overstated. If the property has been placed in the living trust, there are no probate fees at either death. Alternatively, there are only minimal fees to transfer the property to the surviving beneficiary (or beneficiaries). The total probate fee savings, in California, thus could be as much as $58,600 ($20,300 + $38,300), but are more likely to be to be around $20,000. Although this example assumes a marital living trust, a living trust would also reduce probate fees for the estate of a single person.

living trust

A popular term for a revocable *inter vivos trust* whose primary purpose is to avoid probate.

http://

Read about Living Trusts at the American Association of Retired Persons Web site at **http://www.aarp.org/ estate_planning/Articles/ a2002-08-12-Estate PlanningLivingTrusts**

There are costs involved when creating the trust, when transferring title to the property into the trust, when managing the trust, and when making its final distributions. Attorney and certified public accountant (CPA) fees may be incurred at every stage. In addition, probate fees are a deductible expense on the decedent's final income tax filing, and so the amount of savings by using the trust is somewhat overstated. Other reductions in probate fees can be made through waiving executor's fees (which is common) and negotiating attorney fees below the statutory maximum. What the living trust does require is advance planning about fees that may be triggered upon death.

As a special caution, living trusts are marketed in ways that can lead to abuse. For example, the living trust is often sold in hotel seminars as a magic, painless way to save money for one's heirs. Sellers often overcharge for a form trust, failing to spend sufficient time with the client determining whether a living trust makes sense for that individual's estate plan, to appropriately transfer property into the trust, to provide for monitoring of the trust, and to arrange for how the settlors will have their future questions about the trust answered. While a living trust may be a good idea for some, it is not automatically a good idea for everyone. Unless you are a sophisticated investor and estate planner, you should obtain competent professional advice about your particular situation.

The simple living trust discussed here makes the most sense for unconditional gifts to family members. The trustee is expected to be the settlor. (In a marital living trust, both spouses are joint trustees, with the surviving spouse being the successor trustee). The trustee's duties are expected to be simple; the most important and complex of these is the distribution of the property. But the trust must be kept current, with title to property kept in the name of the trust. That can be an annoying burden to some persons. Valuations that are a normal part of probate and are certain to occur are often forgotten in private trust administration. Failure to appraise trust property and to obtain stepped-up valuations for assets can lead to significantly higher income taxes for heirs when inherited assets are ultimately sold.

The following situations are among those that suggest extreme caution in the creation of a living trust and necessitate the advice of an attorney.

- **A minor child is among the beneficiaries.** Special attention must be taken for the care of the minor child, and property should remain subject to the trust at least until the minor reaches majority.
- **Long-term care of the settlors is contemplated** (e.g., a senior center or nursing home). This situation contemplates planning for the best and most appropriate use of your assets to allow for maximum healthcare while preserving property for your heirs.
- **Long-term care of a beneficiary is contemplated** (e.g., a developmentally disabled child or a spouse who is mentally incapacitated). This situation contemplates a more complex trust and significant long-term responsibilities.
- **Conditional gifts to beneficiaries are contemplated** (e.g., in the Lee case, property to Kelly if she graduates from college). Conditional gifts create increased responsibilities for the trustee. If the trustee has discretionary powers, conflict between the beneficiary and the trustee is possible.
- **The value of the estate is significant, and estate taxes are to be paid** (e.g., a significant amount might be $1,800,000). Note that the estate tax exemption continues to increase through the year 2009. Depending on whether the estate is liquid (i.e., cash, stocks, and bonds) or not (i.e., real property, most partnership interests, or a sole proprietorship business), determining and accumulating the money to pay the death taxes may complicate the duties of the trustee.
- **You have or expect to have a substantial number of unsecured debts.** One of the advantages of probate is the provision for an orderly method of paying debtors of the decedent—a living trust does not extinguish the debts of the settlor. Creditors expect

to be paid, and without probate the process may be awkward. Secured property (e.g., real property with a mortgage or an automobile with a secured interest) will be transferred subject to its indebtedness. Unsecured creditors have a claim against all property of the decedent. If the amount of debt is small, there will be little difficulty; if debts are significant, then careful plans should be made to pay them. Creditor claims complicate the trustee's duties and can cloud the title to property for intended beneficiaries for some time.

- **You are in business and your personal trust assets are used from time to time as security for business loans.** Private lenders will inspect your trust documents and may well require changes be made to the trust terms. If you later require additional financing, a second lender may also desire changes to the trust documents, which require approval of the first lender if it is willing. In any case, it gets complicated and the settlor loses control of the terms of the trust. This caution applies also to nonbusiness situations where you intend that trust property act as security for a loan.

None of these situations makes a living trust inappropriate. Indeed, the same or similar problems arise when there is no trust. However, if they or other complications are likely, then how the estate planner wishes these complications to be addressed should be considered in deciding whether a trust is appropriate and, if so, how it should be drafted.

TESTAMENTARY TRUSTS

A trust created in a will is called a **testamentary trust.** Although it is created when the will is made, the trust does not take effect until the settlor's death. If the will setting up a testamentary trust is invalid, then the trust will also be invalid. The property that was supposed to be in the trust will then pass according to intestacy laws, not according to the terms of the trust. Since the property is part of the decedent's estate, a testamentary trust does not avoid estate taxes or probate fees, nor provide the privacy of *inter vivos* trusts.

MARITAL LIFE ESTATE TRUSTS

Don and Pat may wish to reduce federal death taxes on their estate. The living trust discussed earlier does not accomplish that goal. A **marital life estate trust,** also called an *A and B trust,* can, however, significantly reduce death taxes to the ultimate benefit of the beneficiaries if it is created before the first spouse dies. In this trust, once the first spouse dies, the surviving spouse receives a life interest in the property and someone else (the designated beneficiary) has a **remainder interest** (the interest remaining after the life interest). An owner of a life interest can use the property for life, but cannot transfer it away by contract or will. At the death of the owner of the life interest, the owner of the remainder interest (usually a child or children) automatically becomes the sole owner of the property. This trust, whether created *inter vivos* or by will, does restrict the freedom of the surviving spouse to use the property as he or she might wish. The person(s) owning the remainder interest is (are) therefore protected from diversion and unjustified dispersion of the trust property.

The effect of the trust is to reduce the size of the estate transferred upon the death of the second spouse. The net tax savings can be considerable. The larger the estate is, the larger the potential savings. There are, of course, additional costs of creating and maintaining the trust and a loss of deductions on the decedent's final tax return. Actual predicted savings for an individual should be determined in consultation with tax and estate planning advisors. The general admonition is to seek competent legal and tax advice for any kind of trust, which has significant, sometimes undesirable consequences to the settlors. Fortunately, such trusts are

testamentary trust

Trust created by a valid will.

marital life estate trust

Reciprocal trust executed by a husband and wife with the other spouse as a life beneficiary. These trusts are also called *A and B trusts.*

remainder interest

Any interest that is left after another interest in the property ends.

http://

See the information on Marital Trusts from CPA firm Kern, DeWenter, Viere at **http://www.kdv.com/ nonprofit-articles/ maritaltrust.html** usually revocable by either settlor before either dies. Thus, the trust can be revoked or amended if circumstances or wishes change before either one of them dies.

THE RULE AGAINST PERPETUITIES

As noted at the beginning of this chapter, there is an old saying that "you can't take it with you." The law cannot get around that truism, but instruments such as trusts and wills do the next best thing: they legitimately avoid probate fees and death taxes. Moreover, they allow a person to control who is to receive the property upon her or his death, and to instruct and/or restrict how that property may be used. However, the **rule against perpetuities** limits this control as it applies to trusts and other legal instruments that restrict the use and free transferability of property in the future. Under this rule, title in property must vest (i.e., some beneficiary must get full and unrestricted possession and ownership of the property) no later than a life or lives in being, plus 21 years.

The details of this rule are very complicated and beyond the scope of this text. But the purpose of the rule is simple and understandable. The rule against perpetuities is meant to prevent a trust from accumulating and compounding income for perhaps ten generations, by which time a small sum may have grown to a prodigious amount. It also keeps assets under the control of living persons rather than straitjacketed by donors long since dead. The rule does not generally apply to charitable gifts. A gift of real property to a church, so long as no alcohol is served on the property, would not violate the rule. Such a restriction can last for hundreds of years, whereupon a violation (i.e., liquor is served on the land) could lead to a reversion of the property to the donor's heirs (who may well be hard to find and who will be surprised to learn of their interest).

TAXATION OF GENERATION-SKIPPING TRUSTS

There are special rules to tax certain large generation-skipping transfers of wealth. Trusts are usually used for such transfers. For example, in a **generation-skipping trust,** a father (first generation) creates a trust under which his daughter (second generation) receives the income while she lives. When she dies, the principal goes to her child, a son (third generation). There is a death tax when the father dies, but no second tax when the daughter dies. The daughter's generation has been skipped as to estate tax liability because the daughter never received or controlled the principal. (Of course, when her child dies, any property from the trust still in his possession would be part of his estate for tax purposes.) This technique of tax avoidance is effective only for a trust that, on the death of the second generation member (the daughter in our example), has a value of less than $1.1 million. The $1.1 million exemption increases to $1.5 million in 2004, to $2 million in 2006, and to $3.5 million in 2009. Then in 2010, the exemption is for 12 months, until 2011 when it falls back to only $1.1 million (as indexed for inflation). Any value in excess of the exemption amount is taxed.[26]

ARE THERE OTHER USES OF TRUSTS?

LEGAL FOCUS—PROBLEM

H. Pauline Amesbury dearly loves her husband, who is fifteen years her senior and in his 80s. She is terminally ill and afraid that when she dies first, as is likely, he will be unable to manage the family estate alone. He might be talked into foolish investments, or

---

rule against perpetuities

A rule that requires remainder interests in property to *vest* (i.e., to take effect) no later than a life or any number of identified lives in being, plus twenty-one years.

generation-skipping trust

A trust created whereby the settlors of the first generation (parents) arrange for their child(ren) (the second generation) to receive the income while they are alive, but not the principal, which is reserved for the grandchild(ren) (the third generation) after the death of the second generation.

worse, into remarriage to someone interested only in his money. What can Amesbury do to protect her husband against such developments?

She can create an *inter vivos* or testamentary trust, specifying that he shall receive the income during his lifetime and that the trustee may use the principal, if necessary, for his welfare. When he dies, the property will not appear in his estate, where it would boost his estate tax. Instead, it will be distributed as prescribed in Amesbury's trust, perhaps to go to their children, or even held for their grandchildren. The effect is the same as in the marital life estate trust, even if only one spouse creates the trust, as long as the settlor spouse is the first to die.

The trust instrument could name charities or other beneficiaries selected by H. Pauline Amesbury herself, or designated by Mr. Amesbury if he is given a **power of appointment**—a designation in a will or trust giving him the power to decide who gets the money or property or to designate how the money or property will be used. This useful estate-planning tool allows the trust to postpone deciding which child or children or other beneficiaries receive what gifts. In these ways, a trust can frustrate would-be fortune hunters who prey on wealthy and unsophisticated beneficiaries.

Sometimes trusts make sense when the beneficiary is ill, mentally retarded, or very old. Settlors may even create a trust naming themselves as the beneficiaries and a bank or trust company as the trustees, to spare themselves the burden of managing their estate. One may also create a trust and name it as beneficiary of insurance policies on one's life. This arrangement is often preferable to allowing the insurance proceeds to go as a lump sum to a beneficiary unequipped to handle such a sum.

A **discretionary sprinkling and accumulation trust** may be appropriate when flexibility is vital to meet the changing needs of family-member beneficiaries. The trustee is authorized to decide who among the designated beneficiaries is to receive periodic payments of income, or principal, or both. Beneficiaries who need more can be given more; those who need less get less. To help the trustee distribute the trust funds, the trust specifies guidelines, which might include maintaining a stated standard of living or comfort and general welfare for beneficiaries and allowing special payment for educational or medical fees. Income not paid is accumulated and ultimately distributed as part of the principal.

A trust designed for the benefit of a segment of the public or of the public in general is a **charitable trust.** It differs from a private trust in that the identities of the beneficiaries are uncertain. Usually, to be deemed a charitable trust, a trust must be created for charitable, educational, religious, or scientific purposes.

A trust created to provide for the maintenance of a beneficiary by preventing his or her improvidence with the bestowed funds is a **spendthrift trust.** Essentially, the beneficiary receives or is permitted to draw only a certain portion of the total amount of which he or she is the beneficial owner. Most states permit spendthrift trust provisions that prohibit creditors from taking possession of the assets of the trust before they are distributed to the beneficiaries.

A special type of trust created when one person deposits money in a bank in his or her own name as a trustee for another is a **Totten trust.** This trust is tentative in that it is revocable at will until the depositor dies or completes the gift in his or her lifetime by some unequivocal act or declaration (for example, delivery of the funds to the intended beneficiary). If the depositor should die before the beneficiary dies and if the depositor has not revoked the trust expressly or impliedly, a presumption arises that an absolute trust has been created for the benefit of the beneficiary. At the death of the depositor, the beneficiary obtains property rights to the balance on hand.

---

power of appointment

Authority given to a person (the donee) under a trust or will to designate or appoint the person(s) who shall receive specified assets after a specified event such as death of the donee.

discretionary sprinkling and accumulation trust

A trust where the trustee is authorized to decide who among the designated beneficiaries is to receive periodic payments of income or principal, and when.

charitable trust

A trust designed for the benefit of a segment of the public or of the public in general.

spendthrift trust

A trust created to provide for the maintenance of an improvident beneficiary by limiting his or her control of the corpus (the principal of the trust) and by barring access by creditors.

Totten trust

A trust for bank depositors whereby they deposit money in a bank in the settlor's own name as a trustee for another person.

I S JOINT TENANCY AN EFFECTIVE WAY TO AVOID PROBATE?

Joint tenancy (or the similar tenancy by the entireties between spouses in some states) is a form of ownership for two or more persons to hold real and personal property (see Chapter 12). One of the most important aspects of joint tenancy is its *survivorship feature*.

LEGAL FOCUS—PROBLEM

Al Brumley and Beth Alvarez own a house in joint tenancy. If Alvarez dies, Brumley automatically becomes the sole owner of the house immediately and without probate. Full title passes to Brumley even if Alvarez left a will that attempted to give her interest in the house to her mother, Sue Smith. Surviving joint tenants automatically receive the interests of a deceased joint-tenancy owner. As Brumley's interest is perfected at the moment of Alvarez's death, there is no interest left to convey by will.

Depending on the circumstances and desires of the co-owners, this survivorship feature is either a reason to own property in joint tenancy or a reason not to own property in this manner. Because the ownership transfers automatically at the death of a joint tenant to the remaining tenant(s), joint-tenancy property is not subject to probate. Indeed, it is an effective way to avoid probate. However, like most living trusts, a transfer by joint tenancy will not reduce death taxes because the transfer itself may be subject to such taxes because of its value. Other disadvantages to holding title to property in joint tenancy include:

- Either joint tenant can secretly terminate the tenancy while alive by conveying his or her interest to another person. The owner of the conveyed interest will not be a joint tenant but a tenant in common with the other joint owner(s).
- Creditors may terminate the tenancy by claims against the interest of one of the tenants. Such a claim may require sale of the asset to satisfy the claim. Such actions can tie up and cloud title to the property, even though the creditor's claim is generally good only against the debtor's interest in the property.
- The establishment of joint tenancy in property other than a bank account might be considered a gift. To the extent that its value exceeds $11,000 in a given year, the gift is a federal taxable event.
- Following the death of a joint tenant, there may be adverse capital gains treatment for the surviving tenant when the property is subsequently sold. Explanation of such complex tax consequences is beyond the scope of this text. The moral is as follows: If you are dealing with significant financial interests, seek legal and tax advice as to the most appropriate manner of joint ownership for you and your co-owners.

W HAT ARE CONSERVATORSHIPS AND GUARDIANSHIPS?

LEGAL FOCUS—PROBLEM

Peter White, age 78, is a millionaire who sometimes acts in a way his family considers eccentric. His son Ed has been particularly disturbed since Peter bought a large sailboat and announced his intention to sail to the South Pacific with an all-female crew. Ed contacted an attorney to inquire how he might stop his father from squandering the family fortune. Can Ed tie up his father's money?

Not unless there is more to the story. Peter White appears to be capable of handling his own affairs, including his personal needs and financial resources. However, if he were physically or mentally unable to handle his affairs (including the sailboat!), his son could petition the court to declare a **conservatorship.** A responsible person would be named the *conservator,* to manage the assets and personal affairs of the *conservatee.* The conservator will make periodic reports to the court showing the business and personal transactions that have occurred. Although the conservatee is without authority to handle his or her own affairs, he or she ordinarily can still make, or modify, a last will. A conservatorship cannot and will not be declared simply to stop an eccentric person from overspending and thereby dissipating his or her estate.

An alternative procedure, called a **guardianship,** is available for those who, for any reasons, are unable to care for themselves or their estates. Usually a guardianship is created to provide for a minor whose parents are dead, but an adult who is infirm may be judicially declared incompetent and placed in a guardianship. The person subject to a guardianship is called a *ward.* The person in charge of the ward's personal and financial affairs is called the *guardian.*

Under a typical guardianship statute, in order to declare one a ward, proof must show that the person is substantially unable to provide for his or her own personal needs (food, clothing, shelter, medical care)—in other words, to manage his or her finances. Isolated incidents of negligence or improvidence will not suffice as evidence of substantial inability. The alleged incompetent has the right to appear at the court hearing and to oppose the petition with the aid of counsel. A proposed conservatee has similar rights, and either party may call for a jury trial if provided by state law. If the petition is granted, the court monitors the activities of the person in charge, requiring periodic reports. Both guardianships and conservatorships are usually costly to the estate of the protected party.

PRINCIPAL ELEMENTS OF ESTATE PLANNING

Although you probably have little personal need for an estate plan at this early stage of your life, the following guidelines may be valuable in the future, and perhaps now for members of your family. Also see Exhibit 14-5 for a useful checklist.

1. Prepare a personal or family balance sheet to show assets and liabilities. Keep accurate records of dates along with evidence of the acquisition costs of assets, including real property and its improvements (with receipts, for future tax purposes). Prepare a budget to monitor your earnings, spending, saving, and investing on a monthly and annual basis.
2. Consider life insurance if appropriate for the needs of beneficiaries. (Be sure you understand the difference between term and ordinary life policies.) Select a suitable settlement option for each policy.
3. Consider creation of trusts (*inter vivos* or testamentary, or both). Consider using a living trust to avoid probate and death taxes.
4. You (and your spouse, if married) should prepare a will specifying the recipients of all your possessions. Prepare a will even if you use a trust to avoid probate. Let your heirs celebrate if there is insufficient property to require probate because you effectively and economically transferred your estate by other means.

conservatorship

A legal relationship created by a court to allow a person, the *conservator,* to manage the assets and personal affairs of another, the *conservatee,* who is not competent to manage his or her affairs.

http://

The California Advocates for Nursing Home Reform (CANHR) Web site is not directly related to our text discussion, but this important Web site for people with loved ones in nursing home care can be found at
http://www.canhr.org/

guardianship

A court-established arrangement whereby an adult guardian is appointed to take care of the person and/or the estate of a minor.

http://

A new area of practice is elder law, well represented at the Elder Law Section of the New York State Bar Association Web site at **http://www.nysba.org/ MSTemplate.cfm? MicrositeID=53**

http://

Read some estate planning strategies from the Financial Planning Association, James Muse CFP **http://www.bevbank.com/ library/0602/plan_strat.pdf**

EXHIBIT 14-5: **Trust Arrangement**

WHERE TO FIND MY IMPORTANT PAPERS

Name _____ Social Security Number _____

My valuable papers re stored locations (address plus where to look):

A. Residence _____

B. Safe-deposit box(es) _____

C. Other _____

	A	B	C		A	B	C
Items				**Items**			
My will (original)	___	___	___	Retirement papers	___	___	___
Powers of appointment	___	___	___	Deferred compensation;			
				IRA papers	___	___	___
Spouse's will (original)	___	___	___	Titles and deeds	___	___	___
Location and combination				Notes (mortgages)	___	___	___
of safe	___	___	___				
Trust agreements				List of stored & loaned items			
As settlor	___	___	___	(item, bailee, and address)	___	___	___
As beneficiary	___	___	___	Motor vehicle ownership			
				records	___	___	___
Life insurance policy(ies)	___	___	___	Birth certificates (mine, spouse's			
Insurance policy(ies)	___	___	___	and children's)	___	___	___
Homeowner's insurance				Military enlistment and			
policy	___	___	___	discharge papers	___	___	___
Motor vehicle and				Marriage certificate(s)	___	___	___
other insurance							
policy(ies) (including boats)	___	___	___				
Employment contract(s)	___	___	___	Divorce/separation records	___	___	___
Partnership agreement(s)	___	___	___	Contract(s)	___	___	___
List of checking, savings				Important receipts*	___	___	___
accounts	___	___	___				
List of credit cards with				Important warranties	___	___	___
numbers	___	___	___				
Brokerage account records	___	___	___	Other	___	___	___
Stock certificates	___	___	___		___	___	___
Bonds	___	___	___		___	___	___
Notes receivabale	___	___	___		___	___	___
Notes payable	___	___	___				

* Including receipts for capital improvements to residence.

IMPORTANT NAMES, ADDRESSES AND PHONE NUMBERS

Beneficiaries under my will (list)

_____

_____

_____

_____

_____

Attorney _____

Accountant _____

Insurance agent _____

Stock broker _____

Medical doctor _____

Date prepared _____

People to whom copies have been given _____

1. _____

2. _____

3. _____

4. _____

5. Write a letter of or record your final instructions. Leave a version of Exhibit 14-5 explaining where important records and assets are located.
6. Consider donating your body organs at death and prepare appropriate documents. Make your intentions known to others (e.g., on a card in your wallet, as such information should be immediately accessible).
7. Consider execution of a living will and/or a durable power of attorney to permit implementation of your wishes if you become terminally ill or incapacitated.
8. Consider the transfer of certain assets into joint tenancy so that they will pass to the surviving joint tenant, avoiding probate. If married and living in a community property state, consider holding your jointly owned property as community property.
9. Make tax-free *inter vivos* gifts to reduce the size of your estate and thus reduce the level of income taxes and death taxes that will have to be paid upon your death. A salutary side effect is to help the donees when they need the money most and not years later when unpredictable destiny forces a distribution by death.
10. Review pension plans to determine how much retirement income you can expect from these sources, including social security.
11. Consider investments in annuities to supplement a fixed income expected from pensions. Annuities can be created from the lump-sum proceeds of cash surrender values of life insurance policies.
12. Keep in mind the possible assistance obtainable from workers' compensation insurance and social security in case of accidental injury or death on the job, and from unemployment insurance, in case of forced idleness.
13. If one of your major assets is a stock in a closely held corporation, prepare and execute a buy-sell agreement coupled with qualified plans for deferred compensation through profit sharing or company pension plans.
14. If one of your major assets is an interest in a partnership, prepare and execute a suitable buy-sell agreement and arrange for life insurance or some other means of providing cash to fund the purchase.
15. If one of your major assets is a sole proprietorship, provide a funded plan that will provide for the continuation of the company or a liquidation under favorable circumstances.
16. Review and update your plan anytime there is a change in your personal status, or at least every few years. An outdated plan may be worse than no plan.

CASE

ESTATE OF DOROTHY SOUTHWORTH V. NORTH SHORE ANIMAL LEAGUE

Court of Appeal, 51 Cal. App. 4th 564, 59 Cal. Rptr. 2d 272 (California, 1996)

Dorothy Southworth requested information from the North Shore Animal League (NSAL) about its lifetime pet care program. NSAL sent Dorothy the information, included a request that Dorothy return an enclosed pet care registration card, and told Dorothy to contact her attorney about including a bequest to NSAL in her estate. Dorothy did not return the registration card to NSAL; however, after additional correspondence she did return a donor card to NSAL. In a blank space following the printed words, "I am not taking action now, but my

intention is," Dorothy wrote, "my entire estate is to be left to North Shore Animal League" and she signed and dated the donor card. On January 14, 1994, Dorothy Southworth died without a will. NSAL asked that the donor card be admitted to probate as a holographic will and the trial court ruled in its favor, stating that the card "substantially complies with all the Probate Code requirements for a holographic will." The intestate heirs, suppressing their natural love for animals, appealed.

GILBERT, Associate Justice

Facts

Decedent never married and had no children. On March 4, 1986, in response to decedent's request for information, NSAL sent a letter to her describing its lifetime pet care program and explaining how to register for it. NSAL asked that she return its enclosed pet care registration card, contact her attorney to include her bequest to NSAL in her estate and send a copy of the bequest to NSAL. NSAL informed her that "[e]ven if you don't currently have a will, we'll accept your Registration on good faith and maintain an Active file on your pet while you're arranging the Bequest." Decedent never returned the registration card to NSAL.

NSAL sent a donor card to the decedent. It stated: "Your newest gift to the North Shore Animal League will help get more homeless dogs and cats out of cages and into new homes." The donor card thanked her "for your interest in making a bequest to the League." It explained that she could change her life insurance policy or provide for animals in her will by calling her attorney. It sought gifts and legacies and asked her to complete and return the donor card.

On April 19, 1989, she returned the donor card to NSAL. [There had been other occasional contact in the inter-

vening 3 years.] The card provided three options: a. naming NSAL as a beneficiary of a life insurance policy, b. changing one's will to leave securities or cash to NSAL, or c. not taking immediate action, but stating her intentions.

On the card, the decedent circled printed option (c) which states: "I am not taking action now, but my intention is [in the blank space provided she wrote] My entire estate is to be left to North Shore Animal League."

The donor card also included a printed statement which reads, "The total amount that the animal shelter will someday receive is [she wrote in the blank space] $500,000." The card then stated, "I would like the money used for:

"Food and shelter for the animals
"Adoption Fund to advertise for new owners
"Spaying and Neutering Program
"Unrestricted use[.]"

Decedent placed an "x" next to the food and spaying options listed. She signed and dated the donor card.

On May 10, 1989, NSAL sent a thank you letter to decedent for "letting us know that you will remember the North Shore Animal League in your will." The letter requested that decedent "have your attorney send us a copy of your will[.]"

The Neptune Society [where she had arranged for her cremation] asked for additional information to complete the death certificate, pursuant to amendments to the Probate Code. Decedent returned Neptune's supplemental form and stated that there are "[n]o living relatives" and to "[p]lease notify North Shore Animal League." She included NSAL's address, telephone numbers and the name of the executive director of NSAL. She signed the supplemental form and dated it October 20, 1989.

On September 2, 1992, NSAL sent a letter to decedent acknowledging that in March 1989 she wrote NSAL to state that she intended to take action leading to its becoming one of the beneficiaries of her estate. NSAL requested a meeting with decedent, thanking her for her "kind thoughts and generous support." She never responded to this request.

Jeanette Southworth, Jack Southworth, Michael Hulse and Arthur Hulse assigned part of their alleged interests in the estate to [Francis V.] See. Jeanette and Jack are the surviving half-siblings of decedent. Michael and Arthur Hulse are the children of another half-sister of decedent who predeceased her.

The See contestants argued that the donor card should be denied admission into probate as a holographic will because not all of its material provisions are in the handwriting of the decedent and there is no showing of testamentary intent at the time she signed the card. NSAL argued that the donor card reflected decedent's testamentary intent and satisfied the statutory requirements for a holographic will.

The trial court concluded that decedent's handwritten statement on the donor card that "[m]y entire estate is to be left to North Shore Animal League" substantially complies with all the Probate Code requirements for a holographic will. The court viewed the preprinted parts of the donor card and the $500,000 sum written in to be immaterial. The court interpreted the preprinted words stating that "I am not taking action now, but my intention is . . ." to mean that she did not want to immediately transfer her funds to NSAL, but intended to bequeath them upon her death. The trial court admitted the donor card to probate as the last will of the decedent. Jeanette and Jack Southworth, and Francis V. See, appeal from the judgment.

Discussion

The facts are stipulated. "Where, as here, there is no conflict in the evidence, the validity of the holographic instrument must be determined entirely by reference to the applicable statutes and principles of law." Interpretation of statutes is a question of law and our fundamental task is to ascertain the intent of the Legislature.

Former Civil Code section 1277 stated that "[a] [h]olographic will is one that is entirely written, dated and signed by the hand of the testator himself. It is subject to no other form, . . . and need not be witnessed." (Emphasis added.) Section 1277 was strictly construed.

In 1931, the Legislature reenacted former Civil Code section 1277 as section 53 of the Probate Code and added a third sentence . . . "No address, date or other matter written, printed or stamped upon the document, which is not incorporated in the provisions which are in the handwriting of the decedent, shall be considered as any part of the will."

In Estate of Black, the decedent wrote out her will on three identical, commercially-printed one-page will forms. In the blanks provided, she wrote her signature and place of domicile, and on the third page she inserted the name and gender of her executor, the date of the instrument and the city and state where she executed it. She either struck out or ignored other printed language regarding residuary gifts, the

appointment of an executor, attesting witnesses and a testimonium clause.

"Using virtually all of the remaining space on each of the three pages, testatrix expressed in her own handwriting a detailed testamentary disposition of her estate, including specific devises and legacies to individuals and a charitable institution and a bequest of her residuary estate."

The trial court denied probate because the testatrix incorporated some of the printed language, even though it concerned perfunctory procedural matters in the form will. Our Supreme Court reversed because "none of the incorporated material is either material to the substance of the will or essential to its validity as a testamentary disposition. . . ." (Estate of Black, 181 Cal.Rptr. 222.)

The Black court explained that "[t]he policy of the law is toward a construction favoring validity, in determining whether a will has been executed in conformity with statutory requirements." Moreover, we affirmed ([in the] Estate of Baker) "the tendency of both the courts and the Legislature . . . toward greater liberality in accepting a writing as an holographic will. . . ." "Substantial compliance with the statute, and not absolute precision is all that is required. . . ." Courts are to use common sense in evaluating whether a document constitutes a holographic will.

The Black court recognized that "[i]f testators are to be encouraged by a statute like ours to draw their own wills, the courts should not adopt, upon purely technical reasoning, a construction which would result in invalidating such wills in half the cases." That sensible admonition is no less appropriate today. The law recognizes that such wills are generally made by people without legal training. The primary purpose of the statutory holographic will provisions is to prevent fraud. Because counterfeiting another's handwriting "is exceedingly difficult," these statutes require the material provisions of holographic wills to be in the testator's handwriting.

Whether a document should be admitted to probate as a holographic will depends on proof of its authorship and authenticity, and whether the words establish that it was intended to be the author's last will and testament at the time she wrote it.

Our high court explained that four questions are pertinent in evaluating whether a document should be invalidated as a holographic will due to printed language in the document: "Was the particular provision relevant to the substance of the will? Was it essential to the will's validity? Did the testator intend to incorporate the provision? Would invalidation of the holograph defeat the testator's intent?"

Accordingly, in 1983, the year after our Supreme Court decided Black, our Legislature replaced Probate Code section 53 with Probate Code section 6111. Section 6111 provides, in pertinent part, that "(a) A will ... is valid as a holographic will, whether or not witnessed, if the signature and the material provisions are in the handwriting of the testator." In 1990, the Legislature added subdivision (c) which provides that "Any statement of testamentary intent contained in a holographic will may be set forth either in the testator's own handwriting or as part of a commercially printed form will."

There is no question that the handwriting on the document at issue is that of Dorothy Southworth, and that she signed and dated it. Unlike Black, however, the document is not a commercially-printed will form. It is a donor card for a charity. It was not drafted to serve as a will. The card provides the option of informing NSAL that the donor has or intends to instruct one's attorney to change his or her will.

Furthermore, the printed language Southworth incorporated from the donor card does not evince her present testamentary intent. Instead of striking the material printed words which state "I am not taking action now, but my intention is," she chose to incorporate those words with her handwritten statement, "My entire estate is to be left to North Shore Animal League." The material printed language together with her handwriting evince a future intent; not present testamentary intent.

Although other extrinsic evidence, such as her letter to NSAL of September 4, 1987, and the supplemental Neptune form she signed on October 20, 1989, shows that Southworth desired to leave her estate to NSAL, neither the donor card at issue nor the handwriting on it substantially complies with probate code requirements for holographic wills. Although

courts may consider statements made before and after a holographic will is made and the surrounding circumstances, evidence of present testamentary intent provided by the instrument at issue is paramount.

Here, Southworth incorporated printed language stating that she was not taking any action when she executed it. It does not establish her testamentary intent at the time she executed it. It only states her intention to make a will in the future.

The judgment is reversed. The parties are to bear their own costs.

For Critical Analysis

1. What were the appellate court's reasons in holding there was no valid holographic will? Do you agree with the court? Explain.

2. What could NSAL have done, if anything, to increase its chances of inheriting from Ms. Southworth?

3. Identify the heirs who are claiming Ms. Southworth's estate and their relation to Ms. Southworth. Why had Ms. Southworth told the Neptune Society she had no "living relatives"?

4. Are the rules for holographic wills too technical? Explain your answer. ■

McConnell v. Beverly Enterprises-Connecticut, Inc.

Supreme Court of Connecticut, 209 Conn. 692, 553 A.2d 596 (Connecticut, 1989)

The husband and children of a comatose, terminally ill patient brought an action seeking to terminate life-support services being provided to Carol M. McConnell by a private nursing home, Danbury Pavilion Healthcare. Carol McConnell was the 57-year-old wife of the plaintiff John E. McConnell and the mother of the three other co-plaintiffs. By profession, she was a registered nurse. Her last nursing positions were as head nurse and manager of the emergency room at Danbury Hospital. On January 18, 1985, Mrs. McConnell sustained a severe head injury as the result of an automobile accident. She had not regained consciousness, despite excellent medical care. She was in an irreversible persistent vegetative state with no prospect of improvement. In the opinion of her attending physician, her con-

dition was terminal. Her life was sustained by means of a gastrostomy tube through which she received nutrition and hydration. The Superior Court entered judgment for patient's husband and children, and the state attorney general and the patient's guardian ad litem took appeal.

Chief Justice Peters wrote the opinion: This case concerns the right of a family, on behalf of a patient who is presently in a terminal coma, to implement the patient's clearly expressed wish for the removal of a gastrostomy tube that is artificially providing nutrition and hydration for the patient.

[T]he Removal of Life Support Systems Act in which the legislature, cognizant of a common law right of self-determination and of a constitutional right to privacy, sought to provide a statutory mechanism to implement these important rights. We must decide what role this act plays in the present litigation. The trial court held that the plaintiffs were entitled to relief without regard to the act, which the court construed to be nonexclusive. The defendants, by contrast, maintain that the act governs and precludes the relief sought by the plaintiffs. There is, however, a middle ground, a construction of the act that is consistent with the plaintiffs' affirmative claims for relief.

Although the United States Constitution does not expressly provide a right to privacy, the United States Supreme Court has recognized a right to privacy in the penumbra of the Bill of Rights, specifically in the protection of the First, Third, Fourth and Fifth amendments. "[T]he Court has recognized that a right of personal privacy, or a guarantee of certain areas or zones of privacy, does exist under the Constitution." Justice Brandeis has referred to this right as "the right to be let alone—the most comprehensive of rights and the right most valued by civilized men." Although the court has recently construed this right to privacy narrowly; it has held that personal rights that are "implicit in the concept of ordered liberty"; or "deeply rooted in this Nation's history and tradition" are included in this guarantee of personal privacy. The court has found that contraception, procreation, marriage, and education implicate privacy rights.

The right to refuse medical treatment has been specifically recognized as a subject of constitutional protection. "This court has also long held that '[e]very human being of adult years and sound mind has a right to determine what shall be done with his own body....'" Court after court has recognized the existence of a right, in principle and in properly guarded circumstances, to the removal of medical treatments that artificially prolong life.

Many of the cases upholding a right of self-determination for terminally ill individuals have urged legislatures to enact guidelines for appropriate private decision-making in these heart-rending dilemmas. When the legislature has attempted to respond to this urgent request for statutory assistance, we have an obligation to pursue the applicability of statutory criteria before resorting to an exploration of residual common law rights, if any such rights indeed remain. We must therefore decide whether a reasonable construction of our act ever permits the removal of a gastrostomy tube.

Careful examination of our act discloses that the legislature approached the appropriate treatment for very sick patients by establishing three guiding principles. First, if a patient, in the eyes of his or her attending physician, is not in a terminal condition, "beneficial medical treatment and nutrition and hydration must be provided." Second, if a patient, to the contrary, is deemed by his or her physician to be in a ter-

minal condition, life sustaining technology may be removed, in the exercise of the physician's best medical judgment, when that judgment has received the informed consent of the patient's next of kin or guardian and when it coincides with the expressed wishes of the patient. Third, even the removal of life sustaining technology must be done in a manner consistent with providing "comfort care and pain alleviation" for the patient. Under the act, the patient's attending physician must deem "the patient to be in a terminal condition." For the purposes of the act, "'[t]erminal condition' means the final stage of an incurable or irreversible medical condition which, in the opinion of the attending physician, will result in death." Dr. Robert Ruxin serves as Mrs. McConnell's attending physician and he testified that he deemed her to be in a terminal condition. While there was testimony to the contrary on this issue, the act places the responsibility for reaching the conclusion with the attending physician, contemplating a decision to discontinue treatment reached after consultation between the attending physician and the family or next of kin, unimpeded by courts, other medical experts or ethicists.

Ruxin reached his conclusion after numerous examinations of Mrs. McConnell. He deemed her to be in an incurable, irreversible, persistent vegetative state, a condition that ultimately will lead to her death. The trial court found Ruxin's testimony credible and we have discovered nothing in the trial transcripts to warrant disturbing this finding.

The Statute requires that the attending physician obtain the informed consent of the patient's next of kin prior to removing a life support system. The fact that the rest of the McConnell family (husband John, daughters Kathleen and Amy, and son James), all over the age of majority, have brought this action indicates that they consent to the removal of the gastrostomy tube. Furthermore, the testimony of all four demonstrates positively that they reached their decision out of love and concern for their mother and wife and respect for her wishes. There is not a hint in the trial court testimony of any ulterior motive on the part of any of the plaintiffs.

Finally, pursuant to the act, the attending physician must consider "the patient's wishes as expressed by the patient directly, through his next of kin or legal guardian...." The trial court found clear and convincing evidence that Mrs. McConnell had expressed "forcefully and without wavering" that artificial means should not be employed to prolong her life. We conclude that the trial court did not err in this finding.

That Mrs. McConnell desired that her family not prolong her life should she ever suffer an injury that left her in a vegetative state could not have been clearer. She worked as a registered nurse in an emergency room, and therefore often saw the tragedy that befell those who suffered severe head injuries. The court heard testimony from a co-worker, Marie Kornhaas, that Mrs. McConnell did not believe in the use of respirators, feeding tubes or other life-sustaining systems, and that if she were ever placed on such a system, she hoped that Kornhaas would do what she could to stop it.

The trial court heard testimony from all of Mrs. McConnell's immediate family that she was extremely concerned about head injuries, warning her children often about the dangers of motorcycles and small cars. Her husband described her as having "a phobia about head injury." She had also been adamant that her own mother, when dying of cancer, not be placed on any life support system. Finally, each member of her immediate family testified absolutely, without hesitation, that Mrs. McConnell did not believe in life support systems, including gastrostomy tubes, for herself, that she would want the tube removed from her and that they sought to carry out her wishes. We therefore conclude that the record sustains those findings of fact by the trial court that are required by the act to be shown as a condition for the withdrawal of life support systems.

III

In his brief, the Attorney General raises the specter of suicide, claiming that the state has a compelling interest in preventing it and that to allow Mrs. McConnell to carry out her wish to discontinue food and nutrition would be to allow her to commit suicide. We are not persuaded that a suicide would occur in this case.

It is well-established that the state may not base a criminal prosecution on the exercise of a constitutional right. Because we hold that the legislature in enacting the Removal of Life Support Systems Act sought to establish a workable mechanism by which individuals may implement their common law and constitutional rights, it follows that by exercising these rights, the individual cannot become criminally liable.

Furthermore, we agree with the majority of jurisdictions that have addressed this issue in holding that the removal of a gastrostomy tube is not the "death producing agent," set in motion with the intent of causing her own death. In exercising her right of self-determination, Mrs. McConnell merely seeks to be free of extraordinary mechanical devices and to allow nature to take its course. Thus, death will be by natural causes underlying the disease, not by self-inflicted injury.

There is no error.

In this opinion CALLAHAN, GLASS and COVELLO, J.J., concur.

For Critical Analysis

1. Why did the State Attorney General oppose the family's wishes? Was it appropriate that they do so?

2. What does this sentence mean? "The trial court held that the plaintiffs were entitled to relief without regard to the act, which the court construed to be nonexclusive."

3. Do you agree with the doctor's diagnosis that the Mrs. McConnell was in a "terminal condition"? Remember this diagnosis was made before removal of the gastrostomy tube—after removal it is clear she would be. How would Mrs. McConnell's situation be any more terminal than that of anyone else, including you?

4. Assume a person makes a conscious decision to stop taking nutrition and hydration (eating and drinking). Is that suicide? Is it illegal? At some time the person would become unconscious before death; would it be wrongful to provide hydration and nutrition by a feeding tube against the person's wishes? If it were administered could the person demand removal upon regaining consciousness?

CHAPTER QUESTIONS AND PROBLEMS

1. Joe Mariano never made a will. Now he is flat on his back in a hospital bed after being injured in a crash of his private plane. Both his arms are in casts and he has extensive internal injuries. But his mind is alert and he can talk. Realizing that the prognosis is bad, he calls for his lawyer. Can they prepare a formal, witnessed will, even though Mariano cannot write his name?

2. When Pauline Puffington died, she left her entire estate of $3 million to a trust for the care of her 12 dogs and 14 cats. After the pets' deaths, the principal was to be paid to a designated society for the prevention of cruelty to animals. Relatives challenged the will, proving not only that she was eccentric and senile when she made it, but also that she was insane when she died. Can the will be enforced?

3. Mary Dorsett was convinced that making a will was tantamount to writing one's own death warrant. Even after she married and had given birth to the twins, she did nothing to ensure the economical transfer of her estate to

her family after her death. She was a hard-working dentist and had acquired an estate of $250,000 by age 30. Then she suddenly died of a heart attack. Under the state's law of intestacy, her husband received one-third of her separate property and the twins, age 5, shared the balance equally. What expenses and burdens might she have avoided for her widower?

4. Richard Kalfus murdered his wife, Domenica. He pled guilty and was sentenced to prison. Her husband and two infant children survived Domenica. She left no will. Under New Jersey's law of intestate succession, a husband is entitled to a one-third share of personal property if children also survive the deceased parent. The statute made no reference to the effect of wrongful acts by an heir. Is Richard entitled to his intestate share of Domenica's estate? [*Estate of Kalfus v. Kalfus,* 81 N.J. Super. 435, 195 A.2d 903 (N.J., 1963).]

5. Harry Gordon died at the age of 83. The sole beneficiary in his will was a charitable organization. The attorney who drafted Gordon's will was the regional vice president of the organization and his practice was located in the same building as the charity. All witnesses to the will were officers of the corporation, as were the executors. The original of the will was kept in the charity's offices. The will was executed seven years before Gordon's death. Would there be a presumption of undue influence? Was undue influence present? [*Herman v. Kogan,* 487 So.2d 48 (Fla., 1986).]

6. The will of Warren E. Burger, Chief Justice of United States from 1969 until 1986, is included as Exhibit 14-2 in this chapter. He prepared the will himself. Is it a holographic will? What improvements to his will could you advise?

7. Discuss some of the situations in which a directive to physician would apply. A durable power of attorney? What ethical dilemmas do these instruments create?

8. What is the difference between a revocable and an irrevocable trust? Identify a circumstance where each would be appropriate.

9. First Virginia Bank of Tidewater was the trustee of a testamentary marital trust. In the course of the bank's service as trustee, it invested $40,000 in real estate investment trusts (REIT). The investment became worthless. The beneficiaries of the trust brought suit, complaining that the bank had violated the Virginia statutory "prudent man rule," which guided trustees in careful investment of trust assets. The bank defended, alleging the settlor had granted the bank broad discretion, obviating the "prudent man rule." Language in the will authorized real estate investments and to hold or sell investments "...without liability on the part of any fiduciary for depreciation in the value...." Can a settlor supersede a statutory standard for a trustee? Did the testator settlor do so in this case? [*Hoffman v. First Virginia Bank of Tidewater,* 220 Va. 834, 263 S.E. 402 (Va., 1980).]

10. J. T. Payne executed a valid will on June 29, 1934. On April 24, 1956, a will with singed edges was offered to the probate court. Three of his children challenged the will, contending the deceased had revoked it. A witness at the trial testified that in July of 1934, J. T. Payne said, "I am going to get rid of this damn will right now," and he threw it on live coals in the fireplace. Payne's wife rescued the document and, with it still smoking on one end, put it into her apron. No language of the will offered in probate was obliterated or obscured. Can this be considered a valid will? [*Payne v. Payne,* 3213 Ga. 613, 100 S.E.2d 450 (Ga., 1957).]

11. Sung Fong had two strong obsessions during a long, eventful life: to become a millionaire and to "go it alone." He never married and now, at age 90, has a net worth of more than $10 million, almost all in stocks and bonds. He has no enemies, explaining with a chuckle that he's outlived them all. He has no true friends and no known relatives. With his health failing rapidly, he's added a third goal: to pay no death tax to the government. "Not one cent," he repeats. Can you tell him how to accomplish this last strange goal?

12. Answer each of the following questions. Check your answer with answers provided by experts conducting an Internet search of estate planning Web sites.
    a. Why should I prepare a will?
    b. What happens if I die without a will?
    c. Does a will cover all my property?
    d. How do I change my will after it's been signed?
    e. What is probate? How can I avoid it?
    f. What does it mean when a will is contested?
    g. What does it mean to be an executor?

Case Brief

Case briefing is a long-used method of studying law. Its purpose is to have students identify the rules of law found in court cases and analyze how courts apply these rules of law to the facts of a case in an objective and rational manner. Case briefing hones analytic skills and heightens understanding of the role of courts in defining, interpreting, and applying law. This appendix explains one way to brief cases. There is no single standard for case briefing, but the structure below is common and will serve you well, both in studying the law now and in using the law in the future. It is worthwhile mastering. After explaining a how a brief is constructed, a sample brief the of case *Eric J. v. Betty M.,* appearing at the end of Chapter 1, is provided.

P URPOSES OF A BRIEF

1. Establishes a useful means of bringing the facts of a case back to memory in a short time, for whatever purpose, including classroom discussion.
2. Allows you to extract from a judicial decision its future value as precedent. In other words, it helps you find the principles of law that the case sets forth.
3. Allows for easier and smoother review of an area of law. Each brief takes a complex and long document (the case) and reduces it to its key facts, holding, and rationale (the brief). A collection of briefs can provide a comprehensive summary of an area of law.

E LEMENTS OF A BRIEF

A brief is primarily a self-teaching tool; as such, you should structure them to meet your own needs. Many formats have been proposed by various writers. The method to use is the one that makes the most sense to you. For an introductory law class, the purpose of a brief is more limited than for either a law student or a lawyer. Also, a brief should be brief! A long brief eliminates the most important role of a brief: the boiling down of a complex case to its essence.

Several basic components of a brief are present in almost all brief styles. If your brief style includes the following elements, you should do well:

- Facts
- Issue or issues
- Holding, including the rule of law
- Rationale

FACTS

State the facts of the case *in your own words*. Indicate which facts are operative, and which bear on the issues to be decided. Do not just repeat the judge's words. Be brief. Often a sign of how well you understand the case is your ability to identify the relative importance of facts. Some cases may have many extraneous facts that do not need to be in your brief. Most certainly, some facts will be more important than others. Your task is to frame the problem by describing the facts that count, the ones that matter.

ISSUE

Issue spotting is the skill of recognizing in the facts a pattern that implies a certain type of issue. For instance, facts that describe two people both claiming ownership rights over a chair should spotlight an issue of ownership of personal property. In reading cases, often the parties and the court do this work for you. Ask yourself what legal questions are posed by the appealing party. The appealing party is alleging that an error of law was made. What is that error? What question is the court answering? Sometimes a court will see the issue differently than the parties and present a different twist on the issue. State the issue cleanly and crisply. Avoid stating it in technical or procedural terms. Some believe that beginning your issue statement with "Whether" will allow you to focus your statement.

Example: Whether Smith established legal ownership of the chair by physically possessing it for seven years.

HOLDING

What is the ruling by the court? Who won? Answering these questions forces you to identify the outcome of the case. You must understand the procedural setting enough to know what happens as a result of the decision. For instance, if the court rules "in favor of the appellants," what does this mean? More importantly, you need to find the holding on the issue itself. How did the court decide the issue? What rule of law is provided by the case? Using the chair ownership example from above, a holding that resolves the issue might be:

Example: The court found that Smith had not established ownership of the chair by virtue of possessing the chair for seven years.

Notice how the above statement ignores who owns the chair. A newspaper headline would be more focused on the personal story: "Smith Loses Chair to Green." In briefing a case, however, you are not a reporter; you are a student of the law. For that reason you must stick to the issue and its resolution as the primary focus.

RATIONALE

The length of each part of the case brief need not be evenly distributed. In fact, the rationale section is usually the longest section. In the rationale section you explain why the court ruled the way that it did. This means that you need to describe the court's reasoning, sometimes even quoting the court's choice of words. You also must explain which facts the court depended upon and which ones it discounted or ignored. You should also note what prior decisions it looked at and whether it chose to follow them, overrule them, or differentiate them. The court might also interpret or cite particular statutes or other laws in reaching its decision. Finally, notice whether the court relies upon public policy to reach its decision. Thus the potential components to a court's rationale include:

- Facts: which ones were dispositive and which ones not
- Prior cases that were followed, differentiated, or overruled
- Statutory law and how it was interpreted
- Public policy principles

Your task is to organize these components and explain how the court used them to reach its decision. You are trying to find the rule of law that may flow from this case. The rule of law is the "why" of the decision, not the "what." This is very important, as unless you can determine the why of a case, it is very difficult to use the case to predict the outcome of similar disputes when they arise.

Returning to the chair ownership issue above, the holding does not tell us the "why" and, as such, it is not really that useful. The rationale of the court, however, might describe how the court relied upon a long history that ownership is not automatically determined by mere possession, but instead depends on how possession and control was lost by a previous owner.

REMEMBER

Note that almost all cases are appellate cases. Think about which appellate court they are from: state or federal? Is it a final court of appeal or an intermediate court? Consider when the case was decided—recently, or many years ago? Has the passage of time eroded the soundness of the decision? Finally, but also important, what do you think of the decision? Is it logical, just, fair, or otherwise? How does it fit with a textbook chapter or topic? Briefing cases can teach you about courts, moral viewpoints, and the seam between ethical values and the law.

Ⓑ RIEF OF THE CASE OF Eric J. v. Betty M.

Here is a sample brief of the case of *Eric J. v. Betty M.* (Cal. Appellate Case 1999), which you read at the end of Chapter 1. *Note that Facts and Rationale make up the bulk of the case brief. The facts have been retold in the author's own words. Not all facts were recited. The Rationale explains the court's holding and what it means as a rule of law. It cites the case law as well as the public policy that the court applied. The Rationale also explains how the court dealt with a possible contrary case.*

FACTS

Robert brought home his new girlfriend, Helen, and her eight-year-old son, Eric, to meet his mother, father, brothers, and sister and their spouses. The relationship between Robert and Helen continued and Helen and Eric were guests several times in different family homes. No family member told Helen about Robert's criminal history of felony child molestation. It was later discovered that Robert sexually molested Eric during some of these visits at the family homes all the while Robert was on parole for child molestation. Robert was convicted of molesting Eric and sent back to prison. Helen filed suit against Robert's family claiming they had a duty to warn her about Robert's criminal past and the potential danger to her child, and failing that duty they were liable for money damages for the harm suffered by Eric. The trial court dismissed the case on a nonsuit motion.

ISSUE

Whether the trial court properly dismissed the negligence claim based on the premise that family members of a convicted child molester have no affirmative duty to disclose that information to the molester's girlfriend who has an eight-year-old boy.

HOLDING

The appellate court affirmed the trial court, holding that the family members had no affirmative duty to disclose the information.

RATIONALE

The appellate court placed great weight upon the "no duty to aid" rule, developed "over the centuries" in courts. The court noted that a special relationship is required to create a duty to warn, give aid, or otherwise help another. Ultimately, the court found that no such special relationship existed and found no other reason to suggest that the family members had a duty to warn the girlfriend. The court cited several cases, including a California Supreme Court case, *Williams v. State of California,* that establish the "no duty to aid" rule. In short, a person who has not created the danger or risk is not liable simply for failing to take an affirmative action unless there is "some relationship" that creates a "duty to act." The court rejected a case that seemed to rule the other way, *Soldano v. O'Daniels,* by explaining that the facts in that case clearly showed that the defendant had actually prevented someone else from rendering aid. The court also noted that any decision to find a duty to aid in this case would interfere with family relationships by creating "intolerable conflicts of interest." Impliedly, this went against public policy.

Declaration of Independence

In Congress, July 4, 1776

The Unamimous Declaration of the thirteen united States of America

When in the Course of human Events, it becomes necessary for one people to dissolve the political bands which have connected them with another, and to assume among the powers of the earth, the separate and equal station to which the Laws of Nature and of Nature's God entitle them, a decent respect to the opinions of mankind requires that they should declare the causes which impel them to the separation.

We hold these Truths to be self-evident, that all men are created equal, that they are endowed by their Creator with certain unalienable Rights, that among these are Life, Liberty, and the Pursuit of Happiness—That to secure these rights, Governments are instituted among Men, deriving their just powers from the consent of the governed, That whenever any Form of Government becomes destructive of these ends, it is the Right of the People to alter or to abolish it, and to institute new Government, laying its Foundation on such principles, and organizing its powers in such form, as to them shall seem most likely to effect their Safety and Happiness. Prudence, indeed, will dictate that Governments long established should not be changed for light and transient causes; and accordingly all experience hath shewn, that mankind are more disposed to suffer, while evils are sufferable, than to right themselves by abolishing the forms to which they are accustomed. But when a long train of abuses and usurpations, pursuing invariably the same Object, evinces a design to reduce them under absolute Despotism, it is their Right, it is their duty, to throw off such Government, and to provide new Guards for their future security. Such has been the patient sufferance of these Colonies; and such is now the Necessity which constrains them to alter their former Systems of Government. The history of the present King of Great-Britain is a history of repeated injuries and usurpations, all having in direct object the establishment of an absolute Tyranny over these States. To prove this, let facts be submitted to a candid World.

He has refused his Assent to Laws, the most wholesome and necessary for the public good.

He has forbidden his Governors to pass Laws of immediate and pressing importance, unless suspended in their operation till his Assent should be obtained; and when so suspended, he has utterly neglected to attend to them.

The spelling, capitalization, and punctuation as provided by the U.S. government Archives is used.

He has refused to pass other Laws for the accommodation of large districts of people, unless those people would relinquish the right of Representation in the Legislature, a right inestimable to them, and formidable to Tyrants only.

He has called together legislative bodies at places unusual, uncomfortable, and distant from the depository of their public Records, for the sole Purpose of fatiguing them into compliance with his Measures.

He has dissolved Representative Houses repeatedly, for opposing with manly firmness his invasions on the rights of the people.

He has refused for a long time, after such dissoulutions, to cause others to be elected; whereby the Legislative powers, incapable of Annihilation, have returned to the People at large for their exercise; the State remaining in the mean time exposed to all the dangers of invasion from without, and convulsions within.

He has endeavoured to prevent the population of these States; for that purpose obstructing the Laws for Naturalization of Foreigners; refusing to pass others to encourage their migrations hither, and raising the conditions of new Appropriations of Lands.

He has obstructed the Administration of Justice, by refusing his Assent to Laws for establishing Judiciary powers.

He has made Judges dependent on his Will alone, for the tenure of their offices, and the amount and payments of their salaries.

He has erected a multitude of New Offices, and sent hither swarms of Officers to harrass our people, and eat out their substance.

He has kept among us, in times of peace, Standing Armies, without the consent of our legislatures.

He has affected to render the Military independent of and superior to the Civil power.

He has combined with others to subject us to a jurisdiction foreign to our constitution, and unacknowledged by our laws; giving his Assent to their Acts of pretended Legislation:

For Quartering large bodies of armed troops among us:

For protecting them, by a mock Trial, from punishment for any Murders which they should commit on the Inhabitants of these States:

For cutting off our Trade with all parts of the world:

For imposing Taxes on us without our Consent:

For depriving us, in many cases, of the benefits of Trial by Jury:

For transporting us beyond Seas to be tried for pretended offences:

For abolishing the free System of English Laws in a neighbouring Province, establishing therein an arbitrary government, and enlarging its Boundaries, so as to render it at once an example and fit instrument for introducing the same absolute rule into these Colonies:

For taking away our Charters, abolishing our most valuable Laws, and altering fundamentally the Forms of our Governments:

For suspending our own Legislatures, and declaring themselves invested with power to legislate for us in all cases whatsoever.

He has abdicated Government here, by declaring us out of his Protection and waging War against us.

He has plundered our seas, ravaged our Coasts, burnt our towns, and destroyed the lives of our people.

He is, at this time, transporting large Armies of foreign Mercenaries to compleat the Works of death, desolation, and tyranny, already begun with circumstances of Cruelty and perfidy, scarcely paralleled in the most barbarous ages, and totally unworthy the Head of a civilized nation.

He has constrained our fellow Citizens taken Captive on the high Seas to bear Arms against their Country, to become the executioners of their friends and Brethren, or to fall themselves by their Hands.

He has excited domestic insurrections amongst us, and had endeavoured to bring on the inhabitants of our frontiers, the merciless Indian Savages, whose known rule of warfare, is an undistinguished destruction, of all ages, sexes and conditions.

In every stage of these Oppressions We have Petitioned for Redress in the most humble terms: Our repeated Petitions have been answered only by repeated injury. A Prince, whose character is thus marked by every act which may define a Tyrant, is unfit to be the ruler of a free people.

Nor have we been wanting in attentions to our British Brethren. We have warned them from time to time of attempts by their legislature to extend an unwarrantable jurisdiction over us. We have reminded them of the circumstances of our emigration and settlement here. We have appealed to their native justice and magnanimity, and we have conjured them by the ties of our common kindred to disavow these usurpations, which would inevitably interrupt our connections and correspondence. They too have been deaf to the voice of justice and of consanguinity. We must, therefore, acquiesce in the necessity, which denounces our Separation, and hold them, as we hold the rest of mankind, Enemies in War, in Peace Friends.

We, therefore, the Representatives of the United States of America, in General Congress Assembled, appealing to the Supreme Judge of the World for the Rectitude of our intentions, do, in the Name, and by Authority of the good People of these Colonies, solemnly publish and declare, That these United Colonies are, and of Right ought to be, Free and Independent States; that they are absolved from all Allegiance to the British Crown, and that all political connection between them and the State of Great-Britain, is and ought to be totally dissolved; and that as Free and Independent States they have full Power to levy War, conclude Peace, contract Alliances, establish Commerce, and to do all other Acts and Things which Independent States may of right do. And for the support of this Declaration, with a firm reliance on the protection of divine Providence, we mutually pledge to each other our Lives, our Fortunes, and our sacred Honor.

John Hancock, MASSACHUSETTS

GEORGIA, *Button Gwinnett, Lyman Hall, Geo. Walton.*

NORTH-CAROLINA, *Wm. Hopper, Joseph Hewes, John Penn.*

SOUTH-CAROLINA, *Edward Rutledge, Thos Heyward, junr., Thomas Lynch, junr., Arthur Middleton.*

MARYLAND, *Samuel Chase, Wm. Paca, Thos. Stone, Charles Carroll of Carrollton.*

VIRGINIA, *George Wythe, Richard Henry Lee, Ths. Jefferson, Benja. Harrison, Thos. Nelson, jr., Francis Lightfoot Lee, Carter Braxton.*

PENNSYLVANIA, *Robert Morris, Benjamin Rush, Benja. Franklin, John Morton, Geo. Clymer, Jas. Smith, Geo. Taylor, James Wilson, Geo. Ross.*

DELAWARE, *Caesar Rodney, Geo. Read, Thomas McKean.*

NEW-YORK, *Wm. Floyd, Phil. Livingston, Frank Lewis, Lewis Morris.*

NEW-JERSEY, *Richd. Stockton, Jno. Witherspoon, Fras. Hopkinson, John Hart, Abra. Clark.*

NEW-HAMPSHIRE, *Josiah Bartlett, Wm. Whipple, Matthew Thornton.*

MASSACHUSETTS-BAY, *Saml. Adams, John Adams, Robt. Treat Paine, Elbridge Gerry.*

RHODE-ISLAND AND PROVIDENCE, *C. Step. Hopkins, William Ellery.*

CONNECTICUT, *Roger Sherman, Saml. Huntington, Wm. Williams, Oliver Wolcott.*

Constitution of the United States of America

We the People of the United States, in Order to form a more perfect Union, establish Justice, insure domestic Tranquility, provide for the common defence, promote the general Welfare, and secure the Blessings of Liberty to ourselves and our Posterity, do ordain and establish this Constitution for the United States of America.

A RTICLE I

Section 1. All legislative Powers herein granted shall be vested in a Congress of the United States, which shall consist of a Senate and House of Representatives.

Section 2. The House of Representatives shall be composed of Members chosen every second Year by the People of the several States, and the Electors in each State shall have the Qualifications requisite for Electors of the most numerous Branch of the State Legislature.

No Person shall be a Representative who shall not have attained to the Age of twenty five Years, and been seven Years a Citizen of the United States, and who shall not, when elected, be an Inhabitant of that State in which he shall be chosen.

Representatives and direct (Taxes)[1] shall be apportioned among the several States which may be included within this Union, according to their respective Numbers (which shall be determined by adding to the whole Number of free Persons, including those bound to Service for a Term of Years, and excluding Indians not taxed, three fifths of all other Persons).[2] The actual Enumeration shall be made within three Years after the first Meeting of the Congress of the United States, and within every subsequent Term of ten Years, in such Manner as they shall by Law direct. The Number of Representatives shall not exceed one for every thirty Thousand, but each State shall have at Least one Representative; and until such enumeration shall be made, the State of New Hampshire shall be entitled to chuse three, Massachusetts eight, Rhode Island and Providence Plantations one, Connecticut five, New York six, New Jersey four, Pennsylvania eight, Delaware one, Maryland six, Virginia ten, North Carolina five, South Carolina five, and Georgia three.

When vacancies happen in the Representation from any State, the Executive Authority thereof shall issue Writs of Election to fill such Vacancies.

The spelling, capitalization, and punctuation of the original have been retained here. Parentheses indicate passages that have been altered by amendments to the Constitution.

The House of Representatives shall chuse their Speaker and other Officers; and shall have the sole Power of Impeachment.

Section 3. The Senate of the United States shall be composed of two Senators from each State (chosen by the Legislature thereof),[3] for six Years; and each Senator shall have one Vote.

Immediately after they shall be assembled in Consequence of the first Election, they shall be divided as equally as may be into three Classes. The Seats of the Senators of the first Class shall be vacated at the Expiration of the second Year, of the second Class at the Expiration of the fourth Year, and of the third Class at the Expiration of the sixth Year, so that one third may be chosen every second Year (and if Vacancies happen by Resignation, or otherwise, during the Recess of the Legislature of any State, the Executive thereof may make temporary Appointments until the next Meeting of the Legislature, which shall then fill such Vacancies).[4]

No Person shall be a Senator who shall not have attained to the Age of thirty Years, and been nine Years a Citizen of the United States, and who shall not, when elected, be an Inhabitant of that State for which he shall be chosen.

The Vice President of the United States shall be President of the Senate, but shall have no Vote, unless they be equally divided.

The Senate shall chuse their other Officers, and also a President pro tempore, in the Absence of the Vice President, or when he shall exercise the Office of President of the United States.

The Senate shall have the sole Power to try all Impeachments. When sitting for that Purpose, they shall be on Oath or Affirmation. When the President of the United States is tried, the Chief Justice shall preside: And no Person shall be convicted without the Concurrence of two thirds of the Members present.

Judgment in Cases of Impeachment shall not extend further than to removal from Office, and disqualification to hold and enjoy any Office of honor, Trust or Profit under the United States; but the Party convicted shall nevertheless be liable and subject to Indictment, Trial, Judgment and Punishment, according to Law.

Section 4. The Times, Places and Manner of holding Elections for Senators and Representatives, shall be prescribed in each State by the Legislature thereof; but the Congress may at any time by Law make or alter such Regulations, except as to the Places of chusing Senators.

(The Congress shall assemble at least once in every Year, and such Meeting shall be on the first Monday in December, unless they shall by Law appoint a different Day.)[5]

Section 5. Each House shall be the Judge of the Elections, Returns and Qualifications of its own Members, and a Majority of each shall constitute a Quorum to do Business; but a smaller Number may adjourn from day to day, and may be authorized to compel the Attendance of absent Members, in such Manner, and under such Penalties as each House may provide.

Each House may determine the Rules of its Proceedings, punish its Members for disorderly Behaviour, and, with the Concurrence of two thirds, expel a Member.

Each House shall keep a Journal of its Proceedings, and from time to time publish the same, excepting such Parts as may in their Judgment require Secrecy; and the Yeas and Nays of the Members of either House on any question shall, at the Desire of one fifth of those Present, be entered on the Journal.

Neither House, during the Session of Congress, shall, without the Consent of the other, adjourn for more than three days, nor to any other Place than that in which the two Houses shall be sitting.

Section 6. The Senators and Representatives shall receive a Compensation for their Services, to be ascertained by Law, and paid out of the Treasury of the United States.[6] They shall in all Cases, except Treason, Felony and Breach of the Peace, be privileged from Arrest during their Attendance at the Session of their respective Houses, and in going to and returning from the same; and for any Speech or Debate in either House, they shall not be questioned in any other Place.

No Senator or Representative shall, during the Time for which he was elected, be appointed to any civil Office under the Authority of the United States, which shall have been created, or the Emoluments whereof shall have been encreased during such time; and no Person holding any Office under the United States, shall be a Member of either House during his Continuance in Office.

Section 7. All Bills for raising Revenue shall originate in the House of Representatives; but the Senate may propose or concur with Amendments as on other Bills.

Every Bill which shall have passed the House of Representatives and the Senate, shall, before it becomes a Law, be presented to the President of the United States; If he approve he shall sign it, but if not he shall return it, with his Objections to the House in which it shall have originated, who shall enter the Objections at large on their Journal, and proceed to reconsider it. If after such Reconsideration two thirds of that House shall agree to pass the Bill, it shall be sent, together with the Objections, to the other House, by which it shall likewise be reconsidered, and if approved by two thirds of that House, it shall become a Law. But in all such Cases the Votes of both Houses shall be determined by yeas and Nays, and the Names of the Persons voting for and against the Bill shall be entered on the Journal of each House respectively. If any Bill shall not be returned by the President within ten Days (Sundays excepted) after it shall have been presented to him, the Same shall be a Law, in like Manner as if he had signed it, unless the Congress by their Adjournment prevent its Return, in which Case it shall not be a Law.

Every Order, Resolution, or Vote to Which the Concurrence of the Senate and House of Representatives may be necessary (except on a question of Adjournment) shall be presented to the President of the United States; and before the Same shall take Effect, shall be approved by him, or being disapproved by him, shall be repassed by two thirds of the Senate and House of Representatives, according to the Rules and Limitations prescribed in the Case of a Bill.

Section 8. The Congress shall have Power To lay and collect Taxes, Duties, Imposts and Excises, to pay the Debts and provide for the common Defence and general Welfare of the United States; but all Duties, Imposts and Excises shall be uniform throughout the United States;

To borrow money on the credit of the United States;

To regulate Commerce with foreign Nations, and among the several States, and with the Indian Tribes;

To establish a uniform Rule of Naturalization, and uniform Laws on the subject of Bankruptcies throughout the United States;

To coin Money, regulate the Value thereof, and of foreign Coin, and fix the Standard of Weights and Measures;

To provide for the Punishment of counterfeiting the Securities and current Coin of the United States.

To establish Post Offices and Post Roads;

To promote the Progress of Science and useful Arts, by securing for limited Times to Authors and Inventors the exclusive Right to their respective Writings and Discoveries;

To constitute Tribunals inferior to the supreme Court;

To define and punish Piracies and Felonies committed on the high Seas, and Offences against the Law of Nations;

To declare War, grant Letters of Marque and Reprisal, and make Rules concerning Captures on Land and Water;

To raise and support Armies, but no Appropriation of Money to that Use shall be for a longer Term than two Years;

To provide and maintain a Navy;

To make Rules for Government and Regulation of the land and naval Forces;

To provide for calling forth the Militia to execute the Laws of the Union, suppress Insurrections and repel Invasions;

To provide for organizing, arming, and disciplining the Militia, and for governing such Part of them as may be employed in the Service of the United States, reserving to the States respectively, the Appointment of the Officers, and the Authority of training the Militia according to the discipline prescribed by Congress;

To exercise exclusive Legislation in all Cases whatsoever, over such District (not exceeding ten Miles square) as may, by Cession of Particular States, and the Acceptance of Congress, become the Seat of the Government of the United States, and to exercise like Authority over all Places purchased by the Consent of the Legislature of the State in which the Same shall be, for the Erection of Forts, Magazines, Arsenals, dock-Yards, and other needful Buildings;—And

To make all Laws which shall be necessary and proper for carrying into Execution the foregoing Powers, and all other Powers vested by this Constitution in the Government of the United States, or in any Department or Officer thereof.

Section 9. The Migration or Importation of Such Persons as any of the States now existing shall think proper to admit, shall not be prohibited by the Congress prior to the Year one thousand eight hundred and eight, but a Tax or duty may be imposed on such Importation, not exceeding ten dollars for each Person.

The Privilege of the Writ of Habeas Corpus shall not be suspended, unless when in Cases of Rebellion or Invasion the public Safety may require it.

No Bill of Attainder or ex post facto Law shall be passed.

(No Capitation, or other direct, Tax shall be laid, unless in Proportion to the Census or Enumeration herein before directed to be taken.)[7]

No Tax or Duty shall be laid on Articles exported from any State.

No Preference shall be given by any Regulation of Commerce or Revenue to the Ports of one State over those of another; nor shall Vessels bound to, or from, one State, be obliged to enter, clear, or pay Duties in another.

No Money shall be drawn from the Treasury, but in Consequence of Appropriations made by Law; and a regular Statement and Account of the Receipts and Expenditures of all public Money shall be published from time to time.

No Title of Nobility shall be granted by the United States; And no Person holding any Office of Profit or Trust under them, shall, without the Consent of the Congress accept of any present, Emolument, Office, or Title, of any kind whatever, from any King, Prince, or foreign State.

Section 10. No state shall enter into any Treaty, Alliance, or Confederation; grant Letters of Marque and Reprisal; coin Money; emit Bills of Credit; make any Thing but gold and silver Coin a Tender in Payment of Debts; pass any Bill of Attainder, ex post facto Law, or Law impairing the Obligation of Contracts, or grant any Title of Nobility.

No State shall, without the Consent of the Congress, lay any Imposts or Duties on Imports or Exports, except what may be absolutely necessary for executing its inspection

Laws; and the net Produce of all Duties and Imposts, laid by any State on Imports or Exports, shall be for the Use of the Treasury of the United States; and all such Laws shall be subject to the Revision and Controul of the Congress.

No State shall, without the Consent of Congress, lay any Duty of Tonnage, keep Troops, or Ships of War in time of Peace, enter into any Agreement or Compact with another State, or with a foreign Power, or engage in War, unless actually invaded, or in such imminent Danger as will not admit of delay.

ARTICLE II

Section 1. The executive Power shall be vested in a President of the United States of America. He shall hold his Office during the Term of four Years, and, together with the Vice President, chosen for the Same Term, be elected, as follows:

Each State shall appoint, in such Manner as the Legislature thereof may direct, a Number of Electors, equal to the whole Number of Senators and Representatives to which the State may be entitled in the Congress; but no Senator or Representative, or Person holding an Office of Trust or Profit under the United States, shall be appointed an Elector.

(The Electors shall meet in their respective States and vote by Ballot for two Persons of whom one at least shall not be an Inhabitant of the same State with themselves. And they shall make a List of all the Persons voted for, and of the Number of Votes for each; which List they shall sign and certify, and transmit sealed to the Seat of the Government of the United States, directed to the President of the Senate. The President of the Senate shall, in the Presence of the Senate and House of Representatives, open all the Certificates, and the Votes shall then be counted. The Person having the greatest Number of Votes shall be the President, if such Number be a Majority of the whole Number of Electors appointed; and if there be more than one who have such Majority, and have an equal Number of Votes, then the House of Representatives shall immediately chuse by Ballot one of them for President; and if no Person have a Majority, then from the five highest on the List the said House shall in like Manner chuse the President. But in chusing the President, the Votes shall be taken by States, the Representation from each State having one Vote; A quorum for this Purpose shall consist of a Member or Members from two thirds of the States, and a Majority of all the States shall be necessary to a Choice. In every Case, after the Choice of the President, the Person having the greater Number of Votes of the Electors shall be the Vice President. But if there should remain two or more who have equal Votes, the Senate shall chuse from them by Ballot the Vice President.)[8]

The Congress may determine the Time of chusing the Electors, and the Day on which they shall give their Votes; which Day shall be the same throughout the United States.

No person except a natural born Citizen, or a Citizen of the United States, at the time of the Adoption of this Constitution, shall be eligible to the Office of President; neither shall any Person be eligible to that Office who shall not have attained to the Age of thirty five Years, and been fourteen Years a Resident within the United States.

(In Case of the Removal of the President from Office, or of his Death, Resignation, or Inability to discharge the Powers and Duties of the said Office, the Same shall devolve on the Vice President, and the Congress may by Law provide for the Case of Removal, Death, Resignation or Inability, both of the President and Vice President, declaring what Officer shall then act as President, and such Officer shall act accordingly, until the Disability be removed, or a President shall be elected.)[9]

The President shall, at stated Times, receive for his Services, a Compensation, which shall neither be encreased nor diminished during the Period for which he shall have been elected, and he shall not receive within that Period any other Emolument from the United States, or any of them.

Before he enter on the Execution of his Office, he shall take the following Oath or Affirmation: "I do solemnly swear (or affirm) that I will faithfully execute the Office of President of the United States, and will to the best of my Ability, preserve, protect and defend the Constitution of the United States."

Section 2. The President shall be Commander in Chief of the Army and Navy of the United States, and of the Militia of the several States, when called into the actual Service of the United States; he may require the Opinion, in writing, of the principal Officer in each of the Executive Departments, upon any Subject relating to the Duties of their respective Offices, and he shall have Power to grant Reprieves and Pardons for Offences against the United States, except in Cases of Impeachment.

He shall have Power, by and with the Advice and Consent of the Senate, to make Treaties, provided two thirds of the Senators present concur; and he shall nominate, and by and with the Advice and Consent of the Senate, shall appoint Ambassadors, other public Ministers and Consuls, Judges of the Supreme Court, and all other Officers of the United States, whose Appointments are not herein otherwise provided for, and which shall be established by Law; but the Congress may by Law vest the Appointment of such inferior Officers, as they think proper, in the President alone, in the Courts of Law, or in the Heads of Departments.

The President shall have Power to fill up all Vacancies that may happen during the Recess of the Senate, by granting Commissions which shall expire at the End of their next Session.

Section 3. He shall from time to time give to the Congress Information of the State of the Union, and recommend to their Consideration such Measures as he shall judge necessary and expedient; he may, on extraordinary Occasions, convene both Houses, or either of them, and in Case of Disagreement between them, with Respect to the Time of Adjournment, he may adjourn them to such Time as he shall think proper; he shall receive Ambassadors and other public Ministers; he shall take Care that the Laws be faithfully executed, and shall Commission all the Officers of the United States.

Section 4. The President, Vice President and all civil Officers of the United States, shall be removed from Office on Impeachment for, and Conviction of, Treason, Bribery, or other high Crimes and Misdemeanors.

Ⓐ RTICLE III

Section 1. The judicial Power of the United States, shall be vested in one supreme Court, and in such inferior Courts as the Congress may from time to time ordain and establish. The Judges, both of the supreme and inferior Courts, shall hold their Offices during good Behaviour, and shall, at stated Times, receive for their Services, a Compensation, which shall not be diminished during their Continuance in Office.

Section 2. The judicial Power shall extend to all Cases, in Law and Equity, arising under this Constitution, the Laws of the United States, and Treaties made, or which shall be made, under their Authority;—to all Cases affecting Ambassadors, other public Ministers and Consuls;—to all Cases of admiralty and maritime Jurisdiction;—to Controversies to which the United States shall be a Party;—to Controversies between two or more States; (—between a State and Citizens of another State;—)[10] between Citizens of different States,—between Citizens of the same State claiming Lands under the Grants of different States, (and between a State, or the Citizens thereof, and foreign States, Citizens or Subjects).

In all Cases affecting Ambassadors, other public Ministers and Consuls, and those in which a State shall be a Party, the supreme Court shall have original Jurisdiction. In all the other Cases before mentioned, the supreme Court shall have appellate Jurisdiction, both as to Law and Fact, with such Exceptions, and under such Regulations as the Congress shall make.

The Trial of all Crimes, except in Cases of Impeachment, shall be by Jury; and such Trial shall be held in the State where the said Crimes shall have been committed; but when not committed within any State, the Trial shall be at such Place or Places as the Congress may by Law have directed.

Section 3. Treason against the United States, shall consist only in levying War against them, or in adhering to their Enemies, giving them Aid and Comfort. No Person shall be convicted of Treason unless on the Testimony of two Witnesses to the same overt Act, or on Confession in open Court.

The Congress shall have Power to declare the Punishment of Treason, but no Attainder of Treason shall work Corruption of Blood, or Forfeiture except during the Life of the Person attainted.

ARTICLE **IV**

Section 1. Full Faith and Credit shall be given in each State to the public Acts, Records, and judicial Proceedings of every other State. And the Congress may by general Laws prescribe the Manner in which such Acts, Records and Proceedings shall be proved, and the Effect thereof.

Section 2. The Citizens of each State shall be entitled to all Privileges and Immunities of Citizens in the several States.

A Person charged in any State with Treason, Felony, or other Crime, who shall flee from Justice, and be found in another State, shall on Demand of the executive Authority of the State from which he fled, be delivered up, to be removed to the State having Jurisdiction of the Crime.

(No Person held to Service or Labour in one State, under the Laws thereof, escaping into another, shall, in Consequence of any Law or Regulation therein, be discharged from such Service or Labour, but shall be delivered up on Claim of the Party to whom such Service or Labour may be due.)[11]

Section 3. New States may be admitted by the Congress into this Union; but no new State shall be formed or erected within the Jurisdiction of any other State; nor any State be formed by the Junction of two or more States, or Parts of States, without the Consent of the Legislatures of the States concerned as well as of the Congress.

The Congress shall have Power to dispose of and make all needful Rules and Regulations respecting the Territory or other Property belonging to the United States; and nothing in this Constitution shall be so construed as to Prejudice any Claims of the United States, or of any particular State.

Section 4. The United States shall guarantee to every State in this Union a Republican Form of Government, and shall protect each of them against Invasion, and on Application of the Legislature, or of the Executive (when the Legislature cannot be convened) against domestic Violence.

ARTICLE V

The Congress, whenever two thirds of both Houses shall deem it necessary, shall propose Amendments to this Constitution, or, on the Application of the Legislatures of two thirds of the several States, shall call a Convention for proposing Amendments, which, in either Case, shall be valid to all Intents and Purposes, as Part of this Constitution, when ratified by the Legislatures of three fourths of the several States, or by Conventions in three fourths thereof, as the one or the other Mode of Ratification may be proposed by the Congress; Provided that no Amendment which may be made prior to the Year One thousand eight hundred and eight shall in any Manner affect the first and fourth Clauses in the Ninth Section of the first Article; and that no State, without its Consent, shall be deprived of its equal Suffrage in the Senate.

ARTICLE VI

All Debts contracted and Engagements entered into, before the Adoption of this Constitution, shall be as valid against the United States under this Constitution, as under the Confederation.

This Constitution, and the Laws of the United States which shall be made in Pursuance thereof; and all Treaties made, or which shall be made, under the Authority of the United States, shall be the supreme Law of the Land; and the Judges in every State shall be bound thereby, any Thing in the Constitution or Laws of any State to the Contrary notwithstanding.

The Senators and Representatives before mentioned, and the Members of the several State Legislatures, and all executive and judicial Officers, both of the United States and of the several States, shall be bound by Oath or Affirmation, to support this Constitution: but no religious Test shall ever be required as a Qualification to any Office or public Trust under the United States.

ARTICLE VII

The Ratification of the Conventions of nine States, shall be sufficient for the Establishment of this Constitution between the States so ratifying the Same.

done in Convention by the Unanimous Consent of the States present the Seventeenth Day of September in the Year of our Lord one thousand seven hundred and Eighty seven and of the Independence of the United States of America the Twelfth. In witness whereof we have hereunto subscribed our Names,

Go. WASHINGTON
Presid't. and deputy from Virginia

Attest
William Jackson
Secretary

Delaware
Geo Read
Gunning Bedford jun
John Dickinson
Richard Basset
Jaco. Broom

Massachusetts
Nathaniel Gorham
Rufus King

Connecticut
Wm. Saml. Johnson
Roger Sherman

New York
Alexander Hamilton

New Jersey
Wh. Livingston
David Brearley.
Wm. Paterson.
Jona Dayton

Virginia
John Blair
James Madison Jr.

North Carolina
Wm. Blount
Richd. Dobbs Spaight.
Hu. Williamson

South Carolina
J. Rutledge
Charles Cotesworth Pinckney
Charles Pinckney
Pierce Butler.

Georgia
William Few
Abr. Baldwin

New Hampshire
John Langdon
Nicholas Gilman

Pennsylvania
B. Franklin
Thomas Mifflin
Robt. Morris
Geo. Clymer
Thos. FitzSimons
Jared Ingersoll
James Wilson.
Gouv. Morris

Maryland
James McHenry
Dan of St. Thos. Jenifer
Danl Carroll

AMENDMENT I[12]

Congress shall make no law respecting an establishment of religion, or prohibiting the free exercise thereof; or abridging the freedom of speech, or of the press; or the right of the people peaceably to assemble, and to petition the Government for a redress of grievances.

AMENDMENT II

A well regulated Militia, being necessary to the security of a free State, the right of the people to keep and bear Arms, shall not be infringed.

AMENDMENT III

No Soldier shall, in time of peace be quartered in any house, without the consent of the Owner, nor in time of war, but in a manner to be prescribed by law.

AMENDMENT IV

The right of the people to be secure in their persons, houses, papers, and effects, against unreasonable searches and seizures, shall not be violated, and no Warrants shall issue, but upon probable cause, supported by Oath or affirmation, and particularly describing the place to be searched, and the persons or things to be seized.

AMENDMENT V

No person shall be held to answer for a capital, or otherwise infamous crime, unless on a presentment or indictment of a Grand Jury, except in cases arising in the land or naval forces, or in the Militia, when in actual service in time of War or public danger; nor shall any person be subject for the same offence to be twice put in jeopardy of life or limb; nor shall be compelled in any criminal case to be a witness against himself, nor be deprived of life, liberty, or property, without due process of law; nor shall private property be taken for public use, without just compensation.

AMENDMENT VI

In all criminal prosecutions, the accused shall enjoy the right to a speedy and public trial, by an impartial jury of the State and district wherein the crime shall have been committed, which district shall have been previously ascertained by law, and to be informed of the nature and cause of the accusation; to be confronted with the witnesses against him; to have compulsory process for obtaining witnesses in his favor, and to have the Assistance of Counsel for his defence.

AMENDMENT VII

In Suits at common law, where the value in controversy shall exceed twenty dollars, the right of trial by jury shall be preserved, and no fact tried by jury, shall be otherwise re-examined in any Court of the United States, than according to the rules of the common law.

AMENDMENT VIII

Excessive bail shall not be required, nor excessive fines imposed, nor cruel and unusual punishments inflicted.

AMENDMENT IX

The enumeration in the Constitution, of certain rights, shall not be construed to deny or disparage others retained by the people.

AMENDMENT X

The powers not delegated to the United States by the Constitution, nor prohibited by it to the States, are reserved to the States respectively, or to the people.

AMENDMENT XI (RATIFIED ON FEBRUARY 7, 1795)

The Judicial power of the United States shall not be construed to extend to any suit in law or equity, commenced or prosecuted against one of the United States by Citizens of another State, or by Citizens or Subjects of any Foreign State.

AMENDMENT XII (RATIFIED ON JUNE 15, 1804)

The Electors shall meet in their respective states, and vote by ballot for President and Vice-President, one of whom, at least, shall not be an inhabitant of the same state with themselves; they shall name in their ballots the person voted for as President, and in distinct ballots the person voted for as Vice-President, and they shall make distinct lists of all persons voted for as President, and of all persons voted for as Vice-President, and of the number of votes for each, which lists they shall sign and certify, and transmit sealed to the seat of the government of the United States, directed to the President of the Senate;—The President of the Senate shall, in the presence of the Senate and House of Representatives, open all the certificates and the votes shall then be counted;—The person having the greatest number of votes for President, shall be the President, if such number be a majority of the whole number of Electors appointed; and if no person have such majority, then from the persons having the highest numbers not exceeding three on the list of those voted for as President, the House of Representatives shall choose immediately, by ballot, the President. But in choosing the President, the votes shall be taken by states, the representation from each state having one vote; a quorum for this purpose shall consist of a member or members from two-thirds of the states, and a majority of all the states shall be necessary to a choice. (And if the House of Representatives shall not choose a President whenever the right of choice shall devolve upon them, before the fourth day of March next following, then the Vice-President shall act as President, as in the case of the death or other constitutional disability of the President.)[13] The person having the greatest number of votes as Vice-President, shall be the Vice-President, if such number be a majority of the whole number of Electors appointed, and if no person have a majority, then from the two highest numbers on the list, the Senate shall choose the Vice-President; a quorum for the purpose shall consist of two-thirds of the whole number of Senators, and a majority of the whole number shall be necessary to a choice. But no person constitutionally ineligible to the office of President shall be eligible to that of Vice-President of the United States.

AMENDMENT XIII (RATIFIED ON DECEMBER 6, 1865)

Section 1. Neither slavery nor involuntary servitude, except as a punishment for crime whereof the party shall have been duly convicted, shall exist within the United States, or any place subject to their jurisdiction.

Section 2. Congress shall have power to enforce this article by appropriate legislation.

AMENDMENT XIV (RATIFIED ON JULY 9, 1868)

Section 1. All persons born or naturalized in the United States, and subject to the jurisdiction thereof, are citizens of the United States and of the State wherein they reside. No State shall make or enforce any law which shall abridge the privileges or immunities of citizens of the United States; nor shall any State deprive any person of life, liberty, or property, without due process of law; nor deny to any person within its jurisdiction the equal protection of the laws.

Section 2. Representatives shall be apportioned among the several States according to their respective numbers, counting the whole number of persons in each State, excluding Indians not taxed. But when the right to vote at any election for the choice of electors for President and Vice President of the United States, Representatives in Congress, the Executive and Judicial offices of a State, or the members of the Legislature thereof, is denied to any of the male inhabitants of such State, being (twenty-one)[14] years of age, and citizens of the United States, or in any way abridged, except for participation in rebellion, or other crime, the basis of representation therein shall be reduced in the proportion which the number of such male citizens shall bear to the whole number of male citizens (twenty-one)[15] years of age in such State.

Section 3. No person shall be a Senator or Representative in Congress, or elector of President and Vice President, or hold any office, civil or military, under the United States, or under any State, who having previously taken an oath, as a member of Congress, or as an officer of the United States, or as a member of any State legislature, or as an executive or judicial officer of any State, to support the Constitution of the United States, shall have engaged in insurrection or rebellion against the same, or given aid or comfort to the enemies thereof. But Congress may by a vote of two-thirds of each House, remove such disability.

Section 4. The validity of the public debt of the United States, authorized by law, including debts incurred for payment of pensions and bounties for services in suppressing insurrection or rebellion, shall not be questioned. But neither the United States nor any State shall assume or pay any debt or obligation incurred in aid of insurrection or rebellion against the United States, or any claim for the loss or emancipation of any slave, but all such debts, obligations and claims shall be held illegal and void.

Section 5. The Congress shall have power to enforce, by appropriate legislation, the provisions of this article.

AMENDMENT XV (RATIFIED ON FEBRUARY 3, 1870)

Section 1. The right of citizens of the United States to vote shall not be denied or abridged by the United States or by any State on account of race, color, or previous condition of servitude.

Section 2. The Congress shall have power to enforce this article by appropriate legislation.

AMENDMENT XVI (RATIFIED ON FEBRUARY 3, 1913)

The Congress shall have power to lay and collect taxes on incomes, from whatever source derived, without apportionment among the several States, and without regard to any census or enumeration.

AMENDMENT XVII (RATIFIED ON APRIL 8, 1913)

The Senate of the United States shall be composed of two Senators from each State, elected by the people thereof, for six years; and each Senator shall have one vote. The electors in each State shall have the qualifications requisite for electors of the most numerous branch of the State legislatures.

When vacancies happen in the representation of any State in the Senate, the executive authority of such State shall issue writs of election to fill such vacancies: Provided, That the legislature of any State may empower the executive thereof to make temporary appointments until the people fill the vacancies by election as the legislature may direct.

This amendment shall not be so construed as to affect the election or term of any Senator chosen before it becomes valid as part of the Constitution.

AMENDMENT XVIII (RATIFIED ON JANUARY 16, 1919)

Section 1. After one year from the ratification of this article the manufacture, sale, or transportation of intoxicating liquors within, the importation thereof into, or the exportation thereof from the United States and all territory subject to the jurisdiction thereof for beverage purposes is hereby prohibited.

Section 2. The Congress and the several States shall have concurrent power to enforce this article by appropriate legislation.

Section 3. This article shall be inoperative unless it shall have been ratified as an amendment to the Constitution by the legislatures of the several States, as provided in the Constitution, within seven years from the date of the submission hereof to the States by the Congress.[16]

AMENDMENT XIX (RATIFIED ON AUGUST 18, 1920)

The right of citizens of the United States to vote shall not be denied or abridged by the United States or by any State on account of sex.

Congress shall have power to enforce this article by appropriate legislation.

AMENDMENT XX (RATIFIED ON JANUARY 23, 1933)

Section 1. The terms of the President and Vice President shall end at noon on the 20th day of January, and the terms of Senators and Representatives at noon on the 3d day of January, of the years in which such terms would have ended if this article had not been ratified, and the terms of their successors shall then begin.

Section 2. The Congress shall assemble at least once in every year, and such meeting shall begin at noon on the 3d day of January, unless they shall by law appoint a different day.

Section 3. If, at the time fixed for the beginning of the term of the President, the President elect shall have died, the Vice President elect shall become President. If the President shall not have been chosen before the time fixed for the beginning of his term, or if the President elect shall have failed to qualify, then the Vice President elect shall act as President until a President shall have qualified; and the Congress may by law provide for the case wherein neither a President elect nor a Vice President elect shall have qualified, declaring who shall then act as President, or the manner in which one who is to act shall be selected, and such person shall act accordingly until a President, or Vice President shall have qualified.

Section 4. The Congress may by law provide for the case of the death of any of the persons from whom the House of Representatives may choose a President whenever the right of choice shall have devolved upon them, and for the case of the death of any of the persons from whom the Senate may choose a Vice President whenever the right of choice shall have devolved upon them.

Section 5. Sections 1 and 2 shall take effect on the 15th day of October following the ratification of this article.

Section 6. This article shall be inoperative unless it shall have been ratified as an amendment to the Constitution by the legislatures of three-fourths of the several States within seven years from the date of its submission.

AMENDMENT XXI (RATIFIED ON DECEMBER 5, 1933)

Section 1. The eighteenth article of amendment to the Constitution of the United States is hereby repealed.

Section 2. The transportation or importation into any State, Territory, or possession of the United States for delivery or use therein of intoxicating liquors, in violation of the laws thereof, is hereby prohibited.

Section 3. This article shall be inoperative unless it shall have been ratified as an amendment to the Constitution by conventions in the several States, as provided in the Constitution, within seven years from the date of the submission hereof to the States by the Congress.

AMENDMENT XXII (RATIFIED ON FEBRUARY 27, 1951)

Section 1. No person shall be elected to the office of the President more than twice, and no person who has held the office of President, or acted as President, for more than two years of a term to which some other person was elected President shall be elected to the office of President more than once. But this Article shall not apply to any person holding the office of President when this Article was proposed by the Congress, and shall not prevent any person who may be holding the office of President, or acting as President, during the term within which this Article becomes operative from holding the office of President or acting as President during the remainder of such term.

Section 2. This article shall be inoperative unless it shall have been ratified as an amendment to the Constitution by the legislatures of three-fourths of the several States within seven years from the date of its submission to the States by the Congress.

AMENDMENT XXIII (RATIFIED ON MARCH 29, 1961)

Section 1. The District constituting the seat of Government of the United States shall appoint in such manner as the Congress may direct:

A number of electors of President and Vice President equal to the whole number of Senators and Representatives in Congress to which the District would be entitled if it were a State, but in no event more than the least populous State; they shall be in addition to those appointed by the states, but they shall be considered, for the purposes of the election of President and Vice President, to be electors appointed by a State; and they shall meet in the District and perform such duties as provided by the twelfth article of amendment.

Section 2. The Congress shall have power to enforce this article by appropriate legislation.

AMENDMENT XXIV (RATIFIED ON JANUARY 23, 1964)

Section 1. The right of citizens of the United States to vote in any primary or other election for President or Vice President, for electors for President or Vice President, or for Senator or Representative in Congress, shall not be denied or abridged by the United States or any State by reason of failure to pay any poll tax or other tax.

Section 2. The Congress shall have power to enforce this article by appropriate legislation.

AMENDMENT XXV (RATIFIED ON FEBRUARY 10, 1967)

Section 1. In case of the removal of the President from office or of his death or resignation, the Vice President shall become President.

Section 2. Whenever there is a vacancy in the office of the Vice President, the President shall nominate a Vice President who shall take office upon confirmation by a majority vote of both Houses of Congress.

Section 3. Whenever the President transmits to the President pro tempore of the Senate and the Speaker of the House of Representatives his written declaration that he is unable to discharge the powers and duties of his office, and until he transmits to them a written declaration to the contrary, such powers and duties shall be discharged by the Vice President as Acting President.

Section 4. Whenever the Vice President and a majority of either the principal officers of the executive departments or of such other body as Congress may by law provide, transmit to the President pro tempore of the Senate and the Speaker of the House of Representatives their written declaration that the President is unable to discharge the powers and duties of his office, the Vice President shall immediately assume the powers and duties of the office as Acting President.

Thereafter, when the President transmits to the President pro tempore of the Senate and the Speaker of the House of Representatives his written declaration that no inability exists, he shall resume the powers and duties of his office unless the Vice President and a majority of either the principal officers of the executive department or of such other body as Congress may by law provide, transmit within four days to the President pro tempore of the Senate and the Speaker of the House of Representatives their written declaration that the President is unable to discharge the powers and duties of his office. Thereupon Congress shall decide the issue, assembling within forty-eight hours for that purpose if not in session. If the Congress, within twenty-one days after receipt of the latter written declaration, or, if Congress is not in session, within twenty-one days after Congress is required to assemble, determines by two-thirds vote of both Houses that the President is unable to discharge the powers and duties of his office, the Vice President shall continue to discharge the same as Acting President; otherwise, the President shall resume the powers and duties of his office.

AMENDMENT XXVI (RATIFIED ON JULY 1, 1971)

Section 1. The right of citizens of the United States, who are eighteen years of age or older, to vote shall not be denied or abridged by the United States or by any State on account of age.

Section 2. The Congress shall have power to enforce this article by appropriate legislation.

AMENDMENT XXVII (RATIFIED ON MAY 7, 1992)

No law, varying the compensation for the services of the Senators and Representatives, shall take effect, until an election of Representatives shall have intervened.

Legal Research

Understanding the Law, Fourth Edition, presents legal rules that help to solve a variety of problems that people commonly confront in their personal and business relations. When a legal problem or question arises, the law or laws applying to that particular situation in that particular jurisdiction must be determined. In our discussion of general rules of law, a rule presented may or may not apply in your particular state. Sometimes the rules of different states on a given matter may differ even fundamentally. If differences do exist, the decisive rule is the one that applies in the particular state involved.

Both lawyers and students of law conduct legal research to find the legal rule(s) that apply to specific problems, as well as those that form the body of a larger area of law. Legal research over the years has been conducted as library research, but today much research is conducted through computer terminals accessing proprietary databases or legal research sites on the Internet.

Legal research is the search for authority to determine what the applicable law is, or to support your legal arguments; it is the search for primary law. **Primary law** consists of established rules from constitutions, statutes, administrative agency regulations and rules, treaties, and judicial decisions. Primary law is law stated without interpretation by commentators. It is law issued directly from an authoritative source, such as Congress or an appellate court. In important legal matters, one cites existing primary law in support of contentions made; if primary law of the appropriate jurisdiction is not available, one may present primary law from other jurisdictions or discussions of applicable law from secondary sources.

Law from other than primary sources is gathered from **secondary materials,** which include encyclopedias and other books that present some writer's opinion of what the law is or should be. This textbook is a secondary source. Secondary materials also assist a researcher in finding primary law and in understanding broad areas of the law.

Here we discuss how to begin legal research, sources for primary law, database legal research, some types of secondary materials, and Internet research.

Ⓦ HERE TO BEGIN

There are many ways to begin legal research. Among the benefits of a formal legal education is knowledge about how and where to look for answers to legal questions. For example, a person may want to know if the cost of repairing a flood-damaged home is a deductible expense for income tax purposes. This is a legal question. The inquirer is interested in applicable federal statutes and regulations, and in administrative interpretations and court enforcement of those laws. Once the answer is obtained for federal income taxes, a similar inquiry may be necessary if state income taxes are also payable. State law may or may not treat the expense in the same way.

While there are several good methods to begin a search for the answer to a legal problem, the index/descriptive word approach suggested by the West Publishing Company is among the most helpful. Most legal materials, with the exception of court cases, are indexed by topics. Identifying appropriate index topics can quickly take the researcher to a discussion of the law that is of interest. The key to the index approach is the identification of multiple index possibilities. Note that legal materials are generally indexed according to the historical descriptions of legal issues, which are not always obvious. For example, a problem involving a child under the age of eighteen might lead you to think logically of such terms as "child," "minor," or "youth." However, the term *legal description of a minor* historically was *infant,* and that is often how the information you now seek is indexed. The more index possibilities you identify at the beginning of your search, the more likely you are to find the information you seek. Indexing the key words, phrases, and issues can be aided by following this time-tested method from *West's Research Techniques.*

When analyzing your fact situation for the purpose of searching for cases or statutes in point (i.e., that apply), it is helpful to ask yourself, "What words describe the parties concerned; the places or things involved; the basis of the action or issue; the possible defense or defenses; and the relief sought?"

PARTIES Persons of a particular class, occupation, or relation; e.g., children, collectors, heirs, or any person who is either directly or indirectly necessary to a proper determination of the action.

PLACES AND THINGS Objects that necessarily must exist before any cause of action or dispute can arise; objects perceptible through the senses; e.g., automobiles, sidewalks, derricks, or garages are words describing the places or things that must exist before a cause of action alleging negligent use or defective condition can arise regarding them.

BASIS OF ACTION OR ISSUE Some wrong suffered by reason of another's neglect of duty; e.g., loss (of goods); some affirmative wrong—boycott, ejection, assault; some legal obligation ignored—stop, look, and listen; or the violation of some statutory or constitutional provision—eight-hour law, the Civil Rights Act, or restriction of free speech.

DEFENSE Some reason in law or fact why the plaintiff should not recover; e.g., failure of consideration, act of God, assumption of risk, infancy.

RELIEF SOUGHT Legal remedy sought; e.g., restraining order, restitution, damages, annulment.

THE SEARCH FOR PRIMARY LAW

Primary law consists of court opinions, constitutions, statutes, and administrative regulations.

STATE COURT DECISIONS

For most state trial court cases, the judges do not write opinions, and decisions are not published. New York and a few other states do publish selected opinions of their trial courts, but generally decisions of the state trial courts are filed in the office of the clerk of the court, where they are available for public inspection. These decisions include findings of fact and conclusion of law but do not have the authority or "*stare decisis* effect" of appellate court decisions and related opinions.

Written decisions of the appellate courts are published and distributed. They generally include opinions that give reasons for the judgments. The reported appellate decisions are published in volumes called *Reports,* which are numbered consecutively. State appellate court decisions are found in the state reports of that particular state. More and more states are now making appellate court opinions available on the Internet. At this time, however, most older cases still are available only in books and on private databases.

Additionally, state court opinions appear in regional units of the *National Reporter System,* published by West Publishing Company. Most lawyers and libraries have the West reporters because they report cases more quickly and are distributed more widely than the state-published reports. In fact, many states (e.g., Texas) have eliminated their own official reports in favor of West's *National Reporter System.* The *National Reporter System* divides the states into geographical areas: Atlantic (A. or A.2d), South Eastern (S.E. or S.E.2d), South Western (S.W. or S.W.2d), North Western (N.W. or N.W.2d), North Eastern (N.E. or N.E.2d), Southern (So. or So.2d), and Pacific (P. or P.2d).

After appellate decisions have been published, they are normally referred to (cited) by the name of the case; the volume, name, and page of the state's official reporter (if different from West's *National Reporter System*); the volume, unit, and page number of the *National Reporter;* and the volume, name, and page number of any other selected reporter. (Citing a reporter by volume number, name, and page number, in that order, is common to all citations.) This information is included in what is called the **citation.** When more than one reporter is cited for the same case, each reference is called a *parallel citation.* For example, consider the following case: *People v. Segal,* 54 N.Y.2d 58, 429 N.E.2d 107 (New York, 1981). We see that the opinion in this case may be found in volume 54 of the official *New York Reporter,* Second Series, on page 58. The parallel citation is to Volume 429 of the *North Eastern Reporter,* Second Series, on page 107. In reprinting appellate opinions in this text, in addition to the citation, we give the state of the court hearing the case and the year of the court's decision (New York, 1981).

A few states—including those with intermediate appellate courts, such as California, Illinois, and New York—have more than one reporter for opinions given in their courts.

FEDERAL COURT DECISIONS

Federal trial court decisions are published unofficially in West's *Federal Supplement* (F.Supp.), and decisions of the circuit courts of appeal are reported unofficially in West's *Federal Reporter* (F. or F.2d). Cases concerning federal bankruptcy law are published unofficially in West's *Bankruptcy Reporter* (Bankr.). Decisions of the United States Supreme Court are reported in West's *Supreme Court Reporter* (S.Ct.) and in the *United States Reports* (U.S.).

The *United States Reports* is the official edition of all decisions of the United States Supreme Court for which there are written opinions. Published by the federal government, the series includes reports of Supreme Court cases dating from the term of August 1791, although originally many of the decisions were not reported in the early volumes.

West's *Supreme Court Reporter* is an unofficial edition dating from the Court's term in October 1882. Preceding each of its case reports is a summary of the case with *headnotes* (brief editorial statements of the law involved in the case, numbered to correspond to numbers in the report). The headnotes are also given classification numbers that serve to cross-reference each headnote to other headnotes on similar points throughout the *National Reporter System* and other West publications. This facilitates research of all relevant cases on a given point. This is important because, as may be evident from the doctrine of *stare decisis,* a lawyer's goal in undertaking legal research is to find an authority that is similar "on all fours": where the facts are very close and the same questions of law are involved.

CASE TITLES

In the title of a case, such as *Ardmeyer v. Rau,* the *v.* or *vs.* stands for versus, which means "against." In the trial court, Ardmeyer was the plaintiff—the person who filed the suit. Rau was the defendant. If the case is appealed, however, the appellate court will sometimes place the name of the party appealing the decision first, so that the case may be called *Rau v. Ardmeyer.* Since some appellate courts retain the trial court order of names, it is often impossible to distinguish the plaintiff from the defendant by the title of a reported appellate court decision. The student must carefully read the facts of each case in order to identify the legal status of each party. Otherwise, the discussion by the appellate court is difficult to understand.

TERMINOLOGY

The following terms and phrases are frequently encountered in court opinions and legal publications. Because it is important to understand what these terms and phrases mean, we define and discuss them here.

DECISIONS AND OPINIONS Most decisions reached by reviewing, or appellate, courts are explained in writing. A *decision* contains the opinion (the court's reasons for its decision), the rules of law that apply, and the judgment (outcome). There are four possible types of written *opinions* for any particular case decided by an appellate court. When all justices agree on an opinion, it is written for the entire court and is called a **unanimous opinion.** When there is not a unanimous opinion, a **majority opinion** is written, outlining the views of the majority of the justices deciding the case. Often, a justice who feels strongly about making or emphasizing a point that was not made or emphasized in the unanimous or majority opinion will write a **concurring opinion.** That means that the judge or justice agrees (concurs) with the judgment given in the unanimous or majority opinion, but for different reasons. In other than unanimous opinions, a judge or justice who does not agree (i.e., dissents) with the majority reasoning or holding often writes a **dissenting opinion.** The dissenting opinion is important because it may form the basis of the arguments used years later in overruling the precedent of the majority opinion.

JUDGES AND JUSTICES The terms *judge* and *justice* are usually synonymous and represent two designations given to judges in various courts. All members of the U.S. Supreme Court, for example, are referred to as justices. And justice is the formal title usually given to judges of appellate courts, although this is not always so. Thus, in New York, a justice is a trial judge of the trial court (which is called the Supreme Court), whereas a member of the Court of Appeals (the state's highest court) is called a judge. The term *justice* is commonly abbreviated to J., and *justices* to JJ. A Supreme Court case might refer to Justice Kennedy as Kennedy, J.; or to Chief Justice Rehnquist as Rehnquist, C. J.

APPELLANTS AND APPELLEES The **appellant** is the party who appeals a case to another court or jurisdiction from the court or jurisdiction in which the case was originally brought. Sometimes, an appellant who appeals from a judgment is referred to as the **petitioner.** The **appellee** is the party against whom the appeal is taken. Sometimes, an appellee is referred to as the **respondent.**

UPDATING CASE LAW RESEARCH

Case law is printed chronologically, by its decision date. One can never know by reading the case itself whether it has been subsequently reheard by the same court, reversed by a later higher court, or even whether the doctrines declared in the opinion have been rendered moot for later disputants by an act of the legislature. Yet that information is critical for one relying upon the holding of a court opinion. Imagine a lawyer's embarrassment (and perhaps malpractice) when citing an apparently leading dispositive case, when he or she is told by the opposing counsel that "the case was overruled two months ago."

Although other sources exist, *Shepard's Citations* or *Citators* provide the primary protection against such errors as an overruled case. These publications track and then report when and where reported cases are cited. Assume you are interested in the case of *Boyson v. Thorn* cited in 98 Cal. 578. You can find the case citation in *Shepard's Citators,* where accompanying the citation is a list of every published case in the U.S. that has cited *Boyson* since it was issued. *Shepard's* also notes whether the case has been overruled, criticized, or followed. The primary limitation of *Shepard's* is the delay between the publication of updated *Citators* and brand-new cases. For example, if a case was overruled last week, *Shepard's Citators* will not show that—except on a database service where the information is often available within hours of the issuance of a new case through a computer search. (Fortunately, most leading cases are not overruled.)

CONSTITUTIONAL LAW

The federal government and the states have separate constitutions that define the general organization, powers, and limits of governments. The U.S. Constitution is the supreme law of the land. A law in violation of the Constitution, no matter what its source, will be declared unconstitutional and will not be enforced. Similarly, unless it conflicts with the U.S. Constitution, every state constitution is supreme within the borders of that state. The U.S. Constitution defines the powers and limitations of the federal government. All powers not granted to the federal government are retained by the states or by the people.

Constitutions are published and available for research in the same publications that provide the text of federal and state **codes** (systematic collections of law, rules, or regulations).

STATUTORY LAW

Statutes enacted by the U.S. Congress and the various state legislative bodies are another source of law, generally called **statutory law.** Statutory law also includes the ordinances passed by cities and counties. Today, legislative bodies and regulatory agencies exercise an ever-increasing role in lawmaking. Much of the work of modern courts is interpreting what the rulemakers meant when a statute was enacted and applying it to a particular set of facts. When Congress passes laws, and the president signs them, they are collected in a publication titled *United States Statutes at Large.* When state legislatures pass laws, and state governors sign them, they are collected in similar state publications. These publications arrange laws chronologically by date of enactment. Most frequently, however, laws are cited in their codified form—that is, the form in which they appear in the federal and state codes.

In these codes, laws are compiled by subject. For example, the *United States Code* (U.S.C.) arranges all existing federal laws of a public and permanent nature by 50 subjects. Each of the subjects into which U.S.C. arranges the laws has a title number and a title. For example, laws relating to commerce and trade are collected in Title 15, which is titled "Commerce and Trade." (Titles may be divided into chapters and subchapters. Within Title 15, for instance, Chapter 1 includes laws concerning monopolies.) Within each subdivision, statutes are assigned numbers, which are referred to as section numbers. A U.S.C. citation includes titles and section numbers. Thus, a reference to "15 U.S.C. Section 1" means that the statute can be found in Section 1 of Title 15. ("Section" may also be designated by the symbol §.)

Sometimes, a citation includes the abbreviation *et seq.*—e.g., 15 U.S.C. Section 1 *et seq.* (Latin: *et sequens,* "and the following.") This is a reference to sections that concern the same subject as the numbered section and follow it in sequence.

State codes follow the U.S.C. pattern of law arranged by subject. They may be called Codes, Revisions, Compilations, Consolidations, General Statutes, or Statutes, depending on the preference of the specific state. In some codes, subjects are designated by number. In others, they are designated by name. For example, "13 Pennsylvania Consolidated Statutes Section 1101" means the statute can be found in Section 1101 of Title 13 of the Pennsylvania code. "California Commercial Code Section 1101" means the statute can be found in Section 1101 under the commercial heading of the California code. Abbreviations may be used. For example, "13 Pennsylvania Consolidated Statutes Section 1101" may be abbreviated "13 Pa. C.S. § 1101," and "California Commercial Code Section 1101" may be abbreviated "Cal. Com. Code § 1101."

Commercial publications of these laws and regulations are available and are often more helpful than the official publications. For example, West Publishing Company publishes the *United States Code Annotated* (U.S.C.A.). U.S.C.A. contains the complete text of laws included in U.S.C., as well as notes of short summaries of court decisions that interpret and apply specific sections of the statutes, plus the text of presidential proclamations and executive orders. U.S.C.A. also includes research aids, such as cross-references to related statutes, historical notes, and library references. A citation to U.S.C.A. is similar to a citation to U.S.C. (e.g., 15 U.S.C.A. Section 1.)

Commercial publishers provide comparable publications for state statutes. For example, in California two private compilations of California statutory law exist, West's *Annotated Codes* and Deering's *Codes Annotated.* Each provides helpful features similar to those found in U.S.C.A.

UPDATING STATUTORY LAW RESEARCH

There are two major benefits to placing statutes into organized codes. It is easier to index the law and thus to help those researchers who wish to find a specific provision of the law when they do not know the appropriate legal citation. The second benefit is provided by *pocket-parts.* Once a code is published, it is almost immediately out of date. When the legislature passes a new statute or amends an existing one, the code must be changed. Publishing a new set of books each year so as to be temporarily current is wasteful and expensive beyond reason. Pocket-parts meet the need of accuracy and efficiency. Several times during the course of the year, the publisher issues to purchasers of its book supplements that update the main text. These supplements are commonly placed in a pouch or pocket in the back inside cover of the book. They are indexed to correspond to the sections in the main body of the work.

To find an appropriate statute in the main text and then fail to check and examine any pocket-part is a critical error in legal research. In annotated codes or constitutions, these pocket-parts also provide summaries of new recent cases that have interpreted statutes listed in the main text.

ADMINISTRATIVE LAW

Rules and regulations adopted by federal administrative agencies are compiled in the *Code of Federal Regulations* (C.F.R.). Like U.S.C., C.F.R. is divided into fifty titles. Rules within each title are assigned section numbers. A full citation to C.F.R. includes title and section numbers. For example, a reference to "17 C.F.R. Section 230.504" means the rule can be found in Section 230.504 of Title 17.

State administrative offices generally also have their regulations listed in a state administrative code.

UPDATING ADMINISTRATIVE LAW RESEARCH

The procedure for updating administrative law research is as follows: Check each book to see if it provides pocket-parts; if so, consult them. If the publication does not provide pocket-parts, check the publication date; the older it is, the less confidence you can have in any source you have identified therein. State administrative regulations are sometimes available in loose-leaf form. If so, check the date on the page consulted and check the beginning of the volume to see when the last loose-leaf additions were made available to the library.

COMPUTER-ASSISTED LEGAL RESEARCH

INTERNET

Throughout this textbook we have made references to Internet sites which give you additional, background, or follow-up information about the topics we are discussing. If you went to the referenced site you engaged in legal research. If you wish to research your own topic, using an Internet search engine will be helpful. You can use your favorite search engine to find the information you seek or you can try some of our favorites. Use the Index/Descriptive word approach discussed on page 725.
- Law.com: http://www.law.com/
- Internet Legal Resource Guide: http://www.ilrg.com/
- 'Lectric Library: http://www.lectlaw.com/
- Findlaw: http://www.findlaw.com/
- Hieros Gamos: http://www.hg.org/
- The World Wide Web Virtual Law Library: http://www.law.indiana.edu/v-lib/
- Cornell Law School Legal Information Institute: http://www.law.cornell.edu/
- LawCrawler: http://lawcrawler.findlaw.com/
- The Meta-Index for U.S. Legal Research: http://gsulaw.gsu.edu/metaindex/
- Yahoo: http://www.yahoo.com/law/

DATABASES

Computers have made possible the streamlining of the legal research techniques used by businesses, lawyers, and members of the judiciary. Today a number of databases—collections of information useful to anyone doing legal research—can be accessed through several high-speed data-delivery systems. The two most common systems are Westlaw and LexisNexis. Westlaw, http://www.westlaw.com, is a computer-assisted legal research service of West Publishing Company. LexisNexis, http://www.lexisnexis.com, is a similar service of Reed Elsevier, Inc. Each system has database-access software that makes it possible for the researcher to interact with the delivery system. These providers also allow for Internet access. Users can purchase a subscription to these databases or pay per transaction or per hour.

A user can search these databases for a specific case, statute, or administrative regulation. Cases can be retrieved by either case citation or case name, and cross-checked to see if they have been cited as precedent in later cases or overruled. The databases can also be searched by topic by using descriptive or key words. The resulting documents can be saved as a file or printed. There are many advantages to using a legal database:

1. Users need not duplicate large libraries available on the database systems.
2. Data systems allow researchers to speed up the research effort.
3. The database may identify source material that manual research might overlook.
4. Updating and checking for accuracy is tedious and boring. This effort can be automated and time spent on the effort reduced.
5. Data services can track the time spent on each project, allowing for ease in billing to a particular client.
6. Staying at your desk with computer and proper software minimizes time spent in traffic and parking problems.

Much of the research for this textbook was completed using a home computer and both Westlaw and LexisNexis. These systems are still expensive for most private users, although they have become more reasonable in recent years. Many university libraries provide access privileges for currently enrolled students to one or more of these databases.

In short, Westlaw, LexisNexis, and similar computerized data-search systems allow access to virtually all cases, statutes, and federal regulations. Access is almost immediate and requires a minimum of physical effort. Often the latest cases can be found through a database before they are available at a local law school or law office library.

CD-ROM

Most hard-copy legal publications are now available on CD-ROM. An amazing amount of information can be coded on this easy-to-retrieve format. Index searches using correct combinations of terms can be conducted in nanoseconds to retrieve on-point (relevant) information. Unlike database services, CD-ROMs (like print publications) do require updating for changes in law occurring after publication. Frequently updating CDs or manually updating using database services or hard-copy sources can overcome some problems inherent in the use of this format. CD-ROMs can be purchased or leased. In either option, most users pay a flat fee for the materials or a usage fee similar to the one charged when accessing either Lexis-Nexis or Westlaw.

Ⓢ ECONDARY SOURCES OF LEGAL INFORMATION

There are numerous legal publications that meet different needs of lawyers, judges, and others interested in the law. Some provide general discussions of the law; others provide excellent methods to find the appropriate and important primary law sources. The following are major secondary sources of law.

DICTIONARIES

Dictionaries provide definitions of terms and pronunciation guides. The leading authoritative legal dictionaries are *Ballentine's Law Dictionary* and *Black's Law Dictionary*. West Publishing Company also publishes an elaborate dictionary called *Words and Phrases*. The definitions are taken from actual court opinions and feature pocket-parts to keep the publication current.

LEGAL ENCYCLOPEDIAS

Encyclopedias report the whole of the law without commentary or analysis. Some encyclopedias are national in scope (*American Jurisprudence* and *Corpus Juris Secundum*); others are statewide (*California Jurisprudence*). These books are very useful starting points when you want a general overview of almost any important legal topic. They also often provide useful citations to important cases and statutes. When using an encyclopedia, be sure to check applicable pocket-parts or supplemental books.

TOPICAL PUBLICATIONS

Publishers offer topical publication in areas of legal practice where great detail and current status may be critical. Taxation, employment law, and securities regulation exemplify areas where topical publications are available. The publications are often loose-leaf, to facilitate insertion of current supplements. Again, when using topical publications check for pocket-parts or supplemental books.

RESTATEMENTS OF THE LAW

A *Restatement* is a product of extensive consultation and research by scholars, judges, and practitioners on specific areas of law, such as torts, contracts, and agency. Each *Restatement* includes a synthesis of state black letter law (i.e., principles accepted by appellate courts and/or included in statutes), commentaries, and examples of the application of listed rules of law to specific problems. Although a *Restatement* has no binding force of law, courts often cite *Restatement* provisions because of their clarity and precision in stating the law. Such citation gives the quoted *Restatement* rule the force of law in that particular jurisdiction. Here again, when using *Restatements,* check for pocket-parts and supplemental volumes.

TREATISES AND TEXTS

Treatises are books, limited in topical content, that cover either one area of law or a group of closely related areas of law. Treatises are usually more comprehensive than encyclopedias in their discussion of a given topic. They often contain critical commentary in addition to the expository text treatment. Other texts that serve this purpose are also available.

DIGESTS

Digests are elaborate indexes to court decisions. They provide a short synopsis of parts of the court opinions (usually the headnotes) and are arranged and indexed by topic and subtopic. Digests exist for federal court opinions (*Federal Digest* and *Supreme Court Digest*), for all state opinions (*American Digest System*), and for some populous states. Check the pocket-parts.

ANNOTATED REPORTS

Annotated reports are publications of selected cases accompanied by a thorough discussion, summary, and synthesis of other reported cases on the same or similar topic. They provide a very valuable source for finding citations of similar cases. Annotated reports are updated, but by different means depending on the policy of the publisher. Consult the source on how to find updated information.

ANNOTATED CODES

Annotated codes are private publications that generally contain the entire applicable federal or state code and constitution, along with summary capsule annotations to cases that have construed or interpreted the statutes. Also included are references to legislative history and cross-references to related statutes. Check for pocket-parts.

LAW JOURNALS

Law journals are periodicals that contain scholarly articles on the law written by professors, judges, practitioners, and sometimes law students. Leading law schools usually publish them, although professional associations such as the American Bar Association also sponsor such learned journals.

SELF-HELP BOOKS

A growing number of books are published by commercial publishers and professional organizations advising laypersons how to perform legal tasks. The quality of these books varies widely, but Nolo Press in Berkeley, California (http://www.nolopress.com), has earned a reputation for providing high-quality self-help books at reasonable prices. Great care should be exercised in using self-help books. Pay particular attention to their publication dates.

PRACTICE BOOKS

Some books are published to assist lawyers in procedural requirements for performing certain legal tasks. They are often provided by continuing education organizations and give very specific directions on how to perform certain legal tasks in areas such as criminal procedure, family law, and wills and trusts. The books are usually too complicated for use by laypersons.

SOURCES TO ASSIST YOU IN YOUR LEGAL RESEARCH

The following excellent books present more detailed information on legal research:

- Morris Cohen and Kent Olson, *Cohen's Legal Research in a Nutshell,* 7th ed. (Belmont, CA: West Wadsworth, 2000), ISBN: 0314238859
- Steven Elias and Susan Levinkind, *Legal Research: How to Find & Understand the Law,* 10th ed., (Berkeley, CA: Nolo Press, 2002), ISBN: 0-87337-835-0
- Marjorie Dick Rombauer, *Legal Problem Solving, Analysis, Research and Writing,* 5th ed. (St. Paul, MN: West Publishing Co., 1991)
- William Statsky, *Legal Research and Writing,* 5th ed. (Clifton Park, NY: Delmar Learning, 1998), ISBN: 0314129014
- *West's Law Finder: A Legal Research Manual* (St. Paul, MN: West Publishing Co., 1991)
- Roy M. Mersky and Donald J. Dunn, *Fundamentals of Legal Research,* 8th ed. (New York: Foundation Press, 2002), ISBN: 1587780666

Chapter I

1. *Black's Law Dictionary,* 6th ed. (St. Paul, MN: West Group, 1990).

2. The HyperSoar was designed by aerospace engineer Preston Carter of the Livermore National Laboratory, who announced that his design requires further analysis by the U.S. Air Force and university aeronautic engineers. See David Perlman, "Californian Designs Plane of the Future," *San Francisco Chronicle,* 11 September 1998.

3. Gerald Celente, director of Trends Research Institute in Rhinebeck, New York, quoted in Dale Russakofff, "The 'Millennium Generation' Is Making Its Mark," *Washington Post,* 4 October 1998.

4. Michael Kitei, president of Small Talk, a marketing consulting firm that specializes in influencing children's spending, quoted in Russakoff, "The 'Millennium Generation' Is Making Its Mark."

5. Although the life expectancy of a person born in the year 2000 is expected to be nearly 80 years, much medical opinion suggests that there is no inherent reason why life expectancy should not reach 100 years in the early part of the twenty-first century.

6. Alice Kessler-Harris, *Women Have Always Worked: A Historical Perspective* (New York: Feminist Press, 1981).

7. Much of the trivia about the turn of the twentieth century is from David Traxel, 1898, *The Birth of the American Century* (New York: Alfred A. Knopf, 1998).

8. Ashley H. Grant, "Overkill? Indianapolis Schools Screen Elementary School Pupils for Guns," Associated Press, 5 May 1998.

9. Linda Deutsch, "New Legal Rules in Gang Cases Raise Civil Liberties Concern," Associated Press, 17 August 1998.

10. *Plessy v. Ferguson,* 163 U.S. 537, 16 S.Ct. 1138 (1896).

11. *Brown v. Board of Education,* 347 U.S. 483, 74 S.Ct. 686 (1954).

12. *Powell v. Alabama,* 287 U.S. 45, 53 S.Ct. 55 (1932).

13. *Roe v. Wade,* 410 U.S. 113, 93 S.Ct. 705 (1973).

14. Roscoe Pound, "Studying Law," in Arthur Vanderbilt, ed., *Introduction to American Law* (New York: New York University Press, 1955), p. 396.

15. Wolfshead Through the Ages: A History of Robin Hood," at http://www.geocities.com/puckrobin/rh/robages.html.

16. Sir Thomas Erskine May, quoted in Theodore F. T. Plucknett, *A Concise History of the Common Law,* 5th ed. (Boston: Little, Brown, 1956).

17. "Justice Kline Defends His Dissent," *California Lawyer,* September 1998, p. 25.

18. This incident prompted congress to force Amtrak to modernize. Some Amtrak trains then converted human waste into a liquid that was sprayed onto the railroad tracks as a fine mist when the trains exceeded 35 miles per hour. Associated Press, Washington, 23 November 1991.

19. Some state courts have the power to render advisory opinions to the legislature. Federal courts are required to only consider matters involving a case and controversy by the U.S. Constitution, Article III, section 2.

20. Dennis D. Dorin, review of *Judicial Activism-Bulwark of Liberty or Precarious Security?* rev. ed. by Christopher Wolfe, *The Law and Politics Book Review* 8 no. 4 (April 1998), pp. 165–167; http://www.unt.edu/lpbr/subpages/newrevs/wolfe.htm.

21. J. Frug, "Why Courts Are Always Making Law," *Fortune,* 25 September 1989, p. 245.

22. The U.S. Supreme Court agreed with the District Court, holding there was no medical-necessity exception to the Controlled Substances Act's prohibitions on manufacturing and distributing marijuana. *United States v. Oakland Cannabis Buyers' Cooperative,* 532 U.S. 483, 121 S.Ct. 1711 (2001).

23. A hypothetical situation based on the U.S. Copyright Law of 1976.

24. Based on an event reported by Brian Macquarrie, *Boston Globe,* 18 September 1998.

25. Associated Press, Las Vegas, 9 September 1998.

26. In 1999 Nevada passed a statute making it a misdemeanor to fail to report a violent or sexual crime committed against a child twelve or younger, Nevada Revised Statutes Annotated § 202.882. In 2000 California added a similar law, Cal Pen Code § 152.3. Thus California and Nevada joined Florida, Massachusetts, Minnesota, Ohio, Rhode Island, Vermont, Washington, and Wisconsin in requiring some level of reporting to authorities. Vermont, Wisconsin and Minnesota have laws that go farther and require some duty to assist.

27. *San Francisco Chronicle* wire reports, 17 September 1998.

28. http://www.pbs.org/newshour/bb/military/jan-june99/trial_3-4.html

29. Associated Press, Santa Ana, 15 September 1998.

30. Based on an article by Tim Malloy, Associated Press, 15 March 1998.

31. Richard Wydick and Rex R. Perschbacher, *California Legal Ethics* 2nd ed. (West Publishing Company, College & School Division, 1997), citing the *American Heritage Dictionary of the English Language* (Houghton Mifflin, 1978); *Webster's Third New International Dictionary* (Merriam-Webster, 1986) and *The Random House Dictionary of the English Language* (Random House, 1968).

32. Ibid.

33. See generally A.M. Rosenthal, *Thirty-Eight Witnesses: The Kitty Genovese Case* (New York City: McGraw-Hill, 1964); *Hughes v. State* 719 S.W. 2d 560, 565 (Tex. Ct. App. 1986) (Teague, J., concurring).

34. Michael Josephson, "What Is Ethics Anyway?" in *Making Ethical Decisions* (Josephson Institute of Ethics, 1996; rev. June 2001 online at http://www.josephsoninstitute.org/MED/MED-whatisethics.htm).

35. J.M. McClosky, "A Non-Utilitarian Approach to Punishment," in Michael D. Boyles, ed., *Contemporary Utilitarianism* (Anchor Doubleday, 1968), pp. 244–249.

36. Jean Piaget, *The Moral Judgment of the Child,* trans., Marjorie Grabain, (The Free Press, 1965).

37. Manuel G. Velasquez, *Business Ethics,* 3d ed. (Prentice-Hall, 1992), p. 34.

38. This hypothetical is based on an event reported by Ralph Montano, "Student Death Probed in Sutter," *Sacramento Bee,* 30 April 20002, p. B1.

Chapter 2

1. Giovanni Sartori, "Constitutionalism: A Preliminary Discussion," *The American Political Science Review,* December 1962.

2. *Webster's Third New International Dictionary* (Chicago: Encyclopedia Britannica, Inc., 1981).

3. *Elwood Investors Co. v. Behme,* 79 Misc.2d 910, 361 N.Y.S.2d 488 (New York, 1974).

4. *Youngstown Sheet and Tube Co. v. Sawyer,* 343 U.S. 579, 72 S.Ct. 863 (1952).

5. E. Corwin, *The "Higher Law" Background of American Constitutional Law* (Ithaca, N.Y.: Cornell University Press, 1967).

6. John Locke, *Two Treatises of Government* (London: Cambridge University Press, 1967).

7. *The Federalist,* No. 51.

8. Thomas Paine, *Political Writings,* (1837), pp. 45–46.

9. *The Federalist,* No. 78.

10. Ibid.

11. *Marbury v. Madison,* 1 Cranch 137 (1803).

12. *Plessy v. Ferguson,* 163 U.S. 537, 16 S.Ct. 1138 (1896).

13. *Brown v. The Board of Education of Topeka,* 347 U.S. 483, 74 S.Ct. 686 (1954).

14. See U.S. Constitution, Art. I, Art. II, and Art. III.

15. *The Federalist,* No. 51.

16. *United States v. Eichman* and *United States v. Haggerty,* 496 U.S. 310, 110 S.Ct. 2404 (1990).

17. A hypothetical situation based on *Clinton v. City of New York,* 524 U.S. 417, 118 S.Ct. 2091 (1998).

18. U.S. Constitution, Art. I, § 8.

19. U.S. Constitution, Twentieth Amendment, 1933; Twenty-Second Amendment, 1951; Twenty-Fifth Amendment, 1967.

20. U.S. Constitution, Art. II, § 2.

21. *Prize cases,* 67 U.S. 635 (1863).

22. U.S. Constitution, Art. II, § 2.

23. Ibid.

24. U.S. Constitution, Art. III, § 1.

25. "Impeachment of U.S. District Judge," Facts on File Yearbook Publication for 1986 (New York: Facts on File Inc., 1987).

26. Impeachment of Judge Harry E. Claiborne, House of Representatives Report 99-688.

27. http://www.ajs.org/lcji/cji_impeachment.asp.

28. J. Specter, "Impeachment: Another Look," *The National Law Journal,* 12 January 1989, p. 1.

29. Harriet Chiang, "Public Reprimand for Federal Judge," *San Francisco Chronicle,* 19 August 1998.

30. U.S. Constitution, Art. III, § 1 and *United States v. Will,* 449 U.S. 200, 101 S.Ct. 471 (1980).

31. The American Bar Association, "Independence of the Judiciary: Judicial Compensation," updated April 15, 2002. http://www.abanet.org/poladv/priorities/judcom.html.

32. U.S. Constitution, Art. I, § 8.

33. U.S. Constitution, Art. II, § 2.

34. U.S. Constitution, Tenth Amendment, 1791.

35. U.S. Constitution, Art. I, § 9.

36. As discussed in Chapter 1, Nevada passed a statute making it a misdemeanor to fail to report a violent or sexual crime committed against a child age twelve or younger, Nevada Revised Statutes Annotated § 202.882. The statute does not require that the bystander assist the minor.

37. Fred Krinsky and Gerald Rigby, *Theory and Practice of American Democracy* (Belmont, CA: Dickenson Publishing Co., 1967), p. 105.

38. James MacGregor Burns, J.W. Peltason, and Thomas E. Cronin, *Government by the People* (Englewood Cliffs, NJ: Prentice-Hall, 1989), p. 606.

39. *The Federalist,* No. 51.

40. *Miller v. Schoene,* 276 U.S. 272, 48 S.Ct. 246 (1928).

41. *The Federalist,* No. 51.

42. U.S. Constitution, Art. I, § 8.

43. U.S. Constitution, Art. VI.

44. *Martin v. Hunters Lessee,* 1 Wheaton 304 (1816) and *Cohens v. Virginia,* 6 Wheaton 264 (1821).

45. *McCulloch v. Maryland,* 4 Wheaton 316 (1819). See also U.S. Constitution, Art. III, § 1.

46. U.S. Constitution, Art. I, § 8.

47. Masha Herbst, "Conn. Tool Maker Stanley Works at Center of Tax Haven Debate," The Associated Press State & Local Wire, 9 May 2002.

48. Ibid.

49. *Wickard v. Filburn,* 317 U.S. 111, 63 S.Ct. 82 (1942).

50. Eun-Kyung Kim, Associated Press, 21 August 1997.

51. *Beskind v. Easley,* 197 F.Supp.2d 464 (W.D.N.C.2002) and Jacqueline L. Salmon, "Law on Virginia Wine Sales Struck Down," Washington Post, Apr 2002.

52. For example, see the statute of Oregon allowing reciprocity (O.R.S. Chapter 511; § 471.229 approved June 29, 1989, effective October 3, 1989)(¶ 7078).

53. *Barron v. Baltimore,* 7 Pet. 243, 32 U.S. 243 (1833).

54. U.S. Constitution, Thirteenth Amendment, 1865.

55. *Gitlow v. New York,* 268 U.S. 652, 49 S.Ct. 625 (1925).

56. *Palko v. Conn.,* 302 U.S. 319, 58 S.Ct. 149 (1937).

57. *Milk Wagon Drivers Union v. Meadowmoor Dairies,* 312 U.S. 287, 60 S.Ct. 259 (1941).

58. *Near v. Minnesota,* 283 U.S. 697, 51 S.Ct. 625 (1931) and *Bridges v. California,* 314 U.S. 252, 62 S.Ct. 190 (1941). See also *DeJonge v. Oregon,* 299 U.S. 353, 57 S.Ct. 255 (1937) and *Cox v. Louisiana,* 379 U.S. 536, 85 S.Ct. 466 (1965).

59. *Schenk v. United States,* 249 U.S. 47, 39 S.Ct. 247 (1919).

60. *Abrams v. United States,* 250 U.S. 616, 40 S.Ct. 17 (1919).

61. *United States v. Carolene Products,* 304 U.S. 141, 58 S.Ct. 778 (1938).

62. *Dennis v. United States,* 341 U.S. 494, 71 S.Ct. 857 (1951).

63. *Coates v. Cincinnati,* 402 U.S. 611, 91 S.Ct. 1686 (1971).

64. "Judge Decries How-to Book for Murderers," *Los Angeles Times* (Richmond, VA), 8 May 1997. "Publisher Can Be Sued for Killings," Chronicle News Service, 11 November 1997.

65. *Hazelwood School District v. Kuhlmeir,* 484 U.S. 260, 108 S.Ct. 562 (1988) and *Frisby v. Shultz,* 487 U.S. 474, 108 S.Ct. 2495 (1988).

66. *United States v. Haggerty* and *United States v. Eichman,* 496 U.S. 310, 110 S.Ct. 2404 (1990).

67. *Metromedia Inc. v. City of San Diego,* 453 U.S. 490, 101 S.Ct. 2882 (1981).

68. Based on a report by Wendy Hower, *Raleigh News & Observer,* 15 March 1998.

69. *Tinker v. Des Moines School District,* 393 U.S. 503, 89 S.Ct. 733 (1969).

70. Bill Workman, "Ban on Hate Speech Struck Down," *San Francisco Chronicle,* 1 March 1995, Final Ed.

71. Ibid.

72. *R.A.V. v. City of St. Paul,* 505 U.S. 377, 112 S.Ct. 2538 (1969).

73. Ibid.

74. *Wisconsin v. Mitchell,* 508 U.S. 476, 113 S.Ct. 2194 (1993).

75. *Chaplinsky v. New Hampshire,* 315 U.S. 568, 62 S.Ct. 766 (1942).

76. *New York Times,* 13 June 1998.

77. *Miller v. California,* 413 U.S. 15, 93 S.Ct. 2607 (1973).

78. *Barnes v. Glen Theater, Inc.,* 501 U.S. 560, 111 S.Ct. 2456 (1991).

79. Associated Press, 20 September 1997.

80. Nat'l Telecomm. & Info. Admin., "A Nation Online: How Americans Are Expanding Their Use of the Internet" (February 2002), available at http://www.ntia.doc.gov/ntiahome/dn/.

81. http://www.statistics.com/content/datapages/data5.html.

82. 47 U. S. C. A. § 223.

83. 18 U.S.C. § 2251 et seq.

84. *Reno v. A.C.L.U.,* 521 U.S. 844, 117 S.Ct. 2329 (1997).

85. 20 U.S.C. § 9134(f) and 47 U.S.C. § 254(h)(6).

86. *Everson v. Board of Education of the Town of Ewing,* 330 U.S. 1, 67 S.Ct. 504 (1947).

87. *Engel v. Vitale,* 370 U.S. 421, 82 S.Ct. 1261 (1962).

88. Ibid.

89. *Wallace v. Jaffree,* 472 U.S. 38, 105 S.Ct. 2479 (1985).

90. Church doctrine regarding polygamy was changed in 1890. See D. Michael Quinn, "LDS Church Authority and New Plural Marriages, 1890–1904;" http://www.lds-mormon.com/quinn_polygamy.shtml.

91. 20 U.S.C. § 4071-4074.

92. 42 U.S.C.A. § 2000bb et seq.

93. 42 U.S.C.A. § 2000bb (a) (3).

94. *Board of Education of the Westside Community Schools v. Mergens,* 496 U.S. 226, 110 S.Ct. 2356 (1990).

95. Joan Lowy, Scripps Howard News Service, 1 March 1998. See also the case of *Good News Club, et al., v. Milford Central School,* 533 U.S. 98, 121 S.Ct. 2093 (2001).

96. *Cheema v. Thompson,* 67 F.3d 883 (C.A.9 1995).

97. *Lewis v. United States,* 445 U.S. 55, 100 S.Ct. 915 (1980).

98. *Adams v. Williams,* 407 U.S. 143, 92 S.Ct. 1921 (1972).

99. Quoting from the government's brief, Linda Greenhouse, "U.S., in a Shift, Tells Justices Citizens Have a Right to Guns," *The New York Times,* 8 May 2002, Late Edition - Final, Sec. A; p. 1.

100. *Wolf v. Colorado,* 338 U.S. 25, 69 S.Ct. 1359 (1949).

101. *Mapp v. Ohio,* 367 U.S. 643, 81 S.Ct. 1684 (1961).

102. Ibid.

103. *Malloy v. Hogan,* 378 U.S. 1, 84 S.Ct. 1489 (1964), and *Miranda v. Arizona,* 384 U.S. 436, 86 S.Ct. 1602 (1966). *Miranda* is discussed in Chapter 6.

104. *Klopher v. North Carolina,* 386 U.S. 213, 87 S.Ct. 988 (1967).

105. *In re Oliver,* 333 U.S. 257, 69 S.Ct. 499 (1948).

106. *Parker v. Gladden,* 385 U.S. 363, 87 S.Ct. 468 (1966) and *Duncan v. Louisiana,* 391 U.S. 145, 88 S.Ct. 1444 (1968).

107. *Washington v. Texas,* 388 U.S. 14, 87 S.Ct. 1920 (1967).

108. *Argersinger v. Hamblin,* 407 U.S. 25, 92 S.Ct. 2006 (1972) and *Gideon v. Wainwright,* 372 U.S. 335, 83 S.Ct. 792 (1963).

109. Ibid.

110. *Brown v. Board of Education of Topeka,* 347 U.S. 483, 74 S.Ct. 686 (1954).

111. *Brown v. Board of Education of Topeka,* 349 U.S. 294, 75 S.Ct. 753 (1955).

112. *Runyon v. McCrary,* 427 U.S. 160, 96 S.Ct. 2586 (1976).

113. *Board of Education of Oklahoma City v. Dowell,* 498 U.S. 237, 111 S.Ct. 630 (1991).

114. *United States v. Fordice,* 505 U.S. 717, 112 S.Ct. 2727(1992).

115. *Steelworkers v. Weber,* 443 U.S. 193, 99 S.Ct. 2721 (1979) and *Sheet Metal Workers v. Equal Employment Opportunity Commission,* 478 U.S. 501, 106 S.Ct. 3063 (1986).

116. *Wygant v. Jackson Board of Education,* 476 U.S. 267, 106 S.Ct. 1842 (1986).

117. *Griswold v. Connecticut,* 381 U.S. 479, 85 S.Ct. 1678 (1965).

118. *Eisenstady v. Baird,* 405 U.S. 438, 92 S.Ct. 1029 (1972); *Loving v. Virginia,* 388 U.S. 87, S.Ct. 1817 (1967); *Roe v. Wade,* 410 U.S. 113, 93 S.Ct. 705 (1973); *Doe v. Bolton,* 410 U.S. 179, 93 S.Ct. 739 (1973); and *Stanley v. Georgia,* 394 U.S. 557, 87 S.Ct. 1243 (1969).

119. *Paris Adult Theater I v. Slayton,* 413 U.S. 49, 93 S.Ct. 2628 (1973).

120. *Bowers v. Hardwick,* 478 U.S. 186, 106 S.Ct. 284 (1986).

121. *The Wall Street Journal,* 23 June 1989.

122. Carolyn Said, "Software Firm Skirts U.S. Law on Encryption," *San Francisco Chronicle,* 20 March 1998.

123. Title 18, U.S. Code.

124. *Schmerber v. California,* 384 U.S. 757, 86 S.Ct. 1826 (1966).

125. "Drug Testing Becomes a Corporate Mine Field," *The Wall Street Journal,* 21 December 1989.

126. William G. Ross, "Bush v. Gore Has Not Wounded the U.S. Supreme Court," May 2, 2002 Jurist Discussion Forum, http://jurist.law.pitt.edu/forum/forumnew53.php#discuss.

Chapter 3

1. "Novanglus Papers," *Boston Gazette,* 1774, No. 7. "Novanglus" was a pseudonym used by John Adams, signer of the Declaration of Independence and, later, second president of the United States.

2. Alexis de Tocqueville, *Democracy in America,* ed. J.P. Mayer and Max Lerner (New York: Harper and Row, 1966), p. 93.

3. *Richmond Newspapers v. Virginia,* 448 U.S. 555, 100 S.Ct. 2814 (1980).

4. *Maryland v. Cottman Transmissions, Inc.,* 75 Md. App. 647, 542 A.2d 859 (Md., 1988).

5. *International Shoe v. Washington,* 326 U.S. 310, 66 S.Ct. 154 (1945).

6. An example of such an activity is production of a product or material in a foreign state that is used or consumed by a person in the state where jurisdiction is sought. Florida's general long-arm statute is a representative long-arm statute and is found at West's F.S.A. § 48.193.

7. *Young v. New Haven,* 184 Fed.Supp.2d 498 (W.D.Vir., 2001).

8. *Morantz, Inc., v. Hang & Shine Ultrasonics, Inc.,* 79 F.Supp.2d 537 (E.D. Penn. 1999).

9. 18 USC § 1201.

10. 28 USC. §§ 1331 & 1332

11. *Erie Railroad v. Tompkins,* 304 U.S. 64, 58 S.Ct. 817 (1938).

12. "The Supreme Court," Supreme Court Historical Society, 1992, p. 11.

13. *Minneapolis and St. Louis R.R. Co. v. Bombolis,* 241 U.S. 211, 36 S.Ct. 595 (1916).

14. *Duncan v. Louisiana,* 391 U.S. 145, 88 S.Ct. 1444 (1968) and *Baldwin v. New York,* 399 U.S. 66, 90 S.Ct. 1886 (1970).

15. *US News & World Report,* 20 September 1982. Found in *Simpson's Contemporary Quotations,* compiled by James B. Simpson. 1988.

16. The Jury Selection and Service Act of 1968, 28 U.S.C. §§ 1861–1974.

17. As of 1992, twenty-six states have no exemptions for professionals. Robert Litan, "Verdict: Assessing the Civil Jury System" (Washington D.C., The Brookings Institution, 1993), p. 380.

18. Federal statute protects jurors from being discharged, intimidated, or coerced by their permanent employer based on federal jury service. 28 U.S.C. § 1875.

19. *Commonwealth of Mass. v. Geagan,* 339 Mass. 487, 159 N.E.2d 870 (1959).

20. After a second three-month trial, the second jury also deadlocked as to the guilt or innocence of the last remaining defendant, Raymond Buckey. The Los Angeles county district attorney decided to not retry the case. *American Bar Association Journal* (April, 1990), p. 28.

21. *U.S. v. Araujo,* 62 F.3d 930 (7th Cir. 1995).

22. *Colgrove v. Battin,* 413 U.S. 149, 93 S.Ct. 2448 (1973).

23. *Williams v. Florida,* 399 U.S. 78, 90 S.Ct. 1893 (1970), a non-capital criminal case, and *Colgrove v. Battin,* a civil case.

24. *Ballew v. Georgia,* 435 U.S. 223, 98 S.Ct. 1029 (1978).

25. Woolf and Williams, *Juries, Justice for a Generation* (Plenary Sessions American Bar Association, The Senate of the Inns of Court and the Bar. The Law Society of England and Wales, 1985), p. 9.

26. *Apodaca v. Oregon,* 406 U.S. 404, 92 S.Ct. 1628 (1972).

27. *Apodaca v. Oregon.* Also see *Johnson v. Louisiana,* 406 U.S. 356, 92 S.Ct. 1620 (1972). The Oregon plan allows ten to twelve verdicts (i.e., ten out of twelve votes) in all cases except capital ones (those cases calling for the death penalty), which require unanimity.

28. *Burch v. Louisiana,* 441 U.S. 130, 99 S.Ct. 1623 (1979).

29. *Blanton v. North Las Vegas,* 489 U.S. 538, 109 S.Ct. 1289 (1989).

30. Delaware's Court of Chancery still provides an example of the separation of courts of law and equity. The Delaware Court of Chancery may not hear any case in which a sufficient remedy may be had by common law or statute. 10 Del. C. § 341 and Del. Const. Art. IV, § 7 and § 10.

31. *West's Summary of American Law,* annual update (St. Paul, MN: West Publishing, 1990), p. 63.

32. David Rouella, "Is Criminal Contempt Overkill?" *National Law Journal,* 11 May 1998, p. A6.

33. *Ruiz v. Estelle,* 679 F.2d 115 (1982).

34. This verdict was rendered in a different venue (Santa Monica) than the criminal trial (downtown Los Angeles) and by a different and predominately Caucasian jury. A news report on the jury verdict can be found in *USA Today,* 5 February 1997.

Chapter 4

1. Ethics 2000 Commission Final Report, Executive Summary, American Bar Association, June 2001.

2. Richard Posner, *Overcoming Law* (Cambridge: Harvard University Press, 1997). Judge Posner reaches back to the guilds of medieval Europe as a platform for an economic evaluation of the legal profession today, which he concludes reflects an industrialization of service. The "transformation of the profession is the proximate consequence of a surge in demand for legal services" (p. 64).

3. Warren Burger, Chief Justice of the U.S. Supreme Court, in a speech to the American Law Institute, May 1978, as reported in *ABA Journal* 64 (1978), p. 847.

4. Jonathan Harr, *A Civil Action* (New York: First Vintage Books Edition, 1996), p. 295.

5. B. Curran, "Survey of the Public's Legal Needs," ABA Journal 61 (June 1978), p. 848.

6. Ken Meyers, *National Law Journal,* 17 June 1991, 13.

7. *Sacramento Bee,* 9 February 1977.

8. See http://www.azbar.org/FindingLawyer/bls.asp.

9. Jerome Carlin, *Lawyer's Ethics* (New York: Russell Sage Foundation, 1966).

10. A copy of the published quotation is available (contact authors), although the source cannot be identified.

11. http://www.lsc.gov/.

12. Revised Model Rule of Professional Conduct 6.1.

13. Brian Heid, "Note: The Group Legal Plan Revolution: Bright Horizon of Dark Future?" *Hofstra Labor & Employment Law Journal* 18 (2000), p. 33.

14. Judith L. Maute, "Symposium: Prepaid and Group Legal Services: Thirty Years After the Storm" *Law Review* 70 (2001), p. 915.

15. Excerpt from the Model Rules of Professional Conduct, American Bar Association, adopted August 1983.

16. *Maryland State Bar Assoc. v. Agnew,* 271 Md. 543, 318 A.2d 811 (Md., 1974).

17. E. Schnapper, "The Myth of Legal Ethics," *ABA Journal* 64 (Feb. 1978), p. 202.

18. ABA Model Rules of Professional Conduct (2002) Rule 4.2: Communication With Person Represented By Counsel.

19. For both views, see Harry Subin, "The Criminal Lawyer's 'Different Mission': Reflections on the 'Right' to Present a False Case," and John Mitchell, "Reasonable Doubts Are Where You Find Them: A Response to Professor Subin's Position on the Criminal Lawyer's 'Different Mission,'" *Georgetown Journal of Legal Ethics,* 1 (1987), p. 125.

20. Geoffrey Hazard and William Hodes, *The Law of Lawyering* (Englewood Cliffs, NJ: Prentice-Hall, 1989), § 90.2.

21. United States v. Leventhal; see also, *Blackman v. United States,* C.A.9 (Or.) 1995, 72 F.3d 1418, certiorari denied 519 U.S. 911, 117 S.Ct. 275 (1996).

22. ABA Model Rule of Professional Conduct 1.7.

23. http://www.philabar.org/public/ethics/displayethics.asp?id=774532002.

24. ABA Model Rule of Professional Responsibility 1.6.

25. Federal Rule of Civil Procedure 11; 28 U.S.C.A. 1927 (1988); *Chambers v. NASCO Inc.* 501 US 32 111 S.Ct. 2123 (1991).

26. Ibid.

27. Thomas D. Morgan, "Titanic Lessons: Toward a New Perspective on Legal Ethics," *Oregon State Bar Bulletin* 61 (2001) pp. 15, 18 n. 19.

28. Ray August, "The Mythical Kingdom of Lawyers," *ABA Journal* 78 (September 1992), p. 72. An interesting rebuttal to lawyers as political fodder can be found in Charles Epp, "Let's Not Kill All the Lawyers," *The Wall Street Journal,* 9 July 1992.

29. Harvey Rubenstein, "On Being a Private Practitioner," *ABA Journal* 78 (December 1992), p. 78.

30. *Bates v. State Bar of Arizona,* 433 U.S. 350, 97 S.Ct. 2691 (1977).

31. *Shapero v. Kentucky Bar Association,* 486 U.S. 466, 108 S.Ct. 1916 (1988).

32. *Peel v. Attorney Registration and Disciplinary Commission of Illinois,* 496 U.S. 917, 110 S.Ct. 2281 (1990).

33. ABA Model Rule of Professional Responsibility 7.1.

34. ABA Model Rule of Professional Conduct 1.5(c).

35. ABA Model Rule 1.5 Comment (4).

36. American Bar Association Formal Opinion 94-389: American Bar Association Committee on Ethics and Professional Responsibility.

37. NJ R Gen Application R. 1:21-7.

38. Calif. Bus. & Prof. Code § 6146.

39. Darlene Ricker, "The Vanishing Hourly Fee," *ABA Journal* 90 (March 1984), p. 90.

40. *Baron v. Mare,* 47 Cal.App.3d 304, 120 Cal.Rptr. 675 (Ca.,1975).

41. 13 ALR3d 701 (1967).

42. *State of Kansas v. Mayes,* 216 Kan. 38, 531 P.2d 102 (Kan., 1975).

43. *Bushman v. State Bar,* 111 Cal.3d 558, 522 P.2d 312, 13 Cal.Rptr. 904 (1974) and *Florida Bar v. Winn,* 208 So.2d 809 (Fla., 1968).

44. Cal. Bus. & Prof. Code Sec. 6200 (c).

45. ABA Model Rule of Professional Responsibility 1.8 (e) 1, 2.

46. ABA Model Rule of Professional Conduct 1.8 (e), Model Code Comparison.

47. *The Wall Street Journal,* 22 November 1989.

48. American Jurisprudence 2d § 3.

49. J. Shannon, *Texaco and the $10 Billion Jury* (Englewood Cliffs, NJ: Prentice-Hall, 1988).

50. Kristina Horton Flaherty, "Bar Cites 21 for Pro Bono Work," *California State Bar Journal,* Nov., 2002.

51. *In re Thompson,* 574 S.W.2d 365 (Mo., 1978).

52. Ellen Yamshon, "Disabilities Act Doesn't Have to Be Bad for Business," *Sacramento Bee,* 13 November 1994.

53. Roger Fisher, William Ury, and Bruce Patton, *Getting to Yes: Negotiating Agreement Without Giving In* (New York: Penguin Books, 1992).

54. For example, "Model Standards of Conduct for Mediators," approved by the American Arbitration Association, the Litigation Section and the Dispute Resolution Section of the American Bar Association, and the Society of Professionals in Dispute Resolution (now part of the merged Association for Conflict Resolution). A copy can be found at the AAA website http://www.adr.org/index2.1.jsp.

55. For example, see *In re First Merit Bank,* N.A. 52 S.W.3d 749 (Texas, 2001).

56. James F. Henry & Jethro K. Lieberman, *The Managers Guide to Resolving Legal Disputes: Better Disputes Without Litigation* (1985), p. 41.

57. William Ewart Gladstone, (1809–1898), British Statesman.

58. Warren E. Burger, "Our Vicious Legal Spiral," *Judges' Journal* 16 (1977), pp. 22, 49.

Chapter 5

1. See e.g., *INS v. Chadha,* 462 U.S. 919, 103 S.Ct. 2764 (1983).

2. 5 U.S.C. §§ 552 et seq.

3. 15 U.S.C. §§ 77 et seq.

4. 7 U.S.C. §§ 2 et seq.

5. 12 U.S.C. §§ 221 et seq.

6. 15 U.S.C. §§ 21 et seq.

7. 29 U.S.C. §§ 151 et seq.

8. 42 U.S.C. §§ 2000 et seq.

9. 40 C.F.R § 1.

10. 42 U.S.C. §§ 7134.

11. 42 U.S.C. §§ 2011 et seq.

12. 15 U.S.C. §§ 41 et seq.

13. 5 U.S.C. § 551(4).

14. 40 C.F.R. § 238.30.

15. 5 U.S.C. § 553(b).

16. 5 U.S.C. § 553(c).

17. 5 U.S.C. §§ 561-574.

18. Facts on File, *Transportation* (1979), p. 420.

19. See *Camara v. Municipal Court,* 387 U.S. 523, 87 S.Ct. 1727 (1967), and *Marshall v. Barlow's Inc.,* 436 U.S. 307, 98 S.Ct. 1816 (1978).

20. *Payton v. New York,* 445 U.S. 573, 100 S.Ct. 1371 (1980).

21. See, e.g. *Donovan v. Dewey,* 452 U.S. 594, 101 S.Ct. 2354 (1981).

22. See, e.g. *Wyman v. James,* 400 U.S. 309, 91 S.Ct. 381(1971).

23. See, e.g. *Marshall v. Barlow's Inc.,* 436 U.S. 307, 98 S.Ct. 1816 (1978).

24. *CNN Live Event Special* 09:39 am ET April 30, 1998; Transcript # 98043001V54. Content and programming copyright 1998 Cable News Network. Transcribed under license by Federal Document Clearing House, Inc.

25. 5 U.S.C. §§ 571-84.

26. 5 U.S.C. § 573.

27. "When Fines Collapse," *The National Law Journal,* December 4, 1989.

28. 5 U.S.C. § 556.

29. Henry Friendly, *Some Kind of Hearing, University of Pennsylvania Law Review* 123 (1975) p. 1289.

30. 5 U.S.C. § 552.

31. 5 U.S.C. § 552B.

32. 5 U.S.C. § 561 et seq.

33. 5 U.S.C. § 557.

Chapter 6

1. Mel Byrd, Director of Applied Research, North Carolina State University.

2. White House Office of National Drug Control Policy, as reported by Jeff Barnard, Associated Press, 27 July 1998.

3. For a history of private management of prisons, and the differing legal immunities that are applicable to public versus private guards, see *Richardson v. McKnight,* 521 U.S. 399, 117 S.Ct. 2100 (1997).

4. William Glaberson, *New York Times,* 24 May 1998.

5. Jim Robinson, "Internet as the Scene of Crime," speech delivered before the International Computer Crime Conference in Oslo, Norway, 29–31, 2000. http://www.cybercrime.gov/roboslo.htm.

6. *San Francisco Chronicle,* 23 June 1990.

7. *U.S. v. Koon,* 833 F.Supp. 769 (1993).

8. *People v. Jones,* 86 Ill.App.3d 278, 407 N.E.2d 1121 (Illinois, 1980).

9. C. Goodyear, *San Francisco Chronicle,* 20 October 1998.

10. *People v. Municipal Court,* 88 Cal.App.3d 206, 151 Cal.Rptr. 861 (1979).

11. Illinois Code of Corrections, § 1005-8-1.

12. 17 Cal.Jur.III § 71.

13. Illinois Code of Corrections, § 1005-5-3.2.

14. *Commonwealth v. Noble,* 417 Mass. 341, 629 N.E.2d 1328 (Mass., 1994).

15. *State v. Tesack,* 181 W.Va. 422, 383 S.E.2d 54 (West Virginia, 1989).

16. *People v. Caldwell,* 36 C.3d 210, 681 P.2d 274, 203 Cal.Rptr. 433 (1984); *People v. Aurelio R.,* 167 Cal.App.3d 52, 212 Cal.Rptr. 868 (1985).

17. See, for example, *Commonwealth ex.rel. Smith v. Myers,* 438 Pa. 218, 261 A.2d 550 (Pennsylvania, 1970); *Alvarez v. Dist. Ct. for Denver,* 186 Colo. 37, 525 P.2d 1131 (Colorado, 1974); *People v. Wood,* 8 N.Y.2d 48, 167 N.E.2d 736 (New York, 1960); *State v. Harrison,* 90 N.M. 437, 564 P.2d 1321 (New Mexico, 1977).

18. See, for example, California Penal Code, § 187. In *People v. Davis,* 30 Cal.Rptr. 2d 50, 872 P.2d 591 (1994), the California Supreme Court held that the fetus need only have progressed beyond the embryonic stage of seven to eight weeks for the murder statute to apply.

19. *Roe v. Wade,* 410 U.S. 113, 93 S.Ct. 705 (1973); *Webster v. Reproductive Health Services,* 492 U.S. 490, 109 S.Ct. 3040 (1989).

20. Associated Press, 15 November 1997.

21. *National Law Journal,* 26 October 1992, 3.

22. *San Francisco Chronicle,* 2 March 1994, A7.

23. *Battle v. State,* 287 Md. 675, 414 A.2d 1266 (Maryland, 1980); *State v. Way,* 297 N.C. 293, 254 S.E.2d 760 (North Carolina, 1979).

24. Chronicle News Service, New York, 13 December 1997.

25. See 31 Am.Jur.2d, Extortion, Blackmail, and Threats, § 1.

26. California Penal Code §§ 203 and 204.

27. *People v. Valdez,* 175 Cal.App.3d 103, 220 Cal.Rptr. 538 (1985).

28. Richard A. Serrano, "Hate Groups on the Rise Across America," *Los Angeles Times,* 4 March 1998.

29. Associated Press, Washington, October 1997.

30. Associated Press, Santa Monica, 5 March 1998.

31. Patrick O'Driscoll, "Man Charged with Setting Arizona Wildfire," *USA Today,* 1 July, 2002.

32. A hypothetical situation based on an actual case reported by the Los Angeles Daily News Service, 1 January 1999. In that reported case, the victim spent more than 500 hours and $10,000 attempting to clear her name.

33. From the Federal Trade Commission Website http://www.ftc.gov/bcp/conline/pubs/general/idtheftfact.htm.

34. Illicit Drug Policies: Selected Laws from the 50 States (2002) p. 22. A publication of The ImpacTeen Illicit Drug Team, which is a collaborative research group with investigators from Andrews University, RAND, and The MayaTech Corporation as well as other research institutions. http://www.andrews.edu/BHSC/impacteen-illicitdrugteam/main.php.

35. Associated Press, Los Angeles, 6 March 1998.

36. *United States v. Oakland Cannabis Buyers' Cooperative,* 532 U.S. 483, 121 S.Ct. 1711 (2001).

37. Associated Press, 16 April 1998.

38. The states and the punishments: Alabama (one year/$2,000), Florida (sixty days/$500), Idaho (five years to life), Louisiana (five years/$2,000), Mississippi (ten years), North Carolina (ten years/discretionary fine), Puerto Rico (ten years), South Carolina (five years/$500), Utah (six months/$1,000), and Virginia (one to five years). Source: American Civil Liberties Union, http://www.aclu.org.

39. According to a New York State Attorney General's survey in March 1998, of those responding 92 percent favored Megan's Law. However, fewer (79 percent) favored putting the information on the Internet, a tactic that has been done in over half of the states.

40. Hans Greimel, "Neighbors Keep Molester Away by Buying His Home," Associated Press, *San Francisco Chronicle,* 13 August 1998.

41. *Chaplinski v. State of New Hampshire,* 315 U.S. 568, 62 S.Ct. 766 (1942).

42. *San Francisco Chronicle,* 28 March 1989.

43. *The Wall Street Journal,* 18 February 1994.

44. *New York Times,* 6 May 1997.

45. *National Law Journal,* 13 September 1993, 8.

46. "Porn figure Sturman dies in prison at 73," *Las Vegas Review-Journal* 29 October 1997.

47. *National Organization for Women, Inc., v. Scheidler,* 510 U.S. 249, 114 S.Ct. 798 (1994).

48. *Terrell v. Childers,* 836 F.Supp. 468 (N.D. Illinois, 1993).

49. *San Francisco Chronicle,* 15 May 1997.

50. *Maine Statutes,* Chapter 5, Section 103(A).

51. *San Francisco Chronicle,* 29 March 1994.

52. *National Law Journal,* 9 March 1992, p. 13.

53. *People v. Segal,* 54 N.Y.2d 58, 429 N.E.2d 107 (New York, 1981).

54. Judith Schoolman, New York, reported in *San Francisco Chronicle,* 16 March 1998.

55. Reuters, Ottawa, 8 August 1992.

56. http://www.courttv.com/trials/falater/062599_jurors_ctv.html.

57. *People v. Barraza,* 23 Cal.3d 675, 591 P.2d 947, 153 Cal.Rptr. 459 (1979).

58. *People v. Slatton,* 173 Cal.App.3d 487, 219 Cal.Rptr. 70 (1985); *People v. Kelley,* 158 Cal.App.3d 1085, 205 Cal.Rptr. 283 (1984).

59. Proclamation signed by then-President Ronald Reagan when declaring the first annual Crime Victims' Week, April 1981.

60. *Simon & Schuster, Inc. v. Members of New York State Crime Victims Bd.,* 502 U.S. 105, 112 S.Ct. 501 (1991).

61. Associated Press, 14 July 1998.

62. Associated Press, Los Angeles, 25 August 1998.

63. *United States v. Leon,* 468 U.S. 897, 104 S.Ct. 3405 (1984); *United States v. Peltier,* 422 U.S. 531, 95 S.Ct. 2313 (1975).

64. *Michigan Dept. of State Police v. Sitz,* 496 U.S. 444, 110 S.Ct. 2481 (1990).

65. Press release, Colorado Department of Transportation (CDOT), 2 July, 2001.

66. *National Law Journal,* 7 February 1994, p. 42.

67. *National Law Journal,* 7 February 1994, p. 6.

68. *U.S. v. Penny-Feeney,* 773 F.Supp. 220 (D.Hawaii, 1991).

69. *United States v. Rodriquez,* 592 F.2d 553 (1979); *United States v. Ramsey,* 431 U.S. 606, 97 S.Ct. 1972 (1977); *United States v. Olcott,* 568 F.2d 1173 (1978).

70. *U.S. v. Knights,* 534 U.S. 112, S.Ct. 122 (2001).

71. *Wilson v. Jones,* 251 F.3d 1340 (C.A.11 (Ala.), 2001).

72. New York Criminal Procedure Law, § 510.30 et. seq.

73. *National Law Journal,* 19 April 1993, 6, discussing the case of *Alme v. Commonwealth,* 414 Mass. 667, 611 N.E.2d 2941 (1993).

74. The Bail Reform Act of 1984, 18 U.S.C. 3142(d). But see also *United States v. Salerno,* 481 U.S. 739, 107 S.Ct. 2095 (1987) for standards.

75. *United States v. Blackwell,* 694 F.2d 1325 (1982).

76. *Miranda v. Arizona,* 384 U.S. 436, 86 S.Ct. 1602 (1966).

77. Associated Press, Springfield Mass., 30 January 1999.

78. *Brady v. Maryland,* 373 U.S. 83, 83 S.Ct. 1194 (1963).

79. *North Carolina v. Pearce,* 395 U.S. 711, 89 S.Ct. 2072 (1969).

80. U.S. Constitution's Article 1 Section 9, states in part, "No Bill of Attainder or ex post facto Law shall be passed," and Section 10 says: '... pass any ex post facto Law....'"

81. *San Francisco Chronicle,* 29 June 1993.

82. *Frye v. United States,* 293 F.2d 1013 (D.C., 1923).

83. "Whoever, except in cases and under circumstances expressly authorized by the Constitution or Act of Congress, willfully uses any part of the Army or Air Force as a posse comitatus or otherwise to execute the laws shall be fined under this title or imprisoned not more than two years, or both." 18 USC 1385.

84. *See* Department of Defense Authorization Act, 1982, Pub. L. No. 97-86, § 905, 95 Stat. 1099, 1114-16 (1981).

85. Definition from the Council on Foreign Relations, http://www.terrorismanswers.com/responses/tribunals.html.

86. 18 USC 801 et. al.

87. *Daubert v. Merrell Dow Pharmaceuticals, Inc.,* 509 U.S. 579, 113 S.Ct. 2786 (1993).

88. Illinois Code of Corrections, § 1005-5-3.2.

89. Illinois Code of Corrections, § 1005-8-1.

90. *State of Indiana v. Rowold,* 629 N.E.2d 1285 (Indiana, 1994).

91. *Los Angeles Daily News,* 10 July 1998.

92. *Los Angeles Times,* 10 July 1998.

93. Associated Press, 28 January 1999.

94. Associated Press, Jackson, New Jersey, 26 November 1998.

95. *National Law Journal,* 27 July 1992, 17.

96. *United States v. Mistretta,* 488 U.S. 361, 109 S.Ct. 647 (1989).

97. *United States v. Bradley,* 917 F.2d 601 (1990); *United States v. Seluk,* 873 F.2d 15 (1989).

98. *National Law Journal,* 21 February 1994, 38.

99. Associated Press, Boston, 27 August 1998.

100. Jerry Gray, *New York Times,* 29 January 1994.

101. *Harmelin v. Michigan,* 501 U.S. 957, 111 S.Ct. 2680 (1991).

102. *Furman v. Georgia,* 408 U.S. 238, 92 S.Ct. 1133 (1980).

103. *Gregg v. Georgia,* 428 U.S. 153, 96 S.Ct. 2909 (1976).

104. *Godfrey v. Georgia,* 446 U.S. 420, 100 S.Ct. 1759 (1980).

105. *Maynard v. Cartwright,* 486 U.S. 356, 108 S.Ct. 1853 (1988).

106. *State v. Breton,* 212 Conn. 258, 562 A.2d 1060 (Connecticut, 1989).

107. Illinois Criminal Code, § 9-1.

108. *Elledge v. Florida,* 525 U.S. 944, 119 S.Ct. 366 (1998).

109. Bill Blum, "Dead Woman Walking," *California Lawyer,* May 2002, p. 24.

110. *Callins v. Collins,* 510 U.S. 1141, 114 S.Ct. 1127 (1994).

Chapter 7

1. Associated Press, 9 October 1997. Because verdicts are subject to appeal and often settled "out of court," the final amount paid may differ widely from the jury's award.

2. Associated Press, 12 June 2002, *Bullock v. Phillip Morris,* No. BC249171, Superior Court of Los Angeles County, Central, Ca., 10-4-2002.

3. *National Law Journal,* 2 November 1998.

4. *National Law Journal,* 7 February 1994, 6.

5. Associated Press, New York, 3 July 1997.

6. Based on an article in the *Wall Street Journal,* "A Car Salesman's Bizarre Prank May End Up Backfiring In Court," May 4, 1995.

7. 15 USC 1692.

8. Associated Press, San Diego, 25 December 1996.

9. *Restatement of the Law of Torts,* 2d edition, (St. Paul, MN: American Law Institute Publishers, 1934), § 570–575.

10. Associated Press, Poughkeepsie, N.Y., 10 October 1998.

11. Sarah Lyall, *New York Times,* 20 June 1997.

12. *New York Times v. Sullivan,* 376 U.S. 254, 84 S.Ct. 710 (1964); and *Philadelphia Newspapers, Inc. v. Hepps,* 475 U.S. 767, 106 S.Ct. 1558 (1986).

13. *Gertz v. Robert Welch, Inc.,* 418 U.S. 323, 94 S.Ct. 2997 (1974); *Milkovich v. Lorain Journal Co.,* 497 U.S. 1, 110 S.Ct. 2695 (1990).

14. Restatement of Torts, § 652-A-E.

15. *Nader v. General Motors Corporation,* 298 N.Y.S.2d. 137, 31 A.D.2d 392 (New York, 1969).

16. *Carson v. Here's Johnny Portable Toilets* 698 F.2d 831 (6th cir., 1983).

17. *Matthew v. Page,* 354 So.2d 458 (Florida, 1978); *North Carolina National Bank v. McCarley & Co., Inc.,* 34 N.C.App. 689, 239 S.E.2d 583 (North Carolina, 1977); *Masterson v. McCroskie,* 194 Co. 460, 573 P.2d 547 (Colorado, 1978); *A&M Records, Inc. v. Heilman,* 75 Cal.App.3d 554, 142 Cal.Rptr. 390 (1977).

18. *San Francisco Chronicle,* 18 September 1989

19. On appeal, the award of compensatory damages was upheld, but the punitive damage award was reduced to $1,000,000. 703 F.2d 1152 (10th cir., 1983).

20. Charlie Goodyear, *San Francisco Chronicle,* 13 December 1997.

21. *Rodio v. Allstate Insurance Co.,* 123 N.J. 345, 587 A.2d 621 (New Jersey, 1991).

22. *Ledingham v. Blue Cross Plan for Hospital Care,* 29 Ill. App. 3d 339, 330 N.E.2d 540 (Illinois, 1975); *Grand Sheet Metal Products Co. v. Protection Mutual Insurance Co.,* 34 Conn.Supp. 46, 375 A.2d 428 (Connecticut, 1977); *McEvoy v. Group Health Cooperative of Eau Claire,* 570 N.W.2d 397 (Wisconsin, 1997).

23. O.C.G.A. § 33-4-6.

24. For an interesting discussion of the effect of bad-faith lawsuits on auto insurance claims, see "How Do Third-Party, Bad Faith Bodily Injury Claims Affect Automobile Insurance Costs and Compensation?" RAND Research Brief, Rand Institute for Civil Justice RB-9036-ICJ (2001).

25. *Thompson v. County of Alameda* 27 Cal. 3d 741, 614 P.2d 728, 167 Cal.Rptr. 70 (California, 1980).

26. Edward J. Kionka, *Torts in a Nutshell* (St. Paul, MN: West Publishing Co., 1992), 50.

27. *Wisniewski v. Great Atlantic & Pacific Tea Co.,* 226 Pa.Super. 574, 323 A.2d 744 (Pennsylvania, 1974).

28. Henry Campbell Black et al., *Black's Law Dictionary, 5th ed.* (St. Paul, MN: West Publishing Co., 1979).

29. William Prosser and Page Keeton, *Prosser and Keeton on Torts,* 5th ed. (St. Paul, MN: West Publishing Co., 1979), 43.

30. Leon Green, "The Casual Relation Issue in Negligence Law," *Michigan Law Review* 60 (1962), p. 543. See also *Weirum v. RKO General Inc.,* 15 Cal.3d 40, 539 P.2d 36 (California, 1975).

31. Restatement of Torts, § 328A.

32. Stephen Kiehl, *Boston Globe,* 3 September 1998.

33. *County of Sacramento v. Lewis,* 523 U.S. 833, 118 S.Ct. 1708 (1988); John Schwartz, *Washington Post,* 27 May 1998.

34. Hilary MacGregor, *Los Angeles Times,* 25 January 1998.

35. *U.S. v. DeVane,* 306 F.2d, 182 (5th cir., 1962).

36. *Romanesk v. Rose,* 248 Md. 420, 237 A.2d 12, (Maryland, 1968).

37. Randolph Stuart Sergent, *Gross, Reckless, Wanton, and Indifferent: Gross Negligence In Maryland Civil Law,* UBALR 30 (2000) p. 1.

38. *The Wall Street Journal,* 1 March 1990.

39. *Chase v. Luce,* 239 MN 364, 58 N.W.2d 565 (Minnesota, 1953); *Selby v. Tolbert,* 56 N.M. 718, 249 P.2d 498 (New Mexico, 1952); *Hooks v. City of Detroit,* 31 Mich.App. 662, 187 N.W.2d 901 (Michigan, 1971).

40. Reuters, Hartford, Conn., 5 November 1998.

41. Nanette van der Laan, "France Debates Right Not to Be Born," *Christian Science Monitor,* 7 December 2001. http://www.csmonitor.com/2001/1207/pls3-woeu.html.

42. Dave Reynolds, "French Parliament Makes 'Wrongful Birth' Lawsuits a Thing of the Past," *Inclusion Daily Express,* 19 February 2002.

43. *Brown v. Kendrick,* 192 So.2d 49 (Florida, 1996); *Abrams v. Woods,* 316 N.Y.S.2d 750, 64 Misc.2d 1093 (New York, 1970); *Mercer v. Band,* 484 S.W.2d 117 (Texas, 1972).

44. Se e.g., *Franklin v. Gibson,* 138 Cal.App.3d 340, 188 Cal.Rptr, 23 (California, 1982); *Yocco v. Barris,* 16 Ill.3d 113, 305 N.E.2d 584 (Illinois, 1973).

45. *Greenman v. Yuba Power Products, Inc.,* 59 Cal.2d 57, 377 P.2d 897, 27 Cal.Rptr. 697 (California, 1962).

46. Restatement of Torts, § 402A.

47. Associated Press, 10 November 1998.

48. *Los Angeles Times,* 2 December 1998.

49. Chronicle News Service, Los Angeles, 11 November 1998 and 21 November 1998.

50. Kenneth Howe, *San Francisco Chronicle,* 27 November 1998.

51. Mealey's Litigation Report: April 4, 2002. *Marie Schwartz v. Philip Morris Companies Inc.,* No. 0002-01376, Ore. Cir., Multnomah Co.

52. "Philip Morris U.S.A. Will Appeal Oregon Award to Smoker's Estate," Philip Morris Companies press release, May 9, 2002.

53. Study of 1.25 million Chinese jointly by Oxford and Cornell Universities and the Chinese Academies of Preventative Medicine, Emma Ross, Associated Press, 20 November 1998.

54. CDC, National Center for Injury Prevention and Control, National Vital Statistics Reports, Deaths 1999, Volume 49, Number 8 (2002).

55. Henry K. Lee, *San Francisco Chronicle,* 10 November 1998.

56. *Hanflik v. Ratchford,* 848 F.Supp. 1539 (N.D. Ga., 1989); *Craven v. Lowndes County Hospital Authority,* 263 Ga. 656, 437 S.E.2d 308 (Georgia, 1993).

57. This example based on the case of *Dinh v. Rust International Corporation,* 974 F.2d 500 (4th cir., 1992).

58. *Sealey v. Hicks,* 309 Or. 387, 788 P.2d 435 (Oregon, 1990).

59. *Olsen v. Freeman,* 117 Idaho 706, 791 P.2d 1285. (Idaho, 1990).

60. Jim Doyle, *San Francisco Chronicle,* 27 June 1997.

61. *Black's Law Dictionary.*

62. *Grimshaw v. Ford Motor Co.,* 119 Cal.App.3d 757, 174 Cal.Rptr. 348 (California, 1981); *Penner v. Falk,* 153 Cal.App.3d 858, 200 Cal.Rptr. 661 (California, 1964); *Taylor v. Superior Court,* 24 Cal.3d 890, 598 P.2d 854, 157 Cal.Rptr. 693 (California, 1979).

63. *Gordon v. Florida,* 585 So.2d 1033 (Florida, 1991), *Decision Approved by Gordon v. State,* 608 So.2d 800 (Florida, 1992) *Certiorari Denied by Gordon v. Florida,* 507 U.S. 1005, 113 S.Ct. 1647 (1993).

64. *General Resources v. Deadman,* 932 S.W.2d 485 (Texas, 1996).

65. Sam Zuckerman, *San Francisco Chronicle,* 13 November 1998. There are both state and federal "whistleblower" statutes. See e.g., 31 U.S.C.A. 5328

66. *San Francisco Chronicle,* 8 April 1989 and 22 April 1989.

Chapter 8

1. *Restatement of the Law of Contracts,* 2nd ed., (St. Paul, MN: American Law Institute Publishers, 1981), § 1.

2. John Donne, "Devotions upon Emergent Occasions," Number 17, 1624.

3. Uniform Commercial Code (UCC) (St. Paul, MN: American Law Institute Publishers, 1987), § 2-206(1)(a). See also Restatement of Contracts, 2 § 30.

4. Adams v. Lindsell, 106 Eng. Rep. 250 (K.B., 1818).

5. Restatement of Contracts, § 3b.

6. Restatement of Contracts, § 48.

7. Restatement of Contracts, § 37.

8. Pride has also violated a federal criminal statute, 49 U.S.C.A. § 32701 et seq., and undoubtedly state criminal statutes as well (e.g. West's Ann.Cal.Vehicle Code § 11713) that regulate the sale of vehicles.

9. "Bogus 'Rebate' Offers Violate Federal Law," Federal Trade Commission news release, 5 August 2002.

10. The Ten Commandments, or Decalogue, and the other precepts spoken by God to Israel, delivered to Moses on Mount Sinai. The Bible: Exodus 20, Deuteronomy 5.

11. Consumer Credit Protection Act of 1968, 15 U.S.C. § 1601 et seq.

12. Foreign Corrupt Practices Act of 1977, 2 U.S.C. § 241 et seq.

13. Statute of Frauds and Perjuries, 29 Car. II, c. 3.

14. UCC, § 2-106(1).

15. UCC, § 2-105(1).

16. UCC, § 2-201(3).

17. UCC, § 2-201(2).

18. UCC, § 1-206(1).

19. UCC, §§ 2-201, 8-319, 9-203.

20. Restatements of Contracts 2d, § 302(l)(b).

21. Restatements of Contracts 2d, § 302(1)(a).

22. Restatements of Contracts 2d, §§ 423, 430.

23. UCC § 2-615.

24. *San Francisco Chronicle,* 1 December 1989.

25. Press Release from the Consumer Product Safety Commission news release, January 1998.

26. Upton Sinclair, *The Jungle* (New York: Penguin Edition, 1985), p. 163.

27. Copies of the complaint and stipulated final order, as well as consumer education material associated with "Project $cholar$cam," are available from the FTC's Web site at http://www.ftc.gov and also from the FTC's Consumer Response Center, Room 130, 6th Street and Pennsylvania Avenue, N.W., Washington, D.C. 20580; 202-FTC-HELP (202-382-4357); TDD for the hearing impaired 202-326-2502.

28. UCC § 2-104(1).

29. UCC § 2-719(3) and § 2-302.

30. UCC § 2-318.

31. Restatement of Contracts 2d, § 213.

32. Magnuson-Moss Consumer Product Warranty and Guaranty Act, 15 U.S.C. § 2301 et seq.

Chapter 9

1. Don Lattin, *San Francisco Chronicle,* 23 May 1998.

2. *Ankenbrandt v. Richards,* 504 U.S. 112 S.Ct. 2206 (1992).

3. *Rubin v. Smith,* 817 F.Supp. 987 (D. N. H., 1993); *Lannan v. Maul,* 979 F.2d 627 (8th Circuit, 1992).

4. Rayner Pike, Associated Press, 28 February 1998.

5. Amy Argetsinger, *Washington Post,* 15 October 1998.

6. Texas Family Code Annotated, § 1.91.

7. *Jennings v. Hurt,* 160 App.Div.2d 576, 554 N.Y.S.2d 220 (New York, 1990).

8. *Marvin v. Marvin,* 122 Cal.App. 3d 871, 176 Cal.Rptr. 555 (California, 1981).

9. *Levar v. Elkins,* 604 P.2d 602 (Alaska, 1980); *Carroll v. Lee,* 148 Ariz. 101, 712 P.2d 923 (Arizona, 1986); *Boland v. Catalano,* 202 Conn. 333, 521 A.2d 142 (Connecticut, 1987); *Donovan V. Scuderi,* 51 Md. App. 217, 443 A.2d 121 (Maryland 1981); *Eaton v. Johnson,* 235 Kan. 323, 681 P.2d 606 (Kansas, 1984); *Hierholzer v. Sardy,* 128 Mich. App. 259, 340 N.W.2d 91 (Michigan, 1983); *Hay v. Hay,* 100 Nev. 196, 678 P.2d 672 (Nevada, 1984); *Morone v. Morone,* 50 N.Y. 2d 481, 418 N.E.2d 1154 (New York, 1980); *Watts v. Watts,* 137 Wis.2d 506, 405 N.W.2d 303 (Wisconsin, 1987).

10. *Hewitt v. Hewitt,* 77 Ill.2d 49, 394 N.E.2d 1204 (Illinois, 1979)

11. http://www.hrc.org/worknet/dp/index.asp.

12. Elaine Hersher, *San Francisco Chronicle,* 5 November 1998.

13. Vermont H.847 (2000).

14. 15 V.S.A. chapter 23 Sec. 1201 (2).

15. *Rosengarten v. Downes,* 802 A.2d 170 (Conn.App., 2002).

16. For example New York Domestic Relations Law Section 236 (B)(1)(d). Note that gifts received during marriage from a spouse are considered marital property.

17. *Stringfellow v. Sorrels,* 18 S.W. 689 (Texas, 1891).

18. *Brandal v. Shangin,* 36 P.3d 1188 (Alaska, 2001).

19. *Szesny v. Szesny,* 197 Ill.App.3d 966, 557 N.E.2d 222 (Ill. 1990).

20. Checkoway, "Marital Property and Creditor's Rights," *Maine Bar Journal* 4 (1989), p. 254.

21. *The Wall Street Journal,* 2 February 1994.

22. *Barnes v. Barnes,* 603 N.E.2d 1337 (Indiana, 1992).

23. *Dellapenta v. Dellapenta,* 838 P.2d 1153 (Wyoming, 1992).

24. *Bonte v. Bonte,* 136 N.H.286, 616 A.2d 464 (New Hampshire, 1992).

25. *Richard v. Richard,* 599 So.2d 135 (Florida, 1992).

26. *Renko v. McLean,* 697 A.2d 468 (Maryland, 1997). See also *Bushey v. Northern Assur. Co. of America,* 766 A.2d 598 (Maryland, 2001).

27. *Simmons v. Simmons,* 773 P.2d 602 (Colorado, 1988); *Van Meter v. Van Meter,* 328 N.W. 2d 497 (Iowa, 1983); *Vance v. Vance,* 41 Md. App. 130, 396 A.2d 296 (Maryland 1979); *Davis v. Bostick,* 282 Or. 667, 580 P.2d 544 (Oregon 1978); *Noble v. Noble,* 761 P.2d 1369 (Utah, 1988); *Stuart v. Stuart,* 143 Wis.2d 347, 421 N.W.2d 505 (Wisconsin, 1988).

28. *Harris v. McDavid,* 553 So.2d 567 (Alabama 1989); *Richard P. v. Superior Court,* 202 Cal.App.3d 1089, 249 Cal.Rptr. 246, (California, 1988); *Whittington v. Whittington,* 766 S.W.2d 73 (Kentucky, 1989); *Wiener v. Wiener,* 84 A.D.2d 814, 444 N.Y.S.2d 130 (New York, 1981); *Pickering v. Pickering,* 434 N.W.2d 758 (South Dakota, 1989).

29. *South Coast Today,* 26 January 1998, http://www.s-t.com/daily/01-98/01-26-98/zzzwnppl.htm.

30. *Roe v. Wade,* 410 U.S. 113, 93 S.Ct. 705 (1973).

31. *Webster v. Reproductive Health Services,* 492 U.S. 490, 109 S.Ct. 3040 (1989).

32. *Ohio v. Akron Center for Reproductive Health,* 493 U.S. 802, 110 S.Ct. 39 (1990); *Hodgson v. Minnesota,*497 U.S. 417, 1110 S.Ct. 2926 (1990).

33. *Planned Parenthood v. Casey,* 505 U.S. 833, 112 S.Ct. 2791 (1992).

34. *Stenberg v. Carhart,* 530 U.S. 914 120 S.Ct. 2597 (2000).

35. Kaye and Kanwischer, "Admissibility of Genetic Testing in Paternity Litigation: A Survey of State Statutes," *Family Law Quarterly* 22 (1988), p. 109. For representative cases dealing with rebuttal of the presumption of legitimacy, see *Scheland v. Chilldres,* 852 S.W.2d 791 (Arkansas, 1993); *In re M.C.,* 844 P.2d 1313 (Colorado App., 1992); *Miller v. Kirschner,* 225 Conn 185, 621 A.2d 1326 (Connecticut, 1993); *In re Cooper,* 608 N.E.2d 1386 (Indiana, 1993); *Jensen v. Runft,* 252 Kan. 76, 843 P.2d 191 (Kansas, 1992); *Johnson v. Van Blaricom,* 480 N.W.2d 138 (Minn. Ct. App., 1992); *In re Tamara B.,* 585 N.Y.S.2d 757, (New York, 1992).

36. *State v. Hogan,* 613 So.2d 681 (Louisiana, 1993).

37. Lance Williams, *San Francisco Examiner,* 11 January 1998.

38. *Gomez v. Perez,* 409 U.S. 535, 93 S.Ct. 872 (1990).

39. *Levy v. Louisiana,* 391 U.S. 69, 88 S.Ct. 1509 (1968).

40. *Weber v. Aetna Casualty,* 406 U.S. 164, 92 S.Ct. 1400 (1972).

41. The states that bar or severely limit the enforceability of surrogate contracts are Arizona, Indiana, Kentucky, Louisiana, Michigan, New York, and Utah. See *Idaho Law Review* 29 (1992–93), p. 383.

42. Section 801 Uniform Parentage Act (2000).

43. See Appendix 8 to the Uniform Parentage Act (2000) for a list of states that have statutes or case law allowing or disallowing gestation contracts.

44. Gina Kolata, "Clinics Selling Embryos Made for Adoption," *New York Times,* 23 November 1997.

45. Lisa M. Krieger, "Life on Ice: Frozen Embryos Proliferate," *San Francisco Examiner,* 9 May 1997.

46. Florida Statute § 63.042(3).

47. *Lofton v. Kearney,* 157 F.Supp.2d 1372 (S.D.Fla., 2001).

48. *Wisconsin v. Yoder,* 406 U.S. 205, 92 S.Ct. 1526 (1972); *Santosky v. Kramer,* 455 U.S. 745, 102 S.Ct. 1388 (1982).

49. See e.g., California Penal Code, § 272; *Williams v. Garcetti,* 5 Cal.4th 363, 853 P.2d 507, 20 Cal.Rptr.2d 341 (California, 1993); New York Penal Law, § 260.10(2); *People v. Scully,* 134 Misc.2d 906, 513 N.Y.S.2d 625 (New York, 1987); Kentucky Revised Statutes Ann. § 530.060(1).

50. *Restatement of the Law of Torts,* 2d edition (St. Paul, MN: American Law Institute Publishers, 1934), § 316.

51. *The Wall Street Journal* 28 September 1992.

52. In the following paragraphs there are a sprinkling of quotations, all of which, unless otherwise indicated, are from Jeremy Rifkin, *The Biotech Century* (New York: Tarcher/Putnam, 1998).

53. For a discussion of the Human Genome project see, Elizabeth Pennisi, "The Human Genome," *Science,* Feb 16, 2001, pp. 1177–1180.

54. "Cloned Pigs May Offer Humans Transplant Organs," Associated Press, Washington, D.C., 22 August 2002.

55. Nicholas Wade, Biotech Firm Touts Potential of Cow-Human Hybrid Cells," *New York Times,* 13 November 1998.

56. Rick Weiss, *Washington Post,* 19 May 1998.

57. William Wright, *Born That Way: Genes, Behavior, Personality* (New York: Knopf, 1998).

58. Theodore Roosevelt to Charles B. Davenport, January 1913, *Charles B. Davenport Papers,* Department of Genetics, Cold Spring Harbor, NY

59. Rifkin, *The Biotech Century,* 128.

60. Brian Macquarrie, *Boston Globe,* 5 September 1998.

61. James O. Hill, director of the Colorado Clinical Nutrition Research Unit at the University of Colorado, quoted by Associated Press, 15 June 1998.

62. *New York Times,* 18 January 1998.

63. The House passed H.R. 2505 (265-162), The bill criminalizes both therapeutic and reproductive cloning.

64. Two of the bills to follow are S 1899 and S 1758.

65. Human Fertilization and Embryology Act of 1990.

66. "Doctor Challenges UK Cloning Ban," CNN.com, 5 November 2001.

67. The distinctions and much of this paragraph's language are taken from http://www.religioustolerance.org/cloning.htm.

68. California Civil Code §§ 1714.1 & 3; Education Code § 48904; Government Code § 38772 & 53069.5, and Pend Code § 490.5.

69. *San Francisco Chronicle,* 18 June 1998.

70. Associated Press, 12 May 1998.

71. *San Francisco Chronicle,* 12 May 1997.

72. *National Law Journal,* 2 November 1998 and 9 November 1998.

73. *The National Law Journal,* 6 September 1993, 1A.

74. Andrea J. Sedlak, Ph.D., and Diane D. Broadhurst, M.L., "Executive Summary of The Third National Incidence Study of Child Abuse and Neglect," by the U.S. Department of Health and Human Services Administration for Children and Families; Administration on Children, Youth and Families; National Center on Child Abuse and Neglect (1996).

75. *Coy v. Iowa,* 487 U.S. 1012, 108 S.Ct. 2798 (1988).

76. *Maryland v. Craig,* 497 U.S. 836, 110 S.Ct. 3157 (1990).

77. *San Francisco Chronicle,* January 20, 1990, *Time,* August 6, 1990, p. 28.

78. The variance in numbers comes from a variance in studies. Philip A. May, Ph.D. and J. Phillip Gossage, Ph.D. "Estimating the Prevalence of Fetal Alcohol Syndrome." National Institute on Alcohol Abuse and Alcoholism (2002).

79. Gregg Aamot, Associated Press, 24 May 1998.

80. Judy Pasternak, *Los Angeles Times,* 4 May 1998.

81. Ga. Code Ann. Sec. 19-7-5(b)(3) (Supp. 1998).

82. *Family Law Quarterly* 20 (1987), p. 444.

83. *Time,* 1 October 1990.

84. *Time,* 18 August 1997.

85. Title 25, Arizona Revised Statutes, Chapter 7 (1998).

86. http://patriot.net/~crouch/artj/tvshow.html#anchor1530365.

87. *Hanson v. Hanson,* 404 N.W.2d 460 (North Dakota, 1987); *Renfro v. Renfro,* 848 P.2d 830 (Alaska, 1993).

88. *Orr v. Orr,* 440 U.S. 268, 99 S.Ct. 1102 (1979).

89. *Murphy v. Murphy,* 470 S.2d 1297 (Alabama, 1985); *In re the Marriage of Wilson.*

90. *Bliss v. Bliss,* 66 N.Y.2d 344, 497 N.Y.S.2d 344, 488 N.E.2d 90 (New York, 1985).

91. Alabama, California, Georgia, Illinois, Louisiana, Maryland, New York, Ohio, Pennsylvania, Tennessee, and Utah permit modification in such cases. See *The Family Law Quarterly* 23 (1990), p. 546.

92. In 1983, Illinois adopted Section 510(b) of its Marriage and Dissolution Act, which terminates alimony if the former spouse cohabits with another person.

93. Alaska (Statutes § 25-25.24.160(3)) , Florida (Statutes Annotated § 61-08), Kansas (Statutes Annotated § 60-1610(b)(2)), Louisiana (Civil Code, article 160), Maine (Revised Statutes Annotated § 19-721), Michigan (Compiled Laws Annotated § 552.23), Nevada (Revised Statutes Annotated § 125.150) , New Mexico (Statutes Annotated § 40-4-7), North Carolina (General Statutes § 50-16.1), Ohio (Revised Code § 3105.18), Oregon (Revised Statutes § 107-105), South Carolina (Code of Laws § 20-3-130), Virginia (Code § 20-107.1), West Virginia (Code § 48-2-15), and Wyoming (Statutes Annotated § 20-2-114. List compiled by Nolo Press.

94. New Mexico Statutes Chapter 40 Sec. 4-7.

95. *McCarty v. McCarty,* 453 U.S. 210, 101 S.Ct. 2728 (New York, 1981).

96. 10 U.S.C. 1409.

97. *McGowan v. McGowan,* 142 A.D.2d 355, 535 N.Y.S.2d 990 (New York, 1988).

98. *Dorton v. Dorton,* 77 N.C.App. 667, 336 S.E.2d 415 (North Carolina, 1986).

99. *Lovett v. Lovett,* 688 S.W.2d 329 (Kentucky, 1985).

100. See e.g., *In re Marriage of Aufmuth,* 89 Cal.App.3d 446, 152 Cal.Rptr. 668 (1979); *In re Marriage of Washburn,* 101 Wash.2d 168, 677 P.2d 152 (Washington, 1984); *Lowery v. Lowery,* 262 Ga. 20, 413 S.E.2d 73 (Georgia, 1992).

101. *Sorensen v. Sorensen,* 839 P.2d 774 (Utah, 1992).

102. *Guzman v. Guzman,* 827 S.W.2d 445 (Texas, 1992).

103. *In re Francis,* 442 N.W.2d 59 (Iowa, 1989); *Wilson v. Wilson,* 434 N.W.2d 742 (S. Dakota, 1989).

104. The case has continued in the courts for examples see *Wendt v. Wendt,* 757 A.2d 1225 (Conn.App., 2000) and back again in *Wendt v. Wendt,* 2001 WL (Conn.Super. 2001).

105. In Chapter 1 it was noted that some opinions are ordered "not published" and therefore cannot be used as legal precedent. This case was so ordered. Nonetheless, the case binds the parties and their preembryos. Also reported in *The National Law Journal,* 15 June 1992, p. A3.

106. *Aster v. Gross,* 7 Va.App. 1, 371 S.E.2d 833 (Virginia, 1988); but see *Pommerenke v. Pommerenke,* 7 Va.App. 241, 372 S.E.2d 630 (Virginia, 1988), where the court approved giving less than 10 percent of the assets to an adulterous wife.

107. See e.g., *Smith v. Smith,* 331 S.E.2d 682 (North Carolina, 1985).

108. *Bradley v. Bradley,* 336 S.E.2d 658 (North Carolina, 1985).

109. Charles H. Whitebread, "The Uniform Probate Code's Nod to the Partnership Theory of Marriage: The 1990 Elective Share Revisions," 11 *Probate Law Journal* 125 (1992), p. 134.

110. *In re marriage of Sullivan,* 37 Cal.3d 762, 691 P.2d 1020 (California, 1984).

111. Texas Family Code Annotated, § 3.63.

112. *Newberry v. Newberry,* 745 S.W.2d 796 (Missouri, 1988).

113. *Veazey v. Veazey,* 560 P.2d 382 (Alaska, 1977); *DeMontigny v. DeMontigny,* 70 Wis. 2d 131, 233 N.W.2d 463 (Wisconsin, 1975).

114. *Family Law Quarterly* 27 (Winter 1994), p. 503.

115. Paquin, "Protecting the Interests of Children in Divorce Proceedings," *The Journal of Family Law* 26 (1987–88), p. 303.

116. California Civil Code, § 4607.

117. *The National Law Journal,* 16 August 1993, p. 1.

118. 42 U.S.C. Section 666 (1988).

119. Public Law No. 102-521, 106 Stat. 3403, 18 U.S.C. 228 (1992).

120. *Greenwald v. Greenwald,* 154 Wis. 2d 767, 454 N.W.2d 34 (Wisconsin, 1990); *Pendleton v. Fireman,* 24 Cal.4th 39, 5 P.3d 839, 99 Cal.Rptr.2d 278, (Cal. 2000).

121. There are exceptions, however, where states have rejected the illegal-consideration (sexual favors) doctrine. See, e.g., *Latham v. Latham,* 547 P.2d 144 (Oregon, 1976) and *Cook v. Cook,* 142 Ariz. 573, 691 P.2d 664 (Arizona, 1984).

Chapter 10

1. Judy Crichton, *America 1900: The Turning Point* (New York: Henry Holt & Company, 1998), 262.

2. Ibid.

3. 15 U.S.C. 2301 et seq.

4. A "lemon" has been defined as "something or someone that proves to be unsatisfactory or undesirable: DUD, FAILURE . . ." *John v. John Deere Co.,* 306 N.W.2d 231 (South Dakota, 1981).

5. UCC §§ 2-601, 2-602, and 2-607.

6. UCC § 2-608(1)(b) and (2).

7. For examples of lemon laws see Arizona Rev. Stat. Ann. §§ 44-1261 to 1265; California Civil Code § 1793.2; Colorado Rev. Stat. §§ 42-12-101 to 107; Florida Stat. Ann. § 681.10-108; Illinois Rev. Stat. Ch. 121 1/2, § 1201-08, Indiana Code § 24-5-13-1 to 24; Kansas Stat. Ann. § 50-645; Michigan Comp. Laws Ann. § 257.1401; Minnesota Stat. Ann. § 325F.665; Ohio Rev. Code Ann. §§ 1345.71 to .77; Washington Revised Code §§ 19.118.010-070; N.Y. General Business Law § 198-a; and Wisconsin Stat. Ann. § 218.015.

8. A short but useful discussion of automobile leasing versus buying exists in the April 2001 issue of *Consumer Reports* pp. 21–22. A comparison of leasing versus purchasing has been included in the April Annual Auto issue for several years. [but not 2002!]

9. UCC § 2A-103 (e).

10. The original version of UCC Article 2A-103(e) provided for a maximum amount but in August 2002 the National Conference of Commissioners on Uniform Laws deleted the reference to a maximum. See "Legislative Note: Present Article 2A has a bracketed provision allowing States to insert a dollar cap on leases designated as consumer leases, amended Article 2 defines 'consumer contract' and does not include a dollar cap in the definition. Some States have not included a dollar cap in present Article 2A and States which have adopted a dollar cap have stated varying amounts. If a State wishes to include a dollar cap, the cap should be inserted here. Any cap probably should be set high enough to bring within the definition most automobile leasing transactions for personal, family, or household use." Amendment to Uniform Commercial Code Article 2a - Leases National Conference of Commissioners on Uniform State Laws, July 26–August 2, 2002.

11. Statement of Michael P. Jackson Deputy Secretary of Transportation before the Subcommittees on Telecommunications, Trade and Consumer Protection and Oversight and Investigation of the Committee on Energy and Commerce U. S: House of Representatives, 19 June 2001.

12. "88 Deaths Linked to Recalled Tires: Venezuelan Agency Wants Criminal Charges," *USA Today,* 1 September 2001. The difference in the numbers are deaths attributed to the tires in other countries.

13. *The Wall Street Journal,* 29 April 1994. In one of these cases, the trial court awarded the plaintiffs $105 million after a young man died in a fiery crash. The verdict was later overturned on appeal. *General Motors Corp. v. Moseley,* 447 S.E. 2d 302 (Georgia, 1994). The case was settled (along with three others) in 1995 for an undisclosed sum. *National Law Journal,* 25 September 1945, A6. The trial is the subject of a Court TV television program available to the professor from West Publishing for classroom use.

14. Based on the case of *Shimoda v. Bundy,* 142 P. 109 (California, 1914).

15. *Lee v. State,* 187 Kan. 566, 358 P.2d 765 (Kansas, 1961).

16. For example, see Calif. Vehicle Code § 17709, for 15/30/5 liability amounts.

17. See, for example, Calif. Civil Code § 1714.1.

18. *Lovett v. Hitchcock,* 192 Cal. App. 2d 806, 14 Cal. Rptr. 117 (California, 1961).

19. North Carolina General Statute § 90-21.14.

20. North Carolina General Statute § 90-21.14.

21. See *Ney v. Yellow Cab Co.,* 2 Ill.2d 74, 117 N.E.2d 74 (Illinois, 1954) and Hergenrether v. East, 61 Cal.2d 440, 393 P.2d 164, 39 Cal.Rptr. 4 (California, 1964).

22. *Sacramento Bee,* 21 February 1990.

23. *Wanna v. Miller,* 136 N.W.2d 563 (North Dakota, 1965).

24. *Coulter v. Superior Court,* 21 Cal.3d 144, 577 P.2d 669, 145 Cal.Rptr. 534 (California, 1978). This case, along with California's dramshop liability, was later abrogated by statute. See California Business and Professional Code § 25602 and Civil Code § 1714(C).

25. Some representative states with some form of guest statute are Alabama, Idaho, Indiana, Ohio, and Texas.

26. Idaho Code Title 49-§2415.

27. *Tisko v. Harrison,* 500 S.W.2d 565 (Texas, 1973).

28. D. Foley, *Stop DWI: Successful Community Responses to Drunk Driving,* (Lexington MA: Lexington Books, 1986).

29. "Traffic Safety Facts 2000," National Highway Traffic Safety Administration.

30. *Rath v. Bankston,* 101 Cal. App. 274 281 P. 1081 (California, 1929).

31. National Traffic and Motor Vehicle Safety Act of 1966, Title 15 § 1381 et seq.

32. "The Seat Belt Defense," *American Jurisprudence Trials* 35 p. 349.

33. California Business and Professional Code § 22325.

34. *Rathbun v. Ocean Accident & Guarantee Corporation,* 299 Ill. 562, 132 N.E. 754 (Illinois, 1921).

35. *McNeill v. Durham C. R. Co.,* 135 N.C. 682, 47 S.E. 765 (North Carolina, 1904).

36. A California jury held a bus company negligent for failure to equip buses with safety belts. *Greyhound Lines v. Superior Court,* 3 Cal. App. 3d 356, 83 Cal.Rptr. 343 (California, 1970).

37. *Lopez v. Southern California Rapid Transit Dist.,* 40 Cal.3d 780, 710 P.2d 907, 221 Cal.Rptr. 840 (California, 1985).

38. *Finken by Gutknecht v. Milwaukee County,* 120 Wis.2d 69, 353 N.W.2d 827 (Wisconsin, 1984).

39. *Insurance Facts* (New York: Insurance Information Institute, 1987), p. 104fn.

Chapter 11

1. Traxel, 1898: *The Birth of the American Century* (New York: Alfred A. Knopf, 1998), p. 21.

2. Ibid.

3. Judy Crichton, *America 1900* (New York: Henry Holt Co. 1998), p. 22.

4. Andy Furillo, "From Dreams to Decay," *Sacramento Bee,* 15 September 2002.

5. The first publicized application of the FCC rule occurred in 1988. Associated Press, Washington, 21 November 1998.

6. Charles Burress, *San Francisco Chronicle,* 2 January 1999. See California Civil Code § 1954.52 (C).

7. Public Law No. 100-430, 102 Statutes 1619 (1988) amending 42 U.S.C. § 3601-3619.

8. Unruh Civil Rights Act, California Civil Code, § 51 et. seq.

9. Sandra Tan "Landlords Blame Tenants, Demand More Accountability," *The Buffalo News,* 4 June 2002.

10. Uniform Residential Landlord and Tenant Act (URLTA). 12 Strict liability established by *Becker v. IRM Corp.,* 38 Cal.3d 454, 698 P.2d 116, 213 Cal.Rpt. 213 (California, 1985) and disapproved by *Peterson v. Superior Court,* 10 Cal.4th 1185, 899 P.2d 905, 43 Cal.Rptr.2d 836 (California, 1995).

11. In a similar case ten years after *Becker,* strict liability was disapproved. See *Peterson v. Superior Court,* 10 Cal.4th 1185, 899 P.2d 905, 43 Cal.Rptr.2d 836 (California, 1995).

12. See, e.g., Washington statutes, Landlord and Tenant, § 59.18.130.

13. See, e.g., *Yee v. Weiss,* 877 P.2d 510, 110 Nev. 657 (Nevada, 1994) and *Barton v. MTB Enterprises, Inc.,* 889 P.2d 476 (Utah App., 1995).

14. California Civil Code, § 1941.3.

15. Minnesota, Statutes, § 504 .183.

Chapter 12

1. From the New Hampshire Department of Justice Website http://www.state.nh.us/nhdoj/Consumer/mhp.html.

2. *Guimont v. Clarke,* 121 Wash.2d 586, 854 P.2d 1 (Washington, 1993).

3 New Hampshire Title XVIII Housing and Redevelopment Chapter 205—A Regulation pf Manufactured Housing Parks.

4. National Manufactured Housing Construction & Safety Standards Act of 1974, 42 U.S.C. § 5402 *et. seq.*

5. *The National Law Journal,* 8 February 1993, p. 20.

6. Kenneth R. Harney, "Homeowners Concierge Service Is Latest Thing," *San Francisco Examiner,* 31 January 1999.

7. California Civil Code, § 1102 *et. seq.*

8. *Skendzel v. Marshall,* 261 Ind. 226, 301 N.E.2d 641 (Indiana, 1973). A leading case on protecting buyers under installment-land contracts.

9. Todd Juchau, "Is 'Title Insurance' Insurance?" Thesis for Master's in Business Administration, California State University, Sacramento, 1994.

10. Nolo Press publishes books on self-help legal topics, including neighbor law. For information, visit their Web site at http://www.nolo.com.

11. Peoria, Illinois County Code, § 5-19.

12. Albany, California Municipal Ordinance, § 10-3.6.

13. *San Francisco Chronicle,* 3 May 1994.

14. See, e.g., California Civil Code, § 3346; Maine Revised Statutes Ann., Title 14, § 7552; Alabama Code, § 35-14-1.

15. Michigan Comp. Laws Ann., § 750.382, California Penal Code, § 384(a).

16. See, e.g., California Civil Code, § 841.4; Maine Revised Statutes, Title 17, § 280l; Massachusetts Gen. Laws Ann., § 49.21; Mich. Comp. Laws Ann., § 561.02; New Hampshire Rev. Stat. Ann., § 476.1; Rhode Island Gen. Laws, § 34-10-20, and Wisconsin Stat. Ann., § 844.10.

Chapter 13

1. Jon Krakauer, *Into Thin Air,* (New York: Villard, 1997).

2. Fair Labor Standards Act of 1938, 29 U.S.C. § 201 *et seq.* (AKA Wages and Hours Act). Similar legislation in many states governs intrastate commerce.

3. Civil Rights Act of 1964 (notably Title VII) as amended, 42 U.S.C. § 2000e *et seq.* There is similar legislation in most states governing intrastate commerce.

4. *McGowan v. Maryland,* 366 U.S. 420, 81 S.Ct. 1101 (1961) and *Braunffeld v. Brown,* 366 U.S. 599, 81 S.Ct. 1144 (1961).

5. Occupational Safety and Health Act of 1970, 29 U.S.C. § 651 *et seq.*

6. Fair Labor Standards Act of 1938, 29 U.S.C. § 201 *et seq.*

7. National Labor Relations Act of 1935, 29 U.S.C. § 151 *et seq.* (Wagner Act); and National Labor-Management Relations Act of 1947, 29 U.S.C. § 141 *et seq.* (Taft-Hartley Act).

8. Social Security Act of 1935, 42 U.S.C. § 301 *et seq.*

9. *Restatement of the Law of Agency* 2d, § 1.

10. *Sacramento Bee,* 18 September 1998.

11. P.L. Posner, Associate Director, General Accounting Office, quoted in *Insight,* 12 June 1989, 24.

12. See IRS Publication 926, "Household Employer's Tax Guide."

13. Civil Rights Act of 1964, 42 U.S.C. § 703(a)(l).

14. *International Brotherhood of Teamsters v. United States,* 431 U.S. 324, 97 S.Ct. 1843, (1977).

15. *United States v. Meyers,* 906 F.Supp. 1494 (Wyoming, 1995).

16. *Texas Department of Community Affairs v. Burdine,* 450 U.S. 248, 101 S.Ct. 1089 (1981), and *McDonnell Douglas Corp. v. Green,* 411 U.S. 792, 93 S.Ct. 1817 (1973).

17. 42 U.S.C.A. § 2000e-5(k). In the case of *Parton v. GTE North, Inc.,* 971 F2d 150 (8th Cir., 1992), an award of attorneys' fees under Title VII was upheld, even though the plaintiff was awarded only $1 in nominal damages for her claim of hostile environment sexual harassment.

18. *Christianburg Garment v. EEOC,* 434 US 412 (1978).

19. *EEOC v. Waffle House, Inc.,* 534 U.S. 279, 122 S.Ct. 754 (2002).

20. "EEOC Comments on Supreme Court Ruling in Waffle House Case," EEOC press release, 15 January 2002.

21. "Portrait of a Company Behaving Badly," *Time,* 16 March 1998.

22. Greg Winter, "Coca-Cola Settles Racial Bias Case," *New York Times* on the Web, November 17, 2000.

23. *Griggs v. Duke Power Co.,* 401 U.S. 424, 91 S.Ct. 849 (1971).

24. *Wards Cove Packing Company, Inc. v. Atonio,* 490 U.S. 642, 109 S. Ct. 2115 (1989).

25. *Watkins v. Scott Paper Co.,* 530 F.2d 1159, (11th Cir., 1976) cert. denied, 429 U.S. 861, 97 S.C. 163 (1976).

26. 29 U.S.C. § 1802.

27. *Odima v. Westin Tucson Hotel,* 53 F.3d 1484 (9th cir., 1995).

28. "ADC, ACLU File Lawsuits against United, Continental, American Airlines," American-Arab Anti-Discrimination Committee press release, 4 June 2002; Alexandra Marks, "Neew Lawsuits Aim to Curb Racism Aboard Airplanes," *Christian Science Monitor,* 5 June 2002.

29. *Mann v. Frank,* 7 F.3d 1365, 1370 (8th Cir., 1993).

30. *Ansonia Bd. of Educ. v. Philbrook,* 479 U.S. 60, 67, 107 S.Ct. 367 (1986).

31. *Silo v. CHW Medical Foundation,* 27 Col. 4th 1097, 119 Cal.Rptr.2d 698 (California, 2002). Note, however, that this case deals with a comparable state law rather than the Civil Rights Act.

32. *Independent Union of Flight Attendants v. Pan American World Airways, Inc.,* Case #84-4600, Federal District Court, San Francisco, Nov. 27, 1989.

33. EEOC Guidelines for Sexual Harassment.

34. *Weeks v. Baker & McKenzie,* 63 Cal.App.4th 1128, 74 Cal.Rptr.2d 510 (California, 1998). For additional information, see *National Law Journal,* 12 September 1999, A4 (col. 1); *National Law Journal,* 14 November 1994, A4

(col. 1); *National Law Journal,* 18 May 1998, A5 (col.1); and *National Law Journal,* 14 September 1998, A4 (col. 2).

35. *Cotran v. Rollins Hudig Hall Int'l Inc.,* 17 Cal.4th 93, 948 P.2d 412, (California, 1998).

36. *Newport News Shipbuilding & Dry Dock Co. v. EEOC,* 462 U.S. 669, 103 S.Ct. 262, (1983).

37. Institute for Women's Policy Research, "The Status of Women in the States," 2nd ed. 1998–99, http://www.iwpr.org/.

38. Age Discrimination in Employment Act of 1967, an Amendment of Title VII of the Civil Rights Act of 1964, 29 U.S.C. § 630(b).

39. 29 U.S.C. § 630(f).

40. 29 U.S.C. § 631(c).

41. 29 U.S.C. § 623.

42. *United Steelworkers of America v. Weber,* 444 U.S. 889, 99 S.Ct. 2721 (1979).

43. Civil Rights Act of 1991 Sec. 13.

44. *The Coalition for Economic Equity v. Wilson,* 122 F.3d 692 (9th cir., 1997), Cert. Denied 522 U.S.963, 118 S.Ct. 397 (1997).

45. *Hopwood v. State of Tex.,* 999 F.Supp. 872 (W.D.Tex., 1998), *Hopwood v. State of Texas,* 236 F.3d 256(C.A.5 Tex., 2000), *Texas v. Hopwood,* 533 U.S. 929, 121 S.Ct. 2550 (2001).

46. *Gratz v. Bollinger* and the 6th circuit opinion citation is *Gutter v. Bollinger,* 288 F.3d 732 (6th cir., 2002).

47. Employment Opportunity Commission "The ADA: Questions and Answers," http://www.eeoc.gov/facts/adaqa1.html.

48. http://www.eeoc.gov/facts/qanda.html.

49. 42 U.S.C. § 12114(a), (b), and (c); *Salley v. Circuit City Stores, Inc.,* 160 F.3d 977 (3rd Cir., 1998).

50. *Chevron USA, Inc. v. Echazabel,* 536 U.S. 73, 122 S.Ct. 2045 (2002).

51. Equal Employment Opportunity Commission, http://www.eeoc.gov.

52. *Douglas v. Aztec Petroleum Corp.,* 695 S.W.2d 312 (Texas, 1985).

53. Lewis Maltby, Director of the American Civil Liberties Union National Task Force on Civil Liberties in the Work Place, the *National Law Journal,* 14 October 1991, p. 1.

54. Occupational Safety and Health Association, "OSHA Vital Facts 1997."

55. OSHA Region 2 News Release: NY 225, 8 December 1998.

56. Social Security Act of 1935.

57. Employment Retirement Income Security Act (ERISA), 29 U.S.C. § 1001 *et seq.*

58. Pension Benefit Guaranty Corp., http://www.pbgc.gov/

59. Durango pension plan may also be found on the Trusteed Plans Info section of the PBGC Web site, http://www.pbgc.gov.

60. James T; Madore, "Enron Employees See 401(k)s Wiped Out," Newsday, November 30, 2001 Pg. A75; Paul Katzeff, "401(k) Reform Compromise Is Likely Next Step: Senate Action Leading D.C. Bills Similar on Diversification, Differ on Lockdown-Period Rules," *Investor's Business Daily,* 15 May 2002; David Nicklaus, "Many 401(k)s Took the Gas When Enron Stock Hit Bottom," St. Louis Post-Dispatch, 1 December 2001, Saturday Five Star Lift Edition.

61. *Douglas v. E.G. Baldwin & Associates,* 150 F.3d 604 (6th cir., 1998).

62. *Rebel v. Unemployment Compensation Board of Review,* 555 Pa. 114, 723 A.2d 156 (Penn., 1988).

63. *Smyth v. The Pillsbury Co.,* 914 F.Supp. 97 (E.D. Pennsylvania, 1996).

64. *Commonwealth v. Pullis* (Philadelphia Cordwainers Case). Philadelphia Mayor's Court, 3 Commons and Gilmore (1806).

65. *Commonwealth v. Hunt,* 45 Mass. (4 Met.) 111, 38 Am. Dec. 316 (1842).

66. *Thornhill v. Alabama,* 310 U.S. 88, 60 S. Ct. 736 (1940) and *Frisby v. Schultz,* 487 U.S. 474, 108 S.Ct. 2495 (1988).

67. Anti-Injunction Act of 1932, 29 U.S.C. § 101 *et seq.*

68. National Labor Relations Act of 1935, 29 U.S.C. § 151 *et seq.*

69. National Labor-Management Relations Act of 1947, 29 U.S.C. §§ 141-197.

70. Labor-Management Reporting and Disclosure Act of 1959, 29 U.S.C. § 401 *et seq.*

71. Labor statistics can be found on-line at http://stats.bls.gov/data/home.htm.

72. *NLRB v. Fansteel Metallurgical Corporation,* 306 U.S. 240, 59 S.Ct. 490 (1939).

73. Examples of cases denying arbitration include *Prudential Ins. Co. of America v. Lai,* 42 F.3d 1299 (9th cir., 1994); and *Renteria v. Prudential Ins. Co. of America,* 113 F.3d 1104 (9th cir., 1997). Examples of cases upholding arbitration include *Cole v. Burns Int'l. Security Serv.,* 105 F.3d 1465, (D.C. cir., 1997); *Brookwood v. Bank of America* 45 Cal.App.4th 1667, 53 Cal.Rptr.2d 515 (California, 1996); and *Piper Funds v. Piper Cap. Mgmt.,* 71 F.3d 298 (8th cir., 1995).

74. Statement by the American Arbitration Association, http://www.adr.org/.

75. *Circuit City Stores v. Adams,* 532 U.S. 105, 121 S.Ct 1302 (2001).

76. *EEOC v. Waffle House, Inc.,* 534 U.S 279, 122 S.Ct. 754 (2002).

77. *Circuit City Stores v. Adams,* 279 F.3d 889 (Ca. 9th, 2002) Cert. denied 122 S.Ct. 2329 (2002).

78. *Cole v. Burns Int'l Security Services,* 105 F.3d 1465, 1482 (D.C. Cir. 1997).

Chapter 14

1. *Washington v. Glucksberg,* 521 U.S. 702, 117 S.Ct. 2258, (1997).

2. Internal Revenue Code, § 26 U.S.C. 2001.

3. *San Francisco Chronicle,* 17 March 1989.

4. Colorado Statutes §§ 15-11-503 and Calif. Probate Code § 6111.

5. Dear Abby, *San Francisco Chronicle,* 19 June 1989.

6. *Stone v. Stephens,* 155 Ohio St. 595, 99 N.E.2d 766 (Ohio, 1951).

7. *The Guide to American Law,* Supplement 1991 (St. Paul, Minn: West Publishing, 1991), 405.

8. T. Zickefoose, "Videotaped Wills: Ready for Primetime," *Probate Law Journal* 9 (1989), p. 139.

9. "Probate Texas Style," *National Law Journal,* 22 May 1989.

10. Calif. Probate Code § 10800.

11. Dave Kindred "Ted Williams Saga: A Cryonic Shame," Sporting News .Com 22 July 2002, and similar articles.

12. The Uniform Probate Code locator can be found at http://www.law.cornell.edu/uniform/probate.html.

13. For example see Montana Code Annotated § 72-2-523.

14. Forms and individual state requirements are available from Partnership for Caring, 475 Riverside Drive, Suite 1852, New York, NY 10115, http://www.partnership forcaring.org/.

15. PL 101-508, 42 U.S.C. § 1395cc(a)(1).

16. Forms and individual state requirements are available from Partnership for Caring, 475 Riverside Drive, Suite 1852, New York, NY 10115. http://www.partnershipforcaring.org/.

17. Ore. Rev. Stat. § § 127.800 *et seq.* http://detroitsuburbs.miningco.com/library/weekly/aa020298.htm. See *Lee v. Oregon,* 107 F.3d 1382 (9th Cir., 1997), for a discussion of early litigation to stop operative use of the act.

18. http://www.ord.uscourts.gov/rulings/01-1647Opinion.pdf.

19. Also see *Vacco, Attorney General of New York et al. v. Quill et al.,* 521 U.S. 793 S.Ct. 2293, 117 S.Ct. 2293 (1997).

20. *Wash. Rev. Code* § 70.122.070(1).

21. *Washington et al. v. Glucksberg et al.*

22. *Idem.*

23. Alaska H. B. 371 (1996); Ariz. S. B. 1007 (1996); Cal. A. B. 1080, A. B. 1310 (1995); Colo. H. B. 1185 (1996); Colo. H. B. 1308 (1995); Conn. H. B. 6298 (1995); Ill. H. B. 691, S. B. 948 (1997); Iowa Code Ann. §§ 707A.2, 707A.3 (Supp. 1997); Me. H. P. 663 (1997); Me. H. P. 552 (1995); Md. H. B. 474 (1996); Md. H. B. 933 (1995); Mass. H. B. 3173 (1995); Mich. H. B. 6205 (1996); Mich. S. B. 556 (1996); Mich. H. B. 4134 (1995); Miss. H. B. 1023 (1996); N. H. H. B. 339 (1995); N. M. S. B. 446 (1995); N. Y. S. B. 5024 (1995); N. Y. A. B. 6333 (1995); Neb. L. B. 406 (1997); Neb. L. B. 1259 (1996); R. I. Gen. Laws §§ 11-60-1, 11-60-3 (Supp. 1996); Vt. H. B. 109 (1997); Vt. H. B. 335 (1995); Wash. S. B. 5596 (1995); Wis. A. B. 174, S. B. 90 (1995); Senate of Canada, Of Life and Death, Report of the Special Senate Committee on Euthanasia and Assisted Suicide A-156 (June 1995) (describing unsuccessful proposals, between 1991-1994, to legalize assisted suicide). Also, on April 30, 1997, President Clinton signed the Federal Assisted Suicide Funding Restriction Act of 1997, which prohibits the use of federal funds in support of physician assisted suicide. Pub. L. 105-12, 111 Stat. 23 (codified at 42 U.S.C. § 14401 *et seq*).

24. Judy Crichton, *America 1900: The Turning Point* (New York: Henry Holt and Company, 1998), 64.

25. Internal Revenue Code, 26 U.S.C. § 671-677.

26. Internal Revenue Code, 26 U.S.C. §§ 2631 and 2601 *et seq.*

Appendix C

1. Modified by the Sixteenth Amendment.

2. Modified by the Fourteenth Amendment.

3. Repealed by the Seventeenth Amendment.

4. Modified by the Seventeenth Amendment.

5. Changed by the Twentieth Amendment.

6. Modified by the Twenty-seventh Amendment.

7. Modified by the Sixteenth Amendment.

8. Changed by the Twelfth Amendment.

9. Changed by the Twenty-fifth Amendment.

10. Modified by the Eleventh Amendment.

11. Affected by the Thirteenth Amendment.

12. The first ten amendments were passed by Congress on September 15, 1789, and were ratified on December 15, 1791. Collectively they are referred to as the Bill of Rights.

13. Changed by the Twentieth Amendment.

14. Changed by the Twenty-sixth Amendment.

15. Ibid.

16. Modified by the Twenty-seventh Amendment.

A and B trust

A husband-and-wife trust wherein after the first spouse dies, the surviving spouse receives a life interest in the trust property, and someone else (the designated beneficiary) has a remainder interest. An A and B trust is also called a *marital life estate trust.*

abandoned property

Property discarded by the true owner, who has no intention of reclaiming the property.

abandonment

When a tenant leaves rented premises with no intent to return or honor legal obligations under the lease.

abatement

Temporary suspension of a tenant's duty to pay rent because the rented premises have become uninhabitable.

abettor

One who encourages, incites, persuades, or sets another on to commit a crime. Also called an *aider.*

abortion, illegal

Termination of a human pregnancy in a manner that violates the law of the state in which it occurs (for example, during the minority of the female without prior notification to one or more of her parents or, in the alternative, without the consent of a judge).

abortion, legal

Termination of a human pregnancy in conformity with the law of the state in which it occurs (for example, by a licensed physician during the first trimester, i.e., three months from conception).

absolute liability

A theory of liability in which the victim need not prove negligence or wrongful intent.

absolute privilege

A total right under the law to do or not do some act.

absolute privilege to defame

Total protection from liability for defamation. Legislators enjoy it for statements made during official sessions, and judges and others enjoy it during judicial proceedings. See also "conditional (or qualified) privilege to defame."

abstract of title

A chronological history of recorded documents that affect the title to a parcel of real property.

acceleration clause

A clause in a note that declares the unpaid balance of the loan to be immediately due and payable upon the occurrence of any of a number of specified events called "events of default." Typical events that will accelerate a mortgage loan are sale of the home, default in monthly payments, or failure to maintain casualty insurance. See also "right of reinstatement."

acceptance

Affirmative response to the terms of an offer, creating a contract. See also "offer."

accession

"Adding on" to the value of personal property by either labor or materials.

accessories after the fact

Persons who harbor, conceal, or otherwise voluntarily and intentionally aid a known perpetrator of a crime to escape arrest or punishment. They are guilty of criminal conduct, but not of the perpetrator's crime.

accessories before the fact

Persons who encourage or assist a perpetrator of a crime—for example, by planning, advising, or standing guard during its commission. They are as guilty as the perpetrator (principal), but in some states to a lesser degree and with lesser punishment.

accessory

A person who, though not present at the scene of a crime, aided and abetted the principal in its commission. In some states, an accessory is any person who, though not present at the scene of the crime, aided the perpetrator in escaping apprehension.

accident

A sudden, unexpected, unintended happening that causes injury and/or death and/or loss of property. Depending on the circumstances, legal fault may or may not exist.

accomplice

A person who, in cooperation with the principal offender, is associated in a crime before, during, or after its commission. An accomplice is also called an *aider and abettor.* See "aid and abet."

accord and satisfaction

A party agrees (by accord) to accept some substitute for the promised performance of a contract, which is then provided (the satisfaction).

accusation

Formal commencement of a criminal case by a specified public official such as a district attorney or by a grand jury.

accusatory pleading

A document specifying the crime committed and accusing the defendant of its commission.

acquitted

Found not guilty of a crime by judgment of the court following a jury verdict, or by a judge's decision if there is no jury.

actual cause (or causation)

An element of negligence meaning that the negligent person's carelessness is the reason for the loss by the victim; in other words, when injury to person or property results from the tortfeasor's action or failure to act.

ademption

Without revocation, the elimination of a specific gift of property listed in a will because it no longer exists (e.g., a diamond ring is lost, stolen, or destroyed) or because it is transferred in life to the named beneficiary or to someone else.

adhesion contract

A contract drafted by a dominant party and then presented to the other party—the adhering party—on a "take it or leave it" basis.

adjudicate

To hear and decide a dispute in a judicial action or court proceeding.

adjustable-rate mortgage

See "variable-interest-rate mortgage (VIRM)."

administrative agencies

Collectively, sub-branches of the executive branch of federal, state, and local governments. Administrative agencies may possess legislative, executive, and judicial powers in specialized technical areas where appropriate regulation requires action by experts.

administrative hearing

An oral proceeding before an administrative agency to hear and decide some factual question related to agency action.

administrative law

The body of law concerned with the power of administrative agencies. Administrative law consists of rules, regulations, orders, and adjudications. Also the composite body of substantive law created by the various administrative agencies in the performance of their assigned tasks.

administrative law judge

A government employee appointed to hear and decide matters in administrative agency hearings.

Administrative Procedure Act (APA) of 1946

Law that mandates procedures for federal administrative agencies.

administrative process

The administration of law by nonjudicial government agencies.

administrator

A person appointed by a court to supervise disposition of the estate of a decedent who dies without leaving a valid will (i.e., intestate).

ADR

See "alternative dispute resolution (ADR)."

adultery

Sexual intercourse by a married person with someone other than his or her spouse.

advance directive

A general term describing the instructions prepared in advance of a life-threatening condition as to what care should be given or not given in the event of incapacitation (*incapacitation* being the lack of legal capacity to make important decisions). The most common advance directives are called *living wills, directives to physicians, durable powers of attorney,* and *durable powers of attorney for health-care decisions.*

adversary system

The jurisprudential system in which the parties to a legal dispute are opponents. Their attorneys advocate a great variety of theories of benefit to the cause of their clients both before and during the trial, and on any appeal. This system is thought by many to be the best method of eliciting the truth and producing a just result. The judge acts as an independent magistrate rather than prosecutor, as found in many foreign countries that have an inquisitorial system (which see).

adverse possession

The creation of ownership of real property through its possession for a prescribed number of years without the consent of its owner.

affidavit

A signed written statement of facts, confirmed by oath or affirmation of the signer, before a person authorized to administer such oath (e.g., a notary public).

affirmative action

Policies and practices designed to assure employment of women and of minorities until their percentages in the work force approximate their percentages in the community.

affirmative action employment programs

Programs requiring that preference in hiring be given to some statutorily protected group.

affirmed

The confirmation of a lower court's judgment or order because the prior decision is deemed to be correct and free from prejudicial error.

Age Discrimination in Employment Act of 1967

Federal law that added "advanced age" (over age 40) to attributes listed in the Civil Rights Act of 1964 that may not be used negatively in employment decisions.

agency

Relationship in which, by mutual consent, an employee (the agent) is authorized to represent and bind an employer (the principal) in business dealings with third parties. An agent is a fiduciary of the principal.

agency shop

A company or department in which all employees in the bargaining unit must pay union dues (or some comparable fee) irrespective of whether they are union members.

agent

A person employed by a principal to deal with third parties and to make contracts binding the principal to the third parties. An agent is a fiduciary of the principal.

aid and abet

To help or assist another in committing a crime or tort.

alimony

Maintenance payment by one spouse to the other spouse following dissolution of their marriage. Alimony may be rehabilitative (terminates at a specified time) or permanent (indefinite in duration). Alimony is also called *maintenance*.

allegations of fact

Plaintiff's statement of alleged facts, contained in the complaint that serves to commence a civil action.

alternative dispute resolution (ADR)

Term that describes various methods of resolving disputes through means other than the judicial process.

amenities

Features that increase the attractiveness or value of real estate.

American Arbitration Association (AAA)

Private nonprofit organization organized to provide education, training, and administrative assistance to parties who use nonjudicial methods—that is, alternative dispute resolution (ADR)—for resolving disputes.

American Land Title Association insurance policy

A standardized form of extended title insurance coverage that is more comprehensive than the customary policy.

Americans with Disabilities Act (ADA) of 1990

Federal law that bars discrimination in the employment of capable handicapped persons by both private and public employers, and that requires reasonable accommodations for their special needs.

amicus curiae

[Latin for "friend of the court"] One—not a party to a lawsuit—who submits a brief containing arguments in favor of the position of the plaintiff or the defendant. An *amicus curiae* usually appears only at the appellate level when a case has generated broad public interest.

amnesty

Action by a legislature or chief executive to abolish and legally forget a specified offense, generally of a political nature such as alleged treason or desertion by a large group. Contrasted to a *pardon,* which remits or abates punishment imposed on an individual, generally for a felony.

amortization

Repayment of a note secured by mortgage through agreed-upon monthly payments of principal and interest over the life of the loan. A mortgage loan amortizes very slowly during the early years of its term because most of each monthly payment represents interest on the borrowed money. As the unpaid balance decreases, however, an increasing percentage of each monthly payment is used to reduce the principal (because less interest is due on the declining principal), and amortization of the debt thus accelerates.

annualized percentage rate (APR)

The rate of interest a borrower is paying to a mortgage lender when points and lender's fees are considered as interest rather than mere expenses of the transaction. Thus, the contract rate of interest (stated in the note) is always less than the APR, which computationally spreads several one-time charges, such as points, over the life of the loan and recomputes that stated interest rate. This consumer protection device also informs consumers of the true annual costs of loans or credit transactions (e.g., 1.5 percent a month is realistically 18 percent a year).

annulment

A court decree canceling a marriage because of some defect that existed when the marriage was entered. An annulment states that no valid marriage ever existed, whereas a divorce or dissolution terminates a valid marriage.

answer

A document containing a defendant's allegations of fact. It is filed by the defendant, with the clerk of the court, after receiving a summons and complaint. A copy is given to the plaintiff (or the plaintiff's lawyer).

antenuptial agreement

A contract whereby two persons who are contemplating marriage specify certain future mutual rights and obligations as marriage partners. For example, persons entering marriage might specify how they will divide listed assets if a divorce occurs. These binding contracts are also called *premarital agreements* or *prenuptial agreements*.

anti-deficiency law

A state law protecting a homeowner from payment of any deficiency (or unpaid balance) if a mortgage foreclosure sale fails to produce sufficient money to satisfy the underlying debt in full. It applies only to a purchase-money mortgage incurred to buy the home.

Anti-Injunction Act of 1932 (Norris-LaGuardia Act)

Federal law that restricts the issuance of injunctions in labor disputes, outlaws yellow-dog contracts, and exempts unions from legal attack as monopolies.

appeal

Formal request to a higher court to review any action of a lower court.

appellant

The party who appeals to a higher court for review of lower court rulings.

appellate court

Court that reviews decisions of prior courts for substantive and procedural correctness. The court has authority to affirm, modify, or reverse rulings of the lower court. Also known as an *appeals court.*

appellee

The party, on appeal, who defends the earlier court determination. Also called the *respondent.*

appraisal

Professional expert's opinion or estimate of the value of real or personal property.

appraised value

Opinion of a real estate expert "professional appraiser" of the fair market value of property, usually stated in a formal writing.

APR

See "annualized percentage rate (APR)."

arbitrary and capricious

Action taken impulsively or in bad faith and without good or valid reason.

arbitration

Alternative to litigation whereby conflicting parties select a neutral third party (or parties) to hear and decide their dispute. Arbitration can be binding or nonbinding. See also "court-annexed arbitration."

arbitrator

A private person selected by parties in conflict to hear and decide their dispute. Arbitrators are usually selected because of their expertise in the subject area of the dispute.

armed robbery

Robbery committed with the use of a lethal weapon, such as a gun or a knife.

arraignment

The formal charging in a court of law of a person accused of a crime. In this criminal court proceeding, following arrest, the charge is read to the accused. He or she is advised of constitutional rights and must enter a plea (e.g., guilty, not guilty, nolo contendere, not guilty by reason of insanity).

arrest

To take a person into custody in order to charge him or her with commission of a crime. An arrest may be made with or without a warrant, depending on the circumstances.

arson

The intentional and malicious burning of a building or other property for unlawful purposes.

articles of incorporation

Document that, minimally, states the name, address (for service of legal process), purpose(s), and capital structure of a proposed profit-seeking corporation. When dated and signed by the incorporator(s), it is filed in the proper state office, at which moment the corporation comes into existence.

as is

Property sold without warranty as to quality or condition.

assault, civil

The tort of creating apprehension in the mind of the victim that he or she is about to be touched in a harmful or offensive way. There is no requirement that the actor have the present ability to inflict actual harm.

assault, criminal

The crime of unlawful attempt, coupled with present ability, to commit a battery. There is no touching required in an assault.

assessed value

The value assigned to real property by a local official called an *assessor* for the purpose of levying a property tax. In some states, the assessed value is a designated fraction (e.g., one-fourth) of the appraised or full cash value.

asset

Anything of value that is owned. An asset is distinguished from a *liability,* which is indebtedness.

assigned risk

A high-risk applicant seeking automobile liability insurance who is rejected by an insurance company and is then directed, by random rotating choice, to a designated insurer from a pool that includes all insurers in the state. Minimal coverage must be provided, although higher premiums are usually charged.

assignment

(a) The transfer of some or all rights under a contract to another person. (b) The transfer by a tenant of his or her leasehold interest for its unexpired time. See also "sublease."

assumption fee

A one-time charge made by the lender of an existing mortgage loan for accepting a new debtor (usually a buyer who has agreed to take over, or assume, the unpaid balance of the seller's existing loan). The fee, which is agreed upon in the note, often is six months' interest— a substantial amount.

assumption of loan

An agreement by one person (usually a buyer) to *assume* (i.e., take upon himself or herself) all the obligations of an existing loan of another person (usually the seller). In periods of rising interest rates, it is sometimes desirable for a buyer to assume an existing loan on a house to be purchased rather than to obtain new financing at a higher interest rate.

assumption of risk

When a plaintiff with knowledge of the facts of a dangerous condition voluntarily exposes himself or herself to the particular risk of injury.

attempt

Intention of the accused to commit a crime and a substantial step toward its commission. This is a crime in itself. However, evil thought and even simple preparation are not enough to constitute an attempt—a substantial step toward the crime must be taken. If the crime is completed, the attempt "merges" into the crime.

attestation

The act of witnessing the signing of a document and thereafter signing, as evidence that you have witnessed it.

attorney at law

A person licensed to practice law, and usually called a *lawyer, attorney, counsel,* or *counselor.* In England such a person is called a *solicitor,* or a *barrister* if engaged in conducting trials.

attorney–client privilege

The right of a client to keep communications with his or her attorney confidential and free from disclosure.

attractive-nuisance doctrine

The doctrine under which minors who trespass may collect damages if attracted onto the defendant's premises where they are injured by a manmade instrumentality that has special appeal to children (such as a railroad turntable or an unfenced swimming pool).

at will

A term used, for example, to indicate that an employment contract may be terminated at any time by either the employee or the employer without any liability (beyond payment for services rendered up to the time of departure or discharge).

auction sale

Public sale in which an auctioneer solicits offers, or bids; normally the goods are sold to the highest bidder.

automated teller machine (ATM)

Machine that allows bank customers to transact certain business without the direct help of bank employees. ATMs receive deposits, dispense funds from checking and savings accounts, make credit card advances, and receive payments.

automobile insurance

Insurance against hazards flowing directly from the ownership and operation of motor vehicles.

automobile medical payments coverage

Automobile insurance that pays the medical expenses of the insured and of other occupants of the insured's vehicle who are injured in an accident, regardless of who caused the accident.

award

The final decision of an arbitrator or other nonjudicial officer in the resolution of a dispute.

bad faith

The deliberate failure to fulfill some duty or contractual obligation owed to another (e.g., a purposeful failure by an insurance company to pay a lawful claim).

bail

Security posted with the court to assure that the accused, if released before trial, will voluntarily return for further criminal proceedings.

bail bond

A document signed by both the accused and a bail bondsman, binding the bail bondsman to pay a specified sum of money to the state if the accused fails to appear in court as directed.

bailee

One who rightfully receives temporary possession of personal property from another, the bailor, in a bailment.

bailment

A delivery of personal property to another by which that person has the right to temporary possession. Often, though not always, bailment is created by contract.

bailor

One who transfers temporary possession of personal property to another, the bailee.

balloon payment

The unpaid balance of a mortgage loan due in one payment at the end of an agreed-upon period of time. A loan might require interest-only payments for three years and then a balloon payment of the entire amount of principal originally borrowed.

bankruptcy

Proceedings under federal law whereby all assets of a debtor (excluding certain exempt property) are distributed to his or her creditors. The debtor is then "discharged," or excused from the legal obligation to pay most of the debts. See also "Chapter 7 bankruptcy," "Chapter 11 reorganization," and "Chapter 13 adjustment of debts."

bar association

A professional organization of attorneys who are licensed to practice law.

bar examination

Test given to otherwise qualified lawyer candidates (generally law school graduates), the purpose of which is to assure possession of minimum standards of knowledge of the law before engaging in its practice.

bargaining unit

The department of a company, or other group of employees, that is deemed appropriate (by the National Labor Relations Board) for collective-bargaining purposes, based on common or related skills and duties.

battery

Any harmful or offensive touching of another human being without excuse or consent. Usually (but not necessarily) battery involves violent infliction of injury.

beneficiary

(a) The person designated by the insured to receive the proceeds of an insurance policy. (b) The person (also called a donee) designated by the settlor (or testator or donor) to receive the benefit of property in a trust. (c) A third party who receives the benefit of a contract between two other persons. (d) The creditor under a deed of trust.

benefit of the bargain

The respective consideration that each party in a contractual agreement is entitled to receive.

bequest

A gift of personal property by will. See "devise."

Better Business Bureau

A voluntary private agency, sponsored by the Chamber of Commerce, whose purpose is to encourage ethical business practice and to inform consumers of fraudulent sales schemes.

beyond a reasonable doubt

A term applied in a criminal trial to a quantum of evidence that fully satisfies and entirely convinces the jury that the defendant is guilty as charged.

bias

A preconceived belief about some person or fact that makes it difficult to be neutral, dispassionate, or fair in evaluating that person's rights and duties, guilt or innocence.

bigamy

The crime of willfully and knowingly contracting a second marriage while still lawfully married to another spouse.

bilateral contract

Agreement in which both parties exchange binding promises.

bilateral mistake

See "mutual mistake."

bill of attainder

Act of the legislature inflicting capital punishment upon a named person or member of a specific group without trial and conviction. Such a law is forbidden by the U.S. Constitution.

Bill of Rights

The first ten amendments to the U.S. Constitution.

blackmail

Obtaining property through the use of either oral or written threats.

blight

An extremely adverse condition affecting the value of real property such as disrepair or garbage in the yard.

blue-collar crime

Crimes committed by persons of comparatively lower social status and economic wealth, often involving violence (such as robbery and battery), in contrast to white-collar crimes such as income tax evasion and fraudulent sales practices.

blue laws

Statutes that regulate or prohibit commercial activities and amusements on Sundays.

blue sky laws

Statutes that regulate the sale of corporate securities. They seek to prevent fraudulent promotion and sale of highly speculative or worthless stock and other securities.

board of directors

A group of usually three or more persons elected by the stockholders to set basic company policies and to appoint the top executives who actively manage a business corporation. The board also declares dividends, to distribute profits to stockholders.

bodily injury and property damage insurance

Automobile insurance that protects against the risk of liability for injuring or killing another or damaging her/his property as a result of negligence.

bona fide occupational qualification (BFOQ)

Selection criteria that serve a legitimate business interest, which is justified although the selection has a discriminatory impact.

bond

(a) A written obligation to pay a sum of money upon the happening of a specified event. (b) A written promise by a borrower to pay a lender a fixed sum of interest for a prescribed time, and to repay the principal of a loan on a stated date. (If payable within a year, it may be referred to as a *promissory note*.)

booking

Administrative practice that occurs when an arrested person is brought to a police station following arrest but before incarceration in jail. Booking typically includes recording of name, address, and alleged crime, as well as fingerprinting, photographing, and blood testing for alcohol.

breach of contract

Failure without legal excuse to perform a promise made in a legally binding agreement.

breach of legal duty

Failure to act as an ordinary prudent person is required by law to act, under the given circumstances.

briefs

Written arguments addressed to the appellate court by counsel for appellant and by counsel for appellee, including points of law and what they claim to be authoritative case support for their respective positions.

broker, real estate

A person licensed by the state to engage in the business of negotiating the buying and selling of real property, and to employ licensed real estate sales agents to assist in this business.

burden of proof

The duty to produce evidence as a trial progresses. In a civil case, alleged facts must be proved by a preponderance of the evidence. In a criminal case, the required measure of proof is that alleged guilt must be proved beyond a reasonable doubt and to a moral certainty.

burglary

The crime of unlawfully entering premises, structures, and vehicles with intent to commit larceny (theft) or any other felony.

business invitee

A person who is expressly or impliedly invited onto the premises by the occupier of land for business purposes designed to produce a profit.

busing

Compulsory movement of children by bus to particular public schools to achieve a higher level of racial integration. Less controversial purposes include safety of the children and economy in the utilization of facilities.

but-for test

A test to determine causation in negligence by asking, "But for" the defendant's negligence, would the accident have occurred?

buy-and-sell agreement

A contract under which business partners (or stockholders in a closely held corporation) reciprocally agree to sell and buy their interests in the firm to the remaining member(s) upon the death or disability of any one of the owners.

bylaws

Private rules for the internal government of a business corporation. Normally adopted by the board of directors of the corporation.

cancellation (of contract)

Termination of a contract by a buyer with return of the parties to their original status, because of a breach of contract by the seller. The buyer may still sue for damages suffered. The reciprocal is also true if the buyer breaches the contract.

canon law

Generally codified law of a church and more specifically law of the Roman Catholic Church and in Great Britain law of the Anglican Church.

cap

The maximum interest rate that a variable-interest-rate mortgage can reach. There is an "overall" cap that is the highest amount the variable rate may become during the entire life of the loan. A "periodic" cap is the maximum amount the interest rate may increase in any one jump. Usually interest rates may "trigger" every six months, or every year, and rise or fall in sync with index levels, unless capped or limited at some lesser level by prior agreement.

capital

(a) Money and credit used to start and continue a business. (b) Total assets of a business. (c) Owner's equity in a corporation, consisting of common (and sometimes preferred) stock and retained earnings.

capital crime

A crime for which the death penalty may be imposed in states where authorized and at the federal level.

capital gain

The profit realized from the sale or exchange of a capital asset (i.e., generally a thing of value owned). In other words, the *gain* is the difference between (a) what was originally paid for the property (to buy or build) minus accumulated depreciation (in the case of investment property), plus accumulated costs of major improvements, and (b) its net sales price.

capital punishment

Death penalty for a crime.

carjacking

Taking a motor vehicle from a person by force and violence or by intimidation.

carryback mortgage financing

A credit sale of real property where the seller takes a promissory note and security in the property (mortgage) from the buyer.

case

A controversy brought before a court for decision. There are two broad categories of cases: See "case at law" and "case in equity."

case at law

A case in which the relief sought is monetary damages, and in which a jury may be used to decide questions of fact.

case citation

A reference that identifies a legal case and indicates where it may be found in a reporter system that publishes opinions of appellate cases. For example: *Commonwealth of Mass. v. Geagan,* 339 Mass. 487, 159 N.E.2d 870 (1959).

case-in-chief

The case presented by each party in a trial. It includes calling witnesses and introducing into evidence documents, photographs, or whatever else is relevant to the issues in a trial.

case in equity

A case in which the plaintiff seeks specific performance, an injunction, an accounting, dissolution of marriage, or other nonmonetary relief because the remedy at law is inadequate or unavailable. The judge, alone, decides questions of fact as well as those of law.

case law

All reported judicial decisions; the law that comes from judges' opinions in lawsuits.

case or controversy

U.S. constitutional requirement that federal courts may decide only cases in which an actual conflict between persons exists.

causation

The act or means by which a specified effect is produced. See also "actual causation" and "proximate causation."

cause of action

An existing right to seek and to receive judicial relief, assuming the factual allegations of the plaintiff are true.

caveat emptor

[Latin for "let the buyer beware"] A phrase meaning that before purchase a buyer should investigate and then rely on his or her own judgment regarding obvious or readily discoverable shortcomings of the goods or services.

caveat venditor

[Latin for "let the seller beware"] A phrase meaning that a seller should exercise appropriate care to assure that goods sold (or services rendered) are of fair value and suitable for human use, or be subjected to possible legal sanctions.

CC&Rs

See "covenants, conditions, and restrictions (CC&Rs)."

cease and desist

A command from an administrative agency that the subject party refrain from specified activities.

certificate of incorporation

See "charter."

certificate of ownership

A legal document issued by a state government showing who owns a vehicle (i.e., has legal and/or equitable title to it).

certificate of registration

A legal document issued by a state government permitting operation of a motor vehicle on the highways of the state.

certiorari

[Latin for "to be informed of"] A writ or order by which the U.S. Supreme Court exercises its discretionary power to decide which lower court cases it will hear.

challenge (of juror)

Any prospective trial juror may be challenged *for cause* if his or her bias or prejudice is indicated. Statutes also provide that prospective trial jurors may be challenged *peremptorily* for any reason other than their race or gender. The decision to exclude a juror for cause is made by the judge; the decision to exclude a juror peremptorily is made by a party acting through his or her attorney. Peremptory challenges are limited in number.

champerty

An illegal agreement with a party to a suit for a portion of any recovery in exchange for paying the litigant's lawsuit expenses.

Chapter 7 bankruptcy

Voluntary or involuntary proceeding (also called *straight bankruptcy*) whereby a debtor surrenders all property, excluding certain exempt property, to the court for liquidation. Proceeds are distributed to creditors and most debts are discharged.

Chapter 11 reorganization

Voluntary or involuntary proceeding whereby the debtor remains in possession and control of the business. The creditors and the debtor agree on a plan that permits the business to continue after creditors accept a portion of their claims as payment in full. Owners also accept less for their equity in the business.

Chapter 13 adjustment of debts

Bankruptcy court–approved plan whereby an individual or a small business is shielded against involuntary bankruptcy while unsecured creditors receive at least as much as they would in Chapter 7 liquidation bankruptcy. Payments are normally made over a period of up to three years, but no longer than five years.

charitable trust

A trust designed for the benefit of a segment of the public or of the public in general.

charter (of corporation)

A permit issued by the government to do business as a corporation. In some states, a *certificate of incorporation* and *articles of incorporation* serve the same purpose.

chattel

See "property."

check-off

An agreement between an employer and a union whereby the employer deducts union dues from employees' pay and forwards the funds directly to the union.

citation

(a) An abbreviation that refers to the written decision of a published appellate court case, usually including its name, volume and page numbers, and year of publication. (b) Accusation that an infraction has occurred, as in *traffic citation*.

citizen's arrest

The taking into custody by a private citizen of a person who allegedly committed a felony in the citizen's presence, or of a person who allegedly committed a misdemeanor that constitutes a breach of the peace then in progress.

civil action or civil dispute

A lawsuit commenced for the purpose of resolving a civil conflict. Distinguished from a criminal action.

civil law

(a) The branch of law dealing with civil rights and civil duties and their enforcement. (b) The total system of law embracing civil and criminal matters, used in the ancient Roman Empire and copied on the continent of Europe in modern times. In ancient times the law was defined by experts and imposed from above by the emperor. Roman civil law is contrasted to English *common law*.

civil rights

See "rights, civil."

Civil Rights Act of 1964

Federal law (specifically Title VII) that makes it unlawful for employers of fifteen or more persons, engaged in interstate commerce, to discriminate with respect to employment against any individual because of such person's race, color, religion, sex, or national origin.

class action

When all members of a group of persons who have suffered the same or similar injury join together in a single lawsuit against the alleged wrongdoer. The group must be so numerous that it is impracticable to bring all members before the court individually. Therefore, they are collectively represented by only one or a few members. However, all members must have a definable common interest in the disputed situations of law and fact, and all are bound to the court's decision.

clemency

A formal act of kindness, mercy, and leniency by a governor or the president in commuting (i.e., reducing) a criminal penalty or granting a pardon.

client

One who employs an attorney to provide legal advice or other assistance.

close corporation

A corporation whose stock is owned by one person or very few persons. Also known as a *closely held corporation* or a *family corporation*.

closed shop

A place of employment where workers must join a union before they can be hired. Made illegal by the Taft-Hartley Act.

closely held corporation

A corporation in which the common stock is owned by only one or a small number of shareholders. Also known as a *close corporation* or a *closed corporation*.

close of escrow

The time when all required monies and documents from all interested persons are distributed by the escrow agent to the appropriate persons in connection with the sale/purchase of real property.

closing costs

Charges for various services that arise in connection with the purchase and sale of a home. The charges are paid upon close of escrow by the buyer and seller in accordance with the terms of their agreement and escrow instructions. Examples of closing costs are termite-inspection charges, loan fees, title insurance premiums, notary public fees, and transfer taxes.

cloud on title

Any dormant or actively pursued claim to the possession of or title to real property that is unresolved or contested. An unresolved claim may be evidenced by a written document, whether recorded or not, or by some physical characteristic, such as a ditch.

code of ethics

A systematic statement of agreed-upon moral rules for a profession, business, or group.

codes

Compilations of statutes that are grouped together by subject matter, e.g., a vehicle code.

codicil

A document prepared to change but not revoke an existing will.

cohabitation

Living together as husband and wife. It is *notorious cohabitation* if done without complying with the legal formalities of marriage.

cohabitation agreement

An agreement between notoriously cohabiting persons concerning financial or property matters.

collateral

Money or other property made available as security by a debtor to a creditor, through physical possession or legal right, to guarantee repayment of a loan.

collaterals

Relatives who are brother, sister, uncle, aunt, cousins, and so forth. See also "lineals."

collective bargaining

The process of negotiation by representative(s) of the employees' union and representative(s) of an employer for an employment contract that provides terms and conditions of employment.

collision insurance

Automobile insurance that protects against the risk of loss from damages to one's own automobile in a collision regardless of who is at fault.

commerce

The exchange of goods or commodities for payment in cash, credit, services, or other goods, often between parties separated from each other in time and space, and usually accomplished by means of legal contracts.

commerce clause

A part of the U.S. Constitution that provides Congress with the power to pass laws to provide for trade with foreign countries and among states.

commercial impracticability

When performance as agreed is rendered impracticable by occurrence of a contingency, the nonoccurrence of which was a basic assumption of the parties when they made the contract.

commercial property

Property used in trade or commerce, contrasted to *residential.*

commercial speech

Oral, written, and other forms of communication used in advertising and in other business activities. It is protected to some extent by the First Amendment.

commingling

The mixing together of community property and separate property to the extent that the properties cannot be traced back to their original status. Commingled property becomes totally community property.

commission, real estate

The compensation a home seller agrees to pay the listing sales agent if a ready, willing, and able buyer is found. The commission rate is negotiable and is calculated as a percentage of the sales price of the home, not the seller's equity in the home.

common area

Any area available for use by all the residents of a multifamily residential development, such as sidewalks, swimming pools, landscaping, parking spaces, hallways, and recreation rooms.

common carrier

A carrier that transports for payment all persons who apply for passage, assuming space is available and there is no legal excuse for refusal.

common law

(a) The total system of law that originated in medieval England and was adopted by the United States at the time of the American Revolution. Expressed originally in opinions and judgments of the courts, it is judge-made law that reflects the customs and usages of the people. Contrasted to Roman *civil law,* it is found throughout the English-speaking world. (b) That law which comes from the common courts as opposed to a legislature or court of equity. Common law is also called unwritten law.

common-law marriage

The bond formed when a man and a woman live together in the manner of a husband and a wife for the number of years prescribed by state laws, though without observing the legal formalities of marriage. This is a legal form of marriage in some states.

common stock

Shares representing ownership in a business corporation. They have no contractual rate or amount of dividend payment but are usually coupled with the right to vote for directors.

community property

All property acquired (in a community-property state) by the husband or the wife during marriage other than by gift or inheritance, and other than as profits or income from separate property. See also "separate property."

commutation

Reduction, by a state governor or by the U.S. president, of punishment for a crime—for example, changing a death sentence to life imprisonment.

company union

A union formed, sponsored, or financed by the employer of its members, and thus subject to possible domination or control by that employer. The National Labor Relations Act of 1935 banned such unions.

comparable-worth theory

The theory that the same wage or salary should be paid for jobs that have equal societal and economic value based on such factors as required preparation, skill, effort, responsibility, and working conditions.

comparative negligence

Negligence of the plaintiff that does not bar recovery of damages but may reduce the amount of recovery proportionally.

compensatory damages

Amount awarded by a court to make good or replace the actual loss suffered by a plaintiff. In the case of a breach of contract, this amount is equivalent to the actual dollar loss suffered because the defendant did not perform as promised. See also "general damages" and "special damages."

competent parties

Parties who are legally qualified (i.e., have the *capacity*) to make a binding contractual agreement.

complaint, civil

A document filed by the plaintiff with the court and served on the defendant to inform her or him of the facts constituting an alleged cause of action.

complaint, criminal

(a) A written statement filed by the complainant containing facts that indicate a crime has been committed and that the accused committed it. (b) An accusation of a misdemeanor.

composition of creditors

A plan whereby all or most of the creditors of a defaulting debtor mutually agree to accept less than the full amount due each. In some plans, the time for payment is extended.

comprehensive insurance

Automobile insurance that protects against losses from having one's car stolen or damaged other than by collision (e.g., by falling trees, sandstorm).

compulsory arbitration

See "arbitration."

compulsory process

(a) The right guaranteed by the Sixth Amendment to every person accused of a crime to require witnesses to appear in his or her favor, by court order. (b) Official action to force a person to appear as a witness in court, in an administrative hearing, or before a legislature.

conciliation and mediation of labor disputes

Process by which a neutral third party attempts to negotiate a voluntary settlement of a labor dispute.

concurrent jurisdiction

Power of more than one court to hear a case.

concurring opinion

A written opinion wherein a judge agrees (concurs) with the result reached by another judge, but does so for different reasons than those stated by the other judge.

conditional (or qualified) privilege to defame

Protection from liability for defamation extended, for example, to employers who, in good faith and without negligence, critically discuss employee qualifications with third parties. See "absolute privilege to defame."

condominium

A residential or business building in which individuals own, and receive title to, separate units or apartments. Each owner is responsible for financing his or her own purchase. Common areas (such as the land, entry hall, and elevators) are owned in common and managed collectively by all owners of the individual units through a community association.

conflict of interest

In a situation where if one party were obligated to represent another, a real, perceived, or potential situation exists where the interests of the representing party and represented party are opposed. Conflict of interest can occur in attorney–client situations or where a member of the board of directors of a corporation is representing a corporation in such a way as to receive personal benefit.

confusion

Mixing of one person's personal property with another's resulting in the goods becoming indistinguishable.

consanguinity

The blood relationship of persons who are descended from a common ancestor.

consequential damages

Amount awarded by a court to make good or replace indirect but foreseeable economic loss resulting from a party's breach of contract (e.g., the value of an expected crop that was not produced because of seed that did not conform to agreed-upon specifications).

conservatorship

A legal relationship created by a court to allow a person, the *conservator*, to manage the assets and personal affairs of another, the *conservatee*, who is not competent to manage his or her affairs.

consideration

The price or inducement (for example, reciprocal promises) to enter a contract.

consortium

The reciprocal legal right of companionship, cooperation, aid, affection, and sexual relations of each spouse from and to the other.

conspiracy

An agreement by two or more persons to commit a crime. In most states, one or more of the conspirators must commit an overt act in furtherance of the criminal plan.

constitution

A written document defining fundamental legal principles for governance of the people within the country or state. It may include grants of power and limitations of power.

constitutionalism

The principles of constitutional government; adherence to them, including, notably, restrictions and limitations on government power.

construction loan

A short-term real estate loan, secured by mortgage, intended to finance building costs. Upon completion, when long-term financing is obtained, the loan is paid.

constructive delivery

Acts that are the equivalent of actual delivery such as delivering the key to the safety deposit box with the present intent to give the person the contents of that box.

constructive eviction

Indirect eviction of a tenant by means of the landlord's failure to correct an intolerable interference or defect in the premises, which effectively drives the tenant out. For example, a landlord's failure to prevent neighboring tenants from making outrageous noises throughout the night can constitute constructive eviction.

Consumer Credit Protection Act

Federal law requiring full disclosure to borrowers or consumers of the cost of credit as an annual percentage rate (APR) and in total dollars. This act is also known as the Truth in Lending Act.

Consumer Product Safety Commission

Independent federal agency charged with implementing the Consumer Product Safety Act of 1972 by setting safety standards for most potentially dangerous consumer products.

contempt of court

Willful defiance of the authority of a court, affront to its dignity, or willful disobedience of its lawful orders.

contingent fee

A fixed percentage of the monetary recovery obtained by a lawyer for a client. It is agreed on in advance and accepted in full payment for services rendered. If the representation produces no recovery, no fee is due under the contingent-fee agreement.

continuation agreement

Contract between partners to permit continuation of a partnership business after dissolution, thus avoiding the winding-up period and forestalling termination. See also *"winding-up period."*

contract

A legally enforceable agreement to do or not to do a specified thing.

contract for deed

An installment sales contract whereby the buyer, although in possession of the premises, promises to make monthly payments for years before title is conveyed from the seller by deed.

contributing to the delinquency of a minor

Any conduct by an adult that encourages or assists a person under the age of eighteen in any unlawful activity.

contributory negligence

The negligence of a plaintiff that helped to cause a tort. In states accepting the doctrine a contributory negligence plaintiff is usually barred or restricted from claiming damages if injured.

conventional loan

A home-purchase mortgage the repayment of which is not guaranteed by an agency of the federal government. The lender relies exclusively upon the value of the collateral and the creditworthiness of the borrower in making the loan.

conversion

Unauthorized taking of the personal property of another and wrongfully exercising rights of ownership. Conversion is an intentional tort.

convicted

Found guilty of a crime by a judgment of the court following a jury verdict or the judge's decision. See also "acquitted."

cooling-off period, in business transactions

Three-day period during which a person who borrows money on the security of a second mortgage on his or her home may rescind. Most states also permit a three-day cancellation period for door-to-door sales and for home-improvement contracts.

cooling-off period, in labor

A period of time in which unions cannot strike and a company cannot engage in a lockout. Other conduct by the parties may be forbidden as well. The president is authorized under the Taft-Hartley Act to enjoin labor activities to "cool off" for up to eighty days.

cooperative apartment

An apartment building owned by a corporation formed to acquire land and erect the building. Interested persons buy shares in the corporation to obtain the right to live in one of the units.

corporation

A legal entity with rights of a human person, created by compliance with applicable law for some designated purpose. A corporation may or may not seek profits. It is generally characterized by unlimited life, transferable shares, limited liability for owners, and centralized management.

corpus (of a trust)

[Latin for "body"] The principal or capital sum, as distinguished from income, of the trust estate.

corpus delicti

[Latin for "body of a crime"] The two essential elements of every crime: evidence that (a) harm has occurred, (b) most probably because of a criminal act. Such evidence may be provided by a corpse with gunshot wounds or by a burned building with lingering gas fumes, for example.

corrective advertising

Advertisements required by order of the Federal Trade Commission to inform the public of errors or misstatements in earlier advertisements by the same company.

court

(a) A government body that administers justice by applying laws to civil controversies and criminal offenses. Under the control of the judge(s), it also includes attorneys, clerks, and others to conduct and facilitate its proceedings. (b) The place where trials are held. (c) Sometimes the term is used as a synonym for *judge(s)*.

court-annexed arbitration

A type of nonbinding arbitration required by some courts before the parties may proceed to trial.

court costs

Fees charged by the court to cover some of the administrative costs of processing the paperwork (e.g., filing a complaint) connected with litigation.

covenant

A formal promise or binding agreement.

covenant marriage

A type of marriage where couples agree to certain marital promises and limitations on their ability to terminate the marriage. States allowing covenant marriage provide it as optional.

covenant not to compete

A promise not to engage in a competing business or profession. Such covenants are generally illegal unless part of an otherwise enforceable contract for the sale of a business or for employment. In such case, they are legal only if they are drafted to be reasonable regarding time, scope, and geographic area, and are necessary to protect the interests of the contracting parties.

covenant of good faith and fair dealing

Agreement implied under the Uniform Commercial Code that contracting merchants shall always act with honesty and observe standards of fair dealing in the trade.

covenant of quiet enjoyment

See "implied covenant of quiet enjoyment."

covenants, conditions, and restrictions (CC&Rs)

A written set of limitations, in deeds or other recorded documents, on the future use of real property. For example, for residential use, they may require minimum-sized homes, with specified fencing, and so forth. Enforcement is often delegated to a homeowners' association (HOA). See also "deed restrictions."

creative financing

Any financing for the purchase of a home in which the seller accepts a note secured by mortgage for all or part of the purchase price. Creative financing is also called *seller's financing*.

credit

Legal right given by one person (the creditor) to another (the debtor) to incur a debt, coupled with a promise to pay it later, usually with interest.

credit card

A small card, usually made of plastic, identifying the holder by signature (and sometimes by photograph), issued by banks, stores, and other agencies to permit the holder to obtain goods, services, or money on credit up to a specified limit.

Credit Card Act of 1970

Federal law that regulates issuance and enforcement of credit cards.

crime

An offense against the public resulting from violation of a criminal statute.

criminal action, case, or dispute

A trial before a jury (if demanded by either party) in which the government (state or federal) prosecutes a person charged with a crime.

criminal facilitation

The crime of assisting the commission of a crime by another person.

criminal intent

The guilty state of mind [Latin *mens rea*, "guilty mind"] necessary for a person to be held responsible for a particular crime.

criminal law

The branch of law dealing with crimes and their punishment.

criminal negligence

Conduct that is without criminal intent and yet is so careless, or occurs in such reckless disregard of another's safety, that criminal penalties are prescribed by statute.

cruel and unusual punishment

Criminal punishment in which the duration of sentence in jail is totally disproportionate to the offense, or the prisoner is subjected to inhuman torture or merciless abuse, or the method of the punishment is unacceptable to society, or the punishment is arbitrary. Cruel and unusual punishment is prohibited by the Eighth Amendment to the U.S. Constitution.

cure a default

To bring current any past-due payments of rent or of monthly payments on a home-purchase mortgage, or to correct any other default, such as removing a dog from rented premises where animals are prohibited.

custom-built home

A home built according to specifications (e.g., floor plan, building materials, interior design) selected by its buyer. Custom-built homes are usually constructed on subdivision lots or sometimes on rural acreage.

damages

Money awarded by a court to a plaintiff for injury or economic loss caused by the defendant. There are various types, including compensatory, consequential, general, incidental, liquidated, nominal or token, punitive or exemplary, special, and treble. See each of these entries.

dangerous instrumentality

A gun or other object that may cause harm when given to a child without instruction as to its proper use.

dangerous propensity

A child's harmful habit that may result in injury to others, such as throwing rocks at automobiles.

date rape

Nonconsensual sexual intercourse by a friend or acquaintance.

death taxes

Taxes imposed on the estate of the decedent (that is, an *estate* tax on the privilege of giving) and on the gifts received by the donee(s) (that is, an *inheritance* tax on the privilege of receiving).

Death with Dignity Act

A state statute that allows competent, terminally ill adult patients to obtain a physician's prescription for drugs to end their life.

decedent

A deceased person.

deceit

Fraudulent misrepresentation made knowingly to mislead another person who is thereby misled and injured. Deceit is also called *fraud*.

decisional law

The written decisions of appellate courts, also referred to as the common law and case law.

declaratory judgment

A judicial action where a court states the rights and duties of parties without specifically ordering that anything be done. Declaratory judgment is also called *declaratory relief*.

decree of dissolution

A court judgment ending a marriage.

deductible clause

A provision in an insurance policy whereby the insured bears modest losses up to a prescribed sum (e.g., $50, $100, or a little more) in exchange for reduced premiums. Typically there is no deduction from full coverage when the loss is substantial.

deductive logic

A method of logical reasoning from two or more propositions to a conclusion. Inferences are drawn from a general premise to a specific premise. The conclusion is valid if the propositions on which the conclusion is based are true.

deed

Any document used to transfer any ownership interest in real property. Many types of deeds are used in a variety of property transfers. For example, *grant deeds* and *warranty deeds* are commonly used in the sale of homes; they include certain guarantees by the transferor that are implied by law. A *trustee's deed* transfers ownership to the purchaser of property at a foreclosure sale. See also "deed of reconveyance," "deed of trust," and "quitclaim deed."

deed of reconveyance

A deed used by a trustee to return title to real property to the trustor (borrower) when he or she pays off a loan that was secured by a trust deed. See also "deed."

deed of trust

A deed used by a borrower (called *trustor*) to transfer the legal title to real property to a disinterested stakeholder (the trustee) to hold as security or collateral for the benefit of the lender (the *beneficiary*). When the loan is paid in full, the legal title is reconveyed to the trustor. Also called a *trust deed*. See also "deed of reconveyance."

deed restrictions

A clause included within a deed that restricts the future use of the real property that is being conveyed. For example, property can be conveyed subject to the restriction that it be used only for residential purposes. Covenants, conditions, and restrictions (CC&Rs) may be included within a deed, incorporated by reference into a deed, or

contained in a separate document that, like a deed, is recorded and legally restricts the future use of the property.

de facto

[Latin for "in fact" or "actually"] A situation that exists in fact whether or not it is lawful (e.g., the term *de facto segregation* is often used to refer to a separation of races caused by social selection, living patterns, and economic conditions). See also *"de jure."*

defamation

False statement, either oral (called *slander*) or written (called *libel*), that tends to injure the reputation of the victim. It may be civil (a tort) as well as criminal (a crime).

default

Failure of a party to do what is legally required (e.g., failing to keep a contractual promise, or failing to file an answer to a complaint).

default judgment

Court-awarded judgment based on the defendant's failure to answer the summons and complaint or to appear at the trial to contest the claim of the plaintiff.

defective (or voidable) marriage

A marriage that may be legally nullified by the innocent party through court action, thereby restoring both parties to the legal status of persons who have never been married to each other.

defendant

(a) In a civil trial, the person from whom money damages or other relief is sought by the plaintiff. (b) In a criminal trial, the accused.

defense

Some reason in law or fact why the plaintiff should not recover in a civil action (e.g., failure of consideration, act of God, assumption of risk) or why the defendant is not guilty as charged in a criminal action.

deficiency judgment

Judgment against a debtor for the unpaid balance still due after repossession and resale of goods that were sold on credit, or after judicial foreclosure of a real estate mortgage.

defined benefit plans

Retirement plans that provide for the payment of definitely determinable income benefits by a predetermined formula.

de jure

[Latin for "by law" or "lawfully"] Of right; done in compliance with law; legitimate; lawful, whether or not such is true in actual fact (e.g., the term *de jure segregation* is often used to refer to officially sanctioned racial discrimination). See also *"de facto."*

delegation

Transfer of some or all contractual duties to another person.

deliberate

The jury's review, discussion, and weighing of evidence presented at a trial.

democracy

[Greek for "rule by the people"] System of government in which power is vested in the people and exercised by them directly, or indirectly as through a system of representation involving free elections.

demurrer

A motion filed by a defendant in response to a summons and complaint when allegations of the complaint, even if true, are insufficient to state a cause of action. In federal courts, and in many states, the same result is achieved by a motion to dismiss.

de novo review

An entirely new hearing (including witnesses and other evidence) as contrasted to an appeal (limited to a review of the law as applied).

deposition

Questioning of a witness or adverse party to an action, under oath, by the opposing attorney before the trial. Depositions are conducted in the presence of a court reporter and the person's own counsel. They are the principal type of discovery procedure.

deposit receipt

Idiom for a legally binding contract to purchase and sell a specific parcel of real property. See also "purchase agreement and deposit receipt."

depreciated value

The value of property after deduction of a percentage of its original value because of aging and/or use.

depreciation

(a) In tax law, a tax deduction allowed by law for taxpayers who own certain kinds of assets. Such a tax deduction permits a taxpayer to pay a smaller income tax than otherwise would be due; for example, apartment house owners are entitled to large income tax deductions for depreciation. (b) In other than tax law, a decline in value, or the opposite of appreciation in value.

detention

The brief stopping of a suspicious person by a police officer for the limited purpose of determining if a crime has been or is being committed in the proximity of the detainee.

devise

A gift of real property by will.

dictum (pl. dicta)

[Latin for "remark(s)"] Any part of a court opinion that is unnecessary to the resolution of dispute before the court. Such digression by a judge is not binding on later courts.

diminished capacity

Reduced ability to exercise one's freedom of will or to choose between right and wrong. Possibly delusion induced by drugs, diminished capacity may negate the presence of specific criminal intent required for first-degree murder.

directive to physicians

A signed document communicating the signer's wishes regarding the use of life-support systems in the treatment of a terminal illness.

director (of corporation)

One of a group of persons (called a *board*) legally charged with the determination of major policies for management of a business corporation, appointment of top executives, and the declaration of dividends.

disability insurance

A form of insurance that provides replacement income for a person who is unable to work because of a disability (illness or injury).

disbarment

Revocation of an attorney's license to practice law. A disbarred attorney may seek reinstatement at a future date.

discharge of contract

Completion of contractual obligation(s).

disclaimer

(a) A written or oral statement stating that a warranty does not exist. (b) Refusal of an insurer to accept certain types of liability. (c) Rejection of an estate or right offered to a person. (d) Renunciation of a claim or power. (e) Negation or limitation of a warranty in the sale of goods.

discovery procedures

Methods used under court order during the period between commencement of a lawsuit and the date of trial to learn facts about the dispute. See also "deposition," "motion to produce," "request for admission of facts," and "interrogatories."

discretionary sprinkling and accumulation trust

A trust where the trustee is authorized to decide who among the designated beneficiaries is to receive periodic payments of income or principal, and when.

disparate-impact

A facially neutral employment criterion that has an adverse discriminatory impact upon a protected group.

disparate-treatment

Less favorable treatment than others because of race, color, religion, gender, age, or national origin.

disputants

Opposing parties in conflict.

dissenting opinion

A written opinion by a judge or judges who vote(s) contrary to the majority opinion and holding of the court.

dissolution

Termination of marriage relationship by court judgment. Dissolution is called *divorce* in some states.

diversity of citizenship

A basis of jurisdiction in federal courts. It requires that plaintiff and defendant be involved in an actual controversy and be citizens of different states, and that a minimum of $75,000 be sought in damages.

divided interest

Interest in property such as a parcel of land, held by a person either separately or in severalty—for example, by the owner of a condominium.

dividend

(a) Profit of a corporation distributed proportionally to stockholders by order of the board of directors. (b) Refund of overpaid premiums by an insurance company.

divorce

Termination of a marriage relationship by court judgment. Divorce is called dissolution in some states.

divorce from bed and board

A modification of the spousal relationship in which the parties are forbidden to cohabit but do not dissolve the marriage. Support may be paid, and property is divided as in a divorce. See also "separate Maintenance."

doctrine of supremacy

The constitutional doctrine that applies whenever the United States and a state or local government enact conflicting laws on the same subject. Under this constitutional doctrine, the federal law prevails.

domestic law

The laws of the United States, as distinguished from the laws relating to foreign nations. Sometimes also refers to the law of domestic relations, i.e., family law.

domestic partnership

Unmarried couples who live together and seek economic and noneconomic benefits available to married couples.

domestic torts

Torts based on negligent or intentional conduct by one spouse causing bodily injury or property damage to the other.

donative intent

Present intent to make a gift.

donee

The person to whom a gift is made in life or by will.

donor

A person who makes a gift in life or by will.

double jeopardy

A second criminal prosecution against a person for the same single offense, after the person has been found innocent of the crime in the prior trial.

double taxation of corporate income

After corporate net income has already been taxed, it is taxed again as personal income if it is distributed to the shareholders as dividends.

dower and curtesy

Dower is the common-law right of a married woman to a life estate in the property of her husband upon his death. Curtesy is the comparable right of a husband to property of his wife upon her death. Dower and curtesy have no application in community-property jurisdictions and have been abolished or modified in most other states.

down payment

The purchase price of a home less the net amount of funds that can be borrowed equals the amount of cash the buyer will have to deposit into escrow to complete the purchase—i.e., the down payment. Broadly, the amount paid in cash for real or personal property as contrasted to the debt incurred for the balance due.

dramshop statute

A state law making it a crime for a tavern proprietor or employee to serve intoxicants to an obviously inebriated customer.

driving under the influence (DUI)

Violating the law by driving while one's judgment and ability to react are impaired by alcohol or other mind-altering drugs.

due-on-sale clause

A clause found in most promissory notes secured by home-purchase mortgages that accelerates the due date of the loan to the date the home is sold. A due-on-sale clause is one variety of *acceleration clause,* the purpose of which is to *call* an existing loan (legally demand its payment in full) because of some act of the borrower, such as selling the collateral, e.g., the home.

due process of law

The requirement that legal proceedings (including arrest, civil and criminal trials, and punishment) comply with the U.S. Constitution and other applicable substantive and procedural laws.

durable power of attorney

A document authorizing another person to make health-care (and sometimes other) decisions for a person even after he/she has become incapacitated. See also "power of attorney."

duress

Any threat of, or actual, physical harm that deprives a person of the freedom of will to choose and decide.

duty-based ethics

The doctrine that actions are morally correct if they comply with existing obligations owed another or oneself.

duty, legal

The obligation enforceable in court to recognize and respect the person, property, and rights of others. Legal duty is the reciprocal of *legal right.*

easement

The right to use the real property of another for a limited purpose (e.g., access to a beach or public road).

economic strike

A strike in which workers seek a change in wages, hours, and/or conditions of employment. See also "unfair labor practice strike."

Electronic Fund Transfer Act

Federal law that authorizes financial institutions to transfer funds through accounts without the use of paper instruments (e.g., checks or drafts).

emancipated minor

A minor meeting certain legal requirements allowing her or him to handle their own financial affairs.

emancipation

Parental consent to a minor to handle her or his own financial affairs. It normally also ends parental duties of supported care.

embezzlement

The crime of stealing property that, before the theft, was lawfully in the possession of the thief (e.g., when a cashier steals money from the company cash register).

eminent domain

The constitutional power of the government to take private property for public use upon payment of just compensation.

employee

A person who agrees by contract to perform work as directed and controlled by an employer in exchange for compensation (usually consisting of wages or salary and fringe benefits).

employee stock ownership plans (ESOPs)

Plans encouraged by federal income tax benefits whereby employees become owners of stock in the corporation that employs them.

Employment Act of 1946

Federal law committing the federal government to encourage employment for all persons able to, willing to, and seeking to work.

employment at will

Typical employment contract under which both the employee and the employer may end the relationship at any time without liability (other than payment for services already rendered, generally).

Employment Retirement Income Security Act (ERISA)

Federal legislation regulating private pension plans that supplement social security.

enabling statute

A statute that authorizes an administrative agency to perform specified actions. The statute that creates the agency typically empowers it to act.

enact

To establish a law by proper vote of members of the legislative branch of government and (normally) with executive approval (i.e., by signature of the president or responsible governor).

encroachment

Construction (e.g., building or fence) or vegetation (e.g., tree limb or ground cover) that physically intrudes upon or overlaps the real property of another. An encroachment can be a *nuisance,* enjoinable by court judgment.

endorsements, policy

Clauses that supplement standard policies of insurance. May be printed forms added to policies.

entrapment

A defense to criminal charges if the crime was induced by police encouragement, but not if police merely provided an opportunity for the accused to commit the criminal act.

entrepreneur

One who organizes, owns, and manages a business.

environmental impact statement (EIS)

A report required by law before any major federal action that might affect the environment can be taken. The report analyzes the effects of the proposed development or action on the surrounding natural and fabricated environment in accordance with the National Policy Act of 1969.

environmental law

Federal, state, and local statutory and administrative laws designed to protect the environment.

Equal Credit Opportunity Act of 1974

Federal law that forbids discrimination in the extension of credit because of sex, marital status, race, or other specified qualities of the applicant.

Equal Employment Opportunity Act (EEOA) of 1972

Federal law that created the Equal Employment Opportunity Commission.

Equal Employment Opportunity Commission (EEOC)

Federal agency created by the Equal Employment Opportunity Act of 1972 that authorized the federal government to use its resources to enforce the Civil Rights Act of 1964 for private persons.

Equal Pay Act (1963)

Federal law that mandates the same wage or salary for women and men for equal work done in jobs performed under similar conditions. Different wages are permitted when justified by such factors as seniority, quality and quantity of output, and any basis (such as night shift) other than gender.

equal-pay laws

Statutes that prohibit discrimination in wages for equal work because of the gender of the employee. The federal Equal Pay Act of 1963 was the first law of this type.

equal-protection clause

The clause in the Fourteenth Amendment to the U.S. Constitution declaring that "no state shall . . . deny to any person within its jurisdiction the equal protection of the laws." The thrust of the mandate is to prohibit unreasonable discrimination. This clause is the basis for much civil rights litigation by minorities and women.

equitable distribution

The division and distribution by the court of marital property to the spouses upon divorce or dissolution—not applicable in community-property states, where each spouse owns one-half of all community property.

equitable maxims

General rules applied by courts to cases in equity (e.g., "Those who seek equity, must do equity" and "Equity aids the vigilant and not those who sleep on their rights").

equitable owner

An owner who has possession and use of the property although someone else may retain the legal title.

equitable title

Title possessed by the beneficial owner of goods who has possession and use, as in installment (on-credit) sales where the seller retains the legal title as security until paid in full.

equity

(a) The body of law that developed in Courts of Chancery as an alternative to English Common Law courts. This law provided an alternate set of principles based on characteristics of fairness and provided remedies for wrongs not adequately provided for by the common law. (b) The net interest of a homeowner in the property, representing the excess of the value of the property over loans or other legal claims outstanding against it.

equity, action in

A civil trial held without a jury when relief sought by the plaintiff is equitable in nature, such as an injunction, or a divorce or dissolution of a marriage.

escrow

[from Old French for "roll of writings"] An arrangement common in real estate transactions whereby the buyer and seller (and/or the borrower and lender) designate a neutral third party as an agent to carry out instructions for gathering and distributing documents and funds as instructed.

escrow agent

A person paid to perform all the administrative tasks necessary to close a real estate escrow. Escrow agents are similar to stakeholders, but are not fiduciaries. They merely carry out instructions received from buyers and sellers, who cannot rely upon escrow agents for information about their real estate transactions.

estate

The totality of interest(s) that a person has in property.

estate planning

The process of arranging a person's property and estate, taking into account the laws of wills, taxes, insurance, property, and trusts so as to gain maximum benefit of all laws while carrying out the person's wishes for use of the property during his or her lifetime and disposition of the property upon his or her death.

estate tax

A tax imposed by the federal government and some states on the privilege of giving property to another person after death of the donor.

estate tax exemption

A sum of money that can be transferred without tax implications. Once that amount is met, tax liability begins on any additional transferred amount.

ethics

Norms of just and morally correct conduct.

estray statutes

Laws requiring finders of lost personal property to report their discovery to authorities.

euthanasia

The act of allowing one to die by withholding extraordinary medical measures, or putting to death by painless means a person suffering from an incurable disease or condition of an extremely painful nature. Euthanasia is also called *mercy killing*.

evict

The act of expelling a tenant from rented premises.

eviction, legal

The legal process by which landlords expel tenants who are in breach of their lease contracts. Because eviction is considered a draconian remedy, legal proceedings to evict require prior notice to the tenant, who must be given opportunity to be heard in court.

eviction, wrongful

Any unlawful conduct by the landlord designed to evict a tenant for any reason. An example is changing locks on doors.

evidence

Everything presented by disputing parties and witnesses that the "finder of fact" is entitled to consider in arriving at a determination of the facts.

exclusionary rule

The court-made rule that precludes the use in criminal court proceedings of any evidence improperly obtained by the prosecution.

exclusive-agency listing

Employment contract between an owner of real property and a licensed agent in which the owner may find a buyer and sell the property without liability for payment of commission, but must pay the listing agent if that agent—or any other licensed agent—finds the buyer.

exclusive listing

Employment contract in which the owner of real property agrees to pay a licensed agent a certain commission regardless of who finds the buyer to whom the property is sold. Also called an *exclusive right to sell.*

exculpatory clause

Provision in a contractual agreement (e.g., a lease) by which a party agrees not to hold the other party responsible for his or her negligence.

executed contract

A contract that has been fully performed by both parties.

executive branch

The government officials responsible for execution or effectuation of constitutional mandates and statutes enacted by the legislative branch. See "judicial branch" and "legislative branch."

executive clemency

A formal act of kindness, mercy, and leniency by a governor, or by the president, in commuting a criminal penalty or granting a pardon.

executive order (or directive)

A lawful order by the president of the United States, the governor of a state, or the head of a local government given without the concurrence of the legislative branch. An example is the 1990 executive order of President George H. Bush calling certain units of the U.S. military reserve to active duty in the Middle East for the Persian Gulf War.

executive privilege

The right of the president of the United States to refuse to disclose information because of national security considerations, provided that there is no overriding reason for disclosure as determined by judicial review.

executor

A person named by a testator to dispose of her or his estate after death as directed in the will and in compliance with law.

executory contract

A valid contract in which something remains to be done by either or both parties.

exhaustion of remedies

A doctrine requiring that a person attempt all available options within an administrative agency before taking a claim to a court.

exemplary damages

See "punitive damages."

exempt assets

Property that a debtor can protect against seizure resulting from execution of judgment by a judgment creditor or a trustee in a bankruptcy distribution.

ex parte

[Latin for "for/with one party"] Term usually used in conjunction with some legal action occurring after only one side of the dispute has been heard.

expert fact-finding

Neutral expert fact-finding is a nonbinding process in which an appointed expert investigates or hears facts on selected issues. At the conclusion, he or she makes findings of fact.

expert witness

Anyone qualified by knowledge and skill, experience, training, or education to offer a credible and useful opinion upon some material issue in a trial.

ex post facto law

[Latin for "after the fact"] A statute that retroactively makes previously lawful conduct a crime. Such a statute is unconstitutional.

express contract

An agreement stated in words, spoken or written.

express powers

The powers specifically delegated to the U.S. government by the Constitution.

express warranty

A warranty given by a seller to a buyer orally or in writing.

extended coverage title insurance

Coverage for title defects as described within the American Land and Title Insurance form of insurance contract.

extortion

The crime of obtaining money or other property by wrongful use of actual or threatened force or violence to the victim or the victim's family. The threat may be to accuse the victim of a crime or to expose any secret tending to subject the victim to hatred, contempt, or ridicule.

fair comment

A privilege that legitimates certain statements on matters of public concern that might otherwise be considered defamatory. See "privileged communication."

Fair Credit Billing Act of 1974

A federal law that permits users of credit cards to challenge correctness of charges, without penalty.

Fair Credit Reporting Act of 1970

A federal law that enables consumers to check and correct credit information about themselves in the files of credit-reporting companies.

Fair Debt Collection Practices Act of 1977

A federal law that outlaws certain unreasonably harsh collection practices previously used by professional debt collectors.

Fair Labor Standards Act of 1938 (FLSA)

A New Deal statute that mandated worker protections, including the maximum eight-hour workday, forty-hour workweek, and protection of child labor.

false arrest

Taking custody of another, without proper legal authority, to be held or restrained in order to answer a civil claim or criminal charge. Because this action restrains the person's liberty, it is also *false imprisonment.*

false imprisonment

The wrongful restraint of the personal liberty of another.

Family and Medical Leave Act of 1993 (FMLA)

A federal law requiring employers with fifty or more employees to grant employees leave for certain family purposes related to child care and family health.

family-purpose doctrine

A law in some states that holds the owner of a motor vehicle vicariously responsible whenever a member of his or her immediate family or household drives and a third party is injured because of the negligence of the driver.

family-settlement agreement

A law of probate in some states allowing family members to agree to settle among themselves the distribution of a decedent's assets.

Fannie Mae

The nickname for the Federal National Mortgage Association, a corporation created by the National Housing Act to establish a secondary mortgage market by purchasing existing home-purchase mortgages. The cash paid for existing mortgages thus becomes available to lenders for new mortgage loans.

featherbedding

Causing or attempting to cause an employer to pay for services by employees that are not actually performed or are not to be performed, such as requiring unneeded extra workers (e.g., brakemen on modern trains).

federal

Refers to the U.S. government and its activities. The United States is a federation of fifty sovereign states.

Federal Housing Administration (FHA)

A federal agency in the U.S. Department of Housing and Urban Development (HUD). The FHA insures (guarantees) the repayment of home-purchase mortgages and provides housing subsidies, thus making financing available to home buyers, and to owners and developers of housing projects.

Federal Housing Administration loan

A loan in which the lender is insured by the Federal Housing Administration, with the borrower paying the mortgage insurance premium.

Federal Insurance Contribution Act (FICA)

A federal law authorizing a tax to finance social security benefits (unemployment, disability, retirement, and survivors' benefits payments). FICA deductions are automatically made by employers from employees' paychecks.

federalism

A government consisting of a union of more or less self-governing states under an umbrella of federal government.

federal law

Includes the U.S. Constitution, statutes enacted by Congress, international treaties, presidential orders, rules promulgated by federal agencies, and decisions of federal courts.

Federal Register

The official publication of the federal government for promulgating all agency rules and regulations.

Federal Reporter

Volumes containing decisions and opinions of U.S. courts of appeals.

Federal Savings and Loan Insurance Corporation (FSLIC)

The federal agency charged with assuring the collectibility of deposits and savings accounts (up to $100,000 per covered account) in savings and loan associations (S&Ls). The failure of hundreds of these associations led Congress to create and fund the Resolution Trust Corporation in 1990, an agency responsible for liquidating and selling off insolvent S&Ls.

Federal Trade Commission (FTC)

A federal agency charged with regulating business to prevent unfair competition and to protect consumers against false advertising and other unfair trade practices.

fee (or fee simple)

Complete ownership of real property. A fee simple is distinguished, for example, from a life estate, which is ownership limited in its duration.

felon

Person convicted of a felony.

felony

A serious crime (such as murder) that is punishable by death or imprisonment for more than one year.

felony-murder rule

A rule in some states mandating that all participants in a dangerous felony are guilty of murder in the first degree if a killing occurs during its commission (e.g., the driver of a getaway car in a bank robbery where one of the robbers was killed by a guard).

fictitious name

A name other than the true name(s) [i.e., the forename(s) and family surname(s)] used to identify a sole proprietorship or partnership. State statutes generally require filing with the county clerk the true name(s) along with the assumed name(s) to inform the public of the facts.

fidelity bond

A bond insuring against losses caused by a fraudulent performance of duties by a personal representative (for example, an executor or guardian).

fiduciary relationship

A relationship between two persons wherein one has an obligation to perform services with scrupulous good faith and honesty (e.g., an attorney toward a client, a trustee toward a beneficiary in a trust, and a partner toward another partner in a partnership have a fiduciary relationship).

field sobriety test

A simple test used to determine the reactions of a motor vehicle driver who is suspected of driving under the influence of alcohol or another drug. The test is administered at the scene of the arrest.

financial-responsibility law

A statute requiring that after an automobile accident of specified severity, any driver not covered by insurance must post specified cash or equivalent bond (e.g., $35,000 in California) or lose his or her driver's license and vehicle registration until released from the potential liability for damages.

financial statement

A written summary of the financial condition or operating results of a business (most commonly the balance sheet and income statement).

financing package

A presentation of prearranged loan terms that are available for qualified (in terms of creditworthiness) borrowers who desire to purchase a home.

firm offer

A written offer signed by a merchant that remains open for a specified time, up to three months. It is binding even though the offeree does not pay for the right (i.e., the option to buy the goods at the stated price).

first degree

A measurement in law of the degree of culpability (blameworthiness) of the perpetrator of a crime. A perpetrator of first-degree murder, for example, is guilty of the highest culpability known in the law.

first-degree murder

Premeditated murder perpetrated with malice aforethought; e.g., by an explosive device or poison, or while lying in wait, or during commission of a specified dangerous felony such as robbery, rape, or arson.

fixed-rate mortgage

A traditional home-purchase mortgage in which the interest rate and the monthly payment do not fluctuate during the life of the loan.

fixer-upper

A house that needs extensive work and repair, usually of a cosmetic nature, before it can be sold at a higher price. When major structural repairs are necessary, the substantial costs may not be covered or recouped through the rise in its fair market value.

for cause

See "challenge (of juror)."

forcible eviction

An illegal eviction technique by which a landlord confronts a tenant, forcibly removes all personal items, and changes locks on the unit.

foreclosure

Process by which secured real property is confiscated at the direction of the unpaid creditor and sold to the highest bidder. Cash proceeds go to retire or reduce the unpaid debt. There are two kinds of foreclosure. Judicial foreclosure is accomplished through court proceedings much as other litigation. Nonjudicial foreclosure, the more commonly occurring, is accomplished without resort to courts or lawyers. It takes place through a private sale conducted by a trustee under the direction of the unpaid creditor.

foreclosure, judicial

The forced sale, following a court proceeding, of an owner's real property to raise money to satisfy the creditor's claim for the unpaid balance of the loan that is in default.

foreclosure, nonjudicial

The involuntary sale, without court proceedings, of an owner's real property to raise money to satisfy the unpaid balance of the loan that is in default.

foreclosure sale

Sale of a debtor's real property to raise cash with which to reduce or retire the unpaid debt. A foreclosure sale may be of two varieties, by a court official following judicial foreclosure or by a trustee following nonjudicial foreclosure.

foreseeability

The ability of a reasonably prudent person to anticipate in advance that injury to person and/or property is likely to result from a specified act or failure to act. Foreseeability is an essential element of the tort of negligence.

formal contract

Agreement that uses prescribed language.

formal will

A typewritten or computer-printed will executed in compliance with law and signed or acknowledged by the testator in the presence of witnesses who also sign the document.

form prescribed by law

Any written expression or particular language that may be required for a valid, fully enforceable contract (e.g., a promissory note).

401(k) plan

Retirement savings account taking its name from the Internal Revenue Code of 1978. The plan is funded by employee contributions and (often) matching contributions from the employer. Contributions are taken from pre-tax salary, and the funds grow tax-free until withdrawn.

franchise

(a) The right obtained by a person or group through contract with a manufacturer or distributor to sell a branded item in a given location. (b) The right granted by government to conduct certain activities (such as the sale of gas or electricity throughout a county) as monopolies. (c) The right to vote for candidates for public office.

franchisee

A person or group who obtains a franchise from a manufacturer or distributor-franchisor.

franchisor

A manufacturer or distributor who grants a franchise to a franchisee.

fraud

A knowingly false representation of a material fact, made through words or conduct, with intent to deceive a victim, who is induced to contract in reliance on the lie, and who is thereby injured. Fraud is also called *deceit*.

Freddie Mac

The nickname for the Federal Home Loan Mortgage Corporation, a corporation that participates in the secondary mortgage market by buying and selling conventional, FHA, and VA (Veterans Administration) mortgages.

Freedom of Information Act (FOIA)

A federal law requiring the federal government to disclose most public records to any person on request.

free speech

The right to express any opinion in public without censorship or restraint by the government.

fringe benefits

Direct and indirect compensation, other than in money wages, to employees by an employer for services rendered. Examples include health and life insurance, vacations, and stock purchase plans.

full cash value

The appraised value of real property determined for the purpose of calculating the annual property tax.

fungible

Each item of personal property is identical to every other item.

future interest

Any possessory or ownership interest in real property that will *vest* (become perfected) at some future date. For example, the owners of the remainder interest following a life estate have future interests in the property that will vest upon the death of the life tenant.

garnishment

A legal proceeding in which a plaintiff-creditor gets a court order compelling a third party (such as the employer of the defendant-debtor) to pay monies earned by the defendant to the plaintiff. Garnishment is a type of *attachment*.

general damages

Amount awarded by a court to pay the plaintiff for nonmonetary losses (e.g., pain and suffering) that resulted from an injury, without reference to any special circumstances of the plaintiff. General damages are a type of compensatory damages.

general intent

In criminal law, the intent to do the prohibited act without necessity of proving intent to cause the precise harm.

general jurisdiction

Authorization of a court to hear and decide virtually any type of case occurring within the political boundaries of the geographical area in which it is located.

general partner

A partner who manages the firm, shares equally with other general partners in its profits and losses (unless otherwise agreed), and is liable to third parties without limit for partnership debts.

general partnership

A partnership in which all members are general partners. See also "limited partnership."

generation-skipping trust

A trust created whereby the settlors of the first generation (parents) arrange for their child(ren) (the second generation) to receive the income while they are alive, but not the principal, which is reserved for the grandchild(ren) (the third generation) after the death of the second generation.

genuine assent

When consent of both parties to be bound by a contract is freely given and is not negated by fraud, duress, undue influence, and/or certain mistakes.

gerrymandering

The intentional drawing of a political district by a political party that is in power so as to give itself or a useful minority a majority of voters in as many districts as possible while concentrating the voting power of the other party into as few districts as possible. With this technique, an incumbent party may control a legislature even though it generates only the same number of votes as the other party. In some cases, the result would be the same even if the incumbent party generates fewer votes for its candidates.

gift tax

A tax imposed on donors at the federal and state levels on the value of certain gifts made by living persons, with the exception of gifts to charities.

gift

A voluntary transfer of property ownership by one under no duty to transfer ownership.

Ginnie Mae

The nickname for the Government National Mortgage Association, a federal corporation that purchases mortgages in the secondary mortgage market.

good faith

A general obligation imposed by the Uniform Commercial Code on both sellers and buyers to practice honesty in business conduct and contracts.

goods

Tangible, movable personal property.

Good Samaritan

Reference to a biblical story where a person (a Samaritan) came to the aid of a stranger in desperate need. Refers to statutes today that protect volunteers from liability for ordinary negligence while aiding persons in need.

goodwill, business

Intangible asset of a business that is developed through supplier confidence and customer satisfaction with sales and service, stimulating future sales and profits.

Government-in-the-Sunshine Act

A federal law requiring that most meetings of federal agencies be open for public observation and that advance notice be given of agency meetings, listing the expected topics of discussion.

grace period

A period of time during which a tardy payment on a debt, a home-purchase mortgage, or rent will be accepted without penalty. The grace period is the time between the due date of a payment and the delinquent date, following which a penalty may be assessed.

graduated-payment mortgage

A home-purchase mortgage and promissory note that features artificially low monthly payments for the initial few years as an inducement for borrowers whose incomes and creditworthiness are expected to improve in the future.

grandfather clause

Any provision in a statute that exempts a specified class of persons from some change or new requirement in the law.

grand jury

An appointed body of citizens formed both to investigate the operations of government and to issue indictments against persons suspected of criminal conduct. Indictments are one procedure to instigate either state or federal criminal proceedings.

grand theft

Theft of personal property of substantial value, as declared by statute. Because of the substantial value of the stolen property, grand theft is a felony. However, sometimes theft of a specific type of property is grand theft regardless of its value, as, for example, theft of a horse or hunting dog.

grant deed

A document that conveys the ownership of real property, and impliedly warrants that the grantor has not previously conveyed the property to another and that the property is free from undisclosed encumbrances.

guardian

A person appointed by the court (in a guardianship proceeding) to supervise and take care of the person and/or the estate of another.

guardian ad litem

[Latin for "for the suit"] A guardian appointed by the court to prosecute or defend any action for a minor as party.

guardianship

A court-established arrangement whereby an adult guardian is appointed to take care of the person and/or the estate of a minor.

guest

A person who rides for free in another person's vehicle.

guest statute

Law that pertains to guests of a driver of a motor vehicle. In some states a guest cannot sue the driver if injured, unless the driver is guilty of intoxication, willful misconduct, or gross negligence that causes the accident and resulting injury or death. In other states a guest may sue the driver for ordinary negligence.

habeas corpus

[Latin for "you have the body"] A legal writ or court order to release a prisoner from allegedly unlawful confinement so that he or she can appear before a court for proper remedial action. The petitioner seeks release.

habitability, implied warranty of

See "implied warranty of habitability."

hate crime

Any crime the motivation for which was persecution of a victim because of race, religion, sexual orientation, or political beliefs. Hate crimes usually result in enhancement of the penalty otherwise imposed. In some instances, hate crimes are treated as separate offenses with specified penalties.

hate speech

Words spoken, written, or symbolized (e.g., by placing burning crosses on private lawns) that express irrational and false ideas that insult and demean certain persons or classes of persons. Such speech, often illegal, may encourage violent attacks on innocent people.

hearsay evidence

Evidence not based on personal observation or knowledge of the witness, but consisting of repetition of what someone else has said. Hearsay is generally not admissible to prove a fact, but exceptions exist.

hedonic damages

Monetary damages for the future loss of the pleasures of life suffered by a deceased or severely injured victim.

heirs

Persons designated by law to receive the estate of a decedent who leaves no will (i.e., dies intestate).

holder of mortgage

The present owner of a mortgage loan, to whom monthly payments are made by the homeowner. Mortgage loans are often transferred from one holder to another investor.

holographic will

An unwitnessed will. States that allow such a will usually require it to be written in longhand by the testator, signed, and dated.

home equity loan

A loan for any purpose (e.g., to pay off credit card balances that carry higher interest rates, or to pay for college tuition, a new car, a vacation, or home improvements) that is collateralized by a mortgage on the borrower's home. Although the mortgage securing a home equity loan typically incurs higher interest than a home-purchase mortgage, its interest is deductible from federal and state income taxes, which helps explain its popularity.

home inspection services

Professional businesses that inspect residential properties to discover any defects that might influence the decision of a prospective buyer either to buy or to offer a lower price. They can also alert prospective sellers to needed repairs.

homeowners' association (HOA)

Association of people who own homes, condominiums, or cooperatives in a given area, formed for the purpose of improving or maintaining the quality of that area. HOAs are often formed by the developers/ builders of planned unit developments to manage and maintain the property in which all owners have a common, undivided interest. Such associations commonly supervise the property deed CC&Rs.

homeowner's policy of insurance

Insurance that typically covers losses of the homeowner's property from specified casualties, such as fire and water damage, as well as the possible liability of the owner for specified damages he or she may cause to another person through negligent behavior (other than with a motor vehicle or boat). A casualty-loss homeowner's policy (e.g., coverage of fire losses) does not necessarily include liability protection for the homeowner, however.

homestead exemption

An exemption for the homeowner from the valid claims of creditors who otherwise could take substantially all of the debtor's assets in satisfaction of debts. The exemption protects a specified amount of the equity in the homeowner's residence from levy and execution by a creditor.

homicide

The killing of a human being by another human being.

hostile environment

Conduct by others in the workplace that has the purpose or effect of unreasonably interfering with an individual's work performance or creating an intimidating, hostile, or offensive working environment.

hung jury

A jury that cannot reach a verdict because of inability or unwillingness of a sufficient number of jurors to agree on disputed facts.

immaterial evidence

Evidence that is not important or essential to the proof of facts in dispute. Counsel may successfully object to its introduction by the opponent.

immunity from prosecution

The granting by a court of freedom from liability for a specified crime. A person who has been granted this immunity possesses no privilege against self-incrimination and may be compelled to testify about the event in question.

impeach

(a) To discredit, dispute, disparage, or contradict a witness's testimony. (b) Proceeding against a political figure for a crime or misfeasance before the proper political forum.

implied covenant of quiet enjoyment

(a) An implied obligation of a landlord to maintain reasonably comfortable living conditions for the tenant in the rented premises, without disturbance by hostile claimants. (b) An implied promise by the seller of real property that he or she will defend against claims or lawsuits by others who may challenge the buyer's title to the property.

implied-in-fact contract

Contractual agreement manifested by conduct or body language (e.g., purchase of items from vendors in noisy stadiums during sporting events).

implied-in-law contract

Not a true contract, but an obligation imposed on one party to prevent unjust enrichment of another. Also called "quasi-contract."

implied powers

The authority of Congress to make such laws as are "necessary and proper" for effective performance of duties under its powers that are expressly granted.

implied warranty

A warranty implied by actions or law whether or not it is specifically mentioned in a contract. See also "warranty."

implied warranty against encumbrances

An implied warranty in the sale of goods that goods are delivered free from any security interest or other lien of which the buyer has no knowledge.

implied warranty of habitability

(a) An implied guarantee in a lease that there are no concealed defects in the rented premises existing at the beginning of the lease term. (b) An implied obligation upon a landlord to maintain leased premises in a condition fit for use and enjoyment by the tenant through the term of the lease.

impossibility

When it is impossible through no fault of the obligor to perform an obligation as promised in a contract.

impound account

An account held by a mortgage lender in which to accumulate sufficient funds to pay all annual property taxes and property and liability insurance premiums. The funds are taken from the borrower's monthly mortgage payment and accumulated until the periodic taxes and insurance premiums are due.

incapacity

Lack of legal capacity to make important decisions. Minority is an example of incapacity to make contracts.

incest

Sexual intercourse between relatives who are *lineals* (grandparents, parents, children, etc.) or *collaterals* (brothers/sisters, aunts/uncles, etc.) of those degrees of closeness in which marriage is prohibited by state law.

incidental damages

Amount awarded by a court after a breach of a sales contract to cover reasonable expenses incurred by a party (e.g., to inspect, transport, and care for goods rightfully rejected by a buyer).

incompetent evidence

Evidence that the court will not permit counsel to present during trial because of some defect in the qualification of the witness or in the nature of the evidence.

incorporation doctrine

The Supreme Court's utilization of the Fourteenth Amendment to find Bill of Rights limitations on state and local governments.

indemnification

Payment by one person (e.g., an employer) to another person (e.g., an employee) to make up for a loss suffered by the latter in performance of the job.

independent contractor

A person who is hired to do a specific job, and who retains control over how that job is done.

independent regulatory agency

An administrative body empowered to regulate some policy area led by officials who cannot be dismissed by the president of the United States except for good cause.

indeterminate sentence law

A statute that provides for a range (such as one to five years) rather than a specific period of incarceration for a crime, the exact time to be determined by a designated authority after confinement begins.

indict

The act by a grand jury of declaring, after an evidentiary hearing, that there is probable cause that a named person has committed a specific crime and should stand trial to determine his or her guilt or innocence. The official declaration of a grand jury is an *indictment*.

indictment

An accusation of felony filed by a grand jury. See also "information."

Individual Retirement Account (IRA)

Federally authorized private pension plans supplementing social security whereby qualified employees contribute a certain percentage of their income, tax-free, to their retirement accounts until retirement. The money is then normally distributed in installments beginning by April 1 following the year the employee reaches age $70^1/_2$, when it is subject to the personal income tax.

information

An accusation of a criminal offense. Unlike an indictment by a grand jury, it is issued following a preliminary hearing before a judge who decides if the defendant should be required to stand trial or be released.

informed consent

(a) Actual and complete knowledge by a person of risks involved in a situation. (b) Agreement of a patient to undergo surgical procedures or administration of experimental drugs after full disclosure of the risk involved and available alternatives.

infraction

Any minor crime (e.g., parking violation) that is not punishable by incarceration, but only by fine. Accordingly, trial by jury is not required or permitted.

inheritance tax

A tax imposed by most states on the privilege of receiving property from a decedent.

initiative

An electoral process for making new statutes or changing the constitution by filing appropriate formal petitions to be voted upon by legislature (and governor) or by the total electorate. The initiative is not available in all states.

injunction

An order of a court of equity forbidding an action that is considered injurious to the plaintiff. Injunctions are used when dollar damages are unavailable or would be an inadequate remedy (e.g., to restrain the scope of picketing when violence is threatened in a strike).

in loco parentis

[Latin for "in the place of a parent"] Term meaning that a person other than a parent is charged with a parent's rights, duties, and responsibilities.

in personam jurisdiction

The power of a court over a person, usually obtained by personal service of a summons on the defendant while he or she is within the boundaries of the state in which the suit is commenced.

in propria persona

[Latin for "in one's own proper person"] Term meaning that the person represents herself or himself in a legal action without the appearance of an attorney.

inquisitorial system

A legal system used in some countries that allows the judge to investigate, question witnesses, and seek out evidence during a trial.

in rem jurisdiction

The power of a court to declare rights against the world rather than solely against the named defendant(s). If the legal question involves ownership of real property located in Alaska, for example, the court with authority to hear the case would be the appropriate trial court in Alaska.

insanity, legal

Mental disease or defect that causes the accused to lack substantial and sufficient capacity either to appreciate the criminality (wrongfulness) of his or her conduct or to conform his or her conduct to the requirements of the law. Definitions of insanity vary among the states.

in severalty

Form of ownership under which a sole person owns an interest in real property. The term is confusing because it appears to be related to the word *several*. Actually, it relates to the word *separate*.

installment land contract

A method of selling real property in which the seller retains title during the years that the buyer in possession is making monthly payments. Equitable title passes to the buyer after all or most payments have been made. This contract is also called a *contract for deed*.

insurable interest

A sufficient interest in property to where its loss or destruction would cause an economic loss to the owner or possessor. Required to enforce an insurance policy.

intangible property

Property recognized by law even though it has no physical existence. Warranty rights under a contract to buy an automobile and ownership of shares in a corporation are examples of intangible personal property. The legal right of the telephone company to bury and maintain telephone lines across your property is an intangible real property interest, called an *easement*.

intentional infliction of mental distress

Outrageous conduct that causes mental, if not immediate physical, suffering by the victim.

intentional tort

Where the tortfeasor deliberately performs a wrongful act that injures an innocent victim.

interest

The price, usually expressed as an annualized rate (percentage), for use of a sum of money (principal) obtained from a lender.

interference with an economically advantageous relationship

A knowing and wrongful interference with the promised performance of another person's contract. The term may also refer to violations of antitrust laws and to other unfair competitive practices.

international law

The branch of law governing relations between and among sovereign nations.

interpleader

A legal proceeding to resolve conflicting claims (e.g., to funds in an escrow account).

interrogatories

A form of discovery used by attorneys, consisting of written questions directed to a party or witness who is expected to reply with written answers under oath.

interspousal immunity

The traditional ban on lawsuits between spouses to avoid possible resulting disruption of family harmony. The modern trend is to allow such lawsuits.

interstate commerce

Commercial trading or transportation between or among two or more states. The U.S. Constitution (Article I) delegates to Congress power to regulate such commerce.

intervening cause

A cause of an accident or other injury that legally excuses the wrongdoer who originally sets a series of events in motion.

intervenor

A neutral third party who assists parties in resolving their private conflicts (e.g., *conciliator* or *mediator*) or acts as a decision maker in such conflicts (e.g., *arbitrator*).

inter vivos

[Latin for "between the living"] A term applied to a gift or trust. An *inter vivos gift* is made from one living person to another. This is a way to transfer title to personal property. An *inter vivos trust* is created during the life of the trustor to take effect during her or his lifetime. Such a trust contrasts with a *testamentary trust*, which takes effect upon the death of the trustor or testator.

intestate (or intestacy)

The status of a person who has died without leaving a valid will.

intestate law

Statutory prescription for distribution, among heirs, of the estate of a decedent who has died leaving no will.

intrastate commerce

Commercial trading or transportation within any one state. Under the Tenth Amendment of the U.S. Constitution, the power to regulate intrastate commerce is reserved to the respective concerned states.

invidious discrimination

Discrimination by a government or private business against a person based on ethnicity, religion, or national origin, for which there is a legal remedy.

invitee

One who enters another's land with the permission (implied or express) of the owner or occupier, for a matter of business benefiting the owner or occupier.

involuntary manslaughter

The unintentional killing of another person because of gross negligence, or as a result of dangerous and unlawful conduct (e.g., killing a pedestrian while speeding).

irrelevant evidence

Evidence that does not relate to or have a bearing upon a question of fact in dispute during a trial. The objection of "Irrelevant" may be made to a question during a trial.

irresistible impulse

The motivation whereby an accused, because of a diseased mind, could not avoid committing a criminal act even if he or she knew it was wrong. An acceptable test of legal insanity in a few states.

irrevocable trust

A trust that cannot be terminated or revoked by the trustor who created it.

issue arbitration

Only part of a dispute is submitted to arbitration and thereafter decided by the arbitrator.

J

joint and several liability

Responsibility both together and individually. Joint and several liability applies in contracts (as when two or more persons sign a promissory note as makers) and in torts (as when two or more wrongdoers cause the injury together). Of course, the plaintiff is entitled to only one full recovery of his or her total damages.

joint custody

Responsibility shared by both parents, following a divorce, annulment, or separation, to guide and support their child(ren).

joint tenancy

A method of co-ownership of property by two or more persons. Upon the death of any co-owner, his or her percentage interest goes to the surviving joint tenant(s) regardless of the decedent's last will. This right of survivorship is the basic incident of joint-tenancy ownership.

joint tortfeasors

Two or more persons who together commit a tort.

judge

The official who presides over a trial court. See also "court."

judgment

The final determination or decision of the court as to the rights and duties of the parties in a lawsuit.

judgment creditor

A person who has won a judgment but has not been fully paid.

judgment debtor

A person against whom a judgment for payment of money has been entered but who has not yet made or completed that payment.

judgment non obstante veredicto (or n.o.v.)

[Latin for "notwithstanding the verdict"] A decision by a judge that overrules the verdict of the jury.

judgment-proof

Financial condition of a person who lacks the assets to pay any judgment rendered against him or her.

judicial activist

A judge or court that is readily willing to announce or apply new rules of law through interpretation without regard to precedents or legal trends.

judicial branch

Judges who are the government officials responsible for determining the constitutionality of legislative and executive actions and adjudicating rights and duties of persons involved in disputes. They interpret and apply the laws. See also "executive branch" and "legislative branch."

judicial foreclosure

See "foreclosure."

judicial process

The administration of law by the courts.

judicial review

Power of the U.S. Supreme Court to declare unconstitutional an act of Congress, a presidential order, or a state law.

jurisdiction

The power of a court to decide a controversy and to award appropriate relief. Jurisdiction may also refer to the geographic area in which the court has authority and the types of cases it has power to hear.

jury

A group of men and women selected according to pre-established procedures to ensure lack of bias, who are sworn under oath to inquire of certain matters of fact and declare the truth based on evidence presented to them. A jury is also referred to as a trier of fact.

jury deliberation

A thoughtful and thorough discussion by jury members of the facts of a case in light of the applicable law before determining their verdict.

jury instructions

Rules of law and charges provided by the judge to the jury for guidance in reaching a verdict. The instructions include essential facts that must be proved by the prevailing party; they also state the law applicable to the cause of action.

jury nullification

The power of a jury in a criminal trial to disregard the law and unanimously find the defendant innocent, although there is ample evidence to support a verdict of guilty. Although a judge can set aside a guilty verdict in a criminal case, the judge cannot reverse a finding of innocent. A judge can order a mistrial upon a showing of jury misconduct, but refusing to find an accused guilty is not juror misconduct. "The jury has the power to bring in a verdict in the teeth of both law and facts."

jury, trial

A group, usually consisting of twelve adults, but sometimes a smaller number, who are selected and sworn to review evidence in civil and criminal trials, and to return a verdict consistent with their view of the evidence. Also *petit* [French for "small"] *jury*.

just cause

An action based on reasonable grounds and fair treatment; lawful reasons for taking an action. Term used in labor contracts to restrict employer discretion to terminate or discipline an employee.

justices

Judges in appellate courts.

juvenile court

A court with special jurisdiction of a parental nature over delinquent, dependent, and neglected children.

Keogh plan

Federally authorized private pension plan whereby self-employed persons may contribute a percentage of their earnings, tax-free, to a trust account until retirement.

kidnapping

The crime of unlawful seizure and movement of a victim from one place to another against his or her will.

Labor Management Relations Act

See "National Labor Management Relations Act of 1947."

Labor-Management Reporting and Disclosure Act of 1959 (Landrum-Griffin Act)

Federal law that mandates open, democratic internal government of unions.

Labor Relations Act

See "National Labor Relations Act of 1935."

laches, doctrine of

A doctrine that bars *stale* (old) lawsuits in civil cases in courts of equity. The doctrine of laches may be applied by the court to bar a claim when the petitioner has unreasonably delayed his or her pursuit of the claim, and this delay has prejudiced or harmed the case of the respondent. The doctrine of laches may bar a claim that is otherwise timely under the *statute of limitations*.

land contract

An agreement by an owner of real property to sell to a buyer who takes possession immediately but does not obtain legal title until all or most payments have been made to the seller. See also "installment land contract."

landlord

The owner of residential property who leases it to a tenant, or renter, in exchange for rent.

landlord's lien

A statutory lien in favor of an unpaid landlord that provides a mechanism for storage of the tenant's belongings and ultimate sale of them to pay unpaid rent (plus storage costs).

larceny

The crime of stealing property from another who is not then present. Larceny is also called *theft*.

larceny by trick

Theft accomplished by deceit or subterfuge wherein the victim turns over property, especially money, to the perpetrator.

last will

See "will."

law

A body of rules of conduct prescribed by controlling authority and having binding legal force. General principles and detailed rules of human conduct that are enforceable in civil and criminal courts and by administrative agencies.

lawyer

See "attorney at law."

lease

A contract, usually written, by which the relationship of landlord and tenant is created. Leases are also called *rental agreements*.

leasehold

The legal interest a tenant has in residential property leased from the landlord. A leasehold is usually created by a written contract called a *lease*.

legacy

A disposition of personal property by will. Also called a "bequest."

legal assistants

Persons qualified through education, training, and/or work experience to be employed or retained by a lawyer, law office, government agency, or other entity in a capacity or function that involves the performance, under the ultimate direction and supervision of an attorney, of specifically delegated substantive legal work. This work, for the most part, requires sufficient knowledge of legal concepts that, absent such assistants, the attorney would perform the task. Legal assistants are also called "paralegals."

legal owner

An owner who has legal title, for example, as security for repayment of a loan or payment of the purchase price of real property or personal property, such as an automobile. Legal title is transferred to the equitable owner when the debt is paid in full.

legal separation

A court order permitting spouses to live apart with necessary related orders for child custody and child support, support of the wife (or husband), and division of property (as in dissolution), but the marriage endures.

legal service plans

Insurance plans designed to make legal services available to members of unions or other organizations, such as business firms.

Legal Services Corporation (LSC)

A federally funded corporation that distributes federal tax dollars to state programs that provide legal assistance in noncriminal proceedings to persons financially unable to afford such services.

legislative branch

The government officials who are responsible for enacting statutory laws. See also "executive branch" and "judicial branch."

legislative veto

A legislative device whereby Congress may include within a statute a means for congressional review of the executive branch's implementation of the law.

legitimate

Status of a person who is the issue of his or her natural, married parents. The child of an unmarried mother is *illegitimate*.

legitimation

Irrevocable acknowledgment by a natural father that, although not married to the mother of a child, he is the male parent.

lemon

Something, usually a product such as an automobile, that proves to be unsatisfactory because of serious defects that remain after repeated attempts to correct them.

lemon laws

State statutes designed to assist the buyer of seriously defective goods to obtain a replacement or full refund.

lessee

A party to a lease who pays rent to the landlord in exchange for the possession and use of real property, such as a person who rents an apartment.

lessor

A party to a lease who receives rent from a tenant in exchange for the possession and use of real property by the tenant. The lessor is more commonly called the *landlord*.

letter of last instructions

A document prepared by a person instructing his or her personal representative (executor or administrator) as to the nature and location of assets and liabilities and suggesting appropriate action to be taken after death. Such letters are useful but not legally binding.

liability

Any legal obligation or debt (e.g., money owed).

libel

The customary written or printed form of defamation. It may also be committed by defamatory pictures, statues, or signs—all of which are more durable than spoken defamatory words (slander).

license

Permission, often formal, to do something specific (e.g., to drive or to enter property).

licensee

Person who holds a license. Includes a person who enters another's land with permission (implied or express) of the owner or possessor, for the visitor's convenience.

licensor

Organization or person who grants a license to another.

lien

A formal, legal claim to a possessory or ownership interest in the real property of another.

life estate

An ownership interest in property characterized by the right to its possession for the duration of the owner's life. At the death of the owner (called the *life tenant*) possession may (a) revert to the person (called the *grantor*) who created the life estate, (b) go to a designated person (called the *remainderman*), or (c) go to a successor life tenant. Upon death of a life tenant, the value of the life estate is extinguished, and therefore no death taxes are payable. A life estate may be created by deed or will, and it may be created so as to continue until the death of someone other than the life tenant.

limited jurisdiction

Limitation on a court as to the types of cases it can hear and decide.

limited liability company (LLC)

A variation of the S-type corporation but with no limit on the number of owners (or members) or on the nature of the financial structure. The liability of the owners is limited to the amount of their investment in the company, and they are not subject to double taxation of their profits, as are owners of stock in conventional corporations.

limited liability of stockholders

Refers to the fact that regardless of the number of shares owned, a stockholder is normally not liable for the debts of the corporation beyond the extent of his or her investment. This limited liability is considered a primary advantage of corporate ownership.

limited liability partnership (LLP)

A variation of the general partnership in which if the firm (of lawyers, for example) is sued by a client for malpractice, only the lawyer(s) actually guilty of the tortious conduct is (are) liable without limit. Of course, firm assets and firm professional liability insurance would first be exhausted.

limited partner

Partner whose liability for partnership debts extends only to his or her capital investment. Substantial limitations exist as to the extent such partners may participate in management of the partnership.

limited partnership

A partnership form authorized by state statute in which at least one member is a general partner who manages the firm and has unlimited liability for its debts, but the liability of the other partner(s) is limited to the amount of their capital investment(s). See also "general partnership."

lineals

Relatives who are in a direct line of descent, as parents, children, and grandchildren. See also "collaterals."

line item veto

Selective veto, by the executive, of a specific proposed expenditure as it appears on a separate line in a fiscal budget, without vetoing the entire budget or legislative bill.

liquidated damages

Amount of damages that contracting parties have previously agreed would be fair payment in case of breach. This amount will be unacceptable by a court if it is so large as to constitute a penalty.

list

As a verb, the act by a prospective seller of hiring a real estate agent to hunt for a buyer for his or her real property. For example, "I am going to list my house with ABC Realty." The document that establishes the employment relationship is called a *listing*. See "listing agreement."

listing agreement

An employment contract between the owner of real property and a licensed agent authorizing the latter to hunt for a buyer of the property on specified terms. Preprinted types of listing agreement forms include exclusive, exclusive-agency, net, and open listings. See each of these entries.

litigation

Any pending lawsuit.

litigious

Excessively inclined to resolve disputes and claims through lawsuits rather than by negotiation or other methods.

living trust

A popular term for a revocable *inter vivos trust* whose primary purpose is to avoid probate. See "*inter vivos*."

living will

A document, usually authorized by state statute, that directs any attending physician to comply with the wishes of the drafter regarding the use of life-support systems in the treatment of a terminal illness. Also called a *directive to physicians*.

loan-origination fee

A lump-sum fee paid by a mortgage borrower to the lender, who in turn pays all or a portion of it to the mortgage broker who introduced the borrower to the lender. Often the fee is called *points* when it is charged to the borrower and a *loan-origination fee* when paid by the lender to the mortgage broker.

loan ratio

The ratio of a prospective loan amount to the appraised value of a home. For example, a buyer who needed to borrow $100,000 to buy a home with an appraised value of $125,000 would ask the lender to accept a loan ratio of 80 percent ($100,000/125,000 = 80%). Also called the *loan-to-value ratio*.

loan shark

A person who charges usurious (exorbitantly as well as illegally high) interest for the loan of money and commonly threatens or uses violence to compel payment.

loan underwriting

The process of evaluating the acceptability of a prospective borrower's loan application. Underwriters adhere to rules, policies, and company practices to determine whether a specific loan ought to be made or denied.

lobbying

Efforts by individuals and representatives of special-interest groups to persuade legislators (and sometimes administrators) to enact, amend, or rescind specified laws.

lockout

A shutdown of operations by an employer in response to union demands or to achieve other changes in an employment contract.

long-arm statute

A state law authorizing a court to hear cases brought against nonresidents under specified circumstances. It requires certain minimal contacts with the defendant, such as involvement in an automobile accident while driving in the state, or conducting business within the state that claims to have jurisdiction.

lost property

Property that is involuntarily left and forgotten.

magistrates

(a) State judges of the justice court or other lower courts with jurisdiction over relatively minor offenses and small claims. (b) U.S. officials who perform specified judicial services in the prosecution of federal crimes.

Magnuson-Moss Warranty Act of 1975

Federal law that protects ultimate consumers of personal, family, and household goods by defining effects of full and limited warranties.

maintenance

(a) Financial support or promotion of litigation in which one has no legitimate interest. See also "champerty." (b) Term used interchangeably with alimony.

majority opinion

A written opinion by a judge outlining the views of the majority of the judges of the court deciding the case.

maker

The creator of a promissory note.

malice

Evil intent; a desire to inflict injury or suffering; a cold-blooded state of mind.

malice aforethought

The highest degree of criminal culpability, characterized by a cold and malignant heart and a mental predetermination to do the wrongful act without legal justification or excuse.

malicious prosecution

A sham lawsuit brought for the purpose of vexing, harassing, or forcing the payment of money from the defendant.

malpractice

Violation of a duty of due care by a professional person.

manslaughter

The unlawful killing of another person without malice aforethought. Usually classified as voluntary or involuntary, depending on the degree of culpability involved. Vehicular manslaughter is a special category for negligent killing by automobile.

manufactured home

Single-family house constructed entirely in a controlled factory environment, built to the federal Manufactured Home Construction and Safety Standards.

marital deduction

A tax deduction allowing a surviving spouse to receive an estate from the deceased spouse free of federal estate tax.

marital fault

The legal basis necessary in some states to obtain a divorce, such as repeated infidelity. In those states where marital fault is not a prerequisite for divorce, it is irrelevant.

marital life estate trust

Reciprocal trust executed by a husband and wife with the other spouse as a life beneficiary. These trusts are also called *A and B trusts*.

marital property

Property acquired during marriage in a marital property state.

market value

The price property would bring if offered for sale in a fair market (not at auction or in a forced sale) by a willing and fully informed (but not compelled) seller, after ample time to find a willing and fully informed (but not compelled) buyer. The price is such as would be fixed by negotiation and mutual agreement. Market value is distinguished from market price, which is what the property might actually be sold for at a given time.

marriage

Legal union as husband and wife. Usually requiring a license, medical tests, and a ceremony.

material alteration

Any deliberate, *unilateral* (by one of the parties), important change that is made in a written contract, without legal excuse.

mayhem

The crime of unlawfully depriving the victim of some member of his or her body; disfiguring, disabling, or rendering the member useless or otherwise permanently disfiguring the body.

mechanic's lien

A legal claim of a contractor or worker who helped construct, improve, or repair a building (or repair a product, such as a car). It may be asserted against the property itself for any sum unpaid. A similar claim is given by law to suppliers of materials for construction projects.

med-arb

An alternative dispute resolution (ADR) process that combines mediation and arbitration. The intervenor is appointed to mediate the dispute. If the mediation is unsuccessful, the intervenor is authorized to resolve the dispute by arbitration with a binding award.

mediation

The use of a neutral third party to assist parties in voluntarily resolving their dispute(s).

medical-payments insurance

Coverage available in conjunction with automobile insurance—for example, to pay medical, surgical, dental, and funeral expenses suffered by the insured or any member of the insured's household who is injured while occupying or being struck by an automobile. Coverage may be extended to other persons occupying the owned automobile.

mens rea

[Latin for "guilty mind"] The intent necessary to be convicted of most criminal acts.

merchant

A businessperson who regularly deals in goods of the kind involved in a sales contract.

meretricious

A relationship between cohabiting, but unmarried, persons that includes sexual relations. Usage of the term is decreasing.

mini-trial

A nonbinding version of alternative dispute resolution (ADR) where the disputing parties, usually sizable business organizations, participate in an informal trial-like proceeding. Each side agrees to the procedural rules, including an exchange of information and selection of a neutral advisor. The presentation is made before officials of the parties who possess authority to settle disputes.

minor

A person below the age of legal competence. For most purposes, in most states, minority ends at age eighteen. For some purposes, such as the purchase and consumption of alcoholic beverages, it may end later, up to the age of twenty-one.

Miranda warnings

Warnings directed to a suspect by police before a *custodial* (while in custody) interrogation may occur. The warnings include disclosure of the right to remain silent, of the fact that anything said can and will be used against the person in court, and of the right to have a lawyer present during the questioning.

misdemeanor

A crime punishable by fine or by incarceration in a county jail up to a year, or by both.

mislaid property

Property that has been voluntarily placed somewhere by the owner and then forgotten.

misrepresentation

A false statement made intentionally, knowing it is not true. A negligent misrepresentation is a false statement made carelessly. See also "deceit" and "fraud."

mistrial

A trial that has failed to conclude properly because of some defect or because of the inability of the proper number of jurors to concur in a verdict. For example, inflammatory remarks by an attorney to a jury may result in a mistrial before the jury returns a verdict. A new trial is usually scheduled to follow a mistrial.

mobile home

A compact movable home, available for a relatively low price, and generally securely set down in a "mobile home park" and not removed thereafter.

Model Business Corporations Act

A model act concerning the corporation form of business, first drafted in 1933. Although not adopted in full by any state, it has significantly influenced the corporation codes of most states.

money

Coins and paper currency authorized by the federal government as a medium of exchange and as legal tender for payment of debts.

moot question

A question (a) open to argument and not settled by court decision, (b) purely hypothetical or academic, or (c) no longer important.

morals

Values concerning right and wrong.

moral problem solving

Conflict resolution process aimed at solving conflicts involving moral dilemmas through communication, education, and negotiation. A broad term that describes interrelational rather than individual process.

moral reasoning

A rational thought process directed at testing whether action is right or wrong. The conclusion is a determination of moral responsibility or culpability.

mortgage (or real mortgage)

The contract in which the buyer of real property typically gives a lender a lien or claim against the real property which serves as collateral for a loan of money, often borrowed to pay part of the purchase price. As borrower, the buyer signs a related contract— a promissory note—for the amount of the loan. Foreclosure and forced sale of the real property may follow if payments are not made as promised. In some states the same results are achieved with a *deed of trust.*

mortgage banker

A business that makes real estate loans with its own capital, as well as with institutional funds, and then sells the loans in the secondary mortgage market.

mortgage broker

A person licensed to engage in the business of bringing together borrowers and lenders of mortgage funds. Mortgage brokers typically are paid a commission based upon the volume of loans they originate.

mortgagee

The lender of funds secured by a mortgage. In states where deeds of trust are used instead of mortgages, the lender of funds (creditor) is called the *beneficiary.*

mortgagor

The borrower of funds secured by a mortgage. In states where deeds of trust are used instead of mortgages, the borrower (debtor) is called the *trustor.*

Mosaic Code

The Ten Commandments, or Decalogue, delivered to Moses on Mount Sinai. Some ethicists believe the commandments include a succinct statement of the *natural law.*

motion

A formal request by counsel addressed to a court or other tribunal for a particular decision or act (e.g., motion for directed verdict).

motion for change of venue

Request to a judge by counsel to transfer the trial to a different geographic location within the jurisdiction of the court.

motion for directed verdict

Request to a judge by counsel to enter a particular verdict instead of allowing the jury to do so because there are insufficient facts to allow any other verdict.

motion for summary judgment

Request to a judge by counsel to award judgment because there are no significant questions of fact in the lawsuit.

motion in limine

An application to a court requesting that the court make a pretrial decision, usually about excluding evidence expected to be introduced by the party opposing the motion.

motion to dismiss

See "demurrer."

motion to produce

Request to a judge by counsel to compel the opposing party to provide specified evidence to the court. This is a type of discovery procedure.

motive

A reason for doing, or not doing, an act. Motive is not synonymous with criminal intent. Intent is essential for proof of crime; motive is not. However, a good motive is no excuse for criminal conduct.

moving party

The party making a request of a court.

multiple-listing service

An organization of real estate brokers who exchange information about listings of property they have obtained. All member brokers (and their sales agents) may seek buyers for any of the multiple-listed properties. Any agent who finds a ready, willing, and able buyer of a listed property shares the commission earned with the agent who obtained the original listing agreement with the seller.

murder

The unlawful killing of a human being with malice aforethought. Usually classified as first-degree (or capital murder) or second-degree (or noncapital murder), depending on the degree of culpability involved. In some states murder includes the unlawful killing of a fetus.

mutual assent

A proper exchange of an offer and its acceptance by the parties forming a contract.

mutual mistake

Where both parties to a contract labor under the same error about an important fact in their agreement. Also called a *bilateral mistake.*

National Labor Management Relations Act of 1947 (Taft-Hartley Act)

A federal law that lists unfair labor practices of unions. It outlaws the closed shop and the secondary boycott.

National Labor Relations Act of 1935 (Wagner Act)

A federal law that recognizes the right of workers to organize into unions of their own choice, and the duty of employers to bargain collectively with the unions over wages, hours, and conditions of employment. It provides a list of unfair labor practices by management.

Natural Death Act

A statute that allows a person with a terminal condition to request a physician who may honor the request for removal of life support without criminal prosecution.

natural law

The higher law believed by some ethicists to be above and beyond man's power to change.

natural rights

Inalienable rights of every human being that exist by virtue of natural law, notably to life, liberty, and property.

necessaries

Goods and services ordinarily required by and appropriate to an incompetent person's station in life, yet not available and/or not provided by parent or guardian.

negative amortization

A monthly increase in the unpaid principal balance of a mortgage loan resulting when the borrower does not make the required monthly interest payments in full. Unpaid monthly interest is converted (called *capitalized*) into unpaid principal, causing the unpaid principal balance to increase each month. When a cap prevents the monthly payment of an adjustable-rate mortgage from rising to the amount required by the index rate of interest, the borrowers pay only the capped amount each month. But the amount of interest accruing each month continues, resulting in negative amortization.

negative injunction

An order of a court of equity forbidding specified action (e.g., continued sale of goods manufactured in violation of a patent owned by the plaintiff).

negligence

Failure to act as a reasonable, careful person would act under the same or similar circumstances, thereby causing injury that was foreseeable.

negligence per se

[Latin for "of itself"] (a) The unexcused violation of a statute or ordinance which is automatically deemed to be negligent conduct without argument or proof as to the particular surrounding circumstances. (b) Certain conduct that is deemed negligent because of its obvious breach of duty (e.g., driving a vehicle on a residential street at 90 mph is negligence per se).

negotiated rulemaking

A process to bring together representatives of a rulemaking agency and stakeholders to jointly prepare the text of a proposed rule in a consensus-seeking negotiation before the agency formally submits the rule to the formal rulemaking process.

negotiation

Communication between disputing parties for the purposes of persuasion and settlement without litigation. Negotiation is bargaining.

neighborhood dispute centers

Private or public organizations that provide trained mediators to assist parties in resolving consumer and neighbor disputes.

neighbor law

The body of laws and rules found in state statutes; in county and city ordinances; in covenants, conditions, and restrictions (CC&Rs); and in court decisions that govern the legal issues that arise between residential neighbors.

net listing

Employment contract in which the owner of real property agrees that, as compensation for finding a ready, willing, and able buyer, the licensed agent will retain all sums received by the seller that are in excess of a specified net amount.

net worth

The difference between total assets and total liabilities of a person or organization. (If liabilities exceed assets, the negative difference is called a *deficit*. In a corporation, a deficit is the excess of liabilities and capital stock over assets.)

neutral

An unbiased third party who assists others in the resolution of their disputes. Includes arbitrators, mediators, and ombudspersons.

neutral expert fact-finding

A nonbinding alternative dispute resolution (ADR) process in which an appointed third-party expert investigates and/or hears facts on selected issues and makes advisory findings of fact.

NIMBY

"Not in my back yard." A response that planners often hear to the location of less than desirable social programs or buildings.

no-fault

A type of automobile insurance, generally mandatory for all motorists in adopting states, that provides benefits to the insured, regardless of fault of parties to the accident.

no-fault divorce

A divorce granted by a court without either party having to prove fault in the other party. Traditional divorce used to be granted only to an innocent spouse, on proof that the other spouse was guilty of some misconduct, such as infidelity, mental cruelty, or desertion.

nolo contendere, plea of

[Latin for "I will not contest it"] Equivalent to a plea of guilty, but it cannot be regarded as admission of guilt in any subsequent civil trial against the defendant.

nominal (or token) damages

Insignificant amount (such as $1) awarded by a court when the defendant has violated the rights of the plaintiff but no monetary loss has been suffered or can be proved.

nonbinding arbitration

A form of arbitration in which the arbitrator's finding is not binding on the parties.

noncapital crime

A homicide for which the death penalty may not be imposed even if such penalty is authorized for other crimes by the state in which the crime is committed.

nonjudicial foreclosure

See "foreclosure."

non-normative statements

Statements that reflect no value judgment.

non-owned automobile

An automobile or trailer not owned by, or furnished for, the regular use of the named insured.

nonsupport

Failure to contribute money, in accordance with one's ability, to the maintenance of a parent or child as required by law.

normative statements

Statements that prescribe what should be or how one should act.

notarized

Signed in the presence of a person licensed by the state to perform identification services as a notary public. Most real estate documents, such as deeds, deeds of trust, mortgages, and written easements, must be notarized before they can be recorded in the official records of the county in which the property is located.

note

A written contract which is the best evidence of the existence of a debt. A note contains all of the essential terms of the loan, including the dollar amount, interest rate, signature of the borrower, due date, and other important matters. Also called *promissory note*.

notice of default

Notice used to inform the public (including the debtor) of an impending private foreclosure sale under a real estate mortgage and to commence the statutory time period that must elapse before a sale can take place.

novation

A three-party agreement in which a creditor accepts a new party who agrees to assume the debt and to release the prior debtor.

nuisance

Any unreasonable and continuous interference with the use and enjoyment of real property. For example, an overhanging tree that threatens the safety of a neighbor is a nuisance. Intangibles, such as sound, also can be a nuisance if unreasonable and continuous.

nullification of marriage

A court judgment terminating a defective or voidable marriage (for example, one involving a person below the age of legal consent).

nuncupative will

An oral will.

objective theory of contracts

A theory that the words and conduct of an offeror mean whatever a reasonable person in the offeree's position would think they mean, as opposed to what the offeror may have actually meant.

obscene

Material or conduct is obscene if, considered as a whole, its predominant appeal is to prurient interest, i.e., a morbid interest in nudity, sex, or excretion. Community standards, as distinguished from national standards, are used by the jury in applying this definition to material or conduct alleged to be obscene.

Occupational Safety and Health Administration (OSHA)

A federal agency charged with defining and enforcing minimum standards of health and safety in the workplace. Assisted in some states by state OSHA officials.

offer

A promise by one person (the offeror) to do or to give consideration (something of value) in exchange for sought-for consideration through acceptance by another person (the offeree). See also "acceptance."

offeree

In contracts, the party to whom an offer is made by the offeror.

offeror

In contracts, the party who makes an offer.

officers (of corporation)

Persons selected by directors and given delegated authority to manage the day-to-day business affairs of a corporation. Officers typically include a president, vice-president(s), secretary, and treasurer.

ombudsperson

A proactive neutral party who investigates and determines facts and suggests resolutions to disputes.

opening statements

Summaries by counsel of plaintiff and of defendant indicating what they expect to prove in the ensuing trial.

open listing

Employment contract in which the owner of real property agrees to pay a commission only to the real estate agent who produces a ready, willing, and able buyer. Thus, an owner may sign several open listings, each with a different agent, and pay only one commission. The owner may also sell the property without the aid of any agents and pay no commission.

open shop

A company or department where union membership is not required to get or keep a job.

option

The right to purchase property at an established price at any time within a specified period. The optionee (potential buyer) pays option money to the owner in exchange for this right.

option contract

An agreement concerning the right to buy or sell something to another at a certain price within a certain time. It often refers to rights to buy or sell real or personal property.

order of examination

A judicially authorized inquiry as to the assets of a judgment debtor.

ordinance

A written law enacted by a city or county. An example is a zoning ordinance that governs the use of land.

ordinary care

The standard of care that would have been exercised by an ordinary, reasonably prudent person under the same or similar circumstances.

ordinary wear and tear

Deterioration in a residential rental property that is attributable to the passage of time (e.g., fading of draperies) and not to abuse by the tenant.

outrageous conduct

Intentional conduct that does not involve assault or battery yet inflicts extreme emotional trauma on the victim.

owner

A person who has legal and/or equitable title to property, with related rights and duties, or benefits and burdens. See also "equitable owner" and "legal owner."

paralegal

A person qualified to perform a wide range of legal tasks under the guidance of an attorney. See also "legal assistant."

pardon

Release of a convicted criminal from all punishment for his or her crime through an act of the governor of the state or president of the United States.

parole

Release from a prison on specified conditions involving good behavior. If these conditions are violated, the prisoner is returned to prison to complete the original sentence.

parol-evidence rule

The rule that when contracting parties have put their complete agreement into writing, no prior or contemporaneous oral or written terms may be unilaterally added later to change the written contract, absent proof of fraud, mistake, or illegality.

participating preferred stock

Shares of preferred stock, the owners of which are entitled to receive additional dividends (beyond the regular agreement amount) when payments are made to common stockholders of the corporation.

parties

Persons of a particular class, occupation, or relation (e.g., children, creditors, heirs), or any persons who are either directly or indirectly necessary to a proper determination of the legal action before a court.

partnering

A teambuilding process designed to improve contract performance and reduce or eliminate contract litigation through common understanding of goals and improved communication. The process is used in large, complicated and expensive contracts with its roots in the construction industry.

partnership

An association of two or more persons to carry on, as co-owners, a business for a profit. Also known as a "general partnership."

paternity

Establishing the father of a child. Often determined by a lawsuit to prove that a named person is the father of a child.

paternity action

A lawsuit to determine whether or not the defendant is the natural father of a child.

payee

Person in whose favor a check, draft, or promissory note is drawn.

peaceful eviction

An improper eviction technique by which a landlord surreptitiously enters the absent tenant's apartment, removes the tenant's belongings, and changes locks to the unit. It is peaceable in the sense that no eye-to-eye, person-to-person confrontation takes place, as in a forcible eviction.

Pension Benefit Guaranty Corporation (PBGC)

Created under the Employee Retirement Income Security Act to assure financial soundness of specified private pension plans.

peremptory challenge

See "challenge (of juror)."

performance

That which each party to a contract promises to do.

periodic tenancy

A leasehold interest that continues indefinitely for successive periods (usually monthly) until properly terminated by either the lessor (landlord) or lessee (tenant).

perjury

Lying about material facts when testifying under oath.

personal-liability insurance

Contract that protects the insured from civil liability that may arise from his or her action in causing injury or death to another person.

personal property

All property that is not *real property,* i.e., property other than land and things permanently attached to it.

petition

A written request to a court asking it to take a particular action.

petitioner

(a) In many courts, term used interchangeably with the term *plaintiff* to mean the moving party in a lawsuit. (b) Moving party in an action in equity. (c) Used synonymously with the term *appellee.* (d) Moving party in an arbitration case.

petty larceny

Theft of personal property of a value less than that specified by statute. If the value exceeds the statutory minimum, often $500, the crime becomes grand larceny.

petty theft

Theft of a thing of little value, as specified by statute. Because of the small value, the crime is a misdemeanor.

picketing

Patrolling by strikers or sympathizers, generally at the entrances to a business plant, during a labor dispute. Pickets usually carry placards urging workers to join the strikers and urging suppliers and customers to refuse to deal with the employer.

pilferage

Stealing of small goods from storage, usually by employees of the owner or of the warehouse operator.

pimping

The crime of enticing a female to engage in prostitution. Also called *pandering* and *procuring.*

PITI

An acronym for *principal, interest, taxes,* and *insurance,* which represent the four basic repetitive expenses of buying real property with borrowed funds. Lenders qualify prospective borrowers upon their ability to make the monthly payment of PITI.

plaintiff

In trial, the person trying to recover money damages or other relief from a defendant.

planned unit development (PUD)

A subdivision that is designed and built functionally integrated, featuring common areas (such as private roadways, parks, and landscaping), uniformity of aesthetically attractive building design, and ongoing regulation by a homeowners' association (HOA).

plea

Response of the accused to criminal charges. In most states it may be (a) guilty, (b) not guilty, (c) nolo contendere, or (d) not guilty by reason of insanity.

plea bargain

A binding agreement in which an accused agrees to plead guilty (or nolo contendere) if the court agrees to a specified punishment in advance. Plea bargains avoid the time, expense, and outcome uncertainty of a trial.

pleadings

The complaint of the plaintiff and answer of the defendant in a lawsuit.

PMI

See "private mortgage insurance (PMI)."

points

A one-time charge made by a lender when a home loan is originated. One point is 1 percent of the loan.

police power

The inherent power of the government to make laws and impose reasonable regulations for the health, safety, morals, or general welfare of the public, even when this limits individual freedom.

polygraph (tests)

"Lie detector" tests using an electromechanical device for recording dramatic changes in body functions during interrogation.

portfolio lender

A lender of home-purchase funds that does not expect to sell its mortgages in the secondary mortgage market. Because such lenders keep their loans within their own portfolio of loans, they can be more flexible (liberal) in the terms of the loans they offer prospective home buyers.

positive law

Law enacted by governmental authority, such as legislatures, courts, and administrative agencies, as distinguished from natural law.

possession

The custody and control of property coupled with the right to use it.

possessory lien

A lien that empowers a creditor to retain possession of the collateral until the debt is paid or until it is sold to the highest bidder in accordance with law. Typically a mechanic has a possessory lien on the automobile that is repaired. On the other hand, an attorney does not have a possessory lien on the client's files.

power of appointment

Authority given to a person (the donee) under a trust or will to designate or appoint the person(s) who shall receive specified assets after a specified event (such as death of the donee or death of the testator).

power of attorney

A document authorizing another person to act as one's agent. A general power of attorney authorizes the agent (called the *attorney-in-fact*) to do all acts not prohibited by law for another (called the *principal*). A special power of attorney authorizes the attorney-in-fact to do a limited and specified class of acts for the principal.

power of sale

A clause found in a mortgage or deed of trust that, upon a default in monthly payments, authorizes the creditor (mortgagee or beneficiary) to cause the collateral for the loan (i.e., the debtor's home) to be sold to the highest bidder at a private sale. Without a power-of-sale clause, foreclosing creditors would be required to file a court action for foreclosure, a time-consuming and costly process, before the collateral could be sold.

precedent

A court decision on a question of law that gives authority or direction on a similar question of law in a later case with similar facts. See also "*stare decisis.*"

preemption

Assertion by the federal government of authority to regulate a field (such as certain labor relations). States cannot enforce conflicting laws in such fields. (The same principle applies between state and local governments.) Preemption is also called *supremacy.*

preferred stock

Shares that represent ownership in a business corporation and whose holders are entitled to dividends of a fixed amount before any payment is made to shareholders of common stock.

Pregnancy Discrimination Act (1978)

Federal law that requires employers to treat women affected by pregnancy or related medical conditions just as they would treat other temporarily disabled employees (e.g., regarding accrual of seniority status and return to work). This act is an amendment to the Civil Rights Act of 1964.

preliminary hearing

An examination in open court by a judge to determine whether sufficient evidence exists to hold the accused for trial. Preliminary hearings are not used when a grand jury issues an indictment.

prenuptial

Occurring prior to the commencement of marital status. Prenuptial agreements are made before marriage but concern property matters during marriage. These binding agreements are also called *antenuptial agreements* and *premarital agreements.*

preponderance of evidence

Standard of determining civil liability, that the weight of the evidence offered to prove a matter is more probable than not.

prescriptive easements

Easements, usually of access, over the land of another person, created by a continuous, open (visible) use without the consent of the landowner for a long period of time, usually five years or more in most states.

presumption

A rule of law permitting one to assume a fact is true until such time as there is a greater weight of evidence that disproves or outweighs the assumed fact.

pretermitted heir

A child who was not specifically provided for in life and was not mentioned in his or her parent's will. Statutes typically declare that such a child, or the issue of a deceased child, shares in the estate as though the testator had died intestate.

pretermitted heir statute

A statute giving rights of inheritance to a testator's children (or grandchildren) when they are not named in the will and not provided for by settlement in life.

pretrial proceeding (conference or hearing)

In the months before a civil trial is scheduled to begin, several pretrial proceedings may occur. One type is a settlement conference attended by the attorneys, parties, and judge to determine if the case can be amicably settled without a trial. Another type is a conference attended by the attorneys and the judge to formalize the issues to be determined at trial and to decide whether to have a jury, among other matters.

prima facie

[Latin for "on first appearance"] Term describing a fact presumed to be true unless disproved by some contrary evidence. With reference to a legal case, such fact will prevail unless and until contradicted and overcome by other evidence.

primary law

Law stated without interpretation by commentators. Primary law consists of established rules from constitutions, statutes, administrative agency regulations and rules, treaties, and judicial decisions.

principal

(a) The person who empowers an agent to enter contract(s) on her or his behalf. (b) In criminal law, one who is present and participates in a crime or persuades another to commit a crime.

prior restraint

(a) Legal measures to prevent anticipated illegal conduct before it takes place, such as the banning of a parade expected to cause a riot. (b) Constitutional—First Amendment—prohibition of restraints on a publication before it is actually published. Exceptions to the rule include certain obscene publications, certain publications that invade personal privacy, and publications that create clear and present danger to the public.

privacy, invasion of right of

Violation of the fundamental right of every person who has done no wrong to be simply left alone.

private judging

The use of a legally trained arbitrator who follows formal judicial procedures in hearing a case outside a court. The final award is entered as a judgment in many states with the right of judicial appeal allowed.

private law

That body of law regulating the rights and duties that exist between private persons (including private corporations). Contract law is an example of private law.

private mortgage insurance (PMI)

Insurance to protect a lender in the event that a borrower defaults in the repayment of a mortgage loan. Premiums for PMI are paid monthly by the borrower along with the monthly mortgage payment.

privilege

A legal right to do or refrain from doing something enjoyed by only some persons or classes (e.g., immunity of judges from liability for defamation for statements made during judicial proceedings).

privilege against self-incrimination

The right of any person, including one accused of a crime, to remain silent when what might be said could indicate guilt. The Fifth Amendment to the U.S. Constitution provides that "No person . . . shall be compelled in any criminal case to be a witness against himself. . . ."

privileged communication

A right and duty one has to withhold communications from legal proceedings because of some special relationship (e.g., attorney-client, physician-patient, husband-wife, priest-penitent).

privity of contract

Applies to a direct contractual relationship between parties, as exists, for example, with a consumer-buyer dealing with the retail-seller but not with the wholesaler or manufacturer of the goods (who are farther away in the chain of distribution).

probate

The process of proving the validity of a will in court, coupled with the related matter of administering the decedent's estate. Involves payment of debts to creditors and distribution of remaining assets to heirs and/or named beneficiaries.

probation

Release of a convicted criminal before sentence begins on condition of good behavior and under supervision of a probation officer. If this condition is violated, incarceration begins.

pro bono publico

[Latin for "for the public good"] When an attorney provides legal services free of charge to poor but worthy clients or causes.

procedural law

General principles and detailed rules that define the methods of administering substantive law.

process

Legal documents or writs (orders issued from a court) used to compel a defendant in a lawsuit to answer a complaint and appear in court.

process server

A person who serves (delivers) a copy of the summons and complaint, or other legal document, upon a party or witness at the request of the opposing party to civil litigation.

product liability

A general area of law holding manufacturers and sellers of goods liable to buyers, users, and perhaps bystanders for harm caused when goods are defective.

professional ethics

Written rules of prohibited conduct that are adopted by and binding upon members of a professional group.

profit

(a) The excess of revenues or receipts of a business over costs or expenses. The profit is also called *net income.* (b) A right to enter the land of another and take something from the land such as oil, minerals, and timber (more formally called *profit-a-pendre*).

promisee

The person to whom a contractual promise has been made. See also "offeree."

promisor

The person who makes a contractual promise. See also "offeror."

promissory note, negotiable

A written promise to pay to a named person or to the bearer of the note a certain sum of money in the future. The note may contain the terms of the loan, such as the due date, repayment schedule, interest rate, and so forth. To be a negotiable promissory note, it must comply with Article III of the Uniform Commercial Code.

property

Anything that may be owned. Classified broadly as real and personal property. See *"personal property"* and *"real property."*

property-damage insurance

Contract that protects the insured with coverage for liability arising from his or her damaging the property of another.

property-tax rate

The factor that, when multiplied by the assessed value of a parcel of taxable real property, produces the amount of annual property tax the owner must pay. The factor is computed annually by local government officials who divide the county budget by the assessed value of all taxable real property in the county [e.g., assuming this factor to be 1.25 percent (.0125), the annual tax on a home assessed at $150,000 would be $1,875 (since .0125 x 150,000 = 1,875)].

pro se

[Latin for "for himself or herself"] See *"in propria persona."*

prosecutor

An attorney employed by the government to pursue legal proceedings against persons accused of crime. The prosecutor represents the state, or the people, in criminal trials.

prospectus

A formal report published prior to the issuance of securities by a corporation, containing basic important facts about the company and its operations.

protected class

A classification of persons defined by one or more of these criteria: race, color, gender, national origin, age, or religion.

provocative-act rule

The rule that all participants in a dangerous felony are guilty of murder in the first degree if a lawful killing occurs in response to some threatening act by one of the felons. An example is a killing of an innocent bystander by a police officer who fires in response to gun-waving by one of the fleeing felons.

proximate cause (or causation)

An action that, in natural and continuous sequence, unbroken by an intervening force or cause, produces the injury, and without which the effect or result would not have occurred. Furthermore, the result is not entirely outside the range of expectation or probability.

proxy

A written power of attorney signed by a shareholder authorizing another person to vote on her or his behalf at a meeting of the stockholders of the corporation.

publication of defamatory material

Communicating defamatory material about a person(s) to one or more other persons.

public defender

A lawyer provided by the community for a person who is accused of a serious crime (felony) and cannot afford to hire counsel.

public-interest law firm

A nonprofit law firm that offers assistance in areas such as employment, minority rights, civil rights, political rights, family law, and environmental law.

public law

That body of law directly concerned with public rights and obligations, such as constitutional, administrative, criminal, and international law.

public policy

A fundamental guideline under which courts condemn or validate actions depending on whether the conduct is deemed to be contrary to or supportive of the commonweal or good of society.

published

A legal rule of wills in some states requiring a declaration by the maker of the will to the witnesses that the document they are about to sign is indeed his or her will.

puffing

Seller's talk; claims about the quality of goods, usually exaggerated; not considered fraud.

punitive (or exemplary) damages

Amount awarded by a court, to the victim of an intentional tort, in addition to compensatory damages; designed to punish the tortfeasor and serve as an example to others.

purchase agreement and deposit receipt

A contract by which a seller agrees to sell, and the buyer agrees to buy, a specified parcel of real property at a specified price and upon specified terms.

purchase-money mortgage

A loan the proceeds of which are used to purchase a home. The lender retains a nonpossessory equitable interest in the home as security for repayment of the loan.

quasi

[Latin for "as if"] A term used in conjunction with other words to mean having a legal status only by operation or construction of law. For example, "quasi-contract" means an agreement that resembles a contract and may be enforced as one even when some essential element of a contract is missing. Designed to prevent unjust enrichment of one of the parties.

questions of fact

Circumstances or matters surrounding and involved in a case that is being tried by a court. These questions refer to events that allegedly took place in the past and are now in dispute. The jury decides if the information provided is true.

questions of law

Principles and rules of human conduct determined by the judge to be applicable in a case being tried by a court. For example, the definition of murder is a question of law within the province of the judge and not the jury.

quid pro quo

[Latin: "this for that"] Expression often is used in sexual harassment situations when sexual favors or demands are a term or condition of an individual's employment, or the basis for employment decisions affecting such individual. Also used as a synonym for consideration.

quiet enjoyment

The sense of ownership, such as freedom from interference by others (who claim a superior legal right to occupy the premises) that a tenant is entitled to receive as an implied incident of a lease.

quiet title action

Action "against the world" initiated by a person who claims ownership of a particular parcel of real property. The action forces any person in the world who has a claim to ownership or possession of the property either to step forward and assert the claim or to lose it forever.

quitclaim deed

A deed to real property in which the transferor conveys whatever ownership interest he or she may possess, which may be none. The transferor makes no warranties and therefore cannot be held liable if the title transferred proves to be faulty. A quitclaim deed is commonly used to correct errors in recorded titles. See also "deed."

racial quota

Required hiring of specific numbers of minorities and/or women to rectify past discrimination. Affirmative action programs are legal but the U.S. Supreme Court has rejected quotas.

Racketeer Influenced and Corrupt Organization Act (RICO) of 1970

A federal law passed to control attempts by organized crime to invest money gained from illegal racketeering in legitimate business activities. The scope of this law is broad and creates both civil and criminal remedies for activities defined as racketeering, which include twenty-six types of federal crimes and nine state felonies.

rape, forcible

An unlawful act of sexual intercourse, against the will of the victim. Consent obtained by trick or threat or through the use of intoxicants or narcotics is not considered true consent.

rape-shield statute

A statute that protects victims from courtroom questioning about prior sexual experiences with persons other than the defendant.

real estate agent

A person licensed by the state to negotiate the buying and selling of real property while employed and supervised by a licensed real estate broker.

real estate broker

One licensed by the state to act as an intermediary for real estate transactions on behalf of others for a fee or commission.

real estate owned (REO)

Institutional lenders, such as banks and savings and loan associations, sometimes receive title to properties secured by loans that are in default, following foreclosure sales. Typically these lenders then offer the reclaimed properties, called REOs, for sale.

real property

Land and things permanently attached to it. Includes air space above, surface water, and subsurface waters, gases, and minerals.

reasonable accommodation

Expression in some employment statutes requiring an employer to make modifications in workplace or job requirements to accommodate an employee.

reasonable person

A hypothetical person used in the law as a standard for reasonable conduct. For example, failure to act as a reasonable person under given circumstances is usually deemed to be negligence. This may result in liability to others for injuries caused thereby.

recall

A democratic process for removing public officials from their elective positions by a vote of the people taken after filing of a petition signed by the required number of qualified voters.

receiving stolen property

The crime of knowingly receiving stolen property. Proof of knowledge may be inferred from the circumstances.

recidivist

A criminal who is a repeat offender. Violation of statutes against recidivism may increase a lesser penalty to life imprisonment.

recognizance

A written promise by the accused that if released without posting bail, he or she will return voluntarily for further criminal proceedings. See also "bail."

recordation

The act or process of recording title to real property in a public registry.

redlining

An illegal lending practice derived from identifying minority or low-income neighborhoods where repayment histories have been poor and then denying or restricting loans to persons in that area.

referendum

A democratic process whereby a state legislature submits (refers) proposed laws, or existing laws, to the electorate for approval or rejection.

refinance loan

A loan, secured by mortgage, the proceeds of which are used primarily to pay off, or retire, an existing mortgage loan. Refinancing occurs when interest rates drop, encouraging homeowners to pay off existing high-interest-rate loans with new lower-interest-rate loans.

registered buyer-owner

The buyer of a car on credit, who, as the equitable owner, gets possession and use of the vehicle while making payments. The seller (or lender) remains the legal owner until the car is paid for in full. See also "owner."

regulations

Rules promulgated by an administrative agency under authority given to the agency by the enabling statute.

Regulatory Flexibility Act

Federal law requiring federal agencies to consider the effects of their regulatory actions on small businesses and other small entities and to minimize any undue disproportionate burden.

regulatory offense

A violation of a rule promulgated by an administrative agency.

rehabilitative alimony

Financial support paid by one former spouse to the other for a definite period of time during which the recipient is expected to prepare for financial independence (e.g., by vocational education).

reinstatement of mortgage

A procedure in which, upon payment to a foreclosing creditor of all delinquent sums and related fees within a prescribed period of time, the original loan terms are reinstated as if no default had occurred. The right of reinstatement belongs to the debtor or her or his assigns. See also "right of reinstatement."

relevant evidence

Evidence that is related to the facts in dispute. See also "irrelevant evidence."

remainderman

The person designated to receive complete ownership of property upon termination of a life estate. For example, when a man, in his will, leaves real property to his widow for her life, and then to their children, the children are called remaindermen. See also "life estate."

remainder interest

Any interest that is left after another interest in the property ends.

remainder trust

A trust that distributes (gives) the remaining property interest to an identified beneficiary (or beneficiaries) after the termination of a life estate.

remanded

The status of a case sent back to a lower court from which it had been appealed, with binding instructions as to its disposal or further required proceedings.

remedies

Relief provided by courts to redress wrongs and to enforce rights. Examples are monetary damages, orders for specific performance, injunctions, and other appropriate relief.

rent

Money paid by a renter to the landlord in exchange for the possession and use of rental property. Rent may also take the form of personal services, or the transfer of any asset in lieu of money.

rental agreement

A contract, usually written, between a landlord and tenant. Technically it is a lease. See also "lease."

rental unit

One unit in a multi-unit residential structure that is available to be rented. Urban apartments that are owned by their occupants are technically condominiums.

rent control

Government regulation of how much rent a landlord may charge for the possession and use of rental premises. Rent controls have not been imposed on commercial properties.

renter

(a) One who receives payment in exchange for the use of one's property by another. (b) One who pays rent for the use of another's property; a tenant.

REO

See "real estate owned (REO)."

replevin

Legal action to recover possession of goods (personal property) wrongfully taken or retained by a defendant.

reporter

A set of books that contain the written opinions of justices of specified appellate courts. These volumes contain the decisional or unwritten law. Volumes in the reporters and the cases they contain are arranged in chronological order and accessible by case name or subject matter index.

reprieve

Postponement, or stay of execution (i.e., of enforcement) of the judgment, after conviction for a crime.

republic

A system of government with the supreme power in the people, who exercise it by representatives chosen through the votes of qualified voters (i.e., qualified by age, citizenship, and registration).

request for admission of facts

A request submitted to counsel by the opposing attorney before trial for the acknowledgment of facts that are not in dispute and yet are relevant and material. This is a type of discovery procedure.

rescission

An equitable remedy that annuls a contract and returns the parties to the relationship they had before the contract was made.

residual powers

Any powers not expressly delegated to the United States by the U.S. Constitution nor prohibited by it to the states, and hence reserved to the states, or to the people.

residuary clause

Any part of a will which disposes of property not expressly disposed of by other provisions of the will.

res ipsa loquitur

[Latin for "the thing speaks for itself"] A doctrine under which negligence is inferred when the instrumentality causing the injury was under control of the defendant and an injury occurred that normally would not occur in the absence of negligence by the defendant. This doctrine is frequently relied on by victims of medical malpractice. To avoid liability the defendant must prove he or she was not negligent.

Resolution Trust Corporation (RTC)

A corporation created by Congress to salvage savings and loan companies and thrift institutions from insolvencies that resulted from imprudent lending practices during the 1980s. The RTC takes full control of such insolvent institutions and auctions their real estate holdings to raise money with which to reimburse depositors.

respondeat superior

[Latin for "let the master answer"] A legal doctrine holding employers liable for injuries caused third persons by their employees who were negligent while acting in the course and within the scope of their employment.

respondent

(a) The person against whom an appeal is taken. See also "appellee." (b) The person against whom a *motion* is filed. (c) Party who is notified to respond and proceed to arbitration.

Restatement of the Law

A series of authoritative volumes on major areas of law (e.g., contracts, agency, and torts) written by scholars of the nonprofit American Law Institute.

restitution

Return of what has been received or stolen, as when a contract is rescinded or when a thief repays stolen money or returns other stolen property.

retainer fee

(a) A sum of money paid to an attorney for a promise to remain available to the client for consultation when needed and requested. (b) Fees paid in advance that are held in a trust account to be drawn down (taken) by the attorney as work progresses.

retaliatory eviction

An eviction carried out by a landlord primarily for revenge, or retaliation, against a particular tenant who has in some way angered the landlord.

reverse discrimination

Label given to the results of affirmative action programs by opponents who claim that such programs discriminate against male and white workers.

reversionary interest

(a) Something of value (such as the right to borrow against the policy) that a life insurance policyholder may retain when giving the policy to another person. (b) The future interest in real property retained by the grantor of a life estate.

revocable trust

A trust that may be terminated or revoked by the trustor who created it.

right of redemption

Right of a debtor to recover, within one year, the property sold at a judicial foreclosure sale. The debtor must reimburse the purchaser of the foreclosure sale and must retire any unpaid amount owing the

original unpaid creditor who initiated the sale. A right of redemption is in the nature of a real property interest and is freely saleable.

right of reinstatement

The right of a defaulting debtor to reinstate the loan by payment of all money due for prior months including late charges, even though the note and mortgage declare that the *entire* unpaid balance is immediately due in full upon any default.

right of retraction

A defense against libel favoring certain publications, such as newspapers. Even if a paper defames someone, prompt publication of a retraction, or admission of error, may be a complete or partial defense against a claim for damages.

rights, civil

Rights that a person has as a human being and by virtue of U.S. citizenship. These rights are found in constitutions and state and federal civil rights laws. They include the rights to equal protection of the law and to due process of law.

rights, fundamental

Basic rights that a person has under the U.S. Constitution, such as the rights of freedom of speech, press, religion, and assembly.

rights, legal

Rights to recognition and protection of one's person, property, and other interests, enforceable in court. Legal rights may include civil, natural, and political rights. They are the reciprocal of legal duties.

rights, natural

Rights that a person has by virtue of being human, such as the right to life, liberty, and the pursuit of happiness.

rights, political

Rights that citizens share in government, including the right to vote and to hold public office.

right-to-know law

Statute that requires informing workers of the hazards from chemicals that they are likely to be exposed to on the job.

right-to-work laws

Statutes enacted in about twenty states that provide that a person cannot be required to join a union as a condition of receiving or retaining a job. Most of them also ban any obligation to pay dues to a union.

robbery

The crime of stealing property from another person in his or her immediate presence through the use of force or fear.

Roman civil law

See "civil law."

Roth IRA

A form of Individual Retirement Account authorized by federal law that allows a taxpayer to save after-tax dollars and pay no federal income taxes on the earnings even when withdrawn.

rule against perpetuities

A rule that requires remainder interests in property to vest (i.e., to take effect) no later than a life or any number of identified lives in being, plus twenty-one years.

rule of law

Holds that decisions should be made by the application of established laws without the intervention of individual discretion.

sale

A contract in which title (ownership) of property passes from seller to buyer. Possession usually transfers at the time of sale.

same-sex marriage

The bond formed when persons of the same sex live together as spouses though without the legal formalities. Same-sex marriages are not legal in the U.S., but are legal in some countries (e.g., Denmark, Norway, and Sweden).

satisfaction of judgment

Proof that a debt created by a judgment of the court has been paid by the defendant.

S corporation

A closely held corporation that is treated as a partnership for federal tax purposes. Income is regarded as taxable personal income to the stockholders, whether distributed or retained in the business. One effect is avoidance of the customary double taxation of corporate net income.

search and seizure

A phrase that describes any search of one's person or property and the process of taking evidence into custody by an officer of the law. Evidence obtained by police in an unreasonable search and seizure (e.g., without a proper warrant) is tainted with illegality and may not be used against the accused under the so-called *exclusionary rule*.

secondary boycott

Occurs when striking workers picket or use other pressure against a neutral third party who supplies or buys from the struck employer.

secondary materials

Law from other than *primary sources;* books that present some writer's opinion of what the law is or should be, such as encyclopedias, dictionaries, treatises, and texts.

secondary mortgage market

A financial market in which existing mortgages are bought and sold. The market is composed of investors, private institutions (such as pension funds and insurance companies), and government agencies, which purchase mortgages, thereby making funds available for new mortgages.

second degree

A measurement in law of the degree of culpability of the perpetrator of a crime—less than first degree.

second mortgage

A loan secured by a mortgage that is originated subsequent to an existing mortgage. In real estate, "first in time is first in right." Upon default and sale of property to satisfy indebtedness, a first mortgagee must be paid in full (or the creditor-mortgagee may accept the collateralized home, free and clear of all debt) before the holder of the second mortgage is entitled to receive anything.

secured loan

Money borrowed in exchange for a pledge by the borrower of specific assets that may be forfeited if repayment is not made as promised.

secured transaction

Any transaction, regardless of form, that is intended to create a security interest in personal property.

security

Collateral for loan, available to the creditor if the debtor should default. In home-purchase loans, the home is the security for repayment of the mortgage debt.

security deposit

A lump sum of cash paid by a tenant to his or her new landlord as security that the tenant will pay rent as agreed and will not damage the rented premises.

seduction

The criminal act of enticing a person to engage in sexual intercourse by means of a false promise (as of marriage), but without physical force.

segregation

Isolation or separate treatment, usually unequal, on the sole basis of race, color, creed, or national origin.

self-defense

The legal right to use whatever force appears to be reasonably necessary to protect oneself (or specified others) from great and imminent bodily injury by an assailant.

self-help

A common-law rule that, under certain circumstances, a person can legally take action to resolve a problem without resort to a court or the legal system (e.g., to trespass for the purpose of recovering stolen property, or to tear down an encroaching fence). Generally, self-help is no longer a lawful remedy; an aggrieved person must resort to peaceful judicial alternatives.

self-incrimination

See "privilege against self-incrimination."

separate maintenance

A partial termination of marriage in which the spouses live apart while support is paid. Property normally is not divided. See also "divorce from bed and board" and "legal separation."

separate property

Property, real or personal, either brought into a marriage at the outset or acquired during marriage by gift or inheritance, together with the profits there from. To retain this status, it must be treated as such, in formal records, for example. See also "community property."

separation

The status of spouses who are by judicial decree living apart, i.e., no longer cohabiting.

separation agreement

A contract between spouses who are contemplating a divorce. See also "antenuptial agreement."

separation of powers

The constitutional doctrine dividing and confining certain powers of the U.S. government into the legislative, the executive, and the judicial branches.

SEPs

See "simplified employee pension plans (SEPs)."

Service Corps of Retired Executives (SCORE)

A sizable group of experienced retired business executives who provide expert counselling and training to new small-business entrepreneurs without charge, under the auspices of the federal Small Business Administration.

settlor

A person who establishes a trust. A settlor is also called a *trustor*.

severalty

Separate or individual ownership of property by one person or ownership as separate property by a married person. See "in severalty."

sex perversion

Criminal violation of state laws prohibiting sodomy, oral copulation, and/or lewd or lascivious acts with a child.

sexual harassment

A form of illegal gender discrimination wherein (a) job opportunities, promotions, and the like are given on the basis of sexual favors or (b) the employee is subjected to a work environment where the employee must put up with sexual comments, jokes, or physical contact that is sexually offensive.

shareholder

See "stockholder."

shares

See "stock."

shoplifting

Surreptitiously stealing merchandise from displays in a retail store.

shopkeeper's privilege

Legal right of a storekeeper to detain suspected shoplifters for a reasonable time in a reasonable way when there is probable cause to believe a theft has taken place.

short sale

(a) The sale of property (such as a home) for less than the unpaid balance of a loan in which the property serves as security. (b) The sale of securities, commodities, or foreign currency not actually owned by the seller, who hopes to "cover" (i.e., buy back at a lower price) contracts for the goods previously sold—and thus earn a profit.

simple contracts

All oral and written contracts that are not classified as formal contracts which require a specified form to be enforceable (e.g., contracts under seal).

simplified employee pension plans (SEPs)

Private employee pension plans authorized by federal law whereby employers contribute to their employees' Individual Retirement Accounts.

sitdown strike

Illegal strike in which strikers remain in their places of employment but refuse to work.

situational ethics

Term used disparagingly to describe an "end justifies the means" maxim supplanting duty or obligation.

slander

Oral defamation. See "defamation."

slander per se

Slander in itself; words not requiring proof of special damages.

Small Business Administration (SBA)

Federal administrative agency that provides information, advice, and financial assistance to business managers and qualified small-business firms.

small claims court

A court with jurisdiction to decide civil controversies of a relatively minor or insignificant nature as far as society in general is concerned.

sobriety checkpoint

A method used by police authorities of stopping automobiles at random locations and inspecting the drivers to determine whether they are guilty of DUI (driving under the influence of alcohol or drugs).

social contract

(a) An agreement setting forth rights, duties, and obligations of government officials and the people governed (e.g., a constitution). (b) In political philosophy, a theory that human beings associate together for mutual protection and well-being, and the government rests on and depends on their consent.

sole proprietorship

A business owned and typically operated by one person, who receives all profits and is liable for all losses.

solicitation

The crime of assisting or encouraging another person to commit a crime.

"Son of Sam" law

A law that limits the ability of a criminal offender to receive profits from the recounting of his or her crime.

sovereign immunity

Traditional legal rule that "the king can do no wrong," hence, government is not liable for the torts of its agents and employees. The modern trend is away from recognition of such immunity.

special damages

Amount awarded by a court to pay for monetary out-of-pocket losses resulting from the specific or special circumstances of the plaintiff (e.g., for medical expenses, loss of wages, and destruction of property). Special damages are a type of compensatory damages.

specific performance

Remedy available in a court of equity for a buyer to get possession and title to real property and to goods that are unique, when the seller refuses to deliver under a valid sales contract. Dollar damages that are the customary remedy are deemed inadequate.

specious lawsuit

(a) Any lawsuit brought against the authors of this text. (b) A lawsuit which on its face may appear to have validity but is in fact totally without merit.

spendthrift trust

A trust created to provide for the maintenance of an improvident beneficiary by limiting his or her control of the corpus (the principal of the trust) and by barring access by creditors. Only a small portion is given to the beneficiary at any one time, and major expenses may be paid directly by the trustee.

spite fence

A fence erected primarily to vex, annoy, or "spite" a neighbor. Such fences usually block the targeted neighbor's view or access, or are constructed so shabbily as to detract from the value of the neighbor's property.

spousal immunity

A doctrine of the common law that tort actions between spouses are prohibited because of a public policy to protect the harmony of the marital relationship from adversarial and disruptive legal proceedings.

stalking

An unwelcome or intrusive long-term pattern of threat or harassment directed repeatedly toward a specific individual which triggers fear or concern in that person.

standard of care

The legal duty to behave as a hypothetical reasonably prudent person would behave under the same or similar circumstances.

standard title insurance

Customary title insurance coverage that does not include the special coverage included within the more expensive American Land Title Association policy, which includes physical inspection of the premises as well as a review of the official records in a title search.

standing to sue doctrine

A person's right or capacity to bring a lawsuit because he or she has a legally protectible interest at stake in the litigation.

stare decisis

[Latin for "to stand by decided cases"] The common-law doctrine that binds an inferior (subordinate) court to follow and apply decisions and interpretations of higher courts when similar cases arise. Also called the *doctrine of precedents*.

state action

The limitations provided in the Constitution are limitations on governmental action. If a behavior is questioned as violating an individual's constitutional rights, the party so complaining must show the action was by government or an agent of government.

state law

Includes state constitutions, statutes enacted by state legislatures, rules promulgated by state agencies, and the decisions of state courts.

statute of frauds

A state statute requiring certain types of contracts to be evidenced in writing and to be signed by the party to be charged, or by her or his authorized agent.

statute of limitations

A statute that bars civil or criminal proceedings unless brought within a specified period of time after the act occurred. Note that there is no statute of limitations for murder. See also "statute of repose."

statute of repose

A type of statute of limitations that specifies an absolute time from the date of sale during which a cause of action must be brought to collect damages for defects in the product.

statutes

Laws enacted by Congress or by state legislatures.

statutory rape

Sexual intercourse between a male, usually eighteen or older, and a consenting female, usually seventeen or younger. State statutes vary the penalties depending on the age of the victim. Also called *unlawful intercourse*.

statutory will

A form will authorized by state law with blanks to be completed by the testator.

stock

Certificate of ownership of a share or interest in a business corporation. May be common or preferred, with further subdivisions depending on related rights.

stock dividend

A distribution declared by directors of a corporation in the form of shares of the corporation's stock rather than cash. An appropriate accounting transfer is made from "earned surplus" to "capital." The dividend is not taxable to the recipient unless a share received is sold and a profit is realized.

stockholder

A person who owns one or more shares of the capital stock of a profit-seeking corporation. The stockholder's liability for losses is normally limited to the amount of the capital investment made through purchase and retention of the stock.

stock split

Occurs when directors of a corporation divide each share of stock into a larger number of shares. There is no accounting transfer from "earned surplus" to "capital" as in a stock dividend. However, if the stock has par value or stated value, such values are accordingly changed. There is no tax due from the stockholder unless a share is sold and a profit is realized.

strict constructionist

A judge or court that is reluctant to create new rules by departing from clear precedent, leaving the creation of new laws primarily to the legislative branch of government.

strict liability

A legal theory applicable when a defective or hazardous product is sold and a user-victim is injured. The victim need not prove negligence, wrongful intent, breach of warranty, or privity of contract.

strike, labor

A concerted refusal by employees to perform the services for which they were hired, generally in order to gain recognition of a union, or improvements in wages, hours, or conditions of employment.

strike, sympathy

A strike called by workers in a company or department where there is no labor dispute in order to support striking workers employed elsewhere.

strikebreakers

Persons hired to take the place of workers who are out on strike. If it is an economic strike, the strikebreakers may be retained as permanent replacements.

subdivision home

Any home built in a tract of land that previously has been subdivided into lots. Most homes in a subdivision are built by one builder following three or four floor plans.

subject-matter jurisdiction

The power of a court to hear and decide cases of the general class to which the subject in question belongs, e.g., probate matters or domestic relations.

sublease

The transfer by a tenant of less than the full, unexpired term of the lease to a subtenant.

subornation of perjury

Crime of persuading another person to commit perjury.

subpoena

An order directing a person to appear at a certain time and place for the purpose of giving testimony as a witness.

subpoena duces tecum

[Latin for "under penalty bring with you"] A judicial order to bring specified documents or physical evidence to court.

subrogation

The substitution of a third party for the creditor in a claim against a debtor. For example, an insurance company may pay the claim of its insured against the defendant, and then sue the defendant in the name of the insured for damages resulting from an auto accident.

subsequent illegality

When terms of a contract, legal at inception, cannot be performed legally.

substantial performance

When a party to a contract honestly performs most essentials of the contract, but there is some minor omission or deviation that can be corrected, or compensated for in a reduction of the price.

substantive law

General principles and detailed rules that define legal rights and duties. Substantive law is contrasted to *procedural law.*

suffrage

The right to vote in political elections.

suicide

The intentional killing of oneself.

summary jury trial

A nonbinding alternative dispute resolution (ADR) process in which parties present their cases to a private mock jury, which then gives the parties an advisory verdict.

summation

The review of the evidence presented to the court by each lawyer in oral argument at the close of the trial, before the jury retires and before the judge renders a decision.

summons

A document issued by a clerk of the court at the request of the plaintiff when a complaint is filed. After service on the defendant, judgment will be taken if the complaint is not answered within the statutory time (e.g., fifteen or thirty days). A summons is prepared by the plaintiff's attorney. See also "complaint."

supremacy doctrine

The judicial doctrine that holds that any state or federal law that is inconsistent with the U.S. Constitution is null and void.

surrogate mother

A female who is artificially inseminated, carries the fetus to term, and then relinquishes her parental rights to the biological father. Surrogacy services are performed pursuant to a contract in return for money.

survivor statutes

Law allowing a lawsuit even after the death of the victim, perhaps permitting recovery for damages to the victim.

sustain

Agreement by the judge with an argument by an attorney. For example, if an attorney objects to the introduction of certain evidence and the judge agrees to the objection, the judge sustains the objection.

syllogism

A pattern of deductive logic that contains a major or general premise, a minor or specific premise, and a conclusion, always in that order. The conclusion follows from the premises but is not a premise itself.

symbolic speech

Communication of ideas by conduct and/or use of material objects, without the use of words. The expression may be deemed a form of speech protected by the First Amendment (e.g., use of black arm bands to protest the war in Vietnam).

tangible property

Property that has physical existence and can be touched. An automobile is tangible personal property; a house is tangible real property.

tax deductibility

Legal right to exclude an expense or expenditure from gross income, thereby reducing taxable income and its concomitant tax.

tax evasion

The intentional and illegal violation of federal and state tax laws. In contrast, tax avoidance is legitimate and an ongoing concern of accountants and tax lawyers under pressure from their clients.

temporary insanity

A passing or temporal mental disease or defect.

tenancy at sufferance

A tenant remaining in possession of real property without permission of the landlord after the expiration of a lawful term.

tenancy at will

A lawful possession of a tenancy without a definite duration. Tenancy at will can be terminated by either the landlord or the tenant at any time. (Statutes may require a short advance notice by landlords.)

tenancy by the entirety

A form of co-ownership of property between husband and wife in some states. As with joint-tenancy ownership, the spouses have a right of survivorship. See also "joint tenancy."

tenancy for years

A leasehold interest that expires at a specified time. It need not actually be for years in duration.

tenancy in common

A form of co-ownership of property by two or more persons. Upon the death of any co-owner, his or her percentage interest passes by intestate succession or by last will. Unlike joint tenancy, there is no right of survivorship by co-owners.

tenant

A party to a lease who pays rent to the landlord in exchange for the possession and use of real property (e.g., a person who rents an apartment).

testamentary trust

Trust created by a valid will.

testate

The legal status of a person who dies leaving a valid will.

testator

(a) Person who makes a valid will. (b) Person who dies leaving a valid will.

theft

The crime of stealing property from another who is not then present. Depending on the nature or value of the property stolen, it is either petty theft (*misdemeanor*) or grand theft (*felony*).

third-party beneficiary

One who is not a party to a contract, yet benefits from it. May be (a) a donee beneficiary, a third party who receives the benefit as a gift; or (b) a creditor beneficiary named because of an existing enforceable claim against one of the parties; or (c) an incidental beneficiary who may benefit from the contract but has no legally enforceable rights under it.

title

Full and complete ownership of property. It may be separated into *legal title* (ownership) and *equitable title* (possession). For example, the purchaser of a home may agree to make payments for years before receiving full ownership from the seller. While waiting for legal title from the seller, the buyer is enjoying possession (equitable ownership) of the home. See also "equitable title" and "legal title."

title insurance

A variety of insurance designed to insure against loss suffered by a homeowner or mortgage lender if title to the property is not as described by the insurer. Unlike most insurance, the premium is paid in total at the beginning of the period to be covered, it is measured in amount by the value of the property rather than by the risk of its loss, and it extends for as long as the insured continues to own the property, be it a week or fifty years or more.

Title VII

Literally refers to number 7, but its usual use is to refer to one of the operative parts of the Civil Rights Act of 1964.

TOD (Transfer on Death)

A method authorized by state statute allowing for the transfer of registered securities to a named beneficiary free of probate under the Uniform Transfer-on-Death Security Registration Act.

token damages

See "nominal (or token) damages."

tort

A private wrong committed by one person (the tortfeasor) that injures another (the victim) in person and/or property, and for which society allows the legal remedy of monetary damages.

tortfeasor

A wrongdoer who commits a private injury to another person by breaching a duty recognized by law.

Totten trust

A trust for bank depositors whereby they deposit money in a bank in their own name as a trustee for another person. It is revocable at will until the depositor dies or completes the gift in his or her lifetime by some unequivocal act or declaration.

treble damages

Amount of compensatory damages as determined by a jury or judge, multiplied by three, in order to punish the wrongdoers and serve as an example to others. Treble damages are available, for example, by statute for victims of certain violations of federal antitrust laws.

trespass

Wrongful interference with the real or personal property of another. Trespass commonly refers to entry onto another's rural land without authority or permission (implied or express).

trespass to chattel

A brief, temporary, unauthorized interference with the personal-property rights of another.

trial

Formal procedure before a court conducted to resolve disputed questions of fact and of law.

trial courts

Tribunals that conduct trials, as distinguished from courts that conduct appeals of cases decided by trial courts.

trial *de novo*

A new trial that takes place as if the first trial had not occurred.

trier of fact

See "jury."

trust

A legal relationship in which one party (called trustor, settlor, or donor) transfers legal title in property to a second party (trustee) for the benefit of a third party (beneficiary, or donee).

trustee

A person who holds property in a trust for the benefit of another, the beneficiary.

trustee's deed

A deed from a trustee, under a deed of trust provided to the successful bidder at a nonjudicial foreclosure sale.

trustee's sale

Auction-type sale conducted by a trustee under the direction of the unpaid creditor (called the beneficiary) of a mortgage (or deed of trust).

trustor

The person who creates a trust. The trustor is also called a *settlor* or *donor*.

Truth in Lending Act

See "Consumer Credit Protection Act."

unanimous opinion

A written opinion of the court wherein all judges agree on the holding and the stated reasons for it.

unconscionable contract

A contract in which one party is treated unfairly, oppressively, and with bad faith. The court may refuse to enforce the contract, or may modify it to eliminate the part that is unconscionable.

undue influence

Wrongful persuasion, often by a fiduciary or other trusted individual, that deprives the victim of freedom of will in making a contract.

unenforceable contract

A contract that was initially valid but can no longer be enforced, e.g., because of the running out of a statute of limitations.

unfair labor practice

Certain practices of employers, and also certain practices of unions, that are prohibited by federal or state law.

unfair labor practice strike

A strike in which the workers are protesting an unfair labor practice of their employer. See "economic strike."

unified estate and gift tax

A federal tax levied on the transfer of property through an estate at the time of death or on a taxable transfer by gift. The estate or the donor is responsible for payment of the tax. A unified credit is available to be applied against the transfer tax.

Uniform Commercial Code (UCC)

One of several uniform laws drafted by the National Conference of Commissioners of Uniform State Laws. It covers a wide range of commercial activity and has been generally adopted by all states.

Uniform Residential Landlord and Tenant Act (URLTA)

A uniform law modernizing common-law rules that govern the landlord-tenant relationship. In general, the act adopts contract principles and imposes implied duties upon landlords.

unilateral contract

A contract in which the promisor seeks performance of a requested act. Upon performance of the act, the contract is formed and the promisor is obligated to fulfill his or her promise.

unilateral mistake

A situation in which one of the parties to a contract labors under some error about an important fact in the agreement.

uninsured motorist insurance

Automobile insurance that protects against the risk of loss from bodily injury (and in some states, from property damage) suffered by an insured driver because of the negligence of either an uninsured driver or a hit-and-run driver.

union

Association of workers formed to bargain collectively with employers over wages, hours, and conditions of employment.

union shop

A place of employment where newly hired workers must join the union within thirty days of being hired.

unlawful detainer

A statutory remedy for a landlord to evict a renter who has defaulted in the payment of rent or who has broken the terms of the lease in some other manner. It is a summary judicial proceeding (i.e., not a full-blown trial on all issues before a jury). In some states it is called a *dispossessory-warrant proceeding* or a *forcible-entry proceeding*.

unwritten law

Laws that are enforced by courts and are included in their written opinions (cases) but not in statutes or ordinances. Also called "common law."

usury

Interest charged for the use of borrowed money that exceeds the maximum rate allowed by state law. Institutional lenders are commonly exempt from usury laws.

utilitarianism

An ethical doctrine holding that determining right conduct is based on consequences; that the purpose of the behavior should be the greatest happiness of the greatest number.

valid

Legally enforceable (for example, a proper contract).

valid contract

An agreement that complies with all requisites of the law for enforceability.

variable-interest-rate mortgage (VIRM)

A home-purchase mortgage and promissory note in which the interest rate may fluctuate, up or down, in sync with a published index. This type of mortgage is also called an *adjustable-rate mortgage*.

vehicular manslaughter

The wrongful killing of another person by a perpetrator driving a vehicle in a reckless and dangerous manner (e.g., in some cases while under the influence of alcohol or other drug). Some states have created, by statute, this special category of vehicular manslaughter to embrace all wrongful conduct involving the operation of automobiles resulting in homicide. Other states govern homicides by automobiles under their all-encompassing manslaughter statutes.

venue

[French for "to come"] The local place, within the geographical boundaries of a larger jurisdiction, where a case is generally most appropriately tried.

venue, change of

Transfer of a case for trial to another county or judicial district within the same jurisdiction, usually because of local prejudice against the defendant.

verdict

The expressed decision of the jury on questions of fact submitted to it for determination, based on evidence presented during trial.

Veterans Administration (VA) loan

A home-purchase mortgage loan made to any eligible veteran by the federal Veterans Administration. The VA was established in 1944 by the Serviceman's Readjustment Act to assist veterans in becoming homeowners.

vicarious liability

The responsibility of one person for the wrongful acts of another. For example, the owner of a vehicle is vicariously liable for the damages caused by the negligence of the driver.

vicarious-murder rule

A rule holding that an aider and abettor of a murder may also be guilty of the crime even though another person was the actual killer.

victim

The person who is the object of a crime or tort.

victimless crime

Any crime that allegedly hurts only the wrongdoer, if anyone (e.g., unusual sexual practices by consenting adults in private, prostitution, public drunkenness, use of marijuana and other hard drugs, usury, and illegal gambling). Reformers contend that such acts should be decriminalized, although participants frequently suffer painful consequences such as disease and loss of money, and society is often burdened with resulting costs of medical care, family decline, and welfare support.

violation

The act of disobeying or breaking a law or rule. Violation is also the act of doing harm to another person's rights, and of seducing or ravishing.

voluntary manslaughter

The wrongful and intentional killing of another person during the heat of passion, or under the influence of alcohol or drugs, or while engaged in some reckless and dangerous activity (such as driving while under the influence of a drug).

void

Without legal force or binding effect.

voidable contract

An agreement that may be legally enforced or may be rejected by a party. For example, a contract between a minor and an adult is voidable or valid at the option of the minor.

void agreement

A misnomer, because such attempted contract is a nullity. One or more essential elements of a valid contracts are missing in the attempt to make a contract.

voir dire

[Old French for "to speak the truth"] Process of questioning prospective jurors to ascertain whether they have any bias that would make difficult or unlikely their impartiality in determining questions of fact during a trial.

voluntary arbitration

See "arbitration."

voluntary rescission

When both parties voluntarily agree to return to the status quo as it existed before a contract was made. See also "rescission."

wage-earner receivership

A plan under which a court-appointed trustee collects all nonexempt wages of the debtor and distributes them pro rata to the creditors, who meanwhile may not garnish wages or repossess goods of the debtor.

waive

To give up a right, such as the constitutional right to a trial by jury.

ward

A person, usually a child, subject to a guardianship.

warrant

A written authorization of a judge or magistrate to arrest or search a specific person and/or place.

warranty

Assurance given by the seller of goods concerning the title to, or the quality or performance of, the product sold. A warranty may be express (oral or written) or *implied* by law even if not mentioned by the seller.

warranty against encumbrances

An implied warranty that goods will be delivered free of liens and encumbrances that are not otherwise noted.

warranty against infringement

An implied warranty by a merchant-seller that goods are free of any rightful claim, such as a patent.

warranty deed

A type of deed with several warranties implied by law to protect the buyer.

warranty of fitness for particular purpose

A warranty that arises when the buyer, having stated the intended use of the goods, relies on the seller's selection of goods.

warranty of merchantability

An implied warranty in a sale by a merchant that the goods are of fair, average quality and fit for the ordinary purpose(s) for which such goods are used.

warranty of title

An implied warranty to a buyer that the seller has and is transferring good title.

waste

Conduct that is destructive to real property and that is perpetrated by an owner/debtor, life tenant, or renter who is in possession. The conduct is wrongful because it damages or reduces the value of property for others who have a beneficial interest in it. The wronged party can sue the party in tort, for damages for waste. Damage by a trespasser, although wrongful, is considered not waste but trespass.

whistleblowers

A person who makes a disclosure about improper conduct by an organization or organization officer or official.

white-collar crime

Illegal acts committed usually without violence by persons of comparatively high social status and economic wealth. Examples are embezzlement, fraudulent sale of securities, and tax evasion. White-collar crime is contrasted to blue-collar crime, such as robbery and battery.

wildcat strike

An unlawful strike of union members that takes place without the approval of the union leaders.

will

Legal expression (usually in writing, signed and witnessed) of a person's directions as to how property owned is to be disposed of after death. A will is also called the *last will and testament.*

winding-up period

After dissolution of a partnership, the time during which outstanding debts are paid, assets are sold, and partners' investments are returned if possible. The partnership is then legally terminated. The term may also be applied to the winding-up process of liquidating a corporation.

Worker Adjustment and Retraining Notification Act (WARN) of 1989

A federal law that requires business managers to give employees sixty days' advance notice of a plant closing or mass layoff.

workers' compensation

Medical treatment, rehabilitation benefits, and disability payments for workers injured on the job. It is paid for by employer-financed insurance.

work furlough

A rehabilitative program for prisoners under which they may participate in part-time gainful employment even while they are serving time in a prison or jail.

writ of *certiorari*

A procedural document whereby an appellate court exercises its discretionary power to accept jurisdiction of a pending case.

writ of execution

Order of the court directing the sheriff to confiscate property of the defendant. The property is then sold to satisfy the award of dollar damages given to the plaintiff at a trial.

writ of *habeas corpus*

[Latin: "you have the body"] A judicial command to bring a prisoner to court for further legal proceedings.

written interrogatories

See "interrogatories."

written law

The statutes and ordinances of federal, state, and local governments, and the published rules of administrative agencies.

wrongful-death statute

A law allowing the heirs of a deceased person to sue whoever caused the decedent's death, and to collect any court-awarded damages. The damage sued for is the damage to the heirs for the loss of the loved one's life.

wrongful discharge

The wrongful dismissal of a permanent employee (i.e., discharge without good cause). Wrongful discharge is a tort.

yellow dog contract

An employment contract in which a worker agrees not to join a union. This type of contract was outlawed by the Anti-Injunction Act of 1932.

Note: Footnote material is denoted by an "*f*" following the page number.